기출하프 + 파생하프 + 복습모의고사

성정혜 기적사 하프 모의고사

강파이널편

결국엔 성정혜 영어 하프모의고사 기적사

INTRO 들어가며

기적사는 수험생이 아닌 합격생을 만듭니다.
시험장에서의 확실한 출력을 위한 객관적 모의고사

- **합격생 추천 1위**

    수많은 합격생들이 엄지를 들어 올리며 추천하는 기적사의 본질은 교재나 강의가 아닙니다.
    합격으로 가는 시스템입니다.
    매일 10문항, 기적사는 개인의 의견이 아닌 객관적인 기출 DATA로 무장했습니다. 당신이 노베이스에서 시작할지라도 매일 책상을 향해 몸을 당기게 하는, 나의 노력이 바로 다음날 반영될 수 있도록 설계되었습니다.

- **주관이 아닌 객관을 담은 5일 반복 시스템**

    사실의 반대는 거짓이 아닌 의견입니다.
    기적사는 철저하게 개인의 의견을 배제하였습니다.
    기출문제의 객관적인 사실을 철저하게 분석하고 수치화해 설계한 문항이 수록되어있습니다.
    세상에 모의고사는 많습니다. 하지만 기적사는 무작위로 문항이 반복되지 않습니다.
    기출문제를 기반으로 출제 포인트가 주 5회 반복되도록 구성되어 실전 난도부터 시작해 점점 난도가 높아지도록 설계되었습니다. 이는 시험장에서 어떠한 빈틈이나 매력적인 오답에도 수험생이 흔들리지 않고 정답만을 마킹하게 하기 위함입니다.

- **기적사**

    기출을 적용해 합격으로 가는 길이 바로 '기적사'입니다.
    기적은 알아서 찾아오는 것이 아니라, 내가 끝내 찾아가는 것임을 지금 이 글을 마주하는 당신은 알고 있습니다. 우리는 기적을 찾아 수많은 날을 책상 앞에서 잠과 사투할 것이고, 피곤함을 이기고 책을 펼쳐낼 것입니다. 우리가 매일 함께하는 모든 하루의 끝에 바라는 결과가 있음을 알기에 오늘도 기적사와 함께 성실한 하루를 보낼 당신께 경의를 표합니다.

성정혜

System 기적사 시스템

• 회차별 구성

Day 1	핵심 기출 하프
Day 2	기출 파생 신출 하프 1
Day 3	기출 파생 신출 하프 2
Day 4	기출 파생 신출 하프 3
Day 5	기출 파생 신출 하프 4
동형	복습 동형 모의고사

[Day별 구성]

어휘 3 + 생활영어 1 + 문법 3
+ 독해 3 = 10문항

[1세트]

핵심 기출 하프 1회
+ 기출 파생 신출 하프 4회
→ 총 16세트, 80회 구성
+ 동형 복습 모의고사 8회

• 회차별 특징

- **기출 하프 모의고사** : 방대한 기출 DATA에서 핵심 기출만 뽑아 구성된 하프 모의고사입니다.

- **기출 파생 하프 모의고사** : 기출 하프에서 학습한 핵심 출제포인트를 담아 파생 제작한 신출 하프 모의고사입니다. 기출 주요 포인트를 신출 문제로 반복 학습해 핵심 기출 포인트 반복 학습과 동시에 신규 문항에 포인트를 적용하는 훈련까지 할 수 있습니다.

- **동형 복습 모의고사** : 10회차의 하프 모의고사에서 오답률이 가장 높았던 문항과 꼭 다시 풀어봐야하는 문항을 20문항 선별해 동형 모의고사로 구성하였습니다. 무작위로 많은 양의 문제를 푸는 것이 아닌 출제포인트와 함께 최적의 문항들로 복습할 수 있도록 구성하였습니다.

결국엔 성정혜 영어 하프모의고사 기적사

Structure 교재 구성

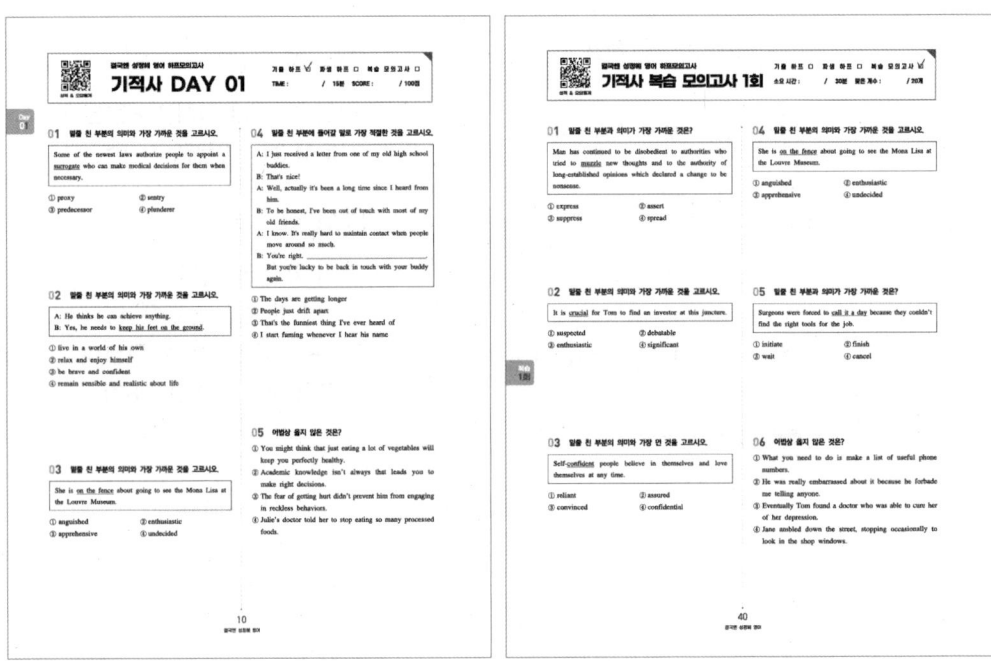

3·3·3·1 + 복습모의고사, 실전에 강한 균형 잡힌 학습

어휘 3문항, 생활영어 1문항, 문법 3문항, 독해 3문항으로 구성해 영어 전 영역을 균형 있게 학습할 수 있도록 배치하였습니다. 핵심 기출 문제, 핵심 기출 포인트를 반복 학습할 수 있는 기출 파생 문제, 그리고 실시간 성적&오답률 통계로 강점은 더욱 강화하고 약점은 확실하게 보완할 수 있습니다. 또한 10회차 단위로 구성된 복습 모의고사를 20문항으로 구성하여 실전 시험에서의 적응력을 높일 수 있도록 구성하였습니다.

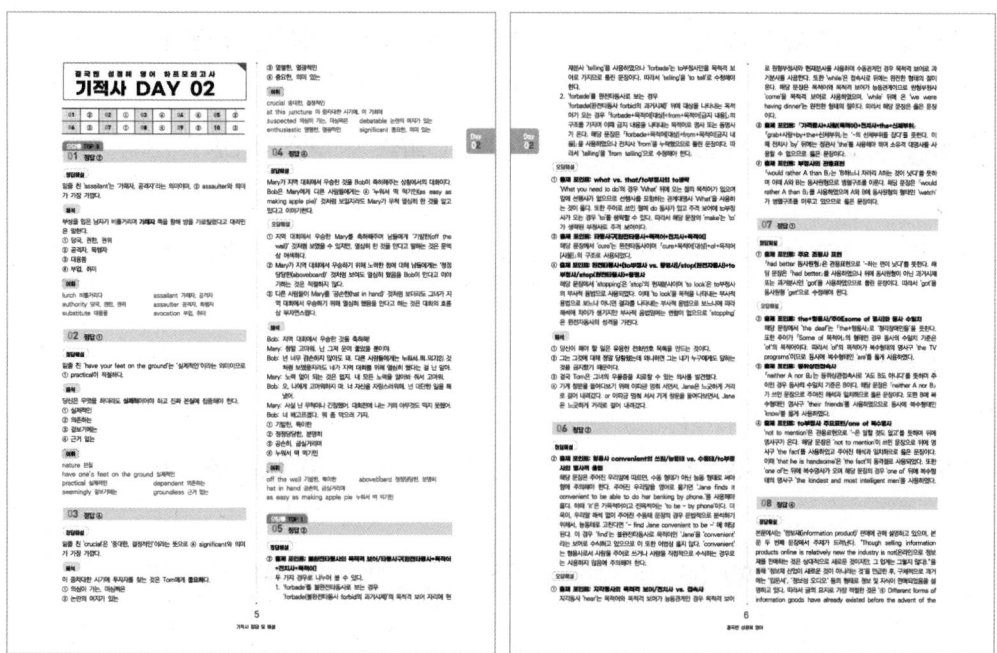

친절&꼼꼼한 해설 + 특별 부록 어휘 Handbook까지

효율적인 개인 학습을 위해 꼼꼼하고 상세한 해설을 담았습니다. 어휘와 생활영어는 핵심 어휘와 관용 표현을 함께 정리하였습니다. 문법은 출제포인트를 먼저 제시하여 학습 방향을 제시하고 정답해설 뿐만 아니라 오답해설까지 상세하고 꼼꼼하게 기재하여 읽는 것만으로도 학습이 될 수 있도록 구성하였습니다. 독해는 해석뿐만 아니라 정답을 찾아가는 과정과 근거를 명확히 제시하여 단순히 문제를 푸는 것이 아닌 논리적 사고력을 향상시킬 수 있도록 하였습니다. 또한 각 문항의 어휘는 특별 부록 Handbook으로 구성하여 어휘만 따로 정리하는 시간을 절약하고 효율적으로 학습할 수 있도록 구성하였습니다.

결국엔 성정혜 영어 하프모의고사 기적사

CONTENTS 목차

기출	기적사 DAY 01	10	기출	기적사 DAY 11	46
파생	기적사 DAY 02	13	파생	기적사 DAY 12	49
파생	기적사 DAY 03	16	파생	기적사 DAY 13	52
파생	기적사 DAY 04	19	파생	기적사 DAY 14	55
파생	기적사 DAY 05	22	파생	기적사 DAY 15	58
기출	기적사 DAY 06	25	기출	기적사 DAY 16	61
파생	기적사 DAY 07	28	파생	기적사 DAY 17	64
파생	기적사 DAY 08	31	파생	기적사 DAY 18	67
파생	기적사 DAY 09	34	파생	기적사 DAY 19	70
파생	기적사 DAY 10	37	파생	기적사 DAY 20	73
동형	복습 모의고사 1회	40	동형	복습 모의고사 2회	76

기출	기적사 DAY 21	82	기출	기적사 DAY 31	118
파생	기적사 DAY 22	85	파생	기적사 DAY 32	121
파생	기적사 DAY 23	88	파생	기적사 DAY 33	124
파생	기적사 DAY 24	91	파생	기적사 DAY 34	127
파생	기적사 DAY 25	94	파생	기적사 DAY 35	130
기출	기적사 DAY 26	97	기출	기적사 DAY 36	133
파생	기적사 DAY 27	100	파생	기적사 DAY 37	136
파생	기적사 DAY 28	103	파생	기적사 DAY 38	139
파생	기적사 DAY 29	106	파생	기적사 DAY 39	142
파생	기적사 DAY 30	109	파생	기적사 DAY 40	145
동형	복습 모의고사 3회	112	동형	복습 모의고사 4회	148

결국엔 성정혜 영어 하프모의고사 기적사

CONTENTS 목차

기출	기적사 DAY 41	154	기출	기적사 DAY 51	190
파생	기적사 DAY 42	157	파생	기적사 DAY 52	193
파생	기적사 DAY 43	160	파생	기적사 DAY 53	196
파생	기적사 DAY 44	163	파생	기적사 DAY 54	199
파생	기적사 DAY 45	166	파생	기적사 DAY 55	202
기출	기적사 DAY 46	169	기출	기적사 DAY 56	205
파생	기적사 DAY 47	172	파생	기적사 DAY 57	208
파생	기적사 DAY 48	175	파생	기적사 DAY 58	211
파생	기적사 DAY 49	178	파생	기적사 DAY 59	214
파생	기적사 DAY 50	181	파생	기적사 DAY 60	217
동형	복습 모의고사 5회	184	동형	복습 모의고사 6회	220

기출	기적사 DAY 61	226		기출	기적사 DAY 71	262
파생	기적사 DAY 62	229		파생	기적사 DAY 72	265
파생	기적사 DAY 63	232		파생	기적사 DAY 73	268
파생	기적사 DAY 64	235		파생	기적사 DAY 74	271
파생	기적사 DAY 65	238		파생	기적사 DAY 75	274
기출	기적사 DAY 66	241		기출	기적사 DAY 76	277
파생	기적사 DAY 67	244		파생	기적사 DAY 77	280
파생	기적사 DAY 68	247		파생	기적사 DAY 78	283
파생	기적사 DAY 69	250		파생	기적사 DAY 79	286
파생	기적사 DAY 70	253		파생	기적사 DAY 80	289
동형	복습 모의고사 7회	256		동형	복습 모의고사 8회	292

기적사 DAY 01

01 밑줄 친 부분의 의미와 가장 가까운 것을 고르시오.

Some of the newest laws authorize people to appoint a surrogate who can make medical decisions for them when necessary.

① proxy
② sentry
③ predecessor
④ plunderer

02 밑줄 친 부분의 의미와 가장 가까운 것을 고르시오.

A: He thinks he can achieve anything.
B: Yes, he needs to keep his feet on the ground.

① live in a world of his own
② relax and enjoy himself
③ be brave and confident
④ remain sensible and realistic about life

03 밑줄 친 부분의 의미와 가장 가까운 것을 고르시오.

She is on the fence about going to see the Mona Lisa at the Louvre Museum.

① anguished
② enthusiastic
③ apprehensive
④ undecided

04 밑줄 친 부분에 들어갈 말로 가장 적절한 것을 고르시오.

A: I just received a letter from one of my old high school buddies.
B: That's nice!
A: Well, actually it's been a long time since I heard from him.
B: To be honest, I've been out of touch with most of my old friends.
A: I know. It's really hard to maintain contact when people move around so much.
B: You're right. _____.
But you're lucky to be back in touch with your buddy again.

① The days are getting longer
② People just drift apart
③ That's the funniest thing I've ever heard of
④ I start fuming whenever I hear his name

05 어법상 옳지 않은 것은?

① You might think that just eating a lot of vegetables will keep you perfectly healthy.
② Academic knowledge isn't always that leads you to make right decisions.
③ The fear of getting hurt didn't prevent him from engaging in reckless behaviors.
④ Julie's doctor told her to stop eating so many processed foods.

06 우리말을 영어로 잘못 옮긴 것을 고르시오.

① 나는 매달 두세 번 그에게 전화하기로 규칙을 세웠다.
  → I made it a rule to call him two or three times a month.
② 그는 나의 팔을 붙잡고 도움을 요청했다.
  → He grabbed me by the arm and asked for help.
③ 폭우로 인해 그 강은 120cm만큼 상승했다.
  → Owing to the heavy rain, the river has risen by 120cm.
④ 나는 눈 오는 날 밖에 나가는 것보다 집에 있는 것을 더 좋아한다.
  → I prefer to staying home than to going out on a snowy day.

07 우리말을 영어로 잘못 옮긴 것을 고르시오.

① 그를 당황하게 한 것은 그녀의 거절이 아니라 그녀의 무례함이었다.
  → It was not her refusal but her rudeness that perplexed him.
② 부모는 아이들 앞에서 그들의 말과 행동에 대해 아무리 신중해도 지나치지 않다.
  → Parents cannot be too careful about their words and actions before their children.
③ 환자들과 부상자들을 돌보기 위해 더 많은 의사가 필요했다.
  → More doctors were required to tend sick and wounded.
④ 설상가상으로, 또 다른 태풍이 곧 올 것이라는 보도가 있다.
  → To make matters worse, there is a report that another typhoon will arrive soon.

08 글의 제목으로 가장 적절한 것은?

Economists say that production of an information good involves high fixed costs but low marginal costs. The cost of producing the first copy of an information good may be substantial, but the cost of producing(or reproducing) additional copies is negligible. This sort of cost structure has many important implications. For example, cost-based pricing just doesn't work: a 10 or 20 percent markup on unit cost makes no sense when unit cost is zero. You must price your information goods according to consumer value, not according to your production cost.

① Securing the Copyright
② Pricing the Information Goods
③ Information as Intellectual Property
④ The Cost of Technological Change

09 밑줄 친 부분이 지칭하는 대상이 다른 것은?

Dracula ants get their name for the way they sometimes drink the blood of their own young. But this week, ① the insects have earned a new claim to fame. Dracula ants of the species Mystrium camillae can snap their jaws together so fast, you could fit 5,000 strikes into the time it takes us to blink an eye. This means ② the blood-suckers wield the fastest known movement in nature, according to a study published this week in the journal Royal Society Open Science. Interestingly, the ants produce their record-breaking snaps simply by pressing their jaws together so hard that ③ they bend. This stores energy in one of the jaws, like a spring, until it slides past the other and lashes out with extraordinary speed and force—reaching a maximum velocity of over 200 miles per hour. It's kind of like what happens when you snap your fingers, only 1,000 times faster. Dracula ants are secretive predators as ④ they prefer to hunt under the leaf litter or in subterranean tunnels.

10 글의 흐름상 빈칸에 들어갈 말로 가장 적절한 것은?

A country's wealth plays a central role in education, so lack of funding and resources from a nation-state can weaken a system. Governments in sub-Saharan Africa spend only 2.4 percent of the world's public resources on education, yet 15 percent of the school-age population lives there. _____, the United States spends 28 percent of all the money spent in the world on education, yet it houses only 4 percent of the school-age population.

① Nevertheless ② Furthermore
③ Conversely   ④ Similarly

01 밑줄 친 부분의 의미와 가장 가까운 것을 고르시오.

The proxy says that the wounded man lurched across the room at his <u>assailant</u>.

① authority ② assaulter
③ substitute ④ avocation

02 밑줄 친 부분의 의미와 가장 가까운 것을 고르시오.

You must <u>have your feet on the ground</u> whatever you do and focus on true nature.

① practical ② dependent
③ seemingly ④ groundless

03 밑줄 친 부분의 의미와 가장 가까운 것을 고르시오.

It is <u>crucial</u> for Tom to find an investor at this juncture.

① suspected ② debatable
③ enthusiastic ④ significant

04 밑줄 친 부분에 들어갈 말로 가장 적절한 것을 고르시오.

Bob: Congratulations on winning first prize in the regional contest!
Mary: Thank you so much. I was just lucky.
Bob: You don't have to be so modest. I know you studied really hard for it although it seemed _____ to others.
Mary: Nothing comes without effort. Thank you for recognizing all my effort.
Bob: Oh, don't thank me. Be proud of yourself. You've done an amazing job.
Mary: I was actually terribly nervous. I barely ate anything before the contest.
Bob: You must be hungry. Let's go grab something to eat.

① off the wall
② aboveboard
③ hat in hand
④ as easy as making apple pie

05 어법상 옳지 않은 것은?

① What you need to do is make a list of useful phone numbers.
② He was really embarrassed about it because he forbade me telling anyone.
③ Eventually Tom found a doctor who was able to cure her of her depression.
④ Jane ambled down the street, stopping occasionally to look in the shop windows.

06 우리말을 영어로 잘못 옮긴 것을 고르시오.

① 나는 우리가 저녁을 먹고 있는 동안 그녀가 들어오는 소리를 들었다고 생각했다.
→ I thought I heard her come in while we were having dinner.

② Jane은 전화로 은행 업무를 할 수 있는 것이 편리하다고 생각한다.
→ Jane is found convenient to be able to do her banking by phone.

③ 나는 강도의 멱살을 잡고 방에서 끌어냈다.
→ I grabbed the robber by the collar and dragged him out of the room.

④ 나는 영어로 더빙된 영화를 보느니 차라리 자막이 있는 영화를 보는 것이 낫다.
→ I would rather watch a film with subtitles than watch one dubbed into English.

07 우리말을 영어로 잘못 옮긴 것을 고르시오.

① Jane은 빨리 여기에 오는 것이 좋겠다. 그렇지 않으면 그녀는 그 개막식을 놓칠 것이다.
→ Jane had better got here soon, or she'll miss the opening ceremony.

② 일부 TV 프로그램은 청각장애인들을 위해 자막과 함께 방송된다.
→ Some of the TV programs are broadcasted with subtitles for the deaf.

③ 그들의 가족도 친구도 그들이 결혼한다는 것을 알지 못한다.
→ Neither their families nor their friends know that they are getting married.

④ Tom이 잘생겼다는 사실은 말할 것도 없고, 그는 내가 아는 가장 친절하고 똑똑한 남자들 중 한 명이다.
→ Tom is one of the kindest and most intelligent men I know, not to mention the fact that he is handsome.

08 다음 글의 요지로 가장 적절한 것은?

Before we dive into digital publishing specifically, let's take a step back and look at the information marketing and information publishing industry as a whole. Though selling information products online is relatively new, the industry is not. The idea of packaging knowledge, information, and expertise into a sellable product has been around for ages. When print publishing first appeared, people would write "how-to" books, and when audio cassette technology became available, they would record their information in the form of audios. That is to say, the idea of creating informative content and packaging it into something you can vend isn't entirely new and the idea of being able to do it online just opened up access to this industry to many more people and made the opportunity much more accessible.

① The information products industry has been rapidly growing.
② Creating information products and selling them online is never easy.
③ Not until the Internet was invented did information products emerge.
④ Different forms of information goods have already existed before the advent of the Internet.

09 Bulldog ant에 관한 다음 글의 내용과 일치하는 것은?

The most dangerous ant in the world is the bulldog ant (Myrmecia pyriformis) found in coastal regions in Australia. In attack it uses its sting and jaws simultaneously. There have been at least three human fatalities since 1936, the latest of whom was a Victorian farmer in 1988. The bulldog ant earned its name because of its ferocity and determination during an attack. It is extremely aggressive and shows little fear of human beings, stinging a number of times in quick succession and therefore injecting more venom with each bite. In an attack, the ant will hold on to its victim with long, toothed mandibles, curl its body underneath and thrust its long barbless sting into the skin. On a few occasions this sting has been enough to kill adults within 15 minutes.

① It is recorded as the world's most dangerous insect.
② No one has been killed because of its attack since 1989.
③ It was named based on its physical appearance.
④ It uses either its mandibles or poisoned sting to make an attack.

10 빈칸에 들어갈 표현으로 가장 적절한 것은?

Prior to the nineteenth century, systematic investment in human resources was not considered specially important in any country. Expenditures on schooling, on-the-job training, and other similar forms of investment were quite small. This began to change radically with the application of science to the development of new goods and more efficient methods of production, first in the United Kingdom, and then gradually in other countries. During the twentieth century, education, skills, and the acquisition of knowledge have become crucial determinants of a person's and a nation's productivity. The primary determinant of a country's standard of living is how well it succeeds in developing and utilizing the skills and knowledge, and furthering the health and educating the majority of its population. In the sense, one can even call the twentieth century the "_____."

① Age of Craft Skills
② Era of Technology
③ Age of Human Capital
④ Era of Economic Development

기적사 DAY 03

01 밑줄 친 부분의 의미와 가장 가까운 것을 고르시오.

Shareholders are blaming the company's problems on the lassitude of the planning department.

① weariness ② instruction
③ sentry ④ interrogation

02 밑줄 친 부분의 의미와 가장 가까운 것을 고르시오.

Therefore, it is no use in remaining sensible to remain indifferent towards the victim.

① reasonable ② impartial
③ empirical ④ illogical

03 밑줄 친 부분의 의미와 가장 가까운 것을 고르시오.

In Chinese myth, the dragon and the tiger was seen as a powerful almighty king.

① ambivalent ② omnipotent
③ anguished ④ casual

04 밑줄 친 부분에 들어갈 말로 가장 적절한 것을 고르시오.

Tobe: What are you doing here?
Sharon: I was writing down my new-years resolution on my new planner.
Tobe: Oh, is that your new planner?
Sharon: Yes it is. I bought it today. I also made some plans for the new year.
Tobe: Well done! Plans are essential. However there are moments in which you have no other choice but to _____.
Sharon: I know, that happens. But knowing that I have a plan makes me feel safer even when I have to make adjustments.

① go bananas
② beat a dead horse
③ change horses in the middle of the stream
④ look like the cat that swallowed the canary

05 어법상 옳지 않은 것은?

① The beautiful beach makes this a highly popular area with tourists.
② A secretary was hired to relieve Tom of some of the administrative work.
③ What makes football fun is that we all have different ways of looking at it.
④ She said she would consider to unseal some documents after the jury is chosen.

06 우리말을 영어로 잘못 옮긴 것을 고르시오.

① 모든 대출자들은 더 높은 금리를 받아들일 수밖에 없었다.
   → All borrowers had no choice but accept higher interest rates.

② Jane은 남편이 술을 너무 많이 마셨음에도 불구하고 남편을 사랑했다.
   → Jane loved her husband in spite of the fact that he drank too much.

③ 내가 말을 걸었던 많은 학생들은 그들 주변에서 무슨 일이 일어나고 있는지 믿기 어렵다는 것을 깨달았다.
   → Many students I spoke to found it hard to believe what was happening around them.

④ 그들 중 두 명은 Tom의 팔을 잡고 있었고 다른 한 명은 그가 어떤 것도 말할 필요가 없다고 말했다.
   → Two of them were holding Tom by the arms while another said he didn't have to say anything.

07 우리말을 영어로 잘못 옮긴 것을 고르시오.

① 위원회가 살펴봐야 할 한 가지 측면은 장애인들을 위한 접근성이다.
   → One aspect the committee needs to look at is access for the disabled.

② 날씨가 더 추워지면 식물을 안으로 가져오는 것이 낫다.
   → It would be better to bring the plants inside when the weather gets colder.

③ Tom은 프랑스어도 독일어도 하지 않고, 그 둘을 이상하게 섞어서 말한다.
   → Tom speaks neither French nor German, and a strange mixture of the two.

④ 쉽게 말해, 1980년대 노인의 생존전략은 소득 유지에 초점이 맞춰져 있었다.
   → To put it in a nutshell, older people's survival strategies during the 1980s focused on maintaining their income.

08 밑줄 친 (A), (B)에 들어갈 말로 가장 적절한 것은?

Many of the unique pricing and market structure questions in IT industries stem from a specific unusual cost structure: high fixed costs of production, but near-zero or zero variable costs of production. This cost structure characterizes a class of technology products that are collectively termed information goods. ___(A)___, the cost of producing the first unit of an information good is very high, and yet the cost of producing each additional unit is virtually nothing. ___(B)___, Microsoft spends hundreds of millions of dollars on developing each version of its Windows operating system. Once this first copy of the OS has been developed, however, it can be replicated costlessly.

	(A)	(B)
①	Nevertheless	For example
②	In brief	Otherwise
③	Hence	In summary
④	Put differently	To take an instance

09 다음 글의 제목으로 가장 적절한 것은?

If you're looking for queen ants for your pet ant colonies in the United States, you're better off catching one rather than buying them online. The sale of queen ants is frowned upon by the United States Department of Agriculture (USDA), which has banned it for an important ecological reason. If you buy a queen ant and it escapes and establishes a colony in an area where it isn't naturally found, it could put plenty of stress on the local ecosystem. Invasive ant species cause harm to the natural biodiversity. Take the example of the infamous red imported fire ants. These are native to South America but found their way to the United States through shipping crates. Having no natural predators here, they spread throughout the southern states, causing irreparable economic and ecological damage. For this reason, USDA prohibits the sale of queen ants in the United States. You can still buy them in Europe and other countries but this is being debated now.

① How Ants Make Good Pets
② Why You Can't Buy Queen Ants in the US
③ How Invasive Species Impact the Environment
④ The Important Roles of Queen Ants in Ecosystem

10 밑줄 친 부분 중 글의 흐름상 가장 어색한 것은?

Marketization of higher education helps to relate higher education closely to the market and society and this accelerates the reform of higher education, and promotes the innovation of the education system. ① It also helps to change the traditional enclosed mode of school running into an open society-oriented model. ② It changes the policy of higher education institutions from creating conditions that will meet the various needs of students to focusing on the requirements and regulations of the government. ③ Of course, it is not that the basic spirit of the pursuit of knowledge and truth of higher education has changed in a modern society with a market economy. ④ But the development of higher education has been closely linked with social development, and higher education institutions must survive and develop in a competitive market economy. The main advantage of this market model is that it can continuously stimulate the higher education institutions to adapt to the changing economic and social situation.

01 밑줄 친 부분의 의미와 가장 가까운 것을 고르시오.

This movie shows the Biblical seven deadly sins of pride, envy, lust, gluttony, sloth, avarice and wrath.

① calling
② vocation
③ avidity
④ plunderer

02 밑줄 친 부분의 의미와 가장 먼 것을 고르시오.

Self-confident people believe in themselves and love themselves at any time.

① reliant
② assured
③ convinced
④ confidential

03 밑줄 친 부분의 의미와 가장 가까운 것을 고르시오.

The government has been assiduous in the fight against deflation.

① ambivalent
② apprehensive
③ industrious
④ avocational

04 밑줄 친 부분에 들어갈 말로 가장 적절한 것을 고르시오.

Clerk: What can I help you with?
Customer: I'd like to get a refund for a product I bought just a few days ago.
Clerk: Sure, you've come to the right place. What is the product you purchased?
Customer: It's a wireless earphone.
Clerk: And what is the reason for your refund?
Customer: I received _____. The sound is too small even when the sound is at its maximum volume.
Clerk: Oh, we're very sorry. Please fill out this form.

① a lemon
② an act of god
③ four-letter word
④ the best thing since sliced bread

05 어법상 옳지 않은 것은?

① William admitted feeling hurt by what I had said before.
② What he does possess is the ability to get straight to the core of a problem.
③ It is considered bad manners in European cultures to speak with your mouth full of food.
④ His legal advisers persuaded him mentioning the names of the people involved in the robbery.

06 우리말을 영어로 잘못 옮긴 것을 고르시오.

① Tom은 명령에 복종해야 했기 때문에 군대에 있는 것을 싫어했다.
→ Tom hated being in the army because he had to obey commands.

② 우리의 최선의 노력에도 불구하고, 그와 접촉하는 것은 불가능하다는 것으로 드러났다.
→ In spite of our best endeavors, it has proven impossible to contact him.

③ 의사가 가자마자 William은 아들의 볼에 가볍게 입을 맞추었다.
→ As soon as the doctor went, William kissed his son lightly on his cheek.

④ 만약 당신이 폭력으로 공격당하면, 당신은 폭력으로 대응하지 않을 수 없다.
→ If you are attacked with violence, you cannot choose but respond with violence.

07 우리말을 영어로 잘못 옮긴 것을 고르시오.

① William은 결코 폭력적인 영화에 관심을 가지지 않을 사람이다.
→ William is the last person to be interested in violent movies.

② 그것은 그의 몸을 이완시켰을 뿐만 아니라, 그의 자존감을 북돋웠다.
→ Not only has it relaxed his body, but it has also boosted his ego.

③ 누가 내 가방을 훔칠지도 모르니 거기에 두고 가지 않는 것이 좋다.
→ I had not better leave my bag there because someone might steal it.

④ 부유한 학생들에게 가난의 정신을 사랑하고 가난한 사람들로 살라고 요구하는 것은 비현실적이다.
→ It is unrealistic to ask rich students to love the spirit of poverty and live as the poor.

08 다음 글의 밑줄 친 부분 중 문맥상 단어의 쓰임이 적절하지 않은 것은?

Info products provide several ① benefits, but the most significant benefit is the ability to productize your business so you can leverage your time and focus on growing your business. This helps you avoid the pitfalls of entrepreneurial burnout, and once you ramp up to a ② well-oiled productizing machine, you can continue the growth by hiring a virtual assistant. Moreover, there's limitless inventory with info products, which means your sales potential is ③ restricted and your order fulfillment process is streamlined and automatic. In other words, by selling a digital product, you do all the legwork in advance and only need ④ minimal maintenance — mainly marketing — on the back-end. Once your storefront is set up, your customers can purchase as many info products as they'd like without you having to fulfill orders manually.

09 주어진 문장이 들어갈 위치로 가장 적절한 것은?

The fungus thereby benefits because infectious spores are released onto the ground below, where they can infect other foraging ants.

Researchers at Penn State University released new information about one of Earth's weirdest natural phenomena: zombie ants. (①) These are carpenter ants in tropical locations, infiltrated and controlled by *Ophiocordyceps unilateralis sensu lato*, sometimes called zombie ant fungus. (②) This fungal body-snatcher forces ants to a forest understory and compels them to climb vegetation and bite into the underside of leaves or twigs, where the ants die. (③) The invasion culminates with the sprouting of a spore-laden fruiting body from a dead ant's head. (④) The new research shows the fungal parasite accomplishes all this without infecting the ants' brains. Instead, according to the study, the zombie ant fungus surrounds and invades muscle fibers throughout the ant's body.

10 다음 글의 내용과 일치하는 것은?

Across OECD countries, expenditures per full-time-equivalent (FTE) student at the elementary/secondary level were generally higher in 2015 than in 2005. Countries with the highest expenditures per FTE student at the elementary/secondary level in 2015 generally had the highest expenditures in 2005, and vice versa. In 2015, the average of OECD countries' expenditures per FTE student at the elementary/secondary level was $9,500, compared with $7,700 in 2005. Of the 27 OECD countries with data available in both years, the average expenditures per FTE student at the elementary/secondary level were higher in 2015 than in 2005 in 23 countries, including the United States. Three countries (Iceland, Greece, and Slovenia) had expenditures per FTE student at the elementary/secondary level that were lower in 2015 than in 2005. In Mexico, expenditures per FTE student at the elementary/secondary level were nearly the same in 2015 as in 2005 (both $3,300).

① Nations with the lowest expenditures per FTE student at elementary/secondary level in 2015 generally had the lowest expenditures in 2005.
② The average amount of expenditures per FTE student at the elementary/secondary level has declined over the past ten years in every OECD countries.
③ The United States spent $9,500 on elementary/secondary education in 2015.
④ In 2015, expenditures per FTE student at the elementary/secondary level of Iceland were lower than those of the United States.

01 밑줄 친 부분의 의미와 가장 가까운 것을 고르시오.

Those who watched the match on television must have observed it with dismay.

① euthanasia ② predecessor
③ disappointment ④ torture

02 밑줄 친 부분의 의미와 가장 가까운 것을 고르시오.

In the modern arts, the realistic style and meticulous observation of the artist are well represented.

① relaxing ② pragmatic
③ infeasible ④ impractical

03 밑줄 친 부분의 의미와 가장 가까운 것을 고르시오.

The Enforcement Ordinance prohibits unions from using payroll-deducted funds for political purposes.

① subtracted ② dedicated
③ defeated ④ undecided

04 밑줄 친 부분에 들어갈 말로 가장 적절한 것을 고르시오.

Ned: Have you been to another country?
Luke: Yeah, I love traveling overseas. How about you?
Ned: I've never been abroad. I was always curious about what it is like to go on a trip to another land.
Luke: It's doubtlessly a valuable experience. To put it into words, you'll realize that you were _____. There are so many interesting things in other parts of the world.
Ned: I can't imagine what it would be like. But hearing from you now, I think it would be a great opportunity to broaden my perspective.
Luke: Exactly. You'll learn a lot from your trip.

① thumbs up
② Alpha and Omega
③ a pretty kettle of fish
④ a big fish in a little pond

05 어법상 옳지 않은 것은?

① I told Jane to drive more slowly, but she chose to ignore my advice.
② We have to dissuade Congress from cutting funds for health programs.
③ John is thought costing the software company millions of dollars a year.
④ What is extraordinary is that Tom left without making a public statement about the incident.

06 우리말을 영어로 잘못 옮긴 것을 고르시오.

① 연방 규제 기관들과 미국의 대출 기관들은 5년 동안 금리를 동결하기로 합의했다.
   → Federal regulators and US lenders agreed to freeze interest rates for five years.

② 그 부검은 살인범이 쇠막대기로 그녀의 머리를 때린 것임을 밝혔다.
   → The autopsy revealed that her murderer had struck her on the head with an iron bar.

③ John이 쓰기, 말하기, 생각의 자유에 대해 말할 때, 나는 웃지 않을 수 없다.
   → When John talks of the freedom of writing, speaking, or thinking, I can do no other than laugh.

④ 희생자들은 텔레비전에 나오는 한일 친선 축구 경기를 보는 동안 공격받았다.
   → The victims were attacked during they watched a friendly soccer match between Korean and Japan on television.

07 우리말을 영어로 잘못 옮긴 것을 고르시오.

① 그 붉은 꽃들은 프랑스인들에 의해 대중화되면서, 많은 시럽에서 사용된다.
   → The red flowers are used in many syrups, popularized by the French.

② Tom은 자신이 재판에 회부되거나 아니면 석방되어야 한다는 것을 요구하고 있었다.
   → Tom was demanding that he should be either put on trial or set free.

③ 아이들이 정원에서 뛰어놀 때 자유시간을 갖도록 하는 것이 좋을 것이다.
   → It would be better to let the children have free time when they run around in the garden.

④ 우리 선수들 중 두 명이 아팠고, 설상가상으로, 우리의 주요 득점원은 발목이 부러졌다.
   → Two of our players were ill, and to make matters bad, our main scorer broke his ankle.

08 주어진 문장이 들어갈 위치로 가장 적절한 것은?

Instead, there are several somewhat different products some of which are close substitutes.

Digital materials typically have the property that it is very costly to produce the first copy and very cheap to produce subsequent copies. It is often said, for example, that the "first copy costs" are more than 70% of the cost of an academic journal. (①) Cost structures of this form pose special problems for pricing. The first problem is that it is very difficult to sustain a competitive market with this sort of cost structure. (②) Economists define a purely competitive market to be one where there are "several" producers of an identical commodity. The markets for wheat, corn, shares of IBM stock, etc. are all examples of purely competitive markets. (③) The market for automobiles is not purely competitive because there are not multiple producers of identical products. (④) Economists call this a situation of monopolistic competition. The market for academic journals (or other sorts of information goods) tends to be much more like the automobile market than the wheat market. The high-fixed-cost/low-incremental-cost structure forces this outcome.

09 밑줄 친 부분 중 글의 흐름상 가장 어색한 것은?

With a name like "Dracula ant," it's probably no surprise that the species' signifying characteristic is its predilection for feeding on the blood of its young. ① Fifteen years ago in a pile of rotting leaves in Madagascar, an entomologist discovered the species and their unique feeding style. ② Unlike most ants which practice "social food transfer" behavior — each colony's workers' sharing food and carrying it to the queen — Dracula ants opt for "nondestructive cannibalism." ③ Since the original discovery, six species of Dracula ants have been discovered. ④ Worker ants scratch the skin of the larvae in their own colony's nursery, making them bleed. Then, they chew on the larvae, drink the blood and regurgitate it to the queen — leaving the larvae alive, but scarred.

10 다음 글의 요지로 가장 적절한 것은?

In Costa Rica just 23 percent of adults go on to be educated at tertiary level. And those who do so are likely to really notice the benefits. Tertiary-educated adults there earn around double that of their peers with lower levels of educational attainment. Younger Costa Ricans who have received a tertiary education experienced unemployment rates five or more percentage points lower in 2017 than in 2007. Actually, it is in respect of the gender gap where the benefits are perhaps the most visible. In Costa Rica the earnings of tertiary-educated women are closest to their male counterparts - although they are still seven percent lower.

① Costa Rican women earn less than men in most sectors.
② In Costa Rica, less than half of students decide to pursue higher education.
③ It is expensive for young Costa Ricans to go to college after graduating from high school.
④ In Costa Rica, people with higher education experience more advantages than others with lower education level.

기적사 DAY 06

01 밑줄 친 부분과 의미가 가장 가까운 것은?

Man has continued to be disobedient to authorities who tried to muzzle new thoughts and to the authority of long-established opinions which declared a change to be nonsense.

① express ② assert
③ suppress ④ spread

02 밑줄 친 부분과 의미가 가장 가까운 것은?

Don't be pompous. You don't want your writing to be too informal and colloquial, but you also don't want to sound like someone you're not—like your professor or boss, for instance, or the Rhodes scholar teaching assistant.

① presumptuous ② casual
③ formal ④ genuine

03 밑줄 친 부분과 의미가 가장 가까운 것은?

Surgeons were forced to call it a day because they couldn't find the right tools for the job.

① initiate ② finish
③ wait ④ cancel

04 대화 중 가장 어색한 것은?

① A: I'd like to make a reservation for tomorrow, please.
  B: Certainly. For what time?
② A: Are you ready to order?
  B: Yes, I'd like the soup, please.
③ A: How's your risotto?
  B: Yes, we have risotto with mushroom and cheese.
④ A: Would you like a dessert?
  B: Not for me, thanks.

05 밑줄 친 부분 중 어법상 가장 옳지 않은 것은?

His survival ① over the years since independence in 1961 does not alter the fact that the discussion of real policy choices in a public manner has hardly ② never occurred. In fact, there have always been ③ a number of important policy issues ④ which Nyerere has had to argue through the NEC.

06 밑줄 친 부분 중 어법상 가장 옳지 않은 것은?

I'm ① pleased that I have enough clothes with me. American men are generally bigger than Japanese men so ② it's very difficult to find clothes in Chicago that ③ fits me. ④ What is a medium size in Japan is a small size here.

07 밑줄 친 부분 중 어법상 가장 옳지 않은 것은?

Blue Planet II, a nature documentary ① produced by the BBC, left viewers ② heartbroken after showing the extent ③ to which plastic ④ affects on the ocean.

08 글의 흐름상 빈칸에 들어갈 말로 가장 적절한 것은?

"Highly conscientious employees do a series of things better than the rest of us," says University of Illinois psychologist Brent Roberts, who studies conscientiousness. Roberts owes their success to "hygiene" factors. Conscientious people have a tendency to organize their lives well. A disorganized, unconscientious person might lose 20 or 30 minutes rooting through their files to find the right document, an inefficient experience conscientious folks tend to avoid. Basically, by being conscientious, people _____ they'd otherwise create for themselves.

① deal with setbacks ② do thorough work
③ follow norms ④ sidestep stress

09 글의 흐름상 빈칸에 들어갈 말로 가장 적절한 것은?

Climate change, deforestation, widespread pollution and the sixth mass extinction of biodiversity all define living in our world today—an era that has come to be known as "the Anthropocene". These crises are underpinned by production and consumption which greatly exceeds global ecological limits, but blame is far from evenly shared. The world's 42 wealthiest people own as much as the poorest 3.7 billion, and they generate far greater environmental impacts. Some have therefore proposed using the term "Capitalocene" to describe this era of ecological devastation and growing inequality, reflecting capitalism's logic of endless growth and _____.

① the better world that is still within our reach
② the accumulation of wealth in fewer pockets
③ an effective response to climate change
④ a burning desire for a more viable future

10 글의 흐름상 빈칸에 들어갈 말로 가장 적절한 것은?

Ever since the time of ancient Greek tragedy, Western culture has been haunted by the figure of the revenger. He or she stands on a whole series of borderlines: between civilization and barbarity, between _____ and the community's need for the rule of law, between the conflicting demands of justice and mercy. Do we have a right to exact revenge against those who have destroyed our loved ones? Or should we leave vengeance to the law or to the gods? And if we do take action into our own hands, are we not reducing ourselves to the same moral level as the original perpetrator of murderous deeds?

① redemption of the revenger from a depraved condition
② divine vengeance on human atrocities
③ moral depravity of the corrupt politicians
④ an individual's accountability to his or her own conscience

01 밑줄 친 부분과 의미가 가장 가까운 것은?

When we find the grave, we take out the dirt and eventually clean the body, document it, and exhume it.

① explore ② exploit
③ express ④ excavate

02 밑줄 친 부분과 의미가 가장 가까운 것은?

It's going to be the most frigid day of the winter today, with temperatures dipping to minus 12 degrees in Seoul and even lower in some other cities and made frostier by a heavy wind chill, weather forecasters said.

① fake ② fallible
③ formal ④ freezing

03 밑줄 친 부분과 의미가 가장 가까운 것은?

The next administration needs to first have emphasis on abolishing regulations to lay the ground for brisk investment.

① surrender ② hesitate
③ initiate ④ stress

04 대화 중 가장 어색한 것은?

① A: Would you like some drink?
  B: Yes, could I have some soda please?
② A: Do you know where my coat is?
  B: I hung it on the hanger.
③ A: My father taught me valuable lessons.
  B: Historical lessons should be passed on to the next generation.
④ A: We should be more careful when handling this car.
  B: You are right. But it's not as easy as it seems.

05 밑줄 친 부분 중 어법상 가장 옳지 않은 것은?

A Harvard education that currently costs $100,000 may therefore end up ① costing half a million dollars for an infant born today. ② Millions of workers who retired with pensions ③ for the 1960s and 1970s found that inflation pushed up costs far beyond their ④ expected expenses.

06 밑줄 친 부분 중 어법상 가장 옳지 않은 것은?

The linkage between systems and services is ① critical to any discussion of infrastructure. Although it is the performance of the hardware ② what is of immediate concern ③ following an earthquake, it is actually the loss of services that these systems provide that ④ is the real loss to the public.

07 밑줄 친 부분 중 어법상 가장 옳지 않은 것은?

Feelings may ① affect various aspects of your eating, ② including your motivation to eat, your food choices, ③ where and with whom you eat, and the speed ④ which you eat.

08 밑줄 친 (A), (B)에 들어갈 말로 가장 적절한 것은?

Hogan and Hogan (1993) suggested that the relationship between conscientiousness and performance may vary by job type and hypothesized that conscientiousness would be negatively related to performance in occupations where creativity is important. ___(A)___, Chamorro-Premuzic (2006) found that conscientiousness was positively related to conventional, well-defined academic measures such as written examination and negatively related to less conventional measures such as an original research study, which were better predicted by creative thinking. But ___(B)___, empirical studies investigating the relationship between creative performance and conscientiousness have found mixed results, with some showing a positive relationship (e.g., McCrae, 1987), some showing a negative relationship (e.g., Wolfradt & Pretz, 2001), and some showing no relationship.

	(A)	(B)
①	Likewise	as a result
②	Conversely	on the whole
③	Similarly	overall
④	For example	unfortunately

09 다음 글의 요지로 가장 적절한 것은?

During the International Geological Congress held in Cape Town, a group of scientists announced the Anthropocene, an epoch in the earth's history defined most prominently by human activity. One piece of evidence, that scientists believe future archaeologists would use to recognize this era, is the prevalence of fossilized chicken bones; according to them, the global domestication of a vast number of chickens is one of the defining features of the Anthropocene. In the last 50 years, livestock populations have exploded. Chickens, cows and pigs now number in the billions, far outnumbering the human population. This change has had clear and dramatic consequences for the world we live in, not least through the emission of massive amounts of climate-altering greenhouse gases (GHGs). Estimates vary, but a conservative calculation provided by the United Nations Food and Agriculture Organization suggests that livestock production is responsible for 18 percent of global anthropogenic GHGs. Assuming this calculation to be correct, livestock produces more GHGs than the entire global transport system directly contributes.

① The global livestock industry produces more GHGs than any other sector.
② The announcement of the Anthropocene as a new geological epoch has lead to intensive debates.
③ The emergence of a new epoch has partly been brought about by increased livestock populations.
④ GHGs are one of the largest contributors to climate change and to the more frequent extreme weather events.

10 다음 글의 요지로 가장 적절한 것은?

Historically, there are two schools of thought on revenge. The Bible, in Exodus 21:23, instructs us to "give life for life, eye for eye, tooth for tooth, hand for hand, foot for foot" to punish an offender. But more than 2,000 years later, Martin Luther King Jr., responded, "The old law of 'an eye for an eye' leaves everybody blind." Which is right? As psychologists explore the mental machinery behind revenge, it turns out both can be, depending on who and where you are. If you're a power-seeker, revenge can serve to remind others you're not to be trifled with. If you live in a society where the rule of law is weak, revenge provides a way to keep order. But revenge comes at a price. Instead of helping you move on with your life, it can leave you dwelling on the situation and remaining unhappy, psychologists' research finds.

① Pursuing revenge is human nature.
② Revenge can have either positive or negative effects.
③ People who seek revenge are driven by anger and violence.
④ Taking your own revenge is necessary if the law is not strong enough.

기적사 DAY 08

01 밑줄 친 부분과 의미가 가장 가까운 것은?

Recently, NASA <u>initiated</u> a project called "Ultra Space Program" to understand how space affects human's dermal health.

① asserted ② coordinated
③ loitered ④ launched

02 밑줄 친 부분과 의미가 가장 가까운 것은?

Although most spam messages, usually of a commercial nature sent out in bulk, are <u>innocuous</u> and easy to delete, some are not.

① harmless ② venenose
③ casual ④ malicious

03 밑줄 친 부분과 의미가 가장 가까운 것은?

She doesn't want to <u>make up to</u> people to gain their trust at any private end.

① flatter ② migrate
③ notify ④ cancel

04 대화 중 가장 어색한 것은?

① A: How do you motivate yourself?
　B: I want to be motivated so that I can make great achievements.
② A: Do you believe in superstitions?
　B: No, superstitions are not based on scientific evidence.
③ A: I wish I had a friend in the neighborhood.
　B: Maybe you should go outside and find someone of an age with you to get along with.
④ A: It's been years since I went to the movie theatre.
　B: It seems like you need some time to catch up with the new releases.

05 밑줄 친 부분 중 어법상 가장 옳지 않은 것은?

① <u>During</u> her childhood years, the artist Tammy Rahr spent a lot of time outdoors ② <u>making</u> things from flowers and dirt. Then Tammy and her family ③ <u>moved from</u> the woodlands of New York State to an urban city outside of Los Angeles, California. The experience made her more ④ <u>aware</u> what was going on in the world.

06 밑줄 친 부분 중 어법상 가장 옳지 않은 것은?

① Building in regular "your time," however, can provide numerous benefits, all of which ② help to make life a little bit sweeter and a little bit more manageable. Unfortunately, many individuals ③ struggle reaching goals ④ due to an inability to prioritize their own needs.

07 밑줄 친 부분 중 어법상 가장 옳지 않은 것은?

Still, many believe ① that we will eventually ② reach a point ③ at which conflict with the finite nature of resources ④ are inevitable.

08 주어진 문장이 들어갈 위치로 가장 적절한 것은?

There is such a thing as being too organized, however.

The positive effect of conscientiousness is related to the fact that it provides continuity and predictability of action. (①) It also helps you organize and plan ahead so that you don't need to try everything on the fly. (②) Pedantry, a neurotic adherence to routine and perfectionism are extreme examples of conscientiousness. (③) All things must always be done in a particular way and perfectly. (④) A supervisor can become a painful micro-manager. In the worst case, decisions take longer, and the ability to improvise and prioritize is lost. Extreme conscientiousness can also expose you to rapid burnout.

09 빈칸 (A), (B)에 들어갈 표현으로 가장 적절한 것은?

"Anthropocene" is a widely proposed term for the geological epoch that covers human impact on our planet. But it is not ____(A)____ with "climate change," nor can it be covered by "environmental problems." Bigger and more shocking, the Anthropocene encapsulates the evidence that human pressures became so profound around the middle of the 20th century that we blew a planetary gasket. Hello, new Earth System. Hello, Anthropocene. The phrase "Earth System" refers to the entirety of our planet's interacting physical, chemical, biological, and human processes. Enabled by new data-collecting technologies like satellites and ever more powerful computer modeling, Earth System science reframes how we understand our planet. Climate is just one element of this system; if we focus on that alone, we will ____(B)____ the complexity of the danger. The term "environment" helps us understand ourselves as part of ecosystems, but fails to capture the newness of our current situation. We have always lived in the environment; only very recently just as Asia began its skyrocketing development, did we begin living in the altered Earth System of the Anthropocene.

	(A)	(B)
①	unanimous	mistake
②	anonymous	misplace
③	continuous	misbelieve
④	synonymous	misunderstand

10 다음 글의 내용과 일치하는 것은?

In June 2010, the usually mild-mannered Derrick Bird went on a gun rampage in Cumbria, killing 12 people, injuring 11 others and, finally, shooting himself. Bird had set out from his house with a double-barrelled, sawn-off shotgun and a .22 rifle. His first victims were his twin brother, David, and their family solicitor, Kevin Commons, who he wrongly believed were plotting to send him to prison for tax evasion. Next were fellow taxi drivers who'd taunted him over his bald head and disheveled clothes. Darren Rewcastle was the first. Bird pulled up at the taxi rank in Whitehaven, beckoned him over, and then shot him in the face and stomach. He died where he fell. Bird also shot and injured three other cabbies. After that, Bird began firing indiscriminately at passers-by before finally driving to nearby woods and shooting himself. At an inquest into the deaths, psychologist Dr. Adrian West said that the 'bitter and resentful' Bird blamed society for his own shortcomings, and took revenge rather than just killing himself.

① A total of 13 people died because of Bird's killing spree.
② Bird had been insulted about his appearance by his siblings.
③ Bird thought his fellow drivers were planning to put him in jail.
④ All of Bird's victims were his original targets.

기적사 DAY 09

01 밑줄 친 부분과 의미가 가장 가까운 것은?

It had the right to open preliminary investigations, an inquiry into unfamiliar or questionable activities, and to interrogate people officially.

① spread
② intrigue
③ question
④ intimidate

02 밑줄 친 부분과 의미가 가장 가까운 것은?

The realistic style and meticulous observation, the act of making and recording a measurement, of the artist is well represented.

① malleable
② precise
③ genuine
④ mischievous

03 밑줄 친 부분과 의미가 가장 가까운 것은?

Without sheets of the music; the sounds produced by singers or musical instruments we could not pass down our music to future generations.

① compel
② wait
③ dispatch
④ transfer

04 대화 중 가장 어색한 것은?

① A: Do you have any sibling?
   B: I have two older sisters.
② A: I am looking for a recipe book for beginners.
   B: You should go and search the right corner.
③ A: Don't forget to look both sides when you cross the street.
   B: Sure, I should also make sure the green light is on.
④ A: It was a bad choice to take the subway during the rush hour.
   B: You might get caught in the traffic jam in the rush hour.

05 밑줄 친 부분 중 어법상 가장 옳지 않은 것은?

① Despite the number of books he owned in total ② is simply unknown, an episode about his passion for books is well-known: he carried ③ so many books that he was able to pull book after book out of his pocket when a student tried ④ to show off his knowledge of Greek writers.

06 밑줄 친 부분 중 어법상 가장 옳지 않은 것은?

When we want something ① badly for our children, so badly that we behave in ways ② that aren't helpful for our kids, it can mean we're trying to fulfill a need for ourselves. ③ It's normal to feel good when your child wins, it's normal to want him to win, ④ and when you need him to win in order to feel good about yourself, you have a problem.

07 밑줄 친 부분 중 어법상 가장 옳지 않은 것은?

Once we ① arrive the refuge at ② about 10:00 am, we will begin our six-hour hike, ③ searching for birds and ④ learning about the plants and animals of the refuge.

08 주어진 문장 다음에 이어질 글의 순서로 가장 적절한 것은?

There are obvious benefits that come with being conscientious, such as the ability to more easily achieve one's goals due to their self-discipline and determination.

(A) One study found that those who were described as conscientious at a young age by their parents and teachers lived longer lives, while another found connections between this personality trait and lower blood pressure, lower rate of diabetes and stroke, and fewer joint problems.

(B) But there also are additional ones which are certainly worth noting as they pertain to one's health: according to Harvard Health, conscientiousness is linked most consistently to good health.

(C) Now, why are consciousness individuals also healthier individuals? Scientists say the answer is simple and obvious. They have better health habits. People who possess this quality are less likely to adopt harmful behaviors, such as smoking or heavy drinking, and more likely to take to healthy ones.

① (A) - (B) - (C) ② (A) - (C) - (B)
③ (B) - (A) - (C) ④ (B) - (C) - (A)

09 주어진 문장 다음에 이어질 글의 순서로 가장 적절한 것은?

The chemical and biological signatures of our species are everywhere.

(A) In this newly designated epoch, our species' impact on the oceans, the land, and the atmosphere has become an inescapable feature of the Earth.

(B) Transported around the globe by fierce atmospheric winds, relentless ocean currents, and the capacious cargo-holds of millions of fossil-fuel-powered vehicles, nowhere on Earth is free from humanity's imprint. Pristine nature has permanently blinked out of existence.

(C) These planetary changes have been characterized by geographers, geologists, and climate scientists as the end of one geological epoch—the Holocene—and the start of the next, the Anthropocene.

① (B) - (A) - (C)
② (B) - (C) - (A)
③ (C) - (B) - (A)
④ (C) - (A) - (B)

10 밑줄 친 (A), (B)에 들어갈 말로 가장 적절한 것은?

Kevin Carlsmith and his colleagues set up a group investment game with college students where if everyone cooperated, everyone would benefit equally, whereas if someone refused to invest his or her money, that person would benefit at the group's expense. A secret experimenter (called a free rider) in each group convinced the group members to invest equally. But when it came time to put up the money, the free riders didn't go along with the agreed-upon plan. ___(A)___, the free riders earned an average of $5.59, while the other players earned around $2.51. Here's the revenge part. Carlsmith offered some groups a way to get back at the free rider: They could spend some of their own earnings to financially punish the group's defector. Everyone who was given the chance for revenge took it, and they predicted that they would feel much better after they got their revenge. ___(B)___, the results showed that the students who got revenge reported feeling worse than those who didn't.

	(A)	(B)
①	Hence	Furthermore
②	As a result	However
③	Nevertheless	Consequently
④	For instance	On the other hand

기적사 DAY 10

01 밑줄 친 부분과 의미가 가장 가까운 것은?

A cold and snowy snap persisted for a couple of weeks in the country in mid-February this year.

① relieved ② refrained
③ persevered ④ suppressed

02 밑줄 친 부분과 의미가 가장 가까운 것은?

Some people just get irritated for no apparent reason, and it might be better to avoid all their triggers in daily life and get them proper counseling by specialists.

① bothered ② interested
③ probed ④ presumptuous

03 밑줄 친 부분과 의미가 가장 가까운 것은?

By the advent of the GPS system, drivers rely on this navigation device to reach their destination quickly and properly.

① resort ② resume
③ cease ④ regain

04 대화 중 가장 어색한 것은?

① A: The elevator stops on every floor.
  B: That's why it takes so long.
② A: Excuse me, do you have any pain killer?
  B: Pain can cause great amount of stress.
③ A: I need to buy a Christmas present for my cousin.
  B: Do you need any recommendations on what to buy?
④ A: Do you remember when we used to hang out in the playground after school?
  B: Of course. I can never forget the days back then.

05 밑줄 친 부분 중 어법상 가장 옳지 않은 것은?

"Sit there until you finish" may be ① how we learned, and may also be the only way you feel able to achieve your goal, but think about it: the experience of eating ② a pile of unwanted cabbage until they feel sick is hardly ③ never going to make children ④ jump for joy the next time it is served.

06 밑줄 친 부분 중 어법상 가장 옳지 않은 것은?

For this reason, ① recognizing that our first impressions of others also may be perceptual errors. To help avoid ② committing these errors, engage in perception checking, which ③ means that we consider a series of questions to confirm or challenge our perceptions of ④ others and their behaviors.

07 밑줄 친 부분 중 어법상 가장 옳지 않은 것은?

Seeing the hero ① battle obstacles and overcome crises ② engage the viewer in an emotional struggle ③ in which the drama's storyline and its conclusion events carry an emotional impact that would otherwise be ④ missing.

08 다음 글의 요지로 가장 적절한 것은?

The "Big Five" personality traits do seem to get at something meaningful about human personality. They certainly don't capture everything, but Openness to Experience, Conscientiousness, Extraversion, Agreeableness, and Neuroticism are traits that can be measured with a high degree of stability from one test to the next. One of these traits — conscientiousness — is, unsurprisingly, strongly related to how people perform at work. But why, and in what settings? A paper published in PNAS used the data from more than 2,500 studies to summarize what we know about conscientiousness. Unexpectedly, the authors find that conscientiousness scores make less of a difference to people's performance when they're in high-complexity jobs such as a doctor, social worker, and attorney. Instead, they mainly seem to matter in low- or moderate-complexity jobs such as a factory worker, salesperson, and call center operator.

① It is impossible to measure a person's personality.
② Conscientiousness may matter less in certain careers.
③ Conscientiousness is the most important trait among the Big Five personality traits.
④ Conscientiousness is closely linked to one's job performance regardless of job types.

09 다음 글의 밑줄 친 부분 중 문맥상 단어의 쓰임이 적절하지 않은 것은?

Most of us agree that human use of the earth's natural resources has caused environmental effects ① extreme enough to require a new era. But what to call it? The term "Anthropocene" has been used by environmental scientists and scholars to ② designate a new epoch, but does the term have the force to name the political critique of climate change that such a moment demands? Jason W. Moore introduced the term "Capitalocene" to provide more analytical focus, arguing that "Anthropocene" does not name the system that produces modern environmental ③ catastrophes: capitalism. By focusing on the "anthro," we maintain the delusion that all humans are equal participants in this global change, ④ acknowledging the idea that human-caused climate change is largely driven by the consumption of resources within developed countries fed by an economic system structured around compounding economic growth.

10 글의 흐름상 빈칸에 들어갈 말로 가장 적절한 것은?

In the third one they will either decide to forgive, hold a grudge but do nothing – or take or plot revenge.

The desire to take revenge is hardwired into us from a young age. (①) In other words, to want to take revenge is instinctive behavior. (②) In a society, it prevents people from harming others for fear of reprisal and it dates back to long before biblical times. (③) Explaining revenge, Ann Macaskill, professor of health psychology at Sheffield Hallam University, said: When individuals are attacked in some way that feels unjust, they go through these psychological stages: a shock phase, an adjustment phase and a reaction phase. (④) In fact, vengefulness is quite normal in many circumstances and evolutionary psychologists suggest that the ability to take revenge is part of human nature.

기적사 복습 모의고사 1회

01 밑줄 친 부분과 의미가 가장 가까운 것은?

Man has continued to be disobedient to authorities who tried to muzzle new thoughts and to the authority of long-established opinions which declared a change to be nonsense.

① express ② assert
③ suppress ④ spread

02 밑줄 친 부분의 의미와 가장 가까운 것을 고르시오.

It is crucial for Tom to find an investor at this juncture.

① suspected ② debatable
③ enthusiastic ④ significant

03 밑줄 친 부분의 의미와 가장 먼 것을 고르시오.

Self-confident people believe in themselves and love themselves at any time.

① reliant ② assured
③ convinced ④ confidential

04 밑줄 친 부분의 의미와 가장 가까운 것을 고르시오.

She is on the fence about going to see the Mona Lisa at the Louvre Museum.

① anguished ② enthusiastic
③ apprehensive ④ undecided

05 밑줄 친 부분과 의미가 가장 가까운 것은?

Surgeons were forced to call it a day because they couldn't find the right tools for the job.

① initiate ② finish
③ wait ④ cancel

06 어법상 옳지 않은 것은?

① What you need to do is make a list of useful phone numbers.
② He was really embarrassed about it because he forbade me telling anyone.
③ Eventually Tom found a doctor who was able to cure her of her depression.
④ Jane ambled down the street, stopping occasionally to look in the shop windows.

07 Bulldog ant에 관한 다음 글의 내용과 일치하는 것은?

The most dangerous ant in the world is the bulldog ant (Myrmecia pyriformis) found in coastal regions in Australia. In attack it uses its sting and jaws simultaneously. There have been at least three human fatalities since 1936, the latest of whom was a Victorian farmer in 1988. The bulldog ant earned its name because of its ferocity and determination during an attack. It is extremely aggressive and shows little fear of human beings, stinging a number of times in quick succession and therefore injecting more venom with each bite. In an attack, the ant will hold on to its victim with long, toothed mandibles, curl its body underneath and thrust its long barbless sting into the skin. On a few occasions this sting has been enough to kill adults within 15 minutes.

① It is recorded as the world's most dangerous insect.
② No one has been killed because of its attack since 1989.
③ It was named based on its physical appearance.
④ It uses either its mandibles or poisoned sting to make an attack.

08 밑줄 친 부분 중 어법상 가장 옳지 않은 것은?

For this reason, ① recognizing that our first impressions of others also may be perceptual errors. To help avoid ② committing these errors, engage in perception checking, which ③ means that we consider a series of questions to confirm or challenge our perceptions of ④ others and their behaviors.

09 글의 제목으로 가장 적절한 것은?

Economists say that production of an information good involves high fixed costs but low marginal costs. The cost of producing the first copy of an information good may be substantial, but the cost of producing(or reproducing) additional copies is negligible. This sort of cost structure has many important implications. For example, cost-based pricing just doesn't work: a 10 or 20 percent markup on unit cost makes no sense when unit cost is zero. You must price your information goods according to consumer value, not according to your production cost.

① Securing the Copyright
② Pricing the Information Goods
③ Information as Intellectual Property
④ The Cost of Technological Change

10 밑줄 친 부분 중 글의 흐름상 가장 어색한 것은?

Marketization of higher education helps to relate higher education closely to the market and society and this accelerates the reform of higher education, and promotes the innovation of the education system. ① It also helps to change the traditional enclosed mode of school running into an open society-oriented model. ② It changes the policy of higher education institutions from creating conditions that will meet the various needs of students to focusing on the requirements and regulations of the government. ③ Of course, it is not that the basic spirit of the pursuit of knowledge and truth of higher education has changed in a modern society with a market economy. ④ But the development of higher education has been closely linked with social development, and higher education institutions must survive and develop in a competitive market economy. The main advantage of this market model is that it can continuously stimulate the higher education institutions to adapt to the changing economic and social situation.

11 밑줄 친 부분에 들어갈 말로 가장 적절한 것을 고르시오.

> Tobe: What are you doing here?
> Sharon: I was writing down my new-years resolution on my new planner.
> Tobe: Oh, is that your new planner?
> Sharon: Yes it is. I bought it today. I also made some plans for the new year.
> Tobe: Well done! Plans are essential. However there are moments in which you have no other choice but to _____.
> Sharon: I know, that happens. But knowing that I have a plan makes me feel safer even when I have to make adjustments.

① go bananas
② beat a dead horse
③ change horses in the middle of the stream
④ look like the cat that swallowed the canary

12 대화 중 가장 어색한 것은?

① A: How do you motivate yourself?
　B: I want to be motivated so that I can make great achievements.
② A: Do you believe in superstitions?
　B: No, superstitions are not based on scientific evidence.
③ A: I wish I had a friend in the neighborhood.
　B: Maybe you should go outside and find someone of an age with you to get along with.
④ A: It's been years since I went to the movie theatre.
　B: It seems like you need some time to catch up with the new releases.

13 우리말을 영어로 잘못 옮긴 것을 고르시오.

① 그를 당황하게 한 것은 그녀의 거절이 아니라 그녀의 무례함이었다.
→ It was not her refusal but her rudeness that perplexed him.
② 부모는 아이들 앞에서 그들의 말과 행동에 대해 아무리 신중해도 지나치지 않다.
→ Parents cannot be too careful about their words and actions before their children.
③ 환자들과 부상자들을 돌보기 위해 더 많은 의사가 필요했다.
→ More doctors were required to tend sick and wounded.
④ 설상가상으로, 또 다른 태풍이 곧 올 것이라는 보도가 있다.
→ To make matters worse, there is a report that another typhoon will arrive soon.

14 우리말을 영어로 잘못 옮긴 것을 고르시오.

① Tom은 명령에 복종해야 했기 때문에 군대에 있는 것을 싫어했다.
→ Tom hated being in the army because he had to obey commands.
② 우리의 최선의 노력에도 불구하고, 그와 접촉하는 것은 불가능하다는 것으로 드러났다.
→ In spite of our best endeavors, it has proven impossible to contact him.
③ 의사가 가자마자 William은 아들의 볼에 가볍게 입을 맞추었다.
→ As soon as the doctor went, William kissed his son lightly on his cheek.
④ 만약 당신이 폭력으로 공격당하면, 당신은 폭력으로 대응하지 않을 수 없다.
→ If you are attacked with violence, you cannot choose but respond with violence.

15 밑줄 친 (A), (B)에 들어갈 말로 가장 적절한 것은?

Kevin Carlsmith and his colleagues set up a group investment game with college students where if everyone cooperated, everyone would benefit equally, whereas if someone refused to invest his or her money, that person would benefit at the group's expense. A secret experimenter (called a free rider) in each group convinced the group members to invest equally. But when it came time to put up the money, the free riders didn't go along with the agreed-upon plan. ____(A)____, the free riders earned an average of $5.59, while the other players earned around $2.51. Here's the revenge part. Carlsmith offered some groups a way to get back at the free rider: They could spend some of their own earnings to financially punish the group's defector. Everyone who was given the chance for revenge took it, and they predicted that they would feel much better after they got their revenge. ____(B)____, the results showed that the students who got revenge reported feeling worse than those who didn't.

	(A)	(B)
①	Hence	Furthermore
②	As a result	However
③	Nevertheless	Consequently
④	For instance	On the other hand

16 글의 흐름상 빈칸에 들어갈 말로 가장 적절한 것은?

"Highly conscientious employees do a series of things better than the rest of us," says University of Illinois psychologist Brent Roberts, who studies conscientiousness. Roberts owes their success to "hygiene" factors. Conscientious people have a tendency to organize their lives well. A disorganized, unconscientious person might lose 20 or 30 minutes rooting through their files to find the right document, an inefficient experience conscientious folks tend to avoid. Basically, by being conscientious, people _____ they'd otherwise create for themselves.

① deal with setbacks ② do thorough work
③ follow norms ④ sidestep stress

17 다음 글의 요지로 가장 적절한 것은?

During the International Geological Congress held in Cape Town, a group of scientists announced the Anthropocene, an epoch in the earth's history defined most prominently by human activity. One piece of evidence, that scientists believe future archaeologists would use to recognize this era, is the prevalence of fossilized chicken bones; according to them, the global domestication of a vast number of chickens is one of the defining features of the Anthropocene. In the last 50 years, livestock populations have exploded. Chickens, cows and pigs now number in the billions, far outnumbering the human population. This change has had clear and dramatic consequences for the world we live in, not least through the emission of massive amounts of climate-altering greenhouse gases (GHGs). Estimates vary, but a conservative calculation provided by the United Nations Food and Agriculture Organization suggests that livestock production is responsible for 18 percent of global anthropogenic GHGs. Assuming this calculation to be correct, livestock produces more GHGs than the entire global transport system directly contributes.

① The global livestock industry produces more GHGs than any other sector.
② The announcement of the Anthropocene as a new geological epoch has lead to intensive debates.
③ The emergence of a new epoch has partly been brought about by increased livestock populations.
④ GHGs are one of the largest contributors to climate change and to the more frequent extreme weather events.

18 다음 글의 밑줄 친 부분 중 문맥상 단어의 쓰임이 적절하지 않은 것은?

Info products provide several ① benefits, but the most significant benefit is the ability to productize your business so you can leverage your time and focus on growing your business. This helps you avoid the pitfalls of entrepreneurial burnout, and once you ramp up to a ② well-oiled productizing machine, you can continue the growth by hiring a virtual assistant. Moreover, there's limitless inventory with info products, which means your sales potential is ③ restricted and your order fulfillment process is streamlined and automatic. In other words, by selling a digital product, you do all the legwork in advance and only need ④ minimal maintenance — mainly marketing — on the back-end. Once your storefront is set up, your customers can purchase as many info products as they'd like without you having to fulfill orders manually.

19 주어진 문장이 들어갈 위치로 가장 적절한 것은?

Instead, there are several somewhat different products some of which are close substitutes.

Digital materials typically have the property that it is very costly to produce the first copy and very cheap to produce subsequent copies. It is often said, for example, that the "first copy costs" are more than 70% of the cost of an academic journal. (①) Cost structures of this form pose special problems for pricing. The first problem is that it is very difficult to sustain a competitive market with this sort of cost structure. (②) Economists define a purely competitive market to be one where there are "several" producers of an identical commodity. The markets for wheat, corn, shares of IBM stock, etc. are all examples of purely competitive markets. (③) The market for automobiles is not purely competitive because there are not multiple producers of identical products. (④) Economists call this a situation of monopolistic competition. The market for academic journals (or other sorts of information goods) tends to be much more like the automobile market than the wheat market. The high-fixed-cost/low-incremental-cost structure forces this outcome.

20 주어진 문장 다음에 이어질 글의 순서로 가장 적절한 것은?

There are obvious benefits that come with being conscientious, such as the ability to more easily achieve one's goals due to their self-discipline and determination.

(A) One study found that those who were described as conscientious at a young age by their parents and teachers lived longer lives, while another found connections between this personality trait and lower blood pressure, lower rate of diabetes and stroke, and fewer joint problems.

(B) But there also are additional ones which are certainly worth noting as they pertain to one's health: according to Harvard Health, conscientiousness is linked most consistently to good health.

(C) Now, why are consciousness individuals also healthier individuals? Scientists say the answer is simple and obvious. They have better health habits. People who possess this quality are less likely to adopt harmful behaviors, such as smoking or heavy drinking, and more likely to take to healthy ones.

① (A) - (B) - (C) ② (A) - (C) - (B)
③ (B) - (A) - (C) ④ (B) - (C) - (A)

MEMO

01 밑줄 친 부분과 의미가 가장 가까운 것을 고르시오.

Tuesday night's season premiere of the TV show seemed to be trying to strike a balance between the show's convoluted mythology and its more human, character-driven dimension.

① ancient ② unrelated
③ complicated ④ otherworldly

02 밑줄 친 부분과 의미가 가장 가까운 것을 고르시오.

By the time we wound up the conversation, I knew that I would not be going to Geneva.

① initiated ② resumed
③ terminated ④ interrupted

03 밑줄 친 부분에 들어갈 말로 가장 적절한 것은?

A police sergeant with 15 years of experience was dismayed after being _____ for promotion in favor of a young officer.

① run over ② asked out
③ carried out ④ passed over

04 밑줄 친 부분에 들어갈 말로 가장 적절한 것을 고르시오.

A: How do you like your new neighborhood?
B: It's great for the most part. I love the clean air and the green environment.
A: Sounds like a lovely place to live.
B: Yes, but it's not without its drawbacks.
A: Like what?
B: For one, it doesn't have many different stores. For example, there's only one supermarket, so food is very expensive.
A: _____
B: You're telling me. But thank goodness. The city is building a new shopping center now. Next year, we'll have more options.

① How many supermarkets are there?
② Are there a lot of places to shop there?
③ It looks like you have a problem.
④ I want to move to your neighborhood.

05 밑줄 친 부분 중 어법상 옳은 것은?

Last week I was sick with the flu. When my father ① heard me sneezing and coughing, he opened my bedroom door to ask me ② that I needed anything. I was really happy to see his kind and caring face, but there wasn't ③ anything he could do it to ④ make the flu to go away.

06 어법상 옳은 것은?

① A week's holiday has been promised to all the office workers.
② She destined to live a life of serving others.
③ A small town seems to be preferable than a big city for raising children.
④ Top software companies are finding increasingly challenging to stay ahead.

07 우리말을 영어로 잘못 옮긴 것은?

① 예산은 처음 기대했던 것보다 약 25퍼센트 더 높다.
→ The budget is about 25% higher than originally expecting.
② 시스템 업그레이드를 위해 해야 될 많은 일이 있다.
→ There is a lot of work to be done for the system upgrade.
③ 그 프로젝트를 완성하는 데 최소 한 달, 어쩌면 더 긴 시간이 걸릴 것이다.
→ It will take at least a month, maybe longer to complete the project.
④ 월급을 두 배 받는 그 부서장이 책임을 져야 한다.
→ The head of the department, who receives twice the salary, has to take responsibility.

08 글의 흐름상 가장 적절하지 않은 문장은?

It seems to me possible to name four kinds of reading, each with a characteristic manner and purpose. The first is reading for information—reading to learn about a trade, or politics, or how to accomplish something. ① We read a newspaper this way, or most textbooks, or directions on how to assemble a bicycle. ② With most of this material, the reader can learn to scan the page quickly, coming up with what he needs and ignoring what is irrelevant to him, like the rhythm of the sentence, or the play of metaphor. ③ We also register a track of feeling through the metaphors and associations of words. ④ Courses in speed reading can help us read for this purpose, training the eye to jump quickly across the page.

09 <보기>의 문장이 들어갈 위치로 가장 적절한 것은?

<보기>
In this situation, we would expect to find less movement of individuals from one job to another because of the individual's social obligations toward the work organization to which he or she belongs and to the people comprising that organization.

Cultural differences in the meaning of work can manifest themselves in other aspects as well. (①) For example, in American culture, it is easy to think of work simply as a means to accumulate money and make a living. (②) In other cultures, especially collectivistic ones, work may be seen more as fulfilling an obligation to a larger group. (③) In individualistic cultures, it is easier to consider leaving one job and going to another because it is easier to separate jobs from the self. (④) A different job will just as easily accomplish the same goals.

10 글을 문맥에 가장 어울리는 순서대로 배열한 것은?

㉠ To navigate in the dark, a microbat flies with its mouth open, emitting high-pitched squeaks that humans cannot hear. Some of these sounds echo off flying insects as well as tree branches and other obstacles that lie ahead. The bat listens to the echo and gets an instantaneous picture in its brain of the objects in front of it.

㉡ Microbats, the small, insect-eating bats found in North America, have tiny eyes that don't look like they'd be good for navigating in the dark and spotting prey.

㉢ From the use of echolocation, or sonar, as it is also called, a microbat can tell a great deal about a mosquito or any other potential meal. With extreme exactness, echolocation allows microbats to perceive motion, distance, speed, movement, and shape. Bats can also detect and avoid obstacles no thicker than a human hair.

㉣ But, actually, microbats can see as well as mice and other small mammals. The nocturnal habits of bats are aided by their powers of echolocation, a special ability that makes feeding and flying at night much easier than one might think.

① ㉠-㉢-㉡-㉣
② ㉡-㉣-㉠-㉢
③ ㉡-㉢-㉣-㉠
④ ㉠-㉣-㉢-㉡

01 밑줄 친 부분과 의미가 가장 가까운 것을 고르시오.

Korea's education system is globally renowned for its high rigor and standards which makes Korean the powerhouse about IT, the branch of engineering that deals with the use of computers and telecommunications.

① prestigious ② relative
③ quarrelsome ④ otherworldly

02 밑줄 친 부분과 의미가 가장 가까운 것을 고르시오.

Police also arrested another suspect staying nearby and have been interrogating him about how he had made away with the bag.

① interrupted ② reconciled
③ stolen ④ nullified

03 밑줄 친 부분에 들어갈 말로 가장 적절한 것은?

Owning a pet helps us learn to _____ or take care of something other than ourselves.

① look after ② run over
③ make out ④ make up for

04 밑줄 친 부분에 들어갈 말로 가장 적절한 것을 고르시오.

A: What are you planning to do after graduation?
B: I've made several plans. Before I start work, I want to live abroad for at least a year.
A: A year? Why is that?
B: I want to improve my English. If I reside in an English-speaking country, I'll naturally learn to speak and write like a native.
A: That's interesting. Unlike you, I want to start working right away.
B: What's the reason for that?
A: As far as I heard, I should _____ when I can. If I get delayed, I think I'm going to lose my motivation.
B: I've also heard that a lot.

① set a ceiling on
② get the ball rolling
③ drive you up the wall
④ have my back to the wall

05 밑줄 친 부분 중 어법상 옳은 것은?

We feel little curiosity upon watching ① a Pony Express rider to deliver mail at the next outpost, but we feel great curiosity ② via suspense if that same rider is a Western hero ③ whose loses his horse to a hostile environment, overcomes rattlesnake bites, outsmarts evil-minded outlaws, ④ and otherwise fight his way triumphantly to the next outpost.

06 어법상 옳은 것은?

① Tom found it frustrated that Jane could not figure out the questions.
② Women's status in traditional society was clearly inferior than that of men.
③ William was allowed access to the prison for the first time a few days ago.
④ All the police officers equipped with shields to defend themselves against the rioters.

07 우리말을 영어로 잘못 옮긴 것은?

① 우리는 그녀의 증거가 과민성의 정도에 근거되어지고 있다는 것을 발견한다.
→ We find her evidence to base on a degree of oversensitivity.

② Tom이 경기 운영과 관련된 많은 것들을 평준화하는 데 한 시간이 걸렸다.
→ It took Tom an hour to equalize many things concerning the run of play.

③ 그녀는 물 한잔을 마시기 위해 문을 열었고 Tom이 현관에 서 있는 것을 발견했다.
→ She opened the door to drink a glass of water and found Tom standing in the hall.

④ 월요일에 발견된 그의 유골은 골목에 있는 쓰레기봉투에 넣어져 있었다.
→ His ashes, which were found on Monday, had been placed in a rubbish bag in an alley.

08 빈칸 (A), (B)에 들어갈 표현으로 가장 적절한 것은?

How to Read a Book by Mortimer J. Adler and Charles Van Doren is one of the most celebrated classic works in the reading literature. It was first published in 1940 and then revisited and updated in an edition that was released in 1972. Since its publication millions of copies have been sold and is still widely circulating among education circles as a required reading text. It's true that the book was conceived in a 'pre-digital' era but its content is still ___(A)___ even today when the digital text is predominantly prevalent. In *How to Read A Book*, Van Doren and Mortimer talked about four main levels of reading: elementary reading, inspectional reading, analytical reading, and syntopical reading. Note here that the authors deliberately named them levels and not kinds because, according to them, kinds can be distinct from one another while levels denote a notion of embeddedness with lower levels included in higher ones. In other words, levels of reading are ___(B)___.

	(A)	(B)
①	valid	separate
②	extraneous	transient
③	relevant	cumulative
④	esoteric	complicated

09 주어진 문장이 들어갈 위치로 가장 적절한 것은?

Individualist cultures stress the importance of each person taking care of his or her self without depending on others for assistance.

Workers in an individualist culture are more likely to value their own well-being over the good of the group. (①) Contrast this with a collectivist culture where people might sacrifice their own comfort for the greater good of everyone else. (②) Such differences can affect nearly every aspect of behavior ranging from the career a person chooses, the products they buy, and the social issues that they care about. (③) Approaches to health care, for example, are influenced by these tendencies. (④) Those in collectivist cultures may instead stress sharing the burden of care with the group as a whole.

10 밑줄 친 부분 중 글의 흐름상 가장 어색한 것은?

The Malayan flying fox is hailed as the largest bat in the world. This endangered bat is a megaspecies that has made its home in the tropical region of Southeast Asia. ① This bat is a superb flyer and can navigate towering canopies with no problems. ② However, when it comes to landing, they crash and fumble into their destination, often smashing into bundles of branches and piles of forest foliage just to grab a bite to eat. ③ Also, unlike their smaller, microbat kin, the flying fox is a large mammal with excellent eyesight. ④ The darkness of the night doesn't stop this nocturnal animal from getting where it needs to go, and it finds food using squeaks and chirps to map out the area. Instead of using sound waves to pinpoint where they are and what's around them, they use their well-developed peepers to scour their terrain.

01 밑줄 친 부분과 의미가 가장 가까운 것을 고르시오.

The director who received an Oscar was extremely reticent about his personal life.

① prestigious ② ancient
③ placid ④ mutual

02 밑줄 친 부분과 의미가 가장 가까운 것을 고르시오.

In this case, how can you make up with your ideal with reality?

① flatter ② terminate
③ notify ④ reconcile

03 밑줄 친 부분에 들어갈 말로 가장 적절한 것은?

The fact of the matter is, drug abuse is a primary factor to _____ your work performance and mental ability.

① make up to ② mess up
③ pass over ④ pass down

04 밑줄 친 부분에 들어갈 말로 가장 적절한 것을 고르시오.

Tom: Who is the person you respect the most?
Eva: It's a cliche answer, but my dad is the most respectable person to me.
Tom: Why do you say so?
Eva: He's a _____. He keeps all his promises.
Tom: That's not an easy thing to do although it does seem so.
Eva: I know. There's a lot to learn from him.

① con artist ② rank and file
③ a man of his word ④ a man of the world

05 밑줄 친 부분 중 어법상 옳은 것은?

After an hour, ① my frustration reached to its climax, when I ② saw a man to ride a pony with a brand-new saddle. When he looked at our door, he just passed by, which ③ caused me break into tears. Then, he said, "Kid, do you know ④ a boy named Lennie Steffens?" "That's me," I replied in tears.

06 어법상 옳은 것은?

① She thinks she is morally superior as the rest of us.
② On a hot day, it is lovely to hear the chink of ice in a glass.
③ When this pore space is completely filled with water, the soil saturates.
④ If everyone is made carry ID cards, it will foster the idea that we are all under suspicion.

07 우리말을 영어로 잘못 옮긴 것은?

① 지속적인 관심이 필요한 그 여자는 친척들에 의해 보살핌을 받는다.
  → The woman, who needs constant attention, is cared for by relatives.
② John이 그녀를 구하기 위해 땅속에 굴을 파는 데 몇 시간이 더 걸렸다.
  → It took several more hours John to dig a tunnel in the ground to rescue her.
③ 네 명의 사진작가가 찍은 이 작품들은 영화 역사상 가장 눈부신 시간을 떠올리게 한다.
  → These works, taken by four photographers, recall the most dazzling time in movie history.
④ 즉각적 만족이 일반적인 사회에서, 인내는 우리 아이들이 배워야 할 가치다.
  → In a society where instant gratification is the norm, patience is a value our children need to learn.

08 다음 글의 요지로 가장 적절한 것은?

Skimming is sometimes referred to as gist reading. It may help in order to know what the text is about at its most basic level. You might typically do this with a magazine or newspaper and this would help you mentally and quickly list those articles which you might consider for a deeper read. You might also skim to search for a name in a telephone directory. You can reach a speed count of even 700 words per minute if you train yourself well in some particular methods. Comprehension is of course very low and understanding of overall content is very superficial. It will certainly save you a lot of time, but for the reason stated above, it is not the best way to read. However, skimming is useful when your goal is to preview the text to get a better idea of what it's about. It will help prepare you for deeper learning.

① Skimming skills can be developed through training.
② Skimming is the most important skill of speed reading.
③ Skimming enables readers to fully understand the text.
④ Skimming is a good way to get an overview of the text.

09 다음 글의 요지로 가장 적절한 것은?

While individualism/collectivism can be measured in any culture, much of the research on individualism/collectivism so far has been carried out on East Asian and Western cultures. Researchers have found that Western cultures tend to be more individualistic while East Asian cultures tend to be more collectivistic. However, it's important to remember that many factors can influence individualism/collectivism, so individuals within a culture can also differ in their levels of independence/interdependence. Individualism/collectivism can even be affected by the situational context. For example, one study found that individuals from two different cultural backgrounds became more individualistic when shown images relating to an individualistic culture and more collectivistic when shown images relating to a collectivistic culture. In other words, as humans, we switch between cultural frames depending on the context.

① Each culture should be respected.
② Individualism and collectivism are relative.
③ Wider research on individualism/collectivism is necessary.
④ Western people are individualistic and East Asians are collectivistic.

10 주어진 문장이 들어갈 위치로 가장 적절한 것은?

As a result, bats exhaust critical stores of fat they need to get through the winter, which leads to starvation.

Over the past decade, an epidemic called white-nose syndrome has devastated bat populations in the eastern United States and Canada. More than 6 million bats have died. (①) Some species may go extinct. (②) The culprit is the invasive fungus *Pseudogymnoascus destructans (Pd.)*, which is not native to North America. (③) It infects cave-dwelling bats, damages their wings, causes them to wake more frequently and raises their metabolism during winter hibernation. (④) Most caves where the fungus has appeared have seen bat die-offs of 90 percent or more.

01 밑줄 친 부분과 의미가 가장 가까운 것을 고르시오.

The future of our country is quite bright since robust and affirmative signs are being seen in many parts of its economy.

① unrelated　　② sturdy
③ placid　　　④ mutual

02 밑줄 친 부분과 의미가 가장 가까운 것을 고르시오.

The official who revealed the content of confidential documents was subjected to a severe punishment.

① settled　　　② restrained
③ resumed　　④ disclosed

03 밑줄 친 부분에 들어갈 말로 가장 적절한 것은?

Some girls are _____ with losing weight and they have unhealthy eating habits.

① compelled　　② asked out
③ dispatched　④ obsessed

04 밑줄 친 부분에 들어갈 말을 순서대로 나열한 것을 고르시오.

A: Have you heard the news about Micheal Jackson?
B: You mean the news about his hidden son who is a pianist?
A: Yes, Micheal Jackson died several years ago. It's a bolt from the _____ sky to see his son all of a sudden.
B: I know. I didn't believe it at first. It just doesn't make sense.
A: Right. Micheal Jackson never mentioned his pianist son when he was alive.
B: Maybe the article we read was just _____ journalism.
A: What an awful reporter! He shouldn't mess with Micheal Jackson. He is still one of the most popular and renowned musicians around the world.
B: I agree with you. Everywhere he went, people rolled out the _____ carpet.

① blue － yellow － red　　② black － white － red
③ red － yellow － white　　④ blue － green － black

05 밑줄 친 부분 중 어법상 옳은 것은?

To prepare for the race, both Zach and Tony bought a specially made swimming suit that could minimize resistance against water and ① help them swimming faster. But they found out that ② this type of the special suit had not been allowed in previous races. Both Zach and Tony asked the swimming coach ③ that they could wear it. He said that ④ he would let them know before the race.

06 어법상 옳은 것은?

① Rationing has made easier to find some products like butter and meat.
② It points to a date posterior than the conquest of Alexander the Great.
③ The competition would expect to force the banks to reduce their costs.
④ The company was set up to buy and sell shares on behalf of investors.

07 우리말을 영어로 잘못 옮긴 것은?

① William이 2권을 완성하는 데 2년이 걸렸다.
  → It has taken William two years to complete two volumes.
② Jane은 주목받는 것을 좋아하는 그러한 사람들 중 한 명이다.
  → Jane is one of those people who loves to be the center of attention.
③ William은 Tom이 탈출할 수 없다고 확신하면서, 열쇠를 꺼내 문을 잠갔다.
  → William took out a key and locked the door, ensuring that Tom couldn't escape.
④ 테러 행위를 효과적으로 예방하고 저지할 수 있는 메커니즘을 개선할 필요가 있다.
  → There is a need to improve mechanisms to effectively prevent and deter acts of terrorism.

08 빈칸에 들어갈 표현으로 가장 적절한 것은?

In terms of outcomes, longitudinal research, the kind that follows kids for decades, tells a sad story. If your child is experiencing reading failure, it is almost as if he has contracted a chronic and debilitating disease. Kids who are not reading at grade level in first grade almost invariably remain poor fourth grade readers. Seventy four percent of struggling third grade readers still struggle in ninth grade, which in turn makes it hard to graduate from high school. It won't surprise you to know that kids who struggle in reading grow up to be adults who struggle to hold on to steady work; they are more likely to experience periods of prolonged unemployment, require welfare services, and are more likely to end up in jail. Reading experts call them "_____." Most of them don't have neurological problems. Their schools and, specifically, their primary school teachers have failed them.

① social misfits
② gifted readers
③ incompetent students
④ instructional casualties

09 빈칸에 들어갈 표현으로 가장 적절한 것은?

We think that _____.
This assumption derives support from the following considerations. First, individualist versus collectivist orientations have been found to influence pro-environmental behavior. Roughly, collectivist individuals are more likely to engage in a variety of pro-environmental behavior than are those with individualist tendencies, including resource conservation and green purchasing behavior. Further, a survey conducted in New Zealand by Semenova found that the more environmentally active group was more collectivist in its value orientation than was the less environmentally active group. Similar findings were also reported by Jia et al., who demonstrated that environmental activists were more likely to endorse self-transcendent values, while non-activists were more likely to endorse self-interest values. In addition, several studies within the framework of cultural worldview have suggested that individualist's worldviews are negatively related with concern about climate change, willingness to behave in climate-friendly ways, and acceptance of related policy measures.

① neither individualism nor collectivism is related to climate change inaction
② collectivism is more related to climate change inaction than is individualism
③ individualism is more related to climate change inaction than is collectivism
④ both individualism and collectivism are equally related to climate change inaction

10 다음 글의 주제로 가장 적절한 것은?

Bats can help an area get rid of pests and bugs. Each bat is known to feast on 6,000 to 8,000 insects in one night, with the capacity to eat 1,200 mosquitoes or mosquito-sized insects in one hour. They also eat flies, gnats, cucumber beetles, and crop-destroying moths like the codling moth that affects 99 percent of the world's walnut crops. Their ability to provide a natural pest control has made them popular with farmers. Another reason to thank these nocturnal mammals is chocolate. In Indonesia, when it was estimated what the cacao yield would be if they exterminated the bats, the result was a drastic drop of 22 percent which would run into a loss of hundreds of millions of dollars.

① benefits of bats
② dangers of bats
③ bats' natural habitat
④ bats' physical features

01 밑줄 친 부분과 의미가 가장 가까운 것을 고르시오.

The nation's countless sedulous people are once again facing many uncertainties in the new generation.

① industrious
② sensual
③ sensible
④ complicated

02 밑줄 친 부분과 의미가 가장 가까운 것을 고르시오.

Ministry of Defense is aiding the nation with the situation, and it ruled out the possibility of the terror.

① initiated
② solicited
③ excluded
④ leaked

03 밑줄 친 부분에 들어갈 말로 가장 적절한 것은?

The animals are believed to have _____ on the island after being left there by some sailors who were passing by.

① settled down
② been carried out
③ been set store by
④ seeped out

04 밑줄 친 부분에 들어갈 말로 가장 적절한 것을 고르시오.

Nancy: Why were you absent yesterday?
Kevin: I was so tired from the family trip that I just fell asleep.
Nancy: Oh, that's why you _____(A)_____.
Kevin: Yes, it was such a _____(B)_____.
Nancy: Well, how was the trip?
Kevin: It was awesome. I had nothing to worry about there. I had all the time to myself.
Nancy: Sometimes, people definitely need to _____(C)_____ from the reality.
Kevin: I strongly agree with you.

① (A) cut corners
  (B) a long day
  (C) take a break
② (A) cut corners
  (B) a soap opera
  (C) stack the deck
③ (A) took the French leave
  (B) a long day
  (C) take a break
④ (A) took the French leave
  (B) a long day
  (C) lead a dog's life

05 밑줄 친 부분 중 어법상 옳은 것은?

He later ① told me it before he experienced the embarrassment of ② being had a flat, he "planned on ③ getting it fixed when he had the time". If he would have only taken a few minutes to ④ get the nail removing, he most likely would not have received a flat tire on that particular day.

06 어법상 옳은 것은?

① Jane bought some new shoes which are very similar to ones she had before.
② The court was also ordered to pay £260 in compensation and £70 costs by William.
③ Tom is found ludicrous that nothing has been done to protect passengers from fire.
④ The police was sent to keep order because there would be many children that would need their help.

07 우리말을 영어로 잘못 옮긴 것은?

① 그 집에 사는 다른 사람들은 정말 친절하다.
→ The other people who live in the house are really friendly.
② 우리가 질문해야 할 진짜 질문은 무엇이 악이고 무엇이 선인가이다.
→ The real question we need to ask is what is evil and what is good.
③ 그 헤어스타일은 정확히 그녀가 자신의 주차 티켓에 대해 드는 시간의 양만큼 걸린다.
→ The haircut takes just exactly the amount of time that she has on her car park ticket.
④ 그녀는 최근에 매우 비슷한 사진을 찍었기 때문에 이것을 특징으로 삼은 포스터가 눈에 띄었다.
→ A poster featured this caught her eye, because she recently took a very similar photograph.

08 밑줄 친 (A), (B)에 들어갈 말로 가장 적절한 것은?

In real life, people read a variety of texts for both information and pleasure. Reading materials differ in content, style and purpose, and we adjust our reading style accordingly. To become efficient readers, we train ourselves to read different texts in different ways. ___(A)___, we do not read a novel and a textbook in preparation for an examination in the same way. When we are reading a novel, we do not need to pay attention to every detail the way we do when reading a textbook and read more quickly: most speed reading involves a process called chunking. Instead of reading each word, the reader takes words in "chunks," — ___(B)___, groups of words that make a meaningful unit, such as phrases, clauses or even whole sentences. And, as adults, most of our reading is silent. When we read silently, we save the time spent on articulating words, and read in chunks or sense groups instead of one word at a time.

	(A)	(B)
①	On the contrary	indeed
②	For instance	that is
③	Therefore	however
④	Otherwise	in other words

09 밑줄 친 (A), (B)에 들어갈 말로 가장 적절한 것은?

Through globalization, Japanese society has been influenced by European American cultures. This is especially true for the aspects of Japanese society adopting the individualistic systems imported from European American cultures. However, it has been argued that individualism in Japan might be qualitatively different from that in the European American cultural contexts. Individualism in these cultural contexts means being independent from others but still actively making social relationships. _____(A)_____, to be independent and achieve "individualism," the Japanese might feel the need to distance themselves from interdependent relationships. Indeed, connotations of individualism in Japan are more negative than are those in the U.S. _____(B)_____, in the U.S. individualism is perceived to be unique or independent, while in Japan individualism is regarded as being selfish and feeling lonely.

	(A)	(B)
①	Similarly	As a result
②	On the other hand	Apart from that
③	Thus	For example
④	By contrast	Specifically

10 다음 글의 내용과 일치하는 것은?

It's not hard to find bats for sale in the marketplaces of Bolivia. They're usually tucked away in pungent shoeboxes, some with as many as 20 bats jammed together, the live ones crawling over those that have already succumbed to disease or stress. People buy them so they can drink bat blood for its purported healing properties — particularly, they think, to help manage epilepsy. "The belief is well-rooted within our society, mainly in the Andes," explains bat specialist Luis F. Aguirre. However, there's no proof of any medicinal benefit from drinking bat blood. In addition, bat hunting is officially illegal. Bolivian law forbids the killing or sale of any wild animal without proper permitting, and the offense is punishable with up to six years in prison. Yet the belief — and killings — persist.

① Bats are discreetly traded in Bolivian markets.
② Only bats that are alive are being sold.
③ People put bat blood on their body expecting some curative effects.
④ The belief about bat blood's medical benefits is groundless.

기적사 DAY 16

01 밑줄 친 부분과 의미가 가장 가까운 것은?

Ethical considerations can be an integral element of biotechnology regulation.

① key
② incidental
③ interactive
④ popular

02 밑줄 친 부분과 의미가 가장 가까운 것은?

If the area of the brain associated with speech is destroyed, the brain may use plasticity to cause other areas of the brain not originally associated with this speech to learn the skill as a way to make up for lost cells.

① accuracy
② systemicity
③ obstruction
④ suppleness

03 빈칸에 들어갈 단어로 가장 적절한 것은?

Mephisto demands a signature and contract. No mere _____ contract will do. As Faust remarks, the devil wants everything in writing.

① genuine
② essential
③ reciprocal
④ verbal

04 빈칸에 들어갈 것으로 가장 적절한 것은?

A: You don't know about used cars, Ned. Whew! 70,000 miles.
B: Oh, that's a lot of miles! We have to take a close look at the engine, the doors, the tires, everything.
A: It's too expensive, Ned. _____
B: You have to watch these used car salesmen.

① Let's buy it.
② I'll dust it down.
③ What model do you want?
④ I don't want to get ripped off.

05 밑줄 친 부분 중 어법상 가장 옳지 않은 것은?

When you find your tongue ① twisted as you seek to explain to your ② six-year-old daughter why she can't go to the amusement park ③ that has been advertised on television, then you will understand why we find it difficult ④ wait.

06 밑줄 친 부분 중 어법상 가장 옳지 않은 것은?

Lewis Alfred Ellison, a small-business owner and ① a construction foreman, died in 1916 after an operation to cure internal wounds ② suffering after shards from a 100-lb ice block ③ penetrated his abdomen when it was dropped while ④ being loaded into a hopper.

07 어법상 가장 옳은 것은?

① If the item should not be delivered tomorrow, they would complain about it.
② He was more skillful than any other baseball players in his class.
③ Hardly has the violinist finished his performance before the audience stood up and applauded.
④ Bakers have been made come out, asking for promoting wheat consumption.

08 밑줄 친 인물(Marcel Mauss)에 대한 설명으로 가장 옳지 않은 것은?

Marcel Mauss (1872-1950), French sociologist, was born in Épinal (Vosges) in Lorraine, where he grew up within a close-knit, pious, and orthodox Jewish family. Emile Durkheim was his uncle. By the age of 18 Mauss had reacted against the Jewish faith; he was never a religious man. He studied philosophy under Durkheim's supervision at Bordeaux; Durkheim took endless trouble in guiding his nephew's studies and even chose subjects for his own lectures that would be most useful to Mauss. Thus Mauss was initially a philosopher (like most of the early Durkheimians), and his conception of philosophy was influenced above all by Durkheim himself, for whom he always retained the utmost admiration.

① He had a Jewish background.
② He was supervised by his uncle.
③ He had a doctrinaire faith.
④ He was a sociologist with a philosophical background.

09 글의 문맥에 가장 어울리는 순서대로 배열한 것은?

ⓐ Today, however, trees are being cut down far more rapidly. Each year, about 2 million acres of forests are cut down. That is more than equal to the area of the whole of Great Britain.

ⓑ There is not enough wood in these countries to satisfy the demand. Wood companies, therefore, have begun taking wood from the forests of Asia, Africa, South America, and even Siberia.

ⓒ While there are important reasons for cutting down trees, there are also dangerous consequences for life on earth. A major cause of the present destruction is the worldwide demand for wood. In industrialized countries, people are using more and more wood for paper.

ⓓ There is nothing new about people cutting down trees. In ancient times, Greece, Italy, and Great Britain were covered with forests. Over the centuries those forests were gradually cut back. Until now almost nothing is left.

① ⓐ-ⓑ-ⓒ-ⓓ
② ⓓ-ⓐ-ⓑ-ⓒ
③ ⓑ-ⓐ-ⓒ-ⓓ
④ ⓓ-ⓐ-ⓒ-ⓑ

10 글의 내용과 일치하는 것은?

A family hoping to adopt a child must first select an adoption agency. In the United States, there are two kinds of agencies that assist with adoption. Public agencies generally handle older children, children with mental or physical disabilities, or children who may have been abused or neglected. Prospective parents are not usually expected to pay fees when adopting a child from a public agency. Fostering, or a form of temporary adoption, is also possible through public agencies. Private agencies can be found on the Internet. They handle domestic and international adoption.

① Public adoption agencies are better than private ones.
② Parents pay huge fees to adopt a child from a foster home.
③ Children in need cannot be adopted through public agencies.
④ Private agencies can be contacted for international adoption.

기적사 DAY 17

01 밑줄 친 부분과 의미가 가장 가까운 것은?

Still, it's certain that many in the Pacific region are vigilant for stormy seas.

① unsure
② alert
③ popular
④ null

02 밑줄 친 부분과 의미가 가장 가까운 것은?

Despite its violation of the act, EU, in reality, doesn't seem ready to willingly abandon its hegemonistic ambitions.

① infringement
② vulnerability
③ suppleness
④ viability

03 빈칸에 들어갈 단어로 가장 적절한 것은?

In many countries around the world, the tap water is _____ to drink due to contamination and disease.

① cautious
② verbal
③ unsafe
④ unwitting

04 빈칸에 들어갈 것으로 가장 적절한 것은?

A: It seems like your cold is worsening.
B: I've been to the hospital but it was just ___(A)___. The hospital charged me $50 for a simple check-up.
A: You must have felt really angry. Did you take any over-the-counter medicine?
B: Yeah, I just went to the drug store and took some pills for fever.
A: Did it work on you?
B: Well, I'm not sure. But at least I didn't have any ___(B)___.

① (A) a rip-off   (B) side effect
② (A) a rip-off   (B) hue and cry
③ (A) a dark horse   (B) side effect
④ (A) a shot in the dark (B) chalk and cheese

05 밑줄 친 부분 중 어법상 가장 옳지 않은 것은?

Stable patterns are necessary ① lest we live in chaos; however, they make it difficult ② to abandon entrenched behaviors, even those ③ that are no longer useful, constructive, or health creating. And fear can keep you from changing ④ during you don't want to risk a step into unknown territory.

06 밑줄 친 부분 중 어법상 가장 옳지 않은 것은?

What story could be harsher than ① that of the Great Auk, the large black-and-white seabird that in northern oceans ② taking the ecological place of a penguin? Its tale rises and falls like a Greek tragedy, with island populations savagely ③ destroyed by humans until almost all were ④ gone.

07 어법상 가장 옳은 것은?

① If you should decide not to go on the trip, you get a full refund.
② I've always believed that happiness counts more than any other things.
③ The people were made to wait outside while the committee reached its decision.
④ Hardly the demonstration had started when trouble broke out and the police moved in to arrest people.

08 빈칸에 들어갈 표현으로 가장 적절한 것은?

While it is probably as a teacher that Marcel Mauss' influence was greatest, the courses that he taught and the way he taught them can only be understood in terms of his participation in another enterprise - the publication of the *Annie sociologique*. This journal was founded by Emile Durkheim in 1898, and was dedicated to the promulgation of doctrines which have come to be known as French sociology. From the beginning Mauss was an integral member of the tightly knit group which published this journal, and after Durkheim's death it was Mauss who succeeded him as director. As an indication of the close collaboration between the members of this group, it is worth noting that practically all of Mauss's early work was written in conjunction with another. Due to the close cooperation between the members of this group and their sharing of so many ideas, it is _____ any particular contribution made by Mauss to the development of theory in this early period.

① easy to pinpoint
② difficult to disregard
③ necessary to confirm
④ impossible to distinguish

09 빈칸에 들어갈 표현으로 가장 적절한 것은?

A new study finds that simply paying landowners in the developing world not to cut down trees can significantly reduce carbon in the atmosphere. It may also be a very cost-effective way to help meet goals such as the Paris Accord targets. The study, published today in the journal *Science*, found that in Uganda, _____ cut deforestation in half. Because the amounts of money involved are fairly small, it was estimated 10 to 50 times more effective per dollar spent than many energy efficiency programs in the U.S. Annie Duflo, Executive Director of Innovations for Poverty Action, said that this study will be key to informing future conservation programs in the developing world. "Good science like this helps us understand how to combat climate change and preserve endangered habitats, while also helping poor farmers."

① paying local people to plant more trees
② persuading landowners to stop selling wood
③ offering small financial incentives to landowners
④ raising awareness among landowners of climate change

10 다음 글의 내용과 일치하지 않는 것은?

The incredible story of Samantha Futerman and Anais Bordier, identical twins who were separated at birth then found each other after 25 years, made headlines a few years ago. They were born in South Korea in 1987 and were adopted by different families shortly after birth. Futerman, who grew up in a large family in Los Angeles, is outgoing and has always been happy with her life because it was full of love and joy, while the more introspective Bordier who grew up in Paris as a single child felt more lonely and was often hurt when peers made fun of her asking why she looked different from her Caucasian parents. The two, who did not know of the other's existence, dramatically found each other through social networking services in 2013 and immediately embraced each other into their lives.

① Samantha Futerman did not know that she has a twin sister for about 25 years.
② They were raised in the same country but in different cities.
③ Futerman had more family members than Bordier.
④ Based on the story, it can be concluded that personality is determined by the environment.

기적사 DAY 18

01 밑줄 친 부분과 의미가 가장 가까운 것은?

It faces a possibly raucous tussle with other domestic IT companies.

① interactive
② uproarious
③ flamboyant
④ extended

02 밑줄 친 부분과 의미가 가장 가까운 것은?

The other thing that they had in common and kept in their mind was this: They fully embraced vulnerability.

① infringement
② weakness
③ obstruction
④ viability

03 빈칸에 들어갈 단어로 가장 적절한 것은?

The temperature in the tunnel is maintained at a _____ level regardless of the season or the weather.

① vulnerable
② reciprocal
③ constant
④ splendid

04 빈칸에 들어갈 것으로 가장 적절한 것은?

A: I heard you went to the debating contest! How did it go?
B: You're right! I was actually very lucky because I won the winning prize!
A: Wow, congratulations! I'm so proud that you are my friend!
B: Thanks. I was ____(A)____ because the opposing team had strong refuting points.
A: How did you manage to overcome it?
B: I tried to stay ____(B)____.

	(A)	(B)
①	under fire	sour grapes
②	under fire	cool as a cucumber
③	in a nutshell	cool as a cucumber
④	an apple of discord	behind the eight ball

05 밑줄 친 부분 중 어법상 가장 옳지 않은 것은?

My ① five-years-old son couldn't go to bed one night until he wrote "I love you Mom" on a piece of paper. Pajamas on, red crayon in hand, he was very determined. A ② few mixed-up letters, a couple of ③ crumpled papers, and some help from Daddy later, he handed ④ me his heart on the page.

06 밑줄 친 부분 중 어법상 가장 옳지 않은 것은?

After ① returned to New York State with her family, Tammy faced another ② lesson in growing up. A gifted student, she ③ was sent to college when she was just 14. Tammy was able to earn her high school diploma and some college credit before trying her hand at ④ a number of different jobs.

07 어법상 가장 옳은 것은?

① The children were let to do whatever they wanted.
② William knows much more about movies than the other man does.
③ You should wish to use the Internet, there will be a code available at the reception desk.
④ Jane had no sooner started cooking than there was a power cut and she had no electricity.

08 다음 밑줄 친 단어가 가리키는 대상이 나머지 넷과 다른 것은?

In 1895 Emile Durkheim encountered the work of Robertson Smith and had the illumination that sacrifice (or rituals of sacrifice) is the foundation of social life. ① He would pursue this idea for the following decades. However, ② he needed to properly substantiate his ideas, and had neither the time nor the necessary ethnographic knowledge to do so. ③ He therefore directed Marcel Mauss towards working on the question of sacrifice, and would constantly pressure ④ him to deliver. This only intensified after Durkheim published *Suicide* in 1897. The 'Essay on the Nature and Function of Sacrifice', co-authored by Hubert and Mauss, was completed in 1898, under the watchful 'guidance' of him, who wanted to ensure that the analysis was pushed in the 'right' direction.

09 다음 밑줄 친 단어가 가리키는 대상이 나머지 넷과 다른 것은?

① A Bucks County man faces a quarter-million dollar fine and community service for cutting down 22 trees on a neighboring property to get a better view from his backyard. Prosecutors announced that David Topel, 62, of Solebury Township, has been ordered to pay $261,211.07 to the township, serve five years probation and perform community service for hiring an arborist to chop down the trees in the fall of 2014. Topel said ② he'd submit a check for the full amount of the fine, which authorities say represents the cost of the trees. ③ The defendant recently moved to his new house in Solebury from Florida and wanted a more scenic view from the back deck of his home. According to the Bucks County District Attorney's Office, Topel, a retired lawyer, told ④ the man whom he employed that he believed the trees, some of which were 100-150 years old, were on his property. The trees, however, were on a wooded area owned by 11 members of a local home owner's association, authorities say.

10 빈칸에 들어갈 표현으로 가장 적절하지 않은 것은?

The requirements for adoption are different depending on the type of adoption, the agency you work with and the place you are adopting from. When you adopt domestically, you must meet the requirements of the state and the agency. One example of this could be meeting minimum age requirements. International adoption is typically more _____. Some countries have marriage requirements and others have higher age limits. Unfortunately, many countries still do not allow LGBTQ couples to adopt. Is it easier to adopt internationally or domestically? The difficulty of meeting requirements will depend on your unique situation. Generally speaking, however, you will have a greater chance of facing more demanding requirements when adopting from a different country.

* LGBTQ: 성 소수자

① lenient
② rigid
③ stringent
④ tight

01 밑줄 친 부분과 의미가 가장 가까운 것은?

People out at sea have been warned of the impending heavy rain warning from Meteorological Office.

① imminent
② incidental
③ constant
④ splendid

02 밑줄 친 부분과 의미가 가장 가까운 것은?

People do not know about religions that much, but the enthusiasm for someone special and eagerness of their followers is amazing.

① empathy
② anguish
③ ardor
④ systemicity

03 빈칸에 들어갈 단어로 가장 적절한 것은?

_____ sunscreen is recommended because it will outlast sweating and water activities.

① Hollow
② Essential
③ Watertight
④ Neurological

04 빈칸에 들어갈 것으로 가장 적절한 것은?

Visitor: Excuse me, where is the information desk?
Security: The information desk is closed at the moment. It's open from 9 am to 8 pm.
Visitor: Oh, that's too bad. I ran here ____(A)____ as soon as I realized my phone was lost.
Security: Did you lose your cellphone? Isn't it ____(B)____? It holds all your private information.
Visitor: Yes, that's why I came here all the way. Unfortunately though, I'll have no other choice but to come back here tomorrow.
Security: In case someone returns your phone, I'll ____(C)____ the lost and found.
Visitor: Thank you so much. I'll return your favor ____(D)____.
Security: No problem. I'm just doing my job.

① (A) like water off a duck's back
  (B) goose bumps
  (C) keep an eye on
  (D) in on time

② (A) like water off a duck's back
  (B) the apple of your eye
  (C) stand up for
  (D) at all costs

③ (A) like a chicken with its head off
  (B) the apple of your eye
  (C) keep an eye on
  (D) at all costs

④ (A) like a chicken with its head off
  (B) the apple of your eye
  (C) stand up against
  (D) at all costs

05 밑줄 친 부분 중 어법상 가장 옳지 않은 것은?

A school of ① fish will split in two to avoid a predator and then quickly regroup behind it. A herd of zebras can become a ② dazzling display of black and white stripes, ③ make it more difficult for a lion ④ to see where one zebra ends and another begins.

06 밑줄 친 부분 중 어법상 가장 옳지 않은 것은?

After enjoying a few ① years of comparative safety, disaster of a different kind ② striking the Great Auk. Volcanic activity caused the island refuge ③ to sink completely beneath the waves, and surviving individuals ④ were forced to find shelter elsewhere.

07 어법상 가장 옳은 것은?

① I was made wait for four hours before I was examined by a doctor.
② You'll never guess what happened as soon as Tom had left his room.
③ Do you think Australia is a much democratic country than any other country?
④ If the Prime Minister were to resign, there would have to be a general election within 30 days.

08 주어진 문장이 들어갈 위치로 가장 적절한 것은?

Mauss shows us that in many tribal and native cultures, this is not necessarily true.

In his *The Gift*, Marcel Mauss attempts to explain and understand gifts in primitive societies. (①) Mauss first decides to show that the motives behind giving gifts are more complicated than they are commonly believed to be. (②) In modern day society, gifts are often thought of as something given out of good will and without the expectancy of something in return. (③) In discussing the Maori, he says, "They had a kind of exchange system, or rather one of giving presents that must ultimately either be reciprocated or given back." (④) The principle of gift giving is governed by the concept of mana, which is the authority, honor, and prestige derived from the wealth and glory of being a superior gift giver. One must give gifts in order to maintain and increase mana and reciprocates them in order to prevent oneself from losing it.

09 다음 글의 요지로 가장 적절한 것은?

Forests are feeling the heat. In places like the American West, rising temperatures and drought mean less water for trees. Now, scientists have found that thinning early in forest growth creates tougher trees that can endure climate change. What's more, these thinned forests can suck carbon out of the air just as fast as dense forests. As trees grow, they convert carbon dioxide to food and store it in their leaves, trunks, and roots. U.S. forests capture between 10 percent and 20 percent of U.S. emissions each year. But if trees get too crowded, they compete for light and water — and stressed trees are more susceptible to drought and insect attacks. Removing some trees can ease the competition, letting the remaining trees grow big and healthy.

① Trees can help reduce air pollution.
② More trees are needed in U.S. forests.
③ Trees compete with one another to survive.
④ Cutting down some trees can be good for nature.

10 주어진 문장 다음에 이어질 글의 순서로 가장 적절한 것은?

A multitude of issues may arise when children become aware that they have been adopted.

(A) Children may feel grief over the loss of a relationship with their birth parents or the loss of the cultural and family connections that would have existed with those parents.

(B) Such grief feelings may be triggered at many different times throughout the child's life including when they first learn of their adoption, during the turbulent teen years, upon the death of other family members, or even as becoming a spouse or parent.

(C) This feeling of loss may be especially intense in closed or semi-open adoptions where little or no information or contact is available with birth parents.

① (A) - (B) - (C)   ② (A) - (C) - (B)
③ (B) - (A) - (C)   ④ (B) - (C) - (A)

기적사 DAY 20

01 밑줄 친 부분과 의미가 가장 가까운 것은?

It was the first time for the nation to win two consecutive World Cups since 2000.

① deserted ② archaeological
③ successive ④ key

02 밑줄 친 부분과 의미가 가장 가까운 것은?

Despite the apparent indolence of his attitude I could know that he was keenly alert.

① idleness ② determinism
③ transformation ④ accuracy

03 빈칸에 들어갈 단어로 가장 적절한 것은?

According to the U.S. _____ Survey, there are about 1,500 potentially active volcanoes worldwide, not including the continuous belt of volcanoes on the ocean floor.

① Isolated ② Hollow
③ Genuine ④ Geological

04 빈칸에 들어갈 것으로 가장 적절한 것은?

Chris: I saw the movie 'The Great Gatsby' on the weekend.
Ray: That's a classic. Did you like it?
Chris: Well, the life of Gatsby was really shocking to me. He could lead his life in whatever way he wanted. It must feel like being ____(A)____.
Ray: It's hard to imagine what life would be like if I were Gatsby. He's a character ____(B)____.
Chris: You're right. Do you remember the ending?
Ray: Yeah, it was tragic. Despite Gatsby's sacrifice for his love, Daisy, there was no one left ____(C)____ in his funeral.
Chris: Watching that scene, I realized wealth is meaningless in the moment of death.

① (A) up a tree
   (B) six feet under
   (C) for a song
② (A) on cloud nine
   (B) six feet under
   (C) in the doghouse
③ (A) a turkey shoot
   (B) born with a silver spoon in his mouth
   (C) at the eleventh hour
④ (A) on cloud nine
   (B) born with a silver spoon in his mouth
   (C) at the eleventh hour

05 밑줄 친 부분 중 어법상 가장 옳지 않은 것은?

It is not hard ① to see that a strong economy, where opportunities are plentiful and jobs go begging, ② helps break down social barriers. ③ Biased employers may still dislike hiring members of one group or another, but when nobody else is available, discrimination most often gives way to the basic need to get the work ④ do.

06 밑줄 친 부분 중 어법상 가장 옳지 않은 것은?

In the early 1950s, Imo, a ① one-year-old female macaque, somehow ② hit upon the idea of washing her sweet potatoes in a stream before eating them. Soon ③ that was hard to find a Koshima macaque who wasn't careful to wash off her sweet potato before ④ eating it.

07 어법상 가장 옳은 것은?

① William had had a phone from Jane the moment he got home.
② It is a wrong thing that people are had to work long hours.
③ No other writing has influenced as many readers as his writing.
④ We were to give up the fight, it would mean the end of democracy in our country.

08 다음 글의 주제로 가장 적절한 것은?

Durkheim's intellectual influence on Mauss can hardly be overstated. The earliest fruit of their collaboration was the study *Primitive Classification*. Its assemblage of factual materials reflects Mauss's more empirical bent, and the theoretical interpretation is largely Durkheim's. Considered a pioneering effort to uncover the origins of such classifications as space, time, number, and hierarchy in the social structure, *Primitive Classification* theorizes from data gathered from studies of Australian aborigines and the American Zuñi, as well as from traditional Chinese culture. The work's methodology, which seeks to establish formal correspondences between social and symbolic classifications, reflects Durkheim's lifelong insistence on the unity of all social phenomena. Although *Primitive Classification* has met with substantial criticism over the years, it remains an important and influential theoretical contribution.

① Mauss's major work
② A co-written publication
③ Criticism on Durkheim's work
④ Durkheim's influence on Mauss

09 밑줄 친 (A), (B)에 들어갈 말로 가장 적절한 것은?

A common method of logging in Canada is clear cutting – the harvesting and removal of an entire stand of trees. Although efficient, clear cutting poses a variety of environmental problems. It can increase the harmful impact of wind and rain on local ecosystems; destroy the valuable wildlife habitat used by pine martens, caribou, and other animals; and cause soil to become dry and overheated, which may in turn increase the risk of fire or interfere with seedling growth. _____(A)_____ such logging operations can alter the chemical and physical makeup of nearby bodies of water and affect the health of fish and other aquatic species. _____(B)_____ professional foresters and loggers argue that clear cutting mimics natural disturbances, such as forest fires and insect infestations, and is a sustainable way to harvest trees when managed properly.

	(A)	(B)
①	As a consequence	Nevertheless
②	Also	However
③	That is to say	Simply put
④	But	For instance

10 밑줄 친 부분 중 글의 흐름상 가장 어색한 것은?

Those interested in becoming foster parents must be at least 21 years of age and becoming a foster family requires an extensive background check. ① Most children are in foster care for a short time, with the majority of children returning to their family of origin. ② To make sure of the child's safety, the agency will conduct a criminal record check and child abuse clearance on everyone in your home, age 14 and over. ③ Foster families do not need to be well-off financially. ④ However, the home approval process will require an in-depth evaluation of your total family picture and history, including financial stability. The physical features of your home will also be evaluated to ensure that there is adequate space for a child and that all safety requirements are met.

기적사 복습 모의고사 2회

01 밑줄 친 부분과 의미가 가장 가까운 것은?

Ethical considerations can be an <u>integral</u> element of biotechnology regulation.

① key ② incidental
③ interactive ④ popular

02 밑줄 친 부분과 의미가 가장 가까운 것을 고르시오.

Korea's education system is globally <u>renowned</u> for its high rigor and standards which makes Korean the powerhouse about IT, the branch of engineering that deals with the use of computers and telecommunications.

① prestigious ② relative
③ quarrelsome ④ otherworldly

03 밑줄 친 부분과 의미가 가장 가까운 것을 고르시오.

Ministry of Defense is aiding the nation with the situation, and it <u>ruled out</u> the possibility of the terror.

① initiated ② solicited
③ excluded ④ leaked

04 밑줄 친 부분에 들어갈 말로 가장 적절한 것은?

A police sergeant with 15 years of experience was dismayed after being _____ for promotion in favor of a young officer.

① run over ② asked out
③ carried out ④ passed over

05 어법상 가장 옳은 것은?

① The children were let to do whatever they wanted.
② William knows much more about movies than the other man does.
③ You should wish to use the Internet, there will be a code available at the reception desk.
④ Jane had no sooner started cooking than there was a power cut and she had no electricity.

06 어법상 옳은 것은?

① She thinks she is morally superior as the rest of us.
② On a hot day, it is lovely to hear the chink of ice in a glass.
③ When this pore space is completely filled with water, the soil saturates.
④ If everyone is made carry ID cards, it will foster the idea that we are all under suspicion.

07 우리말을 영어로 잘못 옮긴 것은?

① 우리는 그녀의 증거가 과민성의 정도에 근거되어지고 있다는 것을 발견한다.
→ We find her evidence to base on a degree of oversensitivity.

② Tom이 경기 운영과 관련된 많은 것들을 평준화하는 데 한 시간이 걸렸다.
→ It took Tom an hour to equalize many things concerning the run of play.

③ 그녀는 물 한잔을 마시기 위해 문을 열었고 Tom이 현관에 서 있는 것을 발견했다.
→ She opened the door to drink a glass of water and found Tom standing in the hall.

④ 월요일에 발견된 그의 유골은 골목에 있는 쓰레기봉투에 넣어져 있었다.
→ His ashes, which were found on Monday, had been placed in a rubbish bag in an alley.

08 밑줄 친 부분 중 어법상 가장 옳지 않은 것은?

It is not hard ① to see that a strong economy, where opportunities are plentiful and jobs go begging, ② helps break down social barriers. ③ Biased employers may still dislike hiring members of one group or another, but when nobody else is available, discrimination most often gives way to the basic need to get the work ④ do.

09 빈칸에 들어갈 것으로 가장 적절한 것은?

A: It seems like your cold is worsening.
B: I've been to the hospital but it was just ____(A)____. The hospital charged me $50 for a simple check-up.
A: You must have felt really angry. Did you take any over-the-counter medicine?
B: Yeah, I just went to the drug store and took some pills for fever.
A: Did it work on you?
B: Well, I'm not sure. But at least I didn't have any ____(B)____.

① (A) a rip-off   (B) side effect
② (A) a rip-off   (B) hue and cry
③ (A) a dark horse   (B) side effect
④ (A) a shot in the dark (B) chalk and cheese

10 밑줄 친 부분에 들어갈 말을 순서대로 나열한 것을 고르시오.

A: Have you heard the news about Micheal Jackson?
B: You mean the news about his hidden son who is a pianist?
A: Yes, Micheal Jackson died several years ago. It's a bolt from the _____ sky to see his son all of a sudden.
B: I know. I didn't believe it at first. It just doesn't make sense.
A: Right. Micheal Jackson never mentioned his pianist son when he was alive.
B: Maybe the article we read was just _____ journalism.
A: What an awful reporter! He shouldn't mess with Micheal Jackson. He is still one of the most popular and renowned musicians around the world.
B: I agree with you. Everywhere he went, people rolled out the _____ carpet.

① blue – yellow – red   ② black – white – red
③ red – yellow – white   ④ blue – green – black

11 주어진 문장 다음에 이어질 글의 순서로 가장 적절한 것은?

A multitude of issues may arise when children become aware that they have been adopted.

(A) Children may feel grief over the loss of a relationship with their birth parents or the loss of the cultural and family connections that would have existed with those parents.
(B) Such grief feelings may be triggered at many different times throughout the child's life including when they first learn of their adoption, during the turbulent teen years, upon the death of other family members, or even as becoming a spouse or parent.
(C) This feeling of loss may be especially intense in closed or semi-open adoptions where little or no information or contact is available with birth parents.

① (A) - (B) - (C) ② (A) - (C) - (B)
③ (B) - (A) - (C) ④ (B) - (C) - (A)

12 〈보기〉의 문장이 들어갈 위치로 가장 적절한 것은?

〈보기〉
In this situation, we would expect to find less movement of individuals from one job to another because of the individual's social obligations toward the work organization to which he or she belongs and to the people comprising that organization.

Cultural differences in the meaning of work can manifest themselves in other aspects as well. (①) For example, in American culture, it is easy to think of work simply as a means to accumulate money and make a living. (②) In other cultures, especially collectivistic ones, work may be seen more as fulfilling an obligation to a larger group. (③) In individualistic cultures, it is easier to consider leaving one job and going to another because it is easier to separate jobs from the self. (④) A different job will just as easily accomplish the same goals.

13 다음 글의 주제로 가장 적절한 것은?

Bats can help an area get rid of pests and bugs. Each bat is known to feast on 6,000 to 8,000 insects in one night, with the capacity to eat 1,200 mosquitoes or mosquito-sized insects in one hour. They also eat flies, gnats, cucumber beetles, and crop-destroying moths like the codling moth that affects 99 percent of the world's walnut crops. Their ability to provide a natural pest control has made them popular with farmers. Another reason to thank these nocturnal mammals is chocolate. In Indonesia, when it was estimated what the cacao yield would be if they exterminated the bats, the result was a drastic drop of 22 percent which would run into a loss of hundreds of millions of dollars.

① benefits of bats   ② dangers of bats
③ bats' natural habitat   ④ bats' physical features

14 밑줄 친 부분 중 글의 흐름상 가장 어색한 것은?

The Malayan flying fox is hailed as the largest bat in the world. This endangered bat is a megaspecies that has made its home in the tropical region of Southeast Asia. ① This bat is a superb flyer and can navigate towering canopies with no problems. ② However, when it comes to landing, they crash and fumble into their destination, often smashing into bundles of branches and piles of forest foliage just to grab a bite to eat. ③ Also, unlike their smaller, microbat kin, the flying fox is a large mammal with excellent eyesight. ④ The darkness of the night doesn't stop this nocturnal animal from getting where it needs to go, and it finds food using squeaks and chirps to map out the area. Instead of using sound waves to pinpoint where they are and what's around them, they use their well-developed peepers to scour their terrain.

15 밑줄 친 인물(Marcel Mauss)에 대한 설명으로 가장 옳지 않은 것은?

Marcel Mauss (1872-1950), French sociologist, was born in Épinal (Vosges) in Lorraine, where he grew up within a close-knit, pious, and orthodox Jewish family. Emile Durkheim was his uncle. By the age of 18 Mauss had reacted against the Jewish faith; he was never a religious man. He studied philosophy under Durkheim's supervision at Bordeaux; Durkheim took endless trouble in guiding his nephew's studies and even chose subjects for his own lectures that would be most useful to Mauss. Thus Mauss was initially a philosopher (like most of the early Durkheimians), and his conception of philosophy was influenced above all by Durkheim himself, for whom he always retained the utmost admiration.

① He had a Jewish background.
② He was supervised by his uncle.
③ He had a doctrinaire faith.
④ He was a sociologist with a philosophical background.

16 다음 글의 내용과 일치하는 것은?

It's not hard to find bats for sale in the marketplaces of Bolivia. They're usually tucked away in pungent shoeboxes, some with as many as 20 bats jammed together, the live ones crawling over those that have already succumbed to disease or stress. People buy them so they can drink bat blood for its purported healing properties — particularly, they think, to help manage epilepsy. "The belief is well-rooted within our society, mainly in the Andes," explains bat specialist Luis F. Aguirre. However, there's no proof of any medicinal benefit from drinking bat blood. In addition, bat hunting is officially illegal. Bolivian law forbids the killing or sale of any wild animal without proper permitting, and the offense is punishable with up to six years in prison. Yet the belief — and killings — persist.

① Bats are discreetly traded in Bolivian markets.
② Only bats that are alive are being sold.
③ People put bat blood on their body expecting some curative effects.
④ The belief about bat blood's medical benefits is groundless.

17 다음 글의 요지로 가장 적절한 것은?

Skimming is sometimes referred to as gist reading. It may help in order to know what the text is about at its most basic level. You might typically do this with a magazine or newspaper and this would help you mentally and quickly list those articles which you might consider for a deeper read. You might also skim to search for a name in a telephone directory. You can reach a speed count of even 700 words per minute if you train yourself well in some particular methods. Comprehension is of course very low and understanding of overall content is very superficial. It will certainly save you a lot of time, but for the reason stated above, it is not the best way to read. However, skimming is useful when your goal is to preview the text to get a better idea of what it's about. It will help prepare you for deeper learning.

① Skimming skills can be developed through training.
② Skimming is the most important skill of speed reading.
③ Skimming enables readers to fully understand the text.
④ Skimming is a good way to get an overview of the text.

18 밑줄 친 (A), (B)에 들어갈 말로 가장 적절한 것은?

A common method of logging in Canada is clear cutting – the harvesting and removal of an entire stand of trees. Although efficient, clear cutting poses a variety of environmental problems. It can increase the harmful impact of wind and rain on local ecosystems; destroy the valuable wildlife habitat used by pine martens, caribou, and other animals; and cause soil to become dry and overheated, which may in turn increase the risk of fire or interfere with seedling growth. ___(A)___ such logging operations can alter the chemical and physical makeup of nearby bodies of water and affect the health of fish and other aquatic species. ___(B)___ professional foresters and loggers argue that clear cutting mimics natural disturbances, such as forest fires and insect infestations, and is a sustainable way to harvest trees when managed properly.

	(A)	(B)
①	As a consequence	Nevertheless
②	Also	However
③	That is to say	Simply put
④	But	For instance

19 빈칸에 들어갈 표현으로 가장 적절한 것은?

A new study finds that simply paying landowners in the developing world not to cut down trees can significantly reduce carbon in the atmosphere. It may also be a very cost-effective way to help meet goals such as the Paris Accord targets. The study, published today in the journal *Science*, found that in Uganda, _____ cut deforestation in half. Because the amounts of money involved are fairly small, it was estimated 10 to 50 times more effective per dollar spent than many energy efficiency programs in the U.S. Annie Duflo, Executive Director of Innovations for Poverty Action, said that this study will be key to informing future conservation programs in the developing world. "Good science like this helps us understand how to combat climate change and preserve endangered habitats, while also helping poor farmers."

① paying local people to plant more trees
② persuading landowners to stop selling wood
③ offering small financial incentives to landowners
④ raising awareness among landowners of climate change

20 빈칸에 들어갈 표현으로 가장 적절한 것은?

In terms of outcomes, longitudinal research, the kind that follows kids for decades, tells a sad story. If your child is experiencing reading failure, it is almost as if he has contracted a chronic and debilitating disease. Kids who are not reading at grade level in first grade almost invariably remain poor fourth grade readers. Seventy four percent of struggling third grade readers still struggle in ninth grade, which in turn makes it hard to graduate from high school. It won't surprise you to know that kids who struggle in reading grow up to be adults who struggle to hold on to steady work; they are more likely to experience periods of prolonged unemployment, require welfare services, and are more likely to end up in jail. Reading experts call them "_____." Most of them don't have neurological problems. Their schools and, specifically, their primary school teachers have failed them.

① social misfits
② gifted readers
③ incompetent students
④ instructional casualties

MEMO

01 밑줄 친 부분에 들어갈 가장 적절한 것을 고르시오.

Given our awesome capacities for rationalization and self-deception, most of us are going to measure ourselves _____: I was honest with that blind passenger because I'm a wonder person. I cheated the sighted one because she probably has too much money anyway.

① harshly
② leniently
③ honestly
④ thankfully

02 밑줄 친 ㉠과 ㉡에 공통으로 들어갈 가장 적절한 것은?

- In Korea, the eldest son tends to ___㉠___ a lot of responsibility.
- The same words ___㉡___ different meaning when said in different ways.

① take over
② take down
③ take on
④ take off

03 밑줄 친 표현과 의미가 가장 가까운 것은?

We need to iron out a few problems first.

① conceive
② review
③ solve
④ pose

04 밑줄 친 부분에 가장 적절한 것은?

A: I saw the announcement for your parents' 25th anniversary in yesterday's newspaper. It was really neat. Do you know how your parents met?
B: Yes. It was really incredible, actually, very romantic. They met in college, found they were compatible, and began to date. Their courtship lasted all through school.
A: No kidding! That's really beautiful. I haven't noticed anyone in class that I could fall in love with!
B: _____. Oh, well, maybe next semester!

① Me neither
② You shouldn't blame me
③ It is up to your parents
④ You'd better hang about with her

05 밑줄 친 부분 중 어법상 옳지 않은 것을 고르시오.

The corals are the foundation of an ecosystem ① increasingly damaging by fishing nets, but scientists know ② very little about the ③ slow-growing life-forms because they are somewhat difficult ④ to reach.

06 어법상 옳지 않은 것을 고르시오.

① I met a student yesterday in the cafeteria who said she knew you.
② Even though Tim is your friend, he isn't to be trusted with other people's money.
③ We suggest you to take a copy of the final invoice along with your travel documents.
④ Surprisingly, she didn't have any objections to make to the proposal.

07 우리말을 영어로 잘못 옮긴 것은?

① 많은 사람들이 아파서 회의가 취소되었다.
   → With many people ill, the meeting was cancelled.
② 이것은 우리가 예상했던 것만큼 그렇게 간단한 문제는 아니다.
   → It is not so straightforward a problem as we expected.
③ 학생들이 몇 개의 가방을 가지고 탑승할 건가요?
   → How many bags are the students carrying on board with them?
④ 아무런 해명도 없었다. 사과는 말할 것도 없고.
   → No explanation was offered, still more an apology.

08 글의 제목으로 가장 적절한 것은?

After analyzing a mass of data on job interview results, a research team discovered a surprising reality. Did the likelihood of being hired depend on qualifications? Or was it work experience? In fact, it was neither. It was just one important factor: did the candidate appear to be a pleasant person. Those candidates who had managed to ingratiate themselves were very likely to be offered a position; they had charmed their way to success. Some had made a special effort to smile and maintain eye contact. Others had praised the organization. This positivity had convinced the interviewers that such pleasant and socially skilled applicants would fit well into the workplace, and so should be offered a job.

① To Get a Job, Be a Pleasant Person
② More Qualifications Bring Better Chances
③ It Is Ability That Counts, Not Personality
④ Show Yourself As You Are at an Interview

09 글의 내용과 일치하지 않는 것은?

Most writers lead double lives. They earn good money at legitimate professions, and carve out time for their writing as best they can: early in the morning, late at night, weekends, vacations. William Carlos Williams and Louis-Ferdinand Céline were doctors. Wallace Stevens worked for an insurance company. T.S. Elliot was a banker, then a publisher. Don DeLilo, Peter Carey, Salman Rushdie, and Elmore Leonard all worked for long stretches in advertising. Other writers teach. That is probably the most common solution today, and with every major university and college offering so-called creative writing courses, novelists and poets are continually scratching and scrambling to land themselves a spot. Who can blame them? The salaries might not be big, but the work is steady and the hours are good.

① Some writers struggle for teaching positions to teach creative writing courses.
② As a doctor, William Carlos Williams tried to find the time to write.
③ Teaching is a common way for writers to make a living today.
④ Salman Rushdie worked briefly in advertising with great triumph.

10 글의 흐름상 가장 어색한 문장은?

One of the largest celebrations of the passage of young girls into womanhood occurs in Latin American and Hispanic cultures. This event is called La Quinceañera, or the fifteenth year. ① It acknowledges that a young woman is now of marriageable age. The day usually begins with a Mass of Thanksgiving. ② By comparing the rites of passage of one culture with those of another, we can assess differences in class status. The young woman wears a full-length white or pastel-colored dress and is attended by fourteen friends and relatives who serve as maids of honor and male escorts. ③ Her parents and godparents surround her at the foot of the altar. When the Mass ends, other young relatives give small gifts to those who attended, while the Quinceañera herself places a bouquet of flowers on the altar of the Virgin. ④ Following the Mass is an elaborate party, with dancing, cake, and toasts. Finally, to end the evening, the young woman dances a waltz with her favorite escort.

결국엔 성정혜 영어 하프모의고사

기적사 DAY 22

기출 하프 ☐　파생 하프 ☑　복습 모의고사 ☐

소요 시간 :　　/ 15분　맞은 개수 :　　/ 10개

---

01 밑줄 친 부분에 들어갈 가장 적절한 것을 고르시오.

What's wrong with Sally? She's got a _____ face this morning.

① long　　　　② honest
③ blue　　　　④ sluggish

02 밑줄 친 부분에 들어갈 가장 적절한 것을 고르시오.

His wife _____ him on the trip.

① accompanied　② annihilated
③ took on　　　④ took off

03 밑줄 친 표현과 의미가 가장 가까운 것은?

Italian referendum can only abrogate all or part of existing laws, not insert new language.

① administer　② benefit
③ repeal　　　④ pose

04 밑줄 친 부분에 가장 적절한 것은?

A: I heard you had a meeting this morning.
B: Yes, I came here to meet you as soon as it ended.
A: Thanks for coming all the way here. How did the meeting go?
B: It didn't go so smooth. Today was the first meeting we had with the new employees and one of them was such _____.
A: Tell me all about it. What did he do?
B: First, he was late and second, he had rude attitude during the whole conference.
A: That must have been harsh. Cheer up!
B: Thank you for your encouragement.

① a real McCoy　　② a walk of life
③ a wet blanket　　④ an act of God

05 밑줄 친 부분 중 어법상 옳지 않은 것을 고르시오.

Last week's lunch is difficult ① to remember because your brain has filed ② it away with all the other lunches you've ever ③ eaten as just another ④ lunches.

06 어법상 옳지 않은 것을 고르시오.

① Despite warned to be on time William and Jane arrived late.
② No evidence suggests that she courted danger for her children.
③ William rang them yesterday to check when they were arriving.
④ By the time they got there, there had hardly been any food left.

07 우리말을 영어로 잘못 옮긴 것은?

① 이러한 소음이 계속되어서, 나는 숙제를 할 수가 없다.
 → With this noise going on, I can't do my homework.
② 우리는 동남아시아 여행 중에 매우 매력적인 장소를 방문했다.
 → We visited so a fascinating place on our trip through Southeast Asia.
③ 그곳은 가장 가까운 해변에서 길어야 10분인 아름다운 오두막이다.
 → It's a beautiful cottage not more than ten minutes from the nearest beach.
④ 요금이 얼마나 빨리 오를 수 있도록 허용되어야 하는지에 대한 정치적인 의문이 있다.
 → There is a political question about how fast fares ought to be allowed to rise.

08 다음 글의 요지로 가장 적절한 것은?

Regardless of how nervous you are, it is essential to portray confidence during your interview, because around 20 percent of interviewers said that candidates who sat with their arms crossed during their meetings were not considered for the roles, because of their body language that reflected their lack of confidence. Eye contact is also crucial for portraying confidence and around 65 percent of interviewers said that candidates who failed to make eye contact didn't get the roles that they were applying for. In fact, nearly 40 percent of interviewers stated that an interviewee's overall confidence was a reason for selecting, or not selecting, the candidate for the position.

① There is a lot of body language that reflects confidence.
② Portraying confidence in a job interview can be a challenge.
③ Interviewers prefer candidates who are obedient and dedicated.
④ Confidence is an important factor when it comes to job candidates being successful.

09 빈칸에 들어갈 표현으로 가장 적절한 것은?

When Caitriona Lally won the Rooney Prize for Literature for her debut novel Eggshells, the media focus was on her day job. She is a cleaner at Trinity College Dublin, scrubbing and mopping in the small hours of the morning so that the "paying gig" is over early and the business of writing can begin. For outsiders and for the press, this is incongruous and something to be remarked upon, discussed, and dissected. For insiders, the interesting detail is that Lally is open about the less-than-prestige work that has paid, and will continue to pay, the bills — despite the €10,000 prize set aside mainly for childcare — as she diligently writes the next book, and the next. Many writers and artists in this country and indeed throughout the world _____; the question is whether to admit to it or not.

① are broke
② are unhealthy
③ lack originality
④ are overestimated

10 주어진 문장이 들어갈 위치로 가장 적절한 것은?

That is, according to Korean traditional beliefs, a woman is the former while the number fifteen is the latter.

At a coming-of-age ceremony for young women of marriageable age, they put their hair up in a chignon and fixed it in place with a hair rod. (①) The coming-of-age ceremony for girls in Joseon society took place when they were fifteen years old or arranged to be married. (②) Even after a coming-of age ceremony, girls were expected to behave like children under the care of their parents until their marriage. (③) The ceremony was held at the age of fifteen because girls of that age represented harmony between yin and yang. (④) Under another theory, the ceremony should be held for fifteen-year-old girls because the moon becomes full on the fifteenth day of the month by the lunar calendar.

01 밑줄 친 표현과 의미가 가장 가까운 것을 고르시오.

When the spectators protested firmly, the incident developed into the riot.

① harshly ② audaciously
③ assiduously ④ adamantly

02 밑줄 친 부분에 들어갈 가장 적절한 것을 고르시오.

He has been forced to _____ his schedule.

① adjust ② admire
③ take over ④ take off

03 밑줄 친 표현과 의미가 가장 가까운 것은?

Some forms of life adapt to change more readily than others.

① acclimate ② adopt
③ solve ④ pose

04 밑줄 친 부분에 가장 적절한 것은?

Wendy: You look fancy tonight! I really like your blue shirt! It looks pretty good on you.
David: Thanks. Well, I'm quite nervous.
Wendy: Why? Where are you headed?
David: I'm meeting someone special. It's a secret.
Wendy: Then let me guess. Are you going on _____ _____?
David: How did you know? It's my first time meeting her.
Wendy: It was just a good guess. I hope it turns out well.
David: I hope so too.

① double date ② a blind date
③ a pipe dream ④ monkey business

05 밑줄 친 부분 중 어법상 옳지 않은 것을 고르시오.

If the solar surface, not the center, ① was as hot as this, the radiation ② emitted into space would be ③ so great that the whole Earth would be vaporized within a few ④ minutes.

06 어법상 옳지 않은 것을 고르시오.

① He tried not to laugh, since she looked pretty angry just now.
② I tried taking tablets for the stomachache but they didn't have no effect.
③ I propose that we send a delegation to Los Angeles to discuss our concerns.
④ Despite the fact that Friday was her busiest day, Jane seemed to enjoy herself.

07 우리말을 영어로 잘못 옮긴 것은?

① 우리가 제공하는 서비스는 얼마나 적절하고 효과적인가?
→ How appropriate and effective are the services we offer?
② Tom이 선생님이 되기에 적합하지 않은 것은 내가 성직자가 되기에 적합하지 않은 것과 같다.
→ Tom is no more fit to be a teacher as I am fit to be a priest.
③ William은 창밖을 응시하며, 양손을 싱크대에 올려놓은 채로 서 있었다.
→ William stood with his hands on the sink, staring out the window.
④ 너무 어려운 시험이라 나는 끝내 완전히 지쳐버렸다.
→ It was such a difficult exam that I was completely exhausted at the end.

08 주어진 문장이 들어갈 위치로 가장 적절한 것은?

> It was these entirely novel institutions that created what we've come to think of as "a job."

From cavemen until about the time of the Civil War, your ancestors didn't have jobs and didn't go on job interviews. Instead, your folks in the "Old Country" grew up, lived, and worked within 10 miles of where they were born. (①) Almost everyone that they met was from their own tribes. And like everybody else, they worked for the king, the church, or the army, or, most likely, were farmers, serfs, or slaves. (②) Until around 1860, farmers made up two-thirds of the U.S. workforce. (③) It was only after the Civil War and industrialization that enormous new factories producing steel, shoes, railroad cars, or pork bellies rose up across the country. (④) Statistically, then, it was not until your great-grandparents' time that your forebears started going on job interviews.

09 다음 글의 내용과 일치하는 것은?

Long before his well-documented work as a freelance journalist and legal clerk in a London law office, 12-year-old Charles Dickens worked in a factory pasting labels onto pots of boot polish. Working 10 hours a day, he earned a weekly wage of six shillings — equivalent to around £16 today. He later recalled how he had worked alongside "two or three other boys who were kept at similar duty downstairs on similar wages", one of whom had shown him around on his first day in the job. "His name was Bob Fagin," Dickens later told his friend and biographer John Forster, "and I took the liberty of using his name in my story, long afterwards."

① Charles Dickens had two jobs before setting out on his career as a writer.
② Charles Dickens worked as a boot polisher.
③ Charles Dickens received 16 shilling per month.
④ Bob Fagin joined the factory before Charles Dickens started his work there.

10 다음 글의 주제로 가장 적절한 것은?

In the Brazilian Amazon, young boys belonging to the indigenous Sateré-Mawé tribe mark their coming of age when they turn 13 in a Bullet and Ant Initiation. The tradition goes as so: they search the jungle for bullet ants which will be sedated with a herbal solution by a leader. The ants are then woven into gloves with the stingers pointed inwards. An hour or so later, the ants wake up angrier than ever, and the initiation begins. Each boy has to wear the gloves for ten minutes. Enduring the pain demonstrates the boys' readiness for manhood, and crying out as doing so demonstrates weakness. Each boy will eventually wear the gloves 20 times over the span of several months before the initiation is complete.

① The dangers of bullet ants
② The Sateré-Mawé tribe's hunting methods
③ A rite of passage from the Sateré-Mawé tribe
④ An important role of the leader in the Sateré-Mawé tribe

기적사 DAY 24

01 밑줄 친 부분에 들어갈 가장 적절한 것을 고르시오.

Most people think that as humans age, they become less _____ at performing routine tasks.

① ambivalent ② adept
③ lenient ④ odd

02 밑줄 친 부분에 들어갈 가장 적절한 것을 고르시오.

He expressed his readiness to _____ the reform bill.

① appease ② take down
③ take off ④ adopt

03 밑줄 친 표현과 의미가 가장 가까운 것은?

He thinks the tax is impossible to administer.

① adjust ② review
③ apologize ④ host

04 밑줄 친 (A), (B), (C)에 들어갈 가장 적절한 것은?

A: There was an important notice from the school cafeteria.
B: What is it about?
A: The school is planning to ____(A)____ food waste.
B: That seems like a reasonable measure considering the planet.
A: I think so too. There is a growing trend for supporting the protection of Earth.
B: I know. Now the school is trying to ____(B)____ the environmentally-friendly movements.
A: It's certainly an urgent issue in the current society.
B: Yeah, global warming is why we should ____(C)____ preserving our precious natural resources.

① (A) cut down on (B) give in to (C) zero in on
② (A) boil down to (B) catch up with (C) zero in on
③ (A) cut down on (B) catch up with (C) zero in on
④ (A) cut down on (B) catch up with (C) drop out of

05 밑줄 친 부분 중 어법상 옳지 않은 것을 고르시오.

Other ① deep-rooted cultural characteristics of races and racial subgroups are much more difficult ② to change. These are the cultural patterns that ③ are so resistant to alteration ④ which they have the appearance of being inherent.

06 어법상 옳지 않은 것을 고르시오.

① The little boy you have seen a moment ago was my nephew.
② I suggested to William that we go out for a meal with his colleagues.
③ There is no provision for any of these costs to be met out of public funds.
④ Although a new drug was good news for patients, it had to be paid for in cash.

07 우리말을 영어로 잘못 옮긴 것은?

① 어떻게 William은 그렇게 짧은 시간에 그것을 성취할 수 있었을까?
→ How could William achieve it in so short a time?
② 피고는 어떤 죄로 기소되고 있는가?
→ What crimes is the defendant being charged with?
③ 표를 사는 사람이 천 명이나 되었다.
→ There were no less than a thousand people buying tickets.
④ Jane은 그의 어깨에 머리를 기대고 잠이 들었었다.
→ Jane had been fallen asleep with her head against his shoulder.

08 글의 주제로 가장 적절한 것은?

Company culture refers to a company's personality. Every company has its own culture. For instance, some companies have a culture of working late or overtime to make sure everything gets done, while other companies have a culture of leaving at 5 p.m. on the dot. Some companies have a culture of teamwork and socializing with colleagues. At other companies, on the other hand, employees work individually most of the time. Whatever your company's culture is, you have to think about how candidates will fit in. When your new employee is a good cultural fit, he or she will be happier and more satisfied at work, which helps reduce turnover.

① How to build a positive corporate culture
② Different interview processes in different cultures
③ A factor to consider when making a hiring decision
④ Company cultures that today's job seekers want to join

09 다음 글의 제목으로 가장 적절한 것은?

Although Louisa May Alcott's best known work, Little Women, was published under her own name, the American writer frequently used the ambiguous nom de plume A.M. Barnard to write sensational gothic thrillers with subject matter deemed 'unladylike' for a late 19th century female writer. Alcott's works written under A.M. Barnard included A Long Fatal Love Chase, a dark love story written two years prior to Little Women, and the novella Behind a Mask, with themes of social class and manipulation. In the 1940s, her secret male pseudonym was discovered by rare book dealer Madeleine B. Stern and librarian Leona Rostenberg.

① Louisa May Alcott's Most Famous Work
② A Female Author Who Used A Male Pen Name
③ Those Who Discovered Louisa May Alcott's Talent
④ General Characteristics of Male and Female Writers

10 빈칸 (A), (B)에 들어갈 표현으로 가장 적절한 것은?

Among the Irish Celts, the coming-of-age ritual was very important for boys. It was a highly religious event that was supposed to turn a boy into a warrior and, as a subsequent, a man. The ritual consisted of a quest, though the nature of it differed depending on the tribe. Some boys were sent out into the forest on a scavenger hunt. They had to come back with certain items to show that they were _____(A)_____ and capable. Others had to head far into the wilderness on longer expeditions. This would show how well they could _____(B)_____ themselves. To manage this, the Celts believed that the boy would be able to evoke help from a god or goddess, an important part of transitioning into an adult. Sometimes, girls would also undertake this quest, though it was not as necessary for them as it was for boys.

	(A)	(B)
①	self-conscious	stand up for
②	self-reliant	take care of
③	self-respecting	put up with
④	self-satisfied	get away with

01 밑줄 친 부분에 들어갈 가장 적절한 것을 고르시오.

But people who see the world through shades of gray are more _____.

① ambivalent ② harsh
③ abrasive ④ casual

02 밑줄 친 부분에 들어갈 가장 적절한 것을 고르시오.

I'm not sure I can _____ to save for my retirement.

① bail ② take down
③ take on ④ afford

03 밑줄 친 표현과 의미가 가장 가까운 것은?

The new law was designed to appease the concerns of farmers.

① soothe ② conceive
③ apologize ④ attempt

04 밑줄 친 (A), (B)에 들어갈 가장 적절한 것은?

Mentor: Do you have any problem in mind?
Mentee: Well, I do have something I want to talk about. I have an opportunity to meet with the board of directors of an enterprise I want to work at.
Mentor: What's the problem with that? Isn't that a good thing?
Mentee: Yeah, it sure is once-in-a-lifetime chance. But I'm afraid I might ___(A)___.
Mentor: Don't be. If you ___(B)___ preparing for the meeting, I'm sure you'll do fine.
Mentee: I feel much more confident now than before.

	(A)	(B)
①	blow it	call it a day
②	blow it	go at full tilt
③	come off second best	call it a day
④	cut from the same cloth	go at full tilt

05 밑줄 친 부분 중 어법상 옳지 않은 것을 고르시오.

The typical scenario in the ① less developed world is one ② in which a very few commercial ③ agriculturalists are technologically advanced ④ on the other hand the vast majority are incapable of competing.

06 어법상 옳지 않은 것을 고르시오.

① I see no reason for us to depart from our usual practice.
② Jane demanded that he returns the books he borrowed from her.
③ Even though he hadn't really got the time, he still offered to help.
④ Tom has earned his own living since he was seven, doing all kinds of jobs.

07 우리말을 영어로 잘못 옮긴 것은?

① Jane은 그와 말도 하지 않을 것이며, 하물며 그와 함께 일하지 않을 것이다.
→ Jane won't even talk to him, much less work with him.
② William은 Jane이 자신을 뒤따르게 한 채 버스 정류장까지 걸어갔다.
→ William walked back to the bus stop, with Jane followed him.
③ 그는 자신이 무엇을 했는지 깨닫자마자, 당황해서 얼굴이 빨개졌다.
→ He turned scarlet from embarrassment, once he realized what he had done.
④ 그것이 원작만큼 좋은 소설일 수 없는 분명한 이유는 없었다.
→ There was no obvious reason why it could not be as good a novel as the original.

08 주어진 문장 다음에 이어질 글의 순서로 가장 적절한 것은?

Usually people think that they are putting a lot of effort in writing a cover letter and therefore it demands to be read with patience.

(A) According to the rule, no application has to be given any more than forty seconds, which means that members of the selection committee would only have enough time to glance through the applications before rounding up the final bunch.
(B) But the reality is exactly the opposite; the interview selection process has to be completed as quickly as possible since employers would not want too many days wasted on granting employment and keeping work on stand-by.
(C) Due to this reason and the innumerable number of applications, most employers have set a golden rule of forty seconds to make things faster and more convenient.

① (A) - (B) - (C)　　② (B) - (A) - (C)
③ (B) - (C) - (A)　　④ (C) - (A) - (B)

09 다음 글의 요지로 가장 적절한 것은?

It's a fact that female writers still battle with stereotypes. The gender bias revealed in an analysis of some 10,000 book reviews by Andrew Piper and Richard Jean So is sufficient evidence of such assertions. As far as reviewers for The New York Times and Sunday Book Review are concerned, "women write about family, men write about war". The results of this study are frustrating. Reviewers favor terms like "husband", "marriage", and "beauty" when describing female books, "theory" and "argument" when critiquing men. Piper and So concluded that "women are still being defined by their 'sentimental' traits and a love of writing about maternal issues, while men are most often being defined by their attention to matters of science and the state."

① Male writers have successfully defied stereotypes.
② Women are better at writing about love than men.
③ Male authors outnumber their female counterparts.
④ There exists prejudice against female authors to this day.

10 다음 글의 내용과 일치하는 것은?

The bar mitzvah and bat mitzvah are coming of age ceremonies for Jewish boys and girls, respectively. Under Jewish Law, individuals are only required to formally observe the commandments once they reach a specific age (12 for girls, 13 for boys). While this change occurs automatically once the child reaches that age, a bar or bat mitzvah is often held to celebrate the boy or girl's coming-of-age and publicly mark the individual's right to now participate in religious ceremonies, count in the minyan, or form contacts. While the ceremony does not indicate that the child is physically an adult, it does so mentally and emotionally with the emphasis on the individual's increased culpability and responsibility. The name itself "bar" or "bat mitzvah", translates into son or daughter of the mitzvah, since from that point on the individual must abide by the mitzvahs (also known as commandments or laws) of the Torah.

*Torah: 유대교의 율법

① The bar mitzvah is for girls and the bat mitzvah is for boys.
② Jewish boys celebrate their coming of age earlier than girls.
③ Without having a coming-of-age ceremony, a Jewish boy over 13 cannot take part in any religious events.
④ Completing the bat mitzvah does not mean a person's physical maturity.

기적사 DAY 26

01 밑줄 친 부분에 들어갈 가장 적절한 것은?

Most people acknowledge that being ethical means being fair and reasonable and not being _____.

① greedy
② altruistic
③ weary
④ skeptical

02 밑줄 친 부분과 의미가 가장 가까운 것을 고르시오.

Reforms enacted in some states have already taken effect, whereas in other states, reformed legislation is shelved.

① pending
② hasty
③ precise
④ divisible

03 밑줄 친 부분과 의미가 가장 가까운 것을 고르시오.

There is no need to make the final decision today. Why don't you go home and sleep on it?

① take a day off to sleep late
② take time to think about it
③ take it for granted
④ take a good rest

04 밑줄 친 부분에 가장 적절한 것은?

A: Did you see Steve this morning?
B: Yes. But why does he _____?
A: I don't have the slightest idea.
B: I thought he'd be happy.
A: Me too. Especially since he got promoted to sales manager last week.
B: He may have some problem with his girlfriend.

① have such a long face
② step into my shoes
③ jump on the bandwagon
④ play a good hand

05 밑줄 친 부분 중 어법상 옳은 것은?

Russian military vehicles crossed the border into Ukraine on Thursday, ① prompted a skirmish between Ukrainian and Russian forces, acting Ukrainian Interior Minister Arsen Avakov said. According to Avakov, tanks crossed the border at a checkpoint ② controlled by pro-Russian separatists in the Luhansk region of eastern Ukraine. Armored vehicles and artillery were part of the columns, Avakov said, ③ cited Ukrainian intelligence. The incident ④ was occurred in the midst of Ukrainian leaders' campaign of violence against people living in the largely pro-Russian east.

06 우리말을 영어로 가장 잘 옮긴 것은?

① 이 가벼운 골프 카트는 접어서 내 차량 트렁크에 넣을 수 있다.
→ This lightweight golf cart will fold and fit in the trunk of my car.

② 아놀드는 새로운 사업 아이디어들을 가지고 있는 소수의 젊은이들 중 하나이다.
→ Arnold is one of handful youngsters with ideas for a new business.

③ 교육 문제는 사회구성원들의 합의에 바탕을 두어 해결되어야 한다.
→ Educational problems should solve upon the agreement of the society members.

④ 그 강의 시리즈는 재무 문제를 다루는 데 익숙하지 않은 사람들을 대상으로 한다.
→ The lecture series are intended for those who are not used to deal with financial issues.

07 우리말을 영어로 잘못 옮긴 것은?

① 남에게 의존하지 말고 너 자신이 직접 그것을 하는 것이 중요하다.
→ It is important that you do it yourself rather than rely on others.

② 은행 앞에 주차된 내 차가 불법 주차로 인해 견인되었다.
→ My car, parked in front of the bank, was towed away for illegal parking.

③ 토요일까지 돈을 갚을 수 있다면, 돈을 빌려줄게.
→ I'll lend you with money provided you will pay me back by Saturday.

④ 만약 태풍이 접근해오지 않았었더라면 그 경기가 열렸을 텐데.
→ The game might have been played if the typhoon had not been approaching.

08 주어진 문장이 들어갈 위치로 가장 적절한 곳은?

> He dismally fails the first two, but redeems himself in the concluding whale episode, where he does indeed demonstrate courage, honesty, and unselfishness.

Disney's work draws heavily from fairy tales, myths, and folklore, which are profuse in archetypal elements. (①) Pinocchio is a good example of how these elements can be emphasized rather than submerged beneath a surface realism. (②) Early in the film, the boy/puppet Pinocchio is told that in order to be a "real boy," he must show that he is "brave, truthful, and unselfish." (③) The three principal episodes of the movie represent ritualistic trials, testing the youth's moral fortitude. (④) As such, like most of Disney's works, the values in Pinocchio are traditional and conservative, an affirmation of the sanctity of the family unit, the importance of a Higher Power in guiding our destinies, and the need to play by society's rules.

09 글의 내용과 일치하지 않는 것은?

Stanislavski was fortunate in many ways. He was the son of a wealthy man who could give him the advantages of a broad education, the opportunity to see the greatest exponents of theatre art at home and abroad. He acquired a great reputation because he had set high goals and never faltered along the hard road leading to them. His personal integrity and inexhaustible capacity for work contributed to making him a professional artist of the first rank. Stanislavski was also richly endowed by nature with a handsome exterior, fine voice and genuine talent. As an actor, director and teacher, he was destined to influence and inspire the many who worked with him and under him or who had the privilege of seeing him on the stage.

① Stanislavski was born with attractive features.
② Stanislavski remained uninfluential on his colleagues throughout his life.
③ Stanislavski's father was affluent enough to support his education.
④ Stanislavski became a top-ranked artist by the aid of his upright character and untiring competence.

10 글의 제목으로 가장 적절한 것은?

Character is a respect for human beings and the right to interpret experience differently. Character admits self-interest as a natural trait, but pins its faith on man's hesitant but heartening instinct to cooperate. Character is allergic to tyranny, irritable with ignorance and always open to improvement. Character is, above all, a tremendous humility before the facts — an automatic alliance with truth even when that truth is bitter medicine.

① Character's Resistance to Truth
② How to Cooperate with Characters
③ The Ignorance of Character
④ What Character Means

01 밑줄 친 부분에 들어갈 가장 적절한 것은?

The Seigneur had a _____ veto power and the right to appoint most of the island's officers.

① suspensive ② crooked
③ eloquent ④ skeptical

02 밑줄 친 부분과 의미가 가장 가까운 것을 고르시오.

The law allows a suspected patient who refuses to be isolated to be quarantined forcibly.

① competent ② boundless
③ dubious ④ divisible

03 밑줄 친 부분과 의미가 가장 가까운 것을 고르시오.

Fit people are better able to cope with stress.

① count on ② deal with
③ cut at ④ sleep on

04 밑줄 친 부분에 가장 적절한 것은?

A: Your fingernails are bleeding!
B: Ouch! No wonder it hurts. I have this bad old habit of biting my fingernails.
A: I've seen many people who have such a habit. But it's not very good for your health.
B: I know. I've been trying really hard to _____ _____ my bad habit but it's not easy.
A: I totally understand. Why don't you keep yourself distracted from your fingernails?
B: You're right. Maybe I should go out and play soccer instead.

① get rid of ② give birth to
③ get the better of ④ keep close tabs on

05 밑줄 친 부분 중 어법상 옳지 않은 것은?

On 2 July 1982, American truck driver Lawrence Richard Walters, nicknamed 'Lawnchair Larry', ① built a homemade airship. Using his lawn chair, 45 helium weather balloons, a Citizens' Band radio, and a pellet gun, he flew to 15,000 feet over ② controlled airspace near Los Angeles International Airport. After 45 minutes, ③ aware that he had breached commercial airspace, he shot several balloons and began his descent. He lost his pellet gun overboard and eventually got caught in power lines, ④ caused a twenty-minute blackout in Long Beach.

06 우리말을 영어로 가장 잘 옮긴 것은?

① 아이들이 거리에서 놀도록 허용되어서는 안 된다.
  → Children shouldn't allow to play in the street.
② Tom은 Jane에게 한 아름의 튤립을 선물하며 청혼했다.
  → Tom proposed Jane, presenting her an armful of tulips.
③ 그 지역의 많은 작은 마을들은 분명히 방문할 가치가 있다.
  → A lot of the small villages in the area are definitely worth visiting.
④ Tom이 의자에 칠했던 페인트가 벌써 벗겨지기 시작하는 중이다.
  → The paint which Tom applied to the chairs are already starting to peel.

07 우리말을 영어로 잘못 옮긴 것은?

① 그가 너의 처남이라는 것이 너의 결정에 영향을 미쳐서는 안 된다.
  → It should not affect your decision that he is your brother-in-law.
② Tom은 그것을 자기 것이라고 주장하며, 그 책을 돌려줄 것을 요구했다.
  → Tom demanded to return the book, claiming that it belonged to him.
③ 나는 Tom에게 예산이 발표될 때까지 기다릴 것을 제안한다.
  → I propose Tom that we wait until the budget has been announced.
④ 만약 그녀가 시험을 잘 봤다면, 그녀는 3월에 대학에 갔을 것이다.
  → If she had done well in her exams, she would have been going to college in March.

08 빈칸에 들어갈 표현으로 가장 적절한 것은?

The bell tower of a cathedral is not the most obvious place to find your one true love, but Quasimodo somehow manages to achieve this. Despite saving the woman he loves, the beautiful Esmeralda, from the stake, however, the Hunchback ends up sadly spurned for another - significantly more good looking - man. On the face of it, the story tells us that it is wrong to despise others for being different, in this case someone with a deformity. It also shows that those with deformities, or disabilities, are just as likely to be good and brave people as anyone else - and that tyrants will meet a sticky end. But a more cynical reading shows that despite Quasimodo's transformation from 'freak' to hero, his physical unattractiveness still prevents him from bagging the girl of his dreams. In short, it shows _____ _____.

① right always prevails in the end
② nothing is stronger than true love
③ the handsome guy always gets the girl
④ the warmhearted person is liked by everyone

09 다음 글의 요지로 가장 적절한 것은?

The Stanislavski system, also called the Stanislavski method, requires that an actor utilize, among other things, his emotional memory (i.e., his recall of past experiences and emotions). The actor's entrance onto the stage is considered to be not a beginning of the action or of his life as the character but a continuation of the set of preceding circumstances. The actor has trained his concentration and his senses so that he may respond freely to the total stage environment. Through empathic observation of people in many different situations, he attempts to develop a wide emotional range so that his onstage actions and reactions appear as if they were a part of the real world rather than make-believe ones.

① Emotion is an important factor in acting.
② The Stanislavski system has been widely practiced.
③ Today's audiences prefer natural and believable stories.
④ The Stanislavski method helps actors build realistic characters.

10 다음 글의 요지로 가장 적절한 것은?

We are accustomed to judge of a man's character by his behavior, that is to say, by the manner in which he reacts to the countless vicissitudes of everyday existence. In our experience these reactions differ according to the individual, and we interpret this variability of response by saying that the characters of the individuals affected are correspondingly diverse. Although character is an attribute of the man himself, it can only be known by the man's actions, and is a rough description of the mental and nervous constitution on which the reactions depend. This constitution is partly inborn and partly acquired. The pattern of the cells and nerve paths which make up the central nervous system is already laid down before birth, but the resistance which any impulse meets with in its passage through the central nervous system is the resultant not only of the inherited pattern, but also of experience.

① Everyone has different characters for genetic reasons.
② Making accurate character judgments is a difficult task.
③ Upbringing influences an individual's character the most.
④ A person's character is determined by both genes and environmental factors.

01 밑줄 친 부분에 들어갈 가장 적절한 것은?

The _____ man stood no nonsense from people.

① criminal ② controversial
③ weary ④ conscientious

02 밑줄 친 부분과 의미가 가장 가까운 것을 고르시오.

Thousands of years ago, human beings lived in dark, dank caves.

① debatable ② deciduous
③ precise ④ humid

03 밑줄 친 부분과 의미가 가장 가까운 것을 고르시오.

Citizens hope to cut off offenders from the outside world completely.

① shut off from
② make a commitment
③ take a day off to sleep late
④ take time to think about it

04 밑줄 친 (A), (B)에 들어갈 가장 적절한 것은?

Ned: What are your plans for the winter vacation?
Ian: I'm going on a ski trip with my family. How about you?
Ned: Oh, a ski trip? That sounds fun. I'm also going on a ski trip with my friends but we have some problems with the transportation.
Ian: Why is that?
Ned: No one has a driver's license. But the only way we can get there is by driving. So I am going to ask my parents if they can give us ____(A)____.
Ian: If your parents say they can't drive you there, I would like to give you ____(B)____.
Ned: Thank you so much for your offer. That's very nice of you.
Ian: It's my pleasure.

	(A)	(B)
①	a lift	a ring
②	a shot	a lift
③	a lift	a hand
④	a ring	a hand

05 밑줄 친 부분 중 어법상 옳지 않은 것은?

But economics is not a laboratory science. Economists test their theories using real-world data, which ① are generated by the actual operation of the economy. In this rather ② bewildering environment, "other things" do change. ③ Although the development of complex statistical techniques designed to hold other things equal, control is less than perfect. As a result, economic principles are less certain and less precise than ④ those of laboratory sciences. That also means they are more open to debate than many scientific theories.

06 우리말을 영어로 가장 잘 옮긴 것은?

① 오염된 음식 한 스푼이면 당신을 매우 아프게 하기에 충분할지도 모른다.
→ One spoonful contaminated food may be enough to make you very ill.

② 수공예로 만든 흔드는 당나귀들은 미국 전역에서 잘 팔렸다.
→ The handcrafting rocking donkeys have sold well across the United States.

③ 폭력으로 공격받으면, 폭력으로 대응하지 않을 수 없다.
→ If we are attacked with violence, we cannot help to respond with violence.

④ SRI 펀드가 사회적으로 책임 있는 투자를 하기 위해 사용하는 기준을 스크린이라고 한다.
→ The criteria that SRI funds use to make socially responsible investments are called screens.

07 우리말을 영어로 잘못 옮긴 것은?

① 나는 Jane이 Tom을 만나자고 요구하는 것을 듣고도 놀라지 않았다.
→ I was not surprised to hear Jane to demand to see Tom.

② 누구도 John을 돕고 싶어 한다는 것은 믿을 수 없는 일이었다.
→ It was unbelievable that anyone should want to help John.

③ 당신은 매우 숙련된 사람에게 그렇게 낮은 봉급을 줄 수 없다.
→ You can't offer such a low salary to someone who is so highly skilled.

④ 소량만 복용했다면 그 약은 아무런 폐해도 끼치지 않았을 텐데.
→ If taken in small doses, the drug would have had no harmful effects.

08 다음 밑줄 친 단어가 가리키는 대상이 나머지 넷과 다른 것은?

Born in Chicago in 1901 and raised in Missouri, Walt Disney was the fourth son among five siblings. His father, Elias, was a domineering figure who was allegedly abusive as ① he tried, unsuccessfully, to make ends meet for the family. In order to escape from ② his stressful circumstances, young Disney found solace in drawing. Still, ③ he'd watch his older brothers, one by one, run off from home to escape from their father, and soon ④ he'd follow suit by lying about his age to become an ambulance driver during World War I. When his father died, he reportedly refused to cut a business trip short and therefore missed his dad's funeral.

09 주어진 문장이 들어갈 위치로 가장 적절한 것은?

So as a young adult he adopted a stage name - Stanislavski - so he could keep his performances a secret.

Konstantin Sergeievich Alexeiev was born in 1863 to a wealthy Russian family living in Moscow. He was brought up immersed in drama and the arts, as his father built a stage for Konstantin and his siblings to perform plays on. (①) The family would also regularly attend the ballet and the opera. (②) Konstantin's parents did not, however, want their son to pursue a career in the theater. (③) He became a well known amateur actor in Russia, and also began to direct. (④) In 1898 Stanislavski co-founded the Moscow Art Theater with writer Vladimir Nemirovich-Danchenko. The theater was a success, with Stanislavski's method for training and directing the actors described as "genius" by fellow actor and director Vsevolod Meyerhold. His system is still used to train method actors today.

10 주어진 문장이 들어갈 위치로 가장 적절한 것은?

Everything we do, even if it's helping others, is done because in one way or another it makes us feel good.

A virtue is a trait or quality that is deemed to be morally good. (①) Examples of this are things like honesty, courage, compassion, generosity, and integrity. We all have a natural obligation to benefit ourselves. (②) The virtue of human character is the central focus of Socrates' perspective. Good living through good character was the holy grail of Socrates' ideal of the examined life. (③) Socrates believed that knowledge is the fundamental good and the governing dynamic of all human action. (④) The ability to allow knowledge to influence our world view and behavior is the fundamental good that makes all other human good stand up and live. It is necessary to practice seeking knowledge and seek improvement of our human character for the rest of our lives.

기적사 DAY 29

01 밑줄 친 부분에 들어갈 가장 적절한 것은?

Thus whether or not CPTED is actually effective at reducing crime is _____.

① debatable ② altruistic
③ meticulous ④ humid

02 밑줄 친 부분과 의미가 가장 가까운 것을 고르시오.

He looks as old as a person who's in his 60s and totally decrepit.

① eloquent ② hasty
③ discreet ④ impotent

03 밑줄 친 부분과 의미가 가장 가까운 것을 고르시오.

However, we usually go through a variety of hardships during our lifetime.

① get above ourselves
② take a day off to sleep late
③ pass through
④ hand over

04 밑줄 친 부분에 가장 적절한 것은?

Amy: Hi, Trevor. Have you been to Spain?
Trevor: Yeah, I've been there when I was about five years old. Why do you ask?
Amy: My brother lives in Madrid, Spain, and I want to spend the New Years day with him there.
Trevor: That sounds like an exciting plan! Feel free to ask me anything.
Amy: Well, I actually want to travel nearby countries, such as Portugal.
Trevor: That's a common route. Why do you hesitate?
Amy: I have to travel all by myself because my brother has to work. But I'm not sure I _____ that.
Trevor: How about asking some of your friends to go with you?
Amy: I should try that.

① have a say in
② have a soft spot for
③ have had enough of
④ have the nerve to do

05 밑줄 친 부분 중 어법상 옳지 않은 것은?

The institutions and incentive structures of society ① operation largely in accordance with Bentham's claim and thus are missing out on some of the most profound motivators of human behavior. What Bentham and the rest of us typically overlook is ② that humans are wired with another set of interests that are just as ③ basic as physical pain and pleasure. We are wired to be social. We are ④ driven by deep motivations to stay connected with friends and family. We are naturally curious about what is going on in the minds of other people.

06 우리말을 영어로 가장 잘 옮긴 것은?

① 우리의 생각은 그가 그 규칙을 지키도록 해야 한다는 것이었다.
→ Our idea was that he must be made comply with the rules.

② 그 냉장고를 문으로 통과시키는 것은 불가능했다.
→ There was no getting the refrigerator through the door.

③ William의 여행 가이드는 잘 읽히고 매우 유익하다.
→ William's travel guide reads well and is very uninformative.

④ 두 명의 강도가 보석상에서 값비싼 반지를 몇 개 훔쳤다.
→ Two robbers stole a handful of expensive rings of a jewellery store.

07 우리말을 영어로 잘못 옮긴 것은?

① 경제 상황이 호전될 것으로 예측되었다.
→ It predicted that the economic situation would improve.

② William은 자기 딸에게 천과 건초를 사용해서 예쁜 인형을 만들어 주었다.
→ William made his daughter a pretty doll, using some cloth and hay.

③ 네가 나를 위해 내 컴퓨터를 고쳤더라면 너에게 20파운드를 주었을 텐데.
→ I would have given you twenty pounds if you had fixed my computer for me.

④ 그는 일반 청중에게 연설할 때 자신의 의견을 굽히지 않는 용기가 필요하다.
→ He needs the courage to stick to his opinion when addressing a general audience.

08 다음 글의 요지로 가장 적절한 것은?

Over the years, the Disney company has become expert at crafting stories that tug at your heartstrings and stay with you long. Why are Disney stories so memorable and popular? It's because they focus on shared desires. Walt Disney knew a lot about people: he recognized that there were certain common struggles and desires that all humans experience. I'm not just talking about the longing for more money or a better job. I'm talking about the deeper and more hidden desires like the desire for belonging, for true love, or for discovering you're a part of something bigger than yourself. The Disney company crafts stories that specifically focus on shared human experiences. Think of Remy, the rat in *Ratatouille*, who has a dream that seems so far out of his reach, or Hercules, who literally sings, "I will go most anywhere to find where I belong." These characters provide a mouthpiece to the thoughts and feelings we all have.

① Disney stories are popular worldwide.
② Disney stories give us long-lasting impressions.
③ We like Disney stories because we empathize with them.
④ Disney movies deliver unrealistic and utopian messages to us.

09 다음 글의 주제로 가장 적절한 것은?

An Actor Prepares is the most famous acting training material ever to have been written and the work of Stanislavski has inspired generations of actors and trainers. This translation was the first to introduce Stanislavski's 'system' to the English speaking world and has stood the test of time in acting classes to this day. Here Stanislavski deals with the inward preparation an actor must undergo in order to explore a role to the full. He introduces the concepts of the 'magic if' units and objectives, of emotion memory, of the super-objective and many more now famous rehearsal aids. This volume is an essential read for actors, directors and anyone interested in the art of drama.

① a play by Stanislavski
② a book by Stanislavski
③ an actor's autobiography
④ Stanislavski's training system

10 빈칸 (A), (B)에 들어갈 가장 적절한 것은?

Humor is observed in all cultures and at all ages. But only in recent decades has experimental psychology respected it as an essential, fundamental human behavior. Historically, psychologists framed humor negatively, suggesting it demonstrated superiority, vulgarity, Freudian id conflict, or a defense mechanism to hide one's true feelings. In this view, an individual used humor to demean or disparage others, or to inflate one's own self-worth. ___(A)___, it was treated as an undesirable behavior to be avoided. And psychologists tended to ignore it as worthy of study. ___(B)___ research on humor has recently come to light, with humor now viewed as a character strength. Positive psychology, a field that examines what people do well, notes that humor can be used to make others feel good, to gain intimacy, or to help buffer stress.

	(A)	(B)
①	Nevertheless	In the end
②	Therefore	Likewise
③	Hence	However
④	Otherwise	But

01 밑줄 친 부분에 들어갈 가장 적절한 것은?

A saint is a person who gets credit for having _____ holiness or goodness by living an extremely virtuous life.

① greedy
② frigid
③ executive
④ exceptional

02 밑줄 친 부분과 의미가 가장 가까운 것을 고르시오.

In this particular case, we decided, you know, that we would have no gratuitous violence.

① pending
② groundless
③ gregarious
④ hospitable

03 밑줄 친 부분과 의미가 가장 가까운 것을 고르시오.

We will need to keep close tabs on whether any further delays emerge because postponing the launch will worsen the company's competitive position.

① look forward to
② have our eyes on
③ make against
④ sleep on

04 밑줄 친 (A), (B), (C)에 들어갈 가장 적절한 것은?

Rudy: Hi, Melissa. Are you free this afternoon?
Melissa: Sorry, but no. I have to finish my group assignment. The due date is tomorrow.
Rudy: That's too bad. How is it going with your team members?
Melissa: They're not very active participants. Sometimes, they even ___(A)___ other team members by refusing to complete their assigned work.
Rudy: Oh, that must be a great burden on you. Why don't you ___(B)___ about that with your group members?
Melissa: Well, I don't mean to ___(C)___ them. My hopes may be too high for them to reach. They might be trying their best.

① (A) go in for　　(B) talk big　(C) get along with
② (A) go in for　　(B) speak out (C) find fault with
③ (A) pass the buck to (B) talk big　(C) get away with
④ (A) pass the buck to (B) speak out (C) find fault with

05 밑줄 친 부분 중 어법상 옳지 않은 것은?

People weep during funeral rituals, for instance, in every culture except in Bali, and even there people weep in mourning—tearless funerals are made ① possible only by postponing the rites until two full years after the death. However much the rules ② governing emotional display may vary from time to time and place to place, adults weep for myriad reasons and sometimes, a few ③ claims that they weep for no reason at all. In American culture, even those rare people (usually male) who claim they never cry can remember ④ doing so as children.

06 우리말을 영어로 가장 잘 옮긴 것은?

① Tom은 그것이 시행될 수 없다면 금지해봐야 아무 소용없다고 말한다.
→ Tom says it's of no use having a ban if it can't be enforced.

② 그녀는 장작을 한 아름 들고 오두막에서 나왔다.
→ She came out of her cottage, carried an armful of firewood.

③ 전 세계 여자들이 안도의 한숨을 크게 내쉬는 소리가 들렸다.
→ Women around the world were heard heave a huge sigh of relief.

④ Tom과 John은 연극에서 아버지와 아들로 출연하는데, 그 연극이 오늘 밤에 개봉된다.
→ Tom and John star as father and son in the play, which opens tonight.

07 우리말을 영어로 잘못 옮긴 것은?

① 우리는 누군가에게 그 마을로 가는 길을 물어봐야 할 것이다.
→ We'll have to ask someone the way to the village.

② 당신이 의사가 되고 싶었다면 대학에 갔어야 했는데.
→ You should have gone to college if you had wanted to be a doctor.

③ 그 사고의 장기적인 영향이 어떨지 예측하기 어렵다.
→ It is difficult to predict what the long-term effects of the accident will be.

④ 이것이 잘못된 질문임을 암시하면서, 그의 표정은 우레와 같은 양상을 띠게 된다.
→ His expression, suggesting this be the wrong question to ask, takes on a thunderous aspect.

08 밑줄 친 (A), (B)에 들어갈 말로 가장 적절한 것은?

In November 1966, doctors discovered that Disney, a longtime smoker, had lung cancer. He died at a Burbank hospital the following month, on December 15, at age 65. Not long after his death, stories began circulating in the tabloid press that the filmmaker had been cryogenically preserved. _____(A)_____, he'd been frozen with the hope that science might one day make it possible for him to be brought back to life. In spite of the persistent rumors concerning Disney and cryonics, he was, _____(B)_____, cremated and his ashes were interred in a mausoleum at Forest Lawn Cemetery in Glendale, California. The first person to be frozen cryogenically was an American university professor in January 1967. Since that time, more than a hundred others have been cryopreserved, including baseball great Ted Williams, who died in 2002.

	(A)	(B)
①	On the other hand	unfortunately
②	To take an example	accordingly
③	That is to say	in fact
④	As a result	in addition

09 밑줄 친 부분 중 글의 흐름상 가장 어색한 것은?

Stanislavski's Magic If may be one of the most useful tools available to actors today. ① This device is used to get actors to open up their imaginations to discover new and interesting things about the characters they are playing. In utilizing it, an actor simply asks himself a 'what if' question about the character. ② Let's say he is playing a young man whose objective is to leave his family forever. ③ After getting as much information as he can about the character from the text of the play, there will still be aspects of his character's back story and present situation which are cloudy or simply not answered by the text. ④ Stanislavski emphasizes the importance of the actor's completely understanding the text of the play. As an example, if the character knows close to nothing about his father and it would be useful to have such information, then 'what if' questions about the father may prove to be helpful. Questions such as what if the character's father beat him, what if his father ran off, or what if the father died before the character was born may be appropriate.

10 빈칸에 들어갈 표현으로 가장 적절한 것은?

Nothing that has ever happened is quite without influence at this moment. The present is simply the past rolled up and concentrated in this second of time. You, too, are your past; often your face is your autobiography; you are what you are because of what you have been; because of your heredity stretching back into forgotten generations; because of every element of environment that has affected you, every man or woman that has met you, every book that you have read, every experience that you have had; all these are accumulated in your memory, your body, your character, and your soul. So with a city, a country, or a race; it is its past, and cannot be understood without it. It is the present, not the past, that dies; this present moment, to which we give so much attention, is forever flitting from our eyes and fingers into that pedestal and matrix of our lives which we call the past. _____.

① Let the past go to move on
② It is only the past that lives
③ Your past determines your character
④ The present is more important than anything else

기적사 복습 모의고사 3회

01 밑줄 친 표현과 의미가 가장 가까운 것은?

The new law was designed to appease the concerns of farmers.

① soothe ② conceive
③ apologize ④ attempt

02 밑줄 친 표현과 의미가 가장 가까운 것은?

We need to iron out a few problems first.

① conceive ② review
③ solve ④ pose

03 밑줄 친 부분과 의미가 가장 가까운 것을 고르시오.

Fit people are better able to cope with stress.

① count on ② deal with
③ cut at ④ sleep on

04 밑줄 친 부분에 들어갈 가장 적절한 것은?

Most people acknowledge that being ethical means being fair and reasonable and not being _____.

① greedy ② altruistic
③ weary ④ skeptical

05 다음 글의 내용과 일치하는 것은?

Long before his well-documented work as a freelance journalist and legal clerk in a London law office, 12-year-old Charles Dickens worked in a factory pasting labels onto pots of boot polish. Working 10 hours a day, he earned a weekly wage of six shillings — equivalent to around £16 today. He later recalled how he had worked alongside "two or three other boys who were kept at similar duty downstairs on similar wages", one of whom had shown him around on his first day in the job. "His name was Bob Fagin," Dickens later told his friend and biographer John Forster, "and I took the liberty of using his name in my story, long afterwards."

① Charles Dickens had two jobs before setting out on his career as a writer.
② Charles Dickens worked as a boot polisher.
③ Charles Dickens received 16 shilling per month.
④ Bob Fagin joined the factory before Charles Dickens started his work there.

06 어법상 옳지 않은 것을 고르시오.

① I see no reason for us to depart from our usual practice.
② Jane demanded that he returns the books he borrowed from her.
③ Even though he hadn't really got the time, he still offered to help.
④ Tom has earned his own living since he was seven, doing all kinds of jobs.

07 다음 글의 제목으로 가장 적절한 것은?

Although Louisa May Alcott's best known work, Little Women, was published under her own name, the American writer frequently used the ambiguous nom de plume A.M. Barnard to write sensational gothic thrillers with subject matter deemed 'unladylike' for a late 19th century female writer. Alcott's works written under A.M. Barnard included A Long Fatal Love Chase, a dark love story written two years prior to Little Women, and the novella Behind a Mask, with themes of social class and manipulation. In the 1940s, her secret male pseudonym was discovered by rare book dealer Madeleine B. Stern and librarian Leona Rostenberg.

① Louisa May Alcott's Most Famous Work
② A Female Author Who Used A Male Pen Name
③ Those Who Discovered Louisa May Alcott's Talent
④ General Characteristics of Male and Female Writers

08 밑줄 친 부분 중 어법상 옳지 않은 것을 고르시오.

If the solar surface, not the center, ① was as hot as this, the radiation ② emitted into space would be ③ so great that the whole Earth would be vaporized within a few ④ minutes.

09 주어진 문장이 들어갈 위치로 가장 적절한 것은?

It was these entirely novel institutions that created what we've come to think of as "a job."

From cavemen until about the time of the Civil War, your ancestors didn't have jobs and didn't go on job interviews. Instead, your folks in the "Old Country" grew up, lived, and worked within 10 miles of where they were born. (①) Almost everyone that they met was from their own tribes. And like everybody else, they worked for the king, the church, or the army, or, most likely, were farmers, serfs, or slaves. (②) Until around 1860, farmers made up two-thirds of the U.S. workforce. (③) It was only after the Civil War and industrialization that enormous new factories producing steel, shoes, railroad cars, or pork bellies rose up across the country. (④) Statistically, then, it was not until your great-grandparents' time that your forebears started going on job interviews.

10 밑줄 친 부분 중 글의 흐름상 가장 어색한 것은?

Stanislavski's Magic If may be one of the most useful tools available to actors today. ① This device is used to get actors to open up their imaginations to discover new and interesting things about the characters they are playing. In utilizing it, an actor simply asks himself a 'what if' question about the character. ② Let's say he is playing a young man whose objective is to leave his family forever. ③ After getting as much information as he can about the character from the text of the play, there will still be aspects of his character's back story and present situation which are cloudy or simply not answered by the text. ④ Stanislavski emphasizes the importance of the actor's completely understanding the text of the play. As an example, if the character knows close to nothing about his father and it would be useful to have such information, then 'what if' questions about the father may prove to be helpful. Questions such as what if the character's father beat him, what if his father ran off, or what if the father died before the character was born may be appropriate.

11 밑줄 친 부분에 가장 적절한 것은?

A: I heard you had a meeting this morning.
B: Yes, I came here to meet you as soon as it ended.
A: Thanks for coming all the way here. How did the meeting go?
B: It didn't go so smooth. Today was the first meeting we had with the new employees and one of them was such _____.
A: Tell me all about it. What did he do?
B: First, he was late and second, he had rude attitude during the whole conference.
A: That must have been harsh. Cheer up!
B: Thank you for your encouragement.

① a real McCoy
② a walk of life
③ a wet blanket
④ an act of God

12 밑줄 친 부분에 가장 적절한 것은?

Amy: Hi, Trevor. Have you been to Spain?
Trevor: Yeah, I've been there when I was about five years old. Why do you ask?
Amy: My brother lives in Madrid, Spain, and I want to spend the New Years day with him there.
Trevor: That sounds like an exciting plan! Feel free to ask me anything.
Amy: Well, I actually want to travel nearby countries, such as Portugal.
Trevor: That's a common route. Why do you hesitate?
Amy: I have to travel all by myself because my brother has to work. But I'm not sure I _____ that.
Trevor: How about asking some of your friends to go with you?
Amy: I should try that.

① have a say in
② have a soft spot for
③ have had enough of
④ have the nerve to do

13 다음 글의 내용과 일치하는 것은?

The bar mitzvah and bat mitzvah are coming of age ceremonies for Jewish boys and girls, respectively. Under Jewish Law, individuals are only required to formally observe the commandments once they reach a specific age (12 for girls, 13 for boys). While this change occurs automatically once the child reaches that age, a bar or bat mitzvah is often held to celebrate the boy or girl's coming-of-age and publicly mark the individual's right to now participate in religious ceremonies, count in the minyan, or form contacts. While the ceremony does not indicate that the child is physically an adult, it does so mentally and emotionally with the emphasis on the individual's increased culpability and responsibility. The name itself "bar" or "bat mitzvah", translates into son or daughter of the mitzvah, since from that point on the individual must abide by the mitzvahs (also known as commandments or laws) of the Torah.

* Torah: 유대교의 율법

① The bar mitzvah is for girls and the bat mitzvah is for boys.
② Jewish boys celebrate their coming of age earlier than girls.
③ Without having a coming-of-age ceremony, a Jewish boy over 13 cannot take part in any religious events.
④ Completing the bat mitzvah does not mean a person's physical maturity.

14 우리말을 영어로 가장 잘 옮긴 것은?

① 이 가벼운 골프 카트는 접어서 내 차량 트렁크에 넣을 수 있다.
→ This lightweight golf cart will fold and fit in the trunk of my car.
② 아놀드는 새로운 사업 아이디어들을 가지고 있는 소수의 젊은 이들 중 하나이다.
→ Arnold is one of handful youngsters with ideas for a new business.
③ 교육 문제는 사회구성원들의 합의에 바탕을 두어 해결되어야 한다.
→ Educational problems should solve upon the agreement of the society members.
④ 그 강의 시리즈는 재무 문제를 다루는 데 익숙하지 않은 사람들을 대상으로 한다.
→ The lecture series are intended for those who are not used to deal with financial issues.

15 우리말을 영어로 잘못 옮긴 것은?

① 많은 사람들이 아파서 회의가 취소되었다.
   → With many people ill, the meeting was cancelled.
② 이것은 우리가 예상했던 것만큼 그렇게 간단한 문제는 아니다.
   → It is not so straightforward a problem as we expected.
③ 학생들이 몇 개의 가방을 가지고 탑승할 건가요?
   → How many bags are the students carrying on board with them?
④ 아무런 해명도 없었다. 사과는 말할 것도 없고.
   → No explanation was offered, still more an apology.

16 빈칸에 들어갈 표현으로 가장 적절한 것은?

Nothing that has ever happened is quite without influence at this moment. The present is simply the past rolled up and concentrated in this second of time. You, too, are your past; often your face is your autobiography; you are what you are because of what you have been; because of your heredity stretching back into forgotten generations; because of every element of environment that has affected you, every man or woman that has met you, every book that you have read, every experience that you have had; all these are accumulated in your memory, your body, your character, and your soul. So with a city, a country, or a race; it is its past, and cannot be understood without it. It is the present, not the past, that dies; this present moment, to which we give so much attention, is forever flitting from our eyes and fingers into that pedestal and matrix of our lives which we call the past. _____.

① Let the past go to move on
② It is only the past that lives
③ Your past determines your character
④ The present is more important than anything else

17 빈칸에 들어갈 표현으로 가장 적절한 것은?

When Caitriona Lally won the Rooney Prize for Literature for her debut novel Eggshells, the media focus was on her day job. She is a cleaner at Trinity College Dublin, scrubbing and mopping in the small hours of the morning so that the "paying gig" is over early and the business of writing can begin. For outsiders and for the press, this is incongruous and something to be remarked upon, discussed, and dissected. For insiders, the interesting detail is that Lally is open about the less-than-prestige work that has paid, and will continue to pay, the bills − despite the €10,000 prize set aside mainly for childcare − as she diligently writes the next book, and the next. Many writers and artists in this country and indeed throughout the world _____; the question is whether to admit to it or not.

① are broke
② are unhealthy
③ lack originality
④ are overestimated

18 주어진 문장 다음에 이어질 글의 순서로 가장 적절한 것은?

Usually people think that they are putting a lot of effort in writing a cover letter and therefore it demands to be read with patience.

(A) According to the rule, no application has to be given any more than forty seconds, which means that members of the selection committee would only have enough time to glance through the applications before rounding up the final bunch.

(B) But the reality is exactly the opposite; the interview selection process has to be completed as quickly as possible since employers would not want too many days wasted on granting employment and keeping work on stand-by.

(C) Due to this reason and the innumerable number of applications, most employers have set a golden rule of forty seconds to make things faster and more convenient.

① (A) - (B) - (C)
② (B) - (A) - (C)
③ (B) - (C) - (A)
④ (C) - (A) - (B)

19 다음 글의 요지로 가장 적절한 것은?

We are accustomed to judge of a man's character by his behavior, that is to say, by the manner in which he reacts to the countless vicissitudes of everyday existence. In our experience these reactions differ according to the individual, and we interpret this variability of response by saying that the characters of the individuals affected are correspondingly diverse. Although character is an attribute of the man himself, it can only be known by the man's actions, and is a rough description of the mental and nervous constitution on which the reactions depend. This constitution is partly inborn and partly acquired. The pattern of the cells and nerve paths which make up the central nervous system is already laid down before birth, but the resistance which any impulse meets with in its passage through the central nervous system is the resultant not only of the inherited pattern, but also of experience.

① Everyone has different characters for genetic reasons.
② Making accurate character judgments is a difficult task.
③ Upbringing influences an individual's character the most.
④ A person's character is determined by both genes and environmental factors.

20 다음 밑줄 친 단어가 가리키는 대상이 나머지 넷과 다른 것은?

Born in Chicago in 1901 and raised in Missouri, Walt Disney was the fourth son among five siblings. His father, Elias, was a domineering figure who was allegedly abusive as ① he tried, unsuccessfully, to make ends meet for the family. In order to escape from ② his stressful circumstances, young Disney found solace in drawing. Still, ③ he'd watch his older brothers, one by one, run off from home to escape from their father, and soon ④ he'd follow suit by lying about his age to become an ambulance driver during World War I. When his father died, he reportedly refused to cut a business trip short and therefore missed his dad's funeral.

MEMO

결국엔 성정혜 영어 하프모의고사
기적사 DAY 31

01 밑줄 친 부분에 들어갈 가장 적절한 것은?

The Secretary General said the U.N. will put forward several action plans to _____ the multilateral nuclear security and safety. He said toughening financial sanctions are necessary to prevent the spread of weapons of mass destruction and nuclear terrorism.

① beef up   ② dispense with
③ damp down   ④ scratch off

02 밑줄 친 부분에 들어갈 가장 적절한 것을 고르시오.

The satellite image shows "brown clouds" over eastern China. The noxious cocktail of soot, smog and toxic chemicals is _____ the sun, fouling the lungs of millions of people in large parts of Asia.

① blotting out   ② poring over
③ catering to   ④ resorting to

03 밑줄 친 부분에 들어갈 가장 적절한 것을 고르시오.

A hypnotized person _____ a kind of trance, a state in which someone can move and speak but is not conscious in a normal way.

① looms on   ② lapses into
③ levels at   ④ laps against

04 밑줄 친 부분에 들어갈 표현으로 가장 적절한 것을 고르시오.

A: Look at this letter.
B: Ah yes, I thought it was something official looking. You're being fined for exceeding the speed limit, it says. Why weren't you fined on the spot?
A: _____.
B: They're installing more and more of them around here. You're going to have to be more careful in future.
A: You're not kidding. The fine is $60.

① Because the spot was too busy to be fined
② Because I could not find any camera to take it
③ Because I already paid for it when I was fined
④ Because I was photographed by one of speed cameras

05 밑줄 친 부분 중 어법상 옳지 않은 것을 고르시오.

The Netherlands now ① becomes the only country in the world to allow the mercy killing of patients, though there are some strict conditions. ② Those who want medical assistance to die ③ must be undergone unbearable suffering. Doctor and patient must also agree there is no hope of remission. And ④ a second physician must be consulted.

06 밑줄 친 부분 중 어법상 옳지 않은 것을 고르시오.

① Unable to do anything or go anywhere while my car ② was repairing at my mechanic's garage, I suddenly ③ came to the realization that I had become ④ overly dependent on machines and gadgets.

07 밑줄 친 부분 중 어법상 옳지 않은 것을 고르시오.

A Civil Service career is your chance ① to begin a journey ② where the things that you accomplish on a daily basis can make a difference in the world. From improving trade opportunities for U.S. businesses, to monitoring human rights issues, and ③ to providing management supervision, you can use your skills in a Civil Service career to directly impact foreign policy issues or uphold the business practices and processes ④ involving in supporting the U.S. Department of State's diplomatic efforts.

08 글의 주제로 가장 적절한 것은?

Children who under-achieve at school may just have poor working memory rather than low intelligence. Researchers from a university surveyed more than 3,000 primary school children of all ages and found that 10 % of them suffer from poor working memory, which seriously impedes their learning. Nationally, this equates to almost 500,000 children in primary education being affected. The researchers also found that teachers rarely identify poor working memory and often describe children with this problem as inattentive or less intelligent.

① children's identification with teachers at school
② low intelligence of primary school children
③ influence of poor working memory on primary school children
④ teachers' efforts to solve children's working-memory problem

09 글의 내용과 일치하는 것은?

A new study by Harvard researchers may provide a compelling reason to remove canned soup and juice from your dining table. People who ate one serving of canned food daily over the course of five days, the study found, had significantly elevated levels — more than a tenfold increase — of bisphenol-A, or BPA, a substance that lines most food and drink cans. Public health officials in the United States have come under increasing pressure to regulate it. Some of the research on BPA shows that it is linked to a higher risk of cancer, heart disease, and obesity. Some researchers, though, counter that its reputation as a health threat to people is exaggerated. The new study published in The Journal of the American Medical Association is the first to measure the amounts of BPA that are ingested when people eat food that comes directly out of a can.

① 하버드의 새로운 연구가 통조림 음식의 안전성을 입증하였다.
② 비스페놀 A와 암, 심장병, 비만의 연관성이 과장되었다는 데에 모든 학자들이 동의한다.
③ 통조림 음식으로부터 사람의 몸에 유입된 비스페놀 A의 양이 아직 측정되지 않았다.
④ 미국의 보건 관리들은 비스페놀 A를 규제하라는 압력을 점점 더 받고 있다.

10 주어진 글 다음에 이어질 글의 순서로 가장 적절한 것은?

All animals have the same kind of brain activation during sleep as humans. Whether or not they dream is another question, which can be answered only by posing another one: Do animals have consciousness?

(A) These are three of the key aspects of consciousness, and they could be experienced whether or not an animal had verbal language as we do. When the animal's brain is activated during sleep, why not assume that the animal has some sort of perceptual, emotional, and memory experience?

(B) Many scientists today feel that animals probably do have a limited form of consciousness, quite different from ours in that it lacks language and the capacity for propositional or symbolic thought.

(C) Animals certainly can't report dreams even if they do have them. But which pet owner would doubt that his or her favourite animal friend has perception, memory, and emotion?

① (A) − (B) − (C)
② (A) − (C) − (B)
③ (B) − (C) − (A)
④ (C) − (B) − (A)

결국엔 성정혜 영어 하프모의고사
기적사 DAY 32

01 밑줄 친 부분에 들어갈 가장 적절한 것은?

The data were so hard to analyze that we couldn't _____ what they tried to show to us.

① make up with ② dispense with
③ damp down   ④ make out

02 밑줄 친 부분에 들어갈 가장 적절한 것을 고르시오.

Usually, blue rock thrush birds do not _____ to other areas and mainly inhabit near the coast.

① cater   ② perpetrate
③ migrate   ④ oblige

03 밑줄 친 부분에 들어갈 가장 적절한 것을 고르시오.

This _____ the way for his success as a trunk designer and finally, he opened his own shop in 1854.

① paved   ② loomed on
③ mended   ④ dispatched

04 밑줄 친 부분에 들어갈 표현으로 가장 적절한 것을 고르시오.

A: What job do you wish to have in the future?
B: I want to become a CEO.
A: Wow, that's a venerable occupation. Why did you decide you want to become a CEO?
B: It looks like a job which is _____ by many people.
A: You're right. In fact, according to survey conducted last year, CEO is one of the most respected jobs among high school students.
B: Oh, that's something I didn't know.

① hitting upon   ② living up to
③ looked up to   ④ out of season

05 밑줄 친 부분 중 어법상 옳지 않은 것을 고르시오.

Most people who live in direct contact with the environment and employ relatively little technology in the acquisition of food actually ① work harder than simply picking low-hanging fruit, but ② gather what grows wild in the environment is a form of production. Production ③ refers to any human action intended to convert resources in the environment ④ into food.

06 밑줄 친 부분 중 어법상 옳지 않은 것을 고르시오.

The injured student received more help ① when wearing a shirt of the participant's favorite team ② as when wearing either of the other kinds of ③ shirts. People who are fans of the same soccer team ④ form an ingroup.

07 밑줄 친 부분 중 어법상 옳지 않은 것을 고르시오.

Prior to ① coming on board at the hospital, he had worked as an independent contractor. At the hospital he took a position that was ② newly created because the hospital believed change was needed in how painting services were provided. ③ Upon beginning his job, Mark did a 4-month analysis of the direct and indirect costs of painting services. His findings supported the perceptions of his administrators that painting services were ④ inefficiently and costly.

08 빈칸에 들어갈 표현으로 가장 적절한 것은?

The part of the brain responsible for working memory is also responsible for _____. Here, working memory skills help kids to remember what they need to be paying attention to. Take, for example, doing a long division problem. Your child needs working memory not only to come up with the answer, but also to zero in on all of the steps involved in getting there. Children with weak working memory skills have trouble staying on task to get to the end result. It is like that you walk into a room and then forget what you came in to get.

① storing visual and auditory memory
② maintaining focus and concentration
③ solving complex and difficult problems
④ developing children's learning capacities

09 다음 글의 제목으로 가장 적절한 것은?

In 2013, scientists from Brigham and Women's Hospital published findings showing that bisphenol A (BPA) exposure can affect abnormal egg maturation in humans. A review of previous studies, published in 2015, found evidence that BPA can interfere with endocrine function involving the hypothalamus and the pituitary gland. The researchers suggested that this type of action can affect puberty and ovulation, and that it may lead to infertility. The authors add: "The detrimental effects on reproduction may be lifelong and transgenerational." Male impotence may be affected, according to a study that looked at the effect of men's exposure to BPA at work. Findings indicated that high-level exposure may increase the risk of erectile dysfunction and problems with sexual desire and ejaculation.

* hypothalamus: 시상하부 ** pituitary gland: 뇌하수체

① The Chemical We Cannot Live Without: BPA
② Male Health Issues That Can Be Caused By BPA
③ Positive and Negative Effects of BPA on Human Beings
④ Relation Between Exposure to BPA and Reproductive Disorders

10 빈칸에 들어갈 가장 적절한 것을 고르시오.

In the West, consciousness was long thought to be a divine gift bestowed solely on humans. Western philosophers historically conceived of nonhuman animals as unfeeling automatons. Even after Darwin demonstrated our kinship with animals, many scientists believed that the evolution of consciousness was a recent event. They thought the first mind sparked awake sometime after we split from chimpanzees and bonobos. This notion that consciousness was of recent vintage began to change in the decades following the Second World War, when more scientists were systematically studying the behaviors and brain states of Earth's creatures. Now each year brings a raft of new research papers, which, taken together, suggest that _____.

① humans are closely related to primates
② consciousness is an exclusive human trait
③ a great many animals are conscious like humans
④ even human beings were not conscious until recently

01 밑줄 친 부분에 들어갈 가장 적절한 것은?

The Pacific _____ about 46 percent of the Earth's water surface.

① beefs up   ② makes up
③ damps down   ④ makes over

02 밑줄 친 부분에 들어갈 가장 적절한 것을 고르시오.

During the period of Ramadan, Muslim people _____ from eating and drinking during daylight hours.

① refrain   ② pore
③ mediate   ④ regard

03 밑줄 친 부분에 들어갈 가장 적절한 것을 고르시오.

Although he was immediately taken to a nearby hospital, he wasn't able to _____ consciousness.

① revoke   ② level at
③ regain   ④ lap against

04 밑줄 친 부분에 들어갈 표현으로 가장 적절한 것을 고르시오.

A: I'm thinking of changing jobs.
B: What? Are you serious?
A: Yes, I've been thinking about that for a quite long time.
B: What's the issue?
A: Well, things are not turning out so well with my co-workers. One of my co-workers likes to ____(A)____.
B: That must be quite stressful. It seems like you ____(B)____.
A: Exactly. You ____(C)____.

① (A) go off the deep end
  (B) get to the point
  (C) got somewhere

② (A) go off the deep end
  (B) have a chip on your shoulder
  (C) got the picture

③ (A) boss people around
  (B) have a chip on your shoulder
  (C) got somewhere

④ (A) boss people around
  (B) have a chip on your shoulder
  (C) got the picture

05 밑줄 친 부분 중 어법상 옳지 않은 것을 고르시오.

① Born in Massachusetts to a Quaker farm family, Abby Kelley Foster was the seventh daughter in a time ② which farmers prayed for boys. She was ③ raised in the town of Worcester, completed grammar school, and was one of the rare girls to go on to higher education, at a Quaker school in Providence, Rhode Island. She alternated studying ④ with spells of teaching children to earn her way.

06 밑줄 친 부분 중 어법상 옳지 않은 것을 고르시오.

The personalities of people in groups ① speaking different languages often ② can be diverged. A study revealed that personality tests ③ taken by English-speaking Americans and Spanish-speaking Mexicans ④ differ reliably.

07 밑줄 친 부분 중 어법상 옳지 않은 것을 고르시오.

Some organizations do have policies which allow either men or women ① to take career breaks to look after children. However, not only ② have very few fathers actually availed themselves of such opportunities but anecdotal evidence also suggests that if they had done so, their careers would have been 'ruined' for life. Indeed, the knowledge of this ③ may well be a cause of the low take-up of such schemes by men. Organizations, therefore, not only need to establish the structures which allow careers to be more flexible but they also need to change attitudes which typically ④ remain thorough traditional.

08 다음 글의 밑줄 친 부분 중 문맥상 단어의 쓰임이 적절하지 않은 것은?

Probably the most widely known fact about working memory is that it can only hold around seven chunks of information (between 5 and 9). However, this tells us little about the limits of working memory because the size of a chunk is ① determinate. 1 2 3 4 5 6 7 are seven different chunks - if you remember each digit ② separately (as you would, for example, if you were not familiar with the digits - as a young child isn't). But for those of us who are only too ③ well-versed in our numbers, 1 through to 7 could be a single chunk. Recent research suggests, however, that it is not the number of chunks that is important. What may be important may be how ④ long it takes you to say the words (information is usually held in working memory in the form of an acoustic code). It seems that you can only hold in working memory what you can say in 1.5 — 2 seconds. Slow speakers are thus penalized.

09 다음 글의 요지로 가장 적절한 것은?

Small amounts of bisphenol A (BPA) may remain in polycarbonate products and epoxy linings after curing, and be released into food and beverages. Canned foods and liquids stored or heated in polycarbonate containers and epoxy-lined cans appear to be the main source of exposure to BPA. Infants may have greater exposure to BPA than others because their diet may consist largely of infant formula from epoxy-lined cans. Infants may also be given infant formula and other liquids in polycarbonate baby bottles. As very low levels of BPA have been detected in human breast milk, infant exposure from breastfeeding is expected to be lower compared to exposure from formula packaged in epoxy-lined cans and using polycarbonate baby bottles.

① BPA can be more harmful to children than adults.
② It is advised to use BPA free products for your babies.
③ Breastfeeding can help little kids be less affected by BPA.
④ Infant formula manufacturers must stop using epoxy-lined cans.

10 다음 글의 요지로 가장 적절한 것은?

Animal welfare science is a relatively new field based on the belief that animals are conscious, but has grown rapidly to encompass different disciplines. A large body of published research on farm animal welfare addresses topics ranging from basic biological principles of welfare assessment to applications for evaluating and improving housing, husbandry, transport, and slaughter. This research has influenced legislation and standards setting, but concerns have been raised about its applicability in commercial settings. Most animal welfare research has been conducted in small-scale experimental settings, which are often very different from the "real world" of commercial animal production in terms of scale, complexity, automation, and variability.

① Animal welfare must be the primary concern in all countries.
② Despite its growth, whether animal welfare science can be applied to real situations is doubtable.
③ Commercial animal production can be developed through the application of animal welfare science.
④ Animal welfare science has contributed to many significant improvements in the welfare of animals.

기적사 DAY 34

01 밑줄 친 부분에 들어갈 가장 적절한 것은?

The toxic vapour then _____ and found its way to its victims.

① canceled
② seeped out
③ excluded
④ scratched off

02 밑줄 친 부분에 들어갈 가장 적절한 것을 고르시오.

He has never _____ the opinions of critics because they didn't have any effect on sales of his book.

① blotted out
② pored over
③ catered to
④ set store by

03 밑줄 친 부분에 들어갈 가장 적절한 것을 고르시오.

Just _____ the seeds in the summer and you can see the beautiful flowers in the fall.

① sew
② sow
③ loom on
④ lapse into

04 밑줄 친 부분에 들어갈 표현으로 가장 적절한 것을 고르시오.

Interviewer: Why did you apply for our company?
Interviewee: Above all, I really liked this company's motto. 'Selection and concentration' is also the motto of my life.
Interviewer: A motto can sure help you throughout hardship. Could you please tell me about your previous work experience?
Interviewee: I used to work at an insurance enterprise. So I had to meet with many customers in person. Through such experiences, I can assure you that I learned to treat customers skillfully.
Interviewer: Our company is looking forward to working with someone who is capable of dealing with his or her clients in a proficient manner.
Interviewee: I'm very confident in that. I _____ _____ in satisfying my customers.

① make believe
② make a scene
③ know the ropes
④ pull myself together

05 밑줄 친 부분 중 어법상 옳지 않은 것을 고르시오.

Many firms have turned their attention to ① building a continuing long-term relationship between the organization ② so the customer as the ultimate objective of a successful marketing strategy. They are taking action ③ to increase lifetime customer value — the present value of a stream of revenue that can ④ be produced by a customer over time.

06 밑줄 친 부분 중 어법상 옳지 않은 것을 고르시오.

Ornstein and Ehrlich relate the large-scale threats ① we face to what they call the ② "boiled frog syndrome." Frogs placed in a pan of water that ③ is slowly heated cannot detect ④ the gradual rising in temperature.

07 밑줄 친 부분 중 어법상 옳지 않은 것을 고르시오.

Diversity without any ① shared values and goals is likely to break a group apart; however, shared values and goals may lead to ② that Irving Janis has termed groupthink. Groupthink describes what happens when groups ③ converge on a single answer to a problem and, rather than critically evaluate the solution, they convince themselves and each other ④ that the solution they came up with is the best one.

08 다음 글의 요지로 가장 적절한 것은?

New research on children with attention deficit hyperactivity disorder(ADHD) might show some tasks can improve working memory in general, and could help children with the condition. Torkel Klingberg ran a randomized controlled trial of 53 children with ADHD in which half of the participants practiced working-memory tasks that gradually increased in difficulty. The other half completed tasks that did not get harder as the children became better at them. The children who practiced with increasingly difficult memory tasks performed better on two working memory tests, which were different from the practice tasks, than the control group. In addition, the parents of children with memory training reported a reduction in their children's hyperactivity and inattention three months after the intervention, while the parents of the control group participants did not.

① ADHD can cause children to have poor working memory.
② ADHD symptoms can be reduced effectively by medication.
③ ADHD patients tend to have difficulty with completing a task.
④ Increasing working memory capacity can have a positive impact on kids with ADHD.

09 주어진 문장 다음에 이어질 글의 순서로 가장 적절한 것은?

The tolerable daily intake, or TDI, is an internationally established safe level for chemicals like BPA.

(A) For example, a nine month old baby weighing 9kg would have to eat more than 1kg of canned baby custard containing BPA every day to reach the TDI, assuming that the custard contained the highest level of BPA found in a survey by CHOICE.

(B) It's a conservative estimate of a safe level of BPA which applies to the whole population and estimates the amount of BPA in food that can be ingested daily over a lifetime without appreciable health risk.

(C) In other words, it's the amount that can be safely consumed per day, every day. Extremely large amounts of foods and beverages would need to be consumed to reach the TDI for BPA.

① (A) - (C) - (B)
② (B) - (A) - (C)
③ (B) - (C) - (A)
④ (C) - (A) - (B)

10 주어진 문장이 들어갈 위치로 가장 적절한 것은?

Yet many societies display a parallel tendency to brand animals as lesser beings, or even automatons, locked into the lower rungs of a great chain of being where humans are at the apex.

Humans' curiosity about other animals, and the seeming impossibility of knowing what it is like in their minds, if they have them, has persisted for the whole history of our species. (①) Animist spirituality, the first human philosophy, posits open channels of communication between predator and prey. (②) Medieval Europeans made animals stand trial for crimes and misdemeanors, but did not grant them souls or access to heaven. (③) To this day, we worry about our dogs getting bored while we are at work, but think nothing of feeding them the exact same food every day of their lives. (④) This ambivalence points to our own uncertainty and fear when confronted with the possibility of minds unlike our own.

01 밑줄 친 부분에 들어갈 가장 적절한 것은?

Recent flight incidents, particularly the disappearance of a Malaysian jetliner last March, _____ widespread demand for an improved global airplane tracking system.

① spurred
② damped down
③ supervised
④ dispensed with

02 밑줄 친 부분에 들어갈 가장 적절한 것을 고르시오.

Koreans _____ from Japan's brutalities, and independence activists were jailed, tortured, or killed.

① resorted
② subtracted
③ suffered
④ prompted

03 밑줄 친 부분에 들어갈 가장 적절한 것을 고르시오.

The government has _____ its redevelopment plan in response to resident protests.

① suspended
② terrified
③ emphasized
④ loomed

04 밑줄 친 부분에 들어갈 표현으로 가장 적절한 것을 고르시오.

A: Congratulations on winning first prize in the race! I knew you would do it!
B: Thank you so much. I could never have finished the race without your support.
A: It was nothing. Thinking about the first time you ran the track, I never imagined you would win.
B: Me neither. I did _____ from baby steps to a runner.
A: I know! Good for you! We should go and celebrate your championship.
B: Thank you again. I'll never forget your commitment.

① wrap up
② break the ice
③ buy the farm
④ come a long way

05 밑줄 친 부분 중 어법상 옳지 않은 것을 고르시오.

When we speak of the political organization of a particular cultural system, frequently we ① are left with the impression ② that political boundaries and cultural boundaries are the same. But the boundaries of a polity, or politically ③ organized unit, may or may not ④ correspond the boundaries of a particular way of life.

06 밑줄 친 부분 중 어법상 옳지 않은 것을 고르시오.

One way ① in which children and youth can achieve better status among their peers is ② to be perceived as physically competent. However, a problem that ③ is persisted in physical education is the inability to provide equitable learning experiences ④ for less-skilled children and youth.

07 밑줄 친 부분 중 어법상 옳지 않은 것을 고르시오.

I once attended a seminar ① where the speaker's slide—a map of North America—was upside down. The speaker quickly said, "This is ② what North America looks like from the Southern Hemisphere," which got a good laugh. A year or so later, I was speaking and my map of Brazil was backwards, so I said, "Here's what Brazil looks like when ③ seen from the center of the earth." It took ④ for them a minute to get it, but they laughed at this one too.

08 밑줄 친 부분 중 글의 흐름상 가장 어색한 것은?

Working memory is critical for academic performance as it is an important part of executive functioning (e.g. planning, initiating, task monitoring, organizing, etc.). At school, the areas of learning that are greatly affected by poor working memory are: maths, reading comprehension, complex problem solving, and test taking. ① The biggest impact on school work occurs from difficulties with the first two areas. ② Working memory is much like a bucket that you can keep filling up using a glass of water. ③ It can be improved through simple games and day-to-day activities. ④ Every drop that you add remains in it unless over time memory evaporates through lack of repeated use. In children with poor working memory, it is much like the bucket has a hole in the bottom. You can keep tipping in glasses of water (information/ knowledge) but it continually drains out.

09 빈칸 (A), (B)에 들어갈 표현으로 가장 적절한 것은?

Two studies have thrown the controversial compound bisphenol A (BPA) back into the limelight. One study found that the chemical is readily absorbed through the skin, while a second study found that those who routinely touch BPA-laden till receipts have higher than average levels of the chemical in their bodies. Taken together, the findings _____(A)_____ calls for tougher regulation of the chemical, which is widely used in plastics manufacturing. BPA is detectable in most people in Western countries. Animal studies have confirmed that high doses are harmful, but some evidence that it may also be harmful at low doses has yet to _____(B)_____ regulators to take decisive action against the compound.

	(A)	(B)
①	abate	encourage
②	fortify	dissuade
③	blunt	permit
④	strengthen	convince

10 다음 글의 내용과 일치하는 것은?

"Almost all other animals are clearly observed to partake in sleep, whether they are aquatic, aerial, or terrestrial," wrote Aristotle in his work *On Sleep and Sleeplessness*. But do other animals dream? On that the Greek philosopher also had an opinion. In *The History of Animals*, he wrote: "It would appear that not only do men dream, but horses also do, and dogs, and oxen; aye, and sheep, and goats, and all viviparous quadrupeds; and dogs show their dreaming by barking in their sleep." His research methods may lack sophistication, but Aristotle may not have been too far off the mark. Still today, we certainly can't ask animals if they dream, but we can at least observe the evidence that they might. There are two ways in which scientists have gone about this seemingly impossible task. One is to look at their physical behavior during the various phases of the sleep cycle. The second is to see whether their sleeping brains work similarly to our own sleeping brains.

① Aristotle thought fishes don't sleep.
② Aristotle believed that all animals dream.
③ According to Aristotle, dogs bark while sleeping because they are dreaming.
④ Aristotle had an opposite opinion about sleep in nonhuman animals from today's scientists.

01 밑줄 친 부분에 들어갈 가장 적절한 것은?

There are several places in the world that are famous for people who live a very long time. These places are usually in mountainous areas, far away from modern cities. Doctors, scientists, and public health experts often travel to these regions to solve the mystery of long, healthy life; the experts hope to bring to the modern world the secrets of _____.

① longevity ② security
③ innovation ④ loyalty

02 밑줄 친 부분과 의미가 가장 가까운 것은?

The metabolic machinery of the cell functions in a completely <u>analogous</u> fashion, with its own version of master plans, working blueprints, transfer agents, and all the rest.

① delicate ② weird
③ similar ④ novel

03 밑줄 친 부분에 공통으로 들어갈 가장 적절한 것은?

- Many experts criticized the TV and radio networks as being too biased to _____ the race fairly.
- I got these tires from your guys two months ago. Will the warranty _____ the cost of the repair?

① cover ② cast
③ charge ④ claim

04 밑줄 친 부분에 들어갈 표현으로 가장 적절한 것을 고르시오.

Tom: Frankly, I don't think my new boss knows what he is doing.
Jack: He is young, Tom. You have to give him a chance.
Tom: How many chances do I have to give him? He's actually doing terribly.
Jack: _____.
Tom: What? Where?
Jack: Over there. Your new boss just turned around the corner.

① Speak of the devil ② I wish you good luck
③ Keep up the good work ④ Money makes the mare go

05 어법상 옳은 것은?

① The elite campus-based programs which he will be taking it next semester are scheduled to be extremely difficult.
② That happens in a particular period does not have any significant effects on the long-term investors in the stock market.
③ The newly built conference room, though equipped with more advanced facilities, accommodates fewer people than the old one.
④ With such a diverse variety of economical appliances to choose from, it's important to decide what it is best.

06 우리말을 영어로 바르게 옮긴 것은?

① 우리가 공항에 도착할 무렵, 비행기는 이미 이륙했다.
　→ By the time we had arrived at the airport, the flight already took off.
② 당신이 바쁘지 않으면 오늘 저녁에 당신 집에 들르겠다.
　→ I'll drop by your place this evening lest you should be busy.
③ 그녀가 콘서트에 왔었다면 좋아했을 것이다.
　→ Had she come to the concert, she would have enjoyed it.
④ 그는 의사로서 자질이 없다.
　→ He is cut out to be a doctor.

07 우리말을 영어로 잘못 옮긴 것은?

① 그는 빚을 갚고 나니 먹고 살아갈 수가 없게 되었다.
　→ The payment of his debts left him nothing to live on.
② 사람의 가치는 재산보다도 오히려 인격에 있다.
　→ A person's value lies not so much in what he is as in what he has.
③ 나이를 먹음에 따라, 이 속담의 의미를 분명히 알게 될 것이다.
　→ As you grow older, you will come to realize the meaning of this saying clearly.
④ 그들은 물이 부족했으므로 가능한 한 적게 마셨다.
　→ They were short of water, so that they drank as little as possible.

08 밑줄 친 부분에 들어갈 말로 가장 적절한 것을 고르시오.

> There's a knock at your door. Standing in front of you is a young man who needs help. He's injured and is bleeding. You take him in and help him, make him feel comfortable and safe and phone for an ambulance. This is clearly the right thing to do. But if you help him just because you feel sorry for him, according to Immanuel Kant, _____ _____. Your sympathy is irrelevant to the morality of your action. That's part of your character, but nothing to do with right and wrong. Morality for Kant wasn't just about what you do, but about why you do it. Those who do the right thing don't do it simply because of how they feel: the decision has to be based on reason, reason that tells you what your duty is, regardless of how you happen to feel.

① that wouldn't be a moral action at all
② your action is founded on reason
③ then you're exhibiting ethical behavior
④ you're encouraging him to be an honest person

09 밑줄 친 부분에 들어갈 말로 가장 적절한 것을 고르시오.

A group of tribes and genera of hopping reptiles, small creatures of the dinosaur type, seem to have been pushed by competition and the pursuit of their enemies towards the alternatives of extinction or adaptation to colder conditions in the higher hills or by the sea. Among these distressed tribes there was developed a new type of scale — scales that were elongated into quill-like forms and that presently branched into the crude beginnings of feathers. These quill-like scales lay over one another and formed a heat-retaining covering more efficient than any reptilian covering that had hitherto existed. So they permitted an invasion of colder regions that were otherwise uninhabited. Perhaps simultaneously with these changes there arose in these creatures a greater solicitude for their eggs. Most reptiles are apparently quite careless about their eggs, which are left for sun and season to hatch. But some of the varieties upon this new branch of the tree of life were acquiring a habit of guarding their eggs and _____. With these adaptations to cold, other internal modifications were going on that made these creatures, the primitive birds, warm-blooded and independent of basking.

① hatching them unsuccessfully
② leaving them under the sun on their own
③ keeping them warm with the warmth of their bodies
④ flying them to scaled reptiles

10 내용의 흐름상 적절하지 못한 문장은?

Of equal importance in wars of conquest were the germs that evolved in human societies with domestic animals. ① Infectious diseases like smallpox, measles, and flu arose as specialized germs of humans, derived by mutations of very similar ancestral germs that had infected animals. ② The most direct contribution of plant and animal domestication to wars of conquest was from Eurasia's horses, whose military role made them the jeeps and Sherman tanks of ancient warfare on that continent. ③ The humans who domesticated animals were the first to fall victim to the newly evolved germs, but those humans then evolved substantial resistance to the new disease. ④ When such partly immune people came into contact with others who had had no previous exposure to the germs, epidemics resulted in which up to 99 percent of the previously unexposed population was killed. Germs thus acquired ultimately from domestic animals played decisive roles in the European conquests of Native Americans, Australians, South Africans, and Pacific islanders.

01 밑줄 친 부분에 들어갈 가장 적절한 것은?

The _____ and implementation of the exams are conducted by the College Board, a non-profit company in the United States.

① excellence   ② superstition
③ supervision   ④ loyalty

02 밑줄 친 부분과 의미가 가장 가까운 것은?

Only a handful of the planets and moons found have the suitable conditions for water and life.

① malicious   ② strict
③ similar   ④ appropriate

03 밑줄 친 부분에 들어갈 가장 적절한 것은?

The skeleton _____ to be the unidentified one on the list.

① claimed   ② trespassed
③ took over   ④ turned out

04 밑줄 친 부분에 들어갈 표현으로 가장 적절한 것을 고르시오.

Reader: Hello, it's an honor to meet you in person.
Author: It's my pleasure to earn this precious opportunity to share my thought with the readers.
Reader: Thank you. Your book was amazing! Time went by so fast while reading your book.
Author: That's the best compliment I've ever heard. Do you have any questions about the book?
Reader: I've had plenty. How do you feel now that you've become an author of a best-seller.
Author: I can't believe it! I was actually a bit worried when the book may seem _____ to the readers.
Reader: Not at all. I've never read such a creative story.

① in season   ② bold as brass
③ cut and dried ④ off the record

05 어법상 옳은 것은?

① That he wanted to find out first was how long it was going to take.
② It is what I would have shown it to you if I had got round to the thing.
③ The house, which completed in 1850, was famous for its huge marble staircase.
④ Her jeans and checked shirt, though old and well worn, looked clean and of good quality.

06 우리말을 영어로 바르게 옮긴 것은?

① 나는 그가 아마 약간 매력이 부족하다고 생각한다.
→ I think he is perhaps a little wanting in charm.

② William은 누가 자기를 보지 않도록 창밖으로 몸을 돌렸다.
→ William turned away from the window although anyone see him.

③ 전화벨이 울리고 있었지만 Tom이 실내에 들어섰을 때쯤, 전화가 멈춰 있었다.
→ The phone was ringing but by the time Tom got indoors, it stopped.

④ 투어를 하기 전에 끝냈더라면 훨씬 더 좋은 기록이었을 텐데.
→ If we finished it before we went on the tour, it would have been a much better record.

07 우리말을 영어로 잘못 옮긴 것은?

① William은 John에게 그 차가 월요일에 준비될 것이라고 약속했다.
→ William promised John the car would be ready on Monday.

② 나는 사실 그 애를 아들이라기보다 아주 좋은 친구로 생각한다.
→ I don't really think of him as a son so much as a very good friend.

③ 우리가 가장 피하고 싶은 것은 그것이 상부 구조가 되는 것이다.
→ What we are most anxious to avoid is that that becomes a superstructure.

④ 그 회의는 월요일에 열리기로 되어 있었는데 우리는 그것을 연기해야만 했다.
→ The meeting was supposed to be taken place on Monday, but we've had to postpone it.

08 주어진 문장이 들어갈 위치로 가장 적절한 것은?

> Moreover, everyone had an incentive to obey such rules.

In order to understand Kant's moral philosophy, it's crucial to be familiar with the issues he, and other thinkers of his time, were dealing with. From the earliest recorded history, people's moral beliefs and practices were grounded in religion. (①) Scriptures, such as the bible and the Quran, laid out moral rules that believers thought to be handed down from God: Don't kill. Don't steal. Don't commit adultery, and so on. (②) The fact that they supposedly came from a divine source of wisdom gave them their authority. (③) They were not simply someone's arbitrary opinion; they were God's opinion, and as such, they offered humankind an objectively valid code of conduct. (④) If you "walked in the ways of the Lord," you would be rewarded, either in this life or the next. If you violated the commandments, you'd be punished. As a result, any sensible person brought up in such a faith would abide by the moral rules their religion taught.

09 밑줄 친 부분 중 글의 흐름상 가장 어색한 것은?

Egg-laying and nest-building behaviors vary widely among reptiles. ① These behaviors range from the "casual" dropping of the eggs in a relatively suitable site to the preparation of an elaborate nest, and in a few groups parental care may also occur. Interestingly, some reptiles may bear their young alive. ② This mode, called viviparity, is widespread and has evolved independently dozens of times in the squamate reptiles (that is, the lizards and snakes). No living crocodiles, turtles, or tuatara are live-bearers. ③ During periods of high stress and other relatively unusual conditions (such as in captivity), females have been known to generally retain eggs in their oviducts for weeks to months. ④ However, in the squamate reptiles, live-bearing ranges from retention of unshelled eggs in the oviducts to the development of placentae between the mother and her fetuses. The evolutionary steps from egg laying to placental development are demonstrated by extant species.

10 주어진 문장이 들어갈 위치로 가장 적절한 것은?

This can happen if the mother is newly infected with the parasite while pregnant or just before she becomes pregnant.

Toxoplasmosis is a common disease found in birds and mammals across North America. (①) The infection is caused by a protozoa parasite called Toxoplasma gondi and affects 10 to 20 out of every 100 people in North America by the time they are adults. (②) The concern is greatest for pregnant women as the growing fetus can become infected with the toxoplasmosis parasite. (③) Infection in the unborn child during pregnancy can result in miscarriage, poor growth, early delivery or stillbirth. (④) If a child is born with toxoplasmosis, he/she can experience eye problems, hydrocephalus (water on the brain), convulsions or mental disabilities.

* Toxoplasmosis: 톡소플라스마증(톡소플라스마 원충에 의한 사람과 동물의 공통 전염병)

01 밑줄 친 부분에 들어갈 가장 적절한 것은?

Believing that something good or bad will happen without proof is called the _____.

① excellence   ② superstition
③ innovation   ④ antipathy

02 밑줄 친 부분과 의미가 가장 가까운 것은?

His argument to me was completely specious.

① novel   ② scarce
③ stern   ④ superficial

03 밑줄 친 부분에 들어갈 가장 적절한 것은?

In every restaurant in the world, waiters and waitresses _____ diners and serve them food.

① assuage   ② charge
③ withdraw ④ wait on

04 밑줄 친 부분에 들어갈 표현으로 가장 적절한 것을 고르시오.

Nina: What are you guys doing here?
John: It's a secret. We're preparing a surprise birthday party for Danny.
Nina: Wow, Danny must be really happy once he finds out about all this.
John: I really hope so. We've been planning this for over two weeks. Would you like to join?
Nina: Sure, I'd love to. If anyone asks what we are doing, I'll just ___(A)___ to keep Danny from discovering the truth.
John: I trust you. If anyone ___(B)___, Danny will find out right away.

① (A) go to my head   (B) plays it by ear
② (A) hold my tongue   (B) plays it by ear
③ (A) hold my tongue   (B) spills the beans
④ (A) live from hand to mouth (B) spills the beans

05 어법상 옳은 것은?

① What really concerned her was how unhappy was the child.
② It is interesting is that they are interested in what is made you fun.
③ Tom found a huge nest which is what he assumes was the magpie house.
④ The house, though imposing from the outside, are in fact a very comfortable size.

06 우리말을 영어로 바르게 옮긴 것은?

① 그녀의 행동은 국회의원에 대한 기대에 어긋났다.
   → Her conduct was consistent with what is expected of a congressman.
② 시간이 충분했다면 직장에 가져갈 샌드위치를 만들었을 텐데.
   → Did I have enough time, I would have made a sandwich to take to work.
③ 그녀는 소수에게만 알려져 있긴 하지만, 그들 사이에서 그녀에 대한 평판은 매우 좋다.
   → Although she is known to only a few, her reputation among them is very great.
④ 내가 암탉들에게 먹이를 주기 위해 그것을 열었을 때쯤, 그는 현관 밖을 내다보고 있었다.
   → By the time I had opened it to feed the hens, he had been looking out the front door.

07 우리말을 영어로 잘못 옮긴 것은?

① 나는 그의 아이들을 박물관에 데려가기 위해 그에게 10파운드를 빌려주어야 했다.
   → I had to borrow him ten pounds to take his children to the museum.
② 노래나 영화 테이프에 대한 작은 흠집은 대단한 문제는 아닐 것이다.
   → A small blemish on the tape of a song or movie may not be much of a problem.
③ 새 대통령은 즉각 소년범을 단속하는 법을 발표했다.
   → The new president promptly announced a law to crack down on juvenile criminals.
④ 외무부 장관은 그 나라의 상황에 대해 여전히 걱정하고 있다고 인정했다.
   → The foreign minister admitted she was still anxious about the situation in the country.

08 주어진 문장 다음에 이어질 글의 순서로 가장 적절한 것은?

Consider the case of someone who contemplates relieving a financial crisis by borrowing money from someone else, promising to repay it in the future while in fact having no intention of doing so.

(A) The entire practice of lending money on promise presupposes at least the honest intention to repay; if this condition were universally ignored, the false promises would never be effective as methods of borrowing.

(B) Since the universalized maxim is contradictory in and of itself, no one could will it to be law, and Kant concluded that we have a perfect duty (to which there can never be any exceptions whatsoever) not to act in this manner.

(C) The maxim of this action would be that it is permissible to borrow money under false pretenses if you really need it. But as Kant pointed out, making this maxim into a universal law would be clearly self-defeating.

① (A) - (B) - (C)   ② (B) - (A) - (C)
③ (B) - (C) - (A)   ④ (C) - (A) - (B)

09 밑줄 친 (A), (B)에 들어갈 말로 가장 적절한 것은?

Birds lay eggs with hard shells, whereas some reptile species lay soft-shelled eggs. Why might this be the case? If a mother cannot lay a hard-shelled egg at its full size, it could lay a soft-shelled egg instead allowing the egg to expand after laying. _____(A)_____, a soft shell has the capacity to absorb moisture from the atmosphere and ground. For some reasons, birds have evolved such that their eggs don't need additional moisture, which is not the case for some species of reptiles. Another reason some reptiles lay soft-shelled eggs is because of the way they are incubated. Birds will sit on their eggs and use the warmth of their bodies; _____(B)_____ reptiles tend to utilize the natural heat of vegetation or the earth to incubate their eggs. As reptile eggs don't have to be strong enough to protect the unborn contents from the full weight of their parents, they can be soft-shelled.

	(A)	(B)
①	Thus	by contrast
②	Additionally	on the other hand
③	However	accordingly
④	Besides	furthermore

10 밑줄 친 (A), (B)에 들어갈 말로 가장 적절한 것은?

Farm animals including cows, sheep, pigs, chickens and goats, can pass diseases to people since they are not like house pets and do not have places to rest or eat that are away from where they excrete feces and urine. _____(A)_____, you should thoroughly wash your hands with running water and soap after contact with them or after touching things such as fences, buckets, and straw bedding that have been in contact with farm animals, and adults should carefully watch children who are visiting farms and help them wash their hands well. Different types of farm animals can carry different diseases. _____(B)_____, cows and calves can carry the bacterium *Escherichia coli*, often called *E. coli*. This germ can cause bloody diarrhea in people. In addition, children can develop kidney failure due to *E. coli* infection. Pigs can carry the bacterium *Yersinia enterocolitica* which causes the disease yersiniosis. Chickens can carry bacteria such as Salmonella, which causes the disease salmonellosis. Many of these germs are in farm animal manure.

	(A)	(B)
①	However	Likewise
②	That is	Furthermore
③	Therefore	For instance
④	Moreover	On the other hand

01 밑줄 친 부분에 들어갈 가장 적절한 것은?

The _____ unites the whole organization to focus on solving the problem.

① empathy ② anguish
③ angst ④ security

02 밑줄 친 부분과 의미가 가장 가까운 것은?

The once dilapidated neighborhood was thus reborn as "Street of Artists".

① tactile ② devastated
③ delicate ④ extended

03 밑줄 친 부분에 들어갈 가장 적절한 것은?

Fast food businesses must _____ in a highly volatile market.

① cast ② compete
③ counterfeit ④ commit

04 밑줄 친 부분에 들어갈 표현으로 가장 적절한 것을 고르시오.

Andy: Hi, Hannah. What did you do on parents' day?
Hannah: Hey, Andy. I bought a cake and a present for my parents. What about you?
Andy: I took my parents out for dinner at a fancy restaurant.
Hannah: Did your parents like it?
Andy: Yeah, they said they never expected such a thing. I'm just giving back what I received from them.
Hannah; What a nice thought! I also realized that I should not _____.
Andy: Me too. I am really grateful for their sacrifice.

① act my age ② go high gear
③ take it for granted ④ take a long chance

05 어법상 옳은 것은?

① What they call a fun situation is actually not a fun situation.
② Her story of what happened that night didn't correspond the witness's version.
③ This practice, though sacred in the eyes of their ancestors, is appeared ridiculous to them.
④ William spent the night in the house of the evil spirits which was no longer able to live there.

06 우리말을 영어로 바르게 옮긴 것은?

① William은 그의 사업이 어떻게 운영되는지에 대해 매우 까다롭다.
 → William is very particular about how his business is run.

② 그가 더 많은 사람들에게 그것에 대한 일을 하도록 시켰다면, 그는 그 일을 더 빨리 끝냈을 텐데.
 → If he had had more people to work on it, he would have got the job done quicker.

③ 자신을 만족시키기 위해 살을 빼려고 하지 않는 한, 의욕을 유지하는 것은 어렵다.
 → Unless you are not trying to lose weight to please yourself, it's hard to stay motivated.

④ 그의 아버지는 아들이 상자 안으로 뛰어드는 것을 보았을 때쯤 방 안의 고양이를 수술하고 있었다.
 → His father was operating on a cat in the room by the time he saw his son hurtle into the box.

07 우리말을 영어로 잘못 옮긴 것은?

① 지난주 시내 중심부의 주차 제한 조치가 시행되었다.
 → Parking restrictions in the town centre have come into force last week.

② Jane은 그를 비난하지 않았고 그것에 대해 언급조차도 하지 않았다.
 → Jane had not reproached him and never so much as mentioned it.

③ 독자들은 당신의 복잡하지 않은 성공을 제외하고는 어떤 것도 용서할 것이다.
 → Readers will forgive you anything except your uncomplicated success.

④ 그것은 멋진 것이 아니라 우리가 부끄러워하거나 당황해야 할 것이다.
 → It is not a wonderful thing but something we should be ashamed of or embarrassed about.

08 다음 글의 주제로 가장 적절한 것은?

Sarah Holtman, a professor of philosophy, sees Kant's political philosophy, not as an attempt to prescribe specific laws, but rather as a general framework of principles for determining what counts as justice. "What counts as justice doesn't change," she says, "but how we realize justice will vary over time and in different circumstances." But how do we realize justice today on the theory of justice Holtman attributes to Kant? It's a question that Holtman seeks to answer, relating Kant's theory of justice to issues that Kant himself never considered, such as civic virtue, the prison system, and the death penalty. Through the application of the general principles of Kant's theory of justice to these issues, Holtman believes one comes away with a conception that is not antiquated but productive and laudable. Far from a mere artifact of the eighteenth century, Kant's political writings offer, according to Holtman, an appealing theory for grappling with twenty-first-century problems.

① Realizing justice for convicts
② Applying Kant's theory today
③ Criticizing Kant's theory of justice
④ Comparing Kant's and Holtman's theories

09 다음 글의 요지로 가장 적절한 것은?

Why have birds not "advanced" beyond egg laying and begun to bear their young alive like mammals? People have claimed that viviparity (live-bearing) is incompatible with flight, but bats disprove that hypothesis. Daniel Blackburn of Vanderbilt University and Howard Evans of Cornell point out that the evolutionary path to viviparity usually involved retaining eggs for longer and longer periods until they finally hatch within the female's body. Blackburn and Evans argue that egg retention would offer little advantage to birds, and several disadvantages. Among the latter are a loss of productivity — since females obviously could not retain many eggs until they hatched — and increased risk to the mother associated with the added burden of weight. In addition, in many species, the contribution of the male to the care of offspring would be lost and it has recently been suggested that a female bird's body may be too hot for proper egg development. It seems likely, therefore, that evolving viviparity would be a step backward for birds.

① Different birds take care of their eggs in different ways.
② It is more effective for birds to lay eggs than live-bearing.
③ Birds and mammals have some characteristics in common.
④ The egg-laying mode of reproduction is more primitive than viviparity.

10 다음 글의 요지로 가장 적절한 것은?

Dogs roll in the mud. They sniff feces and other questionable substances. Then they track countless germs into our homes on their paws, snouts and fur. And if the recent research on pets and human health is correct, that cloud of dog-borne microbes may be working to keep us healthy. Epidemiological studies show that children who grow up in households with dogs have a lower risk for developing autoimmune illnesses like asthma and allergies — and that it may be a result of the diversity of microbes that these animals bring inside our homes. According to the so-called hygiene hypothesis, spending over 90 percent of our time in the bacteria-poor environment indoors, as we do (especially early in life, when our immune systems are being formed), can cause our bodies to overreact to harmless substances later on, making us sick.

① Dogs can carry harmful bacteria that can cause illness in humans.
② Exposure to a rich array of indoor germs may actually be salutary.
③ It is important to keep your homes as clean as possible to raise your children healthy.
④ Illnesses such as asthma and allergies can be prevented by using simple home remedies.

기적사 DAY 40

01 밑줄 친 부분에 들어갈 가장 적절한 것은?

Due to the economic recession, many school districts have experienced cuts to their _____.

① budget
② longevity
③ plasticity
④ heredity

02 밑줄 친 부분과 의미가 가장 가까운 것은?

These days, there are many educational computer programs, games, and tools <u>available</u>.

① similar
② attainable
③ waterproof
④ neurological

03 밑줄 친 부분에 들어갈 가장 적절한 것은?

He _____ to me this morning, but I was too angry to accept it.

① accused
② covered
③ apologized
④ possessed

04 밑줄 친 부분에 들어갈 표현으로 가장 적절한 것을 고르시오.

Jake: I heard you went to a concert last weekend.
Lena: Yes I did. It was awesome. I went there alone but it was the most exciting concert I've ever been to.
Jake: I'm glad you enjoyed it. Weren't you lonely at all?
Lena: When I first arrived there, I felt a bit lonely. But once the concert started, I kept singing along with the crowd.
Jake: No wonder your voice sounds different. It seems like you _____.
Lena: You're right. I kept jumping up and down and shouted in the crowd for nearly three hours.
Jake: Wow! You must have really enjoyed the concert!
Lena: I really did!

① get the ax
② smell a rat
③ lose the day
④ have a frog in your throat

05 어법상 옳은 것은?

① If you told me what was wrong, I could have helped.
② What she needs to do is make a list of useful phone numbers.
③ You must have your own work area which can cut off from the rest of the house.
④ Tom, though too often telling us that we have known already, was competent in his work.

06 우리말을 영어로 바르게 옮긴 것은?

① Jane은 이제 자신의 버려진 사건에 대한 낭비된 비용에 대해 책임이 있다.
→ Jane is now liable for the wasting costs of her abandoned case.

② 개가 짖지 않았다면, 우리는 정원에 누군가가 있다는 것을 몰랐을 텐데.
→ If the dog hadn't barked, we would have known there was someone in the garden.

③ 그가 고등학생이 되었을 때쯤, 그의 가족 모두는 고기를 먹지 않기로 결정했다.
→ By the time he became a high school student, his whole family had decided not to eat meat.

④ 만약 당신이 언짢은 상황에 대한 해결책을 강구한다면 당신은 당신 자신에 대해 훨씬 더 좋게 느낄 것이다.
→ You'll feel a lot better about yourself although you work on solutions to your upsetting situations.

07 우리말을 영어로 잘못 옮긴 것은?

① 나는 하루 종일 그를 볼 수조차도 없다.
→ I cannot so much as catch sight of him all day long.

② 유언장에서 그녀는 자신의 모든 아이들에게 적은 액수의 돈을 남겨두었다.
→ In her will, she left all her children a small sum of money.

③ Tom은 이번 시즌에 대한 실망스러운 출발을 만회하기를 갈망할 것이다.
→ Tom will be anxious to make up for a disappointing start to the season.

④ 그들의 부상은 건물에서 떨어진 것과 일치한다.
→ Their injuries are inconsistent with having fallen from the building.

08 밑줄 친 부분 중 글의 흐름상 가장 어색한 것은?

Immanuel Kant stresses that a society can only function politically in relation to the state if fundamental rights, laws and entitlements are given and enhanced by the state. ① As Kant teaches, these "righteous laws" are founded upon three rational principles: (1) the liberty of every member of the society as a man, (2) the equality of every member of the society with every other, as a subject, (3) the independence of every member of the commonwealth as a citizen. ② An interesting aspect of these principles is that they are not given by the state, but are fundamental in the creation and acceptance of a state by the people of the state. ③ In this sense Kant believes these principles are necessary above all, not only for the founding of "righteous laws", but for the state to function in the first place. ④ Everyone needs to have the same rights within the state so that laws can be evaluated and applied in the same and "equal" manner for everyone. This is so because without the acceptance of the people a state would not exist, and therefore rights are needed within the state to keep the support of the people of the state.

09 빈칸에 들어갈 표현으로 가장 적절한 것은?

Birds are closely related to reptiles — most closely to crocodiles. To understand this, we should look at some history. The first groups of reptiles evolved about 300 million years ago. About 40 million years later, (very quickly by geologic standards), a group of reptiles called therapsids branched off, which eventually became modern mammals. Other groups of reptiles split off over the next 120 million years, and one branch called the dinosaurs were very successful. These dinosaurs were only distantly related to modern snakes, lizards, and turtles, groups that had split off at different times. But 65 million years ago there was a massive extinction event, and all dinosaurs were killed except for a single group of _____ dinosaurs. These evolved over the next 65 million years into modern birds. So birds aren't just closely related to dinosaurs; they really are dinosaurs!

① gigantic
② scaled
③ feathered
④ petite

10 다음 글의 내용과 일치하지 않는 것은?

Many different types of animals can carry harmful germs, such as bacteria, fungi, parasites, and viruses. These are then shared with humans and cause illness. Zoonotic diseases, also called zoonoses, range from mild to severe, and some can even be fatal. Zoonotic diseases are widespread both in the U.S. and worldwide. The World Health Organization (WHO) estimates that 61 percent of all human diseases are zoonotic in origin, while 75 percent of new diseases discovered in the last decade are zoonotic. Before the introduction of new hygiene regulations about 100 years ago, zoonotic diseases such as bovine tuberculosis, bubonic plague, and glanders caused millions of deaths. They are still a major problem in developing countries.

① A variety of animals can transmit diseases to humans.
② Certain zoonotic illnesses can cause human fatalities.
③ Over seventy percent of human diseases were originated from animals.
④ Around a century has passed since some action was taken to address hygiene issues.

01 밑줄 친 부분과 의미가 가장 가까운 것은?

The metabolic machinery of the cell functions in a completely <u>analogous</u> fashion, with its own version of master plans, working blueprints, transfer agents, and all the rest.

① delicate ② weird
③ similar ④ novel

02 밑줄 친 부분과 의미가 가장 가까운 것은?

His argument to me was completely <u>specious</u>.

① novel ② scarce
③ stern ④ superficial

03 밑줄 친 부분에 들어갈 가장 적절한 것을 고르시오.

Koreans _____ from Japan's brutalities, and independence activists were jailed, tortured, or killed.

① resorted ② subtracted
③ suffered ④ prompted

04 밑줄 친 부분에 들어갈 가장 적절한 것은?

The Secretary General said the U.N. will put forward several action plans to _____ the multilateral nuclear security and safety. He said toughening financial sanctions are necessary to prevent the spread of weapons of mass destruction and nuclear terrorism.

① beef up ② dispense with
③ damp down ④ scratch off

05 밑줄 친 부분에 들어갈 가장 적절한 것을 고르시오.

During the period of Ramadan, Muslim people _____ from eating and drinking during daylight hours.

① refrain ② pore
③ mediate ④ regard

06 우리말을 영어로 잘못 옮긴 것은?

① 지난주 시내 중심부의 주차 제한 조치가 시행되었다.
  → Parking restrictions in the town centre have come into force last week.
② Jane은 그를 비난하지 않았고 그것에 대해 언급조차도 하지 않았다.
  → Jane had not reproached him and never so much as mentioned it.
③ 독자들은 당신의 복잡하지 않은 성공을 제외하고는 어떤 것도 용서할 것이다.
  → Readers will forgive you anything except your uncomplicated success.
④ 그것은 멋진 것이 아니라 우리가 부끄러워하거나 당황해야 할 것이다.
  → It is not a wonderful thing but something we should be ashamed of or embarrassed about.

07 우리말을 영어로 바르게 옮긴 것은?

① 우리가 공항에 도착할 무렵, 비행기는 이미 이륙했다.
  → By the time we had arrived at the airport, the flight already took off.
② 당신이 바쁘지 않으면 오늘 저녁에 당신 집에 들르겠다.
  → I'll drop by your place this evening lest you should be busy.
③ 그녀가 콘서트에 왔었다면 좋아했을 것이다.
  → Had she come to the concert, she would have enjoyed it.
④ 그는 의사로서 자질이 없다.
  → He is cut out to be a doctor.

08 어법상 옳은 것은?

① What really concerned her was how unhappy was the child.
② It is interesting is that they are interested in what is made you fun.
③ Tom found a huge nest which is what he assumes was the magpie house.
④ The house, though imposing from the outside, are in fact a very comfortable size.

09 다음 글의 제목으로 가장 적절한 것은?

In 2013, scientists from Brigham and Women's Hospital published findings showing that bisphenol A (BPA) exposure can affect abnormal egg maturation in humans. A review of previous studies, published in 2015, found evidence that BPA can interfere with endocrine function involving the hypothalamus and the pituitary gland. The researchers suggested that this type of action can affect puberty and ovulation, and that it may lead to infertility. The authors add: "The detrimental effects on reproduction may be lifelong and transgenerational." Male impotence may be affected, according to a study that looked at the effect of men's exposure to BPA at work. Findings indicated that high-level exposure may increase the risk of erectile dysfunction and problems with sexual desire and ejaculation.

* hypothalamus: 시상하부 ** pituitary gland: 뇌하수체

① The Chemical We Cannot Live Without: BPA
② Male Health Issues That Can Be Caused By BPA
③ Positive and Negative Effects of BPA on Human Beings
④ Relation Between Exposure to BPA and Reproductive Disorders

10 주어진 글 다음에 이어질 글의 순서로 가장 적절한 것은?

All animals have the same kind of brain activation during sleep as humans. Whether or not they dream is another question, which can be answered only by posing another one: Do animals have consciousness?

(A) These are three of the key aspects of consciousness, and they could be experienced whether or not an animal had verbal language as we do. When the animal's brain is activated during sleep, why not assume that the animal has some sort of perceptual, emotional, and memory experience?

(B) Many scientists today feel that animals probably do have a limited form of consciousness, quite different from ours in that it lacks language and the capacity for propositional or symbolic thought.

(C) Animals certainly can't report dreams even if they do have them. But which pet owner would doubt that his or her favourite animal friend has perception, memory, and emotion?

① (A) − (B) − (C) ② (A) − (C) − (B)
③ (B) − (C) − (A) ④ (C) − (B) − (A)

11 밑줄 친 부분에 들어갈 표현으로 가장 적절한 것을 고르시오.

A: Look at this letter.
B: Ah yes, I thought it was something official looking. You're being fined for exceeding the speed limit, it says. Why weren't you fined on the spot?
A: _____.
B: They're installing more and more of them around here. You're going to have to be more careful in future.
A: You're not kidding. The fine is $60.

① Because the spot was too busy to be fined
② Because I could not find any camera to take it
③ Because I already paid for it when I was fined
④ Because I was photographed by one of speed cameras

12 밑줄 친 부분에 들어갈 표현으로 가장 적절한 것을 고르시오.

Nina: What are you guys doing here?
John: It's a secret. We're preparing a surprise birthday party for Danny.
Nina: Wow, Danny must be really happy once he finds out about all this.
John: I really hope so. We've been planning this for over two weeks. Would you like to join?
Nina: Sure, I'd love to. If anyone asks what we are doing, I'll just ___(A)___ to keep Danny from discovering the truth.
John: I trust you. If anyone ___(B)___, Danny will find out right away.

① (A) go to my head   (B) plays it by ear
② (A) hold my tongue   (B) plays it by ear
③ (A) hold my tongue   (B) spills the beans
④ (A) live from hand to mouth (B) spills the beans

13 다음 글의 내용과 일치하지 않는 것은?

Many different types of animals can carry harmful germs, such as bacteria, fungi, parasites, and viruses. These are then shared with humans and cause illness. Zoonotic diseases, also called zoonoses, range from mild to severe, and some can even be fatal. Zoonotic diseases are widespread both in the U.S. and worldwide. The World Health Organization (WHO) estimates that 61 percent of all human diseases are zoonotic in origin, while 75 percent of new diseases discovered in the last decade are zoonotic. Before the introduction of new hygiene regulations about 100 years ago, zoonotic diseases such as bovine tuberculosis, bubonic plague, and glanders caused millions of deaths. They are still a major problem in developing countries.

① A variety of animals can transmit diseases to humans.
② Certain zoonotic illnesses can cause human fatalities.
③ Over seventy percent of human diseases were originated from animals.
④ Around a century has passed since some action was taken to address hygiene issues.

14 밑줄 친 부분 중 글의 흐름상 가장 어색한 것은?

Working memory is critical for academic performance as it is an important part of executive functioning (e.g. planning, initiating, task monitoring, organizing, etc.). At school, the areas of learning that are greatly affected by poor working memory are: maths, reading comprehension, complex problem solving, and test taking. ① The biggest impact on school work occurs from difficulties with the first two areas. ② Working memory is much like a bucket that you can keep filling up using a glass of water. ③ It can be improved through simple games and day-to-day activities. ④ Every drop that you add remains in it unless over time memory evaporates through lack of repeated use. In children with poor working memory, it is much like the bucket has a hole in the bottom. You can keep tipping in glasses of water (information/ knowledge) but it continually drains out.

15 밑줄 친 부분 중 어법상 옳지 않은 것을 고르시오.

Some organizations do have policies which allow either men or women ① to take career breaks to look after children. However, not only ② have very few fathers actually availed themselves of such opportunities but anecdotal evidence also suggests that if they had done so, their careers would have been 'ruined' for life. Indeed, the knowledge of this ③ may well be a cause of the low take-up of such schemes by men. Organizations, therefore, not only need to establish the structures which allow careers to be more flexible but they also need to change attitudes which typically ④ remain thorough traditional.

16 밑줄 친 부분에 들어갈 말로 가장 적절한 것을 고르시오.

There's a knock at your door. Standing in front of you is a young man who needs help. He's injured and is bleeding. You take him in and help him, make him feel comfortable and safe and phone for an ambulance. This is clearly the right thing to do. But if you help him just because you feel sorry for him, according to Immanuel Kant, _____ _____. Your sympathy is irrelevant to the morality of your action. That's part of your character, but nothing to do with right and wrong. Morality for Kant wasn't just about what you do, but about why you do it. Those who do the right thing don't do it simply because of how they feel: the decision has to be based on reason, reason that tells you what your duty is, regardless of how you happen to feel.

① that wouldn't be a moral action at all
② your action is founded on reason
③ then you're exhibiting ethical behavior
④ you're encouraging him to be an honest person

17 빈칸에 들어갈 가장 적절한 것을 고르시오.

In the West, consciousness was long thought to be a divine gift bestowed solely on humans. Western philosophers historically conceived of nonhuman animals as unfeeling automatons. Even after Darwin demonstrated our kinship with animals, many scientists believed that the evolution of consciousness was a recent event. They thought the first mind sparked awake sometime after we split from chimpanzees and bonobos. This notion that consciousness was of recent vintage began to change in the decades following the Second World War, when more scientists were systematically studying the behaviors and brain states of Earth's creatures. Now each year brings a raft of new research papers, which, taken together, suggest that _____.

① humans are closely related to primates
② consciousness is an exclusive human trait
③ a great many animals are conscious like humans
④ even human beings were not conscious until recently

18 다음 글의 요지로 가장 적절한 것은?

New research on children with attention deficit hyperactivity disorder(ADHD) might show some tasks can improve working memory in general, and could help children with the condition. Torkel Klingberg ran a randomized controlled trial of 53 children with ADHD in which half of the participants practiced working-memory tasks that gradually increased in difficulty. The other half completed tasks that did not get harder as the children became better at them. The children who practiced with increasingly difficult memory tasks performed better on two working memory tests, which were different from the practice tasks, than the control group. In addition, the parents of children with memory training reported a reduction in their children's hyperactivity and inattention three months after the intervention, while the parents of the control group participants did not.

① ADHD can cause children to have poor working memory.
② ADHD symptoms can be reduced effectively by medication.
③ ADHD patients tend to have difficulty with completing a task.
④ Increasing working memory capacity can have a positive impact on kids with ADHD.

19 밑줄 친 (A), (B)에 들어갈 말로 가장 적절한 것은?

Birds lay eggs with hard shells, whereas some reptile species lay soft-shelled eggs. Why might this be the case? If a mother cannot lay a hard-shelled egg at its full size, it could lay a soft-shelled egg instead allowing the egg to expand after laying. _____(A)_____, a soft shell has the capacity to absorb moisture from the atmosphere and ground. For some reasons, birds have evolved such that their eggs don't need additional moisture, which is not the case for some species of reptiles. Another reason some reptiles lay soft-shelled eggs is because of the way they are incubated. Birds will sit on their eggs and use the warmth of their bodies; _____(B)_____ reptiles tend to utilize the natural heat of vegetation or the earth to incubate their eggs. As reptile eggs don't have to be strong enough to protect the unborn contents from the full weight of their parents, they can be soft-shelled.

(A)	(B)
① Thus	by contrast
② Additionally	on the other hand
③ However	accordingly
④ Besides	furthermore

20 주어진 문장이 들어갈 위치로 가장 적절한 것은?

Moreover, everyone had an incentive to obey such rules.

In order to understand Kant's moral philosophy, it's crucial to be familiar with the issues he, and other thinkers of his time, were dealing with. From the earliest recorded history, people's moral beliefs and practices were grounded in religion. (①) Scriptures, such as the bible and the Quran, laid out moral rules that believers thought to be handed down from God: Don't kill. Don't steal. Don't commit adultery, and so on. (②) The fact that they supposedly came from a divine source of wisdom gave them their authority. (③) They were not simply someone's arbitrary opinion; they were God's opinion, and as such, they offered humankind an objectively valid code of conduct. (④) If you "walked in the ways of the Lord," you would be rewarded, either in this life or the next. If you violated the commandments, you'd be punished. As a result, any sensible person brought up in such a faith would abide by the moral rules their religion taught.

MEMO

기적사 DAY 41

01 밑줄 친 부분에 들어갈 말로 가장 적절한 것을 고르시오.

Our main dish did not have much flavor, but I made it more _____ by adding condiments.

① palatable ② dissolvable
③ potable ④ susceptible

02 밑줄 친 부분과 의미가 가장 가까운 것을 고르시오.

During both World Wars, government subsidies and demands for new airplanes vastly improved techniques for their design and construction.

① financial support ② long-term planning
③ technical assistance ④ non-restrictive policy

03 밑줄 친 부분에 들어갈 말로 가장 적절한 것을 고르시오.

The two cultures were so utterly _____ that she found it hard to adapt from one to the other.

① overlapped ② equivalent
③ associative ④ disparate

04 두 사람의 대화 중 가장 어색한 것은?

① A: What time are we having lunch?
   B: It'll be ready before noon.
② A: I called you several times. Why didn't you answer?
   B: Oh, I think my cell phone was turned off.
③ A: Are you going to take a vacation this winter?
   B: I might. I haven't decided yet.
④ A: Hello. Sorry I missed your call.
   B: Would you like to leave a message?

05 우리말을 영어로 가장 잘 옮긴 것은?

① 너는 내게 전화해서 일에 늦을 거라고 알렸어야 했다.
   → You were supposed to phone me and let me know you were going to be late for work.
② 내가 축구 경기를 시청하는 동안, 내 남편은 다른 TV로 영화를 보았다.
   → While I watched a soccer match, my husband has watched a movie on the other TV.
③ 그녀의 감정을 상하게 하지 않으려고, 그는 독감으로 매우 아팠다고 말했다.
   → He said he was very sick with a flu, so as not hurting her feelings.
④ 상관이 생각하는 것과는 반대로, 절대 이 프로젝트를 일주일에 끝낼 수 없다.
   → Contrary to what the boss thinks, there is no way we can't get this project done in a week.

06 밑줄 친 부분 중 어법상 옳지 않은 것은?

Princeton University offers a tuition-free, nine-month "Bridge Year" in which students can elect ① to do a service project outside of the U.S. The University of North Carolina at Chapel Hill and Tufts University have similar programs, while ② ones run by the New School in New York City offers up to a year's worth of academic credit to participants. But in the last five years, the idea has been ③ gaining more traction in the U.S.—particularly among Americans ④ admitted to selective colleges and universities.

07 어법상 옳은 것은?

① Little did we think three months ago that we'd be working together.
② I would love to see you tonight if you will have finished your work.
③ When I had a problem with my new apartment, I wondered who should I go and talk to.
④ This book has been the best seller for weeks, but it hasn't come in any paperback yet, is it?

08 다음 글의 요지로 가장 적절한 것은?

My students often believe that if they simply meet more important people, their work will improve. But it's remarkably hard to engage with those people unless you've already put something valuable out into the world. That's what piques the curiosity of advisers and sponsors. Achievements show you have something to give, not just something to take. In life, it certainly helps to know the right people. But how hard they go to bat for you, how far they stick their necks out for you, depends on what you have to offer. Building a powerful network doesn't require you to be an expert at networking. It just requires you to be an expert at something. If you make great connections, they might advance your career. If you do great work, those connections will be easier to make. Let your insights and your outputs — not your business cards — do the talking.

① Sponsorship is necessary for a successful career.
② Building a good network starts from your accomplishments.
③ A powerful network is a prerequisite for your achievement.
④ Your insights and outputs grow as you become an expert at networking.

09 다음 글에 나타난 화자의 심경으로 가장 적절한 것은?

My face turned white as a sheet. I looked at my watch. The tests would be almost over by now. I arrived at the testing center in an absolute panic. I tried to tell my story, but my sentences and descriptive gestures got so confused that I communicated nothing more than a very convincing version of a human tornado. In an effort to curb my distracting explanation, the proctor led me to an empty seat and put a test booklet in front of me. He looked doubtfully from me to the clock, and then he walked away. I tried desperately to make up for lost time, scrambling madly through analogies and sentence completions. "Fifteen minutes remain," the voice of doom declared from the front of the classroom. Algebraic equations, arithmetic calculations, geometric diagrams swam before my eyes. "Time! Pencils down, please."

① nervous and worried
② excited and cheerful
③ calm and determined
④ safe and relaxed

10 주어진 문장 다음에 이어질 글의 순서로 가장 적절한 것은?

Devices that monitor and track your health are becoming more popular among all age populations.

(A) For example, falls are a leading cause of death for adults 65 and older. Fall alerts are a popular gerotechnology that has been around for many years but have now improved.
(B) However, for seniors aging in place, especially those without a caretaker in the home, these technologies can be lifesaving.
(C) This simple technology can automatically alert 911 or a close family member the moment a senior has fallen.

* gerotechnology: 노인을 위한 양로 기술

① (B) − (C) − (A)   ② (B) − (A) − (C)
③ (C) − (A) − (B)   ④ (C) − (B) − (A)

01 밑줄 친 부분과 의미가 가장 가까운 것을 고르시오.

Several types of sugar, such as white sugar and brown sugar, make foods palatable and add a smooth flavor to bitter drinks, such as coffee.

① saline
② insipid
③ pungent
④ delectable

02 밑줄 친 부분과 의미가 가장 가까운 것을 고르시오.

The Seoul mayor recently announced that the city will provide living allowances to approximately 50,000 citizens who have failed to receive the central government's support due to legal loopholes.

① parley
② backing
③ rupture
④ endowment

03 밑줄 친 부분과 의미가 가장 가까운 것을 고르시오.

Countries that have adopted democracy follow this ideal and try to provide equal opportunities in their societies.

① indign
② lopsided
③ equivalent
④ analogous

04 두 사람의 대화 중 가장 어색한 것은?

① A: I have bruises all over my leg.
　B: What's wrong? Did you trip over something?
② A: Could you please do me a favor?
　B: My favorite book is Harry Potter.
③ A: There's a fire truck all over the town.
　B: I heard the sound of sirens a few minutes ago.
④ A: I checked the weather forecast this morning.
　B: Good for you! Will it rain today?

05 우리말을 영어로 가장 잘 옮긴 것은?

① 지난 50년 동안 일반 노동자의 실질 임금이 약 10%까지 증가했다.
　→ The real wage of the average worker increases by about 10% in the last 50 years.
② 나는 시대에 뒤떨어지지 않기 위해 매일 아침 인터넷에서 검색하는 것을 규칙으로 삼는다.
　→ I make it a rule to search on the internet every morning so as not to get behind the times.
③ 그 노트북은 너무 심하게 손상되어서 그것 안에 저장된 자료는 좀처럼 복구될 수 없다.
　→ The notebook was so badly damaged that the data stored in it could not scarcely be recovered.
④ 스마트폰은 그것을 소유한 개인이 정보에 접근할 수 있는 능력을 만들어 낸다.
　→ Smart phone has created the ability for an individual who has it to have an access to information.

06 밑줄 친 부분 중 어법상 옳지 않은 것은?

People in reasonably good health at the age of 60 can now expect ① to live close to thirty more years. These can be the happiest years of their lives, since the ② pressures of earning a living, building a career, and ③ rising a family are behind them. Workers can use their "golden years" to do many of the things they had always hoped ④ to do, but never had the opportunity to do because of their 40-plus-hour workweeks.

07 어법상 옳은 것은?

① It has been over thirty years since you performed together, has it?
② Before negotiating for your monthly salary, you have to first know where you stand.
③ If I should fail in finding a job this time, I would not have another chances next year.
④ Little Tom knew that it would be one of the things representing Korea's pop culture.

08 글의 흐름상 빈칸에 들어갈 단어로 가장 적절한 것은?

How do people who aren't fond of networking get ahead in their careers? There's the hope — backed by some evidence — that producing good work will _____ most of the need to network at all. Cal Newport, a computer scientist who explores how people reach elite levels in knowledge-based careers, interviewed several Rhodes Scholars in the course of his research, and discovered that the path to success for many of them is often misreported. He wrote, "Rhodes Scholars invest a large amount of energy in doing a small number of things (usually two) extremely well rather than depend on connections or chance." It's the results of work — and not necessarily exposing yourself to as many people as possible — that attracts more and varied opportunities outside of that work.

* Rhodes Scholar: 로즈 장학생(영국 옥스퍼드 대학에서 공부하는 미국·독일·영연방 공화국 출신 학생들에게 주어지는 로즈 장학금(Rhodes scholarship)을 받는 학생)

① aggravate
② attenuate
③ awaken
④ slay

09 다음 글의 주제로 가장 적절한 것은?

You can enter the exam room within one hour of the official start time, with permission from the exam supervisor. However, late students will not be given any extra time beyond the scheduled end time for the exam. If you arrive after the first hour, you will not be permitted to enter the exam room. In this situation you can apply to defer your examination; however a deferred exam will only be granted under exceptional circumstances such as illness or circumstances beyond your control. To apply, you must complete the examination deferral form. Forms can be submitted before or no later than three University working days after the date of your exam. Your application must include appropriate supporting documents.

① How to apply for an exam
② Breaches of the exam rules
③ Exam policy for late arrivals
④ Penalties for being late for an exam

10 밑줄 친 (A), (B)에 들어갈 말로 가장 적절한 것은?

According to the American Association of Retired Persons(AARP), almost 90 percent of seniors would like to stay in their homes as they age. This idea of aging in place — growing older where you already live, typically not in a health-care environment — continues to be a popular choice among seniors able to live without a lot of assistance. ____(A)____, as this population ages in homes that have been designed for their old lifestyles, there are considerable risks to elderly people's health and safety. Many seniors aging in place may not have access to caretakers or health-care professionals on a day-to-day basis. Accidents and falls are a major concern for elderly people living alone. ____(B)____, gerontechnology today can help seniors live in their homes with ease and safety. This can include smart home automation, wearable tech, activity sensors, etc.

* age in place: 살던 곳에서 노후를 맞이하다
* gerontechnology: 노인을 위한 양로 기술

	(A)	(B)
①	Accordingly	In a word
②	Similarly	For instance
③	However	Fortunately
④	Consequently	Hence

01 밑줄 친 부분과 의미가 가장 가까운 것을 고르시오.

The new technology is made of a dissolvable material, meaning that when it is placed onto the skin it will dissolve straight away.

① erodible   ② resolvable
③ solidified   ④ vaporizable

02 밑줄 친 부분과 의미가 가장 가까운 것을 고르시오.

The "Seoul Digital Basic Plan 2020" will include the city's digital policy vision and scheme for five years, starting in 2016.

① bulletin   ② planning
③ engagement   ④ extemporization

03 밑줄 친 부분과 의미가 가장 가까운 것을 고르시오.

The colorful plastic bricks are very simple, but have endless possibilities when stacked together.

① reversed   ② separated
③ overlapped   ④ segmented

04 두 사람의 대화 중 가장 어색한 것은?

① A: Where did you put your socks?
   B: It's in the laundry. Why do you ask?
② A: I want to see you in your new clothes.
   B: I'll try them out when the weather gets warmer.
③ A: I know the fastest route to the train station.
   B: The map doesn't show the fastest route.
④ A: Why do you keep sneezing? Are you allergic to cats?
   B: I've had it since I was young.

05 우리말을 영어로 가장 잘 옮긴 것은?

① William은 자신의 역사 수업에 늦지 않도록 서둘렀다.
   → William made haste lest he should not be late for his history class.
② Tom과 Jane은 누가 엿듣지 못하도록 언제나 조용히 이야기한다.
   → Tom and Jane always speak quietly so as not to being overheard by anybody.
③ 그 연구원은 6,500만 년 전에 포유류가 번성하였고 영장류가 출현했다고 말했다.
   → The researcher has suggested that mammals prospered and primates appeared 65 million years ago.
④ 다른 이들이 새로운 어떤 것을 배우도록 돕는 것에 서툴기 때문에 그는 교사로서의 자질이 없다.
   → He is not cut out to being a teacher because he is poor at helping others to learn something new.

06 밑줄 친 부분 중 어법상 옳지 않은 것은?

Lone animals ① rely on their own senses to defend themselves, but an animal in a group benefits by having a lot of other animals' eyes, ears, and noses on the alert for danger. An animal in a group also has a smaller chance of being the unlucky individual ② picked out by a predator. In addition, a group of ③ animals fleeing from a predator can create confusion. This makes ④ a predator harder to focus on one animal to catch.

07 어법상 옳은 것은?

① Tom is hardly likely to admit he was wrong, is he?
② Hardly the whole process has been conducive to the stability of central government.
③ Some people ask why do we tolerate a popular culture that celebrates violence and depravity.
④ If we were to provide more money with local government, it would solve this problem more easily.

08 빈칸에 들어갈 표현으로 가장 적절한 것은?

At the present day networking has become an essential aspect of your job search. Even if you are well established in your current job and have no plans of moving or advancing your career soon, networking has proven to be a valuable tool. Today, studies have shown that up to 80 percent of jobs are never advertised; instead, they are filled by word of mouth. Thus, it is _____ that matters. You must develop relationships and connections so that you can have more opportunities to advance your career. Attending meetings and social events hosted by your professional association is one of the greatest ways to connect with people in your field.

① who you work with and for
② what you do and how you do it
③ who you know and who knows you
④ where and how you meet new people

09 다음 글의 밑줄 친 부분 중 문맥상 단어의 쓰임이 적절하지 않은 것은?

If a student does not appear during the scheduled examination period or is ① unable to take the examination during the scheduled examination time, the student must notify a dean as soon as possible but no ② earlier than 24 hours after the scheduled start time of the examination. If the student fails to notify a dean within 24 hours of the scheduled start time of the examination, the student will not be allowed to take the examination and will receive an "F" on the examination, unless the student makes a ③ separate showing of extraordinary circumstances beyond the student's control, and the dean finds the reasons ④ justifying such late notice. The term "extraordinary circumstances beyond the student's control" used herein includes but is not limited to health emergency or immediate family emergency.

10 빈칸에 들어갈 표현으로 가장 적절한 것은?

Various types of technology are specifically designed to support aging in place, such as emergency help systems, vital signs monitoring, and fall detection systems. These technologies are sometimes referred to as Smart Home technology. Additionally, there is e-Health, which encompasses a broad range of technologies, including online tools to support seniors' self-management of chronic conditions. But these technologies have not been implemented on a large scale for various reasons. One of the reasons is older adults' _____ _____ these types of technology. On the one hand, they recognize that such technologies could support independent living of the older population, while on the other hand, they do not feel that they themselves personally need them.

* aging in place: 살던 곳에서 노후 맞기

① vigilant approach to
② general preference for
③ prevalent ignorance of
④ ambivalent attitude towards

기적사 DAY 44

01 밑줄 친 부분과 의미가 가장 가까운 것을 고르시오.

They are equipped with water purification machines and evaporators capable of producing more than 100,000 gallons of drinkable water per day.

① potable
② stewable
③ digestible
④ comestible

02 밑줄 친 부분과 의미가 가장 가까운 것을 고르시오.

Supporting poor people in this way is better because these organizations can provide a proper amount of assistance that will encourage people not to be lazy.

① halt
② tribute
③ seizure
④ succor

03 밑줄 친 부분과 의미가 가장 가까운 것을 고르시오.

Some of the tasks tested the dogs' associative learning skills while others tested the dogs' creativity at solving problems.

① poignant
② eradicable
③ reminiscent
④ crystallizable

04 두 사람의 대화 중 가장 어색한 것은?

① A: I have a headache.
　B: Migraine is one kind of headache.
② A: Can I borrow your shirt?
　B: Sure, but I don't know if it will fit you.
③ A: Did you pack all your socks already?
　B: I packed it as soon as I woke up.
④ A: I want to spend the rest of the weekend with my mom.
　B: Did you make any plan with your mom?

05 우리말을 영어로 가장 잘 옮긴 것은?

① William은 소리를 내지 않으려고 구두를 벗었다.
→ William took off his shoes in order not to make any noise.
② 그가 범행을 저질렀다는 것을 모르는 사람은 아무도 없다.
→ There is no one but doesn't know that he committed a crime.
③ 그는 10살 이후 어머니에게 선물을 사드리기 위해 돈을 모으는 중이었다.
→ He was saving money to buy a present for his mother since he was ten years old.
④ 근육 손실을 보충하기 위해 적당량의 단백질을 섭취해야 한다.
→ You should take in an appropriate amount of protein to make up to the loss of muscles.

06 밑줄 친 부분 중 어법상 옳지 않은 것은?

A planning discussion can be fairly complex and fast-paced, ① causing us to forget things. Take the time to summarize what's supposed to ② be happened. It could sound something like this: "Let me see if I got this right. Tom, you'll prepare the nine copies of the report ③ stapled with a standard company cover sheet for the meeting Tuesday at 2 p.m. Is that right?" Tom would probably say, "Right," and then you could ask him whether there is anything else that you haven't talked about ④ that might cause a problem.

07 어법상 옳은 것은?

① Jane couldn't help but wondering what Tom was thinking.
② Not only did he listen to the music, but also wrote what he had listened.
③ The leadership training with Mr. William begins at eleven o'clock, hasn't it?
④ If I were to stay in my current job, I would gain more experience in the negotiations between labor and management.

08 다음 글에서 필자가 주장하는 것으로 가장 적절한 것은?

There's an old adage that if you throw spaghetti against the wall and it sticks, the pasta is done. Over the years, this phrase has evolved to mean that when you throw enough activity or ideas at a situation or problem, eventually something will stick; that is, eventually you will find the answer. So when you're told you need to network to help you be successful, those of you who are ambitious tackle the problem with this approach. You throw a lot of activity at the issue and hope for the best. You go to lots of networking events and conferences, collect and hand out hundreds of business cards. You establish an online presence and build a large group of followers. Unfortunately, these don't result in the type of network that supports your career advancement because they have no specific and clear purpose or intention. To create the type of network that supports your ambitions, your networking activity needs to be strategic and focused and your efforts must be purposeful and intentional.

① A reliable network is a must for success.
② When networking, quality is more important than quantity.
③ If you do not give up, you will get what you want in the end.
④ You should not limit your network to the people in your field.

09 밑줄 친 (A), (B)에 들어갈 말로 가장 적절한 것은?

In 2011, Macquarie University was the first Australian university to debate the abolition of exams, that is, no exams in any subject, at any year level. At the time it was suggested that exams fail to develop "questioning, self-sufficient learners".   (A)   , critics often argue that exams promote a superficial understanding of topics, and that they are inauthentic: in other words, they fail to represent the kinds of things students will be asked to do "in the real world".   (B)   , this is taking a narrow view of the benefits of exams. Good assessment programs can provide a balanced and fair evaluation of each student. Rather than abolishing exams, we should instead be asking what mix of assessment tasks is most appropriate for each subject.

	(A)	(B)
①	Otherwise	But
②	Nevertheless	Moreover
③	For example	As a result
④	Also	However

10 다음 글의 밑줄 친 부분 중 문맥상 단어의 쓰임이 적절하지 않은 것은?

Gerontechnology has traditionally focused on improving ① physical health, with the development and promotion of medication monitoring apps and safety alert systems. In recent years, however, there has been a ② shift to promote mental health and adopt a holistic approach to aging. By ③ diminishing seniors' social life and connectivity, gerontechnology are helping seniors avoid depression, boredom, and loneliness. Chaiwoo Lee, a researcher at the AgeLab, notes that people are trying to move away from ④ medicalizing health and that "older adults care more about being connected to family and staying productive." Through her research on caregivers, Chaiwoo has found that one of their most time-consuming tasks is "keeping older adults company and managing emotional burdens."

* gerontechnology: 노인을 위한 양로 기술

01 밑줄 친 부분과 의미가 가장 가까운 것을 고르시오.

The country's aging population is also a factor because the elderly are more susceptible to air quality-related illnesses.

① dull
② nimble
③ feeble
④ impressionable

02 밑줄 친 부분과 의미가 가장 가까운 것을 고르시오.

This trend is causing some politicians to question the value of Korea's policy of not including women in its policy of compulsory military service.

① tactic
② doctrine
③ edification
④ stratagem

03 밑줄 친 부분과 의미가 가장 가까운 것을 고르시오.

They connect disparate information, and they bring it together in a way that a security analyst doesn't expect.

① seely
② intricate
③ homogeneous
④ heterogeneous

04 두 사람의 대화 중 가장 어색한 것은?

① A: I'm really thirsty.
   B: There is a water fountain in the hallway.
② A: How much is the fee for this club?
   B: You have to pay thirty dollars annually.
③ A: Do not drive too fast on the highway!
   B: I'll keep that in mind. Don't worry!
④ A: The woman who lives next door said that she is thinking of starting a new business.
   B: People are running out of business these days. But I don't know why.

05 우리말을 영어로 가장 잘 옮긴 것은?

① 우리는 이 섬 주위를 항해하던 중에 이 유적지를 발견했다.
   → We discovered this historic site while we were sailing around the island.
② 다른 나라들은 음식물 쓰레기를 처리하는 것에 대해 그 나라를 비난할 수 없을 것이다.
   → There is no way other countries can't criticize the country for disposing of its food waste.
③ 그 국제 항공사는 사법권이 없다고 말하면서, 승객들을 적극적으로 단속하지 않는다.
   → The international airline does not actively crack down for passengers, saying it has no judicial power.
④ 등산할 때는 길을 잃지 않도록 지도와 나침반을 가지고 가는 편이 낫다.
   → You had better to take a map and compass with you so as not to lose your way when you go climbing.

06 밑줄 친 부분 중 어법상 옳지 않은 것은?

Obviously, one of the judgments the public has of us is ① if or not our telephone service is good. Technically, if they get their calls through, efficiently and promptly, they get ② what they want. That, however, is not all they want. They want to have the service ③ rendered to them in a manner that pleases them; they want not only efficiency ④ but courtesy and consideration; and they are in a position to get what they want.

07 어법상 옳은 것은?

① It gets very cold there this time of the year, doesn't it?
② Seldom aren't books returned to their right place on the shelves.
③ Tom did not know why did the animals follow him, for he rarely had anything to give them.
④ If you should go to the department, William would hope you to return to your original department.

08 밑줄 친 부분 중 글의 흐름상 가장 어색한 것은?

Jordan Harbinger, one of the most successful podcasters on the planet, says that you need to create the relationships beforehand. ① We've all been on the receiving end of an email that "pretends" to check on you, when the person is just buttering you up for an ask. This is the wrong way to lean on a network. The right way is to build up social capital over time. ② When asking a favor of someone in your network, it's better to do so face to face and not through email. Check in with people consistently, not just when you need something. It's too late if you start to look for people when you need them. ③ Relationships get deeper over time, so planting seeds early makes all the difference. "Creating relationships before you ever need them is key," says Harbinger. ④ In fact, he recommends assuming you'll never need them. "It's like putting a tire in the trunk of your car before you get a flat," he says. You don't plan to get a flat. And, in the best case scenario, you never use the spare.

* podcaster: 팟캐스터
(인터넷망을 통해 제공되는 다양한 콘텐츠를 제작하는 사람)

09 다음 글의 요지로 가장 적절한 것은?

High-stakes exams often determine the future of learners: transition, graduation, or entrance to higher education, to better schools, or to better jobs. These exams do not only have high stakes for students, but also for teachers, schools and families, as the test results can influence funding, recognition and reputation. In some cases, the stakes are so high that examinations can dominate thinking about the purpose and nature of schooling. Students are constantly preparing for examinations, students and their parents are continually anxious about academic success, and the pressure on students to do well can lead to stress, anxiety, depression as well as school violence and even suicide. Furthermore, the focus on 'high scores' may be undermining other fundamental aspects of learning that are often not captured in tests and examinations and questions whether education systems have lost sight of the true value and purpose of education.

① High-stakes exams are effective and necessary to improve schooling and learning.
② High-stakes exams should be abandoned because they are causing a variety of problems.
③ Scoring well on high-stakes exams can make a significant difference in a student's future.
④ Although high-stakes exams have some advantages, they also can produce negative effects.

10 주어진 문장이 들어갈 위치로 가장 적절한 것은?

Furthermore, physical and mental decline might make it even more difficult for them to use these new technologies.

There are relevant challenges concerning gerontechnology applications. Firstly, the acceptance of the new technologies by older people is questionable. Not every older person will be enthusiastic to have cameras and microphones in bath or bedrooms. Of course, these cameras and microphones are just sensors that should be analyzing their data immediately, without any recording functionality. (①) But some feeling of being watched (and some uncertainty what the technology is doing in reality) might be highly uneasy. (②) Secondly, the technologies might be too complex for older people to handle. (③) Today's older people grew up in a time, where technology use was less computerized and less complicated. (④) Thirdly, the technologies are most probably expensive, so many people may not be able to buy such technologies, and even if so the maintenance costs might be rather high as well. Thus, these new technologies may exacerbate social inequalities that already exist.

* gerontechnology: 노인을 위한 양로 기술

01 밑줄 친 부분과 의미가 가장 먼 것을 고르시오.

As a prerequisite for fertilization, pollination is essential to the production of fruit and seed crops and plays an important part in programs designed to improve plants by breeding.

① crucial ② indispensable
③ requisite ④ omnipresent

02 글의 흐름상 빈칸에 들어갈 단어로 가장 옳은 것은?

Mr. Johnson objected to the proposal because it was founded on a _____ principle and also was _____ at times.

① faulty — desirable
② imperative — reasonable
③ conforming — deplorable
④ wrong — inconvenient

03 빈칸에 들어갈 단어로 가장 적절한 것은?

The company and the union reached a tentative agreement in this year's wage deal as the two sides took the company's _____ operating profits seriously amid unfriendly business environments.

① deteriorating ② enhancing
③ ameliorating ④ leveling

04 대화의 흐름으로 보아 빈칸에 들어갈 가장 적절한 것은?

A: Why don't you let me treat you to lunch today, Mr. Kim?
B: _____.

① No, I'm not. That would be a good time for me
② Good. I'll put it on my calendar so I don't forget
③ OK. I'll check with you on Monday
④ Wish I could but I have another commitment today

05 밑줄 친 부분 중 어법상 가장 옳지 않은 것은?

There is a more serious problem than ① maintaining the cities. As people become more comfortable working alone, they may become ② less social. It's ③ easier to stay home in comfortable exercise clothes or a bathrobe than ④ getting dressed for yet another business meeting!

06 밑줄 친 부분 중 어법상 가장 옳지 않은 것은?

This Abstract, which I now publish, must necessarily be imperfect. I cannot here give references and authorities for my several statements; and I must ① trust to the reader reposing some confidence in my accuracy. No ② doubt errors will have crept in, though I hope I have always been cautious in trusting to good authorities alone. I can here give only the general conclusions at which I have arrived, with a few facts in illustration, but which, I hope, in most cases will ③ be sufficed. No one can feel more sensible than I do of the necessity of hereafter publishing in detail all the facts, with references, on which my conclusions have been grounded; and I hope in a future work to do this. For I am well aware that scarcely a single point is discussed in this volume on which facts cannot be ④ adduced, often apparently leading to conclusions directly opposite to those at which I have arrived. A fair result can be obtained only by fully stating and balancing the facts and arguments on both sides of each question; and this cannot possibly be here done.

07 밑줄 친 부분 중 어법상 가장 옳지 않은 것은?

In the fifteenth century, an alphasyllabic Korean script was invented. Linguists admire it as it ① symbolizes the speech sounds in a ② sophisticated and very elegant way. The script, called Hangul, can be used in tandem with the Chinese characters but can also replace them altogether. Slowly, Hangul has ③ been taken over. In North Korea, only Hangul is used, while in South Korea, Chinese characters still ④ occur in particular contexts.

08 밑줄 친 부분에 들어갈 말로 가장 적절한 것을 고르시오.

The secret of successful people is usually that they are able to concentrate totally on one thing. Even if they have a lot in their head, they have found a method that the many commitments don't impede each other, but instead they are brought into a good inner order. And this order is quite simple: _____. In theory, it seems to be quite clear, but in everyday life it seems rather different. You might have tried to decide on priorities, but you have failed because of everyday trivial matters and all the unforeseen distractions. Separate off disturbances, for example, by escaping into another office, and not allowing any distractions to get in the way. When you concentrate on the one task of your priorities, you will find you have energy that you didn't even know you had.

① the sooner, the better
② better late than never
③ out of sight, out of mind
④ the most important thing first

09 다음 글의 제목으로 가장 적절한 것은?

With the help of the scientist, the commercial fishing industry has found out that its fishing must be done scientifically if it is to be continued. With no fishing pressure on a fish population, the number of fish will reach a predictable level of abundance and stay there. The only fluctuation would be due to natural environmental factors, such as availability of food, proper temperature, and the like. If a fishery is developed to take these fish, their population can be maintained if the fishing harvest is small. The mackerel of the North Sea is a good example. If we increase the fishery and take more fish each year, we must be careful not to reduce the population below the ideal point where it can replace all of the fish we take out each year. If we fish at this level, called the maximum sustainable yield, we can maintain the greatest possible yield, year after year. If we catch too many, the number of fish will decrease each year until we fish ourselves out of a job. Examples of severely overfished animals are the blue whale of the Antarctic and the halibut of the North Atlantic. Fishing just the correct amount to maintain a maximum annual yield is both a science and an art. Research is constantly being done to help us better understand the fish population and how to utilize it to the maximum without depleting the population.

① Say No to Commercial Fishing
② Sea Farming Seen As a Fishy Business
③ Why Does the Fishing Industry Need Science?
④ Overfished Animals: Cases of Illegal Fishing

10 밑줄 친 (A), (B)에 들어갈 말로 가장 적절한 것은?

Does terrorism ever work? 9/11 was an enormous tactical success for al Qaeda, partly because it involved attacks that took place in the media capital of the world and the actual capital of the United States, ____(A)____ ensuring the widest possible coverage of the event. If terrorism is a form of theater where you want a lot of people watching, no event in human history was likely ever seen by a larger global audience than the 9/11 attacks. At the time, there was much discussion about how 9/11 was like the attack on Pearl Harbor. They were indeed similar since they were both surprise attacks that drew America into significant wars. But they were also similar in another sense. Pearl Harbor was a great tactical success for Imperial Japan, but it led to a great strategic failure: Within four years of Pearl Harbor the Japanese empire lay in ruins, utterly defeated. ____(B)____, 9/11 was a great tactical success for al Qaeda, but it also turned out to be a great strategic failure for Osama bin Laden.

	(A)	(B)
①	thereby	Similarly
②	while	Therefore
③	while	Fortunately
④	thereby	On the contrary

결국엔 성정혜 영어 하프모의고사
기적사 DAY 47

01 밑줄 친 부분과 의미가 가장 가까운 것을 고르시오.

A country's legal voting age means the age that citizens can begin voting for political leaders that will make crucial decisions for their nation.

① trifling
② intrinsic
③ immaterial
④ momentous

02 밑줄 친 부분과 의미가 가장 가까운 것을 고르시오.

By showing that Jane had made a faulty assumption, all of John's arguments became more convincing.

① unerring
② unsound
③ impaired
④ regainable

03 밑줄 친 부분과 의미가 가장 가까운 것을 고르시오.

Their significant contributions to ecology and conservation have made a powerful difference across rapidly deteriorating ecosystems and restored wildlife habitats.

① unscathed
② aggravating
③ obsolescing
④ ameliorative

04 대화의 흐름으로 보아 빈칸에 들어갈 가장 적절한 것은?

A: Oh my gosh! It's raining so hard outside!
B: Wow! I think it's been years since it rained this much.
A: Right. People were worried it was a drought.
B: I know. But the bad news is that I forgot to bring my umbrella. I didn't check the weather forecast this morning.
A: Don't worry. I have two umbrellas. You can borrow mine.
B: Thank you so much! You're my savior.
A: Oh, you're welcome. Anyways, if it rains this much, there might be a _____ sooner or later today.
B: Oh no! I should prepare my flashlight.

① big deal
② black out
③ showdown
④ backseat driver

05 밑줄 친 부분 중 어법상 가장 옳지 않은 것은?

In each of the five ① selected countries, it is predicted ② that the life expectancy of women will be higher than ③ those of men. In the case of women, life expectancy in the Republic of Korea is expected to be the highest among the five countries, ④ followed by that in Austria.

06 밑줄 친 부분 중 어법상 가장 옳지 않은 것은?

Parents are quick to inform friends and relatives as soon as their infant holds her head up, reaches for objects, sits by herself, and walks alone. Parental enthusiasm for these motor accomplishments ① is not at all misplaced, for they are, indeed, milestones of development. With each additional skill, babies gain control over their bodies and the environment in a new way. Infants who are able to sit alone ② are granted an entirely different perspective on the world than are those who spend much of their day on their backs or stomachs. Coordinated reaching opens up a whole new avenue for exploration of objects, and when babies can move about, their opportunities for independent exploration and manipulation are multiplied. No longer ③ do they restrict to their immediate locale and to objects that others place before them. As new ways of controlling the environment are achieved, motor development provides the infant ④ with a growing sense of competence and mastery, and it contributes in important ways to the infant's perceptual and cognitive understanding of the world.

07 밑줄 친 부분 중 어법상 가장 옳지 않은 것은?

There is strong research evidence ① that children perform better in mathematics if music is incorporated in it. It has ② been shown that mathematics is related with music in various known ways so much that not putting the relationship ③ to good use in and out of school could only be to our disadvantage. Researchers at a Los Angeles school found that 136 second year elementary school pupils who learned to play the piano and read music ④ improving their numeracy skills.

08 주어진 문장이 들어갈 위치로 가장 적절한 것은?

Nor is it likely to be any number of random busy assignments at home or work that won't be appreciated by your family, reflected on your annual goal, or noticed by anyone but yourself.

We live in a world of distraction, of short attention spans, and ever-changing priorities. Do not fall victim to the swirling deluge of triviality. (①) Do not get lost in the weeds of random tangents and unimportant tasks. (②) As you navigate the day, ask yourself, "What is the most important thing?" (③) Chances are, the most important thing is not browsing YouTube for the latest silly cat video. (④) The most important thing is whatever makes the most difference and brings the most value either to yourself or others. While there are no guarantees in life, doing what's most important is the best we can do, and working toward the most important things often brings what's best for us.

09 밑줄 친 (A), (B)에 들어갈 말로 가장 적절한 것은?

Scientific research shows that climate change impacts on the ocean have already affected fisheries. While abundance of several cold water species is reducing, some tropical species are appearing on our coasts. In future decades ocean warming and acidification can affect growth and reproduction processes of many marine organisms, which may reduce stocks available for many significant commercial species. _____(A)_____, shellfish such as oysters and mussels are especially sensitive to acidification. Climate change is also going to impact bacterial and phytoplankton communities, which are key to the marine food web. _____(B)_____, if we keep on producing greenhouse gases at the current pace, changes expected before the end of the century in terms of biodiversity could be similar to those that occurred during the prior 20 or 30 million years.

	(A)	(B)
①	Consequently	By contrast
②	That is	However
③	As an example	Nevertheless
④	For instance	Eventually

10 빈칸에 들어갈 표현으로 가장 적절한 것은?

We examined 90 groups to determine whether _____.
Half of the groups we studied used terrorism to achieve their ends, and the other half used peaceful means. To choose the 90 groups, we identified 45 pairs of groups operating in the same country or region in relatively the same time period. For instance, in Chile during the rule of autocratic dictator Augusto Pinochet from 1973 to 1990, people organized to end his rule. One group, Chile's Concertación, sought to bring Pinochet down using a referendum. Meanwhile, the Manuel Rodriguez Patriotic Front opposed Pinochet with bombings, shootings, kidnappings and assassinations. Through our research, we found only six of the 45 terror groups – that's 13.3 percent – accomplished their broader goals; the others did not. Meanwhile, among the 45 groups that chose not to use terrorism, 26 – or 57.8 percent – reached their objectives.

① terrorism can be justified
② terrorism works to achieve a group's goals
③ terrorist attacks can be prevented in advance
④ terrorists share specific psychological or psychiatric traits

01 밑줄 친 부분과 의미가 가장 가까운 것을 고르시오.

Soy is an indispensable part of the Argentine economy that is regarded as a major factor for lifting the country out of an economic crisis in 2001.

① petty
② banal
③ swing
④ imperative

02 밑줄 친 부분과 의미가 가장 가까운 것을 고르시오.

Speed limits exist because they provide safe and reasonable driving conditions on roads and highways.

① sane
② consonant
③ indecent
④ imprudent

03 밑줄 친 부분과 의미가 가장 가까운 것을 고르시오.

It is said that two gymnasts, Yang Hak-seon and Son Yeon-jae have been busy shooting image-enhancing campaign commercials for certain companies since their return from London.

① fixating
② intensifying
③ replenishing
④ undermining

04 대화의 흐름으로 보아 빈칸에 들어갈 가장 적절한 것은?

Son: Mom, is the smell coming from the kitchen? It smells like apple pie.
Mom: I thought you were coming home late today. So I was going to bake it for you as a surprise.
Son: Thanks, mom! I love your apple pie! Is it still in the oven?
Mom: Yes. It's not ready yet. It's too bad I couldn't surprise you as I planned.
Son: It's like a surprise gift to me. I can't wait to taste it!
Mom: Be careful! Don't touch the oven, it's really hot.
Son: Oh, I almost touched the oven! I want to look inside to see if the pie is baking well.
Mom: _____. I don't want you to get hurt.

① Enough is enough
② Now you're talking
③ Curiosity killed the cat
④ You can say that again

05 밑줄 친 부분 중 어법상 가장 옳지 않은 것은?

Your strengths are ① more important than your passions. Studies show that the best career choices tend to ② be grounded in things which you're ③ good, more so than your interests and passions. Ideally, you want to find a convergence of your strengths and your values with a career path ④ that is in demand.

06 밑줄 친 부분 중 어법상 가장 옳지 않은 것은?

When we see a happy face (or an angry one), it subtly generates the corresponding emotion in us. To the degree which we ① take it on the pace, posture, and facial expression of another person, we start to inhabit their emotional space; as our body mimics the other's, we begin to experience emotional matching. Our nervous system is automatically set to ② engage in this emotional empathy. But how well we use this capacity is largely a learned ability. Animals — and people — who have ③ been raised in extreme social isolation are poor at reading emotional cues in those around them not because they lack the basic circuitry for empathy ④ but because, lacking emotional tutors, they have never learned to pay attention to these messages and so haven't practiced this skill.

07 밑줄 친 부분 중 어법상 가장 옳지 않은 것은?

One reason many people keep ① delaying things they should do ② is that they fear they will do them wrong or ③ poor, so they just don't do them at all. For example, one of the best ways to write a book is to write it as quickly as possible, ④ getting your thoughts onto paper without regard to style. Then, you can go back to revise and polish your writing.

08 다음 글의 요지로 가장 적절한 것은?

Imagine that you have a pile of sand, a pile of big rocks, and a jar into which you must put both piles. Let's say you filled the jar first with the sand; you might find that it took up so much space that you ultimately didn't have room for the big rocks. But, let's say you instead first filled the jar with big rocks, and then put in the sand; the sediment will settle in the cracks of the big rocks, allowing you to fit everything in from both piles. Your life is like the jar. The sand is the urgent, but less important things in your life. The big rocks are the most important things in your life: activities that don't have hard deadlines but help you achieve your principle goals. When you tackle life's "big rocks" first, you end up having time for everyday life maintenance tasks, as well as for relaxation and fun. But when you put the sand first, the more important things in life get crowded out.

① Balancing your life between work and play is important.
② Urgent matters should be given your immediate attention.
③ Take care of the most important things first and the rest will follow.
④ There is always a solution to a problem no matter how complicated it is.

09 다음 글의 요지로 가장 적절한 것은?

Some kinds of fishing gear can be even more destructive when they become lost or forgotten in the water because they continue to catch animals, a phenomenon known as "ghost fishing." This is particularly wasteful and destructive because the gear can ensnare tons of animals that aren't being harvested or used in any way. Diamondback terrapins provide a case study of how ghost fishing can impact animal populations. These turtles inhabit salt marshes along the East Coast where people also fish for blue crabs. Blue crabs are caught using a crab pot, a metal cage that is dropped to the floor of the marsh and tied to a buoy that floats along the surface. If the buoy becomes detached, fishermen may not be able to find the gear, and it becomes a "ghost pot." Terrapins as well as blue crabs swim into the pots, attracted by the bait in the middle. Because they are social animals, when several turtles are in a pot, it often draws in other individuals, leading the ghost pot to catch more and more turtles over time. A single ghost pot was discovered in Georgia that contained more than 130 deceased turtles.

* Diamondback terrapin: 후미거북

① Turtles are the biggest victims of ocean debris.
② Derelict fishing equipment is threatening some marine animals.
③ State-of-the-art fishing gear makes it possible to catch several species at the same time.
④ Diamondback terrapins are in danger because of a decrease in the number of blue crabs.

10 다음 글의 내용과 일치하는 것은?

As the sun set on 12 February 1894, the Café Terminus at the Gare Saint-Lazare was full of young Parisians listening to an orchestra when the music stopped abruptly. A fireball consumed everything in sight: the world went black. When the survivors came round, there was a jigsaw of body parts around them, and people were on fire, running, and screaming. It was the work of a smartly dressed 20-year-old French accountant called Emile Henry. He had placed a bomb in a metal workman's lunchbox and hurled it at the orchestra. It was the first time a private individual had randomly blown up civilians. He was captured at the scene of the bombing. He said he had one regret: that he didn't kill more "bourgeois." If only he had a bomb big enough, he boasted, he would have blown up the whole of Paris. After Henry was executed at the age of 21, a series of revenge bombings staged by anarchists ripped through France.

① The attack on 12 February was carried out by an anarchist group.
② An attacker threw a hidden bomb at the musicians.
③ Emile Henry managed to leave the bombing scene without being caught.
④ Emile Henry regretted accidentally killing innocent people.

01 밑줄 친 부분과 의미가 가장 가까운 것을 고르시오.

We're really lucky that we have the requisite neural machinery to process music and to appreciate it and enjoy it.

① binding
② fastidious
③ incumbent
④ superfluous

02 밑줄 친 부분과 의미가 가장 가까운 것을 고르시오.

Although racism is deplorable, and the student is a terrible person for posting such sensitive remarks, the student's punishment is wrong.

① haughty
② vaunting
③ lamentable
④ magnificent

03 밑줄 친 부분과 의미가 가장 가까운 것을 고르시오.

Currently, developers can mitigate or obviate adverse impacts by providing or supporting ameliorating actions or developments, such as provision for public transport.

① refining
② deforming
③ regressing
④ aggravating

04 대화의 흐름으로 보아 빈칸에 들어갈 가장 적절한 것은?

Jamie: Alex, did you watch the soccer match yesterday?
Alex: Of course! It was the most exciting soccer game I've ever seen lately. Did you watch it too?
Jamie: I stayed up all night to watch it. Which team did you cheer for?
Alex: I cheered for Tottenham. When Son took away the ball from the opposing team, I screamed _____(A)_____.
Jamie: Same here. But Son seemed to _____(B)_____. He was breathing really hard.
Alex: I saw that too. But he kept running all across the field. I was amazed by his passion.
Jamie: Right. I realized once again that he is doubtlessly _____(C)_____.
Alex: No wonder all the major soccer teams want to scout him.

① (A) out of the blue sky
   (B) be in the red
   (C) a blue blood
② (A) out of the blue sky
   (B) be short of breath
   (C) a big bug
③ (A) at the top of my lungs
   (B) be in the black
   (C) a blue blood
④ (A) at the top of my lungs
   (B) be short of breath
   (C) a big bug

05 밑줄 친 부분 중 어법상 가장 옳지 않은 것은?

You will see how much better ① <u>it</u> feels to praise yourself rather than put down ② <u>yourself</u>. With this good feeling, you can do more for yourself and others ③ <u>than</u> you could ever do with the negative energy of self-criticism. Choose ④ <u>to see</u> the good. The choice is yours alone.

06 밑줄 친 부분 중 어법상 가장 옳지 않은 것은?

One of the most demanding, and at the same time inspiring, ① <u>aspects</u> of translating for children is the potential for such creativity that ② <u>arises</u> from what Peter Hollindale has called the 'childness' of children's texts: 'the quality of being a child — dynamic, imaginative, experimental, interactive and unstable'. The 'unstable' qualities of childhood that Hollindale cites require a writer or translator ③ <u>to have</u> an understanding of the freshness of language to the child's eye and ear, the child's affective concerns and the linguistic and dramatic play of early childhood. Translating sound, for example, whether in the read-aloud qualities of books for the younger child, in animal noises, children's poetry or in nonsense rhymes, ④ <u>demand</u> imaginative solutions — as indeed does working with visual material. Such multi-faceted creativity has, at times, placed children's literature at the forefront of imaginative experimentation.

07 밑줄 친 부분 중 어법상 가장 옳지 않은 것은?

When people interact with someone ① <u>whom</u> they do not foresee meeting again, they have little reason to search for positive qualities. In fact, doing so may be ② <u>depressed</u>, given that they may not have the opportunity to get ③ <u>to know</u> the person better in future interactions. Indeed, people are sometimes ④ <u>motivated</u> to find negative qualities in individuals whom they do not expect to see again.

08 주어진 문장 다음에 이어질 글의 순서로 가장 적절한 것은?

People who overeat are often described as having 'eyes bigger than their stomachs'.

(A) The equivalent in time management is the person who takes on more and more projects that look inviting and exciting, with a total disregard for existing work commitments.

(B) To regain control over your workload, a reality check is essential. Prioritize everything on your things-to-do list and then estimate how long each task needs in order to be completed.

(C) This behavior is typical of a Type A working style and the end result is 'plate spinning' – dashing from one unfinished task to another, putting in short bursts of effort and hoping that none of the plates crashes to the floor. Not only is this a very ineffective way of working, it is also a very stressful.

*Type A: A형 행동 양식(의 사람)
(긴장하고 성급하며 경쟁적인 것이 특징)

① (A) - (B) - (C)   ② (A) - (C) - (B)
③ (B) - (C) - (A)   ④ (C) - (A) - (B)

09 빈칸에 들어갈 표현으로 가장 적절한 것은?

Long-lining is one of the most widespread fishing methods. Ships unreel up to 50 miles of line bristling with hundreds of thousands of baited hooks. These are dragged behind the boat at varying depths or kept afloat by buoys and left overnight, luring any animal in the area to grab a free meal. Once hooked, some animals drown or bleed to death in the water, and many others struggle for hours until the boat returns to reel them in. Large fish such as swordfish and yellowfin tuna, weighing hundreds of pounds each, are pulled toward the boat by the baited line. Fishers sink pickaxes into the animals' fins, sides, and even eyes — any part that will allow them to haul the animals aboard without ripping out the hook. _____ fishing practices like this kill hundreds of thousands of sea turtles, dolphins, birds, sharks, other untargeted fish, and other marine animals every year in U.S. territories alone.

*long-lining: 주낙 어업, 주낙 낚시질
(긴 낚싯줄에 여러 개의 낚시를 달아 물속에 늘어뜨려 고기를 잡는 것)

① Indiscriminate
② Sympathetic
③ Scrupulous
④ Indifferent

10 다음 글의 요지로 가장 적절한 것은?

The jihadi bombings in Sri Lanka on Easter Sunday are the latest reminder that no one in this global world can be free from terrorist attacks. One reason why such terrorist attacks keep taking place is that the U.S.-led global war on terrorism has failed — and that is because it has focused on eliminating terrorists and their networks, not on defeating the radical jihadi ideology that inspires suicide attacks around the world. When it comes to radical Islamist terrorism, the ideological roots can most often be traced back to Wahhabism, an extreme form of Sunni Islam promoted by Saudi Arabia. Wahhabism legitimizes violent jihad with its call for a war on "infidels." According to the Saudi Muslim scholar Ali al-Ahmed, it advocates that nonbelievers are "to be hated, to be persecuted, and even killed." The bombings in a place as unlikely as Sri Lanka — a country with no history of radical Islamist terrorism — underscore how far militaristic theology can spread and why the world needs to tackle it at its roots.

* Wahhabism: (이슬람) 와하브파의 교리, 와하비즘

① Terrorist attacks cannot be completely stopped from occurring however hard we try.
② Suicide bombing attacks take place everywhere in the world regardless of religious roots.
③ Young and vulnerable people around the world are easily lured by the radical jihadi ideology.
④ The war on terrorism strategy needs to focus on discrediting the ideology that attracts terrorists.

01 밑줄 친 부분과 의미가 가장 가까운 것을 고르시오.

On the tour, William was omnipresent, not because he wanted to monitor me but because he was responsible for everything that happened.

① banal
② sparse
③ peculiar
④ ubiquitous

02 밑줄 친 부분과 의미가 가장 가까운 것을 고르시오.

We are all prone to forgetfulness, which can range from mildly annoying to very inconvenient in our daily lives.

① cozy
② sticky
③ tenacious
④ apathetic

03 밑줄 친 부분과 의미가 가장 가까운 것을 고르시오.

Some people said it was leveling out, but the so called experts changed their minds the day after and it is all spiraling down again.

① equalizing
② consolidating
③ abnormalizing
④ differentiating

04 대화의 흐름으로 보아 빈칸에 들어갈 가장 적절한 것은?

Eugene: Did you hear about the old lady who lives downtown?
Vanessa: No, I didn't. Who is she?
Eugene: She was an extremely rich woman who lived alone all her life. But she is ____(A)____ now.
Vanessa: Oh that's too bad. What happened to her? Did she make wrong investment?
Eugene: Exactly. She ____(B)____.
Vanessa: That was quite a risk. It would have been safer if she had made diversified investment.
Eugene: Right. I sincerely hope she ____(C)____.
Vanessa: Me too. I'm sure she will become a stronger person after she overcomes all this hardship.

① (A) a couch potato
　(B) put all her eggs in one basket
　(C) lays an egg
② (A) a couch potato
　(B) put all her eggs in one basket
　(C) loses heart
③ (A) dead broke
　(B) hit the nail on the head
　(C) keeps body and soul together
④ (A) dead broke
　(B) put all her eggs in one basket
　(C) keeps body and soul together

05 밑줄 친 부분 중 어법상 가장 옳지 않은 것은?

Consumers like a bottle of wine more if they are told it cost ninety dollars a bottle ① as if they are told it cost ten. Belief ② that the wine is more expensive ③ turns on the neurons in the medial orbitofrontal cortex, an area of the brain ④ associated with pleasure feelings.

06 밑줄 친 부분 중 어법상 가장 옳지 않은 것은?

Some might think self-confidence is innate, or ① it is enough to feel it once and charge through the difficulties of life without hesitation. Bad news. Self-confidence is certainly not innate and there is no universal confidence. Practice and active repetition make the master. Standing up for myself once did start a change in me, but it didn't ② grant me unlimited and never-ending confidence. It was just a start, a proof that I could be there for myself. If you have this belief, that you're there for yourself, every situation ③ is seemed more bearable, achievable or in my case, survivable. The more times you prove to yourself ④ that you are there for yourself, and you're enough to handle the situation, the more confident you'll be.

07 밑줄 친 부분 중 어법상 가장 옳지 않은 것은?

Some psychologists believe that insight is the result of a restructuring of a problem after a period of non-progress ① which the person is believed to be too focused on past experience and get stuck. A new manner ② to represent the problem is suddenly discovered, leading to a different path to a solution heretofore ③ unpredicted. It has ④ been claimed that no specific knowledge, or experience is required to attain insight in the problem situation.

08 다음 밑줄 친 단어가 가리키는 대상이 나머지와 다른 것은?

Time is a unique resource in that everyone is given an equal amount — a gift of 24 hours each day. How you invest that gift is a major factor in how you feel about your life. Think of ① it as one of the tools that you have available to reach your goals. As with many tools, if you want to use ② it effectively, it may require some training (or retraining), determination and practice. Even though time management is said a great deal, there really is no such thing as ③ it. Using time effectively is actually a matter of your own personal management. ④ It goes by at the same rate no matter what you do. You can't speed it up or slow it down. Unlike the other resources that you manage, there is no way to control it. The best that you can do is take charge of yourself in the framework of time, investing yourself in those things that matter most in your life.

09 주어진 글 다음에 이어질 글의 순서로 가장 적절한 것은?

Many of the world's major fishing areas have already been fished beyond their natural limits. Different approaches to the problem of overfishing are under consideration to help prevent the collapse of the world's fisheries.

(A) The scallop population recovered within five years, reaching levels in excess of the original population, and parts of the bay could be reopened for scallop fishing.

(B) But other species in Georges Bank continue to decline. Rapid and direct replenishment is not possible for slow-growing species that take years to reach maturity.

(C) For example, Georges Bank, once one of the most fertile fishing grounds in the North Atlantic, is now closed and is considered commercially extinct. This area underwent strict controls for scallop fishing in 1996, which proved to be a viable remedy for that species in that locale.

① (A) - (B) - (C)
② (B) - (A) - (C)
③ (B) - (C) - (A)
④ (C) - (A) - (B)

10 주어진 문장이 들어갈 위치로 가장 적절한 것은?

Given these complexities, the psychology of terrorism is marked more by theory and opinion than by good science, researchers admit.

Determining what drives people to terrorism is not an easy task. (①) For one thing, terrorists aren't likely to volunteer as experimental subjects, and examining their activities from afar can lead to erroneous conclusions. (②) What's more, one group's terrorist is another group's freedom fighter, as the millions of Arabs who support Palestinian suicide bombers will attest. (③) But a number of psychologists are starting to put together reliable data. (④) They're finding that it is generally more useful to view terrorism in terms of political and group dynamics and processes than individual ones. And universal psychological principles — such as our subconscious fear of death and our desire for meaning and personal significance — may also help explain some aspects of terrorist actions and our reactions to them.

기적사 복습 모의고사 5회

01 밑줄 친 부분과 의미가 가장 가까운 것을 고르시오.

Their significant contributions to ecology and conservation have made a powerful difference across rapidly deteriorating ecosystems and restored wildlife habitats.

① unscathed ② aggravating
③ obsolescing ④ ameliorative

02 밑줄 친 부분과 의미가 가장 먼 것을 고르시오.

As a prerequisite for fertilization, pollination is essential to the production of fruit and seed crops and plays an important part in programs designed to improve plants by breeding.

① crucial ② indispensable
③ requisite ④ omnipresent

03 밑줄 친 부분과 의미가 가장 가까운 것을 고르시오.

Although racism is deplorable, and the student is a terrible person for posting such sensitive remarks, the student's punishment is wrong.

① haughty ② vaunting
③ lamentable ④ magnificent

04 밑줄 친 부분에 들어갈 말로 가장 적절한 것을 고르시오.

Our main dish did not have much flavor, but I made it more _____ by adding condiments.

① palatable ② dissolvable
③ potable ④ susceptible

05 밑줄 친 부분에 들어갈 말로 가장 적절한 것을 고르시오.

The two cultures were so utterly _____ that she found it hard to adapt from one to the other.

① overlapped ② equivalent
③ associative ④ disparate

06 어법상 옳은 것은?

① Tom is hardly likely to admit he was wrong, is he?
② Hardly the whole process has been conducive to the stability of central government.
③ Some people ask why do we tolerate a popular culture that celebrates violence and depravity.
④ If we were to provide more money with local government, it would solve this problem more easily.

07 다음 글의 내용과 일치하는 것은?

As the sun set on 12 February 1894, the Café Terminus at the Gare Saint-Lazare was full of young Parisians listening to an orchestra when the music stopped abruptly. A fireball consumed everything in sight: the world went black. When the survivors came round, there was a jigsaw of body parts around them, and people were on fire, running, and screaming. It was the work of a smartly dressed 20-year-old French accountant called Emile Henry. He had placed a bomb in a metal workman's lunchbox and hurled it at the orchestra. It was the first time a private individual had randomly blown up civilians. He was captured at the scene of the bombing. He said he had one regret: that he didn't kill more "bourgeois." If only he had a bomb big enough, he boasted, he would have blown up the whole of Paris. After Henry was executed at the age of 21, a series of revenge bombings staged by anarchists ripped through France.

① The attack on 12 February was carried out by an anarchist group.
② An attacker threw a hidden bomb at the musicians.
③ Emile Henry managed to leave the bombing scene without being caught.
④ Emile Henry regretted accidentally killing innocent people.

08 밑줄 친 부분 중 어법상 가장 옳지 않은 것은?

One reason many people keep ① delaying things they should do ② is that they fear they will do them wrong or ③ poor, so they just don't do them at all. For example, one of the best ways to write a book is to write it as quickly as possible, ④ getting your thoughts onto paper without regard to style. Then, you can go back to revise and polish your writing.

09 다음 글의 제목으로 가장 적절한 것은?

With the help of the scientist, the commercial fishing industry has found out that its fishing must be done scientifically if it is to be continued. With no fishing pressure on a fish population, the number of fish will reach a predictable level of abundance and stay there. The only fluctuation would be due to natural environmental factors, such as availability of food, proper temperature, and the like. If a fishery is developed to take these fish, their population can be maintained if the fishing harvest is small. The mackerel of the North Sea is a good example. If we increase the fishery and take more fish each year, we must be careful not to reduce the population below the ideal point where it can replace all of the fish we take out each year. If we fish at this level, called the maximum sustainable yield, we can maintain the greatest possible yield, year after year. If we catch too many, the number of fish will decrease each year until we fish ourselves out of a job. Examples of severely overfished animals are the blue whale of the Antarctic and the halibut of the North Atlantic. Fishing just the correct amount to maintain a maximum annual yield is both a science and an art. Research is constantly being done to help us better understand the fish population and how to utilize it to the maximum without depleting the population.

① Say No to Commercial Fishing
② Sea Farming Seen As a Fishy Business
③ Why Does the Fishing Industry Need Science?
④ Overfished Animals: Cases of Illegal Fishing

10 밑줄 친 부분 중 글의 흐름상 가장 어색한 것은?

Jordan Harbinger, one of the most successful podcasters on the planet, says that you need to create the relationships beforehand. ① We've all been on the receiving end of an email that "pretends" to check on you, when the person is just buttering you up for an ask. This is the wrong way to lean on a network. The right way is to build up social capital over time. ② When asking a favor of someone in your network, it's better to do so face to face and not through email. Check in with people consistently, not just when you need something. It's too late if you start to look for people when you need them. ③ Relationships get deeper over time, so planting seeds early makes all the difference. "Creating relationships before you ever need them is key," says Harbinger. ④ In fact, he recommends assuming you'll never need them. "It's like putting a tire in the trunk of your car before you get a flat," he says. You don't plan to get a flat. And, in the best case scenario, you never use the spare.

* podcaster: 팟캐스터
(인터넷망을 통해 제공되는 다양한 콘텐츠를 제작하는 사람)

11 대화의 흐름으로 보아 빈칸에 들어갈 가장 적절한 것은?

Son: Mom, is the smell coming from the kitchen? It smells like apple pie.
Mom: I thought you were coming home late today. So I was going to bake it for you as a surprise.
Son: Thanks, mom! I love your apple pie! Is it still in the oven?
Mom: Yes. It's not ready yet. It's too bad I couldn't surprise you as I planned.
Son: It's like a surprise gift to me. I can't wait to taste it!
Mom: Be careful! Don't touch the oven, it's really hot.
Son: Oh, I almost touched the oven! I want to look inside to see if the pie is baking well.
Mom: _____. I don't want you to get hurt.

① Enough is enough
② Now you're talking
③ Curiosity killed the cat
④ You can say that again

12 두 사람의 대화 중 가장 어색한 것은?

① A: I have bruises all over my leg.
　 B: What's wrong? Did you trip over something?
② A: Could you please do me a favor?
　 B: My favorite book is Harry Potter.
③ A: There's a fire truck all over the town.
　 B: I heard the sound of sirens a few minutes ago.
④ A: I checked the weather forecast this morning.
　 B: Good for you! Will it rain today?

13 우리말을 영어로 가장 잘 옮긴 것은?

① William은 소리를 내지 않으려고 구두를 벗었다.
　→ William took off his shoes in order not to make any noise.
② 그가 범행을 저질렀다는 것을 모르는 사람은 아무도 없다.
　→ There is no one but doesn't know that he committed a crime.
③ 그는 10살 이후 어머니께 선물을 사드리기 위해 돈을 모으는 중이었다.
　→ He was saving money to buy a present for his mother since he was ten years old.
④ 근육 손실을 보충하기 위해 적당량의 단백질을 섭취해야 한다.
　→ You should take in an appropriate amount of protein to make up to the loss of muscles.

14 밑줄 친 부분 중 어법상 가장 옳지 않은 것은?

Parents are quick to inform friends and relatives as soon as their infant holds her head up, reaches for objects, sits by herself, and walks alone. Parental enthusiasm for these motor accomplishments ① is not at all misplaced, for they are, indeed, milestones of development. With each additional skill, babies gain control over their bodies and the environment in a new way. Infants who are able to sit alone ② are granted an entirely different perspective on the world than are those who spend much of their day on their backs or stomachs. Coordinated reaching opens up a whole new avenue for exploration of objects, and when babies can move about, their opportunities for independent exploration and manipulation are multiplied. No longer ③ do they restrict to their immediate locale and to objects that others place before them. As new ways of controlling the environment are achieved, motor development provides the infant ④ with a growing sense of competence and mastery, and it contributes in important ways to the infant's perceptual and cognitive understanding of the world.

15 밑줄 친 (A), (B)에 들어갈 말로 가장 적절한 것은?

Scientific research shows that climate change impacts on the ocean have already affected fisheries. While abundance of several cold water species is reducing, some tropical species are appearing on our coasts. In future decades ocean warming and acidification can affect growth and reproduction processes of many marine organisms, which may reduce stocks available for many significant commercial species. ___(A)___, shellfish such as oysters and mussels are especially sensitive to acidification. Climate change is also going to impact bacterial and phytoplankton communities, which are key to the marine food web. ___(B)___, if we keep on producing greenhouse gases at the current pace, changes expected before the end of the century in terms of biodiversity could be similar to those that occurred during the prior 20 or 30 million years.

	(A)	(B)
①	Consequently	By contrast
②	That is	However
③	As an example	Nevertheless
④	For instance	Eventually

16 글의 흐름상 빈칸에 들어갈 단어로 가장 적절한 것은?

How do people who aren't fond of networking get ahead in their careers? There's the hope — backed by some evidence — that producing good work will _____ most of the need to network at all. Cal Newport, a computer scientist who explores how people reach elite levels in knowledge-based careers, interviewed several Rhodes Scholars in the course of his research, and discovered that the path to success for many of them is often misreported. He wrote, "Rhodes Scholars invest a large amount of energy in doing a small number of things (usually two) extremely well rather than depend on connections or chance." It's the results of work — and not necessarily exposing yourself to as many people as possible — that attracts more and varied opportunities outside of that work.

* Rhodes Scholar: 로즈 장학생(영국 옥스퍼드 대학에서 공부하는 미국·독일·영연방 공화국 출신 학생들에게 주어지는 로즈 장학금(Rhodes scholarship)을 받는 학생)

① aggravate   ② attenuate
③ awaken   ④ slay

17 빈칸에 들어갈 표현으로 가장 적절한 것은?

Various types of technology are specifically designed to support aging in place, such as emergency help systems, vital signs monitoring, and fall detection systems. These technologies are sometimes referred to as Smart Home technology. Additionally, there is e-Health, which encompasses a broad range of technologies, including online tools to support seniors' self-management of chronic conditions. But these technologies have not been implemented on a large scale for various reasons. One of the reasons is older adults' _____ _____ these types of technology. On the one hand, they recognize that such technologies could support independent living of the older population, while on the other hand, they do not feel that they themselves personally need them.

* aging in place: 살던 곳에서 노후 맞기

① vigilant approach to
② general preference for
③ prevalent ignorance of
④ ambivalent attitude towards

18 다음 글의 요지로 가장 적절한 것은?

High-stakes exams often determine the future of learners: transition, graduation, or entrance to higher education, to better schools, or to better jobs. These exams do not only have high stakes for students, but also for teachers, schools and families, as the test results can influence funding, recognition and reputation. In some cases, the stakes are so high that examinations can dominate thinking about the purpose and nature of schooling. Students are constantly preparing for examinations, students and their parents are continually anxious about academic success, and the pressure on students to do well can lead to stress, anxiety, depression as well as school violence and even suicide. Furthermore, the focus on 'high scores' may be undermining other fundamental aspects of learning that are often not captured in tests and examinations and questions whether education systems have lost sight of the true value and purpose of education.

① High-stakes exams are effective and necessary to improve schooling and learning.
② High-stakes exams should be abandoned because they are causing a variety of problems.
③ Scoring well on high-stakes exams can make a significant difference in a student's future.
④ Although high-stakes exams have some advantages, they also can produce negative effects.

19 주어진 문장이 들어갈 위치로 가장 적절한 것은?

Given these complexities, the psychology of terrorism is marked more by theory and opinion than by good science, researchers admit.

Determining what drives people to terrorism is not an easy task. (①) For one thing, terrorists aren't likely to volunteer as experimental subjects, and examining their activities from afar can lead to erroneous conclusions. (②) What's more, one group's terrorist is another group's freedom fighter, as the millions of Arabs who support Palestinian suicide bombers will attest. (③) But a number of psychologists are starting to put together reliable data. (④) They're finding that it is generally more useful to view terrorism in terms of political and group dynamics and processes than individual ones. And universal psychological principles — such as our subconscious fear of death and our desire for meaning and personal significance — may also help explain some aspects of terrorist actions and our reactions to them.

20 주어진 문장 다음에 이어질 글의 순서로 가장 적절한 것은?

People who overeat are often described as having 'eyes bigger than their stomachs'.

(A) The equivalent in time management is the person who takes on more and more projects that look inviting and exciting, with a total disregard for existing work commitments.

(B) To regain control over your workload, a reality check is essential. Prioritize everything on your things-to-do list and then estimate how long each task needs in order to be completed.

(C) This behavior is typical of a Type A working style and the end result is 'plate spinning' — dashing from one unfinished task to another, putting in short bursts of effort and hoping that none of the plates crashes to the floor. Not only is this a very ineffective way of working, it is also a very stressful.

* Type A: A형 행동 양식(의 사람)
(긴장하고 성급하며 경쟁적인 것이 특징)

① (A) - (B) - (C) ② (A) - (C) - (B)
③ (B) - (C) - (A) ④ (C) - (A) - (B)

MEMO

01 밑줄 친 부분에 들어갈 말로 가장 적절한 것을 고르시오.

Penicillin can have an _____ effect on a person who is allergic to it.

① affirmative   ② aloof
③ adverse   ④ allusive

02 밑줄 친 부분과 의미가 가장 가까운 것은?

No one is very comfortable making a large investment while the currency values fluctuate almost daily.

① sway   ② linger
③ duplicate   ④ depreciate

03 밑줄 친 부분과 의미가 가장 가까운 것을 고르시오.

If these explanations seem too frivolous for the reader, I can only think of one other alternative.

① complex   ② polite
③ shallow   ④ inclusive

04 밑줄 친 부분에 들어갈 말로 가장 적절한 것을 고르시오.

A: Where do you want to go for our honeymoon?
B: Let's go to a place that neither of us has been to.
A: Then, why don't we go to Hawaii?
B: _____

① I've always wanted to go there.
② Isn't Korea a great place to live?
③ Great! My last trip there was amazing!
④ Oh, you must've been to Hawaii already.

05 밑줄 친 부분 중 어법상 옳은 것은?

Risk is a fundamental element of human life in the sense ① how risk is always a factor in any situation where the outcome is not precisely known. In addition, the necessary calculations that we make about the probability of some form of harm resulting from an action that we take ② are generally a given in our decision processes. Whether the risk assessment involves decisions about a major corporate initiative or just making the decision ③ walk down the street, we are always anticipating, identifying, and evaluating the potential risks involved. In that respect, we can be said to be constantly managing risk in everything ④ what we do.

06 밑줄 친 부분 중 어법상 옳지 않은 것은?

Yawning is ① catching. One person's yawn can trigger yawning among an entire group. People who are more empathic are believed to be more ② easily influenced to yawn by others' yawns; brain imaging studies have shown that ③ when humans watch other people yawn, brain areas known to be involved in social function are activated. Even dogs yawn in response to seeing their owners or even strangers ④ to yawn, and contagious yawning has been noted in other animals as well.

07 우리말을 영어로 잘못 옮긴 것은?

① 모든 정보는 거짓이었다.
   → All of the information was false.
② 토마스는 더 일찍 사과했어야 했다.
   → Thomas should have apologized earlier.
③ 우리가 도착했을 때 영화는 이미 시작했었다.
   → The movie had already started when we arrived.
④ 바깥 날씨가 추웠기 때문에 나는 차를 마시려 물을 끓였다.
   → Being cold outside, I boiled some water to have tea.

08 다음 글의 내용과 일치하지 않는 것은?

We entered a new phase as a species when Chinese scientists altered a human embryo to remove a potentially fatal blood disorder — not only from the baby, but all of its descendants. Researchers call this process "germline modification." The media likes the phrase "designer babies." But we should call it what it is, "eugenics." And we, the human race, need to decide whether or not we want to use it. Last month, in the United States, the scientific establishment weighed in. A National Academy of Sciences and National Academy of Medicine joint committee endorsed embryo editing aimed at genes that cause serious diseases when there is "no reasonable alternative." But it was more wary of editing for "enhancement," like making already-healthy children stronger or taller. It recommended a public discussion, and said that doctors should "not proceed at this time." The committee had good reason to urge caution. The history of eugenics is full of oppression and misery.

※ eugenics: 우생학

① Doctors were recommended to immediately go ahead with embryo editing for enhancement.
② Recently, the scientific establishment in the U.S. joined a discussion on eugenics.
③ Chinese scientists modified a human embryo to prevent a serious blood disorder.
④ "Designer babies" is another term for the germline modification process.

09 주어진 문장이 들어갈 위치로 가장 적절한 것은?

If neither surrendered, the two exchanged blows until one was knocked out.

The ancient Olympics provided athletes an opportunity to prove their fitness and superiority, just like our modern games. (①) The ancient Olympic events were designed to eliminate the weak and glorify the strong. Winners were pushed to the brink. (②) Just as in modern times, people loved extreme sports. One of the favorite events was added in the 33rd Olympiad. This was the pankration, or an extreme mix of wrestling and boxing. The Greek word pankration means "total power." The men wore leather straps with metal studs, which could make a terrible mess of their opponents. (③) This dangerous form of wrestling had no time or weight limits. In this event, only two rules applied. First, wrestlers were not allowed to gouge eyes with their thumbs. Secondly, they could not bite. Anything else was considered fair play. The contest was decided in the same manner as a boxing match. Contenders continued until one of the two collapsed. (④) Only the strongest and most determined athletes attempted this event. Imagine wrestling "Mr. Fingertips," who earned his nickname by breaking his opponents' fingers!

10 밑줄 친 부분에 들어갈 말로 가장 적절한 것은?

In our time it is not only the law of the market which has its own life and rules over man, but also the development of science and technique. For a number of reasons, the problems and organization of science today are such that a scientist does not choose his problems; the problems force themselves upon the scientist. He solves one problem, and the result is not that he is more secure or certain, but that ten other new problems open up in place of the single solved one. They force him to solve them; he has to go ahead at an ever-quickening pace. The same holds true for industrial techniques. The pace of science forces the pace of technique. Theoretical physics forces atomic energy on us; the successful production of the fission bomb forces upon us the manufacture of the hydrogen bomb. We do not choose our problems, we do not choose our products; we are pushed, we are forced — by what? By a system which has no purpose and goal transcending it, and which _____.

① makes man its appendix
② creates a false sense of security
③ inspires man with creative challenges
④ empowers scientists to control the market

01 밑줄 친 부분과 의미가 가장 가까운 것을 고르시오.

Her affirmative mindset of loving herself has become a true inspiration to the next generation.

① bleak
② skeptical
③ sanguine
④ misanthropic

02 밑줄 친 부분과 의미가 가장 가까운 것은?

The government should not be given unlimited power to influence and sway the minds of its people through the manipulation of information.

① wage
② induce
③ embellish
④ relinquish

03 밑줄 친 부분과 의미가 가장 가까운 것을 고르시오.

Now, scientists believe that special facial recognition does not always need a complex brain.

① lucid
② fancy
③ artless
④ unfussy

04 밑줄 친 부분에 들어갈 말로 가장 적절한 것을 고르시오.

A: Did you understand today's lecture?
B: Oh, do you mean the economics class?
A: Yes. Wasn't it quite difficult?
B: It was very hard to understand. I couldn't get hold of what the professor was trying to explain.
A: It was about 'capitalism' and the 'invisible hand' which keeps the capital flowing.
B: 'The invisible hand'? I totally _____. I thought today's lecture was on a completely different topic.
A: If you go home and review what you learned today, I'm sure you'll catch up with other classmates.

① got to the point
② cut a fine figure
③ kicked the bucket
④ got the wrong end of the stick

05 밑줄 친 부분 중 어법상 옳지 않은 것은?

Textiles and clothing have functions ① that go beyond just protecting the body. Dress and textiles alike are used as a means of nonverbal communication. Obvious examples would be the use of uniforms to communicate a particular social role and the modern white wedding dress Western cultures use ② it to mark this rite of passage. Both types of ③ clothing communicate important information nonverbally to the onlooker. The female wearing the white dress is about to be married and change her status and role in society. The person in the uniform has some ④ specialized function in society, such as police officer, nurse, or soldier.

06 밑줄 친 부분 중 어법상 옳지 않은 것은?

We are pleased to introduce our company's ① recently launched emergency training program for teachers. Our CPR class is the most common option for a school. We make ② teachers easy to participate in CPR training at a time to suit your school's schedule. Our class offers you full life-saving expertise ③ that you can then use to deliver vital support in emergencies. With the proper training, you will be able to perform CPR quickly and effectively and ④ improve a sufferer's chances of survival.

07 우리말을 영어로 잘못 옮긴 것은?

① Tom은 자기 자식들의 결혼 모두가 너무나 갑작스러웠다고 말했다.
→ Tom said all of his children's marriages were very sudden.

② 우리는 몇 시간 전에 그 사고를 막았을 수도 있다.
→ We should have prevented the accident a few hours beforehand.

③ William은 그 배가 이미 떠난 것을 알고 실망했다.
→ William was disappointed to find that the ship had already left.

④ 12시였기 때문에, 의장은 회의를 중단하길 갈망했다.
→ It being twelve o'clock, the chairman was anxious to adjourn the meeting.

08 주어진 문장 다음에 이어질 글의 순서로 가장 적절한 것은?

Eugenicists insisted that parents from "good stock" produced healthier and intellectually superior children.

(A) However, eugenicists were able to persuade the Carnegie Institution and prestigious universities to support their work, thus legitimizing it and creating the perception that their philosophy was, in fact, science.

(B) They believed that "traits" like poverty, shiftlessness, criminality and poor work ethic were inherited and that people of Nordic ancestry were inherently superior to other peoples, despite an obvious lack of evidence and scientific proof.

(C) The eugenics movement became widely seen as a legitimate way to improve society and was supported by such people as Winston Churchill, Margaret Sanger, Theodore Roosevelt and John Harvey Kellogg. Eugenics also became an academic discipline at many prominent colleges including Harvard University.

① (A) - (B) - (C)　　② (B) - (A) - (C)
③ (B) - (C) - (A)　　④ (C) - (A) - (B)

09 다음 글의 내용과 일치하는 것은?

Only men, boys and unmarried girls were allowed to watch the ancient Olympic Games. Married women were barred. If they were caught sneaking in, they could be thrown off the side of a mountain as punishment. However, married women could still own horses in the chariot races at the Olympics. Even though married women were not allowed at the Olympic Games, one story tells of a mother so keen to see her son compete that she broke the no-women rule and got in disguised as a man. Meanwhile, unmarried women had their own festival at Olympia. This was called the Heraia and was held in honor of Hera, Zeus's wife, every four years. Winners of the Heraia Games were awarded crowns of sacred olive branches, the same as men.

① Some females were able to spectate at the Olympic Games.
② Women who owned horses could compete in the chariot races.
③ A woman disguised herself as a man to play at the Olympic Games.
④ All women could participate in the Heraia Games.

10 다음 글의 제목으로 가장 적절한 것은?

Science as a collective institution focuses on producing more and more accurate natural explanations of how the natural world works, what its components are, and how the world got to be the way it is now. Classically, science's main goal has been building knowledge and understanding, regardless of its potential applications — for instance, investigating the chemical reactions that an organic compound undergoes to learn about its structure. However, increasingly, scientific research is undertaken with the explicit goal of solving a problem or developing a technology, and along the path to that goal, new knowledge and explanations are constructed. For example, a chemist might try to produce an antimalarial drug synthetically and in the process, discover new methods of forming bonds that can be applied to making other chemicals.

① The Aims of Science
② The Impacts of Science
③ The Necessity of Science
④ The Mysteries of Science

01 밑줄 친 부분과 의미가 가장 가까운 것을 고르시오.

Some people wanted to be close to you but they felt that you were aloof.

① pally
② overt
③ callous
④ clandestine

02 밑줄 친 부분과 의미가 가장 가까운 것은?

The emission of greenhouse gases is detrimental in the long-term since it will linger in the air for centuries and carbon dioxide will continuously warm up the air by trapping heat.

① abide
② wobble
③ deviate
④ ensnare

03 밑줄 친 부분과 의미가 가장 가까운 것을 고르시오.

In Jordan, it is usually a polite attitude to decline the offer of a meal three times before accepting it.

① splendid
② complaisant
③ impertinent
④ dispassionate

04 밑줄 친 부분에 들어갈 말로 가장 적절한 것을 고르시오.

Wendy: Do you know how Alex is doing these days?
Max: Not at all. I _____(A)_____ him because I haven't heard from him in a while.
Wendy: From what I heard lately, he's become a military officer.
Max: Wow! That is an unexpected news. But I think it fits him quite well.
Wendy: Me too. But I'm not sure if that's true. I just heard from Nancy.
Max: I remember Nancy. I should really keep in touch with my high school friends.
Wendy: Why don't you _____(B)_____? I'm sure they'll be really glad to hear from you.
Max: Thanks. I should try that.

① (A) do not know beans about
　(B) drop them a line
② (A) do not know beans about
　(B) get on their nerves
③ (A) give him a piece of your mind
　(B) drop them a line
④ (A) give him a piece of your mind
　(B) get on their nerves

05 밑줄 친 부분 중 어법상 옳은 것은?

Everybody has moments of doubt about something or other from time to time; it is a natural process. The challenge is not to let those moments accumulate and ① affect your self-belief. You will always face the challenge of other people's comments and opinions. There are people ② what you feel good being around and others you don't. Some people give you positive energy because they believe in you. You feel it and you ③ raise to the occasion. Others may always have a negative comment to make about ④ that you are doing or talking about. Don't let these comments rock your self-belief.

06 밑줄 친 부분 중 어법상 옳지 않은 것은?

"That's why so many insights happen ① during warm showers," Subhra Bhattacharya, a ② well-known psychologist, says. "For many people, it's the most relaxing part of the day." It's not until we're being massaged by warm water, ③ unable to check our e-mail, that we're finally able to hear the quiet voices in the backs of our heads ④ to tell us about the insight.

07 우리말을 영어로 잘못 옮긴 것은?

① Tom이 잠이 든 사이에 도둑이 든 게 틀림없다.
  → Tom must have been burgled while he was asleep.
② 어제 눈이 많이 와서, 그는 하루 종일 집에 있었다.
  → Snowing heavily yesterday, he stayed at home all day long.
③ 그들의 일 대부분이 시상식 연회에 음식을 공급하는 것과 관련이 있다.
  → Most of their work involves catering for the award banquet.
④ 우리는 이미 정해진 범위 내에서 작업을 해야 했다.
  → We had to work within the scope that had already been established.

08 다음 글의 내용과 일치하지 않는 것은?

Adam Nash is considered to be the first designer baby, born in 2000 using in vitro fertilization with pre-implantation genetic diagnosis, a technique used to choose desired characteristics. When Adam was still an embryo, living in a dish in the lab, scientists tested his DNA to make sure it was free of Fanconi anemia, the rare inherited blood disease from which his sister Molly suffered. They also checked his DNA for a marker that would reveal whether he shared the same tissue type. Molly needed a donor match for stem cell therapy, and her parents were determined to find one. Adam was conceived so the stem cells in his umbilical cord could be the lifesaving treatment for his sister. Adam's conception and birth received both praise and criticism because of the ethical issues.

① Adam Nash's genes were chosen by his parents.
② Adam Nash had the genes for Fanconi anemia.
③ Molly did not have a matched donor until Adam was born.
④ Molly's parents gave birth to Adam in order to use his umbilical cord to save their daughter.

09 밑줄 친 부분 중 글의 흐름상 가장 어색한 것은?

The competitors of the ancient Olympics were always naked. Their bodies were designed to perfection through the training and the nakedness symbolized eternal beauty as well as the symbiosis of body and soul. Also, the athletes kept impeccable hygiene and body care. This is little known fact. ① From when they got to high school, the institution where they were taught and coached, they would begin to learn to take care of their hygiene, since they were naked. ② Only men were allowed to compete in the games and women were forbidden to watch the games as the competitors were in the nude. ③ The whole process would include olive oil and a layer of dust with fine sand that athletes rubbed into the skin. ④ It would protect them not only from the sun, but also from the occasional hits from their coaches when they got the set task done. Upon completion of the training, the layer had to be taken off with water and a sponge. And this was also done each time before the competition.

10 주어진 문장 다음에 이어질 글의 순서로 가장 적절한 것은?

There are many excellent science studies which are based on well-designed experiments and which make reasoned claims based on the assembled experimental data.

(A) Sometimes this is not the fault of the scientists, for the media can take a small observation or a statement that is written in a guarded way as a possibility, and turn this into established facts. For example, a "cure for all types of cancer" is one of the most common (and misleading) headlines.

(B) While the majority of scientific findings and papers issued each year offer valid findings and make a contribution to the body of knowledge, there are, unfortunately, many cases of bad science out there.

(C) There are multiple reasons for bad science: poor research, poorly designed experiments, misconduct by researchers, and accidental or deliberate misinterpretation of data.

① (A) - (B) - (C)   ② (B) - (A) - (C)
③ (B) - (C) - (A)   ④ (C) - (A) - (B)

01 밑줄 친 부분과 의미가 가장 가까운 것을 고르시오.

It seems that the adverse effects of the low birthrate continue to appear year after year.

① stuffy
② cynical
③ upbeat
④ detrimental

02 밑줄 친 부분과 의미가 가장 가까운 것은?

Despite the help of state-of-the-art scientific equipment and modern technology, scientists just couldn't duplicate the process.

① dally
② emulate
③ replicate
④ fluctuate

03 밑줄 친 부분과 의미가 가장 가까운 것을 고르시오.

One hypothesis predicts that shallow water can confuse whales and disturb their navigational ability.

① shoal
② feeble
③ tortuous
④ heterogeneous

04 밑줄 친 부분에 들어갈 말로 가장 적절한 것을 고르시오.

A: As partners of this team project, we should discuss what we want as our topic.
B: Well, I've been thinking about it over the weekend and I came up with the idea of 'the fourth industrial revolution'.
A: That's a very interesting topic! How about mentioning the 'Artificial Intelligence(AI)' as well?
B: Good point! There are so much news related to those technological advancements these days.
A: I know. We should _____ by making a presentation on the recent developments.
B: Yeah, it's a good way to keep up with the trend.

① bury the hatchet
② work against the clock
③ jump on the bandwagon
④ put the cart before the horse

05 밑줄 친 부분 중 어법상 옳은 것은?

Thank you for your question about how to donate children's books for our book drive. The event will ① be taken place for one week from September 10th to 16th. Books can be dropped off 24 hours a day during this period. There are two locations ② designating for donations: Adams Children's Library and Aileen Community Center. At each location, there are blue donation boxes at the main entrance. If you are unable to visit these locations, books can be mailed directly to our organization. Your donations will help ③ support children in our community ④ which may not be able to afford books. We hope this information makes your donation easier.

06 밑줄 친 부분 중 어법상 옳지 않은 것은?

In the summer of 1972, the actor Anthony Hopkins was signed to play a leading role in a film based on George Feifer's novel The Girl from Petrovka. That is ① why he traveled to London to buy a copy of the book. Unfortunately, none of the main London bookstores ② didn't have a copy. Then, on his way home, ③ waiting for an underground train at Leicester Square tube station, he saw a ④ discarded book lying on the seat next to him.

07 우리말을 영어로 잘못 옮긴 것은?

① 바다가 잔잔해서, 우리는 잠수하기로 결정했다.
  → The sea being calm, we decided to go diving.
② 나는 기다리면서 찬물 한 잔을 들이켰다.
  → I drank a cup of cold water while I was waiting.
③ 난 오늘 밤 그 결혼식에 참석할 필요가 없었는데.
  → I need not have participated in the wedding tonight.
④ 많은 사람들이 그녀의 배가 들어오기 직전에 부두를 떠났다.
  → Many a man have left the dock just before her ship came in.

08 다음 글의 제목으로 가장 적절한 것은?

Today, the World Anti-Doping Agency (WADA) has a new hurdle to overcome — that of gene doping. This practice is defined as the nontherapeutic use of cells, genes, or genetic elements to enhance athletic performance. Gene doping takes advantage of cutting-edge research in gene therapy that involves the transfer of genetic material to human cells to treat or prevent disease. Because gene doping increases the amount of proteins and hormones that cells normally make, testing for genetic performance enhancers will be very difficult, and a new race is on to develop ways to detect this form of doping. The potential to alter genes to build better athletes was immediately realized with the invention of so-called "Schwarzenegger mice" in the late 1990s. These mice were given this nickname because they were genetically engineered to have increased muscle growth and strength.

① Doping in Various Sports
② A New Threat to Fair Play in Sport
③ Why Athletes Should Be Doping Tested
④ Gene Doping: Advantages and Disadvantages

09 빈칸에 들어갈 표현으로 가장 적절한 것은?

As long as there has been sport, _____.
In the ancient Olympics, competitors ate exotic meats that supposedly gave them strength. Before chromosome testing, the Greeks competed naked to prevent women from pretending to be men. In 1807, Abraham Wood claimed that he used laudanum to stay awake for twenty-four hours while racewalking against the great Captain Barclay. In the 1904 Olympic marathon, the American Thomas J. Hicks downed several doses of strychnine and egg whites, followed by a large glass of brandy, given to him by his "trainer," Charles Lucas. Although he finished second, he was declared the winner when it was discovered that the first-place finisher, Fred Lorz, had been driven in a car for at least three miles. Afterward, Lucas bragged that "the marathon race demonstrated that drugs are of much benefit to athletes along the road."

① there has been cheating
② there has been coaching
③ there has been sports fan
④ there has been sport gambling

10 주어진 문장이 들어갈 위치로 가장 적절한 것은?

If denialists had evidence disproving global warming or evolution, they could submit it to scientific conferences and journals, inviting analysis by scientists.

From evolution to global warming to vaccines, science is under assault from denialists — those who dismiss well-tested scientific knowledge as merely one of many competing ideologies. Science requires conclusions about how nature works to be rooted in evidence-based testing. Sometimes progress is slow. But through a difficult and often frustrating process, we learn more about the world. (①) Science denialism works differently. Creationists are unmoved by the wealth of fossil, molecular, and anatomical evidence for evolution. Global-warming denialists are unimpressed by mountains of climate data. (②) Denialists ignore overwhelming evidence, focusing instead on a few hoaxes. (③) For denialists, opinion polls and talk radio are more important than thousands of peer-reviewed journal articles. (④) But, knowing their arguments don't hold water, they spread misinformation in arenas not subject to expert scrutiny: mass-market books, newspapers, talk radio, and blogs.

결국엔 성정혜 영어 하프모의고사
기적사 DAY 55

01 밑줄 친 부분과 의미가 가장 가까운 것을 고르시오.

His poems are highly allusive and capable of many different interpretations.

① blunt
② smug
③ connotative
④ supercilious

02 밑줄 친 부분과 의미가 가장 가까운 것은?

Since the agreement of the G-20 meeting was to reconfirm an existing principle, experts predicted that the yen would depreciate further.

① revalue
② detract
③ impugn
④ disparage

03 밑줄 친 부분과 의미가 가장 가까운 것을 고르시오.

Cooperation within the international community is so important for inclusive and sustainable global economic growth.

① sweeping
② amenable
③ determinate
④ metaphysical

04 밑줄 친 부분에 들어갈 말로 가장 적절한 것을 고르시오.

Serena: I'm so exhausted! I really need some time to relax.
Jaden: You look like you had a very harsh day. What's wrong?
Serena: I got a part-time job at a coffee shop lately but I really don't like my boss.
Jaden: You must feel really stressed out. Did he do something to you?
Serena: I really didn't want to say this, but my boss is _____.
Jaden: It sounds like he's unfriendly and full of greed. Am I right?
Serena: Right. He never allows us to sit down while working. But he keeps seated and keeps an eye on us all the time from right behind where we work.
Jaden: Oh, that must be much more stressful than I imagined.

① a cash cow
② bread and butter
③ doubting Thomas
④ a dog in the manger

05 밑줄 친 부분 중 어법상 옳은 것은?

Next Monday, Nature's Beauty Gardens will have the pleasure of hosting very important guests for the annual "Toddler Trek" event. We ① want that this event will be fun, educational, and most importantly safe for the toddlers. Parents and children participating in it ② are going to spend time enjoying outdoor activities and having a picnic lunch. ③ That is therefore very important to check the garden for potential dangers. Managers of each department must make sure ④ of all dangerous equipment and machinery are safely stored.

06 밑줄 친 부분 중 어법상 옳지 않은 것은?

Research has shown that ① when people who feel helpless fail to take control, they experience negative emotional states such as anxiety and depression. ② Like stress, these negative emotions can damage the immune response. We can see from this ③ what health is not linearly related to control. For optimum health, people should be encouraged ④ to take control to a point but to recognize when further control is impossible.

07 우리말을 영어로 잘못 옮긴 것은?

① 택시가 없어서, 나는 어제 집에 갈 수 없었다.
→ There being no taxi, I couldn't go home yesterday.
② 유명 가수가 떠난 후, 사람들은 흩어졌다.
→ After the famous singer had gone, the crowd dissolved.
③ 그는 눈에 띄지 않도록 좀 더 조심했어야 했는데.
→ He could have been more careful to keep out of sight.
④ 카레라이스는 전 세계의 모두를 위한 간단한 식사입니다.
→ Curry and rice is an easy meal for everyone in the world.

08 밑줄 친 (A), (B)에 들어갈 말로 가장 적절한 것은?

A designer baby is a baby genetically engineered in vitro for specially selected traits, which can vary from lowered disease-risk to gender selection. Before the advent of genetic engineering and in vitro fertilization, designer babies were primarily a science fiction concept. However, the rapid advancement of technology before and after the turn of the twenty-first century makes designer babies an increasingly real possibility. ____(A)____, designer babies have become an important topic in bioethical debates, and in 2004 the term "designer baby" even became an official entry in the Oxford English Dictionary. Designer babies represent an area within embryology that has not yet become a practical reality, but ____(B)____ draws out ethical concerns about whether or not it will become necessary to implement limitations regarding designer babies in the future.

	(A)	(B)
①	On the other hand	otherwise
②	As a result	nonetheless
③	Moreover	accordingly
④	For instance	unfortunately

09 주어진 문장이 들어갈 위치로 가장 적절한 것은?

The distance of the modern marathon was standardized as 26 miles 385 yards or 42.195 km in 1908 when the Olympic Games were held in London.

The marathon was not an event of the ancient Olympic games. (①) It is a modern event that was first introduced in the Modern Olympic Games of 1896 in Athens, a race from Marathon northeast of Athens to the Olympic Stadium, a distance of 40 kilometers. (②) The race commemorates the run of Pheidippides, an ancient "day-runner" who carried the news of the Persian landing at Marathon of 490 B.C. to Sparta (a distance of 149 miles) in order to enlist help for the battle. (③) According to the fifth century B.C. ancient Greek historian Herodotus, Pheidippides delivered the news to the Spartans the next day. (④) It was the exact measurement between Windsor Castle, the start of the race, and the finish line inside White City Stadium.

10 다음 글의 주제로 가장 적절한 것은?

Scientific researchers face perpetual struggle to secure and sustain funding. While the scientific workforce is increasing, the funding in most countries has been on a decline over the past decade. The situation is particularly for early career researchers who find it difficult to compete for funds with senior researchers. This extreme competition is also impacting the way science is conducted. The respondents of the Vox survey pointed out that since most grants are allotted only for a couple of years, researchers tend to opt for short-term projects, which can sometimes be insufficient to study complex research questions. This means researchers make choices based on what would keep the funding bodies and their institutions happy. However, the consequences of these choices are an increasing number of published papers with substandard quality and low research impact.

① How to obtain funds for a study
② The financial short in the field of science
③ High competitions between new and senior scientists
④ The importance of scientific research and publication

01 밑줄 친 부분과 의미가 가장 가까운 것은?

As a salesman, you should remember that your cardinal rule is to do everything you can do to satisfy a customer.

① definitive
② gigantic
③ potential
④ principal

02 밑줄 친 부분과 의미가 가장 가까운 것은?

The audio of the surreptitious recording clearly indicates that the participants did not want to be recorded.

① clandestine
② statutory
③ forthright
④ seraphic

03 밑줄 친 부분과 의미가 가장 가까운 것은?

After three years of desultory wandering, the old man came to Andalusia, the region in southern Spain.

① purposeful
② miserable
③ ascetic
④ disconnected

04 다음 대화의 흐름으로 보아 밑줄 친 부분에 가장 적절한 것은?

A: Do you have any vacancies?
B: I'm sorry. _____
A: I should have made reservation.
B: That would have helped.

① How many people are there in your company?
② We're completely booked.
③ We have plenty of rooms.
④ What kind of room would you like?

05 어법상 가장 옳지 않은 것은?

① The boss wants our team to go the documents through before the board of directors begins.
② Not only has the number of baseball players increased but so have the values of the players.
③ Bob tends to borrow more money from the bank than he can pay back.
④ A huge research fund was given to a local private university by the Ministry of Education.

06 밑줄 친 부분 중 어법상 가장 옳지 않은 것은?

To a music lover watching a concert from the audience, it would be easy to believe that ① a conductor has one of easiest jobs in the world. There he stands, ② waving his arms in time with the music, and the orchestra produces glorious sounds, to all appearances quite spontaneously. ③ Hidden from the audience-especially from the musical novice-are the conductor's abilities to read and interpret all of the parts at once, to play several instruments and understand the capacities of many more, to organize and coordinate the disparate parts, ④ to motivate and communicate with all of the orchestra members.

07 어법상 ㉠~㉢에 들어갈 말로 가장 적절한 것은?

Supplements on the market today ___㉠___ those that use natural herbs or synthetic ingredients. Experts point out that when choosing between multivitamins, those ___㉡___ natural herbs may not necessarily be better than those with synthetic ingredients. The body recognizes the molecular weight and structure of each vitamin and mineral for their functions regardless of ___㉢___ the vitamins come from synthetic or natural sources.

	㉠	㉡	㉢
①	include	contained	if
②	include	containing	whether
③	includes	containing	if
④	includes	contained	whether

08 다음 글의 내용과 일치하는 것은?

Soils of farmlands used for growing crops are being carried away by water and wind erosion at rates between 10 and 40 times the rates of soil formation, and between 500 and 10,000 times soil erosion rates on forested land. Because those soil erosion rates are so much higher than soil formation rates, that means a net loss of soil. For instance, about half of the top soil of Iowa, the state whose agriculture productivity is among the highest in the U.S., has been eroded in the last 150 years. On my most recent visit to Iowa, my hosts showed me a churchyard offering a dramatically visible example of those soil losses. A church was built there in the middle of farmland during the 19th century and has been maintained continuously as a church ever since, while the land around it was being farmed. As a result of soil being eroded much more rapidly from fields than from the churchyard, the yard now stands like a little island raised 10 feet above the surrounding sea of farmland.

① A churchyard in Iowa is higher than the surrounding farmland.
② Iowa's agricultural productivity has accelerated its soil formation.
③ The rate of soil formation in farmlands is faster than that of soil erosion.
④ Iowa has maintained its top soil in the last 150 years.

09 다음 글의 흐름상 가장 어색한 문장은?

Whether you've been traveling, focusing on your family, or going through a busy season at work, 14 days out of the gym takes its toll—not just on your muscles, but your performance, brain, and sleep, too. ① Most experts agree that after two weeks, you're in trouble if you don't get back in the gym. "At the two week point without exercising, there are a multitude of physiological markers that naturally reveal a reduction of fitness level," says Scott Weiss, a New York-based exercise physiologist and trainer who works with elite athletes. ② After all, despite all of its abilities, the human body (even the fit human body) is a very sensitive system and physiological changes (muscle strength or a greater aerobic base) that come about through training will simply disappear if your training load dwindles, he notes. Since the demand of training isn't present, your body simply slinks back toward baseline. ③ More protein is required to build more muscles at a rapid pace in your body. ④ Of course, how much and how quickly you'll decondition depends on a slew of factors like how fit you are, your age, and how long sweating has been a habit. "Two to eight months of not exercising at all will reduce your fitness level to as if you never exercised before," Weiss notes.

10 다음 글의 내용과 일치하지 않는 것은?

Before the fifteenth century, all four characteristics of the witch (night flying, secret meetings, harmful magic, and the devil's pact) were ascribed individually or in limited combination by the church to its adversaries, including Templars, heretics, learned magicians, and other dissident groups. Folk beliefs about the supernatural emerged in peasant confessions during witch trials. The most striking difference between popular and learned notions of witchcraft lay in the folk belief that the witch had innate supernatural powers not derived from the devil. For learned men, this bordered on heresy. Supernatural powers were never human in origin, nor could witches derive their craft from the tradition of learned magic, which required a scholarly training at the university, a masculine preserve at the time. A witch's power necessarily came from the pact she made with the devil.

① The folk and learned men had different views on the source of the witch's supernatural powers.
② According to the folk belief, supernatural powers belonged to the essential nature of the witch.
③ Four characteristics of the witch were attributed by the church to its dissident groups.
④ Learned men believed that the witch's power came from a scholarly training at the university.

01 밑줄 친 부분과 의미가 가장 가까운 것은?

John found underlined(definitive) proof that when Leonardo da Vinci painted the original portrait, he included Mona Lisa's lashes.

① hazy
② plain
③ muddy
④ inchoate

02 밑줄 친 부분과 의미가 가장 가까운 것은?

More clandestine ways will keep showing up, as malware keeps evolving to get around those vaccine programs or firewalls.

① furtive
② blatant
③ exoteric
④ conspicuous

03 밑줄 친 부분과 의미가 가장 가까운 것은?

The crimes in the information technology sector aren't disconnected with other types of crimes happening in other areas.

① decent
② external
③ indecent
④ pertinent

04 다음 대화의 흐름으로 보아 밑줄 친 부분에 가장 적절한 것은?

A: I want to go on a trip with my friends before school starts.
B: What a good idea! I really want to ___(A)___ too.
A: Why don't we go together with some of our other friends?
B: Yeah, I'd love that. I didn't have any time for travelling this vacation.
A: Me too. It will feel like I'm ___(B)___ if I travel with my friends.
B: ___(C)___! I'm sure we can make unforgettable memories during our whole trip!
A: We should make plans right away.
B: Sure, let's get started!

① (A) hit the road
  (B) in seventh heaven
  (C) Tell me about it
② (A) hit the road
  (B) the tip of the iceberg
  (C) Give me a break
③ (A) lose the day
  (B) in seventh heaven
  (C) Every dog has its day
④ (A) lose the day
  (B) the tip of the iceberg
  (C) Every dog has its day

05 어법상 가장 옳지 않은 것은?

① The actual cost to restore the building destroyed by Hurricane Katrina was higher than we expected.
② William had to study hard to get through this exam because he made many mistakes in the last exam.
③ Not only were the number of measures taken to alleviate the problem, but also many bills were passed to ease off it.
④ Jane was given exemption from the final examination as she suffered injury to the left occipital area in a traffic accident.

06 밑줄 친 부분 중 어법상 가장 옳지 않은 것은?

Richard Porson, one of Britain's most notable classical ① scholars, was born on Christmas in 1759. His talents were recognized early, and he was sent to Eton College by wealthy sponsors at 15. Four years later, he ② entered Cambridge University. He significantly improved Greek texts and edited four plays written by Euripides. In 1806, he was elected Principal Librarian at the newly ③ founding London Institution. ④ During his lifetime, he collected a great many books on classical literature.

07 어법상 ㉠~㉢에 들어갈 말로 가장 적절한 것은?

____㉠____ English by watching movies, he soon managed to translate his jokes for the American audience. In 1948, Victor Borge became an American citizen and a few years later ____㉡____ offered a show of his own, Comedy in Music. The show ____㉢____ the longest-running one-man show in Broadway history.

	㉠	㉡	㉢
①	Learning	was	remains
②	Learning	were	is remained
③	Learned	were	remains
④	Learned	was	is remained

08 빈칸에 들어갈 표현으로 가장 적절한 것은?

Thai farmers usually have low formal education and lack of knowledge on soil quality improvement and proper use of fertilizers. After a few years of farming, they try to trespass in conserved forest areas because of soil deterioration in their own limited expanses of farmland and because they believe soils in the conserved area are _____ than soils in their own farms. Consequently, most of them are arrested, creating individual and family problems. To address this issue, a recent project compared the physical and chemical properties of soils from farmlands and soils from the conserved area. The results showed that soil nutrients from both were not significantly different in nearly all parameters of analysis except that soils from the conserved area have more organic matters and nitrogen content. The analysis data were informed to the farmers and suggested to them improving their farmlands using appropriate organic matters to get more productivity.

① more fertile
② more sterile
③ more barren
④ less arable

09 다음 글의 제목으로 가장 적절한 것은?

When we exercise, our muscles process insulin and absorb the resulting glucose as energy. Reduce that energy expenditure, and your muscles will adapt physiologically to become a little less insulin sensitive, says John Thyfault, a researcher at the University of Kansas. Losing insulin sensitivity means that your body converts sugar into fat rather than using it as energy to power your movements. And while that adaptation helped our hunter-gatherer ancestors survive a feast-or-famine lifestyle, it's bad news for the modern desk jockey, because improper regulation of insulin can prompt your cells to store some of what's not used in muscle movement as fat. This change puts you at greater risk for the development of other conditions, such as Type 2 diabetes and inflammation.

① Why Are Muscles Important?
② Ways to Increase Energy Levels for Better Health
③ One Thing That Happens When You Quit Working Out
④ Insulin Sensitivity: How to Improve It Naturally And Quickly

10 다음 글의 요지로 가장 적절한 것은?

There is no question that some of the economic and social, and demographic developments that occurred in early modern Europe aggravated the personal tensions that underlay many witchcraft accusations. Inflation, an increase in poverty, pressure by a growing population on a limited supply of resources, the growth of the unattached female population, and changes in the structure of the family all played some part in encouraging witchcraft accusations. Some women may have been accused of witchcraft because they were most adversely affected by such changes or, with respect to the advent of capitalism, most resistant to it. In addition, specific economic crises, such as famine, outbreaks of epidemic disease, and dislocations caused by war, may have helped trigger many individual witch-hunts.

① Witch-hunts can be caused for many reasons such as religion and superstitions.
② The European witch-hunts are one of the most bizarre phenomena of Western history.
③ The European witch-hunts may be considered as the product of social and economic changes.
④ Witch-hunts resulted in the torture and execution of tens of thousands of victims, most of whom were women.

01 밑줄 친 부분과 의미가 가장 가까운 것은?

Located in California, the park is best known for its gigantic waterfalls, deep valleys, and a variety of wild animals and plants.

① puny   ② titanic
③ effete   ④ timorous

02 밑줄 친 부분과 의미가 가장 가까운 것은?

Nowhere on the planet have all the debtors been bailed out in excess of what their statutory entitlements were.

① illicit   ② felonious
③ legitimate   ④ conspiratorial

03 밑줄 친 부분과 의미가 가장 가까운 것은?

We cannot bear a pointless torment, but we can endure great pain if we believe that it's intended.

① adrift   ② apathetic
③ purposeful   ④ undirected

04 다음 대화의 흐름으로 보아 밑줄 친 부분에 가장 적절한 것은?

A: Long time no see!
B: Oh my gosh! It's been such a long time since I met you!
A: I know! How have you been doing?
B: I've been doing just fine. How about you? Are things going all right?
A: Yeah, do you have some time?
B: Right now? Yes, I have some spare time. Why?
A: Well, then let's go in somewhere and _____.
B: Good idea. We have a lot to talk about.

① talk the talk   ② shoot the breeze
③ rob Peter to pay Paul   ④ speak the same language

05 어법상 가장 옳지 않은 것은?

① Can we get the book written by Milton out by the end of the year?
② The baseball star was said that rest should be imperative for weeks.
③ I am interested in your system, but it is so much more expensive than your competitors'.
④ A number of simplifications have been made to the welfare system by a number of civic movements.

06 밑줄 친 부분 중 어법상 가장 옳지 않은 것은?

A sleeping mother has the ability ① to identify the particular cry of her own baby. This is one of the bonding factors that ② has been forgotten because of the way in which we live today. Typically, there is now only one newborn baby in any family house or apartment, so there is no way to test this ability. In an ancient tribe, however, ③ living in small huts in a tiny village settlement, a mother would have been able to hear any of the babies ④ to cry in the night.

07 어법상 ㉠~㉢에 들어갈 말로 가장 적절한 것은?

The saola stays at higher elevations ㉠ the wetter summer season, when streams at these altitudes have plenty of water, and ㉡ down to the lowlands in winter, when the mountain streams dry up. They are said to travel mostly in groups of two or three animals. Hunting and the loss of forest habitat due to logging and conversion to farmland ㉢ its survival.

*saola: 사올라(1992년 베트남에서 발견된 솟과의 포유류)

	㉠	㉡	㉢
①	for	move	threatens
②	during	moves	threaten
③	for	moves	threatens
④	during	move	threaten

08 주어진 문장이 들어갈 위치로 가장 적절한 것은?

To build homes and roadways, the top soil is stripped and subsoil compacted to create a firm foundation.

Soils develop over hundreds to thousands of years. (①) However, as it is buried beneath our feet, its complex structure and ecosystem are difficult to see and appreciate. (②) Productive soils which support plant growth contain pore spaces with interconnected pathways that bring air and water to roots, insects, and microbes. (③) The soil that took nature thousands of years to develop from its parent material can be destroyed in a matter of hours with excavation equipment. (④) Once disturbed and compacted, it takes decades to centuries for natural forces to recreate the different layers, aggregates and interconnected pores of soil. Piling up a bunch of dirt does not make it soil.

09 다음 글의 요지로 가장 적절한 것은?

When you exercise, your body does not actually create new muscles. Instead, your existing muscles grow larger and stronger, and the number of capillaries — the networked blood vessels between arterioles and venules — increases. With regular exercise, muscles also develop more mitochondria — this is where biochemical processes of respiration and energy production occur in the cell. The result is larger, more defined muscle mass, not newly created muscle tissue. Adopting a sedentary — or inactive — lifestyle has the opposite effect on your muscles. The increased blood flow previously needed to fuel your cells during exercise is no longer required, and your body begins to contract and reduce the size of your capillaries. You may be afraid that muscles turn to fat or disappear if you stop working out, but instead all they do is shrink and decrease in mass. Fat may be produced if your diet provides your body with more calories than you require for the level of activity you maintain, but your body doesn't magically transform muscle into fat.

* mitochondria: 미토콘드리아
(진핵(眞核)생물의 세포질 속에 있는 호흡을 관장하는 소기관)

① You should not avoid consuming fat after working out.
② Your muscles do not just go away even if you stop exercising.
③ Stopping exercise can have immediate health effects such as gaining weight.
④ Maintaining proper diet and exercise routines is necessary to ward off illness.

10 다음 글의 내용과 일치하는 것은?

The infamous Salem witch trials started during the spring of 1692, after two young girls in Salem Village, Massachusetts, named Elizabeth Hubbard and Dorothy Good, claimed to be possessed by the devil and accused several local women of witchcraft. As a wave of hysteria spread throughout colonial Massachusetts, a special court convened in Salem to hear the cases; the first convicted witch, Bridget Bishop, was hanged that June. Eighteen others followed Bishop to Salem's Gallows Hill, while more than 150 men, women and children were accused over the next several months. By September 1692, the hysteria had begun to abate and public opinion turned against the trials. Although the Massachusetts General Court later annulled guilty verdicts against accused witches and granted indemnities to their families, bitterness lingered in the community, and the painful legacy of the Salem witch trials would endure for centuries.

① The trials began after Elizabeth Hubbard and Dorothy Good had been charged with witchcraft.
② Eighteen people were executed by hanging.
③ A number of people were accused of witchcraft regardless of gender and age.
④ The trials had had the support of the general public for years.

01 밑줄 친 부분과 의미가 가장 가까운 것은?

The U.S. law requires an automaker to notify the government of it within five business days when a potential safety defect is found.

① latent ② manifest
③ equivocal ④ quiescent

02 밑줄 친 부분과 의미가 가장 가까운 것은?

The Senior Secretary to the President for Civil Affairs, who directly reports to the president, must be absolutely forthright.

① sly ② candid
③ impromptu ④ disingenuous

03 밑줄 친 부분과 의미가 가장 가까운 것은?

In 1833, when he returned to his previous master, he witnessed the miserable lives of slaves again.

① rosy ② ruddy
③ abject ④ grievous

04 다음 대화의 흐름으로 보아 밑줄 친 부분에 가장 적절한 것은?

A: Hey, you look sick. Are you feeling okay?
B: I can't say I'm completely fine. I'm half asleep right now.
A: Did you have trouble sleeping last night?
B: It wasn't just last night. I haven't been getting enough sleep for the last two weeks.
A: Oh, that's why you looked so sick. Why did you sleep wrong?
B: I was overloaded with too much work. I had no other choice but to _____.
A: You should prioritize your health above anything else. Work can really ruin your health.
B: You're right. I should go home and take a nap.

① make a shift ② stick to my guns
③ burn the midnight oil ④ blow my own trumpet

05 어법상 가장 옳지 않은 것은?

① It was believed that people could be possessed by evil spirits.
② There's nothing worse as going out in the cold with wet hair.
③ Poor trading figures put back our plans for expansion so we cannot help but revise them.
④ Little did she know that she was fueling her daughter with a passion that would last for a lifetime.

06 밑줄 친 부분 중 어법상 가장 옳지 않은 것은?

Human farmers and their ① <u>domesticated</u> plants and animals made a grand bargain, though the farmers did not realize it at the time. Consider maize. Domestication made it ② <u>dependent</u> on man. But its association with humans also carried maize far beyond its origins as a little-known Mexican grass, so that it is now one of ③ <u>most</u> widely planted crops on earth. From mankind's point of view, meanwhile, the domestication of maize ④ <u>made</u> available an abundant new source of food.

07 어법상 ㉠~㉢에 들어갈 말로 가장 적절한 것은?

The price that the farmer gets from the wholesaler ___㉠___ much more flexible from day to day than the price that the retailer charges consumers. If, for example, bad weather ___㉡___ to a poor potato crop, then the price that supermarkets have to pay to their wholesalers for potatoes will go up ___㉢___ this will be reflected in the prices they mark on potatoes in their stores.

	㉠	㉡	㉢
①	is	leading	but
②	are	leading	and
③	are	leads	but
④	is	leads	and

08 다음 글의 내용과 일치하지 않는 것은?

The U.S. Natural Resources Conservation Service (NRCS) has classified soils into capability groupings that indicate their general suitability for most kinds of farming. The groupings are based upon composition and limitations of the soils, the risk of damage when they are used, and the way they respond to treatment. Under the NRCS system, there are eight capability classes ranging from Class I to Class VIII. In general, Class I soils are more arable and suitable for cropland; Class II soils have some limitations that reduce the choice of plants that can be grown, or require moderate conservation practices to reduce the risk of damage when used; Class III soils have severe limitations that reduce the choice of plants, require special conservation practices, or both, but may be productive with careful management. The soils in the remaining classes have progressively greater natural limitations for cropland, but may be used for pasture, grazing, woodland, wildlife, recreation, and esthetic purposes.

① The NRCS took multiple factors into account when grouping soils.
② Some crops that can be grown in Class I land may not be able to survive in Class III land.
③ Class II soils require more care and treatment than Class III soils.
④ There are five soil classes that are not recommended for cropland.

09 다음 글의 내용과 일치하지 않는 것은?

Exercise and physical activity are great ways to feel better, boost your health and have fun. For most healthy adults, the Department of Health and Human Services recommends at least 140 minutes a week of moderate aerobic activity or 70 minutes a week of vigorous aerobic activity, or a combination of moderate and vigorous activity. The guidelines suggest that you spread this exercise throughout the week. Examples include running, walking or swimming. Even small amounts of physical activity are helpful, and accumulated activity throughout the day adds up to providing similar health benefits. It also recommends strength training exercises for all major muscle groups at least two times a week. Examples include lifting free weights, using weight machines or doing body-weight training. Spread your activities throughout the week. If you want to lose weight, meet specific fitness goals or get even more benefits, you may need to ramp up your moderate aerobic activity to 280 minutes or more a week.

① Doing vigorous swimming for 70 minutes a week is equivalent to doing 140 minutes' moderate swimming a week.
② Twenty minutes of daily moderate walking can be good for an healthy adult.
③ Doing a ten-minute workout six times a day is less beneficial than exercising nonstop for an hour.
④ Body-weight training is recommended twice a week at the least.

10 다음 글의 제목으로 가장 적절한 것은?

People would usually seek culprits responsible for their misfortune first and foremost in their immediate environment. Behringer claims that a basic set of beliefs about anti-social people who try to inflict harm by mystical means, mostly on their relatives or neighbors, is common to the ancient world, medieval and early modern Europe and present-day Africa, south-east Asia, Australia and Americas. Especially close neighbors with whom people were in everyday contacts represented the most threatening source of harm and the most obvious targets of witchcraft accusations almost everywhere. Macfarlane argued that accusations of witchcraft in Essex trials from 1560-1599 were mostly made between people who not only came from the same village, but even from the same part of the village and knew each other intimately and that the accusations were limited to the area of intense relationships between individuals. Also in the 19th century, in the Dutch province of Drenthe, suspicions of witchcraft mainly fell on (female) neighbors.

① The Enemy near the Door
② Witch Hunting Around The World
③ Solving a Dispute with a Neighbor
④ The History of Witchcraft Accusations

01 밑줄 친 부분과 의미가 가장 가까운 것은?

As owners or managers of the local palace, they were makers and shapers of a principal community attraction.

① petty
② staple
③ shabby
④ immaterial

02 밑줄 친 부분과 의미가 가장 가까운 것은?

There was a man who was extolled as a hero in history and his seraphic sacrifice was known to everyone.

① sublime
② plebeian
③ ludicrous
④ outlandish

03 밑줄 친 부분과 의미가 가장 가까운 것은?

William is extroverted and fun-loving in school, while John who is his brother is ascetic and strict in school.

① lavish
② prodigal
③ sybaritic
④ abstinent

04 다음 대화의 흐름으로 보아 밑줄 친 부분에 가장 적절한 것은?

Kevin: What did you do on Christmas?
Helena: I spent Christmas with my family. How about you?
Kevin: I was travelling in Canada. It was a very white Christmas there.
Helena: It must have been so nice! I'm jealous of you.
Kevin: I'll hold on to those memories forever. Did you give your younger brother a Christmas gift?
Helena: Yeah, I kept it hidden behind the Christmas tree and he _____ before he found it.
Kevin: He must have felt disappointed when he saw the space under the tree was empty.
Helena: So I gave him a hint of where the present was placed.

① saved face
② faced the music
③ pulled a long face
④ had a corner on the market

05 어법상 가장 옳지 않은 것은?

① It is said that the corruption in the organization is acute.
② It is important to properly prepare, cook, and put away foods.
③ Not speaking the language proved to be a bigger handicap than I had imagined.
④ Only when national security is guaranteed we can turn our attention to the concept of civil rights.

06 밑줄 친 부분 중 어법상 가장 옳지 않은 것은?

The development and improvement of transportation was one of the most important factors in allowing modern tourism ① to develop on a large scale and become a regular part of the lives of billions of people around the world. Technological advances ② providing the basis for the explosive expansion of local, regional, and global transportation networks and made travel faster, easier, and cheaper. This not only created new tourist-generating and tourist-receiving regions but also ③ prompted a host of other changes in the tourism infrastructure, such as accommodations. As a result, the availability of transportation infrastructure and services has been ④ considered a fundamental precondition for tourism.

07 어법상 ㉠~㉢에 들어갈 말로 가장 적절한 것은?

I used to train with a world-class runner who ㉠_____ constantly hooking himself up to pulse meters and pace keepers. He spent hours ㉡_____ data that he thought would help him improve. In fact, a good 25 percent of his athletic time was devoted to externals other than working out. Sports became ㉢_____ complex for him that he forgot how to enjoy himself.

	㉠	㉡	㉢
①	were	collecting	too
②	was	to collect	too
③	was	collecting	so
④	were	to collect	so

08 다음 글의 제목으로 가장 적절한 것은?

The earth's soil stores a lot of carbon from the atmosphere, and managing it with the climate in mind may be an important part of reducing greenhouse gas emissions to curb global warming, according to a paper published in the journal Nature. About three times the carbon currently in the atmosphere is stored in the earth's soil — up to 2.4 trillion metric tons. Much of that is locked up in land used for agriculture. Cropland soil stores atmospheric carbon in organic matter such as manure, roots, fallen leaves and other pieces of decomposing plants. The study says that if all the earth's farmers were to manage their fields so the soil stored more carbon, impacts of the greenhouse gases emitted from burning fossil fuels annually could be cut by between half and 80 percent.

① Impacts of Carbon on Crops and Plants
② Global Warming and Agricultural Productivity
③ Farmland Could Help To Combat Climate Change
④ Farmers' Continuous Battles Against Soil Pollution

09 주어진 문장 다음에 이어질 글의 순서로 가장 적절한 것은?

Body dysmorphic disorder is a psychological disorder in which you are excessively concerned about a perceived defect in your physical features, such as your arm or leg muscles being too small or your waistline not being thin enough.

* body dysmorphic disorder: 신체변형장애(자신의 외모 중 마음에 들지 않거나 원하지 않는 특징 혹은 상상으로 만든 신체 결함에 집착하고 걱정하며 염려하는 증상)

(A) You may turn to cycling, marathoning, bodybuilding or any other activity which uses the same muscles over and over again to try to hammer away at your perceived defect, even when it comes to the detriment of your joints or health.

(B) Typically, this type of thinking and activity can begin in adolescence or early adulthood, but can stay with you in your entire life as you wish for the "perfect body".

(C) Often, you might justify this behavior by believing that you are a serious athlete who can never work too hard or too long at your sport, and this can often lead to immoderate and addictive, and even socially isolated exercise in an attempt to "repair the defect."

① (A) - (B) - (C)
② (A) - (C) - (B)
③ (B) - (A) - (C)
④ (B) - (C) - (A)

10 주어진 문장이 들어갈 위치로 가장 적절한 것은?

That is, heroes and heroines are allowed to kill witches, ogres, and sorceresses, even stepmothers, but never their own parents.

Whereas in most stories the witch dies at the hands of the hero or heroine, the witch in Perrault's The Sleeping Beauty in the Woods dies by her own hand. (①) Frustrated by her failure to execute her evil plan, the mother-in-law commits suicide by jumping into the vat filled with "toads, vipers, snakes, and serpents." (②) Hence, Perrault's story is one of the few fairy tales in which the witch takes her own life. There is a reason for this. (③) A cardinal rule in fairy tales mandates that children are not permitted to destroy their own flesh and blood. (④) If the prince destroyed the witch in Perrault's story, he would be committing matricide. By having the ogress-mother take her own life, Perrault avoids an ending that might be overly disturbing to young readers.

01 밑줄 친 부분과 의미가 가장 가까운 것을 고르시오.

In Jordan, it is usually a polite attitude to decline the offer of a meal three times before accepting it.

① splendid ② complaisant
③ impertinent ④ dispassionate

02 밑줄 친 부분과 의미가 가장 가까운 것은?

The Senior Secretary to the President for Civil Affairs, who directly reports to the president, must be absolutely forthright.

① sly ② candid
③ impromptu ④ disingenuous

03 밑줄 친 부분과 의미가 가장 가까운 것은?

The audio of the surreptitious recording clearly indicates that the participants did not want to be recorded.

① clandestine ② statutory
③ forthright ④ seraphic

04 밑줄 친 부분에 들어갈 말로 가장 적절한 것을 고르시오.

Penicillin can have an _____ effect on a person who is allergic to it.

① affirmative ② aloof
③ adverse ④ allusive

05 어법상 가장 옳지 않은 것은?

① Can we get the book written by Milton out by the end of the year?
② The baseball star was said that rest should be imperative for weeks.
③ I am interested in your system, but it is so much more expensive than your competitors'.
④ A number of simplifications have been made to the welfare system by a number of civic movements.

06 어법상 ㉠~㉢에 들어갈 말로 가장 적절한 것은?

The price that the farmer gets from the wholesaler ㉠_____ much more flexible from day to day than the price that the retailer charges consumers. If, for example, bad weather ㉡_____ to a poor potato crop, then the price that supermarkets have to pay to their wholesalers for potatoes will go up ㉢_____ this will be reflected in the prices they mark on potatoes in their stores.

	㉠	㉡	㉢
①	is	leading	but
②	are	leading	and
③	are	leads	but
④	is	leads	and

07 우리말을 영어로 잘못 옮긴 것은?

① Tom이 잠이 든 사이에 도둑이 든 게 틀림없다.
  → Tom must have been burgled while he was asleep.
② 어제 눈이 많이 와서, 그는 하루 종일 집에 있었다.
  → Snowing heavily yesterday, he stayed at home all day long.
③ 그들의 일 대부분이 시상식 연회에 음식을 공급하는 것과 관련이 있다.
  → Most of their work involves catering for the award banquet.
④ 우리는 이미 정해진 범위 내에서 작업을 해야 했다.
  → We had to work within the scope that had already been established.

08 밑줄 친 부분 중 어법상 옳은 것은?

Risk is a fundamental element of human life in the sense ① how risk is always a factor in any situation where the outcome is not precisely known. In addition, the necessary calculations that we make about the probability of some form of harm resulting from an action that we take ② are generally a given in our decision processes. Whether the risk assessment involves decisions about a major corporate initiative or just making the decision ③ walk down the street, we are always anticipating, identifying, and evaluating the potential risks involved. In that respect, we can be said to be constantly managing risk in everything ④ what we do.

09 다음 대화의 흐름으로 보아 밑줄 친 부분에 가장 적절한 것은?

A: I want to go on a trip with my friends before school starts.
B: What a good idea! I really want to ___(A)___ too.
A: Why don't we go together with some of our other friends?
B: Yeah, I'd love that. I didn't have any time for travelling this vacation.
A: Me too. It will feel like I'm ___(B)___ if I travel with my friends.
B: ___(C)___! I'm sure we can make unforgettable memories during our whole trip!
A: We should make plans right away.
B: Sure, let's get started!

① (A) hit the road
   (B) in seventh heaven
   (C) Tell me about it
② (A) hit the road
   (B) the tip of the iceberg
   (C) Give me a break
③ (A) lose the day
   (B) in seventh heaven
   (C) Every dog has its day
④ (A) lose the day
   (B) the tip of the iceberg
   (C) Every dog has its day

10 밑줄 친 부분에 들어갈 말로 가장 적절한 것을 고르시오.

A: Did you understand today's lecture?
B: Oh, do you mean the economics class?
A: Yes. Wasn't it quite difficult?
B: It was very hard to understand. I couldn't get hold of what the professor was trying to explain.
A: It was about 'capitalism' and the 'invisible hand' which keeps the capital flowing.
B: 'The invisible hand'? I totally _____.
   I thought today's lecture was on a completely different topic.
A: If you go home and review what you learned today, I'm sure you'll catch up with other classmates.

① got to the point
② cut a fine figure
③ kicked the bucket
④ got the wrong end of the stick

11 주어진 문장 다음에 이어질 글의 순서로 가장 적절한 것은?

Body dysmorphic disorder is a psychological disorder in which you are excessively concerned about a perceived defect in your physical features, such as your arm or leg muscles being too small or your waistline not being thin enough.

* body dysmorphic disorder: 신체변형장애(자신의 외모 중 마음에 들지 않거나 원하지 않는 특징 혹은 상상으로 만든 신체 결함에 집착하고 걱정하며 염려하는 증상)

(A) You may turn to cycling, marathoning, bodybuilding or any other activity which uses the same muscles over and over again to try to hammer away at your perceived defect, even when it comes to the detriment of your joints or health.
(B) Typically, this type of thinking and activity can begin in adolescence or early adulthood, but can stay with you in your entire life as you wish for the "perfect body".
(C) Often, you might justify this behavior by believing that you are a serious athlete who can never work too hard or too long at your sport, and this can often lead to immoderate and addictive, and even socially isolated exercise in an attempt to "repair the defect."

① (A) - (B) - (C)   ② (A) - (C) - (B)
③ (B) - (A) - (C)   ④ (B) - (C) - (A)

12 주어진 문장이 들어갈 위치로 가장 적절한 것은?

If denialists had evidence disproving global warming or evolution, they could submit it to scientific conferences and journals, inviting analysis by scientists.

From evolution to global warming to vaccines, science is under assault from denialists — those who dismiss well-tested scientific knowledge as merely one of many competing ideologies. Science requires conclusions about how nature works to be rooted in evidence-based testing. Sometimes progress is slow. But through a difficult and often frustrating process, we learn more about the world. (①) Science denialism works differently. Creationists are unmoved by the wealth of fossil, molecular, and anatomical evidence for evolution. Global-warming denialists are unimpressed by mountains of climate data. (②) Denialists ignore overwhelming evidence, focusing instead on a few hoaxes. (③) For denialists, opinion polls and talk radio are more important than thousands of peer-reviewed journal articles. (④) But, knowing their arguments don't hold water, they spread misinformation in arenas not subject to expert scrutiny: mass-market books, newspapers, talk radio, and blogs.

13 다음 글의 제목으로 가장 적절한 것은?

Today, the World Anti-Doping Agency (WADA) has a new hurdle to overcome — that of gene doping. This practice is defined as the nontherapeutic use of cells, genes, or genetic elements to enhance athletic performance. Gene doping takes advantage of cutting-edge research in gene therapy that involves the transfer of genetic material to human cells to treat or prevent disease. Because gene doping increases the amount of proteins and hormones that cells normally make, testing for genetic performance enhancers will be very difficult, and a new race is on to develop ways to detect this form of doping. The potential to alter genes to build better athletes was immediately realized with the invention of so-called "Schwarzenegger mice" in the late 1990s. These mice were given this nickname because they were genetically engineered to have increased muscle growth and strength.

① Doping in Various Sports
② A New Threat to Fair Play in Sport
③ Why Athletes Should Be Doping Tested
④ Gene Doping: Advantages and Disadvantages

14 밑줄 친 부분 중 글의 흐름상 가장 어색한 것은?

The competitors of the ancient Olympics were always naked. Their bodies were designed to perfection through the training and the nakedness symbolized eternal beauty as well as the symbiosis of body and soul. Also, the athletes kept impeccable hygiene and body care. This is little known fact. ① From when they got to high school, the institution where they were taught and coached, they would begin to learn to take care of their hygiene, since they were naked. ② Only men were allowed to compete in the games and women were forbidden to watch the games as the competitors were in the nude. ③ The whole process would include olive oil and a layer of dust with fine sand that athletes rubbed into the skin. ④ It would protect them not only from the sun, but also from the occasional hits from their coaches when they got the set task done. Upon completion of the training, the layer had to be taken off with water and a sponge. And this was also done each time before the competition.

15 다음 글의 내용과 일치하지 않는 것은?

The U.S. Natural Resources Conservation Service (NRCS) has classified soils into capability groupings that indicate their general suitability for most kinds of farming. The groupings are based upon composition and limitations of the soils, the risk of damage when they are used, and the way they respond to treatment. Under the NRCS system, there are eight capability classes ranging from Class I to Class VIII. In general, Class I soils are more arable and suitable for cropland; Class II soils have some limitations that reduce the choice of plants that can be grown, or require moderate conservation practices to reduce the risk of damage when used; Class III soils have severe limitations that reduce the choice of plants, require special conservation practices, or both, but may be productive with careful management. The soils in the remaining classes have progressively greater natural limitations for cropland, but may be used for pasture, grazing, woodland, wildlife, recreation, and esthetic purposes.

① The NRCS took multiple factors into account when grouping soils.
② Some crops that can be grown in Class I land may not be able to survive in Class III land.
③ Class II soils require more care and treatment than Class III soils.
④ There are five soil classes that are not recommended for cropland.

16 다음 글의 내용과 일치하는 것은?

Only men, boys and unmarried girls were allowed to watch the ancient Olympic Games. Married women were barred. If they were caught sneaking in, they could be thrown off the side of a mountain as punishment. However, married women could still own horses in the chariot races at the Olympics. Even though married women were not allowed at the Olympic Games, one story tells of a mother so keen to see her son compete that she broke the no-women rule and got in disguised as a man. Meanwhile, unmarried women had their own festival at Olympia. This was called the Heraia and was held in honor of Hera, Zeus's wife, every four years. Winners of the Heraia Games were awarded crowns of sacred olive branches, the same as men.

① Some females were able to spectate at the Olympic Games.
② Women who owned horses could compete in the chariot races.
③ A woman disguised herself as a man to play at the Olympic Games.
④ All women could participate in the Heraia Games.

17 다음 글의 주제로 가장 적절한 것은?

Scientific researchers face perpetual struggle to secure and sustain funding. While the scientific workforce is increasing, the funding in most countries has been on a decline over the past decade. The situation is particularly for early career researchers who find it difficult to compete for funds with senior researchers. This extreme competition is also impacting the way science is conducted. The respondents of the Vox survey pointed out that since most grants are allotted only for a couple of years, researchers tend to opt for short-term projects, which can sometimes be insufficient to study complex research questions. This means researchers make choices based on what would keep the funding bodies and their institutions happy. However, the consequences of these choices are an increasing number of published papers with substandard quality and low research impact.

① How to obtain funds for a study
② The financial short in the field of science
③ High competitions between new and senior scientists
④ The importance of scientific research and publication

18 다음 글의 내용과 일치하지 않는 것은?

Exercise and physical activity are great ways to feel better, boost your health and have fun. For most healthy adults, the Department of Health and Human Services recommends at least 140 minutes a week of moderate aerobic activity or 70 minutes a week of vigorous aerobic activity, or a combination of moderate and vigorous activity. The guidelines suggest that you spread this exercise throughout the week. Examples include running, walking or swimming. Even small amounts of physical activity are helpful, and accumulated activity throughout the day adds up to providing similar health benefits. It also recommends strength training exercises for all major muscle groups at least two times a week. Examples include lifting free weights, using weight machines or doing body-weight training. Spread your activities throughout the week. If you want to lose weight, meet specific fitness goals or get even more benefits, you may need to ramp up your moderate aerobic activity to 280 minutes or more a week.

① Doing vigorous swimming for 70 minutes a week is equivalent to doing 140 minutes' moderate swimming a week.
② Twenty minutes of daily moderate walking can be good for an healthy adult.
③ Doing a ten-minute workout six times a day is less beneficial than exercising nonstop for an hour.
④ Body-weight training is recommended twice a week at the least.

19 빈칸에 들어갈 표현으로 가장 적절한 것은?

Thai farmers usually have low formal education and lack of knowledge on soil quality improvement and proper use of fertilizers. After a few years of farming, they try to trespass in conserved forest areas because of soil deterioration in their own limited expanses of farmland and because they believe soils in the conserved area are _____ than soils in their own farms. Consequently, most of them are arrested, creating individual and family problems. To address this issue, a recent project compared the physical and chemical properties of soils from farmlands and soils from the conserved area. The results showed that soil nutrients from both were not significantly different in nearly all parameters of analysis except that soils from the conserved area have more organic matters and nitrogen content. The analysis data were informed to the farmers and suggested to them improving their farmlands using appropriate organic matters to get more productivity.

① more fertile
② more sterile
③ more barren
④ less arable

20 밑줄 친 부분에 들어갈 말로 가장 적절한 것은?

In our time it is not only the law of the market which has its own life and rules over man, but also the development of science and technique. For a number of reasons, the problems and organization of science today are such that a scientist does not choose his problems; the problems force themselves upon the scientist. He solves one problem, and the result is not that he is more secure or certain, but that ten other new problems open up in place of the single solved one. They force him to solve them; he has to go ahead at an ever-quickening pace. The same holds true for industrial techniques. The pace of science forces the pace of technique. Theoretical physics forces atomic energy on us; the successful production of the fission bomb forces upon us the manufacture of the hydrogen bomb. We do not choose our problems, we do not choose our products; we are pushed, we are forced — by what? By a system which has no purpose and goal transcending it, and which _____.

① makes man its appendix
② creates a false sense of security
③ inspires man with creative challenges
④ empowers scientists to control the market

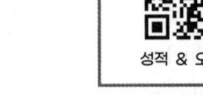

기적사 DAY 61

01 밑줄 친 부분과 의미가 가장 가까운 것은?

There are some diseases your doctor will rule out before making a diagnosis.

① trace ② exclude
③ instruct ④ examine

02 밑줄 친 부분과 의미가 가장 가까운 것을 고르시오.

I am not made of money, you know!

① needy ② thrifty
③ wealthy ④ stingy

03 밑줄 친 부분과 의미가 가장 가까운 것을 고르시오.

Experienced salespeople claim there is a difference between being assertive and being pushy.

① thrilled ② brave
③ timid ④ aggressive

04 밑줄 친 부분에 들어갈 말로 가장 적절한 것을 고르시오.

A: What are you getting Ted for his birthday? I'm getting him a couple of baseball caps.
B: I've been _____ trying to think of just the right gift. I don't have an inkling of what he needs.
A: Why don't you get him an album? He has a lot of photos.
B: That sounds perfect! Why didn't I think of that? Thanks for the suggestion!

① contacted by him ② sleeping all day
③ racking my brain ④ collecting photo albums

05 우리말을 영어로 잘못 옮긴 것은?

① 대다수의 기관에서 가장 중요한 것은 유능한 관리자들을 두는 것이다.
→ What matters most in the majority of organizations is having competent managers.
② 많은 진료소들이 치료법을 안내하기 위해 유전자 검사를 이용하고 있다.
→ Many clinics are using therapy to guide gene tests.
③ 요즘에는 신문들이 광고에서 훨씬 더 적은 돈을 번다.
→ Nowadays, newspapers make much less money from advertisements.
④ 통화의 가치는 대개 한 국가 경제의 힘을 반영한다.
→ A currency's value usually reflects the strength of a country's economy.

06 밑줄 친 부분 중 어법상 옳지 않은 것은?

According to a recent report, three quarters of Airbnb listings in New York City were illegal. It also ① founded that commercial operators—not the middle-class New Yorkers in the ads—were making millions renting spaces exclusively to Airbnb guests. In a letter sent to ② elected officials last week, Airbnb said that most of its local ③ hosts—87 percent—were residents who rented their spaces infrequently "to pay their bills and ④ stay in their homes."

07 어법상 옳은 것은?

① This book is intended for educators, new or veteran, interested in enhancing student understanding and design more effective curricula.
② Darwin knew far less about the various species he collected on the Beagle voyage than do experts in England at the time who classified these organisms for him.
③ A challenge in reading a text is to gain a deep understanding of what the text might mean, despite of the obstacles of one's assumptions and biases.
④ The software developer works to maximize user-friendliness and to reduce bugs that impede results.

08 글의 흐름상 빈칸에 들어갈 표현으로 가장 옳은 것은?

Contemporary art has in fact become an integral part of today's middle class society. Even works of art which are fresh from the studio are met with enthusiasm. They receive recognition rather quickly—too quickly for the taste of the surlier culture critics. _____, not all works of them are bought immediately, but there is undoubtedly an increasing number of people who enjoy buying brand new works of art. Instead of fast and expensive cars, they buy the paintings, sculptures and photographic works of young artists. They know that contemporary art also adds to their social prestige. _____, since art is not exposed to the same wear and tear as automobiles, it is a far better investment.

① Of course – Furthermore
② Therefore – On the other hand
③ Therefore – For instance
④ Of course – For example

09 글의 내용과 가장 부합하는 속담은?

It is one thing to believe that our system of democracy is the best, and quite another to impose it on other countries. This is a blatant breach of the UN policy of non-intervention in the domestic affairs of independent nations. Just as Western citizens fought for their political institutions, we should trust the citizens of other nations to do likewise if they wish to. Democracy is also not an absolute term — Napoleon used elections and referenda to legitimize his hold on power, as do leaders today in West Africa and Southeast Asia. States with partial democracy are often more aggressive than totally unelected dictatorships which are too concerned with maintaining order at home. The differing types of democracy make it impossible to choose which standards to impose. The U.S. and European countries all differ in terms of restraints on government and the balance between consensus and confrontation.

① The grass is always greener on the other side of the fence.
② One man's food is another's poison.
③ There is no rule but has exceptions.
④ When in Rome, do as the Romans do.

10 글의 흐름상 빈칸에 들어갈 표현으로 가장 옳은 것은?

The idea of clowns frightening people started gaining strength in the United States. In South Carolina, for example, people reported seeing individuals wearing clown costumes, often hiding in the woods or in cities at night. Some people said that the clowns were trying to lure children into empty homes or the woods. Soon, there were reports of threatening-looking clowns trying to frighten both children and adults. Although there were usually no reports of violence, and many of the reported sightings were later found to be false, this _____.

① benefited the circus industry
② promoted the use of clowns in ads
③ caused a nationwide panic
④ formed the perfect image of a happy clown

01 밑줄 친 부분과 의미가 가장 가까운 것은?

This project combines population genetics with molecular biology to trace the migration of humans.

① bolt ② expel
③ debar ④ chase

02 밑줄 친 부분과 의미가 가장 가까운 것을 고르시오.

Through the program, people can donate money to needy families.

① posh ② opulent
③ destitute ④ pernicious

03 밑줄 친 부분과 의미가 가장 가까운 것을 고르시오.

They were thrilled to watch this magnificent show, which turned the sun into a near perfect ring of fire.

① hyper ② callous
③ benign ④ sedate

04 밑줄 친 부분에 들어갈 말로 가장 적절한 것을 고르시오.

Charles: What did you do during the last summer vacation?
Chloe: I visited Vietnam with my high school friends.
Charles: That must have been fun! How was it?
Chloe: Everything was fun except for just one thing.
Charles: Oh, what was that one thing?
Chloe: When we visited the local market, the merchants who were trying to sell items tried to _____ _____.
Charles: Oh, really? What a bad experience! But that happens very often to tourists.

① rip us off ② talk turkey
③ strike it rich ④ kiss and make up

05 우리말을 영어로 잘못 옮긴 것은?

① 나는 웃지 않으려고 무진 애를 썼지만, 웃을 수밖에 없었다.
→ I tried hard not to laugh, but I could not help but laugh.
② Jane이 자기 결정에 내포되는 의미를 심사숙고해 보도록 두었다.
→ Jane was left to reflect on the implications of her decision.
③ 지금 우리에게 필요한 것은 공격적이어야 한다는 것이 아니라 방어적이어야 한다는 것이라고 말할 수 있나요?
→ Can you say what we need now is not to be defensive but to be offensive?
④ 군사적 개입은 두 국가 간의 갈등을 훨씬 더 악화시킬 뿐이다.
→ Military intervention will only aggravate the conflict between the two countries even further.

06 밑줄 친 부분 중 어법상 옳지 않은 것은?

Some empires were big, but the rigid social ① controls required to hold an empire together was not beneficial to science, just as it was not beneficial to reason. The early nurturing and later flowering of science required a large and ② loosely structured, competitive community to support original thought and freewheeling incentive. The rise in commerce and the decline of authoritarian religion ③ allowed science to follow reason in ④ seventeenth-century Europe.

07 어법상 옳은 것은?

① Prior to come on board at the hospital, he had worked as an independent contractor.
② They saw a wilderness that was filled with seemingly infinite abundance, but untamed, having no plowed fields, fences, or farm houses.
③ According to the statistics, in 2005, more than 3 percent of employees left their jobs each month, most of them took a job with another employer.
④ It leads to a better life for the present generation and survival for generations to come, enhancing their ability to cope the world that they will inherit.

08 빈칸에 들어갈 표현으로 가장 적절한 것은?

One of the benefits of Contemporary art is that it allows individuals _____.
Through painting, sculpture, and performance art, anyone can reveal themselves in a way that will be safely observable for others. Likewise, the perspectives that are exhibited are valuable for society because it gives a unique window into the minds and thoughts of the artist. Moreover, just as the making of art is a way to reveal oneself, so is the selection and display of art in someone's office or home décor. By selecting art pieces that appeal personally, an individual can exercise their own choice and express elements of their own minds and thoughts, even if they have no personal artistic talent or interest in making art. Others also can quickly gain an understanding about the person based on the artistic choices.

① a place with no judgment
② a glimpse into our daily lives
③ a means of personal expression
④ a chance to express their artistic skills

09 다음 글의 요지로 가장 적절한 것은?

A common view is that one of the main goals for nations should be to be a democracy. However, nations should not be satisfied when they had achieved democratic status. One of the subsequent goals ought to be to establish and maintain a high degree of quality of democracy. Of course this goal also applies to well-established democracies. For the legitimacy of a democratic system, it can be seen that a high degree of quality of democracy is important, and a low degree of quality of democracy can be seen as a serious democratic problem. For example, political participation through voting can be seen as a cornerstone in a democratic system. If voter turnout is low, the legitimacy of the election and the democratic system can come into question.

① Democracy can be beneficial.
② Not all democracy is the same.
③ It is difficult to reach high-quality democracy.
④ Voting is the most important act in a democratic society.

10 다음 밑줄 친 단어가 가리키는 대상이 나머지와 다른 것은?

Many professions have their own codes of conduct. Even though clowns seldom find ① themselves facing the ethical dilemmas of, say, a doctor or lawyer, ② they too need to abide by a list of rules. These "clown commandments" mainly seek to preserve the clown as someone who exclusively spreads laughter, which is an important goal, considering the creepy associations many people have with clowns. While ③ they are fairly detailed, the main points involve professional conduct and appearance. Clowns should never drink or smoke while in clown outfits, for instance. ④ They should never be intoxicated while working. They should change out of their garb as soon as possible to avoid anything that might reflect badly on clowns. Clowns may make a living being funny, but they are quite serious about not being taken seriously.

기적사 DAY 63

01 밑줄 친 부분과 의미가 가장 가까운 것은?

They argue that homeschooler's eclectic curriculum often <u>excludes</u> important subjects.

① scratches ② condones
③ subsumes ④ condemns

02 밑줄 친 부분과 의미가 가장 가까운 것을 고르시오.

Discount stores have cheap products for <u>thrifty</u> shoppers.

① canny ② spartan
③ imprudent ④ offhand

03 밑줄 친 부분과 의미가 가장 가까운 것을 고르시오.

The bravest act you can do when you are not <u>brave</u> is to profess courage and act accordingly.

① puny ② scant
③ gallant ④ cowardly

04 밑줄 친 (A), (B)에 들어갈 말로 가장 적절한 것을 고르시오.

A: Are you sick? You don't seem to be feeling well.
B: No, I'm not sick at all. Actually, it's because of a serious problem I have.
A: Oh, what's wrong? I'm always here to help you.
B: Well, I was preparing to open my own clothing store but I failed to. I feel like I ___(A)___.
A: I don't know what to say. Can I ask why you are not opening your clothing shop?
B: My parents are very unpleasant with the idea. They want me to concentrate on studying.
A: That's too bad because I think you can earn a lot of money from the business. If you don't open your store, it's like ___(B)___.
B: I know. But sadly, there's no other choice.

① (A) lost my head
　(B) making a mountain out of a molehill
② (A) lost my head
　(B) killing the goose that laid the golden egg
③ (A) went on a wild goose chase
　(B) making a mountain out of a molehill
④ (A) went on a wild goose chase
　(B) killing the goose that laid the golden egg

05 우리말을 영어로 잘못 옮긴 것은?

① 그들의 우월한 경제력이 그들에게 엄청난 이점을 준다.
→ Their superior economic strength gives them a huge advantage.

② William과 John은 바람으로부터 스스로를 보호하기 위해 함께 옹송그리며 모여 있었다.
→ William and John huddled together to protect themselves from the wind.

③ 이틀 전에 발생한 사고에 대한 훨씬 더 많은 소식이 있었다.
→ There were even more news of the accident that happened two days ago.

④ 우리가 경영이라고 부르는 것은 직원들이 일하기 어렵게 만드는 것으로 구성되어 있다.
→ What we call management consists of what makes it difficult for the employees to work.

06 밑줄 친 부분 중 어법상 옳지 않은 것은?

After making a choice, the decision ultimately changes our ① estimated pleasure, enhancing the expected pleasure from the selected option and ② decreasing the expected pleasure from the rejected option. If we were not inclined to ③ updating the value of our options rapidly ④ so that they concur with our choices, we would second-guess ourselves to the point of insanity.

07 어법상 옳은 것은?

① The students typically get fewer opportunities to practice and have less success than do their peers.

② These finds are usually cleaned, identify, and cataloged in the field before being packed for transport to the laboratory.

③ Since then, the pineapple was internationally recognized as a symbol of hospitality and a sign of friendliness, warmth, and cheer.

④ When we speak of the political organization of a particular cultural system, we get the impression what political boundaries and cultural boundaries are the same.

08 주어진 글 다음에 이어질 글의 순서로 가장 적절한 것은?

Modern art is that which was created sometime between the 1860s and the late 1960s. Art was called "modern" because it did not build on what came before it or rely on the teachings of the art academies.

(A) Many art historians consider Édouard Manet to have been the first modern artist not only because he was depicting scenes of modern life but also because he broke with tradition when he made no attempt to mimic the real world by way of perspective tricks.

(B) While this shocked audiences and critics, it inspired his peers and the next several generations of artists, each of whom, whether in abstract works or representational, experimented with how to draw more attention to their medium.

(C) He, instead, drew attention to the fact that his work of art was simply paint on a flat canvas and that it was made by using a paint brush which sometimes left its mark on the surface of the composition.

① (A) - (B) - (C)   ② (A) - (C) - (B)
③ (B) - (A) - (C)   ④ (B) - (C) - (A)

09 주어진 문장이 들어갈 위치로 가장 적절한 것은?

All modern democracies hold elections, but not all elections are democratic.

Elections are the central institution of democratic representative governments because in a democracy, the authority of the government derives solely from the consent of the governed. (①) The principal mechanism for translating that consent into governmental authority is the holding of free and fair elections. (②) Right-wing dictatorships, Marxist regimes, and single-party governments stage elections to give their rule the aura of legitimacy. (③) In such elections, there may be only one candidate or a list of candidates, with no alternative choices. (④) Some elections may offer several candidates for each office, but ensure through intimidation or rigging that only the government-approved candidate is chosen. Other elections may offer genuine choices — but only within the incumbent party. These are not democratic elections.

10 밑줄 친 부분 중 글의 흐름상 가장 어색한 것은?

In the Cheyenne tribes of North America, a certain type of warrior called a contrary could well be considered that particular culture's clown. The contraries communicated always in opposites – for instance shaking their heads to mean 'yes', and nodding to mean 'no'. If they wanted to warn about a shortage of firewood, they said, "We have lots of wood! Don't bring any more." This reversal extended beyond communication as well. ① They would wear their clothes backwards, bathe in dirt, and were even known to dry themselves with water. ② The reason a warrior might choose to become such a figure was to overcome fear. ③ A warrior was viewed by the people not as a maker of war but as a protector and leader, and warriors gained rank by performing and accumulating various acts of bravery in battle. ④ A contrary used a lance as a weapon that was said to make the bearer invulnerable to lightning. So people with a fear of thunder or lightning could become the tribe's clown warrior and conquer their phobia.

01 밑줄 친 부분과 의미가 가장 가까운 것은?

This material serves to <u>instruct</u> and encourage civilians to engage in activities that would support their compatriots fighting abroad.

① oust ② acquit
③ impeach ④ mandate

02 밑줄 친 부분과 의미가 가장 가까운 것을 고르시오.

She was a <u>wealthy</u> Russian industrialist and supporter of the arts.

① stark ② blunt
③ tactful ④ opulent

03 밑줄 친 부분과 의미가 가장 가까운 것을 고르시오.

A <u>timid</u> person prefers spicy and salty food while an extrovert likes bland food.

① astute ② mousy
③ affable ④ cunning

04 밑줄 친 부분에 들어갈 말로 가장 적절한 것을 고르시오.

Mom: How are you feeling today?
Son: I'm starting to get a bit nervous. I have an important audition tomorrow.
Mom: Oh, really? I didn't know that. What are you auditioning for?
Son: I haven't told anyone yet. I am auditioning for the lead singer position in the school band.
Mom: Wow! That's wonderful! Son, don't worry too much. You have a heavenly voice. You doubtlessly _____ _____ in the audition.
Son: Thank you, mom. You are my biggest support.

① break a leg ② make a killing
③ stand a chance ④ blow hot and cold

05 우리말을 영어로 잘못 옮긴 것은?

① 해외에서 돌아오니 집이 텅 비어 있었다.
→ I returned from abroad to find the house empty.
② 경찰은 실제로 발생했던 것을 알아내기 위해 애쓰는 중이다.
→ The police are trying to ascertain what really happened.
③ Tom은 그 궁전을 전보다 훨씬 더 호화로운 규모로 재건했다.
→ Tom rebuilt the palace on an even more lavish scale than before.
④ 완전 회복 가능성은 그가 입은 부상의 심각성에 달려 있을 것이다.
→ The chances of a full recovery will be depended on the severity of his injuries.

06 밑줄 친 부분 중 어법상 옳지 않은 것은?

Tourism allows people from different places and cultures ① to come together, and then tourists and host communities learn about each other's differences and similarities. They also learn new tastes and ways of thinking, ② which may lead to a better understanding between hosts and tourists. Another positive effect of tourism is the aid that it ③ is provided for the survival of a society's culture, especially the culture's art forms. The ④ opportunity to sell native artworks to tourists or perform folk dances for them encourages local artists to preserve traditional art forms.

08 밑줄 친 부분 중 글의 흐름상 가장 어색한 것은?

Buying a piece of art made of items that one can find at the supermarket for ten times less is baffling for many of us. Two types of reactions generally follow: anger or a complete self-doubt of one's judgment capacities. Do they take me for a fool? Or: who am I to say it is not art after all? ① How did we get to such an advanced state of miscommunication between art and its audience? ② The origin of this phenomenon, as everybody well knows, is Marcel Duchamp's act to take a urinal, turn it upside-down and call it a "fountain". ③ However, the show committee insisted that it was not art, and rejected it from the show, which led Duchamp to resign from the board of the Independent Artists. This was the beginning of the "readymade". ④ By doing so, the artist transformed an ordinary manufactured object into a piece of art. Now, an object is no longer "represented", as it used to be in classical genres like still life, but directly "presented" to the public.

07 어법상 옳은 것은?

① The speaker quickly said this is that North America looks like from the Southern Hemisphere.
② Thought of as a relationship, leadership becomes a process of collaboration that occurs between leaders and followers.
③ Inequality doesn't offer benefits to anyone except the elite and is harmful to the whole society because the unnecessary conflicts it creates.
④ If we will think that people and relationships are like complex machines, we will probably see their problems as malfunctions in the machinery.

09 밑줄 친 (A), (B)에 들어갈 말로 가장 적절한 것은?

News reports over the past few months paint a bleak picture of the state of democracy in Asia. ____(A)____ a severe crackdown on political dissidents has been imposed by the prime minister in Cambodia and the closing of the last independent newspaper suggests that democracy is crumbling well before next year's general elections. In the Philippines, President Rodrigo Duterte's anti-drug crusade has led to thousands of victims in a spate of extrajudicial killings. And in Myanmar, one of the international community's most prominent defenders of democracy and human rights, Aung San Suu Kyi, has received harsh criticism from around the globe for failing to act on the ongoing Rohingya crisis. ____(B)____, the bigger picture actually tells another story. Over the past ten years, net democratic progress has increased significantly. Democratic gains have surpassed the rollbacks and the agenda for "government of the people, by the people, for the people" is gaining momentum.

	(A)	(B)
①	Therefore	However
②	To take some examples	As a consequence
③	To be specific	In short
④	For instance	On the other hand

10 다음 글의 요지로 가장 적절한 것은?

Do you think that red nosed jokers only belong in the circus? Think again. Medical clowning speeds up patients' overall healing and is successfully turning children's cries into giggles around the world. You know what they say, laughter is the best form of medicine. This idea is now being applied to hospital practices as new research indicates that "clown therapy" reduces stress and anxiety in patients. Different from the painted faces of your nightmares, these clowns use jokes and pranks to provoke laughter and release endorphins in their patients, reducing the need for painkillers and improving general health. In Israel, medical clowning has become an established practice that is not to be laughed at. These Dream Doctors help cheer and heal patients in hospital wards and are even present during surgeries. One Israeli study showed that the presence of clowns helps increase a woman's chances of getting pregnant during IVF fertility treatment from 20.2 percent to 36.4 percent.

* IVF: 체외 수정(in vitro fertilization)
* fertility treatment: 불임 치료, 임신 촉진 치료

① Circus clowns can be as funny as they can be terrifying.
② Certain clowns are playing positive roles in the medical world.
③ Clown therapy should be encouraged both in child and adult patients.
④ Medical clowns must be properly educated and trained to help patients.

01 밑줄 친 부분과 의미가 가장 가까운 것은?

He says that the results of the research can be used to examine this in more detail.

① thrust ② plunge
③ canvass ④ insinuate

02 밑줄 친 부분과 의미가 가장 가까운 것을 고르시오.

The country should not be stingy in inviting talented foreign students for educational purposes.

① provident ② sagacious
③ extravagant ④ parsimonious

03 밑줄 친 부분과 의미가 가장 가까운 것을 고르시오.

Collision sports like hockey, football, and rugby feature aggressive tackling and extremely physical styles of play.

① vicious ② uptight
③ revengeful ④ peripheral

04 밑줄 친 부분에 들어갈 말로 가장 적절한 것을 고르시오.

A: Did you hear about the recent political issue?
B: No, I was too busy to check the news this morning. Was there anything serious?
A: North Korea fired a missile at South Korea late last night.
B: What? Are you serious? Was anyone hurt?
A: Fortunately, there were no injuries. But I was very upset to hear the news.
B: I feel the same. We must do something to stop their brutality.
A: Definitely. We should no longer _____. It's time that we take action.

① hold water ② clear the air
③ sit on the fence ④ scratch the surface

05 우리말을 영어로 잘못 옮긴 것은?

① 네가 그녀를 보기 위해 간다면, 그녀가 아주 기뻐할 것이다.
→ If you went to see her, she would be delighted.
② 당신은 호텔에서 현지 통화를 달러로 환전할 수 있다.
→ You can exchange local currency for dollars in the hotel.
③ 은행의 실수로 인해, 내 계좌에는 돈이 훨씬 적게 들어 있었다.
→ Due to an oversight by my bank, there was even fewer money in my account.
④ 그녀를 사진가로서 주목하게 만들었던 것은 순간을 포착하는 그녀의 기량이었다.
→ What made her remarkable as a photographer was her skill in capturing the moment.

06 밑줄 친 부분 중 어법상 옳지 않은 것은?

If you've ever seen the bank of flashing screens at a broker's desk, you have a sense of the information overload ① what they are up against. When ② deciding whether to invest in a company, for example, they may take into account the people at the helm; the current and potential size of its market; net profits; and its past, present, and future stock value, among other pieces of information. Weighing all of these factors can ③ take up so much of your working memory ④ that it becomes overwhelmed.

07 어법상 옳은 것은?

① Education is an investment in the young, and is universally recognized as part of the duty of the state.
② He became one of young artists in the mid-1850s and were particularly friendly with John, who influenced his painting.
③ Although the fact that sport is a salient part of our daily lives, it has, until recently, received little serious study by sociologists.
④ Leaders who carefully choose which seminars and conferences to attend helps themselves increase their contribution to their personal developmental goals.

08 다음 글의 제목으로 가장 적절한 것은?

Contemporary art can often be dismissed as being a bit pointless and lacking in skill. The clichéd "my five-year-old kid could do this" phrase is mentioned if an artist's work looks too simple. Yes, a lot of contemporary artworks do seem a bit basic at first glance, but it doesn't mean that they don't contain complex concepts — in fact, the ideas contained within these works are frequently more profound than those in much older, but more popular, paintings. And surely the more recent the artwork, the more relevant the message is for the modern viewer, right? Rachel Maclean's recent exhibition at HOME is an example of this. It was quite simple and not to everyone's taste, but the message it expressed of our relationship with social media and technology really struck a chord. There seems to be this ongoing belief that art should be a visual pleasure and nothing more. But art should conjure up emotions and provoke thoughts, even if it isn't pretty and complicated. In this sense, contemporary art deserves our appreciation and it's time it lost its undeserved bad reputation.

① Anyone Can Be a Contemporary Artist
② Is Contemporary Art Worth Looking At?
③ How Does Contemporary Art Affect Society?
④ Why Does Contemporary Art Look So Simple?

09 다음 글의 내용과 일치하지 않는 것은?

The U.S. has been demoted from a full democracy to a flawed democracy for the first time, according to the Economist Intelligence Unit. Every year, the firm's Democracy Index provides a snapshot of global democracy by scoring countries on five categories: electoral process and pluralism; civil liberties; the functioning of government; political participation; and political culture. Nations are then classified under four types of governments: full democracy, flawed democracy, hybrid regime and authoritarian regime. America's score fell to 7.98 in 2016 from 8.05 in the previous year, below the 8.00 threshold for a full democracy. That put the world's largest economy on the same footing as Italy, a country known for its fractious politics. A flawed democracy is a country with free elections but weighed down by weak governance, an underdeveloped political culture and low levels of political participation. Other flawed democracies in 2016 included Japan, France, Belgium, South Korea and India, all of which were deemed flawed democracies in 2015 as well.

① The U.S. had always been rated a full democracy before 2016.
② The Economist Intelligence Unit evaluates countries in multiple categories.
③ In 2015, the U.S. received a lower score than Belgium.
④ Italy had the title of a flawed democracy in 2016.

10 다음 글의 주제로 가장 적절한 것은?

We all know that some people have a fear of clowns, or coulrophobia, which can vary from finding the faces unsettling to feeling outright terror at the sight of them. Researchers have been trying to explain the phenomenon and their main hypothesis for that is the "uncanny valley" effect. This effect refers to the unsettling nature of images that look nearly — but not quite — human. It originally exclusively covered robots designed to look like people. When looking at a robot meant to resemble a human, brains have to push harder to interpret what they're seeing, compared with just viewing a plainly inanimate robot or a natural human. The aversion to the sight may stem from an instinctive repulsion to one other nearly-human sight: corpses. The uncanny valley effect can kick in with figures besides robots, such as paintings, or video game characters — or clowns. Your brain expects to see a person, but the distorted and colored features of the clown look just enough unlike a person to be quite disturbing.

① A way to get over coulrophobia
② Common features of clowns and robots
③ Various symptoms of the fear of clowns
④ A probable reason why clowns are feared

01 다음 중 밑줄 친 단어와 뜻이 가장 가까운 것은?

Parents must not give up on kids who act rebellious or seem socially awkward; this is a normal stage most youngsters go through and eventually outgrow.

① passive
② delirious
③ disobedient
④ sporadic

02 다음 중 밑줄 친 단어와 뜻이 가장 가까운 것은?

He was born to a wealthy family in New York in 1800s. This circumstance allowed him to lead a prodigal existence for much of his life.

① perjury
② unstable
③ pernicious
④ lavish

03 다음 중 밑줄 친 단어와 뜻이 가장 가까운 것은?

Perhaps the brightest spot in the contemporary landscape of American higher education is the resurgence of interest in engaging students in civic life beyond campus.

① comeback
② disappearance
③ motivation
④ paucity

04 다음 빈칸에 가장 적합한 것은?

A: Kate, I am too tired. It's only 7:30 in the morning! Let's take a rest for a few minutes.
B: Don't quit yet. Push yourself a little more. When I started jogging, it was so hard for me, too.
A: Have pity on me then. This is my first time.
B: Come on, Mary. After you jog another three months or so, you will ready for the marathon.
A: Marathon! How many miles is the marathon?
B: It's about thirty miles. If I jog every day, I'll be able to enter it in a couple of months.
A: _____ I am exhausted now after only half a mile. I am going to stop.

① Count me out!
② Why shouldn't I enter the marathon?
③ Why didn't I think of that?
④ I don't believe so.
⑤ Look who is talking!

05 밑줄 친 부분 중 어법상 가장 옳지 않은 것은?

The growth of foreign markets and competition, most notably those in China and India, ① is having a tremendous impact on the manner in which companies conduct business all over the globe. In fact, the advent of outsourcing and off-shoring(the shifting of production to sites outside the United States), which helped place China and India on the economic map, has created quite a debate in the United States and abroad as to ② whether economic globalization is a good or an evil. Many, however, suggest that globalization is a good thing, and that outsourcing and off-shoring are simple manifestations of the economic theory of comparative advantage, ③ which holds that everyone gains when each country specializes in ④ that it does best.

06 밑줄 친 부분 중 어법상 가장 옳지 않은 것은?

① Beginning in October, as the expedition ② made its way through present northern South Dakota, it passed numerous abandoned villages, composed of earth-lodge dwellings and cultivated fields. Some of the fields, ③ unless unattended, still had squash and corn growing in them. ④ These had once been home to the mighty Arikara tribe.

07 밑줄 친 부분 중 어법상 가장 옳지 않은 것은?

Losing just a couple hours of sleep at night makes you angrier, especially in ① frustrated situations, according to new research. While the results may ② seem intuitive, the study is one of the first to ③ provide evidence that sleep loss causes anger. The research also provides new insight on our ability to adjust ④ to irritating conditions when tired.

08 <보기> 문장이 들어갈 곳으로 가장 적절한 것은?

<보기>
If you are unhappy yourself, you will probably be prepared to admit that you are not exceptional in this.

(①) Animals are happy so long as they have health and enough to eat. Human beings, one feels, ought to be, but in the modern world they are not, at least in a great majority of cases. (②) If you are happy, ask yourself how many of your friends are so. (③) And when you have reviewed your friends, teach yourself the art of reading faces; make yourself receptive to the moods of those whom you meet in the course of an ordinary day. (④)

09 글의 흐름상 가장 적절하지 않은 문장은?

Tighter regulations on cigarette products have spilled over to alcohol, soda and other consumer products, which has restricted consumer choices and made goods more expensive. ① Countries have taken more restrictive measures, including taxation, pictorial health warnings and prohibitions on advertising and promotion, against cigarette products over the past four decades. ② Regulatory measures have failed to improve public health, growing cigarette smuggling. ③ Applying restrictions first to tobacco and then to other consumer products have created a domino effect, or what is called a "slippery slope", for other industries. ④ At the extreme end of the slippery slope is plain packaging, where all trademarks, logos and brand-specific colors are removed, resulting in unintended consequences and a severe infringement of intellectual property rights.

10 글의 흐름상 빈칸에 들어갈 가장 적절한 것은?

Language changes when speakers of a language come into contact with speakers of another language or languages. This can be because of migration, perhaps, because they move to more fertile lands, or because they are displaced on account of war or poverty or disease. It can also be because they are invaded. Depending on the circumstances, the home language may succumb completely to the language of the invaders, in which case we talk about replacement. _____, the home language might persist side-by-side with the language of the invaders, and depending on political circumstances, it might become the dominant language.

① Typically
② Consistently
③ Similarly
④ Alternatively

01 다음 중 밑줄 친 단어와 뜻이 가장 가까운 것은?

The common belief was that men should be aggressive and work outdoors while women should be passive and stay indoors.

① meek
② feisty
③ privative
④ assertive

02 다음 중 밑줄 친 단어와 뜻이 가장 가까운 것은?

The dessert is a work of art: assorted berries, crushed pistachios, dark chocolate, and mint leaves delicately garnish this lavish dessert.

① dour
② stark
③ austere
④ sumptuous

03 다음 중 밑줄 친 단어와 뜻이 가장 가까운 것은?

Due to the paucity of his upbringing, his illiteracy, and his lack of control over his own fate, he is chiefly remembered as a tragic figure in the history of the Joseon Period.

① dearth
② surfeit
③ satiety
④ plenitude

04 다음 빈칸 (A), (B)에 가장 적합한 것은?

Jane: I'm really bored these days.
Steve: Oh, I thought you were busy with your part-time job.
Jane: I quit my part-time job a month ago. Now, I'm just enjoying my hobby.
Steve: Good for you! What's your hobby?
Jane: I love watching movies. So I'm watching a lot of movies at home.
Steve: Could you recommend some _____(A)_____ movies that you liked?
Jane: Sure! My recommendation is <Inception>.
Steve: I watched that movie! It was _____(B)_____ when it was released.
Jane: In fact, it recorded the largest number of audience.
Steve: Wow! That's amazing. It's one of my favorite movies.

① (A) up to date   (B) smash hit
② (A) up to date   (B) top notch
③ (A) carrot and stick (B) smash hit
④ (A) carrot and stick (B) a spitting image

05 밑줄 친 부분 중 어법상 가장 옳지 않은 것은?

The term "biological control" has been used, at times, in a broad context to cover a full spectrum of biological organisms and biologically based products. This has been spectacularly successful in many instances, with a number of pest problems permanently ① resolved by importation and successful establishment of natural enemies. These importation successes have been limited largely to certain types of ② the ecosystems and/or pest situations such as introduced pests in perennial ecosystems. On the other hand, this approach has met with limited success for major pests of row crops or other ephemeral systems. In these situations, the problem is often not the lack of effective natural enemies ③ but management practices and a lack of concerted research on factors that ④ determine the success or failure of importation attempts in the specific agro-ecosystem setting.

06 밑줄 친 부분 중 어법상 가장 옳지 않은 것은?

We drift, ① <u>driven by the winds</u> of circumstance and tossed about by the waves of tradition and custom. Eventually, most men find they must ② <u>be satisfied with</u> "any port in a storm." Sailors ③ <u>who select</u> a port because they are driven to it can scarcely have one chance ④ <u>of being dropped</u> anchor.

07 밑줄 친 부분 중 어법상 가장 옳지 않은 것은?

For example, do you ① <u>feel like having</u> a child who is a winner proves you're a worthwhile parent? Do you ② <u>crave the recognition</u> of being the parent of a star athlete? If you can answer yes to ③ <u>either questions</u>, you may be ④ <u>trying to feel</u> good about yourself through your child's athletic accomplishments.

08 밑줄 친 (A), (B)에 들어갈 말로 가장 적절한 것은?

The variation in how happiness is accepted across different cultures is evident in language. Words like 'happiness' and 'happy' carry different connotations in Eastern and Western cultures and can't always be directly translated. For example, Mandarin has multiple words for "happiness" that aren't a perfect equivalent to the English concept, since they can mean anything from "good mood" to "having meaning in life" or "having a good life". (A) , in Mandarin, happiness is also defined as "having a good death", which would be rather unthinkable in English-speaking cultures. In addition, the way happiness is defined in different languages points at how differently it's experienced across cultures. For instance, the Danish concept of "lykke" is translated as "happiness", but has very little to do with the way happiness is experienced in the United States, where it involves a state of celebration. (B) , the word for happiness in Hong Kong's Cantonese is linked to low arousal states and its meaning is closer to calm and relaxation rather than to celebration.

	(A)	(B)
①	Therefore	Likewise
②	However	That is
③	In fact	Similarly
④	Accordingly	By contrast

09 다음 글의 요지로 가장 적절한 것은?

In 2016, the Food and Drug Administration finalized regulations asserting regulatory authority over e-cigarettes. E-cigarette use has boomed in recent years, fueled largely by current and former smokers. Many cigarettes users have learned that they can satisfy their nicotine craving while doing less damage to their lungs. Because e-cigarettes compete with traditional cigarettes — and many e-cigarettes and vaping products are made by small startup companies — major tobacco companies, such as Altria (a.k.a. Philip Morris), have sought to clamp down on this market. The Big Tobacco companies have created or acquired e-cigarette brands while also pushing for regulation that will make it more difficult for little guys to compete. With the new FDA rules, Big Tobacco got just what it wanted.

① E-cigarettes have been competing with traditional cigarettes.
② The FDA's new e-cigarette regulations were a gift to Big Tobacco.
③ The FDA should regulate e-cigarettes more strictly to protect public health.
④ The e-cigarette market has been growing significantly despite the new regulations.

10 밑줄 친 (A), (B)에 들어갈 말로 가장 적절한 것은?

Language contact often occurs along borders or as a result of migration. However, it has been taking place in different ways as technology has advanced. In recent decades, the internet has brought many languages in contact, and thus they are influencing one another. ___(A)___, only a few languages dominate the web, influencing the others significantly. English by far predominates, along with Russian, Korean and German. Even languages spoken by multiple millions, such as Spanish and Arabic, have, ___(B)___, little representation on the internet. As a result, English words are influencing other languages worldwide at a far greater rate as a direct result of internet use. In France, for example, the English term "cloud computing" has come into common use despite efforts to get French speakers to adopt "informatique en nuage."

	(A)	(B)
①	Also	in a word
②	Still	by comparison
③	So	for instance
④	But	likewise

01 다음 중 밑줄 친 단어와 뜻이 가장 가까운 것은?

It was a sentiment shared by tens of thousands of <u>delirious</u> fans in pubs all across Bournemouth.

① torpid ② supine
③ listless ④ rapturous

02 다음 중 밑줄 친 단어와 뜻이 가장 가까운 것은?

You start to think about various solutions to solve that problem, even if the problem is <u>pernicious</u> and as intractable as racism.

① dainty ② capital
③ exquisite ④ succulent

03 다음 중 밑줄 친 단어와 뜻이 가장 가까운 것은?

They filled their times with these dreams and consequently people were able to have more <u>motivation</u> to work and achieve things in life.

① daring ② impetus
③ audacity ④ momentum

04 다음 빈칸에 가장 적합한 것은?

A: Have you ever made an investment?
B: Sure. I don't know a lot about stock investments, but I do have some experience with making investments. Are you thinking of making investments?
A: Well, I recently invested in a global IT company. When I checked the stock status this morning, I was very disappointed.
B: Why? Did it _____?
A: Yes it did. Should I just wait until it rises again?
B: I suggest you wait a little longer.

① beef up ② take a nosedive
③ sell like hot cakes ④ rain cats and dogs

05 밑줄 친 부분 중 어법상 가장 옳지 않은 것은?

What do you think can make you a good tennis player? Suppose there are two different tennis pros ① <u>giving</u> you tennis lessons. The first pro says things like "good shot" and "good swing" all the time to encourage you. The second one says "good swing" only when you make a good swing. If just hearing "good swing" ② <u>gives</u> you a reward, then you will prefer the first instructor. But ③ <u>if</u> you want is to get better at tennis, you will prefer the second instructor. That's because the second instructor's feedback to you is much more informative than the first one's. You're not after "good swing" rewards but you're after a better tennis game. So feedback that simply makes you ④ <u>feel</u> great will not help you develop tennis skills in the long run.

06 밑줄 친 부분 중 어법상 가장 옳지 않은 것은?

① Knowing how dangerous chemical poisoning is, I think it's important that you adequately warn customers not to microwave the bowl. I suggest you ② to use bold print on the outside of the box. Clarify that the notice of harmful chemicals ③ is a warning, not just a characteristic of the clay. Please consider this so that unnecessary poisoning ④ does not occur.

07 밑줄 친 부분 중 어법상 가장 옳지 않은 것은?

It should ① note, though, that no development in the Internet job age ② has reduced the importance of ③ the most basic job search skill: self-knowledge. Even in the Internet age, the job search starts with identifying individual job skills, sector interests, and ④ preferred workplace environment and interests.

08 주어진 글 다음에 이어질 글의 순서로 가장 적절한 것은?

The idea that people want to be happy seems obvious to laypeople and has been confirmed in cross-cultural empirical research. But, paradoxically, a growing body of research indicates that pursing happiness actually impairs well-being.

(A) For instance, happiness in an individualistic culture like the United States may be defined in highly self-oriented ways, whereas happiness in collectivist cultures found in regions such as East Asia may be defined in terms of social engagement.

(B) However, most research on the pursuit of happiness and well-being has been conducted in the United States, leaving open the possibility that this relationship depends on culture.

(C) Since social connection is a robust predictor of well-being, it may be that pursuit of happiness leads to higher well-being in cultures where happiness is defined in more socially engaged ways, leading people to engage in social behaviors — like spending more time with friends and family — in the pursuit of happiness.

① (A) - (B) - (C) ② (B) - (A) - (C)
③ (B) - (C) - (A) ④ (C) - (A) - (B)

09 주어진 문장이 들어갈 위치로 가장 적절한 것은?

Now that this is a federal law, all states will have to comply.

The US Food and Drug Administration has officially raised the minimum age to buy tobacco products like cigarettes, electronic cigarettes, and vaping products that contain nicotine from 18 to 21. (①) By raising the age to buy tobacco products, the federal government is replicating what a number of states have been doing. (②) Nineteen states around the US plus Washington, DC, have already raised the minimum age to buy tobacco to 21. (③) The change could save thousands of lives. (④) Research shows it's important to try to prevent teens from smoking or vaping nicotine products, because they are the most likely to become addicted.

10 다음 글의 요지로 가장 적절한 것은?

Language change is not a goal of speakers. Rather it is what is called an 'epiphenomenon' – something which happens but which is not intentional. In linguistic terms, an epiphenomenon means that change occurs for internal or external reasons – or a combination of both – but the change is not intended by the speakers. A comparison with a traffic jam might help to illustrate the point: if every car brakes to avoid hitting the one in front, the result is a traffic jam, but the jam is not the goal of any driver; it arises as a consequence of the compression of the traffic which results from stopping and starting. Thus the traffic jam is an epiphenomenon resulting from the behavior of the drivers.

① Language changes because society changes.
② Language change happens in every language.
③ Language change is an unintentional process.
④ Traffic jams can be caused by careful driving habits.

기적사 DAY 69

01 다음 중 밑줄 친 단어와 뜻이 가장 가까운 것은?

Some people are concerned that teachers would have difficulties controlling problematic or <u>disobedient</u> students at schools.

① genial
② cordial
③ amiable
④ truculent

02 다음 중 밑줄 친 단어와 뜻이 가장 가까운 것은?

Korea's <u>unstable</u> economic and political circumstances have prevented large companies from investing in facilities or recruiting staff.

① wobbly
② ruinous
③ rambling
④ interminable

03 다음 중 밑줄 친 단어와 뜻이 가장 가까운 것은?

A Oxford University report published in 2013 predicts the <u>disappearance</u> of 47 percent of present jobs within the next 20 years.

① exile
② expiry
③ passing
④ omission

04 다음 빈칸 (A), (B), (C)에 가장 적합한 것은?

Clara: Hi, David! You look furious.
David: I'm very angry right now because there is a problem with the team project in progress.
Clara: You must be stressed out. What's bothering you?
David: One of my teammates wouldn't participate at all. So I told her very politely to be more responsible.
Clara: How did she behave after you told her so?
David: She ___(A)___. I have no idea why she got mad.
Clara: Oh, it sounds like your teammate is someone who ___(B)___ her duties.
David: Well, I agree with you. She should ___(C)___ behave that way.

① (A) went Dutch
　(B) makes little of
　(C) fall prey to
② (A) hit the roof
　(B) makes little of
　(C) fall prey to
③ (A) hit the roof
　(B) makes little of
　(C) know better than to
④ (A) went Dutch
　(B) comes to terms with
　(C) know better than to

05 밑줄 친 부분 중 어법상 가장 옳지 않은 것은?

A couple of years ago, I became interested in ① what we call hardship inoculation. This is the idea that struggling with a mental puzzle — trying to remember a phone number or deciding what to do on a long Sunday afternoon — ② inoculate you against future mental hardships just as vaccinations inoculate you against illness. There is good evidence to support the idea that small doses of mental hardship are good for us. Young adults do much better on tricky mental puzzles when they've solved ③ difficult rather than easy ones earlier. Adolescent athletes also thrive on challenges: we've found, for example, ④ that college basketball teams do better when their preseason schedules are more demanding.

06 밑줄 친 부분 중 어법상 가장 옳지 않은 것은?

This recommendation ① is based on the assumption that this change is welcomed, but laws banning texting while walking ② failed in Toronto, Arkansas, Illinois, Nevada, New Jersey and New York. Meanwhile, high-tech firms are developing technological solutions to the problem, ③ offered a transparent screen that allows pedestrians to see ④ what is going on in front of them while texting.

07 밑줄 친 부분 중 어법상 가장 옳지 않은 것은?

According to a ① renowned French scholar, the growth in the size and complexity of human populations ② were the driving force in the evolution of science. Early, small communities had to concentrate all their physical and mental effort on survival; their thoughts ③ were focused on food and religion. As communities became larger, some people had time ④ to reflect and debate.

08 다음 글에서 필자가 주장하는 것으로 가장 적절한 것은?

Browsing social media and being confronted with friends scoring dream jobs, creating perfect families and sunning themselves on beaches can create the impression that everyone else is in some unending state of euphoria. And there you are, laying on the sofa with one hand in a bag of crisps and the other holding your phone, an hour into a scrolling session. Social media is making us unsatisfied. It's likely that everyone around us is always happy. But such constant happiness is overrated. Not only is it overrated, but it's totally unachievable. If we expect to be constantly happy, we judge that to feel any other emotion is wrong and therefore we internalize that we are bad if we feel sad, angry, frustrated, and so on. But in actual fact in order to feel truly happy, we need to accept other emotions. That's why experiencing sadness or miserableness can sometimes be useful. In the long term, unhappiness might just be the key to happiness.

① Social media is full of fake happiness.
② Feeling unhappy can be good for you.
③ Express your emotions to those who love you.
④ To be happy, try not to compare yourself to others.

09 주어진 문장 다음에 이어질 글의 순서로 가장 적절한 것은?

With tobacco smoking being the leading cause of preventable deaths, Australia enacted its plain packaging regulations for cigarettes and tobacco products in December 2012 to discourage people from using tobacco products.

(A) According to the National Health Survey 2014-2015 of Australian Bureau of Statistics, the rate of smoking in the country declined by more than 10% between 2001 (28.2%) and 2015 (16.3%) due to a number of initiatives including the implementation of plain packaging.

(B) The effectiveness of plain packaging, however, was refuted by the leading tobacco companies in the country. They claimed the decrease in smoking rates to be insignificant and that plain packaging boosted the illegal tobacco market.

(C) The regulations required the majority of the packaging to be covered in health warnings to increase their effectiveness and remove any brand names and logos to make the packaging less attractive for the consumers.

① (A) - (C) - (B)
② (B) - (A) - (C)
③ (B) - (C) - (A)
④ (C) - (A) - (B)

10 빈칸에 들어갈 표현으로 가장 적절한 것은?

Everyone knows that language changes. It is easy to pick out words that have only been recently introduced (bromance, YOLO, derp) or sentence constructions that have gone out of style (How do you do? Have you a moment?), but we are constantly in the middle of language change that _____. Some of the biggest and most lasting changes to language happen slowly and imperceptibly. The Great Vowel Shift, for instance, was a series of pronunciation changes occurring over 350 years, and not really noticed for over 100 years after that. It resulted in an intelligibility gap between Modern and Middle English and created the annoying misalignment between English pronunciation and spelling. But it was impossible to see while it was going on.

① may be influenced by foreign languages
② may not be used for long periods of time
③ may be triggered by social and cultural factors
④ may not be noticeable for decades or even centuries

01 다음 중 밑줄 친 단어와 뜻이 가장 가까운 것은?

There was sporadic fighting involving English and Germany soccer fans in various parts of the city before the match.

① amenable ② scattered
③ relentless ④ implacable

02 다음 중 밑줄 친 단어와 뜻이 가장 가까운 것은?

The government is planning to establish laws to allow prosecutors to forcibly summon suspects and to punish those who commit perjury.

① parole ② felony
③ jailbird ④ mendacity

03 다음 중 밑줄 친 단어와 뜻이 가장 가까운 것은?

It was bought by a dealer who was convinced that the tapestries would make a comeback in the vast new homes being built for billionaires.

① respite ② resurgence
③ deferment ④ suspension

04 다음 빈칸 (A), (B)에 가장 적합한 것은?

Student: Good afternoon, professor. Is it your office hours right now?
Professor: Good afternoon. Yes it is my office hours now. You are welcome to come in.
Student: Thank you. I want to talk to you about the internship program you mentioned during class.
Professor: Oh, are you interested in applying for it next semester?
Student: Yeah. But I just have one concern. I was thinking of going abroad as an exchange student next semester. I can't decide which side to take.
Professor: Well, there are certainly ____(A)____ to both choices. But I think the internship program will offer a better opportunity to get some hands-on work experience.
Student: You're right. I'll ____(B)____ this concern. Thank you for your time, professor.
Professor: You're welcome. You can visit me anytime during my office hours.

① (A) pros and cons (B) mull over
② (A) the bottom line (B) mull over
③ (A) pros and cons (B) run short of
④ (A) the bottom line (B) run short of

05 밑줄 친 부분 중 어법상 가장 옳지 않은 것은?

Often the ① difference between feeling fulfilled at work and feeling empty, lost, annoyed, and burned out is all about ② if or not you're learning anything. This is another reason to listen. It's amazing how much more you learn when you pause, quiet your mind, and listen to what others say. This is true for peers to your left and right as well as the very teams you lead. Sometimes it's hard ③ to listen to your boss or an executive, especially if you don't agree 100 percent of the time. In some cases, you may not even like them. I get it. Remember, they're in their roles for a reason, and they just might know a few things. Be open and willing to listen to ④ what they say. You may not agree with everything you hear, but at least you listened.

06 밑줄 친 부분 중 어법상 가장 옳지 않은 것은?

Buildings arouse an empathic reaction in us through these ① projected experiences, and the strength of these reactions ② are determined by our culture. They tell stories, for their form and spatial organization ③ give us hints about how they should be used. Their physical layout encourages some uses and inhibits others; we do not go backstage in a theater ④ unless especially invited.

07 밑줄 친 부분 중 어법상 가장 옳지 않은 것은?

Like ① that of an actor, his or her interpretation is full of subtle timings and inflections. Performers project ② to an audience a mixture of their own feelings and the composer's intentions. Critics sometimes ③ are said about a particularly ④ convincing interpretation that a performer is identified with a work and its composer.

08 다음 글의 주제로 가장 적절한 것은?

A new study found that happiness has no effect on how long a person will live. University of Oxford researchers found the exact opposite of the common belief that sadness and tension cause poor health. Instead, they found that neither happiness nor sadness impacted a person's lifespan. "Many still believe that stress or unhappiness can directly cause disease, but they are simply confusing cause and effect," Richard Peto of the University of Oxford said. "Of course people who are ill tend to be unhappier than those who are well, but the UK Million Women Study shows that happiness and unhappiness do not have any direct effect on death rates." The findings showed that happiness may not prolong a person's life, and feeling blue doesn't predispose a person to health problems that can cause death.

① The impacts of happiness on mental health
② The cause and effect of stress and depression
③ Tips for avoiding deadly diseases and living a longer life
④ The relationship between someone's mood and his or her lifespan

09 밑줄 친 (A), (B)에 들어갈 말로 가장 적절한 것은?

Known as the leading cause of preventable deaths worldwide, smoking places people at risk of several tobacco-related diseases including lung cancer and heart disease. Unfortunately, while many people wish to stop smoking, they do not find it easy to do so. ___(A)___, according to studies, up to 70 percent of smokers wish to stop smoking, and up to 50 percent have reported attempting to quit within the past year but failing to do so. This challenge is due to the addictive nature of smoking. ___(B)___, smokers often need to follow a specific treatment plan for smoking cessation, which refers to the process of quitting the habit of smoking, in order to successfully stop smoking. Primarily due to the nicotine content that makes cigarettes highly addictive, the deeper and longer their attachment to cigarettes is, the harder the process of smoking cessation will be.

(A)	(B)
① However	Therefore
② Subsequently	That is
③ In addition	On the other hand
④ In fact	Thus

10 주어진 문장 다음에 이어질 글의 순서로 가장 적절한 것은?

Language changes very subtly whenever speakers come into contact with each other.

(A) Also, even if your family has lived in the same area for generations, you can probably identify a number of differences between the language you use and the way your grandparents speak.

(B) No two individuals speak identically: people from different geographical places clearly speak differently, but even within the same small community there are variations according to a speaker's gender, ethnicity, and social and educational background.

(C) Through our interactions with these different speakers, we encounter new words, expressions and pronunciations and integrate them into our own speech. In this way, we are making our own small contribution to language change.

① (A) - (B) - (C) ② (A) - (C) - (B)
③ (B) - (A) - (C) ④ (B) - (C) - (A)

기적사 복습 모의고사 7회

01 밑줄 친 부분과 의미가 가장 가까운 것은?

They argue that homeschooler's eclectic curriculum often excludes important subjects.

① scratches ② condones
③ subsumes ④ condemns

02 다음 중 밑줄 친 단어와 뜻이 가장 가까운 것은?

Parents must not give up on kids who act rebellious or seem socially awkward; this is a normal stage most youngsters go through and eventually outgrow.

① passive ② delirious
③ disobedient ④ sporadic

03 다음 중 밑줄 친 단어와 뜻이 가장 가까운 것은?

You start to think about various solutions to solve that problem, even if the problem is pernicious and as intractable as racism.

① dainty ② capital
③ exquisite ④ succulent

04 밑줄 친 부분과 의미가 가장 가까운 것을 고르시오.

Experienced salespeople claim there is a difference between being assertive and being pushy.

① thrilled ② brave
③ timid ④ aggressive

05 다음 글의 요지로 가장 적절한 것은?

A common view is that one of the main goals for nations should be to be a democracy. However, nations should not be satisfied when they had achieved democratic status. One of the subsequent goals ought to be to establish and maintain a high degree of quality of democracy. Of course this goal also applies to well-established democracies. For the legitimacy of a democratic system, it can be seen that a high degree of quality of democracy is important, and a low degree of quality of democracy can be seen as a serious democratic problem. For example, political participation through voting can be seen as a cornerstone in a democratic system. If voter turnout is low, the legitimacy of the election and the democratic system can come into question.

① Democracy can be beneficial.
② Not all democracy is the same.
③ It is difficult to reach high-quality democracy.
④ Voting is the most important act in a democratic society.

06 어법상 옳은 것은?

① The speaker quickly said this is that North America looks like from the Southern Hemisphere.
② Thought of as a relationship, leadership becomes a process of collaboration that occurs between leaders and followers.
③ Inequality doesn't offer benefits to anyone except the elite and is harmful to the whole society because the unnecessary conflicts it creates.
④ If we will think that people and relationships are like complex machines, we will probably see their problems as malfunctions in the machinery.

07 밑줄 친 부분 중 어법상 가장 옳지 않은 것은?

It should ① note, though, that no development in the Internet job age ② has reduced the importance of ③ the most basic job search skill: self-knowledge. Even in the Internet age, the job search starts with identifying individual job skills, sector interests, and ④ preferred workplace environment and interests.

08 다음 글의 제목으로 가장 적절한 것은?

Contemporary art can often be dismissed as being a bit pointless and lacking in skill. The clichéd "my five-year-old kid could do this" phrase is mentioned if an artist's work looks too simple. Yes, a lot of contemporary artworks do seem a bit basic at first glance, but it doesn't mean that they don't contain complex concepts — in fact, the ideas contained within these works are frequently more profound than those in much older, but more popular, paintings. And surely the more recent the artwork, the more relevant the message is for the modern viewer, right? Rachel Maclean's recent exhibition at HOME is an example of this. It was quite simple and not to everyone's taste, but the message it expressed of our relationship with social media and technology really struck a chord. There seems to be this ongoing belief that art should be a visual pleasure and nothing more. But art should conjure up emotions and provoke thoughts, even if it isn't pretty and complicated. In this sense, contemporary art deserves our appreciation and it's time it lost its undeserved bad reputation.

① Anyone Can Be a Contemporary Artist
② Is Contemporary Art Worth Looking At?
③ How Does Contemporary Art Affect Society?
④ Why Does Contemporary Art Look So Simple?

09 글의 흐름상 빈칸에 들어갈 표현으로 가장 옳은 것은?

The idea of clowns frightening people started gaining strength in the United States. In South Carolina, for example, people reported seeing individuals wearing clown costumes, often hiding in the woods or in cities at night. Some people said that the clowns were trying to lure children into empty homes or the woods. Soon, there were reports of threatening-looking clowns trying to frighten both children and adults. Although there were usually no reports of violence, and many of the reported sightings were later found to be false, this _____.

① benefited the circus industry
② promoted the use of clowns in ads
③ caused a nationwide panic
④ formed the perfect image of a happy clown

10 빈칸에 들어갈 표현으로 가장 적절한 것은?

Everyone knows that language changes. It is easy to pick out words that have only been recently introduced (bromance, YOLO, derp) or sentence constructions that have gone out of style (How do you do? Have you a moment?), but we are constantly in the middle of language change that _____. Some of the biggest and most lasting changes to language happen slowly and imperceptibly. The Great Vowel Shift, for instance, was a series of pronunciation changes occurring over 350 years, and not really noticed for over 100 years after that. It resulted in an intelligibility gap between Modern and Middle English and created the annoying misalignment between English pronunciation and spelling. But it was impossible to see while it was going on.

① may be influenced by foreign languages
② may not be used for long periods of time
③ may be triggered by social and cultural factors
④ may not be noticeable for decades or even centuries

11 밑줄 친 부분에 들어갈 말로 가장 적절한 것을 고르시오.

Mom: How are you feeling today?
Son: I'm starting to get a bit nervous. I have an important audition tomorrow.
Mom: Oh, really? I didn't know that. What are you auditioning for?
Son: I haven't told anyone yet. I am auditioning for the lead singer position in the school band.
Mom: Wow! That's wonderful! Son, don't worry too much. You have a heavenly voice. You doubtlessly _____ in the audition.
Son: Thank you, mom. You are my biggest support.

① break a leg
② make a killing
③ stand a chance
④ blow hot and cold

12 다음 빈칸 (A), (B), (C)에 가장 적합한 것은?

Clara: Hi, David! You look furious.
David: I'm very angry right now because there is a problem with the team project in progress.
Clara: You must be stressed out. What's bothering you?
David: One of my teammates wouldn't participate at all. So I told her very politely to be more responsible.
Clara: How did she behave after you told her so?
David: She ___(A)___ . I have no idea why she got mad.
Clara: Oh, it sounds like your teammate is someone who ___(B)___ her duties.
David: Well, I agree with you. She should ___(C)___ behave that way.

① (A) went Dutch
  (B) makes little of
  (C) fall prey to
② (A) hit the roof
  (B) makes little of
  (C) fall prey to
③ (A) hit the roof
  (B) makes little of
  (C) know better than to
④ (A) went Dutch
  (B) comes to terms with
  (C) know better than to

13 밑줄 친 부분 중 어법상 가장 옳지 않은 것은?

Often the ① difference between feeling fulfilled at work and feeling empty, lost, annoyed, and burned out is all about ② if or not you're learning anything. This is another reason to listen. It's amazing how much more you learn when you pause, quiet your mind, and listen to what others say. This is true for peers to your left and right as well as the very teams you lead. Sometimes it's hard ③ to listen to your boss or an executive, especially if you don't agree 100 percent of the time. In some cases, you may not even like them. I get it. Remember, they're in their roles for a reason, and they just might know a few things. Be open and willing to listen to ④ what they say. You may not agree with everything you hear, but at least you listened.

14 우리말을 영어로 잘못 옮긴 것은?

① 대다수의 기관에서 가장 중요한 것은 유능한 관리자들을 두는 것이다.
  → What matters most in the majority of organizations is having competent managers.
② 많은 진료소들이 치료법을 안내하기 위해 유전자 검사를 이용하고 있다.
  → Many clinics are using therapy to guide gene tests.
③ 요즘에는 신문들이 광고에서 훨씬 더 적은 돈을 번다.
  → Nowadays, newspapers make much less money from advertisements.
④ 통화의 가치는 대개 한 국가 경제의 힘을 반영한다.
  → A currency's value usually reflects the strength of a country's economy.

15 다음 글의 내용과 일치하지 않는 것은?

The U.S. has been demoted from a full democracy to a flawed democracy for the first time, according to the Economist Intelligence Unit. Every year, the firm's Democracy Index provides a snapshot of global democracy by scoring countries on five categories: electoral process and pluralism; civil liberties; the functioning of government; political participation; and political culture. Nations are then classified under four types of governments: full democracy, flawed democracy, hybrid regime and authoritarian regime. America's score fell to 7.98 in 2016 from 8.05 in the previous year, below the 8.00 threshold for a full democracy. That put the world's largest economy on the same footing as Italy, a country known for its fractious politics. A flawed democracy is a country with free elections but weighed down by weak governance, an underdeveloped political culture and low levels of political participation. Other flawed democracies in 2016 included Japan, France, Belgium, South Korea and India, all of which were deemed flawed democracies in 2015 as well.

① The U.S. had always been rated a full democracy before 2016.
② The Economist Intelligence Unit evaluates countries in multiple categories.
③ In 2015, the U.S. received a lower score than Belgium.
④ Italy had the title of a flawed democracy in 2016.

16 다음 글의 주제로 가장 적절한 것은?

A new study found that happiness has no effect on how long a person will live. University of Oxford researchers found the exact opposite of the common belief that sadness and tension cause poor health. Instead, they found that neither happiness nor sadness impacted a person's lifespan. "Many still believe that stress or unhappiness can directly cause disease, but they are simply confusing cause and effect," Richard Peto of the University of Oxford said. "Of course people who are ill tend to be unhappier than those who are well, but the UK Million Women Study shows that happiness and unhappiness do not have any direct effect on death rates." The findings showed that happiness may not prolong a person's life, and feeling blue doesn't predispose a person to health problems that can cause death.

① The impacts of happiness on mental health
② The cause and effect of stress and depression
③ Tips for avoiding deadly diseases and living a longer life
④ The relationship between someone's mood and his or her lifespan

17 밑줄 친 (A), (B)에 들어갈 말로 가장 적절한 것은?

The variation in how happiness is accepted across different cultures is evident in language. Words like 'happiness' and 'happy' carry different connotations in Eastern and Western cultures and can't always be directly translated. For example, Mandarin has multiple words for "happiness" that aren't a perfect equivalent to the English concept, since they can mean anything from "good mood" to "having meaning in life" or "having a good life".   (A)   , in Mandarin, happiness is also defined as "having a good death", which would be rather unthinkable in English-speaking cultures. In addition, the way happiness is defined in different languages points at how differently it's experienced across cultures. For instance, the Danish concept of "lykke" is translated as "happiness", but has very little to do with the way happiness is experienced in the United States, where it involves a state of celebration.   (B)   , the word for happiness in Hong Kong's Cantonese is linked to low arousal states and its meaning is closer to calm and relaxation rather than to celebration.

	(A)	(B)
①	Therefore	Likewise
②	However	That is
③	In fact	Similarly
④	Accordingly	By contrast

18 밑줄 친 부분 중 글의 흐름상 가장 어색한 것은?

In the Cheyenne tribes of North America, a certain type of warrior called a contrary could well be considered that particular culture's clown. The contraries communicated always in opposites – for instance shaking their heads to mean 'yes', and nodding to mean 'no'. If they wanted to warn about a shortage of firewood, they said, "We have lots of wood! Don't bring any more." This reversal extended beyond communication as well. ① They would wear their clothes backwards, bathe in dirt, and were even known to dry themselves with water. ② The reason a warrior might choose to become such a figure was to overcome fear. ③ A warrior was viewed by the people not as a maker of war but as a protector and leader, and warriors gained rank by performing and accumulating various acts of bravery in battle. ④ A contrary used a lance as a weapon that was said to make the bearer invulnerable to lightning. So people with a fear of thunder or lightning could become the tribe's clown warrior and conquer their phobia.

19 주어진 문장이 들어갈 위치로 가장 적절한 것은?

Now that this is a federal law, all states will have to comply.

The US Food and Drug Administration has officially raised the minimum age to buy tobacco products like cigarettes, electronic cigarettes, and vaping products that contain nicotine from 18 to 21. (①) By raising the age to buy tobacco products, the federal government is replicating what a number of states have been doing. (②) Nineteen states around the US plus Washington, DC, have already raised the minimum age to buy tobacco to 21. (③) The change could save thousands of lives. (④) Research shows it's important to try to prevent teens from smoking or vaping nicotine products, because they are the most likely to become addicted.

20 주어진 문장 다음에 이어질 글의 순서로 가장 적절한 것은?

Language changes very subtly whenever speakers come into contact with each other.

(A) Also, even if your family has lived in the same area for generations, you can probably identify a number of differences between the language you use and the way your grandparents speak.

(B) No two individuals speak identically: people from different geographical places clearly speak differently, but even within the same small community there are variations according to a speaker's gender, ethnicity, and social and educational background.

(C) Through our interactions with these different speakers, we encounter new words, expressions and pronunciations and integrate them into our own speech. In this way, we are making our own small contribution to language change.

① (A) - (B) - (C) ② (A) - (C) - (B)
③ (B) - (A) - (C) ④ (B) - (C) - (A)

01 밑줄 친 부분과 의미가 가장 가까운 것을 고르시오.

One of the immutable laws of television is that low ratings inevitably lead to cancellation.

① unchanging ② provisional
③ drastic ④ irresponsible

02 밑줄 친 부분과 의미가 가장 가까운 것을 고르시오.

Canny investors are starting to worry that the stock market might be due for a sharp fall.

① shrewd ② prestigious
③ impudent ④ curious

03 밑줄 친 부분과 의미가 가장 가까운 것을 고르시오.

Electric cars also are a key part of China's efforts to curb its unquenchable appetite for imported oil and gas, which communist leaders see as a strategic weakness.

① infallible ② aesthetic
③ adolescent ④ insatiable

04 밑줄 친 부분에 들어갈 말로 가장 적절한 것을 고르시오.

A: So, Mr. Wong, how long have you been living in New York City?
B: I've been living here for about seven years.
A: Can you tell me about your work experience?
B: I've been working at a pizzeria for the last three years.
A: What do you do there?
B: I seat the customers and wait on them.
A: How do you like your job?
B: It's fine. Everyone's really nice.
A: _____
B: It's just that I want to work in a more formal environment.
A: Okay. Is there anything else you would like to add?
B: I am really good with people. And I can also speak Italian and Chinese.
A: I see. Thank you very much. I'll be in touch shortly.
B: I hope to hear from you soon.

① So, what is the environment like there?
② Then, why are you applying for this job?
③ But are there any foreign languages you are good at?
④ And what qualities do you think are needed to work here?

05 우리말을 영어로 잘못 옮긴 것은?

① 내일 아침 일찍 저를 반드시 깨워주세요.
  → Be sure to wake me up early tomorrow morning.
② 사람들은 우리가 파산할 것으로 여겼으나, 우리는 그럭저럭 견뎌 나갔다.
  → People thought we would go bankrupt, but we managed to get by.
③ 수요가 공급을 초과하면 가격이 오르고 그 반대가 되면 내린다.
  → Prices go up when demand exceeds supply, and vice versa.
④ 나는 그가 그렇게 유명한 음악가가 되리라고는 전혀 생각하지 못했다.
  → Hardly did I dream before he became such a famous musician.

06 밑줄 친 부분 중 어법상 옳지 않은 것은?

Environmentalists argue that no system of waste disposal can be absolutely safe, ① either now or in the future. Governments and the nuclear industry have tried ② to find acceptable solutions. But in countries ③ where popular opinion is taken into consideration, no mutually acceptable solution has been found. As a result, most ④ spending fuel has been stored in the nuclear power plants where it was produced.

07 어법상 옳지 않은 것은?

① Because of its perfect cone shape and proximity to the beautiful Albay Gulf, Mount Tarn is a popular tourist attraction.
② Its base is 80 miles wide in circumference, and it stands a dramatic 8,077 feet tall.
③ The volcano locates in the center of Gulf National Park, where many people come to camp and climb.
④ Authorities hope that by issuing early warnings, they will help avoid major destruction and danger.

08 글의 흐름상 빈칸에 들어갈 가장 적절한 것은?

The notion that a product tested without branding is somehow being more objectively appraised is entirely _____. In the real world, we no more appraise things with our eyes closed and holding our nose than we do by ignoring the brand that is stamped on the product we purchase, the look and feel of the box it comes in, or the price being asked.

① correct
② reliable
③ misguided
④ unbiased

09 <보기> 글의 제목으로 가장 적절한 것은?

<보기>
Many visitors to the United States think that Americans take their exercise and free time activities too seriously. Americans often schedule their recreation as if they were scheduling business appointments. They go jogging every day at the same time, play tennis two or three times a week, or swim every Thursday. Foreigners often think that this kind of recreation sounds more like work than relaxation. For many Americans, however, their recreational activities are relaxing and enjoyable, or at least worthwhile, because they contribute to health and physical fitness.

① Health and fitness
② Popular recreational activities in the United States
③ The American approach to recreation
④ The definition of recreation

10 <보기> 글의 요지로 가장 적절한 것은?

<보기>
Feelings of pain or pleasure or some quality in between are the bedrock of our minds. We often fail to notice this simple reality because the mental images of the objects and events that surround us, along with the images of the words and sentences that describe them, use up so much of our overburdened attention. But there they are, feelings of myriad emotions and related states, the continuous musical line of our minds, the unstoppable humming of the most universal of melodies that only dies down when we go to sleep, a humming that turns into all-out singing when we are occupied by joy, or a mournful requiem when sorrow takes over.

① Feelings are closely associated with music.
② Feelings are composed of pain and pleasure.
③ Feelings are ubiquitous in our minds.
④ Feelings are related to the mental images of objects and events.

결국엔 성정혜 영어 하프모의고사
기적사 DAY 72

01 밑줄 친 부분과 의미가 가장 가까운 것을 고르시오.

> William passionately maintained that street vendors were not only dangerous but <u>irresponsible</u>.

① torpid   ② slothful
③ feckless   ④ strenuous

02 밑줄 친 부분과 의미가 가장 가까운 것을 고르시오.

> The shepherds who found a strange thing in the shed were <u>curious</u> about its softness.

① stony   ② uneven
③ inquisitive   ④ impassive

03 밑줄 친 부분과 의미가 가장 가까운 것을 고르시오.

> Members on both sides of Congress seem to show an <u>insatiable</u> appetite for debating European affairs.

① chaste   ② decent
③ prodigious   ④ unappeasable

04 밑줄 친 부분에 들어갈 말로 가장 적절한 것을 고르시오.

> A: What did you do yesterday?
> B: I went to celebrate my best friend's birthday. The party was held at a buffet.
> A: Oh, it must have been very fun! Did you enjoy the food?
> B: Yeah, _____.
> I ate so much that I was very full.
> A: It sure sounds like you really had a delicious meal.
> B: Indeed. I especially like the spaghetti and the chicken.

① I kept my shirt on
② I burned my fingers
③ I had butterflies in my stomach
④ my eyes were bigger than my stomach

05 우리말을 영어로 잘못 옮긴 것은?

① 권장량을 초과하는 것은 매우 위험하므로 권장량을 확인해야 한다.
→ It is too dangerous to exceed the recommending dose that you must check it.

② Tom이 사무실에 도착하자마자 그녀는 불평하기 시작했다.
→ Hardly had Tom arrived at the office when she started complaining.

③ 그것은 외견상으로 매우 좋은 생각인 것 같지만 분명히 문제가 있다.
→ It seems like a very good idea on the surface but there are sure to be problems.

④ 비록 그녀는 급여를 받지 못하게 되겠지만, 그녀는 자신이 어떻게든 간신히 그럭저럭 살아가게 될 것이라고 믿었다.
→ Although she would miss the paycheck, she believed that she would somehow manage to get by.

06 밑줄 친 부분 중 어법상 옳지 않은 것은?

New media may also include aromas, such as Disney's "Soaring Over California" attraction at the California Adventure theme park, ① where audiences smell orange orchards and pine forests while ② enjoying a simulated hang-gliding experience across the countryside. Makers of emerging forms of entertainment will likely continue to experiment with ways ③ how they can simulate and manipulate reality by ④ stimulating our senses.

07 어법상 옳지 않은 것은?

① I couldn't get him to do what I wanted him to do.
② Each of the students voiced his or her own complaints.
③ Tom knew that although the team would lose, they played with tremendous spirit.
④ The 35-years-old national captain says he needs a new challenge after 10 years in New York.

08 주어진 문장 다음에 이어질 글의 순서로 가장 적절한 것은?

Brand equity is the added value a product acquires as a result of past investments in the marketing activity for the brand.

(A) The simplest way to understand what it is is to understand the typical results of product sampling and comparison tests.
(B) When consumers report different opinions about branded and unbranded versions of identical products, it must be the case that knowledge about the brand has changed their perceptions, because consumers' perceptions of product performance are highly dependent on their impressions of the brand that goes along with it.
(C) One such test is blind taste test in which consumers sample a product without knowing the brand that they consume and then consume the same product knowing the brand.

① (A) - (B) - (C)   ② (A) - (C) - (B)
③ (B) - (A) - (C)   ④ (B) - (C) - (A)

09 빈칸 (A), (B)에 들어갈 표현으로 가장 적절한 것은?

Americans may not be too ___(A)___ to exercise after all. A new RAND Corporation study finds that Americans average more than 5 hours of free time each day. But instead of being physically active during their free hours, Americans report they spend most of that time looking at screens (televisions, phones or other devices). "There is a general perception among the public and even public health professionals that a lack of leisure time is a major reason that Americans do not get enough physical activity," said Dr. Deborah Cohen, co-author of the study. "But we found no evidence for those beliefs." These findings suggest getting Americans to devote at least 20 or 30 minutes each day to physical activity is ___(B)___. Increasing the public's awareness of how they actually use their time and creating messages that encourage Americans to reduce their screen time may help people become more physically active.

	(A)	(B)
①	indolent	ideal
②	busy	feasible
③	occupied	inevitable
④	lazy	possible

10 주어진 문장이 들어갈 위치로 가장 적절한 것은?

For instance, just thinking about something threatening can trigger an emotional fear response.

A feeling is a mental portrayal of what is going on in your body when you have an emotion and is the byproduct of your brain perceiving and assigning meaning to the emotion. Feelings are the next thing that happens after having an emotion, involve cognitive input, usually subconscious, and cannot be measured precisely. (①) They are sparked by emotions and colored by the thoughts, memories, and images that have become subconsciously linked with that particular emotion for you. (②) But it works the other way around too. (③) While individual emotions are temporary, the feelings they evoke may persist and grow over a lifetime. (④) Because emotions cause subconscious feelings which in turn initiate certain emotions and this goes on and on, your life can become a never-ending cycle of painful and confusing emotions, which produce negative feelings, which cause more negative emotions.

기적사 DAY 73

01 밑줄 친 부분과 의미가 가장 가까운 것을 고르시오.

This could lead to drastic consequences for the climate, biodiversity, and the global economy.

① lofty ② meek
③ sublime ④ submissive

02 밑줄 친 부분과 의미가 가장 가까운 것을 고르시오.

It would be impudent of you to make enemies of those who can help you.

① rash ② wary
③ remiss ④ assiduous

03 밑줄 친 부분과 의미가 가장 가까운 것을 고르시오.

According to the report, over 70 percent of parents with adolescent children have good relationships with each other.

① mellow ② caustic
③ juvenile ④ pungent

04 밑줄 친 부분에 들어갈 말로 가장 적절한 것을 고르시오.

Mom: I was looking for you! Where were you?
Daughter: I went on my morning workout to the gym. Do you need anything?
Mom: No, I went to your room and saw that you weren't in bed. I was just worried.
Daughter: Oh, I didn't want to wake you up when I left home. I'm sorry to worry you.
Mom: It's okay. How was your workout in the gym?
Daughter: I _____. I have no energy now.

① blew my top ② caught on fire
③ burned myself out ④ came to my senses

05 우리말을 영어로 잘못 옮긴 것은?

① 그녀가 수화기를 내려놓기가 무섭게 초인종이 울렸다.
→ She had scarcely put the phone down when the doorbell rang.
② 그 상품은 고객의 요구에 부응하여 개발될 것이다.
→ Customer demand will be developed in response to the product.
③ 그 축구팀은 이번 주에 경기를 잘하면 상황 악화를 간신히 중단시킬 수가 있을 것이다.
→ The soccer team will manage to stop the rot if they play well this week.
④ 그것들을 우편으로 발송한다면, 우편이 배달되는 시간을 반드시 고려해야 합니다.
→ If you mail them in, be sure to factor in the time for the mail to be delivered.

06 밑줄 친 부분 중 어법상 옳지 않은 것은?

For many years now, mediated entertainment ① such as TV and film has been able to stimulate our optical and auditory senses with sights and sounds. Some forms of new media, however, even ② engage our senses of touch and smell. The view which the wearer of some special device sees ③ it is projected on the screen behind him. Wearers become ④ immersed in the computerized scene and use the gloves to pick up and move simulated objects.

07 어법상 옳지 않은 것은?

① Jane liked her new hat so much that she wouldn't take it off.
② In case of they continue destroying the environment, their life will be affected.
③ When Tom entered the room, he found the cat lying motionless on the floor.
④ There was some very interesting news on the radio this morning about the earthquake.

08 다음 글의 요지로 가장 적절한 것은?

In 1975, many participants were invited for a blind taste test between Pepsi and Coca-Cola, and to no surprise people chose Pepsi, as they found Pepsi was sweeter; however in 2003, Neuroscientist Read Montague raised a question: if most of the people prefer Pepsi, why aren't its sales dominating the market? To get to the bottom of this, he called up some consumers and took them to the MRI scan to track brain activities. Half of the participants said they preferred Pepsi. His team found that a brain region called ventral putamen, associated with seeking reward, was active when people drank their favorite drink. However things changed when consumers were told what they were drinking. The ratio shifted to 3:1 in favor of Coke. This time they noticed a different part of the brain was active - medial prefrontal cortex which associates with higher thinking. At that point he concluded that brain was recalling ideas from Coke's commercials, and the emotions attached with the brand were overriding the product's actual quality.

* ventral putamen: 배 쪽 피각
* medial prefrontal cortex: 내측 전전두피질

① The importance of brand marketing should not be overlooked.
② Coke is still dominating the market although Pepsi won a blind taste test.
③ A positive brand image may be more important than a product's high quality.
④ Coca-Cola managed to maintain its market share against Pepsi by improving its taste.

09 다음 글의 내용과 일치하지 않는 것은?

Watching TV is America's favorite leisure activity, according to the Census Bureau data. Sitting in front of a television took up 2.7 hours daily, just over half of the total free time Americans have each day. The survey found that American men spend 5.5 hours watching TV on an average day — compared to women who spent 4.8 hours doing so. The survey also broke down how long people watched by age, employment status and more. Older people took more time out of their day for TV — those 65 and older watched more than four hours daily on average. On the other hand, the 15-44 age group watched the least, about two hours daily on average. The unemployed also spent more time watching daily on average — 3.78 hours — than those with either full-time or part-time jobs on average — 2.10 hours. This means even people with jobs are spending a lot of their free time, on average, watching some kind of television shows.

① Americans have on average less than 6 hours of free time each day.
② Males spend more time watching TV than females do.
③ Children under 15 watched TV more than those between 15 and 44 years of age did.
④ The 65 and older age group watched less hours than the unemployed group.

10 다음 밑줄 친 단어가 가리키는 대상이 나머지와 다른 것은?

The concept of feelings and emotions is fascinating by itself, but one of the most interesting parts of it is the phenomenon of gut feeling. Gut feeling is unconscious, irrational and intuitive. ① It can be either positive or negative. You might feel you can trust someone without actually knowing them, or you might feel in danger when, rationally speaking, there is no reasons to be afraid. The weirdest part is that sometimes ② it is actually right. Many attempts have been made to explain gut feeling. Some suggest ③ it can be explained by our previous experiences. It is like all of a sudden all your knowledge and experience manifests with no effort from your side. ④ It, of course, makes perfect sense. Having said that, you can also probably think of a time when gut feeling can't be explained by having previous experiences when it is correct.

01 밑줄 친 부분과 의미가 가장 가까운 것을 고르시오.

When it was not possible to lead the independence movement in Tibet, Dalai Lama left for India and set up the provisional government.

① casual ② callous
③ abiding ④ ephemeral

02 밑줄 친 부분과 의미가 가장 가까운 것을 고르시오.

The designer took first place at MIT's extremely prestigious annual science design competition.

① petty ② interim
③ authentic ④ prominent

03 밑줄 친 부분과 의미가 가장 가까운 것을 고르시오.

Recently, German researchers studied the images and aesthetic qualities of famous monuments in Europe to determine their values.

① shrill ② tasteful
③ mellifluous ④ cacophonous

04 밑줄 친 부분에 들어갈 말로 가장 적절한 것을 고르시오.

A: How do I look in this dress?
B: You look beautiful! The color looks really good on you.
A: Thank you so much. I bought this two days ago, but I'm not sure if I look okay in it.
B: You look just fine. Have some more confidence.
A: Don't I look fatter?
B: Not at all. Believe me, you look awesome. I _____ _____.

① step on it ② mean business
③ lose my temper ④ hit the bull's eye

05 우리말을 영어로 잘못 옮긴 것은?

① Tom이 그것을 말하자마자 그녀는 울음을 터트렸다.
→ No sooner had Tom said it than she burst into tears.
② 포도주 값은 산지에 따라 다르다.
→ The price of wine varies depending on where it comes from.
③ 매우 극소수의 사람들이 간신히 일과 학업을 병행할 수 있기 때문에 그들은 존경받을 만하다고 여겨진다.
→ They consider respectable because very few people manage to maintain a job and go to school.
④ 약물 치료를 받는 동안은, 병원에서 의사가 일러 준 금기 사항을 반드시 지키세요.
→ While you're on medication, be sure to observe the restrictions the doctor told you about at the hospital.

06 밑줄 친 부분 중 어법상 옳지 않은 것은?

When the harmony is broken, the body sends us ① informations, signals and symptoms, in very direct and obvious ways. ② It is necessary that we pay attention to these signals instead of ③ viewing them as burdens in our life. If we ignore or suppress health symptoms, they will become progressively louder and more extreme ④ as the body attempts to capture our attention.

07 어법상 옳지 않은 것은?

① A number of people in exile lives under the threat of assassination.
② Doing fieldwork was one of the common methods used by anthropologists.
③ William did not arrive on time because he had worked late the night before.
④ For many decades, people have been trying to find out if the alien really exists.

08 다음 글의 제목으로 가장 적절한 것은?

Blind testing aims to assess a product based on its intrinsic merits by hiding any reference to the wider brand. This avoids results being influenced by any halo effect or negative associations set up by previous experiences. This approach is effective in giving market researchers a clear picture of the test product's absolute appeal relative to those of competitors or previous versions of that item. For brands struggling for appeal, this can be useful in establishing whether issues are rooted in a brand's image or the products themselves. For brands with high appeal, it's helpful to understand whether their products are actually 'good' or ratings are flattered by brand halo.

① What Is Blind Testing for?
② Why Is Blind Testing Pointless?
③ How Is Blind Testing Undertaken?
④ How Are Blind and Branded Testing Different?

09 밑줄 친 부분 중 글의 흐름상 가장 어색한 것은?

When the French government instituted a policy that would allow employees to disconnect from work email while they're not in the office in 2017, many American workers may have looked across the ocean with jealousy. ① Though the new French law didn't set any hard-and-fast rules, it was designed to help workers limit the amount of time that work email infringes upon leisure time. ② It's just an example of the many labor laws and norms that tend to leave European workers with a more even work-life balance than their U.S. counterparts. For instance, in 2015, the French worked an average of 1,482 hours a year, while American workers worked about 1,790 hours. ③ Meanwhile, U.S. workers — who receive about 15 days off per year — also get less vacation time than their European counterparts, who get about 30. ④ Also, American workers like to spend even their leisure time doing something productive, whereas Europeans prefer doing something fun and stress-free. What's more, while American employees take about 73 percent of their allotted vacation time, German and French workers take nearly all of the vacation time allowed.

10 다음 글에서 필자가 주장하는 것으로 가장 적절한 것은?

We use the words "emotions" and "feelings" interchangeably, to mean the same thing. However, emotions and feelings are distinct. They are just highly related things like two sides of the same coin. One side of the coin is an emotion: a physical response to change that is almost hard-wired and universal. The other side of the coin is your feeling: mental associations and other reactions to an emotion that are personal and gained through experience. Despite seeming the same, emotions actually proceed to feelings. Emotions are more predictable and easily understood than feelings, which are often idiosyncratic and confusing. Whereas emotions are inborn and common to us all, the meanings they acquire and the feelings they prompt are very personal. Feelings are shaped by individual temperament and experience; they vary enormously from person to person and from situation to situation. There are so many ways to feel a particular emotion.

① Emotions are subjective and feelings are objective.
② Emotions are instinctual and feelings are acquired.
③ Emotions and feelings are universal across cultures.
④ Emotions are mental states and feelings are physical sensations.

기적사 DAY 75

01 밑줄 친 부분과 의미가 가장 가까운 것을 고르시오.

When there are big life changes, unchanging traditions can help you stay strong and carry on.

① volatile ② turbulent
③ perdurable ④ tempestuous

02 밑줄 친 부분과 의미가 가장 가까운 것을 고르시오.

She has suffered so many hardships since she was a child that she has become shrewd.

① dim ② astute
③ murky ④ radiant

03 밑줄 친 부분과 의미가 가장 가까운 것을 고르시오.

I soon found an infallible way to draw a red herring across the path if she became too excited.

① inept ② strong
③ clumsy ④ efficacious

04 밑줄 친 부분에 들어갈 말로 가장 적절한 것을 고르시오.

Adele: Evan, you look so concerned!
Evan: I lost my wallet, which I got returned this morning. But someone took all the cash inside it.
Adele: Oh no, what a mean person! How much cash did you have in your wallet?
Evan: I carried about $100. It was for my textbook.
Adele: I feel really sorry for you. The person who took the money should have some _____.
Evan: I hope so.

① a close call ② a double take
③ the pang of conscience ④ the long and short of it

05 우리말을 영어로 잘못 옮긴 것은?

① 그녀는 도착하자마자 병이 났다.
 → She had no sooner arrived when she fell ill.
② Tom은 틀림없이 언론계에서 명성을 날릴 것이다.
 → Tom is sure to make himself famous in journalism.
③ 주요 전기 공급은 허리케인 Sandy에 의해 끊긴 상태였다.
 → The main electricity supply was cut off by Hurricane Sandy.
④ 그 회사는 고등법원에서 간신히 파산 선고를 받았다.
 → The company managed to be declared bankrupt in the High Court.

06 밑줄 친 부분 중 어법상 옳지 않은 것은?

① Whether or not we can catch up on sleep on the weekend ② is a hotly debated topic among sleep researchers; the latest evidence suggests that while it isn't ideal, it ③ help. When Peter Liu, a UCLA sleep researcher, brought chronically sleep-restricted people into the lab for a weekend of sleep during ④ which they slept about 10 hours per night, they showed improvements in the ability of insulin to process blood sugar.

07 어법상 옳지 않은 것은?

① You shouldn't touch anything unless you know what you're doing.
② She doesn't mind spending money on training if it improves productivity.
③ Since the business was known to everybody, many similar stores had been opened.
④ A novel that was serialized in the newspaper is going to be published in book form.

08 다음 글의 밑줄 친 부분 중 문맥상 단어의 쓰임이 적절하지 않은 것은?

Consumers determine their preferences for products and services based on ① various factors like the product's attributes and their personal attitudes toward the product. However, another factor that plays a key role is the shared and unique aspects of the products in the relevant choice set they are ② facing. Thus, the process of determining what product to buy takes into account the shared characteristics of the product like its quality and its unique characteristics like brand name. The decision also involves the ③ indistinctiveness of the purchaser. Examples of such factors include the personal characteristics of the purchaser like socio-economic level, individual characteristics like personality and situational characteristics like the purpose of the purchase. Furthermore, the ④ interaction between these characteristics can also have an effect on this choice. This task of choosing a product can be even more complicated when many different types of characteristics are involved.

09 다음 글의 요지로 가장 적절한 것은?

As recently as the 19th century, 30 percent of all the energy used in the American workplace was provided by human muscle power; today, the percentage is minuscule. In most ways, the transition from an agricultural economy to an industrial society to today's information age has been a great boon. But something has also been lost. America has become a nation of spectators. About 30 percent of adults are entirely sedentary and another 45 percent don't get enough physical activity, which means only a quarter of all Americans get the exercise they need. The real situation may be even worse. Most people who say they exercise report walking as their only regular physical activity. But when researchers from the CDC evaluated more than 1,500 people who said they were walkers, they found that only 6 percent walked often enough, far enough, or briskly enough to meet the current standards for health. Even people who report intense activity often overstate their efforts.

① Walking is an ideal exercise for most people in the U.S.
② Generally speaking, people in the U.S. are not physically active enough.
③ Most people actually do not work out as intensely as they think they do.
④ The American workforce has dramatically changed since the 19th century.

10 빈칸에 들어갈 표현으로 가장 적절한 것은?

Over many years, Antonio Damasio investigated patients who had sustained injuries to the frontal lobe, the area responsible for tasks related to reasoning, attention, planning, sequencing, and reorientation of behavior, and suffered changes to behavioral aspects _____.
For example, Phineas Gage worked for the railway industry. One day, an iron rod was driven into the left side of his face and destroyed part of his frontal lobe. Surprisingly, he survived this experience and, although he was able to recover most of his mental functions, he was no longer himself. He became irascible, moody, and impatient. Also, Elliot, a successful lawyer, suffered a brain tumor on the top of his forehead. It was surgically removed but, similarly to Gage, there were drastic changes in his behavior. Intellectually he was brilliant as always but he was completely indifferent not only to what had happened to him, but to tragedies in general.

* frontal lobe: 전두엽

① linked to intelligence
② connected to emotions
③ associated with memory
④ relevant to mental functions

기적사 DAY 76

01 밑줄 친 부분과 뜻이 가장 유사한 단어를 고르면?

The name England is derived from the Angles, one of the Germanic tribes which established monarchies in lowland Britain in the 5th century, after the final withdrawal of the Romans in 409.

① collapse ② invasion
③ surrender ④ retreat

02 밑줄 친 부분과 뜻이 가장 유사한 단어를 고르면?

The distinguished businesswoman finds herself unable to jettison her lower-middle-class prejudices.

① discard ② digress
③ denounce ④ deny

03 문맥상 빈칸에 들어갈 가장 적절한 것은?

Usually several skunks live together; however, adult male striped skunks are _____ during the summer.

① nocturnal ② solitary
③ predatory ④ dormant

04 다음 대화 중 어색한 것은?

① A: I'm going to China next month.
   B: Where in China?
② A: I have some good news.
   B: What is it?
③ A: Get me some wine from your trip to Brazil.
   B: You bet.
④ A: I like winter sports.
   B: I envy you.
⑤ A: May I have seconds?
   B: Help yourself.

05 어법상 가장 옳지 않은 것은?

① Culture shock is the mental shock of adjusting to a new country and a new culture which may be dramatically different from your own.
② A recent study finds that listening to music before and after surgery helps patients cope with related stress.
③ By brushing at least twice a day and flossing daily, you will help minimize the plaque buildup.
④ The existence of consistent rules are important if a teacher wants to run a classroom efficiently.

06 밑줄 친 부분 중 어법상 가장 옳지 않은 것은?

I ① convinced that making pumpkin cake ② from scratch would be ③ even easier than ④ making cake from a box.

07 어법상 가장 옳지 않은 문장은?

① Born in Genoa, Italy, Piccolo Paganini was one of the greatest composers of the nineteenth century. ② While he widely acclaimed as a violinist, Paganini had other musical talents which included tuning, arranging, and composing. ③ More often than not, he turned to the viola and the piano, and in his last years began to practice as an orchestra conductor. ④ But above all he left many beautiful scores for the violin concerto.

08 〈보기〉 글의 분위기로 가장 적절한 것은?

<보기>
I go to the local schoolyard, hoping to join in a game. But no one is there. After several minutes of standing around, dejected under the netless basketball hoops and wondering where everybody is, the names of those I expected to find awaiting me start to fill my mind. I have not played in a place like this for years. What was that? What was I thinking of, coming here? When I was a child, a boy, I went to the schoolyard to play. That was a long time ago. No children here will ever know me. Around me the concrete is empty except for pebbles, bottles, and a beer can that I kick, clawing a scary noise out of the pavement.

① calm and peaceful   ② festive and merry
③ desolate and lonely ④ horrible and scary

09 <보기> 글의 내용과 일치하는 것은?

<보기>
In the American Southwest, previously the Mexican North, Anglo-America ran into Hispanic America. The meeting involved variables of language, religion, race, economy, and politics. The border between Hispanic America and Anglo-America has shifted over time, but one fact has not changed: it is one thing to draw an arbitrary geographical line between two spheres of sovereignty; it is another to persuade people to respect it. Victorious in the Mexican-American War in 1848, the United States took half of Mexico. The resulting division did not ratify any plan of nature. The borderlands were an ecological whole; northeastern Mexican desert blended into southeastern American desert with no prefiguring of nationalism. The one line that nature did provide — the Rio Grande — was a river that ran through but did not really divide continuous terrain.

① The borderlands between America and Mexico signify a long history of one sovereignty.
② While nature did not draw lines, human society certainly did.
③ The Mexican-American War made it possible for people to respect the border.
④ The Rio Grande has been thought of as an arbitrary geographical line.

10 <보기> 글을 문맥에 가장 어울리게 순서대로 배열한 것은?

<보기>
㉠ The trigger for the aggressive driver is usually traffic congestion coupled with a schedule that is almost impossible to meet.
㉡ Unfortunately, these actions put the rest of us at risk. For example, an aggressive driver who resorts to using a roadway shoulder to pass may startle other drivers and cause them to take an evasive action that results in more risk or even a crash.
㉢ As a result, the aggressive driver generally commits multiple violations in an attempt to make up time.
㉣ Aggressive driving is a traffic offense or combination of offenses such as following too closely, speeding, unsafe lane changes, failing to signal intent to change lanes, and other forms of negligent or inconsiderate driving.

① ㉠-㉢-㉡-㉣
② ㉠-㉣-㉢-㉡
③ ㉣-㉠-㉢-㉡
④ ㉣-㉡-㉢-㉠

01 밑줄 친 부분과 뜻이 가장 유사한 단어를 고르면?

The article published in the New York Times predicates that the market collapse was caused by weakness of the dollar.

① truce ② turmoil
③ disruption ④ retardation

02 밑줄 친 부분과 뜻이 가장 유사한 단어를 고르면?

Although they were divided by different ideologies, they didn't deny their common ethnicity.

① rescind ② eschew
③ forswear ④ repudiate

03 밑줄 친 부분과 뜻이 가장 유사한 단어를 고르면?

Scientists believe the animal to have been nocturnal, like other mammals of the time were thought to be.

① dusky ② diurnal
③ luminous ④ noctivagant

04 다음 대화 중 어색한 것은?

① A: I appreciate your support.
   B: It's no big deal.
② A: Can I borrow your pencil sharpener?
   B: Here you go. It's my pencil.
③ A: The weather is so nice! I want to go on a picnic.
   B: I think so, too. Why don't we take some food and drinks when we go on a picnic?
④ A: If you have a problem, please contact me right away.
   B: Don't worry. I'll make sure everything is alright.

05 어법상 가장 옳지 않은 것은?

① It takes for him a while to adjust to living alone.
② A helicopter was scrambled to help rescue five young climbers.
③ The research suggests that listening to soporific music while driving is dangerous.
④ To be conscious that we are perceiving or thinking is to be conscious of our own existence.

06 밑줄 친 부분 중 어법상 가장 옳지 않은 것은?

I am also ① convinced that users should be protected ② from corrupt knowledge by intermediary services. There ③ needs to be some forms of guides and filters ④ provided by responsible individuals and organizations.

07 어법상 가장 옳지 않은 문장은?

① Leaders with positive emotional states of mind are like human magnets. ② People naturally gravitate to them and want to follow them. ③ Such leaders inspire enthusiasm in their organizations and attract the best people to work for them. ④ Conversely, leaders who emit negative emotional states of mind, which are irritable and bossy, repel people and have few followers.

08 다음 글에 나타난 화자의 심경으로 가장 적절한 것은?

Wandering through my old town, peering into closed shops, sauntering through desolate playgrounds and parks, and watching the lights in upstairs windows slowly extinguished as time ticked by were an extraordinary experience for me. There are so many moments that make up a person's life, and ones are added with each passing second, but how many of us ever take the time to languish in the cottony folds of memory? How many of us really want to? I think we all do. I think there is always a tiny box somewhere, filled with a moment you would relive over and over again. But do we ever shrink ourselves down to size so we can fit inside it? Most of us don't. We grow larger and more complicated each year, and the box seems smaller and smaller, until one day it becomes impossible to find, so that it is permanently, but unknowingly filed away, lost in the constant reshuffling of life and time. But that night I felt like I had found all my little boxes and I was in the mood for opening them all.

① skeptical and wary   ② lonely and depressed
③ pleased and delighted   ④ alarmed and distressed

09 주어진 문장 다음에 이어질 글의 순서로 가장 적절한 것은?

History has blurred the details, but the tale hangs on a boozy dispute, angry words, a scuffle and a gunshot.

(A) Some say John Weller struck Andrew Gray in the jaw; others say he tried to strangle Andrew Gray, but in both accounts, Andrew Gray shot John Weller in the thigh. The border survey, less than a year old, was a mess.

(B) It was October 1849. Commissioner John Weller and surveyor Andrew Gray had been sent to the border of the United States and Mexico to mark a line that existed only on maps, and the work was not going well.

(C) This dispute was just one of many problems that cropped up while the U.S. struggled to define its southern border after the Mexican-American War. Finally, a line had been drawn, but the border was far from settled.

① (A) - (B) - (C) ② (B) - (A) - (C)
③ (B) - (C) - (A) ④ (C) - (A) - (B)

10 다음 글의 제목으로 가장 적절한 것은?

The National Highway Traffic Safety Administration defines aggressive driving as occurring when "an individual commits a combination of moving traffic offenses so as to endanger other persons or property." Most people drive aggressively from time to time and many drivers are not even aware they are doing it. Many psychological factors are at play in aggressive driving. Human beings are naturally prone to territoriality and have the tendency to view their vehicle as an extension of their personal domain. They feel threatened by other vehicles and respond aggressively or out of an instinct to self-protection. Driving may also lead some to feel a sense of power behind the wheel. Someone normally courteous and polite might become aggressive when driving. Our natural competitive instinct can also be a factor in aggressive driving. Some drivers respond to being overtaken by another vehicle as a challenge. This, in turn may lead drivers to make risky overtaking maneuvers.

① Who Drives Aggressively?
② What Causes Aggressive Driving?
③ How Is Aggressive Driving Defined?
④ Why Is Aggressive Driving Dangerous?

01 밑줄 친 부분과 뜻이 가장 유사한 단어를 고르면?

He is remembered as the hero who saved Korea from Japanese invasion during the Imjin War in the Joseon period.

① coup ② chink
③ rupture ④ encroachment

02 밑줄 친 부분과 뜻이 가장 유사한 단어를 고르면?

The Seoul Plaza is the citizens' place used to denounce authoritarian regime in quest for democracy in the past.

① expel ② acquit
③ recount ④ condemn

03 밑줄 친 부분과 뜻이 가장 유사한 단어를 고르면?

Solitary drinking without a friend can make you more sad and confused.

① sole ② surly
③ dubious ④ convivial

04 다음 대화 중 어색한 것은?

① A: I have to wake up early tomorrow.
   B: Do you have an early schedule?
② A: Look out the window! It's snowing!
   B: Wow! It's the first snow of the year.
③ A: It's too dim here. Could you please turn on the light?
   B: Sure. Where is the switch?
④ A: Don't walk on the ice. It might not be frozen even if it looks so.
   B: I like walking on frozen ice.

05 어법상 가장 옳지 않은 것은?

① Every person has to decide what is right for him or her.
② The operation, which spanned eleven countries, resulted in 300 arrests.
③ She was seen enter the building about the time the crime was committed.
④ The injury made it impossible for him to think of becoming a professional baseball player.

06 밑줄 친 부분 중 어법상 가장 옳지 않은 것은?

If from this land, which ① is your property, you would cultivate daily as many feet ② as you cover with your lazy body, you would reap every year ③ very more corn ④ than you see upon the cart here.

07 어법상 가장 옳지 않은 문장은?

① Our essentially subtropical body isn't well suited to life in the Arctic because we don't have the fur of polar bears or the thick, insulating fat of sea mammals. ② But we can make fur clothing, shelters to contain warmth, and weapons with which we hunt and defend ourselves. ③ These items are good examples of cultural adaptation, which show how culture uses to survive the natural world. ④ Keep in mind, though, that people must also survive the cultural world they inhabit.

08 다음 글의 요지로 가장 적절한 것은?

Most of us have memories of playing outdoors. Even if growing up in the city, there was usually a park or green area where children could congregate to play and use their imagination. Unfortunately, as new developments go up, it seems our children are being forgotten. Children spend a lot of time in enclosed spaces nowadays, at home, in school and inside a car traveling between the two, but they are also on stricter time schedules with less free time to enjoy playing outside. However, giving children the space and freedom to play outdoors will bring many benefits such as health benefits and opportunities to build various relationships and appreciate nature. Children learn by experience and through their senses. When indoors, your children's senses are more limited to sight and sound, but when outdoors, their development and educational potential can be maximized. This is why we need green spaces, parks and gardens in our local neighborhoods where our children can go and enjoy the outdoors.

① Through play, kids can make true friends.
② Big cities lack green space due to buildings.
③ There are advantages to children playing outside.
④ Compared to the past, today's children mostly play indoors.

09 다음 글의 제목으로 가장 적절한 것은?

When rains fall and creeks rise, residents of this small city in the state's south know which streets to avoid as floodwaters race toward its namesake river just a few hundred feet downslope. Now, with a steel border fence as high as 30 feet slated to be built between the city and the Rio Grande — which in Texas doubles as the U.S.-Mexico border — locals worry that flooding will worsen, just as it has in other border communities where fences and waterways intersect. During heavy rains, the creeks carry debris and trash. The fence could trap this material, blocking the water's natural path and sending it through streets and into homes. Scientists who have researched the possible damage are particularly concerned about effects in the Lower Rio Grande Valley, one of the most ecologically diverse regions along the entire 1,954-mile U.S.-Mexico border and home to scores of farms and towns. The consequences could be dire for both the local economy and the environment.

① Floodwaters Contain Hidden Dangers
② How to Prepare for Flash Flooding in Texas
③ Along the Border, Fences Are Being Erected
④ Planned Barriers Could Cause More Severe Flooding

10 다음 글의 주제로 가장 적절한 것은?

When narcissists feel their needs aren't met, when they feel shamed or criticized, or when they feel others' behaviors impose on them in some way, this can trigger what is referred to as "narcissistic rage," even on the road. Although all of us can become frustrated or angry when sitting in traffic, or when we're in a hurry and someone is driving too slowly in front of us, for most people the frustration is temporary. It's also unaccompanied by the need to punish those around us. And despite temporary anger or frustration, most people care enough about their passengers to place their safety above the thirst for vengeance. This is not the case for narcissistic drivers, however. In general, narcissists lack empathy, are insolent, and believe that they are not bound by the normal rules; these qualities extend to narcissists' driving behaviors. Specifically, narcissists are more likely to drive aggressively and engage in dangerous driving behaviors.

① the characteristics and behaviors of narcissists
② the reasons why you should avoid narcissistic drivers
③ the connection between narcissism and aggressive driving
④ the causes of narcissism and narcissistic personality disorder

기적사 DAY 79

01 밑줄 친 부분과 뜻이 가장 유사한 단어를 고르면?

The textbook published in 1979 specified independence was the result of not only Japan's <u>surrender</u>, but also the efforts of independence fighters.

① sanction
② resignation
③ capitulation
④ acquiescence

02 밑줄 친 부분과 뜻이 가장 유사한 단어를 고르면?

If you allow me to <u>digress</u> for a moment, I explain what happened previously.

① trim
② deck
③ deviate
④ ramble

03 밑줄 친 부분과 뜻이 가장 유사한 단어를 고르면?

The white shark dates back more than 50 million years and is the world's largest <u>predatory</u> fish.

① raptorial
② rapacious
③ herbivorous
④ omnivorous

04 다음 대화 중 어색한 것은?

① M: Do you know how to swim?
　W: I'm actually really good at swimming.
② M: Where should I hang my clothes?
　W: You should hang them in the balcony.
③ M: What do you want to have for lunch?
　W: I have no appetite these days. You should pick the menu.
④ M: I really want to see your childhood photos.
　W: I went through a lot of things during my childhood.

05 어법상 가장 옳지 않은 것은?

① Keeping early hours is a doorway to health.
② Cotton clothings allow your skin to breathe.
③ This year's fashions are quite different from those of last year.
④ It is essential that your sign appear on your loan application form.

06 밑줄 친 부분 중 어법상 가장 옳지 않은 것은?

For my son and me, it was a ① lovely gift to start off the new year. She ② reminded me that life is too short to not lend a ③ helping hand when the opportunity ④ is arisen.

07 어법상 가장 옳지 않은 문장은?

① This is now causing its own problems as storage ponds designing to store a few years' waste become filled or overflowing. ② One avenue that has been explored is the reprocessing of spent fuel to remove the active ingredients. ③ Some of the recovered material can be recycled as fuel. ④ The remainder must be stored safely until it has become inactive.

08 빈칸에 들어갈 표현으로 가장 적절한 것은?

One of the major sociocultural factors that negatively affect children's play opportunities is the increasing trend amongst parents _____.
As they perceive the outside environment as dangerous or harmful for various reasons, they adopt a risk averse attitude by keeping children indoors or allowing them to play in predesignated places that are known to be safe – such as the school yard or certain playgrounds. The reasons for such overprotectiveness can vary in degree from place to place and from parent to parent. However Singer et al. revealed through their survey of mothers across sixteen countries in Asia, Europe, Africa, South, and North America, that fear of traffic accidents, germs, violence, gangs and possible abduction were commonplace among mothers' globally – which they cite as a possible cause for the reduction in children's spontaneous play over the last two decades in the studied countries.

① to be excessively protective of themselves
② to be with their children most of the time
③ to raise their children naturally and simplistically
④ to be overly solicitous about their children's safety

09 주어진 문장이 들어갈 위치로 가장 적절한 것은?

In fact, this policing wasn't always aimed at keeping them out.

Donald Trump's decision to send National Guard troops to the U.S.-Mexican border is only the latest in a long history of U.S. militarization of its national boundaries. Indeed, America's southern border — which has shifted multiple times with U.S. expansion — was arguably formed through violence. (①) Texas and American militias used force to establish that border in the 1830s and 1840s, capturing modern-day states like California, Texas, and all of the American southwest from Mexico. (②) In the decades after, the both official and vigilante groups violently regulated the movement of people across that border — be they Native Americans, escaped slaves, Chinese immigrants, or Mexicans. (③) The Native Americans forced out of Texas had lived either in the area or further east before European colonizers violently pushed them West. (④) Enslaved people from Africa were another group whose movement vigilantes tried to police. Slave catchers who monitored the border weren't trying to keep anyone out — they were trying to keep enslaved people in.

10 밑줄 친 부분 중 글의 흐름상 가장 어색한 것은?

Driving lawfully and cautiously is one of the most important things that we do every day. Our lives, as well as the people we share the road with, depend on us making careful decisions behind the wheel. ① You can never count on other drivers to always do the right thing, so sometimes driving defensively is an important part of being a safe driver. ② A defensive driver is one who is always alert and ready to make an adjustment necessary to accommodate an unforeseen circumstance. ③ Using defensive driving practices will put everyone's safety first, but sometimes the line between defensive and aggressive driving can get blurry. A defensive driver knows that anything can happen any time, like when driving defensively around semis. ④ The flow of traffic, weather, and road conditions can change in an instant and require immediate adjustments to stay safe while driving. A defensive driver is ready to make those changes while always keeping their composure. A defensive driver is also always ready to react to another driver's mistake.

결국엔 성정혜 영어 하프모의고사
기적사 DAY 80

기출 하프 □ 파생 하프 ☑ 복습 모의고사 □
소요 시간 : / 15분   맞은 개수 : / 10개

01 밑줄 친 부분과 뜻이 가장 유사한 단어를 고르면?

> But according to the results of a newly published study, these advances have recently been showing signs of <u>retreat</u>.

① asylum   ② upsurge
③ recession   ④ sanctuary

02 밑줄 친 부분과 뜻이 가장 유사한 단어를 고르면?

> When they are no longer hot, peel them, <u>discard</u> the seeds and stem, and cut them lengthwise into strips.

① bin   ② spurn
③ retain   ④ loathe

03 밑줄 친 부분과 뜻이 가장 유사한 단어를 고르면?

> Some plants evade dry seasons through their seed which can even be <u>dormant</u> for several years.

① incidental   ② bouncy
③ judicious   ④ diapausing

04 다음 대화 중 어색한 것은?

① A: Have you done your assignment?
   B: I stayed up all night to finish it.
② A: Did you submit your work online?
   B: Yes, I barely met the deadline.
③ A: Don't step on the pedal too hard.
   B: I won't. The pedal is too weak to withstand the pressure.
④ A: Check for any signs of fever before visiting the hospital.
   B: She must have spring fever as she kept getting drowsy.

05 어법상 가장 옳지 않은 것은?

① Each of the toys has a variety of colors and shapes.
② The jacket, with the blue tie you bought, looks really nice.
③ The opposition party demanded the persons involved in the incidents step down.
④ A test for color blindness is so a familiar thing that most people take it for granted.

06 밑줄 친 부분 중 어법상 가장 옳지 않은 것은?

The idea of a fish in a freshwater lake ① struggling to accumulate salts inside ② their body ③ to mimic the ocean ④ reminds the other great contradiction of the biosphere.

07 어법상 가장 옳지 않은 문장은?

① That's because being a good writer is about more than writing. ② Clear writing is a sign of clear thinking. ③ Good writers know how to communicate. ④ They are made things easy to understand.

08 다음 글의 밑줄 친 부분 중 문맥상 단어의 쓰임이 적절하지 않은 것은?

Currently, one of the most ① concerning aspects of raising children is the amount of time they spend in front of screens. When children focus their attention onto a screen, it is a very ② passive form of learning or entertainment. Instead of using their own imaginations to learn about the world and create something, children are mere recipients of visual and auditory stimulation that may or may not require some response using fine motor skills. This is a very ③ unartificial way of learning and does not engage children in a kinesthetic manner using their entire bodies. Imaginative and creative play is a more ④ natural way for children to learn about the world and does involve the whole body. Children manipulate and touch various play materials. They express themselves through play both verbally and non-verbally. They use all of their muscles and senses to move around. Actively using their large and small muscles as well as their different senses in play, children develop healthy, strong, and complete neurological connections in their brains.

09 다음 글의 밑줄 친 부분 중 문맥상 단어의 쓰임이 적절하지 않은 것은?

The leading cause of war in history involves territorial disputes such as competition over Alsace-Lorraine, Kashmir, the Golan Heights, and the Beagle Channel. Territorial disputes occur when official representatives of one country make ① explicit statements claiming sovereignty over a specific piece of territory that is claimed or administered by another country. The Issue Correlates of War (ICOW) Project has identified over 800 territorial disputes globally since 1816. Territorial disputes lead to militarized conflict more ② frequently than other types of diplomatic disputes. Countries that share ③ contiguous borders are more likely to fight wars with each other than distant states, especially if they have ④ agreements over specific pieces of territory. Territory that is more valuable because of natural resources, religious sites, or historical homeland claims generates more violence.

10 주어진 문장이 들어갈 위치로 가장 적절한 것은?

Many employee driving safety programs take the approach that aggressive driving starts and stops with the person behind the wheel.

We've all seen the effects of aggressive driving and road rage. Many companies with extensive fleets conduct some sort of driver safety training. (①) Most of these fleet safety programs focus on the what, where and when of driver safety. But all too often they miss out on an important question — who? (②) Most of the time, however, truckers and other professional drivers aren't the initial cause of road rage. (③) Instead, how they drive is influenced by other drivers. (④) Drivers may begin the workday with the best intentions of driving safely, but as the day goes on, conflicts and frustration with other drivers can set in. The combination of these factors can leave the drivers much more likely to drive aggressively.

기적사 복습 모의고사 8회

01 밑줄 친 부분과 뜻이 가장 유사한 단어를 고르면?

Although they were divided by different ideologies, they didn't <u>deny</u> their common ethnicity.

① rescind ② eschew
③ forswear ④ repudiate

02 밑줄 친 부분과 의미가 가장 가까운 것을 고르시오.

The shepherds who found a strange thing in the shed were <u>curious</u> about its softness.

① stony ② uneven
③ inquisitive ④ impassive

03 밑줄 친 부분과 뜻이 가장 유사한 단어를 고르면?

The name England is derived from the Angles, one of the Germanic tribes which established monarchies in lowland Britain in the 5th century, after the final <u>withdrawal</u> of the Romans in 409.

① collapse ② invasion
③ surrender ④ retreat

04 밑줄 친 부분과 의미가 가장 가까운 것을 고르시오.

<u>Canny</u> investors are starting to worry that the stock market might be due for a sharp fall.

① shrewd ② prestigious
③ impudent ④ curious

05 밑줄 친 부분과 뜻이 가장 유사한 단어를 고르면?

Some plants evade dry seasons through their seed which can even be <u>dormant</u> for several years.

① incidental ② bouncy
③ judicious ④ diapausing

06 어법상 가장 옳지 않은 것은?

① It takes for him a while to adjust to living alone.
② A helicopter was scrambled to help rescue five young climbers.
③ The research suggests that listening to soporific music while driving is dangerous.
④ To be conscious that we are perceiving or thinking is to be conscious of our own existence.

07 어법상 옳지 않은 것은?

① I couldn't get him to do what I wanted him to do.
② Each of the students voiced his or her own complaints.
③ Tom knew that although the team would lose, they played with tremendous spirit.
④ The 35-years-old national captain says he needs a new challenge after 10 years in New York.

08 우리말을 영어로 잘못 옮긴 것은?

① 그녀가 수화기를 내려놓기가 무섭게 초인종이 울렸다.
→ She had scarcely put the phone down when the doorbell rang.

② 그 상품은 고객의 요구에 부응하여 개발될 것이다.
→ Customer demand will be developed in response to the product.

③ 그 축구팀은 이번 주에 경기를 잘하면 상황 악화를 간신히 중단시킬 수가 있을 것이다.
→ The soccer team will manage to stop the rot if they play well this week.

④ 그것들을 우편으로 발송한다면, 우편이 배달되는 시간을 반드시 고려해야 합니다.
→ If you mail them in, be sure to factor in the time for the mail to be delivered.

09 다음 글의 제목으로 가장 적절한 것은?

Blind testing aims to assess a product based on its intrinsic merits by hiding any reference to the wider brand. This avoids results being influenced by any halo effect or negative associations set up by previous experiences. This approach is effective in giving market researchers a clear picture of the test product's absolute appeal relative to those of competitors or previous versions of that item. For brands struggling for appeal, this can be useful in establishing whether issues are rooted in a brand's image or the products themselves. For brands with high appeal, it's helpful to understand whether their products are actually 'good' or ratings are flattered by brand halo.

① What Is Blind Testing for?
② Why Is Blind Testing Pointless?
③ How Is Blind Testing Undertaken?
④ How Are Blind and Branded Testing Different?

10 주어진 문장 다음에 이어질 글의 순서로 가장 적절한 것은?

History has blurred the details, but the tale hangs on a boozy dispute, angry words, a scuffle and a gunshot.

(A) Some say John Weller struck Andrew Gray in the jaw; others say he tried to strangle Andrew Gray, but in both accounts, Andrew Gray shot John Weller in the thigh. The border survey, less than a year old, was a mess.

(B) It was October 1849. Commissioner John Weller and surveyor Andrew Gray had been sent to the border of the United States and Mexico to mark a line that existed only on maps, and the work was not going well.

(C) This dispute was just one of many problems that cropped up while the U.S. struggled to define its southern border after the Mexican-American War. Finally, a line had been drawn, but the border was far from settled.

① (A) - (B) - (C)   ② (B) - (A) - (C)
③ (B) - (C) - (A)   ④ (C) - (A) - (B)

11 다음 대화 중 어색한 것은?

① A: I have to wake up early tomorrow.
   B: Do you have an early schedule?

② A: Look out the window! It's snowing!
   B: Wow! It's the first snow of the year.

③ A: It's too dim here. Could you please turn on the light?
   B: Sure. Where is the switch?

④ A: Don't walk on the ice. It might not be frozen even if it looks so.
   B: I like walking on frozen ice.

12 밑줄 친 부분에 들어갈 말로 가장 적절한 것을 고르시오.

A: How do I look in this dress?
B: You look beautiful! The color looks really good on you.
A: Thank you so much. I bought this two days ago, but I'm not sure if I look okay in it.
B: You look just fine. Have some more confidence.
A: Don't I look fatter?
B: Not at all. Believe me, you look awesome. I _____ _____.

① step on it
② mean business
③ lose my temper
④ hit the bull's eye

13 밑줄 친 부분 중 어법상 가장 옳지 않은 것은?

If from this land, which ① is your property, you would cultivate daily as many feet ② as you cover with your lazy body, you would reap every year ③ very more corn ④ than you see upon the cart here.

14 주어진 문장이 들어갈 위치로 가장 적절한 것은?

For instance, just thinking about something threatening can trigger an emotional fear response.

A feeling is a mental portrayal of what is going on in your body when you have an emotion and is the byproduct of your brain perceiving and assigning meaning to the emotion. Feelings are the next thing that happens after having an emotion, involve cognitive input, usually subconscious, and cannot be measured precisely. (①) They are sparked by emotions and colored by the thoughts, memories, and images that have become subconsciously linked with that particular emotion for you. (②) But it works the other way around too. (③) While individual emotions are temporary, the feelings they evoke may persist and grow over a lifetime. (④) Because emotions cause subconscious feelings which in turn initiate certain emotions and this goes on and on, your life can become a never-ending cycle of painful and confusing emotions, which produce negative feelings, which cause more negative emotions.

15 밑줄 친 부분 중 글의 흐름상 가장 어색한 것은?

Driving lawfully and cautiously is one of the most important things that we do every day. Our lives, as well as the people we share the road with, depend on us making careful decisions behind the wheel. ① You can never count on other drivers to always do the right thing, so sometimes driving defensively is an important part of being a safe driver. ② A defensive driver is one who is always alert and ready to make an adjustment necessary to accommodate an unforeseen circumstance. ③ Using defensive driving practices will put everyone's safety first, but sometimes the line between defensive and aggressive driving can get blurry. A defensive driver knows that anything can happen any time, like when driving defensively around semis. ④ The flow of traffic, weather, and road conditions can change in an instant and require immediate adjustments to stay safe while driving. A defensive driver is ready to make those changes while always keeping their composure. A defensive driver is also always ready to react to another driver's mistake.

16 다음 글에 나타난 화자의 심경으로 가장 적절한 것은?

Wandering through my old town, peering into closed shops, sauntering through desolate playgrounds and parks, and watching the lights in upstairs windows slowly extinguished as time ticked by were an extraordinary experience for me. There are so many moments that make up a person's life, and ones are added with each passing second, but how many of us ever take the time to languish in the cottony folds of memory? How many of us really want to? I think we all do. I think there is always a tiny box somewhere, filled with a moment you would relive over and over again. But do we ever shrink ourselves down to size so we can fit inside it? Most of us don't. We grow larger and more complicated each year, and the box seems smaller and smaller, until one day it becomes impossible to find, so that it is permanently, but unknowingly filed away, lost in the constant reshuffling of life and time. But that night I felt like I had found all my little boxes and I was in the mood for opening them all.

① skeptical and wary ② lonely and depressed
③ pleased and delighted ④ alarmed and distressed

17 글의 흐름상 빈칸에 들어갈 가장 적절한 것은?

The notion that a product tested without branding is somehow being more objectively appraised is entirely _____. In the real world, we no more appraise things with our eyes closed and holding our nose than we do by ignoring the brand that is stamped on the product we purchase, the look and feel of the box it comes in, or the price being asked.

① correct ② reliable
③ misguided ④ unbiased

18 빈칸 (A), (B)에 들어갈 표현으로 가장 적절한 것은?

Americans may not be too ___(A)___ to exercise after all. A new RAND Corporation study finds that Americans average more than 5 hours of free time each day. But instead of being physically active during their free hours, Americans report they spend most of that time looking at screens (televisions, phones or other devices). "There is a general perception among the public and even public health professionals that a lack of leisure time is a major reason that Americans do not get enough physical activity," said Dr. Deborah Cohen, co-author of the study. "But we found no evidence for those beliefs." These findings suggest getting Americans to devote at least 20 or 30 minutes each day to physical activity is ___(B)___. Increasing the public's awareness of how they actually use their time and creating messages that encourage Americans to reduce their screen time may help people become more physically active.

	(A)	(B)
①	indolent	ideal
②	busy	feasible
③	occupied	inevitable
④	lazy	possible

19 〈보기〉 글의 내용과 일치하는 것은?

<보기>
In the American Southwest, previously the Mexican North, Anglo-America ran into Hispanic America. The meeting involved variables of language, religion, race, economy, and politics. The border between Hispanic America and Anglo-America has shifted over time, but one fact has not changed: it is one thing to draw an arbitrary geographical line between two spheres of sovereignty; it is another to persuade people to respect it. Victorious in the Mexican-American War in 1848, the United States took half of Mexico. The resulting division did not ratify any plan of nature. The borderlands were an ecological whole; northeastern Mexican desert blended into southeastern American desert with no prefiguring of nationalism. The one line that nature did provide — the Rio Grande — was a river that ran through but did not really divide continuous terrain.

① The borderlands between America and Mexico signify a long history of one sovereignty.
② While nature did not draw lines, human society certainly did.
③ The Mexican-American War made it possible for people to respect the border.
④ The Rio Grande has been thought of as an arbitrary geographical line.

20 다음 글의 내용과 일치하지 않는 것은?

Watching TV is America's favorite leisure activity, according to the Census Bureau data. Sitting in front of a television took up 2.7 hours daily, just over half of the total free time Americans have each day. The survey found that American men spend 5.5 hours watching TV on an average day — compared to women who spent 4.8 hours doing so. The survey also broke down how long people watched by age, employment status and more. Older people took more time out of their day for TV — those 65 and older watched more than four hours daily on average. On the other hand, the 15-44 age group watched the least, about two hours daily on average. The unemployed also spent more time watching daily on average — 3.78 hours — than those with either full-time or part-time jobs on average — 2.10 hours. This means even people with jobs are spending a lot of their free time, on average, watching some kind of television shows.

① Americans have on average less than 6 hours of free time each day.
② Males spend more time watching TV than females do.
③ Children under 15 watched TV more than those between 15 and 44 years of age did.
④ The 65 and older age group watched less hours than the unemployed group.

기적사 DAY 01

결국엔 성정혜 영어 하프모의고사

01	①	02	④	03	④	04	②	05	②
06	④	07	③	08	②	09	③	10	③

오답률 TOP 1
01 정답 ①
17 지방직

정답해설

밑줄 친 'surrogate'는 '대리인'이라는 의미이며, ① proxy와 동일한 의미를 가진다.

해석

가장 최신 법률들 중 일부는 사람들이 필요한 경우에 그들을 위해 의료 결정을 할 수 있는 **대리인**을 지정하는 것을 허가한다.
① 대리인
② 보초(감시)병
③ 전임자
④ 약탈자

어휘

authorize 허가하다, 승인하다   surrogate 대리인
proxy 대리인   sentry 보초(감시)병
predecessor 전임자   plunderer 약탈자

02 정답 ④
17 지방직

정답해설

밑줄 친 'keep his feet on the ground'는 '현실적이다, 들떠있지 않다'라는 의미로, ④ remain sensible and realistic about life와 가장 유사하다.

해석

A: 그는 그가 무엇이든 이룰 수 있다고 생각해.
B: 맞아, 그는 **현실적일** 필요가 있어.
① 그만의 세계에서 살다
② 긴장을 풀고 마음껏 즐기다
③ 용감하고 자신 있다
④ 삶에 대해 분별 있고 현실감 있는 상태로 남다

어휘

keep one's feet on the ground 현실적이다, 들떠있지 않다
confident 자신 있는, 확신하는   sensible 분별 있는, 현명한
realistic 현실적인, 실제적인

03 정답 ④
17 지방직

정답해설

밑줄 친 'on the fence'는 '결정하지 못하여'의 의미이며, ④ undecided와 동일한 의미를 가진다.

해석

그녀는 루브르 박물관에 있는 모나리자를 관람하러 가야 하는 것에 대해 **결정을 못 하고** 있다.
① 번민의, 고뇌에 찬
② 열광적인
③ 불안한
④ 결정하지 못한

어휘

on the fence 결정하지 못하여   anguished 번민의, 고뇌에 찬
enthusiastic 열광적인   apprehensive 불안한
undecided 결정하지 못한

04 정답 ②
17 지방직

정답해설

밑줄 친 부분 전 대화에서 A가 연락을 유지하기는 참 어렵다고 말하자 B가 이에 동의했다. 그러므로 ② '사람들은 멀어지기 마련이야(People just drift apart).'라고 하는 것이 문맥상 가장 적절하다.

오답해설

① 대화의 내용과 상관이 없으므로 적절하지 않다.
③ B가 A의 말이 웃기다고 생각했다면, 앞서 '네 말이 맞아(You're right)'라고 하며 A의 말에 수긍하지 않았을 것이다.
④ B는 그(A의 친구)와 아는 사이가 아니다.

해석

A: 나 방금 오랜 고등학교 친구들 중 한 명에게 편지를 받았어.
B: 잘됐다!
A: 그게, 사실 그에게서 소식을 들은 건 꽤 오랜만이야.
B: 솔직히 말하면, 나는 오래된 친구들과 대부분 연락이 끊겼는걸.
A: 나도 알지. 모두들 여기저기로 이사를 다니는 와중에 연락을 유지하기는 참 어려운 일이야.
B: 네 말이 맞아. 사람들은 멀어지기 마련이야. 그렇지만 너는 그 친구와 연락이 다시 닿아서 참 다행이야.
① 낮이 점점 길어지고 있어
② 사람들은 멀어지기 마련이야
③ 그 말은 내가 여태 들어본 말 중에 가장 웃겨
④ 나는 그의 이름을 듣기만 하면 화가 치밀어 오르기 시작해

어휘

out of touch with ~와의 접촉 없이
drift apart 사이가 멀어지다   fume (화가 나서) 씩씩대다

오답률 TOP 3
05 정답 ②
17 지방직

정답해설

② 출제 포인트: what vs. that
'leads'를 'that' 이하의 관계대명사절의 동사로 본다면 그에 맞는 선행사를 찾을 수 없기 때문에 'leads'는 주절의 동사임을 알 수 있다. 'leads'는 일반 동사이므로 부정문을 사용할 때 be동사가 아닌 do동사를 사용해야 한다. 올바르게 고친 문장은 that을 삭제한 'Academic knowledge doesn't always lead you to make right decisions.'이다. 혹은 'is'의 보어에 해당하는 명사가 없고 'leads'의 주어가 없으므로 'that'을 선행사를 포함한 관계대명사 'what'으로 바꿔 'what leads you to make ~'로 수정할 수 있다.

오답해설

① 출제 포인트: 불완전타동사의 목적격 보어
종속절인 'that' 이하의 절의 동사인 'keep'은 「keep+목적어+목적격 보어」

의 형태를 가진다. 목적격 보어는 형용사인 'healthy'이고 이를 부사인 'perfectly'가 수식하고 있는 형태이다.

③ **출제 포인트: 타동사구[완전타동사+목적어+전치사+목적어]**
「prevent A from B」는 'A가 B하는 것을 막다[방지하다]'라는 뜻으로 B에는 명사나 동명사가 와야 한다. 해당 문장에서는 전치사 'from' 뒤에 동명사 'engaging'이 올바르게 사용되었으며 'engage in'은 '~에 관여하다, 참여하다'를 뜻한다.

④ **출제 포인트: 완전타동사+[to부정사 vs. 동명사]**
'stop'은 목적어로 오직 동명사만을 갖는다. 「stop+-ing」는 '~하는 것을 멈추다'는 의미이고, 「stop+to부정사」의 경우 to부정사는 정확히는 목적어가 아니라 부정사의 부사적 용법 중 목적에 해당하는 '~하기 위해 멈추다'라는 의미이다. 해당 문장에서는 'stop'의 목적어로 동명사 'eating'이 사용되었으므로 옳은 문장이다.

해석
① 당신은 단지 채소를 많이 먹는 것이 당신을 완벽히 건강하게 유지할 것이라고 생각할지도 모른다.
② 학문적 지식이 항상 당신이 올바른 결정을 내리도록 이끌지는 않는다.
③ 다칠지 모른다는 두려움은 그가 무모한 행동들을 하는 것을 막지는 못했다.
④ Julie의 담당의는 너무 많은 가공식품을 섭취하는 것을 중단하라고 말했다.

오답률 TOP 2
06 정답 ④   17 지방직

정답해설
④ **출제 포인트: 부정사의 관용표현**
「prefer A to B」는 'B보다 A를 선호하다'라는 뜻으로 A와 B는 병렬구조가 되어야 한다. 그러므로 바르게 고치면 'I prefer staying home to going out on a snowy day.'가 된다. 동명사 대신 to부정사를 사용하고 싶다면 'I prefer to stay home rather than (to) go out on a snowy day.'로 고쳐도 된다.

오답해설
① **출제 포인트: to부정사의 명사적 용법**
'~하는 것을 규칙으로 세우다'라는 의미를 지닌 「make it a rule to R」 관용표현이 사용되었다. 이때 'it'은 가목적어이며 'to R'은 진목적어에 해당한다. 또한 부정관사가 기간을 나타내는 단어 앞에 와서 '~ 마다'라는 뜻으로 쓰이기도 한다. 여기에서 'a month'는 '매달'이라는 뜻으로 알맞게 쓰였다.

② **출제 포인트: 「가격동사+사람(목적어)+전치사+the+신체부위」**
'grab, catch, pull, take, seize, hold' 등의 동사는 「목적격 + by + 정관사 + 신체부위」의 형태로 쓴다. 이때 주의할 것은 'by my arm'이 아니라 정관사 'the'를 사용해 'by the arm'으로 쓴다는 것이다.

③ **출제 포인트: 전치사 vs. 접속사/ 타동사로 착각하기 쉬운 자동사**
'owing to'는 전치사구이다. 그러므로 다음에 명사구인 'the heavy rain'이 온 것은 적절하다. 또한 완전자동사 'rise'의 현재완료인 'has risen'이 옳게 사용되었으며 문장의 마지막 전치사 'by'는 정도 혹은 차이를 나타내기 위해 사용된 것으로 적절하다.

07 정답 ③   17 지방직

정답해설
③ **출제 포인트: the+형용사**
'tend'는 '돌보다, 보살피다'라는 뜻의 타동사로 목적어가 필요하다. 형용사(sick and wounded)가 목적어가 되기 위해서는 명사로 바꾸어야 한다. 「the+형용사」는 '~한 사람들'이라는 뜻으로 해당 문장에서는 'sick and wounded'를 'the sick and the wounded'로 바꿔야 목적어 자리에 오는 명사 역할을 할 수 있다.

오답해설
① **출제 포인트: It ~ that 강조용법/등위상관접속사**
「It ~ that」 강조용법으로 'not ~ rudeness'를 강조하고 있다. 또한 여기서 「not A but B」 구문이 사용되었는데, 여기에서 'her refusal'과 'her rudeness'가 각각 명사로 병렬구조를 이루고 있으므로 적절하다.

② **출제 포인트: 주요 조동사 표현**
「cannot be too+형용사」의 형태로 '아무리 ~해도 지나치지 않다'라는 의미이다. 해당 문장은 '아무리 신중해도 지나치지 않다'라는 해석과 'cannot be too careful'이 일치하므로 옳다.

④ **출제 포인트: to부정사 주요표현/동격의 접속사 that**
'To make matters worse'는 '설상가상으로'라는 의미의 관용표현이다. 또한, 이어지는 문장에서 'that'은 'a report'를 설명하는 동격절을 이끄는 접속사이다.

08 정답 ②   19 서울시

정답해설
글의 도입에서 'production of an information goods(정보재 생산)'에 대해서 먼저 언급하고 있다. 이런 정보재의 특징은 고정비용은 크지만, 한계비용이 낮은 점이 일반재와는 다른 점을 명확히 명시하고 있다. 글의 후반부 'You must price your information goods according to consumer value, not according to your production cost(당신은 당신의 생산비가 아닌 소비자 가치에 따라 당신의 정보 상품의 가격을 책정해야 한다).'를 통해서 'information goods(정보재)'는 '생산비에 따라 값을 매기는 것이 아니라 소비자의 가치에 따라 가격을 매겨야 한다.'고 설명하고 있으므로 글의 제목으로 가장 적절한 것은 ② Pricing the Information Goods(정보재 가격 책정)가 가장 적절한 제목이다.

오답해설
① 본문에서 저작권을 언급하고 있지 않다.
③ 정보재 가격 책정이 글의 주된 내용이지 지적재산에 대해서는 서술하고 있지 않다.
④ 글에서 언급하고 있지 않다.

해석
경제학자들은 정보재의 생산은 높은 고정비용과 낮은 한계비용을 수반한다고 말한다. 정보 재화의 첫 번째 사본 제작비용은 상당할 수 있지만, 추가 사본을 제작(또는 복제)하는 비용은 무시할 수 있다. 이런 종류의 비용 구조는 많은 중요한 의미를 가지고 있다. 예를 들어, 생산비에 바탕을 둔 가격 책정은 작동을 안 할 수가 있다: 단가가 0일 때 단가를 10% 또는 20% 인상하는 것은 말이 되지 않는다. 당신은 당신의 생산비가 아닌 소비자 가치에 따라 당신의 정보 상품의 가격을 책정해야 한다.
① 저작권 확보
② 정보재 가격 책정
③ 지적재산으로서의 정보
④ 기술 변화의 비용

어휘
high fixed cost 높은 고정비용   marginal cost 한계비용
substantial 상당한   negligible 무시할 수 있는
implication 의미   markup 인상
unit cost 단가   make no sense 말이 되지 않다
production cost 생산비   intellectual property 지적재산

09 정답 ③
19 서울시

정답해설
글에서 소재는 'Dracula ants(드라큘라 개미)'임을 글 초반부에 명백히 제시하고 있다. 'Dracula ants(드라큘라 개미)'를 지칭하지 않는 선택지를 고르는 문제로, ③의 'they'는 바로 직전의 'their jaws(그들의 턱들)'를 지칭하는 표현에 해당된다. ①,②,④의 'Dracula ants(드라큘라 개미)'를 가리키는 나머지와 대상이 다르므로, 정답은 ③이다.

오답해설
나머지 보기들은 'Dracula ants'를 지칭하고 있으므로 오답이다.

해석
드라큘라 개미는 때때로 자기 새끼의 피를 마시는 방법으로 이름을 얻는다. 하지만 이번 주에, ① 이 곤충들은 명성에 대한 권리를 얻게 되었다. 미스트리움 카밀레 종의 드라큘라 개미는 그들의 턱을 아주 빠르게 맞부딪칠 수 있고, 당신은 우리가 눈을 깜빡이는 데 걸리는 시간에 5,000번의 타격을 맞출 수 있다. 이번 주 Royal Society Open Science지에 발표된 한 연구에 따르면 이것은 ② 이 흡혈 곤충들이 자연에서 가장 빠르게 알려진 움직임을 행한다는 것을 의미한다. 흥미롭게도, 개미들은 그들의 턱을 너무 세게 눌러서 ③ 그들이 구부러지는 것만으로도 기록을 깨는 스냅을 만들어 낸다. 이는 용수철처럼 이것(턱)이 반대쪽(턱)을 최고 시속 200마일에 달하는 엄청난 속도와 힘으로 미끄러져 강타할 때까지 한쪽 턱에 에너지를 저장한다. 당신이 손가락을 튕길 때 일어나는 일과 비슷한데, 단지 1,000배 정도 더 빠를 뿐이다. 드라큘라 개미는 ④ 그들이 낙엽 밑에서 또는 지하 터널에서 사냥하는 것을 선호하기 때문에 비밀스러운 포식자들이다.

어휘
claim 권리
blood-sucker 흡혈하는 것
lash out 후려갈기다
snap 딱 소리를 내다, 부러지다
leaf litter 낙엽
fame 명성
slide 미끄러지다
velocity 속도
secretive 비밀스러운, 숨기는
subterranean 지하의

10 정답 ③
19 서울시

정답해설
교육 예산을 미국과 아프리카라는 지역을 들어 비교하는 글이다. 빈칸 이전에 'Governments in sub-Saharan Africa spend only 2.4 percent of the world's public resources on education,(사하라 이남의 아프리카에 있는 정부에서 교육에 대해 쓰는 돈은 단지 2.4%이다,)'라고 서술하고 있는 반면에 'the United States spends 28 percent of all the money spent in the world on education,(미국에서는 28%를 교육과 관련된 비용으로 지출하고 있다,)'고 하였으므로 서로 교육 예산이 눈에 띄게 상반됨을 알 수 있다. 따라서 '역으로'라는 뜻인 ③ Conversely가 빈칸에 적절한 표현이다.

① 그럼에도 불구하고
② 더욱이
③ 반대로
④ 유사하게

어휘
wealth 부
lack 부족
nation-state 국민국가
furthermore 더욱이
similarly 유사하게
central 중심적인
resource 자원
nevertheless 그럼에도 불구하고
conversely 역으로

오답해설
빈칸을 사이에 두고 대조되는 내용이 서술되고 있으므로 나머지 보기들은 글의 흐름상 적절하지 않다.

해석
한 나라의 부는 교육에서 중심적인 역할을 수행하므로 국민국가로부터의 자본과 자원의 부족은 시스템을 약하게 할 수 있다. 사하라 이남의 아프리카 정부들은 교육에 대해 세계의 공공 자원의 단지 2.4퍼센트를 지출한다, 하지만 학령기 인구의 15퍼센트가 거기에 살고 있다. 역으로 미국은 교육에 대해 세계에서 소비하는 모든 돈의 28퍼센트를 소비한다. 하지만 학령기 인구의 단지 4퍼센트만이 거주하고 있다.

기적사 DAY 02

결국엔 성정혜 영어 하프모의고사

| 01 | ② | 02 | ① | 03 | ④ | 04 | ④ | 05 | ② |
| 06 | ② | 07 | ① | 08 | ④ | 09 | ② | 10 | ③ |

오답률 TOP 3

01 정답 ②

정답해설

밑줄 친 'assailant'는 '가해자, 공격자'라는 의미이며, ② assaulter와 의미가 가장 가깝다.

해석

부상을 입은 남자가 비틀거리며 **가해자** 쪽을 향해 방을 가로질렀다고 대리인은 말한다.
① 당국, 권한, 권위
② 공격자, 폭행자
③ 대용품
④ 부업, 취미

어휘

lurch 비틀거리다
authority 당국, 권한, 권위
substitute 대용품
assailant 가해자, 공격자
assaulter 공격자, 폭행자
avocation 부업, 취미

02 정답 ①

정답해설

밑줄 친 'have your feet on the ground'는 '실제적인'이라는 의미이므로 ① practical이 적절하다.

해석

당신은 무엇을 하더라도 **실제적**이어야 하고 진짜 본질에 집중해야 한다.
① 실제적인
② 의존하는
③ 겉보기에는
④ 근거 없는

어휘

nature 본질
have one's feet on the ground 실제적인
practical 실제적인
seemingly 겉보기에는
dependent 의존하는
groundless 근거 없는

03 정답 ④

정답해설

밑줄 친 'crucial'은 '중대한, 결정적인'이라는 뜻으로 ④ significant와 의미가 가장 가깝다.

해석

이 중차대한 시기에 투자자를 찾는 것은 Tom에게 **중요하다**.
① 의심이 가는, 미심쩍은
② 논란의 여지가 있는
③ 열렬한, 열광적인
④ 중요한, 의미 있는

어휘

crucial 중대한, 결정적인
at this juncture 이 중차대한 시기에, 이 기회에
suspected 의심이 가는, 미심쩍은
enthusiastic 열렬한, 열광적인
debatable 논란의 여지가 있는
significant 중요한, 의미 있는

04 정답 ④

정답해설

Mary가 지역 대회에서 우승한 것을 Bob이 축하해주는 상황에서의 대화이다. Bob은 Mary에게 다른 사람들에게는 ④ '누워서 떡 먹기인(as easy as making apple pie)' 것처럼 보일지라도 Mary가 무척 열심히 한 것을 알고 있다고 이야기한다.

오답해설

① 지역 대회에서 우승한 Mary를 축하해주며 남들에게 '기발한(off the wall)' 것처럼 보였을 수 있지만, 열심히 한 것을 안다고 말하는 것은 문맥상 어색하다.
② Mary가 지역 대회에서 우승하기 위해 노력한 점에 대해 남들에게는 '정정당당한(aboveboard)' 것처럼 보여도 열심히 했음을 Bob이 안다고 이야기하는 것은 적절하지 않다.
③ 다른 사람들이 Mary를 '공손한(hat in hand)' 것처럼 보더라도 그녀가 지역 대회에서 우승하기 위해 열심히 했음을 안다고 하는 것은 대화의 흐름상 부자연스럽다.

해석

Bob: 지역 대회에서 우승한 것을 축하해!
Mary: 정말 고마워. 난 그저 운이 좋았을 뿐이야.
Bob: 넌 너무 겸손하지 않아도 돼. 다른 사람들에게는 누워서 떡 먹기인 것처럼 보였을지라도 네가 지역 대회를 위해 열심히 했다는 걸 난 알아.
Mary: 노력 없이 되는 것은 없지. 내 모든 노력을 알아봐 줘서 고마워.
Bob: 오, 나에게 고마워하지 마. 너 자신을 자랑스러워해. 넌 대단한 일을 해냈어.
Mary: 사실 난 무척이나 긴장했어. 대회전에 나는 거의 아무것도 먹지 못했어.
Bob: 너 배고프겠다. 뭐 좀 먹으러 가자.
① 기발한, 특이한
② 정정당당한, 분명히
③ 공손히, 굽실거리며
④ 누워서 떡 먹기인

어휘

off the wall 기발한, 특이한
hat in hand 공손히, 굽실거리며
as easy as making apple pie 누워서 떡 먹기인
aboveboard 정정당당한, 분명히

오답률 TOP 1

05 정답 ②

정답해설

② **출제 포인트: 불완전타동사의 목적격 보어/타동사구[완전타동사+목적어+전치사+목적어]**

두 가지 경우로 나누어 볼 수 있다.
1. 'forbade'를 불완전타동사로 보는 경우
   'forbade(불완전타동사 forbid의 과거시제)'의 목적격 보어 자리에 현

재분사 'telling'을 사용하였으나 'forbade'는 to부정사만을 목적격 보어로 가지므로 틀린 문장이다. 따라서 'telling'을 'to tell'로 수정해야 한다.

2. 'forbade'를 완전타동사로 보는 경우
'forbade(완전타동사 forbid의 과거시제)' 뒤에 대상을 나타내는 목적어가 오는 경우 「forbade+목적어[대상]+from+목적어[금지 내용]」의 구조를 가지며 이때 금지 내용을 나타내는 목적어로 명사 또는 동명사가 온다. 해당 문장은 「forbade+목적어[대상]+from+목적어[금지 내용]」을 사용하였으나 전치사 'from'을 누락했으므로 틀린 문장이다. 따라서 'telling'을 'from telling'으로 수정해야 한다.

(오답해설)

① **출제 포인트: what vs. that/to부정사의 to생략**
'What you need to do'의 경우 'What' 뒤에 오는 절의 목적어가 없으며 앞에 선행사가 없으므로 선행사를 포함하는 관계대명사 'What'을 사용하는 것이 옳다. 또한 주어로 쓰인 절에 do 동사가 있고 주격 보어에 to부정사가 오는 경우 'to'를 생략할 수 있다. 따라서 해당 문장의 'make'는 'to'가 생략된 부정사로 주격 보어이다.

③ **출제 포인트: 타동사구[완전타동사+목적어+전치사+목적어]**
해당 문장에서 'cure'는 완전타동사이며 「cure+목적어[대상]+of+목적어[사물]」의 구조로 사용되었다.

④ **출제 포인트: 완전타동사+[to부정사 vs. 동명사]/stop(완전자동사)+to부정사/stop(완전타동사)+동명사**
해당 문장에서 'stopping'은 'stop'의 현재분사이며 'to look'은 to부정사의 부사적 용법으로 사용되었다. 이때 'to look'을 목적을 나타내는 부사적 용법으로 보느냐 아니면 결과를 나타내는 부사적 용법으로 보느냐에 따라 해석에 차이가 생기지만 부사적 용법임에는 변함이 없으므로 'stopping'은 완전자동사의 성격을 가진다.

(해석)
① 당신이 해야 할 일은 유용한 전화번호 목록을 만드는 것이다.
② 그는 그것에 대해 정말 당황했는데 왜냐하면 그는 내가 누구에게도 말하는 것을 금지했기 때문이다.
③ 결국 Tom은 그녀의 우울증을 치료할 수 있는 의사를 발견했다.
④ 가게 창문을 들여다보기 위해 이따금 멈춰 서면서, Jane은 느긋하게 거리로 걸어 내려갔다. or 이따금 멈춰 서서 가게 창문을 들여다보면서, Jane은 느긋하게 거리로 걸어 내려갔다.

06 정답 ②

(정답해설)

② **출제 포인트: 형용사 convenient의 쓰임/능동태 vs. 수동태/to부정사의 명사적 용법**
해당 문장은 주어진 우리말에 따르면, 수동 형태가 아닌 능동 형태로 써야 함에 주의해야 한다. 주어진 우리말을 영어로 옮기면 'Jane finds it convenient to be able to do her banking by phone.'을 사용해야 옳다. 이때 'it'은 가목적어이고 진목적어는 'to be ~ by phone'이다. 더욱이, 우리말 해석 없이 주어진 수동태 문장의 경우 문법적으로 분석하기 위해서, 능동태로 고친다면 '~ find Jane convenient to be ~'에 해당된다. 이 경우 'find'는 불완전타동사로 목적어인 'Jane'을 'convenient'라는 보어로 수식하고 있으므로 이 또한 어법상 옳지 않다. 'convenient'는 형용사로서 사람을 주어로 쓰거나 사람을 직접적으로 수식하는 경우로는 사용하지 않음에 주의해야 한다.

(오답해설)

① **출제 포인트: 지각동사의 목적격 보어/전치사 vs. 접속사**
지각동사 'hear'는 목적어와 목적격 보어가 능동관계인 경우 목적격 보어로 원형부정사와 현재분사를 사용하며 수동관계인 경우 목적격 보어로 과거분사를 사용한다. 또한 'while'은 접속사로 뒤에는 완전한 형태의 절이 온다. 해당 문장은 목적어와 목적격 보어가 능동관계이므로 원형부정사 'come'을 목적격 보어로 사용하였으며, 'while' 뒤에 온 'we were having dinner'는 완전한 형태의 절이다. 따라서 해당 문장은 옳은 문장이다.

③ **출제 포인트: 「가격동사+사람(목적어)+전치사+the+신체부위」**
「grab+사람+by+the+신체부위」는 '~의 신체부위를 잡다'를 뜻한다. 이때 전치사 'by' 뒤에는 정관사 'the'를 사용해야 하며 소유격 대명사를 사용할 수 없으므로 옳은 문장이다.

④ **출제 포인트: 부정사의 관용표현**
「would rather A than B」는 'B하느니 차라리 A하는 것이 낫다'를 뜻하며 이때 A와 B는 동사원형으로 병렬구조를 이룬다. 해당 문장은 「would rather A than B」를 사용하였으며 A와 B에 동사원형의 형태인 'watch'가 병렬구조를 이루고 있으므로 옳은 문장이다.

07 정답 ①

(정답해설)

① **출제 포인트: 주요 조동사 표현**
「had better 동사원형」은 관용표현으로 '~하는 편이 낫다'를 뜻한다. 해당 문장은 「had better」를 사용하였으나 뒤에 동사원형이 아닌 과거시제 또는 과거분사인 'got'을 사용하였으므로 틀린 문장이다. 따라서 'got'을 동사원형 'get'으로 수정해야 한다.

(오답해설)

② **출제 포인트: the+형용사/주어[some of 명사]와 동사 수일치**
해당 문장에서 'the deaf'는 「the+형용사」로 '청각장애인들'을 뜻한다. 또한 주어가 「Some of 목적어」의 형태인 경우 동사의 수일치 기준은 'of'의 목적어이다. 따라서 'of'의 목적어가 복수형태의 명사구 'the TV programs'이므로 동사에 복수형태인 'are'를 옳게 사용하였다.

③ **출제 포인트: 등위상관접속사**
「neither A nor B」는 등위상관접속사로 'A도 B도 아니다'를 뜻하며 주어인 경우 동사의 수일치 기준은 B이다. 해당 문장은 「neither A nor B」가 쓰인 문장으로 주어진 해석과 일치하므로 옳은 문장이다. 또한 B에 복수형태인 명사구 'their friends'를 사용하였으므로 동사에 복수형태인 'know'를 옳게 사용하였다.

④ **출제 포인트: to부정사 주요표현/one of 복수명사**
'not to mention'은 관용표현으로 '~은 말할 것도 없고'를 뜻하며 뒤에 명사구가 온다. 해당 문장은 'not to mention'이 쓰인 문장으로 뒤에 명사구 'the fact'를 사용하였고 주어진 해석과 일치하므로 옳은 문장이다. 이때 'that he is handsome'은 'the fact'의 동격절로 사용되었다. 또한 'one of'는 뒤에 복수명사가 오며 해당 문장의 경우 'one of' 뒤에 복수형태의 명사구 'the kindest and most intelligent men'을 사용하였다.

08 정답 ④

(정답해설)

본문에서는 '정보재(information product)' 판매에 관해 설명하고 있으며, 본문 두 번째 문장에서 주제가 드러난다. "Though selling information products online is relatively new the industry is not(온라인으로 정보재를 판매하는 것은 상대적으로 새로운 것이지만, 그 업계는 그렇지 않다)."을 통해 '정보재 산업이 새로운 것이 아니라는 것'을 언급한 후, 구체적으로 과거에는 '입문서', '정보성 오디오' 등의 형태로 정보 및 지식이 판매되었음을 설명하고 있다. 따라서 글의 요지로 가장 적절한 것은 '④ Different forms of information goods have already existed before the advent of the

Internet(인터넷의 출현 이전에도 다른 형태의 정보재가 이미 존재해 왔다).'이다.

오답해설
① '정보재 산업의 빠른 성장'에 관해서는 본문에 언급되지 않는다.
② 본문에서 언급되지 않는 내용이다.
③ 본문에서는 '온라인으로 정보재를 판매하는 것은 상대적으로 새로운 것이지만, 그 업계는 그렇지 않다'라고 설명하고 있으므로, '인터넷이 발명된 후에야 비로소 정보재가 등장했다'는 본문의 내용과 반대되는 문장이다.

해석
우리가 구체적으로 디지털 출판계로 뛰어들기 전에, 한 걸음 물러서서 정보 마케팅과 정보 출판 산업을 전체적으로 살펴보자. 온라인으로 정보재를 판매하는 것은 상대적으로 새로운 것이지만, 그 업계는 그렇지 않다. 지식, 정보, 그리고 전문 지식을 판매가 가능한 제품으로 제작한다는 아이디어는 오랫동안 존재해 왔다. 인쇄 출판이 최초로 등장했을 때 사람들은 "입문"서를 집필했고, 오디오 카세트 기술이 이용 가능해졌을 때 그들은 그들의 정보를 오디오 및 기타 형식으로 녹음했다. 다시 말해서, 정보를 제공하는 콘텐츠를 만들고 그것을 당신이 판매할 수 있는 무언가로 제작한다는 아이디어는 완전히 새로운 것이 아니며, 그것을 온라인상에서 할 수 있다는 아이디어는 단지 더 많은 사람들에게 이 업계에 대한 접근성을 열어주었고, 그 기회를 더욱더 이용하기 쉽게 만들어 주었다.
① 정보재 산업은 빠르게 성장하고 있다.
② 정보재를 만들고 온라인으로 판매하는 것은 결코 쉽지 않다.
③ 인터넷이 발명된 후에야 비로소 정보재가 등장했다.
④ 인터넷의 출현 이전에도 다른 형태의 정보재가 이미 존재해 왔다.

어휘
relatively 상대적으로
expertise 전문 지식[기술]
how-to 입문서의, 초보적인
vend 판매하다
accessible 접근 가능한, 이용하기 쉬운
emerge 나타나다, 드러나다
package 꾸리다, 포장하다, 제작하다
sellable 판매할 수 있는
that is to say 다시 말해서, 즉
access 접근[성]
advent 출현, 도래, 등장

오답률 TOP 2

09 정답 ②

정답해설
본문은 '세계에서 가장 위험한 개미(The most dangerous ant in the world)'인 '불독개미(bulldog ant)'에 관하여 서술하고 있다. 세 번째 문장 "There have been at least three human fatalities since 1936, the latest of whom was a Victorian farmer in 1988(1936년 이래로 최소 3명의 사망자가 발생했으며, 가장 최근의 사망자는 1988년 빅토리아 지방의 농부였다)."에서 '가장 최근의(마지막) 사망자는 1988년 발생했음'을 알 수 있으므로, 1989년 이후로는 사망자가 나오지 않은 것을 유추할 수 있다. 따라서 글의 내용과 일치하는 것은 '② No one has been killed because of its attack since 1989(1989년 이후로 그것의 공격에 의해 사망한 사람은 없다).'이다.

오답해설
① 본문은 '세계에서 가장 위험한 개미(The most dangerous "ant" in the world)'에 관해 언급하고 있고, '세계에서 가장 위험한 곤충(The most dangerous "insect" in the world)'은 이보다 더 범위가 큰 부문이다. 'bulldog ant'가 실제로 '가장 위험한 곤충'인지 여부는 본문을 통해서는 알 수 없으므로 글의 내용과 일치하지 않는다.
③ "The bulldog ant earned its name because of its ferocity and determination during an attack(불독개미는 그것의 사나움과 공격 중 집요함 때문에 이름을 얻었다)."을 통해 '불독개미의 이름은 성향 또는 행동 때문에 생겼다'는 것을 알 수 있으므로, 외양과는 상관이 없음을 알 수 있다. 따라서 오답이다.
④ "stinging a number of times in quick succession and therefore injecting more venom with each bite(연달아 여러 번 침을 찌르고 그에 따라 한 번 물때마다 더 많은 독을 주입한다)."를 통해 침에 독이 있다는 것을 알 수 있다. 그러나 본문 두 번째 문장 "In attack it uses its sting and jaws simultaneously(공격을 할 때 그것은 침과 턱을 동시에 사용한다)."와 본문 후반 "In an attack, the ant will hold on to its victim with long, toothed mandibles, curl its body underneath and thrust its long barbless sting into the skin(공격을 할 때, 그 개미는 길고 이가 나 있는 아래턱뼈를 이용해 그것의 희생양을 꽉 붙잡고 몸을 아래쪽으로 구부려 길고 미늘이 없는 침을 피부로 찔러 넣는다)."을 통해, 불독개미는 공격 시 '아래턱뼈로 공격 대상을 붙잡고, 몸을 둥글게 말아 아랫부분의 침으로 피부를 찌른다'는 것을 알 수 있다. 따라서 '아래턱뼈와 침을 동시에 사용'하여 공격한다는 사실을 알 수 있으므로, 본문의 내용과 일치하지 않는다.

해석
세계에서 가장 위험한 개미는 호주의 해안 지대에서 발견되는 불독개미(Myrmecia pyriformis)이다. 공격을 할 때 그것은 침과 턱을 동시에 사용한다. 1936년 이래로 최소 3명의 사망자가 발생했으며, 가장 최근의 사망자는 1988년 빅토리아 지방의 농부였다. 불독개미는 그것의 사나움과 공격 중 집요함 때문에 이름을 얻었다. 그것은 극도로 공격적이며 인간에 대한 두려움을 거의 보이지 않으며, 연달아 여러 번 침을 찌르고 그에 따라 한 번 물때마다 더 많은 독을 주입한다. 공격을 할 때, 그 개미는 길고 이가 나 있는 아래턱뼈를 이용해 그것의 희생양을 꽉 붙잡고 몸을 아래쪽으로 구부려 길고 미늘이 없는 침을 피부로 찔러 넣는다. 일부의 경우에 이 침은 성인을 15분 안에 사망에 이르게 할 만큼 충분했다.
① 그것은 세계에서 가장 위험한 곤충으로 기록되어 있다.
② 1989년 이후로 그것의 공격에 의해 사망한 사람은 없다.
③ 그것의 신체적 외모 때문에 이름이 붙었다.
④ 그것은 공격을 하기 위해 아래턱뼈 또는 독이 있는 침 중 하나를 사용한다.

어휘
simultaneously 동시에
ferocity 사나움
aggressive 공격적인
venom 독
thrust 찌르다, 쑤셔 넣다
appearance 외모
fatality 사망자
determination 투지, 결의
in quick succession 연달아
mandible 아래턱뼈
barbless 미늘[바늘]이 없는
either A or B A, B 둘 중 하나

10 정답 ③

정답해설
본문 첫 문장에서 "Prior to the nineteenth century, systematic investment in human resources was not considered specially important in any country(19세기 이전 인적 자원에 대한 조직적인 투자는 어느 나라에서도 특별히 중요하게 여겨지지 않았다)."라고 언급하며, 과거에는 '인적 자원에 대한 투자가 적었다'고 언급한 후, 세 번째 문장에서 "This began to change radically ~(이것은 급격히 변화하기 시작했다)"라고 언급하며, '인적 자원에 대한 투자가 증가하기 시작했음'을 설명하고 있다. 이후, 20세기에 '교육, 기술, 지식 획득' 등이 매우 중요하게 대두되었음을 언급하고, 해당 요소들을 잘 활용하는지 여부가 개인과 국가의 생활 수준을 결정짓는 주요한 요인이라고 설명하고 있다. 즉, '20세기에 대두되기 시작한 교육과 훈련 등 '사람'에게 투자하는 것의 중요성'에 대해 언급하고 있으므로, 20세기를 명명할 수 있는 대표적인 표현이 들어가야 하는 빈칸에 가장 적절한 것은 '③ Age of Human Capital(인적 자본의 시대)'이다.

오답해설
① 본문에서 '공예 기술(Craft Skills)'을 특정하여 언급하고 있지 않기 때문에 빈칸에 적절하지 않다.
② 세 번째 문장 "with the application of science to the development of new goods and more efficient methods of production(새로운 제품과 더 효율적인 제작 방식 개발에 과학을 적용시키는 것과 함께)"을 통해 '기술 발전으로 인해 인적 자원에 대한 투자의 중요성이 더욱 증가했다'는 것을 알 수 있으며, 본문은 '기술(technology) 자체에 초점이 맞추어진 글이 아니므로 빈칸에 적절하지 않다.
④ '경제 발전(Economic Development)'에 대해서는 본문에 언급되지 않는다.

해석
19세기 이전 인적 자원에 대한 조직적인 투자는 어느 나라에서도 특별히 중요하게 여겨지지 않았다. 학교 교육과 실습 훈련에 대한 지출, 그리고 기타 유사한 형태의 투자는 다소 적었다. 이것은 최초로 영국에서, 이후 점진적으로 다른 국가들에서 새로운 제품과 더 효율적인 제작 방식 개발에 과학을 적용시키는 것과 함께 급격히 변화하기 시작했다. 20세기에 교육, 기술, 그리고 지식의 획득은 한 사람의 그리고 한 국가의 생산성의 중요한 결정 요인이 되었다. 한 국가의 생활 수준의 주요 결정 요인은 기술과 지식을 개발하고 활용하며, 번영을 촉진하고 인구의 대다수를 교육하는 것에 얼마나 성공을 거두느냐이다. 이러한 의미에서, 우리는 심지어 20세기를 "인적 자본의 시대"라고 부를 수도 있을 것이다.
① 공예 기술의 시대
② 기술의 시대
③ 인적 자본의 시대
④ 경제 발전의 시대

어휘
expenditure 지출
radically 급진적으로
acquisition 획득
determinant 결정 요인
standard of living 생활 수준
further 조장[촉진]하다, 조성[증진]하다
craft 공예
on-the-job 실지[실습]로 배우는
gradually 점진적으로, 차차
crucial 중대한, 결정적인
productivity 생산성
utilize 이용하다, 활용하다
health (국가·사회 등의) 활력, 번영

결국엔 성정혜 영어 하프모의고사
기적사 DAY 03

| 01 | ① | 02 | ① | 03 | ② | 04 | ③ | 05 | ④ |
| 06 | ① | 07 | ③ | 08 | ④ | 09 | ② | 10 | ② |

오답률 TOP 1

01 정답 ①

정답해설
밑줄 친 'lassitude'는 '무기력, 노곤함'의 뜻으로 ① weariness와 의미가 가장 가깝다.

해석
주주들은 그 회사의 문제를 기획부의 **무기력함** 탓으로 돌리고 있다.
① 권태, 피로, 지루함
② 교육, 지시, 방법, 설명
③ 보초(감시)병
④ 질문, 심문, 의문

어휘
lassitude 무기력, 노곤함
instruction 교육, 지시, 방법, 설명
interrogation 질문, 심문, 의문
weariness 권태, 피로, 지루함
sentry 보초(감시)병

02 정답 ①

정답해설
밑줄 친 'sensible'은 '분별력 있는'의 뜻으로 ① reasonable과 의미가 가장 가깝다.

해석
그러므로, 희생자에 대해서 무관심한 채로 남는 것은 **분별력 있는** 상태를 유지해도 소용없다.
① 합리적인
② 치우치지 않는
③ 경험적인
④ 비논리적인

어휘
sensible 분별력 있는
impartial 치우치지 않는
illogical 비논리적인
reasonable 합리적인
empirical 경험적인

03 정답 ②

정답해설
밑줄 친 'almighty'는 '전능한'이라는 뜻으로 ② omnipotent와 의미가 가장 가깝다.

해석
중국 신화에서, 용호를 강력하고 **전능한** 왕으로 보았습니다.
① 상반되는
② 전능한
③ 번민의, 고뇌에 찬

④ 평상시의, 격의 없는, 우연한

어휘

the dragon and the tiger 용호(龍虎)
almighty 전능한　　　　　　　ambivalent 상반되는
omnipotent 전능한　　　　　　anguished 번민의, 고뇌에 찬
casual 평상시의, 격의 없는, 우연한

04 정답 ③

정답해설

Sharon이 새해 계획을 적고 있는 상황에서 Tobe와 나눈 대화의 내용이다. Tobe는 계획은 중요하지만 ③ '어려운 순간에 계획을 바꿀(change horses in the middle of the stream)' 수밖에 없는 순간들이 있다고 말한다.

오답해설

① Tobe와 Sharon은 계획을 수립하는 것에 관해 대화를 나누면서 Tobe가 계획은 중요하지만 '열광할 (go bananas)' 수밖에 없는 순간들이 있다고 말하는 것은 문맥상 부자연스럽다.
② Tobe는 계획은 중요하나 '헛수고할(beat a dead horse)' 수밖에 없는 순간들이 있다고 이야기하는 것은 적절하지 않다.
④ 계획을 세우는 것의 중요성을 인정하지만, Tobe는 '의기양양할(look like the cat that swallowed the canary)' 수밖에 없는 순간들이 있다고 하는 것은 빈칸에 들어갈 말로 적합하지 않다.

해석

Tobe: 너 여기서 뭐 하고 있어?
Sharon: 나는 새 다이어리에 내 새해 소원을 적고 있었어.
Tobe: 오, 그거 네 새 다이어리야?
Sharon: 응 맞아. 오늘 샀어. 그리고 새해 계획도 좀 세워봤어.
Tobe: 잘했네! 계획은 중요하지. 근데 어려운 순간에 계획을 바꿀 수밖에 없는 순간들이 있어.
Sharon: 알아, 그럴 때가 있지. 그런데 내가 계획이 있다는 것을 알면 내가 조정을 해야 하더라도 더 안정감을 느끼게 해줘.

① 열광하다
② 헛수고하다
③ 어려운 순간에 계획을 바꾸다
④ 의기양양하다

어휘

adjustment 조정　　　　　　　go bananas 열광하다
beat a dead horse 헛수고하다
change horses in the middle of the stream 어려운 순간에 계획을 바꾸다
look like the cat that swallowed the canary 의기양양하다

05 정답 ④

정답해설

④ **출제 포인트: 완전타동사+[to부정사 vs. 동명사]**
'consider'는 완전타동사의 경우 목적어로 동명사를 사용할 수 있으나 to부정사는 사용할 수 없다. 해당 문장은 'consider'의 목적어로 to부정사 'to unseal'을 사용하였으므로 틀린 문장이다. 따라서 'to unseal'을 동명사 'unsealing'으로 수정해야 한다.

오답해설

① **출제 포인트: 불완전타동사의 목적격 보어**
'make'는 불완전타동사로 쓰일 때 「make+목적어+목적격 보어[명사(구)]」

의 구조를 가지며 '~을 ~로 만들다'를 뜻한다. 해당 문장에서는 명사구 'a highly popular area'가 목적격 보어로 옳게 사용되었다.
② **출제 포인트: 타동사구[완전타동사+목적어+전치사+목적어]**
「relieve+목적어[대상]+of+목적어[사물]」은 '~에게서 ~을 덜어주다'를 뜻한다. 이때 'some of the administrative work'는 목적어[사물]에 해당하는 명사(구)이다.
③ **출제 포인트: what vs. that**
'What makes football fun'의 경우 'What' 뒤에 오는 절의 주어가 없으며 앞에 선행사가 없으므로 선행사를 포함하는 관계대명사 'what'을 사용하는 것이 옳다. 또한 'we all have different ways of looking at it'의 경우 완전한 형태의 절이므로 앞에 접속사 'that'을 사용하는 것이 옳다.

해석

① 그 아름다운 해변은 이곳을 관광객들에게 매우 인기 있는 지역으로 만든다.
② Tom에게서 행정 업무의 일부를 덜어주기 위해 비서 한 명이 고용되었다.
③ 축구를 재미있게 만드는 것은 우리 모두가 그것을 보는 다른 방식을 가지고 있다는 것이다.
④ 그녀는 배심원단이 선정된 후에 몇 가지 서류를 공개하는 것을 고려하겠다고 말했다.

06 정답 ①

정답해설

① **출제 포인트: 부정사의 관용표현**
「have no choice but to 동사원형」은 관용표현으로 '~하지 않을 수 없다'를 뜻한다. 해당 문장은 「have no choice but」의 과거형인 'had no choice but'을 사용하였으나 뒤에 'to+동사원형'이 아닌 동사원형 'accept'를 사용하였으므로 틀린 문장이다. 따라서 'accept'를 'to accept'로 수정해야 한다.

오답해설

② **출제 포인트: 전치사 vs. 접속사**
'in spite of'는 전치사이므로 뒤에 명사(구)가 온다. 해당 문장은 'in spite of' 뒤에 명사(구) 'the fact'를 사용하였으므로 옳은 문장이다. 또한 해당 문장에서 'that'은 'the fact'와 명사절 'he drank too much'가 동격 관계임을 나타내는 접속사이며 주절과 시제 일치하여 'drank'는 'drink'의 과거형으로 썼다.
③ **출제 포인트: 가목적어 it**
'find'는 불완전타동사의 경우 「find+목적어+목적격 보어[(to be)+형용사]」의 구조를 가진다. 이때 목적어가 긴 경우 가목적어 'it'을 사용하며 진목적어는 목적격 보어 뒤로 이동한다. 해당 문장은 불완전타동사 'find'의 과거시제 'found'를 사용하였으며 목적어(to believe what was happening around them)가 긴 경우에 해당하므로 가목적어 'it'을 사용하였고 진목적어는 목적격 보어 'hard' 뒤로 이동하였다.
④ **출제 포인트: 「가격동사+사람(목적어)+전치사+the+신체부위」**
「hold+사람+by+the+신체부위」는 '~의 신체부위를 잡다'를 뜻한다. 이때 전치사 'by' 뒤에는 정관사 'the'를 사용해야 하며 소유격 대명사를 사용할 수 없다.

오답률 TOP 2

07 정답 ③

정답해설

③ **출제 포인트: 등위상관접속사**
「neither A nor B but C」는 등위상관접속사로 'A도 B도 아닌 C'를 뜻한다. 해당 문장은 동사 「neither A nor B」를 사용하였으나 뒤에 'but

Day 03

C'를 'and C'로 사용하였으므로 틀린 문장이다. 따라서 'and'를 'but'으로 수정해야 한다. 이때 A(French), B(German), C(a strange mixture of the two)는 동사 'speaks'의 목적어이다.

오답해설

① **출제 포인트: the+형용사/목적격 관계대명사 생략**
해당 문장에서 'the disabled'는 「the+형용사」로 '장애인들'을 뜻하며 「형용사+복수명사」인 'disabled people'로 바꿔 쓸 수 있다. 또한 'One aspect'와 'the committee' 사이에는 목적격 관계대명사 'which' 또는 'that'이 생략되어 있다.

② **출제 포인트: 주요 조동사 표현**
「It would be better to 동사원형」은 관용표현으로 '~하는 것이 낫다'를 뜻한다. 또한 'get'은 불완전자동사의 경우 주격 보어로 형용사를 사용할 수 있으며 해당 문장에서 비교급 형용사 'colder'는 'gets'의 주격 보어이다.

④ **출제 포인트: to부정사 주요표현/during vs. for**
'To put it in a nutshell'은 관용표현으로 '쉽게 말해, 간단명료하게 말하면'을 뜻한다. 또한 전치사 'during'은 특정 기간을 목적어로 가지며 해당 문장에서 'the 1980s'는 특정 기간에 해당한다.

08 정답 ④

정답해설

(A) 빈칸 이전에서 "high fixed costs of production, but near-zero or zero variable costs of production. This cost structure characterizes a class of technology products that are collectively termed information goods(제작의 높은 고정비용, 그러나 거의 0에 가까운 또는 0인 변동비용. 이 비용 구조는 집합적으로 정보재라 일컬어지는 기술 재화 부류의 특징이다)."라고 언급하며, '정보재의 특징은 높은 고정비용과 낮은 변동비용'이라는 것을 설명하고 있다. (A) 이후 문장의 내용은 "the cost of producing the first unit of an information good is very high, and yet the cost of producing each additional unit is virtually nothing(한 정보재의 첫 번째 제품을 제작하는 비용은 매우 높지만, 각각의 추가적인 제품을 제작하는 비용은 사실상 무(無)이다.'로, 사실상 (A) 이전에 언급되었던 것과 거의 동일한 내용을 재차 언급해 주고 있다. 따라서 (A)에는 '재서술, 요약'에 사용되는 'In brief(간단히 말해)' 또는 'Put differently(달리 말하면)'가 사용될 수 있다.

(B) 이전에서는 '높은 고정비용과 낮은 변동비용'에 관해 설명하고 있으며, (B) 이후에서는 'Microsoft사의 윈도우 운영 체제 개발'에 대해 설명하며 앞서 언급된 내용에 대한 구체적인 예시를 들고 있다. 따라서 빈칸에 가장 적절한 것은 '예시'를 나타내는 'For example(예를 들어)' 또는 'To take an instance(예를 들면)'이다. 따라서 정답은 '④ Put differently(달리 말하면) – To take an instance(예를 들면)'이다.

오답해설

① (A) 전후 내용이 사실상 동일한 내용이므로, '양보, 역접'을 나타내는 'Nevertheless(그럼에도 불구하고)'는 빈칸에 적절하지 않다.
② (B) 이후 내용이 (B) 이전 내용에 대한 반대 상황을 가정하는 것이 아니기 때문에 'Otherwise(그렇지 않으면)'는 빈칸에 적절하지 않다.
나머지 보기는 문맥상 어색하므로 오답이다.

해석

IT 업계에서의 독특한 가격 책정 및 시장 구조에 대한 질문들 중 많은 것들이 특이한 특정 비용 구조에서 기인한다: 바로 제작의 높은 고정비용, 그러나 거의 0에 가까운 또는 0인 변동비용. 이 비용 구조는 집합적으로 정보재라 일컬어지는 기술 재화 부류의 특징이다. (A) 달리 말하면, 한 정보재의 첫 번째 제품을 제작하는 비용은 매우 높지만, 각각의 추가적인 제품을 제작하는 비용은 사실상 무(無)이다. (B) 예를 들면, Microsoft사는 윈도우 운영 체제의 각각의 버전을 개발하는 데 수억 달러를 지출했다. 그러나 OS의 최초 원본이 일단 개발되면, 그것은 비용이 들지 않고 복제될 수 있다.

(A)	(B)
① 그럼에도 불구하고	예를 들어
② 간단히 말해	그렇지 않으면
③ 그래서	요약하면
④ 달리 말하면	예를 들면

어휘

pricing 가격 책정
fixed cost 고정비용, 고정 원가
characterize …의 특징이 되다
unit (제품) 한 개[단위]
operating system(OS) 운영 체제
stem from …에서 기인하다
variable cost 변동비용, 변동 원가
collectively 집합적으로, 총괄적으로
virtually 사실상
replicate 복제하다

09 정답 ②

정답해설

본문에서는 'The sale of queen ants is frowned upon by the United States Department of Agriculture (USDA), which has banned it for an important ecological reason(미농무부(USDA)는 여왕개미 판매를 못마땅해 하고 있으며, 중요한 생태학적 이유로 그것을 금지시켰다.)'라고 설명하며, 그 이유는 '침입종이 생태계를 교란시키는 것을 방지하기 위한 것'이라는 것을 언급하고 있다. 따라서 글의 제목으로 가장 적절한 것은 '② Why You Can't Buy Queen Ants in the US(당신이 미국에서 여왕개미를 살 수 없는 이유)'이다.

오답해설

① 본문과 관련이 없는 제목이다.
③ 본문에서는 '침입 개미 종이 생태계에 끼치는 악영향'에 대해 언급하고 있으나, 타 침입종에 관해서는 언급하고 있지 않으며, 또한, '그러한 악영향으로 인해 여왕개미 거래가 금지되어 있다'는 것이 본문의 주요 내용이므로, 글의 제목으로는 적절하지 않다.
④ 여왕개미의 중요한 역할에 대해서는 구체적으로 설명하고 있지 않다.

해석

만일 당신이 미국에서 애완 개미 군락을 위한 여왕개미를 찾고 있다면, 당신은 온라인에서 그것들을 구매하는 것보다 한 마리를 잡는 것이 더 나을 것이다. 미농무부(USDA)는 여왕개미 판매를 못마땅해 하고 있으며, 중요한 생태학적 이유로 그것을 금지시켰다. 만일 당신이 여왕개미를 구매하고, 그것이 탈출하여 그것이 자연적으로 발견되지 않는 지역에 군락을 형성한다면, 그것은 지역의 생태계에 많은 스트레스를 줄 수 있다. 침입 개미 종은 자연적인 생물 다양성에 해를 끼친다. 악명 높은 붉은불개미를 예로 들어보자. 이것들은 남미가 원산지이지만 운송 나무 상자를 통해 미국으로 오는 길을 찾았다. 이곳에는 천적이 없기 때문에, 그것들은 남부 주들로 퍼져나갔고, 돌이킬 수 없는 경제적, 생태학적 피해를 야기하고 있다. 이러한 이유로 USDA는 미국 내에서 여왕개미를 판매하는 것을 금한다. 당신은 여전히 유럽과 다른 국가에서 그것들을 구매할 수 있지만, 이것은 현재 논의가 되고 있는 중이다.
① 개미가 어떻게 좋은 애완동물이 되는가
② 당신이 미국에서 여왕개미를 살 수 없는 이유
③ 침입종이 환경에 어떻게 영향을 미치는가
④ 생태계에 있어서 여왕개미의 중요한 역할

어휘

be better off ~ing ~하는 것이 더 낫다[좋다]
frown upon ~에 눈살을 찌푸리다[~을 못마땅해 하다]

ban 금지하다
ecosystem 생태계
biodiversity 생물 다양성
red imported fire ant 붉은불개미
crate (물품 운송용 대형 나무) 상자
irreparable 돌이킬 수 없는
debate 논쟁하다, 논의하다
ecological 생태학의
invasive 침입의
infamous 악명 높은
native to … 토종의[원산의]
predator 포식자
prohibit 금지하다

오답률 TOP 3
10 정답 ②

정답해설

본문은 '고등 교육의 자유 시장화(Marketization of higher education)'의 이점에 대해 설명하는 글이다. 본문에 따르면 '고등 교육의 자유 시장화는 고등 교육의 개혁과 교육 시스템 혁신에 도움이 되고, 폐쇄적 학교 운영 방식을 개방적 사회 지향적 모델로 변화시킬 수 있으며, 빠르게 발전하는 사회 및 경제 상황에 고등 교육기관이 더욱더 잘 적응하고 그에 따라 발전할 수 있도록 지속적으로 자극을 준다'고 설명한다. 그런데 '② It changes the policy of higher education institutions from creating conditions that will meet the various needs of students to focusing on the requirements and regulations of the government(그것은 학생들의 다양한 요구를 충족시키는 환경을 만드는 것으로부터 정부의 요구와 규제에 초점을 맞추는 것으로 정책을 변화시킨다).'에서는 '자유 시장적인 모델(학생들의 다양한 요구를 충족시키는 자유롭고 개방적인 환경)에서 정부의 요구와 규제에 집중하는 폐쇄적인 모델로의 변화'를 설명하고 있다. 즉, 본문에서 언급하는 '고등 교육의 자유 시장화의 특징'과는 정반대의 내용을 언급하고 있으므로, 글의 전체 흐름과 부합하지 않는다. 따라서 정답은 ②이다.

오답해설

①에서 '고등 교육의 자유 시장화가 전통적인 학교 운영 방식을 변화시키는 데 도움이 된다'고 언급한 후, ③, ④에서 '비록 고등 교육의 기본 정신은 변화하지 않았으나, 사회가 발전함에 따라 고등 교육 또한 발맞추어 발전해야 할 필요성이 있다'고 언급하여, 앞서 ①에서 언급한 '변화'의 필요성에 대해 설명한다. 글의 흐름상 자연스럽게 이어지므로, 나머지 보기는 오답이다.

해석

고등 교육의 자유 시장화는 고등 교육이 시장 및 사회에 밀접하게 관련되도록 도와주고, 이것이 고등 교육의 개혁을 가속화하고 교육 시스템의 혁신을 촉진한다. ① 그것은 또한 전통적인 폐쇄적 학교 운영 방식을 개방적인 사회 지향적인 모델로 변화시키는 것에 도움이 된다. ② 그것은 학생들의 다양한 요구를 충족시키는 환경을 만드는 것으로부터 정부의 요구와 규제에 초점을 맞추는 것으로 정책을 변화시킨다. ③ 물론 시장 경제가 존재하는 현대 사회에서의 고등 교육의 지식과 진리 추구의 기본 정신이 변화한 것은 아니다. ④ 그러나 고등 교육의 발전은 사회 발전과 밀접한 관련이 있고, 고등 교육기관은 경쟁적인 시장 경제 안에서 살아남고 발전해 나가야 한다. 이 시장 모델의 주된 이점은 그것이 고등 교육기관들이 변화하는 경제적 사회적 상황에 적응하도록 지속적으로 자극할 수 있다는 것이다.

어휘

marketization 자유 시장 경제로 전환, 자유 시장화
accelerate 가속화하다
running 운영, 경영
meet 충족시키다
pursuit 추구
stimulate 자극하다
enclosed 단절된, 폐쇄된
-oriented -지향적인, -중심의
various 다양한
competitive 경쟁의, 경쟁이 심한
adapt 적응하다

결국엔 성정혜 영어 하프모의고사
기적사 DAY 04

| 01 | ③ | 02 | ④ | 03 | ③ | 04 | ① | 05 | ④ |
| 06 | ③ | 07 | ③ | 08 | ③ | 09 | ④ | 10 | ① |

01 정답 ③

정답해설

밑줄 친 'avarice'는 '탐욕'의 뜻으로 ③ avidity와 의미가 가장 가깝다.

해석

이 영화는 자만, 시기, 음욕, 탐식, 나태, **탐욕**, 그리고 분노 등 성경에 나오는 죽음에 이르는 일곱 가지 대죄를 보여준다.
① 소명
② 직업
③ 탐욕
④ 약탈자

어휘

envy 시기
gluttony 탐식
avarice 탐욕
calling 소명
avidity 탐욕
lust 음욕
sloth 나태
wrath 분노
vocation 직업
plunderer 약탈자

오답률 TOP 1
02 정답 ④

정답해설

밑줄 친 'confident'는 '자신감 있는, 확신하는'이라는 의미로 사용되었고, 유의어가 아닌 것은 ④ confidential이다.

해석

자신감 있는 사람들은 그들 스스로를 믿고 항상 그들 스스로를 사랑한다.
① 확신하는
② 확신하는
③ 확신하는
④ 기밀의

어휘

confident 자신감 있는, 확신하는
assured 확신하는
confidential 기밀의
reliant 확신하는
convinced 확신하는

오답률 TOP 2
03 정답 ③

정답해설

밑줄 친 'assiduous'는 '근면한, 성실한'의 뜻으로 ③ industrious와 의미가 가장 가깝다.

해석

정부는 디플레이션을 잡는데 **끈기 있어**왔다.
① 상반되는

② 우려하는, 이해가 빠른
③ 근면한
④ 취미의, 여가 활동의

어휘

assiduous 끈기 있는, 근면한, 성실한 ambivalent 상반되는
apprehensive 우려하는, 이해가 빠른 industrious 근면한
avocational 취미의, 여가 활동의

04 정답 ①

정답해설

'무선 이어폰(wireless earphone)' 환불을 받고 싶은 손님과 안내원의 대화이다. 안내원이 손님에게 환불을 받고자 하는 이유를 묻자 손님은 "The sound is too small even when the sound is at its maximum volume(음량 크기가 최대로 되어 있는데도 소리가 너무 작아요)."라며 환불의 이유에 대해 말한다. 손님이 말하는 이유로 보아 손님이 받은 무선 이어폰은 ① '품질이 좋지 않은 물건(a lemon)'임을 알 수 있다.

오답해설

② 손님이 며칠 전에 구입한 제품을 환불받고 싶은 이유를 이야기하는 상황에서 '불가항력(an act of god)'을 받았기 때문이라고 말하는 것은 맥락상 부적절하다.
③ 손님이 제품을 환불받고 싶어 하는 이유가 '욕(four-letter word)'이라고 답변하는 것은 문맥상 어색하다.
④ 안내원이 손님이 환불받고 싶어 하는 이유를 묻자 손님이 '최고의 것(the best thing since sliced bread)'을 받았기 때문이라는 답변은 대화의 흐름상 부자연스럽다.

해석

안내원: 무엇을 도와드릴까요?
손님: 며칠 전에 구매한 제품을 환불받고 싶습니다.
안내원: 네, 잘 찾아오셨네요. 구매하신 제품이 뭔가요?
손님: 무선 이어폰입니다.
안내원: 그리고 환불받고 싶으신 이유가 뭔가요?
손님: 품질이 좋지 않은 물건을 받았어요. 음량 크기가 최대로 되어있는데도 소리가 너무 작아요.
안내원: 오, 정말 죄송합니다. 이 서류를 작성해주세요.
① 품질이 좋지 않은 물건
② 불가항력
③ 욕
④ 최고의 것

어휘

a lemon 품질이 좋지 않은 물건
an act of god 불가항력
four-letter word 욕
the best thing since sliced bread 최고의 것

05 정답 ④

정답해설

④ **출제 포인트**: 불완전타동사[불완전타동사+목적어+to 동사원형]
'persuade'가 불완전타동사로 사용되는 경우 「persuade+목적어[대상]+to 동사원형」의 구조를 가지며 '~을 설득하여 …하게 하다'를 뜻하나 해당 문장에서는 'to mention'이 아닌 'mentioning'을 사용했으므로 옳지 않다. 따라서 'mentioning'을 'to mention'으로 수정해야 한다.

오답해설

① **출제 포인트**: 완전타동사+[to부정사 vs. 동명사]
'admit'은 완전타동사로 동명사를 목적어로 가지며 to부정사를 목적어로 가질 수 없다. 해당 문장은 'admit'의 과거시제인 'admitted'를 사용하였으며 동명사 'feeling'을 목적어로 가지므로 옳은 문장이다. 또한 해당 문장에서 동명사 'feeling'은 불완전자동사의 성격을 가지므로 주격 보어로 과거분사 'hurt'를 옳게 사용하였다.
② **출제 포인트**: what vs. that/강조의 조동사 do
'What he does possess'에서 'What' 뒤에 오는 절의 목적어가 없으며 앞에 선행사가 없으므로 선행사를 포함하는 관계대명사 'What'을 사용하는 것이 옳다. 또한 'does'는 'possess'를 강조하는 강조의 조동사 'do'의 역할을 하고 있다.
③ **출제 포인트**: 불완전타동사의 목적격 보어/with 분사구문
해당 문장은 불완전타동사 'consider'가 수동태로 쓰인 문장으로 'bad manners'는 목적격 보어에 해당하며 'to speak with your mouth full of food'는 진주어로 사용된 to부정사구이다. 이때 'with your mouth full of food'는 'with 분사구문'으로 「with+목적어+(being)+형용사(구)」의 형태로 사용되었다.

해석

① William은 전에 내가 말했던 것 때문에 상처받았다는 것을 인정했다.
② 그가 정말 지니고 있는 것은 문제의 핵심으로 들어가는 능력이다.
③ 입에 음식을 가득 물고 말하는 것이 유럽 문화권에서는 실례로 여겨진다.
④ 그의 법률 고문들은 그를 설득하여 강도 사건에 연루된 사람의 이름을 언급하게 했다.

오답률 TOP 3

06 정답 ③

정답해설

③ **출제 포인트**: 「가격동사+사람(목적어)+전치사+the+신체부위」
「kiss+사람+on+the+신체부위」는 '~의 신체부위에 입을 맞추다'를 뜻한다. 이때 전치사 'on' 뒤에는 정관사 'the'를 사용해야 하며 소유격 대명사를 사용할 수 없다. 해당 문장은 「kiss+사람+on」을 사용하였으나 뒤에 정관사 'the'가 아닌 소유격 대명사 'his'를 사용하였으므로 틀린 문장이다. 따라서 'his cheek'을 'the cheek'으로 수정해야 한다.

오답해설

① **출제 포인트**: 전치사 vs. 접속사
'because'는 종속접속사로 뒤에 원인을 나타내는 부사절이 온다. 해당 문장은 'because'를 사용하였으며 뒤에 오는 'he had to obey commands'는 원인을 나타내는 부사절에 해당하므로 옳은 문장이다. 또한 해당 문장에서 'being'은 동명사로 'hated'의 목적어이다.
② **출제 포인트**: to부정사의 명사적 용법
해당 문장에서 'it'은 가주어이며 'to contact him'은 진주어에 해당한다. 또한 'proven'은 불완전자동사이며 'impossible'은 주격 보어이다.
④ **출제 포인트**: 부정사의 관용표현
「cannot choose but 동사원형」은 관용표현으로 '~하지 않을 수 없다'를 뜻한다. 해당 문장은 「cannot choose but」 뒤에 동사원형 'respond'를 사용하였으므로 옳은 문장이다.

07 정답 ③

정답해설

③ 출제 포인트: 주요 조동사 표현
「had better 동사원형」의 부정형은 「had better not 동사원형」이다. 해당 문장은 「had better 동사원형」의 부정형을 사용하였으나 'not'이 'better' 앞에 위치하고 있으므로 옳지 않은 문장이다. 따라서 'not'을 동사원형 'leave' 앞으로 이동시켜 'had not better leave'를 'had better not leave'로 수정해야 한다.

오답해설

① 출제 포인트: to부정사 주요표현
'the last person to 동사원형'은 관용표현으로 '결코 ~하지 않을 사람'을 뜻한다.

② 출제 포인트: 등위상관접속사/부정부사 도치
등위상관접속사 「not only A but also B」를 사용하여 절과 절을 연결하고 있다. 이때 'Not only' 뒤에 오는 어순은 의문문 어순으로 「be동사/조동사+주어 ~」이다. 해당 문장은 절과 절을 「not only A but also B」를 통해 연결하고 있으며, 'Not only' 뒤에 의문문 어순으로 'has it'를 사용하였으므로 옳은 문장이다.

④ 출제 포인트: to부정사의 명사적 용법/불완전타동사/the+형용사
해당 문장에서 'to ask ~ the poor'를 주어로 사용하였으나 길이가 긴 경우에 해당하므로 주어 자리에 가주어 'It'을 사용하고 'to ask ~the poor'는 문미로 이동하였다. 또한 'ask'는 불완전타동사의 경우 「ask+목적어+목적격 보어[to+동사원형]」의 형태를 가지며 'the poor'는 「the+형용사」로 '가난한 사람들'을 뜻한다. 이때 'the poor'는 「형용사+복수명사」인 'poor people'로 바꿔 쓸 수 있다.

08 정답 ③

정답해설

본문의 내용에 따르면, '정보재에는 여러 이점이 있는데 그중 가장 중요한 것은 사업을 제품화하는 것이며, 제품화된 정보재의 재고는 무제한적이고 정보재의 주문 처리 또한 능률적, 자동적으로 이행될 수 있다.' 즉, 재고가 무한하다는 것은 제품을 판매할 수 있는 잠재력(가능성) 또한 무한하다는 것을 의미한다고 볼 수 있는데, ③에서 'which means your sales potential is ③ restricted'라고 언급하는 것은 본문에서 주장하는 것과는 반대되는 내용이다. 따라서 '③ restricted(제한적인)'는 'unrestricted(제한이 없는)'로 바뀌어야 문맥상 자연스러우므로, 정답은 ③이다.

오답해설

① 전체적인 본문 내용이 '정보재의 이점'에 관해 언급하고 있으므로, ① benefits는 문맥상 적절하다.

② '성장을 지속할 수 있는' 상태가 되는 것은 '능률적으로 제품화할 수 있는 단계까지 성장했을 경우'에 해당하는 것이므로, 'well-oiled(능률적인, 순조로운)'는 문맥상 자연스럽다.

④ 'you do all the legwork in advance(당신은 모든 발품 파는 일을 미리 진행하고)'라고 언급한 후, 초반에 비해 말기에는 주로 마케팅과 같은 '최소한의(minimal)' 유지만 필요하다고 서술하는 것은 문맥상 자연스럽다. 따라서 오답이다.

해석

정보재는 여러 가지 ① 이점을 제공하지만, 그것들 중 가장 중요한 것은 당신이 시간을 충분히 활용하고 사업을 성장시키는 데 집중할 수 있도록 당신의 사업을 제품화할 수 있는 능력이다. 이것은 당신이 사업가로서의 기력 소진의 위험을 피할 수 있도록 도와주고, 일단 당신이 ② 능률적인 제품화 기계로까지 성장한다면, 당신은 가상의 비서를 고용함으로써 성장세를 이어갈 수 있다. 게다가, 정보재에는 무제한적인 재고가 있으며, 이는 당신의 판매 잠재력은 ③ 제한적이고(→제한이 없고) 당신의 주문 이행 절차는 능률적이고 자동적이라는 것을 의미한다. 다시 말해, 디지털 상품을 판매함으로써, 당신은 모든 발품 파는 일을 미리 진행하고, 말기에는 ④ 최소한의 유지 - 주로 마케팅 - 만을 필요로 한다는 것이다. 일단 당신의 온라인 상점이 마련되면 당신이 수동으로 주문을 처리할 필요 없이 당신의 손님들은 그들이 원하는 만큼의 정보재를 구매할 수 있다.

어휘

significant 주요한
productize 제품화하다
leverage 활용하다, 강화하다
pitfall 위험, 곤란
entrepreneurial 사업가의
burnout (마음·체력의) 쇠진, (스트레스에 의한) 정신·신경의 쇠약, 기력 소진
ramp up 성장하다, 증가시키다
well-oiled 능률적인, 순조로운
virtual assistant (인공지능) 가상의 비서
inventory 재고
sales potential 판매 잠재력, 세일즈 포텐셜(잠재수요 중 기업이 얻을 수 있는 점유율)
maintenance 유지
back-end 말기
manually 수동으로

09 정답 ④

정답해설

본문은 '좀비 개미 균(zombie ant fungus)'이 어떻게 목수 개미를 감염시키고 통제하는지 설명해주고 있다. 주어진 문장의 "The fungus thereby benefits ~"로 보아, 좀비 개미 균이 이득을 얻게 되는 지점이 바로 이전에 언급되어야 하는 것을 알 수 있다. ④ 이전 문장 "The invasion culminates with the sprouting of a spore-laden fruiting body from a dead ant's head."에서 '포자가 든 자실체(spore-laden fruiting body)'가 싹튼다고 언급하고 있으므로, 이 싹튼 자실체로부터 '전염성 있는 포자(infectious spores)'가 확산된다는 것을 알 수 있다. 따라서 주어진 문장이 들어갈 가장 적절한 위치는 ④이다.

오답해설

③ 이전 문장에서 'compels them to climb vegetation and bite into the underside of leaves or twigs(그들에게 식물을 타고 올라가 잎 또는 작은 가지의 밑 부분을 물도록 명령하는데)'라고 언급하며 '지면과 떨어진 윗부분'에서 개미가 죽는다는 것을 설명하고 있으므로, '포자가 밑에 있는 땅(the ground below)으로 떨어진다'는 주어진 문장이 이어질 수도 있을 것이라 생각될 수도 있지만, '포자가 든 자실체가 싹을 틔운다'는 내용이 ③ 이후에 이어지므로, 그 뒤에 '(자실체 안의) 포자가 확산된다'고 연결되는 것이 문맥상 자연스럽다. 따라서 ③은 오답이다.

나머지 보기는 문맥상 어색하므로 오답이다.

해석

Penn State University의 연구진은 지구상에서 가장 이상한 자연 현상 중 하나인 좀비 개미에 관한 새로운 정보를 공개했다. (①) 그것들은 열대 지방의 목수 개미인데, 때때로 좀비 개미 균이라 불리는 Ophiocordyceps unilateralis sensu lato에 의해 침투되어 조종받는다. (②) 이 균성의 신체 도둑은 개미가 산림의 하층 식물 군락으로 가도록 강제하고, 그들에게 식물을 타고 올라가 잎 또는 작은 가지의 밑 부분을 물도록 명령하는데, 그곳에서 개미는 죽는다. (③) 이 침입은 죽은 개미의 머리에 포자가 든 자실체를 싹틔우는 것으로 마무리된다. (④ **그 균은 그렇게 함으로써 이득을 얻는데, 왜냐하면 전염성의 포자가 아래에 있는 땅으로 떨어지고, 그곳에서 그것들이 먹이를 찾아다니는 다른 개미들을 감염시킬 수 있기 때문이다.**) 새로운 연구는 그 균성의 기생충이 개미의 뇌를 감염시키지 않고 이 모든 것을 행한다는

것을 보여준다. 대신에, 연구에 따르면, 좀비 개미 균은 개미의 몸 전체의 근섬유를 에워싸며 침입한다.

어휘

fungus 균류
infectious 전염성의
forage (특히 동물이) 먹이를 찾다
infiltrate 침투시키다
snatcher 낚아채는 사람, (시체) 도둑
understory (식물 군락의) 하층, 하층 식생
compel 강요하다, 명령하다
twig 작은 가지
culminate with …로 끝나다
spore-laden 포자가 가득한[든]
thereby 그것에 의해
spore 포자
phenomenon 현상
fungal 균성의
vegetation 식물
invasion 침입, 침범
sprouting 싹 틔움
fruiting body (균류의) 자실체

10 정답 ①

정답해설

본문은 '2005년과 2015년의 OECD 회원국의 초/중등 단계의 정규 교육을 받는 학생당 지출을 조사한 결과'를 설명하는 글이다. 두 번째 문장 "Countries with the highest expenditures per FTE student at the elementary/secondary level in 2015 generally had among the highest expenditures in 2005, and vice versa(2015년에 초/중등 단계의 정규 교육을 받는 학생당 지출이 가장 많았던 국가들은 대개 2005년에도 가장 많은 지출을 했으며, 그 반대도 마찬가지였다)."에서 '2015년 지출이 가장 많았던 국가들이 2005년에도 지출이 가장 많았으며, 그 반대 또한 마찬가지다'라고 언급하고 있으므로, '2015년 지출이 가장 적었던 국가들이 2005년에도 지출이 가장 적었음'을 유추할 수 있다. 따라서 글의 내용과 일치하는 것은 '① Nations with the lowest expenditures per FTE student at elementary/secondary level in 2015 generally had among the lowest expenditures in 2005(2015년에 초/중등 단계의 정규 교육을 받는 학생당 지출이 가장 적었던 국가들은 대개 2005년에도 가장 적은 지출을 했다).'이다.

오답해설

② 본문 세 번째 문장 "In 2015, the average of OECD countries' expenditures per FTE student at the elementary/secondary level were $9,500, compared with $7,700 in 2005(2015년 OECD 회원국의 초/중등 단계의 정규 교육을 받는 학생당 평균 지출액은 2005년 7,700달러와 비교하여 9,500달러였다)."를 통해, 2005년보다 2015년의 평균 지출이 더 많은 것을 알 수 있으므로, 모든 OECD국가에서 감소하지 않았음을 알 수 있다. 따라서 글의 내용과 일치하지 않는다.

③ 9,500달러라는 금액은 2015년 OECD 회원국들의 평균치이며, 미국의 지출 금액은 본문에서 언급되지 않는다. 따라서 오답이다.

④ 미국과 아이슬란드의 지출을 직접적으로 비교하는 내용은 본문에 등장하지 않는다.

해석

OECD 회원국에서, 초/중등 단계의 정규 교육을 받는 학생당 지출이 일반적으로 2005년보다 2015년에 더 많았다. 2015년에 초/중등 단계의 정규 교육을 받는 학생당 지출이 가장 많았던 국가들은 대개 2005년에도 가장 많은 지출을 했으며, 그 반대도 마찬가지였다. 2015년 OECD 회원국의 초/중등 단계의 정규 교육을 받는 학생당 평균 지출액은 2005년 7,700달러와 비교하여 9,500달러였다. 두 해의 데이터가 모두 이용 가능한 27개의 OECD 회원국들 중, 미국을 포함한 23개국에서 초/중등 단계의 정규 교육을 받는 학생당 지출이 2005년보다 20015년에 더 많았다. 세 국가들(아이슬란드, 그리스, 슬로베니아)은 초/중등 단계의 정규 교육을 받는 학생당 지출이 2005년보다 2015년에 더 적었다. 멕시코에서는 2015년의 초/중등 단계의 정규 교육을 받는 학생당 지출이 2005년과 거의 동일했다 (두 해 모두 3,300달러).

① 2015년에 초/중등 단계의 정규 교육을 받는 학생당 지출이 가장 적었던 국가들은 대개 2005년에도 가장 적은 지출을 했다.
② 모든 OECD국가들에서 초/중등 단계의 정규 교육을 받는 학생당 지출의 평균 액수는 지난 10년 동안 감소해왔다.
③ 미국은 2015년에 초/중등 교육에 9,500달러를 지출했다.
④ 2015년 아이슬란드의 초/중등 단계의 정규 교육을 받는 학생당 지출은 미국의 지출보다 더 적었다.

어휘

expenditure 지출, 소비, 비용
full-time-equivalent 임의의 업무에 투입된 노동력을 전일 종사 노동자 수로 측정하는 방법
vice versa 역(逆)도 또한 같음
decline 감소하다, 줄다
generally 대개, 일반적으로

결국엔 성정혜 영어 하프모의고사
기적사 DAY 05

01	③	02	②	03	①	04	④	05	③
06	④	07	④	08	④	09	③	10	④

01 정답 ③

정답해설

밑줄 친 'dismay'는 '실망, 경악'이라는 뜻으로 ③ disappointment와 의미가 가장 가깝다.

해석

그 경기를 텔레비전에서 지켜보았던 사람들은 그것을 **실망**하며 보았음이 틀림없다.
① 존엄사
② 전임자
③ 실망
④ 고문

어휘

dismay 실망, 경악
predecessor 전임자
torture 고문
euthanasia 존엄사
disappointment 실망

02 정답 ②

정답해설

밑줄 친 'realistic'은 '실용적인'이라는 뜻으로 ② pragmatic과 의미가 가장 가깝다.

해석

현대예술에서, 그 예술가의 **실용적인** 스타일과 섬세한 관찰은 잘 표현된다.
① 편한, 마음을 느긋하게 해주는
② 실용적인
③ 실행 불가능한
④ 실행할 수 없는

어휘

realistic 실용적인
relaxing 편한, 마음을 느긋하게 해주는
infeasible 실행 불가능한
meticulous 섬세한, 꼼꼼한
pragmatic 실용적인
impractical 실행할 수 없는

오답률 TOP 2

03 정답 ①

정답해설

밑줄 친 'deducted'는 'deduct(공제하다, 감하다)'의 과거분사로 'subtract(공제하다, 빼다)'의 과거분사인 ① subtracted와 의미가 가장 가깝다.

해석

그 시행령은 노동조합들이 정치적인 목적으로 급여가 **공제된** 자금을 사용하는 것을 금지한다.
① 감해진, 공제된
② 헌신적인, 전념하는
③ 패배한
④ 결정하지 못한

어휘

deducted 공제된
dedicated 헌신적인, 전념하는
undecided 결정하지 못한
subtracted 감해진, 공제된
defeated 패배한

04 정답 ④

정답해설

Ned와 Luke는 해외여행을 가는 것에 관한 대화를 나눈다. 해외여행 가는 것을 좋아하냐고 묻는 Luke에게 Ned는 해외에 가본 적이 없다며 다른 나라로 여행을 가보는 것이 어떨지 항상 궁금했었다고 답한다. 이에 Luke는 해외여행이 값진 경험이며 Ned가 ④ '우물 안 개구리(a big fish in a little pond)'였다는 것을 깨닫게 될 것이라고 이야기한다.

오답해설

① Luke는 해외여행이 값진 경험이었다며 Ned에게 그도 해외여행이 '긍정의 표시(thumbs up)'였다는 것을 깨닫게 될 것이라고 말하는 것은 문맥상 자연스럽지 않다.
② Ned에게 Luke는 해외여행에 관해 이야기하며 값진 경험이었고 말로 하자면 Ned가 '시작과 끝(Alpha and Omega)'이었다는 점을 깨닫게 되리라는 것은 빈칸에 들어갈 말로 적절하지 않다.
③ Luke는 해외여행을 다녀오는 것이 값진 경험이라고 묘사하며 Ned가 '아수라장(a pretty kettle of fish)'이라는 것을 깨닫게 될 것이라고 말하는 것은 대화의 흐름상 어색하다.

해석

Ned: 너 다른 나라 가본 적 있어?
Luke: 응, 나 해외여행 가는 거 좋아해. 너는 어때?
Ned: 나 해외에 가본 적이 한 번도 없어. 다른 나라로 여행 가보는 것이 어떨지 항상 궁금했었어.
Luke: 그것은 의심할 여지 없이 귀중한 경험이었어. 말로 하자면, 너는 네가 우물 안 개구리였다는 것을 깨닫게 될 거야. 세계의 다른 지역에는 굉장히 흥미로운 것들이 많아.
Ned: 어떨지 상상할 수가 없어. 근데 너한테 지금 듣고 보니 내 시야를 넓힐 멋진 기회일 것 같아.
Luke: 정확해. 너는 여행하면서 많은 것을 배우게 될 거야.
① 긍정의 표시
② 시작과 끝
③ 아수라장
④ 우물 안 개구리

어휘

thumbs up 긍정의 표시
a pretty kettle of fish 아수라장
a big fish in a little pond 우물 안 개구리
Alpha and Omega 시작과 끝

05 정답 ③

정답해설

③ **출제 포인트: 불완전타동사의 목적격 보어/불완전타동사의 수동태**

'think'는 불완전타동사의 경우 목적격 보어로 to부정사를 사용할 수 있으나 현재분사는 사용할 수 없다. 해당 문장은 불완전타동사 'think'가 수동태로 사용되었으나 목적격 보어에 현재분사 'costing'을 사용하였으므로 틀린 문장이다. 따라서 'costing'을 to부정사 'to cost'로 수정해야 한다.

오답해설

① **출제 포인트: 불완전타동사의 목적격 보어/완전타동사+[to부정사 vs. 동명사]**
'tell'은 불완전타동사의 경우 목적격 보어에 to부정사를 사용하며 'choose'는 완전타동사의 경우 목적어에 to부정사를 사용한다. 해당 문장은 'told(불완전타동사 tell'의 과거시제)'의 목적격 보어로 to부정사 'to drive'를 사용하였으며, 'chose(완전타동사 choose의 과거시제)'의 목적어로 to부정사 'to ignore'를 사용하였으므로 옳은 문장이다.

② **출제 포인트: 타동사구[완전타동사+목적어+전치사+목적어]**
'dissuade+목적어[대상]+from+목적어[명사/동명사]'는 타동사구로 '~하지 않도록 ~을 설득하다'를 뜻한다. 해당 문장에서는 전치사 'from' 뒤에 동명사 'cutting'을 사용하였으므로 옳은 문장이다.

④ **출제 포인트: what vs. that**
'What is extraordinary'의 경우 'What' 뒤에 오는 절의 주어가 없으며 앞에 선행사가 없으므로 선행사를 포함하는 관계대명사 'what'을 사용하는 것이 옳다. 또한 'Tom left without making a public statement about the incident'의 경우 완전한 형태의 절이므로 앞에 접속사 'that'을 사용하는 것이 옳으며 'left'는 'leave'의 과거형으로 완전자동사로 쓰였다.

해석

① 나는 Jane에게 좀 더 천천히 운전하라고 말했지만 그녀는 내 충고를 무시하기로 결정했다.
② 우리는 건강 프로그램을 위한 기금을 삭감하지 않도록 의회를 설득해야 한다.
③ John은 그 소프트웨어 회사에 연간 수백만 달러의 비용을 지불하는 것으로 생각된다.
④ 이상한 것은 Tom이 그 사고에 대해 공개 성명을 하지 않고 떠났다는 것이다.

오답률 TOP 3
06 정답 ④

정답해설

④ **출제 포인트: 전치사 vs. 접속사**
'during'은 전치사로 뒤에 명사(구)가 오며 명사절이 올 수 없다. 해당 문장은 'during'을 사용하였으나 뒤에 명사절을 사용하였으므로 틀린 문장이다. 따라서 'during'을 접속사 'while'로 수정해야 한다. 또한 주어진 우리말 해석에 따라 'during they watched'를 'while they were watching'으로 수정하는 것도 가능하다.

오답해설

① **출제 포인트: to부정사의 명사적 용법**
'to freeze'는 to부정사의 명사적 용법으로 사용되었으며 'agreed(완전타동사 agree의 과거시제)'의 목적어이다.

② **출제 포인트: 「가격동사+사람(목적어)+전치사+the+신체부위」**
「strike+사람+on+the+신체부위」는 '~의 신체부위를 때리다'를 뜻한다. 이때 전치사 'on' 이후에는 정관사 'the'를 사용해야 하며 소유격 대명사는 사용할 수 없다.

③ **출제 포인트: 부정사의 관용표현**
「can do no other than 동사원형」은 관용표현으로 '~하지 않을 수 없다'를 뜻한다. 해당 문장은 「can do no other than」 이후에 동사원형 'laugh'를 사용하였으므로 옳은 문장이다.

07 정답 ④

정답해설

④ **출제 포인트: to부정사 주요표현**
'to make matters worse'는 관용표현으로 '설상가상으로'를 뜻한다. 해당 문장은 주어진 해석이 '설상가상으로'나 'to make matters bad'를 사용하였으므로 틀린 문장이다. 따라서 'bad'를 'worse'로 수정해야 한다.

오답해설

① **출제 포인트: the+형용사**
'the French'는 'the+형용사'로 '프랑스인들'을 뜻하며 「형용사+복수명사」인 'French people'로 바꿔 쓸 수 있다. 또한 해당 문장에서 생략된 주어 'The red flowers'와 'popularize'가 수동관계이므로 과거분사 'popularized'로 시작하는 분사구문을 사용하는 것이 옳다.

② **출제 포인트: 등위상관접속사**
과거분사구 'put on trial'과 'set free'가 등위상관접속사 「either A or B」를 통해 병렬구조를 이루고 있다. 이때 'set'은 불완전타동사 'set'의 과거분사이며 뒤에 목적격 보어로 형용사 'free'를 사용하였다.

③ **출제 포인트: 주요 조동사 표현**
「It would be better to 동사원형」은 관용표현으로 '~하는 것이 좋다'를 뜻한다. 또한 사역동사 'let'은 목적격 보어로 원형부정사를 가진다. 해당 문장에서 원형부정사 'have'는 'let'의 목적격 보어로 목적어 'the children'과 능동관계이다.

오답률 TOP 1
08 정답 ④

정답해설

본문은 '디지털 자료(digital material)'의 특징 중 '특수한 가격 구조(high-fixed-cost/low-incremental-cost structure, 높은 고정비용/낮은 증분 비용)'가 디지털 자료 시장을 '순수 경쟁 시장(purely competitive market)'이 아닌 '독점적 경쟁(monopolistic competition)'으로 이끈다고 설명하고 있다. 주어진 문장은 '유사한 대체품인 다소 다른 종류의 제품들이 존재하는 상황'에 관해 언급하고 있다. ③ 이전 문장에서는 동일한 제품을 거래하는 '밀, 옥수수, 주식 지분'과 같은 '순수 경쟁 시장'에 대해 언급하고 있으며, ④ 이전 문장에서는 '동일하지 않은 제품을 거래'하는 '자동차' 시장과 같은 '비 순수 경쟁 시장'에 대해 언급하고 있다. 주어진 문장에서 설명하고 있는 '유사한 대체품인 몇 가지 다소 다른 종류의 제품(several somewhat different products some of which are close substitutes)'이라 함은 '밀, 옥수수' 보다는 '자동차'를 설명하기에 더욱 적합한 표현이다. 따라서 주어진 문장은 '자동차 시장(market for automobiles)'에 대한 설명이라는 것을 알 수 있으므로, ④에 주어진 문장이 들어가는 것이 가장 자연스럽다.

오답해설

나머지 보기는 문맥상 어색하므로 오답이다.

해석

디지털 자료는 일반적으로 첫 번째 사본을 제작하는 것은 비용이 매우 많이 들고, 그 후 사본을 제작하는 것은 매우 저렴하다는 특징을 가지고 있다. 예를 들어, 한 학술지 발행 비용의 70% 이상이 "초판 발행 비용"이라고 종종 말한다. (①) 이러한 형태의 비용 구조는 가격 책정에 있어서 특수한 문제를 제기한다. 첫 번째 문제는 이러한 종류의 비용 구조로는 경쟁 시장을 유지하기 매우 어렵다는 것이다. (②) 경제학자들은 순수 경쟁 시장을 동일한 제품에 대한 "다수의" 생산자들이 있는 형태로 정의한다. 밀, 옥수수, IBM 주식의 지분 등이 모두 순수 경쟁 시장의 예시이다. (③) 자동차 시장은 동일한 제품에 대한 다수의 생산자가 없기 때문에 순수 경쟁적이지 않다. (④ **대신에,**

유사한 대체품인 몇 가지 다소 다른 종류의 제품들이 있다.) 경제학자들은 이것을 독점적 경쟁 상황이라고 부른다. 학술지 (또는 다른 종류의 정보재) 시장은 밀 시장보다는 자동차 시장에 훨씬 가까운 경향이 있다. 높은 고정비용/낮은 증분 비용 구조가 이러한 결과를 야기한다.

어휘

somewhat 다소, 약간
property 특징, 특성
academic journal 학술지
pricing 가격 책정
identical 동일한, 같은
share 지분, 주식
monopolistic competition 독점적 경쟁
incremental cost 증분 원가[비용]
substitute 대체재
subsequent 다음의, 그 후의
pose (질문 등) 제기하다
sustain 유지하다, 지탱하다
commodity 상품
stock 주식
outcome 결과

09 정답 ③

정답해설

본문은 '새끼의 피를 마시는 드라큘라 개미의 특이한 식성'에 대해 설명하는 글이다. ①에서 드라큘라 개미와 그것의 식성이 최초로 발견된 시기에 대해 언급한 후, ②에서 '다른 개미'와 비교하여 '드라큘라 개미만의 특이한 식성을 구체적으로 설명하고, ②에서 언급한 "nondestructive cannibalism(비 파괴적인 카니발리즘)"에 대해 구체적으로 설명(유충의 피부를 긁어 피를 낸다)하고 있는 ④가 이어진 후, 마지막으로 피를 마시는 방식에 대해 자세히 언급하는 내용이 이어지는 것이 문맥상 자연스럽다. ③은 '최초 발견 이래로 6가지 종의 드라큘라 개미가 발견되었다'는 내용으로, '드라큘라 개미의 식성'과는 거리가 먼 내용이므로 글의 흐름상 적절하지 않다. 따라서 정답은 ③이다.

오답해설

나머지 보기는 문맥상 자연스러우므로 오답이다.

해석

"드라큘라 개미"와 같은 이름으로 보아, 그 종의 중요한 특징이 새끼의 피를 먹는 것을 매우 좋아하는 것이라는 것은 그렇게 놀라운 것은 아닐 것이다. ① 한 곤충학자가 15년 전 Madagascar의 부패한 잎 더미에서 그 종과 그것들의 특이한 섭식 방식을 발견했다. ② 각 군락의 일개미들이 먹이를 공유하고 여왕개미에게 가져다주는 "사회적 먹이 수송" 행위를 수행하는 대부분의 개미와는 달리 드라큘라 개미는 "비 파괴적인 카니발리즘"을 택한다. ③ **최초의 발견 이래로, 6종의 드라큘라 개미가 발견되었다.** ④ 일개미들은 자신들의 군락의 육아실에 있는 유충의 피부를 긁어서 피가 나게 만든다. 그러고 나서 그들은 유충을 깨물어 피를 마시고 그것을 역류시켜서 여왕개미에게 주고, 유충은 살려두지만 상처를 남긴다.

어휘

signify 중요하다, 의미가 되다
pile (쌓아 올린) 더미
nondestructive 비 파괴적인
cannibalism 카니발리즘, 동족끼리 서로 잡아먹음
larva 유충, 애벌레 (pl. larvae)
regurgitate (삼킨 음식물을 입 안에 다시) 역류시키다
predilection 기호, 애호, 매우 좋아함
rot 썩다, 부패하다
nursery 육아실

10 정답 ④

정답해설

본문은 '코스타리카에서 3차 교육을 받는 사람들은 상대적으로 적으나, 그러한 사람들에게는 '더 높은 급여, 더 높은 취업률, 성별에 따른 더 낮은 급여 격차' 등 여러 이점(benefit)이 주어진다'고 설명하고 있다. 따라서 글의 요지로 가장 적절한 것은 '④ In Costa Rica, people with higher education experience more advantages than others with lower education level(코스타리카에서, 고등 교육을 받은 사람들은 더 낮은 교육 수준의 사람들보다 더 많은 이점을 경험한다).'이다.

오답해설

① 남성과 여성 간 급여 격차는 본문 마지막에 언급되기는 하지만, 글 전체를 아우르는 내용이 아니므로 오답이다.
② 첫 번째 문장 "In Costa Rica just 23 percent of adults go on to be educated at tertiary level(코스타리카에서 절반 이하의 학생들이 고등 교육을 추구하기로 결정한다)."에서 언급되는 사실과 일치하는 보기이나 이는 단순한 사실 제시이며 이후에는 '고등 교육을 받은 사람들이 경험하는 이점'에 대해 집중적으로 설명하고 있으므로, 글 전체의 요지로는 적절하지 않다.
③ 대학 진학 비용에 대해서는 본문에 언급되지 않는다.

해석

코스타리카에서 성인 중 오직 23퍼센트만이 3차 단계의 교육을 받는다. 그리고 그렇게 하는 사람들은 진정으로 이점을 알아차릴 가능성이 있다. 그곳에서 3차 교육을 받은 성인은 더 낮은 교육 수준을 지닌 그들의 또래보다 약 두 배를 번다. 3차 교육을 받은 젊은 코스타리카인들은 2007년보다 2017년에 5퍼센트 포인트 이상 더 낮은 실업률을 겪었다. 사실, 이점이 아마도 가장 두드러지는 분야는 성별에 따른 격차에 관한 것이다. 코스타리카에서 3차 교육을 받은 여성들의 수입은, 비록 여전히 7퍼센트 더 낮긴 하지만, 그들의 남성 동료들의 수입에 가장 근접하다.
① 대부분의 분야에서 코스타리카의 여성들은 남성들보다 더 적게 번다.
② 코스타리카에서 절반 이하의 학생들이 고등 교육을 추구하기로 결정한다.
③ 젊은 코스타리카인들이 고등학교 졸업 후 대학을 가는 것은 비용이 많이 든다.
④ 코스타리카에서, 고등 교육을 받은 사람들은 더 낮은 교육 수준의 사람들보다 더 많은 이점을 경험한다.

어휘

tertiary 제3의, 3차의
educational attainment 교육 정도[수준]
in respect of …에 대한
counterpart 상대, 대응 관계에 있는 사람
pursue 추구하다
peer 또래, 동배
visible 뚜렷한, 두드러지는

結국엔 성정혜 영어 하프모의고사

기적사 DAY 06

| 01 | ③ | 02 | ① | 03 | ② | 04 | ③ | 05 | ② |
| 06 | ③ | 07 | ④ | 08 | ① | 09 | ② | 10 | ④ |

01 정답 ③
18 서울시

정답해설

밑줄 친 'muzzle'은 '입막음하다, (말하는 것 등을) 억누르다'라는 의미로, ③ suppress와 의미가 가장 유사하다.

해석

인간은 새로운 생각을 **억압하려고** 시도했던 정부 당국, 그리고 변화는 허튼수작이라고 선언했던 오래전부터 확립된 견해라는 권위에 대해 계속해서 반항해 왔다.
① 표현하다
② 주장하다
③ 억누르다
④ 펼치다, 퍼뜨리다

어휘

disobedient 반항하는, 거역하는
muzzle 입막음하다, (말하는 것 등을) 억누르다
nonsense 허튼수작, 터무니없는 생각
express 표현하다   assert 주장하다
suppress 억누르다   spread 펼치다, 퍼뜨리다

02 정답 ①
18 서울시

정답해설

밑줄 친 'pompous'는 '(글이나 문체가) 과시적인, 거만한'의 의미를 가지고 있다. 선지 중에서는 ① presumptuous가 의미상 가장 가깝다. 'pompous'의 뜻을 모를 경우에는 'like your professor or boss'의 예시를 참고하면 답 선택에 도움이 된다. 즉, 이들은 상하관계에서 '상'에 해당되는 계층이며, 이들에 대한 부정적인 특징으로 답을 유추할 수도 있다.

해석

과시하려 하지 말라. 당신은 당신의 글이 너무 격식이 없고 구어체인 것을 원하지 않지만, 당신은 또한 당신이 아닌 누군가처럼, 즉 당신의 교수, 상관, 또는 예를 들어 Rhodes 장학생 교육 조교처럼 들리는 것도 원하지 않을 것이다.
① 과시하는
② 평상시의, 우연한
③ 공식적인
④ 진실된, 진짜의

어휘

pompous (글이나 문체가) 과시적인, 거만한
colloquial 구어의, 일상적인 대화체의   presumptuous 과시하는
casual 평상시의, 우연한   formal 공식적인
genuine 진실된, 진짜의

03 정답 ②
18 서울시

정답해설

밑줄 친 'call it a day'는 '하던 일을 그만두다'라는 의미이므로 ② finish와 의미가 가장 유사하다.

해석

외과의들은 그 일에 적합한 도구들을 찾을 수 없었기 때문에 어쩔 수 없이 **그만두게** 되었다.
① 시작하다
② 끝내다
③ 기다리다
④ 취소하다

어휘

call it a day 하던 일을 그만두다   initiate 시작하다
finish 끝내다   wait 기다리다
cancel 취소하다

04 정답 ③
18 서울시

정답해설

A의 "리조또는 어떻습니까?(How's your risotto?)"라는 질문에 대한 답으로 'Yes' 또는 'No'로 답하는 것은 알맞지 않으며, 뒤의 내용인 "저희는 버섯과 치즈가 들어간 리조또가 있어요(we have risotto with mushroom and cheese)."도 알맞은 응답이 아니다.

오답해설

④ '디저트'를 권하는 표현에 대해서, 거절하는 표현으로 'Not for me(저는 괜찮아요)'는 자연스럽다.
나머지 선지는 문맥상 자연스러우므로 오답이다.

해석

① A: 내일로 예약하고 싶어요.
   B: 네. 몇 시를 원하세요?
② A: 주문하시겠어요?
   B: 네, 수프로 할게요.
③ A: 리조또는 어떻습니까?
   B: 네, 저희는 버섯과 치즈가 들어간 리조또가 있어요.
④ A: 디저트 드시겠어요?
   B: 저는 괜찮아요, 감사해요.

어휘

reservation 예약   certainly (대답)알았습니다; 물론이지

05 정답 ②
18 서울시

정답해설

② **출제 포인트: 이중부정 금지**
  현재완료 형태에서 부정부사인 'hardly'는 「have hardly+p.p.」의 형태로 나타낸다. 이렇게 부정부사를 포함한 동사 형태에 부정부사인 'never'를 사용하면 이중부정이 되므로 'never'를 삭제하는 것이 옳다.

오답해설

① **출제 포인트: 전치사의 쓰임**
  기간 명사 앞에 쓰인 'over'는 '~동안'이라는 의미로 옳게 사용되었다.

③ 출제 포인트: a number of vs. an amount of
'a number of'는 복수 가산명사를 수식하므로 복수 가산명사 'important policy issues' 앞에 쓰인 'a number of'는 옳은 표현이다.
④ 출제 포인트: 목적격 관계대명사
'which' 이후 문장에서 'argue'의 목적어가 없으므로 밑줄 친 'which'는 'issues'를 선행사로 하는 목적격 관계대명사이다.

해석
1961년 독립 이후 여러 해 동안의 그의 생존은 공식적인 방식에서 진정한 정책 선택에 대한 논의가 거의 일어나지 않았다는 사실을 바꾸지 않는다. 사실, Nyerere가 NEC를 통해 논의했어야 하는 많은 중요한 정책 이슈들이 항상 있어 왔다.

어휘
independence 독립	alter 바꾸다
manner 방식, 태도

06 정답 ③
18 서울시

정답해설
③ 출제 포인트: 주격 관계대명사절의 동사 수일치
주격 관계대명사 'that'의 선행사는 'Chicago'가 아닌 복수명사인 'clothes'이다. 따라서 복수명사인 선행사를 받는 주격 관계대명사절의 동사는 복수동사가 되어야 하므로 'fits'를 'fit'으로 수정하는 것이 옳다.

오답해설
① 출제 포인트: 현재분사 vs. 과거분사
감정형 분사가 사람의 감정 상태를 나타낼 때는 과거분사를 사용한다. 밑줄 친 'pleased'는 사람을 나타내는 주어 'I'를 수식하고 있으므로 옳다.
② 출제 포인트: 가주어 it
진주어 'to find ~ fits me'를 대신하는 가주어 'it'으로 적절하게 사용되었다.
④ 출제 포인트: what vs. that
밑줄 친 'What'의 선행사가 없고 뒤따라오는 절이 주어가 없는 불완전한 형태이므로 선행사를 포함한 관계대명사 'What'이 주어로 쓰인 옳은 문장이다.

해석
나는 내가 충분한 옷을 가지고 있어서 기쁘다. 미국 남성들은 보통 일본 남성들보다 크기 때문에, 시카고에서 나에게 맞는 옷을 찾는 것은 어렵다. 일본에서 중간 사이즈인 것이 여기에서는 작은 사이즈이다.

어휘
clothes 옷, 의복	fit 맞다
medium 중간의

오답률 TOP 1
07 정답 ④
18 서울시

정답해설
④ 출제 포인트: 자동사로 착각하기 쉬운 완전타동사
'affect(영향을 미치다)'는 타동사이기 때문에 뒤에 전치사(on)를 사용하지 않고 바로 목적어가 와야 한다. 따라서 'affects on the ocean'에서 'on'을 삭제해 'affects the ocean'으로 수정하거나 'affects'를 'have an effect[influence](~에 영향을 미치다)' 구문으로 대체해 3인칭 단수주어의 인칭을 반영하여 'has an effect[influence] on the ocean'으로 수정하는 것이 옳다.

오답해설
① 출제 포인트: 현재분사 vs. 과거분사
완전자동사 'produce'의 과거분사인 'produced' 뒤에 목적어가 아닌 전명구 'by the BBC'가 왔으며 수식하는 대상 'a nature documentary'와 수동관계이다. 따라서 과거분사 'produced'를 사용하는 것이 옳다.
② 출제 포인트: 현재분사 vs. 과거분사
밑줄 친 'heartbroken'은 불완전타동사로 쓰인 'left'의 목적격 보어로 사용되었다. 따라서 'viewers(시청자들)'의 마음이 '슬픔에 잠기게 된' 것이므로 감정의 상태를 나타내는 과거분사 'heartbroken'이 적절하다.
③ 출제 포인트: 전치사+관계대명사
밑줄 친 「전치사+관계대명사」는 선행사를 'the extent'로 갖고 있다. 이후의 문장은 'plastic affects the ocean'으로 완전한 문장이므로 적절하다.

해석
BBC에 의해 제작된 자연 다큐멘터리 *Blue Planet II*는 플라스틱이 바다에 영향을 미치는 정도를 보여준 후 시청자들을 슬픔에 잠기게 만들었다.

어휘
planet 행성	heartbroken 슬픔에 잠긴
documentary 다큐멘터리	extent 정도

오답률 TOP 2
08 정답 ④
19 서울시

정답해설
주어진 지문의 핵심어인 'conscientious'의 경우 '양심적인' 또는 '성실한'의 의미로 주로 쓰이게 되는데, 해당 지문에서는 일의 효율성과 관련된 지문이므로 '성실한'의 의미로 해석하는 것이 적절하다. 'conscientious employees (성실한 직원들)'가 일의 효율성을 중요시하는 반면에, 빈칸 이전에 제시된 'disorganized, unconscientious person(정리되지 않은, 성실하지 않은 사람)'은 이에 상대적인 개념으로 제시되고 있다. 결국 빈칸의 내용 이후에 'otherwise'에 주목해서 '그렇지 않으면' 즉 '성실하지 않으면' 만들어 낼 '부정적인 측면'에 대한 서술이 빈칸에 들어가야 함을 유추할 수 있다. 따라서 '성실한 사람들이 성실하지 않았으면 스스로 만들어 낼 ④ 스트레스를 피한다 (sidestep stress)'가 적절하다.

오답해설
주어진 빈칸은 '타동사 술어+목적어'로 이뤄져 있으며 빈칸과 'they' 사이에는 목적격관계대명사가 생략되었음을 인지하고, 빈칸에 해당되는 목적어는 'create'의 목적어이자 선행사임에 주의하고 해당 문제에 접근해야 한다.
① 본문에서 '좌절(setbacks)'의 예를 언급하고 있지 않으므로 '좌절을 극복하다(deal with setbacks)'는 적절하지 않다.
② '철저한 일(through work)'의 경우 성실하지 않았으면 만들어 낼 만한 일이 아니기에 적절하지 않다.
③ '표준(norms)' 역시 성실하지 않았으면 만들어 낼 만한 일이 아니기에 적절하지 않다. 또한 술어가 'follow'이므로 '표준을 따르다(follow norms)'는 더욱이 어색하다.

해석
"고도로 성실한 직원들은 우리보다 일련의 일을 더 잘합니다."라고 성실성을 연구하는 일리노이 대학의 심리학자인 Brent Roberts는 말한다. Roberts는 그들의 성공을 "위생" 요인에 돌린다. 성실한 사람들은 자신의 삶을 잘 정리하는 경향이 있다. 체계적이지 못하고 성실하지 않은 사람은 올바른 문서를 찾기 위해 파일을 찾아 헤매면서 20분 혹은 30분을 낭비할지도 모른다, 성실한 사람들은 피하는 경향이 있는 비효율적인 경험들 말이다. 기본적으로, 성실하게 됨으로써, 사람들은 그렇지 않다면 그들이 스스로 만들어 낼 수 있는 스트레스를 회피한다.

① 좌절을 극복하다
② 철저한 일을 하다
③ 표준을 따르다
④ 스트레스를 회피하다

어휘

conscientious 성실한, 양심적인 conscientiousness 성실, 양심
hygiene 위생 factor 요인
tendency 경향 disorganized 체계적이지 못한
unconscientious 성실하지 못한, 비양심적인
root through 찾아 헤매다 inefficient 비효율적인
folk 사람들 setback 좌절
thorough 철저한 norm 표준, 기준
sidestep 회피하다

09 정답 ②
19 서울시

정답해설

주어진 지문은 두 단락으로 나뉜다. 생물학적 기후변화와 환경 파괴 등의 전 지구적인 위험을, 경제적인 관점에서 과량 생산과 소비로 전환하는 두 단락이 그것이다. 이를 각각 'the Anthropocene'이라고 제시하고, 또, 'Capitalocene'으로 제시하고 있다. 이는 합성어로, 인간이 지배하는 '인류세' 그리고 자본의 논리가 지배하는 '자본세'를 각각 나타낸다. 빈칸 이전에서 자본주의의 논리로 부유한 사람에게 더 많은 자본이 몰리는 'growing inequality(증가하는 불평등)' 문제를 이야기하고 있고, 따라서 빈칸은 'endless growth(끝없는 성장)'와 '자본의 편중'을 지적하는 것이 적절하다. 즉 부익부 빈익빈(소수가 사회 대부분의 부를 가져가는 것)과 상통하는 것은 ② 'the accumulation of wealth in fewer pockets(소수의 주머니에 부의 축적)'이다. 따라서 정답은 ②이다. 여기에서 'fewer pockets'는 소수의 자본가들의 주머니를 상징하고 있다.

오답해설

나머지 선지는 자본주의의 논리와 연관이 없는 내용이거나 반대되는 내용이므로 빈칸에 적합하지 않다.

해석

기후변화, 삼림 벌채, 광범위한 오염, 그리고 생물 다양성의 6번째 대량 멸종은 모두 오늘날 우리 세계에 살고 있는 것을 정의한다 - "인류세"로 알려진 시대. 이러한 위기는 세계 생태계의 한계를 크게 초과하는 생산과 소비에 의해 뒷받침되지만, 비난은 균등하게 공유되는 것과는 거리가 멀다. 세계에서 가장 부유한 42명이 가장 가난한 37억 명의 재산을 소유하고 있으며, 그들은 훨씬 더 큰 환경적 영향을 초래한다. 따라서 일부에서는 끝없는 성장과 소수의 주머니 안의 부의 축적에 대한 자본주의의 논리를 반영하여 생태적 황폐화와 증가하는 불평등의 이 시대를 묘사하기 위해 "자본론"이라는 용어를 사용할 것을 제안하였다.
① 우리의 도달 범위 안에 여전히 있는 더 나은 세상
② 소수의 주머니에 부의 축적
③ 기후변화에 대한 효과적인 반응
④ 더욱더 실행 가능한 미래를 위한 타오르는 욕구

어휘

deforestation 삼림 벌채 mass extinction 대량 멸종
biodiversity 생물 다양성 Anthropocene 인류세
underpin 뒷받침하다 exceed 초과하다
ecological 생태학적인 evenly 공평하게
generate 발생하다 Capitalocene 자본론
devastation 황폐화 inequality 불평등
accumulation 축적 viable 실행 가능한

오답률 TOP 3

10 정답 ④
19 서울시

정답해설

본문은 개인적 복수 즉, 사적 복수의 정당성이 글의 소재이다. 이는 우리가 사회적 그리고 개인적 입장에서의 경계선에 있음을 명시하고 있다. 본문 빈칸 주위의 세 번 제시된 'between'에 주목해야 한다. 이는 빈칸 앞의 'between' 구(문명과 야만)와 빈칸 뒤의 'between' 구(정의(처벌)와 자비(용서))가 모두 반대 개념의 나열인 것으로 보아 빈칸에는 빈칸 이하의 '법치에 대한 지역사회의 요구'(the community's need for the rule of law)와 반대가 되는 '개인'에 대한 욕구가 제시되는 것이 적절하다. 따라서 정답은 ④ 'an individual's accountability to his or her own conscience(그 혹은 그녀 자신의 양심에 대한 개인적 책임)'로 보아야 적절하다.

오답해설

①, ②, ③ 공동체의 법이 아닌 양심에 대한 개인적인 책임감에 대한 것이 빈 칸에 가장 적절하므로 개인적인 복수와 타락은 빈칸에 적절하지 않다.

해석

고대 그리스 비극 시대부터 서양 문화는 복수자의 형상에 시달려 왔다. 그 또는 그녀는 문명과 야만, 그 혹은 그녀 자신의 양심에 대한 개인적 책임과 법치 주의에 대한 공동체의 필요 사이, 정의와 자비의 상반된 요구 사이에서, 완전한 일련의 경계선에 서 있다. 우리가 사랑하는 사람을 파괴한 자들에 대한 복수를 정확히 할 권리가 있는가? 아니면 복수심을 법에 맡겨야 할까, 신에게 맡겨야 할까? 그리고 만약 우리가 스스로 행동을 취한다면, 우리는 살인을 한 원래 가해자와 같은 도덕적 수준으로 우리 스스로를 낮추는 것은 아닌가?
① 타락한 상태로부터 복수하는 사람의 구원
② 인간의 잔혹 행위들에 대한 성스러운 복수
③ 부패한 정치인들의 도덕적인 타락
④ 그 혹은 그녀 자신의 양심에 대한 개인적 책임

어휘

tragedy 비극 be haunted by ~에 시달리다
revenger 복수하는 사람 borderline 경계(선)
barbarity 야만(적 행위) conflicting 상충되는
justice 정의 mercy 자비
exact 요구하다 revenge 복수
vengeance 복수, 보복
take into one's hands 마음대로 하다
moral 도덕적인 perpetrator 가해자
murderous 살인의, 흉악한 deed 행동, 행위
redemption 되찾기, 상환, 구원 depraved 부패한, 타락한
divine 신의, 신성한 atrocity 악행, 포악
depravity 타락, 부패 corrupt 부패한
politician 정치인 accountability 책임, 의무
conscience 양심

기적사 DAY 07

결국엔 성정혜 영어 하프모의고사

01	④	02	④	03	④	04	③	05	③
06	②	07	④	08	③	09	③	10	②

01 정답 ④

정답해설

밑줄 친 'exhume'은 '발굴하다, 파내다'라는 뜻으로 ④ excavate와 의미가 가장 가깝다.

해석

우리가 무덤을 찾아냈을 때, 우리는 흙을 제거하고 최종적으로는 시신을 정리하고, 그것을 기록하고, 그것을 **발굴한다**.
① 탐험하다
② 활용하다, 착취하다
③ 표현하다
④ 발굴하다, 출토하다

어휘

document 기록하다 exhume 발굴하다, 파내다
explore 탐험하다 exploit 활용하다, 착취하다
express 표현하다 excavate 발굴하다, 출토하다

02 정답 ④

정답해설

밑줄 친 'frigid'는 '몹시 추운'의 의미로 ④ freezing과 의미가 가장 가깝다.

해석

오늘 서울은 기온이 영하 12도까지 떨어지고 그 이상으로 떨어지는 도시들도 있는 데다 차가운 강풍으로 인해 체감온도가 더욱 떨어져 올겨울 들어 가장 **추운** 날이 될 것이라고 일기 예보관들이 말했다.
① 위조의
② 잘못을 저지르기 쉬운
③ 공식적인
④ 몹시 추운, 영하의

어휘

frigid 몹시 추운 fake 위조의
fallible 잘못을 저지르기 쉬운 formal 공식적인
freezing 몹시 추운, 영하의

03 정답 ④

정답해설

'have emphasis on'은 '강조하다'의 의미로 'stress(강조하다, 역설하다)'와 뜻이 가장 가깝다.

해석

차기 정부는 활발한 투자를 위한 초석을 다지기 위해 규제를 폐지하는 것을 우선적으로 **강조할** 필요가 있다.
① 항복하다, 포기하다, 인도하다
② 주저하다, 망설이다
③ 시작하다
④ 강조하다, 역설하다

어휘

have emphasis on 강조하다 brisk 활발한
surrender 항복하다, 포기하다, 인도하다
hesitate 주저하다, 망설이다 initiate 시작하다
stress 강조하다, 역설하다

04 정답 ③

정답해설

아버지가 '귀중한 교훈(valuable lessons)'을 가르쳐 주셨다는 A의 말에 대한 답변으로 B가 '역사적 교훈(Historical lessons)'은 다음 세대에 전달되어야 한다고 말하는 것은 대화의 흐름상 어색하다.

오답해설

① A는 B에게 '음료(drink)'를 권하고 B는 '탄산음료(soda)'를 달라고 이야기한다. 이는 자연스러운 대화이다.
② A가 자신의 코트가 어디 있는지 묻자 B는 자신이 옷걸이에 걸어놨다고 말한다. B는 A의 물음에 적절한 답변을 제시했다.
④ A는 "이 차를 다룰 때 더 조심해야 한다. (We should be more careful when handling this car)"라고 말하자 B는 A의 말에 동의하며 '보는 것만큼 쉽지 않다(it's not as easy as it seems)'고 얘기한다. B의 답변은 A의 말에 적합한 반응이다.

해석

① A: 음료 좀 드릴까요?
  B: 네, 탄산음료 좀 주시겠습니까?
② A: 내 코트가 어디 있는지 알아?
  B: 내가 옷걸이에 걸었어.
③ A: 우리 아버지는 귀중한 교훈을 가르쳐 주셨어.
  B: 역사적인 교훈들은 다음 세대에 전달되어야 해.
④ A: 우리는 이 차를 다룰 때 더 조심해야 해.
  B: 네 말이 맞아. 근데 보는 것만큼 쉽지 않네.

오답률 TOP 3

05 정답 ③

정답해설

③ 출제 포인트: 전치사의 쓰임
전치사 'for'는 뒤에 불특정 기간을 나타내는 명사(구)가 오며, 전치사 'during'은 뒤에 특정 기간을 나타내는 명사(구)가 온다. 해당 문장은 'for'를 사용하였으나 뒤에 특정 기간을 나타내는 명사(구) 'the 1960s and 1970s'가 왔으므로 틀린 문장이다. 따라서 'for'를 'during'으로 수정해야 한다.

오답해설

① 출제 포인트: 동명사 관용표현
'end up ~ing'는 관용표현으로 '결국 ~하게 되다'를 뜻하며, 해당 문장에서 밑줄 친 'costing'이 -ing에 해당한다.

② 출제 포인트: 수 단위명사
「수 단위명사[복수형태] of 명사[복수형태]」와 「기수+수 단위명사[단수형태]+명사[복수형태]」를 묻는 문제이다. 해당 문장에서 수 단위명사가 복수형태인 'Millions'이며 앞에 기수가 없고 뒤에 'of 명사[복수형태]'인 'of workers'가 있으므로 옳은 문장이다.

④ **출제 포인트: 과거분사**

'expected'는 완전타동사 'expect'의 과거분사로 수식하는 대상 'expenses'와 수동관계이다.

해석

현재 10만 달러가 드는 하버드 대학교의 교육은 오늘 태어난 아기에게는 결국 50만 달러가 들게 될지도 모른다. 1960년대와 1970년대 동안에 연금을 받으며 은퇴한 수백만 명의 노동자들은 인플레이션이 그들의 예상되는 지출을 훨씬 넘어서도록 비용을 올린다는 것을 알게 되었다.

어휘

end up -ing 결국 ~하게 되다   infant 유아, 아기
pension 연금, 생활보조금   inflation 인플레이션

06 정답 ②

정답해설

② **출제 포인트: that vs. what/It ~ that 강조용법**

'Although the performance of the hardware is of immediate concern following an earthquake'에서 'the performance of the hardware'를 강조하기 위해 It ~ that 강조용법을 사용하였으나, 'that'의 자리에 'what'을 사용하였으므로 틀린 문장이다. 따라서 'what'을 'that'으로 수정해야 하며 이때 'that'은 'which'로 바꾸어 사용할 수 있다.

오답해설

① **출제 포인트: 형용사 vs. 부사**

해당 문장에서 'critical'은 불완전자동사 'is'의 주격 보어로 옳게 사용되었다.

③ **출제 포인트: 현재분사 vs. 과거분사**

'following'은 완전타동사 'follow'의 현재분사로 수식하는 대상 'concern'과 능동관계이다. 또한 'following'을 전치사로 보고 'an earthquake'를 'following'의 목적어로 보아도 된다.

④ **출제 포인트: It ~ that 강조용법/주어와 동사의 수일치**

해당 문장은 'the loss of services that these systems provide'를 강조하는 'It ~ that 강조용법'이 쓰인 문장이다. 이때 밑줄 친 'is'의 주어는 단수형태인 'the loss'이므로 옳게 사용되었다.

해석

시스템과 서비스의 결합은 기반 시설에 대한 어떤 논의에도 대단히 중요하다. 비록 지진에 뒤이어 즉각적인 염려는 하드웨어의 작동이지만 대중에게 진짜 손실이 되는 것은 사실상 이러한 시스템들이 제공하는 서비스의 상실이다.

어휘

linkage 연결, 결합   infrastructure 기반 시설, 인프라
performance 실행, 수행, 공연, 실적, 성과
follow ~의 뒤를 잇다, ~의 뒤를 따라가다

07 정답 ④

정답해설

④ **출제 포인트: 전치사+관계대명사**

밑줄 친 'which'는 'the speed'를 선행사로 하는 관계대명사이다. 이때 'which'를 'eat'의 목적어로 보는 경우 '속도를 먹다'가 되므로 해석이 어색해진다. 따라서 문맥상 '그 속도로 먹다'가 자연스러우므로 'which' 앞에 전치사 'at'을 사용해 'which'를 'at which'로 수정하고 'eat'은 완전자동사로 보아야 한다.

오답해설

① **출제 포인트: 자동사로 착각하기 쉬운 완전타동사**

'affect'는 완전타동사로 전치사 없이 목적어를 가진다.

② **출제 포인트: 전치사의 쓰임**

밑줄 친 including은 전치사로 쓰여 '~을 포함하여'를 뜻하며 목적어로 'your motivation'을 갖는다.

③ **출제 포인트: 간접의문문/의문부사**

밑줄 친 'where' 이후 'you eat'이라는 문장이 의문사 두 종류와 함께하고 있다. 첫 번째 의문사인 밑줄 친 'where'과 두 번째 「전치사+의문대명사」인 'with whom'으로 두 의문사는 병렬구조를 이루고 있다. 'with whom'에서 'whom'은 의문대명사 중 사람을 나타내는 목적격 의문사이므로 전치사 'with'와 함께 쓸 수 있다. 따라서 의문부사 'where'는 적절하게 사용되었다.

해석

감정은 여러분의 식사 동기, 여러분의 음식 선택, 어디에서 누구와 여러분이 식사할지, 그리고 여러분이 식사하는 속도를 포함하여, 여러분의 식사의 여러 측면에 영향을 줄지도 모른다.

어휘

aspect 측면, 양상   including ~을 포함하여
motivation 동기

오답률 TOP 1

08 정답 ③

정답해설

본문은 '성실성과 성과의 관계(the relationship between conscientiousness and performance)'를 조사한 연구의 결과를 소개하는 글이다. 본문 첫 문장에서는 '창의성이 중요시되는 직업군에서는 성실성과 성과가 부정적 관계에 있다'는 주장을 설명하고 있다. 그리고 (A) 이후에서도 또한 "~ negatively related to less conventional measures such as an original research study, which were better predicted by creative thinking(창의적 사고로 더 잘 예측될 수 있는 독창적 연구 조사와 같은 덜 틀에 박힌 기준들과는 부정적인 관계에 있다)"이라고 언급하며 '성실성과 창의성의 부정적 관계'를 주장하는 연구 결과에 대해 서술하고 있다. (A) 전후로 유사한 내용이 전개되므로, 빈칸에 가장 적절한 것은 'Likewise(마찬가지로)' 또는 'Similarly(유사하게)'이다. (B) 이후 문장에서는 앞서 '부정적인 관계'를 강조한 것과는 달리, '긍정적 관계, 부정적 관계, 또는 관계없음 등 엇갈린 결과를 보여주는 여러 실증 연구들이 있음'을 언급하며, 해당 분야에 대한 연구 결과의 '전반적인' 추세에 대해 설명하고 있다. 따라서 빈칸에 가장 적절한 표현은 'on the whole(전체적으로 보아)' 또는 'overall(전반적으로)'이다. 그러므로 정답은 '③ Similarly(유사하게) - overall(전반적으로)'이다.

오답해설

① (B) 이후 문장이 이전 문장의 '결과'를 나타내고 있지 않으므로, 'as a result(결과적으로)'는 빈칸에 적절하지 않다.

② (A) 전후의 내용이 '대조' 관계에 있지 않으므로 'Conversely(반대로)'는 빈칸에 적절하지 않다.

나머지 보기는 문맥상 어색하므로 오답이다.

해석

Hogan과 Hogan(1993년)은 성실성과 성과의 관계는 직업 유형에 따라 달라진다고 말하고 창의성이 중요한 직업군에서는 성실성이 성과에 부정적으로 관련되어 있을 수 있다고 가정했다. (A) 유사하게 Chamorro-Premuzic(2006년)은 성실성이 필기시험과 같은 틀에 박히고 명확한 학문적인 평가 기준들과는 긍정적인 관계에 있고 창의적 사고로 더 잘 예측될 수 있는 독창적 연구

조사와 같은 덜 틀에 박힌 기준들과는 부정적인 관계에 있다는 것을 발견했다. 그러나 (B) 전반적으로 창의적 성과와 성실성의 관계를 조사하는 실증 연구들은, 일부는 긍정적인 관계를 보여주고(예를 들어 McCrae, 1987년), 일부는 부정적인 관계를 보여주고(예를 들어 Wolfradt & Pretz, 2001년) 다른 일부는 관계가 없음을 보여주며 엇갈린 결과를 내놓고 있다.

(A)	(B)
① 마찬가지로	결과적으로
② 반대로	전체적으로 보아
③ 유사하게	전반적으로, 종합적으로
④ 예를 들어	안타깝게도

어휘

conscientiousness 성실성, 양심 hypothesize 가정하다, 가설을 세우다
conventional 틀에 박힌, 진부한, 전통적인
well-defined 명확한, 알기 쉬운
measure (판단·평가·비교 따위의) 기준, 표준, 척도
original 독창적인 empirical 경험적인, 실증적인
mixed 엇갈린, 혼합된 conversely 반대로, 역으로
on the whole 전체적으로 보아, 전반적으로

오답률 TOP 2
09 정답 ③

정답해설

본문은 '인류세(Anthropocene)' 선포에 대한 근거에 대해 설명하는 글로, 본문 중반 "according to them, the global domestication of a vast number of chickens is one of the defining features of the Anthropocene(그들에 의하면 수많은 닭의 전 세계적인 사육은 인류세를 정의하는 특징 중 하나이다)."을 통해 '수많은 닭(가축)이 인류세의 특징 중 하나'라는 것을 알 수 있다. 또한, 인류세가 선포된 이유는 '인류의 행위(human activity)'로 인해 지질학적 특징이 변하였기 때문이며, 그중 하나가 '기후변화(climate change)'인데, 이러한 기후변화를 일으키는 주요 원인 중 하나인 '온실가스(GHGs)'가 '증가한 가축 사육'으로 인해 다량으로 배출되고 있다고 언급하고 있는 것 또한 '증가한 가축의 수가 '인류세'의 등장에 부분적으로 영향을 미쳤다'는 것을 유추할 수 있는 근거가 될 수 있다. 따라서 글의 요지로 가장 적절한 것은 '③ The emergence of a new epoch has partly been brought about by increased livestock populations(새로운 시기의 등장은 부분적으로 증가한 가축의 수에 의해 야기되었다).'이다.

오답해설

① 본문 마지막 문장 "Assuming this calculation to be correct, livestock produces more GHGs than the entire global transport system directly contributes(이 계산이 정확하다고 가정한다면, 가축은 전 세계의 전체 운송 시스템이 직접적으로 영향을 미치는 것보다 더 많은 GHGs를 생산한다)."에서, '가축 사육과 운송 분야'에 관해서만 비교하고 있으며, '가축 사육이 가장 많은 온실가스를 배출한다'는 내용은 본문 어디에도 언급되지 않으므로, 전체 글의 요지로 적절하지 않다.
② 본문은 '인류세(Anthropocene)' 선포에 대해 언급하고 있으나, 그것이 논쟁을 불러일으켰는지 여부에 대해서는 언급하고 있지 않으므로 글의 요지로 적절하지 않다.
④ 본문의 주요 내용은 인간에 의한 가축 사육 증가에 따른 온실가스(GHGs)를 배출의 증가에 대한 것이며, 기후변화와 극단적 날씨의 원인에 대해 설명하는 글이 아니기 때문에 오답이다.

해석

Cape Town에서 개최된 International Geological Congress에서 한 과학자 집단이 지구의 역사에서 인류의 행위에 의해 현저하게 정의되는 시기인 인류세를 발표했다. 과학자들이 미래의 고고학자들이 이 시기를 인식하기 위해 사용할 것이라 믿는 증거 중 하나는 많은 화석화된 닭의 뼈이다. 그들에 의하면 수많은 닭의 전 세계적인 사육은 인류세를 정의하는 특징 중 하나이다. 지난 50년 동안 가축의 수는 폭등했다. 현재 닭, 소, 그리고 돼지의 수는 수십억 마리이며, 이는 인류의 인구를 훨씬 웃도는 수치이다. 이러한 변화는 특히 기후를 변화시키는 온실가스(GHGs)의 대량 배출을 통해 우리가 사는 세계에 분명하고 극적인 결과를 낳았다. 추정치는 다양하지만, UN 식량농업기구가 제공한 보수적 계산에 따르면 가축에 의한 생산은 전 세계적인 인류 발생 GHGs의 18퍼센트를 발생시킨다. 이 계산이 정확하다고 가정한다면, 가축은 전 세계의 전체 운송 시스템이 직접적으로 영향을 미치는 것보다 더 많은 GHGs를 생산한다.
① 전 세계 가축 산업은 다른 어떤 분야보다 더 많은 GHGs를 생산한다.
② 새로운 지질학적 시기로서의 인류세 발표는 격렬한 논쟁으로 이어졌다.
③ 새로운 시기의 등장은 부분적으로 증가한 가축의 수에 의해 야기되었다.
④ GHGs는 기후변화와 더 빈히 발생하는 극단적 날씨 상황에 가장 많이 영향을 끼치는 요소 중 하나이다.

어휘

Anthropocene 인류세 epoch 시기, 시대, 세
prominently 현저하게, 두드러지게 archaeologist 고고학자
prevalence 널리 퍼짐 fossilized 화석화된
domestication 사육, 가축화
outnumber …보다 수가 더 많다, 수적으로 우세하다
consequence 결과 not least 특히
emission 배출 vary 다르다, 다양하다
conservative 보수적인, 적게 잡은 anthropogenic 인류 발생의
geological 지질학의 intensive 격렬한, 강한
debate 논쟁 bring about 야기하다

10 정답 ②

정답해설

본문은 '복수(revenge)'에 관한 두 가지 견해를 소개하며, '복수의 역할'에 대해 설명하고 있다. 본문 초반에서 '복수를 장려하는 성경'과 '복수에 대한 부정적인 견해'를 보인 'Martin Luther King Jr.'에 대해 언급한 후, 본문 중반 "As psychologists explore the mental machinery behind revenge, it turns out both can be, depending on who and where you are(심리학자들이 복수 뒤에 있는 정신적인 시스템을 탐구함에 따라, 당신이 누구이고 어디에 있는지에 따라 둘 다 옳을 수 있다는 것이 밝혀졌다)."라고 언급하며, '상황에 따라 둘 다 옳을 수 있다'라고 언급하고 있다. 이후, 복수의 '긍정적인 영향'과 '부정적인 영향'에 대해 각각 설명하고 있으므로, 글의 요지로 가장 적절한 보기는 '② Revenge can have either positive or negative effects(복수는 긍정적인 효과를 낼 수도, 부정적인 효과를 낼 수도 있다).'이다.

오답해설

① 복수와 인간의 본성의 관계에 대해서는 본문에서 언급되지 않으므로 오답이다.
③ 분노와 폭력에 관해서는 본문에서 언급되지 않는다.
④ 본문 후반 "If you live in a society where the rule of law is weak, revenge provides a way to keep order(만일 당신이 법규가 빈약한 사회에 살고 있다면, 복수는 질서를 유지할 수 있는 방법을 제공할 수 있다)."라고 '법이 빈약한 사회에서는 복수의 필요 가능성을 언급하고 있으며, 이후, 'But revenge comes at a price(그러나 복수에는 대가가 따른다).'라고 '복수의 부정적 영향'에 대해서도 동시에 언급하고 있다. 따라서 전체 글의 요지로는 적절하지 않다.

해석

역사적으로, 복수에 대한 두 가지 학설이 존재한다. 성경은 출애굽기 21장 23절에서 우리에게 범죄자를 벌하기 위해 "목숨에는 목숨, 눈에는 눈, 이에는 이, 손에는 손, 발에는 발을 주어라"라고 가르친다. 그러나 약 2,000년 이상 이후에 Martin Luther King Jr.는 "'눈에는 눈'이라는 구법이 모든 사람을 장님으로 만든다."라고 답했다. 어느 것이 옳은가? 심리학자들이 복수 뒤에 있는 정신적인 시스템을 탐구함에 따라, 당신이 누구이고 어디에 있는지에 따라 둘 다 옳을 수 있다는 것이 밝혀졌다. 만일 당신이 권력을 추구하는 사람이라면, 복수는 사람들에게 당신이 하찮게 볼 사람이 아니라는 것을 상기시켜주는 도구로 사용될 수 있다. 만일 당신이 법규가 빈약한 사회에 살고 있다면, 복수는 질서를 유지할 수 있는 방법을 제공할 수 있다. 그러나 복수에는 대가가 따른다. 당신이 삶을 계속해서 이어 나가도록 도와주는 대신에, 당신이 그 상황을 계속해서 곱씹도록 만들고 불행하게 할 수 있다는 것을 심리학자들의 연구는 밝힌다.

① 복수를 추구하는 것은 인간의 본성이다.
② 복수는 긍정적인 효과를 낼 수도, 부정적인 효과를 낼 수도 있다.
③ 복수를 추구하는 사람들은 분노와 폭력에 의해 움직인다.
④ 만일 법이 충분히 강력하지 않다면 스스로 복수를 하는 것이 필요하다.

어휘

school of thought 학설, 학파
offender 범죄자
trifle with …을 우습게[하찮게] 보다
punish 벌하다, 응징하다
revenge 복수, 보복
dwell on 곱씹다

결국엔 성정혜 영어 하프모의고사
기적사 DAY 08

| 01 | ④ | 02 | ① | 03 | ① | 04 | ① | 05 | ④ |
| 06 | ③ | 07 | ④ | 08 | ② | 09 | ④ | 10 | ① |

01 정답 ④

정답해설

밑줄 친 'initiated'는 '시작했다, 착수시켰다'의 의미로 ④ launched와 뜻이 가장 가깝다.

해석

최근, 나사는 우주가 어떻게 인간의 피부 건강에 영향을 끼치는지 이해하기 위해 "Ultra Space Program"이라는 프로젝트를 **시작했다**.
① 주장했다
② 조정했다, 조직했다, 협력했다
③ 빈둥거렸다, 게으름 피웠다
④ 시작했다, 개시했다

어휘

initiate 시작하다, 착수시키다
assert 주장하다
coordinate 조정하다, 조직하다, 협력하다
loiter 빈둥거리다, 게으름 피우다
dermal 피부의
launch 시작하다, 개시하다

02 정답 ①

정답해설

밑줄 친 'innocuous'는 '무해한, 악의 없는'의 뜻으로 ① harmless와 의미가 가장 가깝다.

해석

대부분의 스팸 메시지는, 일반적으로 사업적인 본질을 가지고 대량으로 보내진, **무해하고** 지우기가 쉽지만 일부는 그렇지 않다.
① 무해한, 악의 없는
② 해로운, 유독한
③ 평상시의, 우연한
④ 악의 있는

어휘

innocuous 무해한, 악의 없는
venenose 해로운, 유독한
malicious 악의 있는
harmless 무해한, 악의 없는
casual 평상시의, 우연한

03 정답 ①

정답해설

'make up to'는 '~에게 아첨하다'의 의미로 ① flatter와 의미가 가장 가깝다.

해석

그녀는 어떤 사적 목적으로도 그들의 신용을 얻기 위해 사람들에게 **아첨하는** 것은 원치 않는다.
① 아첨하다, 알랑거리다
② 이동하다, 이주하다

③ 통보하다, 알리다
④ 취소하다

어휘

make up to ~에게 아첨하다 flatter 아첨하다, 알랑거리다
migrate 이동하다, 이주하다 notify 통보하다, 알리다
cancel 취소하다

04 정답 ①

정답해설

A는 B에게 '자기 자신에게 동기부여 하는 방법'을 묻고 있지만, B는 '자신이 큰 성취를 이룰 수 있게 동기 부여되고 싶다'라고 답변한다. B의 답변은 A의 물음에 대한 답으로 적절하지 않다.

오답해설

② A는 B에게 미신을 믿는지 묻고, B는 미신은 과학적인 근거를 기반으로 하고 있지 않기 때문에 믿지 않는다고 답변한다. 이는 자연스러운 대화의 흐름이다.
③ A는 이웃 동네에 친구가 있었으면 좋겠다고 이야기한다. 이에 대해 B는 A에게 밖에 나가서 비슷한 나이대의 함께 놀 친구를 찾아보라고 권한다. 이는 문맥상 적합하다.
④ A는 영화관에 간 지 수년이 지났다고 말한다. B는 새로운 출시작들을 따라잡을 시간이 필요해 보인다고 대답한다. B는 A의 말에 적합한 답변을 했다.

해석

① A: 넌 어떻게 너 자신을 동기 부여해?
   B: 나는 내가 큰 성취를 이룰 수 있게 동기부여 되고 싶어.
② A: 너 미신을 믿어?
   B: 아니, 미신은 과학적 증거에 근거해 있지 않잖아.
③ A: 난 이웃 동네에 친구가 있었으면 좋겠어.
   B: 밖에 나가서 함께 놀 네 또래의 친구를 찾아봐.
④ A: 내가 영화관에 간 지 수년이 지났어.
   B: 새로운 출시작들을 따라잡을 시간이 필요해 보이네.

어휘

motivate ~에게 동기 부여하다 superstition 미신
catch up with ~을 따라잡다

오답률 TOP 3
05 정답 ④

정답해설

④ **출제 포인트: aware of+명사구 vs. aware that+명사절**
'aware' 뒤에 'of'가 오는 경우 명사구가 오며, 'that'이 오는 경우 명사절이 온다. 또한 'what'이 이끄는 관계대명사절은 형용사 절로 앞에 선행사에 해당하는 명사(구)가 생략되어 있다고 보아야 한다. 해당 문장은 'aware' 뒤에 'what'이 이끄는 관계대명사절이 왔으므로 틀린 문장이다. 따라서 'aware' 뒤에 전치사 'of'를 사용해야 한다. 단, 참고로 비격식체 또는 구어체에서 'of'를 생략하는 경우도 있다. (※ aware of+(생략된 선행사)+what+절)

오답해설

① **출제 포인트: 전치사의 쓰임**
전치사 'during'은 뒤에 특정 기간을 나타내는 명사(구)가 온다. 해당 문장은 전치사 'During' 뒤에 특정 기간을 나타내는 명사(구) 'her childhood years'가 왔으므로 옳은 문장이다.

② **출제 포인트: 동명사의 쓰임**
「spend+시간+~ing」는 관용표현으로 '~하는 데 시간을 보내다'를 뜻한다. 해당 문장에서는 'making'이 '~ing'에 해당하므로 옳게 사용되었다.

③ **출제 포인트: 완전자동사**
해당 문장에서 'move'는 완전자동사로 전치사 없이는 목적어를 가질 수 없다. 해당 문장은 'move' 뒤에 전치사 'from'을 사용하여 목적어를 가지므로 옳은 문장이다.

해석

예술가 Tammy Rahr는 그녀의 어린 시절에, 꽃과 흙으로 이것저것을 만들면서 많은 시간을 야외에서 보냈다. 그리고 나서 Tammy와 그의 가족은 뉴욕주의 삼림 지대에서 캘리포니아 LA의 외곽에 있는 도심으로 이사했다. 그 경험은 그녀가 세상에서 일어나는 일을 더 많이 알게 해주었다.

어휘

spend+시간+~ing ~하는 데 시간을 보내다
dirt 흙, 먼지, 때 woodland 삼림 지대

오답률 TOP 1
06 정답 ③

정답해설

③ **출제 포인트: 타동사로 착각하기 쉬운 완전자동사**
'struggle'이 타동사로 쓰이는 경우 '~을 허덕이며 나르다'를 의미하며, 자동사로 쓰이는 경우 '분투하다, 노력하다'를 뜻한다. 해당 문장에서는 문맥상 "목표에 도달하는 일로 '분투하다(노력하다)'"의 의미가 자연스러우므로 'struggle'은 완전자동사로 쓰였다는 것을 알 수 있다. 완전자동사로 쓰인 'struggle'은 전치사 없이 목적어를 가질 수 없다. 해당 문장은 'struggle'을 사용하였으나 뒤에 전치사 없이 목적어 'reaching goals'가 왔으므로 틀린 문장이다. 따라서 'struggle' 뒤에 전치사 'with'를 사용해야 한다.

오답해설

① **출제 포인트: 동명사의 쓰임**
밑줄 친 'Building'은 주어 자리에 쓰인 동명사로 옳게 사용되었다.
② **출제 포인트: 선행사와 관계대명사절 동사의 수일치**
밑줄 친 'help'는 관계대명사절의 동사이며 수일치 기준은 'all of which'이므로 선행사를 찾아야 한다. 이때 선행사는 복수형태인 'numerous benefits'이므로 복수 동사 'help'와 수일치 한다.
④ **출제 포인트: 전치사의 쓰임**
밑줄 친 'due to'는 전치사구로 뒤에 명사구 'an inability'가 목적어로 사용되었다.

해석

그러나 규칙적인 "여러분의 시간"을 구축하는 것은 많은 이득을 제공할 수 있는데, 이 모든 것들이 삶을 좀 더 달콤하고 좀 더 관리하기 쉽게 하는 데 도움을 준다. 안타깝게도, 많은 사람들은 그들 자신만의 필요한 사항에 우선순위를 매기지 못해 목표에 도달하는 일로 분투하고 있다.

어휘

a little bit 조금 struggle with ~로 분투하다, 노력하다
manageable 관리할 수 있는 inability 무능, 불능
prioritize 우선순위를 매기다

07 정답 ④

정답해설

④ 출제 포인트: 주어와 동사의 수일치

밑줄 친 'are'의 주어는 단수형태인 'conflict'이므로 수일치를 위해서 'are'를 단수형태의 동사인 'is'로 수정해야 한다.

오답해설

① 출제 포인트: what vs. that

밑줄 친 'that'은 뒤에 오는 절이 완전한 형태이므로 접속사임을 알 수 있으며 타동사 'believe'의 목적어절을 이끄는 접속사로 옳게 사용되었다.

② 출제 포인트: 자동사로 착각하기 쉬운 완전타동사

'reach'는 완전타동사로 전치사 없이 목적어를 가진다. 따라서 타동사 'reach'의 목적어로 'a point'가 왔으므로 옳게 사용되었다.

③ 출제 포인트: 전치사+관계대명사

밑줄 친 'at which'는 「전치사+관계대명사」로 뒤에 오는 절은 완전한 형태이다. 해당 문장은 'at which' 이후에 완전한 형태의 문장이 왔으므로 'at which'는 옳게 사용되었다.

해석

하지만 많은 이들이 우리가 결국 자원의 유한한 특성과의 갈등이 불가피한 지점에 도달할 것이라고 믿는다.

어휘

conflict 갈등, 충돌 finite 한정된, 유한한
inevitable 불가피한, 필연적인

오답률 TOP 2
08 정답 ②

정답해설

본문 초반에서는 '성실성의 긍정적인 면'에 대해 언급하고 있으나, 본문 중후반에서는 '극단적인 성실성의 부정적 영향'에 대해 언급하고 있다. 주어진 문장의 'however(그러나)'로 보아, 주어진 문장을 기점으로, '성실성의 긍정적 측면에 대한 설명'에서 '성실성의 부정적 측면에 대한 설명'으로 전환되어야 함을 알 수 있다. 첫 번째 문장과 두 번째 문장은 '성실성의 긍정적 영향에 대해 언급하고 있으나, ② 이후 문장부터 '~ extreme examples of conscientiousness(성실함의 극단적인 예시이다.)'라고 언급하며 '극단적인 성실성의 부정적 영향'에 대해 언급하고 있다. 따라서 '내용 전환'의 역할을 해야 하는 주어진 문장은 '성실성의 부정적 영향'이 최초로 언급되기 시작한 ② 이후 문장 바로 이전에 위치해야 한다. 따라서 정답은 ②이다.

오답해설

나머지 위치는 문맥상 자연스럽지 않으므로 오답이다.

해석

성실성의 긍정적 효과는 그것이 행동의 지속성과 예측성을 제공해 준다는 사실과 관련이 있다. (①) 그것은 또한 당신이 모든 것을 급히 처리하지 않도록 미리 정리하고 계획을 세우도록 도와준다. (② **그러나 과도하게 체계적인 것과 같은 것도 존재한다.**) 지나치게 규칙에 얽매이는 것, 정례적인 틀에 과도하게 집착하는 것, 그리고 완벽주의는 성실함의 극단적인 예시이다. (③) 모든 일들이 항상 특정 방식으로 완벽하게 처리되어야만 한다. (④) 관리자는 골치 아프게 사소한 것까지 신경 쓰는 사람이 될 수도 있다. 최악의 경우에, 결정은 더욱 오래 걸리고, 즉각적으로 처리하고 우선순위를 설정하는 능력을 상실하게 된다. 극도의 성실함은 또한 당신을 빠른 기력 소진 상태에 노출시킬 수도 있다.

어휘

organized 체계적인, 조직적인 conscientiousness 성실함, 양심
continuity 지속성 predictability 예측 가능성
on the fly 급히, 대충 그때그때 봐 가며
pedantry 지나치게 규칙을 찾음[세세한 것에 얽매임]
neurotic 신경증의 adherence 고수, 집착
painful 성가신, 귀찮은
micro-manager 사소한 일까지 챙기는 사람
improvise 즉석에서[즉흥적으로] 하다 prioritize 우선순위를 정하다
expose 노출시키다, 경험하게[접하게]하다
burnout 번 아웃, 기력 소진, (신체적 또는 정신적인) 극도의 피로

09 정답 ④

정답해설

본문은 "인류세(Anthropocene)라는 용어는 '기후변화(climate change)'와 같은 환경적 변화분만 아니라 더 넓은 범위를 포괄하는 표현이며, 현재와 같이 '환경(environment)' 측면에만 초점을 맞춘다면 우리는 인류세의 위험성의 복잡성을 제대로 이해할 수 없을 것"이라고 경고하고 있는 글이다. (A) 빈칸에는 "climate change"와 "Anthropocene"이라는 용어를 비교할 수 있는 표현이 들어가야 하므로, 서로 '동일한 의미'가 아니라는 뜻이 될 수 있는 'synonymous'가 가장 적절하다. 그리고 (B)에는 '만일 우리가 '기후'라는 단편적인 요소에만 초점을 맞추면 위험의 복잡성을 제대로 이해할 수 없다'는 의미가 되는 것이 자연스러우므로, 문맥상 빈칸에는 'mistake(잘못 판단하다)', 'misunderstand(잘못 이해하다)'가 적절하다. 따라서 정답은 '④ synonymous (같은 의미의) - misunderstand(잘못 이해하다)'이다.

오답해설

① 'unanimous'는 '만장일치의'라는 의미로, (A) 빈칸에 적절하지 않다.

② 'anonymous'는 '익명의'라는 의미로, (A) 빈칸에 적절하지 않으며, 'misplace'는 '제자리에 두지 않다'라는 의미로 (B) 빈칸에 적절하지 않다.

③ 'continuous'는 '지속적인'이라는 의미로, (A) 빈칸에 적절하지 않으며, 'misbelieve'는 '의심하다'라는 의미로 (B) 빈칸에 적절하지 않다.

해석

"인류세"는 우리의 행성에 미친 인간의 영향을 아우르는 지질학적 시기를 일컫는 널리 제안된 용어이다. 그러나 그것은 "기후변화"와 (A) <u>같은 의미의</u> 것이 아니며, "환경 문제"로도 지칭될 수 없다. 더 거대하고 더 충격적인 인류세는 20세기 중반쯤 인류의 압박이 너무나도 극심해져서 우리가 행성의 뚜껑을 날려버렸다는 증거를 압축하고 있다. 안녕, 새로운 지구 시스템. 안녕, 인류세. "지구 시스템"이라는 구절은 우리 행성이 상호작용하는 물리적, 화학적, 생물적, 그리고 인간적 과정의 전체를 가리킨다. 인공위성 그리고 훨씬 더 강력한 컴퓨터 모델링과 같은 새로운 데이터 수집 기술에 의해 가능해진 지구 시스템 과학은 우리가 어떻게 우리의 행성을 이해하는지를 재구성한다. 기후는 이 시스템의 한 요소일 뿐이다. 만일 우리가 그것 하나에만 초점을 맞춘다면, 우리는 위험성의 복잡성을 (B) <u>잘못 이해할</u> 것이다. "환경"이라는 용어는 우리가 스스로를 생태계의 일부로 이해하도록 도와주지만 우리의 현재 상황의 새로움을 표현하지는 못한다. 우리는 항상 환경에 살아왔다. 아시아가 급격한 발전을 시작한 최근에 들어서야 비로소 우리는 인류세라는 변화된 지구 시스템 속에서 살기 시작한 것이다.

	(A)	(B)
①	만장일치의	잘못 판단하다
②	익명의	제자리에 두지 않다
③	지속적인	의심하다
④	같은 의미의	잘못 이해하다

어휘

Anthropocene 인류세	geological 지질학의
epoch 시기, 세	encapsulate 압축하다, 요약하다
profound 깊은, 극심한	
gasket 개스킷(가스·기름 등이 새어 나오지 않도록 파이프나 엔진 등의 사이에 끼우는 마개)	
skyrocketing 치솟는	altered 바꾼
unanimous 만장일치의	mistake 오해하다, 잘못 판단하다
anonymous 익명인	misplace 제자리에 두지 않다
continuous 끊임없는	misbelieve 의심하다, 믿지 않다
synonymous 같은 뜻의, 동의어의	
misunderstand 오해하다, 잘못 이해하다	

10 정답 ①

정답해설

본문은 2010년 Cumbria에서 발생한 총기 난사 사건에 대한 내용이다. 첫 번째 문장 "In June 2010, the usually mild-mannered Derrick Bird went on a gun rampage in Cumbria, killing 12 people, injuring 11 others and, finally, shooting himself."에 따르면, Bird가 저지른 총기 범죄에 의해 희생된 희생자는 12명이고, 또한 Bird 자신도 총기로 자살을 했다. 따라서 Bird의 총기 난사 사건에 의해 사망한 사람의 수는 Bird 자신을 포함하여 총 13명이므로 글의 내용과 일치하는 보기는 '① A total of 13 people died because of Bird's killing spree(Bird의 한바탕 살인으로 인해 총 13명이 죽었다).'이다.

오답해설

② 본문 중반 "Next were fellow taxi drivers who'd taunted him over his bald head and disheveled clothes(다음은 그의 대머리와 부스스한 옷차림에 대해 조롱하던 동료 택시 기사들이었다)."를 통해, '그의 외모로 그를 놀린 것은 형제들이 아니라 동료 기사'이었음을 알 수 있다. 따라서 오답이다.

③ 세 번째 문장 "His first victims were his twin brother, David, and their family solicitor, Kevin Commons, who he wrongly believed were plotting to send him to prison for tax evasion(그의 첫 번째 희생자는 그의 쌍둥이 형제 David와 그들의 가족 변호사인 Kevin Commons였는데, 그는 그들이 자신을 탈세 혐의로 감옥에 보낼 계획을 음모를 꾸미고 있다고 잘못 생각하고 있었다)."을 통해 'Bird가 자신을 감옥으로 보낼 음모를 꾸미고 있다고 생각한 사람들은 쌍둥이 형제와 가족 변호사였음'을 알 수 있다.

④ 본문 후반 "Bird began firing indiscriminately at passers-by(Bird는 행인들을 향해 무차별적으로 총을 난사하기 시작했다)"를 통해 '애초에 표적으로 정한 쌍둥이 형제와 변호사, 동료 기사들 이외에도 행인들에게 무차별 난사를 했음'을 알 수 있으므로, 글의 내용과 일치하지 않는다.

해석

2010년 6월, 평소 온화한 성격을 지녔던 Derrick Bird가 Cumbria에서 총기를 난사하여 12명을 죽이고 11명을 부상 입혔으며, 끝내 스스로 목숨을 끊었다. Bird는 총신이 짧은 2연발 엽총과 .22구경 소총을 가지고 집에서 출발했다. 그의 첫 번째 희생자는 그의 쌍둥이 형제 David와 그들의 가족 변호사인 Kevin Commons였는데, 그는 그들이 자신을 탈세 혐의로 감옥에 보낼 계획을 음모를 꾸미고 있다고 잘못 생각하고 있었다. 다음은 그의 대머리와 부스스한 옷차림에 대해 조롱하던 동료 택시 기사들이었다. Darren Rewcastle이 첫 번째였다. Bird는 Whitehaven에 있는 택시 승강장에 차를 세우고 그에게 가까이 오라고 손짓한 후, 그의 얼굴과 배에 총을 쐈다. 그는 쓰러진 곳에서 사망했다. Bird는 또한 3명의 다른 택시 기사들을 쏘아 부상을 입혔다. 그 후, 마침내 인근 숲으로 가서 자살을 하기 전에 Bird는 행인들을 향해 무차별적으로 총을 난사하기 시작했다. 사망에 대한 조사에서 심리학자 Adrian West 박사는 '억울해하고 분개한' Bird가 자신의 결점에 대해 사회를 탓했으며, 단순히 자살을 하는 것 대신에 복수를 했다고 말했다.

① Bird의 한바탕 살인으로 인해 총 13명이 죽었다.
② Bird는 형제들에 의해 외모에 대한 모욕을 받아왔다.
③ Bird는 동료 기사들이 자신을 감옥에 보낼 계획을 하고 있다고 생각했다.
④ Bird의 모든 희생자는 그의 초기 표적이었다.

어휘

mild-mannered 온화한, 온순한	rampage 광란
double-barrelled 쌍총신인	sawn-off 한쪽 끝을 (톱으로 잘라) 없앤
solicitor 사무 변호사	plot 음모(모의하다
tax evasion 탈세	taunt 조롱하다, 비웃다
disheveled 단정치 못한, 부스스한	pull up 멈추다, 서다
taxi rank 택시 승강장	beckon 손짓하다, 부르다
cabby 택시 기사	indiscriminately 무차별적으로
passer-by 행인	inquest 조사, 심리
bitter 억울해하는	resentful 분개하는, 분노하는
shortcoming 결점, 결핍	spree 한바탕 저지르기

기적사 DAY 09

결국엔 성정혜 영어 하프모의고사

01	③	02	②	03	④	04	④	05	①
06	④	07	①	08	③	09	②	10	②

01 정답 ③

정답해설

밑줄 친 'interrogate'는 '심문하다, 추궁하다'의 뜻으로 ③ question과 의미가 가장 가깝다.

해석

그것은 생소하거나 의심스러운 활동인 조사, 예비 조사를 시작하고 공식적으로 사람들을 **심문하는** 권한을 가지고 있었습니다.
① 펼치다, 퍼뜨리다
② 음모를 꾸미다, 호기심을 돋우다
③ 질문하다, 심문하다
④ ~을 협박하다

어휘

preliminary 예비의, 최초의,
questionable 의심스러운
spread 펼치다, 퍼뜨리다
question 질문하다, 심문하다
inquiry 조사, 탐구, 연구
interrogate 심문하다, 추궁하다
intrigue 음모를 꾸미다, 호기심을 돋우다
intimidate ~을 협박하다

02 정답 ②

정답해설

밑줄 친 'meticulous'는 '꼼꼼한, 세심한'의 의미로 ② precise와 뜻이 가장 가깝다.

해석

그 예술가의 현실적인 스타일과, 측정을 기록하고 행하는 행동으로서의 **세심한** 관찰이 잘 표현되어 있다.
① (금속 등을) 펴 늘릴 수 있는, 가단성의, 적응성이 있는, 유순한
② 세밀한, 정밀한, 정확한
③ 진실된, 진짜의
④ 짓궂은

어휘

meticulous 꼼꼼한, 세심한
malleable (금속 등을) 펴 늘릴 수 있는, 가단성의, 적응성이 있는, 유순한
precise 세밀한, 정밀한, 정확한
genuine 진실된, 진짜의
mischievous 짓궂은

03 정답 ④

정답해설

밑줄 친 'pass down'은 '~을 물려주다'의 뜻으로 ④ transfer와 의미가 가장 가깝다.

해석

가수나 악기에 의해서 생산된 소리인 음악의 악보 없이 우리는 우리의 음악을 미래 세대들에게 **물려줄** 수 없다.

① 강요하다, ~하게 하다
② 기다리다
③ 파견하다, 보내다
④ 넘겨주다, 물려주다

어휘

pass down ~을 물려주다
wait 기다리다
transfer 넘겨주다, 물려주다
compel 강요하다, ~하게 하다
dispatch 파견하다, 보내다

04 정답 ④

정답해설

A와 B는 '출퇴근 혼잡 시간대(the rush hour)'의 교통 이용에 관한 대화를 나눈다. A는 지하철을 이용하는 것에 대해 말하지만, B는 지하철로 인해서, '교통 체증(the traffic jam)'에 휩싸인 듯이 말하므로 적절하지 않다.

오답해설

① A가 B의 형제 관계에 관해 묻자 B는 두 명의 여자 형제가 있다고 대답하므로 A의 물음에 대한 적합한 답변이다.
② A는 초보자를 위한 조리법 책을 찾고 있다고 말하자 B는 오른쪽 구석에 가서 찾아보라며 위치를 알려준다. 따라서 B는 A의 말에 적절히 대답했다.
③ A가 길을 건널 때 양쪽을 보는 것을 잊지 말라고 말하자, B는 동의하며 초록색 불이 켜져 있다는 것도 확인해야 한다고 말한다. B의 대답은 A의 발언에 알맞은 답변이다.

해석

① A: 너 형제 관계가 어떻게 돼?
   B: 나는 두 명의 여자 형제가 있어.
② A: 나는 초보자를 위한 조리법 책을 찾고 있어.
   B: 오른쪽 모퉁이로 가서 찾아봐.
③ A: 길을 건널 때 양쪽을 보는 것을 잊지 마.
   B: 물론이지, 초록색 불이 켜져 있는 것도 확인해야 해.
④ A: 혼잡 시간대에 지하철을 탄 것은 나쁜 선택이었어.
   B: 혼잡 시간대에는 교통 체증에 갇힐 수도 있어.

어휘

sibling (한 명의) 형제자매[동기]
make sure (...임을)확인하다
traffic jam 교통 체증
look for 찾다, 구하다
rush hour 혼잡 시간대

05 정답 ①

정답해설

① **출제 포인트: 전치사 vs. 접속사**
   'despite'는 전치사로 뒤에 명사(구)가 오며 'although'는 접속사로 뒤에 부사절이 온다. 해당 문장은 'despite'를 사용하였으나 뒤에 절이 왔으므로 틀린 문장이다. 따라서 'Despite'를 'Although'로 수정해야 한다.

오답해설

② **출제 포인트: 주어[the number of 복수명사]와 동사의 수일치**
   주어가 'the number of 복수명사'인 경우 수일치 기준은 단수형태인 'the number'이므로 동사에 단수형태를 사용해야 한다. 해당 문장은 주어 'the number of books'와 동사 'is'가 수일치하므로 옳은 문장이다.

③ **출제 포인트: so+형용사/부사+that+주어+동사 vs. too+형용사/부사+to+동사원형**
   「so+형용사/부사 ~+that+주어+동사 ~」는 '너무 ~해서 ~하다'를 뜻하며 'that'은 부사절을 이끄는 접속사로 옳게 사용되었다.

④ 출제 포인트: 완전타동사+목적어[to부정사 vs. 동명사]

완전타동사 'try'가 to부정사를 목적어로 가지는 경우 '~하려고 하다'를 뜻한다. 해당 문장은 문맥상 '~하려고 했다'가 자연스럽게 사용되었으므로 'tried'의 목적어에 to부정사인 'to show'가 적절하다.

해석

비록 그가 통틀어 소유한 책의 수는 전혀 알려져 있지 않지만, 책에 대한 그의 열정에 관련된 일화는 잘 알려져 있다: 한 학생이 그리스 작가들에 대해 자기가 아는 것을 자랑하려고 할 때 그가 자기 주머니에서 계속해서 책을 꺼낼 수 있을 정도로 매우 많은 책을 가지고 다녔다.

어휘

unknown 알려지지 않은　　　episode 사건, 에피소드
passion 열정
try to 동사원형 ~하려고 하다, ~하려고 애쓰다

오답률 TOP 2
06 정답 ④

정답해설

④ 출제 포인트: 접속사의 쓰임

등위접속사 'and'를 사용하였으나 문맥상 '그러나'가 자연스러우므로 'but'으로 수정해야 한다.

오답해설

① 출제 포인트: 형용사 vs. 부사

밑줄 친 'badly'는 '몹시'를 뜻하는 부사로 동사 'want'를 수식한다.

② 출제 포인트: what vs. that

밑줄 친 'that'은 앞에 선행사 'ways'가 있으며, 뒤따라오는 절의 주어가 없으므로 주격 관계대명사로 사용되었음을 알 수 있다.

③ 출제 포인트: 가주어 it

밑줄 친 부분의 'It'은 가주어로 진주어는 to부정사구 'to feel good'이다.

해석

우리 아이들을 위해 우리가 뭔가를 몹시 원할 때, 참으로 몹시 원해서 아이들에게 도움이 되지 않는 방식으로 우리가 행동할 때, 그것은 우리 스스로를 위한 필요성을 충족시키려고 애쓰고 있다는 것을 의미할 수 있다. 자녀가 승리할 때 기분 좋은 것이 당연하고 자녀가 이기기를 바라는 것이 당연하지만, 여러분 스스로에 대해 좋은 기분을 느끼기 위해 자녀가 이기기를 필요로 할 때는 여러분에게 문제가 있다.

어휘

badly 몹시, 심하게, 서투르게　　behave 처신하다, 행동하다
fulfill 충족시키다, 실행하다

07 정답 ①

정답해설

① 출제 포인트: 타동사로 착각하기 쉬운 완전자동사

'arrive'는 완전자동사로 전치사 없이 목적어를 가질 수 없다. 해당 문장은 'arrive' 뒤에 전치사 없이 목적어 'the refuge'를 사용하였으므로 틀린 문장이다. 따라서 'arrive' 뒤에 전치사 'at'을 사용해야 한다.

오답해설

② 출제 포인트: 전치사 vs. 부사

밑줄 친 'about'은 부사로 사용되었으며 '약, -쯤, -경'을 뜻한다.

③ 출제 포인트: 현재분사 vs. 과거분사

밑줄 친 'searching'은 완전자동사 'search'의 현재분사로 생략된 주어 'we'와 능동관계이다.

④ 출제 포인트: 현재분사 vs. 과거분사

밑줄 친 'learning'은 완전자동사 'learn'의 현재분사로 생략된 주어 'we'와 능동관계이다.

해석

일단 오전 10시경에 보호 구역에 도착하면, 6시간에 걸친 도보 여행을 시작하여 새를 찾고 보호 구역의 식물과 동물에 대해 배우게 됩니다.

어휘

refuge 피난처, 보호 구역　　　hike 도보 여행, 하이킹
search for ~를 찾다　　　　　learn about ~에 대해 배우다

오답률 TOP 3
08 정답 ③

정답해설

주어진 문장에서는 '성실함이 주는 이점'으로 '목표 달성을 할 수 있는 능력'에 대해 언급하고 있다. 이후 이어질 문장으로 가장 적절한 것은 주어진 문장에서 언급된 이점 외에 추가적인 이점인 '좋은 건강(good health)'에 대해 소개하고 있는 (B)가 이어지는 것이 가장 자연스럽다. (B)의 'additional ones'에서 'ones'가 주어진 문장의 'benefits'를 대신하는 표현이라는 것에 주의한다. 이후 추가적인 연구의 결과를 언급하며, (B)에서 언급된 '성실함과 좋은 건강의 관계'에 대해 좀 더 구체적으로 설명하고 있는 (A)가 이어지고, 앞서 설명한 '긍정적인 관계'가 존재하는 '이유'에 대해 'why are ~'로 질문을 던지고 답하며 설명하는 (C)가 연결되는 것이 문맥상 자연스럽다. 따라서 정답은 '③ (B) - (A) - (C)'이다.

오답해설

①, ② 주어진 문장을 제외하고 모두 '성실함과 건강의 관계'에 대해 언급하고 있다는 것을 알 수 있고, (A), (B), (C) 중 '건강'과의 관련성에 대해 최초로 언급하고 있는 보기는 (B)이다. 따라서 (B)가 가장 먼저 등장해야 한다는 것을 알 수 있으므로, 해당 보기는 오답이다.
나머지 선지는 문맥상 부자연스러우므로 오답이다.

해석

자기 절제 및 투지 때문에 자신의 목표를 더욱더 쉽게 달성할 수 있는 능력과 같이 성실함과 동반되는 분명한 이점들이 있다.

(B) 그러나 확실히 주목할 가치가 있는 부차적인 이점들도 또한 존재하는데, 그 이유는 그것들이 건강과 관련되어 있기 때문이다: Harvard Health에 따르면 성실함은 좋은 건강과 가장 꾸준히 연관되어 있다.

(A) 한 연구는 어린 나이에 부모와 교사로부터 성실하다고 묘사된 사람들은 더 오래 살았다는 것을 발견했고, 한편 다른 연구는 이 성격 특성과 낮은 혈압, 낮은 비율의 당뇨와 뇌졸중, 그리고 더 적은 관절 문제 사이의 관련성을 발견했다.

(C) 그렇다면, 왜 성실한 사람들이 또한 더 건강한 사람들인 것인가? 과학자들은 정답이 간결하고 명확하다고 말한다. 그들이 더 나은 건강 습관을 지니고 있다. 이 특성을 지닌 사람들은 흡연 또는 과음과 같은 해로운 행위를 취할 가능성이 더 적고, 건강한 행동을 할 가능성이 더 높다.

어휘

conscientious 성실한, 양심적인　self-discipline 자기 규율[훈련]
determination 투지, 결심　　　trait 특성
diabetes 당뇨병　　　　　　　stroke 뇌졸중
joint 관절　　　　　　　　　　note 주목하다
conscientiousness 성실함, 양심

consistently 꾸준히, 지속적으로, 일관되게
quality 특성, 특징
adopt (특정한 방식이나 자세를) 쓰다[취하다]

오답률 TOP 1

09 정답 ②

정답해설

주어진 문장에서는 '우리 종(인류)의 흔적이 모든 곳에 있다'고 언급하고 있으므로, 이에 대해 구체적으로 '인류의 흔적이 전 세계로 퍼져나가는 경로'에 대해 언급하고 있는 (B)가 주어진 문장 바로 이후에 이어지는 것이 자연스럽다. (B)에서 '인류의 흔적이 전 세계에 퍼져나감'에 따라 'Pristine nature has permanently blinked out of existence(원시적인 자연은 영구적으로 사라졌다).'라고 언급하며, '인류에 의한 자연의 변화'에 대해 언급하고 있으므로, 이러한 변화를 가리키는 (C) "These planetary changes ~"가 이어지는 것이 자연스럽다. 이후에는 (C)의 후반부에 언급된 새로운 시기인 'Anthropocene(인류세)'을 (A)의 'this newly designated epoch'가 가리키고 있으므로, (C) 이후에 (A)가 이어지는 것이 적절하다. 따라서 정답은 '② (B) - (C) - (A)'이다.

오답해설

나머지 보기는 문맥상 어색하므로 오답이다.

해석

우리 종의 화학적, 생물학적 표식은 모든 곳에 있다.
(B) 격렬한 대기의 바람, 끊임없는 해류, 그리고 수백만 척의 화석 연료로 움직이는 운송 수단의 큼지막한 화물 선적실에 의해 전 세계로 운반되는 인류의 흔적으로부터 자유로운 곳은 지구상에 없다. 원시적인 자연은 영구적으로 사라졌다.
(C) 이러한 행성의 변화는 지리학자, 지질학자, 그리고 기후 과학자들에 의해 하나의 지질학적 시기인 완신세의 종료와 다음 시기인 인류세의 시작으로 특징지어졌다.
(A) 이 새롭게 지정된 시기에 해양, 육지, 그리고 대기에 미치는 우리 종의 영향은 지구의 피할 수 없는 특징이 되었다.

어휘

designated 지정된
atmospheric 대기의
current (물, 공기의) 흐름
cargo-hold 화물 적재실, 화물칸
pristine 자연[원래] 그대로의, 오염되지 않은
permanently 영구히
geographer 지리학자
Holocene 완신세
inescapable 피할 수 없는
relentless 끊임없는
capacious 널찍한, 큼직한
imprint 자국
blink 명멸하다, 스러지다
geologist 지질학자
Anthropocene 인류세

10 정답 ②

정답해설

본문은 '일반적으로 복수를 한 후 사람들은 기분이 더 나아질 것이라 생각하지만 실험 결과 복수를 한 후의 기분이 복수를 하지 않은 사람들보다 좋지 않다는 것이 밝혀졌다'라는 내용이다. 본문 초반에서 설명하고 있는 게임의 규칙에 따르면 모든 사람이 동일하게 협조할 시 모두 동일한 이득을 얻을 수 있지만, 한 사람이 배신한다면 배신을 한 사람은 더 큰 이득을 얻고 나머지는 그보다 적은 이득을 얻게 된다. (A) 이전에 '무임 승차자가 합의된 규칙을 따르지 않는다'고 언급한 후, (A) 이후에 '무임 승차자가 타 참가자보다 더 많은 이득을 얻은 상황'에 대해 설명하고 있으므로, 맥락상 '규칙을 따르지 않음으로 인해, 그 결과 더 많은 이득을 얻게 되었다'는 내용이 되어야 한다. 따라서 (A)에는 '인과'를 나타내는 'Hence(그래서)' 또는 '결과'를 나타내는 'As a result(그 결과)'가 적절하다. 또한, (B) 이전에는 '복수를 하기 전 학생들은 자신들의 기분이 나아질 것이라 예측'했으나, (B) 이후에 실제로 복수를 한 후의 기분은 '복수를 하지 않은 사람들보다 더 좋지 않았다'는 내용이 언급되므로, 예측과 실제가 대조적인 상황임을 알 수 있다. 따라서 (B)에는 '역접'을 나타내는 'However(그러나)'가 들어가는 것이 적절하다. 그러므로 정답은 '② As a result(그 결과) - However(그러나)'이다.

오답해설

① (B) 전후 관계가 '첨가'하는 내용이 아니므로, 'Furthermore(게다가)'는 빈칸에 적절하지 않다.
나머지 보기는 문맥상 어색하므로 오답이다.

해석

Kevin Carlsmith와 그의 동료들은 대학생들을 대상으로 만일 모두 협조한다면 모두가 동일하게 이득을 얻게 되는 반면, 누군가 그 또는 그녀의 돈을 투자하길 거부한다면 그 사람은 그 집단에게 손해를 끼치는 대신 이득을 얻게 되는 집단 투자 게임을 준비했다. 각 집단의 (무임 승차자라고 불리는) 비밀 실험자는 집단 구성원들이 동일하게 투자하도록 설득했다. 그러나 돈을 내놓을 시간이 되었을 때, 무임 승차자들은 합의된 계획을 따르지 않았다. (A) 그 결과 무임 승차자들은 평균 5.59달러를 벌었고, 반면 다른 참가자들은 약 2.51달러를 벌었다. 이제 복수 부분이 등장한다. Carlsmith는 일부 집단에게 무임 승차자에게 복수할 수 있는 방법을 제안했다. 그들은 집단의 배신자를 재정적으로 벌하기 위해 자신들의 수입을 일부 사용할 수 있었다. 복수의 기회를 받은 사람들 모두 그것을 받아들였고, 그들은 복수를 한 후 자신들의 기분이 훨씬 나아질 것이라 예측했다. (B) 그러나 결과는 복수를 한 학생들이 하지 않은 학생들보다 기분이 더 좋지 않다고 보고하였다는 것을 보여주었다.

	(A)	(B)
①	그래서	게다가
②	그 결과	그러나
③	그럼에도 불구하고	결과적으로
④	예를 들어	반면에

어휘

at somebody's expense …의 비용[희생]으로
go along with 동조하다, 따르다   get back at 복수하다
defector 배신자

기적사 DAY 10

| 01 | ③ | 02 | ① | 03 | ① | 04 | ② | 05 | ③ |
| 06 | ① | 07 | ② | 08 | ② | 09 | ④ | 10 | ④ |

01 정답 ③

정답해설
밑줄 친 'persisted'는 'persist'의 과거형으로 '계속되다, 지속되다'의 의미를 가진다. 따라서 ③ persevered와 의미가 가장 가깝다.

해석
춥고 눈 오는 일시적인 한파가 금년 2월 중순 국내에서 몇 주간 **계속되었다**.
① 안도시켰다
② 자제했다, 삼갔다
③ 유지하다, 인내했다
④ 억눌렀다

어휘
snap 일시적인 한파
relieve 안도시키다
persevere 유지하다, 인내하다
persist 계속되다, 지속되다
refrain 자제하다, 삼가다
suppress 억누르다

02 정답 ①

정답해설
밑줄 친 'irritated'는 '짜증나게 하는'을 의미한다. 따라서 ① bothered와 의미가 가장 가깝다.

해석
일부 사람들은 분명하지 않은 이유로 단지 **짜증나므로**, 일상에서 그들의 모든 자극 요인들을 피하고 그들이 전문가들에 의한 알맞은 상담을 받을 수 있도록 하는 게 나을지도 모른다.
① 괴롭힘당하는, 성가신
② 흥미가 있는
③ 조사되는, 수사받는
④ 과시하는

어휘
irritated 짜증나게 하는
counseling 상담
interested 흥미가 있는
presumptuous 과시하는
trigger 자극 요인
bothered 괴롭힘당하는, 성가신
probed 조사되는, 수사받는

03 정답 ①

정답해설
밑줄 친 'rely on'은 '기대다, 의존하다'의 뜻으로 ① resort와 의미가 가장 가깝다.

해석
GPS 시스템의 도입에 의해, 운전자들은 그들의 목적지에 빠르고 적절하게 도달하기 위해 이 내비게이션 장치에 **의존한다**.
① 기대다, 의지하다
② 재개하다
③ 끝내다
④ 되찾다, 회복하다

어휘
rely on 기대다, 의존하다
resume 재개하다
regain 되찾다, 회복하다
resort 기대다, 의지하다
cease 끝내다

04 정답 ②

정답해설
A가 B에게 '진통제(pain killer)'가 있는지 질문하자 B는 진통은 많은 스트레스를 유발할 수 있다고 답한다. 이는 A의 질문에 대한 적절한 답변이 아니다.

오답해설
① A가 '엘리베이터가 매 층마다 멈춘다'고 말하자 B는 '매 층마다 멈추기 때문에 오래 걸리는 것이다'라고 답변한다. 이는 A의 말에 대한 적절한 답변이다.
③ A가 '사촌 동생을 위한 크리스마스 선물을 구입해야 한다'고 하자 B는 '어떤 선물을 구입할지에 대한 추천이 필요한지' 묻는다. 이는 A의 발언에 대한 자연스러운 반응이다.
④ A가 B에게 '방과 후 놀이터에서 놀던 과거의 날들이 기억나는지' 묻자 B는 '기억한다'며 '그 당시 과거의 추억을 잊을 수 없다'고 대답한다. B의 말은 A의 질문에 적합하다.

해석
① A: 이 엘리베이터는 층마다 멈추네.
  B: 그게 이렇게 오래 걸리는 이유야.
② A: 실례합니다, 진통제 있으신가요?
  B: 진통은 많은 스트레스를 유발할 수 있죠.
③ A: 저는 사촌 동생을 위해 크리스마스 선물을 사야 해요.
  B: 무엇을 살지 추천이 필요하신가요?
④ A: 우리가 방과 후 놀이터에서 놀던 때 기억나?
  B: 물론이지. 그 시절의 날들을 절대 잊을 수 없어.

어휘
pain killer 진통제
hang out 놀다, 어울리다
recommendation 추천

05 정답 ③

정답해설
③ 출제 포인트: 이중부정 금지
하나의 절 안에 두 개의 부정부사를 사용할 경우 이중부정이 되므로 비문이 된다. 해당 문장은 부정의 뜻을 내포한 빈도부사 'hardly' 뒤에 부정부사 'never'를 사용하였으므로 틀린 문장이다. 따라서 'never'를 삭제해야 한다.

오답해설
① 출제 포인트: 관계부사 how
해당 문장에서 'how'는 관계부사이며 뒤에 오는 절의 동사 'learned'는 완전자동사이다.
② 출제 포인트: a pile of+[가산명사 vs. 불가산명사]
'a pile of'는 '한 무더기의'를 뜻하며 목적어로 가산명사와 불가산명사 모두 사용할 수 있다. 해당 문장은 'a pile of'가 쓰인 문장으로 뒤에 온 'cabbage'는 '양배추'를 뜻하는 불가산명사로 사용되었다.

④ 출제 포인트: 사역동사의 목적격 보어

해당 문장에서 사역동사 'make'는 목적어로 'children'을 갖고 목적격 보어는 동사원형 형태인 원형부정사 'jump'를 갖는다. 이때, 목적어와 목적격 보어의 관계가 능동인 경우 사역동사는 목적격 보어로 원형부정사를 사용하는 것이 적절하다.

해석

"끝낼 때까지 앉아있어."가 우리가 배웠던 방식일지도 모른다. 그리고 또한 당신이 목표를 성취할 수 있다고 느끼는 유일한 방식일지도 모른다. 그러나 생각해보라. 아이들이 메스꺼움을 느낄 때까지 원치 않는 양배추 더미를 먹는 경험은, 다음에 양배추가 제공될 때 아이들이 기뻐 날뛰게 만들 가능성은 거의 없다.

어휘

achieve 성취하다, 달성하다   cabbage 양배추

오답률 TOP 1

06 정답 ①

정답해설

① 출제 포인트: 동사 vs. 준동사

해당 문장에서 'may be'는 접속사 'that'이 이끄는 명사절의 동사이므로 주절의 동사가 없음을 알 수 있다. 따라서 'recognizing'을 동사 'recognize'로 수정해 명령문으로 바꿔야 한다.

오답해설

② 출제 포인트: 완전타동사+목적어[to부정사 vs. 동명사]

해당 문장에서 'help'의 목적어로 온 원형 부정사 'avoid'는 완전타동사로 사용되었으며 동명사를 목적어로 가진다. 따라서 'avoid'의 목적어로 온 밑줄 친 동명사 'committing'은 옳은 표현이다.

③ 출제 포인트: 주격 관계대명사절의 동사 수일치

주격 관계대명사절의 동사는 선행사에 수일치 한다. 밑줄 친 'means'는 주격 관계대명사 'which'가 이끄는 절의 동사로 선행사는 'perception checking'에 해당된다. 따라서 단수형태인 선행사에 따라 단수동사인 'means'를 옳게 사용하였다.

④ 출제 포인트: other vs. others

대명사 'other'는 단독으로 사용할 수 없으며 정관사 'the'와 함께 사용한다. 또한 대명사 'others'는 '다른 사람들'을 뜻하며 단독으로 사용할 수 있다. 해당 문장은 'others'를 단독으로 사용하였으므로 옳은 문장이다.

해석

이런 이유 때문에, 우리의 다른 사람에 대한 첫인상은 또한 인식의 오류일 수 있다는 것을 인식해라. 이런 오류를 범하는 것을 피하는 데 도움을 주기 위해서, 우리가 다른 사람들에 대한 그리고 그들의 행동들에 대한 우리의 인식들을 확인하고 그것들에 문제를 제기해 보기 위해 일련의 질문을 고려한다는 것을 의미하는, 인식의 점검에 들어가라.

어휘

recognize 인식하다, 알아보다   first impression 첫인상
commit 저지르다, 범하다   a series of 일련의

07 정답 ②

정답해설

② 출제 포인트: 주어와 동사의 수일치

주어가 동명사(구)인 경우 단수로 취급하며 동사에 단수형태를 사용한다. 밑줄 친 'engage'의 주어는 동명사(구) 'Seeing ~ crises'이므로 'engage'는 단수형태의 동사인 'engages'로 수정해야 한다.

오답해설

① 출제 포인트: 지각동사의 목적격 보어

지각동사 'see'의 목적격 보어는 원형부정사 또는 현재분사를 사용한다. 해당 문장은 동명사 'seeing'이 사용되었으며 이때 밑줄 친 'battle'은 'seeing'의 목적격 보어인 원형부정사에 해당한다.

③ 출제 포인트: 전치사+관계대명사

밑줄 친 'in which'는 「전치사+관계대명사」로 뒤에 오는 절은 완전한 형태이며 선행사는 'an emotional struggle'이다.

④ 출제 포인트: 현재분사 vs. 과거분사

'missing'은 현재분사 형태의 형용사로 '빠진, 누락된'을 뜻한다. 해당 문장은 문맥상 '그렇지 않았다면 감정적인 영향이 빠졌을 것이다'가 자연스러우므로 'missing'을 사용하는 것이 옳다.

해석

영웅이 장애물과 싸우고 위기를 극복하는 것을 보는 것은 관객들을 감정적 투쟁에 참여하게 하는데, 그런 투쟁 속에서 드라마의 줄거리와 결말에 나오는 사건들은 그렇지 않다면 빠졌을 감정적인 영향을 지닌다.

어휘

obstacle 장애, 장애물   overcome 극복하다
crisis 위기
engage A in B A를 B에 관여하게 하다, 참여하게 하다
missing 빠진, 누락된, 없어진, 실종된

오답률 TOP 3

08 정답 ②

정답해설

본문 초반에서 '"Big Five" personality traits('5가지' 성격 특성)'에 대해 간략히 언급한 후, 그중에서도 업무 성과와 관련이 깊은 'conscientiousness (성실성)'에 대해 집중적으로 설명하고 있다. 한 논문의 연구 결과를 인용하며 "the authors find that conscientiousness scores make less of a difference to people's performance when they're in high-complexity jobs such as a doctor, social worker, and attorney(저자들은 그들이 성실성 지수가 의사, 사회복지사, 그리고 변호사와 같은 고 복잡성 직업에 종사할 때, 사람들의 성과에 더 적은 차이를 만든다는 것을 발견한다)."를 통해 '성실성이 덜 중요시되는 분야'에 대해 언급하고, 이후 "Instead, they mainly seems to matter in low- or moderate-complexity jobs such as a factory worker, salesperson, and call center operator(대신에 그것들은 주로 공장 노동자, 판매원, 그리고 콜센터 직원과 같은 낮은 - 또는 중간 - 복잡성 직업에 있어서 중요한 것처럼 보인다)."를 통해 '성실성이 더 중요시되는 분야'에 대해 언급하며, '성실성이 덜 혹은 더 중요한 직종이 존재함'을 언급하고 있다. 따라서 글의 요지로 가장 적절한 것은 '② Conscientiousness may matter less in certain careers(특정 직종에서는 성실성이 덜 중요할 수도 있다).'이다.

오답해설

① 본문과 관련이 없는 내용이므로 오답이다.
③ 5가지 성격 특성을 서로 비교하며 중요도를 분석하는 내용은 아니므로, 글의 요지로 적절하지 않다.
④ 본문에서는 '고 복잡성 직업에 종사할 때 성실성 지수가 더 적은 차이를 만든다'고 언급하며, 일부 직종에서는 성실성과 업무 성과의 관계가 낮은 사실을 설명하고 있는데, 보기에서는 '직업의 유형에 관계없이(regardless of job types)' 성실성이 업무 성과와 밀접한 관계가 있다고 언급하고 있으므로, 본문의 주장과 반대되는 내용이다. 따라서 오답이다.

해석

"5가지" 성격 특성은 인간의 성격에 대한 의미 있는 무언가에 도달하는 것처럼 보인다. 그것들은 분명 모든 것들을 포착하지는 않지만, 경험에 대한 개방성, 성실성, 외향성, 우호성, 그리고 신경증적 경향성은 한 테스트로부터 다음 테스트를 통해 고도로 안정적으로 측정될 수 있는 특성들이다. 놀랄 것도 없이, 이 특성 중 하나인 – 성실성은 – 사람들이 직장에서 업무를 어떻게 보는지와 깊은 관련이 있다. 그러나 왜, 그리고 어떤 환경에서 그러한 것인가? PNAS에 게재된 한 논문은 우리가 성실성에 대해 아는 것을 요약하기 위해 2,500가지 이상의 연구의 데이터를 활용했다. 뜻밖에도, 저자들은 성실성 지수가 의사, 사회복지사, 그리고 변호사와 같은 고 복잡성 직업에 종사할 때, 사람들의 성과에 더 적은 차이를 만든다는 것을 발견한다. 대신에 그것들은 주로 공장 노동자, 판매원, 그리고 콜센터 직원과 같은 낮은 – 또는 중간 – 복잡성 직업에 있어서 중요한 것처럼 보인다.
① 한 사람의 성격을 측정하는 것은 거의 불가능하다.
② 특정 직종에서는 성실성이 덜 중요할 수도 있다.
③ 성실성은 5가지 성격 특성 중 가장 중요한 특성이다.
④ 성실성은 직업 유형에 관계없이 한 사람의 직업적 성과와 밀접하게 관련되어 있다.

어휘

trait 특성
conscientiousness 성실성, 양심
agreeableness 우호성
stability 안정성
moderate 중간의
get at …에 도달하다[미치다]
extraversion 외향성
neuroticism 신경증적 경향
unexpectedly 뜻밖에

오답률 TOP 2
09 정답 ④

정답해설

본문은 많은 과학자들과 학자들이 인류에 의해 변화된 현시기를 "Anthropocene(인류세)"이라고 명명하는 것에 대한 'Jason W. Moore'의 반박을 소개하며, '모든 인류에 의해 변화한 것이 아닌, 자본주의에 의한 일부 국가들에 의해 변화한 것이므로 "Capitalocene(자본세)"라고 칭해야 한다'고 설명하고 있다. ④ 이전 문장에서, "By focusing on the "anthro," we maintain the delusion that all humans are equal participants in this global change"라고 언급하며, '모든 인류가 동일한 참여자'라는 것이 '착각, 망상(delusion)'이라고 언급하고 있으므로, 이러한 생각은 ④ 이후의 "the idea that human-caused climate change is largely driven by the consumption of resources within developed countries(인류에 의해 발생한 기후변화는 선진국 내에서의 자원 소비에 의해 주로 야기되었다는 생각)"를 '인정(acknowledging)'하는 것이 아닌 '무시(ignoring)'하는 행태라고 보는 것이 적절하다. 따라서 ④는 문맥상 적절하지 않다.

오답해설

① 새로운 시기의 도래를 논의할 정도로 인류가 환경에 커다란 영향을 미치고 있으므로, '극심한(extreme)'은 문맥상 적절하다.
② "Anthropocene"은 '새로운 시기'를 '지정하기(designate)' 위해 과학자들이 사용해온 용어이므로 문맥상 적절하다.
③ 본문 중반에 언급된 "the political critique of climate change that such a moment demands(그러한 순간이 요구하는 기후변화에 대한 정치적 비판)"로 보아, 본문에서 다루는 인류가 미친 환경에의 영향은 '부정적'인 것이라는 것을 유추할 수 있다. 따라서 이러한 것을 '재앙(catastrophes)'이라고 지칭하는 것은 문맥상 자연스럽다.

해석

우리 중 대부분은 인간의 지구의 천연자원 사용이 새로운 시대를 필요로 할 만큼 ① 극심한 환경적인 영향을 야기했다는 것에 동의한다. 하지만 그것을 무엇으로 부를 것인가? 환경 과학자들과 학자들은 새로운 시기를 ② 정하기 위해 "인류세"라는 용어를 사용해왔으나, 그 용어가 그러한 순간이 요구하는 기후변화에 대한 정치적 비판을 명확히 할 수 있는 힘을 지니고 있는가? Jason W. Moore는 더 분석적인 초점을 제공하기 위해 "자본세"라는 용어를 도입하고, "인류세"는 현대의 환경적 ③ 재앙을 일으키는 시스템, 즉 자본주의를 밝히지 않는다고 주장했다. "인류의"에 초점을 맞춤으로써 우리는 모든 인간이 이 세계적 변화에의 동일한 참여자라는 착각에 빠지고, 인류에 의해 발생한 기후변화는 복합 경제 성장을 중심으로 구조화된 경제 시스템에 의해 부양되는 선진국 내에서의 자원 소비에 의해 주로 야기되었다는 생각을 ④ <u>인정한다(→무시한다)</u>.

어휘

Anthropocene 인류세
epoch 시기, 세
catastrophe 재앙, 참사
acknowledge 인정하다
designate 지정하다
Capitalocene 자본세
delusion 망상, 착각
feed 부양하다

---

10 정답 ④

정답해설

본문은 '복수를 하고자 하는 욕망'이 '인간의 본성'이며 '정상적인 감정'이라고 설명하고 있다. 주어진 문장의 "In the third one"으로 보아 주어진 문장 이전에 적어도 세 가지 이상의 대상이 언급되어야 함을 알 수 있다. 본문 중 ④ 이전 문장에서 "they go through these psychological stages: a shock phase, an adjustment phase and a reaction phase(그들은 이러한 심리적인 단계들을 거친다고 말한다: 충격 단계, 적응 단계, 그리고 반응 단계.)."라고 '세 가지 단계'에 대해 언급하고 있는 것으로 보아, 주어진 문장의 'third one'이 'a reaction phase'를 가리킨다는 것을 알 수 있다. 따라서 주어진 문장이 들어갈 가장 적절한 위치는 ④이다.

오답해설

'third one'이 지칭할 수 있는 대상이 본문의 나머지 문장에서는 전혀 등장하지 않기 때문에 나머지 보기는 오답이다.

해석

복수를 하고자 하는 욕망은 어린 시절부터 우리에게 고정되어 있다. (①) 다시 말해, 복수하길 원하는 것은 본능적인 행동이다. (②) 한 사회에서 그것은 보복에 대한 두려움으로 인해 사람들이 타인을 해하는 것을 막아주고, 그것은 성서 시대 훨씬 이전으로 거슬러 올라간다. (③) 복수를 설명하기 위해 Sheffield Hallam University의 건강 심리학 교수 Ann Macaskill은 개인이 부당하다고 느껴지는 방식으로 공격을 당했을 때, 그들은 이러한 심리적인 단계를 거친다고 말한다: 충격 단계, 적응 단계, 그리고 반응 단계. (④ **세 번째 단계에서 그들은 결정 또는 용서하고 원한은 가지고 있지만 아무것도 하지 않기로 결정하거나, 또는 복수를 하거나 복수를 계획할 것이다.**) 사실, 복수심에 불타는 것은 많은 상황에서 꽤 정상적이며 진화 심리학자들은 복수를 하는 능력이 인간 본성의 일부라고 말한다.

어휘

grudge 원한
hardwire 고정화시키다, 굳어버리게하다
instinctive 본능적인
vengefulness 복수심에 불탐, 앙심을 품음
plot 계획하다, 꾀하다
reprisal 보복, 앙갚음

결국엔 성정혜 영어 하프모의고사
기적사 복습 모의고사 1회

01	③	02	④	03	④	04	④	05	②
06	②	07	②	08	①	09	②	10	②
11	③	12	①	13	③	14	③	15	②
16	④	17	③	18	③	19	④	20	③

01 정답 ③   Day 06-01

정답해설

밑줄 친 'muzzle'은 '입막음하다, (말하는 것 등을) 억누르다'라는 의미로, ③ suppress와 의미가 가장 유사하다.

해석

인간은 새로운 생각을 **억압하려고** 시도했던 정부 당국, 그리고 변화는 허튼수작이라고 선언했던 오래전부터 확립된 견해라는 권위에 대해 계속해서 반항해왔다.
① 표현하다
② 주장하다
③ 억누르다
④ 펼치다, 퍼뜨리다

02 정답 ④   Day 02-03

정답해설

밑줄 친 'crucial'은 '중대한, 결정적인'이라는 뜻으로 ④ significant와 의미가 가장 가깝다.

해석

이 중차대한 시기에 투자자를 찾는 것은 Tom에게 **중요하다**.
① 의심이 가는, 미심쩍은
② 논란의 여지가 있는
③ 열렬한, 열광적인
④ 중요한, 의미 있는

03 정답 ④   Day 04-02

정답해설

밑줄 친 'confident'는 '자신감 있는, 확신하는'이라는 의미로 사용되었고, 유의어가 아닌 것은 ④ confidential이다.

해석

자신감 있는 사람들은 그들 스스로를 믿고 항상 그들 스스로를 사랑한다.
① 확신하는
② 확신하는
③ 확신하는
④ 기밀의

04 정답 ④   Day 01-03

정답해설

밑줄 친 'on the fence'는 '결정하지 못하여'의 의미이며, ④ undecided와 동일한 의미를 가진다.

해석

그녀는 루브르 박물관에 있는 모나리자를 관람하러 가야 하는 것에 대해 **결정을 못 하고** 있다.
① 번민의, 고뇌에 찬
② 열광적인
③ 불안한
④ 결정하지 못한

05 정답 ②   Day 06-03

정답해설

밑줄 친 'call it a day'는 '하던 일을 그만두다'라는 의미이므로 ② finish와 의미가 가장 유사하다.

해석

외과의들은 그 일에 적합한 도구들을 찾을 수 없었기 때문에 어쩔 수 없이 **그만두게** 되었다.
① 시작하다
② 끝내다
③ 기다리다
④ 취소하다

06 정답 ②   Day 02-05

정답해설

② 출제 포인트: 불완전타동사의 목적격 보어/타동사구[완전타동사+목적어+전치사+목적어]

두 가지 경우로 나누어 볼 수 있다.
1. 'forbade'를 불완전타동사로 보는 경우
   'forbade(불완전타동사 forbid의 과거시제)'의 목적격 보어 자리에 현재분사 'telling'을 사용하였으나 'forbade'는 to부정사만을 목적격 보어로 가지므로 틀린 문장이다. 따라서 'telling'을 'to tell'로 수정해야 한다.
2. 'forbade'를 완전타동사로 보는 경우
   'forbade(완전타동사 forbid의 과거시제)' 뒤에 대상을 나타내는 목적어가 오는 경우 「forbade+목적어[대상]+from+목적어[금지 내용]」의 구조를 가지며 이때 금지 내용을 나타내는 목적어로 명사 또는 동명사가 온다. 해당 문장은 「forbade+목적어[대상]+from+목적어[금지 내용]」을 사용하였으나 전치사 'from'을 누락했으므로 틀린 문장이다. 따라서 'telling'을 'from telling'으로 수정해야 한다.

해석

① 당신이 해야 할 일은 유용한 전화번호 목록을 만드는 것이다.
② 그는 그것에 대해 정말 당황했는데 왜냐하면 그는 내가 누구에게도 말하는 것을 금지했기 때문이다.
③ 결국 Tom은 그녀의 우울증을 치료할 수 있는 의사를 발견했다.
④ 가게 창문을 들여다보기 위해 이따금 멈춰 서면서, Jane은 느긋하게 거리로 걸어 내려갔다. or 이따금 멈춰 서서 가게 창문을 들여다보면서, Jane은 느긋하게 거리로 걸어 내려갔다.

07 정답 ②   Day 02-09

정답해설

본문은 '세계에서 가장 위험한 개미(The most dangerous ant in the world)'인 '불독개미(bulldog ant)'에 관하여 서술하고 있다. 세 번째 문장 "There have been at least three human fatalities since 1936, the latest of whom was a Victorian farmer in 1988(1936년 이래로 최소 3명의 사망자가 발생했으며, 가장 최근의 사망자는 1988년 빅토리아 지방의 농부였다)."에서 '가장 최근의(마지막) 사망자는 1988년 발생했음'을 알 수 있으므로, 1989년 이후로는 사망자가 나오지 않은 것을 유추할 수 있다. 따라서 글의 내용과 일치하는 것은 '② No one has been killed because of its attack since 1989(1989년 이후로 그것의 공격에 의해 사망한 사람은 없다).'이다.

해석

세계에서 가장 위험한 개미는 호주의 해안 지대에서 발견되는 불독개미 (Myrmecia pyriformis)이다. 공격을 할 때 그것은 침과 턱을 동시에 사용한다. 1936년 이래로 최소 3명의 사망자가 발생했으며, 가장 최근의 사망자는 1988년 빅토리아 지방의 농부였다. 불독개미는 그것의 사나움과 공격 중 집요함 때문에 이름을 얻었다. 그것은 극도로 공격적이며 인간에 대한 두려움을 거의 보이지 않으며, 연달아 여러 번 침을 찌르고 그에 따라 한 번 물때마다 더 많은 독을 주입한다. 공격을 할 때, 그 개미는 길고 이가 나 있는 아래턱뼈를 이용해 그것의 희생양을 꽉 붙잡고 몸을 아래쪽으로 구부려 길고 미늘이 없는 침을 피부로 찔러 넣는다. 일부의 경우에 이 침은 성인을 15분 안에 사망에 이르게 할 만큼 충분했다.
① 그것은 세계에서 가장 위험한 곤충으로 기록되어 있다.
② 1989년 이후로 그것의 공격에 의해 사망한 사람은 없다.
③ 그것의 신체적 외모 때문에 이름이 붙었다.
④ 그것은 공격을 하기 위해 아래턱뼈 또는 독이 있는 침 중 하나를 사용한다.

08 정답 ①   Day 10-06

정답해설

① 출제 포인트: 동사 vs. 준동사
해당 문장에서 'may be'는 접속사 'that'이 이끄는 명사절의 동사이므로 주절의 동사가 없음을 알 수 있다. 따라서 'recognizing'을 동사 'recognize'로 수정해 명령문으로 바꿔야 한다.

해석

이런 이유 때문에, 우리의 다른 사람에 대한 첫인상은 또한 인식의 오류일 수 있다는 것을 인식하라. 이런 오류를 범하는 것을 피하는 데 도움을 주기 위해서, 우리가 다른 사람들에 대한 그리고 그들의 행동들에 대한 우리의 인식들을 확인하고 그것들에 문제를 제기해 보기 위해 일련의 질문을 고려한다는 것을 의미하는, 인식의 점검에 들어가라.

09 정답 ②   Day 01-08

정답해설

글의 도입에서 'production of an information goods(정보재 생산)'에 대해서 먼저 언급하고 있다. 이런 정보재의 특징은 고정비용은 크지만, 한계비용이 낮은 점이 일반재와는 다른 점을 명확히 명시하고 있다. 글의 후반부 'You must price your information goods according to consumer value, not according to your production cost(당신은 당신의 생산비가 아닌 소비자 가치에 따라 당신의 정보 상품의 가격을 책정해야 한다).'를 통해서 'information goods(정보재)'는 '생산비에 따라 값을 매기는 것이 아니라 소비자의 가치에 따라 가격을 매겨야 한다.'고 설명하고 있으므로 글의 제목으로 가장 적절한 것은 ② Pricing the Information Goods(정보재 가격 책정)가 가장 적절한 제목이다.

해석

경제학자들은 정보재의 생산은 높은 고정비용과 낮은 한계비용을 수반한다고 말한다. 정보 재화의 첫 번째 사본 제작비용은 상당할 수 있지만, 추가 사본을 제작(또는 복제)하는 비용은 무시할 수 있다. 이런 종류의 비용 구조는 많은 중요한 의미를 가지고 있다. 예를 들어, 생산비에 바탕을 둔 가격 책정은 작동을 안 할 수가 있다: 단가가 0일 때 단가를 10% 또는 20% 인상하는 것은 말이 되지 않는다. 당신은 당신의 생산비가 아닌 소비자 가치에 따라 당신의 정보 상품의 가격을 책정해야 한다.
① 저작권 확보
② 정보재 가격 책정
③ 지적재산으로서의 정보
④ 기술 변화의 비용

10 정답 ②   Day 03-10

정답해설

본문은 '고등 교육의 자유 시장화(Marketization of higher education)'의 이점에 대해 설명하는 글이다. 본문에 따르면 '고등 교육의 자유 시장화는 고등 교육의 개혁과 교육 시스템 혁신에 도움이 되고, 폐쇄적 학교 운영 방식을 개방적 사회 지향적 모델로 변화시킬 수 있으며, 빠르게 발전하는 사회 및 경제 상황에 고등 교육기관이 더욱더 잘 적응하고 그에 따라 발전할 수 있도록 지속적으로 자극을 준다'고 설명한다. 그런데 '② It changes the policy of higher education institutions from creating conditions that will meet the various needs of students to focusing on the requirements and regulations of the government(그것은 학생들의 다양한 요구를 충족시키는 환경을 만드는 것으로부터 정부의 요구와 규제에 초점을 맞추는 것으로 정책을 변화시킨다).'에서는 '자유 시장적인 모델(학생들의 다양한 요구를 충족시키는 자유롭고 개방적인 환경)에서 정부의 요구와 규제에 집중하는 폐쇄적인 모델로의 변화'를 설명하고 있다. 즉, 본문에서 언급하는 '고등 교육의 자유 시장화의 특징'과는 정반대의 내용을 언급하고 있으므로, 글의 전체 흐름과 부합하지 않는다. 따라서 정답은 ②이다.

해석

고등 교육의 자유 시장화는 고등 교육이 시장 및 사회에 밀접하게 관련되도록 도와주고, 이것이 고등 교육의 개혁을 가속화하고 교육 시스템의 혁신을 촉진한다. ① 그것은 또한 전통적인 폐쇄적 학교 운영 방식을 개방적인 사회 지향적인 모델로 변화시키는 것에 도움이 된다. ② <u>그것은 학생들의 다양한 요구를 충족시키는 환경을 만드는 것으로부터 정부의 요구와 규제에 초점을 맞추는 것으로 정책을 변화시킨다.</u> ③ 물론 시장 경제가 존재하는 현대 사회에서의 고등 교육의 지식과 진리 추구의 기본 정신이 변화한 것은 아니다. ④ 그러나 고등 교육의 발전은 사회 발전과 밀접한 관련이 있고, 고등 교육기관은 경쟁적인 시장 경제 안에서 살아남고 발전해 나가야 한다. 이 시장 모델의 주된 이점은 그것이 고등 교육기관들이 변화하는 경제적 사회적 상황에 적응하도록 지속적으로 자극할 수 있다는 것이다.

11 정답 ③   Day 03-04

정답해설

Sharon이 새해 계획을 적고 있는 상황에서 Tobe와 나눈 대화의 내용이다. Tobe는 계획은 중요하지만 ③ '어려운 순간에 계획을 바꿈(change horses in the middle of the stream)' 수밖에 없는 순간들이 있다고 말한다.

해석

Tobe: 너 여기서 뭐 하고 있어?
Sharon: 나는 새 다이어리에 내 새해 소원을 적고 있었어.
Tobe: 오, 그거 네 새 다이어리야?
Sharon: 응 맞아. 오늘 샀어. 그리고 새해 계획도 좀 세워봤어.
Tobe: 잘했네! 계획은 중요하지. 근데 어려운 순간에 계획을 바꿀 수밖에 없는 순간들이 있어.
Sharon: 알아, 그럴 때가 있지. 그런데 내가 계획이 있다는 것을 알면 내가 조정을 해야 하더라도 더 안정감을 느끼게 해줘.
① 열광하다
② 헛수고하다
③ 어려운 순간에 계획을 바꾸다
④ 의기양양하다

12 정답 ① — Day 08-04

정답해설

A는 B에게 '자기 자신에게 동기부여 하는 방법'을 묻고 있지만, B는 '자신이 큰 성취를 이룰 수 있게 동기 부여되고 싶다'라고 답변한다. B의 답변은 A의 물음에 대한 답으로 적절하지 않다.

해석

① A: 넌 어떻게 너 자신을 동기 부여해?
   B: 나는 내가 큰 성취를 이룰 수 있게 동기부여 되고 싶어.
② A: 너 미신을 믿어?
   B: 아니, 미신은 과학적 증거에 근거해 있지 않잖아.
③ A: 난 이웃 동네에 친구가 있었으면 좋겠어.
   B: 밖에 나가서 함께 놀 네 또래의 친구를 찾아봐.
④ A: 내가 영화관에 간 지 수년이 지났어.
   B: 새로운 출시작들을 따라잡을 시간이 필요해 보이네.

13 정답 ③ — Day 01-07

정답해설

③ 출제 포인트: the+형용사

'tend'는 '돌보다, 보살피다'라는 뜻의 타동사로 목적어가 필요하다. 형용사(sick and wounded)가 목적어가 되기 위해서는 명사로 바뀌어야 한다. 「the+형용사」는 '~한 사람들'이라는 뜻으로 해당 문장에서는 'sick and wounded'를 'the sick and the wounded'로 바꿔야 목적어 자리에 오는 명사 역할을 할 수 있다.

14 정답 ③ — Day 04-06

정답해설

③ 출제 포인트: 「가격동사+사람(목적어)+전치사+the+신체부위」

「kiss+사람+on+the+신체부위」는 '~의 신체부위에 입을 맞추다'를 뜻한다. 이때 전치사 'on' 뒤에는 정관사 'the'를 사용해야 하며 소유격 대명사를 사용할 수 없다. 해당 문장은 「kiss+사람+on」을 사용하였으나 뒤에 정관사 'the'가 아닌 소유격 대명사 'his'를 사용하였으므로 틀린 문장이다. 따라서 'his cheek'을 'the cheek'으로 수정해야 한다.

15 정답 ② — Day 09-10

정답해설

본문은 '일반적으로 복수를 한 후 사람들은 기분이 더 나아질 것이라 생각하지만 실험 결과 복수를 한 후의 기분이 복수를 하지 않은 사람들보다 더 좋지 않다는 것이 밝혀졌다'라는 내용이다. 본문 초반에서 설명하고 있는 게임의 규칙에 따르면 모든 사람이 동일하게 협조할 시 모두 동일한 이득을 얻을 수 있지만, 한 사람이 배신한다면 배신을 한 사람은 더 큰 이득을 얻고 나머지는 그보다 적은 이득을 얻게 된다. (A) 이전에 '무임 승차자가 합의된 규칙을 따르지 않는다'고 언급한 후, (A) 이후에 '무임 승차자가 타 참가자보다 더 많은 이득을 얻은 상황'에 대해 설명하고 있으므로, 맥락상 규칙을 따르지 않음으로 인해, 그 결과 더 많은 이득을 얻게 되었다'는 내용이 되어야 한다. 따라서 (A)에는 '인과'를 나타내는 'Hence(그래서)' 또는 '결과'를 나타내는 'As a result(그 결과)'가 적절하다. 또한, (B) 이전에는 '복수를 하기 전 학생들은 자신들의 기분이 나아질 것이라 예측'했으나, (B) 이후에 실제로 복수를 한 후의 기분은 '복수를 하지 않은 사람들보다 더 좋지 않았다'는 내용이 언급되므로, 예측과 실제가 대조적인 상황임을 알 수 있다. 따라서 (B)에는 '역접'을 나타내는 'However(그러나)'가 들어가는 것이 적절하다. 그러므로 정답은 '② As a result(그 결과) – However(그러나)'이다.

해석

Kevin Carlsmith와 그의 동료들은 대학생들을 대상으로 만일 모두 협조한다면 모두가 동일하게 이득을 얻게 되는 반면, 누군가 그 또는 그녀의 돈을 투자하길 거부한다면 그 사람은 그 집단에게 손해를 끼치는 대신 이득을 얻게 되는 집단 투자 게임을 준비했다. 각 집단의 (무임 승차자라고 불리는) 비밀 실험자는 집단 구성원들이 동일하게 투자하도록 설득했다. 그러나 돈을 내놓을 시간이 되었을 때, 무임 승차자들은 합의된 계획을 따르지 않았다. (A) 그 결과 무임 승차자들은 평균 5.59달러를 벌었고, 반면 다른 참가자들은 약 2.51달러를 벌었다. 이제 복수 부분이 등장한다. Carlsmith는 일부 집단에게 무임 승차자에게 복수할 수 있는 방법을 제안했다. 그들은 집단의 배신자를 재정적으로 벌하기 위해 자신들의 수입을 일부 사용할 수 있었다. 복수의 기회를 받은 사람들 모두 그것을 받아들였고, 그들은 복수를 한 후 자신들의 기분이 훨씬 나아질 것이라 예측했다. (B) 그러나 결과는 복수를 한 학생들이 하지 않은 학생들보다 기분이 더 좋지 않다고 보고하였다는 것을 보여주었다.

	(A)	(B)
①	그래서	게다가
②	그 결과	그러나
③	그럼에도 불구하고	결과적으로
④	예를 들어	반면에

16 정답 ④ — Day 06-08

정답해설

주어진 지문의 핵심어인 'conscientious'의 경우 '양심적인' 또는 '성실한'의 의미로 주로 쓰이게 되는데, 해당 지문에서는 일의 효율성과 관련된 지문이므로 '성실한'의 의미로 해석하는 것이 적절하다. 'conscientious employees(성실한 직원들)'가 일의 효율성을 중요시하는 반면에, 빈칸 이전에 제시된 'disorganized, unconscientious person(정리되지 않은, 성실하지 않은 사람)'은 이에 상대적인 개념으로 제시되고 있다. 결국 빈칸의 내용 이후에 'otherwise'에 주목해서 '그렇지 않으면' 즉 '성실하지 않으면' 만들어 냈을 '부정적인 측면'에 대한 서술이 빈칸에 들어가야 함을 유추할 수 있다. 따라서 '성실한 사람들이 성실하지 않았으면 스스로 만들어 낼 ④ 스트레스를 피한다(sidestep stress)'가 적절하다.

해석

"고도로 성실한 직원들은 우리보다 일련의 일을 더 잘합니다."라고 성실성을 연구하는 일리노이 대학의 심리학자인 Brent Roberts는 말한다. Roberts는 그들의 성공을 "위생" 요인에 돌린다. 성실한 사람들은 자신의 삶을 잘 정리하는 경향이 있다. 체계적이지 못하고 성실하지 않은 사람은 올바른 문서를 찾기 위해 파일을 찾아 헤매면서 20분 혹은 30분을 낭비할지도 모른다, 성실한 사람들은 피하는 경향이 있는 비효율적인 경험들 말이다. 기본적으로, 성실하게 됨으로써, 사람들은 그렇지 않다면 그들이 스스로 만들어 낼 수 있는 스트레스를 회피한다.
① 좌절을 극복하다
② 철저한 일을 하다
③ 표준을 따르다
④ 스트레스를 회피하다

17 정답 ③ Day 07-09

정답해설
본문은 '인류세(Anthropocene)' 선포에 대한 근거에 대해 설명하는 글로, 본문 중반 "according to them, the global domestication of a vast number of chickens is one of the defining features of the Anthropocene(그들에 의하면 수많은 닭의 전 세계적인 사육은 인류세를 정의하는 특징 중 하나이다)."을 통해 '수많은 닭(가축)이 인류세의 특징 중 하나'라는 것을 알 수 있다. 또한, 인류세가 선포된 이유는 '인류의 행위(human activity)'로 인해 지질학적 특징이 변하였기 때문이며, 그중 하나가 '기후변화(climate change)'인데, 이러한 기후변화를 일으키는 주요 원인 중 하나인 '온실가스(GHGs)'가 '증가한 가축 사육'으로 인해 다량으로 배출되고 있다고 언급하고 있는 것 또한 '증가한 가축의 수가 '인류세'의 등장에 부분적으로 영향을 미쳤다'는 것을 유추할 수 있는 근거가 될 수 있다. 따라서 글의 요지로 가장 적절한 것은 '③ The emergence of a new epoch has partly been brought about by increased livestock populations(새로운 시기의 등장은 부분적으로 증가한 가축의 수에 의해 야기되었다).'이다.

해석
Cape Town에서 개최된 International Geological Congress에서 한 과학자 집단이 지구의 역사에서 인류의 행위에 의해 현저하게 정의되는 시기인 인류세를 발표했다. 과학자들이 미래의 고고학자들이 이 시기를 인식하기 위해 사용할 것이라 믿는 증거 중 하나는 많은 화석화된 닭의 뼈이다. 그들에 의하면 수많은 닭의 전 세계적인 사육은 인류세를 정의하는 특징 중 하나이다. 지난 50년 동안 가축의 수는 폭증했다. 현재 닭, 소, 그리고 돼지의 수는 수십억 마리이며, 이는 인류의 인구를 훨씬 웃도는 수치이다. 이러한 변화는 특히 기후를 변화시키는 온실가스(GHGs)의 대량 배출을 통해 우리가 사는 세계에 분명하고 극적인 결과를 낳았다. 추정치는 다양하지만, UN 식량농업기구가 제공한 보수적 계산에 따르면 가축에 의한 생산은 전 세계적인 인류 발생 GHGs의 18퍼센트를 발생시킨다. 이 계산이 정확하다고 가정한다면, 가축은 전 세계의 전체 운송 시스템이 직접적으로 영향을 미치는 것보다 더 많은 GHGs를 생산한다.
① 전 세계 가축 산업은 다른 어떤 분야보다 더 많은 GHGs를 생산한다.
② 새로운 지질학적 시기로서의 인류세 발표는 격렬한 논쟁으로 이어졌다.
③ 새로운 시기의 등장은 부분적으로 증가한 가축의 수에 의해 야기되었다.
④ GHGs는 기후변화와 더 빈번히 발생하는 극단적 날씨 상황에 가장 많이 영향을 끼치는 요소 중 하나이다.

18 정답 ③ Day 04-08

정답해설
본문의 내용에 따르면, '정보재에는 여러 이점이 있는데 그중 가장 중요한 것은 사업을 제품화하는 것이며, 제품화된 정보재의 재고는 무제한적이고 정보재의 주문 처리 또한 능률적, 자동적으로 이행될 수 있다.' 즉, 재고가 무한하다는 것은 제품을 판매할 수 있는 잠재력(가능성) 또한 무한하다는 것을 의미한다고 볼 수 있는데, ③에서 'which means your sales potential is ③ restricted'라고 언급하는 것은 본문에서 주장하는 것과는 반대되는 내용이다. 따라서 '③ restricted(제한적인)'는 'unrestricted(제한이 없는)'로 바꾸어야 문맥상 자연스러우므로, 정답은 ③이다.

해석
정보재는 여러 가지 ① 이점을 제공하지만, 그것들 중 가장 중요한 것은 당신이 시간을 충분히 활용하고 사업을 성장시키는 데 집중할 수 있도록 당신의 사업을 제품화할 수 있는 능력이다. 이것은 당신이 사업가로서의 기력 소진의 위험을 피할 수 있도록 도와주고, 일단 당신이 ② 능률적인 제품화 기계로까지 성장한다면, 당신은 가상의 비서를 고용함으로써 성장세를 이어갈 수 있다. 게다가, 정보재에는 무제한적인 재고가 있으며, 이는 당신의 판매 잠재력은 ③ **제한적이고(→제한이 없고)** 당신의 주문 이행 절차는 능률적이고 자동적이라는 것을 의미한다. 다시 말해, 디지털 상품을 판매함으로써, 당신은 모든 발품 파는 일을 미리 진행하고, 말기에는 ④ 최소한의 유지 - 주로 마케팅 - 만을 필요로 한다는 것이다. 일단 당신의 온라인 상점이 마련되면 당신이 수동으로 주문을 처리할 필요 없이 당신의 손님들은 그들이 원하는 만큼의 정보재를 구매할 수 있다.

19 정답 ④ Day 05-08

정답해설
본문은 '디지털 자료(digital material)'의 특징 중 '특수한 가격 구조(high-fixed-cost/low-incremental-cost structure, 높은 고정비용/낮은 증분 비용)'가 디지털 자료 시장을 '순수 경쟁 시장(purely competitive market)'이 아닌 '독점적 경쟁(monopolistic competition)'으로 이끈다고 설명하고 있다. 주어진 문장은 '유사한 대체품인 다소 다른 종류의 제품들이 존재하는 상황'에 관해 언급하고 있다. ④ 이전 문장에서는 동일한 제품을 거래하는 '밀, 옥수수, 주식 지분'과 같은 '순수 경쟁 시장'에 대해 언급하고 있으며, ④ 이전 문장에서는 '동일하지 않은 제품을 거래'하는 '자동차' 시장과 같은 '비 순수 경쟁 시장'에 대해 언급한다. 주어진 문장에서 설명하고 있는 '유사한 대체품인 몇 가지 다소 다른 종류의 제품(several somewhat different products some of which are close substitutes)'이라 함은 '밀, 옥수수'보다는 '자동차'를 설명하기에 더욱 적합한 표현이다. 따라서 주어진 문장은 '자동차 시장(market for automobiles)'에 대한 설명이라는 것을 알 수 있으므로, ④에 주어진 문장이 들어가는 것이 가장 자연스럽다.

해석
디지털 자료는 일반적으로 첫 번째 사본을 제작하는 것은 비용이 매우 많이 들고, 그 후 사본을 제작하는 것은 매우 저렴하다는 특징을 가지고 있다. 예를 들어, 한 학술지 발행 비용의 70% 이상이 "초판 발행 비용"이라고 종종 말한다. (①) 이러한 형태의 비용 구조는 가격 책정에 있어서 특수한 문제를 제기한다. 첫 번째 문제는 이러한 종류의 비용 구조로는 경쟁 시장을 유지하기 매우 어렵다는 것이다. (②) 경제학자들은 순수 경쟁 시장을 동일한 제품에 대한 "다수의" 생산자들이 있는 형태로 정의한다. 밀, 옥수수, IBM 주식의 지분 등이 모두 순수 경쟁 시장의 예시이다. (③) 자동차 시장은 동일한 제품에 대한 다수의 생산자가 없기 때문에 순수 경쟁적이지 않다. (④ **대신에, 유사한 대체품인 몇 가지 다소 다른 종류의 제품들이 있다.**) 경제학자들은 이것을 독점적 경쟁 상황이라고 부른다. 학술지 (또는 다른 종류의 정보재) 시장은 밀 시장보다는 자동차 시장에 훨씬 가까운 경향이 있다. 높은 고정비용/낮은 증분 비용 구조가 이러한 결과를 야기한다.

20 정답 ③   Day 09-08

정답해설

주어진 문장에서는 '성실함이 주는 이점'으로 '목표 달성을 할 수 있는 능력'에 대해 언급하고 있다. 이후 이어질 문장으로 가장 적절한 것은 주어진 문장에서 언급된 이점 외에 추가적인 이점인 '좋은 건강(good health)'에 대해 소개하고 있는 (B)가 이어지는 것이 가장 자연스럽다. (B)의 'additional ones'에서 'ones'가 주어진 문장의 'benefits'를 대신하는 표현이라는 것에 주의한다. 이후 추가적인 연구의 결과를 언급하며, (B)에서 언급된 '성실함과 좋은 건강의 관계'에 대해 좀 더 구체적으로 설명하고 있는 (A)가 이어지고, 앞서 설명한 '긍정적인 관계'가 존재하는 '이유'에 대해 'why are ~'로 질문을 던지고 답하며 설명하는 (C)가 연결되는 것이 문맥상 자연스럽다. 따라서 정답은 '③ (B) - (A) - (C)'이다.

해석

자기 절제 및 투지 때문에 자신의 목표를 더욱더 쉽게 달성할 수 있는 능력과 같이 성실함과 동반되는 분명한 이점들이 있다.
(B) 그러나 확실히 주목할 가치가 있는 부차적인 이점들도 또한 존재하는데, 그 이유는 그것들이 건강과 관련되어 있기 때문이다: Harvard Health에 따르면 성실함은 좋은 건강과 가장 꾸준히 연관되어 있다.
(A) 한 연구는 어린 나이에 부모와 교사로부터 성실하다고 묘사된 사람들은 더 오래 살았다는 것을 발견했고, 한편 다른 연구는 이 성격 특성과 낮은 혈압, 낮은 비율의 당뇨와 뇌졸중, 그리고 더 적은 관절 문제 사이의 관련성을 발견했다.
(C) 그렇다면, 왜 성실한 사람들이 또한 더 건강한 사람들인 것인가? 과학자들은 정답이 간결하고 명확하다고 말한다. 그들이 더 나은 건강 습관을 지니고 있다. 이 특성을 지닌 사람들은 흡연 또는 과음과 같은 해로운 행위를 취할 가능성이 더 적고, 건강한 행동을 할 가능성이 더 높다.

결국엔 성정혜 영어 하프모의고사
기적사 DAY 11

| 01 | ③ | 02 | ③ | 03 | ④ | 04 | ③ | 05 | ① |
| 06 | ① | 07 | ① | 08 | ③ | 09 | ③ | 10 | ② |

오답률 TOP 1

01 정답 ③   17 지방직

정답해설

밑줄 친 'convoluted'는 '대단히 난해한[복잡한]'이라는 뜻으로 ③ complicated와 의미가 가장 가깝다.

해석

화요일 밤의 그 TV 프로그램의 시즌 첫 방송은 그 쇼의 **복잡한** 신화와 그것의 더 인간적인, 인물 중심적인 관점 사이에서 절충점을 찾으려고 노력한 것으로 보였다.
① 고대의
② 관계없는
③ 복잡한
④ 저승의, 내세의

어휘

premiere 초연, 첫날; 개봉하다   convoluted 대단히 난해한[복잡한]
dimension 관점, 차원   ancient 고대의
unrelated 관계없는   complicated 복잡한
otherworldly 저승의, 내세의

02 정답 ③   17 지방직

정답해설

밑줄 친 'wound up'은 'wind up'의 과거형으로 '마무리 짓다, 끝내다'를 뜻하므로 ③ terminated와 의미가 가장 유사하다.

해석

우리가 그 대화를 **마무리 지을** 때쯤, 나는 내가 제네바로 가지 않을 것을 알았다.
① 시작했다
② 재개했다
③ 종결했다
④ 방해했다, 간섭했다

어휘

wind up 마무리 짓다, 끝내다   initiate 시작하다
resume 재개하다   terminate 종결하다
interrupt 방해하다, 간섭하다

03 정답 ④   17 지방직

정답해설

경사가 당황했다는 내용으로 보아 승진에서 '제외되었다'라고 하는 것이 문맥상 자연스럽다. 따라서 pass over의 수동태 표현이 빈칸에 가장 알맞다.

해석

15년 경력의 경찰 경사는 젊은 경관에 유리하도록 승진에서 **제외된** 이후 당황스러워했다.

① (차에) 치이다
② 초대되다
③ 이행되다
④ 제외되다

어휘

sergeant 경사, 병장
dismay 당황하게 하다, 깜짝 놀라게 하다
run over ~을 치다
ask out 초대하다
carry out 이행하다
pass over 제외하다

04 정답 ③
17 지방직

정답해설

대화에서 A와 B는 B의 새로운 동네에 대한 이야기를 나누고 있다. 밑줄 이전의 대화에서 B는 새로 이사한 곳이 살기에는 좋지만 단점이 없는 것은 아니라고 말하며 상점이 다양하지 않다는 것을 단점으로 말하고 있다. 따라서 A가 이에 동조하는 것이 문맥상 자연스러우므로 정답은 ③ 'It looks like you have a problem(그건 문제인 것 같다).'이다.

오답해설

나머지 보기는 문맥상 적절하지 않다.

해석

A: 새로 이사한 곳은 어때?
B: 대부분 좋아. 맑은 공기와 푸른 환경이 마음에 들어.
A: 참 살기 좋은 곳처럼 들려.
B: 응, 그렇지만 단점이 없는 것은 아니야.
A: 예를 들면?
B: 하나 말하자면, 상점이 다양하지 않아. 예를 들어, 슈퍼마켓이 하나밖에 없어서, 식재료가 정말 비싸.
A: 그건 문제인 것 같다.
B: 네 말이 맞아. 그렇지만 고맙게도, 도시에서 지금 새로운 쇼핑센터를 짓고 있어. 내년에, 우린 더 많은 선택권을 가지게 될 거야.
① 그곳에 슈퍼마켓이 몇 군데 있어?
② 그곳에 쇼핑을 할 곳이 많니?
③ 그건 문제인 것 같다.
④ 너희 동네로 이사 가고 싶어.

어휘

neighborhood 지역, 근처, 이웃
drawback 단점, 결점

05 정답 ①
17 지방직

정답해설

① **출제 포인트: 지각동사의 목적격 보어**
지각동사 'heard'는 목적격 보어로 동사원형과 분사 형태를 모두 가질 수 있다. 문맥상 목적어인 'me'와 목적격 보어가 능동관계이므로 현재분사 'sneezing'과 'coughing'은 어법상 적절하다.

오답해설

② **출제 포인트: 접속사의 쓰임**
의미상 '내가 무엇이 필요한지' 묻기 위해 방문을 연 것이므로 명사절 접속사 'that'은 '~인지 아닌지'의 뜻을 갖는 명사절 접속사 'if' 또는 'whether'로 수정해야 한다.

③ **출제 포인트: 목적격 관계대명사**
'anything'과 'he could do it' 사이에 목적격 관계대명사가 생략된 'anything (that) he could do it'의 문장이다. 이때 목적격 관계대명사인 'that(= anything)'이 동사 'do'의 목적어 역할을 하고 있으므로 'it'은 중복 사용될 수 없다. 따라서 'anything he could do it'에서 'it'을 삭제하고 'anything he could do'로 수정해야 한다.

④ **출제 포인트: 사역동사의 목적격 보어**
사역동사 'make'는 목적어와 목적격 보어의 관계에 따라 목적격 보어로 동사원형과 과거분사가 모두 올 수 있다. 이 문장에서 목적어인 'the flu'와 'go away'가 능동의 관계이므로 목적격 보어로는 'to go away'가 아니라 동사원형 'go away'가 와야 한다.

해석

지난주 나는 독감으로 아팠다. 아버지가 내가 기침과 재채기를 하는 소리를 들었을 때, 그는 내가 필요한 것이 있는지 물어보려 내 침실 문을 열었다. 나는 그의 친절함과 배려하는 얼굴을 보며 정말 행복했지만, 독감을 떨쳐내기 위해 그가 할 수 있었던 것은 아무것도 없었다.

어휘

sneeze 재채기하다
caring 배려하는, 보살피는
go away 없어지다

오답률 TOP 3

06 정답 ①
17 지방직

정답해설

① **출제 포인트: 능동태 vs. 수동태**
'A week's holiday'는 '일주일간의 휴가'라는 의미로 시간을 나타내기 위해 소유격을 사용하였으므로 어법상 적절하다. 또한, 'A week's holiday'가 직원들에게 '약속된' 것이므로 완료 수동태인 'has been promised'도 어법상 적절히 쓰였다.

오답해설

② **출제 포인트: 능동태 vs. 수동태**
'destine'은 '~을 예정해 두다'라는 의미의 타동사이며 수동태로 쓰여 '(운명으로) 정해지다, 운명 짓다'의 의미를 나타낸다. 따라서 능동태인 'destined to live'는 문맥상 수동태인 'is[was] destined to live'로 고쳐야 한다. 「be destined to+동사원형」은 'be to용법'의 '운명'에 해당하는 표현이다.

③ **출제 포인트: 라틴어 비교급**
라틴어 비교급인 'preferable, superior, inferior, senior, major, minor' 등은 'than' 대신에 전치사 'to'를 동반한다. 따라서 'than'이 아닌 'to'를 사용해야 옳다.

④ **출제 포인트: 가목적어 it/to부정사의 명사적 용법**
'find'는 3형식 완전타동사와 5형식 불완전타동사로 쓰인다. 그러나 주어진 문장처럼 「find+형용사」 형태의 불완전타동사로 쓰일 수 없으므로 목적어가 필요하다. 여기서는 'to stay ahead'가 진목적어이며 형용사 'challenging'을 동사 'find'의 목적격 보어로 보아야 한다. 이때 가목적어 'it'을 써서 「find+가목적어(it)+목적격 보어+진목적어(to부정사)」의 5형식 문장이 되어야 하므로 'finding it increasingly challenging to stay ahead'로 고쳐야 한다.

해석

① 일주일간의 휴가가 모든 사무직 근로자들에게 약속되었다.
② 그녀는 남들을 돕는 삶을 살아갈 운명이었다.
③ 아이들 양육을 위해 큰 도시보다는 작은 마을이 더 나은 듯하다.
④ 최고의 소프트웨어 회사들은 앞서는 것이 점점 더 도전적임을 느끼고 있다.

오답률 TOP 2
07 정답 ①
17 지방직

정답해설

① 출제 포인트: 현재분사 vs. 과거분사

'than' 뒤의 'expecting'의 수식을 받는 대상인 'the budget'이 생략된 상태이다. 예산이 '원래 기대되었던 것'보다 25퍼센트 더 높다고 하는 것이 적절하므로 수동형의 과거분사를 사용하는 것이 옳다. 따라서 현재분사 'expecting'을 과거분사 'expected'로 고쳐야 한다. 원문은 '~ than (the budget which is(was)) originally expected'이다.

오답해설

② 출제 포인트: to부정사의 태/to부정사의 형용사적 용법

해당 문장은 유도부사 구문으로 주어 'a lot of work'와 동사 'is'가 올바르게 수일치 되었다. 또한 주어진 해석이 '해야 될'이므로 to부정사의 수동태인 'to be done'을 옳게 사용하였다. 이때 'to be done'은 명사 'work'를 수식하고 있으므로 to부정사의 형용사적 용법으로 쓰였다.

③ 출제 포인트: take 동사의 다양한 쓰임

동사 'take' 다음에 시간 관련 명사가 오면 '(시간이) 걸리다'라는 의미로 「It takes + 시간 (for + 행위 주체) + to동사원형」 또는 「It takes + 행위 주체 + 시간 + to동사원형」의 구조로 표현될 수 있다. 해당 문장은 「It takes + 시간 (for + 행위 주체) + to동사원형」을 사용하되, 행위 주체가 생략된 형태의 문장이다. 또한 'at least'는 '최소한, 적어도'라는 의미로 적절하게 사용되었다.

④ 출제 포인트: 주격 관계대명사/선행사와 주격 관계대명사절 동사의 수일치/주어와 동사의 수일치

주격 관계대명사 'who'는 선행사 'The head'를 수식하고 있는 형태이다. 'The head'는 '우두머리, 부서장'의 의미로 선행사를 사람으로 보고 'who'를 사용하는 것이 옳으며 주격 관계대명사 절 내의 동사 'receives'도 단수형태의 선행사 'The head'에 맞추어 단수형태의 동사로 올바르게 수일치 되었다. 또한 문장의 동사는 'has', 즉 3인칭 단수형으로 주어 'The head of the department'와 수일치하고 있다. 그리고 'twice'는 배수사로 'the salary'를 수식하고 있으므로 올바르다.

08 정답 ③
19 서울시

정답해설

글의 소재로, '독서'에 대한 방식에 대해서 서술하기 시작해서, 두 번째 문장에서 "정보를 위한 읽기(reading for information)"를 구체적으로 설명하는 글임을 알 수 있다. 따라서 이어지는 ①에서 "자전거를 조립하는 방법(how to assemble a bicycle)"을 위한 읽기는 정보를 위한 읽기이다. 이후 ②에서 빠르게 글을 읽으며 "필요한 것(what he needs)"과 "무관한 것(what is irrelevant)"을 구분하는 것도 정보를 위한 읽기이다. 이때 무관한 것으로 'metaphor'를 언급하고 있다. 그러나 ③에서 감정의 자취를 기록("register a track of feeling")하는 것이 'metaphor'와 관련이 있다는 서술은 글 전체의 흐름에서 비껴가므로, 전체적인 글의 소재인 '정보를 위한 읽기'에서 벗어나고 있다. 이후 다시 ④에서 "빠르게 페이지를 읽는 것(to jump quickly across the page)"은 정보를 얻기 위한 기술이므로 적절하다. 따라서 글의 흐름과 관계가 없는 문장은 ③이다.

해석

각각마다 특징적인 방법과 목적이 있는 네 가지의 읽기를 말하는 것은 나에게 가능한 것처럼 보인다. 첫 번째는 무역, 정치 혹은 어떤 것을 어떤 방법으로 이루기 위한 정보에 대한 읽기이다. ① 우리는 이런 방법으로 신문, 대부분의 교과서들 혹은 자전거를 어떻게 조립하는지에 대한 설명서를 읽는다. ② 이런 기록물들의 대부분을 통해, 독자는 그에게 필요한 것을 생각하고 문장의 리듬이나 은유의 작용처럼 상관없는 것을 무시하면서 페이지를 빠르게 훑는 법을 배울 수 있다. ③ <u>우리는 또한 은유와 단어의 연관성들을 통해 감정의 자취를 기록할 수 있다</u>. ④ 속독하는 과정들은 눈이 빠르게 페이지를 읽는 것을 훈련하면서 우리가 이러한 목적을 위해 읽는 것을 도와줄 수 있다.

어휘

name 이름을 붙이다, 명명하다, 이름을 대다
politics 정치(학)
direction 지시, 설명
material 자료, 재료
come up with 생각해내다
irrelevant 무관한
metaphor 비유, 은유
association 연관(성), 연상
accomplish 성취하다
assemble 조립하다
scan 훑어보다
ignore 무시하다
play 작용, 운용, 영향
register 등록하다, 기록하다

09 정답 ③
19 서울시

정답해설

주어진 지문 전체는 집단주의 문화와 개인주의 문화에서의 각각의 이직과 조직에 대한 개인의 성향을 대조와 비교의 방식으로 서술하고 있다. <보기>에서 주목할 부분은 'this situation'과 'less movement'에 해당된다. 즉, "개인의 사회적 의무(social obligations)"때문에 이직이 상대적으로 적다는 내용을 'less movement(더 적은 움직임)'를 통해 지적하고 이것을 "this situation"으로 지칭하고 있다. 따라서 사회적 의무가 개인보다 우선시 된다는 내용이 제시되어지는 부분인 'as fulfilling an obligation to a larger group(더 큰 집단에의 책임을 이행함으로써)'를 제시한 이후인 ③이 적합하다. ③ 이후 문장에서는 대조적으로 'individualistic cultures(개인주의 문화)'에서는 이직이 더 쉽다고 언급하고 있으므로 문맥이 자연스럽다.

오답해설

나머지 위치에는 글의 흐름상 집단주의 문화의 예시를 설명하는 보기 지문이 들어가기에 적절하지 않다.

해석

일의 의미에서의 문화적 차이는 다른 측면에서도 나타날 수 있다. (①) 예를 들어, 미국 문화에서, 일은 돈을 모으고 생계를 꾸리기 위한 수단이라고 단순히 생각하기 쉽다. (②) 다른 문화권, 특히 집단주의 문화권에서는 일이 더 큰 집단에 대한 의무를 이행하는 것으로 보일 수 있다. (③ <u>이러한 상황에서, 우리는 개인이 속한 조직과 그 조직을 구성하는 사람들에 대한 개인의 사회적 의무 때문에 한 직장에서 다른 직장으로의 이동이 줄어들 것으로 예상한다</u>.) 개인주의 문화에서는 자기와 직업을 분리하는 것이 더 쉽기 때문에 한 직업을 버리고 다른 직업을 가는 것을 고려하는 것이 더 쉽다. (④) 다른 직장은 같은 목표를 쉽게 달성할 수 있을 것이다.

어휘

obligation 의무
comprise ~를 구성하다
aspect 측면, 양상
accumulate 축적하다
collectivistic 집단주의의
individualistic 개인주의의
accomplish 달성하다
belong to ~에 속하다
manifest 나타내다
means 수단, 방법
make a living 생계를 꾸리다
fulfill 이행하다, 달성하다, 완수하다
separate 분리시키다

10 정답 ②
19 서울시

정답해설

주어진 지문에서 공통적으로 'microbat'에 관한 내용을 서술하고 있다. 이 중에서 'microbat'이 무엇인지를 설명하는 문단인 ㉡이 시작 문단으로 가장 적합하다. ㉡에서 'microbat'을 설명하는데, 이 동물은 '눈이 작아서 밤에 돌아다니거나 먹이를 찾는 데 눈이 도움이 되지 않을 것'처럼 보인다고 설명한다. ㉣에서는 역접의 접속사인 "But"으로 연결해 앞 문단에서 눈이 도움이 안 되는 것처럼 보인다는 것을 부정한 후, 실제로는 다른 포유동물만큼 잘 볼 수 있음을 설명한다. 그 이후에는 박쥐의 'echolocation'이 밤에 도움이 된다는 것을 언급하며 ㉠에서는 밤에 돌아다니는 데 있어서의 역할을, ㉢에서는 먹이를 찾는 데 있어서의 도움을 각각 설명한다. 따라서 정답은 ② ㉡-㉣-㉠-㉢ 이다.

오답해설

가장 일반적인 진술을 하는 문단이 제일 먼저 나와야 하므로 ㉠이 첫 번째로 오는 것은 적절하지 않다.

해석

㉡ 북아메리카에서 발견되는 작고 곤충을 잡아먹는 박쥐인 마이크로박쥐는 작은 눈을 가지고 있는데, 이 눈은 어둠에서 날아가고 먹잇감을 포착하는 데 좋을 것 같지는 않다.

㉣ 하지만 사실, 마이크로박쥐는 쥐와 다른 작은 포유동물들만큼 잘 볼 수 있다. 박쥐의 야행성 습관은 우리가 생각하는 것보다 훨씬 쉽게 밤에 먹이를 먹고 날 수 있게 하는 반향 위치 추적이라는 특별한 능력에 의해 도움을 받는다.

㉠ 어둠 속에서 날아가기 위해 마이크로박쥐가 입을 벌리고 인간이 들을 수 없는 고음의 꽥꽥거리는 소리를 내뿜으며 날아간다. 이 소리들 중 일부는 나뭇가지들과 앞에 놓여있는 다른 장애물들뿐만 아니라 날아다니는 곤충들에도 메아리친다. 박쥐는 메아리에 귀를 기울이고 그 앞에 있는 물건들의 뇌에 순간적인 그림을 획득한다.

㉢ 초음파, 즉 음파탐지기를 사용하는 것으로부터 마이크로박쥐는 모기나 다른 잠재적인 먹이에 대해 많은 것을 구별할 수 있다. 극도의 정확성으로, 반향 위치 능력은 마이크로 박쥐가 움직임, 거리, 속도, 움직임 및 모양을 인식할 수 있게 한다. 박쥐는 또한 사람의 머리카락보다 두껍지 않은 장애물을 감지하고 피할 수 있다.

어휘

navigate 길을 찾다, 항해하다 emit 내뿜다, 배출하다
high-pitched 고음의 squeak 날카로운 소리
echo off ~에 부딪혀 반향하다 branch 나뭇가지
obstacle 방해물, 장애물 lie 놓여있다
ahead 앞에, 앞서서 instantaneous 즉각적인
object 물체 insect 곤충
spot 발견하다, 찾아내다 prey 먹이
echolocation 반향 위치 측정 sonar 초음파
tell 구별하다 perceive 인식하다, 인지하다
detect 감지하다 avoid 피하다

결국엔 성정혜 영어 하프모의고사
기적사 DAY 12

| 01 | ① | 02 | ③ | 03 | ① | 04 | ② | 05 | ② |
| 06 | ③ | 07 | ① | 08 | ③ | 09 | ④ | 10 | ④ |

01 정답 ①

정답해설

밑줄 친 'renowned'는 '유명한, 명성 있는'의 뜻으로 ① prestigious와 의미가 가장 가깝다. 해당 문장은 실용문으로 작가 또는 화자가 'its high rigor and standard(그것의 높은 엄격함과 기준)'를 '하나의 개념'으로 취급해 주격 관계대명사 'which' 이후에 단수동사 'makes'를 사용하였다.

해석

한국의 교육 체계는 컴퓨터 및 통신의 사용을 다루는 공학 부서로서 한국을 강국으로 만들어 준 그것의 높은 엄격함과 기준으로 세계적으로 **유명하다**.
① 명망 있는, 일류의
② 상대적인
③ 싸우기 좋아하는
④ 저승의, 내세의

어휘

renowned 유명한, 명성 있는 prestigious 명망 있는, 일류의
relative 상대적인 quarrelsome 싸우기 좋아하는
otherworldly 저승의, 내세의

02 정답 ③

정답해설

밑줄 친 'made away with'는 'make away with'의 과거형으로 '~을 훔쳤다'라는 뜻이다. 따라서 ③ stolen과 의미가 가장 가깝다.

해석

경찰은 또한 근처에 있던 또 다른 용의자를 체포했고 어떻게 가방을 **훔쳤는지** 그를 심문하고 있다.
① 방해했다, 간섭했다
② 조정했다, 조화시켰다
③ 훔쳤다, 도둑질했다
④ 무효화했다

어휘

interrogate 심문하다 make away with ~을 훔치다
interrupt 방해하다, 간섭하다 reconcile 조정하다, 조화시키다
steal 훔치다, 도둑질하다 nullify 무효화하다

03 정답 ①

정답해설

문맥상 '돌보다, 신경 쓰다'의 'take care of'와 의미가 유사해야 하므로 빈칸에 들어갈 것으로 가장 적절한 선택지는 '돌보다, 주의를 기울이다'라는 뜻을 가진 ① look after이다.

해석

애완동물을 가지는 것은 우리가 우리 자신 외의 어떤 것을 **돌보거나** 신경 쓰는 것을 배우도록 돕는다.

① 돌보다, 주의를 기울이다
② ~를 치다
③ 이해하다, ~을 만들어 내다
④ 보충하다, 보상하다

어휘

take care of 돌보다, 신경 쓰다   other than ~이외의
look after 돌보다, 주의를 기울이다   run over ~를 치다
make out 이해하다, ~을 만들어 내다   make up for 보충하다, 보상하다

04 정답 ②

정답해설

A와 B는 졸업 후 일정에 관해 대화를 나눈다. B는 졸업 후 영어 실력을 향상시키기 위해 '해외에 거주하고 싶다'고 말하고 A는 '졸업 직후 일을 시작하고 싶다'고 말하고 있다. 이에 B가 그 이유를 묻고 있으므로 빈칸에는 A가 일을 시작하고 싶은 이유가 들어가야 한다. 따라서 ② '일을 시작할(get the ball rolling)' 수 있을 때 하고 싶다고 이야기하는 것이 옳다.

오답해설

① A는 졸업 직후 일을 시작하고 싶은 이유를 설명할 때, 자신이 할 수 있을 때 '상한을 규정해야(set a ceiling on)' 하기 때문이라고 말하는 것은 문맥상 어색하다.
③ A가 졸업 직후에 일을 시작하고 싶은 이유는 할 수 있을 때 '너를 분노하게 해야(drive you up the wall)' 하기 때문이라고 들었다고 하는 것은 빈칸에 들어갈 말로 적절하지 않다.
④ A는 B에게 자신이 일을 졸업한 후 바로 시작하고 싶은 이유를 설명할 때, 자신이 듣기로는 '곤경에 처해야(have my back to the wall)' 하기 때문이라고 말하는 것은 대화의 맥락상 부자연스럽다.

해석

A: 너 졸업 후에 뭐 할 계획이야?
B: 나는 몇 가지 계획을 세웠어. 내가 일을 시작하기 전에 최소 일 년 동안 해외에 살고 싶어.
A: 일 년? 왜 그런 거야?
B: 난 내 영어를 향상시키고 싶어. 영어 사용 국가에 거주하면 자연스레 원어민처럼 말하고 쓰는 것을 배울 수 있을 거야.
A: 흥미롭다. 너와 달리 나는 바로 일을 시작하고 싶어.
B: 그 이유는 뭐야?
A: 내가 들은 바로는, 내가 할 수 있을 때 일을 시작해야 해. 지연되면 내가 동기를 잃게 될 것 같아.
B: 나도 그 얘기 많이 들었어.
① 상한을 규정하다
② 일을 시작하다
③ 너를 분노하게 하다
④ 곤경에 처하다

어휘

plan 계획을 세우다, 계획하다   motivation 동기
set a ceiling on 상한을 규정하다   get the ball rolling 일을 시작하다
drive somebody up the wall ~의 이성을 잃게 하다, 분노하게 하다
have one's back to the wall 곤경에 처하다

05 정답 ②

정답해설

② **출제 포인트: 접속사의 쓰임/that의 쓰임**
문맥상 '같은 배달부가 ~라면'이 자연스러우므로 밑줄 친 접속사 'if'의 쓰임은 옳다. 또한 밑줄 친 'that'은 지시형용사이며 'via'는 전치사로 '~을 통해'를 뜻한다. 'that'을 접속사로 오해하지 않도록 주의해야 한다.

오답해설

① **출제 포인트: 지각동사의 목적격 보어**
지각동사의 목적격 보어는 목적어와 능동관계인 경우 원형부정사와 현재분사를 사용하며 수동관계인 경우 과거분사를 사용한다. 밑줄 친 'to deliver'는 'watching(지각동사 watch의 동명사 형태)'의 목적격 보어에 해당하나 목적어 'a Pony Express rider'와 능동관계이다. 따라서 'to deliver'를 원형부정사 'deliver' 또는 현재분사 'delivering'으로 수정해야 한다.
③ **출제 포인트: 소유격 관계대명사 vs. 주격 관계대명사**
소유격 관계대명사 'whose'는 반드시 무관사 명사와 함께해야 한다. 해당 문장은 뒤에 오는 절의 구조가 「동사+명사(동사의 목적어)」이므로 소유격 관계대명사 'whose'를 문장의 주어를 대신하는 주격 관계대명사 'who'로 수정해야 한다.
④ **출제 포인트: 등위접속사의 병렬구조**
관계대명사절 내의 동사가 등위접속사 'and'를 통해 「A, B, C, and D」의 병렬구조를 이루고 있다. D에 해당하는 밑줄 친 동사 'fight'의 경우 복수형태이나 A(loses), B(overcomes), C(outsmarts)의 경우 선행사 'a Western hero'의 형태에 맞춰 단수형태의 동사를 사용했으므로 'fight'도 단수형태의 동사인 'fights'로 수정해야 한다.

해석

우리는 조랑말 우편 배달부가 다음 지점에 우편물을 배달하는 것을 볼 때 거의 호기심을 느끼지 못하지만, 같은 배달부가 적대적인 환경에 그의 말을 잃고 방울뱀에게 물린 것을 극복하고 악한 마음을 가진 무법자보다 한 수 앞서며 그 외에도 다음 지점으로 의기양양하게 그의 길을 헤쳐 나가는 서부의 영웅이라면 긴장감을 통해 엄청난 호기심을 느끼게 된다.

어휘

curiosity 호기심   via ~을 통해
suspense 서스펜스, 긴장감   hostile 적대적인
outsmart ~보다 한 수 앞서다   outlaw 무법자, 도망자

오답률 TOP 1

06 정답 ③

정답해설

③ **출제 포인트: 능동태 vs. 수동태/시간의 부사구**
'allow'는 수여동사의 경우 「allow+간접목적어+직접목적어」의 구조를 가지며, 수동태로 전환할 경우 「간접목적어+be allowed+직접목적어」의 구조를 가진다. 해당 문장은 수여동사 'allow'의 수동태를 사용하였으며 'access'는 직접목적어에 해당한다. 또한 'a few days ago'는 시간의 부사구로 과거시제 동사와 함께 사용한다.

오답해설

① **출제 포인트: 현재분사 vs. 과거분사/가목적어 it/명사절의 접속사 that**
해당 문장에서 'frustrated'는 'frustrate'의 과거분사로 'found'의 목적격 보어이다. 이때 가목적어 'it'이 가리키는 대상은 명사절의 접속사 'that'이 이끄는 절이며 목적격 보어와 능동관계이므로 'frustrated'를 현재분사 'frustrating'으로 수정해야 한다.

② **출제 포인트: 라틴어 비교급**
라틴어 비교급은 비교 대상 앞에 전치사 'to'를 사용한다. 해당 문장은 라틴어 비교급에 해당하는 형용사 'inferior'를 사용하였으나 'inferior' 뒤에 'than'을 사용하였으므로 틀린 문장이다. 따라서 'than'을 'to'로 수정해야 한다. 또한 해당 문장에서의 'that'은 'status'를 지칭한다.

④ **출제 포인트: 능동태 vs. 수동태**
완전타동사 'equip' 뒤에 전치사 'with'가 오는 경우는 수동태 「be equipped with」뿐이다. 해당 문장은 'equip'의 과거시제 'equipped'를 능동태로 사용하였으나 뒤에 전치사 'with'가 있으므로 틀린 문장이다. 따라서 'equipped with'를 수동태 'were equipped with' 또는 'are equipped with'로 수정해야 한다.

해석
① Tom은 Jane이 그 질문들을 이해할 수 없다는 것이 실망스럽다는 것을 알았다.
② 전통적 사회에서 여성의 지위는 분명히 남성들보다 열등했다.
③ William은 며칠 전 처음으로 교도소 출입을 허락받았다.
④ 모든 경찰관들은 폭도들로부터 스스로를 방어하기 위해 방패를 갖추었다.

07 정답 ①

정답해설

① **출제 포인트: to부정사의 태**
완전타동사 'base' 뒤에 전치사 'on'이 올 수 있는 경우는 수동태 「be based on」뿐이며 '~에 근거하다(근거되어지다)'로 해석한다. 해당 문장은 to부정사의 동사원형 자리에 'base'를 사용하였으나 뒤에 전치사 'on'이 왔으며 주어진 해석이 '~에 근거하다'이므로 틀린 문장이다. 따라서 'base'를 수동태 'be based'로 수정해야 한다.

오답해설

② **출제 포인트: take 동사의 다양한 쓰임**
「It takes+목적어[사람]+목적어[시간]+to부정사」는 관용표현으로 '사람이 ~하는 데 시간이 걸리다'를 뜻한다. 해당 문장은 「It takes+사람+시간+to부정사」를 사용하였으며 주어진 해석과 일치하므로 옳은 문장이다. 또한 'concerning'은 전치사로 사용되었으며 '~에 관하여, ~에 대하여'를 뜻한다.

③ **출제 포인트: 현재분사 vs. 과거분사/불완전타동사의 목적격 보어**
지각동사의 목적격 보어는 목적어와 능동관계인 경우 원형부정사와 현재분사를 사용하며 수동관계인 경우 과거분사를 사용한다. 해당 문장의 'found'는 불완전타동사 'find'의 과거시제로 사용되었다. 따라서 'found'는 목적격 보어로 현재분사 'standing'을 사용하였으며 목적어 'Tom'과 능동관계이므로 옳은 문장이다.

④ **출제 포인트: 주격 관계대명사/선행사와 주격 관계대명사절 동사의 수일치**
해당 문장에서 'which'는 주격 관계대명사이며 선행사는 복수형태의 명사(구) 'His ashes'이다. 따라서 주격 관계대명사절의 동사에 복수형태인 'were'를 사용하는 것이 옳다.

오답률 TOP 3

08 정답 ③

정답해설

(A) 세 번째 문장 "Since its publication millions of copies have been sold and is still widely circulating among education circles as a required reading text(그것의 출간 이래로 수백만 권이 판매되었고, 여전히 교육계에서 필수 독서 교과서로서 널리 유포되고 있다)."를 통해, '현재에도 필수 독서 교재로서 널리 인정된다'는 것을 알 수 있으므로 '디지털 텍스트가 널리 퍼진 오늘날에도 내용이 유의미하다'라는 의미가 될 수 있는 'valid(유효한)' 또는 'relevant(유의미한)'가 빈칸에 들어가는 것이 가장 적절하다.

(B) 이전 문장 "levels denote a notion of embeddedness with lower levels included in higher ones(단계는 하위의 단계가 상위 단계에 포함되어 있는 맞물림의 개념을 의미)"에서 '하위 단계가 상위 단계에 포함되는 것'이라고 언급하고 있으므로, 하위 단계와 상위 단계가 개별적인 것이 아니라 아래에서부터 위로 '축적된다'는 것을 알 수 있다. 따라서 가장 적절한 것은 'cumulative(축적되는)'이다. 따라서 정답은 '③ relevant(유의미한) – cumulative(축적되는)'이다.

오답해설

① (A)에 '책의 내용이 오늘날에도 유효하다(valid)'라는 표현이 들어가는 것은 자연스러우나, (B)에 '개별적인'이라는 의미의 'separate'가 들어가게 되면 본문의 주장과는 반대로 '단계가 개별적이다'라는 의미가 되기 때문에 빈칸에 적절하지 않다.
나머지 보기는 문맥상 어색하기 때문에 오답이다.

해석
Mortimer J. Adler와 Charles Van Doren의 저서 How to Read a Book은 독서 문학 분야에서 가장 저명한 고전 작품 중 하나이다. 그것은 1940년 최초로 출간되었고, 이후 1972년 발간된 판에서 다시 논의되고 갱신되었다. 그것의 출간 이래로 수백만 권이 판매되었고, 여전히 교육계에서 필수 독서 교과서로서 널리 유포되고 있다. 그 책이 '디지털 이전' 시대에 고안된 것은 사실이나, 그것의 내용은 디지털 텍스트가 대부분 널리 퍼져 있는 오늘날에도 여전히 (A) 유의미하다. How to Read A Book에서 Van Doren과 Mortimer는 독서의 네 가지 주요 단계에 대해 이야기했다: 초급 독서, 점검 독서, 분석 독서, 주제별 독서. 여기에서 저자들이 의도적으로 그것들을 종류가 아닌 단계로 명명한 것을 주목하라 왜냐하면, 그들에 따르면, 종류는 서로 별개의 것일 수 있으나, 단계는 하위의 단계가 상위 단계에 포함되어 있는 맞물림의 개념을 의미하기 때문이다. 다시 말해, 독서의 단계는 (B) 축적되는 것이다.

　　(A)　　　　　　　(B)
① 유효한　　　　　　개별적인
② 관련 없는　　　　　일시적인
③ 유의미한, 관련 있는　축적되는
④ 난해한　　　　　　복잡한

어휘
celebrated 유명한, 저명한　　revisit 다시 논의하다
conceive 고안하다, 구상하다, 생각하다
predominantly 대개, 대부분　prevalent 널리 퍼진, 일반적인
inspectional 점검의　　　　syntopical 주제별
deliberately 의도적으로　　denote 의미하다
notion 개념　　　　　　　embeddedness 맞물림, 내재
extraneous 관련 없는　　　transient 일시적인, 순간적인
relevant 유의미한, 관련 있는　cumulative 누적되는
esoteric 난해한, 소수만이 즐기는

09 정답 ④

정답해설

본문은 개인주의 문화와 집단주의 문화에 속한 사람들의 행동적인 차이에 대해 설명하며 글의 초반에는 노동자들의 행동 차이에 관해 언급하고, 글의 중후반에는 사회 정책 중 보건 정책을 바라보는 견해 차이에 대해 설명하고 있다. 주어진 문장의 "Individualist cultures stress the importance of each person taking care of his or her self(개인주의 문화는 각각의 사람

이 자기 자신을 돌보는 것의 중요성을 강조한다)"로 보아 주어진 문장은 '보건(health care)'에 대해 언급된 후에 등장하는 것이 자연스럽다는 것을 알 수 있으므로 ④에 위치할 수 있는데, 마지막 문장의 'instead(대신에)'로 보아, 마지막 문장 이전에 비교하는 문장이 먼저 등장해야 한다. 따라서 주어진 문장이 ④에 들어가는 것이 문맥상 가장 자연스럽다.

오답해설
나머지 위치는 문맥상 어색하므로 오답이다.

해석
개인주의 문화에 속한 노동자들은 집단의 이익보다 자기 자신의 행복을 더 가치 있게 여길 가능성이 있다. (①) 이것을 다른 모든 사람들의 더 큰 이익을 위해 자신들의 안락함을 희생할 수도 있는 집단주의 문화와 대조해보라. (②) 이러한 차이는 한 사람이 선택하는 직업, 그들이 사는 물건, 그리고 그들이 관심을 가지는 사회 문제에까지 이르는 행동의 거의 모든 면에 영향을 미친다. (③) 예를 들어, 보건에 대한 접근법은 이러한 경향에 의해 영향을 받는다. (④ 개인주의 문화는 타인의 도움에 의지하지 않고 각각의 사람이 자기 자신을 돌보는 것의 중요성을 강조한다.) 대신에 집단주의 문화에 속한 사람들은 전체로서 보건의 부담을 집단과 함께 공유하는 것을 강조할 것이다.

어휘
individualist 개인주의자(의) stress 강조하다
collectivist 집단주의자(의) sacrifice 희생하다
tendency 경향

오답률 TOP 2
10 정답 ④

정답해설
본문은 '세계에서 가장 큰 박쥐인 말레이날여우박쥐(Malayan flying fox)'를 소개하는 글이다. ①, ②는 '말레이날여우박쥐'의 비행에 관한 설명으로 '비행과 방향 전환에는 문제가 없으나, 착륙에는 서툴다'라는 맥락으로 문맥상 자연스럽다. ③에서는 '첨가'를 나타내는 'Also(또한)'를 이용해, 말레이날여우박쥐의 또 다른 특징에 대해 설명하고 있으므로 글의 흐름상 자연스럽다. '작은 박쥐류와는 달리 큰 박쥐는 시력이 좋다'고 언급한 후, 시력이 발달한 큰 박쥐가 작은 박쥐류와 같이 '음파(sound waves)'를 이용하지 않고, '눈(peepers)'을 이용해 먹이를 찾고 지형을 파악한다는 내용의 마지막 문장이 이어지는 것이 문맥상 자연스럽다. ④에서 언급된 'squeaks(끽하는 소리)'와 'chirps(찍찍 소리)', 즉 소리(음파)를 이용해 먹이를 탐색하는 것은 작은 박쥐류의 특성이므로, 큰 박쥐에 대해 설명하는 본문의 문맥상 어색하다. 따라서 정답은 ④이다.

오답해설
나머지 보기는 문맥상 자연스러우므로 오답이다.

해석
말레이날여우박쥐(Malayan flying fox)는 세계에서 가장 큰 박쥐라는 축하를 받는다. 이 멸종위기에 처한 박쥐는 동남아시아의 열대 지역에 서식하는 거대 종이다. ① 이 박쥐는 훌륭한 비행사이며 높이 솟은 열대 우림 지붕 사이를 아무 문제 없이 방향 조절할 수 있다. ② 그러나, 착륙에 관한 한 그들은 목적지에 충돌하고 목적지를 더듬더듬 찾고, 단지 먹이를 먹기 위해 종종 나뭇가지 더미와 숲의 나뭇잎 무더기에 정면충돌한다. ③ 또한, 더 작은 박쥐류 동족과는 달리, 날여우박쥐는 훌륭한 시력을 지닌 큰 포유류이다. ④ 밤의 어둠은 이 야행성 포유류가 가야 할 곳으로 가는 것을 막지 못하며, 그것은 주변을 지도화하기 위해 끽하는 소리와 찍찍 소리를 이용해 먹이를 찾아낸다. 그들이 어디에 있고 무엇이 그들 주위에 있는지 정확히 알아내기 위해 음파를 이용하는 대신에, 그들은 그들의 구역을 샅샅이 뒤지기 위해 잘 발달된 눈을 이용한다.

어휘
hail 축하하다, 환호하며 맞이하다
navigate 방향을 읽다
canopy (숲의 나뭇가지들이) 지붕 모양으로 우거진 것
fumble 더듬거리다, 실수하다, 놓치다
grab a bite to eat 간단히 먹다
kin 친족, 동족
nocturnal 야행성의
peeper 안경, 눈
superb 대단히 훌륭한, 최고의
towering 우뚝 솟은
foliage 나뭇잎
microbat 작은 박쥐류
flying fox 날여우 박쥐
squeak 끼익[깩/찍]하는 소리

결국엔 성정혜 영어 하프모의고사
기적사 DAY 13

01	③	02	④	03	②	04	③	05	④
06	②	07	②	08	④	09	②	10	④

오답률 TOP 1
01 정답 ③

정답해설

밑줄 친 'reticent'는 '말이 없는, 과묵한'의 뜻으로 ③ placid와 의미가 가장 가깝다.

해석

오스카상을 수상한 그 감독은 그의 사적인 생활에 관해 과도하게 **침묵했**다.
① 일류의, 명성 있는, 유명한
② 고대의
③ 조용한, 차분한
④ 상호적인, 서로의

어휘

reticent 말이 없는, 과묵한   prestigious 일류의, 명성 있는, 유명한
ancient 고대의   placid 조용한, 차분한
mutual 상호적인, 서로의

오답률 TOP 3
02 정답 ④

정답해설

밑줄 친 'make up with'는 '~와 화해하다'의 의미를 가지며 의미가 가장 가까운 것은 ④ reconcile이다.

해석

이런 상황에서, 당신은 어떻게 현실과 이상을 **화해하게** 할 수 있는가?
① 아첨하다, 아부하다
② 종결하다
③ 통보하다, 알리다
④ 화해시키다, 조화시키다

어휘

make up with ~와 화해하다   flatter 아첨하다, 아부하다
terminate 종결하다   notify 통보하다, 알리다
reconcile 화해시키다, 조화시키다

03 정답 ②

정답해설

밑줄 친 부분에 들어갈 말은 문맥상 '엉망으로 만들다'의 ② mess up을 사용하는 것이 가장 자연스럽다.

해석

그 문제에 있어서 사실은, 약물 남용이 당신의 근무 실적과 정신력을 **엉망으로 만드는** 주요 요인이라는 것이다.
① ~에 아첨하다
② 엉망으로 만들다, 다 망치다
③ 제외하다
④ ~을 물려주다, 전수하다

어휘

drug abuse 약물 남용   make up to ~에게 아첨하다
mess up 엉망으로 만들다, 다 망치다   pass over 제외하다
pass down ~을 물려주다, 전수하다

04 정답 ③

정답해설

Tom과 Eva는 '가장 존경하는 사람'에 관한 주제로 대화를 하고 있다. Eva가 '아버지를 가장 존경하는 이유'를 Tom이 질문하자 Eva는 아버지가 '자신의 말을 지키는 사람(a man of his word)'이기 때문이라고 답변한다.

오답해설

① Eva가 자신의 아버지를 존경하는 이유에 관해 아버지가 '신용 사기꾼(con artist)'이기 때문이라고 말하는 것은 문맥상 자연스럽지 않다.
② 아버지를 존경하는 이유를 묻는 Tom에게 Eva가 아버지는 '일반 직원(rank and file)'이기 때문이라고 답변하는 것은 대화의 흐름상 어색하다.
④ Eva가 자신의 아버지를 '세상 물정에 밝은 사람(a man of the world)'이어서 존경한다고 말하고 난 후 '모든 약속을 다 지킨다'고 말하는 것은 맥락상 부적절하다.

해석

Tom: 네가 가장 존경하는 사람은 누구야?
Eva: 진부한 대답이지만, 나에게는 아버지가 가장 존경하는 분이야.
Tom: 왜 그렇게 말해?
Eva: 그는 자신의 말을 지키는 사람이야. 그는 그가 한 약속들을 모두 지켜.
Tom: 비록 그것이 쉬워 보이지만 전혀 쉽지 않은 일이야.
Eva: 그러니까. 그에게서 배울 점들이 많아.
① 신용 사기꾼
② 일반 직원
③ 자신의 말을 지키는 사람
④ 세상 물정에 밝은 사람

어휘

con artist 신용 사기꾼   rank and file 일반 직원
a man of one's word 자신의 말을 지키는 사람
a man of the world 세상 물정에 밝은 사람

05 정답 ④

정답해설

④ **출제 포인트: 현재분사 vs. 과거분사**
밑줄 친 부분의 'named'는 불완전타동사 'name'의 과거분사로 수식하는 대상 'a boy'와 수동관계이다. 이때 명사 'Lennie Steffens'는 'named'의 목적격 보어이다.

오답해설

① **출제 포인트: 자동사로 착각하기 쉬운 완전타동사**
'reach'는 완전타동사로 전치사 없이 목적어를 가진다. 해당 문장은 'reach'의 과거시제인 'reached'가 능동태로 사용되었으나 목적어 'its climax' 앞에 전치사 'to'를 사용하였으므로 틀린 문장이다. 따라서 'to'를 삭제해야 한다.

② **출제 포인트: 지각동사의 목적격 보어**
지각동사의 목적격 보어는 목적어와 능동관계인 경우 원형부정사와 현재

분사를 사용하며 수동관계인 경우 과거분사를 사용한다. 밑줄 친 'to ride'는 'saw(지각동사 see의 과거시제)'의 목적격 보어에 해당하나 목적어 'a man'과 능동관계이므로 원형부정사 'ride' 또는 현재분사 'riding'으로 수정해야 한다.

③ **출제 포인트: 불완전타동사의 목적격 보어**
문맥상 '그것은 내가 울음을 터트리도록 야기했다'가 자연스럽다. 밑줄 친 'caused'는 불완전타동사 'cause'의 과거시제로 「caused+목적어+목적격 보어(to+동사원형)」의 구조를 가진다. 따라서 목적격 보어로 온 'break'을 'to break'으로 수정해야 한다.

해석
한 시간 후에 내가 어떤 남자가 최신의 안장을 갖춘 조랑말을 타고 오는 것을 보았을 때, 내 좌절감은 최고조에 다다랐다. 그가 우리 집 문을 보았을 때, 그는 그냥 지나쳐 갔는데, 그 때문에 내가 울음을 터트렸다. 그러자 그가 말했다. "얘야, Lennie Steffens라는 남자아이를 아니?" "전데요." 나는 눈물을 흘리며 대답했다.

어휘
pony 조랑말
saddle 안장
brand-new 최신의, 신제품의, 새로운
break into tears 울음을 터트리다

오답률 TOP 2

06 정답 ②

정답해설
② **출제 포인트: 가주어 it/to부정사의 명사적 용법**
해당 문장에서 'it'은 가주어이며 'to hear ~ a glass'는 진주어이다. 이때 'to hear ~ a glass'는 to부정사의 명사적 용법에 해당한다. 또한 'chink'는 '쨍그랑'이라는 의성어 표현이며 명사로 사용되고 있다.

오답해설
① **출제 포인트: 라틴어 비교급**
라틴어 비교급은 비교 대상 앞에 전치사 'to'를 사용한다. 해당 문장은 라틴어 비교급에 해당하는 형용사 'superior'를 사용하였으나 뒤에 'as'를 사용하였으므로 틀린 문장이다. 따라서 'as'를 'to'로 수정해야 한다.

③ **출제 포인트: 능동태 vs. 수동태**
'saturate'는 완전타동사이므로 전치사 없이 목적어를 가진다. 해당 문장은 'saturate'의 3인칭 단수 현재시제인 'saturates'를 사용하였으나 뒤에 목적어가 없으며, 문맥상 '토양이 흠뻑 젖다'가 자연스러우므로 'saturates'를 수동태인 'is saturated'로 수정해야 한다. 더해, 제시된 동사 'saturate'는 2015년 국가직 9급 사책형 16번에 제시된 바 있는 기출 어휘이므로 알아두도록 하자.

④ **출제 포인트: 사역동사의 수동태**
사역동사 'make'는 「make+목적어+목적격 보어[원형부정사]」의 구조를 가지며 수동태는 「목적어+be made+목적격 보어[to부정사]」의 구조를 가진다. 해당 문장은 사역동사 'make'의 수동태를 사용하였으나 목적격 보어에 원형부정사 'carry'를 사용하였으므로 틀린 문장이다. 따라서 'carry'를 to부정사 'to carry'로 수정해야 한다.

해석
① 그녀는 그녀가 도덕적으로 나머지 우리들보다 우월하다고 생각한다.
② 더운 날, 잔에 얼음이 부딪히는 소리를 듣는 것은 기분 좋다.
③ 이 공극이 물로 완전히 채워지면, 그 토양은 흠뻑 젖는다.
    (* 공극: 토양 입자와 입자 사이에 공기나 물로 채워질 수 있는 틈새)
④ 만약 모든 사람들이 신분증을 소지하도록 강요받는다면, 그것은 우리 모두가 의심을 받고 있다는 생각을 키울 것이다.

07 정답 ②

정답해설
② **출제 포인트: take 동사의 다양한 쓰임**
「It takes+목적어[사람]+목적어[시간]+to부정사」는 관용표현으로 '사람이 ~하는 데 시간이 걸리다'를 뜻한다. 이때 목적어[시간]이 목적어[사람] 앞으로 이동하는 경우 「It takes+목적어[시간]+for+목적어[사람]+to부정사」의 구조를 가진다. 해당 문장은 목적어[시간] 'several more hours'가 목적어[사람] 'John' 앞으로 이동하였으나 'John' 앞에 전치사 'for'를 사용하지 않았으므로 틀린 문장이다. 따라서 'John'을 'for John'으로 수정해야 한다.

오답해설
① **출제 포인트: 주격 관계대명사/선행사와 주격 관계대명사절 동사의 수일치/주어와 동사의 수일치**
주절의 주어인 'The woman'은 주격 관계대명사의 선행사이며 단수형태이므로 주격 관계대명사절의 동사와 주절의 동사에 단수형태인 'needs'와 'is'를 옳게 사용하였다. 또한 'is cared for'는 타동사구 'care for'의 수동형태로 옳게 사용되었다.

③ **출제 포인트: 현재분사 vs. 과거분사**
해당 문장에서 'taken by four photographers'는 주어와 동사 사이에 삽입된 분사구문이다. 분사구문을 이끄는 과거분사 'taken'은 생략된 주어 'These works'와 수동관계이므로 옳게 사용되었다.

④ **출제 포인트: 관계부사 vs. 관계대명사/목적격 관계대명사**
해당 문장에서 'where'는 관계부사로 선행사는 'a society'이며 뒤에 오는 절은 완전한 형태이다. 또한 'to learn'은 to부정사의 명사적 용법으로 'need'의 목적어에 해당한다. 이때 'to learn' 뒤에 목적어가 없으므로 수동태로 고쳐야 한다고 생각할 수도 있으나 'to learn'의 목적어는 선행사 'a value'이며 'our children need to learn'은 생략된 목적격 관계대명사가 이끄는 절이므로 'to learn'은 옳은 표현이다.

08 정답 ④

정답해설
본문은 독서의 방법 중 하나인 'Skimming(스키밍)'에 대해 설명하는 글로, 스키밍이란 내용을 빨리 훑어보며 글의 골자를 빠르게 파악하는 방법이다. 본문은 스키밍은 정독을 하기 전 기본 내용을 파악하는 데 도움이 되고 시간을 절약해주는 반면, 독자의 전반적인 글의 이해도는 낮을 수밖에 없다고 스키밍의 전반적인 특징에 대해 설명하고 있다. 그러나 본문의 마지막 부분에서 "However, skimming is useful when your goal is to preview the text to get a better idea of what it's about(그러나 스키밍은 당신의 목표가 텍스트가 무엇인지에 대한 더 나은 아이디어를 얻기 위해 그것을 사전 검토하는 것일 때는 유용하다)."라고 스키밍의 장점을 다시 한번 부각하여 언급해 주고 있으므로, 전체 글의 요지로는 '④ Skimming is a good way to get an overview of the text(스키밍은 텍스트의 개요를 얻는 좋은 방법이다).'가 가장 적절하다.

오답해설
① 본문 중반에서 "You can reach a speed count of even 700 words per minute if you train yourself well in some particular methods(만일 당신이 특정한 방식으로 잘 훈련한다면 당신은 분당 700단어를 읽는 속도에 도달할 수 있다)."라고 '훈련을 통해 스키밍 기술이 발달될 수 있음'을 시사하고 있으나, 이는 단지 스키밍에 대한 소개를 위한 내용의 일부이며 글 전체를 아우르는 내용은 아니므로 글의 요지로는 적절하지 않다.
② 본문 초반 "this would help you mentally and quickly shortlist those articles which you might consider for a deeper read(이것은

당신이 마음속으로 빠르게 정독을 고려하는 기사들의 목록을 작성하도록 도와줄 것이다."를 통해, 스키밍이 '속독(speed reading)'의 일부라고 볼 수도 있으나, 스키밍 기술이 속독 기술 중 가장 중요하다는 내용은 본문에 전혀 언급되지 않으므로 오답이다.

③ 본문 중반 "Comprehension is of course very low and understanding of overall content very superficial(물론 이해도는 매우 낮고 전체적인 내용의 이해는 매우 피상적이다)."에서 '이해도가 낮아진다'고 언급하고 있으므로, 본문의 내용과는 반대되는 문장이다.

해석

스키밍(Skimming)은 때때로 요점 읽기라고 일컬어진다. 그것은 텍스트의 가장 기본 단계에서 그것이 무엇에 대한 것인지 알기 위해 도움이 될 수 있다. 당신은 일반적으로 그것을 잡지 또는 신문을 볼 때 할 수 있으며, 이것은 당신이 마음속으로 빠르게 정독을 고려하는 기사들의 목록을 작성하도록 도와줄 것이다. 당신은 또한 전화번호부에서 이름을 찾기 위해 훑어볼 수도 있다. 만일 당신이 특정한 방식으로 잘 훈련한다면 당신은 분당 700단어를 읽는 속도에 도달할 수 있다. 물론 이해도는 매우 낮고 전체적인 내용의 이해는 매우 피상적이다. 그것은 분명 당신의 많은 시간을 절약해 줄 것이지만, 앞서 언급된 이유로 인해 이것은 최상의 독서법은 아니다. 그러나 스키밍은 당신의 목표가 텍스트가 무엇인지에 대한 더 나은 아이디어를 얻기 위해 그것을 사전 검토하는 것일 때는 유용하다. 그것은 당신이 정독을 준비하는 데 도움이 될 것이다.

① 스키밍 기술은 훈련을 통해 발달될 수 있다.
② 스키밍은 속독에 있어서 가장 중요한 기술이다.
③ 스키밍은 독자가 텍스트를 완전히 이해할 수 있도록 해준다.
④ 스키밍은 텍스트의 개요를 얻는 좋은 방법이다.

어휘

skim 대충 읽다, 훑어보다
directory 명단, 목록
superficial 표면적인, 피상적인
gist 요점
comprehension 이해

09 정답 ②

정답해설

본문은 보편적으로 서구 문화권의 사람들은 '개인주의(individualism)' 성향이 있고, 동아시아 지역의 사람들은 '집단주의(collectivism)' 성향이 있지만, 이는 절대적인 것이 아니며, 개인의 '개인주의/집단주의' 성향은 다양한 요소에 의해 영향을 받고 개개인마다 그 수준이 다르다고 언급하고 있다. 본문 마지막 문장 "In other words, as humans, we switch between cultural frames depending on the context(다시 말해, 인간으로서, 우리는 맥락에 따라 문화적 틀을 전환 시킨다)."를 통해, '맥락(상황)에 따라 인간은 개인주의 혹은 집단주의를 채택한다'고 설명하고 있으므로 '개인주의와 집단주의는 절대적인 것이 아닌 상대적인 것이라는 것을 유추할 수 있다. 따라서 글의 요지로 가장 적절한 보기는 '② Individualism and collectivism are relative(개인주의와 집단주의는 상대적이다).'이다.

오답해설

① 본문과 관련 없는 내용이다.
③ 첫 번째 문장에서 "While individualism/collectivism can be measured in any culture, much of the research so far has been carried out on East Asian and Western cultures(개인주의/집단주의가 어느 문화에서나 측정될 수 있으나, 현재까지의 많은 연구가 동아시아와 서구 문화권을 대상으로 실시되어왔다)."라고 현재까지의 연구의 범위가 '서구'와 '동아시아' 문화권에 집중되어 있었다는 것을 언급하고 있지만, 더 폭넓은 연구의 필요성에 대해서는 본문에 언급되지 않다. 따라서 오답이다.
④ 본문 초반에 "Researchers have found that Western cultures tend to be more individualistic while East Asian cultures tend to be more collectivistic(연구자들은 서구 문화가 더 개인주의적인 반면 동아시아 문화가 더 집단주의적이라는 것을 발견했다)."라고 언급하기는 하지만, 이후 "However, it's important to remember that many factors can influence individualism/collectivism, so individuals within a culture can also differ in their levels of independence/interdependence(그러나, 많은 요소들이 개인주의/집단주의에 영향을 미칠 수 있으므로, 한 문화권 내의 개인 또한 그들의 독립성/상호 의존성 수준이 다를 수 있다는 것을 기억하는 것이 중요하다)."라고 설명하며, 한 문화권 내에서도 '개인주의, 집단주의 수준이 다를 수 있다'고 주장하고 있으므로, 글의 요지로는 적절하지 않다.

해석

개인주의/집단주의가 어느 문화에서나 측정될 수 있으나, 현재까지 개인주의/집단주의에 관한 많은 연구가 동아시아와 서구 문화권을 대상으로 실시되어왔다. 연구자들은 서구 문화가 더 개인주의적인 반면 동아시아 문화가 더 집단주의적인 경향이 있다는 것을 발견했다. 그러나, 많은 요소들이 개인주의/집단주의에 영향을 미칠 수 있으므로, 한 문화권 내의 개인 또한 그들의 독립성/상호 의존성 수준이 다를 수 있다는 것을 기억하는 것이 중요하다. 개인주의/집단주의는 심지어 상황적인 맥락에 의해 영향을 받을 수도 있다. 예를 들어, 한 연구는 다른 두 문화적 배경을 지닌 사람들이 개인주의 문화와 관련된 이미지를 보았을 때는 더 개인주의적이 되고, 집단주의 문화와 관련된 이미지를 보았을 때는 더 집단주의적이 된다는 것을 발견했다. 다시 말해, 인간으로서, 우리는 맥락에 따라 문화적 틀을 전환한다.

① 각각의 문화는 존중받아야 한다.
② 개인주의와 집단주의는 상대적이다.
③ 개인주의/집단주의에 관한 더 폭넓은 연구가 필요하다.
④ 서구 사람들은 개인주의적이고 동아시아인들은 집단주의적이다.

어휘

individualism 개인주의
individualistic 개인주의적인
interdependence 상호 의존
relative 상대적인
collectivism 집단주의
collectivistic 집단주의적인
switch 전환하다, 바꾸다

10 정답 ④

정답해설

본문은 '박쥐괴질(white-nose syndrome)'이라는 전염병으로 인해 박쥐가 어떻게 피해를 입는지 상세히 설명하고 있다. 주어진 문장의 "As a result(그 결과)"로 보아, 주어진 문장 이전에는 주어진 문장이 이끄는 내용이 발생하는 원인을 설명하는 내용이 등장해야 한다. 주어진 문장에서는 'bats exhaust critical stores of fat they need to get through the winter, which leads to starvation(박쥐들은 겨울을 나기 위해 필요한 필수 지방 저장분을 전부 소모하게 되어 굶어 죽는다).'고 설명하고 있으므로, 이전에는 '지방 저장분을 소모하게 되는 이유'를 설명하는 문장이 와야 한다. ④ 이전 문장에서, 'causes them to wake more frequently and raises their metabolism during winter hibernation.(동면 중에 더 빈번하게 잠에서 깨어 신진대사를 높인다).'고 언급하였으므로, 그로 인해 '지방을 소비한다'는 것을 알 수 있다. 따라서 주어진 문장이 들어갈 가장 적절한 위치는 ④이다.

오답해설

나머지 위치는 문맥상 어색하므로 오답이다.

해석

지난 10년 동안 박쥐괴질(white-nose syndrome)이라 불리는 전염병이 미 동부와 캐나다의 박쥐 집단을 파괴했다. 6백만 마리 이상의 박쥐가 죽었다.

(①) 일부 종은 멸종할지도 모른다. (②) 범인은 침습성 균류인 *Pseudogymnoascus destructans (Pd.)*인데, 이것은 북미 토종이 아니다. (③) 그것은 동굴에 사는 박쥐를 감염시키고 그들의 날개를 훼손하고 동면 도중에 더 빈번하게 잠을 깨도록 만들어 그들의 신진대사를 증가시킨다. (④) **그 결과, 박쥐들은 겨울을 나기 위해 필요한 필수 지방 저장분을 전부 소모해 버리고, 그것이 그들을 굶어 죽게 한다.**) 균이 나타난 대부분의 동굴에서는 90퍼센트 또는 그 이상의 박쥐 소멸이 발생했다.

어휘

exhaust 다 써 버리다, 고갈시키다
critical 대단히 중요한
epidemic 전염병, 유행병
devastate 파괴하다, 황폐하게 만들다
culprit 범인
invasive 침습성의
fungus 균류
metabolism 신진대사
hibernation 동면
die-off 종(種)의 급격한 자연 소멸

결국엔 성정혜 영어 하프모의고사
기적사 DAY 14

| 01 | ② | 02 | ④ | 03 | ④ | 04 | ① | 05 | ④ |
| 06 | ④ | 07 | ② | 08 | ④ | 09 | ③ | 10 | ① |

01 정답 ②

정답해설

밑줄 친 'robust'는 '탄탄한, 튼튼한'의 의미로 ② sturdy와 의미가 가장 가깝다.

해석

경제의 많은 부분들에서 **탄탄하고** 긍정적인 조짐이 보이기 때문에 우리나라의 미래는 매우 밝다.
① 관계없는
② 튼튼한, 견고한
③ 평온한, 조용한, 차분한
④ 상호적인, 서로의

어휘

robust 탄탄한, 튼튼한
affirmative 긍정적인
unrelated 관계없는
sturdy 튼튼한, 견고한
placid 평온한, 조용한, 차분한
mutual 상호적인, 서로의

02 정답 ④

정답해설

밑줄 친 'revealed'는 'reveal(밝히다, 누설하다)'의 과거시제로 'disclose(밝히다, 폭로하다)'의 과거시제인 ④ disclosed와 의미가 가장 가깝다.

해석

기밀문서의 내용을 **누설했던** 공무원은 엄벌에 처해졌다.
① 해결했다, 타협을 봤다, 진정시켰다
② 자제했다
③ 재개했다
④ 폭로했다, 밝혔다

어휘

reveal 밝히다, 누설하다
confidential 비밀의, 감추는
punishment 엄벌, 처벌
settle 해결하다, 타협을 보다, 진정시키다
restrain 자제하다
resume 재개하다
disclose 폭로하다, 밝히다

03 정답 ④

정답해설

'(어떤 생각이 사람의 마음을) 사로잡다, 집착하게 하다'의 'obsess'를 활용한 ④ obsessed를 사용하여 '다이어트에 사로잡혀 건강에 좋지 않은 식사 습관을 갖고 있다'라고 하는 것이 문맥상 가장 자연스럽다.

해석

몇몇 여자아이들은 다이어트에 **사로잡혀있고** 건강에 좋지 않은 식사 습관을 갖고 있다.

① 강요된, ~하게 된
② 초대된
③ 파견된
④ ~에게 사로잡힌

어휘

compel 강요하다　　　　　　　ask out 초대하다
dispatch 파견하다
obsess (어떤 생각이 사람의 마음을) 사로잡다, 집착하게 하다

04 정답 ①

정답해설

마이클 잭슨의 숨겨진 아들에 관한 기사를 읽은 A와 B가 대화를 나눈다. 그리고 숨겨진 아들에 관한 이야기가 '예기치 못했던 것(bolt from the blue sky)'이기에 기사가 '황색지(yellow journalism)'였을지도 모른다고 말한다. '황색지'는 이목을 끌기 위해 작성된 사실과 거리가 있는 선정적인 보도를 뜻한다. 그리고 마지막 빈칸에는 마이클 잭슨은 살아생전에 가는 곳마다 사람들이 '특히 환영했기(rolled out the red carpet)'에 그에 대해 함부로 말해서는 안 된다고 이야기한다.

오답해설

② '예기치 못한 일'을 의미하는 관용표현은 'bolt from the blue sky'이기 때문에 'black'은 빈칸에 들어갈 말로 적절하지 않다. 또한, '황색지'를 뜻하는 관용어는 'yellow journalism'이기에 빈칸에 들어갈 단어로 'white'는 부자연스럽다.
③ '예기치 못한 일'을 의미하는 관용표현은 'bolt from the blue sky'이기 때문에 'red'는 빈칸에 들어갈 말로 적절하지 않다. 또한 '특히 환영하다'를 나타내는 관용표현은 'roll out the red carpet'이므로 빈칸에 'white'는 옳지 않다.
④ '황색지, 선정적인 언론'을 뜻하는 관용어는 'yellow journalism'이기에 빈칸에 들어갈 단어로 'green'은 자연스럽지 않다. 또한 '특히 환영하다'를 나타내는 관용표현은 'roll out the red carpet'이므로 빈칸에 'black'은 어색하다.

해석

A: 너 마이클 잭슨에 관한 뉴스 들었어?
B: 그의 숨겨진 피아니스트 아들에 관한 것 말하는 거야?
A: 응, 마이클 잭슨은 수년 전에 죽었어. 그의 아들을 갑자기 보는 것은 <u>예기치 못한 일</u>이야.
B: 그러니까. 난 원래 믿지 않았어. 그냥 말이 안 돼.
A: 맞아. 마이클 잭슨은 살아있을 때 그의 피아니스트 아들을 언급했던 적이 없었어.
B: 아마 우리가 읽었던 그 기사는 그저 <u>황색지</u>였나 봐.
A: 나쁜 기자야. 마이클 잭슨 가지고 장난을 치면 안 되지. 그는 아직도 세계에서 가장 인기 있고 유명한 음악가 중 한 명인데.
B: 나도 네 의견에 동의해. 그가 가는 곳곳마다 사람들은 <u>특히 환영해줬어</u>.

① 파랑 – 노랑 – 빨강
② 검정 – 하양 – 빨강
③ 빨강 – 노랑 – 하양
④ 파랑 – 초록 – 검정

어휘

bolt from the blue sky 예기치 못한 일
roll out the red carpet 특히 환영하다
yellow journalism 황색지, 선정적인 언론

05 정답 ④

정답해설

④ **출제 포인트: 사역동사의 목적격 보어**
사역동사 'let'은 목적격 보어로 원형부정사를 사용한다. 밑줄 친 'know'는 원형부정사이며 사역동사 'let'의 목적격 보어로 옳게 사용되었다. 또한 해당 문장에서 'know'는 완전자동사로 사용되었다.

오답해설

① **출제 포인트: 준사역동사의 목적격 보어**
'help'는 준사역동사의 경우 목적격 보어로 to부정사와 원형부정사를 사용할 수 있으나 현재분사는 사용할 수 없다. 따라서 밑줄 친 'swimming'은 준사역동사 'help'의 목적격 보어이므로 to부정사 'to swim' 또는 원형부정사 'swim'으로 수정해야 한다.
② **출제 포인트: sort/kind/type+of+무관사 명사**
'sort/kind/type+of' 뒤에 오는 명사(구)는 관사 없이 사용해야 한다. 밑줄 친 부분은 'this type of' 뒤에 오는 명사(구)에 정관사 'the'를 사용하였으므로 'the'를 삭제해야 한다.
③ **출제 포인트: 접속사의 쓰임**
문맥상 그들이 그것을 입을 수 있는지 없는지를 물어보는 것이므로 명사절 접속사 'that'을 '~인지 아닌지'의 뜻을 갖는 명사절 접속사 'if' 또는 'whether'로 고쳐야 한다.
※ ask+간접목적어+직접목적어: 직접목적어에 올 수 있는 절은 의문사절, if절, whether절 등이 있다.

해석

그 대회를 준비하기 위해서, Zach와 Tony는 둘 다 물의 저항을 최소화하여 그들이 더 빠르게 수영하는 데 도움을 줄 수 있는 특별 제작된 수영복을 샀다. 하지만 이런 유형의 특별한 수영복이 이전 대회에서는 허용되지 않았다는 것을 알게 되었다. Zach와 Tony는 둘 다 그것을 입을 수 있는지 수영 코치에게 물어보았다. 그는 대회전에 그들에게 알려주겠다고 말했다.

어휘

swimming suit 수영복　　　　　minimize 최소화하다
resistance 저항, 반대

오답률 TOP 3

06 정답 ④

정답해설

④ **출제 포인트: 능동태 vs. 수동태**
「set+목적어+up」 관용표현으로 '~을 설립하다'를 뜻하며 수동태는 「목적어+be set up」이다. 해당 문장은 「set+목적어+up」의 수동태인 「목적어+be set up」을 사용한 옳은 문장이다. 이때 'on behalf of'는 '~을 대신하여'를 뜻한다.

오답해설

① **출제 포인트: 가목적어 it/to부정사의 명사적 용법**
해당 문장은 능동태로 쓰인 'made' 뒤에 목적어 없이 목적격 보어에 해당하는 형용사 'easier'이 왔으므로 옳지 않은 문장이다. 이때 'to find ~ meat'은 진목적어에 해당하며 문맥상 '버터와 고기 같은 몇몇 제품들을 찾는 것을 더 쉽게 만든다.'가 자연스러우므로 형용사 'easier' 앞에 가목적어 'it'을 사용해야 한다.
② **출제 포인트: 라틴어 비교급**
라틴어 비교급은 비교 대상 앞에 전치사 'to'를 사용한다. 해당 문장은 라틴어 비교급에 해당하는 형용사 'posterior'를 사용하였으나 뒤에 'than'을 사용하였으므로 틀린 문장이다. 따라서 'than'을 'to'로 수정해야 한다.

③ **출제 포인트: 능동태 vs. 수동태**
해당 문장은 동사 'expect'를 능동태로 사용하였으나 주어인 'The competition'은 'expect'의 행위 주체가 될 수 없으므로 틀린 문장이다. 따라서 'expect'를 수동태 'be expected'로 수정해야 한다. 다만 'to force(force의 to부정사 형태)'는 불완전타동사로 쓰였으며 목적격 보어로 to 부정사인 'to reduce'를 옳게 사용하였다.

해석
① 배급제는 버터와 고기 같은 몇몇 제품들을 찾는 것을 더 쉽게 만들었다.
② 그것은 알렉산더 대왕의 정복 이후의 날짜를 가리키고 있다.
③ 그 경쟁은 은행들로 하여금 그들의 비용을 줄이게 할 것으로 예상된다.
④ 그 회사는 투자자들을 대신하여 주식을 사고팔기 위해 설립되었다.

07 정답 ②

정답해설
② **출제 포인트: 주격 관계대명사/선행사와 주격 관계대명사절 동사의 수일치**
구조상으로는 옳으나 주어진 해석이 '주목받는 것을 좋아하는 그러한 사람들 중 한 명'이므로 주격 관계대명사 'who'의 선행사가 'those people'임을 알 수 있다. 이때 'those people'은 복수형태이므로 주격 관계대명사절의 동사에 복수형태를 사용해야 한다. 따라서 'loves'를 복수형태인 'love'로 수정해야 한다.

오답해설
① **출제 포인트: take 동사의 다양한 쓰임**
「It takes+목적어[사람]+목적어[시간]+to부정사」는 관용표현으로 '사람이 ~하는 데 시간이 걸리다'를 뜻한다. 해당 문장은 「It takes+사람+시간+to부정사」를 사용하였으며 주어진 해석과 일치하므로 옳은 문장이다.

③ **출제 포인트: 현재분사 vs. 과거분사**
해당 문장의 'ensuring that Tom couldn't escape'는 분사구문이다. 분사구문을 이끄는 현재분사 'ensuring'은 생략된 주어 'William'과 능동 관계이므로 옳게 사용되었다.

④ **출제 포인트: 유도부사구문의 수일치/to부정사의 형용사적 용법**
해당 문장은 유도부사구문으로 주어 'a need'와 동사 'is'가 올바르게 수일치 되었다. 'to improve mechanisms'는 명사(구) 'a need'를 수식하며 'to effectively prevent and deter acts of terrorism'은 명사 'mechanisms'를 수식하므로 둘 다 한정적 역할을 하는 to부정사의 형용사적 용법에 해당한다.

오답률 TOP 1
08 정답 ④

정답해설
본문은 학교에서 읽는 법을 제대로 배우지 못한 아이들이 성인이 될 때까지 읽는 것에 어려움을 느끼며, 그에 따라 안정적인 직업을 얻기 힘들고 범죄를 저질러 감옥에 갈 가능성이 더 높다는 연구 결과를 소개하고 있다. 빈칸에는 이러한 사람들을 칭하는 용어를 설명하는 말이 들어가야 하는데, 빈칸 이후 "Most of them don't have neurological problems. Their schools and, specifically, their primary school teachers have failed them(그들 중 대부분은 신경학적인 문제를 가지고 있지 않다. 그들의 학교 그리고 특히 그들의 초등학교 선생님들이 그들에게 도움이 되지 못한 것이다)."로 보아, 그들은 어떠한 질병 또는 장애 때문에 읽지 못하게 된 것이 아니라 학교와 교사들이 그들에게 도움이 되지 않아 그들이 적절한 교육을 받지 못했기 때문에 이러한 결과가 발생한다는 것을 알 수 있다. 따라서, 빈칸에 가장 적절한 보기는 '④ instructional casualties(교육의 피해자들)'이다.

오답해설
① 어릴 때 읽지 못하는 아이들이 성인이 되어서도 사회에 적응하지 못한다는 내용이 본문에 언급되어 있으나, 빈칸에는 '독서 전문가(Reading expert)'들이 이러한 사람들을 지칭하는 근거로 빈칸 이하의 두 문장을 언급하고 있으므로, '사회 부적응자(social misfit)'라는 표현은 '신경학적인 문제가 없고, 학교와 교사의 도움을 받지 못한 사람들'을 표현하기에는 적절하지 않다. 따라서 오답이다.
② 본문에서는 읽는 데 어려움을 겪는 사람들에 대해 다루고 있으므로, 빈칸에 적절하지 않다.
③ 본문에서는 학생들이 읽는 데 어려움을 겪는 것이 학생들의 책임이 아닌 학교와 교사의 책임으로 보고 있다. 따라서 빈칸에 적절하지 않다.

해석
결과에 있어서, 아이들을 수십 년 동안 추적하는 유형인 종단적 연구는 슬픈 이야기를 해준다. 만일 당신의 아이가 읽지 못하는 것을 경험한다면 그것은 거의 그가 만성적이고 심신을 쇠약하게 하는 질병에 걸린 것과 거의 마찬가지이다. 1학년에 학년 수준으로 읽지 못하는 아이들은 거의 변함없이 잘 읽지 못하는 4학년생이 된다. 읽는 데 어려움을 겪는 3학년생들의 74퍼센트는 9학년에도 여전히 어려움을 겪고, 그것은 결과적으로 고등학교 졸업하는 것을 어렵게 만든다. 읽는 데 어려움을 겪는 아이들이 안정적인 직업을 가지는 데 어려움을 겪는 성인으로 자란다는 것을 알게 되는 것이 당신을 놀라게 하지는 않을 것이다. 그들은 장기적인 실업을 경험할 가능성이 더 높고, 복지서비스를 필요로 할 가능성이 더 높으며, 감옥에 갈 가능성이 더 높다. 독서 전문가들은 그들을 "교육의 피해자들"이라고 부른다. 그들 중 대부분은 신경학적인 문제를 가지고 있지 않다. 그들의 학교 그리고 특히 그들의 초등학교 선생님들이 그들에게 도움이 되지 못한 것이다.

① 사회 부적응자들
② 재능 있는 독서가들
③ 무능한 학생들
④ 교육의 피해자들

어휘
longitudinal 종적인(무엇의 장기적인 변화 과정을 다룬)
contract (병에) 걸리다
chronic 만성의
debilitating 쇠약하게 하는
invariably 변함[예외]없이, 언제나
prolonged 오래 계속되는, 장기적인
neurological 신경학적인, 신경의
misfit 부적응자
casualty 피해자

오답률 TOP 2
09 정답 ③

정답해설
본문의 내용에 따르면, '집단주의 성향을 지닌 사람들이 친환경적인 행동을 할 가능성이 더 높으며, 환경적으로 더 활동적인 집단이 더 집단주의적'이라는 것을 알 수 있다. 즉, 집단주의자들이 기후변화에 더욱 적극적 대응을 할 가능성이 높으며, 개인주의자들이 기후변화에 상대적으로 무관심할 가능성이 높다는 것이다. 또한 마지막 문장 "several studies within the framework of cultural worldview have suggested that individualist worldviews are negatively related with concern about climate change, willingness to behave in climate-friendly ways, and acceptance of related policy measures(문화적 세계관이라는 체제 내의 여러 연구들은 개인주의적 세계관은 기후변화에 대한 염려, 기후 친화적인 방식으로 행동하려는 의지, 그리고 관련된 정책 수용과 부정적으로 관련되어 있다고 밝힌)."를 통해서도, '개인주의적인 세계관은 환경 문제를 해결하고자 하는 노력에 대해 부정적으로 반응할 것'임을 시사하고 있다. 따라서 빈칸에 가장 적절한 표현은 '③ individualism is more related to climate change inaction than

is collectivism(개인주의가 집단주의보다 기후변화에 대한 무대응에 더 관련이 있다)'이다.

오답해설

① 본문에서는 개인주의가 기후변화 무대응과 관련이 있다고 언급하고 있으므로 오답이다.
② 본문의 주장과는 반대되는 내용이므로 오답이다.
④ 본문에서는 집단주의보다 개인주의가 좀 더 기후변화 무대응에 관련이 있다는 것을 시사하고 있으므로 오답이다.

해석

우리는 개인주의가 집단주의보다 기후변화에 대한 무대응에 더 관련이 있다고 생각한다. 이러한 가정은 다음과 같은 사항을 통해 근거를 얻는다. 첫째, 개인주의 대 집단주의 성향은 친환경 행위에 영향을 미치는 것으로 밝혀졌다. 대략적으로, 집단주의적 개인은 개인주의적 경향을 지는 사람들보다 자원 보호와 친환경 구매 행위를 포함한 다양한 친환경 행동에 참여할 가능성이 더 높다. 더 나아가, 뉴질랜드에서 Semenova가 실시한 조사는 가치 지향에 있어서 환경적으로 더 활동적인 집단이 환경적으로 덜 활동적인 집단보다 더 집단주의적이라는 것을 밝혀냈다. 유사한 결과들이 Jia 외 다수에 의해 보고되었는데, 그들은 환경운동가들은 자기초월적인 가치를 지지할 가능성이 더 높은 반면, 비운동가들은 사사로운 가치를 지지할 가능성이 더 높았다는 것을 증명했다. 게다가, 문화적 세계관이라는 체제 내의 여러 연구들은 개인주의적 세계관이 기후변화에 대한 염려, 기후 친화적인 방식으로 행동하려는 의지, 그리고 관련된 정책 수용과 부정적으로 관련되어 있다고 밝혀왔다.

① 개인주의와 집단주의 모두 기후변화에 대한 무대응과 관련이 없다
② 집단주의가 개인주의보다 기후변화에 대한 무대응에 더 관련이 있다
③ 개인주의가 집단주의보다 기후변화에 대한 무대응에 더 관련이 있다
④ 개인주의와 집단주의 모두 동일하게 기후변화에 대한 무대응에 관련이 있다

어휘

assumption 가정   derive 얻다, 끌어내다
individualist 개인주의자(의)   collectivist 집단주의자(의)
orientation 성향   tendency 경향
conservation 보존, 보호   value orientation 가치 지향
et al. (특히 이름들 뒤에 써서) 외, 등   endorse 지지하다
self-transcendent 자기초월적인 inaction 무대책, 무대응

10 정답 ①

정답해설

본문 첫 문장 "Bats can help an area get rid of pests and bugs(박쥐는 한 지역이 해충과 벌레를 제거하도록 도와준다)."를 통해 박쥐의 긍정적 역할에 대해 언급하고 있고, 이후 구체적으로 박쥐가 얼마나 많은 수와 종류의 벌레를 먹어 치울 수 있는지 설명해주고 있다. 또한, 본문 후반에서 박쥐의 먹이 활동으로 인해 인도네시아의 카카오 생산량이 유지될 수 있다고도 설명하고 있으므로, 글의 주제로 가장 적절한 것은 '① benefits of bats(박쥐의 이점)'이다.

오답해설

② 본문은 박쥐가 해충 박멸을 해준다는 긍정적인 내용이므로, '박쥐의 위험성'은 글의 주제로는 적절하지 않다.
③ '박쥐의 자연 서식지'는 본문에 언급되지 않는 내용이다.
④ '박쥐의 신체적 특징'은 본문에 언급되지 않는 내용이다.

해석

박쥐는 한 지역이 해충과 벌레를 제거하도록 도와준다. 각각의 박쥐는 한 시간에 1,200마리의 모기 또는 모기 크기의 곤충을 먹을 수 있는 능력으로 하룻밤에 6,000에서 8,000마리의 곤충을 먹어치우는 것으로 알려져 있다. 그들은 또한 파리, 각다귀, 넓적다리잎벌레, 그리고 전 세계의 호두 작물의 99퍼센트에 영향을 미치는 코들링나방과 같은 작물을 파괴하는 나방을 먹는다. 천연 해충 방제를 제공하는 그들의 능력이 농부들 사이에서 그들을 인기 있게 만들었다. 이 야행성 포유류에게 고마워해야 할 또 하나의 이유는 초콜릿이다. 인도네시아에서, 만일 그들이 박쥐를 퇴치한다면 카카오 수확량이 어떻게 될지가 추정되었을 때, 결과는 수억 달러의 손실을 일으킬 22퍼센트의 큰 하락이었다.

① 박쥐의 이점
② 박쥐의 위험성
③ 박쥐의 자연 서식지
④ 박쥐의 신체적 특징

어휘

pest 해충   gnat 각다귀, 모기
cucumber beetle 넓적다리잎벌레   codling moth 코들링나방
nocturnal 야행성의   yield 수확량
exterminate 몰살하다, 근절하다, 퇴치하다
drastic 극단적인, 급격한

결국엔 성정혜 영어 하프모의고사
기적사 DAY 15

01	①	02	③	03	①	04	③	05	③
06	①	07	④	08	②	09	④	10	④

01 정답 ①

정답해설

밑줄 친 'sedulous'는 '근면한, 정성을 다하는'이라는 뜻으로 ① industrious와 의미가 가장 가깝다.

해석

그 국가의 수없이 많은 **근면한** 사람들은 다시 한번 새로운 세대에서 많은 불확실성에 직면하는 중이다.
① 부지런한, 근면한
② 관능적인, 감각론의
③ 현명한, 합리적인
④ 복잡한

어휘

sedulous 근면한, 정성을 다하는   industrious 부지런한, 근면한
sensual 관능적인, 감각론의   sensible 현명한, 합리적인
complicated 복잡한

02 정답 ③

정답해설

밑줄 친 'ruled out'은 'rule out'의 과거형으로 '제외시키다, 배제하다'라는 의미를 가지고 있다. 따라서 ③ excluded와 의미가 가장 가깝다.

해석

국방부는 이 상황에 대해 그 국가를 돕고 있으며, 테러의 가능성을 **배제했다**.
① 시작했다
② 부탁했다
③ 제외했다, 배제했다
④ 새어 나왔다

어휘

rule out 배재하다   initiate 시작하다
solicit 부탁하다   exclude 제외하다, 배제하다
leak 새어 나오다

03 정답 ①

정답해설

'그곳에 남겨졌다'라는 문맥상 의미로 보아 '정착했다'의 ① settled down을 사용하는 것이 가장 적절하다.

해석

그 동물은 지나가던 선원들에 의해서 거기에 남겨져서 그 섬에 **정착하게 되었다**고 믿어진다.
① 정착했다, 문제를 해결했다, 감정을 차분하게 했다
② 이행했다
③ 중시했다
④ 새어 나왔다

어휘

settle down 정착하다, 문제를 해결하다, 감정을 차분하게 하다
carry out 이행하다   set store by 중시하다
seep out 새어 나오다

04 정답 ③

정답해설

Nancy와 Kevin은 Kevin의 가족여행과 결석에 관해 대화를 나누고 있다. Nancy가 Kevin에게 결석한 이유를 묻자 Kevin은 가족여행으로 인해 힘들어 잠이 들었다고 말한다. 이에 Nancy는 그게 (A) '무단결석한(took the French leave)'이었냐고 말하며 수긍한다. Nancy의 말에 Kevin은 가족여행이 (B) '고단한 하루(a long day)'였다고 말하며 걱정 없이 자신만을 위한 시간을 가질 수 있어 여행이 좋았다고 말한다. 그러자 Nancy는 사람들이 때로는 현실로부터 (C) '휴식을 취해야 할(take a break)' 필요가 있다고 말한다.

오답해설

① (A) Kevin이 결석한 이유가 가족여행으로 인해 피곤해 잠들었기 때문이라고 이야기하는 대화에서 Nancy가 Kevin에게 그것이 '절약한(cut corners)' 이유라고 말하는 것은 맥락상 어색하다.
② (A) Kevin이 결석한 이유가 가족여행으로 인해 피곤해 잠들었기 때문이라고 이야기하는 대화에서 Nancy가 Kevin에게 그것이 '절약한(cut corners)' 이유라고 말하는 것은 맥락상 어색하다. (B) Kevin이 무단결석한 사실에 관해서 '연속극(a soap opera)'이라고 하는 것은 문맥상 부자연스럽다. (C) Nancy가 Kevin의 가족여행 이야기를 들은 후 사람들이 때로는 현실에서 '부정한 방법을 쓸(stack the deck)' 필요가 있다고 답변하는 것은 적합하지 않다.
④ (C) Kevin이 가족여행에서 아무것도 걱정거리가 없었다고 말하자 Nancy는 사람들이 때때로 현실로부터 '비참하게 살(lead a dog's life)' 필요가 있다고 말하는 것은 대화의 흐름상 부적절한 답변이다.

해석

Nancy: 너 왜 어제 결석했어?
Kevin: 나 가족여행 다녀와서 너무 지쳐서 바로 잠들었어.
Nancy: 오, 그래서 네가 (A) <u>무단으로 결석한 거구나</u>.
Kevin: 응, 무척이나 (B) <u>고단한 날</u>이었어.
Nancy: 음, 여행은 어땠어?
Kevin: 굉장했어. 거기서 아무것도 걱정할 것이 없었어. 모든 시간이 온전히 내게 있었지.
Nancy: 때때로, 사람들은 분명히 현실로부터 (C) <u>휴식을 가져야 할</u> 필요가 있어.
Kevin: 난 너에게 전적으로 동의해.
① (A) 절약했다 (B) 고단한 날 (C) 휴식하다
② (A) 절약했다 (B) 연속극 (C) 부정한 방법을 쓰다
③ (A) 무단으로 결석했다 (B) 고단한 날 (C) 휴식하다
④ (A) 무단으로 결석했다 (B) 고단한 날 (C) 비참하게 살다

어휘

cut corners 절약했다   a long day 고단한 날
take a break 휴식하다   a soap opera 연속극
stack the deck 부정한 방법을 쓰다
take the French leave 무단으로 결석하다
lead a dog's life 비참하게 살다

05 정답 ③

정답해설

③ 출제 포인트: 준사역동사의 목적격 보어

준사역동사 'get'의 목적격 보어는 목적어와 능동관계인 경우 to부정사와 현재분사를 사용하며 수동관계인 경우 과거분사를 사용한다. 밑줄 친 'fixed'는 getting(준사역동사 get의 동명사 형태)의 목적격 보어에 해당하며 목적어 'it(a flat을 가리킴)'과 수동관계이다. 따라서 과거분사 'fixed'는 옳은 표현이다.

오답해설

① 출제 포인트: 접속사의 쓰임

해당 문장은 4개의 절이 연결되어있으므로 접속사가 3개가 있어야 하나 접속사는 'before'와 'when' 2개뿐이다. 따라서 접속사가 필요하며 문맥상 'before he ~ the time'이 직접목적어에 해당하므로 'it'을 명사절을 이끄는 접속사 'that'으로 수정해야 한다.

② 출제 포인트: 동명사의 태

동명사 'having'의 수동태인 'being had'를 사용하였으나 뒤에 목적어 'a flat'이 있으므로 틀린 문장이다. 따라서 'being had'를 능동태 동명사인 'having'으로 수정해야 한다.

④ 출제 포인트: 준사역동사의 목적격 보어

준사역동사 'get'의 목적격 보어는 목적어와 능동관계인 경우 to부정사와 현재분사를 사용하며 수동관계인 경우 과거분사를 사용한다. 밑줄 친 'removing'은 'to get(준사역동사 get의 to부정사 형태)'의 목적격 보어에 해당하나 목적어 'the nail'과 수동관계이다. 따라서 현재분사 'removing'을 과거분사 'removed'로 수정해야 한다. 또한 해당 문장은 가정법 과거완료가 사용된 문장으로 'If'절에 동사의 경우 'had taken'으로 표현도 가능하지만 주어의 의지를 나타낼 때 조동사 'would'의 의미를 더해 'would have taken'으로도 표현이 가능함에 주의해야한다.

해석

타이어에 바람이 빠지는 당황스러운 경험을 하기 전에 그는 '시간이 있을 때 그 차를 수리할 계획이었다'라고 나중에 나에게 말했다. 만약에 그가 그 못을 제거하기 위해 몇 분만 시간을 들였더라면, 그는 틀림없이 그날 타이어에 바람이 빠지는 일은 당하지 않았을 것이다.

어휘

embarrassment 당황, 곤란　　flat 바람 빠진[펑크 난] 타이어
plan on ~할 계획이다

오답률 TOP 2
06 정답 ①

정답해설

① 출제 포인트: 선행사와 주격 관계대명사절의 동사 수일치/라틴어 비교급

해당 문장에서 'which'는 주격 관계대명사로 선행사는 복수형태인 'some new shoes'이다. 따라서 주격 관계대명사절의 동사에 복수형태인 'are'를 옳게 사용하였다. 또한 'similar'는 라틴어 비교급 형용사로 비교 대상 앞에 전치사 'to'를 사용한다.

오답해설

② 출제 포인트: 자릿값/능동태 vs. 수동태

주어진 문장의 문맥상 법원이 William에 의해 돈을 지불하라고 명령을 받았다는 것은 어색하며 William이 법원에 의해 돈을 지불하라고 명령을 받았다는 것이 자연스럽다. 따라서 주어 'The court'를 'William'으로 수정해야 하며 'by William'을 'by the court'로 수정해야 한다.

③ 출제 포인트: 능동태 vs. 수동태/가목적어 it

불완전타동사 'find'의 수동태 「be found+목적격 보어[형용사]」를 사용하였으나 뒤에 목적어인 'that+절'이 있으므로 틀린 문장이다. 따라서 수동태 'is found'를 능동태 'finds'로 수정하고 목적격 보어 'ludicrous' 앞에 가목적어 'it'을 사용해야 한다.

④ 출제 포인트: 주어와 동사의 수일치/집합명사

'police'는 집합명사로 복수 취급하며 정관사 'the'와 함께 사용한다. 해당 문장은 주어에 'The police'를 사용하였으나 동사에 단수형태인 'was'를 사용하였으므로 틀린 문장이다. 따라서 'was'를 복수형태인 'were'로 수정해야 한다.

해석

① Jane은 전에 가지고 있던 신발과 매우 비슷한 새 신발을 샀다.
② William은 또한 법원에 의해(법원으로부터) 보상금으로 260파운드와 70파운드의 소송비용을 지불하라는 명령을 받았다.
③ Tom은 승객들을 화재로부터 보호하기 위해 아무 조치도 취해지지 않았다는 것이 터무니없다는 것을 깨달았다.
④ 경찰은 그들의 도움이 필요한 많은 아이들이 있을 것이기 때문에 질서를 지키기 위해 보내졌다.

오답률 TOP 3
07 정답 ④

정답해설

④ 출제 포인트: 현재분사 vs. 과거분사

해당 문장은 과거분사 'featured'를 사용하였으나 수식하는 대상 'A poster'와 능동관계이며 뒤에 목적어인 대명사 'this'가 있으므로 틀린 문장이다. 따라서 과거분사 'featured'를 현재분사 'featuring'으로 수정해야 한다.

오답해설

① 출제 포인트: 주격 관계대명사/선행사와 주격 관계대명사절 동사의 수일치/주어와 동사의 수일치

주절의 주어인 'The other people'은 주격 관계대명사의 선행사이며 복수형태이므로 주격 관계대명사절의 동사와 주절의 동사에 복수형태인 'live'와 'are'를 옳게 사용하였다.

② 출제 포인트: to부정사의 명사적 용법/목적격 관계대명사

'to ask'는 to부정사의 명사적 용법으로 'need'의 목적어에 해당한다. 이때 'to ask' 뒤에 목적어가 없으므로 수동태로 고쳐야 한다고 생각할 수도 있으나, 'to ask'의 목적어는 선행사 'The real question'이며 'we need to ask'는 생략된 목적격 관계대명사가 이끄는 절이다. 따라서 'to ask'는 옳은 표현이다.

③ 출제 포인트: take 동사의 다양한 쓰임/the amount of vs. the number of

해당 문장에서 'takes'는 완전타동사로 「주어+takes+시간」의 구조를 가지며 '주어는 시간이 걸린다.'로 해석한다. 또한 'time'의 경우 불가산명사이므로 앞에 양을 나타내는 'the amount of'를 옳게 사용했다.

08 정답 ②

정답해설

(A) 빈칸 이전에서 "To become efficient readers, we train ourselves to read different texts in different ways(효율적인 독서가가 되기 위해 우리는 다른 텍스트를 다른 방식으로 읽도록 훈련한다)."라고 '다른 방식으로 다른 텍스트를 읽는다'라고 언급한 후, 빈칸 이후에서 '소설(novel)'과 '교과서(textbook)'를 읽는 방식이 다른 것을 구체적으로

예시를 들어 설명하고 있으므로, 빈칸에는 '예시'를 나타내는 'For instance (예를 들어)'가 들어가는 것이 가장 적절하다.
(B) 빈칸 이전에서 설명한 'chunk(덩어리)'가 무엇인지 빈칸 이후에서 구체적으로 설명하고 있는 구조로, 동일한 내용을 '재서술'하고 있으므로 빈칸에는 'that is(즉)' 또는 'in other words(다시 말해)'가 들어갈 수 있다. 따라서 정답은 '② For instance(예를 들어) – that is(즉)'이다.

오답해설
④ (A) 이후 내용이 이전 내용의 반대 상황을 가정하는 것이 아니기 때문에 'Otherwise(그렇지 않으면)'는 빈칸에 적절하지 않다.

해석
실생활에서 사람들은 정보와 즐거움 모두를 위해 다양한 텍스트를 읽는다. 읽을거리는 내용, 스타일, 그리고 목적에 따라 다르며 우리는 그에 따라 우리의 독서 스타일을 조정한다. 효율적인 독서가가 되기 위해 우리는 다른 텍스트를 다른 방식으로 읽도록 훈련한다. (A) 예를 들어, 우리는 소설과 시험 준비를 위한 교과서를 동일한 방식으로 읽지 않는다. 우리가 소설을 읽을 때, 우리는 교과서를 읽을 때의 방법으로 모든 세부 사항에 주의를 기울일 필요가 없으며, 더 빨리 읽는다. 대부분의 속독은 chunking(덩어리로 나누기)이라고 불리는 과정을 포함한다. 각각의 단어를 읽는 것 대신에, 독자는 단어들을 "덩어리" – (B) 즉, 구, 절, 또는 심지어 문장 전체와 같은 의미 단위를 구성하는 단어의 집단 – 으로 받아들인다. 그리고 성인으로서, 우리의 대부분의 독서는 조용하다. 우리가 조용히 읽을 때 우리는 단어를 발음하는 시간을 절약하고 한 번에 한 단어 대신에 덩어리 혹은 의미 단위로 읽는다.

(A)	(B)
① 대조적으로	사실
② 예를 들어	즉
③ 그러므로	그러나
④ 그렇지 않으면	다시 말해

어휘
involve 포함하다, 수반하다
the way (that) ~하는 방법, 처럼, 이므로
chunk 덩어리로 나누기; 덩어리   articulate 또렷이 말하다, 발음하다
sense group 의미 단위

오답률 TOP 1
09 정답 ④

정답해설
(A) 이전에는 '유럽과 미국 문화의 개인주의'에 대해 설명하며, '독립적이면서도 활발한 사회관계 형성을 하는 것'이 특징이라고 말한다. (A) 이후에서는 일본에서의 개인주의는 '상호 의존적인 관계에 관여하지 않아야 한다'는 관념을 바탕으로 두고 있으므로, 유럽과 미국 문화에 기반을 둔 개인주의와는 대조적인 의미를 지니고 있다. 따라서 빈칸에 가장 적절한 표현은 '역접, 대조'를 나타내는 'On the other hand(반면에)' 또는 'By contrast(대조적으로)'이다.
(B) 이전에는 '일본에서의 개인주의는 미국에서보다 더 부정적인 의미를 함축한다'고 언급하며 개괄적인 내용을 제시한 후, (B) 이후에서 미국에서는 '특별하고 독립적(unique and independent)'이라고 여겨지고, 일본에서는 '이기적이고 외롭게(selfish and feeling lonely)' 여겨진다고 구체적인 설명을 제시하고 있으므로, 빈칸에는 구체적인 내용을 제시할 때 사용할 수 있는 'For example(예를 들어)' 또는 'Specifically(구체적으로 말하면)'가 가장 적절하다. 따라서 정답은 '④ By contrast(대조적으로) – Specifically(구체적으로 말하면)'이다.

오답해설
② (B) 'Apart from that'은 '그것과는 별개로'라는 의미로 (B)의 빈칸에는 문맥상 어울리지 않는다.
③ (A) 전후 관계가 '역접, 대조' 관계이므로, '인과, 결과'를 나타내는 'Thus (그래서)'는 (A)에 적절하지 않다.
나머지 보기는 문맥상 어색하므로 오답이다.

해석
세계화를 통해 일본 사회는 유럽과 미국 문화에 영향을 받았다. 이것은 특히 유럽과 미국 문화로부터 도입된 개인주의적인 시스템을 채택하고 있는 일본 사회의 측면에 있어서 사실이다. 그러나 일본의 개인주의는 유럽과 미국 문화적 맥락의 개인주의와는 질적으로 다를 수도 있다는 주장이 있다. 이러한 문화적 맥락에서의 개인주의는 타인으로부터 독립적이지만 여전히 사회관계를 활발히 맺는 것을 의미한다. (A) 대조적으로, 독립적이고 "개인주의"를 달성하기 위해, 일본인들은 상호 의존적인 관계에 관여하지 않을 필요성을 느낄지도 모른다. 실제로, 일본에서 개인주의의 함축적 의미는 미국에서의 함축적 의미보다 더 부정적이다. (B) 구체적으로 말하면, 미국에서 개인주의는 특별하거나 독립적인 것으로 인식되는 반면, 일본에서 개인주의는 이기적이고 외로움을 느끼는 것으로 여겨진다.

(A)	(B)
① 유사하게	그 결과
② 반면에	그것과는 별개로
③ 그래서	예를 들어
④ 대조적으로	구체적으로 말하면

어휘
adopt 채택하다, 차용하다   individualistic 개인주의의
qualitatively 질적으로   distance 관여[개입]하지 않게 하다
interdependent 상호 의존의   connotation 함축(적 의미)
perceive 인지[인식]하다, 여기다

10 정답 ④

정답해설
본문은 '볼리비아에서의 박쥐 판매'에 대해 설명하고 있다. 볼리비아에서의 박쥐 사냥 및 판매가 불법임에도 불구하고 이러한 박쥐 판매가 성행하는 이유는 "People buy them so they can drink bat blood for its purported healing properties — particularly, they think, to help manage epilepsy(사람들은 그들이 생각하기에 특히 간질을 관리하는 데 도움이 되는 치유 능력이 있다고 알려진 박쥐의 피를 마시기 위해 그것들을 산다).", 즉, 치료 효과를 기대하며 박쥐의 피를 마시는 사람들이 많기 때문이다. 그러나 본문 후반에서 언급된 것과 같이 "However, there's no proof of any medicinal benefit from drinking bat blood(그러나 박쥐의 피를 마시는 것의 의학적인 이점에 대한 증거는 없다).", 박쥐 피의 의학적 효능에 대한 증거는 없다. 따라서 글의 내용과 일치하는 보기는 '④ The belief about bat blood's medical benefits is groundless(박쥐 피의 의학적 이점에 대한 믿음은 근거가 없다).'이다.

오답해설
① 본문 초반에 드러난 것과 같이 판매를 위한 박쥐들은 '냄새가 나는 신발 상자에 담겨 있으며, 한 상자에 20마리나 담겨 있는 경우도 있고, 일부 박쥐는 질병 또는 스트레스로 인해 죽어있는 상황'으로 비인도적이며 비위생적인 판매 실태를 알 수 있다. 따라서 '사려 깊게(discreetly)' 거래된다는 것은 본문의 내용과는 거리가 멀다.
② 두 번째 문장 "the live ones crawling over those that have already succumbed to disease or stress(살아있는 것들은 이미 질병 또는 스트레스에 굴복한 박쥐들 위를 기어 다닌다)"를 통해, 살아있는 박쥐와 죽은 박쥐를 함께 판매한다는 것을 알 수 있다.

③ 세 번째 문장 "People buy them so they can drink bat blood for its purported healing properties(사람들은 치유 능력이 있다고 알려진 박쥐의 피를 마시기 위해 그것들을 산다)"를 통해, 박쥐의 피를 몸에 '바르는' 것이 아닌 '마시기' 위해 구매한다는 것을 알 수 있다.

해석

볼리비아의 시장에서 판매를 위한 박쥐를 찾는 것은 어렵지 않다. 그것들은 보통 냄새가 지독한 신발 상자에 처박혀있으며, 일부 상자에는 20마리나 되는 박쥐로 빼곡하게 차 있고, 살아있는 것들은 이미 질병 또는 스트레스에 굴복한 박쥐들 위를 기어 다닌다. 사람들은 그들이 생각하기에 – 특히 간질을 관리하는 데 도움이 되는 – 치유 능력이 있다고 알려진 박쥐의 피를 마시기 위해 그것들을 산다. "그 믿음은 우리의 사회, 주로 안데스 지역에 뿌리 깊이 박혀있다."라고 박쥐 전문가 Luis F. Aguirre는 설명한다. 그러나 박쥐의 피를 마시는 것의 의학적 이점에 대한 증거는 없다. 게다가 박쥐 사냥은 공식적으로는 불법이다. 볼리비아의 법은 적절한 허가 없이 야생 동물을 죽이거나 판매하는 것을 금지하고 있으며, 위반 행위는 최대 6년의 징역형을 받을 수 있다. 그러나 그 믿음과 사냥은 지속되고 있다.
① 볼리비아 시장에서 박쥐는 사려 깊게 거래된다.
② 오직 살아있는 박쥐만이 팔린다.
③ 사람들은 치료 효과를 기대하며 박쥐의 피를 몸에 바른다.
④ 박쥐 피의 의학적 이점에 대한 믿음은 근거가 없다.

어휘

tuck 밀어 넣다, 집어넣다
pungent (맛·냄새가) 톡 쏘는 듯한 [몹시 자극적인]
succumb 굴복하다
purported (사실이 아닐지도 모르지만) …라고 알려진
property 속성, 특성   epilepsy 간질
persist 계속되다, 지속하다   discreetly 신중하게, 사려 깊게
curative 치유력이 있는   groundless 근거 없는

결국엔 성정혜 영어 하프모의고사
기적사 DAY 16

| 01 | ① | 02 | ④ | 03 | ④ | 04 | ④ | 05 | ④ |
| 06 | ② | 07 | ① | 08 | ③ | 09 | ④ | 10 | ④ |

01 정답 ①
18 서울시

정답해설

밑줄 친 'integral'은 '완전한, 필수적인'이라는 의미이다. ① key는 형용사로 쓰일 때 '중요한, 주요한, 핵심적인, 필수적인'이라는 뜻을 나타내므로 'integral'과 의미가 가장 가깝다.

해석

윤리적 고려는 생명 공학 규제의 **필수적인** 요소이다.
① 중요한, 주요한, 핵심적인, 필수적인
② 우연한, 부차적인, 간접적인
③ 상호적인
④ 인기 있는, 유명한

어휘

ethical 윤리적인   biotechnology 생명 공학
key 중요한, 주요한, 핵심적인, 필수적인   incidental 우연한, 부차적인, 간접적인
interactive 상호적인   popular 인기 있는, 유명한

오답률 TOP 3

02 정답 ④
18 서울시

정답해설

밑줄 친 'plasticity'는 '유연성, 적응성'이라는 의미로 이와 유사한 의미를 지닌 어휘는 ④ suppleness이다.

해석

만일 언어와 관련된 뇌의 영역이 손상된다면, 그 뇌는 본래는 말하기와 관련되지 않은 뇌의 다른 부분이 손실된 세포를 보전하기 위한 한 방법으로써 그 (말하기) 기술을 배우도록 **유연성**을 사용할지도 모른다.
① 정확성
② 체계성, 조직성
③ 방해물, 장애물
④ 유순한, 유연함

어휘

plasticity 유연성, 적응성   accuracy 정확성
systemicity 체계성, 조직성   obstruction 방해물, 장애물
suppleness 유순한, 유연함

03 정답 ④
18 서울시

정답해설

서명과 계약을 요구하며 빈칸 뒷부분에는 '서면으로 하는 것을 원한다.'고 했다. 빈칸 앞부분에 부정어 'No'가 제시되었기 때문에 빈칸에는 서면과 반대되는 어휘인 ④ verbal이 오는 것이 적절하다.

해석

메피스토는 서명과 계약을 요구한다. 단지 **구두로만 하는** 계약이 진행되지는

않을 것이다. 파우스트가 언급한 대로, 악마는 모든 것을 서면으로 하는 것을 원한다.
① 진짜의, 진실된
② 필수의, 본질적인
③ 상호 간의, 상응하는
④ 구두의, 말의

어휘
signature 서명
remark 언급하다
essential 필수의, 본질적인
verbal 구두의, 말의
contract 계약
genuine 진짜의, 진실된
reciprocal 상호 간의, 상응하는

04 정답 ④
18 서울시

정답해설
A와 B는 '중고차(used car)'에 대하여 대화를 나누고 있다. A가 빈칸 이전에 '너무 비싸'고 이야기했으므로 바로 뒤의 빈칸에 적절한 것은 '④ I don't want to get ripped off(나는 바가지를 쓰고 싶지 않아).'뿐이다. 'rip off'는 '바가지를 씌우다'는 의미이며 해당 문장에서는 수동태로 'get ripped off'로 사용되고 있다.

오답해설
나머지 보기는 문맥상 적절하지 않다.

해석
A: 너는 중고차에 대해 잘 몰라, Ned. 휴! 70,000마일이야.
B: 오, 많은 마일이구나! 우리는 엔진, 문, 타이어, 모든 것을 자세히 봐야 해.
A: 너무 비싸, Ned. 나는 바가지를 쓰고 싶지 않아.
B: 너는 중고차 판매원들을 잘 지켜봐야 해.
① 그것을 사자.
② 나는 먼지를 털 거야.
③ 너는 무슨 모델을 원하니?
④ 나는 바가지를 쓰고 싶지 않아.

어휘
rip off 바가지를 씌우다

05 정답 ④
18 서울시

정답해설
④ 출제 포인트: 가목적어 it/to부정사의 명사적 용법
해당 문장에서 'find'는 불완전타동사로 사용되었는데 'it'은 가목적어이며 'difficult'는 목적격 보어이다. 따라서 'wait'은 진목적어에 해당하며 목적어에 동사원형을 사용할 수 없으므로 'wait'을 to 부정사인 'to wait'으로 수정해야 한다.

오답해설
① 출제 포인트: 현재분사 vs. 과거분사
해당 문장에서 'find'는 불완전타동사로 사용되었으며 목적어 'your tongue'과 'twisted'가 수동관계이므로 목적격 보어에 과거분사 'twisted'를 사용하는 것이 옳다.

② 출제 포인트: 기수-측정 단위명사[단수 vs. 복수]-형용사
「기수-측정단위명사-형용사」가 한정적 용법으로 사용되는 경우 「기수-측정단위명사[단수]-형용사」의 형태를 가진다. 해당 문장은 「기수-측정단위명사-형용사」가 명사 'daughter'를 수식하는 한정적 용법으로 사용되었으므로 「기수-측정단위명사[단수]-형용사」의 형태인 'six-year-old'는 옳은 표현이다.

③ 출제 포인트: 주격 관계대명사
밑줄 친 'that'은 선행사 'the amusement park'를 가지며 'that' 이하의 절에 주어가 없으므로 주격 관계대명사라는 것을 알 수 있다. 따라서 선행사 'the amusement park'를 수식해주는 주격 관계대명사 'that'은 옳은 표현이다.

해석
당신이 당신의 6살 딸에게 왜 TV에서 광고된 놀이공원에 갈 수 없는지 설명할 이유를 찾으며 당신의 혀가 꼬여 말이 잘 안되는 것을 깨닫게 될 때, 당신은 왜 우리가 기다리기가 어려운지 이해할 수 있을 것이다.

어휘
tongue 혀
amusement park 놀이공원
twist 구부리다, 꼬다, 비틀다

오답률 TOP 2
06 정답 ②
18 서울시

정답해설
② 출제 포인트: 현재분사 vs. 과거분사
밑줄 직전의 'wounds'를 수식하는 분사의 형태를 묻고 있다. 'wounds(상처)'는 'suffer(~을 겪다)'와의 관계가 수동이므로 'suffering'은 과거분사인 'suffered'가 되어야 한다. '~ wounds (which were) suffered ~'로 볼 수도 있다.

오답해설
① 출제 포인트: 부정관사 a의 쓰임
단수가산명사 'foreman'을 수식해주므로 부정관사 'a'의 쓰임은 적절하다. 하나의 인물이 두 가지 직업을 가질 때는 'a/an A and B'와 같이 보통은 관사를 생략하여 한 번 사용하는 것이 일반적이나, 화자의 필자가 주어의 두 가지 직업을 보다 분명히 구분해줄 경우에는 관사를 두 번 사용하기도 한다.

③ 출제 포인트: 동사 vs. 준동사
해당 문장에서 접속사로 쓰인 'after' 이하의 문장에서 주어는 'shards'이고, 'penetrated'가 동사로 알맞게 사용되었다.

④ 출제 포인트: 접속사가 살아있는 분사구문/현재분사 vs. 과거분사
'while being loaded into a hopper'는 접속사 'while'이 생략되지 않은 분사구문이다. 해당 분사구문에서 생략된 주어 'it(= a 100-1b ice block)'과 'load(~을 싣다)'는 수동관계이므로 'being loaded'는 옳은 표현이다. 또한 'while ~ing(~하는 동안에)'라는 구문 표현으로도 볼 수 있다.

해석
작은 회사의 소유자이면서 건설 현장 감독이었던 Lewis Alfred Ellison은 개저선에 싣는 동안에 떨어진 100파운드의 얼음덩어리로부터 나온 파편 조각이 그의 복부를 관통한 후에 겪게 된 내부의 상처들을 치료하는 수술 후 1916년에 죽었다.

어휘
foreman 현장 주임, 감독
shard 파편
abdomen 복부, 배
hopper 개저선
wound 부상
penetrate 관통하다
load A into B A를 B에 싣다

오답률 TOP 1
07 정답 ①
18 서울시

정답해설

① **출제 포인트: 가정법 미래**
「If+주어+should+동사원형 ~, 주어+will/would+동사원형 ~.」은 가정법 미래를 나타내는 표현이다. 해당 문장은 가정법 미래를 나타내는 표현으로 「If+주어+should+동사원형 ~, 주어+would+동사원형 ~.」을 사용하였으므로 옳은 문장이다.

오답해설

② **출제 포인트: 최상급 대용표현**
「비교급+than+any other+단수명사」는 비교급을 이용한 최상급 대용표현이다. 해당 문장은 최상급 대용표현으로 「비교급+than+any other」를 사용하였으나 뒤에 복수형태의 명사(구) 'baseball players'를 사용하였으므로 틀린 문장이다. 따라서 'baseball players'를 단수형태인 'baseball player'로 수정해야 한다. 또한 '~ than any other baseball players ~'를 '~ than the other baseball players ~'로 수정해도 옳은 문장이 된다.

③ **출제 포인트: no sooner 구문**
「Hardly+had+주어+과거분사 ~ when/before+주어+과거시제 동사 ~.」는 no sooner 구문(~하자마자 …하다)에 해당한다. 해당 문장은 「Hardly+had+주어+과거분사 ~ before+주어+과거시제 동사 ~.」를 사용하였으나 'had'의 자리에 'has'를 사용하였으므로 틀린 문장이다. 따라서 'has'를 'had'로 수정해야 한다.

④ **출제 포인트: 사역동사의 수동태**
사역동사 make는 「make+목적어+목적격 보어[원형부정사]」의 형태를 가지며 수동태의 경우 「목적어+be made+목적격 보어[to부정사]」의 형태를 가진다. 해당 문장은 사역동사 'make'의 현재완료 수동태 'have been made'를 사용하였으나 목적격 보어에 원형부정사 'come'을 사용하였으므로 틀린 문장이다. 따라서 'come'을 to부정사 'to come'으로 수정해야 한다.

해석

① 만일 그 물건이 내일까지 배달되지 않는다면, 그들은 이것에 대하여 불평할 것이다.
② 그는 반에서 어떤 다른 야구 선수보다 더 기술적이었다.
③ 그 바이올리니스트가 그의 연주를 끝내자마자 청중들은 일어나서 박수를 쳤다.
④ 제빵업자들은 밀 소비 홍보를 요구하면서 나서게 되었다.

08 정답 ③
18 서울시

정답해설

주어진 지문은 사회학자인 Mauss가 '종교적 유대 가정에서 자랐음에도 불구하고 그 종교를 배척했다'는 서술로 이어진다. 그리고 삼촌의 지도로 철학을 공부한 'Marcel Mauss'에 대해 설명하는 내용이다. ③ He had a doctrinaire faith (그는 교조적인 신념을 가지고 있다)의 경우 "Mauss had reacted against the Jewish faith"(Mauss는 유대적 신앙에 반하는 반응을 보였다) 내용과는 정반대에 해당된다. 따라서 정답은 '③ He had a doctrinaire faith(그는 교조적인 신념을 가지고 있었다).'이다.

오답해설

① 'he grew up within a close-knit, pious, and orthodox Jewish family(그는 긴말하게 맺어진, 독실한 정통파 유대인 가족 내에서 성장했다.)'라는 본문 전반부의 내용과 일치한다.
② Emile Durkheim이 그의 삼촌이었고 본문의 He studied philosophy under Durkheim's supervision.(그는 Durkheim의 감독 하에서 철학을 공부했다.)'라는 것과 일치하는 보기이다.
④ 'Mauss was initially a philosopher.(Mauss는 처음에는 철학자였다.)'라는 본문 후반부의 내용으로 그는 철학을 공부한 사회학자라는 것을 알 수 있다. 따라서 본문과 일치한다.

해석

프랑스 사회학자인 Marcel Mauss(1872-1950)는 Lorraine의 Epinal(Vosges)에서 태어났고, 긴밀하게 맺어진, 독실한 정통파 유대인 가족 내에서 성장했다. Emile Durkheim이 그의 삼촌이었다. 18세 무렵, Mauss는 유대적 신앙에 반하는 반응을 보였다; 그는 결코 종교적 인물이 아니었다. 그는 Bordeaux에서 Durkheim의 감독 하에서 철학을 공부했다; Durkheim은 그의 조카를 이끄는 데 수고를 아끼지 않았고 심지어 Mauss에게 가장 유용할 강의 주제도 선정해줬다. 따라서 Mauss는 처음에는 철학자였고(대부분의 초기 Durkheim 학파들처럼), 철학에 대한 그의 이해는 그가 항상 최고의 존경을 유지했던 Durkheim에게 직접 영향을 받았다.

① 그는 유대인 배경을 가지고 있다.
② 그는 그의 삼촌에 의해 감독을 받았다.
③ 그는 교조적인 신념을 가지고 있었다.
④ 그는 철학 배경을 가진 사회학자였다.

어휘

sociologist 사회학자   pious 독실한
orthodox 정통파의   religious 종교적인, 독실한
supervision 감독   conception 개념
retain 유지하다   doctrinaire 교조적인
take trouble 수고하다, 수고를 아끼지 않다

09 정답 ④
18 서울시

정답해설

첫 번째 제시되어질 문장으로는 가장 일반적인 내용이면서 주제인 '벌목'을 제시하는 ⓓ가 제일 앞에 제시되어야 적합하다. 이후에 고대의 몇몇 국가를 언급한 후에 다시 ⓐ에서 현재와의 비교를 언급하고 있다. 이후에 200만 에이커의 벌목을 제시하고 있으며 이후에 이어질 문단은 이 엄청난 양의 벌목이 미치는 영향을 서술한 ⓒ가 적합하다. ⓒ에서 종이를 더욱더 많이 사용하는 'industrialized countries'(선진국들)를 언급하고 있고, 이후에 다시 ⓑ에서 "these countries" 즉, ⓒ에서 언급된 선진국들을 지칭하면서 벌목 요구량이 충족되지 못하고 있음을 밝히므로 마지막 문단은 ⓑ가 적합하다. 따라서 정답은 ④ ⓓ-ⓐ-ⓒ-ⓑ에 해당된다.

오답해설

① 첫 번째 제시되어질 문장으로 앞서 언급된 것에 대한 역접을 나타내는 'However'가 포함된 ⓐ는 적합하지 않다.
③ ⓑ가 첫 번째로 제시되는 경우 ⓑ에서 지칭하는 'these countries'를 알 수 없으므로 첫 문단으로 ⓑ는 적절하지 않다.

해석

ⓓ 사람들이 벌목을 하는 데는 새로울 것이 없다. 고대에, 그리스, 이탈리아, 영국은 숲으로 덮여있었다. 수 세기 동안, 그 숲들은 점차적으로 벌목되었다. 지금은 남은 것이 거의 없다.
ⓐ 그러나 오늘날 나무는 훨씬 더 빨리 베어지고 있다. 매년, 대략 200만 에이커의 숲이 베어진다. 이것은 영국 전체의 면적보다 더 크다.
ⓒ 벌목하는 중요한 이유들이 있는 반면, 지구상의 생명체에 위험한 영향 또한 있다. 현재 삼림파괴의 주요 원인은 전 세계적인 목재에 대한 수요이다. 선진국에서는, 사람들이 종이를 위해 점점 더 많은 나무를 사용하고 있다.

ⓑ 이 국가들에서는 수요를 충족시킬 만큼 충분한 나무가 없다. 따라서 목재 회사들은 아시아, 아프리카, 남아메리카, 그리고 심지어 시베리아의 숲에서 나무를 가지고 오기 시작했다.

어휘

rapidly 빠르게
cut down 베다
destruction 파괴
be covered with 덮여있다
satisfy 만족하다
consequence 결과
Industrialized country 선진국

10 정답 ④
18 서울시

정답해설

본문 후반부 "Private agencies can be found on the Internet. They handle domestic and international adoption(사설 기관들은 인터넷에서 찾을 수 있다. 그 기관들은 국내외 입양을 다룬다)."으로 보아 선택지 '④ Private agencies can be contacted for international adoption(사설 기관들은 국제 입양을 위해 연락 가능하다.)'은 명확하게 본문과 일치하는 내용인 것을 알 수 있다. 따라서 정답은 ④이다.

오답해설

① 입양기관의 우위에 대해서 언급되지 않았다.
② 위탁 양육 가정에서의 입양을 위해 많은 돈을 내야 한다는 언급은 없다.
③ 본문에서 'Public agencies generally handle older children, children with mental or physical disabilities, or children who may have been abused or neglected(공공 기관들은 보통 어느 정도 나이가 있는 아이들, 정신적 신체적 장애가 있는 아이들, 혹은 학대나 방치당했던 아이들을 주로 다룬다).'라고 하며 공공 기관을 통해 '도움이 필요한 아이들(children in need)'이 입양이 가능하다고 언급되어 있으므로 해당 내용은 옳지 않다.

해석

아이를 입양하기를 원하는 가정은 우선 입양기관을 선택해야 한다. 미국에서는 입양을 도와주는 두 가지 종류의 기관이 있다. 공공 기관들은 보통 어느 정도 나이가 있는 아이들, 정신적 신체적 장애가 있는 아이들, 혹은 학대나 방치당했던 아이들을 주로 다룬다. 입양 희망 부모들은 공공 기관에서 아이를 입양할 때 보통 요금을 지불하지 않는다. 위탁 양육, 즉 일시적인 형태의 입양도 공공 기관을 통해 가능하다. 사설 기관들은 인터넷에서 찾을 수 있다. 그 기관들은 국내외 입양을 다룬다.
① 공공 입양기관들이 사설 기관들보다 더 낫다.
② 부모들은 위탁 양육 가정으로부터 아이를 입양하는데 큰 비용을 지불한다.
③ 도움이 필요한 아이들은 공공 기관을 통해 입양이 불가능하다.
④ 사설 기관들은 국제 입양을 위해 연락 가능하다.

어휘

adopt 입양하다
adoption agency 입양기관
disability 장애
neglect 무시하다, 방임하다
fee 요금
domestic 국내의
select 선택하다
assist 도와주다
abuse 학대하다
prospective 장래의
foster 아이를 맡아 기르다

결국엔 성정혜 영어 하프모의고사
기적사 DAY 17

| 01 | ② | 02 | ① | 03 | ③ | 04 | ① | 05 | ④ |
| 06 | ② | 07 | ③ | 08 | ④ | 09 | ③ | 10 | ② |

오답률 TOP 2

01 정답 ②

정답해설

밑줄 친 'vigilant'는 '경계하는, 방심하지 않는'의 뜻으로 ② alert와 의미가 가장 가깝다.

해석

여전히, 태평양 지역의 대다수가 풍랑이 거센 바다를 **경계하는** 것은 분명하다.
① 불확실한
② 방심하지 않는, 기민한
③ 인기 있는, 유명한
④ 가치 없는

어휘

vigilant 경계하는, 방심하지 않는
unsure 불확실한
popular 인기 있는, 유명한
stormy 폭풍우의, 사나운 날씨의
alert 방심하지 않는, 기민한
null 가치 없는

02 정답 ①

정답해설

밑줄 친 'violation'은 '위반, 침해'의 뜻으로 ① infringement와 의미가 가장 가깝다.

해석

시행법 **위반**에도 불구하고, 현실적으로, EU는 자신의 패권주의적 야심을 기꺼이 포기할 준비가 된 것처럼 보이지 않는다.
① 위반, 위배
② 약점이 있음, 취약성
③ 유순한, 유연함
④ 생존력, 실행 가능성

어휘

violation 위반, 침해
abandon 포기하다, 버리다
ambition 야심
vulnerability 약점이 있음, 취약성
viability 생존력, 실행 가능성
willingly 기꺼이
hegemonistic 패권주의의
infringement 위반, 위배
suppleness 유순함, 유연함

03 정답 ③

정답해설

주어진 지문에서 'due to contamination and disease' 즉, '오염과 질병' 때문이라고 했으므로 빈칸에 들어갈 단어로 가장 적절한 것은 '위험한, 불안한'의 의미를 지닌 ③ unsafe이다.

해석

세계 도처의 많은 나라에서, 수돗물은 오염과 질병 때문에 마시기 **위험하다**.
① 신중한, 조심스러운, 주의를 기울이는
② 구두의, 말의
③ 위험한, 불안한
④ 모르는, 무의식적인

어휘

cautious 신중한, 조심스러운, 주의를 기울이는
contamination 오염   verbal 구두의, 말의
unsafe 위험한, 불안한   unwitting 모르는, 무의식적인

04 정답 ①

정답해설

B가 감기에 걸려 병원을 방문한 것에 관한 대화이다. B는 병원에서 간단한 진찰을 받았지만 B에게 50달러를 청구해 (A) '바가지(a rip-off)'였다고 말한다. 이에 A가 화났겠다고 말하며 '처방전 없이 살 수 있는 약(over-the-counter medicine)'을 먹었는지 묻고 효과가 있는지 묻는다. B는 약국에서 해열제를 먹었는데 효과는 미비했지만 적어도 (B) '부작용(side effect)'은 없었다고 말한다.

오답해설

② (B) A가 B에게 해열제 효과가 있었는지 묻자 B가 적어도 '비난의 목소리(hue and cry)'가 없었다고 말하는 것은 문맥상 부자연스럽다.
③ (A) B가 감기 때문에 병원에 방문했지만 '유력한 경쟁 상대(a dark horse)'였다면서 병원이 간단한 진료에 50달러를 청구한다는 것은 빈칸 (A)에 들어갈 말로 대화의 흐름상 적절하지 않다.
④ (A) B가 병원에 방문했지만 '근거 없는 짐작(a shot in the dark)'이었다며 병원이 B에게 50달러를 청구했다고 얘기한 것은 맥락상 적합하지 않다. (B) B는 해열제를 복용한 후 효과는 잘 모르겠으나 최소한 '전혀 관계없는 것(chalk and cheese)'은 없었다고 말하는 것은 빈칸에 들어갈 말로 어색하다.

해석

A: 너 감기가 더 심해지는 것으로 보여.
B: 병원에 가봤는데 그저 (A) 바가지를 씌웠어. 병원이 간단한 진료에도 50달러를 청구했어.
A: 너 되게 화났었겠다. 처방전 없이 살 수 있는 약은 뭐라도 먹었어?
B: 아, 약국에 가서 해열제를 좀 먹었어.
A: 너한테 효과가 있었어?
B: 음, 잘 모르겠어. 그런데 최소한 (B) 부작용은 없었어.
① (A) 바가지 (B) 부작용
② (A) 바가지 (B) 비난의 목소리
③ (A) 유력한 경쟁 상대 (B) 부작용
④ (A) 근거 없는 짐작 (B) 전혀 관계없는 것

어휘

over-the-counter 처방전 없이 살 수 있는
a rip-off 바가지   side effect 부작용
hue and cry 비난의 목소리   a dark horse 유력한 경쟁 상대
a shot in the dark 근거 없는 짐작
chalk and cheese 전혀 관계없는 것

05 정답 ④

정답해설

④ **출제 포인트: 전치사 vs. 접속사**
'during'은 전치사로 뒤에 명사(구)가 오며 절이 올 수 없다. 해당 문장은 'during' 뒤에 절 'you don't want to risk a step into unknown territory'가 왔으므로 틀린 문장이다. 따라서 'during'을 의미상 '~할 때'를 나타내는 접속사 'as' 또는 'when'으로 수정해야 한다.

오답해설

① **출제 포인트: lest(접속사)+주어+(should)+동사원형**
접속사 'lest'가 '~하면 안 되므로, ~하지 않도록'을 뜻하는 경우 뒤따라오는 절은 '(should)+동사원형'의 형태를 가지며 부정부사 'not' 또는 'never'를 사용하지 않는다. 해당 문장은 해석상 '~하면 안 되므로'가 자연스러우므로 'lest' 뒤에 오는 절에 '(should)+동사원형'을 사용하였고, 부정부사 'not' 또는 'never'를 사용하지 않았으므로 옳은 문장이다.

② **출제 포인트: 가목적어 it/to부정사의 명사적 용법**
불완전타동사 'make'의 목적어에 해당하는 to부정사구 'to abandon ~ health creating'이 긴 경우에 해당하므로 가목적어 'it'을 사용하였고 to부정사구 'to abandon ~ health creating'을 문미로 이동하였으므로 옳은 문장이다.

③ **출제 포인트: 주격 관계대명사**
앞에 선행사 'those'가 있으며 뒤따라오는 절의 주어가 없으므로 밑줄 친 'that'은 주격 관계대명사로 사용되었다는 것을 알 수 있다. 또한 선행사 'those'는 지시대명사로 가리키는 대상은 'behaviors'이다.

해석

우리가 혼돈 속에서 살지 않기 위해서 안정적인 패턴이 필요하다; 그러나 그것은 굳어버린 행동, 심지어는 더 이상 쓸모도 없고, 건설적이지도 않으며, 건강한 상태를 만들어 내지도 않는 행동마저도 버리는 것을 어렵게 만든다. 그리고 두려움은 알려지지 않은 영역으로 위험을 무릅쓰고 발걸음을 내딛고 싶지 않을 때, 여러분이 변하는 것을 막아 줄 수도 있다.

어휘

stable 안정된, 안정적인   chaos 혼돈, 혼란
entrench 단단히 자리 잡게 하다   constructive 건설적인
unknown 알려지지 않은, 무명의   territory 영역, 영토, 지역

06 정답 ②

정답해설

② **출제 포인트: 동사 vs. 준동사**
'that' 앞에 선행사 'seabird'가 있으며 주격 관계대명사 'that'이 이끄는 절의 동사가 없으므로 밑줄 친 'taking'은 본래 동사임을 알 수 있다. 따라서 현재분사 'taking'을 문맥에 맞게 과거시제 동사 'took'으로 수정해야 한다.

오답해설

① **출제 포인트: 비교 대상 일치**
해당 문장은 비교급이 사용되었으며 비교 대상이 단수형인 'story'이므로 'than' 뒤에 단수형태 대명사 'that'을 사용하는 것이 옳다.

③ **출제 포인트: 현재분사 vs. 과거분사**
with 분사구문이 쓰인 문장이며 수식하는 대상 'island populations'와 수동관계이므로 과거분사 'destroyed'를 사용하는 것이 옳다.

④ **출제 포인트: 형용사로 고착된 분사**
'gone'은 과거분사 형태의 형용사로 '사라진'을 뜻한다. 해당 문제를 'going(현재분사) vs. gone(과거분사)'의 구별 문제로 오해하지 않도록 주의해야 한다.

해석

어떤 이야기가 북쪽 대양에서 생태 상 펭귄의 위치를 차지했던 흑백의 대형 바닷새인 큰바다쇠오리의 이야기보다 더 가혹할 수 있을까? 그 새의 이야기는 그리스 비극처럼 융성하고 쇠퇴하는데, 거의 모두가 사라질 때까지 섬의 개체군은 인간에 의해 잔인하게 죽임을 당했다.

어휘

harsh 가혹한, 냉혹한
ecological 생태계의
gone 사라진, 떠난, 끝난
seabird 바닷새
population 개체군, 인구

07 정답 ③

정답해설

③ 출제 포인트: 사역동사의 수동태

사역동사 'make'를 수동태로 사용하는 경우 목적격 보어로 쓰인 원형부정사는 to부정사로 바꾸어 사용해야 한다. 해당 문장은 사역동사 'make'의 수동태를 사용하였으며 목적격 보어에 to부정사인 'to wait'을 사용하였으므로 옳은 문장이다.

오답해설

① 출제 포인트: 가정법 미래

가정법 미래는 「If+주어+should+동사원형 ~, 주어+will/would+동사원형 ~.」로 나타낼 수 있다. 해당 문장은 가정법 미래 「If+주어+should+동사원형 ~, 주어+will/would+동사원형 ~.」을 사용하였으나 'will/would+동사원형' 자리에 현재시제 동사 'get'을 사용하였으므로 틀린 문장이다. 따라서 'get'을 'will get' 또는 'would get'으로 수정해야 한다.

② 출제 포인트: 최상급 대용표현

「비교급+than+any other+명사」는 최상급 대용표현으로 이때 명사는 단수형태를 사용한다. 해당 문장은 「비교급+than+any other+명사」를 사용하였으나 명사에 복수형태인 'things'를 사용하였으므로 틀린 문장이다. 따라서 'things'를 단수형태인 'thing'으로 수정해야 한다. 또한 '~more than any other things.'를 '~ more than (all) the other things'로 수정해도 옳은 문장이 된다.

④ 출제 포인트: no sooner 구문

「주어+had+hardly+과거분사 ~, when/before+주어+과거시제 동사 ~.」는 no sooner 구문으로 '~하자마자 ~했다'를 뜻한다. 이때 'hardly'를 문두로 이동하는 경우 「Hardly+had+주어+과거분사 ~, when/before+주어+과거시제 동사 ~.」의 구조가 된다. 해당 문장은 「Hardly+had+주어+과거분사 ~, when+주어+과거시제 동사 ~.」를 사용하였으나 「had+주어」자리에 「주어+had」인 'the demonstration had'를 사용하였으므로 틀린 문장이다. 따라서 'the demonstration had'를 'had the demonstration'으로 수정해야 한다. 다만 해당 문장에서 'move'는 완전자동사, 'in'은 부사로 옳게 사용되었다. 'in'을 전치사로 오해하지 않도록 유의해야한다.

해석

① 여행을 가지 않기로 결정하면, 전액 환불받을 것입니다.
② 나는 항상 행복이 다른 어떤 것보다 중요하다고 믿어왔다.
③ 위원회가 결정을 내리는 동안 사람들은 밖에서 기다리게 되었다.
④ 시위가 시작되자마자 문제가 발생하였고 경찰들은 사람들을 체포하기 위해 출동했다.

오답률 TOP 1

08 정답 ④

정답해설

본문에 따르면 'Marcel Mauss가 학술지 *Annie sociologique*를 출판하는 조직을 담당하였을 당시, 조직 구성원들 간의 협력과 아이디어 공유가 활발하게 이루어졌음'을 알 수 있다. 본문 중반 "practically all of Mauss' early work was written in conjunction with another(실질적으로 Mauss의 모든 초기 작품은 다른 사람과 함께 쓰였다)."를 통해 '초기 Marcel Mauss의 작품이 공저였음'을 밝히고 있으므로, 초기 시기에 그의 작품을 통해 발전된 이론에 미친 그의 기여도가 정확하게 얼마나 될지는 미지수임을 알 수 있다. 즉, 'Mauss가 미친 기여를 구체적으로 특정할 수 없는 상황'이므로, 빈칸에 가장 적절한 표현은 '④ impossible to distinguish(구별하는 것이 불가능한)'이다.

오답해설

① 본문에서 주장하는 바와 반대되는 표현이므로 빈칸에 적절하지 않다. 나머지 보기는 문맥상 어색하므로 오답이다.

해석

Marcel Mauss의 영향력이 가장 강력했을 시기는 아마도 교사였을 때이나, 그가 가르쳤던 수업과 그가 그것들을 가르친 방식은 다른 사업 - *Annie sociologique*의 출판 - 에의 그의 참여 측면에서만 이해될 수 있을 것이다. 이 학술지는 1898년 Emile Durkheim에 의해 창간되었고 프랑스 사회학으로 알려진 교리의 선포에 전념하였다. 초기부터 Mauss는 이 학술지를 출판하는 유대가 긴밀한 조직의 필수 일원이었으며, Durkheim이 사망한 후, 책임자로서 그의 뒤를 이은 것이 바로 Mauss였다. 이 조직 구성원들 사이의 긴밀한 협력에 대한 지표로서, 실질적으로 Mauss의 모든 초기 작품은 다른 사람과 함께 쓰였다는 것을 알아둘 가치가 있다. 이 조직의 구성원 간 긴밀한 협동과 그들의 매우 많은 아이디어 공유 때문에 이 초기 시기에 이론의 발전에 Mauss가 미친 특정한 기여를 <u>구별하는 것은 불가능하다</u>.

① 정확히 기술하기 쉬운
② 무시하기 어려운
③ 확인할 필요가 있는
④ 구별하는 것이 불가능한

어휘

enterprise 사업, 기업
promulgation 공표, 선포
integral 필수의
in conjunction with …와 함께
pinpoint 정확히 기술[묘사]하다
distinguish 구별하다, 구분하다
be dedicated to …에 전념하다
doctrine 교리, 주의, 원칙
succeed 뒤를 잇다, 승계하다
contribution 기여
disregard 무시하다

오답률 TOP 3

09 정답 ③

정답해설

본문은 '삼림파괴(deforestation)를 방지할 수 있는 새로운 방안'에 대한 연구 결과를 소개하는 글이다. 본문 첫 문장 "A new study finds that simply paying landowners in the developing world not to cut down trees can significantly reduce carbon in the atmosphere(새로운 연구는 단순히 개발도상국의 토지 소유주들에게 나무를 자르지 않도록 돈을 지불하는 것이 대기 중의 탄소를 상당히 줄일 수 있다는 것을 밝힌다)."에 따르면, '개발도상국의 토지 소유주들에게 금전적 지원을 하는 방안'이 효과적이라는 것을 알 수 있다. 이후 빈칸 문장에서는 실제로 우간다에서 실시되었던 실험에 대해 구체적으로 언급하고 있으므로, 토지 소유주들에게 '재정적인 지원'이 투입되었음을 시사하는 표현이 들어가야 적절하다. 따라서 빈칸에 가장 적절한 보기는 '③ offering small financial incentives to landowners(토지 소유주들에게 적은 금액의 재정적 지원금을 제공하는 것)'이다.

오답해설
① 본문에서 나무를 심는 것에 대한 내용은 언급되지 않으므로 오답이다.
② 본문에서 토지 소유주들이 나무를 자르는 이유로 '목재 판매'가 언급되지 않았으며, 연구의 골자는 '금전적 지원 여부에 따른 토지 소유주들의 벌목 여부'이므로 단순히 토지 소유주들을 설득했다는 내용은 글의 흐름상 자연스럽지 않다.
④ 본문에 따르면, 토지 소유주들이 나무를 자르지 않는 이유는 금전적 지원을 받았기 때문이며, 기후변화에 대한 인식 변화에 따른 것이 아니므로 빈칸에 적절하지 않다.

해석
새로운 연구는 단순히 개발도상국의 토지 소유주들에게 나무를 자르지 않도록 돈을 지불하는 것이 대기 중의 탄소를 상당히 줄일 수 있다는 것을 밝힌다. 그것은 또한 파리 협정의 목표와 같은 목적을 달성하는 데 도움이 되는 매우 비용 효율적인 방법이다. 학술지 *Science*에 오늘 게재된 그 연구는, 우간다에서 토지 소유주들에게 적은 금액의 재정적 지원금을 제공하는 것이 삼림 벌채를 절반으로 줄인다는 것을 알아냈다. 동원된 자금의 액수가 상당히 적기 때문에, 미국에서 실시되는 많은 에너지 효율 프로그램들보다 소비된 1달러당 10에서 50배 더 효과적인 것으로 추정되었다. Innovations for Poverty Action의 협회장 Annie Duflo는 이 연구가 개발도상국에서의 향후 보호 프로그램들을 알릴 단서가 될 것이라고 말했다. "이와 같은 좋은 과학이 우리가 어떻게 기후변화에 맞서 싸워야 할지 그리고 어떻게 위기에 처한 서식지를 보호해야 하는지에 대해 이해할 수 있게 도와주며, 또한 빈곤한 농부들을 도와줄 수 있다."
① 더 많은 나무를 심도록 지역 주민들에게 돈을 지불하는 것
② 토지 소유주들이 목재 거래를 중지하도록 설득하는 것
③ 토지 소유주들에게 적은 금액의 재정적 지원금을 제공하는 것
④ 토지 소유주들 사이에서 기후변화에 대한 인식을 고치시키는 것

어휘
cost-effective 비용 효율적인　　accord 협정
deforestation 삼림 벌채[파괴]　　involve 관련[연루]시키다
efficiency 효율성　　inform 알리다, 통지하다
conservation 보존, 보호
combat (방지하기 위해) 싸우다, (좋지 않은 일의 발생이나 악화를) 방지하다
incentive 장려금, 지원금　　awareness 인식

10 정답 ②

정답해설
본문은 '25년 만에 극적으로 재회한 일란성 쌍둥이 Samantha Futerman과 Anais Bordier의 놀라운 이야기'를 소개하고 있다. 본문 중반 "Futerman, who grew up in a large family in Los Angeles,(Los Angeles의 대가족에서 자란 Futerman)"을 통해 'Futerman은 미국의 Los Angeles에서 자란 것'을 알 수 있고, "the more introspective Bordier who grew up in Paris(Paris에서 자란 더 내성적인 Bordier는)"을 통해 'Bordier는 프랑스의 Paris에서 자란 것'을 알 수 있다. 따라서 '② They were raised in the same country but in different cities(그들은 같은 국가의 다른 도시에서 자랐다).'는 글의 내용과 일치하지 않는다.

오답해설
① 본문 첫 문장 "identical twins who were separated at birth then found each other after 25 years(태어나자마자 헤어져 25년 후 서로를 찾아낸 일란성 쌍둥이)"에서 25년 만에 서로를 찾았다는 것을 알 수 있고, 마지막 문장 "The two, who did not know of the other's existence(서로의 존재를 모르고 있었던 두 사람)"에서 '서로의 존재를 전혀 모르고 있었다'는 것을 알 수 있다. 따라서 글의 내용과 일치한다.
③ 본문 중반에서 'Futerman은 대가족에서 자랐고, Bordier는 외동딸로 자랐음'을 언급하고 있으므로, Futerman의 가족 구성원의 수가 Bordier의 가족 구성원의 수보다 더 많았다는 것을 알 수 있다.
④ 본문에 따르면, '대가족 사이에서 자란 Futerman은 외향적이며, 외동으로 자란 Bordier는 내성적'이라는 것을 알 수 있다. 즉, 일란성 쌍둥이라 하더라도 자라온 환경에 의해 성격이 바뀐다는 것을 시사하고 있으므로, 글의 내용과 일치한다.

해석
몇 년 전 태어나자마자 헤어져 25년 후 서로를 찾아낸 일란성 쌍둥이인 Samantha Futerman과 Anais Bordier의 놀라운 이야기가 헤드라인을 장식했다. 그들은 1987년 대한민국에서 태어나 출생 직후 각기 다른 가족에게 입양되었다. Los Angeles의 대가족에서 자란 Futerman은 외향적이고 그녀의 삶이 사랑과 즐거움으로 가득 차 있었기 때문에 항상 행복함을 느꼈던 반면, Paris에서 외동딸로 자란 더 내성적인 Bordier는 더 많이 외로움을 느꼈고, 친구들이 백인 부모와 왜 다르게 생겼냐며 놀릴 때 종종 상처를 받았다. 서로의 존재를 모르고 있었던 두 사람은 2013년 소셜네트워크 서비스를 통해 극적으로 서로를 발견했으며 서로를 즉시 그들의 인생으로 받아들였다.
① Samantha Futerman은 쌍둥이 자매가 있다는 것을 약 25년 동안 모르고 있었다.
② 그들은 같은 국가의 다른 도시에서 자랐다.
③ Futerman의 가족의 수는 Bordier보다 더 많았다.
④ 이야기에 근거하면, 성격은 환경에 의해 결정된다는 결론이 내려질 수 있다.

어휘
outgoing 외향적인, 사교적인　　introspective 내성적인
Caucasian 백인　　embrace 받아들이다, 수용하다

결국엔 성정혜 영어 하프모의고사
기적사 DAY 18

| 01 | ② | 02 | ② | 03 | ③ | 04 | ② | 05 | ① |
| 06 | ① | 07 | ④ | 08 | ④ | 09 | ④ | 10 | ① |

오답률 TOP 1

01 정답 ②

정답해설

밑줄 친 'raucous'는 '시끄러운, 소란스러운'의 뜻으로 ② uproarious와 의미가 가장 가깝다.

해석

그것은 국내의 IT회사들과 함께 아마 **소란스러운** 난투에 직면하고 있다.
① 상호적인
② 시끄러운, 소란
③ 타는 듯한, 현란한
④ 확장된

어휘

tussle 난투, 몸싸움 raucous 시끄러운, 소란스러운
interactive 상호적인 uproarious 시끄러운, 소란
flamboyant 타는 듯한, 현란한 extended 확장된

02 정답 ②

정답해설

밑줄 친 'vulnerability'는 '상처받기 쉬움, 취약함'의 뜻으로 ② weakness와 의미가 가장 가깝다.

해석

그들이 공통으로 가지고 있었고 마음속에 명심하고 있던 다른 한 가지는, 그들은 **취약함**을 완전히 포용했다.
① 위반, 침해
② 약함, 약점
③ 방해물, 장애물
④ 생존력, 실행 가능성

어휘

embrace 포용하다 vulnerability 상처받기 쉬움, 취약함
infringement 위반, 침해 weakness 약함, 약점
obstruction 방해물, 장애물 viability 생존력, 실행 가능성

03 정답 ③

정답해설

주어진 지문에서 계절이나 날씨에 관계없이 온도가 유지된다고 하였으므로 빈칸에는 '일정한, 지속적인, 불변의'의 의미를 가지고 있는 ③ constant가 가장 적절하다.

해석

그 터널 안의 온도는 계절이나 날씨에 관계없이 **일정한** 수준으로 유지된다.
① 취약한
② 상호 간의, 상응하는
③ 불변의, 지속적인
④ 화려한, 멋진

어휘

regardless of ~에 관계없이 vulnerable 취약한
reciprocal 상호 간의, 상응하는 constant 일정한, 지속적인, 불변의
splendid 화려한, 멋진

04 정답 ②

정답해설

A는 B가 토론 대회에서 우승한 것을 축하해주고 있다. B는 A와의 대화에서 토론 대회에서 우승한 후 상대 팀이 강력한 반박 근거들이 있어 (A) '공격을 받았다(under fire)'라고 한다. 그리고 A가 '어떻게 극복했냐'고 묻자 B는 (B) '침착하게(cool as a cucumber)' 있으려고 노력했다고 이야기한다.

오답해설

① (B) 토론 대회에서 우승한 B에게 A가 어떻게 상대 팀의 공격을 극복했는지 질문하자 '패배를 인정하지 않고 오기를 부렸다(sour grapes)'라고 답변하는 것은 문맥상 부자연스럽다.
③ (A) B는 상대 팀이 강력한 반박 근거들을 갖고 있어 자신이 '간단히 말했다(in a nutshell)'라고 한다. 이는 대화의 흐름상 빈칸에 들어갈 말로 적절하지 않다.
④ (A) B는 상대 팀이 가진 강력한 반박 근거들 때문에 자신이 '분쟁의 화두(an apple of discord)'였다고 하는 것은 맥락상 어색하다. (B) 상대방의 공격을 어떻게 극복했는지 묻는 A의 질문에 자신이 '곤경에 빠진(behind the eight ball)' 채 있으려고 했다는 것은 빈칸에 들어갈 말로 적합하지 않다.

해석

A: 난 네가 토론 대회에 나갔다는 소식을 들었어! 어떻게 됐어?
B: 네 말이 맞아! 사실은 나 운이 굉장히 좋았어 왜냐면 우승했거든!
A: 우와, 축하해! 네가 내 친구라는 사실이 자랑스러워!
B: 고마워. 나는 상대 팀이 강력한 반박 근거들을 가져서 (A) 공격을 받았어.
A: 너 어떻게 극복했어?
B: 나는 (B) 침착하게 있으려고 노력했어.

	(A)	(B)
①	공격을 받다	패배를 인정하지 않고 오기를 부리다
②	공격을 받다	침착한
③	간단히 말하자면	침착한
④	분쟁의 화두	곤경에 빠진

어휘

under fire 공격을 받다
sour grapes 패배를 인정하지 않고 오기를 부리다
cool as a cucumber 침착한 in a nutshell 간단히 말하자면
an apple of discord 분쟁의 화두 behind the eight ball 곤경에 빠진

05 정답 ①

정답해설

① **출제 포인트: 기수-측정단위명사[단수 vs. 복수]-형용사**
「기수-측정단위명사-형용사」가 한정적 용법으로 사용되는 경우 「기수-측정단위명사[단수]-형용사」의 형태를 가진다. 해당 문장은 「기수-측정단위명사-형용사」가 명사 'son'을 수식하는 한정적 용법으로 사용되었으므로 「기수-측정단위명사[단수]-형용사」의 형태인 'five-year-old'를 사용하는 것이 옳다. 따라서 'years'를 'year'로 수정해야 한다.

> 오답해설

② **출제 포인트: few vs. little**
뒤에 오는 명사가 복수형태인 'letters'이므로 수를 나타내는 형용사 'few'를 옳게 사용하였다.

③ **출제 포인트: 현재분사 vs. 과거분사**
수식하는 대상 'papers'와 수동 관계이며 해석상 '구겨진 종이'가 자연스러우므로 과거분사 'crumpled'를 사용하는 것이 옳다.

④ **출제 포인트: 수여동사의 간접목적어**
밑줄 친 'me'는 'handed(수여동사 hand의 과거시제)'의 간접목적어로 옳게 사용되었다.

> 해석

5살짜리 내 아들은 어느 날 밤 종이에 "엄마 사랑해요."라는 말을 쓰고서야 비로소 잠자리에 들 수 있었다. 잠옷을 입고, 손에는 빨간색 크레용을 쥐고서 그는 매우 단호했다. 몇 개의 엉킨 글자들, 구겨진 두 장의 종이, 그리고 나중에 아빠로부터 약간의 도움을 받고서, 그는 종이에 적힌 자신의 마음을 나에게 건네주었다.

> 어휘

pajamas 잠옷, 파자마   determined 단호한, 단단히 결심한
crumple 구기다

06 정답 ①

> 정답해설

① **출제 포인트: 현재분사 vs. 과거분사**
'After ~ her family'는 접속사가 살아있는 분사구문이다. 생략된 주어 'Tammy'와 'return'의 관계가 능동이므로 현재분사 'returning'을 사용하는 것이 옳다. 따라서 'returned'를 'returning'으로 수정해야 한다. 또한 'returned'를 과거시제 동사로 보고 앞에 생략된 주어 'Tammy' 또는 'she'를 'After' 뒤에 추가해도 옳은 문장이 된다. 또한 'After'를 전치사로 보고 전치사의 목적어로써 동명사 'returning'이 사용되어 '돌아온 후에'라고 해석될 수도 있다.

> 오답해설

② **출제 포인트: another+단수명사**
'another' 뒤에 명사가 오는 경우 단수형태를 사용한다. 해당 문장은 'another' 뒤에 단수형태의 명사인 'lesson'을 사용하였으므로 옳다.

③ **출제 포인트: 능동태 vs. 수동태**
뒤에 부사 역할을 하는 전치사구 'to college'가 왔으며 해석상 '그녀는 대학으로 보내졌다'가 자연스럽다. 따라서 수동태 'was sent'를 사용하는 것이 옳다.

④ **출제 포인트: a number of vs. the number of**
'a number of'는 '많은 ~'을 뜻하며 'the number of'는 '~의 수'를 뜻한다. 해당 문장은 문맥상 '많은 다른 직업들'이 자연스러우므로 'a number of'를 사용하는 것이 옳다. 따라서 밑줄 친 'a'는 옳게 사용되었다.

> 해석

그녀의 가족과 뉴욕 주로 돌아온 후에, Tammy는 자라면서 또 다른 교훈과 대면했다. 재능이 있는 학생이어서, 그녀는 겨우 14살 때에 대학으로 보내졌다. Tammy는 다양한 일들을 직접 해보기 전에 그녀의 고교 졸업장과 어느 정도의 대학 학점을 딸 수 있었다.

> 어휘

gifted 재능이 있는   diploma 졸업장, 수료증
credit 학점, 신용

> 오답률 TOP 3

07 정답 ④

> 정답해설

④ **출제 포인트: no sooner 구문**
「주어+had+no sooner+과거분사 ~, than+주어+과거시제 동사 ~」는 no sooner 구문으로 '~하자마자 ~했다'를 뜻한다. 해당 문장에 적용된 시제와 접속사는 모두 올바르게 사용되었다. 단, 해당 문장에서는 'no sooner'가 문두로 강조되지 않았으므로 '도치' 현상은 일어나지 않는다.

> 오답해설

① **출제 포인트: 사역동사의 수동태**
사역동사 'let'을 수동태로 사용하는 경우 'allow'로 바꾸어 사용해야 한다. 해당 문장은 사역동사 'let'을 수동태로 사용하였으나 'allow'로 바꾸어 사용하지 않았으므로 틀린 문장이다. 따라서 'let'을 'allowed'로 수정해야 한다.

② **출제 포인트: 최상급 대용표현**
「비교급+than+the other+명사」는 최상급 대용표현으로 이때 명사는 복수형태를 사용한다. 해당 문장은 「비교급+than+the other+명사」를 사용하였으나 명사에 단수형태인 'man'을 사용하였으므로 틀린 문장이다. 따라서 'man'을 복수형태인 'men'으로 수정하고 'does'를 'do'로 수정해야 한다. 즉, 'than the other man does'를 'than the other men do'로 해야 올바르다. 또는 '~ than the other man does'를 '~ than any other man does'로 수정해도 옳은 문장이 된다.

③ **출제 포인트: 가정법 미래**
가정법 미래는 「If+주어+should+동사원형 ~, 주어+will/would+동사원형 ~」로 나타낼 수 있으며 이때 'If'를 생략하는 경우 「Should+주어+동사원형 ~, 주어+will/would+동사원형 ~」의 구조가 된다. 해당 문장은 'if'가 생략된 가정법 미래를 사용하였으나 「Should+주어」자리에 「주어+should」인 'You should'를 사용하였으므로 틀린 문장이다. 따라서 'You should'를 'Should you'로 수정하거나 'If you should'로 수정해야 한다.

> 해석

① 아이들은 그들이 원하는 것은 무엇이든지 할 수 있도록 허락되었다.
② William은 다른 사람들보다 영화에 대해 훨씬 더 많이 안다.
③ 인터넷을 사용하고 싶다면, 접수처에 이용할 수 있는 코드가 있을 것이다.
④ Jane이 요리를 시작하자마자 정전이 되어서 전기가 들어오지 않았다.

08 정답 ④

> 정답해설

본문은 Emile Durkheim에 의한 압박(지도)으로 인해 완성된 저서인 'Essay on the Nature and Function of Sacrifice'에 대해 소개하고 있다. 본문에서 Robertson Smith의 작품을 접한 Emile Durkheim이 '제물'과 관련한 그의 아이디어를 계속해서 추구하려고 하였으나 시간과 지식의 부족으로 인해 Marcel Mauss가 대신 연구를 진행하도록 지휘하였고 그가 기대에 부응하도록 압박했다'라고 언급하고 있다. 본문 중반 'and would constantly pressure ④ him to deliver.'에서 '잘 해내도록 압박을 받은 것'은 Marcel Mauss이므로, ④는 Marcel Mauss를 가리킨다는 것을 알 수 있다. 나머지 보기는 Emile Durkheim을 가리키고 있으므로 정답은 ④이다.

> 오답해설

① 아이디어를 추구하고자 했던 인물은 Emile Durkheim이다.
② 아이디어를 입증해야 했으나 시간과 지식이 부족했던 것은 Emile Durkheim이다.

③ "He therefore directed Marcel Mauss towards working on the question of sacrifice.(그는 Marcel Mauss가 제물에 관한 질문에 대해 연구하도록 지휘했고)"에서 Marcel Mauss에게 연구를 지휘한 것은 Emile Durkheim인 것을 알 수 있다.

해석

1895년 Emile Durkheim은 Robertson Smith의 작품을 접하게 되었고 제물을 바치는 것(또는 제물을 바치는 의식)이 사회생활의 토대라는 깨달음을 얻었다. ① 그는 이후 수십 년 동안 이 아이디어를 추구하고자 했다. 그러나 ② 그는 그의 아이디어를 적절히 입증해야 했고, 그렇게 할 시간도 필요한 민속학적인 지식도 없었다. 그래서 ③ 그는 Marcel Mauss가 제물에 관한 질문에 대해 연구하도록 지휘했고, ④ 그가 잘 해내도록 지속적으로 압박을 가하곤 했다. 이것은 Durkheim이 1897 *Suicide*를 출판한 후 더욱 심화되었다. Hubert와 Mauss가 공동 저술한 'Essay on the Nature and Function of Sacrifice'는 분석이 '올바른' 방향으로 나아간다고 확신하길 원했던 그의 감시 가득한 '지도'하에 1898년 완성되었다.

어휘

encounter 접하다, 마주치다 illumination 깨달음
sacrifice 제물, 희생 ritual 의식
substantiate 입증하다 ethnographic 민족지적인, 민족학상의
deliver […을] 잘 해내다, 기대에 부응하다
intensify 정도를 더하다, 격렬해지다 watchful 감시하는

Day 18

오답률 TOP 2

09 정답 ④

정답해설

본문은 '타인의 나무를 함부로 자른 한 남자가 거액의 벌금과 사회봉사 처분을 받았다'는 내용의 글이다. ④의 "Topel, a retired lawyer, told ④ the man whom he employed that he believed the trees, some of which were 100-150 years old, were on his property.(은퇴 변호사인 Topel은 그가 고용한 ④ 그 남자에게 그 나무들이 그의 토지에 있다고 생각한다고 말했는데, 일부 나무들은 100-150년 된 것이었다)"에서 'Topel'은 '수목 재배가(arborist)'를 고용해 나무를 자르게 한 장본인이며, 밑줄 친 'the man'은 Topel이 고용한 '수목 재배가'인 것을 알 수 있다. 나머지 보기는 모두 Topel을 가리키고 있으므로 정답은 ④이다.

오답해설

① A Bucks County man은 '벌금과 사회봉사명령을 받은 당사자'인 Topel을 가리킨다.
② he가 가리키는 것은 '벌금의 액수에 해당하는 수표를 발행할 인물'이며 이는 Topel이다.
③ The defendant는 '나무를 자른 혐의로 소송을 받은 피고인'을 가리키는 것이므로 Topel에 해당한다.

해석

① Bucks County의 한 남자가 뒤뜰의 전망을 더 좋게 만들기 위해 이웃의 토지에 있는 22그루의 나무를 잘라낸 혐의로 25만 달러의 벌금과 사회봉사명령에 처하게 되었다. 검사는 Solebury Township에 거주하는 62세의 David Topel이 2014년 가을 나무를 자르기 위해 수목 재배가를 고용한 혐의로 군구에 261,211.07달러를 지불하고, 5년의 보호 관찰을 받으며 사회봉사를 수행할 것을 판결받았다고 발표했다. Topel은 ② 그가 벌금 전액에 달하는 수표를 지급하겠다고 말했으며, 당국에 따르면 이는 나무의 가격에 해당한다. ③ 피고는 최근 Florida에서 Solebury에 있는 새집으로 이사했고, 그의 집 뒤편 덱에서 더 멋진 전망을 보길 원했다. Bucks County District Attorney's Office에 따르면, 은퇴 변호사인 Topel은 그가 고용한 ④ 그 남자에게 그 나무들이 그의 토지에 있다고 생각한다고 말했는데, 일부 나무들은 100-150년 된 것이었다. 그러나 그 나무들은 지역 집주인 연합의 11인의 구성원이 소유한 나무가 우거진 지역에 있었다고 당국은 말한다.

어휘

community service 사회[지역]봉사 property 부동산, 토지
prosecutor 검사 probation 보호 관찰
arborist 수목 재배가 authority 당국, 권위자
defendant 피고 scenic 경치가 좋은
deck 덱(집 후면에 마루처럼 달아내어 앉아서 쉴 수 있게 만들어 놓은 곳)
attorney 변호사

10 정답 ①

정답해설

본문은 '국내 입양과 해외 입양 요건'을 비교하고 있다. 본문은 '국내 입양이든 해외 입양이든 개인의 상황에 따라 요건 충족의 가능성이 달라질 것이다'라고 언급한 후, 마지막 문장 "Generally speaking, however, you will have a greater chance of facing more demanding requirements when adopting from a different country(그러나 일반적으로 말해, 당신이 타국에서 입양을 할 때 더 어려운 요건에 부딪힐 가능성이 더 클 것이다)."를 통해, '그러나 보통 해외 입양이 더 까다롭고 엄격한 요건을 요구한다'는 것을 설명하고 있다. 빈칸에는 해외 입양의 요건을 설명하는 표현이 들어가야 하므로 '엄격한'이라는 의미를 가진 표현이 적절한데, '① lenient'는 '관대한, 너그러운'이라는 의미로 본문의 주장과는 반대의 뜻이다. 따라서 빈칸에 적절하지 않은 것은 ①이다.

오답해설

나머지 보기는 모두 '엄격한, 엄중한'이라는 의미를 지니고 있으므로 '해외 입양의 요건이 더 엄격하다'는 내용에 부합한다. 따라서 오답이다.

해석

입양의 요건은 입양의 유형, 당신이 이용하는 기관, 그리고 당신이 아이를 입양하는 곳에 따라 다르다. 국내에서 입양할 때, 당신은 주와 기관의 요건을 충족해야만 한다. 이것의 한 예는 최소 나이 요건을 충족시키는 것이다. 해외 입양은 보통 더 엄격하다. 일부 국가들은 혼인 요건을 갖추고 있고, 다른 국가들은 더 높은 나이 제한이 있다. 안타깝게도 여전히 많은 국가들이 성 소수자 커플이 입양하는 것을 허용하지 않는다. 해외 또는 국내 입양이 더 쉬운가? 요건 충족의 어려움은 당신의 고유한 상황에 따라 다를 것이다. 그러나 일반적으로 말해, 당신이 타국에서 입양을 할 때 더 어려운 요건에 부딪힐 가능성이 더 클 것이다.

① 관대한
② 엄격한
③ 엄중한
④ 엄격한, 꽉 끼는

어휘

requirement (필수) 요건, 필요조건 domestically 국내적으로
face 직면하다, 만나다 lenient 관대한
rigid 엄격한, 융통성 없는 stringent 엄중한, 엄격한
tight 엄격한, 꽉 끼는

기적사 DAY 19

결국엔 성정혜 영어 하프모의고사

| 01 | ① | 02 | ③ | 03 | ③ | 04 | ③ | 05 | ③ |
| 06 | ② | 07 | ④ | 08 | ③ | 09 | ④ | 10 | ② |

오답률 TOP 1
01 정답①

정답해설

밑줄 친 'impending'은 '임박한, 곧 닥칠'의 뜻으로 ① imminent와 의미가 가장 가깝다.

해석

바다에 있는 사람들은 기상청으로부터 **임박한** 호의 주의 경보에 대한 경고를 받아왔다.
① 임박한, 일촉즉발의
② 우연한, 부차적인, 간접적인
③ 불변의, 지속적인
④ 화려한, 멋진

어휘

impending 임박한, 곧 닥칠
imminent 임박한, 일촉즉발의
constant 불변의, 지속적인
meteorological 기상의, 기상학의
incidental 우연한, 부차적인, 간접적인
splendid 화려한, 멋진

02 정답③

정답해설

밑줄 친 'eagerness'는 '열의, 열심'의 뜻으로 ③ ardor과 의미가 가장 가깝다. 해당 문장에서는 작가 또는 화자가 'the enthusiasm ~ their followers'를 하나의 개념으로 보고 있어 단수 동사인 'is'와 함께 쓰이고 있음에 주의하자.

해석

사람들은 종교에 대해 그다지 잘 모르지만, 특별한 누군가에 대한 열정과 신도들의 **열의**가 놀랍다.
① 감정이입
② 격통
③ 열정, 열의, 정열
④ 체계성, 조직성

어휘

enthusiasm 열정
empathy 감정이입
ardor 열정, 열의, 정열
eagerness 열의, 열심
anguish 격통
systemicity 체계성, 조직성

03 정답③

정답해설

땀과 수중 활동에도 불구하고 오래 지속된다고 하였으므로 '방수의'를 뜻하는 ③ Watertight가 가장 적절하다.

해석

그것은 땀을 흘리는 것과 수중 활동보다 오래 지속되기 때문에 **방수** 선크림이 추천되어진다.

① 속이 빈
② 필수의, 본질적인
③ 방수의
④ 신경학상의

어휘

hollow 속이 빈
watertight 방수의
essential 필수의, 본질적인
neurological 신경학상의

04 정답③

정답해설

방문객이 휴대전화를 잃어버린 상황에서 보안관과 대화를 나눈다. 방문객은 (A) '정신없이(like a chicken with its head off)' 달려왔지만 안내대가 닫았고 보안관은 휴대전화가 개인 정보를 모두 담고 있어 (B) '매우 소중한 물건(the apple of your eye)' 아니냐고 묻는다. 그러자 방문객은 내일 다시 방문하겠다고 하고, 보안관은 혹시 누군가 분실물을 들고 올 수 있으니 분실함을 (C) '관찰하고 있겠다(keep an eye on)' 말한다. 방문객은 보안관의 호의에 감사를 표하며 (D) '큰 희생을 치르는 한이 있더라도(반드시)(at all costs)' 은혜를 잊지 않겠다고 이야기한다. 따라서 정답은 ③이다.

오답해설

① (A) 휴대전화를 잃어버렸다는 것을 깨달은 순간 '아무 효과 없이(like water off a duck's back)' 뛰어왔다고 말하는 것은 문맥상 어색하다. (B) 보안관이 휴대전화를 잃어버렸냐고 방문객에게 되물으며 '소름(goose bumps)'이 아닌지 질문하는 것은 대화의 흐름상 적절하지 않다. (D) 방문객을 위해 분실함을 관찰하겠다는 보안관에게 '순식간에(in on time)' 은혜를 갚겠다는 것은 휴대전화를 아직 찾지 못한 방문객의 상황에서 할 말로 적합하지 않다.
② (A) 휴대전화를 잃어버렸다는 것을 깨달은 순간 '아무 효과 없이(like water off a duck's back)' 뛰어왔다고 말하는 것은 문맥상 어색하다. (C) 누군가 분실된 휴대전화를 반납할 수도 있으니 분실함의 '편을 들겠다(stand up for)'라는 것은 자연스럽지 않다.
④ (C) 방문객이 분실한 휴대전화를 누군가 반납할지도 모르니 보안관이 분실함에 '맞서 저항하겠다(stand up against)'라고 이야기하는 것은 대화의 흐름상 어색하다.

해석

방문객: 실례합니다. 안내대가 어디에 있죠?
보안관: 안내대는 현재 닫았어요. 오전 9시부터 저녁 8시까지 열려 있습니다.
방문객: 오, 안타깝네요. 제가 휴대전화를 잃어버렸다는 것을 깨닫자마자 저는 여기로 (A) <u>정신없이</u> 달려왔어요.
보안관: 휴대전화를 분실하셨나요? (B) <u>매우 소중한 물건</u> 아닌가요? 손님의 모든 개인 정보를 담고 있잖아요.
방문객: 네, 그것이 제가 온 힘을 다해 여기까지 온 이유에요. 그런데 불행하게도, 이곳을 내일 다시 오는 수밖에 없겠네요.
보안관: 누군가 손님의 휴대전화를 반납할 수도 있으니, 제가 분실함을 (C) <u>관찰할게요</u>.
방문객: 정말 감사합니다. (D) <u>큰 희생을 치르는 한이 있어도 (반드시)</u> 은혜를 잊지 않을게요.
보안관: 아닙니다. 그저 제 일을 할 뿐입니다.

① (A) 아무 효과 없는 (B) 소름 (C) ~을 관찰하다 (D) 순식간에
② (A) 아무 효과 없는 (B) 매우 소중한 물건 (C) ~의 편을 들다 (D) 큰 희생을 치르는 한이 있어도 (반드시)
③ (A) 정신없이 (B) 매우 소중한 물건 (C) ~을 관찰하다 (D) 큰 희생을 치르는 한이 있어도 (반드시)
④ (A) 정신없이 (B) 매우 소중한 물건 (C) ~에 맞서 저항하다 (D) 큰 희생을 치르는 한이 있어도 (반드시)

어휘

all the way 온 힘을 다해, 줄곧
like water off a duck's back 아무 효과 없는
goose bumps 소름　　　　keep an eye on ~을 관찰하다
in on time 순식간에
the apple of one's eye 매우 소중한 물건
stand up for ~의 편을 들다
at all costs 큰 희생을 치르는 한이 있어도 (반드시)
like a chicken with its head off 정신없이
stand up against ~에 맞서 저항하다

05 정답 ③

정답해설

③ 출제 포인트: 본동사 vs. 준동사/분사구문

밑줄 친 부분을 포함한 문장의 주어는 'A herd of zebras'이며 동사는 'become'이다. 밑줄 친 동사 'make'의 경우 이어지는 연결사인 접속사가 없으므로 동사로 쓰인 것이 잘못되었음을 알 수 있다. 따라서 해당 문장에서 'make'는 분사구문으로 수정하여 'making'으로 사용해야 옳다. 현재분사구문으로써 주절의 주어인 'A herd of zebra'와 동사 'make'의 관계가 능동임에 주의해야한다. 또한 'making' 이후에 'it'의 경우 가목적어로 쓰였으며 진목적어는 'to see ~ begins'에 해당된다.

오답해설

① 출제 포인트: 단수와 복수의 형태가 같은 명사

'a school of'는 '~떼'를 뜻하는 경우 뒤에 오는 명사(구)는 복수형태이어야 한다. 해당 문장은 'A school of' 뒤에 복수형태 명사인 'fish'를 사용하였으므로 옳은 문장이다. 'fish'는 단수형태와 복수형태가 동일함에 주의해야한다.

② 출제 포인트: 형용사로 고착화된 현재분사

'dazzling'은 형용사로 고착화된 현재분사로 '현란한'을 뜻한다. 해당 문장은 'display'를 수식하며 해석상 '현란한 광경'이 자연스러우므로 밑줄 친 'dazzling'은 옳은 표현이다.

④ 출제 포인트: 가목적어 it/to부정사의 명사적 용법

불완전타동사 'make'의 목적어에 해당하는 to부정사구 'to see where one zebra ends and another begins'가 긴 경우에 해당하므로 가목적어 'it'을 사용하였고 진목적어인 to부정사구 'to see where one zebra ends and another begins'를 문미로 이동하였으므로 옳은 문장이다.

해석

물고기 떼는 포식자를 피하기 위해 둘로 나뉘었다가 포식자 뒤에서 재빨리 다시 떼를 지을 것이다. 얼룩말 무리는 검은색과 흰색의 줄무늬들이 이루는 현란한 광경이 될 수 있는데, 이로써 사자가 어디에서 한 마리의 얼룩말이 끝나고 다른 얼룩말이 시작되는지를 알아보는 것을 더 어렵게 만든다.

어휘

school 떼, 무리, 유파, 학교　　split 나뉘다, 분열되다
regroup 재편성하다, 재정비하다　　herd 떼
stripe 줄무늬

06 정답 ②

정답해설

② 출제 포인트: 본동사 vs. 준동사

'disaster'를 주어로 하는 절의 동사가 없으므로 밑줄 친 'striking'은 본래 동사임을 알 수 있다. 따라서 현재분사 'striking'을 문맥에 맞게 과거시제 동사 'struck'으로 수정해야 한다.

오답해설

① 출제 포인트: a few+명사[복수]

'a few'는 뒤에 오는 명사는 복수형태를 사용한다. 따라서 해당 문장에서 'a few' 뒤에 복수형태 명사인 'years'를 옳게 사용하였다.

③ 출제 포인트: 불완전타동사의 목적격 보어

밑줄 친 'to sink'는 불완전타동사 'caused'의 목적격 보어로 옳은 표현이다. 또한 해당 문장에서 'sink'는 '가라앉다, 침몰하다'의 의미의 완전자동사로 사용되었다.

④ 출제 포인트: 주어와 동사 수일치

문맥상 '살아남은 개체들'이 자연스러우므로 주어가 'individuals'임을 알 수 있다. 이때 'individuals'는 복수형태이므로 동사에 복수형태인 'were'를 사용하는 것이 옳다.

해석

몇 년을 비교적 안전하게 즐긴 뒤에 다른 종류의 재난이 큰바다쇠오리에 타격을 주었다. 화산 활동은 그 섬 피난처가 완전히 바다 아래 가라앉게 했고 살아남은 개체들은 다른 피난처를 찾아야 했다.

어휘

comparative 비교적, 상대적인　　strike 타격을 주다
refuge 피난(처), 피신(처)　　surviving 살아남은

오답률 TOP 3

07 정답 ④

정답해설

④ 출제 포인트: 가정법 미래

「If+주어+were to+동사원형 ~, 주어+would+동사원형 ~.」은 가정법 미래를 나타낸다. 해당 문장은 'If'절에 'were to resign'을 사용하였고 주절에 'would have to be'를 사용해 옳게 사용되었다. 조동사 'would' 뒤에 의무를 나타내기 위해 일반동사 중 의무의 의미를 나타내는 'have to'가 동사원형의 형태로 쓰였음에 주의해야 한다.

오답해설

① 출제 포인트: 사역동사의 수동태

사역동사 'make'를 수동태로 사용하는 경우 목적격 보어로 쓰인 원형부정사를 to부정사로 바꾸어 사용해야 한다. 해당 문장은 사역동사 'make'의 수동태를 사용하였으나 목적격 보어에 원형부정사 'wait'을 사용하였으므로 틀린 문장이다. 따라서 'wait'을 to부정사 'to wait'으로 수정해야 한다.

② 출제 포인트: no sooner 구문

「As soon as+주어+과거시제 동사 ~, 주어+과거시제 동사 ~.」는 no sooner 구문과 유사한 의미로 '~하자마자 ~했다'를 뜻한다. 해당 구문에서 'As soon as+주어+과거시제 동사 ~,'는 부사절이기 때문에 그 위치가 자유롭다. 해당 문장은 「주어+과거시제 동사 ~, as soon as+주어+과거시제 동사 ~.」를 사용하였으나 과거시제 동사 자리에 과거완료 'had left'를 사용하였으므로 틀린 문장이다. 따라서 'had left'를 'left'로 수정해야 한다.

③ 출제 포인트: 최상급 대용표현

「비교급+than+any other+명사」는 최상급 대용표현으로 이때 명사는 단수형태를 사용한다. 해당 문장은 「비교급+than+any other+명사」를 사용하였으나 비교급 자리에 원급 부사 'much'를 사용하였으므로 틀린 문장이다. 따라서 'much'를 비교급 부사 'more'로 수정해야 한다. 또한 'any other' 뒤에 오는 명사 'country'는 단수형태이므로 옳게 사용되었다.

해석
① 나는 의사의 진찰을 받기 전 4시간 동안 기다리도록 되어있었다.
② Tom이 방을 나가자마자 무슨 일이 일어났는지 너는 절대 짐작하지 못할 것이다.
③ 호주가 다른 나라보다 더 민주적인 국가라고 생각하십니까?
④ 총리가 사퇴한다면, 30일 이내에 총선이 치러져야 한다.

08 정답 ③

정답해설
본문은 'Marcel Mauss의 저서 The Gift에서 설명하는 원시 사회에서의 선물의 의미'에 대해 설명하고 있다. 주어진 문장의 "this is not necessarily true(이것이 반드시 사실은 아니다)"로 보아, 주어진 문장 전후에는 서로 대조적인 내용이 등장해야 한다는 것을 유추할 수 있다. ③ 이전 문장에서 '현대 사회에서 선물은 대가를 바라지 않고 주어진다'고 언급하고 있는데, ③ 이후 문장에서는 '마오리족 사회에서는 선물은 대가를 바라는 교환의 개념'이라고 대조적인 내용을 언급하고 있으므로, 내용을 전환시키는 역할을 하는 주어진 문장이 ③에 들어가야 한다는 것을 알 수 있다. 따라서 정답은 ③이다.

오답해설
④ 이후에서 설명하는 내용은 ③ 이후에서 언급된 '교환 시스템'에 기반을 둔 선물 증정에 관한 것이므로, 동일한 논점으로 글을 전개하고 있다. 따라서 내용을 전환하는 역할을 하는 주어진 문장이 들어가기에는 어색하다.
나머지 위치는 문맥상 어색하므로 오답이다.

해석
그의 저서 *The Gift*에서 Marcel Mauss는 원시 사회에서의 선물을 설명하고 이해하려고 시도한다. (①) Mauss는 먼저 선물을 주는 것 뒤에 숨은 동기가 일반적으로 생각되는 것보다 더 복잡하다는 것을 보여주려고 결심한다. (②) 현대의 사회에서 선물은 호의로 그리고 대가를 기대하지 않고 주어지는 것으로 종종 여겨진다. (③ **Mauss는 많은 부족 그리고 원주민 문화에서 이것이 반드시 사실이 아니라는 것을 보여준다.**) Maori족에 대해 논의하며 그는 "그들은 일종의 교환 시스템, 또는 더 정확히 말하자면 궁극적으로 보답받거나 돌려받아야 하는 선물 증정 시스템을 가지고 있다"고 말한다. (④) 그 선물 증정 원칙은 권위라는 개념에 의해 지배되는데, 이것은 우월한 선물 증정자가 되는 것의 부와 영광에서 오는 권력, 명예, 위신이다. 한 사람은 권위를 유지하고 증가시키기 위해 선물을 주어야 하고 자신이 그것을 잃는 것을 방지하기 위해 그것들을 보답한다.

어휘
tribal 부족의
(or) rather 더 정확히 말하면
reciprocate 보답하다, 응답하다, 화답하다
mana 권위, 위광
derive 끌어내다, 얻다
expectancy 기대
prestige 위신

09 정답 ④

정답해설
본문은 '기온의 상승과 가뭄으로 인해 나무에게 필요한 물이 부족하며, 이에 따른 나무 간 경쟁이 나무의 성장에 악영향을 끼칠 수 있다'고 주장하며, 마지막 문장 "Removing some trees can ease the competition, letting the remaining trees grow big and healthy(약간의 나무들을 제거하는 것이 이러한 경쟁을 완화시킬 수 있고, 남아있는 나무들이 크고 건강하게 성장할 수 있도록 해준다)."를 통해 '나무를 자르는 것이 오히려 숲에 더 이로운 작용을 할 수 있다'는 점을 시사하고 있다. 따라서 전체 글의 요지로 가장 적절한 것은 '④ Cutting down some trees can be good for nature(나무를 일부 자르는 것이 자연에 좋을 수도 있다).'이다.

오답해설
① 본문 중반 "As trees grow, they convert carbon dioxide to food and store it in their leaves, trunks, and roots(나무가 자라면서 그들은 이산화탄소를 식량으로 전환하고 그것을 잎, 몸통, 뿌리에 저장한다)."에서 '나무가 이산화탄소를 흡수'한다는 점을 들어, 공기 정화에 도움이 된다는 사실을 언급하고 있으나, 이는 '나무가 건강하게 자라는 것의 중요성'에 대해 언급하며, '건강한 나무의 성장을 위해 나무 간 경쟁을 완화해야 한다'고 주장하기 위한 것이므로, 전체 글의 요지로는 적절하지 않다.
② 본문에서는 '나무를 솎아내는 것의 필요성'에 대해 언급하고 있으며, '더 많은 나무가 필요하다'는 것은 본문의 주장과 반대되는 내용이므로 오답이다.
③ 본문 후반 "But if trees get too crowded, they compete for light and water — and stressed trees are more susceptible to drought and insect attacks(그러나 만일 나무가 너무 많다면, 그들은 빛과 물을 얻기 위해 경쟁하고, 스트레스를 받은 나무들은 가뭄과 곤충의 공격에 더욱 예민해진다)."에서 '나무 간 경쟁'에 대해 언급하고 있으나, 이는 '나무 수 조정의 필요성'에 대해 언급하기 위한 근거로 사용된 내용이므로, 전체 글의 요지로는 적절하지 않다.

해석
숲이 열기를 느끼고 있다. 미 서부와 같은 지역에서 상승하는 기온과 가뭄은 나무들에게 더 적은 물을 의미한다. 현재, 과학자들은 숲의 성장에 있어서 초기에 솎아내는 것이 기후변화를 견딜 수 있는 더 강한 나무를 만든다는 것을 발견했다. 게다가, 이렇게 솎아진 나무들은 빽빽한 숲만큼이나 공기 중에서 빠르게 탄소를 흡수할 수 있다. 나무가 자라면서 그들은 이산화탄소를 식량으로 전환하고 그것을 잎, 몸통, 뿌리에 저장한다. 미국의 숲은 매년 미국 배출량의 10에서 20퍼센트 사이를 흡수한다. 그러나 만일 나무가 너무 많다면, 그들은 빛과 물을 얻기 위해 경쟁하고, 스트레스를 받은 나무들은 가뭄과 곤충의 공격에 더욱 예민해진다. 약간의 나무들을 제거하는 것이 이러한 경쟁을 완화시킬 수 있고, 남아있는 나무들이 크고 건강하게 성장할 수 있도록 해준다.
① 나무는 공기 오염을 줄이는 데 도움이 될 수 있다.
② 미국의 숲에는 더 많은 나무가 필요하다.
③ 나무들은 생존하기 위해 서로 경쟁한다.
④ 일부 나무들을 자르는 것이 자연에 좋을 수도 있다.

어휘
drought 가뭄
endure 견디다, 참다
convert 전환시키다
thin (수가) 줄어들다[줄어들게 하다], 솎다
dense 빽빽한, 밀집한
susceptible 민감한, 예민한

오답률 TOP 2
10 정답 ②

정답해설
주어진 문장에서는 '입양 사실을 알게 된 아이들이 겪을 수 있는 많은 문제'에 대해 언급하고 있다. 그러한 다양한 문제 중 "큰 슬픔(grief)"을 느끼는 것에 대해 최초로 언급하는 (A)가 주어진 문장 바로 이후에 이어지는 것이 자연스럽다. 이후, (A)에서 슬픔을 느끼는 이유로 언급된 "the loss of a relationship with their birth parents(친부모와의 관계 상실)"와 "the loss of the cultural and family connections that would have existed with those parents(그 부모와 함께 있었더라면 존재했었을지도 모를 문화적, 가족적 유대감의 상실)"를 (C)의 "This feeling of loss(이러한 상실의 감정)"로 가리키고 있으므로 (A) 이후에는 (C)가 이어지는 것이 옳다. 마지막으로, 앞서 언급된 '슬픔'을 느끼게 되는 시기에 대해 언급해 주고 있는 (B)가 이어지는 것이 자연스럽다. 따라서 정답은 ② (A) - (C) - (B)이다.

오답해설

① (A)에서 'grief'가 언급된 후, (B)에서 'grief feelings'가 언급되는 것이 자연스럽다고 볼 수도 있으나, (C)의 'This feelings of loss'가 가리키는 대상이 (A)에 등장하고, (C)에서 'especially(특히)'를 이용해 (A)에서 설명한 슬픔을 느끼게 되는 상황에 대해 구체적으로 부가 설명을 하는 구조이므로, (A)와 (C)가 연달아 이어지는 것이 더 자연스럽다.
③, ④ (B)의 'Such grief feelings'가 가리키는 대상이 주어진 문장에 등장하지 않으므로, 주어진 문장에 (B)가 바로 이어지는 것은 어색하다.

해석

아이들이 입양되었다는 것을 알게 되었을 때 많은 문제가 발생할 수 있다.
(A) 아이들은 친부모와의 관계 상실 또는 그 부모와 함께 있었더라면 존재했었을지도 모를 문화적, 가족적 유대감의 상실에 대해 큰 슬픔을 느낄 수 있다.
(C) 이러한 상실의 감정은 친부모에 대한 정보 또는 접촉이 적거나 거의 없는 폐쇄 또는 반개방형 입양의 경우에 특히 심할 수 있다.
(B) 이러한 슬픈 감정은 아이의 인생에 걸쳐 그들이 입양에 대해 처음으로 알게 되는 때, 격동의 10대 시기 도중에, 다른 가족 구성원이 사망했을 때, 또는 배우자나 부모가 되는 때를 포함한 많은 다른 시기에 촉발될 수 있다.

어휘

multitude 다수
grief 큰 슬픔, 비통
turbulent 격동의
arise 생기다, 발생하다
trigger 유발하다, 촉발하다
spouse 배우자

기적사 DAY 20

| 01 | ③ | 02 | ① | 03 | ④ | 04 | ④ | 05 | ④ |
| 06 | ③ | 07 | ③ | 08 | ② | 09 | ② | 10 | ① |

01 정답 ③

정답해설

밑줄 친 'consecutive'는 '연속적인'의 뜻으로 ③ successive와 의미가 가장 가깝다.

해석

그 국가가 2000년 이래로 월드컵에서 두 번 **연속** 우승을 거머쥔 것은 처음이었다.
① 버려진, 사람이 살지 않는
② 고고학의
③ 연속적인, 연이은
④ 주요한, 중요한

어휘

consecutive 연속적인, 연속되는
archaeological 고고학의
key 주요한, 중요한
deserted 버려진, 사람이 살지 않는
successive 연속적인, 연이은

02 정답 ①

정답해설

밑줄 친 'indolence'는 '게으름, 나태'의 뜻으로 ① idleness와 의미가 가장 가깝다.

해석

그의 태도의 분명한 **게으름**에도 불구하고, 나는 그가 날카롭게 기민하다는 것을 알 수 있었다.
① 게으름, 나태
② 결정론
③ 변화, 변혁
④ 정확성

어휘

apparent 분명한, 명백한
keenly 날카롭게, 강렬하게
idleness 게으름, 나태
transformation 변화, 변혁
indolence 게으름, 나태
alert 기민한; 경계
determinism 결정론
accuracy 정확성

03 정답 ④

정답해설

화산에 관한 자료를 제시할 만한 것으로 가장 적절한 것은 '지질학 조사'이다. 따라서 정답은 ④ Geological이다.

해석

미국 **지질** 조사국에 따르면, 해저에 있는 지속적인 화산 지대를 포함하지 않고 전 세계에 약 1,500개의 잠재적인 활화산이 있다고 한다.
① 고립된

② 속이 빈
③ 진짜의, 진실된
④ 지질학의

어휘

continuous 연속적인, 지속적인   isolated 고립된
hollow 속이 빈   genuine 진짜의, 진실된
geological 지질학의

04 정답 ④

정답해설

영화 '위대한 개츠비(The Great Gatsby)'를 관람한 후 Chris와 Ray는 영화에 관해 대화를 나눈다. Chris가 개츠비가 자신이 원하는 대로 삶을 이끌 수 있어 (A) '아주 행복할(on cloud nine)' 것 같다고 하자 Ray는 개츠비가 (B) '아주 부유하게 태어난(born with a silver spoon in one's mouth)' 인물이라고 말한다. 그리고 영화의 결말에 대해 이야기하며 Ray는 개츠비의 희생에도 불구하고 (C) '최후의 순간(at the eleventh hour)'에 그의 장례식에는 아무도 남지 않았다고 이야기한다.

오답해설

① (A) 개츠비는 자신이 원하는 대로 삶을 이끌 수 있어 '곤경에 빠진(up a tree)' 것처럼 느낀다는 것은 문맥상 어색하다. (B) 개츠비를 '죽은(six feet under)' 인물이라고 지칭하는 것은 옳지 않다. (C) 개츠비의 장례식에서 '헐값에(for a song)' 아무도 남지 않았다고 말하는 것은 대화의 흐름상 적절하지 않다.
② (B) 개츠비를 '죽은(six feet under)' 인물이라고 지칭하는 것은 옳지 않다. (C) 개츠비의 장례식에서 '어려움에 처한(in the dog house)' 남은 사람들이 없었다는 것은 문맥상 부자연스럽다.
③ (A) 개츠비가 삶을 자신이 원하는 방향대로 이끌 수 있는 것이 충격적이면서도 그것이 '방어가 힘든 쉬운 일(a turkey shoot)'인 것처럼 느낄 것이라고 이야기하는 것은 옳지 않다.

해석

Chris: 나 주말에 영화 '위대한 개츠비'를 봤어.
Ray: 그건 고전이잖아. 영화 좋았어?
Chris: 음, 개츠비의 인생은 나에게 정말 충격적이었어. 그는 그가 원하는 방식이 무엇이든지 그의 인생을 이끌 수 있었어. 그것은 틀림없이 (A) 아주 행복하게 느껴질 거야.
Ray: 만약 내가 개츠비라면 삶이 어떨지 상상하기 어려워. 그는 (B) 아주 부유하게 태어난 인물이야.
Chris: 네 말이 맞아. 너 결말을 기억해?
Ray: 응, 그건 비극이었어. 그의 연인 Daisy를 위한 개츠비의 희생에도 불구하고, (C) 최후의 순간에 그의 장례식에는 아무도 남지 않았어.
Chris: 그 장면을 보면서, 나는 죽음의 순간에 부유함은 무의미하다는 것을 깨달았어.

① (A) 곤경에 빠져 (B) 죽은 (C) 헐값에
② (A) 아주 행복한 (B) 죽은 (C) 어려움에 처한
③ (A) 방어가 힘든 쉬운 일 (B) 부유하게 태어난 (C) 최후의 순간에
④ (A) 아주 행복한 (B) 부유하게 태어난 (C) 최후의 순간에

어휘

sacrifice 희생하다   meaningless 의미가 없는, 무익한
up a tree 곤경에 빠져   six feet under 죽은
for a song 헐값에   on cloud nine 아주 행복한
in the doghouse 어려움에 처한   a turkey shoot 방어가 힘든 쉬운 일
born with a silver spoon in one's mouth 부유하게 태어난
at the eleventh hour 최후의 순간에

05 정답 ④

정답해설

④ 출제 포인트: 준사역동사의 목적격 보어

준사역동사 'get'은 목적어와 목적격 보어의 관계가 능동인 경우 to부정사와 현재분사를 목적격 보어로 사용하며, 목적어와 목적격 보어의 관계가 수동인 경우 과거분사를 사용한다. 해당 문장은 준사역동사 'get'의 목적격 보어에 동사원형인 'do'를 사용하였으므로 옳지 않은 문장이다. 따라서 'get'의 목적어 'the work'와 보어의 관계가 수동 관계이므로 'do'를 과거분사 'done'으로 수정해야 한다.

오답해설

① 출제 포인트: 가주어 It/to부정사의 명사적 용법
밑줄 친 'to see'는 to부정사의 명사적 용법으로 사용되었으며 가주어 'It'이 가리키는 진주어에 해당한다.
② 출제 포인트: 주어와 동사의 수일치
주어가 단수형태인 'a strong economy'이므로 동사에 단수형태인 'helps'를 사용하는 것이 옳다.
③ 출제 포인트: 현재분사 vs. 과거분사
수식하는 대상 'employers'와 수동 관계이며 해석상 '편견에 빠져 있는 고용주'가 자연스러우므로 과거분사 'Biased'를 사용하는 것이 옳다.

해석

기회가 많고 일자리가 남아도는 튼튼한 경제가 사회적 장벽을 무너뜨리는 데 도움이 된다는 것을 아는 것은 어렵지 않다. 편견에 빠져 있는 고용주는 이런저런 무리에 속한 구성원을 고용하기를 여전히 싫어할 수 있지만, 다른 어느 누구도 이용할 수 없다면, 차별은 그 일을 끝내야 한다는 기본적인 필요에 자리를 내주게 된다.

어휘

opportunity 기회   plentiful 풍부한
discrimination 차별

06 정답 ③

정답해설

③ 출제 포인트: 가주어 it/to부정사의 명사적 용법

문맥상 '~ Koshima의 마카크 원숭이를 발견하는 것은 힘들었다'가 자연스러우므로 to부정사구 'to find ~ it'이 진주어임을 알 수 있다. 따라서 'that'은 가주어로 사용할 수 없으므로 'it'으로 수정해야 한다.

오답해설

① 출제 포인트: 기수-측정단위명사[단수 vs. 복수]-형용사
「기수-측정단위명사-형용사」가 한정적 용법으로 사용되는 경우 「기수-측정단위명사[단수]-형용사」의 형태를 가진다. 해당 문장은 「기수-측정단위명사-형용사」가 명사(구) 'female macaque'를 수식하는 한정적 용법으로 사용되었으므로 「기수-측정단위명사[단수]-형용사」의 형태인 'one-year-old'는 옳은 표현이다.
② 출제 포인트: 동사 vs. 준동사
주어가 고유 명사 'Imo'이므로 단수 취급하여 단수동사인 'hits'로 수정해야 한다고 생각할 수 있으나 밑줄 친 'hit'는 밑줄 친 'hit'은 과거시제를 나타내는 'In the early 1950s'가 있으므로 과거시제로 적절하게 사용되었다. 동사 'hit'는 현재형과 과거형이 동일하므로 형태에 주의해야한다.
④ 출제 포인트: 접속사가 살아 있는 분사구문/동명사
'before'를 접속사로 보는 경우 밑줄 친 'eating'은 현재분사이며, 생략된 주어이자 주격 관계대명사 'who'의 선행사인 'a Koshima macaque'와 능동관계이므로 옳게 사용되었다. 또한 'before'를 전치사로 보는 경우

'eating'을 동명사로 보고 뒤에 목적어 'it'이 있으므로 능동형 동명사를 옳게 사용한 것임을 알 수 있다.

해석

1950년대 초에, 한 살짜리 암컷 마카크 원숭이 Imo가 갑자기 먹기 전에 개울에서 고구마를 씻는 것을 생각해냈다. 곧 고구마를 먹기 전에 고구마를 씻지 않는 Koshima의 마카크 원숭이를 발견하기가 힘들었다.

어휘

macaque 마카크(아프리카·아시아산 원숭이의 하나)
hit upon ~을 생각해내다   sweet potato 고구마

오답률 TOP 2
07 정답 ③

정답해설

③ 출제 포인트: 최상급 대용표현

「No other+명사+동사+as+원급+as+목적어」는 부정 주어를 이용한 최상급 대용표현이다.

오답해설

① 출제 포인트: no sooner 구문

「The moment+주어+과거시제 동사 ~, 주어+과거시제 동사 ~.」는 no sooner 구문과 유사한 의미로 '~하자마자 ~했다'를 뜻한다. 해당 구문에서 'The moment (that)~'는 '~ 하자마자'의 의미의 접속사 역할을 하고 있음에 주의해야한다. 또한 'The moment+주어+과거시제 동사 ~'는 부사절이므로 그 위치가 자유롭다. 해당 문장은 「주어+과거시제 동사 ~, the moment+주어+과거시제 동사 ~.」를 사용하였으나 과거시제 동사 자리에 과거완료 'had had'를 사용하였으므로 틀린 문장이다. 따라서 'had had'를 'had'로 수정해야 한다.

② 출제 포인트: 사역동사의 수동태

사역동사 'have'를 수동태로 사용하는 경우 'ask'로 바꾸어 사용해야 한다. 해당 문장은 사역동사 'have'를 수동태로 사용하였으나 'ask'로 바꾸어 사용하지 않았으므로 틀린 문장이다. 따라서 'had'를 'asked'로 수정해야 한다.

④ 출제 포인트: 가정법 미래

가정법 미래는 「If+주어+were to+동사원형 ~, 주어+would+동사원형 ~.」로 나타낼 수 있으며, 이때 'If'를 생략하는 경우 「Were+주어+to+동사원형 ~, 주어+would+동사원형 ~.」의 구조가 된다. 해당 문장은 'If'가 생략된 가정법 미래를 사용하였으나 「Were+주어」자리에 「주어+were」인 'We were'를 사용하였으므로 틀린 문장이다. 따라서 'We were'를 'Were we'로 수정하거나 'If we were'로 수정해야 한다.

해석

① William이 집에 오자마자 Jane으로부터 전화가 왔다.
② 사람들에게 장시간 일하라고 하는 것은 잘못된 것이다.
③ 그의 글만큼 많은 독자들에게 영향을 준 글은 없다.
④ 만약 우리가 싸움을 포기한다면, 그것은 우리나라 민주주의의 종말을 의미할 것이다.

오답률 TOP 1
08 정답 ②

정답해설

본문의 두 번째 문장 "The earliest fruit of their collaboration was the study *Primitive Classification*(그들의 합작의 가장 초기 결실은 연구 *Primitive Classification*이다)."을 통해, *Primitive Classification*이 Durkheim과 Mauss의 합작품이라는 것을 알 수 있으며, 또한 세 번째 문장 "Its assemblage of factual materials reflects Mauss's more empirical bent, and the theoretical interpretation is largely Durkheim's(이것의 사실에 기반을 둔 자료의 집합은 더 경험적인 Mauss의 성향을 반영하고, 이론적인 설명은 주로 Durkheim의 견해이다)."에서도 '해당 저서가 Mauss의 성향과 Durkheim의 이론적 해석을 모두 담고 있음'을 언급하며 두 사람이 공동으로 연구한 저서라는 것을 시사한다. 이후 해당 저서에 사용된 자료의 출처와 자료에서 사용된 방법론, 그리고 저서에 대한 비판 및 현대적 의의에 대해서 설명하고 있으므로, 해당 본문은 Durkheim과 Mauss의 공저서를 소개하는 글이라는 것을 알 수 있다. 따라서 글의 주제로 가장 적절한 것은 '② A co-written publication(공저서)'이다.

오답해설

① 본문에서 소개되는 '*Primitive Classification*'은 Mauss의 개인 작품이 아니며, 또한 Mauss의 대표작인지 여부도 알 수 없다.
③ 본문 후반에서 '*Primitive Classification*이 비판을 받았다'고 언급하고는 있으나, 비판 자체가 글의 주요 내용이 아니므로 글 전체의 주제로는 부적절하다.
④ 본문의 내용을 통해서 Mauss와 Durkheim의 '협업 과정'에 영향을 미친 것임을 알 수 있다. 이를 Mauss라는 사람 자체에 영향을 미쳤다고 보는 것은 적절하지 않다.

해석

Mauss에게 미친 Durkheim의 지적인 영향은 과장될 수 없다. 그들의 합작의 가장 초기 결실은 연구 *Primitive Classification*이다. 이것의 사실에 기반을 둔 자료의 집합은 더 경험적인 Mauss의 성향을 반영하고, 이론적인 설명은 주로 Durkheim의 견해이다. 우주, 시간, 수, 그리고 사회 구조 내의 계층과 같은 범주의 기원을 밝히고자 하는 선구자적인 노력으로 여겨지는 *Primitive Classification*은 전통 중국 문화에서뿐만 아니라 호주 원주민들과 미국의 Zuñi족에 대한 연구로 획득한 자료로부터 이론을 세운다. 사회적 그리고 상징적 범주 사이의 공식적인 관련성 확립을 추구하는 그 작품의 방법론은 모든 사회 현상의 통일성에 대한 Durkheim의 평생 동안의 주장을 반영한다. *Primitive Classification*이 수년 동안 상당한 비판을 받아왔음에도 불구하고 그것은 여전히 중요하고 영향력 있는 이론적 기여로 남아있다.
① Mauss의 대표작
② 한 권의 공저서
③ Durkheim의 작품에 대한 비판
④ Mauss에게 미친 Durkheim의 영향

어휘

overstate 과장하다   assemblage 집합, 모임
factual 사실에 입각한   empirical 경험에 의거한, 실증적인
bent 성향, 취향   interpretation 설명, 해석
hierarchy 계층, 계급   aborigine 원주민
methodology 방법론   correspondence 관련성, 연관성
insistence 주장   unity 통일성, 일치
phenomenon 현상   substantial 상당한
contribution 기여, 공헌

09 정답 ②

정답해설

(A) 이전 문장에서 "It can increase the harmful impact of wind and rain on local ecosystems; destroy the valuable wildlife habitat used by pine martens, caribou, and other animals; and cause soil to become dry and overheated, which may in turn increase the risk of fire or interfere with seedling growth(그것은 지역 생태계에 미치는 바람과 비의 악영향을 증가시킬 수 있고; 소나무 담비, 카리부,

그리고 기타 동물이 사용하는 귀중한 야생 서식지를 파괴할 수 있으며; 토양을 건조하고 과열되게 만들어, 결과적으로 화재의 위험을 증가시키거나 묘목의 성장을 방해할 수도 있다)."라고 '개벌(clear cutting)의 문제점'에 대해 설명한 후, (A) 이후에서 "such logging operations can alter the chemical and physical makeup of nearby bodies of water and affect the health of fish and other aquatic species(그러한 벌목 작업들은 인근 수역의 화학적, 물리적 구성을 변화시킬 수 있으며 물고기와 다른 수중 생물의 건강에 영향을 미칠 수 있다)."라고 '개벌이 야기할 수 있는 또 다른 문제점'에 대해 언급하고 있다. 따라서 빈칸 이후에서 이전에 언급된 것과 동일한 논점의 내용을 추가적으로 제시하고 있으므로 '첨가'를 나타내는 'Also(또한)'가 (A)에 적절하다.

(B) 이전 두 문장에서 제기된 '개벌의 문제점'에 대한 의견으로 (B) 이후에서 "professional foresters and loggers argue that clear cutting mimics natural disturbances, such as forest fires and insect infestations, and is a sustainable way to harvest trees when managed properly(전문 삼림 감독관들과 벌목꾼들은 개벌이 산불과 곤충의 침입과 같은 자연적 교란을 모방하는 것이며, 적절히 관리된다면 나무를 수확하는 지속 가능한 방법이라고 주장한다)."라고 '개벌'을 긍정적으로 바라보는 견해에 대해 언급하고 있으므로, 이전 내용과 대조적인 논점을 제시하고 있다는 것을 알 수 있다. 따라서 빈칸에는 '역접'을 나타내는 'Nevertheless(그럼에도 불구하고)' 또는 'However(그러나)'가 적절하다.

따라서 정답은 '② Also(또한) – However(그러나)'이다.

오답해설

① (A) 이후의 내용이 (A) 이전 내용의 '결과'를 나타내고 있지 않기 때문에 'As a consequence(결과적으로)'는 빈칸에 부적절하다.
나머지 보기는 문맥상 어색하므로 오답이다.

해석

캐나다에서 이용되는 흔한 벌목 방법은 개벌, 즉 전체 입목을 수확하고 제거하는 것이다. 효율적이기는 하지만, 개벌은 다양한 환경 문제를 야기한다. 그것은 지역 생태계에 미치는 바람과 비의 악영향을 증가시킬 수 있고; 소나무 담비, 카리부, 그리고 기타 동물이 사용하는 귀중한 야생 서식지를 파괴할 수 있으며; 토양을 건조하고 과열되게 만들어, 결과적으로 화재의 위험을 증가시키거나 묘목의 성장을 방해할 수도 있다. (A) 또한 그러한 벌목 작업들은 인근 수역의 화학적, 물리적 구성을 변화시킬 수 있으며 물고기와 다른 수중 생물의 건강에 영향을 미칠 수 있다. (B) 그러나 전문 삼림 감독관들과 벌목꾼들은 개벌이 산불과 곤충의 침입과 같은 자연적 교란을 모방하는 것이며, 적절히 관리된다면 나무를 수확하는 지속 가능한 방법이라고 주장한다.

(A)	(B)
① 결과적으로	그럼에도 불구하고
② 또한	그러나
③ 즉	간단히 말해
④ 그러나	예를 들어

어휘

clear cutting 개벌(완전히 베어냄) pose 야기하다
pine marten 소나무 담비
caribou 카리부(북미산 순록) (pl. caribou)
interfere 방해하다 seedling 묘목
body of water 물줄기, 수역 forester 삼림 감독관, 수목 관리원
mimic 모방하다, 흉내를 내다 disturbance 교란, 소동
infestation 침략, 침입 sustainable 지속 가능한

오답률 TOP 3

10 정답 ①

정답해설

본문은 '위탁 부모가 되고 위탁 가정으로 승인을 받기 위한 요건'에 대해 설명하는 글이다. 첫 문장에서 'an extensive background check(광범위한 배경 조사)'를 언급한 후, ②에서 이러한 '배경 조사가 무엇인지' 구체적으로 '범죄 기록 조사, 아동 학대 관련 기록 없음 조사'라고 설명해주고 있으므로, ②가 바로 이어지는 것이 자연스럽다. 이후 나머지 문장 모두 '위탁 가정이 되기 위한 요건'에 대해 설명하고 있으나, ①의 경우 '아이가 위탁 가정에 머무르는 기간'과 '위탁 가정에 머무른 이후의 절차'에 대해 설명하고 있으므로, 글의 흐름상 적절하지 않다. 따라서 정답은 ①이다.

오답해설

③에서 '재정적으로 부유할 필요는 없다'라고 언급한 후 ④문장에서 'However(그러나)'를 이용해 '재정적 안정성을 포함한 가족의 전체적인 상황과 역사에 대한 평가가 이루어질 것이다'라고 설명하며, '재정적 부유함이 필수는 아니지만 평가의 항목에는 포함될 수 있다'고 설명하는 맥락이므로, '위탁 가정이 되기 위한 요건'을 설명하는 글의 맥락상 자연스럽다.
나머지 보기는 문맥상 자연스러우므로 오답이다.

해석

위탁 부모가 되는 것에 관심이 있는 사람들은 최소 21세 이상이어야 하고, 위탁 가정이 되는 것은 광범위한 배경 조사를 필요로 한다. ① *대부분의 아이들은 위탁 가정에 단기간 동안 머무르고, 대부분의 아이들은 원가정으로 돌아간다.* ② 아이의 안전을 확보하기 위해, 기관은 범죄 기록을 확인할 것이고 당신 가정에 있는 14세 이상의 모든 사람이 아동 학대 기록이 없음을 조사할 것이다. ③ 위탁 가정이 재정적으로 부유할 필요는 없다. ④ 그러나 가정 승인 절차는 재정적 안정성을 포함한 당신 가족의 전체적인 상황과 역사에 대한 심층적인 평가를 필요로 할 것이다. 아이를 위한 충분한 공간이 있는지 그리고 모든 안전 요건이 충족되어 있는지 확실히 하기 위해 당신의 집의 물리적인 특성 또한 평가될 것이다.

어휘

foster 위탁… extensive 광범위한
abuse 학대
clearance (깨끗이) 치우기, (방해물 등의) 제거, 일소
well-off 부유한, 유복한 approval 승인
evaluation 평가 picture (전반적인) 상황
evaluate 평가하다 adequate 충분한, 적절한

결국엔 성정혜 영어 하프모의고사
기적사 복습 모의고사 2회

01	①	02	①	03	③	04	④	05	④
06	②	07	①	08	④	09	①	10	①
11	②	12	③	13	①	14	④	15	③
16	④	17	④	18	②	19	③	20	④

01 정답 ①   Day 16-01

정답해설

밑줄 친 'integral'은 '완전한, 필수적인'이라는 의미이다. ① key는 형용사로 쓰일 때 '중요한, 주요한, 핵심적인, 필수적인'이라는 뜻을 나타내므로 'integral'과 의미가 가장 가깝다.

해석

윤리적 고려는 생명 공학 규제의 **필수적인** 요소이다.
① 중요한, 주요한, 핵심적인, 필수적인
② 우연한, 부차적인, 간접적인
③ 상호적인
④ 인기 있는, 유명한

02 정답 ①   Day 12-01

정답해설

밑줄 친 'renowned'는 '유명한, 명성 있는'의 뜻으로 ① prestigious와 의미가 가장 가깝다. 해당 문장은 실용문으로 작가 또는 화자가 'its high rigor and standard(그것의 높은 엄격함과 기준)'를 '하나의 개념'으로 취급해 주격 관계대명사 'which' 이후에 단수동사 'makes'를 사용하였다.

해석

한국의 교육 체계는 컴퓨터 및 통신의 사용을 다루는 공학 부서로서 한국을 강국으로 만들어 준 그것의 높은 엄격함과 기준으로 세계적으로 **유명**하다.
① 명망 있는, 일류의
② 상대적인
③ 싸우기 좋아하는
④ 저승의, 내세의

03 정답 ③   Day 15-02

정답해설

밑줄 친 'ruled out'은 'rule out'의 과거형으로 '제외시키다, 배제하다'라는 의미를 가지고 있다. 따라서 ③ excluded와 의미가 가장 가깝다.

해석

국방부는 이 상황에 대해 그 국가를 돕고 있으며, 테러의 가능성을 **배제했다**.
① 시작했다
② 부탁했다
③ 제외했다, 배제했다
④ 새어 나왔다

04 정답 ④   Day 11-03

정답해설

경사가 당황했다는 내용으로 보아 승진에서 '제외되었다'라고 하는 것이 문맥상 자연스럽다. 따라서 ④ pass over의 수동태 표현이 빈칸에 가장 알맞다.

해석

15년 경력의 경찰 경사는 젊은 경관에 유리하도록 승진에서 **제외된** 이후 당황스러워했다.
① (차에) 치이다
② 초대되다
③ 이행되다
④ 제외되다

05 정답 ④   Day 18-07

정답해설

④ 출제 포인트: no sooner 구문

「주어+had+no sooner+과거분사 ~, than+주어+과거시제 동사 ~.」는 no sooner 구문으로 '~하자마자 ~했다'를 뜻한다. 해당 문장에 적용된 시제와 접속사는 모두 올바르게 사용되었다. 단, 해당 문장에서는 'no sooner'가 문두로 강조되지 않았으므로 '도치' 현상은 일어나지 않는다.

해석

① 아이들은 그들이 원하는 것은 무엇이든지 할 수 있도록 허락되었다.
② William은 다른 사람들보다 영화에 대해 훨씬 더 많이 안다.
③ 인터넷을 사용하고 싶다면, 접수처에 이용할 수 있는 코드가 있을 것이다.
④ Jane이 요리를 시작하자마자 정전이 되어서 전기가 들어오지 않았다.

06 정답 ②   Day 13-06

정답해설

② 출제 포인트: 가주어 it/to부정사의 명사적 용법

해당 문장에서 'it'은 가주어이며 'to hear ~ a glass'는 진주어이다. 이때 'to hear ~ a glass'는 to부정사의 명사적 용법에 해당한다. 또한 'chink'는 '쨍그랑'이라는 의성어 표현이며 명사로 사용되고 있다.

해석

① 그녀는 그녀가 도덕적으로 나머지 우리들보다 우월하다고 생각한다.
② 더운 날, 잔에 얼음이 부딪히는 소리를 듣는 것은 기분 좋다.
③ 이 공극이 물로 완전히 채워지면, 그 토양은 흠뻑 젖는다.
  (* 공극: 토양 입자와 입자 사이에 공기나 물로 채워질 수 있는 틈새)
④ 만약 모든 사람들이 신분증을 소지하도록 강요받는다면, 그것은 우리 모두가 의심 받고 있다는 생각을 키울 것이다.

07 정답 ①   Day 12-07

정답해설

① 출제 포인트: to부정사의 태

완전타동사 'base' 뒤에 전치사 'on'이 올 수 있는 경우는 수동태 「be based on」뿐이며 '~에 근거하다(근거되어지다)'로 해석한다. 해당 문장은 to부정사의 동사원형 자리에 'base'를 사용하였으나 뒤에 전치사 'on'이 왔으며 주어진 해석이 '~에 근거하다'이므로 틀린 문장이다. 따라서 'base'를 수동태 'be based'로 수정해야 한다.

08 정답 ④　　　　　　　　　　　　　　　　Day 20-05

정답해설

④ 출제 포인트: 준사역동사의 목적격 보어
준사역동사 'get'은 목적어와 목적격 보어의 관계가 능동인 경우 to부정사와 현재분사를 목적격 보어로 사용하며, 목적어와 목적격 보어의 관계가 수동인 경우 과거분사를 사용한다. 해당 문장은 준사역동사 'get'의 목적격 보어에 동사원형인 'do'를 사용하였으므로 옳지 않은 문장이다. 따라서 'get'의 목적어 'the work'와 보어의 관계가 수동 관계이므로 'do'를 과거분사 'done'으로 수정해야 한다.

해석

기회가 많고 일자리가 남아도는 튼튼한 경제가 사회적 장벽을 무너뜨리는 데 도움이 된다는 것을 아는 것은 어렵지 않다. 편견에 빠져 있는 고용주는 이런저런 무리에 속한 구성원을 고용하기를 여전히 싫어할 수 있지만, 다른 어느 누구도 이용할 수 없다면, 차별은 그 일을 끝내야 한다는 기본적인 필요에 자리를 내주게 된다.

09 정답 ①　　　　　　　　　　　　　　　　Day 17-04

정답해설

B가 감기에 걸려 병원을 방문한 것에 관한 대화이다. B는 병원에서 간단한 진찰을 받았지만 B에게 50달러를 청구해 (A) '바가지(a rip-off)'였다고 말한다. 이에 A가 화났겠다고 말하며 '처방전 없이 살 수 있는 약(over-the-counter medicine)'을 먹었는지 묻고 효과가 있는지 묻는다. B는 약국에서 해열제를 먹었는데 효과는 미비했지만 적어도 (B) '부작용(side effect)'은 없었다고 말한다.

해석

A: 너 감기가 더 심해지는 것으로 보여.
B: 병원에 가봤는데 그저 (A) 바가지를 씌웠어. 병원이 간단한 진료에도 50달러를 청구했어.
A: 너 되게 화났겠다. 처방전 없이 살 수 있는 약은 뭐라도 먹었어?
B: 아, 약국에 가서 해열제를 좀 먹었어.
A: 너한테 효과가 있었어?
B: 음, 잘 모르겠어. 그런데 최소한 (B) 부작용은 없었어.
① (A) 바가지 (B) 부작용
② (A) 바가지 (B) 비난의 목소리
③ (A) 유력한 경쟁 상대 (B) 부작용
④ (A) 근거 없는 짐작 (B) 전혀 관계없는 것

10 정답 ①　　　　　　　　　　　　　　　　Day 14-04

정답해설

마이클 잭슨의 숨겨진 아들에 관한 기사를 읽은 A와 B가 대화를 나눈다. 그리고 숨겨진 아들에 관한 이야기가 '예기치 못했던 것(bolt from the blue sky)'이기에 기사가 '황색지(yellow journalism)'였을지도 모른다고 말한다. '황색지'는 이목을 끌기 위해 작성된 사실과 거리가 있는 선정적인 보도를 뜻한다. 그리고 마지막 빈칸에는 마이클 잭슨은 살아생전에 가는 곳마다 사람이 '특히 환영했었기(rolled out the red carpet)'에 그에 대해 함부로 말해서는 안 된다고 이야기한다.

해석

A: 너 마이클 잭슨에 관한 뉴스 들었어?
B: 그의 숨겨진 피아니스트 아들에 관한 것 말하는 거야?
A: 응, 마이클 잭슨은 수년 전에 죽었어. 그의 아들을 갑자기 보는 것은 예기치 못한 일이야.
B: 그러니까. 난 원래 믿지 않았어. 그냥 말이 안 돼.
A: 맞아. 마이클 잭슨은 살아있을 때 그의 피아니스트 아들을 언급했던 적이 없었어.
B: 아마 우리가 읽었던 그 기사는 그저 황색지였나 봐.
A: 나쁜 기자야. 마이클 잭슨 가지고 장난을 치면 안 되지. 그는 아직도 세계에서 가장 인기 있고 유명한 음악가 중 한 명인데.
B: 나도 네 의견에 동의해. 그가 가는 곳마다 사람들은 특히 환영해줬어.
① 파랑 – 노랑 – 빨강
② 검정 – 하양 – 빨강
③ 빨강 – 노랑 – 하양
④ 파랑 – 초록 – 검정

11 정답 ②　　　　　　　　　　　　　　　　Day 19-10

정답해설

주어진 문장에서는 '입양 사실을 알게 된 아이들이 겪을 수 있는 많은 문제'에 대해 언급하고 있다. 그러한 다양한 문제 중 "큰 슬픔(grief)"을 느끼는 것에 대해 최초로 언급하는 (A)가 주어진 문장 바로 이후에 이어지는 것이 자연스럽다. 이후, (A)에서 슬픔을 느끼는 이유로 언급된 "the loss of a relationship with their birth parents(친부모와의 관계 상실)"와 "the loss of the cultural and family connections that would have existed with those parents(그 부모와 함께 있었더라면 존재했었을지도 모를 문화적, 가족적 유대감의 상실)"를 (C)의 "This feeling of loss(이러한 상실의 감정)"로 가리키고 있으므로 (A) 이후에는 (C)가 이어지는 것이 옳다. 마지막으로, 앞서 언급된 '슬픔'을 느끼게 되는 시기에 대해 언급해 주고 있는 (B)가 이어지는 것이 자연스럽다. 따라서 정답은 ② (A) – (C) – (B)이다.

해석

아이들이 입양되었다는 것을 알게 되었을 때 많은 문제가 발생할 수 있다.
(A) 아이들은 친부모와의 관계 상실 또는 그 부모와 함께 있었더라면 존재했었을지도 모를 문화적, 가족적 유대감의 상실에 대해 큰 슬픔을 느낄 수 있다.
(C) 이러한 상실의 감정은 친부모에 대한 정보 또는 접촉이 적거나 거의 없는 폐쇄 또는 반개방형 입양의 경우에 특히 심할 수 있다.
(B) 이러한 슬픈 감정은 아이의 인생에 걸쳐 그들이 입양에 대해 처음으로 알게 되는 때, 격동의 10대 시기 도중에, 다른 가족 구성원이 사망했을 때, 또는 배우자나 부모가 되는 때를 포함한 많은 다른 시기에 촉발될 수 있다.

12 정답 ③　　　　　　　　　　　　　　　　Day 11-09

정답해설

주어진 지문 전체는 집단주의 문화와 개인주의 문화에서의 각각의 이직과 조직에 대한 개인의 성향을 대조와 비교의 방식으로 서술하고 있다. 〈보기〉에서 주목할 부분은 'this situation'과 'less movement'에 해당된다. 즉, "개인의 사회적 의무(social obligations)" 때문에 이직이 상대적으로 적다는 내용을 'less movement(더 적은 움직임)'를 통해 지적하며 이것을 "this situation"으로 지칭하고 있다. 따라서 사회적 의무가 개인보다 우선시 된다는 내용이 제시되어지는 부분인 'as fulfilling an obligation to a larger group(더 큰 집단에의 책임을 이행함으로써)'를 제시한 이후인 ③이 적합하다. ③ 이후 문장에서는 대조적으로 'individualistic cultures(개인주의 문화)'에서는 이직이 더 쉽다고 언급하고 있으므로 문맥이 자연스럽다.

해석

일의 의미에서의 문화적 차이는 다른 측면에서도 나타날 수 있다. (①) 예를 들어, 미국 문화에서, 일은 돈을 모으고 생계를 꾸리기 위한 수단이라고 단순히 생각하기 쉽다. (②) 다른 문화권, 특히 집단주의 문화권에서는 일이 더 큰 집단에 대한 의무를 이행하는 것으로 보일 수 있다. (③ **이러한 상황에서, 우리는 개인이 속한 조직과 그 조직을 구성하는 사람들에 대한 개인의 사회적 의무 때문에 한 직장에서 다른 직장으로의 이동이 줄어들 것으로 예상한다.**) 개인주의 문화에서는 자기와 직업을 분리하는 것이 더 쉽기 때문에 한 직업을 버리고 다른 직업을 가는 것을 고려하는 것이 더 쉽다. (④) 다른 직장은 같은 목표를 쉽게 달성할 수 있을 것이다.

지에 충돌하고 목적지를 더듬더듬 찾고, 단지 먹이를 먹기 위해 종종 나뭇가지 더미와 숲의 나뭇잎 무더기에 정면충돌한다. ③ 또한, 더 작은 박쥐류 동족과는 달리, 날여우박쥐는 훌륭한 시력을 지닌 큰 포유류이다. ④ **밤의 어둠은 이 야행성 포유류가 가야 할 곳으로 가는 것을 막지 못하며, 그것은 주변을 지도화하기 위해 끽하는 소리와 찍찍 소리를 이용해 먹이를 찾아낸다.** 그들이 어디에 있고 무엇이 그들 주위에 있는지 정확히 알아내기 위해 음파를 이용하는 대신에, 그들은 그들의 구역을 샅샅이 뒤지기 위해 잘 발달된 눈을 이용한다.

13 정답 ①
Day 14-10

정답해설

본문 첫 문장 "Bats can help an area get rid of pests and bugs(박쥐는 한 지역이 해충과 벌레를 제거하도록 도와준다)."를 통해 박쥐의 긍정적 역할에 대해 언급하고 있고, 이후 구체적으로 박쥐가 얼마나 많은 수와 종류의 벌레를 먹어 치울 수 있는지 설명해주고 있다. 또한, 본문 후반에서 박쥐의 먹이 활동으로 인해 인도네시아의 카카오 생산량이 유지될 수 있다고도 설명하고 있으므로, 글의 주제로 가장 적절한 것은 '① benefits of bats(박쥐의 이점)'이다.

해석

박쥐는 한 지역이 해충과 벌레를 제거하도록 도와준다. 각각의 박쥐는 한 시간에 1,200마리의 모기 또는 모기 크기의 곤충을 먹을 수 있는 능력으로 하룻밤에 6,000에서 8,000마리의 곤충을 먹어치우는 것으로 알려져 있다. 그들은 또한 파리, 각다귀, 넓적다리잎벌레, 그리고 전 세계의 호두 작물의 99퍼센트에 영향을 미치는 코들링나방과 같은 작물을 파괴하는 나방을 먹는다. 천연 해충 방제를 제공하는 그들의 능력이 농부들 사이에서 그들을 인기 있게 만들었다. 이 야행성 포유류에게 고마워해야 할 또 하나의 이유는 초콜릿이다. 인도네시아에서, 만일 그들이 박쥐를 퇴치한다면 카카오 수확량이 어떻게 될지가 추정되었을 때, 결과는 수억 달러의 손실을 일으킬 22퍼센트의 큰 하락이었다.
① 박쥐의 이점
② 박쥐의 위험성
③ 박쥐의 자연 서식지
④ 박쥐의 신체적 특징

14 정답 ④
Day 12-10

정답해설

본문은 '세계에서 가장 큰 박쥐인 말레이날여우박쥐(Malayan flying fox)'를 소개하는 글이다. ①, ②는 '말레이날여우박쥐'의 비행에 관한 설명으로 '비행과 방향 전환에는 문제가 없으나, 착륙에는 서툴다'라는 맥락으로 문맥상 자연스럽다. ③에서는 '첨가'를 나타내는 'Also(또한)'를 이용해, 말레이날여우박쥐의 또 다른 특징에 대해 설명하고 있으므로 글의 흐름상 자연스럽다. '작은 박쥐류와는 달리 큰 박쥐는 시력이 좋다'고 언급한 후, 시력이 발달한 큰 박쥐가 작은 박쥐류와 같이 '음파(sound waves)'를 이용하지 않고, '눈(peepers)'을 이용해 먹이를 찾고 지형을 파악한다는 내용의 마지막 문장이 이어지는 것이 문맥상 자연스럽다. ④에서 언급된 'squeaks(끽하는 소리)'와 'chirps(찍찍 소리)', 즉 소리(음파)를 이용해 먹이를 탐색하는 것은 작은 박쥐류의 특성이므로, 큰 박쥐에 대해 설명하는 본문의 문맥상 어색하다. 따라서 정답은 ④이다.

해석

말레이날여우박쥐(Malayan flying fox)는 세계에서 가장 큰 박쥐라는 축하를 받는다. 이 멸종위기에 처한 박쥐는 동남아시아의 열대 지역에 서식하는 거대한 종이다. ① 이 박쥐는 훌륭한 비행사이며 높이 솟은 열대 우림 지붕 사이로 아무 문제없이 방향 조절할 수 있다. ② 그러나, 착륙에 관한 한 그들은 목적

15 정답 ③
Day 16-08

정답해설

주어진 지문은 사회학자인 Mauss가 '종교적 유대 가정에서 자랐음에도 불구하고 그 종교를 배척했다'는 서술로 이어진다. 그리고 '삼촌의 지도로 철학을 공부'한 'Marcel Mauss'에 대해 설명하는 내용이다. ③ He had a doctrinaire faith (그는 교조적인 신념을 가지고 있다)의 경우 "Mauss had reacted against the Jewish faith"(Mauss는 유대적 신앙에 반하는 반응을 보였다) 내용과는 정반대에 해당된다. 따라서 정답은 '③ He had a doctrinaire faith(그는 교조적인 신념을 가지고 있었다).'이다.

해석

프랑스 사회학자인 Marcel Mauss(1872-1950)는 Lorraine의 Epinal(Vosges)에서 태어났고, 긴밀하게 맺어진, 독실한 정통파 유대인 가족 내에서 성장했다. Emile Durkheim이 그의 삼촌이었다. 18세 무렵, Mauss는 유대적 신앙에 반하는 반응을 보였다; 그는 결코 종교적 인물이 아니었다. 그는 Bordeaux에서 Durkheim의 감독 하에서 철학을 공부했다; Durkheim은 그의 조카를 이끄는 데 수고를 아끼지 않았고 심지어 Mauss에게 가장 유용할 강의 주제들도 선정해줬다. 따라서 Mauss는 처음에는 철학자였고(대부분의 초기 Durkheim 학파들처럼), 철학에 대한 그의 이해는 그가 항상 최고의 존경을 유지했던 Durkheim에게 직접 영향을 받았다.
① 그는 유대인 배경을 가지고 있다.
② 그는 그의 삼촌에 의해 감독을 받았다.
③ 그는 교조적인 신념을 가지고 있었다.
④ 그는 철학 배경을 가진 사회학자였다.

16 정답 ④
Day 15-10

정답해설

본문은 '볼리비아에서의 박쥐 판매'에 대해 설명하고 있다. 볼리비아에서의 박쥐 사냥 및 판매가 불법임에도 불구하고 이러한 박쥐 판매가 성행하는 이유는 "People buy them so they can drink bat blood for its purported healing properties — particularly, they think, to help manage epilepsy(사람들은 그들이 생각하기에 특히 간질을 관리하는 데 도움이 되는 치유 능력이 있다고 알려진 박쥐의 피를 마시기 위해 그것들을 산다).", 즉, 치료 효과를 기대하며 박쥐의 피를 마시는 사람들이 많기 때문이다. 그러나 본문 후반에서 언급된 것과 같이 "However, there's no proof of any medicinal benefit from drinking bat blood(그러나 박쥐의 피를 마시는 것의 의학적인 이점에 대한 증거는 없다).", 박쥐 피의 의학적 효능에 대한 증거는 없다. 따라서 글의 내용과 일치하는 보기는 '④ The belief about bat blood's medical benefits is groundless(박쥐 피의 의학적 이점에 대한 믿음은 근거가 없다).'이다.

해석

볼리비아의 시장에서 판매를 위한 박쥐를 찾는 것은 어렵지 않다. 그것들은 보통 냄새가 지독한 신발 상자에 처박혀있으며, 일부 상자에는 20마리나 되는 박쥐로 빼곡하게 차 있고, 살아있는 것들은 이미 질병 또는 스트레스에 굴복한 박쥐들 위로 기어 다닌다. 사람들은 그들이 생각하기에 – 특히 간질을 관

리하는 데 도움이 되는 - 치유 능력이 있다고 알려진 박쥐의 피를 마시기 위해 그것들을 산다. "그 믿음은 우리의 사회, 주로 안데스 지역에 뿌리 깊이 박혀있다."라고 박쥐 전문가 Luis F. Aguirre는 설명한다. 그러나 박쥐의 피를 마시는 것의 의학적인 이점에 대한 증거는 없다. 게다가 박쥐 사냥은 공식적으로는 불법이다. 볼리비아의 법은 적절한 허가 없이 야생 동물을 죽이거나 판매하는 것을 금지하고 있으며, 위반 행위는 최대 6년의 징역형을 받을 수 있다. 그러나 그 믿음과 사냥은 지속되고 있다.

① 볼리비아 시장에서 박쥐는 사려 깊게 거래된다.
② 오직 살아있는 박쥐만이 팔린다.
③ 사람들은 치료 효과를 기대하며 박쥐의 피를 몸에 바른다.
④ 박쥐 피의 의학적 이점에 대한 믿음은 근거가 없다.

17 정답 ④   Day 13-08

정답해설

본문은 독서의 방법 중 하나인 'Skimming(스키밍)'에 대해 설명하는 글로, 스키밍이란 내용을 빨리 훑어보며 글의 골자를 빠르게 파악하는 방법이다. 본문은 스키밍이 정독을 하기 전 기본 내용을 파악하는 데 도움이 되고 시간을 절약해주는 반면, 독자의 전반적 글의 이해도는 낮을 수밖에 없다고 스키밍의 전반적인 특징에 대해 설명하고 있다. 그러나 본문의 마지막 부분에서 "However, skimming is useful when your goal is to preview the text to get a better idea of what it's about(그러나 스키밍은 당신의 목표가 텍스트가 무엇인지에 대한 더 나은 아이디어를 얻기 위해 그것을 사전 검토하는 것일 때는 유용하다)."라고 스키밍의 장점을 다시 한번 부각하여 언급해 주고 있으므로, 전체 글의 요지로는 '④ Skimming is a good way to get an overview of the text(스키밍은 텍스트의 개요를 얻는 좋은 방법이다).'가 가장 적절하다.

해석

스키밍(Skimming)은 때때로 요점 읽기라고 일컬어진다. 그것은 텍스트의 가장 기본 단계에서 그것이 무엇에 대한 것인지 알기 위해 도움이 될 수 있다. 당신은 일반적으로 그것을 잡지 또는 신문을 볼 때 할 수 있으며, 이것은 당신이 마음속으로 빠르게 정독을 고려하는 기사들의 목록을 작성하도록 도와줄 것이다. 당신은 또한 전화번호부에서 이름을 찾기 위해 훑어볼 수도 있다. 만일 당신이 특정한 방식으로 잘 훈련한다면 당신은 분당 700단어를 읽는 속도에 도달할 수 있다. 물론 이해도는 매우 낮고 전체적인 내용의 이해는 매우 피상적이다. 그것은 분명 당신의 많은 시간을 절약해 줄 것이지만, 앞서 언급된 이유로 인해 이것은 최상의 독서법은 아니다. 그러나 스키밍은 당신의 목표가 텍스트가 무엇인지에 대한 더 나은 아이디어를 얻기 위해 그것을 사전 검토하는 것일 때는 유용하다. 그것은 당신이 정독을 준비하는 데 도움이 될 것이다.

① 스키밍 기술은 훈련을 통해 발달될 수 있다.
② 스키밍은 속독에 있어서 가장 중요한 기술이다.
③ 스키밍은 독자가 텍스트를 완전히 이해할 수 있도록 해준다.
④ 스키밍은 텍스트의 개요를 얻는 좋은 방법이다.

18 정답 ②   Day 20-09

정답해설

(A) 이전 문장에서 "It can increase the harmful impact of wind and rain on local ecosystems; destroy the valuable wildlife habitat used by pine martens, caribou, and other animals; and cause soil to become dry and overheated, which may in turn increase the risk of fire or interfere with seedling growth(그것은 지역 생태계에 미치는 바람과 비의 악영향을 증가시킬 수 있고; 소나무 담비, 카리부, 그리고 기타 동물이 사용하는 귀중한 야생 서식지를 파괴할 수 있으며; 토양을 건조하고 과열되게 만들어, 결과적으로 화재의 위험을 증가시키거나 묘목의 성장을 방해할 수도 있다)."라고 '개벌(clear cutting)의 문제점'에 대해 설명한 후, (A) 이후에서 "such logging operations can alter the chemical and physical makeup of nearby bodies of water and affect the health of fish and other aquatic species(그러한 벌목 작업들은 인근 수역의 화학적, 물리적 구성을 변화시킬 수 있으며 물고기와 다른 수중 생물의 건강에 영향을 미칠 수 있다)."라고 '개벌이 야기할 수 있는 또 다른 문제점'에 대해 언급하고 있다. 따라서 빈칸 이후에서 이전에 언급된 것과 동일한 논점의 내용을 추가적으로 제시하고 있으므로 '첨가'를 나타내는 'Also(또한)'가 (A)에 적절하다.

(B) 이전 두 문장에서 제기된 '개벌의 문제점'에 대한 의견으로 (B) 이후에서 "professional foresters and loggers argue that clear cutting mimics natural disturbances, such as forest fires and insect infestations, and is a sustainable way to harvest trees when managed properly(전문 삼림 감독관들과 벌목꾼들은 개벌이 산불과 곤충의 침입과 같은 자연적 교란을 모방하는 것이며, 적절히 관리된다면 나무를 수확하는 지속 가능한 방법이라고 주장한다)."라고 '개벌'을 긍정적으로 바라보는 견해에 대해 언급하고 있으므로, 이전 내용과 대조적인 논점을 제시하고 있다는 것을 알 수 있다. 따라서 빈칸에는 '역접'을 나타내는 'Nevertheless(그럼에도 불구하고)' 또는 'However(그러나)'가 적절하다. 따라서 정답은 '② Also(또한) - However(그러나)'이다.

해석

캐나다에서 이용되는 흔한 벌목 방법은 개벌, 즉 전체 입목을 수확하고 제거하는 것이다. 효율적이기는 하지만, 개벌은 다양한 환경 문제를 야기한다. 그것은 지역 생태계에 미치는 바람과 비의 악영향을 증가시킬 수 있고; 소나무 담비, 카리부, 그리고 기타 동물이 사용하는 귀중한 야생 서식지를 파괴할 수 있으며; 토양을 건조하고 과열되게 만들어, 결과적으로 화재의 위험을 증가시키거나 묘목의 성장을 방해할 수도 있다. (A) 또한 그러한 벌목 작업들은 인근 수역의 화학적, 물리적 구성을 변화시킬 수 있으며 물고기와 다른 수중 생물의 건강에 영향을 미칠 수 있다. (B) 그러나 전문 삼림 감독관들과 벌목꾼들은 개벌이 산불과 곤충의 침입과 같은 자연적 교란을 모방하는 것이며, 적절히 관리된다면 나무를 수확하는 지속 가능한 방법이라고 주장한다.

	(A)	(B)
①	결과적으로	그럼에도 불구하고
②	또한	그러나
③	즉	간단히 말해
④	그러나	예를 들어

19 정답 ③   Day 17-09

정답해설

본문은 '삼림파괴(deforestation)를 방지할 수 있는 새로운 방안'에 대한 연구 결과를 소개하는 글이다. 본문 첫 문장 "A new study finds that simply paying landowners in the developing world not to cut down trees can significantly reduce carbon in the atmosphere(새로운 연구는 단순히 개발도상국의 토지 소유주들에게 나무를 자르지 않도록 돈을 지불하는 것이 대기 중의 탄소를 상당히 줄일 수 있다는 것을 밝힌다)."에 따르면, '개발도상국의 토지 소유주들에게 금전적 지원을 하는 방안'이 효과적이라는 것을 알 수 있다. 이후 빈칸 문장에서는 실제로 우간다에서 실시되었던 실험에 대해 구체적으로 언급하고 있으므로, 토지 소유주들에게 '재정적인 지원'이 투입되었음을 시사하는 표현이 들어가야 적절하다. 따라서 빈칸에 가장 적절한 보기는 '③ offering small financial incentives to landowners(토지 소유주들에게 적은 금액의 재정적 지원금을 제공하는 것)'이다.

해석

새로운 연구는 단순히 개발도상국의 토지 소유주들에게 나무를 자르지 않도록 돈을 지불하는 것이 대기 중의 탄소를 상당히 줄일 수 있다는 것을 밝힌다. 그것은 또한 파리 협정의 목표와 같은 목적을 달성하는 데 도움이 되는 매우 비용 효율적인 방법이다. 학술지 *Science*에 오늘 게재된 그 연구는, 우간다에서 토지 소유주들에게 적은 금액의 재정적 지원금을 제공하는 것이 삼림 벌채를 절반으로 줄인다는 것을 알아냈다. 동원된 자금의 액수가 상당히 적기 때문에, 미국에서 실시되는 많은 에너지 효율 프로그램들보다 소비된 1달러당 10에서 50배 더 효과적인 것으로 추정되었다. Innovations for Poverty Action의 협회장 Annie Duflo는 이 연구가 개발도상국에서의 향후 보호 프로그램들을 알릴 단서가 될 것이라고 말했다. "이와 같은 좋은 과학이 우리가 어떻게 기후변화에 맞서 싸워야 할지 그리고 어떻게 위기에 처한 서식지를 보호해야 하는지에 대해 이해할 수 있게 도와주며, 또한 빈곤한 농부들을 도와줄 수 있다."

① 더 많은 나무를 심도록 지역 주민들에게 돈을 지불하는 것
② 토지 소유주들이 목재 거래를 중지하도록 설득하는 것
③ 토지 소유주들에게 적은 금액의 재정적 지원금을 제공하는 것
④ 토지 소유주들 사이에서 기후변화에 대한 인식을 고취시키는 것

---

20 정답 ④ Day 14-08

정답해설

본문은 학교에서 읽는 법을 제대로 배우지 못한 아이들이 성인이 될 때까지 읽는 것에 어려움을 느끼며, 그에 따라 안정적인 직업을 얻기 힘들고 범죄를 저질러 감옥에 갈 가능성이 더 높다는 연구 결과를 소개하고 있다. 빈칸에는 이러한 사람들을 칭하는 용어를 설명하는 말이 들어가야 하는데, 빈칸 이후 "Most of them don't have neurological problems. Their schools and, specifically, their primary school teachers have failed them(그들 중 대부분은 신경학적인 문제를 가지고 있지 않다. 그들의 학교 그리고 특히 그들의 초등학교 선생님들이 그들에게 도움이 되지 못한 것이다)."로 보아, 그들은 어떠한 질병 또는 장애 때문에 읽지 못하게 된 것이 아니라 학교와 교사들이 그들에게 도움이 되지 않아 그들이 적절한 교육을 받지 못했기 때문에 이러한 결과가 발생한다는 것을 알 수 있다. 따라서, 빈칸에 가장 적절한 보기는 '④ instructional casualties(교육의 피해자들)'이다.

해석

결과에 있어서, 아이들을 수십 년 동안 추적하는 유형인 종단적 연구는 슬픈 이야기를 해준다. 만일 당신의 아이가 읽지 못하는 것을 경험한다면 그것은 거의 그가 만성적이고 심신을 쇠약하게 하는 질병에 걸린 것과 거의 마찬가지이다. 1학년에 학년 수준으로 읽지 못하는 아이들은 거의 변함없이 잘 읽지 못하는 4학년이 된다. 읽는 데 어려움을 겪는 3학년들의 74퍼센트는 9학년에도 여전히 어려움을 겪고, 그것은 결과적으로 고등학교 졸업하는 것을 어렵게 만든다. 읽는 데 어려움을 겪는 아이들이 안정적인 직업을 가지는 데 어려움을 겪는 성인으로 자란다는 것을 알게 되는 것이 당신을 놀라게 하지는 않을 것이다. 그들은 장기적인 실업을 경험할 가능성이 더 높고, 복지서비스를 필요로 할 가능성이 더 높으며, 감옥에 갈 가능성이 더 높다. 독서 전문가들은 그들을 "교육의 피해자들"이라고 부른다. 그들 중 대부분은 신경학적인 문제를 가지고 있지 않다. 그들의 학교 그리고 특히 그들의 초등학교 선생님들이 그들에게 도움이 되지 못한 것이다.

① 사회 부적응자들
② 재능 있는 독서가들
③ 무능한 학생들
④ 교육의 피해자들

결국엔 성정혜 영어 하프모의고사
기적사 DAY 21

| 01 | ② | 02 | ③ | 03 | ③ | 04 | ① | 05 | ① |
| 06 | ③ | 07 | ④ | 08 | ① | 09 | ④ | 10 | ② |

오답률 TOP 2

01 정답② 13 국가직

정답해설

합리화와 자기기만을 고려한다는 것으로 보아 자기 자신을 '관대하게' 평가한다는 것을 알 수 있다. 이후의 예시에 나온 것처럼 눈이 보이지 않는 사람에게는 정직했지만 눈이 보이는 사람은 속였는데, 그것이 자신이 대단한 사람이어서 그렇다고 하는 것은 자기 합리화, 즉 자신을 '관대하게' 평가한 것이다. 따라서 정답은 ② leniently이다.

해석

합리화와 자기기만에 대한 우리의 대단한 능력을 고려해보면, 우리들 중 대부분은 우리 자신을 **관대하게** 평가할 것이다: 나는 대단한 사람이므로 그 눈이 보이지 않는 승객에게 정직했다. 나는 눈이 보이는 사람은 속였는데 어쨌든 아마도 그녀가 너무 많은 돈이 있었기 때문이었다.

① 엄하게
② 관대하게
③ 정직하게
④ 고맙게도, 다행히도

어휘

rationalization 합리화   self-deception 자기기만
cheat 속이다, 기만하다   harshly 엄하게
leniently 관대하게   honestly 정직하게
thankfully 고맙게도, 다행히도

02 정답③ 13 국가직

정답해설

㉠에는 장남이 많은 책임을 '지다'의 의미가, ㉡에는 같은 단어가 다른 의미를 '나타내다'의 의미가 들어가는 것이 알맞다. 따라서 이 두 가지 의미를 포함하는 표현은 ③ take on이다.

해석

• 한국에서, 장남은 많은 책임을 **지는** 경향이 있다.
• 같은 말도 다른 방식으로 말해질 때 다른 의미를 **나타낸다**.

① 인수하다
② (이야기 등을) 적어두다, (건물 등을) 헐어버리다
③ (책임을) 지다, (색채 등을) 나타내다, (일 등을) 떠맡다, ~을 고용하다
④ 이륙하다, (옷을) 벗다

어휘

responsibility 책임, 의무   take over 인수하다
take down (이야기 등을) 적어두다, (건물 등을) 헐어버리다
take on (책임을) 지다, (색채 등을) 나타내다, (일 등을) 떠맡다, ~을 고용하다
take off 이륙하다, (옷을) 벗다

03 정답 ③
13 국가직

정답해설

밑줄 친 'iron out'은 '해결하다'라는 의미이며 ③ solve와 의미가 가장 가깝다.

해석

우리는 먼저 몇 가지의 문제들을 <u>해결할</u> 필요가 있다.
① 생각하다, 임신하다
② 검토하다, 비평하다
③ 해결하다
④ 포즈를 취하다, 제기하다, 주장하다

어휘

iron out 해결하다 conceive 생각하다, 임신하다
review 검토하다, 비평하다 solve 해결하다
pose 포즈를 취하다, 제기하다, 주장하다

04 정답 ①
14 국가직

정답해설

A의 'I haven't noticed anyone in class that I could fall in love with(난 반에서 사랑에 빠질 누구도 찾지 못했는데)!'에 대한 B의 대답으로 ① 'Me neither(나도 그렇다)'이 가장 적절하다. A가 부정문으로 말했으므로, 그에 대한 동의도 부정어를 포함하여 동의를 표하는 것이 적절하다.

오답해설

② A가 B의 탓을 하고 있지 않으므로 '내 탓을 하면 안 되지(You shouldn't blame me)'는 적절하지 않다.
③ A가 반에서 사랑에 빠질 수 있는 대상자를 찾는 것이 '부모님에게 달려있다(It is up to your parents)'라는 내용은 지문에 제시되어 있지 않다.
④ '그녀'라는 특정 친구를 언급한 적이 없으므로 '그녀와 만나보는 것이 좋을 거야(You'd better hang about with her)'는 A의 말에 대한 B의 대답으로 어색하다.

해석

A: 나 어제 신문에서 너희 부모님의 결혼 25주년 공고를 봤어. 정말 멋지더라. 너희 부모님이 어떻게 만나셨는지 아니?
B: 응. 정말 믿기지 않는 일이야, 진짜 로맨틱하거든. 대학에서 만났고, 서로 잘 맞는다는 걸 알고 데이트를 시작했어. 부모님의 교제는 학교 다니는 동안 내내 계속되었어.
A: 정말? 진짜 아름다워. 난 반에서 사랑에 빠질 누구도 찾지 못했는데!
B: <u>나도 그래.</u> 오, 음, 다음 학기에는 있을 거야!
① 나도 그래
② 내 탓을 하면 안 되지
③ 너희 부모님에게 달렸지
④ 그녀와 많은 시간을 보내는 것이 좋을 거야

어휘

announcement 발표, 소식 anniversary 기념일
compatible (사람이) 사이좋게 지낼 수 있는, (사물이) 양립할 수 있는
courtship (결혼 전의) 교제 (기간) be up to ~에 달려 있다
hang about with 많은 시간을 보내다, ~와 만나다(사귀다)

05 정답 ①
16 국가직

정답해설

① **출제 포인트: 현재분사 vs. 과거분사**
현재분사 'damaging' 이후에 「by+행위자」가 있으며 수식하는 대상 'an ecosystem'과 수동관계이므로 틀린 문장이다. 따라서 현재분사 'damaging'을 과거분사 'damaged'로 수정해야 한다.

오답해설

② **출제 포인트: little vs. few**
해당 문장에서 'little'은 동사 'know'를 수식하는 부사로 사용되었으며 원급 강조 부사 'very'의 수식을 받고 있으므로 옳은 문장이다.
③ **출제 포인트: 현재분사 vs. 과거분사**
밑줄 친 'slow-growing'은 수식하는 대상 'life-forms'와 능동관계이므로 현재분사 'growing'을 사용하는 것이 옳으며 해당 문장에서 'slow'는 현재분사 'growing'을 수식하는 부사로 사용되었다.
④ **출제 포인트: 「It+be+형용사+to+동사원형+목적어」에서 목적어 이동이 가능한 경우(difficult)**
「It+be동사+형용사+to+동사원형+목적어」에서 형용사가 'difficult'인 경우 목적어가 가주어 'It'의 자리로 이동할 수 있다. 해당 문장은 'It is somewhat difficult to reach them.'에서 목적어 'them'이 가주어 'It'의 자리로 이동하여 'They are somewhat difficult to reach.'가 된 것이므로 옳은 문장이다.

해석

산호초들은 고기잡이 그물에 의해 점점 손상을 입고 있는 생태계의 기반이다. 그러나 과학자들은 천천히 자라고 있는 생물 형태에 대해서 거의 알고 있지 않은데 왜냐하면 그것들은 다소 닿기 힘들기 때문이다.(포착하기 힘들기 때문이다.)

어휘

coral 산호, 산호초 foundation 기반, 토대, 설립
ecosystem 생태계 fishing net 고기잡이 그물, 어망

오답률 TOP 3

06 정답 ③
16 국가직

정답해설

③ **출제 포인트: 완전타동사 suggest/주장, 요구, 명령, 제안동사+(that)+주어+(should)+동사원형**
'suggest'는 완전타동사이므로 5형식으로 사용할 수 없다. 해당 문장은 5형식 형태인 「suggest+목적어+목적격 보어[to부정사]」를 사용하였으므로 틀린 문장이며 해당 문장을 3형식으로 수정해야 한다. 이때 'suggest'는 '제안하다'로 해석하는 것이 자연스러우므로 목적어로 사용되는 that절의 형태는 「(that)+주어+(should)+동사원형」이어야 한다. 따라서 'you to take a copy of the final invoice along with your travel documents'를 '(that) you (should) take a copy of the final invoice along with your travel documents'로 수정해야 한다.

오답해설

① **출제 포인트: 시간의 부사(구)/주격 관계대명사**
'yesterday'는 시간의 부사구로 과거시제 동사와 함께 사용한다. 따라서 'meet'의 과거시제인 'met'은 옳은 표현이다. 또한 사람을 나타내는 명사(구) 'a student'를 선행사로 하며 'who' 이후에 오는 절의 주어가 없으므로 주격 관계대명사 'who'는 옳은 표현이다.
② **출제 포인트: to부정사의 태/접속사 vs. 전치사**
'trust'는 완전타동사이므로 수동태로 사용되는 경우 이후에 목적어가 없

다. 해당 문장에서 부정사로 쓰인 'to trust'는 수동태인 'to be trusted' 로 사용되어 이후에 목적어가 아닌 전명구 'with other people's money'가 왔으므로 옳은 문장이다. 또한 해당 문장은 접속사 'Even though' 이후에 절을 사용하였으므로 옳은 문장이다.

④ **출제 포인트: to부정사의 형용사적 용법/이중부정 금지**

to부정사(구) 'to make to the proposal'은 명사(구) 'any objections'를 수식하므로 형용사적 용법으로 사용된 것임을 알 수 있으며, 이때 'to make'와 'any objections'의 관계는 술목관계에 해당한다. 또한 부정부사 'not'이 쓰인 문장에 'no'를 사용하면 이중부정이 되어 비문이 되므로 'any'를 사용하는 것이 옳다. 단, 해당 문장은 동명사 관용표현인 'have an objection to ~ing'에 해당되지 않으므로 주의해야한다.

해석

① 나는 어제 구내식당에서 당신을 알고 있다고 말하는 한 학생을 만났다.
② Tim이 당신의 친구일지라도, 그에게 다른 사람의 돈을 맡겨서는 안 된다.
③ 우리는 당신의 여행 서류와 함께 당신이 최종 청구서의 사본을 가져와야 한다고 제안한다.
④ 놀랍게도, 그녀는 그 제안에 대해서 어떠한 반대도 하지 않았다.

오답률 TOP 1

07 정답 ④   16 국가직

정답해설

④ **출제 포인트: 주의해야 할 비교급 관용표현**

'still more'는 긍정문을 받아서 '더구나 …한'의 의미를 지니며, 'still less'는 부정문을 받아서 '더구나 …은 아닌'의 의미를 지닌다. 해당 문장은 부정어 'No'가 포함된 부정문을 대상으로 한 표현이므로 'still more'를 'still less'로 수정해야 한다.

오답해설

① **출제 포인트: with 분사구문/능동태 vs. 수동태**

해당 문장에서 'With many people ill'은 with 분사구문에 해당하며 형용사 'ill' 앞에 현재분사 'being'이 생략되어 있다. 또한 주어진 해석이 '취소되었다'이므로 수동태 'was cancelled'를 옳게 사용하였다.

② **출제 포인트: 관사의 위치**

'so' 이후에 「부정관사+형용사+명사」 형태의 명사(구)가 오는 경우 「so+형용사+부정관사+명사」의 형태를 가진다. 따라서 'so straightforward a problem'은 옳은 표현이다.

③ **출제 포인트: 직접의문문의 어순**

의문부사 'how'를 사용한 직접의문문으로 「동사+주어」의 도치 어순을 옳게 사용하였다. 또한 주어인 'students'를 수식하는 'carrying'이 현재분사로서 능동의 의미로 사용된 것도 적절하다.

08 정답 ①   16 국가직

정답해설

구직 면접 결과에서 놀라운 사실은, 지원자를 채용할 이유가 '자격 조건'이나 '업무 경험'이 아니라 '호감 가는 사람'이었으므로, 제목으로 가장 적절한 것은 ① 'To Get a Job, Be a Pleasant Person(직업을 얻기 위해, 호감 가는 사람이 돼라)'이다.

오답해설

② 지문과 반대의 의견을 말하고 있으므로 틀리다.
③ 자격 조건에 해당하는 '능력'과 '호감 가는 사람'에 해당하는 '성격'은 언급되었지만, 이 둘의 중요도가 바뀌었으므로 틀리다.
④ 지문에서 언급되지 않았으므로 틀리다.

해석

구직 면접 결과에 대한 많은 양의 자료를 분석한 후에, 한 연구팀은 놀라운 현실을 발견해 냈다. 채용될 가능성이 자격 조건에 의해 좌지우지되었을까? 혹은 업무 경험이었을까? 실은, 둘 다 아니다. 그건 그저 한 가지 중요한 요인 이었다: 지원자가 호감이 가는 사람으로 비쳤는지. 자기 자신을 호감이 가도록 해낸 그러한 지원자들은 고용될 가능성이 매우 컸다; 그들은 그들의 길을 성공으로 이끌었다. 일부 지원자들은 미소를 짓고 눈 맞춤을 유지하려는 특별한 노력을 해왔다. 다른 지원자들은 그 기관(회사)을 침이 마르도록 칭찬했다. 이러한 적극성은 면접자에게 그렇게 호감이 가고 사회적으로 능숙한 지원자들이 직장에 잘 들어맞으며, 그래서 채용될 것이라는 것을 확신시켰다.

① 직업을 얻기 위해, 호감 가는 사람이 돼라
② 더 많은 자격 조건들이 더 좋은 기회를 가져다준다
③ 성격이 아니라 능력이 중요하다
④ 면접에서 자기의 참모습을 보여줘라

어휘

likelihood 가능성, 희망   qualification 자격 조건
pleasant 호감이 가는, 상냥한   candidate 지원자, 후보자
ingratiate 마음에 들게 하다, 환심을 사다
charm 매혹하다

09 정답 ④   16 국가직

정답해설

본문 중반에 언급된 "Don DeLilo, Peter Carey, Salman Rushdie, and Elmore Leonard all worked for long stretches in advertising(DeLilo, Peter Carey, Salman Rushdie, 그리고 Elmore Leonard는 모두 오랫동안 광고업에서 일했다)."으로 보아 Don DeLilo, Peter Carey, Salman Rushdie, 그리고 Elmore Leonard 모두 오랫동안 광고업에서 일을 했다는 것을 알 수 있다. 그러나 ④는 'Salman Rushdie가 광고업에서 큰 성공을 이루면서 잠시 일했다'라고 하였으므로 틀리다.

오답해설

① 본문 후반에 언급된 "novelists and poets are continually scratching ~themselves a spot."을 통해 지문과 일치함을 알 수 있다.
② 본문 초반에 언급된 "carve out time ~ vacations"와 "William Carlos Williams ~ were doctors."를 통해 지문과 일치함을 알 수 있다.
③ "Other writers teach. ~common solution today"를 통해 지문과 일치함을 알 수 있다.

해석

대부분의 작가들은 두 개의 삶을 산다. 그들은 적당한 직업에서 좋은 수입을 얻고, 이른 아침, 늦은 저녁, 주말, 방학과 같이 그들이 할 수 있는 최선으로 그들의 글쓰기를 위해 시간을 쪼갠다. William Carlos Williams와 Louis-Ferdinand Céline는 의사였다. Wallace Stevens는 보험 회사에서 일했다. T.S. Elliot은 은행가였다가, 후에는 출판업자가 되었다. Don DeLilo, Peter Carey, Salman Rushdie, 그리고 Elmore Leonard는 모두 오랫동안 광고업에서 일했다. 다른 작가들은 가르치는 일을 한다. 오늘날 그것(교직에 종사하는 것)은 아마도 가장 흔한 해결법일 것이다, 그리고 소설가들과 시인들은 소위 창작 작문 강좌라 부르는 것을 모든 주요 대학이 제공하기 때문에, 이들 강좌 중 한 자리를 차지하기 위해 계속 다툴 것이다. 누가 그들을 비난할 수 있겠는가? 월급은 많지 않을 수 있지만, 그 일은 안정적이고 시간도 적절하다.

① 일부 작가들은 창작 작문 강좌를 가르치는 교직을 위해 고군분투한다.
② 의사로서, William Carlos Williams는 작문할 시간을 찾기 위해 노력했다.
③ 작가들이 오늘날 생계를 유지하기 위해 가르치는 일을 하는 것은 흔한 일이다.

④ Salman Rushdie는 광고업에서 큰 성공을 하면서 잠시 일했었다.

어휘

carve out 베어내다, 잘라내다
stretch (연속된) 길, 거리, 범위, 일련의 기간
so-called 이른바 course 수업, 과정
scratch 긁다, 할퀴다
scramble 앞을 다투다, 고생하며 나아가다

10 정답 ②
16 국가직

정답해설

이 글은 젊은 여성의 성인식과 같은 라틴 아메리카의 La Quinceañera 풍습에 대한 이야기를 다루고 있다. ②에서 언급한 문화비교를 통해 계급 차이를 알 수 있을 만한 근거는 지문 상 언급되어 있지 않다. 따라서 정답은 ②이다.

오답해설

②에서 언급한 계급 차이를 그 다음 문장에서 언급한 'be attended by(~에 의해 시중받다)'로 연관해서 생각할 수 있다. 마치 시중받는 사람과 시중드는 사람 사이에 계급이 존재한다고 생각이 들기 때문이다. 그러나 이는 단순히 연결된 두 문장만 볼 것이 아니라, 글 전체의 흐름을 보아야 하므로 틀리다. 다른 보기들은 La Quinceañera 행사에 관한 절차이므로 글의 흐름에 부합한다.

해석

젊은 여성이 비로소 여성다운 여성이 되는 과정에 대한 가장 큰 축하들 중 하나는 라틴 아메리카와 히스패닉 문화에서 일어난다. 이러한 행사는 La Quinceañera 또는 열다섯 번째 해로 불린다. ① 그것은 젊은 여성이 이제 결혼 가능한 나이라는 것을 인정한다. 그날은 보통 추수 감사절에 대한 미사로 시작된다. ② <u>한 문화와 다른 문화의 통과의례의 관습을 비교하면서, 우리는 계급의 차이를 가늠해볼 수 있다.</u> 그 젊은 여성이 발끝까지 오는 하얀색 또는 파스텔색의 드레스를 입고 여성 들러리들과 남성 수행원으로 14명의 친구와 친지들에 의해 시중을 받는다. ③ 그녀의 부모와 대부들은 제단 아래에서 그녀들 둘러싼다. 그 미사가 끝날 때, 다른 젊은 친척들은 참석한 사람들에게 작은 선물들을 준다, 그동안에 그 Quinceañera 자신은 부케를 처녀 제단에 놓는다. ④ 그 미사 후에 춤, 케이크 그리고 토스트와 함께 정성들여 만든 파티가 있다. 마지막으로, 그 밤이 끝날 때까지, 그 젊은 여성은 가장 맘에 드는 에스코트하는 남자와 함께 왈츠춤을 춘다.

어휘

passage 통과, 통로, 복도 womanhood 여성
altar 제단 bouquet 부케, 꽃다발
elaborate 정교한, 정성 들인

기적사 DAY 22

결국엔 성정혜 영어 하프모의고사

| 01 | ① | 02 | ① | 03 | ③ | 04 | ③ | 05 | ④ |
| 06 | ① | 07 | ② | 08 | ④ | 09 | ① | 10 | ④ |

01 정답 ①

정답해설

문맥상 Sally가 무슨 일이 있었는지 묻는 표현에 이어지는 말로 빈칸에는 '우울한 얼굴을 하다'의 의미인 'get a ① long face'가 적절하다.

해석

Sally에게 무슨 일이 있었니? 그녀는 오늘 아침에 **우울한** 얼굴이었어.
① 우울한; 긴
② 정직한
③ 파란('우울한'은 'feel blue'라고 표현한다)
④ 느린, 부진한, 게으른

어휘

long face 우울한 얼굴, 슬픈 표정 honest 정직한
blue 파란('우울한'의 경우는 'feel blue'라고 표현한다)
sluggish 느린, 부진한, 게으른

02 정답 ①

정답해설

문맥상 '동반하다, 동행하다'라는 뜻을 가진 'accompany'의 과거 동사 ① accompanied를 사용하여 '그의 아내가 동행했다'고 하는 것이 가장 자연스럽다.

해석

그 여행에는 그의 아내가 그와 **동행했다**.
① 동행했다, 반주했다
② 전멸시켰다, 무효로 했다
③ (책임을) 졌다, (색채 등을) 나타냈다, (일 등을) 떠맡았다, ~을 고용했다
④ 이륙했다, (옷을) 벗었다

어휘

accompany 동행하다, 반주하다 annihilate 전멸시키다, 무효로 하다
take on (책임을) 지다, (색채 등을) 나타내다, (일 등을) 떠맡다, ~을 고용하다
take off 이륙하다, (옷을) 벗다

오답률 TOP 2

03 정답 ③

정답해설

밑줄 친 'abrogate'는 '폐지하다, 철폐하다'의 뜻으로 ③ repeal과 가장 가까운 의미를 지닌다.

해석

이탈리아의 국민투표는 오로지 기존의 법의 전체나 일부를 **폐지할** 수 있고 새로운 문구를 넣지는 못한다.
① 관리하다, 집행하다
② 도움이 되다

③ 폐지하다, 철회하다
④ 포즈를 취하다, 제기하다, 주장하다

어휘

referendum 국민투표
administer 관리하다, 집행하다
repeal 폐지하다, 철회하다
abrogate 폐지하다, 철폐하다
benefit 도움이 되다
pose 포즈를 취하다, 제기하다, 주장하다

Day 22

오답률 TOP 3

04 정답 ③

정답해설

밑줄 친 부분 전 대화에서 A가 '회의가 어떻게 되었냐'고 묻자 B가 '회의가 순탄하지 않았다'고 말하며 그 이유로 '새로운 직원 중에 한 명'에 대한 서술을 하고 있다. 따라서 빈칸에 ③ 'a wet blanket(분위기를 깨는 사람)'이 들어가는 것이 문맥상 가장 적절하다.

오답해설

① B는 아침에 순탄하지 않았던 회의의 원인에 관해 이야기할 때 새로 온 직원 중 한 명이 'a real McCoy(진짜배기)'였기 때문이라고 하는 것은 문맥상 어색하다.
② B가 아침에 참석한 회의가 순탄하지 않았던 이유가 'a walk of life(계층)' 때문이라고 말하는 것은 맥락의 흐름상 부적절하다.
④ 아침 회의에서 새로 온 직원 중 한 명이 'an act of God(천재지변)'이었다는 것은 자연스럽지 않다.

해석

A: 네가 오늘 아침에 회의했다는 사실을 들었어.
B: 응, 끝나자마자 너를 만나려고 여기에 왔어.
A: 여기까지 와줘서 고마워. 회의는 어떻게 됐어?
B: 순탄하지 않았어. 오늘이 새로운 직원들과 함께한 첫 회의였고 그들 중 한 명이 분위기를 깨는 사람이었어.
A: 전부 얘기해줘. 그가 뭘 한 거야?
B: 우선, 그는 지각했어. 그리고 둘째로는, 회의 내내 무례한 태도로 일관했어.
A: 쉽지 않았겠다. 힘내!
B: 응원해줘서 고마워.
① 진짜배기
② 계층
③ 분위기를 깨는 사람
④ 천재지변

어휘

a real McCoy 진짜배기
a wet blanket 분위기를 깨는 사람
a walk of life 계층
an act of God 천재지변

05 정답 ④

정답해설

④ 출제 포인트: another + 명사[단수]
'another' 이후에 명사가 오는 경우 단수 형태를 사용해야 한다. 해당 문장은 'another' 이후에 명사를 사용하였으나 복수 형태인 'lunches'를 사용하였으므로 틀린 문장이다. 따라서 'lunches'를 단수 형태인 'lunch'로 수정해야 한다.

오답해설

① 출제 포인트: 「It + be + 형용사 + to + 동사원형 + 목적어」에서 목적어 이동이 가능한 경우(difficult)
「It + be동사 + 형용사 + to + 동사원형 + 목적어」에서 형용사가 'difficult'인 경우 to부정사의 목적어가 가주어 'It'의 자리로 이동할 수 있다. 해당 문장은 'It is difficult to remember last week's lunch.'에서 목적어 'last week's lunch'가 가주어 'It'의 자리로 이동하여 'Last week's lunch is difficult to remember.'가 된 것이므로 옳은 문장이다.
② 출제 포인트: 대명사 수일치
대명사 'it'이 가리키는 대상이 단수형태의 명사(구) 'Last week's lunch'이므로 대명사 수일치가 옳게 사용되었다.
③ 출제 포인트: 현재분사 vs. 과거분사
해당 문장에서 쓰인 'you've'는 'you have'의 축약형이며 'have'는 과거분사와 결합하여 현재완료를 나타낸다. 따라서 과거분사 'eaten'은 옳은 표현이며 'other lunches'와 'you've eaten' 사이에는 목적격 관계대명사가 생략되어 있다.

해석

여러분의 뇌가 단지 다른 점심처럼 여러분이 먹은 적 있는 모든 다른 점심과 함께 지난주의 점심을 정리해 놓았기 때문에 지난주의 점심은 기억하기 어렵다.

어휘

file away ~을 정리해 놓다

06 정답 ①

정답해설

① 출제 포인트: 접속사 vs. 전치사
'Despite'는 전치사이므로 이후에 명사(구)가 온다. 해당 문장은 'Despite'를 사용하였으나 이후에 과거분사구 'warned to be on time'이 왔으므로 틀린 문장이다. 하지만, 단순하게 'warning'으로 수정하지 말아야 한다. 여기에서 'warn'은 불완전타동사로 「warn + 목적어 + to동사원형」의 구조를 갖으나, 해당 문장에서는 William이 '경고를 받았으므로' 수동형인 'As they were warned to be on time'에서 분사구문의 형태로 'Warned to be on time~'이거나, 또는 접속사가 살아있는 분사구문으로 'Though(Although) warned to be on time~'으로 사용할 수 있다. 따라서 'Despite'를 삭제하거나 접속사 'Although' 또는 'Though'로 수정해야 한다. 또한, 전치사 'Despite'를 이용해 수동 형태의 동명사를 목적어로 갖는 형태인 'Despite being warned to be on time~'도 역시 가능하다.

오답해설

② 출제 포인트: 주장/요구/명령/제안동사 + (that) + 주어 + (should) + 동사원형
해당 문장에서 'suggests'는 '암시하다'로 해석하는 것이 자연스러우므로 목적어인 that절의 동사에 시제를 적용할 수 있다. 따라서 that절의 동사에 'court'의 과거시제인 'courted'를 옳게 사용하였다.
③ 출제 포인트: 시간의 부사(구), 부사절/간접의문문의 어순
'yesterday'는 시간의 부사로 과거시제 동사와 함께 사용한다. 따라서 'ring'의 과거시제인 'rang'은 옳은 표현이다. 또한 'when'은 의문부사로 의문사절을 이끌고 있으며, 'check'의 목적어 역할을 하므로 간접의문문 어순인 「의문사 + 주어 + 동사」를 옳게 사용하였다.
④ 출제 포인트: By the time + 주어 + 동사 ~, 주어 + 동사 ~./이중부정 금지
「By the time + 주어 + 동사 ~, 주어 + 동사 ~.」는 종속절의 동사에 과거시제를 사용하면 주절의 동사에 과거완료를 사용해야 한다. 해당 문장은 「By the time + 주어 + 동사 ~, 주어 + 동사 ~.」가 쓰인 문장으로 종속절

에는 과거시제 동사 'got'을, 주절의 동사에는 과거완료인 'had been'을 사용하였으므로 옳은 문장이다. 또한 부정부사 'hardly'가 쓰인 문장에 'no'를 사용하면 이중부정이 되어 비문이 되므로 'any'를 사용하는 것이 옳다.

해석
① 시간을 잘 지키라고 경고를 받았지만 William과 Jane은 늦게 도착했다.
② 증거는 그녀가 그녀의 아이들을 위해 위험을 자초했다는 것을 암시하지 않는다.
③ William은 그들이 언제 도착하는지 확인하기 위해 어제 그들에게 전화를 했다.
④ 그들이 그곳에 도착했을 때쯤에는 남아 있는 음식이 거의 없었다.

07 정답 ②

정답해설
② 출제 포인트: 관사의 위치
'so' 이후에 「부정관사+분사+명사」 형태의 명사(구)가 오는 경우 「so+분사+부정관사+명사」의 형태를 가진다. 해당 문장은 「so+부정관사+분사+명사」의 형태이므로 틀린 문장이다. 따라서 'so a fascinating place'를 'so fascinating a place'로 수정해야 한다. 또한 'so'를 'such'로 수정해도 옳은 문장이 된다.

오답해설
① 출제 포인트: with 분사구문
해당 문장은 with 분사구문이 쓰인 문장이다. 이때 'go on'은 '계속되다'를 뜻하는 「완전자동사+부사」 형태의 자동사구이다. 따라서 'with'의 목적어로 온 'this noise'와 'go on'의 관계가 능동이므로 목적격 보어 자리에 현재분사 형태인 'going on'을 옳게 사용하였다.

③ 출제 포인트: 주의해야 할 비교급 관용표현
'not more than'은 비교급 관용표현으로 '많아야 ~인(고작)'을 뜻한다. 해당 문장은 주어진 해석 '길어야 10분인'과 'not more than ten minutes'가 일치하므로 옳게 사용되었다.

④ 출제 포인트: 간접의문문의 어순/불완전타동사의 수동태
해당 문장에서 'how fast fares ought to be allowed to rise'는 전치사 'about'의 목적어로 쓰인 간접의문문으로 「의문부사+부사+주어+조동사+동사원형」의 어순을 옳게 사용하였다. 또한 주어진 해석이 '~하도록 허용되다'이므로 불완전타동사 'allow'의 수동태인 'be allowed to+동사원형'을 옳게 사용하였다.

08 정답 ④

정답해설
본문은 면접에서 중요한 요소 중 한 가지인 '자신감(confidence)'에 대해 언급하며, 자신감을 보여주는 것이 왜 중요한지 설명하고 있다. 본문에 따르면, 면접관들은 '팔짱을 끼고 있거나 시선을 맞추지 못하는 등 자신감이 부족해 보이는 지원자를 뽑지 않았다'고 응답하고 있다. 또한 마지막 문장 "nearly 40 percent of interviewers stated that an interviewee's overall confidence was a reason for selecting, or not selecting, the candidate for the position(거의 40퍼센트의 면접관들이 면접자의 전반적인 자신감이 해당 직책을 위해 그 지원자를 선택하는, 또는 선택하지 않는, 이유라고 말했다)."에서 '자신감이 지원자 채용 선택 또는 비 선택의 이유'가 된다고 언급하고 있으므로, 면접에 있어서 자신감이 중요한 요소라는 것을 알 수 있다. 따라서 글의 요지로 가장 적절한 보기는 '④ Confidence is an important factor when it comes to job candidates being successful (일자리 지원자들이 성공하는 것[합격하는 것]에 관한 한 자신감은 중요한 요소이다).'이다.

오답해설
① 본문과 관계없는 내용이므로 오답이다.
② 본문에서 언급되지 않는 내용이므로 오답이다.
③ 본문에서 언급된 면접관들이 선호하는 지원자들은 자신감이 있는 지원자들이며, 순종적이고 헌신적인 지원자들에 관해서는 언급되지 않는다.

해석
당신이 얼마나 긴장했는지에 상관없이, 당신의 면접 중에 자신감을 보여주는 것이 매우 중요한데, 이는 약 20퍼센트의 면접관들이 그들의 면접 도중에 팔짱을 낀 채로 앉아있던 지원자들은 그들의 자신감 부족을 나타내었던 보디랭귀지로 인해 그 직책에 고려되지 않았다고 말했기 때문이다. 자신감을 보여주는 것에 있어서 시선을 마주치는 것 또한 매우 중요하고 약 65퍼센트의 면접관들이 시선을 마주치지 못한 지원자들은 그들이 지원했던 직책을 얻지 못했다고 말했다. 실제로, 거의 40퍼센트의 면접관들이 면접자의 전반적인 자신감이 해당 직책을 위해 그 지원자를 선택하는, 또는 선택하지 않는, 이유라고 말했다.
① 자신감을 나타내는 많은 보디랭귀지가 있다.
② 일자리 면접에서 자신감을 보여주는 것은 어려울 수 있다.
③ 면접관들은 순종적이고 헌신적인 지원자들을 선호한다.
④ 일자리 지원자들이 성공하는 것[합격하는 것]에 관한 한 자신감은 중요한 요소이다.

어휘
portray 보여주다, 나타내다 candidate 지원자, 후보자
reflect 나타내다, 반영하다 apply for …에 지원하다
position 직책, 일자리 obedient 순종적인, 복종하는
dedicated 헌신적인, 전념하는 when it comes to …에 관한 한

오답률 TOP 1

09 정답 ①

정답해설
본문은 '낮에는 청소부로 일하는 작가 Caitriona Lally'에 관한 이야기이다. 'Rooney Prize for Literature'를 수상한 Caitriona Lally가 청소부로 일하는 것은 '외부인들(일반인들)과 언론'에게는 이상한 일이고, '내부인들(업계 종사자들)'은 그녀가 그것을 공공연하게 밝힌다는 것에 흥미를 느낀다. 본문에 따르면, '그녀는 많은 상금을 받았음에도 불구하고 생계를 꾸리기 위해 계속 청소부로 일할 것이다'라는 것을 알 수 있다. 즉, 그녀는 작가로 성공했음에도 불구하고 재정적으로는 빈곤한 상태인 것이다. 빈칸에는 그녀의 경우에 비추어 다른 많은 작가와 예술가들이 처한 상황을 설명할 수 있는 표현이 들어가야 하므로, 가장 적절한 것은 '① are broke(빈털터리이다)'이다.

오답해설
② 건강에 관해서는 본문에 언급되지 않는다.
나머지 보기는 문맥상 어색하므로 오답이다.

해석
Caitriona Lally가 그녀의 데뷔 소설 Eggshells로 Rooney Prize for Literature를 수상했을 때, 미디어의 초점은 그녀의 주간 직업에 맞추어졌다. 그녀는 Trinity College Dublin의 청소부로, "돈벌이가 되는 일"이 일찍 끝나고 글쓰기 작업을 시작할 수 있도록 오전의 짧은 시간에 청소하고 닦는다. 외부인들과 언론에게, 이것은 이상하며, 발언, 논의, 분석되어야 하는 일이다. 내부인들(업계 종사자들)에게, 흥미로운 사항은 Lally가 고지서 요금을 지불해 온, 그리고 주로 보육비로 남겨둔 10,000유로의 상금에도 불구하고 그녀가 열심히 다음 책, 그리고 다음을 집필하면서 계속해서 (고지서 요금을) 지불할, 결코 선망을 얻지 못하는 직업에 대해 숨기지 않는다는 것이다. 이 나라의 그리고 실제로 전 세계의 많은 작가들과 예술가들은 빈털터리이다; 문제는 그것을 인정하느냐 아니냐는 것이다.

① 빈털터리이다
② 건강하지 않다
③ 독창성이 부족하다
④ 과대 평가된다

어휘

scrub (보통 비눗물과 솔로) 문질러 씻다[청소하다]
mop (대걸레로) 닦다
gig (특히 임시로 하는) 일[직업]
incongruous (특정한 상황에서는) 어울리지 않는[이상한]
remark upon …에 관한 의견을 말하다[발언하다]
dissect 해부[분석]하다
less than 조금도[결코] …아닌, …이라고는 (도저히) 말할 수 없는
prestige 선망을 얻는, 명망 있는; 위신, 명망
set aside (다시 필요할 때까지) ~을 한쪽으로 치워 놓다
admit 인정하다
broke 무일푼의, 빈털터리의, 파산한
originality 독창성
overestimate 과대평가하다

10 정답 ④

정답해설

본문은 '조선의 여자 성인식'에 관한 내용이다. 주어진 문장의 'That is(다시 말해)'로 보아, 앞서 언급된 것과 동일한 내용을 재차 설명하고 있다는 것을 알 수 있으며, 'the former(전자)'와 'the latter(후자)'가 지칭하는 두 가지가 주어진 문장 이전에 등장해야 한다는 것을 알 수 있다. ④ 이전 문장 "The ceremony was held at the age of fifteen because girls of that age represented harmony between yin and yang(그 의식은 15세의 나이에 행해졌는데, 왜냐하면 그 나이의 소녀들이 음과 양 사이의 조화를 나타냈기 때문이다)."에서 'yin and yang(음과 양)'을 주어진 문장의 'the former(전자)'와 'the latter(후자)'가 각각 가리키고 있으며, ④ 이전 문장에서 설명하고 있는 '15세의 나이의 소녀가 음과 양 사이의 조화를 나타낸다'는 내용을 주어진 문장에서 다시 한번 설명하고 있으므로 주어진 문장이 들어갈 가장 적절한 위치는 ④이다.

오답해설

① 주어진 문장의 'the number fifteen(그 숫자 15)'으로 보아, 주어진 문장 이전에 'fifteen'이라는 숫자가 등장해야 하는데, ① 이전에는 해당 숫자가 등장하지 않으므로 오답이다.
② 에 들어가기에는 문맥상 어색하다.
③ 이전 문장에는 주어진 문장의 'the former(전자)'와 'the latter(후자)'가 지칭하는 두 가지가 언급되지 않으므로 오답이다.

해석

혼인하기에 알맞은 연령의 어린 여성을 위한 성인식에서 그들은 머리를 올려 쪽을 찌고 비녀로 그것을 제자리에 고정시켰다. (①) 조선 사회에서 소녀들을 위한 성인식은 그들이 15세이거나 결혼 준비가 되었을 때 행해졌다. (②) 성인식 후에도, 소녀들은 결혼하기까지 부모의 보호 하에서 어린아이처럼 행동하도록 기대되었다. (③) 그 의식은 15세의 나이에 행해졌는데, 왜냐하면 그 나이의 소녀들이 음과 양 사이의 조화를 나타냈기 때문이다. (④ **다시 말해, 한국의 전통적인 믿음에 따르면, 여성은 전자이고, 그 숫자 15는 후자이다.**) 다른 이론에 따르면, 달은 음력에 따라 그 달의 15번째 날에 보름달이 되기 때문에 그 의식이 15세의 소녀를 위해 행해져야 했다.

어휘

former 전자
latter 후자
coming-of-age ceremony 성인식
marriageable 혼인하기에 알맞은
chignon 쪽, 시뇽(뒤로 모아 틀어 올린 머리 모양)
in place 제자리에
rod (목재·금속·유리 소재의 기다란) 막대
yin 음
yang 양

기적사 DAY 23

결국엔 성정혜 영어 하프모의고사

01	④	02	①	03	①	04	②	05	①
06	②	07	②	08	④	09	④	10	③

오답률 TOP 1

01 정답 ④

정답해설

문장에서 '단호하게'의 뜻을 가진 'firmly'의 동의어로는 ④ adamantly가 가장 적절하다.

해석

관중이 **단호하게** 저항했을 때, 이 사건은 폭동으로 발전했다.
① 엄하게, 거칠게
② 대담하게, 호기롭게, 넉살 좋게
③ 근면하게, 부지런하게
④ 단호하게

어휘

firmly 단호하게
harshly 엄하게, 거칠게
audaciously 대담하게, 호기롭게, 넉살 좋게
assiduously 근면하게, 부지런하게
adamantly 단호하게

02 정답 ①

정답해설

문맥상 스케줄을 '조정하는 것'이 가장 자연스러우므로, 정답은 ① adjust이다.

해석

그는 자신의 일정을 **조절하도록** 강요받아왔다.
① 조절하다, 순응하다, 조정하다
② 존경하다, 감탄하다
③ 인수하다
④ (옷을) 벗다, ~을 데려가다; 이륙하다

어휘

adjust 조절하다, 순응하다, 조정하다
admire 존경하다, 감탄하다
take over 인수하다
take off 이륙하다; (옷을) 벗다, ~을 데려가다

03 정답 ①

정답해설

'adapt'는 '적응하다, 조정하다'라는 뜻으로 ① acclimate와 의미가 가장 가깝다.

해석

일부 생명체들은 다른 것들보다 더 쉽게 변화에 **적응한다**.
① 순응하다
② 채택하다, 입양하다
③ 해결하다
④ 포즈를 취하다, 제기하다, 주장하다

어휘

adapt 적응하다, 조정하다
acclimate 순응하다
solve 해결하다
readily 쉽게, 기꺼이
adopt 채택하다, 입양하다
pose 포즈를 취하다, 제기하다, 주장하다

04 정답 ②

정답해설

밑줄 친 부분 전 대화에서 Wendy는 David에게 '멋져 보인다'고 칭찬하고 '어디에 가냐'고 묻는다. David는 특별한 사람을 만난다고 하며 비밀이라고 말한다. 이에 이어지는 Wendy의 대답에 David는 '어떻게 알았냐'며 '그녀를 처음 만나는 날'이라고 대답하고 있다. 따라서 빈칸에 ② 'a blind date(소개팅)'가 들어가는 것이 문맥상 가장 적절하다.

오답해설

① 그녀를 만나는 것이 처음이라는 David의 말로 보아 Wendy가 'double date(두 커플이 함께하는 데이트)'를 하냐고 추측하는 것은 문맥상 자연스럽지 않다.
③ 특별한 사람을 만나러 가 멋지게 차려입은 David의 모습을 보고 Wendy가 'a pipe dream(허황된 상상)'을 하는지 묻는 것은 부적절하다.
④ 특별한 사람을 만나러 가는 David에게 Wendy가 'monkey business(수상한 일)'를 한다고 추측하는 것은 맥락의 흐름상 어색하다.

해석

Wendy: 너 오늘 밤 멋있어 보인다! 네 파란 셔츠가 정말 마음에 들어! 너한테 꽤 잘 어울려.
David: 고마워. 음, 나는 꽤 긴장돼.
Wendy: 왜? 너 어디 가?
David: 난 오늘 특별한 사람을 만나. 비밀이야.
Wendy: 그럼 내가 맞춰볼게. 너 소개팅 나가?
David: 너 어떻게 알았어? 그녀를 처음 만나는 날이야.
Wendy: 그냥 잘 추측한 것뿐이야. 잘 됐으면 좋겠다.
David: 나도 그랬으면 좋겠어.
① 두 커플이 함께하는 데이트
② 소개팅
③ 허황된 상상
④ 수상한 일

어휘

double date 두 커플이 함께하는 데이트
a blind date 소개팅
a pipe dream 허황된 상상
monkey business 수상한 일

오답률 TOP 2

05 정답 ①

정답해설

① 출제 포인트: 가정법 과거
가정법 과거에서 종속절인 If절에 be동사가 오는 경우 주어에 상관없이 'were'를 사용해야 한다. 해당 문장은 주절의 'would be'를 통해 가정법 과거가 쓰인 문장임을 알 수 있으나 종속절인 If절의 동사에 'were'가 아닌 'was'를 사용하였으므로 틀린 문장이다. 따라서 밑줄 친 'was'를 'were'로 수정해야 한다.

오답해설

② 출제 포인트: 현재분사 vs. 과거분사
밑줄 친 'emitted'는 완전타동사 'emit'의 과거분사로, 이후에 목적어가 없으며 'the radiation'과 수동관계로 해석상 '우주로 방출되는 방사에너지'가 자연스러우므로 과거분사 'emitted'는 옳은 표현이다. 해당 문장의 본동사는 'would be'이므로 'emitted'를 본동사로 착각하지 않도록 주의해야 한다.
③ 출제 포인트: so+형용사/부사+that+주어+동사 vs. too+형용사/부사+to+동사원형
밑줄 친 'so'는 '너무 ~해서 …하다'의 의미인 「so+형용사/부사+that+주어+동사」 구문의 'so'이다. 해당 문장에서는 밑줄 친 'so'가 형용사 'great'을 수식하고 있으므로 옳게 사용되었다.
④ 출제 포인트: a few+명사[복수]
'a few' 이후에 오는 명사는 복수 형태를 사용해야 하므로 밑줄 친 'minutes'는 옳은 표현이다.

해석

중심이 아니라 태양의 표면이 이만큼 뜨겁다면, 우주로 방출되는 방사에너지는 너무나 커서 몇 분 이내에 지구 전체는 증발될 것이다.

어휘

solar 태양의
radiation 방사선, 복사
vaporize 증발시키다
surface 표면, 외관
emit 내뿜다, 방출하다

06 정답 ②

정답해설

② 출제 포인트: 이중부정 금지
부정어인 'no'는 'not ~any'로 쓰일 수 있으므로, 부정부사 'not'이 쓰인 문장에 'no'를 사용하면 이중부정이 되어 비문이 된다. 해당 문장은 부정 표현 'didn't'와 부정어 'no'를 함께 사용하였으므로 틀린 문장이다. 따라서 'no effect'를 'any effect'로 수정해야 한다.

오답해설

① 출제 포인트: 시간의 부사(구), 부사절/to부정사의 부정 표현
'just now'는 시간의 부사구로 현재시제 동사 또는 과거시제 동사와 사용한다. 따라서 시간의 부사구 'just now'와 함께 쓰인 과거시제 동사 'looked'는 옳은 표현이다. 또한 to부정사의 부정 표현은 「not+to+동사원형」이므로 'not to laugh' 또한 옳게 사용되었다.
③ 출제 포인트: 주장/요구/명령/제안동사+(that)+주어+(should)+동사원형
'propose'는 '제안하다'를 뜻하는 동사로 목적어로 that절이 오는 경우 「(that)+주어+(should)+동사원형」을 사용해야 한다. 따라서 'that'절에 쓰인 'we send'는 'should'가 생략된 표현으로 옳게 사용되었다.
④ 출제 포인트: to부정사의 태/불완전자동사의 주격 보어/접속사 vs. 전치사
'enjoy'는 완전타동사이므로 이후에 목적어를 사용한다. 해당 문장은 to부정사에 'enjoy'를 사용하였으며 이후에 목적어 'herself'가 있으므로 옳은 문장이다. 이때 'to enjoy herself'는 불완전자동사 'seemed'의 주격 보어로 사용되었다. 또한 'Despite'는 전치사이므로 목적어로 명사구인 'the fact'를 옳게 사용하였다.

해석

① 그녀가 방금 상당히 화가 난 것 같았기 때문에, 그는 웃지 않으려고 애썼다.
② 나는 복통을 위해 알약을 먹어 보았지만 효과가 없었다.
③ 나는 우리의 일을 논의하기 위해 대표단을 로스앤젤레스로 보낼 것을 제안한다.

④ 금요일이 그녀의 가장 바쁜 날이라는 사실에도 불구하고, Jane은 즐거운 시간을 보내고 있는 것 같았다.

07 정답 ②

정답해설

② **출제 포인트: 주의해야 할 비교급 관용표현**
'A is no more B than C is D.'는 비교급 관용표현으로 'A가 B가 아닌 것은 C가 D가 아닌 것과 같다.'를 뜻한다. 해당 문장은 'A is no more B than C is D.'에서 'than'의 자리에 'as'를 사용하였으므로 틀린 문장이다. 따라서 'as'를 'than'으로 수정해야 한다.

오답해설

① **출제 포인트: 직접의문문의 어순/목적격 관계대명사의 생략**
해당 문장은 의문부사 'How'가 이끄는 직접의문문으로 「의문부사+형용사+be동사+주어」의 어순을 옳게 사용하였다. 또한 'the services'와 'we' 사이에는 목적격 관계대명사 'that' 또는 'which'가 생략되어 있다.

③ **출제 포인트: with 분사구문/현재분사 vs. 과거분사**
해당 문장에서 'with his hands on the sink'는 with 분사구문에 해당하며 이때 'his hands'와 'on the sink' 사이에는 현재분사 'being'이 생략되어 있다. 또한 'staring out the window'는 현재분사구문으로 생략된 주어 'William'과 능동관계이다.

④ **출제 포인트: 관사의 위치/부사절을 이끄는 접속사 that**
'such' 이후에 「부정관사+형용사+명사」 형태의 명사(구)가 오는 경우 「such+부정관사+형용사+명사」의 형태를 가진다. 따라서 'such a difficult exam'은 옳은 표현이다. 또한 해당 문장에서 접속사 'that'이 이끄는 절은 결과를 나타내는 부사절이다.

08 정답 ④

정답해설

주어진 문장의 'these entirely novel institutions(이러한 완전히 새로운 기관들)'로 보아, 주어진 문장 이전에는 이것이 지칭하는 '새로운 기관'이 등장해야 함을 알 수 있다. ④ 이전 문장에서 "enormous new factories producing steel, shoes, railroad cars, or pork bellies rose up across the country(철강, 제화, 철도 차량, 또는 삼겹살을 생산하는 거대한 신규 공장들이 국가 전역에 설립되었다)"라고 언급하며, '새로운 공장들(new factories)'이 등장하기 시작했음을 알리고 있으므로, ④ 이전 문장에서 언급된 'new factories'를 주어진 문장의 'these entirely novel institutions'가 가리킨다는 것을 알 수 있다. 따라서 정답은 ④이다.

오답해설

①, ②, ③ 이전 문장에서는 새로운 것에 대해 언급되지 않으므로 주어진 문장이 들어갈 위치로 적절하지 않다.

해석

원시인부터 약 남북전쟁 시기까지 당신의 조상들은 직업을 가지고 있지 않았고 일자리 면접에 가지 않았다. 대신에, '옛 국가'의 당신의 조상들은 그들이 태어난 곳의 10마일 이내에서 자라고 살고 일했다. (①) 그들이 만났던 거의 모든 사람들은 그들 자신의 부족 출신이었다. 그리고 다른 모든 사람들과 마찬가지로, 그들은 왕, 교회, 군대를 위해 일하거나, 또는 아마 농부, 농노, 또는 노예였다. (②) 약 1860년까지 농부가 미국 노동 인구의 3분의 2를 구성했다. (③) 남북전쟁과 산업화 이후에야 비로소 철강, 제화, 철도 차량, 또는 삼겹살을 생산하는 거대한 신규 공장들이 국가 전역에 설립되었다. (④) **우리가 "직업"이라고 여기게 된 것을 창조한 것이 바로 이러한 완전히 새로운 기관들이었다.**) 그렇다면 통계학적으로, 당신의 증조부 시대에서야 비로소 당신의 선조들이 일자리 면접에 가기 시작했다.

어휘

novel (이전에 볼 수 없었던) 새로운
caveman 원시인
ancestor 조상
serf 농노
workforce 노동 인구, 총노동력
pork belly 삼겹살
statistically 통계학적으로
institution 기관, 협회
Civil War (미국의) 남북전쟁
folk 사람들, 가족, 친척
likely 아마
enormous 거대한, 매우 큰
rise (up) (건물이) 세워지다
forebear 선조

오답률 TOP 3

09 정답 ④

정답해설

본문은 Charles Dickens의 어린 시절 직업에 관한 내용이다. 본문 후반 "He later recalled how he had worked alongside "two or three other boys who were kept at similar duty downstairs on similar wages", one of whom had shown him around on his first day in the job. "His name was Bob Fagin,~"을 통해, '그는 두세 명의 다른 소년들과 함께 일했는데, 그중 한 명의 이름이 Bob Fagin이었다.'는 것과, Bob Fagin이 Charles Dickens의 공장에서의 첫날에 공장 안내를 해주었다'는 것을 알 수 있다. 이러한 내용으로 미루어보아, Bob Fagin은 Charles Dickens보다 공장에 대해 잘 알고 있었음을 알 수 있으며, Charles Dickens보다 앞서 공장에서 일하기 시작했다는 것을 짐작할 수 있다. 따라서 글의 내용과 일치하는 것은 '④ Bob Fagin joined the factory before Charles Dickens started his work there(Bob Fagin은 Charles Dickens가 그곳에서 일을 시작하기 전에 공장에 취직했다).'이다.

오답해설

① 첫 번째 문장 "Long before his well-documented work as a freelance journalist and legal clerk in a London law office, 12-year-old Charles Dickens worked in a factory pasting labels onto pots of boot polish(프리랜서 저널리스트와 런던의 변호사 사무소에서의 법률 사무소 직원으로서 문서로 남아있는 그의 직업을 갖기 훨씬 이전에, 12살의 Charles Dickens는 구두약 병에 라벨을 붙이며 공장에서 일했다)."를 통해, Charles Dickens는 작가가 되기 전 적어도 3가지 직업을 가졌음을 알 수 있다.

② 첫 번째 문장 "12-year-old Charles Dickens worked in a factory pasting labels onto pots of boot polish(12살의 Charles Dickens는 구두약 병에 라벨을 붙이며 공장에서 일했다)"를 통해, Charles Dickens는 '구두닦이'가 아니라 '구두약 병에 라벨을 붙이는 일'을 했음을 알 수 있다.

③ 두 번째 문장 "Working 10 hours a day, he earned a weekly wage of six shillings — equivalent to around £16 today(하루에 10시간을 일하고 그는 오늘날의 약 16파운드에 해당하는 6실링의 주급을 벌었다)"를 통해, 주급으로 6실링을 받았으며, 이는 오늘날의 16파운드에 해당하는 금액이다. 월급으로 환산하면 약 24실링이 될 것임을 알 수 있다.

해석

프리랜서 저널리스트와 런던의 변호사 사무소에서의 법률 사무소 직원으로서 문서로 남아 있는 그의 직업을 갖기 훨씬 이전에, 12살의 Charles Dickens는 구두약 병에 라벨을 붙이며 공장에서 일했다. 하루에 10시간을 일하고, 그는 오늘날의 약 16파운드에 해당하는 6실링의 주급을 벌었다. 나중에 그는 "비슷한 급여를 받으며 아래층에서 비슷한 일을 하던 두세 명의 다른 소년들"과 어떻게 함께 일했는지 떠올렸는데, 그들 중 한 명이 그가 일을 시작한 첫날에 그에게 안내를 해줬다. "그의 이름은 Bob Fagin이었다,"라고 이후에 Dickens가 그의 친구이자 전기 작가인 John Forster에게 말했다, "그리고 나는 오랜 시간 후에 실례를 무릅쓰고 그의 이름을 나의 이야기에 사용했다."
① Charles Dickens는 작가로서의 경력을 시작하기 전 두 가지의 직업을 가졌다.
② Charles Dickens는 구두닦이로 일했다.
③ Charles Dickens는 한 달에 16실링을 받았다.
④ Bob Fagin은 Charles Dickens가 그곳에서 일을 시작하기 전에 공장에 취직했다.

어휘

well-documented 문서[기록]에 의해 충분히 입증된
clerk 점원, 직원　　　　　　paste (풀로) 붙이다
boot polish 구두약
shilling 실링(영국에서 1971년까지 사용되던 주화)
equivalent (가치·의미·중요도 등이) 동등한[맞먹는]
recall 상기하다, 기억하다, 떠올리다　alongside 함께, 나란히
show … around …에게 (~을) 둘러보도록 안내하다[구경시켜 주다]
biographer 전기 작가
take the liberty of ~ing 제멋대로[무단으로, 실례를 무릅쓰고] …하다
set out on …에 착수[시작]하다　boot polisher 구두닦이

10 정답 ③

정답해설

본문은 '브라질 아마존에 사는 Sateré-Mawé 원주민 부족 소년들의 성인식(Bullet and Ant Initiation)'에 관한 내용이다. 본문에 따르면, '13살이 된 Sateré-Mawé 부족의 소년들은 총알개미가 엮인 장갑을 손에 끼고 고통을 참는 의식'을 수개월 동안 치러야 한다. 해당 부족의 소년들이 반드시 거쳐야 할 절차에 대한 글이므로, 주제로 가장 적절한 보기는 '③ A rite of passage from the Sateré-Mawé tribe(Sateré-Mawé 부족의 통과의례)'이다.

오답해설

① 본문의 내용에 비추어 보아, 총알개미의 침에 쏘이면 고통스럽다는 것을 유추할 수는 있으나 본문 전체의 내용이 총알개미의 위험성에 초점이 맞추어진 것이 아니므로 오답이다.
② 본문과 관련이 없는 내용이다.
④ 본문에서 '총알개미를 마취시키는 것'이 지도자의 역할로 언급되기는 하지만, 본문 전체를 아우르는 내용이 아니므로 오답이다.

해석

브라질 아마존에서 Sateré-Mawé 원주민 부족에 속한 어린 소년들은 그들이 13세가 될 때 Bullet and Ant Initiation에서 그들의 성년을 기념한다. 그 전통은 이렇게 진행된다: 그들은 지도자에 의해 약초 용액으로 진정될 총알개미를 찾아 정글을 수색한다. 이후 개미들은 침이 안쪽으로 향하도록 장갑에 엮어진다. 약 한 시간 후, 개미들은 그 어느 때보다 더 화난 채로 깨어나고, 그 의식은 시작된다. 각각의 소년은 장갑을 10분 동안 껴야 한다. 고통을 견디는 것은 소년이 남자가 될 준비가 되어 있음을 보여주고, 그렇게 하는 동안 비명을 지르는 것은 나약함을 보여준다. 각각의 소년은 의식이 끝나기 전 수개월의 기간에 걸쳐 최종적으로 20번 장갑을 낄 것이다.
① 총알개미의 위험성
② Sateré-Mawé 부족의 사냥법
③ Sateré-Mawé 부족의 통과의례
④ Sateré-Mawé 부족에서 지도자의 중요한 역할

어휘

indigenous 토착의, 원산의　　mark 기념하다, 축하하다
coming of age 성인, 성년　　initiation 의식, 의례
bullet ant 총알개미(독개미의 일종)
sedate (진정제로) 진정시키다, 안정시키다
solution 용액　　　　　　　weave 짜다, 엮다
demonstrate 보여주다, 입증하다
manhood (남자) 성인[어른](인 상태·기간)
cry out 비명을 지르다　　　span 기간, 시간
rite of passage 통과의례

기적사 DAY 24

01	②	02	④	03	④	04	③	05	④
06	①	07	④	08	③	09	②	10	②

오답률 TOP 2
01 정답 ②

정답해설

문맥상 일상적인 일을 수행하는 데 '덜 능숙하다'는 의미의 'less ② adept'가 가장 적절하다.

해석

대부분의 사람들은 나이를 먹으면 일상적인 일을 수행하는 데 덜 **능숙하**다고 생각한다.
① 상반되는
② 능숙한
③ 관대한
④ 이상한

어휘

ambivalent 상반되는 adept 능숙한
lenient 관대한 odd 이상한

오답률 TOP 3
02 정답 ④

정답해설

문맥상 '채택하다'의 뜻을 가진 ④ adopt를 사용하여 '개혁안을 채택한다'라고 하는 것이 가장 자연스럽다.

해석

그는 그 개혁안을 **채택하고** 싶다는 그의 의향을 표명했다.
① 달래다, 진정시키다
② (이야기 등을) 적어두다, (건물 등을) 헐어버리다
③ 이륙하다, (옷을) 벗다
④ 채택하다, 입양하다

어휘

readiness 기꺼이 하려는 상태, 준비가 되어 있음
reform bill 개혁안 appease 달래다, 진정시키다
take down (이야기 등을) 적어두다, (건물 등을) 헐어버리다
take off 이륙하다, (옷을) 벗다 adopt 채택하다, 입양하다

오답률 TOP 1
03 정답 ④

정답해설

'administer'는 '관리하다, 운영하다'의 뜻으로 ④ host와 의미가 가장 가깝다.

해석

그는 그 세금을 **관리하는** 것이 불가능하다고 생각한다.
① 조절하다, 순응하다, 조정하다
② 검토하다, 비평하다
③ 사과하다, 용서를 구하다
④ 관리하다

어휘

administer 관리하다, 운영하다 adjust 조절하다, 순응하다, 조정하다
review 검토하다, 비평하다 apologize 사과하다, 용서를 구하다
host 관리하다

04 정답 ③

정답해설

(A) '학교가 음식물 쓰레기를 ~하려고 계획하고 있다'이므로 빈칸 (A)에 들어갈 가장 적절한 것은 'cut down on(~을 줄이다)'이다.
(B) '학교가 친환경적 추세를 ~하기 위해 노력하고 있다'이므로 빈칸 (B)에 들어갈 가장 적절한 것은 'catch up with(~을 따라잡다)'이다.
(C) '지구 온난화는 우리가 우리의 소중한 자연 자원들을 보호하는 것에 ~해야 하는 이유이다'이므로 빈칸 (C)에 들어갈 가장 적절한 것은 'zero in on(~에 집중하다)'이다.

오답해설

① (B) 학교가 환경 보호에 힘쓰려고 노력한다는 사실에 관해 이야기를 나누며 친환경적인 추세에 '패배를 인정하기(give in to)' 위해 노력하고 있다고 말하는 것은 맥락상 적절하지 않다.
② (A) 학교의 중요한 공지에 따르면 학교가 결국 음식물 쓰레기로 '요약되기(boil down to)' 위해 계획 중이라고 하는 것은 문맥상 어색하다.
④ (C) 환경을 보호하는 것의 중요성에 관해 대화를 나누는 상황에서 지구 온난화는 우리가 우리의 자연 자원들을 보존하는 것을 '중도에 그만둬야(drop out of)' 하는 이유라고 이야기하는 것은 적합하지 않다.

해석

A: 오늘 학교 구내식당에서 중요한 공지가 있었어.
B: 어떤 것에 관한 거였어?
A: 학교가 음식물 쓰레기를 (A) 줄이는 것을 계획하고 있어.
B: 그것은 지구를 고려했을 때 합리적인 조치 같아 보여.
A: 나도 그렇게 생각해. 지구 보호를 지지하기 위한 추세가 커지고 있어.
B: 그러니까. 이제 학교가 친환경적 추세를 (B) 따라잡기 위해 노력하고 있어.
A: 그것이 현재 사회에서 확실히 긴급한 문제이긴 해.
B: 맞아, 지구 온난화는 우리가 우리의 소중한 자연 자원들을 보호하는 것에 (C) 집중해야 하는 이유야.
① (A) 줄이다 (B) ~에 패배를 인정하다 (C) ~에 집중하다
② (A) 결국 ~으로 요약되다 (B) ~을 따라잡다 (C) ~에 집중하다
③ (A) 줄이다 (B) ~을 따라잡다 (C) ~에 집중하다
④ (A) 줄이다 (B) ~을 따라잡다 (C) ~을 중도에 그만두다

어휘

protection 보호
environmentally-friendly 환경친화적인, 환경을 해치지 않는
preserve 보존하다, 보호하다 cut down on 줄이다
give in to ~에 패배를 인정하다 zero in on ~에 집중하다
boil down to 결국 ~으로 요약되다 catch up with ~을 따라잡다
drop out of ~을 중도에 그만두다

05 정답 ④

정답해설

④ 출제 포인트: which vs. that/so+[형용사/부사]+that+주어+동사

'which' 이후에 오는 절이 완전한 형태이며 앞에 'so+형용사'인 'so resistant'가 있으므로 「so+형용사+that+주어+동사」 구조가 사용된 문장임을 알 수 있다. 따라서 'which'를 접속사 'that'으로 수정해야 한다.

오답해설

① 출제 포인트: 현재분사 vs. 과거분사

수식하는 대상 'cultural characteristics'와 수동관계이므로 과거분사 'rooted'를 사용하는 것이 옳으며, 해당 문장에서 'deep'은 과거분사 'rooted'를 수식하는 부사로 사용되었다.

② 출제 포인트: 「It+be+형용사+to+동사원형+목적어」에서 목적어 이동이 가능한 경우(difficult)

「It+be동사+형용사+to+동사원형+목적어」에서 형용사가 'difficult'인 경우 목적어가 가주어 'It'의 자리로 이동할 수 있다. 해당 문장은 'It is much more difficult to change other deep-rooted cultural characteristics of races and racial subgroups.'에서 목적어 'other deep-rooted cultural characteristics of races and racial subgroups'가 가주어 'It'의 자리로 이동하여 'Other deep-rooted cultural characteristics of races and racial subgroups are much more difficult to change.'가 된 것이므로 옳은 문장이다.

③ 출제 포인트: 주격 관계대명사절의 동사 수일치

주격 관계대명사 'that'의 선행사가 복수 형태인 'the cultural patterns'이므로 관계대명사절의 동사에 복수 형태인 'are'를 사용하는 것이 옳다.

해석

민족과 민족적 하위집단의 깊이 뿌리박힌 다른 문화적인 특징은 변화시키기가 훨씬 더 어렵다. 이것들은 변화에 너무 저항적이어서 선천적인 것처럼 보이는 문화 양상이다.

어휘

characteristic 특징; 특유의 deep-rooted 깊이 뿌리박힌
subgroup 하위집단, 소집단 resistant 저항하는
alteration 변화, 개조 inherent 본래의, 타고난, 선천적인

06 정답 ①

정답해설

① 출제 포인트: 시간의 부사(구)/목적격 관계대명사의 생략

해당 문장에서 'a moment ago'는 시간의 부사구로 과거시제 동사와 함께 사용한다. 따라서 현재완료 'have seen'을 과거시제 동사 'saw'로 수정해야 한다. 또한 'The little boy'와 'you' 사이에는 목적격 관계대명사 'whom' 또는 'that'이 생략되어 있다.

오답해설

② 출제 포인트: 주장/요구/명령/제안동사+(that)+주어+(should)+동사원형

해당 문장에서 'suggested'는 '제안했다'로 해석하는 것이 자연스러우므로 목적어인 that절에 「주어+(should)+동사원형」을 사용해야 한다. 따라서 동사원형 'go'는 옳은 표현이다.

③ 출제 포인트: to부정사의 형용사적 용법/to부정사의 태/to부정사의 의미상 주어

to부정사(구) 'to be met out of public funds'는 명사 'provision'을 수식하고 있으므로 형용사적 용법으로 사용된 것임을 알 수 있다. 이때 'for any of these costs'는 to부정사(구)의 의미상 주어에 해당하며 수동관계 이므로 to부정사에 수동태인 'to be met'을 옳게 사용하였다.

④ 출제 포인트: 접속사 vs. 전치사/대명사 수일치/능동태 vs. 수동태

'Although'는 접속사이므로 이후에 절을 사용하는 것이 옳다. 또한 해당 문장에서 대명사 'it'은 단수 형태인 명사(구) 'a new drug'를 가리키며 'pay'와 수동관계이므로 의무를 나타내는 'had to'에 이어서 수동태 'be paid for'를 옳게 사용하였다.

해석

① 네가 조금 전에 본 그 어린 소년은 내 조카이다.
② 나는 William에게 그의 동료들과 식사하러 나가자고 제안했다.
③ 이러한 비용들 중 어느 것도 공적 자금에서 지불된다는 조항은 없다.
④ 비록 새로운 약이 환자들에게 좋은 소식이긴 했지만, 그것은 현금으로 지불되어야 했다.

07 정답 ④

정답해설

④ 출제 포인트: 수동태 불가동사/with 분사구문

'fall asleep'은 「불완전자동사+형용사」이므로 수동태를 사용할 수 없다. 따라서 'had been fallen asleep'을 'had fallen asleep'으로 수정해야 한다. 또한 해당 문장에서 'with her head against his shoulder'는 with 분사구문으로 'her head'와 'against his shoulder' 사이에 현재분사 'being'이 생략되어 있다.

오답해설

① 출제 포인트: 관사의 위치/직접의문문의 어순

'so' 이후에 「부정관사+형용사+명사」 형태의 명사(구)가 오는 경우 「so+형용사+부정관사+명사」의 형태를 가진다. 따라서 'so short a time'은 옳은 표현이다. 또한 해당 문장은 의문부사 'How'가 이끄는 직접의문문으로 「의문부사+조동사+주어+동사원형」의 어순을 옳게 사용하였다.

② 출제 포인트: 직접의문문의 어순

의문형용사 'What'이 이끄는 직접의문문으로 「동사+주어」의 도치 어순을 옳게 사용하였다. 이때 'What'이 수식하는 대상은 명사 'crimes'이며 명사(구) 'What crimes'는 전치사 'with'의 목적어에 해당한다.

③ 출제 포인트: 주의해야 할 비교급 관용표현

'no less than'은 비교급 관용표현으로 '~씩이나'를 뜻한다. 해당 문장은 주어진 해석 '천 명이나'와 의미상 'no less than a thousand people'이 일치하므로 옳게 사용되었다.

08 정답 ③

정답해설

본문은 다양한 '기업 문화(company culture)'에 대해 설명하며, 본문 후반 "Whatever your company's culture is, you have to think about how candidates will fit in(당신의 기업 문화가 무엇이든, 당신은 지원자들이 어떻게 조화가 될 것인지 생각해보아야 한다)."을 통해 '당신의 기업 문화에 맞는 지원자를 택해야 한다'는 것을 암시하고 있다. 따라서 글의 주제로 가장 적절한 것은 '③ A factor to consider when making a hiring decision (고용 결정을 할 때 고려해야 할 요소)'이다.

오답해설

① 본문에서 언급되지 않는 내용이다.
② 본문과 관련 없는 내용이므로 오답이다.
④ 구직자들이 원하는 기업 문화가 무엇인지에 관해서는 언급되지 않는다.

> **해석**

기업 문화는 한 기업의 개성을 지칭한다. 모든 기업은 자신의 문화를 가지고 있다. 예를 들어, 어떤 기업은 모든 일이 마무리되는 것을 확실히 하기 위해 늦게까지 또는 초과 근무를 하는 문화를 가지고 있는 반면, 다른 기업은 오후 5시 정각에 퇴근하는 문화를 가지고 있다. 어떤 기업은 팀워크와 동료들과 교제하는 문화를 가지고 있다. 반면에, 다른 기업에서는 직원들이 보통 개별적으로 일을 한다. 당신의 기업 문화가 무엇이든, 당신은 지원자들이 어떻게 조화가 될 것인지 생각해보아야 한다. 당신의 신입 사원이 문화적으로 잘 어울리는 사람일 때, 그 또는 그녀는 직장에서 더 행복하고 더 만족할 것이며, 이것이 이직률을 줄이도록 도와준다.
① 긍정적인 기업 문화를 형성하는 법
② 다른 문화에서의 다른 면접 절차
③ 고용 결정을 할 때 고려해야 할 요소
④ 오늘날의 구직자들이 함께하고 싶어 하는 기업 문화

> **어휘**

refer to 지칭하다, 나타내다 personality 개성, 성격
overtime 초과[시간 외] 근무, 잔업, 야근
on the dot 정각에 socialize 어울리다, 교제하다
colleague 동료 candidate 지원자, 후보자
fit 어울리다, 조화롭다; 맞는[어울리는] 것
turnover 이직률 process 절차, 과정

09 정답 ②

> **정답해설**

본문은 'Little Women의 작가인 Louisa May Alcott이 남성 필명을 사용해 작품 활동을 했다'는 내용이다. 첫 번째 문장 "the American writer frequently used the ambiguous nom de plume A.M. Barnard to write sensational gothic thrillers with subject matter deemed 'unladylike' for a late 19th century female writer(그 미국인 작가는 19세기 말의 여성 작가에게는 "숙녀답지 않다고" 여겨지던 주제를 가지고 선정적인 고딕 스릴러물을 집필하기 위해 A.M. Barnard이라는 불분명한 필명을 자주 사용했다)."를 통해 '여성 작가인 Louisa May Alcott이 스릴러 장르를 집필할 때는 남성 필명을 사용했음'을 언급한 후, 필명으로 출판한 작품과 필명이 밝혀진 시기에 대해 언급하고 있으므로, 글의 제목으로 가장 적절한 것은 '② A Female Author Who Used A Male Pen Name(남성 필명을 사용한 여성 작가)'이다.

> **오답해설**

① Louisa May Alcott의 대표작인 Little Women이 언급되기는 하지만, 주요 주제가 아니므로 글의 제목으로는 적절하지 않다.
③ 본문과 관련 없는 내용이다.
④ 본문은 특정 작가인 Louisa May Alcott 한 사람에 관한 내용이며, 남성 작가와 여성 작가의 일반적 특성에 관해서는 언급되지 않는다.

> **해석**

비록 Louisa May Alcott의 가장 잘 알려진 작품인 Little Women이 그녀 자신의 이름으로 출판되었지만, 그 미국인 작가는 19세기 말의 여성 작가에게는 '숙녀답지 않다고' 여겨지던 주제를 가지고 선정적인 고딕 스릴러물을 집필하기 위해 A.M. Barnard이라는 불분명한 필명을 자주 사용했다. A.M. Barnard의 이름으로 쓰인 Alcott의 작품은 Little Women보다 2년 앞서 쓰인 암울한 연애 소설인 A Long Fatal Love Chase, 사회 계층과 조작의 주제를 가진 중편 소설 Behind a Mask를 포함했다. 1940년대에 그녀의 비밀스러운 남성 필명은 희귀 도서 판매상 Madeleine B. Stern과 사서 Leona Rostenberg에 의해 발견되었다.
① Louisa May Alcott의 가장 유명한 작품
② 남성 필명을 사용한 여성 작가
③ Louisa May Alcott의 재능을 발견한 사람들
④ 남성과 여성 작가의 일반적 특성

> **어휘**

ambiguous 불명확한, 불분명한, 모호한
nom de plume 필명 sensational 선정적인
subject matter 주제, 소재 deem 여기다, 생각하다
unladylike 숙녀답지 못한, 상스러운 novella 중편 소설
manipulation 조작, 속임수 pseudonym 필명
pen name 필명

10 정답 ②

> **정답해설**

본문은 '아일랜드 켈트족의 성인식'에 관한 내용이다.
(A) 이전의 문장 "Some boys were sent out into the forest on a scavenger hunt. They had to come back with certain items(어떤 소년들은 물건 찾기를 하러 숲으로 보내졌다. 그들은 특정 물건을 가지고 돌아와야 했다)"를 통해 성인식이 행해진 방식 중 하나를 언급하고 있다. (A) 바로 이전 'to show that ~(~을 보여주기 위해)'으로 보아 '숲에서 특정 물건을 찾아서 가지고 오게 하는 의식의 목적'을 설명할 수 있는 표현이 빈칸에 들어가는 것이 적절하므로, (A)에 문맥상 가장 적절한 표현은 'self-reliant(자립성 있는)'이다.
(B) 이전의 문장 "Others had to head far into the wilderness on longer expeditions(다른 소년들은 먼 황야를 향해 더 긴 여행을 떠나야 했다)."에서는 앞서 언급된 '물건 찾기' 의식보다 더욱 심화된 성인식 유형에 대해 언급하고 있으며, '황야로 긴 여행을 떠나는 것'의 목적은 자기 자신을 잘 '돌볼 수' 있는지 보여주는 것이므로, (B)에 가장 적절한 표현은 'take care of(돌보다)'이다.
따라서 정답은 '② self-reliant(자립성 있는) - take care of(돌보다)'이다.

> **오답해설**

나머지 보기는 글의 문맥상 어색하므로 오답이다.

> **해석**

아일랜드 켈트족 사이에서 성인식은 소년들에게 매우 중요했다. 그것은 소년을 전사, 그리고 결과적으로 남자로 바꾸어주는 매우 종교적인 행사였다. 비록 부족에 따라 본질이 다르긴 했으나, 그 의식은 하나의 모험으로 구성되어 있었다. 어떤 소년들은 물건 찾기를 하러 숲으로 보내졌다. 그들은 자신들이 (A) 자립성 있고 능력 있다는 것을 보여주기 위해 특정 물건을 가지고 돌아와야 했다. 다른 소년들은 먼 황야를 향해 더 긴 여행을 떠나야 했다. 이것이 그들이 얼마나 자신들을 잘 (B) 돌볼 수 있는지 보여 줄 것이었다. 이것을 해내기 위해, 켈트족은 소년이 신 또는 여신으로부터 도움을 이끌어 낼 수 있어야 한다고 믿었는데, 이는 성인으로 변화하는 것의 중요한 부분이었다. 때때로, 소녀들도 또한 이 모험을 수행하곤 했으나, 소년들에게만큼 소녀들에게 필수적이지는 않았다.

(A)	(B)
① 남의 시선을 의식하는	지지하다
② 자립성 있는	돌보다
③ 자존심이 있는	참다
④ 자기만족에 빠진	교묘히 모면하다

> **어휘**

coming-of-age ritual 성인식 warrior 전사
ritual 의례, 의식 quest 모험 여행, 원정, 탐구[탐색]
scavenger hunt 물건 찾기, 보물찾기
capable 능력 있는 head 가다, 향하다

wilderness 황무지, 황야, 자연
evoke 이끌어내다, 유발하다, 불러내다
transition 변천[변화]하다
self-conscious 남의 시선을 의식하는, 자의식이 강한
stand up for 지지하다, 옹호하다
self-respecting 자존심이 있는
self-satisfied 자기만족에 빠진
expedition 탐험, 원정, 여행
undertake 하다, 착수하다
self-reliant 자립적인, 독립적인
put up with 참다, 받아들이다
get away with 교묘히 모면하다

결국엔 성정혜 영어 하프모의고사
기적사 DAY 25

| 01 | ① | 02 | ④ | 03 | ① | 04 | ② | 05 | ④ |
| 06 | ② | 07 | ② | 08 | ③ | 09 | ④ | 10 | ④ |

오답률 TOP 1

01 정답 ①

정답해설

주어진 문장은 세상을 바라보는 시각을 묘사하고 있다. 문장 내에 제시된 '회색 색조로 세상을 본다'라는 의미는 어떠한 사람이 가진 경향이 뚜렷하지 않음을 비유적으로 나타낸다. 따라서 빈칸에 들어갈 말로 가장 적절한 것은 '불확실한, 이중적인'의 의미를 지닌 ① ambivalent이다.

해석

그러나 회색 색조로 세상을 보는 사람들은 더 **불확실한** 태도를 지니고 있다.
① 불확실한, 이중적인
② 엄한, 가혹한, 냉혹한
③ 벗겨지는, 쓸리는
④ 편한, 가벼운, 형식이 없는

어휘

ambivalent 불확실한, 이중적인, 상반되는
harsh 엄한, 가혹한, 냉혹한   abrasive 벗겨지는, 쓸리는
casual 편한, 가벼운, 형식이 없는

02 정답 ④

정답해설

문맥상 저축을 할 '여력이 있다'라는 뜻을 가진 ④ afford가 가장 적절하다.

해석

나는 은퇴를 위해 저축을 할 **여력이 될지** 확실치 않다.
① (피고를) 보석하다
② 내리다
③ 흥분하다, 인기를 얻다
④ ~할 여력이 있다

어휘

retirement 은퇴   bail (피고를) 보석하다
take down 내리다   take on 흥분하다, 인기를 얻다
afford ~할 여력이 있다

03 정답 ①

정답해설

밑줄 친 'appease'는 '달래다, 진정시키다'라는 뜻으로 ① soothe와 의미가 가장 가깝다.

해석

그 새로운 법은 농부들의 불안감을 **달래주**도록 고안되었다.
① 달래다, 진정시키다
② 생각하다, 임신하다
③ 사과하다
④ 시도하다

어휘
appease 달래다, 진정시키다
soothe 달래다, 진정시키다
conceive 생각하다, 임신하다
apologize 사과하다
attempt 시도하다

04 정답 ②

정답해설
(A) 대화를 통해 멘티가 자신이 일하고 싶은 기업의 임원들과 만날 기회가 생겼음을 알 수 있으며 '~할까 봐 두렵다'라고 말하고 있으므로 빈칸 (A)에 들어갈 가장 적절한 것은 '망치다(blow it)'이다.
(B) 멘토가 멘티에게 '만남을 준비하는데 ~한다면, 넌 괜찮을 거야'라고 말하고 있으므로 빈칸 (B)에 들어갈 가장 적절한 것은 '전력을 다하다(go at full tilt)'이다.

오답해설
① (B) 멘티가 일하고 싶어 하는 기업의 임원들과 모임을 준비하는 데 '일과를 마치면(call it a day)' 모임이 괜찮을 것이라고 하는 것은 대화의 흐름상 부적절하다.
③ (A) 기업 임원들과 만남이 일생일대의 기회이긴 하지만 자신이 '2위가 될까(come off second best)' 봐 무섭다는 것은 문맥상 자연스럽지 않다.
(B) 멘티가 일하고 싶어 하는 기업의 임원들과 모임을 준비하는 데 '일과를 마치면(call it a day)' 모임이 괜찮을 것이라고 하는 것은 대화의 흐름상 어색하다.
④ (A) 기업 임원들과 만나는 것이 일생일대의 기회인 것이 확실하지만 자신이 '매우 똑같을(cut from the same cloth)'까 봐 두렵다는 것은 맥락상 빈칸에 들어갈 말로 적합하지 않다.

해석
멘토: 마음속에 어떤 걱정이라도 있어?
멘티: 음, 제가 상담하고 싶은 것이 있어요. 제가 일하고 싶은 기업의 임원들과 만날 기회가 있어요.
멘토: 그것의 문제가 뭐야? 좋은 것 아니야?
멘티: 네, 이것은 분명 일생일대의 기회예요. 그런데 제가 (A) 망칠까 봐 두려워요.
멘토: 그러지 마. 네가 만남을 준비하는 데 (B) 전력을 다한다면 넌 괜찮을 거야.
멘티: 전보다 훨씬 자신이 생겼어요.

	(A)	(B)
①	망치다	일과를 마치다
②	망치다	전력을 다하다
③	2위가 되다	일과를 마치다
④	매우 똑같다	전력을 다하다

어휘
enterprise 기업
once-in-a-lifetime 일생에 단 한 번의
confident 자신 있는, 확신하는   blow it 망치다
call it a day 일과를 마치다
go at full tilt 전력을 다하다
come off second best 2위가 되다
cut from the same cloth 매우 똑같다

오답률 TOP 2
05 정답 ④

정답해설
④ 출제 포인트: 접속사 vs. 부사(구)
'on the other hand(반면에)'는 부사(구)이므로 절과 절을 연결할 수 없다. 해당 문장은 'on the other hand'가 절과 절을 연결하고 있으므로 옳지 않은 문장이다. 따라서 'on the other hand'를 유사 의미의 접속사인 'while'로 수정해야 한다.

오답해설
① 출제 포인트: 현재분사 vs. 과거분사
수식하는 대상 'world'와 수동관계이므로 과거분사 'developed'를 사용하는 것이 옳으며 해당 문장에서 'less'는 'little'의 비교급으로 과거분사 'developed'를 수식하는 부사로 사용되었다.
② 출제 포인트: 전치사+관계대명사
「전치사+관계대명사」는 뒤따라오는 절의 형태가 완전하다. 해당 문장은 「전치사+관계대명사」인 'in which' 이후에 오는 절이 완전한 형태이므로 옳게 사용되었다.
③ 출제 포인트: a few + 명사[복수]
'a few' 이후에 오는 명사는 복수 형태를 사용해야 하므로 밑줄 친 'agriculturalists'는 옳은 표현이다.

해석
저개발 세계에서 쓰이는 전형적인 시나리오는 아주 소수의 상업적 농업 경영인들이 기술적으로 발전되어 있는 반면에 대다수는 경쟁할 수 없다는 것이다.

어휘
scenario 시나리오, 각본   commercial 상업의, 상업적인
agriculturalist 농업 경영인

06 정답 ②

정답해설
② 출제 포인트: 주장/요구/명령/제안동사 + (that) + 주어 + (should) + 동사원형
'demand'는 '요구하다'를 뜻하는 동사로 목적어로 that절이 오는 경우 「(that)+주어+(should)+동사원형」을 사용해야 한다. 해당 문장은 'demanded'의 목적어인 that절에 현재시제 동사 'returns'를 사용하였으므로 틀린 문장이다. 따라서 'returns'를 'should return' 또는 'return'으로 수정해야 한다.

오답해설
① 출제 포인트: to부정사의 형용사적 용법/to부정사의 의미상 주어/to부정사의 태
to부정사(구) 'to depart from our usual practice'는 문맥상 명사 'reason'을 수식하고 있으므로 형용사적 용법으로 사용된 것임을 알 수 있다. 이때 'for us'는 to부정사(구)의 의미상 주어에 해당하며 'depart'와 능동관계이므로 to부정사에 능동태인 'to depart'를 옳게 사용하였다.
③ 출제 포인트: 접속사 vs. 전치사/to부정사의 명사적 용법
접속사 'Even though' 이후에 절을 사용하였으므로 옳은 문장이다. 또한 'to help'는 동사 'offered'의 목적어로 명사적 용법에 해당하며 이때 'help'는 완전자동사로 사용되었다.
④ 출제 포인트: 시간의 부사절/현재분사 vs. 과거분사
「since+주어+과거시제 동사」는 시간의 부사절로 주절의 동사에 현재완료를 사용한다. 따라서 'has earned'는 옳은 표현이다. 또한 'doing all kinds of jobs'는 현재분사구문으로 생략된 주어는 'Tom'이며 능동의 의미를 나타내는 현재분사 'doing'을 옳게 사용하였다.

해석

① 나는 우리가 우리의 평상시 관행에서 벗어날 이유가 없다고 본다.
② Jane은 그가 자신에게서 빌려 갔던 책을 돌려줘야 한다고 요구했다.
③ 그가 시간이 정말 없는데도 불구하고, 그는 여전히 도와주겠다고 했다.
④ Tom은 7살 이후로 온갖 일을 하면서, 자신의 생계를 꾸려왔다.

오답률 TOP 3

07 정답 ②

정답해설

② **출제 포인트: with 분사구문/현재분사 vs. 과거분사**

'with ~ him'은 with 분사구문에 해당한다. 과거분사 'followed' 이후에 목적어 'him'이 있으며 주어진 해석 'William은 Jane이 자신을 뒤따르게'로 보아 수식하는 대상 'Jane'과 'follow'는 능동관계임을 알 수 있다. 따라서 과거분사 'followed'를 현재분사 'following'으로 수정해야 한다. 또한 주어진 우리말 해석이 '정류장까지 걸어갔다'이므로 'walked back to the bus stop'에서 'back'을 삭제해야 한다.

오답해설

① **출제 포인트: 주의해야 할 비교급 관용표현**

'much less'는 비교급 관용표현으로 앞에는 부정문이어야 하며 '하물며 전혀 ~아니다'를 뜻한다. 해당 문장은 부정문 이후에 'much less'를 사용하였으며 주어진 해석과 일치하므로 옳은 문장이다.

③ **출제 포인트: 간접의문문의 어순**

해당 문장에서 'what he had done'은 완전타동사 'realized(realize의 과거형)'의 목적어로 쓰인 간접의문문으로 「의문대명사+주어+동사」의 어순을 옳게 사용하였다.

④ **출제 포인트: 관사의 위치**

원급 비교 「as+원급+as」가 쓰인 문장으로 원급자리에 「부정관사+형용사+명사」 형태의 명사(구)가 오는 경우 「형용사+부정관사+명사」의 형태이다. 따라서 'as good a novel as'는 옳은 표현이다.

08 정답 ③

정답해설

주어진 문장에서는 '자기소개서(cover letter)'에 관한 사람들의 일반적인 견해에 대해 언급하고 있다. 이후에는 '실제로 고용 현장에서는 사람들의 기대와는 정반대이다'라는 점을 시사하고 있는 (B)가 이어지는 것이 자연스럽다. 이어서 (C)의 'this reason(이러한 이유)'이 (B)에서 언급된 "the interview selection process has to be completed as quickly as possible since employers would not want too many days wasted on granting employment and keeping work on stand-by(고용인들이 고용을 승인하고 업무를 대기 상태로 두는 데 너무 많은 날을 소비하고 싶어 하지 않기 때문에 면접 선발 절차는 가능한 한 신속하게 끝나야 한다)"를 가리키고 있으므로 (C)가 이어진 후, (A)의 'According to the rule(그 법칙에 따르면)'이 (C)의 'golden rule(기본 법칙)'을 가리키고 있으므로 (A)가 마지막으로 이어지는 것이 가장 자연스럽다. 따라서 정답은 '③ (B) - (C) - (A)'이다.

오답해설

① (A)의 'the rule(법칙)'이 가리키는 것이 주어진 문장에 등장하지 않기 때문에, (A)가 주어진 문장에 이어지는 것은 어색하다.
② (A)의 'According to the rule(그 법칙에 따르면)'로 보아, 해당 법칙이 (A) 이전에 먼저 언급되어야 하는데 (B)에는 'the rule(법칙)'이 가리키는 내용이 없기 때문에 (B)에 (A)가 이어지는 것은 어색하다.
④ 'Due to this reason'이 가리키는 내용이 주어진 문장에 언급되지 않으므로, 주어진 문장에 (C)가 이어지는 것은 어색하다.

해석

보통 사람들은 그들이 자기소개서를 작성하는 데 많은 노력을 쏟으며, 따라서 그것이 인내심을 가지고 읽힐 필요가 있다고 생각한다.
(B) 그러나 현실은 정반대이다. 고용인들이 고용을 승인하고 업무를 대기 상태로 두는 데 너무 많은 날을 소비하고 싶어 하지 않기 때문에 면접 선발 절차는 가능한 한 신속하게 끝나야 한다.
(C) 이러한 이유와 셀 수 없이 많은 수의 지원서들 때문에 대부분의 고용인들은 일을 더 빠르고 더 편리하게 만들기 위해 40초 기본 법칙을 지정했다.
(A) 그 법칙에 따르면, 어떠한 지원서에도 40초 이상의 시간이 주어져서는 안 되는데, 이것은 최종 인원을 선발하기 전 선발 위원회의 구성원들은 오직 지원서를 훑어볼 수 있을 정도의 시간만을 가지고 있다는 것을 의미한다.

어휘

cover letter 자기소개서
application 지원서
glance through 훑어보다, 획획[대충] 읽다
round up …을 (찾아) 모으다
process 과정, 절차
stand-by 대기, 예비
golden rule (행동의) 기본 원리[법칙], 황금률
convenient 편리한
demand 필요로 하다
committee 위원회
bunch (한 무리의) 사람들, 한패
grant 승인하다
innumerable 셀 수 없이 많은, 무수한

09 정답 ④

정답해설

본문은 'Andrew Piper와 Richard Jean So'의 연구 결과에 근거해 '여성 작가에 대한 고정 관념이 여전히 존재한다'는 것을 밝히며 첫 문장 "It's a fact that female writers still battle with stereotypes(여성 작가들이 여전히 고정 관념과 싸우고 있다는 것은 사실이다)."에서 요지를 드러내고 있다. 본문에 따르면, 여성 작가들은 여전히 '정서적' 특성과 모성애에 관한 이슈로 평가된다. 반면에 남성은 '과학, 국가' 등의 관점에서 평가되고 있다. 본문 전체적으로 '남성 작가와 여성 작가에 대한 성 편견이 존재한다'고 설명하고 있으므로, 글의 요지로 가장 적절한 것은 '④ There exists prejudice against female authors to this day(지금까지 여성 작가에 대한 편견이 존재한다).'이다.

오답해설

① 남성 작가가 고정 관념에 저항한다는 내용은 본문에서 언급되지 않는다.
② '여성이 남성보다 사랑에 대해 더 잘 쓴다.'는 것이 바로 본문에서 언급한 '여성 작가에 대한 고정 관념'이므로, 글의 요지로 적절하지 않다.
③ 작가의 성비는 본문에 언급되지 않는다.

해석

여성 작가들이 여전히 고정 관념과 싸우고 있다는 것은 사실이다. Andrew Piper와 Richard Jean So에 의해 실시된 약 10,000편의 서평 분석에서 밝혀진 성 편견은 이러한 주장에 대한 충분한 증거이다. *The New York Times*와 *Sunday Book Review*의 평론가들에 관한 한, "여성은 가족에 관해 쓰고 남성은 전쟁에 관해 쓴다." 이 연구의 결과는 절망적이다. 평론가들은 여성의 책을 묘사할 때 "남편", "결혼", 그리고 "아름다움"과 같은 용어를 선호했고, 남성을 비평할 때는 "이론" 그리고 "주장"을 선호했다. Piper와 So는 "여성은 여전히 그들의 '정서적' 특성과 모성과 관련된 문제에 관해 쓰는 것을 좋아하는 것에 의해 정의되는 반면, 남성은 과학과 국가 문제에 관한 그들의 관심에 의해 대부분 정의된다"고 결론지었다.
① 남성 작가들은 성공적으로 고정 관념에 저항해 왔다.
② 여성이 남성보다 사랑에 대해 더 잘 쓴다.
③ 남성 작가들이 그들의 여성 상대방보다 수가 더 많다.

④ 지금까지 여성 작가에 대한 편견이 존재한다.

어휘

bias 편견
sufficient 충분한
as far as … be concerned …에 관한 한, …로서는
frustrating 좌절시키는, 절망적인
critique 비평[평론]하다
maternal 모성의, 어머니의
outnumber …보다 수가 더 많다, 수적으로 우세하다
counterpart 상대, 대응 관계에 있는 사람[것]
prejudice 편견
reveal 밝히다, 드러내다
assertion 주장
favor 선호하다
trait 특성
defy 저항하다, 반항하다
to this day 지금[이날]까지도

10 정답 ④

정답해설

본문은 '유대인의 성인식'인 'bar mitzvah'와 'bat mitzvah'를 소개하고 있다. 본문 중반의 "While the ceremony does not indicate that the child is physically an adult, it does so mentally and emotionally with the emphasis on the individual's increased culpability and responsibility(그 의식이 아이가 신체적으로 성인이라는 것을 나타내지는 않지만, 그것은 개인의 증가된 책임과 의무의 강조와 함께 정신적 그리고 감정적으로는 그렇다는 것을 나타낸다)."로 보아, 'bar mitzvah'와 'bat mitzvah'는 '신체적 성숙'이 아닌 '정신적 성숙'을 의미하는 의식이라는 것을 알 수 있다. 따라서 글의 내용과 일치하는 것은 '④ Completing the bat mitzvah does not mean a person's physical maturity(bat mitzvah를 마치는 것이 한 사람의 신체적 성숙을 의미하지는 않는다).'이다.

오답해설

① 첫 문장 "The bar mitzvah and bat mitzvah are coming of age ceremonies for Jewish boys and girls, respectively(bar mitzvah와 bat mitzvah는 각각 유대인 소년과 소녀를 위한 성인식이다.)"를 통해, 'bar mitzvah'는 소년, 'bat mitzvah'는 소녀를 위한 것임을 알 수 있다.

② 두 번째 문장 "Under Jewish Law, individuals are only required to formally observe the commandments once they reach a specific age (12 for girls, 13 for boys)(유대교 법에 따라 개인은 특정한 나이(소녀는 12세, 소년은 13세)가 되고 나서야 공식적으로 계율을 준수할 필요가 있다)"를 통해, '소녀는 12세, 소년은 13세에 성인식을 치를 나이가 된다'는 것을 알 수 있으므로, 글의 내용과 일치하지 않는다.

③ 세 번째 문장 "While this change occurs automatically once the child reaches that age, a bar or bat mitzvah is often held to celebrate the boy or girl's coming-of-age and publicly mark the individual's right to now participate in religious ceremonies, count in the minyan, or form contacts(이 변화는 아이가 그 나이가 되면 자동적으로 발생하지만, bar mitzvah 또는 bat mitzvah는 소년 또는 소녀의 성년을 축하하고, 이제 종교의식에 참여하거나, 예배 정족수에 포함되거나, 또는 관계를 형성할 수 있는 개인의 권리를 공개적으로 기념하기 위해 종종 개최된다)."를 통해, '성인식은 아이가 성인이 되어 종교적 권리를 가질 수 있음을 공개적으로 기념하기 위해 개최되는 것이며, 계율을 준수해야 하는 변화는 해당 연령에 도달하면 자동적으로 발생한다'고 언급하고 있으므로, '성인식을 공식적으로 치르지 않더라도 종교 행사에 참여할 수 있는 권리는 주어진다'는 것을 유추할 수 있다. 따라서 글의 내용과 일치하지 않는다.

해석

bar mitzvah와 bat mitzvah는 각각 유대인 소년과 소녀를 위한 성인식이다. 유대교 법에 따라 개인은 특정한 나이(소녀는 12세, 소년은 13세)가 되고 나서야 공식적으로 계율을 준수할 필요가 있다. 이 변화는 아이가 그 나이가 되면 자동적으로 발생하지만, bar mitzvah 또는 bat mitzvah는 소년 또는 소녀의 성년을 축하하고, 이제 종교의식에 참여하거나, 예배 정족수에 포함되거나, 또는 관계를 형성할 수 있는 개인의 권리를 공개적으로 기념하기 위해 종종 개최된다. 그 의식이 아이가 신체적으로 성인이라는 것을 나타내지는 않지만, 그것은 개인의 증가된 책임과 의무의 강조와 함께 정신적 그리고 감정적으로는 그렇다는 것을 나타낸다. bar mitzvah 또는 bat mitzvah라는 명칭 자체는 mitzvah의 아들 또는 딸이라고 번역한다, 왜냐하면 그 순간부터 개인은 율법의 (계율 또는 법이라고도 알려진) mitzvahs에 따라 행동해야 하기 때문이다.

① bar mitzvah는 소녀, bat mitzvah는 소년을 위한 것이다.
② 유대인 소년들은 소녀들보다 성년을 더 일찍 축하한다.
③ 성인식을 하지 않은 13세 이상의 유대인 소년은 어떠한 종교 행사에도 참여할 수 없다.
④ bat mitzvah를 마치는 것이 한 사람의 신체적 성숙을 의미하지는 않는다.

어휘

bar mitzvah 바르미츠바(유대교에서 13세가 된 소년의 성인식)
bat mitzvah 바트미츠바(유대교에서 12세가 된 소녀에 대한 성인식)
coming of age ceremony 성인식
respectively 각각
commandment 계율, 계명
count in 포함시키다, 계산에 넣다
minyan 예배 정족수(유대교의 예배를 하는 데 최저로 필요한 출석자 수)
contact 관계, 연줄
culpability 책임, 질책[비난]받을 일, 유죄성, (범죄, 잘못 등의) 책임을 질 수 있음
responsibility 책임, 의무, 할 일
abide by 따르다, 지키다, …에 따라 행동하다
take part in 참여하다
observe 따르다, 준수하다
mark 기념[축하]하다
indicate 나타내다, 보여주다
maturity 성숙, 성인임

기적사 DAY 26

결국엔 성정혜 영어 하프모의고사

| 01 | ① | 02 | ① | 03 | ② | 04 | ① | 05 | ② |
| 06 | ① | 07 | ③ | 08 | ④ | 09 | ② | 10 | ④ |

01 정답 ①
16 국가직

정답해설

대부분의 사람들이 인정하는 '도덕적인 것'이 공정한 것과 합리적인 것이라면, 그와 반대되는 의미는 ① greedy일 것이다.

해석

대부분의 사람들은 도덕적인 것이 공정하고 합리적인 것을 의미하는 것이지 **욕심이 많은** 것을 의미하지 않는다고 인정한다.
① 욕심이 많은
② 이타주의적인
③ 지친, 지루한
④ 회의적인

어휘

acknowledge 인정하다
fair 공정한
greedy 욕심이 많은
weary 지친, 지루한
ethical 윤리의, 도덕의
reasonable 합리적인
altruistic 이타주의적인
skeptical 회의적인

오답률 TOP 2
02 정답 ①
16 국가직

정답해설

'shelve'는 동사로 '보류하다'의 의미를 가지며, 과거분사형태의 'shelved'는 '미결의' 형용사 뜻으로 사용된다. 따라서 '미결의' 의미를 가지는 ① pending이 정답이다.

해석

일부 주들에서 시행된 개혁들이 이미 효과를 가져왔으나, 다른 주들에서 개혁된 법률은 **보류되**었다.
① 미결의
② 서두르는
③ 정확한
④ 나눌 수 있는

어휘

state 주, 국가, 상태, 정부; 언급하다
legislation 법률, 입법 행위
pending 미결의
precise 정확한
enact 시행하다, 제정하다, 입법하다
shelve 보류하다
hasty 서두르는
divisible 나눌 수 있는

03 정답 ②
16 국가직

정답해설

'sleep on something'은 관용적인 표현으로 '~을 하룻밤 자며 생각하다, ~의 결정을 다음날까지 미루다'의 의미를 가진다. 최종 결정을 오늘 할 필요는 없다고 했으므로 '좀 더 생각해보라'라고 말했을 것임을 유추할 수 있다. 빈칸 문제였다면, ④도 정답의 가능성이 있으나, 밑줄 친 표현의 정확한 의미를 묻는 문제였으므로 정답은 ② take time to think about it뿐이다. 단, ③ 'take it for granted'는 'take it for granted that 주어 동사' 또는 'take it for granted to 동사원형'이 원래 옳은 표현이다.

해석

오늘 최종 결정을 할 필요는 없습니다. 집에 가서 **하룻밤 자며 생각해보시는** 것은 어떨까요?
① 늦잠 잘 수 있도록 하루를 쉬다
② ~을 하룻밤 자며 생각하다
③ 당연한 것으로 그것을 받아들이다
④ 충분히 휴식하다

어휘

sleep on something ~을 하룻밤 자며 생각하다, ~의 결정을 다음날까지 미루다
take a day off 하루 쉬다, 휴가를 내다
take it for granted 당연히 ~일 것이라고 믿다

04 정답 ①
14 국가직

정답해설

B의 말 중에서 '그가 행복할 거라고 생각했다'는 말은 그는 행복해 보이지 않는다는 것이므로 빈칸에는 ① 'have such a long face(그렇게 우울한 얼굴을 하다)'가 적절하다.

오답해설

나머지 보기는 문맥상 적절하지 않으므로 오답이다.

해석

A: 너 아침에 Steve 봤니?
B: 응. 그런데 그가 왜 <u>그렇게 우울한 얼굴을 하고 있는 거야?</u>
A: 조금도 모르겠어.
B: 난 그가 행복해할 거라고 생각했었거든.
A: 나도 그래. 특히, 지난주에 그는 판매부장으로 승진했으니까.
B: 여자 친구랑 문제가 좀 있을지도 모르겠어.
① 그렇게 우울한 얼굴을 하다
② 나의 후임이 되다
③ 시류에 편승하다
④ 멋진 수를 쓰다

어휘

a long face 슬픈 표정, 우울한 얼굴
step into one's shoes ~의 후임이 되다
jump on the bandwagon 시류에 편승하다
play a good hand 멋진 수를 쓰다

05 정답 ②
15 국가직

정답해설

② **출제 포인트: 현재분사 vs. 과거분사**
밑줄 친 'controlled'는 'control'의 과거분사로 수식하는 대상 'a checkpoint'와 수동관계이며 이후에 「by+행위자」인 'by pro-Russian separatists'가 왔으므로 'controlled'는 옳은 표현이다.

오답해설

① **출제 포인트: 동사 vs. 준동사/현재분사 vs. 과거분사**
해당 문장의 본동사는 'crossed'이므로 'prompted'는 분사에 해당되는 자리이다. 단, 과거분사의 경우 수여동사를 제외하고는 목적어가 존재할

수 없으나 해당 문장에서는 목적어 'a skirmish'가 존재하므로 과거분사 구문이라고 볼 수 없다. 따라서 생략된 주어인 주절의 'Russian military vehicles'가 분사구문에서의 동사 'prompt'와 능동관계이므로 밑줄 친 'prompted'를 현재분사 'prompting'으로 수정해야 한다.

③ **출제 포인트: 동사 vs. 준동사/현재분사 vs. 과거분사**
문장의 본동사는 'were'이며 삽입절로 'Avakov said'가 들어갔다. 따라서 'cited'는 과거분사의 형태이나 이후에 목적어가 왔으므로 현재분사의 형태인 'citing'으로 고쳐야 적절하다.

④ **출제 포인트: 수동태 불가동사**
'occur'는 자동사이며 수동태로 쓰이지 않는다. 따라서 'was occurred'를 문맥상 시제를 반영해 능동 형태인 'occurred'로 수정해야 한다.

해석

러시아 군사 차량이 우크라이나와 러시아 군대 사이의 소규모 접전을 촉발하면서 목요일에 국경을 넘어 우크라이나로 들어왔다고 우크라이나 내무장관 대행인 Arsen Avakov가 말했다. Avakov에 따르면, 탱크가 동부 우크라이나 Luhansk 지역의 친러시아 분리주의자가 지배하는 국경의 검문소를 건넜다고 한다. 무장된 차량과 대포가 행렬의 일부였다고 우크라이나 정보국의 말을 인용하여 Avakov가 말했다. 이 사건은 주로 친러시아인 동부지역에 사는 사람들에 대한 우크라이나 지도자들의 폭력 운동 가운데 발생했다.

어휘

border 국경
acting 대행의
forces 군대
prompt 촉발하다, 유도하다
interior minister 내무장관
artillery 대포

오답률 TOP 1

06 정답 ① 15 국가직

정답해설

① **출제 포인트: 자동사/타동사**
'fold'는 '(운반보관이 쉽도록) 접다'를 뜻하는 경우 자동사로 사용될 수 있다. 해당 문장은 'fold'를 자동사로 사용하였으며 주어진 해석이 '(운반보관이 쉽도록) 접다'이므로 옳은 문장이다.

오답해설

② **출제 포인트: 수사/관사 + 단위명사 + of**
'handful'은 단위명사이며 '소수의'를 뜻하는 경우 'a handful of'의 형태로 사용된다. 해당 문장은 주어진 해석이 '소수의'이나 'handful'만 사용하였으므로 틀린 문장이다. 따라서 'handful'을 'a handful of'로 수정해야 한다.

③ **출제 포인트: 능동태 vs. 수동태**
'solve'는 완전타동사이므로 이후에 목적어가 있어야 한다. 해당 문장은 'solve'를 능동태로 사용하였으나 이후에 목적어가 없으며 주어진 해석이 '해결되다'이므로 'solve'를 'be solved'로 수정해야 한다.

④ **출제 포인트: 동명사 관용표현**
「be used to + 목적어[명사/동명사]」는 관용표현으로 '~하는 데 익숙하다'를 뜻한다. 해당 문장은 주어진 해석이 '~하는 데 익숙하다'이나 'to' 이후의 목적어 자리에 동사원형 'deal'을 사용하였으므로 틀린 문장이다. 따라서 'deal'을 동명사 'dealing'으로 수정해야 한다.

07 정답 ③ 15 국가직

정답해설

③ **출제 포인트: 수여동사의 문장구조/시간, 조건의 부사절**
'lend'는 수여동사이므로 「lend + 간접목적어[대상] + 직접목적어[사물]」의

형태로 사용된다. 해당 문장은 'lend'를 사용하였으나 직접목적어 'money' 앞에 전치사 'with'를 사용하였으므로 틀린 문장이다. 따라서 'lend you with money'에서 'with'를 삭제해 'lend you money'로 수정해야 한다. 또한 'provided (that)'은 조건의 부사절을 이끄는 접속사로 'will pay'를 'pay'로 수정해 현재시제로 미래를 나타내는 것이 옳다.

오답해설

① **출제 포인트: 가주어 It/명사절의 접속사 that/비교급 관용표현**
해당 문장에서 'It'은 가주어이며 진주어는 접속사 'that'이 이끄는 명사절 'you do it yourself rather than rely on others'이다. 또한 'A rather than B'는 'B라기보다는 A'라는 의미로 'do'와 'rely'는 병렬구조를 이루고 있다.

② **출제 포인트: 현재분사 vs. 과거분사/주어와 동사의 수일치/능동태 vs. 수동태**
'parked'는 완전자동사 'park'의 과거분사로 생략된 주어 'my car'와 수동관계이며 이후에 목적어가 없으므로 옳은 표현이다. 또한 'was towed'의 경우 주어가 단수 형태인 'My car'이며 주어진 해석이 '견인되다'이므로 단수 형태이자 수동태인 'was towed'를 옳게 사용하였다.

④ **출제 포인트: 가정법 과거완료/수동태 불가동사**
가정법 과거완료는 「If + 주어 + had + 과거분사 ~, 주어 + would/should/could/might + have + 과거분사 ~」의 형태로 사용되며, 「If + 주어 + had + 과거분사 ~」는 부사절이므로 그 위치가 자유롭다. 또한 해당 문장에서 'approach'는 완전자동사로 쓰여 이후에 목적어가 없고 수동태로 사용할 수 없다.

오답률 TOP 3

08 정답 ④ 16 국가직

정답해설

Pinocchio의 도덕적 용기를 시험하는 세 가지(용기, 정직, 그리고 이타심) 시련을 언급한 뒤 Pinocchio가 첫 번째 두 부분에서 실패하게 된다는 주어진 문장이 자연스럽게 이어져야 한다. 또한 그러한 주어진 문장에 가족의 신성함, 운명을 인도하는 초자연적 힘 그리고 사회 규칙의 준수와 같은 첨언이 뒤로 이어짐으로써 이야기가 마무리된다. 따라서 주어진 문장이 들어갈 가장 적절한 곳은 ④이다.

오답해설

② 문장의 "용감하고, 진실되고, 이기적이지 않다"의 부분이 주어진 문장에서 언급한 '그 첫 번째 두 부분'이라는 지칭을 받아 ③의 위치에 주어진 문장이 들어갈 수 있는 가능성이 있다. 그러나 ③ 문장에서 언급한 '그 영화의 세 가지 주요한 에피소드'의 부분은 ② 문장의 "용감하고, 진실되고, 이기적이지 않다"는 것을 각각 보여줄 수 있는 세 가지 에피소드를 지칭하는 것이기 때문에, 그사이에 주어진 문장이 위치하여 ② 문장과 ③ 문장의 유기성을 파괴할 수는 없다.

해석

Disney의 작품은 과도하게 동화, 신화, 그리고 민화를 그리는데, 그것들은 모범적인 요소가 다분한 것들이다. (①) Pinocchio가 피상적인 현실주의 아래 가라앉는 대신에 이러한 요소들이 강조될 수 있는 좋은 예이다. (②) 영화 초반부에, 소년이자 인형인 Pinocchio는 "진짜 소년"이 되기 위해서, 그는 그가 "용감하고, 진실되고, 이기적이지 않다"는 것을 보여주어야만 한다고 듣는다. (③) 그 영화의 세 가지 주요한 에피소드들은 젊은이(Pinocchio)의 도덕적 용기를 시험하는 의례적인 시련들을 나타낸다. (④) <u>그는 첫 번째 두 부분에서 우울하게 실패한다. 그러나 용기, 정직, 그리고 이타심을 실로 입증한 마지막 고래 에피소드에서 그가 그 자신을 만회한다.</u>) 그러한 것으로, Disney의 작품 대부분과 같이, 피노키오 안에서의 가치관들은 전통적이고 보수적이며, 가족의 신성함의 확인이며, 우리의 운명을 인도하는 데에 있어서 초자연적 힘의 중요성이며, 그리고 사회 규칙에 의해 행동해야 하는 필요성이다.

어휘

dismally 우울하게, 음울하게; 쓸쓸하게
unselfishness 이타심
submerge 물속에 가라앉히다, 보이지 않게 하다, 매몰시키다
realism 현실주의
ritualistic 의례적인, 관습적인
fortitude 용기, 인내
conservative 보수적인
redeem 되찾다(만회하다), 회복하다
affirmation 확인
sanctity 신성함

09 정답 ②
16 국가직

정답해설

'he was destined to influence ~ him on the stage.'에 언급된 것처럼, Stanislavski는 그와 함께 일하고 그의 밑에서 일했던 많은 사람에게 영향과 영감을 주었기 때문에 ②의 '그의 동료들에게 일생동안 영향력이 없었다.'는 말은 본문과 일치하지 않는다.

오답해설

① 본문 후반부에 언급된 'Stanislavski was also richly ~ genuine talent.'에서 찾아볼 수 있다.
③ 본문 초반에 언급된 'He was the son of a wealthy man ~ art at home and abroad.'에서 찾아볼 수 있다.
④ 본문 중반부에 언급된 'His personal integrity and ~ artist of the first rank.'에서 찾아볼 수 있다.

해석

Stanislavski는 여러모로 운이 좋았다. 그는 그에게 고국 또는 해외에서 극예술의 위대한 대표 인물들을 볼 수 있는 기회인, 폭넓은 교육 혜택을 줄 수 있었던 부유한 남성의 아들이었다. 그는 높은 목표를 설정하고 목표로 가는 어려운 길 도중에 흔들리지 않았기 때문에 굉장한 명성을 얻었다. 일에 대한 그의 개인 성실성과 고갈될 줄 모르는 능력은 그를 일류의 전문 예술가로 만드는 데에 기여했다. Stanislavski는 잘생긴 외모, 좋은 목소리 그리고 천재적인 재능을 또한 선천적으로 풍부하게 부여받았다. 배우, 감독 그리고 교사로서, 그는 그와 함께 일하고 그의 밑에서 일했던 또는 무대에서 그를 보는 특혜를 가졌던 많은 사람에게 영향과 영감을 주도록 운명 지어졌다.
① Stanislavski는 매력적인 외모를 가지고 태어났다.
② Stanislavski 그의 삶 내내 동료들에게 영향력이 없는 채로 남아 있었다.
③ Stanislavski의 아버지는 그의 교육을 지원해주기 충분할 정도로 부유했다.
④ Stanislavski는 올바른 성격과 지치지 않는 능력(자신감) 덕택으로 상위의 예술가가 되었다.

어휘

theatre art 극예술
falter [용기·결심 등이] 흔들리다, 꺾이다.
integrity 성실, 고결
inexhaustible 지칠 줄 모르는
endow 부여하다, 기부하다
exterior 외모, 겉모습, 외부
genuine 진짜의, 성실한
privilege 특권
affluent 부유한, 유복한
upright 정직한, 올바른, 똑바른
competence 능력, 역량

10 정답 ④
16 국가직

정답해설

'인격'에 대한 추상적인 정의를 내리고 있는 지문이다. 따라서 정답은 ④ 'What Character Means(인격이란 무엇인가)'이다.

오답해설

① 인격이 진실을 저항한다는 내용은 지문에서 언급되지 않았다.
② 인격 자체가 협력(협조)하려는 본능에 믿음이 있다고는 하였지만, 인격과 협력하는 것은 그 주체가 누구인지도 알 수 없으며, 지문에서도 언급되지 않았다.
③ 인격이 '무시'에 대해 화를 낸다고 하였지만, '인격에 대한 무시'는 언급하지 않았다.

해석

'인격'이란 인간에 대한 존경이며, 경험을 다르게 해석할 권리이다. '인격'은 이기심을 천성으로써 인정하나, 인간의 망설이지만 용기를 북돋는 협조적 본능에 절대적으로 믿음을 둔다. '인격'은 '가혹한 행위'와는 맞지 않으며, '무시'에 화를 내고 '개선'에 항상 열려있다. '인격'은 무엇보다도 사실 앞에서의 엄청난 겸손이며 설령 그 진실이 쓴 약일지라도 진실이 있는 반사적인 협력이다.
① 진실에 대한 인격의 저항
② 인격과 협력하는 방법
③ 인격에 대한 무시
④ 인격이란 무엇인가

어휘

interpret ~을 설명하다, 해석하다
hesitant 망설이는, 주저하는
hearten ~을 격려하다, 고무하다
tyranny 가혹행위, 폭정, 횡포
irritable 화를 곧잘 내는
humility 겸손
tremendous 엄청난, 대단한
alliance 동맹, 협력
automatic 반사의, 자동의, 자동적인

기적사 DAY 27

결국엔 성정혜 영어 하프모의고사

01	①	02	③	03	②	04	①	05	④
06	③	07	③	08	③	09	④	10	④

오답률 TOP 1
01 정답 ①

정답해설

문맥상 영주가 가지는 권리인 '거부권'을 수식할 단어로 가장 적절한 것은 '(일시적으로) 중지하는'의 의미를 지니는 ① suspensive이다.

해석

영주는 **(일시적으로) 중지하는** 거부권과 그 섬의 관리들 대부분을 임명할 권리를 가졌다.
① (일시적으로) 중지하는, 미결정의, 확실치 못한
② 구부러진, 굽은
③ 웅변의, 달변의, 설득력 있는
④ 회의적인

어휘

suspensive (일시적으로) 중지하는, 미결정의, 확실치 못한
crooked 구부러진, 굽은   eloquent 웅변의, 달변의, 설득력 있는
skeptical 회의적인

02 정답 ③

정답해설

밑줄 친 'suspected'는 '의심하는, 미심쩍은'이라는 뜻으로 ③ dubious와 의미가 가장 가깝다.

해석

법에서는 격리되는 것을 거부하는 **의심** 환자를 강제적으로 격리하는 것을 허용한다.
① 유능한
② 무한한
③ 의심하는, 수상쩍은
④ 나눌 수 있는

어휘

quarantine 격리하다; 격리   forcibly 힘으로, 강제적으로
suspect ~을 의심하다, (위험·나쁜 일 등) 알아채다
refuse 거절하다, 사절[사퇴]하다   isolate ~을 떼놓다, 분리하다, 격리하다
competent 유능한   boundless 무한한
dubious 의심하는, 수상쩍은   divisible 나눌 수 있는

03 정답 ②

정답해설

밑줄 친 'cope with'는 '처리하다, 대처하다'의 뜻으로 ② deal with와 의미가 가장 가깝다.

해석

건강한 사람들은 스트레스에 더 잘 **대처할** 수 있다.

① 기대하다, 생각하다, 의지하다, 세다
② 처리하다, 다루다
③ 내려치다
④ ~을 하룻밤 자며 생각하다

어휘

cope with 처리하다, 대처하다
count on 기대하다, 생각하다, 의지하다, 세다
deal with 처리하다, 다루다   cut at 내려치다
sleep on ~을 하룻밤 자며 생각하다

04 정답 ①

정답해설

B가 자신의 나쁜 습관을 '~하기 위해 정말로 열심히 노력하고 있지만 쉽지 않다'고 말하고 있으므로 빈칸에 ① 'get rid of(~을 없애다)'가 들어가는 것이 문맥상 가장 적절하다.

오답해설

② A가 손톱을 물어뜯는 것이 건강에 좋지 않다고 말하자 B가 그러한 나쁜 습관이 '원인이 되기(give birth to)' 위해 열심히 노력해 왔다고 하는 것은 문맥상 어색하다.
③ B는 손톱을 물어뜯는 나쁜 습관을 '넘어서기(get the better of)' 위해 열심히 노력했다고 하는 것은 대화의 흐름상 적절하지 않다.
④ A가 B의 손톱 물어뜯는 습관이 건강에 좋지 않다고 하자, B는 자신의 나쁜 습관을 눈여겨보기(keep close tabs on)' 위해 열심히 노력했다는 것은 맥락상 부자연스럽다.

해석

A: 너 손톱에서 피나!
B: 아! 어쩐지 아프더라. 나는 손톱을 물어뜯는 오랜 나쁜 버릇이 있어.
A: 그런 버릇 가진 사람들을 많이 봤어. 근데 그건 네 건강에 별로 좋지 않아.
B: 나도 알아. 내 나쁜 버릇을 없애려고 아주 열심히 노력해봤는데 쉽지 않아.
A: 난 완전히 이해해. 네 손톱에서 관심을 돌려 보는 건 어때?
B: 네 말이 맞아. 대신 밖에 나가서 축구를 해야겠어.

① ~을 없애다
② ~의 원인이 되다
③ ~을 넘어서다
④ ~을 눈여겨보다

어휘

fingernail 손톱
get rid of ~을 없애다
give birth to ~의 원인이 되다
get the better of ~을 넘어서다
keep close tabs on ~을 눈여겨보다

오답률 TOP 3
05 정답 ④

정답해설

④ **출제 포인트: 동사 vs. 준동사/현재분사 vs. 과거분사**

해당 문장은 주절과 종속절로 이루어져 있으며, 종속절의 경우 접속사와 주어 없이 밑줄 친 'caused'로 시작한다. 따라서 'caused'는 과거분사임을 알 수 있으며 이때 'caused' 이후에 목적어 'a twenty-minute blackout'이 왔으므로 과거분사 'caused'를 현재분사 'causing'으로 수정해야 한다.

오답해설

① 출제 포인트: 동사 vs. 준동사
해당 문장에 동사가 없으므로 밑줄 친 'built'는 동사임을 알 수 있으며, 이때 'built'는 완전타동사 'build'의 과거시제로 이후에 목적어 'a homemade airship'이 왔다.

② 출제 포인트: 현재분사 vs. 과거분사
밑줄 친 'controlled'는 완전타동사 'control'의 과거분사로, 수식하는 대상 'airspace'와 수동관계이며 해석상 '통제된 영공'이 자연스러우므로 'controlled'는 옳은 표현이다.

③ 출제 포인트: being 생략 분사구문
밑줄 친 'aware that'은 현재분사 'being'이 생략된 분사구문으로 옳은 표현이다. 해당 분사구문을 원래의 문장으로 고치면 'as he was aware that he had breached commercial airspace'가 된다. 이때 'be aware that+절'과 'be aware of+명사(구)'의 구분에 유의하도록 한다.

해석
1982년 7월 2일, 별명이 'Lawnchair Larry'인 미국 트럭 운전사 Lawrence Richard Walters는 직접 비행선을 만들었다. 그의 접이식 의자, 45 헬륨의 기상 관측 기구들, 개인용 주파수대 라디오 및 공기총을 이용하여, 그는 로스앤젤레스 국제공항 근처의 통제된 영공의 위를 15,000피트의 높이로 비행했다. 45분 후, 그는 상업적 영공을 침범했다는 것을 깨달았고, 여러 개의 풍선들을 쏘고 하강하기 시작했다. 그는 그의 공기총을 배 밖으로 잃어버렸고 결국 송전선에 걸려들게 되어 Long Beach에서 20분간 정전을 유발했다.

어휘
homemade 집에서 만든, 손으로 만든
airship 비행선   lawn chair 접이식 의자
weather balloon 기상 관측 기구
a Citizens' Band radio 개인용 주파수대 라디오
pellet gun 공기총   breach 위반하다, 어기다
power line 송전선   blackout 정전

06 정답 ③

정답해설

③ 출제 포인트: 동명사 관용표현
'be worth -ing'는 관용표현으로 '~할 가치가 있다'를 뜻한다. 해당 문장은 주어진 해석 '분명히 방문할 가치가 있다'와 'are definitely worth visiting'이 일치하므로 옳게 사용되었다.

오답해설

① 출제 포인트: 능동태 vs. 수동태
'allow' 이후에 to부정사가 오는 경우는 불완전타동사 'allow'의 수동태인 「be allowed+목적격 보어[to부정사]」뿐이다. 해당 문장은 'allow' 이후에 to부정사를 사용하였으나 능동태이므로 'allow'를 수동태 'be allowed'로 수정해야 한다.

② 출제 포인트: propose(청혼하다) to+사람/수사, 관사+단위명사+of
'propose'가 '청혼하다'를 뜻하고 이후에 목적어로 사람이 오는 경우 사람 앞에 전치사 'to'를 사용해야 한다. 해당 문장은 주어진 해석이 '청혼했다'이며 'proposed'를 사용하였으나 목적어로 온 사람 앞에 전치사 'to'를 사용하지 않았으므로 틀린 문장이다. 따라서 'Jane'을 'to Jane'으로 수정해야 한다. 또한 해당 문장에서 'an armful of'는 「관사+단위명사+of」의 형태로 이때 'armful'은 단위명사임에 유의해야 한다.

④ 출제 포인트: 주어와 동사의 수일치/목적격 관계대명사/능동형 수동태
주절의 동사에 복수 형태인 'are'를 사용하였으나 주절의 주어가 단수 형태인 'The paint'이므로 'are'를 'is'로 수정해야 한다. 또한 해당 문장에서 'which'는 목적격 관계대명사로 이후에 오는 절의 동사 'applied'('바르다'를 뜻하는 apply의 과거시제')의 목적어에 해당하며, 'peel'은 '벗겨지다'를 뜻하는 자동사로 해당 'peel'의 경우 능동형 수동태로 볼 수 있다.

오답률 TOP 2
07 정답 ③

정답해설

③ 출제 포인트: 수여동사로 착각하기 쉬운 완전타동사/시간, 조건의 부사절
'propose'는 완전타동사이므로 수여동사로 사용할 수 없다. 해당 문장은 'propose'를 수여동사로 사용하였으므로 틀린 문장이다. 따라서 대상을 나타내는 목적어 'Tom' 앞에 전치사 'to'를 사용해야 한다. 또한 시간, 조건의 부사절에서는 미래완료가 쓰일 자리를 현재완료로 대체해서 사용할 수 있으므로 'has been announced'는 옳게 사용되었다.

오답해설

① 출제 포인트: 가주어 it/명사절의 접속사 that
해당 문장에서 'It'은 가주어이며 진주어는 접속사 'that'이 이끄는 명사절 'he is your brother-in-law'이다.

② 출제 포인트: 현재분사 vs. 과거분사/to부정사의 명사적 용법
해당 문장에서 'claiming that it belonged to him'은 분사구문이다. 'claiming'은 현재분사로 생략된 주어 'Tom'과 능동관계이며 'claiming'의 목적어로 'that'이 이끄는 절인 'it ~ him'이 따라오므로 옳은 표현이다. 또한 'demand'는 to부정사를 목적어로 사용할 수 있으므로 'to return'은 옳게 사용되었다.

④ 출제 포인트: 가정법 과거완료
가정법 과거완료는 「If+주어+had+과거분사 ~, 주어+would/should/ould/might+have+과거분사 ~.」의 형태로 사용된다. 해당 문장은 가정법 과거완료가 쓰인 문장으로 'If'절에 'had done', 주절에 'would have been'을 사용하였으므로 옳은 문장이다.

08 정답 ③

정답해설

본문은 '디즈니(Disney)의 노트르담의 꼽추(The Hunchback Of Notre Dame)'가 시사하는 바에 대해 설명하고 있다. 본문에 따르면 해당 작품이 주는 표면적 교훈은 '우리와 다른 사람(기형이 있는 사람)을 멸시하는 것은 잘못된 행동이다'라는 것과, '신체적 요건과 관계없이 누구나 선하고 용감한 행위를 할 수 있다' 등의 도덕적인 내용이다. 그러나 다른 관점에서 본다면 '신체의 기형이 있는 사람이 아무리 용감하게 변화할지라도 결국 최종적으로 원하는 것(해당 작품의 경우 아름다운 여인)을 얻는 것은 신체적으로 더 매력적인(잘생긴) 인물이다'라는 내용을 암시하고 있다. 빈칸이 포함된 문장의 'In short(간단히 말해)'로 보아, 빈칸에는 이전에 언급한 내용인 "But a more cynical reading shows that despite Quasimodo's transformation from 'freak' to hero, his physical unattractiveness still prevents him from bagging the girl of his dreams(그러나 더 냉소적인 해석은 Quasimodo가 '괴물'에서 영웅으로 변화했음에도 불구하고, 그의 신체적인 매력이 없음은 여전히 그가 꿈에 그리던 여자를 차지하지 못하게 한다)."를 요약해주는 표현이 들어가야 하므로, 가장 적절한 보기는 '③ the handsome guy always gets the girl(잘생긴 남자가 항상 여자를 차지한다)'이다.

오답해설

①, ②, ④ 빈칸 이전 'In short(간단히 말해)'를 통해, 빈칸에는 빈칸 이전 내용을 요약하는 내용이 들어가야 한다는 것을 알 수 있다. 따라서 문맥상 적절하지 않으므로 오답이다.

해석

대성당의 종탑은 당신의 하나의 진정한 사랑을 찾을 수 있는 가장 분명한 장소가 아니지만, Quasimodo는 어떻게든 이것을 달성한다. 그러나 그녀가 사랑하는 여자인 아름다운 Esmeralda를 화형대에서 구해주었음에도 불구하고, 그 꼽추는 다른 – 상당히 더 잘생긴 – 남자 때문에 슬프게도 결국 퇴짜를 맞는다. 표면적으로, 그 이야기는 우리에게 다르다는 이유로 타인을, 이 경우에는 기형이 있는 사람을, 멸시하는 것은 잘못되었다는 것을 말한다. 그것은 또한 기형 또는 장애를 가진 사람들도 어느 누구와 마찬가지로 선하고 용감한 사람들이 될 수 있다는 것과, 폭군은 불쾌한 최후를 맞이할 것이라는 것을 보여준다. 그러나 더 냉소적인 해석은 Quasimodo가 '괴물'에서 영웅으로 변화했음에도 불구하고, 그의 신체적인 매력이 없음이 여전히 그가 꿈에 그리던 여자를 차지하지 못하게 한다. 간단히 말해, 그것은 <u>잘생긴 남자가 항상 여자를 차지한다</u>는 것을 보여준다.

① 정의는 결국 항상 승리한다
② 진정한 사랑보다 강한 것은 없다
③ 잘생긴 남자가 항상 여자를 차지한다
④ 마음이 따뜻한 사람은 모든 사람이 좋아한다

어휘

cathedral 대성당
somehow 어떻게든
hunchback 꼽추, 곱사등이
spurn 퇴짜 놓다
deformity 기형
tyrant 폭군, 독재자
cynical 냉소적인
freak 괴물, 괴짜
bag 차지하다
obvious 분명한, 명백한, 확실한
stake 화형대
end up 결국 ~이 되다
despise 경멸하다, 멸시하다
disability 장애
sticky 불쾌한, 힘든
reading 해석, 이해
unattractiveness 매력 없음
prevail 승리하다, 이기다

09 정답 ④

정답해설

본문은 연기 훈련 기법 중 하나인 'Stanislavski system (Stanislavski method)'에 관해 설명하고 있다. 본문에 따르면, 'Stanislavski 시스템은 배우들이 감정적 기억(과거의 기억)을 이용하도록 하여, 배우가 무대에서 하는 연기가 새로운 시작이 아닌 이전부터 계속해서 있었던 것과 같은(실제와 같은) 상황이 지속되는 것처럼 보이게 된다' 또한, 'Stanislavski 시스템'을 통해 배우는 '집중과 감각 훈련을 하여 무대에서 자유롭게 반응할 수 있도록 하고, 평상시 여러 사람에게 감정 이입하여 관찰하면서, 폭넓은 감정의 범위를 발달시켜 무대 위에서의 연기가 실제인 것처럼 보이게 할 수 있다.' 즉, 'Stanislavski 시스템' 훈련을 통해 '연기를 가짜가 아닌 현실 상황인 것처럼 보이도록' 할 수 있다는 것을 알 수 있다. 따라서 글의 요지로 가장 적절한 것은 '④ The Stanislavski method helps actors build realistic characters (Stanislavski 방법은 배우들이 현실적인 캐릭터를 구축하도록 돕는다).'이다.

오답해설

① 본문에서 '폭넓은 '감정'을 이용해 현실적인 연기를 할 수 있다'고 언급하고는 있으나, 본문의 주요 주제는 '(일반적) 연기에 있어서 중요한 요소'가 아닌 'Stanislavski 시스템의 특징'이므로 전체 글의 내용을 아우르는 요지로는 적절하지 않다.
② 본문에서 언급되지 않는 내용이다.
③ 본문에서 'Stanislavski 시스템'이 '현실적인 연기'를 하도록 도와준다는 언급은 있으나, 관중의 입장에서 자연스럽고 그럴듯한 이야기가 더 선호된다는 내용은 언급되지 않으므로, 글의 요지로 적절하지 않다.

해석

Stanislavski 방법이라고도 불리는 Stanislavski 시스템은 배우가 다른 것들 중 그의 감정적 기억(즉, 그의 과거 경험과 감정에 대한 기억)을 활용할 것을 필요로 한다. 배우의 무대 등장은 행위 또는 등장인물로서의 삶의 시작이 아니라 이전 상황들 집합의 지속이라고 여겨진다. 배우는 전체 무대 환경에 자유롭게 반응하도록 그의 집중과 감각을 훈련한다. 많은 다른 상황에서의 사람들에 대한 감정 이입적인 관찰을 통해, 그의 무대 위에서의 행위와 반응이 마치 그것들이 가장이 아니라 실제 세계의 일부인 것처럼 보이도록 하기 위해 그는 폭넓은 감정적 범위를 발달시키려 시도한다.

① 감정은 연기에 있어서 중요한 요소이다.
② Stanislavski 시스템은 널리 실행되어왔다.
③ 오늘날의 관중은 자연스럽고 그럴듯한 이야기를 선호한다.
④ Stanislavski 방법은 배우들이 현실적인 캐릭터를 구축하도록 돕는다.

어휘

utilize 활용[이용]하다
recall 기억
circumstance 상황, 환경
onstage 무대 위에서의, 관객 앞에서의
make-believe 가장, 환상
i.e. 즉
preceding 이전의, 앞선
empathic 감정 이입의

10 정답 ④

정답해설

본문은 '우리가 한 사람의 행위를 통해 그 사람의 성격을 판단한다'고 설명하고 있다. 즉, 한 사람이 행동하는 방식이 그 사람의 성격을 나타낸다는 것이다. 본문에 따르면 '이러한 행위(반응)를 결정하는 정신적, 신경적 구조는 일부는 선천적이고 일부는 후천적'이다. 성격의 발현인 행위가 일부 선천적이고 일부 후천적이라는 것은, 사람의 성격 또한 선천적으로 타고나는 기질과 후천적으로 습득하는 기질이 각각 존재한다는 것을 의미한다. 따라서 글의 요지로 가장 적절한 것은 '④ A person's character is determined by both genes and environmental factors(한 사람의 성격은 유전자와 환경적 요소 모두에 의해 결정된다).'이다.

오답해설

① 본문에서는 '개인의 반응(행위)이 다른 이유는 영향을 미치는 성격이 다르기 때문이며, 개인의 성격을 보여주는 행위를 관장하는 정신적, 신경적 구조는 '선천적 요인'과 '후천적 요인'에 의해 형성된다고 언급하고 있다. 따라서 '유전적 요인'으로 인해 성격이 다르다는 내용은 본문의 주장과 일치하지 않는다.
② 본문에 언급되지 않는 내용이므로 오답이다.
③ 본문 후반 "This constitution is partly inborn and partly acquired(이러한 구조는 일부는 선천적이고, 일부는 후천적이다)."를 통해, '성격을 나타내는 행위를 관장하는 신경적 구조가 일부는 선천적이고 일부는 후천적이라는 것'을 알 수 있으며, 선천적 요인과 후천적 요인 중 어느 것이 더 많은 영향을 미치는지는 본문에 언급되지 않으므로 글의 요지로 적절하지 않다.

해석

우리는 한 사람의 성격을 그의 행위에 의해, 즉 일상생활의 수많은 우여곡절에 대해 그가 반응하는 방식에 의해 판단하는 것에 익숙해져 있다. 우리의 경험에서 이러한 반응들은 개인에 따라 다르고, 우리는 영향을 받은 개인의 성격이 상대적으로 다르다고 말함으로써 이 반응의 가변성을 이해한다. 비록 성격이 그 사람 자체의 속성이지만, 그것은 오직 그 사람의 행동을 통해서만 알 수 있고, 반응이 결정되는 정신적 그리고 신경적 구조에 대한 개략적인 표현이다. 이러한 구조는 일부는 선천적이고, 일부는 후천적이다. 중추 신경계를 구성하는 세포와 신경의 경로의 모양은 출생 전에 이미 정해지지만, 어떠한 자극이 중추 신경계를 통하여 지나는 길에 만나는 저항은 유전적인 모양뿐만 아니라 경험의 결과이기도 하다.
① 모든 사람은 유전적인 이유로 다른 성격을 지니고 있다.
② 정확하게 성격을 판단하는 것은 힘든 일이다.
③ 양육이 개인의 성격에 가장 많은 영향을 미친다.
④ 한 사람의 성격은 유전자와 환경적 요소 모두에 의해 결정된다.

어휘

be accustomed to …에 익숙하다
everyday existence 일상생활
variability 가변성, 변동성
correspondingly 상대적으로, 상응하여
diverse 다른, 다양한
constitution 구조
acquired 후천적인
resistance 저항
passage 통로, 길
inherited 유전의, 계승한
accurate 정확한
vicissitude 우여곡절
interpret 이해하다, 해석하다
attribute 속성, 자질
inborn 선천적인
lay down 정하다
impulse 자극
resultant 결과
genetic 유전적인
upbringing 양육, 훈육

기적사 DAY 28
결국엔 성정혜 영어 하프모의고사

| 01 | ④ | 02 | ④ | 03 | ① | 04 | ③ | 05 | ③ |
| 06 | ④ | 07 | ① | 08 | ① | 09 | ③ | 10 | ② |

오답률 TOP 1

01 정답 ④

정답해설

문맥상 사람들의 터무니없는 짓을 가만히 보고 있지 않는 사람을 수식할 단어로 가장 적절한 것은 '양심적인'의 의미인 ④ conscientious이다.

해석

그 **양심적인** 사람은 사람들의 어리석은 짓을 용납하지 않은 채로 서 있었다.
① 범죄의, 범인
② 논란의, 논쟁의
③ 지친, 지루한
④ 양심적인, 성실한

어휘

no nonsense 어리석은 짓을 용납하지 않는; 간단명료한
criminal 범죄의; 범인
weary 지친, 지루한
controversial 논란의, 논쟁의
conscientious 양심적인, 성실한

02 정답 ④

정답해설

밑줄 친 'dank'는 '눅눅한, 축축한'의 뜻으로 ④ humid와 의미가 가장 가깝다.

해석

수천 년 전, 인간은 어둡고 **축축한** 동굴에 살았다.
① 논란의 여지가 있는, 논쟁할 수 있는
② 탈락성의, 낙엽성의
③ 정확한
④ 습한, 눅눅한

어휘

dank 눅눅한, 축축한
debatable 논란의 여지가 있는, 논쟁할 수 있는
deciduous 탈락성의, 낙엽성의
precise 정확한
humid 습한, 눅눅한

03 정답 ①

정답해설

밑줄 친 'cut off'는 '떼어놓다, 차단하다, 중단하다'의 뜻으로 ① shut off from(떼어놓다)과 의미가 가장 가깝다.

해석

시민들은 범죄자들을 외부 세계에서 완전히 **떼어 놓고** 싶었다.
① 떼어 놓다
② 헌신하다
③ 늦잠 잘 수 있도록 하루를 쉬다
④ 그것에 대해 좀 더 생각해보다

어휘

cut off 중단하다
shut off from 떼어 놓다
make a commitment 헌신하다
take a day off 하루를 쉬다
take time to think about it 그것에 대해 좀 더 생각해 보다

04 정답 ③

정답해설

(A) 대화를 통해 Ned가 친구들과 스키장으로 여행을 갈 계획이지만 운전할 수 있는 사람이 아무도 없으므로 부모님께 부탁하려는 것을 알 수 있다. 따라서 빈칸 (A)에 들어갈 가장 적절한 것은 '태워주기(a lift)'이다.

(B) Ian은 Ned의 부모님이 운전할 수 없다면 '자신이 ~하고 싶다'고 말하고 이에 Ned가 고마움을 표한다. 따라서 빈칸 (B)에 들어갈 가장 적절한 것은 '도움(a hand)'이다.

오답해설

나머지 보기는 문맥상 적절하지 않으므로 오답이다.

해석

Ned: 네 겨울 방학 계획이 뭐야?
Ian: 난 가족들과 스키 여행을 가. 너는 어때?
Ned: 오, 스키 여행? 재밌을 것 같이 들린다. 나도 친구들과 스키 여행을 가는데 교통편에 문제가 좀 있어.
Ian: 그게 뭔데?
Ned: 아무도 운전면허가 없어. 근데 우리가 그곳에 갈 수 있는 방법은 운전하는 것밖에 없어. 그래서 난 부모님께 우리를 (A) 태워다 주실 수 있는지 여쭤보려고 했어.
Ian: 너희 부모님이 태워다 주실 수 없다고 하면 내가 너를 (B) 도와주고 싶어.
Ned: 제안해줘서 정말 고마워. 너 정말 친절하다.
Ian: 별말씀을.

① (A) 태워주기 (B) 전화
② (A) 시도 (B) 태워주기
③ (A) 태워주기 (B) 도움
④ (A) 전화 (B) 도움

어휘

give somebody a lift ~를 태워주다
give somebody a ring ~에게 전화를 하다[걸다]
give ~ a shot ~을 시도하다
give somebody a hand ~를 도와주다

오답률 TOP 3

05 정답 ③

정답해설

③ 출제 포인트: 접속사 vs. 전치사

밑줄 친 'Although'는 접속사이므로 이후에 절이 와야 하나 명사(구) 'the development'가 왔으므로 'Although'를 유사한 의미의 전치사 'Despite(~임에도 불구하고)' 또는 'In spite of(~임에도 불구하고)'로 수정해야 한다. 해당 문장에서 'designed'는 동사가 아닌 'techniques'를 수식하는 과거분사로 사용되었음에 유의해야한다.

오답해설

① 출제 포인트: 주격 관계대명사절의 동사 수일치

밑줄 친 'are'는 주격 관계대명사 'which'가 이끄는 절의 동사로 복수 형태의 선행사 'real-world data'에 수일치 해 복수 형태의 동사를 옳게 사용하였다. 'data'가 단수명사가 아닌 복수명사임에 유의해야한다.

② 출제 포인트: 현재분사 vs. 과거분사

밑줄 친 'bewildering'은 감정 제공 형용사(현재분사)로 '혼란스러운'을 뜻한다.

④ 출제 포인트: 비교 대상 수일치

'less certain and less precise than'을 통해 비교급이 쓰인 문장임을 알 수 있다. 따라서 밑줄 친 대명사 'those'는 비교 대상이며 'those'가 가리키는 대상은 복수 형태인 'principles'이므로 'those'는 옳은 표현이다.

해석

그러나 경제학은 실험실 과학이 아니다. 경제학자들은 그들의 이론을 현실-세계 데이터를 이용하여 실험하고, 이것은 실제 경제 활동에 의해 생성된다. 이러한 다소 혼란스러운 환경에서, "다른 것들"은 변한다. 다른 것들을 동일하게 유지하도록 설계된 복잡한 통계 기술의 발달에도 불구하고, 통제가 완벽하지 않다. 그 결과, 경제학 원리들은 실험실 과학의 원리들보다 덜 확실하고 덜 정확하다. 그것은 또한 그들이 많은 과학적인 이론들보다 더 논란의 여지가 있을 것이라는 점을 의미한다.

어휘

theory 이론, 학설
generate 발생시키다, 만들어내다
precise 정확한, 정밀한
statistical 통계의, 통계적인
bewildering 혼란스러운
debate 논의하다, 토론하다

오답률 TOP 2

06 정답 ④

정답해설

④ 출제 포인트: 능동태 vs. 수동태/목적격 관계대명사

해당 문장은 불완전타동사 'call'의 수동태인 「be called + 목적격 보어[명사]」가 사용된 옳은 문장이다. 이때 'criteria'는 'criterion'의 복수형으로 동사에 복수동사인 'are'를 옳게 사용하였다. 또한 해당 문장에서 'that'은 목적격 관계대명사로 선행사는 'The criteria'이며 뒤따라오는 절의 동사 'use'의 목적어에 해당한다.

오답해설

① 출제 포인트: 수사, 관사 + 단위명사 + of

'one spoonful of'는 「수사 + 단위명사 + of」의 형태로 '한 스푼'을 뜻한다. 해당 문장은 주어진 해석이 '한 스푼'이나 'One spoonful' 이후에 전치사 'of'를 사용하지 않았으므로 틀린 문장이다. 따라서 'One spoonful'을 'One spoonful of'로 수정해야 한다.

② 출제 포인트: 현재분사 vs. 과거분사/능동형 수동태

'handcrafting'은 완전타동사 'handcraft'의 현재분사이나 수식하는 대상 'donkeys'와 수동관계이며 주어진 해석이 '수공예로 만든'이므로 'handcrafting'을 과거분사 'handcrafted'로 수정해야 한다. 또한 해당 문장에서 sold는 '팔리다'를 뜻하는 'sell'의 과거분사로 능동형 수동태에 해당한다.

③ 출제 포인트: 동명사 관용표현

「cannot help -ing」는 관용표현으로 '~하지 않을 수 없다'를 뜻한다. 해당 문장은 주어진 해석이 '~하지 않을 수 없다'이나 'cannot help' 이후에 to부정사를 사용하였으므로 틀린 문장이다. 따라서 'cannot help to respond'를 'cannot help responding'으로 수정해야 한다.

07 정답 ①

정답해설

① 출제 포인트: 지각동사와 목적격 보어/현재분사 vs. 과거분사

지각동사 'hear'는 목적어와의 관계가 능동인 경우 목적격 보어 자리에 현재분사 또는 원형 부정사를 사용한다. 해당 문장에서 'hear'는 지각동사이므로 목적격 보어에 to부정사를 사용할 수 없으며, 목적어 'Jane'과 능동 관계이므로 'to demand'를 현재분사 'demanding' 또는 원형부정사 'demand'로 수정해야 한다. 또한 해당 문장에서 'surprised'는 감정 상태 형용사(과거분사)로 옳게 사용되었다.

오답해설

② 출제 포인트: 가주어 It/명사절의 접속사 that

해당 문장에서 'It'은 가주어이며 진주어는 접속사 'that'이 이끄는 절 'anyone should want to help John'이다.

③ 출제 포인트: 4형식에서 3형식으로 전환/관사의 위치

수여동사 'offer'를 3형식으로 전환하는 경우 「offer+직접목적어[사물]+to+간접목적어[대상]」의 형태로 사용된다. 또한 'such' 이후에 「부정관사+형용사+명사」 형태의 명사(구)가 오는 경우 「such+부정관사+형용사+명사」의 형태를 가진다.

④ 출제 포인트: 가정법 과거완료/접속사가 살아있는 분사구문

해당 문장은 종속절의 'If'와 주절의 'would have had'를 통해 가정법 과거완료가 쓰인 문장임을 알 수 있다. 이때 종속절인 'If'절의 경우 분사구문의 형태로 사용되었으며 과거분사 'taken' 앞에 'having been'이 생략되어 있다. 해당 문장을 원래의 문장으로 고치면 'If it had been taken in small doses, the drug would have had no harmful effects.'가 된다.

08 정답 ①

정답해설

본문은 'Walt Disney의 어린 시절 아버지와의 관계'에 대한 내용이다. 본문에 따르면, Walt Disney의 아버지 'Elias'는 '폭력적이고 고압적인 인물'이었으며, 그로 인해 Walt Disney를 포함한 자식들과의 관계가 좋지 않았다는 것을 알 수 있다. ①의 'he tried, unsuccessfully, to make ends meet for the family'에서 'he'가 가리키는 것은 '가족을 위한 생계를 꾸리는 데 실패한 Walt Disney의 아버지 Elias'이며, 나머지 보기는 'Walt Disney'를 가리키고 있으므로, 정답은 ①이다.

오답해설

② "In order to escape from his stressful circumstances, young Disney found solace in drawing(그의 스트레스가 많은 상황으로부터 도망치기 위해, 어린 Disney는 그림 그리는 것에서 위안을 찾았다)."에서, '그의 스트레스가 많은 상황'이라 함은, '그가 처한 아버지와의 관계'를 언급하고 있으므로, 밑줄 친 his는 Walt Disney를 가리키고 있다는 것을 알 수 있다.

③ "he'd watch his older brothers, one by one, run off from home to escape from their father(그는 그의 형들이 아버지로부터 도망치기 위해 차례차례 떠나는 것을 지켜보았고)"에서 '그의 형들이 차례차례 떠나는 것을 목격한 것'은 Walt Disney이므로, 밑줄 친 he가 가리키는 것은 Walt Disney라는 것을 알 수 있다.

④ "he'd follow suit by lying about his age to become an ambulance driver during World War I(그는 제1차 세계대전 중 구급차 기사가 되기 위해 나이를 속임으로써 형들을 따라 했다)"에서, '형들이 떠난 것처럼 집을 떠난 것'은 Walt Disney이므로, he가 가리키는 것은 Walt Disney라는 것을 알 수 있다.

해석

1901년 Chicago에서 태어나고 Missouri에서 자란 Walt Disney는 5형제 중 넷째 아들이었다. 그의 아버지 Elias는 ① 그가 가족을 위한 생계를 꾸리는 것을 시도하는 것에 실패했을 때 폭력적이었다고 알려진 고압적인 인물이었다. ② 그의 스트레스가 많은 상황으로부터 도망치기 위해, 어린 Disney는 그림 그리는 것에서 위안을 찾았다. 그럼에도 불구하고, ③ 그는 그의 형들이 아버지로부터 도망치기 위해 차례차례 떠나는 것을 지켜보았고, 머지않아 ④ 그는 제1차 세계대전 중 구급차 기사가 되기 위해 나이를 속임으로써 형들을 따라 했다. 그의 아버지가 사망했을 때, 알려진 바에 따르면 그는 출장을 단축하기를 거부했고 그에 따라 그의 아버지의 장례식을 놓쳤다.

어휘

sibling 형제자매
figure 인물
abusive 폭력적인, 학대하는
make ends meet 겨우 먹고 살 만큼 벌다
solace 위안, 위로
follow suit 선례를 따르다, 남을 흉내 내다
reportedly 알려진 바에 따르면
domineering 고압적인, 지배하려 드는
allegedly 주장한[전해진] 바에 의하면

09 정답 ③

정답해설

주어진 문장은 'Stanislavski는 그의 연기를 비밀로 하기 위해 만든 예명'이라고 설명하고 있다. 주어진 문장이 '결과'를 나타내는 'So'로 시작하고 있으므로, 주어진 문장 이전에는 그가 비밀스럽게 연기를 해야만 했던 이유가 등장해야 하는 것이 적절하다. ③ 이전 문장 "Konstantin's parents did not, however, want their son to pursue a career in the theater(그러나 Konstantin의 부모는 그들의 아들이 연극계의 직업을 추구하기를 원하지 않았다)."를 통해 '연기를 하는 것을 부모님이 반대했다'는 것을 알 수 있으므로, 그로 인해 예명을 사용하며 몰래 연기를 해야 했음을 알 수 있다. 따라서 주어진 문장이 들어갈 가장 적절한 위치는 ③이다.

오답해설

①, ② 에서는 'Konstantin의 가정에서 연극을 즐기고 정기적으로 발레와 오페라에 참석했다'고 언급하고 있으므로, 연극에 대한 긍정적인 태도를 보이고 있다. 따라서 비밀스럽게 연기를 해야만 하는 상황이라고 할 수 없으므로, 주어진 문장이 들어가기에 적절하지 않다.
④는 문맥상 어색하므로 오답이다.

해석

Konstantin Sergeievich Alexeiev는 1863년에 Moscow에 사는 부유한 러시아인 가정에서 태어났다. 그의 아버지가 Konstantin과 그의 형제자매들이 연극을 할 수 있는 무대를 설치해줌에 따라, 그는 드라마와 예술에 몰두하며 자랐다. (①) 또한 그 가족은 정기적으로 발레와 오페라에 참석했다. (②) 그러나 Konstantin의 부모는 그들의 아들이 연극계의 직업을 추구하기를 원하지 않았다. (③ <u>그래서, 젊은 성인이 되었을 때 그는 그의 연기를 비밀에 부칠 수 있도록 예명인 Stanislavski를 썼다.</u>) 그는 러시아에서 잘 알려진 아마추어 배우가 되었고, 또한 연출을 시작했다. (④) 1898년 Stanislavski는 작가 Vladimir Nemirovich-Danchenko와 함께 Moscow Art Theater를 공동 설립했다. 동료 배우이자 연출가인 Vsevolod Meyerhold에 의해 '천재'적이라고 묘사된 배우를 훈련하고 지휘하는 Stanislavski의 방법과 함께 극장은 성공이었다. 그의 시스템은 여전히 오늘날 매서드 배우들을 훈련시키는 데 사용된다.

어휘

bring up 양육하다, 기르다
pursue 추구하다
stage name (배우의) 예명
method actor 매서드 배우(자신이 연기할 배역의 생활과 감정을 실생활에서 직접 경험하도록 하는 연기법으로 연기하는 배우), 스타니 슬라프스키 방식으로 연기하는 배우
immerse 몰두하게 하다
adopt 쓰다, 채택하다

10 정답 ②

정답해설

본문은 '인격의 미덕(virtue)의 여러 가지 덕목 중 Socrates가 근본적인 선이라 믿었던 지식(knowledge)'에 대해 설명하고 있다. 주어진 문장에서 '우리가 선행을 하는 이유는, 그것이 우리 자신의 기분을 좋게 하기 때문'이라고 언급하고 있는데, ② 이전 문장 "We all have a natural obligation to benefit ourselves(우리는 모두 스스로에게 이익이 되는 자연적인 의무가 있다)."의 'to benefit ourselves(스스로에게 이익이 되는)'를 구체적으로 설명하는 부분이 주어진 문장의 'it makes us feel good(그것이 우리의 기분을 좋게 하다)'이므로, ② 위치에 주어진 문장이 들어가는 것이 문맥상 가장 자연스럽다.

오답해설

① 이후 문장의 'Examples of this'가 가리키는 대상이 첫 문장 'A virtue'에 등장하므로, 두 문장 사이에 주어진 문장이 들어가는 것은 어색하다.
③, ④ 위치는 '일반적인 선행(미덕)'이 아닌, Socrates가 근본적인 선이라 여겼던 지식에 관한 설명이므로 주어진 문장이 들어가기에는 문맥상 어색하다.

해석

미덕은 도덕적으로 좋다고 여겨지는 특성 또는 자질이다. (①) 이것들의 예는 정직, 용기, 연민, 관대함, 그리고 고결함과 같은 것들이다. 우리는 모두 스스로에게 이익이 되는 자연적인 의무가 있다. (② **우리가 하는 모든 것들은, 비록 그것이 다른 사람들 돕는 것이라 할지라도, 그것이 어떻게 해서든 우리의 기분을 좋게 만들어 주기 때문에 행해지는 것이다.**) 인격의 미덕은 Socrates의 관점의 중심축이다. 좋은 인격을 통한 좋은 삶은 점검된 삶에 대한 Socrates의 이상의 성배였다. (③) Socrates는 지식이 기본적 선이며 모든 인간의 행위를 다스리는 동력이라고 믿었다. (④) 지식이 우리의 세계관과 행동에 영향을 미치도록 하는 능력이 모든 다른 인간적인 선을 일으키고 살아가게 만드는 근본적인 선이다. 우리 여생 동안 지식을 추구하고 우리의 인격 향상을 추구하는 것이 필요하다.

어휘

virtue 미덕, 덕
deem 생각하다, 여기다
integrity 고결함, 정직함
one way or another 어떻게 해서든, 어느 쪽이든지
perspective 관점
examine 점검하다, 조사하다
good 선(善)
trait 특성
compassion 연민, 동정심
obligation 의무
holy grail 성배
fundamental 근본적인, 기초적인

결국엔 성정혜 영어 하프모의고사
기적사 DAY 29

| 01 | ① | 02 | ④ | 03 | ③ | 04 | ④ | 05 | ① |
| 06 | ② | 07 | ① | 08 | ③ | 09 | ② | 10 | ③ |

01 정답 ①

정답해설

주어진 문장은 사실 여부를 다루고 있으므로 문맥상 '논란의 여지가 있는'을 뜻하는 ① debatable이 가장 적절하다.

해석

따라서 범죄예방디자인(Crime Prevention Through Environmental Design)이 실제적으로 범죄를 줄이는 것에 효율적인지에 대한 것은 **논란의 여지가 있다**.
① 논란의 여지가 있는, 논쟁할 수 있는
② 이타주의적인
③ 세심한, 꼼꼼한, 소심한
④ 눅눅한, 습한

어휘

debatable 논란의 여지가 있는, 논쟁할 수 있는
altruistic 이타주의적인
meticulous 세심한, 꼼꼼한, 소심한
humid 눅눅한, 습한

오답률 TOP 1
02 정답 ④

정답해설

밑줄 친 'decrepit'는 '노쇠한, 노후한'의 뜻으로 ④ impotent와 의미가 가장 가깝다.

해석

그는 60세 먹은 노인처럼 보였고 완전히 **노쇠해** 보였다.
① 웅변의, 달변의, 설득력 있는
② 서두르는
③ 신중한, 분별력 있는, 사려 깊은
④ 노쇠한, 무력한

어휘

decrepit 노쇠한, 노후한
hasty 서두르는
impotent 노쇠한, 무력한
eloquent 웅변의, 달변의, 설득력 있는
discreet 신중한, 분별력 있는, 사려 깊은

03 정답 ③

정답해설

밑줄 친 'go through'는 '겪다, 경험하다'의 의미로 ③ pass through와 의미가 가장 가깝다.

해석

하지만, 우리는 대개 일생동안 다양한 고난들을 **겪는다**.
① 분수를 넘다, 자만하다, 우쭐하다
② 늦잠 자기 위해 하루를 쉬다

③ 경험하다
④ 인계하다, ~을 양도하다, 양보하다

어휘

go through 겪다, 경험하다
get above 분수를 넘다, 자만하다, 우쭐하다
take a day off 하루를 쉬다
hand over 인계하다, ~을 양도하다, 양보하다
hardship 고난
pass though 경험하다

오답률 TOP 2

04 정답 ④

정답해설

대화를 통해 Amy는 스페인 마드리드에 거주하는 오빠와 그곳에서 새해를 보내기 위해 스페인을 방문하여 근처 국가들을 여행하고 싶어 하지만 주저하고 있음을 알 수 있다. 따라서 빈칸에 ④ 'have the nerve to do(~하는 용기가 있다)'가 들어가는 것이 문맥상 가장 적절하다.

오답해설

① Amy는 혼자 여행하는 것에 대한 '발언권이 있는지(have a say in)' 잘 몰라서 홀로 여행하는 것이 망설여진다고 하는 것은 대화의 흐름상 어색하다.
② Amy는 홀로 여행하는 것에 '약해서(have a soft spot for)' 망설여진다고 말하는 것은 문맥상 부적절하다.
③ Amy는 오빠가 일해야 해서 혼자 여행하는 것에 '질려(have had enough of)' 홀로 여행하는 것을 망설인다는 것은 맥락상 빈칸에 들어갈 말로 적합하지 않다.

해석

Amy: 안녕, Trevor. 너 스페인 가본 적 있어?
Trevor: 응, 내가 다섯 살 때쯤에 방문했었어. 왜 물어봐?
Amy: 내 오빠가 스페인 마드리드에 사는데 새해를 그곳에서 오빠와 보내고 싶어.
Trevor: 재밌는 계획일 것 같아! 나한테 아무거나 자유롭게 물어봐.
Amy: 음, 사실 나는 포르투갈 같은 주변 국가들을 여행하고 싶어.
Trevor: 그건 흔한 경로지. 왜 망설여?
Amy: 오빠가 일해야 해서 나 혼자 여행해야 해. 근데 내가 그럴 용기가 있는지 잘 모르겠어.
Trevor: 너와 같이 갈 수 있는 친구가 있는지 물어보는 건 어때?
Amy: 한번 그래 봐야겠다.
① ~에 발언권이 있다
② ~에 약하다
③ ~에 질리다
④ ~하는 용기가 있다

어휘

have a say in ~에 발언권이 있다
have a soft spot for ~에 약하다
have had enough of ~에 질리다
have the nerve to do ~하는 용기가 있다

05 정답 ①

정답해설

① **출제 포인트: 자릿값 확인(명사 vs. 동사)**
해당 문장은 두 개의 절이 등위접속사 'and'를 통해 병렬구조를 이루고 있으나 첫 번째 절의 동사가 없다. 따라서 밑줄 친 'operation'은 동사 형태로 고쳐야 하므로, 주어가 'The institutions ~ society'이며 'and' 이후의 'are'와 병렬구조를 이루고 있으므로 복수형태의 동사 'operate'로 수정해야 한다.

오답해설

② **출제 포인트: 명사절의 접속사 that**
밑줄 친 'that'은 'is'의 주격 보어 자리에 위치해 명사절을 이끄는 접속사로 옳게 사용되었다.
③ **출제 포인트: 원급 비교**
「as+원급[형용사/부사]+as」는 원급 비교에 해당한다. 따라서 밑줄 친 'basic'은 원급 형용사이므로 옳은 표현이다. 또한 'basic'은 'is'의 주격 보어 자리에 위치해 형용사로 옳게 사용되었다.
④ **출제 포인트: 현재분사 vs. 과거분사**
과거분사 'driven' 이후에 「by+행위자」인 'by deep motivations'가 왔으며 앞에 be동사 'are'를 사용하였으므로 수동태가 사용되었음을 알 수 있다. 수동태는 「be+과거분사」의 형태이므로 밑줄 친 'driven'은 옳은 표현이다.

해석

사회의 기관들과 유인 구조들은 대개 Bentham의 주장에 따라서 작동하고 그리하여 인간 행동의 가장 심오한 동기부여의 일부를 놓치고 있다. Bentham과 나머지 우리가 전형적으로 간과하고 있는 것은 인간들이 물리적인 고통과 기쁨만큼이나 기본적인 또 다른 관심사들에 연결되어 있다는 것이다. 우리는 사회적으로 연결되어 있다. 우리는 친구들 및 가족들과 연결된 상태를 유지하고자 하는 깊은 동기부여에 의해 이끌린다. 우리는 자연스럽게 다른 사람의 마음에는 무슨 일이 일어나는지를 궁금히 여긴다.

어휘

institution 기관
profound 심오한
wire 연결하다
in accordance with ~에 따라서
overlook 간과하다
drive 이끌다, 몰다

오답률 TOP 3

06 정답 ②

정답해설

② **출제 포인트: 동명사 관용표현**
「There is no (in) -ing」는 관용표현으로 '~하는 것은 불가능하다'를 뜻한다. 해당 문장은 주어진 해석과 일치하므로 옳게 사용되었다.

오답해설

① **출제 포인트: 사역동사의 수동태/능동태 vs. 수동태**
사역동사 'make'의 수동태는 「목적어+be made+목적격 보어[to부정사]」의 형태를 가진다. 해당 문장은 사역동사 'make'의 수동태를 사용하였으나 목적격 보어에 원형부정사 'comply'를 사용하였으므로 틀린 문장이다. 따라서 'comply'를 to부정사 'to comply'로 수정해야 한다.
③ **출제 포인트: 해석 주의/능동형 수동태**
해당 문장은 문법적으로 옳은 문장이나 주어진 해석 '유익하다'와 'uninformative(유익하지 않은)'가 일치하지 않으므로 'uninformative'를 'informative'로 수정해야 한다. 또한 해당 문장에서 'reads'는 '읽히다'를 뜻하는 'read'의 3인칭 단수 현재시제로 능동형 수동태에 해당한다.
④ **출제 포인트: 수사, 관사+단위명사+of**
'steal'은 「steal+목적어[사물]+from+목적어[대상]」의 형태를 가진다. 해당 문장은 전치사 'from'이 들어가야 할 자리에 'of'를 사용하였으므로 틀린 문장이다. 따라서 'of a jewellery store'를 'from a jewellery store'로 수정해야 한다. 또한 해당 문장에서 'a handful of'는 「관사+단위명사+of」의 형태이며 이때 'handful'은 단위명사임에 유의해야 한다.

07 정답 ①

정답해설

① 출제 포인트: 가주어 it/명사절의 접속사 that/능동태 vs. 수동태/해석 주의

해당 문장은 문법적으로 「주어+완전타동사+목적어」 형태의 옳은 문장이나 주어진 해석을 통해 'It'이 가주어이며 that절이 진주어라는 것을 알 수 있다. 따라서 'predicted'의 목적어가 없으므로 'predicted'를 수동태 'was predicted'로 수정해야 한다. 또한 해당 문장에서 'improve'는 자동사로 사용되었다.

오답해설

② 출제 포인트: 수여동사의 문장구조/현재분사 vs. 과거분사

해당 문장에서 'made'는 수여동사 'make'의 과거시제로 'his daughter'는 간접목적어[대상]에 해당하며 'a pretty doll'은 직접목적어[사물]에 해당한다. 또한 해당 문장에서 'using'은 현재분사로 생략된 주어 'William'과 능동관계이며 'using' 이후에 목적어 'some cloth and hay'가 있으므로 옳은 표현이다.

③ 출제 포인트: 가정법 과거완료/수여동사의 문장구조

가정법 과거완료는 「If+주어+had+과거분사 ~, 주어+would/should/could/might+have+과거분사 ~.」의 형태로 사용된다. 「If+주어+had+과거분사 ~」는 부사절이므로 그 위치가 자유롭다. 또한 give는 수여동사의 경우 「give+간접목적어[대상]+직접목적어[사물]」의 형태를 가진다.

④ 출제 포인트: 현재분사 vs. 과거분사/접속사가 생략되지 않은 분사구문

해당 문장은 접속사 'when'이 생략되지 않은 분사구문이 사용된 문장으로 생략된 주어 'he'와 능동관계이며 'addressing' 이후에 목적어 'a general audience'가 있으므로 현재분사 'addressing'은 옳게 사용되었다.

08 정답 ③

정답해설

본문에서는 'Disney 이야기가 우리의 심금을 울리며 오랜 인상을 남긴다'라고 언급한 후, "Why are Disney stories so memorable and popular(왜 디즈니 이야기가 그렇게 기억에 남고 인기 있는가)?"라는 의문을 던지며, 우리가 그러한 인상을 받게 되는 이유에 대해 설명하고 있다. 세 번째 문장 "It's because they focus on shared desires(그것은 그것들이 공유되는 욕구에 초점을 맞추고 있기 때문이다)."를 통해, 'Disney가 다루는 주제는 모두가 공감할 수 있는 공통된 욕구'라는 것을 설명하고, 마지막 문장 "These characters provide a mouthpiece to the thoughts and feelings we all have(이러한 캐릭터들은 우리 모두가 가지고 있는 생각과 감정에 대변자를 제공해 준다)."에서 'Disney 이야기 속의 캐릭터가 우리가 가지고 있는 생각과 감정을 대변해 준다'고 설명하고 있다. 즉, 관중들이 Disney 이야기의 등장인물들에게 공감하기 때문에 그것들이 인기가 많다는 것이다. 따라서 글의 요지로 가장 적절한 보기는 '③ We like Disney stories because we empathize with them(우리는 그것들에 공감하기 때문에 디즈니 이야기를 좋아한다).'이다.

오답해설

①, ② 본문 첫 문장에서 언급되는 사실이지만, 본문에서는 그렇게 인기가 있고 깊은 인상을 남기는 이유에 초점을 맞추어 설명하고 있으므로, 글의 요지로는 적절하지 않다.

④ 본문에서는 '디즈니 이야기가 우리 모두가 가지고 있는 생각과 감정'을 다룬다고 언급하고 있으므로, '비현실적이고 이상적인' 메시지를 전달한다고 말할 수 없다.

해석

수년 동안 디즈니사는 당신의 심금을 울리고 오랫동안 당신과 함께 머무르는 이야기를 만드는 데 숙련되어 왔다. 왜 디즈니 이야기가 그렇게 기억에 남고 인기 있는가? 그것은 그것들이 공유되는 욕구에 초점을 맞추고 있기 때문이다. Walt Disney는 사람들에 대해 많이 알고 있었다: 그는 모든 인간이 경험하는 특정한 공통적인 어려움과 욕구가 있다는 것을 깨달았다. 나는 단지 더 많은 돈이나 더 나은 직업에 대한 갈망에 대해 말하고 있는 것이 아니다. 나는 소속에 대한, 진실한 사랑에 대한, 또는 당신이 자신보다 더 큰 무언가의 일부라는 것을 발견하고자 하는 욕구와 같은 더 깊고, 더 숨겨져 있는 욕구에 대해 말하고 있는 것이다. 디즈니사는 공유되는 인간의 경험에 특별히 초점을 맞추는 이야기를 만든다. 너무 멀리 떨어져 닿을 수 없는 것 같은 꿈을 가지고 있는 *Ratatouille*의 쥐 Remy 또는 문자 그대로 "나는 내가 속한 곳을 찾기 위해 거의 어디든지 갈 것이다."라고 노래하는 Hercules를 생각해보라. 이러한 캐릭터들은 우리 모두가 가지고 있는 생각과 감정에 대변자를 제공해 준다.

① 디즈니 이야기는 세계적으로 인기 있다.
② 디즈니 이야기는 우리에게 오래 지속되는 감명을 준다.
③ 우리는 그것들에 공감하기 때문에 디즈니 이야기를 좋아한다.
④ 디즈니 영화는 우리에게 비현실적이고 이상적인 메시지를 전달한다.

어휘

expert 숙련된, 전문적인　　craft (공들여) 만들다
tug at one's heartstrings …의 감정을 뒤흔들다, 심금을 울리다
struggle 힘든 것[일]　　longing 갈망, 열망
literally 문자[말] 그대로　　most 거의
mouthpiece 대변자　　impression 감명, 인상
empathize 공감하다　　utopian 이상적인

09 정답 ②

정답해설

본문은 'Stanislavski의 저서 An Actor Prepares'를 소개하는 글이다. 본문의 첫 문장 "*An Actor Prepares* is the most famous acting training material ever to have been written(*An Actor Prepares*는 이제껏 써진 것들 중 가장 유명한 연기 훈련 자료이다)"과 마지막 문장 "This volume is an essential read for actors, directors and anyone interested in the art of drama(이 책은 배우, 연출가, 그리고 극예술에 관심이 있는 누구에게 필수적인 읽을거리이다)." 등을 통해, 이 글이 Stanislavski의 '책'에 관해 설명하고 있다는 것을 유추할 수 있다. 'material(자료)', 'volume(책, 권)'과 같은 어휘가 'book(책, 저서)'을 가리키고 있다는 것을 알 수 있어야 한다. 따라서 글의 주제로 가장 적절한 것은 '② a book by Stanislavski(Stanislavski의 저서)'이다.

오답해설

① 본문과 관련이 없는 내용이다.
③ 도서에 관한 내용이나, '*An Actor Prepares*'가 Stanislavski의 자서전은 아니므로 오답이다.
④ 본문은 'Stanislavski의 훈련 시스템'을 소개한 도서인 '*An Actor Prepares*'에 대한 글이므로 오답이다.

해석

*An Actor Prepares*는 이제껏 써진 것들 중 가장 유명한 연기 훈련 자료이며 Stanislavski의 저서는 여러 세대에 걸친 배우들과 트레이너들에게 영감을 주었다. 이 번역은 Stanislavski의 '시스템'을 영어권 국가에 소개하기 위한 최초의 것이며 오랜 세월에도 불구하고 연기 수업에서 지금까지도 건재한다. 여기에서 Stanislavski는 배우가 역할을 최대로 탐구하기 위해 행해야 하는 내면의 준비에 대해 다룬다. 그는 'magic if' 단위와 목표, 정서 기억, 초목표의 개념과 그리고 많은 오늘날 더 유명한 리허설 보조 수단들을 소개한다. 이

책은 배우, 연출가, 그리고 극예술에 관심이 있는 누구에게나 필수적인 읽을거리이다.
① Stanislavski가 쓴 연극
② Stanislavski의 저서
③ 한 배우의 자서전
④ Stanislavski의 훈련 시스템

어휘

stand the test of time 세월의 시험을 견디다 [오랜 세월에도 불구하고 건재하다]
inward 내면의, 마음속의
undergo 겪다
to the full 최대한도로
aid 보조 기구, 보조물
volume 책
read 읽을거리
autobiography 자서전

demonstrate 입증하다, 보여주다
superiority 거만함
vulgarity 상스러움
id 이드 (인간의 원시적·본능적 요소가 존재하는 무의식 부분)
defense mechanism 방어 기제
demean 품위를 손상시키다, 비하하다
disparage 폄하하다
inflate 과장하다, 부풀리다
self-worth 자아 존중감, 자부심
treat 대우하다, 취급하다
undesirable 바람직하지 않은
note 주목[주의]하다
intimacy 친밀함
buffer 완충하다

10 정답 ③

정답해설

(A) 이전의 내용은 '유머가 부정적으로 간주되었다'는 것으로, '유머가 타인을 비하 또는 폄하하거나 자신의 자아 존중감을 과장하기 위해 사용되었다'고 설명하고 있다. (A) 이후에서 '유머는 피해야 할 바람직하지 않은 행위로 대우받았다'고 언급하고 있으므로, (A) 이전에 언급된 '부정적 인식'으로 인해 (A) 이후의 결과가 나타난 것임을 알 수 있다. 따라서 빈칸에는 '인과 관계'를 나타내는 'Therefore(그러므로)' 또는 'Hence(이런 이유로)'가 적절하다.

(B) 이전에서는 '유머가 부정적으로 여겨졌으며, 심리학자들은 유머를 연구 대상으로 여기지 않았다'고 설명하고 있다. 그런데 (B) 이후에서는 이와 대조적인 '최근의 유머에 대한 긍정적 평가'에 대해 언급하고 있으므로, (B)에는 '역접, 대조'를 나타내는 'However(그러나)' 또는 'But(그러나)'이 들어가는 것이 문맥상 자연스럽다.

따라서 정답은 '③ Hence(이런 이유로) - However(그러나)'이다.

오답해설

① (B) 이후의 내용이 (B) 이전 내용의 결과를 나타내는 구조가 아니므로, 'In the end(결국)'는 빈칸에 적절하지 않다.
② (B) 전후 내용이 유사한 내용을 '비교'하는 구조가 아니므로, 'Likewise(유사하게)'는 빈칸에 적절하지 않다.
④ (A) 이후 내용이 (A) 이전 내용의 반대 상황을 가정하는 구조가 아니므로 'Otherwise(그렇지 않으면)'는 빈칸에 적절하지 않다.

해석

유머는 모든 문화와 모든 연령에서 관찰된다. 그러나 최근 몇십 년에 들어서야 비로소 실험 심리학이 그것을 필수적이고 기초적인 인간 행동으로 존중하게 되었다. 역사적으로, 심리학자들은 유머를 부정적으로 표현하며, 그것을 입증된 거만함, 상스러움, 프로이트 학설의 이드 충돌, 또는 한 사람의 진정한 감정을 숨기기 위한 방어 기제라고 말했다. 이러한 관점에서, 개인은 유머를 타인을 비하 또는 폄하하거나 자신의 자아 존중감을 과장하기 위해 사용했다. (A) 이런 이유로, 그것은 피해야 할 바람직하지 않은 행위로 대우받았다. 그리고 심리학자들은 연구 가치가 있는 것으로서의 그것을 무시하는 경향이 있었다. (B) 그러나, 이제 유머가 성격 강점으로 간주되며 유머에 대한 연구가 최근에 부각되었다. 사람들이 잘하는 것을 조사하는 분야인 긍정 심리학은 유머가 타인의 기분을 좋게 만들거나, 친밀감을 형성하거나, 또는 스트레스를 완화하는 데 도움이 되기 위해 사용될 수 있다는 것에 주목한다.

	(A)	(B)
①	그럼에도 불구하고	결국
②	그러므로	유사하게
③	이런 이유로	그러나
④	그렇지 않으면	그러나

결국엔 성정혜 영어 하프모의고사
기적사 DAY 30

| 01 | ④ | 02 | ② | 03 | ② | 04 | ④ | 05 | ③ |
| 06 | ④ | 07 | ④ | 08 | ③ | 09 | ④ | 10 | ② |

오답률 TOP 2
01 정답 ④

정답해설

문맥상 성인을 묘사함에 있어서 'holiness(신성함)'를 수식할 알맞은 단어는 '예외적인, 뛰어난, 이례적일 정도로 우수한'의 의미를 지닌 ④ exceptional이다.

해석

성인이란 극히 도덕적인 삶을 삼으로써 **이례적일 정도로 우수한** 신성함이나 선량함을 인정받은 사람이다.
① 욕심이 많은
② 몹시 추운, 냉담한
③ 행정부의
④ 예외적인, 특별한, 이례적일 정도로 우수한

어휘

get credit for ~의 공적을 인정받다, ~으로 명성을 얻다
holiness 신성함   goodness 선량함
virtuous 도덕적인, 고결한   greedy 욕심이 많은
frigid 몹시 추운, 냉담한   executive 행정부의
exceptional 예외적인, 특별한, 이례적일 정도로 우수한

오답률 TOP 3
02 정답 ②

정답해설

밑줄 친 'gratuitous'는 '이유 없는, 불필요한, 쓸데없는'의 뜻으로 ② groundless와 의미가 가장 가깝다.

해석

이 특별한 경우에, 말하자면, 우리는 **이유 없는** 폭력은 하지 않기로 결정했다.
① 미결의
② 근거[이유, 까닭] 없는
③ 사교적인
④ 대접이 좋은

어휘

you know 말하자면, 그러니까
gratuitous 이유 없는, 불필요한, 쓸데없는
pending 미결의   groundless 근거[이유, 까닭] 없는
gregarious 사교적인   hospitable 대접이 좋은

03 정답 ②

정답해설

밑줄 친 'keep close tabs on'은 '~을 면밀히 감시하다'라는 의미로 ② have our eyes on과 의미가 가장 가깝다.

해석

우리는 출시 지연이 회사의 경쟁력을 악화시킬 것이기 때문에 어떤 추가적인 지연이 발생하는지 여부를 **면밀히 감시할** 필요가 있다.
① ~를 학수고대하다
② ~에 신경 쓰다, 주시하다
③ ~에게 불리하게 작용하다
④ ~을 하룻밤 자며 생각하다

어휘

keep close tabs on ~을 면밀히 감시하다
emerge 나타나다, 드러나다   postpone 연기하다, 미루다
launch 개시, 출시; 시작하다, 출간하다
worsen 악화되다, 악화시키다   competitive 경쟁하는, 경쟁력 있는
look forward to ~를 학수고대하다
have one's eyes on ~에 신경 쓰다, 주시하다
make against ~에게 불리하게 작용하다
sleep on ~을 하룻밤 자며 생각하다

04 정답 ④

정답해설

(A) Melissa가 Rudy에게 '조별 과제의 팀원들이 별로 적극적이지 않으며, 자신이 해야 할 일을 하는 것을 거부하면서 다른 조원들에게 ~한다.'고 말하고 있으므로 빈칸 (A)에 들어갈 가장 적절한 것은 'pass the buck to(~에 책임을 미루다)'이다.
(B) Rudy가 Melissa에게 '부담감이 크니까 조별 과제의 팀원들과 그것에 대해 ~하는 게 어때'라고 말하고 있으므로 빈칸 (B)에 들어갈 가장 적절한 것은 'speak out(솔직하게 이야기하다)'이다.
(C) Melissa가 Rudy에게 '조별 과제의 팀원들을 ~할 의도는 없다'라고 말하고 있으므로 빈칸 (C)에 들어갈 가장 적절한 것은 'find fault with(~을 비난하다)'이다.

오답해설

① (A) Melissa는 자신의 조별 과제 조원들이 적극적이지 않고 오히려 자신이 해야 할 일을 하는 것을 거부하며 다른 팀원들을 '좋아한다(go in for)'라고 하는 것은 대화의 흐름상 어색하다. (B) Melissa가 겪는 조원들과의 문제에 관해 Rudy는 그들과 '중요한 회의(talk big)'를 해보라고 권하는 것은 문맥상 부적절하다. (C) Rudy의 권유에 대해 Melissa는 팀원들은 최선을 다하고 있을 수 있지만, 자신의 기대가 너무 높은 것일 수도 있다면서 그들과 '좋은 관계를 유지할(get along with)' 의도가 없다는 것은 대화의 내용상 빈칸에 들어갈 말로 적합하지 않다.
② (A) Melissa는 자신의 조별 과제 조원들이 적극적이지 않고 오히려 자신이 해야 할 일을 하는 것을 거부하며 다른 팀원들을 '좋아한다(go in for)'라고 하는 것은 대화의 흐름상 부자연스럽다.
③ (B) Melissa가 겪는 조원들과의 문제에 관해 Rudy는 그들과 '중요한 회의(talk big)'를 해보라고 권하는 것은 문맥상 적절하지 않다. (C) Rudy의 권유에 대해 Melissa는 팀원들은 최선을 다하고 있을 수 있지만, 자신의 기대가 너무 높은 것일 수도 있다면서 그들과 '모면할(get away with)' 의도가 없다는 것은 맥락상 부적합하다.

해석

Rudy: 안녕, Melissa. 너 오늘 오후에 시간 있어?
Melissa: 미안하지만 없어. 나는 오늘 조별 과제를 끝내야 해. 제출 기한이 내일까지야.
Rudy: 안타깝다. 네 조원과는 어떻게 돼 가?
Melissa: 그들은 별로 적극적이지는 않아. 심지어는 가끔 자신이 해야 할 일을 하는 것을 거부하면서 다른 조원들에게 (A) 책임을 미루기도 해.

Rudy: 오, 그건 너에게 큰 부담이겠다. 네 조원과 그런 것에 관해 (B) 솔직하게 이야기해 보면 어때?
Melissa: 음, 나는 그들을 (C) 비난할 의도는 없어. 내 기대가 그들이 만족시키기에 너무 높은 것일 수도 있어. 그들은 최선을 다하고 있는 것일 수도 있어.

① (A) ~을 좋아하다 (B) 중요한 회의를 하다 (C) ~와 좋은 관계를 유지하다
② (A) ~을 좋아하다 (B) 솔직하게 이야기하다 (C) ~을 비난하다
③ (A) ~에 책임을 미루다 (B) 중요한 회의를 하다 (C) 모면하다
④ (A) ~에 책임을 미루다 (B) 솔직하게 이야기하다 (C) ~을 비난하다

어휘

go in for ~을 좋아하다　　　　talk big 중요한 회의를 하다
get along with ~와 좋은 관계를 유지하다
speak out 솔직하게 이야기하다　　find fault with ~을 비난하다
pass the buck to ~에 책임을 미루다
get away with 모면하다

오답률 TOP 1

05　정답 ③

정답해설

③ 출제 포인트: 자릿값(명사 vs. 동사)

밑줄 친 'claims' 앞에 'a few'가 있으므로 복수형태의 명사인 'claims'를 옳은 표현으로 오해할 수 있으나 해당 문장은 3개의 절이 등위접속사 'and'를 통해 「A, B, and C」의 병렬구조를 이루고 있는 문장이다. 이때 'claims'는 C절의 동사에 해당하며 주어는 복수 형태인 'a few'이므로 'claims'를 복수 형태 동사인 'claim'으로 수정해야 한다.

오답해설

① 출제 포인트: 불완전타동사의 목적격 보어

밑줄 친 'possible'은 불완전타동사 'make'의 수동태 'are made' 이후에 온 목적격 보어에 해당한다.

② 출제 포인트: 현재분사 vs. 과거분사

밑줄 친 'governing'은 완전타동사 'govern'의 현재분사로 수식하는 대상 'the rules'와 능동관계이며 'governing' 이후에 목적어 'emotional display'가 있으므로 현재분사 'governing'은 옳은 표현이다.

④ 출제 포인트: 완전타동사 + 목적어[to부정사 vs. 동명사]

밑줄 친 'doing'은 완전타동사 'remember'의 목적어로 쓰인 동명사이며 문맥상 '그렇게 했던 것을 기억할 수 있다'가 자연스러우므로 옳은 표현이다. 'remember + ing'는 '(과거에) 했던 것을 기억하다'의 의미를 가진다.

해석

예를 들어, 발리를 제외하고 모든 문화에서 장례 의례 동안 사람들이 울고 심지어 그곳에서도 사람들이 애도하며 운다 – 눈물 없는 장례식들은 오직 이 의식이 죽음 이후 만 2년이 될 때까지 연기됨으로써 가능하다. 감정적 표현을 지배하는 많은 규칙들에도 불구하고 시간에 따라 그리고 장소에 따라 달라질지도 모르고, 성인들은 무수히 많은 이유로 울고 때때로 소수의 사람은 아무 이유 없이 운다고 주장한다. 미국 문화에서, 심지어 그들은 결단코 울지 않는다고 주장하는 그 희한한 사람들도 (대체적으로 남성) 그들이 어렸을 때 그렇게 했던 것을 기억할 수 있다.

어휘

weep 울다, 눈물을 흘리다　　　ritual 의례, 의식 절차
mourning 애도　　　　　　　　myriad 무수한

06　정답 ④

정답해설

④ 출제 포인트: 능동형 수동태/주격 관계대명사 동사 수일치

해당 문장에서 'opens'는 '개봉되다'를 뜻하는 'open'의 3인칭 단수 현재시제로 능동형 수동태에 해당하며 계속적 용법에 해당되는 주격 관계대명사 'which'의 선행사 'the play'와 올바르게 수일치 되었다. 또한 'star as'는 관용표현으로 '~으로 출연하다'를 뜻한다.

오답해설

① 출제 포인트: 동명사 관용표현

'it is no use -ing'와 'it is of no use to 동사원형'은 관용표현으로 '~하는 것은 불가능하다, ~해봐야 소용없다'를 뜻한다. 해당 문장은 주어진 해석이 '~해봐야 소용없다'이나 'it's of no use' 이후에 'having'을 사용하였으므로 옳지 않은 문장이다. 따라서 'having'을 'to have'로 수정해야 한다. 또한 'of no use'를 'no use'로 수정하는 것도 가능하다.

② 출제 포인트: 동사 vs. 준동사/현재분사 vs. 과거분사/수사, 관사 + 단위명사 + of

해당 문장에서 'carried'는 앞에 접속사 없으므로 과거분사로 사용된 것임을 알 수 있다. 이때 생략된 주어 'she'와 능동관계이며 'carried' 이후에 목적어 'an armful of firewood'가 있으므로 'carried'를 현재분사 'carrying'으로 수정해야 한다. 또한 해당 문장에서 'an armful of'는 「관사+단위명사+of」의 형태로 'armful'은 단위명사임에 유의해야 한다.

③ 출제 포인트: 능동태 vs. 수동태/지각동사의 수동태

지각동사 'hear'의 수동태는 「목적어+be heard+목적격 보어[to부정사]」의 형태를 가진다. 해당 문장은 지각동사 'hear'의 수동태를 사용하였으나 목적격 보어에 원형부정사 'heave'를 사용하였으므로 틀린 문장이다. 따라서 'heave'를 to부정사 'to heave'로 수정해야 한다.

07　정답 ④

정답해설

④ 출제 포인트: 주장, 요구, 명령, 제안동사 + that + 주어 + (should) + 동사원형

'suggest'가 '제안하다'를 뜻하는 경우 목적어로 온 절의 동사에 「(should)+동사원형」의 형태를 사용하며, '암시하다'를 뜻하는 경우 목적어로 온 절의 동사에 시제를 적용한다. 해당 문장은 주어진 해석이 '암시하다'이나 현재분사 'suggesting'의 목적어로 온 절의 동사에 동사원형 'be'를 사용하였으므로 틀린 문장이다. 따라서 'be'를 시제에 맞게 'is'로 수정해야 한다.

오답해설

① 출제 포인트: 수여동사의 문장구조

해당 문장에서 'ask'는 수여동사로 'someone'은 간접목적어[대상]에 해당하며 'the way'는 직접목적어[사물]에 해당한다. 또한 해당 문장에서 'have to'는 조동사 대용표현으로 '~해야 한다'를 뜻한다.

② 출제 포인트: 가정법 과거완료/to부정사의 명사적 용법

가정법 과거완료는 「If+주어+had+과거분사 ~, 주어+would/should/could/might+have+과거분사 ~」의 형태로 사용된다. 「If+주어+had+과거분사 ~」는 부사절로 그 위치가 자유롭다. 또한 'want'는 to부정사를 목적어로 가진다.

③ 출제 포인트: 가주어 it/to부정사의 명사적 용법/간접의문문의 어순

해당 문장에서 'It'은 가주어이며 진주어는 to부정사(구) 'to predict what the long-term effects of the accident will be'이다. 또한 해당 문장에서 의문사 'what'이 이끄는 절은 'predict'의 목적어로 사용되었으므로 간접의문문에 해당하며 어순은 「의문사+주어+동사」이다.

08 정답 ③

정답해설

(A) 이전에 언급된 내용 "the filmmaker had been cryogenically preserved(그 영화제작자가 극저온으로 보존되었다)"를 (A) 이후에서 "he'd been frozen with the hope that science might one day make it possible for him to be brought back to life(언젠가 과학이 그가 다시 살아나는 것을 가능하게 해줄 수 있다는 희망을 가지고 그가 냉동되었다는 것이다.)"라고 다시 한번 설명해주고 있으므로, (A)에는 '재서술'을 나타내는 'That is to say(다시 말해)'가 들어가는 것이 가장 적절하다.

(B) 이전에는 'Disney가 냉동 보존되었다는 소문'에 대해 언급하고 있다. 그러나 (B) 이후에는 '(소문과는 달리) 실제로' 그는 '화장되었다'고 설명하고 있으므로, 빈칸에는 방금 한 말에 반대되는 내용을 강조할 때 '실제로, 사실'이라는 뜻으로 사용할 수 있는 'in fact(사실)'가 들어가는 것이 가장 적절하다.

따라서 정답은 '③ That is to say(다시 말해) – in fact(사실)'이다.

오답해설

나머지 보기는 문맥상 어색하므로 오답이다.

해석

1966년 11월, 의사들은 오랜 흡연가였던 Disney가 폐암에 걸린 것을 발견했다. 그는 다음 달 12월 15일에 65세의 나이로 Burbank 병원에서 사망했다. 그가 사망한 지 오래 지나지 않아, 그 영화제작자가 극저온으로 보존되었다는 이야기가 타블로이드신문에서 돌기 시작했다. (A) 다시 말해, 언젠가 과학이 그가 다시 살아나는 것을 가능하게 해줄 수 있다는 희망을 가지고 그가 냉동되었다는 것이다. Disney와 인체 냉동 보존술에 대한 지속적인 소문에도 불구하고, (B) 사실, 그는 화장되었으며 그의 유골은 California, Glendale의 Forest Lawn Cemetery에 있는 묘에 매장되었다. 극저온으로 냉동된 최초의 사람은 1967년 1월의 한 미국인 대학 교수였다. 그때 이후, 2002년에 사망한 야구 명사 Ted Williams를 포함한 100명 이상의 다른 사람들이 저온 보존되었다.

(A)	(B)
① 반면에	안타깝게도
② 예를 들면	그에 따라
③ 다시 말해	사실
④ 그 결과	게다가

어휘

tabloid press 타블로이드신문
preserve 보존하다
cryonics 인체 냉동 보존술
ash 유골, 유해, 재
mausoleum 묘, 능
cryopreserve 저온 보존하다
cryogenically 극저온으로
persistent 지속적인, 끈질긴
cremate 화장하다
inter 매장하다
cemetery 묘지
great 위대한 인물, 명사

09 정답 ④

정답해설

본문은 'Stanislavski의 연기 훈련 기법 중 하나인 'Magic If'에 관해 설명하고 있다. 'Magic If'는 상상력을 발휘하여 배역의 상황 또는 환경에 대해 주어지지 않은 정보를 '만약' 질문을 통해 획득하여 배우가 맡은 배역에 대한 더 깊은 이해를 하도록 도와주는 기법이다. 본문에 따르면, 대본을 숙지한 후에도 여전히 모호한 정보가 있다면, '만일 이러한 상황이라면 어떠할까?'라는 질문들을 하는 것이 부족한 정보에 대한 추가적인 디테일을 발견하도록 도와줄 수 있다고 한다. ③ 문장에서는 '대본을 통해서도 여전히 알 수 없는 정보가 존재한다'고 언급한다. ④는 '대본을 완벽히 숙지하는 것의 중요성'에 대해 언급하고 있는데, ③에서는 '대본을 통해서 얻을 수 없는 정보'에 대해 강조하고 있으므로, ③ 이후 대본 숙지의 중요성이 등장하는 것은 부자연스럽다. 따라서 정답은 ④이다.

오답해설

① 'This device'가 이전 문장의 'Magic If'를 가리키고 있으므로, 문맥상 자연스럽다.
② 이전 문장에서, 'Magic If'를 사용하는 방법에 대해 언급한 후, 구체적인 상황을 예시로 드는 ②가 이어지는 것은 자연스럽다.
③은 문맥상 자연스러우므로 오답이다.

해석

Stanislavski의 Magic If는 오늘날 배우들이 이용 가능한 가장 유용한 도구 중 하나일 것이다. ① 이 방법은 그들이 연기하고 있는 배역에 대한 새롭고 흥미로운 것들을 발견하기 위해 배우들이 그들의 상상력을 열게 하는 데 사용된다. 그것을 이용할 때, 배우는 단순히 스스로에게 배역에 대한 '만약에' 질문을 한다. ② 예를 들어 그가 가족을 영원히 떠나는 것이 목표인 젊은 남자를 연기한다고 생각해보자. ③ 연극의 대본으로부터 배역에 대한 가능한 한 많은 정보를 얻은 후에도, 여전히 분명치 않거나 단순히 대본에 의해 답변이 되지 않는 그의 배역의 뒷이야기와 현 상황의 측면이 있을 것이다. ④ *Stanislavski는 배우가 연극의 대본을 완전히 이해하는 것의 중요성을 강조한다.* 예를 들어, 만일 그 배역이 그의 아버지에 대해 거의 아무것도 모르고 있고 그러한 정보를 가지고 있는 것이 유용하다면, 아버지에 대한 '만약에' 질문은 도움이 될 수도 있을 것이다. 만약에 배역의 아버지가 그를 때렸다면, 만약에 그의 아버지가 도망쳤다면, 또는 만약에 그 배역이 태어나기 전에 아버지가 사망했다면과 같은 질문들이 적절할 것이다.

어휘

device (특정한 결과·효과를 낳는) 방법
utilize 활용[이용]하다
what if …면 어쩌지 […라면 어떻게 될까]
let's say 예를 들면, 이를테면
appropriate 적절한

10 정답 ②

정답해설

본문은 '과거(past)'의 중요성에 대해 설명하고 있다. 본문에 따르면, '현재(present)'는 과거가 축적된 찰나의 순간일 뿐이며, 스쳐 지나가면 현재 또한 과거의 순간이 된다. 그리고 과거에 발생한 모든 것들은 현재에 영향을 미치며, 현재의 '나' 또한 '과거의 나'라고 설명하고 있다. 본문 후반 "It is the present, not the past, that dies(죽는 것은 과거가 아니라 현재이다)"를 통해, '과거는 계속되지만 현재는 사라진다'라는 것을 암시하고 있고, 글의 말미에 본문의 전체 내용을 아우르는 문장이 들어가는 것이 문맥상 적절하므로, 빈칸에 알맞은 표현은 '② It is only the past that lives(생존하는 것은 오직 과거이다)'이다.

오답해설

① 본문에서는 '죽는 것은 과거가 아니라 현재'라고 설명하고 있으므로, 글의 흐름과 어울리지 않는 보기이다.
③ 본문에서는 '과거에 발생한 모든 사건'이 '나'라는 '현재의 존재'를 만든다고 설명하고 있다. 즉, '성격'을 포함한 '나'의 모든 것이 과거로 인해 형성된다고 언급하고 있으므로, '성격'과 '과거'의 관계에 관해서만 언급하는 ③은 지엽적인 내용임을 알 수 있다. 따라서 오답이다.
④ 본문에서는 '현재는 스쳐 지나가는 이 순간에 축적된 과거일 뿐'이라고 일축하고 있으므로, 과거의 중요성을 더 강조하고 있다는 것을 알 수 있다. 따라서 ④는 빈칸에 적절하지 않다.

해석

발생한 것들 중 이 순간에 영향을 완전히 미치지 않는 것은 없다. 현재는 단지 이 순간의 시간에 축적되고 집중된 과거일 뿐이다. 당신 또한 당신의 과거이다. 종종 당신의 얼굴은 당신의 자서전이다. 당신은 당신의 과거의 모습 때문에; 잊힌 세대로 뻗어나가는 당신의 유전적 특성 때문에, 당신에게 영향을 미친 모든 환경 요소, 당신을 만난 모든 남자 또는 여자, 당신이 읽은 모든 책, 당신이 겪은 모든 경험 때문에 당신이다(당신의 현재의 모습이다). 이 모든 것들이 당신의 기억, 신체, 성격, 영혼에 축적되어 있다. 도시, 국가, 또는 인종과도 마찬가지이다. 그것은 그것의 과거이며 그것 없이는 이해될 수 없다. 죽는 것은 과거가 아니라 현재이다; 우리가 너무 많은 관심을 두는 현재의 순간은 영원히 우리의 눈과 손가락으로부터 우리가 과거라고 부르는 우리 삶의 받침대와 행렬 속으로 스쳐 지나간다. <u>생존하는 것은 오직 과거이다</u>.

① 나아가기 위해 과거를 보내주어라
② 생존하는 것은 오직 과거이다
③ 당신의 과거가 당신의 성격을 결정한다
④ 그 어느 것보다 현재가 더 중요하다

어휘

quite 지극히, 더없이, 완전히
autobiography 자서전
accumulate 축적시키다
pedestal 받침대
second (아주) 잠깐
heredity 유전(적 특징)
flit 휙 스치다[지나가다]
matrix 행렬, 매트릭스

결국엔 성정혜 영어 하프모의고사
기적사 복습 모의고사 3회

01	①	02	③	03	②	04	①	05	④
06	②	07	②	08	①	09	④	10	④
11	③	12	④	13	①	14	①	15	④
16	②	17	①	18	③	19	④	20	①

01 정답 ① — Day 25-03

정답해설

밑줄 친 'appease'는 '달래다, 진정시키다'라는 뜻으로 ① soothe와 의미가 가장 가깝다.

해석

그 새로운 법은 농부들의 불안감을 **달래주**도록 고안되었다.
① 달래다, 진정시키다
② 생각하다, 임신하다
③ 사과하다
④ 시도하다

02 정답 ③ — Day 21-03

정답해설

밑줄 친 'iron out'은 '해결하다'라는 의미이며 ③ solve와 의미가 가장 가깝다.

해석

우리는 먼저 몇 가지의 문제들을 **해결할** 필요가 있다.
① 생각하다, 임신하다
② 검토하다, 비평하다
③ 해결하다
④ 포즈를 취하다, 제기하다, 주장하다

03 정답 ② — Day 27-03

정답해설

밑줄 친 'cope with'는 '처리하다, 대처하다'의 뜻으로 ② deal with와 의미가 가장 가깝다.

해석

건강한 사람들은 스트레스에 더 잘 **대처할** 수 있다.
① 기대하다, 생각하다, 의지하다, 세다
② 처리하다, 다루다
③ 내려치다
④ ~을 하룻밤 자며 생각하다

04 정답 ① — Day 26-01

정답해설

대부분의 사람들이 인정하는 '도덕적인 것'이 공정한 것과 합리적인 것이라면, 그와 반대되는 의미는 ① greedy일 것이다.

해석

대부분의 사람들은 도덕적인 것이 공정하고 합리적인 것을 의미하는 것이지 **욕심이 많은** 것을 의미하지 않는다고 인정한다.
① 욕심이 많은
② 이타주의적인
③ 지친, 지루한
④ 회의적인

05 정답 ④   Day 23-09

정답해설

본문은 Charles Dickens의 어린 시절 직업에 관한 내용이다. 본문 후반 "He later recalled how he had worked alongside "two or three other boys who were kept at similar duty downstairs on similar wages", one of whom had shown him around on his first day in the job. "His name was Bob Fagin,~"을 통해, '그는 두세 명의 다른 소년들과 함께 일했는데, 그중 한 명의 이름이 Bob Fagin이었다.'는 것과, Bob Fagin이 Charles Dickens의 공장에서의 첫날에 공장 안내를 해주었다'는 것을 알 수 있다. 이러한 내용으로 미루어보아, Bob Fagin은 Charles Dickens보다 공장에 대해 잘 알고 있었음을 알 수 있으며, Charles Dickens보다 앞서 공장에서 일하기 시작했다는 것을 짐작할 수 있다. 따라서 글의 내용과 일치하는 것은 '④ Bob Fagin joined the factory before Charles Dickens started his work there(Bob Fagin은 Charles Dickens가 그곳에서 일을 시작하기 전에 공장에 취직했다).'이다.

해석

프리랜서 저널리스트와 런던의 변호사 사무실에서의 법률 사무소 직원으로서 문서로 남아 있는 그의 직업을 갖기 훨씬 이전에, 12살의 Charles Dickens는 구두약 병에 라벨을 붙이며 공장에서 일했다. 하루에 10시간을 일하고, 그는 오늘날의 약 16파운드에 해당하는 6실링의 주급을 벌었다. 나중에 그는 "비슷한 급여를 받으며 아래층에서 비슷한 일을 하던 두세 명의 다른 소년들"과 어떻게 함께 일했는지 떠올렸는데, 그들 중 한 명이 그가 일을 시작한 첫날에 그에게 안내를 해줬다. "그의 이름은 Bob Fagin이었다."라고 이후에 Dickens가 그의 친구이자 전기 작가인 John Forster에게 말했다, "그리고 나는 오랜 시간 후에 실례를 무릅쓰고 그의 이름을 나의 이야기에 사용했다."
① Charles Dickens는 작가로서의 경력을 시작하기 전 두 가지의 직업을 가졌다.
② Charles Dickens는 구두닦이로 일했다.
③ Charles Dickens는 한 달에 16실링을 받았다.
④ Bob Fagin은 Charles Dickens가 그곳에서 일을 시작하기 전에 공장에 취직했다.

06 정답 ②   Day 25-06

정답해설

② **출제 포인트: 주장/요구/명령/제안동사 + (that) + 주어 + (should) + 동사원형**

'demand'는 '요구하다'를 뜻하는 동사로 목적어로 that절이 오는 경우 「(that) + 주어 + (should) + 동사원형」을 사용해야 한다. 해당 문장은 'demanded'의 목적어인 that절에 현재시제 동사 'returns'를 사용하였으므로 틀린 문장이다. 따라서 'returns'를 'should return' 또는 'return'으로 수정해야 한다.

해석

① 나는 우리가 우리의 평상시 관행에서 벗어날 이유가 없다고 본다.
② Jane은 그가 자신에게서 빌려 갔던 책을 돌려줘야 한다고 요구했다.
③ 그가 시간이 정말 없는데도 불구하고, 그는 여전히 도와주겠다고 했다.
④ Tom은 7살 이후로 온갖 일을 하면서, 자신의 생계를 꾸려왔다.

07 정답 ②   Day 24-09

정답해설

본문은 'Little Women의 작가인 Louisa May Alcott이 남성 필명을 사용해 작품 활동을 했다'는 내용이다. 첫 번째 문장 "the American writer frequently used the ambiguous nom de plume A.M. Barnard to write sensational gothic thrillers with subject matter deemed 'unladylike' for a late 19th century female writer(그 미국인 작가는 19세기 말의 여성 작가에게는 "숙녀답지 않다"고 여겨지던 주제를 가지고 선정적인 고딕 스릴러물을 집필하기 위해 A.M. Barnard라는 불분명한 필명을 자주 사용했다)."를 통해 '여성 작가인 Louisa May Alcott이 스릴러 장르를 집필할 때는 남성 필명을 사용했음'을 언급한 후, 필명으로 출판한 작품과 필명이 밝혀진 시기에 대해 언급하고 있으므로, 글의 제목으로 가장 적절한 것은 '② A Female Author Who Used A Male Pen Name(남성 필명을 사용한 여성 작가)'이다.

해석

비록 Louisa May Alcott의 가장 잘 알려진 작품인 Little Women이 그녀 자신의 이름으로 출판되었지만, 그 미국인 작가는 19세기 말의 여성 작가에게는 '숙녀답지 않다'고 여겨지던 주제를 가지고 선정적인 고딕 스릴러물을 집필하기 위해 A.M. Barnard라는 불분명한 필명을 자주 사용했다. A.M. Barnard의 이름으로 쓰인 Alcott의 작품은 Little Women보다 2년 앞서 쓰인 암울한 연애 소설인 A Long Fatal Love Chase, 사회 계층과 조작의 주제를 가진 중편 소설 Behind a Mask를 포함했다. 1940년대에 그녀의 비밀스러운 남성 필명은 희귀 도서 판매상 Madeleine B. Stern과 사서 Leona Rostenberg에 의해 발견되었다.
① Louisa May Alcott의 가장 유명한 작품
② 남성 필명을 사용한 여성 작가
③ Louisa May Alcott의 재능을 발견한 사람들
④ 남성과 여성 작가의 일반적 특성

08 정답 ①   Day 23-05

정답해설

① **출제 포인트: 가정법 과거**

가정법 과거에서 종속절인 If절에 be동사가 오는 경우 주어에 상관없이 'were'를 사용해야 한다. 해당 문장은 주절의 'would be'를 통해 가정법 과거가 쓰인 문장임을 알 수 있으나 종속절인 If절의 동사에 'were'가 아닌 'was'를 사용하였으므로 틀린 문장이다. 따라서 밑줄 친 'was'를 'were'로 수정해야 한다.

해석

중심이 아니라 태양의 표면이 이만큼 뜨겁다면, 우주로 방출되는 방사에너지는 너무나 커서 몇 분 이내에 지구 전체는 증발될 것이다.

09 정답 ④   Day 23-08

정답해설

주어진 문장의 'these entirely novel institutions(이러한 완전히 새로운 기관들)'로 보아, 주어진 문장 이전에는 이것이 지칭하는 '새로운 기관'이 등장해야 함을 알 수 있다. ④ 이전 문장에서 "enormous new factories producing steel, shoes, railroad cars, or pork bellies rose up across the country(철강, 제화, 철도 차량, 또는 삼겹살을 생산하는 거대한 신규 공장들이 국가 전역에 설립되었다)"라고 언급하며, '새로운 공장들(new factories)'이 등장하기 시작했음을 알리고 있으므로, ④ 이전 문장에서 언급된 'new factories'를 주어진 문장의 'these entirely novel institutions'가 가리킨다는 것을 알 수 있다. 따라서 정답은 ④이다.

해석

원시인부터 약 남북전쟁 시기까지 당신의 조상들은 직업을 가지고 있지 않았고 일자리 면접에 가지 않았다. 대신에, '옛 국가'의 당신의 조상들은 그들이 태어난 곳의 10마일 이내에서 자라고 살고 일했다. (①) 그들이 만났던 거의 모든 사람들은 그들 자신의 부족 출신이었다. 그리고 다른 모든 사람들과 마찬가지로, 그들은 왕, 교회, 군대를 위해 일하거나, 또는 아마 농부, 농노, 또는 노예였다. (②) 약 1860년까지 농부가 미국 노동 인구의 3분의 2를 구성했다. (③) 남북전쟁과 산업화 이후에야 비로소 철강, 제화, 철도 차량, 또는 삼겹살을 생산하는 거대한 신규 공장들이 국가 전역에 설립되었다. (④ **우리가 "직업"이라고 여기게 된 것을 창조한 것이 바로 이러한 완전히 새로운 기관들이었다.**) 그렇다면 통계학적으로, 당신의 증조부 시대에서야 비로소 당신의 선조들이 일자리 면접에 가기 시작했다.

10 정답 ④   Day 30-09

정답해설

본문은 'Stanislavski의 연기 훈련 기법 중 하나인 'Magic If'에 관해 설명하고 있다. 'Magic If'는 상상력을 발휘하여 배역의 상황 또는 환경에 대해 주어지지 않은 정보를 '만약에' 질문을 통해 획득하여 배우가 맡은 배역에 대한 더 깊은 이해를 하도록 도와주는 기법이다. 본문에 따르면, 대본을 숙지한 후에도 여전히 모호한 정보가 있다면, '만일 이러한 상황이라면 어떠할까?'라는 질문들을 하는 것이 부족한 정보에 대한 추가적인 디테일을 발견하도록 도와줄 수 있다고 한다. ③ 문장에서는 '대본을 통해서도 여전히 알 수 없는 정보가 존재한다'고 언급한다. ④는 '대본을 완벽히 숙지하는 것의 중요성'에 대해 언급하고 있는데, ③에서는 '대본을 통해서 얻을 수 없는 정보'에 대해 강조하고 있으므로, ③ 이후 대본 숙지의 중요성이 등장하는 것은 부자연스럽다. 따라서 정답은 ④이다.

해석

Stanislavski의 Magic If는 오늘날 배우들이 이용 가능한 가장 유용한 도구 중 하나일 것이다. ① 이 방법은 그들이 연기하고 있는 배역에 대한 새롭고 흥미로운 것들을 발견하기 위해 배우들이 그들의 상상력을 열게 하는 데 사용된다. 그것을 이용할 때, 배우는 단순히 스스로에게 배역에 대한 '만약에' 질문을 한다. ② 예를 들어 그가 가족을 영원히 떠나는 것이 목표인 젊은 남자를 연기한다고 생각해보자. ③ 연극의 대본으로부터 배역에 대한 가능한 한 많은 정보를 얻은 후에도, 여전히 분명치 않거나 단순히 대본에 의해 답변이 되지 않는 그의 배역의 뒷이야기와 현 상황의 측면이 있을 것이다. ④ *Stanislavski는 배우가 연극의 대본을 완전히 이해하는 것의 중요성을 강조한다.* 예를 들어, 만일 그 배역이 그의 아버지에 대해 거의 아무것도 모르고 있고 그러한 정보를 가지고 있는 것이 유용하다면, 아버지에 대한 '만약에' 질문은 도움이 될 수도 있을 것이다. 만약에 배역의 아버지가 그를 때렸다면, 만약에 그의 아버지가 도망쳤다면, 또는 만약에 그 배역이 태어나기 전에 아버지가 사망했다면과 같은 질문들이 적절할 것이다.

11 정답 ③   Day 22-04

정답해설

밑줄 친 부분 전 대화에서 A가 '회의가 어떻게 되었냐'고 묻자 B가 '회의가 순탄하지 않았다'고 말하며 그 이유로 '새로운 직원 중에 한 명'에 대한 서술을 하고 있다. 따라서 빈칸에 ③ 'a wet blanket(분위기를 깨는 사람)'이 들어가는 것이 문맥상 가장 적절하다.

해석

A: 네가 오늘 아침에 회의했다는 사실을 들었어.
B: 응, 끝나자마자 너를 만나려고 여기에 왔어.
A: 여기까지 와줘서 고마워. 회의는 어떻게 됐어?
B: 순탄하지 않았어. 오늘이 새로운 직원들과 함께한 첫 회의였고 그들 중 한 명이 분위기를 깨는 사람이었어.
A: 전부 얘기해줘. 그가 뭘 한 거야?
B: 우선, 그는 지각했어. 그리고 둘째로는, 회의 내내 무례한 태도로 일관했어.
A: 쉽지 않았겠다. 힘내!
B: 응원해줘서 고마워.
① 진짜배기
② 계층
③ 분위기를 깨는 사람
④ 천재지변

12 정답 ④   Day 29-04

정답해설

대화를 통해 Amy는 스페인 마드리드에 거주하는 오빠와 그곳에서 새해를 보내기 위해 스페인을 방문하여 근처 국가들을 여행하고 싶어 하지만 주저하고 있음을 알 수 있다. 따라서 빈칸에 ④ 'have the nerve to do(~하는 용기가 있다)'가 들어가는 것이 문맥상 가장 적절하다.

해석

Amy: 안녕, Trevor. 너 스페인 가본 적 있어?
Trevor: 응, 내가 다섯 살 때쯤에 방문했었어. 왜 물어봐?
Amy: 내 오빠가 스페인 마드리드에 사는데 새해를 그곳에서 오빠와 보내고 싶어.
Trevor: 재밌는 계획일 것 같아! 나한테 아무거나 자유롭게 물어봐.
Amy: 음, 사실 나는 포르투갈 같은 주변 국가들을 여행하고 싶어.
Trevor: 그건 흔한 경로지. 왜 망설여?
Amy: 오빠가 일해야 해서 나 혼자 여행해야 해. 근데 내가 그럴 용기가 있는지 잘 모르겠어.
Trevor: 너와 같이 갈 수 있는 친구가 있는지 물어보는 건 어때?
Amy: 한번 그래 봐야겠다.
① ~에 발언권이 있다
② ~에 약하다
③ ~에 질리다
④ ~하는 용기가 있다

13 정답 ④   Day 25-10

정답해설

본문은 '유대인의 성인식'인 'bar mitzvah'와 'bat mitzvah'를 소개하고 있다. 본문 중반의 "While the ceremony does not indicate that the child is physically an adult, it does so mentally and emotionally with the emphasis on the individual's increased culpability and responsibility(그 의식이 아이가 신체적으로 성인이라는 것을 나타내지는 않지만, 그것은 개인의 증가된 책임과 의무의 강조와 함께 정신적 그리고 감정적으로는 그렇다는 것을 나타낸다)."로 보아, 'bar mitzvah'와 'bat mitzvah'는 '신체적 성숙'이 아닌 '정신적 성숙'을 의미하는 의식이라는 것을 알 수 있다. 따라서 글의 내용과 일치하는 것은 '④ Completing the bat mitzvah does not mean a person's physical maturity(bat mitzvah를 마치는 것이 한 사람의 신체적 성숙을 의미하지는 않는다).'이다.

해석

bar mitzvah와 bat mitzvah는 각각 유대인 소년과 소녀를 위한 성인식이다. 유대교 법에 따라 개인은 특정한 나이(소녀는 12세, 소년은 13세)가 되고 나서야 공식적으로 계율을 준수할 필요가 있다. 이 변화는 아이가 그 나이가 되면 자동적으로 발생하지만, bar mitzvah 또는 bat mitzvah는 소년 또는 소녀의 성년을 축하하고, 이제 종교의식에 참여하거나, 예배 정족수에 포함되거나, 또는 관계를 형성할 수 있는 개인의 권리를 공개적으로 기념하기 위해 종종 개최된다. 그 의식이 아이가 신체적으로 성인이라는 것을 나타내지는 않지만, 그것은 개인의 증가된 책임과 의무의 강조와 함께 정신적 그리고 감정적으로는 그렇다는 것을 나타낸다. bar mitzvah 또는 bat mitzvah라는 명칭 자체는 mitzvah의 아들 또는 딸이라고 번역한다, 왜냐하면 그 순간부터 개인은 율법의 (계율 또는 법이라고도 알려진) mitzvahs에 따라 행동해야 하기 때문이다.

① bar mitzvah는 소녀, bat mitzvah는 소년을 위한 것이다.
② 유대인 소년들은 소녀들보다 성년을 더 일찍 축하한다.
③ 성인식을 하지 않은 13세 이상의 유대인 소년은 어떠한 종교 행사에도 참여할 수 없다.
④ bat mitzvah를 마치는 것이 한 사람의 신체적 성숙을 의미하지는 않는다.

14 정답 ①   Day 26-06

정답해설

① 출제 포인트: 자동사/타동사

'fold'는 '(운반보관이 쉽도록) 접다'를 뜻하는 경우 자동사로 사용될 수 있다. 해당 문장은 'fold'를 자동사로 사용하였으며 주어진 해석이 '(운반보관이 쉽도록) 접다'이므로 옳은 문장이다.

15 정답 ④   Day 21-07

정답해설

④ 출제 포인트: 주의해야 할 비교급 관용표현

'still more'는 긍정문을 받아서 '더구나 …한'의 의미를 지니며, 'still less'는 부정문을 받아서 '더구나 …은 아닌'의 의미를 지닌다. 해당 문장은 부정어 'No'가 포함된 부정문을 대상으로 한 표현이므로 'still more'를 'still less'로 수정해야 한다.

16 정답 ②   Day 30-10

정답해설

본문은 '과거(past)'의 중요성에 대해 설명하고 있다. 본문에 따르면, '현재(present)'는 과거가 축적된 찰나의 순간일 뿐이며, 스쳐 지나가면 현재 또한 과거의 순간이 된다. 그리고 과거에 발생한 모든 것들은 현재에 영향을 미치며, 현재의 '나' 또한 '과거의 나'라고 설명하고 있다. 본문 후반 "It is the present, not the past, that dies(죽는 것은 과거가 아니라 현재이다)"를 통해, '과거는 계속되지만 현재는 사라진다'라는 것을 암시하고 있고, 글의 말미에 본문의 전체 내용을 아우르는 문장이 들어가는 것이 문맥상 적절하므로, 빈칸에 알맞은 표현은 '② It is only the past that lives(생존하는 것은 오직 과거이다)'이다.

해석

발생한 것들 중 이 순간에 영향을 완전히 미치지 않는 것은 없다. 현재는 단지 이 순간의 시간에 축적되고 집중된 과거일 뿐이다. 당신 또한 당신의 과거이다. 종종 당신의 얼굴은 당신의 자서전이다. 당신은 당신의 과거의 모습 때문에; 잊힌 세대로 뻗어나가는 당신의 유전적 특성 때문에, 당신에게 영향을 미친 모든 환경 요소, 당신을 만난 모든 남자 또는 여자, 당신이 읽은 모든 책, 당신이 겪은 모든 경험 때문에 당신이다(당신의 현재의 모습이다). 이 모든 것들이 당신의 기억, 신체, 성격, 영혼에 축적되어 있다. 도시, 국가, 또는 인종도 마찬가지이다. 그것은 그것의 과거이며 그것 없이는 이해될 수 없다. 죽는 것은 과거가 아니라 현재이다; 우리가 너무나 많은 관심을 두는 현재의 순간은 영원히 우리의 눈과 손가락으로부터 우리가 과거라고 부르는 우리 삶의 받침대와 행렬 속으로 스쳐 지나간다. 생존하는 것은 오직 과거이다.

① 나아가기 위해 과거를 보내주어라
② 생존하는 것은 오직 과거이다
③ 당신의 과거가 당신의 성격을 결정한다
④ 그 어느 것보다 현재가 더 중요하다

17 정답 ①   Day 22-09

정답해설

본문은 '낮에는 청소부로 일하는 작가 Caitriona Lally'에 관한 이야기이다. 'Rooney Prize for Literature'를 수상한 Caitriona Lally가 청소부로 일하는 것은 '외부인들(일반인들)과 언론'에게는 이상한 일이고, '내부인들(업계 종사자들)'은 그녀가 그것을 공공연하게 밝힌다는 것에 흥미를 느낀다. 본문에 따르면, '그녀는 많은 상금을 받았음에도 불구하고 생계를 꾸리기 위해 계속 청소부로 일할 것이다'라는 것을 알 수 있다. 즉, 그녀는 작가로 성공했음에도 불구하고 재정적으로는 빈곤한 상태인 것이다. 빈칸에는 그녀의 경우에 비추어 다른 많은 작가와 예술가들이 처한 상황을 설명할 수 있는 표현이 들어가야 하므로, 가장 적절한 것은 '① are broke(빈털터리이다)'이다.

해석

Caitriona Lally가 그녀의 데뷔 소설 Eggshells로 Rooney Prize for Literature를 수상했을 때, 미디어의 초점은 그녀의 주간 직업에 맞추어졌다. 그녀는 Trinity College Dublin의 청소부로, "돈벌이가 되는 일"이 일찍 끝나고 글쓰기 작업을 시작할 수 있도록 오전의 짧은 시간에 청소하고 닦는다. 외부인들과 언론에게, 이것은 이상하며, 발언, 논의, 분석되어야 하는 일이다. 내부인들(업계 종사자들)에게, 흥미로운 사항은 Lally가 고지서 요금을 지불해 온, 그리고 주로 보육비로 남겨둔 10,000유로의 상금에도 불구하고 그녀가 열심히 다음 책, 그리고 다음을 집필하면서 계속해서 (고지서 요금을) 지불할, 결코 선망을 얻지 못하는 직업에 대해 숨기지 않는다는 것이다. 이 나라의 그리고 실제로 전 세계의 많은 작가들과 예술가들은 빈털터리이다; 문제는 그것을 인정하느냐 아니냐는 것이다.

① 빈털터리이다
② 건강하지 않다
③ 독창성이 부족하다
④ 과대 평가된다

18 정답 ③   Day 25-08

정답해설

주어진 문장에서는 '자기소개서(cover letter)'에 관한 사람들의 일반적인 견해에 대해 언급하고 있다. 이후에는 '실제로 고용 현장에서는 사람들의 기대와는 정반대이다'라는 점을 시사하고 있는 (B)가 이어지는 것이 자연스럽다. 이어서 (C)의 'this reason(이러한 이유)'이 (B)에서 언급된 "the interview selection process has to be completed as quickly as possible since employers would not want too many days wasted on granting employment and keeping work on stand-by(고용인들이 고용을 승인하고 업무를 대기 상태로 두는 데 너무 많은 날을 소비하고 싶어 하지 않기 때문에 면접 선발 절차는 가능한 한 신속하게 끝나야 한다)"를 가리키고 있으므로 (C)가 이어진 후, (A)의 'According to the rule(그 법칙에 따르면)'이 (C)의 'golden rule(기본 법칙)'을 가리키고 있으므로 (A)가 마지막으로 이어지는 것이 가장 자연스럽다. 따라서 정답은 '③ (B) - (C) - (A)'이다.

해석

보통 사람들은 그들이 자기소개서를 작성하는 데 많은 노력을 쏟으며, 따라서 그것이 인내심을 가지고 읽힐 필요가 있다고 생각한다.
(B) 그러나 현실은 정반대이다. 고용인들이 고용을 승인하고 업무를 대기 상태로 두는 데 너무 많은 날을 소비하고 싶어 하지 않기 때문에 면접 선발 절차는 가능한 한 신속하게 끝나야 한다.
(C) 이러한 이유와 셀 수 없이 많은 수의 지원자들 때문에 대부분의 고용인들은 일을 더 빠르고 더 편리하게 만들기 위해 40초 기본 법칙을 지정했다.
(A) 그 법칙에 따르면, 어떠한 지원서에도 40초 이상의 시간이 주어져서는 안 되는데, 이것은 최종 인원을 선발하기 전 선발 위원회의 구성원들은 오직 지원서를 훑어볼 수 있을 정도의 시간만을 가지고 있다는 것을 의미한다.

19 정답 ④ Day 27-10

정답해설

본문은 '우리가 한 사람의 행위를 통해 그 사람의 성격을 판단한다'고 설명하고 있다. 즉, 한 사람이 행동하는 방식이 그 사람의 성격을 나타낸다는 것이다. 본문에 따르면 '이러한 행위(반응)를 결정하는 정신적, 신경적 구조는 일부는 선천적이고 일부는 후천적'이다. 성격의 발현인 행위가 일부 선천적이고 일부 후천적이라는 것은, 사람의 성격 또한 선천적으로 타고나는 기질과 후천적으로 습득하는 기질이 각각 존재한다는 것을 의미한다. 따라서 글의 요지로 가장 적절한 것은 '④ A person's character is determined by both genes and environmental factors(한 사람의 성격은 유전자와 환경적 요소 모두에 의해 결정된다).'이다.

해석

우리는 한 사람의 성격을 그의 행위에 의해, 즉 일상생활의 수많은 우여곡절에 대해 그가 반응하는 방식에 의해 판단하는 것에 익숙해져 있다. 우리의 경험에서 이러한 반응들은 개인에 따라 다르고, 우리는 영향을 받은 개인의 성격이 상대적으로 다르다고 말함으로써 이 반응의 가변성을 이해한다. 비록 성격이 그 사람 자체의 속성이지만, 그것은 오직 그 사람의 행동을 통해서만 알 수 있고, 반응이 결정되는 정신적 그리고 신경적 구조에 대한 개략적인 표현이다. 이러한 구조는 일부는 선천적이고, 일부는 후천적이다. 중추 신경계를 구성하는 세포와 신경의 경로의 모양은 출생 전에 이미 정해지지만, 어떠한 자극이 중추 신경계를 통하여 지나는 길에 만나는 저항은 유전적인 모양뿐만 아니라 경험의 결과이기도 하다.
① 모든 사람은 유전적인 이유로 다른 성격을 지니고 있다.
② 정확하게 성격을 판단하는 것은 힘든 일이다.
③ 양육이 개인의 성격에 가장 많은 영향을 미친다.
④ 한 사람의 성격은 유전자와 환경적 요소 모두에 의해 결정된다.

20 정답 ① Day 28-08

정답해설

본문은 'Walt Disney의 어린 시절 아버지와의 관계'에 대한 내용이다. 본문에 따르면, Walt Disney의 아버지 'Elias'는 '폭력적이고 고압적인 인물'이었으며, 그로 인해 Walt Disney를 포함한 자식들과의 관계가 좋지 않았다는 것을 알 수 있다. ①의 'he tried, unsuccessfully, to make ends meet for the family'에서 'he'가 가리키는 것은 '가족을 위한 생계를 꾸리는 데 실패한 Walt Disney의 아버지 Elias'이며, 나머지 보기는 'Walt Disney'를 가리키고 있으므로, 정답은 ①이다.

해석

1901년 Chicago에서 태어나고 Missouri에서 자란 Walt Disney는 5형제 중 넷째 아들이었다. 그의 아버지 Elias는 ① 그가 가족을 위한 생계를 꾸리는 것을 시도하는 것에 실패했을 때 폭력적이었다고 알려진 고압적인 인물이었다. ② 그의 스트레스가 많은 상황으로부터 도망치기 위해, 어린 Disney는 그림 그리는 것에서 위안을 찾았다. 그럼에도 불구하고, ③ 그는 그의 형들이 아버지로부터 도망치기 위해 차례차례 떠나는 것을 지켜보았고, 머지않아 ④ 그는 제1차 세계대전 중 구급차 기사가 되기 위해 나이를 속임으로써 형들을 따라 했다. 그의 아버지가 사망했을 때, 알려진 바에 따르면 그는 출장을 단축하기를 거부했고 그에 따라 그의 아버지의 장례식을 놓쳤다.

결국엔 성정혜 영어 하프모의고사
기적사 DAY 31

| 01 | ① | 02 | ① | 03 | ② | 04 | ④ | 05 | ③ |
| 06 | ② | 07 | ④ | 08 | ④ | 09 | ④ | 10 | ③ |

01 정답 ①
15 국가직

정답해설

마지막 문장에서 '핵 테러와 대규모 살상 무기의 확산을 막는다(prevent the spread of weapons of mass destruction and nuclear terrorism)'고 했으므로, 빈칸 다음에 있는 '다각적인 핵 안보와 안전(the multilateral nuclear security and safety)'을 ① 강화한다(beef up)고 하는 것이 문맥상 적절하다.

해석

사무총장은 UN이 다각적인 핵 안보와 안전을 **강화하기** 위한 여러 가지 행동 계획을 제안할 것이라고 말했다. 그는 강력한 경제적 제재가 핵 테러와 대규모 살상 무기의 확산을 막는 데에 필수적이라고 말했다.
① ~을 강화하다, 보강하다
② ~을 생략하다, 없애다, 면제시키다
③ ~을 줄이다, 끄다
④ ~에서 지우다

어휘

multilateral 다각적인, 다자간의   sanction 제재
beef up ~을 강화하다, 보강하다
dispense with ~을 생략하다, 없애다, 면제시키다
damp down ~을 줄이다, 끄다   scratch off ~에서 지우다

오답률 TOP 3
02 정답 ①
15 국가직

정답해설

중국의 안 좋은 황사나 각종 유해 물질을 말하고 있는 것으로 유해 물질들이 태양에게 할 수 있는 것은 태양을 차단하는 것이다. 따라서 가장 적절한 것은 ① blotting out이 가장 적절하다.

해석

위성 이미지는 중국 동부를 덮은 "갈색 구름들"을 보여준다. 아시아의 많은 지역의 수백만의 사람들의 폐를 더럽히면서, 그을음, 스모그 그리고 유독성 화학물질들의 유해한 혼합물은 태양을 **가리고** 있다.
① 가리는, 지우는
② 자세히 조사하는
③ 충족시키는
④ 의지하고 있는

어휘

noxious 유독한, 유해한   cocktail 혼합물
soot 그을음, 검댕   foul 더럽히다, 반칙을 범하다
blot out ~을 가리다, 지우다   pore over ~을 자세히 조사하다
cater to ~을 충족시키다   resort to ~에 의지하다

오답률 TOP 1
03 정답 ②
15 국가직

정답해설

'최면에 걸린 사람은 최면상태에 ~한다'이므로 빈칸에 들어갈 가장 적절한 것은 ② lapses into이다.

해석

최면에 걸린 사람은 최면상태**에 빠진다**, 그 상태란 어떤 사람이 움직일 수 있고 말을 할 수 있지만 정상적인 방법으로 의식이 있는 것은 아니다.
① ~에 나타나다
② ~에 빠지다
③ ~에 비슷하게 하다
④ ~에 철썩거리다

어휘

hypnotize ~에 최면술을 걸다, ~을 매료하다
trance 최면상태, 비몽사몽   conscious 의식이 있는
loom on ~에 나타나다   lapse into ~에 빠지다
level at ~에 비슷하게 하다   lap against ~에 철썩거리다

오답률 TOP 2
04 정답 ④
13 국가직

정답해설

과속 제한에 걸리면 현장에서 (경찰관에 의해 직접) 벌금을 지불할 것을 요구받았을 수 있는데 그렇지 않은 이유를 A가 B에게 묻고 있다. 빈칸 이후의 대화에서 감시 카메라를 더 조심하라고 했기 때문에, (무인) 감시 카메라에 찍혔다는 응답인 ④ 'Because I was photographed by one of speed cameras(속도 감시 카메라 중 하나에 내가 찍혔기 때문이야)가 가장 적절하다.

오답해설

나머지 선지는 문맥상 적절하지 않으므로 오답이다.

해석

A: 이 편지 좀 봐.
B: 아 그래, 공문서 같은 거라고 생각했어. 과속 제한에 걸려서 네가 벌금을 내야 한다고 쓰여 있어. 왜 현장에서 벌금을 부과받지 않았니?
A: 속도 감시 카메라들 중 하나에 내가 찍혔기 때문이야.
B: 점점 더 많은 카메라들이 여기 주위로 설치되고 있어. 넌 앞으로 더 조심해야 할 거야.
A: 농담 아냐. 벌금이 60달러야.
① 그 장소가 너무 붐벼서 벌금을 부과받지 않았기 때문이야
② 그것을 찍을 어떠한 카메라도 찾을 수 없었기 때문이야
③ 벌금을 부과받았을 때 이미 지불했기 때문이야
④ 속도 감시 카메라들 중 하나에 내가 찍혔기 때문이야

어휘

official looking 공식(공무상)으로 보이는
exceed 넘어서다, 초과하다, 능가하다
be fined for ~ ~때문에 벌금을 부과받다
fine 벌금

05 정답 ③
14 국가직

정답해설

③ **출제 포인트: 능동태 vs. 수동태**
'undergo'는 완전타동사이므로 수동태로 사용되는 경우 이후에 목적어가 올 수 없다. 해당 문장은 'undergo'의 수동태인 'be undergone'을 사용하였으나 이후에 목적어 'unbearable suffering'이 있으므로 틀린 문장이다. 따라서 'be undergone'을 능동태인 'undergo'로 수정해야 한다.

오답해설

① **출제 포인트: 주어와 동사의 수일치**
나라명은 형태가 복수일지라도 단수로 취급한다. 해당 문장은 주어에 나라명인 'The Netherlands'를 사용하였으므로 동사에 단수 형태인 'becomes'를 사용하는 것이 옳다.

② **출제 포인트: 주격 관계대명사절의 동사 수일치**
'Those who want'의 경우 'Those'는 'those people'의 의미이다. 이때 'people'은 복수로 주격 관계대명사절의 동사에 복수 형태인 'want'로 수일치하는 것이 옳다.

④ **출제 포인트: a second(다른, 또 하나의) + 단수가산명사**
'a second'는 '다른, 또 하나의'를 뜻하며 이후에 단수가산명사가 온다. 해당 문장은 'a second'가 쓰인 문장으로 이후에 단수가산명사 'physician'이 왔으므로 옳은 문장이다.

해석

네덜란드는 몇몇의 엄격한 조건들이 있기는 하지만 현재 환자의 안락사를 허용하는 세계 유일 국가가 되었다. 죽기 위해서 의학적 도움을 원하는 사람들은 참을 수 없는 고통을 겪고 있어야 한다. 또한 의사와 환자가 완화의 희망이 없다는 사실에 동의를 해야 한다. 그리고 다른 의사와 상담을 받아야 한다.

어휘

mercy killing 안락사
condition 조건, 상태
remission 차도, 완화
strict 엄격한, 엄한
undergo 겪다, 받다
consult 상담하다, 의의하다

06 정답 ②
14 국가직

정답해설

② **출제 포인트: 능동태 vs. 수동태**
'repair'는 완전타동사이므로 이후에 목적어가 온다. 해당 문장은 'repair'의 과거진행형 'was repairing'을 사용하였으나 이후에 전명구 'at my mechanic's garage'가 왔으므로 틀린 문장이다. 따라서 'was repairing'을 수동태 'was repaired'로 수정해야 한다.

오답해설

① **출제 포인트: 분사가 생략된 분사구문**
밑줄 친 'Unable to do anything'은 'Unable' 이전에 현재분사 'being'이 생략된 분사구문으로 생략된 주어는 'I'이다.

③ **출제 포인트: 동사 관용표현**
밑줄 친 'came to the realization'은 이후에 있는 접속사 'that'을 포함하여 'come to realize that(~을 깨닫다)'의 과거형으로 사용된 옳은 표현이다.

④ **출제 포인트: 불완전자동사의 주격 보어/부사 vs. 형용사**
불완전자동사 'become'의 주격 보어로 형용사 'dependent'를 사용하였으며 이때, 부사 'overly'가 형용사 'dependent'를 수식하므로 밑줄 친 'overly dependent'는 옳은 표현이다.

해석

자동차가 카센터에서 수리되고 있는 동안 아무것도 할 수 없고, 아무 데도 갈 수 없던 나는 내가 기계와 장비에 과도하게 의존하게 됐었다는 것을 갑자기 깨닫게 되었다.

어휘

garage 차고, 주차장, 차량 정비소 겸 주유소
come to the realization that + 절 (= come to realize that + 절) ~을 깨닫다
gadget 도구, 장치

07 정답 ④
14 국가직

정답해설

④ **출제 포인트: 현재분사 vs. 과거분사**
밑줄 친 'involving'은 '관련시키다'를 뜻하는 완전타동사 'involve'의 현재분사이나 수식하는 대상 'the business practices and processes'와 수동관계이며 이후에 전명구 'in supporting the U.S. Department of State's diplomatic efforts'가 오므로 현재분사 'involving'을 과거분사 'involved'로 수정해야 한다.

오답해설

① **출제 포인트: to부정사의 형용사적 용법**
밑줄 친 'to begin'은 to부정사로 명사 'chance'를 수식하는 형용사적 용법에 해당한다.

② **출제 포인트: 관계부사 vs. 관계대명사**
밑줄 친 'where'는 'a journey'를 선행사로 갖는 관계부사이며 이후에 오는 절이 완전한 형태이므로 'where'는 옳은 표현이다. 또한 'that you ~ daily basis'는 'where'가 이끄는 관계부사절 내의 주어 'the things'를 선행사로 갖는 목적격 관계대명사 절이다.

③ **출제 포인트: 전치사 관용표현(from A to B)**
밑줄 친 'to providing'은 「전치사 + 목적어[동명사]」 형태로 앞에 있는 'From improving'과 연결되어 'from A to B'의 구조를 이룬다. 이때 해당 문장에서 'from A to B and to B'로 'to B' 전명구가 'to monitoring', 'to providing'으로 두 번 연속 나열된 경우이므로 옳다.

해석

공무원이 된다는 것은 매일 이루는 일들이 세상에서 중요한 차이를 만들어 낼 수 있는 여행을 시작할 기회이다. 미국 기업들을 위한 무역 기회를 향상시키는 것에서부터, 인권 문제를 감시하고, 관리 감독을 제공하는 것에 이르기까지, 공무원 일을 행함에 있어 직접적으로 대외 정책에 영향을 주거나 미 국무부의 외교적 노력을 뒷받침하는 데 관련된 업무 관행 및 절차를 뒷받침하기 위해 당신의 능력을 활용할 수 있다.

어휘

accomplish 해내다, 성취하다
supervision 감독, 관리
diplomatic 외교의
monitor 감시하다, 관찰하다
uphold 옹호하다, 유지시키다

08 정답 ③
16 국가직

정답해설

낮은 성과를 내는 초등학생들은 '지능(intelligence)'이 낮다기보다는 사실 '작동 기억(working memory)'이 부진한 것인데, 이를 교사들이 잘 확인하지 않는다는 내용이다. 따라서 이 글의 주제로는 키워드인 '작동 기억'이 있어야 하며 선지 중 ③ 'influence of poor working memory on primary school children(초등학생들에게 미치는 부진한 작동 기억의 영향)'이 가장 적절하다.

오답해설
① 아이들과 교사 사이의 공감이 부족한 것을 '선생님이 부진한 작동 기억에 대해 확인하지 않고 지능이 낮다고 치부해 버리는 것'에 비유한다면 사실이라고 할 수는 있지만 이 글의 주제로 삼기에는 지엽적이다.
② 단순히 초등학교 아이들의 낮은 지능에 대하여 말한 것이 아니라, 낮은 지능이라고 판단되는 아이들은 사실 작동 기억이 부진한 것이라는 내용이므로 주제로 적절하지 않다.
④ 지문과 반대의 내용이기에 주제로 적절하지 않다.

해석
학교에서 낮은 성과를 내는 아이들은 낮은 지능을 가졌다기보다는 단순히 부진한 작동 기억을 가졌을지도 모른다. 한 대학의 연구진들이 3,000명 이상의 모든 연령의 초등학생들을 조사했는데, 그들 중 10%가 심하게 학습을 방해하는 부진한 작동 기억으로 고생한다는 것을 알아냈다. 전국적으로 이것은 거의 500,000명의 초등 교육을 받는 아이들이 영향을 받는 것과 같다. 그 연구진들은 또한 교사들이 좀처럼 부진한 작동 기억에 대해 확인하려 하지 않으며, 종종 이러한 문제를 가진 아이들을 조심성이 없거나 지능이 낮다고 설명해버린다.
① 학교에서의 아이들의 교사들과의 공감성
② 초등학교 아이들의 낮은 지능
③ 초등학생들에게 미치는 부진한 작동 기억의 영향
④ 아이들의 작동-기억 문제를 해결하기 위한 교사들의 노력

어휘
underachieve 자기 능력 이하의 성적을 내다
working memory 작동[심리] 기억   primary school 초등학교
impede 방해하다, 지체하다   rarely 드물게; 좀처럼 …않다
inattentive 부주의한, 태만한

09 정답 ④ 16 국가직

정답해설
본문 중반 'Public health officials ~ pressure to regulate it.'을 통해 ④가 지문과 일치하는 내용을 서술하고 있음을 알 수 있다.

오답해설
① 본문의 첫 문장에 따르면 오히려 통조림 음식의 위험성을 입증할 이유를 제공할지 모른다고 하였기에 본문과 일치하지 않는다.
② 본문 후반에 모든 학자가 그러한 과장에 동의하는 것은 아니며, 일부 연구자들은 그러한 건강 위협에 대해 반박한다고 서술되어 있다.
③ 본문 후반에 미국 의료 협회 잡지에 실린 새로운 연구에 처음으로 통조림 음식을 먹고 소화되는 BPA양을 측정했다고 서술한다.

해석
Harvard 연구진들에 의한 새로운 연구는 통조림 수프와 주스를 당신의 식탁에서 없앨 설득력 있는 이유를 제공할지도 모른다. 5일에 걸쳐 1인분의 통조림 음식을 먹는 사람들은, 연구에 의하면, 대부분의 음식과 음료수 캔에 설명되어진 물질인 bisphenol-A 또는 BPA의 수치가 10배 이상 증가한 심각한 증가 수치를 보였다. 미국 보건 관리국 관계자들은 그것을 규제하라는 압력을 점점 더 받고 있다. BPA에 관한 일부 연구들은 그것이 암, 심장병, 그리고 비만에 대한 더 높은 위험성과 관련이 있다는 것을 보여준다. 그러나 일부 연구자들은 사람들에게 건강적인 위협으로써의 그것의 명성은 과장된 것이라고 반박한다. 미국 의료 협회 잡지에 실린 새로운 연구는 사람이 통조림에서 직접적으로 나온 음식을 먹을 때 소화되는 BPA의 양을 처음으로 측정한 것이다.

어휘
compelling 설득력 있는, 강력한, 강제적인
serving 1인분   tenfold 10배의
come under [비판·공격·영향 등을] 받다
reputation 명성, 평판   exaggerate 과장하다
ingest 섭취하다; 수집하다; 받아들이다

10 정답 ③ 16 국가직

정답해설
주어진 문장 다음으로 도입을 의미하는 (B)가 오는 것이 적절하다. 또한 (A) 초반에 언급된 'These are three of the key aspects~'의 맨 첫 번째 단어 'These'는 (C) 마지막의 'perception, memory, and emotion'을 가리키므로 (C)다음에 (A)가 와야 적절하다. 따라서 정답은 ③이 적절하다.

오답해설
(B)와 (C)의 유기적인 관계의 정보가 부족하다. 따라서 (B) 다음으로 오게 될 순서에서 오답인 (A)를 선택할 수 있다. 그러나 유기적인 관계의 정보가 부족하다면, 나머지 (C)와 (A)의 순서를 먼저 정하면 된다. (A)는 지시대명사 'These'로 인해 (C) 이후에 존재해야 할 이유가 있으므로 답은 (B) 이후에 (C)가 오는 ③ '(B)-(C)-(A)' 뿐이다.

해석
모든 동물들은 사람처럼 자는 동안 같은 종류의 뇌 활동을 한다. 그들이 꿈을 꾸는지 안 꾸는지는 다른 문제이다. 그것은 단지 또 다른 질문을 취하면서 풀릴 수 있기 때문이다: 동물들은 자각 의식을 가지고 있을까?
(B) 오늘날 많은 과학자들은 동물들이 아마도 계획적이거나 상징적인 생각을 위한 언어와 능력이 부족하다는 관점에서 우리와는 꽤나 다른 제한된 형태의 자각 의식을 가진다고 추측한다.
(C) 동물들은 꿈을 진짜 꾸더라도 당연히 꿈에 대해서 보고 하지 못한다. 그러나 어떤 애완동물 주인이 그들의 가장 친한 동물 친구가 자각과 기억 그리고 감정이 있다는 것에 대해 의심할까?
(A) 이러한 것들은 자각 의식의 세 가지 중요한 면들이다. 그리고 그것들은 동물들이 우리들처럼 구두의 언어를 하든 하지 않든 상관없이 체험할 수 있다. 동물의 뇌가 잠을 잘 동안 활동할 때, 동물들이 일종의 지각, 감정의, 그리고 기억의 경험을 한다고 왜 추정하지 않겠는가?

어휘
activation 활동   consciousness 의식
perceptual 지각의   emotional 감정의, 감정적인
capacity 능력   propositional 계획의, 제기하는
symbolic 상징적인

결국엔 성정혜 영어 하프모의고사
기적사 DAY 32

01	④	02	③	03	①	04	③	05	②
06	②	07	④	08	②	09	④	10	③

오답률 TOP 2
01 정답 ④

정답해설

'자료가 분석하기 너무 어려워 그 자료가 보여주려고 했던 것을 ~할 수 없었다'이므로 문맥상 ④ make out이 가장 적절하다.

해석

그 자료는 분석하기가 너무 어려워서 우리는 그 자료가 우리에게 보여주려 했던 것을 **이해할** 수 없었다.
① ~와 화해하다
② ~을 생략하다, 없애다, 면제시키다
③ ~을 줄이다, 끄다
④ ~을 이해하다, 만들어내다

어휘

analyze 분석하다 make up with ~와 화해하다
dispense with ~을 생략하다, 없애다, 면제시키다
damp down ~을 줄이다, 끄다 make out ~을 이해하다, 만들어내다

02 정답 ③

정답해설

'이동하다, 이주하다'의 ③ migrate를 사용하여 '이동하지 않고 서식한다'라고 하는 것이 자연스럽다.

해석

보통, 바다직박구리새들은 다른 지역으로 **이동하지** 않고, 주로 해안 근처에서 서식한다.
① 음식을 공급하다
② 가해하다
③ 이동하다, 이주하다
④ 강요하다

어휘

blue rock thrush 바다직박구리 inhabit 살다[거주/서식하다]
cater 음식을 공급하다 perpetrate 가해하다
migrate 이동하다, 이주하다 oblige 강요하다

오답률 TOP 1
03 정답 ①

정답해설

'마침내 그의 상점을 열었다'고 하였으므로 '이것'이 성공으로의 '기반을 닦았다' 또는 '길을 열었다'고 하는 것이 자연스럽다. 따라서 'pave'를 활용한 ① paved가 가장 적절하다.

해석

이것이 트렁크 디자이너로서 그의 성공으로의 **길을 열었고**, 마침내 그는 1854년에 그의 상점을 열었다.

① (기반을) 닦았다, (길을) 열었다
② ~에 나타났다
③ ~을 개선했다, 고쳤다
④ ~을 파견했다

어휘

pave (기반을) 닦다, (길을) 열다 loom on ~에 나타나다
mend ~을 개선하다, 고치다 dispatch ~을 파견하다

04 정답 ③

정답해설

A와 B는 장래 희망에 대해 이야기하고 있다. B가 '왜 최고경영자가 되고 싶다고 결정했어?'라는 A의 질문에 '최고경영자가 많은 사람들에 의해 ~하는 직업 같아 보이기 때문'이라고 답하고 있다. 따라서 문맥상 '존경받는 직업'이 자연스러우므로 빈칸에 들어갈 가장 적절한 것은 ③ 'looked up to(존경받는)'이다.

오답해설

① B가 최고경영자가 되고 싶은 이유를 사람들에게 '생각이 나는(hitting upon)' 직업이기 때문이라고 하는 것은 문맥상 부자연스럽다.
② B는 최고경영자가 되고 싶은 이유를 이야기하며, 사람들의 '이상에 따라 움직이는(living up to)' 직업이기 때문이라는 것은 대화의 흐름상 적절하지 않다.
④ A가 B에게 최고경영자가 되고 싶은 이유에 관해 질문하자, B는 그 직업이 '철이 지난(out of season)' 것이기 때문이라고 답변하는 것은 대화의 맥락을 고려했을 때 빈칸에 들어갈 말로 어색하다.

해석

A: 너는 미래에 어떤 직업을 갖고 싶어?
B: 나는 최고경영자가 되고 싶어.
A: 우와 그건 선망받는 직업이야. 너는 왜 최고경영자가 되고 싶다고 결정했어?
B: 많은 사람에게 존경받는 직업 같아 보이잖아.
A: 네 말이 맞아. 사실, 작년에 실시된 설문조사에 의하면, 최고경영자는 고등학생들에게 가장 존경받는 직업 중 하나야.
B: 오, 그건 내가 몰랐던 사실이네.
① 생각이 나는
② ~에 따라 사는
③ 존경받는
④ 철이 지난

어휘

venerable 존경할 만한, 공경할 만한 hit upon 생각이 나다
live up to ~에 따라 사는 look up to ~을 존경하다, 쳐다보다
out of season 철이 지난

오답률 TOP 3
05 정답 ②

정답해설

② **출제 포인트: 동명사의 역할**

'but' 이하의 문장에서 주절의 동사는 'is'이므로 밑줄 친 'gather'는 동사 역할이 아닌 주어 역할을 해야 한다. 따라서 'gather'를 동명사로 고쳐야 하며 이후에 목적어인 'what'절이 오므로 능동형 동명사 'gathering'으로 수정해야 한다.

오답해설

① **출제 포인트: 주어와 동사의 수일치**
주어가 복수 형태인 'Most people'이므로 동사에 복수 형태인 'work'를 옳게 사용하였다. 주어 'Most people'과 동사 'work' 사이의 'who live ~ in the acquisition of food'는 주어 'Most people'을 수식하는 주격 관계대명사 절에 해당한다. 이처럼, 주어와 동사 사이의 거리가 먼 경우 수일치에 주의해야 한다.

③ **출제 포인트: 관용표현(refer to+목적어)**
「refer to+목적어」는 관용표현으로 '~을 말하다'를 뜻한다. 해당 문장은 'refer to'가 쓰인 문장으로 이후에 목적어 'any human action'이 왔으므로 옳은 문장이다.

④ **출제 포인트: 관용표현(convert A into B)**
「convert A into B」는 관용표현으로 'A를 B로 바꾸다[변하게 하다]'를 뜻한다. 해당 문장은 'convert A into B'가 쓰인 문장으로 밑줄 친 전치사 'into'는 옳은 표현이다.

해석

자연환경과 직접 접촉하고 살며 식량 확보에 적은 기술을 이용하는 대부분의 사람들은 사실상 단순히 낮게 매달린 과일들을 줍는 것보다 더 열심히 일하지만, 자연환경에서 야생으로 자라는 것을 수집하는 것은 생산의 한 형태이다. 생산은 자연환경의 자원들을 음식으로 바꾸기 위해 의도되는 인간의 어떠한 행위를 말한다.

어휘

acquisition 획득, 습득
refer to ~을 말하다
gather 모으다
convert A into B A를 B로 바꾸다

06 정답 ②

정답해설

② **출제 포인트: 비교급 비교(비교급 형용사+than+비교 대상)**
명사로 쓰인 'help' 앞에 비교급 형용사 'more'를 사용하였으므로 비교 대상인 'when wearing either of the other kinds of shirts' 앞에 전치사 'as'를 사용할 수 없다. 따라서 'as'를 'than'으로 수정해야 한다.

오답해설

① **출제 포인트: 접속사가 생략되지 않은 분사구문/현재분사 vs. 과거분사**
밑줄 친 'when wearing'은 접속사가 생략되지 않은 분사구문이다. 이때, 생략된 주어 'the injured student'와 능동관계이므로 현재분사 'wearing'은 옳은 표현이다.

③ **출제 포인트: sort/kind/type+of+무관사 명사**
'sort/kind/type of' 이후에 오는 명사는 관사를 사용할 수 없다. 따라서 'the other kinds of' 이후에 온 무관사 형태의 복수명사 'shirts'는 옳은 표현이다.

④ **출제 포인트: 주어와 동사의 수일치**
주절의 주어가 복수명사 'People'이므로 주절의 동사에 복수 형태인 'form'을 사용하는 것이 옳다. 주어 'People'과 동사 'form' 사이의 'who are ~ soccer team'은 주어 'People'을 수식하는 주격관계대명사 절에 해당한다. 이처럼, 주어와 동사 사이의 거리가 먼 경우 수일치에 주의해야 한다.

해석

그 부상입은 학생은 다른 팀의 셔츠를 입었을 때보다 (실험) 참여자가 가장 선호하는 팀의 셔츠를 입었을 때 도움을 더 받았다. 같은 축구팀의 팬인 사람은 내집단을 구성한다.

어휘

injure 부상을 입히다, 손상시키다
ingroup 내집단
help (불가산명사) 도움
either (둘 중) 어느 하나

07 정답 ④

정답해설

④ **출제 포인트: 불완전자동사의 주격 보어/형용사 vs. 부사**
밑줄 친 'inefficiently'는 주격 보어에 해당하는 자리이므로 부사를 사용할 수 없다. 따라서 부사 'inefficiently'를 형용사 'inefficient'로 수정해야 한다. 이때 'costly'는 「명사+-ly」 형태의 형용사임에 유의해야 한다.

오답해설

① **출제 포인트: 관용표현(prior to+목적어)**
「prior to+목적어[명사/동명사]」는 관용표현으로 '~에 앞서'를 뜻한다. 따라서 밑줄 친 'coming'은 동명사로 옳은 표현이다.

② **출제 포인트: 현재분사 vs. 과거분사/형용사 vs. 부사**
'created'는 과거분사로 이후에 목적어가 없으며 수식하는 대상 'a position(주격 관계대명사 'that'의 선행사)'과 수동관계이므로 옳게 사용되었다. 또한 'newly'는 부사로 과거분사 'created'를 수식하므로 밑줄 친 'newly created'는 옳은 표현이다.

③ **출제 포인트: '~하자마자 …했다' 구문**
「Upon -ing ~, 주어+과거시제 동사 ~.」는 '~하자마자 …했다' 구문으로 밑줄 친 'Upon beginning'은 옳은 표현이다.

해석

이 병원에 들어오기 전에, 그는 독립 계약자로 일했다. 병원이 어떻게 페인팅 서비스를 제공할지에 대한 변화가 필요하다고 믿었으므로, 그는 병원에서 새롭게 만들어진 지위를 맡았다. 그의 업무를 시작하자마자, Mark는 페인팅 서비스의 직접적인 그리고 간접적인 비용에 대한 4개월간의 분석을 수행했다. 그의 발견은 페인팅 서비스가 비효율적이고 비용이 많이 든다고 생각하는 관리자의 인식을 뒷받침했다.

어휘

prior to+목적어 ~에 앞서
perception 인식
costly 비용이 많이 드는
contractor 계약자
administrator 관리자

08 정답 ②

정답해설

본문은 '작동 기억(working memory)'에 대해 설명하고 있으며, 빈칸에는 작동 기억을 담당하는 뇌의 부분의 다른 역할을 설명하는 표현이 들어가는 것이 적절하다. 두 번째 문장 "working memory skills help kids to remember what they need to be paying attention to(작동 기억 기술은 아이들이 그들이 주의를 기울여야 할 필요가 있는 것을 기억하도록 도와준다)."를 통해, '작동 기억 기술이 아이들이 집중해야 할 것을 기억하도록 해준다'는 것을 알 수 있고, 이후 제시된 예시에서, '아이들이 나눗셈 문제의 답을 도출하기 위해서 뿐만 아니라, 문제의 답을 도출하기 위한 단계에 집중하기 위해 작동 기억이 필요하다'고 언급하고 있다. 또한, '빈약한 작동 기억을 지닌 아이들이 최종 정답을 도출하기 위해 작업을 지속하는 데 어려움을 겪는다'고 언급하고 있으므로, '빈약한 작동 기억은 즉, 빈약한 집중력을 의미하는 것'이라고 유추할 수 있다. 따라서 빈칸에 가장 적절한 표현은 '② maintaining focus and concentration(주의력과 집중력을 유지하는 것)'이다.

오답해설
① 본문과 관련 없는 내용이다.
③, ④ 본문에서는 '정답 도출 능력(학습 능력)'과는 별개로, 문제해결을 위해 끝까지 문제에 '집중'할 수 있는 능력에 대해 설명하고 있으므로, 문맥상 빈칸에 적절하지 않다.

해석
작동 기억을 담당하는 뇌의 부분은 주의력과 집중력을 유지하는 것 또한 담당한다. 여기서, 작동 기억 기술은 아이들이 그들이 주의를 기울여야 할 필요가 있는 것을 기억하도록 도와준다. 예를 들어, 긴 나눗셈 문제를 푸는 것을 생각해보라. 당신의 아이는 답을 찾아내기 위해서 뿐만 아니라 그곳에 도달하는 데 관련된 모든 단계에 관심을 집중시키기 위해서도 작동 기억이 필요하다. 빈약한 작동 기억 기술을 지닌 아이들은 최종 결과에 도달하기 위해 작업을 계속 지속하는 것에 어려움을 겪는다. 이것은 당신이 방 안에 들어간 후 무엇을 가지러 들어왔는지 잊어버리는 것과 같다.
① 시각적 그리고 청각적 기억을 저장하는 것
② 주의력과 집중력을 유지하는 것
③ 복잡하고 어려운 문제를 해결하는 것
④ 아이들의 학습 능력을 발달시키는 것

어휘
working memory 작동[심리] 기억
come up with (해답·돈 등을) 찾아내다[내놓다]
zero in on …에 모든 관심[신경]을 집중시키다
involved in …에 관련된[연루된]   capacity 능력

09 정답 ④

정답해설
본문은 'bisphenol A (BPA)에의 노출이 미치는 영향'에 대한 다양한 연구 결과를 소개하고 있다. 본문에서 언급된 BPA의 영향에는 '비정상적 난자 성숙(abnormal egg maturation), 사춘기와 배란의 영향 및 그로 인한 불임(~ affect puberty and ovulation, and that it may lead to infertility), 남성 발기부전(Male impotence), 발기부전과 성욕 및 사정 문제의 위험성 증가(increase the risk of erectile dysfunction and problems with sexual desire and ejaculation)' 등이 있으며, 모두 인간의 생식 작용에 관한 내용이고, 부정적인 영향임을 알 수 있다. 따라서 글의 제목으로 가장 적절한 것은 '④ Relation Between Exposure to BPA and Reproductive Disorders(BPA에의 노출과 생식 장애들의 관계)'이다.

오답해설
① 본문과 관련 없는 내용이다.
② 본문에서는 남성의 건강 문제 외에도 여성의 건강 문제(비정상적 난자 성숙, 배란 등)도 언급하고 있으므로, 전체 글의 제목으로 적절하지 않다.
③ 본문에서 BPA가 미치는 긍정적인 영향에 대해서는 언급하지 않으므로 오답이다.

해석
2013년 Brigham and Women's Hospital의 과학자들이 bisphenol A (BPA)에의 노출이 인간의 비정상적 난자 성숙을 일으킬 수 있다는 것을 보여주는 결과를 발표했다. 2015년에 발표된 이전 연구들의 한 리뷰는 BPA가 시상하부와 뇌하수체를 수반하는 내분비 기능을 방해할 수 있다는 증거를 발견했다. 연구원들은 이러한 유형의 효과가 사춘기와 배란에 영향을 미칠 수 있고, 그것이 불임을 야기할 수 있다고 말했다. 저자들은 "생식 작용에 미치는 해로운 영향은 일생동안 지속되며 세대를 망라할 수도 있다"고 덧붙인다. 직장에서의 남성의 BPA에의 노출의 영향을 살펴본 연구에 따르면 남성 발기부전이 영향을 받을 수도 있다. 결과는 높은 수준의 노출은 발기부전과 성욕 및 사정 문제의 위험성을 증가시킬 수 있다는 것을 보여주었다.
① 없이는 우리가 살 수 없는 화학물질: BPA
② BPA에 의해 야기될 수 있는 남성 건강 문제
③ BPA가 인간에게 미치는 긍정적 그리고 부정적 영향
④ BPA에의 노출과 생식 장애들의 관계

어휘
exposure 노출   egg 난자
maturation 성숙   interfere 방해하다, 지장을 주다
endocrine 내분비의, 호르몬의   involve 포함하다, 수반하다
puberty 사춘기   ovulation 배란
infertility 불임   detrimental 해로운
reproduction 생식(작용), 번식   transgenerational 세대를 망라하는
impotence (남성의) 발기부전, 무기력   erectile dysfunction 발기부전
ejaculation (남성의) 사정   reproductive 생식[번식]의
disorder 장애

10 정답 ③

정답해설
본문은 '의식(consciousness)'에 대한 서양의 철학자 및 과학자들의 인식 변화에 대해 설명하고 있다. 과거에 동물들은 감정이 없는 것으로 인식되었으며, 의식은 인간만의 고유한 영역으로 여겨졌다. Darwin의 진화론이 대두된 이후에도, 과학자들은 인간들이 침팬지로부터 진화한 이후에야 의식을 가지기 시작했다고 믿었다. 그러나 본문 후반 "This notion that consciousness was of recent vintage began to change in the decades following the Second World War, when more scientists were systematically studying the behaviors and brain states of Earth's creatures(의식이 최근의 형태라는 개념은 더 많은 과학자들이 지구의 생물들의 행동과 뇌의 상태를 체계적으로 연구하던 제2차 세계대전 이후 수십 년 동안 변화하기 시작했다)."에 따르면, '기존의 개념이 변화하기 시작하였다'고 언급하고 있으며, '지구상의 여러 생물에 관한 체계적인 연구가 실시되어 왔음'을 알 수 있다. 이러한 변화로 인해, 인간만이 가지고 있다고 여겨졌던 '의식'에 대한 인식 변화가 나타났다는 것을 유추할 수 있으므로, 빈칸에 가장 적절한 표현은 '③ a great many animals are conscious like humans(매우 많은 동물들이 인간과 같이 의식이 있다)'이다.

오답해설
① 본문 중반 '침팬지와 난쟁이 침팬지가 침팬지로부터 우리가 분열되었다'고 언급되기는 하지만, 이는 '인간의 의식의 발생'에 관한 과거 과학자들의 주장에 대해 언급하기 위한 내용이며, 오늘날 과학자들이 체계적 연구를 통해 밝히고 있는 내용은 아니기 때문에 빈칸에 적절하지 않다.
② 본문 초반에 '과거에는 의식이 인간만이 가진 신성한 선물'이라 여겼다고 언급하고 있으나, 제2차 세계대전 이후 이러한 개념이 변화하기 시작했다고 설명하고 있으므로, 빈칸에 '의식이 인간만의 배타적인 특징이다'라는 내용이 들어가는 것은 적절하지 않다.
④ '의식의 진화가 최근의 사건'이라는 것은 과거의 과학자들의 의견이었으나, 이후 현재의 과학자들은 체계적 연구를 통해 그와는 다른 결론을 내리고 있으므로, '인간이 최근까지 의식이 없었다'는 내용은 빈칸에 적절하지 않다.

해석
서양에서 의식은 오랫동안 오직 인간에게 부여된 신성한 선물로 여겨졌다. 역사적으로 서양 철학자들은 인간이 아닌 동물들을 무감정의 기계적으로 행동하는 동물로 생각했다. 심지어 Darwin이 동물과 우리의 친족 관계를 입증한 후에도, 많은 과학자들은 의식의 진화는 최근의 사건이라고 생각했다. 그들은 최초의 지성은 우리가 침팬지와 난쟁이 침팬지로부터 분열되고 얼마 후 자각

이 발생했다고 생각했다. 의식이 최근의 형태라는 개념은 더 많은 과학자들이 지구의 생물들의 행동과 뇌의 상태를 체계적으로 연구하던 제2차 세계대전 이후 수십 년 동안 변화하기 시작했다. 이제 매년, 종합하면, <u>매우 많은 동물들이 인간과 같이 의식이 있다</u>는 것을 시사하는 많은 새로운 연구 논문이 발행된다.
① 인간은 영장류와 밀접한 관련이 있다
② 의식은 인간의 배타적인 특징이다
③ 매우 많은 동물들이 인간과 같이 의식이 있다
④ 심지어 인간도 최근까지는 의식이 없었다

어휘

consciousness 의식, 자각　　　divine 신성한
bestow 부여[수여]하다
conceive of ~ ~을 상상하다, 마음에 그리다
automaton 기계적으로 행동하는[로봇 같은] 사람[동물]
kinship 친척 관계, 혈족 관계
spark (갑자기) 불꽃을 일으키다[발생하다]
bonobo 난쟁이 침팬지　　　vintage (어느 해의) 제품, 제작품
systematically 체계적으로, 조직적으로
a raft of 많은　　　primate 영장류
exclusive 배타적인　　　a great many 꽤[아주] 많은

결국엔 성정혜 영어 하프모의고사
기적사 DAY 33

| 01 | ② | 02 | ① | 03 | ③ | 04 | ④ | 05 | ② |
| 06 | ② | 07 | ④ | 08 | ① | 09 | ③ | 10 | ② |

01 정답 ②

정답해설

'46 percent'를 통해 구성 비율을 나타내고 있으므로 빈칸에는 '차지하다'의 의미를 가진 ② makes up을 넣는 것이 문맥상 자연스럽다.

해석

태평양은 지구 수면의 약 46%를 **차지한다**.
① ~을 강화하다, 보강하다
② ~을 구성하다, 화장하다, 차지하다
③ ~을 줄이다, 끄다
④ ~을 양도하다, 고치다

어휘

beef up ~을 강화하다, 보강하다
make up ~을 구성하다, 화장하다, 차지하다
damp down ~을 줄이다, 끄다　　　make over ~을 양도하다, 고치다

02 정답 ①

정답해설

문맥상 '자제하다, 삼가다'를 뜻하는 ① refrain을 사용하여 '먹거나 마시는 것을 삼간다'라고 하는 것이 가장 자연스럽다.

해석

라마단 기간 동안, 무슬림 사람들은 낮 시간 동안에 먹거나 마시는 것을 **삼간다**.
① 자제하다, 삼가다
② 숙고하다, 응시하다
③ 중재하다, 조정하다
④ 관련되다, 간주하다

어휘

daylight 낮; 햇빛　　　refrain 자제하다, 삼가다
pore 숙고하다, 응시하다　　　mediate 중재하다, 조정하다
regard 관련되다, 간주하다

03 정답 ③

정답해설

문맥상 '되찾다, 회복하다'를 뜻하는 ③ regain을 사용하여 '의식을 회복할 수 없었다'고 하는 것이 가장 자연스럽다.

해석

그는 즉시 인근 병원으로 이송되었지만, 의식을 **회복할** 수 없었다.
① 취소하다, 철회하다
② ~에 비슷하게 하다
③ 되찾다, 회복하다
④ ~에 철썩거리다

어휘

immediately 즉시, 바로
revoke 취소하다, 철회하다
regain 되찾다, 회복하다
consciousness 의식, 인식, 정신
level at ~에 비슷하게 하다
lap against ~에 철썩거리다

04 정답 ④

정답해설

(A) A가 '자신의 동료들과 사이가 그렇게 좋지 않으며, 그들 중 한 명이 ~하는 것을 좋아한다.'라고 말하고 있으므로 빈칸 (A)에 들어갈 가장 적절한 것은 'boss people around(사람들을 부려 먹다)'이다.
(B) 'A가 처한 상황에 대해 스트레스받겠다고 말하며, A가 ~한 것으로 보인다.'라고 B가 말하고 있으므로 빈칸 (B)에 들어갈 가장 적절한 것은 'have a chip on your shoulder(안 좋은 감정을 갖다)'이다.
(C) 스트레스받겠다는 B의 말에 '정확해. 너는 ~하다'라고 A가 말하고 있으므로 빈칸 (C)에 들어갈 가장 적절한 것은 'got the picture(상황을 이해했다)'이다.

오답해설

① (A) A는 이직을 고민하는 이유가 동료 중 한 명이 '자제심을 잃는(go off the deep end)' 것을 좋아하기 때문이라고 말하는 것은 문맥상 어색하다. (B) B는 A가 스트레스받을 것 같다고 말하며, A에게 '본론을 말한다(get to the point)'라고 이야기하는 것은 대화의 흐름상 부적절하다. (C) B가 A의 상황에 관해 한 말에 A는 정확하다고 하며, B에게 '성공했다(got somewhere)'라고 이야기하는 것은 빈칸에 들어갈 말로 적합하지 않다.
② (A) A는 이직을 고민하는 이유가 동료 중 한 명이 '자제심을 잃는(go off the deep end)' 것을 좋아하기 때문이라고 말하는 것은 문맥상 어색하다.
③ (C) B가 A의 상황에 관해 한 말에 A는 정확하다고 하며, B에게 '성공했다(got somewhere)'라고 이야기하는 것은 빈칸에 들어갈 말로 적합하지 않다.

해석

A: 나는 이직을 생각 중이야.
B: 뭐? 진심이야?
A: 응, 난 꽤 오랫동안 생각해왔어.
B: 뭐가 문제야?
A: 음, 내 동료들과 사이가 그렇게 좋지 않아. 동료 중 한 명이 (A) 사람들을 부려 먹는 것을 좋아해.
B: 그거 꽤 스트레스받겠다. 네가 (B) 안 좋은 감정이 있는 것으로 보여.
A: 정확해. 네가 (C) 상황을 이해했어.
① (A) 자제심을 잃다 (B) 본론을 말하다 (C) 성공했다
② (A) 자제심을 잃다 (B) 안 좋은 감정을 갖다 (C) 상황을 이해했다
③ (A) ~를 부려 먹다 (B) 안 좋은 감정을 갖다 (C) 성공했다
④ (A) ~를 부려 먹다 (B) 안 좋은 감정을 갖다 (C) 상황을 이해했다

어휘

go off the deep end 자제심을 잃다
get to the point 본론을 말하다
get somewhere 성공하다, 효과가 있다
have a chip on one's shoulder 안 좋은 감정을 갖다
get the picture 상황을 이해하다
boss people around ~를 부려 먹다

05 정답 ②

정답해설

② **출제 포인트: 관계부사 vs. 관계대명사**
관계대명사는 이후에 오는 절의 형태가 불완전하며 관계부사는 이후에 오는 절의 형태가 완전하다. 해당 문장은 관계대명사 'which'를 사용하였으나 뒤따라오는 절의 형태가 완전한 형태이므로 틀린 문장이다. 따라서 선행사가 'Massachusetts'보다는 바로 앞의 'a time'이 문맥상 적절하므로 관계대명사 'which'를 관계부사 'when'으로 수정해야 한다.

오답해설

① **출제 포인트: 현재분사 vs. 과거분사**
밑줄 친 'Born'은 'bear'의 과거분사로 이후에 전명구 'in Massachusetts'가 왔으며 생략된 주어 'Abby Kelley Foster'와 수동관계이므로 과거분사 'Born'은 옳은 표현이다.
③ **출제 포인트: 능동태 vs. 수동태**
'raise'는 완전타동사이므로 수동태의 경우 이후에 목적어가 올 수 없다. 해당 문장은 'raise'의 수동태인 'was raised'가 쓰인 문장으로 이후에 목적어가 아닌 전명구 'in the town of Worcester'가 왔으므로 옳은 문장이다.
④ **출제 포인트: 관용표현(alternate A with B)**
「alternate A with B」는 관용표현으로 'A와 B를 번갈아 하다[교대로 하다]'를 뜻한다. 해당 문장은 'alternate A with B'가 쓰인 문장으로 밑줄 친 전치사 'with'는 옳은 표현이다.

해석

Massachusetts의 Quaker 농장 가정에서 태어났을 때, Abby Kelley Foster는 농부들이 아들을 갖길 기원하던 시절에 일곱 번째 딸로 태어났다. 그녀는 Worcester에서 자랐으며 중등학교를 마쳤고, Rhode Island의 Providence에 위치한 Quaker 학교에서 고등 교육에 진학한 거의 몇 안 되는 소녀 중 한 명이었다. 그녀는 스스로 자립하기 위해 한동안 아이들을 가르치면서 공부를 병행했다.

어휘

pray for ~을 간절히 바라다, ~을 기원하다
raise 기르다, 올리다
alternate A with B A와 B를 번갈아 하다[교대로 하다]
earn one's way 자립하여 살아가다

오답률 TOP 2

06 정답 ②

정답해설

② **출제 포인트: 수동태 불가동사**
'diverge'는 완전자동사인 경우 '갈라져 나오다, 갈라지다'의 의미를 가지며, 타동사인 경우 '~을 벗어나게 하다'의 의미를 갖는다. 해당 문장에서 'diverge'는 문맥상 '갈라지다'의 의미인 완전자동사로 사용되었으므로, 수동태를 사용할 수 없다. 해당 문장에서 밑줄 친 'can be diverged'는 수동태로 옳지 않게 사용되었다. 따라서 밑줄 친 'can be diverged'를 능동태 'can diverge'로 수정해야 한다.

오답해설

① **출제 포인트: speak의 문장구조/현재분사 vs. 과거분사**
'speak'은 완전타동사인 경우 목적어로 언어를 나타내는 명사(구)가 온다. 해당 문장은 완전타동사 'speak'의 현재분사인 'speaking'을 사용하였으며 이후에 언어를 나타내는 명사(구) 'different languages'가 왔으므로 옳은 표현이다.

③ 출제 포인트: 현재분사 vs. 과거분사

밑줄 친 'taken by'의 'taken'은 'take'의 과거분사로 수식하는 대상 'personality tests'와 수동관계이며 이후에 「by+행위자」인 'by English-speaking Americans and Spanish-speaking Mexicans'가 왔으므로 옳은 표현이다.

④ 출제 포인트: 주어와 동사의 수일치/완전자동사/부사 vs. 형용사

주어가 복수 형태인 'personality tests'이므로 동사에 복수 형태인 'differ'를 옳게 사용하였으며 이때, 'differ'는 완전자동사이므로 이후에 목적어를 가질 수 없다. 또한 'reliably'는 부사로 동사 'differ'를 수식하고 있다. 따라서 밑줄 친 'differ reliably'는 옳은 표현이다.

해석

다른 언어를 구사하는 집단의 사람들의 성격은 종종 갈라질 수 있다. 한 연구는 영어를 구사하는 미국인들과 스페인어를 구사하는 멕시코인들에 의해 행해진 성격 검사가 확실히 다르다는 것을 보여주었다.

어휘

personality 성격, 개성 speak+O(언어) (언어)를 말하다
diverge [의견, 성격, 모양 등이] 갈라지다, 달라지다
reveal 드러내다, 밝히다

오답률 TOP 3
07 정답 ④

정답해설

④ 출제 포인트: 형용사 vs. 부사

불완전자동사 'remain'의 주격 보어는 형용사 'traditional'이며 밑줄 친 'thorough'는 형용사로 '철저한, 완전한'을 뜻한다. 따라서 'thorough'는 'traditional'을 수식해야 하므로 부사 'thoroughly'로 수정해야 한다.

오답해설

① 출제 포인트: to부정사의 형용사적 용법/불완전타동사의 목적격 보어

밑줄 친 'to take'는 to부정사로서 불완전타동사 'allow'의 목적격 보어 역할을 한다.

② 출제 포인트: 부정부사(구) 도치

부정부사(구) 'not only'가 문두에 왔으므로 이후에 오는 현재완료시제가 쓰인 절의 어순은 「have+주어+과거분사」가 된다. 따라서 밑줄 친 'have very few fathers'는 「have+주어」에 해당하므로 옳은 표현이다. 또한 'few'는 수량형용사로 이후에 복수형태의 '명사'가 온다.

③ 출제 포인트: 관용표현(may well+동사원형)

「may well+동사원형」은 관용표현으로 '~하는 것은 당연하다'를 뜻한다. 따라서 밑줄 친 'may well be'는 옳은 표현이다.

해석

일부 조직들은 남성들이나 여성들에게 아이를 돌보기 위해 직업 휴식(육아휴직)을 취하는 것을 허락하는 정책들을 가지고 있다. 그러나, 매우 소수의 아버지들만이 이러한 기회들을 스스로 활용할 뿐 아니라, 그런 선택을 한 사례는 그들이 그렇게 하는 경우 그들의 경력을 평생 '망치는' 결과가 될 수 있음을 보여준다. 정말로, 이러한 사실은 남성들의 해당 제도 이용 비율이 낮은 원인이 되는 것이 당연하다. 그러므로, 조직들은 경력을 보다 유연하게 운영할 수 있는 구조를 갖추어야 할 뿐 아니라, 전형적으로 완전히 전통적인 상태로 남아 있는 태도들을 변화시켜야 한다.

어휘

organization 조직, 단체, 기구 ruin 망치다, 파괴하다
avail 활용하다, ~에 도움이 되다 anecdotal 일화의
may well+동사원형 ~하는 것은 당연하다

오답률 TOP 1
08 정답 ①

정답해설

본문은 '작동 기억(working memory)의 한계를 규정하는 단위'에 대해 설명하고 있다. 본문 초반에 언급된 일반적으로 알려진 사실에 따르면, 작동 기억은 일정 개수의 '정보 덩어리'만을 저장할 수 있다고 한다. 이후, '정보 덩어리의 크기'에 대한 설명으로 숫자 1~7의 예시를 들고 있는데, 같은 정보라 할지라도 상황에 따라 해당 정보가 각각의 개별적 정보가 될 수도 있고, 한 덩어리의 단일 정보가 될 수도 있다고 설명하고 있다. 즉, 정보의 크기라는 것이 객관적이지 않으며, 확실히 규정된 사항이 아니라는 것이다. 따라서 정보 크기의 특성을 설명하는 ① 'determinate(확실한)'가 'indeterminate(정확히 규정할 수 없는)'로 바뀌어야 문맥상 자연스럽다.

오답해설

② 숫자 1~7이 7개의 다른 덩어리가 되려면, 각각 '개별적으로' 숫자를 기억해야 하므로, 'separately(개별적으로)'는 문맥상 자연스럽다.

③ 숫자 1~7이 1개의 단일 덩어리가 되려면, 해당 숫자를 기억하는 사람이 해당 숫자를 잘 알아야 하기 때문에, 'well-versed(정통한)'는 문맥상 자연스럽다.

④ 본문에서 새롭게 제시된 작동 기억의 한계를 규정하는 단위는 '단어를 말하는 시간'이다. 따라서 how 'long'(얼마나 오래)은 문맥상 자연스럽다.

해석

작동 기억에 대해 가장 널리 알려진 사실은 아마 그것이 약 7덩어리의 정보(5에서 9 사이)만을 저장할 수 있다는 것일 것이다. 그러나, 덩어리의 크기가 ① 확실하기(→정확히 규정할 수 없기) 때문에 이것은 우리에게 작동 기억의 한계에 대해 거의 설명해주지 않는다. 만일 당신이 각각의 숫자를 ② 개별적으로 기억한다면, 1 2 3 4 5 6 7은 7개의 다른 덩어리이다 (예를 들어, 당신이 어린아이가 그러하듯이 당신이 숫자에 익숙하지 않다면, 당신이 그렇게 하는 것과 같이). 그러나, 우리의 숫자에 매우 ③ 정통한 우리들 중의 사람들에게, 1부터 7은 단일한 덩어리가 될 수 있다. 그러나, 최근의 연구는 중요한 것은 덩어리의 개수가 아니라고 말한다. 중요할지도 모르는 것은 당신이 단어를 말하는 데 얼마나 ④ 오래 걸리는가일 수도 있다 (정보는 보통 음향 코드의 형태로 작동 기억에 저장된다). 당신은 작동 기억에 당신이 1.5초에서 2초 이내에 말할 수 있는 것만을 저장할 수 있는 것처럼 보인다. 따라서 느리게 말하는 사람들이 불리하다.

어휘

working memory 작동[심리] 기억 chunk 덩어리
determinate 확정적인, 확실한 only too 매우, 아주
well-versed 정통한, 잘하는 acoustic 음향의
penalize 불리하게 만들다
indeterminate 정확히 규정할 수 없는, 불확정한

09 정답 ③

정답해설

본문에서는, '폴리카보네이트와 에폭시 안감 등으로 인해 음식 및 음료에 BPA가 배출되며, 특히 캔에 포장된 유동식을 폴리카보네이트로 만든 젖병에 담아 먹는 유아들이 일반 사람들보다 더 많은 빈도로 BPA에 노출된다'고 언급하고 있다. 이후 본문 마지막에서, "As very low levels of BPA have been detected in human breast milk, infant exposure from breastfeeding is expected to be lower compared to exposure from formula packaged in epoxy-lined cans and using polycarbonate baby bottles(인간의 모유에서 매우 낮은 수준의 BPA가 발견되어 왔기 때문에, 유아의 모유 수유로부터의 BPA 노출은 에폭시 안감 처리된 캔에 포장된

유동식과 폴리카보네이트 젖병 사용으로부터의 노출과 비교해 더 낮을 것으로 예상된다)."라고 언급하며, '비록 모유에서도 낮은 수준의 BPA가 발견되기는 하지만, 캔의 유동식과 폴리카보네이트 젖병과 비교하면 모유 수유에 의한 BPA 노출은 적은 수준'이라는 것을 시사하고 있다. 즉, 아이들에게 인스턴트 유동식을 먹이는 것보다 모유를 먹이는 것이 BPA 노출의 위험성을 줄일 수 있다는 것이다. 따라서 글의 요지로 가장 적절한 것은 '③ Breastfeeding can help little kids be less affected by BPA(모유 수유는 어린아이들이 BPA에 의해 덜 영향을 받도록 도와줄 수 있다).'이다.

오답해설
① 본문에서 '유아들이 다른 사람들보다 BPA에 더 많이 노출될 가능성이 있음'을 언급하고 있으나, 이러한 노출이 성인과 유아(어린이)에게 미치는 영향을 각각 비교하는 내용은 언급되지 않으므로, 글의 요지로 적절하지 않다.
② 본문에서 언급되지 않는 내용이므로 오답이다.
④ 본문에서 '에폭시 안감 처리된 캔에 포장된 유동식으로 인해 유아들이 BPA에 더 많이 노출된다'는 점을 시사하고 있지만, 제조사들이 해당 캔 사용을 중지해야 한다는 내용의 주장은 언급되지 않으므로 오답이다.

해석
소량의 bisphenol A (BPA)가 경화 이후에 폴리카보네이트 제품과 에폭시 안감에 남아 있을 수 있고, 음식과 음료로 배출될 수 있다. 폴리카보네이트 용기와 에폭시 안감 처리된 캔에 저장되거나 가열된 통조림 식품과 액체는 BPA에의 노출의 주요 원인인 것처럼 보인다. 유아들은 그들의 식사가 주로 에폭시 안감 처리된 캔에 든 유동식으로 구성되어 있기 때문에 다른 사람들보다 BPA에 더 많은 노출이 되어 있을 수 있다. 유아들은 또한 폴리카보네이트 젖병에 담긴 유아용 유동식과 다른 액체를 제공받는다. 인간의 모유에서 매우 낮은 수준의 BPA가 발견되어 왔기 때문에, 유아의 모유 수유로부터의 BPA 노출은 에폭시 안감 처리된 캔에 포장된 유동식과 폴리카보네이트 젖병 사용으로부터의 노출과 비교해 더 낮을 것으로 예상된다.
① BPA는 성인보다 아이들에게 더 해로울 수 있다.
② 당신의 아기들을 위해 무(無) BPA 제품을 사용하는 것이 권고된다.
③ 모유 수유는 어린아이들이 BPA에 의해 덜 영향을 받도록 도와줄 수 있다.
④ 유아 유동식 제조사들은 에폭시 안감 처리된 캔 사용을 중지해야 한다.

어휘
polycarbonate 폴리카보네이트(창문, 렌즈 등에 쓰이는 투명하고 단단한 합성수지)
epoxy 에폭시 수지(강력 접착제의 일종)
lining 안감, 내벽   curing 경화
epoxy-lined 에폭시 안감 처리된, 내벽에 에폭시가 덧칠된
formula 유아용 유동식   detect 발견하다, 감지하다

10 정답 ②

정답해설
본문은 '동물복지 과학(Animal welfare science)'에 관한 내용으로, 본문 초반에는 '동물복지 과학의 성장 및 기여'에 대해 언급한 후, 본문 후반에서 '동물복지 과학의 적용성'에 관한 우려에 대해 언급하고 있다. 마지막 문장 "Most animal welfare research has been conducted in small-scale experimental settings, which are often very different from the "real world" of commercial animal production in terms of scale, complexity, automation, and variability(대부분의 동물복지 연구는 소규모의 실험적 환경에서 수행되어 왔으며, 이것들은 종종 규모, 복잡성, 자동화 그리고 가변성의 측면에서 상업적 가축 생산의 "실제 세계"와는 매우 다르다)."를 통해 '연구와 실제의 차이점'에 관해 언급하며, 동물복지 과학이 적용 가능한지 여부는 여전히 미지수임을 암시하고 있다. 따라서 전체 글의 요지로 가장 적절한 보기는 '② Despite its growth, whether animal welfare science can be applied to real situations is doubtable(성장에도 불구하고 동물복지 과학이 실제 상황에 적용될 수 있는지는 불확실하다).'이다.

오답해설
① 본문의 내용과 관련이 없으므로 오답이다.
③ 본문 후반에서 '상업적 환경과 실험적 환경의 상이함'에 대해 언급하며, 동물복지 과학의 적용성에 대한 불확실성을 언급하고 있으므로, 본문의 요지로 적절하지 않다.
④ 본문 전반에서 '동물복지 과학의 성장과 입법 및 규범 제정에 미친 영향'에 대해 언급하고 있으나, 본문 후반에서는 '동물복지 과학의 적용성'에 관해 언급하고 있다. 따라서 해당 보기는 본문의 전반부만을 아우르는 내용이므로, 글 전체의 요지로는 적절하지 않다.

해석
동물복지 과학은 동물들이 의식이 있다는 믿음에 기초한 상대적으로 새로운 분야이지만, 빠르게 성장하여 다양한 분야를 망라하게 되었다. 농장 동물복지에 대해 발표된 많은 연구는 복지 평가의 기초적 생물학적 원리에서부터 주거, 축산, 수송, 그리고 도축 평가 및 향상을 위한 응용에 이르는 범위의 주제를 다룬다. 이러한 연구는 입법과 규범 설정에 영향을 미쳤지만, 상업적 환경에서 그것의 적용 가능성에 대한 우려가 제기되어 왔다. 대부분의 동물복지 연구는 소규모의 실험적 환경에서 수행되어 왔으며, 이것들은 종종 규모, 복잡성, 자동화 그리고 가변성의 측면에서 상업적 가축 생산의 "실제 세계"와는 매우 다르다.
① 동물복지는 모든 국가에서 주요 관심사가 되어야 한다.
② 성장에도 불구하고, 동물복지 과학이 실제 상황에 적용될 수 있는지는 불확실하다.
③ 상업적 가축 생산은 동물복지 과학 적용을 통해 발전될 수 있다.
④ 동물복지 과학은 동물의 복지의 많은 주요 발전들에 기여해왔다.

어휘
relatively 상대적으로   conscious 의식하는
grow to 동사원형 (…하게) 되다[되어가다]
encompass 망라하다, 아우르다, 포함하다
discipline 학과, 과목, 분야   address 다루다
principle 원리   assessment 평가
application 응용, 적용   evaluate 평가하다
husbandry (낙농·양계 등을 포함하는) 농업, 축산
slaughter 도축   legislation 입법
applicability 적용[응용] 가능성   conduct 수행하다
in terms of … 면에서   automation 자동화
variability 가변성, 변동성   doubtable 불확실한, 의심스러운
contribute 기여하다, 공헌하다

기적사 DAY 34

결국엔 성정혜 영어 하프모의고사

| 01 | ② | 02 | ④ | 03 | ② | 04 | ③ | 05 | ② |
| 06 | ④ | 07 | ② | 08 | ④ | 09 | ③ | 10 | ② |

01 정답 ②

정답해설

주어가 'The toxic vapour(독성을 띤 증기)'이므로 동사 자리에 들어갈 가장 적절한 것은 '새어나오다'를 뜻하는 'seep out'의 과거시제인 ② seeped out이다.

해석

독성을 띤 증기가 이윽고 **새어 나와** 피해자들에게 이르게 되었다.
① 취소했다
② 새어 나왔다
③ 제외했다
④ ~에서 지웠다

어휘

toxic 유독성의 vapour 증기
victim 피해자, 희생자
cancel 취소하다(cancel-canceled[cancelled]-canceled[cancelled])
seep out 새어나오다 exclude 제외하다
scratch off ~에서 지우다

오답률 TOP 3
02 정답 ④

정답해설

문맥상 '~을 중시하다'를 뜻하는 ④ set store by를 사용하여 '비평가들의 의견들을 중요하게 여긴 적 없다'고 하는 것이 가장 자연스럽다.

해석

비평가들의 의견들은 그의 책 판매량에 어떠한 영향도 미치지 못했기 때문에 그는 결코 그것들을 **중요히 여긴** 적이 없다.
① 막았다
② 자세히 조사했다
③ 충족시켰다
④ ~을 중시했다

어휘

critic 비평가 blot out 막다
pore over 자세히 조사하다 cater to 충족시키다
set store by ~을 중시하다

03 정답 ②

정답해설

목적어로 'the seeds'를 가질 동사로 가장 적절한 것은 '뿌리다'를 뜻하는 ② sow이다.

해석

여름에 씨앗을 **뿌리기**만 하면 당신은 가을에 아름다운 꽃들을 볼 수 있다.
① 바느질하다
② 뿌리다
③ ~에 나타나다
④ ~에 빠지다

어휘

sew 바느질하다 sow 뿌리다
loom on ~에 나타나다 lapse into ~에 빠지다

04 정답 ③

정답해설

한 기업에 지원한 면접 대상자와 면접관의 대화이다. 면접관은 '기업에서는 고객들을 상대하는 일에 능숙한 사람을 찾고 있다'고 하자, 면접 대상자는 자신 있다면서 '고객들을 만족시키는 일에 ~하다'라고 답변한다. 따라서 빈칸에 들어갈 가장 적절한 것은 ③ 'know the ropes(요령을 알다)'이다.

오답해설

① 면접 대상자는 고객들을 대하는 것에 자신이 있다면서 고객들을 만족시키는 '척한다(make believe)'라고 말하는 것은 대화의 흐름상 부자연스럽다.
② 면접 대상자는 고객들을 만족시키는 데 자신이 '난동을 피운다(make a scene)'라고 이야기하는 것은 빈칸에 들어갈 말로 어색하다.
④ 면접관은 고객을 대하는 데 능숙한 사람을 찾고 있다고 하자, 면접 대상자는 자신이 있다며 고객들을 만족하게 하는 데 자신이 '기운을 차린다(pull myself together)'라고 말한다. 이는 문맥상 빈칸에 들어갈 말로 적합하지 않다.

해석

면접관: 이 회사에 지원한 이유가 무엇인가요?
면접 대상자: 우선, 저는 이 회사의 신조가 아주 마음에 들었습니다. '선택과 집중'은 제 인생의 신조이기도 합니다.
면접관: 신조는 힘들 때 자신을 도와주기도 하죠. 당신의 과거 일 경력에 대해 말씀해주시겠습니까?
면접 대상자: 저는 보험 관련 기업에서 일했었습니다. 그래서 저는 많은 고객을 일대일로 만나야 했습니다. 그런 경험들을 통해, 저는 고객들을 능숙하게 상대하는 방법을 배웠다고 확신할 수 있습니다.
면접관: 우리 회사는 고객들을 능숙하게 상대하는 능력을 갖춘 사람과 일하는 것을 기대하고 있습니다.
면접 대상자: 저는 그것에 자신 있습니다. 저는 고객을 만족시키는 일에 <u>요령을 알고 있습니다.</u>
① ~한 척하다
② 난동을 피우다
③ 요령을 알다
④ 기운을 차리다

어휘

apply for ~에 지원하다 insurance 보험
look forward to ~을 기대하다 be capable of ~할 수 있다
deal with 다루다, 대처하다, 대하다 proficient 능숙한, 숙달한
make believe ~한 척하다 make a scene 난동을 피우다
know the ropes 요령을 알다 pull oneself together 기운을 차리다

05 정답 ②

정답해설

② 출제 포인트: 관용표현(between A and B)/등위접속사
「between A and B」는 'A와 B 사이에'를 뜻한다. 해당 문장은 문맥상

'조직과 고객 사이의'가 자연스러우므로 'between A and B'를 사용해야 하나 'and'의 자리에 접속사 'so'를 사용하였으므로 틀린 문장이다. 따라서 'so'를 'and'로 수정해야 한다.

오답해설

① **출제 포인트: 동명사의 역할**
밑줄 친 'building'은 동명사이며 전치사 'to'의 목적어에 해당한다. 또한 'building' 이후에 목적어 'a continuing long-term relationship'이 있으므로 능동형 동명사 'building'은 옳은 표현이다.

③ **출제 포인트: to부정사의 형용사적 용법/to부정사의 부사적 용법**
밑줄 친 'to increase'는 to부정사로 명사 'action'을 수식하는 경우 형용사적 용법으로 볼 수 있으며 또한 동사 'are taking'을 수식하는 경우 부사적 용법으로도 볼 수 있다. 따라서 to부정사로 쓰인 'to increase'는 옳은 표현이다.

④ **출제 포인트: 능동태 vs. 수동태**
밑줄 친 'be produced'는 'produce'의 수동태로 이후에 목적어가 없고 「by+행위자」인 'by a customer'가 왔으므로 옳은 표현이다.

해석

많은 기업들이 성공적인 마케팅 전략의 궁극적인 목적으로써 조직과 고객 사이의 계속적인 장기간 관계를 구축하는 것에 그들의 관심을 돌렸다. 그들은 평생 고객 가치를 늘리는 조치를 취하고 있다 - 긴 시간에 걸쳐 고객에 의해 생산될 수 있는 수익 흐름의 현재 가치를 말이다.

어휘

continuing 계속적인, 연속적인   take action 조치를 취하다
revenue 수익

오답률 TOP 2

06 정답 ④

정답해설

④ **출제 포인트: 자릿값(명사 vs. 명사로 고착화된 동명사)**
'rising'은 동명사나 분사가 아닌, 명사의 의미로는 '봉기, 폭동' 혹은 '(불가산적인) 상승' 등이 있다. 해당 문장의 경우 명사로 쓰이는 것은 옳으나, 문맥상 수량, 비율, 숫자의 가산적 상승 개념으로서 '기온의 점진적 상승'이므로 정확히 명사 'rising'을 명사 'rise(상승, 인상)'로 사용하여, 가산적 상승의 의미를 포함한 명사로 수정해야 한다.

오답해설

① **출제 포인트: 목적격 관계대명사 생략/관용표현(relate A to B)**
밑줄 친 'we face to' 앞에는 명사(구) 'the large-scale threats'를 선행사로 하는 목적격 관계대명사 'that' 또는 'which'가 생략되어 있다. 이때 'to'는 목적격 관계대명사절의 동사 'face'와 연결된 것이 아닌 주절의 동사 'relate'와 연결되어 「relate A to B」의 형태로 사용된 것임에 유의해야 한다.

② **출제 포인트: 현재분사 vs. 과거분사**
과거분사 'boiled'와 수식하는 대상 'frog'가 수동관계이며 해석상 '삶은 개구리'가 자연스러우므로 밑줄 친 'boiled frog'는 옳은 표현이다.

③ **출제 포인트: 능동태 vs. 수동태**
밑줄 친 'is slowly heated'는 주격 관계대명사 'that'이 이끄는 절로 선행사는 'water'이며 해석상 '물이 천천히 가열되다'가 자연스러우므로 옳게 사용되었다.

해석

Ornstein과 Ehrlich는 우리가 직면하는 대규모의 위협들을 그들이 "삶은 개구리 신드롬"이라고 부르는 것과 관련짓는다. 천천히 가열되는 물이 담긴 팬 속의 개구리는 서서히 상승하는 온도를 감지할 수 없다.

어휘

relate A to B A를 B와 관련시키다   face ~을 직면하다, ~을 마주보다
detect ~을 감지하다, 발견하다   rising 봉기, 폭동
rise 상승, 인상

---

07 정답 ②

정답해설

② **출제 포인트: that vs. what**
밑줄 친 'that'은 이후에 오는 절이 목적어가 없는 불완전한 형태이므로 관계대명사임을 알 수 있으나 밑줄 친 'that' 이전에 선행사가 없으므로 'that'을 선행사를 포함한 관계대명사 'what'으로 수정해야 한다. 이때 해당 문장에서 'term'은 불완전타동사로 「term+목적어+목적격 보어[명사]」의 형태로 사용되었음에 유의해야 한다.

오답해설

① **출제 포인트: 현재분사 vs. 과거분사**
밑줄 친 'shared'는 'share'의 과거분사로 수식하는 대상 'values'와 수동관계이며 해석상 '공유된 가치'가 자연스러우므로 과거분사 'shared'는 옳은 표현이다.

③ **출제 포인트: 타동사로 착각하기 쉬운 완전자동사**
밑줄 친 'converge'는 해당 문장에서 완전자동사로 쓰였으며 '완전자동사+전치사' 형태로 사용되어 목적어를 가진다. 따라서 밑줄 친 'converge on'은 옳은 표현이다.

④ **출제 포인트: 명사절을 이끄는 접속사 that**
밑줄 친 'that'은 명사절 'the solution they came up with is the best one'을 이끄는 접속사로 수여동사 'convince'의 직접목적어 역할을 하고 있다. 또한 'that'이 이끄는 절 내의 주어는 'the solution ~ with'로 'they came up with'와 'the solution' 사이에는 목적격 관계대명사 'that' 또는 'which'가 생략되어 있다.

해석

어떤 공유된 가치와 목표가 없는 다양성은 집단을 분열시킬 가능성이 있다. 그러나, 공유된 가치와 목표는 Irving Janis가 집단 사고라고 칭하는 것으로 이어질 수 있다. 집단 사고는 집단들이 하나의 문제에 대해 하나의 답으로 수렴하고, 비판적으로 해결책을 평가하기보다는, 그들이 스스로와 서로에게 그들이 제시한 해결책이 최선이라고 납득시킬 때 일어나는 것을 말한다.

어휘

diversity 다양성   groupthink 집단 사고
lead to ~로 이어지다
term+목적어+목적격 보어[명사] ~을 ~라고 칭하다
converge 모여들다, 집중되다   come up with (해답·돈 등을) 내놓다

---

08 정답 ④

정답해설

본문 첫 문장 "New research on children with attention deficit hyperactivity disorder(ADHD) might show some tasks can improve working memory in general, and could help children with the condition(주의력 결핍 과잉 행동 장애(ADHD)를 앓는 아이들에 대한 새로운 연구는 어떤 과제들이 전반적으로 작동 기억을 향상시킬 수 있으며, 그 질환을 앓는 아이들에게 도움이 될 수 있다는 것을 보여줄 수 있다)"을 통해 전체 글의 요지를 파악할 수 있다. 또한 이후 언급되는 실험의 결과(작동 기억 향상 → 과잉 활동과 부주의의 감소)로 더욱 구체적으로 정답의 힌트를 획득할 수 있다. 즉, 작동 기억 능력이 증가된 아이들은 ADHD 증상의 완화를 경험하였

으므로, 작동 기억 능력의 증가가 아이들에게 긍정적인 영향을 미친 것을 알 수 있다. 따라서 정답은 '④ Increasing working memory capacity can have a positive impact on kids with ADHD(작동 기억 능력을 증가시키는 것이 ADHD를 앓는 아이들에게 긍정적인 영향을 미칠 수 있다)'이다.

오답해설

① 본문의 주요 내용은 'ADHD를 앓는 아이들의 작동 기억이 향상될 수 있으며, 이러한 작동 기억 향상 훈련을 거친 아이들의 ADHD 증상(hyperactivity and inattention)이 완화되었다'는 것이므로, 'ADHD와 빈약한 작동 기억의 관계'를 언급하는 ①은 해당 지문의 요지로 적절하지 않다.
② 본문에서는 약물을 통한 치료에 대해서는 언급되지 않으므로 오답이다.
③ 본문과 관련 없는 내용이므로 오답이다.

해석

주의력 결핍 과잉 행동 장애(ADHD)를 앓는 아이들에 대한 새로운 연구는 어떤 과제들이 전반적으로 작동 기억을 향상시킬 수 있으며, 그 질환을 앓는 아이들에게 도움이 될 수 있다는 것을 보여줄 수 있다. Torkel Klingberg는 ADHD를 앓는 53명의 아이들을 대상으로 참가자의 절반은 난이도가 점차 증가하는 작동 기억 과제를 연습하는 무작위 대조 실험을 실시했다. 나머지 절반은 아이들이 과제를 더 잘하게 되었을 때 더 어려워지지 않는 과제를 풀었다. 점점 더 어려워지는 기억 과제를 수행한 아이들이 연습 과제와는 다른 두 가지 작동 기억 테스트에서 대조군보다 더 나은 성과를 보였다. 게다가, 기억 훈련을 한 아이들의 부모들은 교육 활동을 마친 3개월 후 그들의 아이들의 과잉 활동과 부주의의 감소를 보고한 반면, 대조군 참가자들의 부모들은 그렇지 않았다.
① ADHD는 아이들이 빈약한 작동 기억을 갖도록 유발할 수 있다.
② ADHD 증상은 약물을 통해 효과적으로 줄일 수 있다.
③ ADHD 환자들은 과제를 마치는 데 어려움을 겪는 경향이 있다.
④ 작동 기억 능력을 증가시키는 것이 ADHD를 앓는 아이들에게 긍정적인 영향을 미칠 수 있다.

어휘

attention deficit hyperactivity disorder
주의력 결핍 과잉 행동 장애(ADHD)
randomize 임의[무작위] 추출하다
control (실험 결과를) 대조하다, 조사하여 밝히다
trial 실험, 테스트　　　　　control group 대조군
hyperactivity 과잉[과대] 활동　　inattention 부주의
intervention 개입, 치료, 교육 활동

09 정답 ③

정답해설

주어진 문장은 '1일 허용섭취량(TDI)'을 소개하고 있다. 이후에는 주어진 문장에서 소개된 TDI에 대해 자세히 설명하는 (B)가 이어지는 것이 자연스럽다. 이후, (B)의 "estimates the amount of BPA in food that can be ingested daily over a lifetime without appreciable health risk(주목할 만한 건강상의 위험 없이 평생 동안 하루에 먹을 수 있는 음식에 함유된 BPA의 양을 추정한다)"에서 설명한 내용을 'In other words(다시 말해)'를 이용해 '재서술'하고 있는 (C)가 이어지는 것이 적절하다. (C) 후반부에서 'TDI에 도달하는 것'에 대해 언급되었으므로, 이에 관한 예시를 'For example(예를 들어)'을 이용해 설명하는 (A)가 이어지는 것이 알맞다. 따라서 정답은 '③ (B) - (C) - (A)'이다.

오답해설

② (C)의 'In other words(다시 말해)'로 보아 (C) 이전에는 (C) 전반부에서 언급된 내용과 동일한 내용이 등장해야 하므로, (A) 이후에 (C)가 이어지는 것은 어색하다.

나머지 보기는 문맥상 어색하므로 오답이다.

해석

1일 허용섭취량, 또는 TDI는 국제적으로 확립된 BPA와 같은 화학물질의 안전 수준이다.
(B) 그것은 전체 인구에게 적용되는 BPA의 안전 수준에 대한 보수적인 추정치이며, 주목할 만한 건강상의 위험 없이 평생 동안 하루에 먹을 수 있는 음식에 함유된 BPA의 양을 추정한다.
(C) 다시 말해, 그것은 매일 하루에 안전하게 섭취될 수 있는 양이다. BPA의 TDI에 도달하기 위해서는 극도로 많은 양의 음식과 음료가 섭취되어야 할 것이다.
(A) 예를 들어, 몸무게가 9kg인 9개월 아기는 TDI에 도달하기 위해, 그 커스터드가 CHOICE의 조사에서 발견된 가장 높은 수준의 BPA를 함유하고 있다고 가정할 때, 매일 BPA를 함유한 통조림 아기용 커스터드를 1kg 이상 먹어야 할 것이다.

어휘

tolerable 허용할 수 있는, 참을 수 있는
intake 섭취　　　　　conservative 보수적인, 적게 잡은
ingest 삼키다, 먹다　　appreciable 주목할 만한

10 정답 ②

정답해설

주어진 문장의 'Yet(그러나)'으로 보아, 주어진 문장 이전에는 주어진 문장과는 대조적인 내용이 등장해야 한다는 것을 알 수 있다. 주어진 문장은 '인간이 동물을 하등한 존재로 여겼다'는 내용이므로, 주어진 문장 이전에는 '인간과 동물의 관계가 동등 또는 유사한 위치에 있다'는 내용이 등장하는 것이 자연스러울 것이다. ② 이전 문장에서 '물활론자의 영성(Animist spirituality)'에 관한 예시를 들어, 해당 신앙에서는 'predator[포식자(인간)]'와 'prey[먹이(동물)]' 사이의 의사소통의 개방된 경로를 상정했다고 언급하고 있으므로, 인간과 동물이 서로 동등한 관계에 있다는 것을 가정한 신앙이라는 것을 알 수 있다. 반면 ② 이후의 문장에서는 '중세 유럽인(Medieval Europeans)'에 관한 예시를 들어, '동물을 처벌은 하지만 동물의 영혼 또는 동물이 천국에 들어가는 것을 인정하지 않았다'고 언급하고 있으므로, '동물이 인간보다 하위에 있는 상태'임을 알 수 있다. 따라서 내용을 전환하는 역할을 수행할 수 있는 주어진 문장이 ②에 들어가는 것이 자연스럽다.

오답해설

① 주어진 문장이 '대조, 역접'을 나타내는 'Yet(그러나)'으로 시작하고 있는데, 본문의 첫 번째 문장의 내용과 주어진 문장의 관계가 대조 관계가 아니기 때문에 ①의 위치에 주어진 문장이 들어가는 것은 어색하다.

나머지 위치는 문맥상 어색하므로 오답이다.

해석

다른 동물에 대한 인간의 호기심과, 만일 그들이 생각을 가지고 있다면, 그들의 생각이 무엇과 같은지 아는 것의 외견상 불가능함은 우리 종의 역사 전체 동안 지속되어 왔다. (①) 최초의 인간 철학인 물활론자의 영성은 포식자와 먹이 간의 의사소통의 개방된 경로를 상정한다. (② <u>그러나 많은 사회는 동물을 사람이 정상에 있는 존재의 거대한 사슬의 하위 단계에 갇힌 덜 중요한 존재, 또는 심지어 (감정이 없이) 기계적으로 행동하는 동물로서 낙인을 찍는 유사한 경향을 보여준다</u>.) 중세 유럽인들은 범죄와 경범죄를 이유로 동물들이 재판을 받도록 했으나, 그들에게 영혼이나 천국으로의 접근권을 부여하지는 않았다. (③) 오늘날까지도, 우리는 우리가 일터에 있는 동안 우리의 개가 지루해하는 것에 대해 걱정하지만, 그들의 일생동안 매일 똑같은 사료를

그들에게 먹이는 것에 대해서는 아무 생각이 없다. (④) 이러한 양면 가치는 우리 자신의 것과는 다른 생각의 가능성에 직면했을 때의 우리 자신의 불확실성과 두려움을 암시한다.

어휘

parallel 아주 유사한[병행하는] brand 낙인을 찍다
lesser ~ 보다 중요하지 않은, 뒤떨어진
automation 기계적으로 행동하는 [로봇 같은] 사람[동물]
rung (사회·조직 내 서열상의) 단계 apex 정상, 절정
seeming 외견상의, 겉보기의 persist 지속하다
animist 물활론자, 정령 신앙자 spirituality 정신성, 영성
posit (주장·논의의 근거로 삼기 위해 무엇을) 사실로 상정하다[받아들이다]
medieval 중세의 stand trial 재판을 받다
misdemeanor 경범죄, 비행 grant 주다, 수여하다
ambivalence 양면 가치, 이중 경향, 모순
point to 암시하다, 가리키다 confront 직면하게 만들다

결국엔 성정혜 영어 하프모의고사
기적사 DAY 35

| 01 | ① | 02 | ③ | 03 | ① | 04 | ④ | 05 | ④ |
| 06 | ③ | 07 | ④ | 08 | ③ | 09 | ④ | 10 | ③ |

01 정답 ①

정답해설

'여객기 실종'과 '비행기 추적 체계 개선의 요구' 사이의 인과 관계를 고려하면 '박차를 가하다'를 뜻하는 'spur'이 가장 적절하다. 해당 문장에서는 'spur'의 과거시제 ① spurred가 문맥상 빈칸에 들어가기에 가장 적절하다.

해석

근래의 항공기 사건, 특히 지난 3월 말레이시아 제트 여객기 실종은 개선된 국제적 비행기 추적 체계를 위한 널리 퍼진 요구에 **박차를 가했다**.
① 박차를 가했다
② 줄였다, 껐다
③ 감시했다, 관리했다
④ 생략했다, 없앴다

어휘

incident 사건 disappearance 실종, 사라짐, 소멸
jetliner 제트 여객기 spur 박차를 가하다
damp down 줄이다, 끄다 supervise 감시하다, 관리하다
dispense with 생략하다, 없애다

02 정답 ③

정답해설

문맥상 '고통을 받다'를 뜻하는 'suffer'를 활용한 ③ suffered가 빈칸에 들어가기에 가장 적절하다.

해석

한국인들은 일본의 잔인함에 **고통을 받았고**, 독립운동가들은 투옥되고, 고문을 받거나 죽임을 당했다.
① 의지했다
② 뺐다, 공제했다
③ 고통받았다
④ (대사를) 상기시켜 줬다

어휘

brutality 잔인함, 무자비, 만행 independence 독립, 자립
jail 투옥하다; 교도소, 감옥 torture 고문하다, 괴롭히다; 고문
resort 의지하다 subtract 빼다, 공제하다
suffer 고통받다 prompt (대사를) 상기시켜 주다

오답률 TOP 1
03 정답 ①

정답해설

문맥상 '중단하다, 정지하다'를 뜻하는 'suspend'를 활용하여 '주민들의 반대로 인해 재개발 계획을 중단했다'고 하는 것이 가장 자연스럽다. 따라서 빈칸에는 현재완료의 형태인 'have + p.p.(과거분사)'에 해당되는 과거분사 ① suspended가 가장 적절하다.

| 해석 |

정부는 주민들의 반대로 인해 그것의 재개발 계획을 **중지했다**.
① 중단했다, 정지했다, 유예했다
② 겁나게 했다
③ 강조했다
④ 나타났다

| 어휘 |

redevelopment 재개발, 부흥, 재건   resident 거주자[주민], 투숙객
suspend 중단하다, 정지하다, 유예하다
terrify 겁나게 하다   emphasize 강조하다
loom 나타나다

04 정답 ④

| 정답해설 |

B가 달리기 경주에서 1등을 한 상황에 대해 A와 B가 대화를 나누는 지문이다. A는 '처음 달리기를 했을 때를 생각해보면 B가 이기는 것은 상상하지 못했다'라고 이야기한다. 이에 B는 '자신이 걸음마에서 달리기 선수까지 ~했다'라고 이야기한다. 따라서 빈칸에 들어갈 가장 적절한 것은 ④ 'come a long way(크게 발전하다)'이다.

| 오답해설 |

① B가 달리기 경주에서 우승을 한 상황에서 자신이 걸음마에서 선수가 되기까지 '마무리 지었다(wrap up)'고 이야기하는 것은 문맥상 어색하다.
② 달리기 경주에서 우승한 B가 처음 경기장을 뛰던 시절을 상기하며 걸음마에서 선수가 되기까지 '어색한 분위기를 깼다(break the ice)'라고 말하는 것은 대화의 흐름상 적절하지 않다.
③ 달리기 경주에서 우승을 한 상황에서 B가 걸음마에서 선수가 되기까지 '갑자기 죽었다(buy the farm)'고 하는 것은 맥락상 빈칸에 들어갈 말로 부자연스럽다.

| 해석 |

A: 경주에서 1등한 것을 축하해! 네가 해낼 줄 알았어!
B: 정말 고마워. 네 도움 없이는 경주를 절대 끝낼 수 없었을 거야.
A: 아무것도 아니었어. 네가 처음으로 경기장을 뛰던 것을 생각하면, 네가 이길 거라고는 상상도 못 했어.
B: 나도 마찬가지야. 나는 걸음마에서 달리기 선수까지 <u>크게 발전했어</u>.
A: 그러니까! 잘했어! 우리는 가서 네 우승을 축하해야겠어.
B: 다시 한번 고마워. 네 헌신을 절대 잊지 않을게.
① 마무리 짓다
② 어색한 분위기를 깨다
③ 갑자기 죽다
④ 크게 발전하다

| 어휘 |

celebrate 축하하다   commitment 헌신; 약속; 전념
wrap up 마무리 짓다   break the ice 어색한 분위기를 깨다
buy the farm 갑자기 죽다   come a long way 크게 발전하다

05 정답 ④

| 정답해설 |

④ 출제 포인트: 타동사로 착각하기 쉬운 완전자동사

'correspond'는 완전자동사이므로 이후에 전치사 없이 목적어를 가질 수 없다. 해당 문장은 'correspond' 이후에 전치사 없이 목적어 'the boundaries'를 가지므로 틀린 문장이다. 따라서 'correspond'를 'correspond with' 또는 'correspond to'로 수정해야 한다.

| 오답해설 |

① **출제 포인트: 능동태 vs. 수동태**
밑줄 친 'are left'는 완전타동사 'leave'의 수동태이며 이후에 전명구 'with the impression'이 왔으므로 옳은 표현이다.

② **출제 포인트: 동격의 접속사 that**
밑줄 친 'that'은 명사 'impression'과 명사절 'political boundaries and cultural boundaries are the same'이 동격임을 나타내는 접속사이다.

③ **출제 포인트: 현재분사 vs. 과거분사**
밑줄 친 'organized'는 'organize'의 과거분사로 수식하는 대상 'unit'과 수동관계이며 해석상 '조직된 연합'이 자연스러우므로 과거분사 'organized'는 옳은 표현이다.

| 해석 |

특정 문화 체계의 정치 조직을 말할 때, 우리는 자주 정치적 경계와 문화적 경계가 같다는 인상을 받게 된다. 그러나 정치, 또는 정치적으로 조직된 연합의 그 경계는 삶의 특정 방식의 경계와 일치할 수도 일치하지 않을 수도 있다.

| 어휘 |

organization 조직, 기구   impression 인상, 느낌
boundary 경계   polity 정치
correspond with[to] ~와 일치하다

오답률 TOP 2

06 정답 ③

| 정답해설 |

③ 출제 포인트: 수동태 불가동사

'persist'는 완전자동사이므로 수동태를 사용할 수 없다. 따라서 수동태로 쓰인 'is persisted'를 능동태 'persists'로 수정해야 한다. 이때 'persist'는 주격관계대명사 'that'이 이끄는 절의 동사이므로 선행사 'a problem'에 수일치 해 단수 형태의 동사인 'persists'로 수정하는 것이 옳다.

| 오답해설 |

① **출제 포인트: 전치사 + 관계대명사**
「전치사 + 관계대명사」는 이후에 오는 절의 형태가 완전하다. 밑줄 친 'in which'는 「전치사 + 관계대명사」이며 이후에 오는 절의 형태가 완전하므로 옳은 표현이다.

② **출제 포인트: to부정사의 명사적 용법/to부정사의 태**
밑줄 친 'to be perceived'는 불완전자동사 'is'의 주격 보어로 to부정사의 명사적 용법에 해당한다. 'perceive'는 불완전타동사로 사용되는 경우「perceive+목적어+(as)형용사(구)」의 구조로 쓰여 '~를 …으로 여기다'의 의미로 사용된다. 밑줄 친 'to be perceived'는 'to perceive'의 수동 형태로 쓰여 이후에 바로「as+형용사(구)」인 'as physically competent'가 왔으므로 'to be perceived'는 옳은 표현이다.

④ **출제 포인트: 형용사로 고착화된 과거분사/타동사구[완전타동사 + 목적어 + 전치사 + 목적어]**
'skilled'는 과거분사 형태의 형용사로 '능숙한, 숙련된, 노련한'을 뜻한다. 밑줄 친 'for less-skilled'에서 'less-skilled'가 명사(구) 'children and youth'를 수식하므로 옳게 사용되었으며 이때 'for'는 'provide'와 연결되어「provide+사물+for+대상」의 형태로 사용된 것임에 유의해야 한다.

해석
어린이와 청소년이 그들의 또래 사이에서 더 나은 지위를 얻을 수 있는 방법은 신체적으로 능숙한 것으로 여겨지는 것이다. 그러나, 체육 교육에서 지속되는 문제는 능숙하지 못한 어린이와 청소년들을 위해 공평한 학습 경험을 제공하지 못하는 무능력이다.

어휘
peer 또래, 동료
competent 능숙한
equitable 공평한, 공정한
perceive A as B A를 B로 여기다
persist 지속되다, 계속되다
skilled 능숙한, 숙련된, 노련한

07 정답 ④

정답해설
④ 출제 포인트: take의 관용표현(It + takes + 목적어 + 시간 + to부정사)
「It + takes + 목적어 + 시간 + to부정사」는 관용표현으로 '~가 ~하는 데 시간이 걸리다'를 뜻한다. 해당 문장은 'It took' 이후에 「전치사+목적어」 형태의 'for them'이 왔으므로 밑줄 친 'for them'을 'them'으로 수정해야 한다. 또는 「It+takes+시간+for+목적어+to부정사」의 형태를 이용하여 'It took for them a minute~'을 'It took a minute for them~'으로 수정해도 옳다.

오답해설
① **출제 포인트: 관계부사 vs. 관계대명사**
밑줄 친 'where'는 'a seminar'를 선행사로 하는 관계부사이며 이후에 오는 절이 완전한 형태이므로 옳은 표현이다.

② **출제 포인트: what vs. that**
밑줄 친 'what'은 선행사를 포함한 관계대명사로 선행사가 없으며 밑줄 친 'what' 이후의 문장이 전치사 'like'의 목적어가 없는 불완전한 문장이므로 관계대명사 'what'이 옳게 사용되었다.

③ **출제 포인트: 접속사가 살아있는 분사구문**
밑줄 친 'seen'이 포함된 'when ~ earth'는 접속사 'when'이 생략되지 않은 분사구문으로 생략된 주어 'Brazil'과 수동관계이며 'seen' 이후에 전명구 'from the center'가 오므로 밑줄 친 과거분사 'seen'은 옳은 표현이다.

해석
나는 연설자의 슬라이드인 북미의 지도가 위아래가 뒤집어져 있었던 한 세미나에 참가한 적이 있다. 연설자가 재빨리 말했다, "북미를 남반구에서 보았을 때 이렇게 보이죠." 그리고 이것은 많은 웃음을 자아냈다. 그 후 일 년 정도가 지나, 나는 내 브라질 지도가 뒷면으로 놓인 상태로 연설을 하고 있었고, 그래서 내가 말했다, "지구 중심에서 보았을 때 브라질이 이렇게 보이죠." 그들이 그것을 이해하는 데에 시간이 잠깐 걸렸지만, 그들도 이 말에 웃었다.

어휘
attend 참석하다
hemisphere 반구
upside down 거꾸로
backwards 뒤의; 뒷걸음질하는

오답률 TOP 3
08 정답 ③

정답해설
본문은 '작동 기억(working memory)과 아이들의 학업 성과(academic performance) 간의 관계'에 대해 설명하고 있다. 본문 중반 ② 문장부터 본문의 마지막까지 '작동 기억'을 '양동이(bucket)'에 비유하여 설명하고 있는데, 중간에 ③ 문장에서 '작동 기억을 향상시킬 수 있는 방법'이 언급되는 것은 문맥상 부자연스럽다. 따라서 정답은 ③이다.

오답해설
① 이전 문장에서 언급된 '빈약한 작동 기억에 의해 영향을 받는 영역들' 중 '가장 크게 영향을 받는 영역을 ①에서 강조하여 언급하고 있으므로 문맥상 자연스럽다.

④ 'Every drop that you add(당신이 추가하는 모든 물방울)'가 ②에서 언급된 'a glass of water(물 한 컵)'과 연결되는 내용이므로, ②와 ④가 연달아 이어지는 것이 자연스럽다.

해석
작동 기억은 실행 기능(예를 들어, 계획하기, 착수하기, 과제 관찰하기, 조직하기 등)의 중요한 부분이기 때문에 학업 성과에 있어서 매우 중요하다. 학교에서 빈약한 작동 기억에 의해 크게 영향을 받는 학습 영역은: 수학, 독해, 복잡한 문제해결, 그리고 시험을 보는 것이다. ① 학업에 미치는 가장 큰 영향은 첫 두 영역에서의 어려움으로부터 발생한다. ② 작동 기억은 물 한 컵을 이용해 당신이 계속해서 채울 수 있는 양동이와 매우 유사하다. ③ *그것은 단순한 게임과 매일 행해지는 활동을 통해 향상될 수 있다.* ④ 당신이 추가하는 모든 물방울은 시간이 지나 기억의 반복된 사용의 부족을 통해 증발해버리지 않는 한 양동이 안에 남아 있다. 빈약한 작동 기억을 지닌 아이들에게는, 양동이 바닥에 구멍이 있는 것과 매우 유사하다. 당신은 계속해서 컵 속의 물(정보/지식)을 따라 넣을 수 있지만, 그것은 지속적으로 흘러나간다.

어휘
working memory 작동[심리] 기억
executive 실행하는, 집행상의
bucket 양동이
day-to-day (일이) 매일 행해지는, 그날그날의
evaporate 증발하다, 사라지다
tip (내용물을) 따르다; 기울어지다; 끝부분; 봉사료
drain (물을) 빼내다, (액체를) 따라 내다
critical 중요한; 비판적인
initiate 시작하다, 착수시키다

09 정답 ④

정답해설
(A) 'BPA가 피부로 쉽게 흡수된다', 'BPA가 가득한 영수증을 자주 만지는 사람들의 체내에 평균 이상의 화학물질이 존재한다'는 두 가지 연구 결과로 인해 BPA가 다시 한번 사람들의 관심을 받고 있다는 내용이다. (A) 빈칸 이후 'calls for tougher regulation of the chemical(화학물질에 대한 더 강력한 규제 요구)'로 보아, 빈칸에는 'BPA와 같은 화학물질 규제에 대한 더 강력한 규제 요구'가 '증가했다'라는 의미가 되는 것이 문맥상 자연스러우므로, 'fortify(강화하다)' 또는 'strengthen(강화하다)'이 빈칸에 적절하다.

(B) 빈칸 이전에서 '더 강력한 규제 요구'가 있다고 언급하고 있으므로, 현재는 '더 강력한 규제가 부재함'을 유추할 수 있다. 즉, 소량의 BPA도 유해할 수 있다는 증거가 있음에도 불구하고, 규제 기관들이 해당 화학물질에 대한 단호한 조치를 취하지 않고 있다는 내용이므로, 빈칸에는 '해당 증거가 규제 기관들을 설득하지 못했다'는 내용이 들어가는 것이 적절하다. 단, 빈칸 이전에 'has yet to'는 '아직 ~하지 않았다'라는 부정의 의미가 이미 포함되어있으므로, 문맥상 'encourage(권장하다)' 또는 'convince(설득하다)'가 들어가야 한다.

따라서 정답은 '④ strengthen(강화하다) – convince(설득하다)'이다.

오답해설
① (A) 'abate'는 '약화시키다'라는 의미이므로, 본문의 내용과 반대되는 뜻을 가리킨다. 따라서 빈칸에 적절하지 않다.

② (B)의 'dissuade'는 '단념시키다'라는 의미로 문맥상 적절하지 않다.

③ 문맥상 어색하다.

해석

두 가지 연구가 논란이 많은 합성물인 bisphenol A (BPA)가 다시 세간의 관심을 받도록 했다. 한 연구는 그 화학물질이 피부를 통해 쉽게 흡수된다는 것을 발견했고, 반면에 또 다른 연구는 BPA가 가득한 계산대 영수증을 일상적으로 만지는 사람들이 그들의 몸에 평균적인 화학물질 수준보다 더 많이 가지고 있다는 것을 발견했다. 종합적으로, 그 결과들은 플라스틱 제조에 널리 사용되는 화학물질에 대한 더 강력한 규제 요구를 (A) 강화시킨다. BPA는 서양 국가의 대부분의 사람들에게서 발견할 수 있다. 동물 연구는 고용량이 유해하다는 것을 보여주었지만, 저용량 또한 유해할 수도 있다는 일부 증거는 아직 규제 기관들이 그 복합물에 대한 단호한 조치를 취하도록 (B) 설득하지는 못했다.

(A)	(B)
① 약화시키다	권장하다
② 강화하다	단념시키다
③ 둔화시키다	허용하다
④ 강화하다	설득하다

어휘

controversial 논란이 많은 compound 합성물, 복합물
limelight 각광, 세상의 이목[관심] readily 손쉽게, 순조롭게
absorb 흡수하다[받아들이다] -laden …이 가득한
till (상점의) 계산대 call 요구, 요청
detectable 발견할 수 있는, 탐지할 수 있는
confirm (특히 증거를 들어) 사실임을 보여주다 [확인해 주다]
dose (어느 정도의) 양, 약간
have yet to 동사원형 아직 ~하지 않았다
regulator 규제[단속] 기관[담당자] decisive 단호한, 결단력 있는
abate 약화시키다, 줄이다 fortify (감정·태도를) 강화하다
dissuade 단념시키다, 만류하다 blunt 약화[둔화]시키다
convince 설득하다

10 정답 ③

정답해설

본문은 '동물의 수면과 꿈에 대한 Aristotle의 견해와 오늘날의 연구 방향'에 대해 설명하는 글이다. 네 번째 문장 후반부에서 언급된 동물의 꿈에 관한 Aristotle의 의견 "dogs show their dreaming by barking in their sleep(개는 수면 중 짖음으로써 그들이 꿈을 꾸는 것을 보여준다)"에 따르면, '개가 자면서 짖는 것이 개가 꿈을 꾸는 것을 보여준다'고 한다. 따라서 '③ According to Aristotle, dogs bark while sleeping because they are dreaming(Aristotle에 따르면, 개는 꿈을 꾸고 있기 때문에 잠자는 동안 짖는다).'은 글의 내용과 일치한다.

오답해설

① 첫 번째 문장 "Almost all other animals are clearly observed to partake in sleep, whether they are aquatic, aerial, or terrestrial (그들이 수생(水生)이든, 기생(氣生)이든, 육생(陸生)이든 거의 모든 다른 동물들이 분명히 수면을 취하는 것으로 관찰된다)"를 통해, '수생(水生) 동물, 즉 물고기 또한 잠을 잔다'고 생각했다는 것을 알 수 있다. 따라서 오답이다.

② "It would appear that not only do men dream, but horses also do, and dogs, and oxen; aye, and sheep, and goats, and all viviparous quadrupeds(사람이 꿈을 꿀뿐만 아니라, 말, 개, 그리고 소; 아, 그리고 양, 염소, 그리고 모든 태생의 네발짐승들이 그렇다)"를 통해 'Aristotle은 모든 동물이 아닌 네발짐승이 꿈을 꾼다고 생각했음'을 알 수 있다. 따라서 오답이다.

④ 본문에 따르면, 'Aristotle은 동물들이 잠을 잔다고 믿었으며, 네발짐승은 꿈을 꾼다고 믿었다'. 그리고 현재의 과학자들도 동물들이 잠을 자는 동안 꿈을 꾸는지 여부를 관찰하기 위한 연구를 진행하고 있음을 본문 후반에서 언급하고 있으므로, Aristotle과 오늘날의 과학자들은 동물의 잠과 꿈에 대해 유사한 의견을 지녔음을 알 수 있다. 따라서 오답이다.

해석

Aristotle은 그의 저서 *On Sleep and Sleeplessness*에 "그들이 수생(水生)이든, 기생(氣生)이든, 육생(陸生)이든 거의 모든 다른 동물들이 분명히 수면을 취하는 것으로 관찰된다"고 적었다. 그러나 다른 동물들이 꿈을 꾸는가? 그것에 대해 이 그리스인 철학자 또한 의견이 있었다. *The History of Animals*에서 그는 "사람이 꿈을 꿀뿐만 아니라, 말, 개, 그리고 소; 아, 그리고 양, 염소, 그리고 모든 태생의 네발짐승들이 그렇다; 그리고 개는 수면 중 짖음으로써 그들이 꿈을 꾸는 것을 보여준다"고 적었다. 그의 연구 방법은 정교함이 부족할지 모르지만, Aristotle은 정답에서 그렇게 많이 벗어나지는 않았을 수도 있다. 오늘날에도 여전히, 우리는 분명히 동물들에게 그들이 꿈을 꾸는지 아닌지 물어볼 수는 없다. 그러나 우리는 적어도 그들이 그럴지도 모른다는 증거를 관찰할 수는 있다. 과학자들이 이 불가능해 보이는 일을 하는 두 가지 방법이 있다. 하나는 수면 주기의 다양한 단계 동안 그들의 신체적인 행위를 관찰하는 것이다. 둘째는 그들의 수면 중 뇌가 우리 자신의 수면 중 뇌와 유사하게 활동하는지 아닌지 알아보는 것이다.

① Aristotle은 물고기는 잠을 자지 않는다고 생각했다.
② Aristotle은 모든 동물들이 꿈을 꾼다고 믿었다.
③ Aristotle에 따르면, 개는 꿈을 꾸고 있기 때문에 잠자는 동안 짖는다.
④ Aristotle은 인간 이외의 동물들의 잠에 대해 오늘날의 과학자들과는 정반대의 의견을 지니고 있었다.

어휘

partake 참가하다 aerial 공중의, 기생(氣生)의
terrestrial 지상의, 육생(陸生)의 ox 소 (pl. oxen)
aye 네, 응, 그럼 viviparous 태생의
quadruped 네발짐승 sophistication 정교, 세련, 복잡함
off the mark 표적을 빗나간, 예상이 틀린
go about 계속 …을 (바삐) 하다

기적사 DAY 36

결국엔 성정혜 영어 하프모의고사

| 01 | ① | 02 | ③ | 03 | ① | 04 | ① | 05 | ③ |
| 06 | ③ | 07 | ② | 08 | ① | 09 | ① | 10 | ② |

01 정답 ①
14 국가직

정답해설

지문 첫 문장인 'These are several places ~ who live a very long time'으로 보아 글 전체가 장수에 대한 내용뿐이므로 빈칸에 ① longevity가 들어가는 것이 가장 적절하다.

해석

장수하는 사람들로 유명한 곳이 세계 몇몇 곳이 있다. 이곳들은 보통 현대적 도시에서 멀리 떨어진 산악 지역이다. 의사, 과학자, 그리고 공중 보건 전문가들은 종종 건강한 장수의 미스터리를 해결하기 위해 이 지역들을 여행한다; 그 전문가들은 현대 세계에 **장수**의 비밀들을 가져오기를 바란다.
① 장수
② 안전
③ 혁신
④ 충성

어휘

mountainous 산악의, 산이 많은   longevity 장수
security 안전   innovation 혁신
loyalty 충성

오답률 TOP 1
02 정답 ③
14 국가직

정답해설

밑줄 친 'analogous'는 '유사한'을 뜻하며 ③ similar와 의미가 가장 가깝다.

해석

세포의 물질대사 조직은, 그것 나름대로의 종합 계획, 작용하는 청사진, 이동 매개체, 그리고 다른 나머지 등에서 완전히 **유사한** 방식으로 작용한다.
① 섬세한, 연약한
② 이상한
③ 유사한, 비슷한
④ 새로운

어휘

metabolic 물질[신진]대사의   function 기능; 기능하다, 작용하다
analogous 유사한   in (a) … fashion …방식으로
master plan 기본 설계[종합 계획] blueprints 청사진, 계획
delicate 섬세한, 연약한   weird 이상한
similar 유사한, 비슷한   novel 새로운

오답률 TOP 2
03 정답 ①
14 국가직

정답해설

첫 번째 빈칸의 경우 해당 문장의 해석이 'TV와 라디오 네트워크가 인종을 공정하게 ~하다'이므로 문맥상 '다루다'가 자연스러우며, 두 번째 빈칸의 경우 해당 문장의 해석이 '보증서가 수리비를 ~하다'이므로 문맥상 '포함하다'가 자연스럽다. 따라서 '다루다'와 '포함하다'의 뜻을 모두 가진 ① cover가 빈칸에 가장 적절하다.

해석

• 많은 전문가들은 TV와 라디오 네트워크가 인종을 공정하게 **다루기에는** 지나치게 편견을 가지고 있다고 비판했다.
• 나는 2달 전, 당신들에게서 이 타이어들을 구입했습니다. 보증서가 수리비를 **포함하나요**?
① 포함하다, 다루다
② 던지다, 보내다
③ 요금을 물리다
④ 주장하다

어휘

criticize 비판하다   warranty 보증서, 보증
cover 포함하다, 다루다   cast 던지다, 보내다
charge 요금을 물리다   claim 주장하다

04 정답 ①
13 국가직

정답해설

Tom은 Jack에게 새로 온 상사의 흉을 보고 있다. Jack의 마지막 말로 보아 Tom이 상사의 흉을 보고 있는 와중에 마침 상사가 나타난 상황이므로 빈칸에 적절한 속담은 ① 'Speak of the devil(호랑이도 제 말하면 온다더니)'일 것이다

오답해설

나머지 선지는 문맥상 적절하지 않으므로 오답이다.

해석

Tom: 솔직히 말이야, 새로 온 내 상사는 그가 뭘 하고 있는지 잘 모르는 것 같아.
Jack: 그는 어리잖아, Tom. 그에게 기회를 줘야 해.
Tom: 얼마나 많은 기회를 줘야 하니? 그는 실제로, 정말 형편없어.
Jack: 호랑이도 제 말하면 온다더니.
Tom: 뭐? 어디?
Jack: 저쪽에. 새로 온 너의 상사가 막 코너를 돌았어.
① 호랑이도 제 말하면 온다더니
② 행운을 빌어
③ 지금처럼 계속 열심히 해
④ 돈만 있으면 귀신도 부릴 수 있어

어휘

Speak of the devil 호랑이도 제 말하면 온다
Money makes the mare go 돈이 있으면 귀신도 부린다

오답률 TOP 3
05 정답 ③
13 국가직

정답해설

③ **출제 포인트: 접속사가 생략되지 않은 분사구문/현재분사 vs. 과거분사/주어와 동사의 수일치**

해당 문장에서 'though equipped with more advanced facilities'는 접속사가 생략되지 않은 분사구문이다. 생략된 주어 'The newly built conference room'과 수동관계이므로 과거분사 'equipped'는 옳은 표현이

다. 또한 주절의 주어가 단수형태의 명사(구) 'The newly built conference room'이므로 주절의 동사에 단수 형태인 'accommodates'를 옳게 사용하였다.

오답해설

① **출제 포인트: 관계대명사 + 절(불완전한 형태)/주어와 동사의 수일치**
목적격 관계대명사 'which'를 사용하였으나 이후에 오는 절에 목적어 'it'을 사용하였으므로 틀린 문장이다. 따라서 'it'을 삭제해야 한다. 또한 주절의 주어가 복수형태의 명사(구) 'The elite campus-based programs'이므로 주절의 동사에 복수 형태인 'are'는 옳은 표현이다.

② **출제 포인트: what vs. that**
해당 문장에서 관계대명사 'That' 앞에 선행사가 없으므로 틀린 문장이다. 따라서 선행사가 없고 뒤따라오는 문장 'happens ~ period'가 주어가 없는 불완전한 형태이므로 'That'을 선행사를 포함하는 관계대명사 'What'으로 수정해야 한다.

④ **출제 포인트: 관계대명사 + 절(불완전한 형태)/가주어 it/to부정사의 명사적 용법**
선행사를 포함하는 관계대명사 'what'은 뒤따라오는 문장이 불완전하다. 해당 문장은 'what' 이후에 오는 절이 완전한 형태이므로 틀린 문장이다. 따라서 'it is best'에서 'it'을 삭제해야 한다. 또한 해당 문장에서 'it's important'의 'it'은 가주어이며 진주어는 'to decide ~ best'이다.

해석

① 그가 다음 학기에 수강하게 될 그 엘리트 대학 기반의 프로그램들은 매우 어려울 것으로 예정되어 있다.
② 특정한 기간에 발생한 일은 주식 시장에서 장기 투자자들에 대해 어떠한 중대한 영향력도 가지지 못한다.
③ 비록 더 발전된 시설이 갖춰졌지만, 새롭게 지어진 회의실은 옛날보다 더 적은 사람들을 수용한다.
④ 그토록 다양한 종류의 선택할 만한 경제적인 가전제품들이 있어서, 무엇이 최선일지를 결정하는 것이 중요하다.

06 정답 ③ 13 국가직

정답해설

③ **출제 포인트: 가정법 과거완료/If 생략 가정법**
가정법 과거완료는 「If+주어+had+과거분사 ~, 주어+would/could/should/might+have+과거분사 ~.」의 구조이며 'If'를 생략할 경우 「Had+주어+과거분사 ~, 주어+would/could/ should/might+have+과거분사 ~.」의 구조이다. 해당 문장은 'If'를 생략한 가정법 과거완료가 쓰인 옳은 문장이다.

오답해설

① **출제 포인트: By the time+주어+동사 ~, 주어+동사 ~.**
「By the time+주어+동사 ~, 주어+동사 ~.」는 종속절의 동사에 과거 시제를 사용하면 주절의 동사에 과거완료를 사용해야 한다. 해당 문장은 「By the time+주어+동사 ~, 주어+동사 ~.」가 쓰인 문장으로 종속절엔 과거완료 'had arrived'를, 주절의 동사엔 과거시제 동사인 'took'을 사용하였으므로 틀린 문장이다. 따라서 'had arrived'를 과거시제 동사인 'arrived'로 수정하고 'already took off'를 'had already taken off'로 수정해야 한다.

② **출제 포인트: 접속사의 쓰임**
접속사 lest는 해당 문장에서 '~하지 않도록'을 뜻한다. 해당 문장은 'lest'를 사용하였으나 주어진 해석이 '~하지 않으면'이므로 틀린 문장이다. 따라서 'lest you should be busy'를 'if you are not busy'로 수정하거나 'unless you are busy'로 수정해야 한다.

④ **출제 포인트: 관용표현(be cut out to+동사원형)**
「be cut out to+동사원형」은 관용표현으로 '~하는 데 적격이다, 자질이 있다'를 뜻한다. 해당 문장은 「be cut out to+동사원형」을 사용하였으나 주어진 해석이 '~하는데 자질이 없다'이므로 옳지 않은 문장이다. 따라서 be동사인 'is' 이후에 'not'을 붙여 'is cut out to~'를 'is not cut out to~'로 수정해야 한다.

07 정답 ② 13 국가직

정답해설

② **출제 포인트: 관용표현(not so much A as B)**
'not so much A as B'는 관용표현으로 'A라기보다는 오히려 B인'을 뜻한다. 해당 문장은 'not so much A as B'를 사용하였으나 주어진 해석을 통해 A와 B의 위치가 바뀐 것을 알 수 있다. 따라서 A자리에 있는 'in what he is'를 B의 자리로 이동하고 B자리에 있는 'in what he has'를 A자리로 이동해 'A person's value lies not so much in what he has as in what he is.'로 수정해야한다.

오답해설

① **출제 포인트: 수여동사/to부정사의 형용사적 용법**
해당 문장에서 'left'는 수여동사 'leave'의 과거시제로 이후에 간접목적어 'him'과 직접목적어 'nothing'을 옳게 사용하였다. 또한 'to live on'은 부정대명사 'nothing'을 수식하는 to부정사의 형용사적 용법으로 사용되었으며 이때 'nothing'은 전치사 'on'의 목적어에 해당한다.

③ **출제 포인트: 관용표현(come to realize)/불완전자동사의 주격 보어**
「come to realize」는 관용표현으로 '~을 깨닫다'를 뜻한다. 해당 문장은 'come to realize'가 쓰인 문장으로 주어진 해석과 일치하므로 옳은 문장이다. 또한 해당 문장에서 'grow'는 비교급 형용사 'older'를 주격 보어로 하는 불완전자동사로 사용되었다.

④ **출제 포인트: 관용표현(be short of)/원급 비교**
「be short of」는 관용표현으로 '~이 부족한'을 뜻한다. 해당 문장은 'be short of'의 과거시제인 'were short of'가 쓰인 문장으로 주어진 해석과 일치하므로 옳은 문장이다. 또한 해당 문장에서 'as little as'는 원급 비교를 나타내며 동사 'drank'를 수식해야 하므로 원급 부사 'little'은 옳은 표현이다.

08 정답 ① 16 국가직

정답해설

빈칸에 들어갈 말은 Kant가 생각하는 도덕적인 행동의 의미를 찾으면 된다. 빈칸 이후에 자세히 설명이 되어 있는 것처럼 Kant는 도덕적인 행동은 '행위 자체의 실행'으로 도덕적인 게 아니라 '행위의 이유'로 판단해야만 한다고 하였다. 게다가 도덕적 행동의 이유는 '동정심'이 아니라 '이성'에서 비롯된 '의무감' 때문이어야만 한다는 것이다. 글의 전반부에서 당신이 도움을 필요로 하는 남자를 애석하게 여겨서 도움을 주었다면 Kant의 입장에서는 도덕적인 행동이 아닌 것이다. 따라서 빈칸에 들어갈 가장 적절한 것은 ① 'that wouldn't be a moral action at all (그것은 도덕적인 행동이 전혀 아니다)'이다.

오답해설

② 애석한 기분이 들어 도움을 주었다면 '이성'에서 비롯된 것이 아닌 '동정심'에서 비롯된 것이기 때문에 도움을 준 행동이 '이성'에서 비롯되었다고 할 수 없다.
③ Kant는 도덕성과 동정심이 서로 관계가 없다고 했으므로, 빈칸 앞의 행동을 도덕적이라고 인정하지 않는다.
④ 단순히 도움을 준 것이지, 정직한 사람이 되도록 동기부여를 한 것이 아니다. 또한 지문과 관계없는 내용이다.

해석

당신의 문에 노크 소리가 들린다. 당신 앞에 서 있는 것은 도움을 필요로 하는 젊은 남성이다. 그는 부상을 입었고 피를 흘리고 있다. 당신은 그를 데려와서 그를 도와주고, 그를 편안하게 해주고 안전하게 느끼게 해준다, 그리고 앰뷸런스를 불러준다. 이것은 옳은 일임이 분명하다. 그러나 Immanuel Kant에 의하면 만약 당신이 그에게 애석한 기분이 들었기 때문에 그를 도왔다면, <u>그것은 도덕적인 행동이 전혀 아니다</u>. 당신의 동정심은 당신의 행동의 도덕성과는 관련이 없다. 그것은 당신의 성격의 일부이지만, 옳거나 그른 것과는 관계가 없다. Kant에게 도덕성은 그저 당신이 무엇을 하는 것이 아니라, 당신이 그것을 왜 하는 것이었다. 옳은 행동을 하는 사람들은 단순히 그들이 어떻게 느끼는 지 때문에 그것을 하지 않는다: 그 결정은 어떻게 당신이 느끼게 되어 버린 지와 관계없이 당신의 의무가 무엇인지 말해주는 이성에서 기반 해야만 한다.

① 그것은 도덕적인 행동이 전혀 아니다
② 당신의 행동은 이성에서 비롯된다
③ 그렇다면 당신은 도덕적인 행동을 보여주고 있다
④ 당신은 그를 정직한 사람이 되도록 격려하고 있다

어휘

sympathy 동정심
morality 도덕성
regardless of ~와 관계없이
irrelevant 관련이 없는
character 성격, 특성
ethical 윤리적인, 도덕적인

---

09 정답 ① 〈16 국가직〉

정답해설

대부분의 파충류들이 알에 대해 부주의하다고 했는데 빈칸 바로 앞부분에서 일부 종들이 알을 지키는 습관을 취득하였다고 하였으므로, 등위접속사로 연결된 빈칸의 내용 역시 알을 지키는 습관에 대해서 설명할 것임을 유추할 수 있다. 따라서 정답은 ③ 'keeping them warm with the warmth of their bodies(체온의 온기로 그것들을 따뜻하게 유지하는)'이다.

오답해설

①, ②, ④ 나머지 선지는 알을 지키는 습관에 관한 내용이 아니므로 적절하지 않다.

해석

공룡 유형의 작은 생명체인 바쁘게 돌아다니는 파충류의 한 그룹의 부족과 속은, 경쟁과 그들의 적들의 추적으로 인해 멸종 혹은 더 높은 언덕이나 바다에서의 더 추운 환경에 대한 적응이란 대안으로 밀려난 것처럼 보인다. 곤궁에 처한 부족들 사이에서, 새로운 유형의 비늘이 발생했고 – 그 비늘은 깃 모양의 형태로 길어졌다. 그리고 현재 깃털의 불완전한 시작으로 가지를 뻗었다. 이러한 깃 모양의 비늘은 서로 덮고 지금까지 존재했던 어떠한 파충류의 가죽보다 더 효율적으로 보온을 유지하는 가죽을 만들어냈다. 따라서 그것들은, 없었다면 생존할 수 없었던, 더 추운 지역에 대한 침입을 허용해주었다. 아마도 동시에 이러한 변화들과 함께, 이러한 생명체들에게 그들의 알에 대한 커다란 근심들이 생겨났다. 대부분의 파충류들은 확실히 그들의 알에 대해 꽤 부주의하다, 그들의 알은 부화하기 위해 (단지) 태양과 계절에 맡겨지기 때문이다. 그러나 생명의 나무의 새로운 가지에 있는 일부 종들은 그들의 알을 지키고 체온의 온기로 그것들을 따뜻하게 유지하는 습관을 취득하였다. 추위에 대한 이러한 적응과 함께, 원시 새들, 온혈 동물 그리고 햇빛을 쬐지 않아도 되는 이러한 생명체들을 만든 다른 내부적 변화들이 계속되었다.

① 부화에 실패하는
② 그것들을 태양 아래 혼자 두는
③ 체온의 온기로 그것들을 따뜻하게 유지하는
④ 그것들을 비늘이 있는 파충류들에게 나르는

어휘

genus (생물 분류상의) 속(pl. genera)
pursuit 추적, 추구
distressed 곤궁에 처해 있는, 고민하고 있는
elongate 연장하다
hitherto 지금까지
solicitude 염려, 근심
modification 변경
independent 독립적인, 독립된
quill 깃, 가시
simultaneously 동시에, 일제히
internal 내부의
primitive 초기의, 원시 사회의
bask 쬐다, 일광욕하다

---

10 정답 ② 〈15 국가직〉

정답해설

본문은 병원균과 질병의 유래에 관한 내용이다. ①에서 병원균 이야기를 하고 ②에서 유라시아 말들의 전쟁사를 설명하는 것은 글의 흐름상 부자연스럽다. 또한 이어지는 ③, ④에도 병원균과 질병의 유래에 관한 내용이 이어지므로 ②를 삭제해 ①에 이어 ③이 이어지는 것이 적절하다.

오답해설

②를 제외한 나머지 선지는 병원균과 질병의 유래와 전파과정을 다루고 있으므로 흐름상 적절하다.

해석

길들여진 가축들과 함께 인간 사회 안에서 진화해온 병원균들은 정복 전쟁에 있어서 똑같이 중요한 부분이다. ① 수두, 홍역 그리고 독감과 같은 전염병들은 인간의 특화된 병원균으로서 발병하는데 이것은 동물들을 감염시키는 매우 유사한 조상 병원균의 돌연변이로부터 유래된 것이다. ② *정복 전쟁에 있어서 식물과 동물을 사육한 것에 대한 가장 직접적인 공헌은 유라시아의 말들로부터 유래했다. 그 말들의 군사적 역할은 그들을 그 대륙에 있었던 고대 전쟁사의 셔먼 탱크와 지프로 만들었다.* ③ 동물을 사육했던 인류는 새롭게 진화된 병원균의 첫 번째 희생자가 되었다. 그러나 그들 인류는 새로운 질병에 대해서 상당한 저항력을 진화시켰다. ④ 그러한 부분적으로 면역이 된 사람들이 이전에 병원균에 노출된 적이 없던 다른 사람들과 접촉하게 되었을 때 유행병은 전에 노출이 된 적이 없던 인구의 99%까지를 사망에 이르게 하는 결과를 낳았다. 그렇기에 가축 동물로부터 궁극적으로 얻어진 병원균들은 미국, 호주, 남아프리카, 태평양 제도에 사는 원주민들을 유럽인들이 정복하는 데에 결정적인 역할을 하였다.

어휘

conquest 정복
smallpox 천연두
ancestral 조상의
infectious 전염되는, 전염성의
mutation 돌연변이, 변화, 변형

결국엔 성정혜 영어 하프모의고사
기적사 DAY 37

01	③	02	④	03	④	04	③	05	④
06	①	07	④	08	④	09	③	10	③

01 정답 ③

정답해설

'대학입시위원회(the College Board)'에 의해 실시될 것으로, 선택지 중 가장 적절한 것은 '감독, 관리'의 의미를 가진 ③ supervision이다.

해석

시험의 **감독**과 시행은 미국의 비영리 회사인 대학입시위원회에 의해 실시된다.
① 우수함, 장점
② 미신
③ 감독, 관리
④ 충성

어휘

implementation 이행, 실행
superstition 미신
loyalty 충성
excellence 우수함, 장점
supervision 감독, 관리

02 정답 ④

정답해설

밑줄 친 'suitable'은 '적절한, 적합한'의 뜻으로 ④ appropriate와 의미가 가장 가깝다.

해석

발견된 소수의 행성과 달만이 물과 생명에게 **적합한** 조건들을 가지고 있다.
① 악의 있는, 심술궂은
② 엄격한, 엄중한
③ 유사한
④ 적절한, 적합한

어휘

suitable 적절한, 적합한
strict 엄격한, 엄중한
appropriate 적절한, 적합한
malicious 악의 있는, 심술궂은
similar 유사한

03 정답 ④

정답해설

문맥상 '밝혀지다, 드러나다'를 뜻하는 'turn out'의 과거시제인 ④ turned out을 사용하는 것이 가장 자연스럽다.

해석

그 해골은 그 목록에서 확인되지 않은 유골인 것으로 **밝혀졌다**.
① 주장했다
② 침입했다, 침해했다
③ 인수했다, 양도받았다
④ 밝혀졌다, 나타났다

어휘

claim 주장하다
take over 인수하다, 양도받다
trespass 침입하다, 침해하다
turn out 밝혀지다, 나타나다

04 정답 ③

정답해설

독자와 작가가 만나 대화를 나누는 지문이다. 독자는 '책에 대해 할 질문이 많다'며 '인기도서 책의 작가가 되었을 때 기분이 어땠는지' 묻는다. 이에 작가는 믿을 수 없었다며 '책이 독자들에게 ~한 것처럼 보일까 봐 살짝 걱정됐다'라고 이야기한다. 따라서 빈칸에 들어갈 가장 적절한 것은 ③ cut and dried(독창성 없는)이다.

오답해설

① 작가는 독자들에게 책이 '제철(in season)'인 것처럼 보일까 봐 살짝 걱정됐다고 말하는 것은 대화의 흐름상 자연스럽지 않다.
② 작가가 책에 관해 이야기하며, 자신의 인기도서 책이 독자들에게 '뻔뻔스러운(bold as brass)' 것처럼 보일까 봐 살짝 걱정됐다고 이야기하는 것은 문맥상 어색하다.
④ 인기도서 책의 작가가 된 기분이 어떤지 묻는 독자의 질문에 작가는 자신의 책이 독자들에게 '비공식인(off the record)' 것처럼 보였을까 봐 걱정됐다고 하는 것은 맥락상 빈칸에 들어갈 말로 부적절하다.

해석

독자: 안녕하세요, 직접 만나 뵙게 되어 영광입니다.
작가: 독자들과 제 생각을 공유할 귀중한 기회를 얻게 되어 기쁩니다.
독자: 감사합니다. 당신의 책은 멋졌어요! 책을 읽을 때 시간이 아주 빨리 지나갔어요.
작가: 제가 들어본 최고의 칭찬입니다. 책에 대해 궁금한 것 있으신가요?
독자: 많죠. 인기도서의 작가가 됐으니 지금 기분이 어떠신가요?
작가: 저는 믿기지 않아요! 책이 독자들에게 <u>독창성 없는</u> 것처럼 보일까 봐 살짝 걱정했어요.
독자: 전혀 아니에요. 저는 이렇게 창의적인 이야기를 처음 읽어봐요.
① 제철에
② 뻔뻔스러운
③ 독창성 없는
④ 비공식적인

어휘

in season 제철에
cut and dried 독창성 없는
bold as brass 뻔뻔스러운
off the record 비공식적인

오답률 TOP 3
05 정답 ④

정답해설

④ 출제 포인트: 접속사가 생략되지 않은 분사구문/분사가 생략된 분사구문/불완전자동사의 주격 보어/of+추상명사

해당 문장에서 'though old and well worn'은 접속사가 생략되지 않은 분사구문으로 주어 'Her jeans and checked shirt'와 현재분사 'being'이 생략되어 있는 옳은 표현이다. 또한 불완전자동사 'looked'의 주격 보어로 형용사인 'clean'과 형용사의 의미를 나타내는 「of+추상명사」 형태인 'of good quality'를 옳게 사용하였다.

오답해설

① **출제 포인트: what vs. that/to부정사의 명사적 용법**

관계대명사 'That' 앞에 선행사가 없으므로 틀린 문장이다. 따라서 선행사가 없고 뒤따라오는 문장이 'find out'의 목적어가 없는 불완전한 형태이므로 'That'을 선행사를 포함하는 관계대명사 'What'으로 수정해야 한다. 또한 'to find out'은 'wanted'의 목적어로 옳게 사용되었다.

② **출제 포인트: 관계대명사 + 절(불완전한 형태)/관용표현(get round to)**

관계대명사 'what' 이후에 오는 절이 완전한 형태이므로 틀린 문장이다. 따라서 목적어 'it'을 삭제해야 한다. 또한 「get round to」는 관용표현으로 '~할 시간을 내다'를 뜻하며 해당 문장에서 과거완료시제로 사용되었다.

③ **출제 포인트: 주격 관계대명사/능동태 vs. 수동태/주어와 동사의 수일치**

주격 관계대명사 'which'의 선행사는 'The house'이며 문맥상 '집이 완공되다'가 자연스러우므로 주격 관계대명사절에 수동태를 사용해야 한다. 따라서 능동태 'completed'를 수동태 'was completed'로 수정해야 한다. 또한 주절의 주어가 단수형태의 명사(구) 'The house'이므로 주절의 동사에 단수 형태인 'was'는 옳은 표현이다.

해석

① 그가 먼저 알아내고 싶었던 것은 시간이 얼마나 걸릴 것인가 하는 것이었다.
② 그것은 내가 그 일을 할 시간을 냈다면 너에게 보여주었을 것이다.
③ 1850년에 완공된 이 집은 거대한 대리석 계단으로 유명했다.
④ 그녀의 청바지와 체크무늬 셔츠는, 낡고 해졌지만, 깨끗하고 품질이 좋아 보였다.

오답률 TOP 2

06 정답 ①

정답해설

① **출제 포인트: 관용표현(be wanting in)**

「be wanting in」은 관용표현으로 '~이 부족하다'를 뜻한다. 해당 문장은 'be wanting in'이 쓰인 문장으로 주어진 해석과 일치하므로 옳은 문장이다.

오답해설

② **출제 포인트: 접속사의 쓰임**

접속사 'although'는 '(비록) ~이긴 하지만'을 뜻한다. 해당 문장은 'although'를 사용하였으나 주어진 해석이 '~하지 않도록'이므로 틀린 문장이다. 따라서 'although'를 'lest'로 수정해야 한다.

③ **출제 포인트: By the time + 주어 + 동사 ~, 주어 + 동사 ~.**

「By the time + 주어 + 동사 ~, 주어 + 동사 ~.」는 종속절의 동사에 과거시제를 사용하면 주절의 동사에 과거완료를 사용해야 한다. 해당 문장은 「By the time + 주어 + 동사 ~, 주어 + 동사 ~.」가 쓰인 문장으로 종속절에 과거시제 동사 'got'을 사용하였으나 주절의 동사에 과거시제 동사 'stopped'를 사용하였으므로 틀린 문장이다. 따라서 'stopped'를 과거완료 'had stopped'로 수정해야 한다.

④ **출제 포인트: 가정법 과거완료/비교급 강조 부사**

가정법 과거완료는 「If + 주어 + had + 과거분사 ~, 주어 + would/could/should/might + have + 과거분사 ~.」의 구조를 가진다. 해당 문장은 주절의 'would have been'과 주어진 해석을 통해 가정법 과거완료가 쓰인 문장임을 알 수 있다. 따라서 종속절인 If절에 과거완료를 사용해야 하므로 과거시제 동사 'finished'를 'had finished'로 수정해야 한다. 또한 해당 문장에서 'much'는 비교급 강조부사로 비교급 형용사 'better'를 수식하고 있다.

07 정답 ④

정답해설

④ **출제 포인트: 수동태 불가동사/관용표현(be supposed to + 동사원형)**

'take place'는 수동태 불가동사로 '개최되다, 일어나다'를 뜻한다. 해당 문장은 to부정사의 동사원형 자리에 'take place'의 수동태를 사용하였으므로 틀린 문장이다. 따라서 'be taken place'를 능동태 'take place'로 수정해야 한다. 또한 해당 문장에서 'was supposed to + 동사원형'은 'be supposed to + 동사원형'의 과거형으로 '~하기로 되어 있다'를 뜻한다.

오답해설

① **출제 포인트: 수여동사**

해당 문장에서 'promise'는 수여동사로 간접목적어 'John'과 직접목적어 'the car would be ready on Monday'를 옳게 사용하였다. 이때 직접목적어로 쓰인 절 앞에는 접속사 'that'이 생략되어 있음에 유의해야 한다.

② **출제 포인트: 관용표현(not A so much as B)/관용표현(think of A as B)**

「think of A as B」는 관용표현으로 'A를 B라고 생각하다'를 뜻하며 「not A so much as B」는 관용표현으로 'A라기보다는 오히려 B인'을 뜻한다. 해당 문장은 'think of A as B'와 'not A so much as B'가 결합한 문장으로 주어진 해석과 일치하는 옳은 문장이다.

③ **출제 포인트: 관용표현(be anxious to)/that의 쓰임**

「be anxious to + 동사원형」은 관용표현으로 '~하기를 갈망하다'를 뜻한다. 해당 문장은 'be anxious to + 동사원형'이 쓰인 문장으로 주어진 해석과 일치하므로 옳은 문장이다. 또한 해당 문장에서 'that that'의 경우 첫 번째 'that'은 주격 보어로 쓰인 명사절을 이끄는 접속사이며 두 번째 'that'은 대명사이다.

오답률 TOP 1

08 정답 ④

정답해설

본문은 'Kant 시대의 사람들의 도덕적 규율'에 대해 설명하고 있다. 본문은 'Kant 시대의 도덕적 신념과 관례는 종교에 기반을 둔 것이었으며, 종교의 계율이 도덕적인 행동강령을 제시했다'고 설명한다. 주어진 문장의 'Moreover(게다가)'로 보아, 해당 문장 이전에 규율을 따르는 이유에 관한 내용이 먼저 등장해야 함을 알 수 있다. 또한, "everyone had an incentive to obey such rules(모든 사람들이 이러한 강령을 준수하게 하는 유인이 있었다)"로 보아, 주어진 문장 이후에는 '규율을 따르는 것을 통해 받을 수 있는 이득'을 설명하는 내용이 등장하는 것이 자연스럽다는 것을 알 수 있다. ④ 이후 문장에서 "If you "walked in the ways of the Lord," you would be rewarded, either in this life or the next(만일 당신이 "하느님의 길을 걷는다면", 당신은 이생 또는 후생에 보상을 받을 것이다)."라고 '규율을 따르는 것에 의한 보상'에 대해 언급하고 있으므로, 주어진 문장의 'incentive(유인, 동기, 이득)'가 ④ 이후 문장에서 구체적으로 언급되고 있음을 알 수 있다. 따라서 정답은 ④이다.

오답해설

③ 주어진 문장의 'incentive'가 가리키는 것이 이후 문장에서 명확히 드러나지 않으며, 또한 ③ 이후의 문장과 ④ 이후의 문장이 곧바로 이어지는 것은 문맥상 부자연스러우므로, ③은 오답이다.
나머지 위치는 문맥상 어색하므로 오답이다.

해석

Kant의 도덕 철학을 이해하기 위해, 그와 그의 시대의 다른 사상가들이 다루었던 문제들에 친숙해지는 것이 중요하다. 가장 초기에 기록되었던 역사에서부터, 사람들의 도덕적 신념과 관례는 종교에 근거를 두고 있었다. (①) 성경, 쿠란과 같은 성서들은 신자들이 신으로부터 전해진 것으로 생각하던 도덕적 규율(살인하지 말라. 도둑질하지 말라. 간음하지 말라 등)을 나열해 놓았다. (②) 그것들이 아마도 지성의 신성한 근원으로부터 온 것이라는 사실이 그것들에 권위를 부여했다. (③) 그것들은 단순히 누군가의 독단적인 의견이 아니었다; 그것들은 신의 의견이었으며, 신의 의견으로서 인류에게 객관적으로 유효한 행동강령을 제공했다. (④ **게다가, 모든 사람들이 이러한 강령을 준수하게 하는 유인이 있었다.**) 만일 당신이 "하느님의 길을 걷는다면", 당신은 이생 또는 후생에 보상을 받을 것이다. 만일 당신이 율법을 위반한다면, 당신은 벌을 받을 것이다. 그 결과, 이러한 신앙을 가지고 자란 분별 있는 사람은 그들의 종교가 가르친 도덕적 규율을 준수하곤 했다.

어휘

ground 근거를 두다, 입각하다
Quran 쿠란(코란)(= Koran)
adultery 간통, 간음
divine 신성한
arbitrary 독단적인, 임의적인
as such (선행하는 명사를 받아) 그것으로서, 그러한 자격[지위, 기능 (등)]에 있어서
code of conduct 행동강령
obey 따르다, 준수하다
sensible 분별[양식] 있는, 합리적인
abide by 준수하다, 지키다, …에 따라 행동하다
scripture 성서, 경전
lay out 펼쳐 놓다
supposedly 추정 상, 아마
authority 권위
incentive 자극, 유인, 동기, 이득, 혜택
commandment 율법, 계명
bring up 기르다, 양육하다

09 정답 ③

정답해설

본문은 '파충류의 다양한 산란 방식'에 대해 설명하는 글이며, 특히 세 번째 문장부터 특이하게 '태생(胎生)을 하는 파충류'에 대해 집중적으로 소개하고 있다. 본문에 따르면, 태생을 하는 파충류는 오직 뱀과 도마뱀 같은 비늘이 있는 파충류뿐이며, 태생의 방식도 다양하다. 그런데 ③에서는 태생을 하는 파충류의 경우가 아니라 일반적인 파충류 암컷이 '산란을 하지 않고 난관에 알을 간직하는 경우'에 대해 설명하고 있으므로, 글의 흐름상 부자연스럽다. 따라서 정답은 ③이다.

오답해설

④ 이전 문장 "No living crocodiles, turtles, or tuatara are live-bearers (현존하는 악어, 거북이 또는 큰도마뱀 중 태생을 하는 종은 없다)."에서, '태생을 하지 않는 파충류'에 대해 언급한 후, ④ 이후 문장에서 태생을 하는 파충류에 대해 '역접, 대조'를 나타내는 'However(그러나)'를 이용해 설명하고 있으므로, 글의 구조상 자연스럽다.
나머지 보기는 문맥상 자연스러우므로 오답이다.

해석

파충류 사이에서 산란과 집짓기 행동들은 매우 다양하다. ① 이러한 행동들은 상대적으로 적절한 장소에 알을 '대충' 떨어뜨리는 것에서부터, 정성 들인 집을 준비하는 것까지 다양하고, 일부 집단에서 부모의 양육 또한 발생하기도 한다. 흥미롭게도, 어떤 파충류는 새끼를 살아있는 채로 낳는다. ② 태생(胎生)이라 불리는 이 방식은 널리 퍼져있고, 비늘 파충류(즉, 도마뱀과 뱀) 종에서 수십 번 개별적으로 진화해왔다. 현존하는 악어, 거북이 또는 큰도마뱀 중 태생을 하는 종은 없다. ③ <u>높은 스트레스와 다른 상대적으로 특이한 상황(잡혀있는 것과 같은)의 기간 중에 암컷들은 일반적으로 수주에서 수개월 동안 그들의 난관에 알을 간직하고 있는 것으로 알려져 있다.</u> ④ 그러나, 비늘 파충류 종에서, 태생은 부화하지 않은 알을 난관에 보유하는 것에서부터 어미와 태아 사이의 태반의 발달까지 다양하다. 산란으로부터 태반의 발달로의 진화적 단계는 현존하는 종에 의해 입증된다.

어휘

vary 다르다, 다양하다
suitable 적절한, 알맞은
bear 낳다, 출산하다
viviparity 태생(胎生)
tuatara 큰도마뱀
unshelled 껍질을 벗기지 않은
placenta 태반 (pl. placentae)
placental 태반의
relatively 상대적으로
elaborate 정성 들인, 공들인
young 새끼
squamate 비늘이 있는
retention 보유, 유지
oviduct 난관
fetus 태아
extant 현존[잔존]하는

10 정답 ③

정답해설

본문은 인수 공통 전염병인 'Toxoplasmosis(톡소플라스마증)'에 관한 내용이며, 본문에 따르면 '톡소플라스마증'은 '성인의 약 10~20퍼센트가 톡소플라스마 기생충에 영향을 받으며, 태아의 감염 위험 때문에 특히 임신부에게 위험한 질병'이다. 주어진 문장에서 'This(이것)'가 '엄마가 임신 중 또는 임신 전에 감염이 되면 발생한다'고 언급하고 있으므로, 'This'가 '엄마의 감염에 따른 태아의 감염'을 가리킨다는 사실을 유추할 수 있다. 따라서 주어진 문장의 'This'가 가리킬 수 있는 것은, 문맥상 ③ 이전 문장에서 언급된 "the growing fetus can become infected with the toxoplasmosis parasite(톡소플라스마증 기생충에 의해 자라고 있는 태아가 감염될 수 있다)"라는 것을 알 수 있다. 따라서 정답은 ③이다.

오답해설

④ 주어진 문장에서는 '임신 중(while pregnant)' 또는 '임신 전(just before she becomes pregnant)' 감염에 대해 언급하고 있는데, ④ 이전 문장에서는 '임신 중(during pregnancy)' 감염된 태아에게 미치는 영향에 대해 자세히 설명하고 있으므로, ④ 이전 문장에서 주어진 문장의 'This'가 가리키는 것을 찾을 수 없다. 따라서 오답이다.
나머지 위치는 문맥상 어색하므로 오답이다.

해석

톡소플라스마증은 북미 전역에서 새와 포유류에게서 발견되는 흔한 질병이다. (①) 그 전염병은 Toxoplasma gondii라고 불리는 원생 기생충에 의해 발생되고, 북미에서 그들이 성인이 될 무렵 100명당 10에서 20명의 사람에게 영향을 미친다. (②) 톡소플라스마증 기생충에 의해 자라고 있는 태아가 감염될 수 있기 때문에 임신부에게 있어서 우려가 가장 크다. (③ **이것은 만일 엄마가 임신 중 또는 그녀가 임신을 하기 바로 전에 그 기생충에 새롭게 감염된다면 발생할 수 있다.**) 임신 중 태아의 감염은 유산, 발육 부진, 조기 출산 또는 사산을 야기할 수 있다. (④) 만일 아이가 톡소플라스마증에 걸린 채로 태어난다면, 그/그녀는 시력 문제, 뇌수종 (뇌에 물이 차는 것), 경련, 또는 정신 장애들을 겪을 수 있다.

어휘

infection 전염병; 감염
pregnant 임신한
miscarriage 유산
stillbirth 사산
convulsion 경련, 경기
protozoa parasite 원생 기생충
fetus (특히 임신 8주 이후의) 태아
delivery 출산
hydrocephalus 뇌수종
disability 장애

기적사 DAY 38

결국엔 성정혜 영어 하프모의고사

| 01 | ② | 02 | ④ | 03 | ④ | 04 | ③ | 05 | ③ |
| 06 | ③ | 07 | ① | 08 | ④ | 09 | ② | 10 | ③ |

01 정답 ②

정답해설

'증거 없이 좋거나 나쁜 일이 일어날 것이라고 믿는 것'은 ② superstition 즉, '미신'이다.

해석

증거 없이 좋거나 나쁜 일이 일어날 것이라고 믿는 것은 **미신**이라고 불린다.
① 우수함, 장점
② 미신
③ 혁신
④ 반감

어휘

proof 증거, 증명 excellence 우수함, 장점
superstition 미신 innovation 혁신
antipathy 반감

오답률 TOP 3
02 정답 ④

정답해설

'specious'는 '그럴듯한, 겉만 번드르르한'의 뜻으로 ④ superficial과 의미가 가장 가깝다.

해석

그의 주장은 나에게 있어 완전히 **그럴듯했**다.
① 새로운
② 부족한, 희귀한, 드물게, 적은
③ 엄중한, 강경한
④ 외관상의, 피상적인, 실체 없는

어휘

specious 그럴듯한, 겉만 번드르르한 novel 새로운
scarce 부족한, 희귀한, 드물게, 적은 stern 엄중한, 강경한
superficial 외관상의, 피상적인, 실체 없는

오답률 TOP 2
03 정답 ④

정답해설

주어진 문장에서 장소가 식당이고 목적어로 'diner(식사 손님)'를 받기에 가장 적절한 것은 '응대하다, 시중들다'의 ④ wait on이다.

해석

세계에 있는 모든 식당에서 웨이터와 웨이트리스는 식사 손님들을 **응대하고** 음식을 제공한다.
① 완화하다
② 청구하다, 기소하다, 비난하다
③ 철수하다, 취소하다, 인출하다
④ 시중들다, 응대하다

어휘

diner 식사 손님 assuage 완화하다
charge 청구하다, 기소하다, 비난하다 withdraw 철수하다, 취소하다, 인출하다
wait on 응대하다, 시중들다

---

04 정답 ③

정답해설

(A) 대화를 통해 John이 Danny를 위한 깜짝 생일파티를 열어주기 위해 준비하고 있으며 Nina도 동참하게 된 상황임을 알 수 있다. 이때 Nina가 '누군가 무엇을 하고 있는지 물어보면 Danny가 사실을 알아채지 못하게끔 ~할 것이다'라고 이야기하므로 빈칸 (A)에 들어갈 가장 적절한 것은 'hold my tongue(묵묵부답하다)'이다.

(B) '누군가 ~한다면, Danny는 바로 알게 될 것이다.'라고 John이 말하고 있으므로 빈칸 (B)에 들어갈 가장 적절한 것은 'spills the beans(비밀을 폭로하다)'이다.

오답해설

① (A) Nina는 Danny를 위한 깜짝 비밀 생일파티를 준비하면서 누군가 무엇을 하는지 묻는다면 Danny가 알아내지 못하게끔 자기가 그저 '자만하겠다(go to my head)'고 말하는 것은 대화의 흐름상 어색하다. (B) John은 Nina가 비밀을 유지하겠다고 말한 것에 누군가 '임기응변으로 대처하면(plays it by ear)' Danny가 바로 알게 될 것이라고 이야기하는 것은 문맥상 자연스럽지 않다.

② (B) John은 Nina가 비밀을 유지하겠다고 말한 것에 누군가 '임기응변으로 대처하면(plays it by ear)' Danny가 바로 알게 될 것이라고 이야기하는 것은 문맥상 빈칸에 들어갈 말로 적합하지 않다.

④ (A) Nina는 Danny의 깜짝 비밀 생일파티를 준비하며 누군가 무엇을 하는지 물어본다면 Danny가 사실을 알지 못하도록 자신이 '겨우 삶을 연명하겠다(live from hand to mouth)'라고 얘기하는 것은 대화의 맥락상 부적절하다.

해석

Nina: 너희들 여기서 뭐 해?
John: 이건 비밀이야. Danny를 위한 깜짝 생일파티를 준비 중이야.
Nina: 우와 Danny가 이것에 대해 모두 알게 되면 아주 기쁘겠다.
John: 정말 그랬으면 좋겠어. 우리는 이것을 이 주 넘게 계획했어. 너도 동참할래?
Nina: 물론이지, 난 아주 좋아. 누군가 우리가 뭐 하고 있는지 묻는다면 난 그냥 Danny가 사실을 알게 되지 않게끔 (A) **묵묵부답할게**.
John: 난 널 믿어. 누구든 (B) **비밀을 폭로하면** Danny는 바로 알게 될 거야.
① (A) 자만하다 (B) 임기응변으로 대처하다
② (A) 묵묵부답하고 있다 (B) 임기응변으로 대처하다
③ (A) 묵묵부답하고 있다 (B) 비밀을 폭로하다
④ (A) 겨우 삶을 연명하다 (B) 비밀을 폭로하다

어휘

find out about ~의 존재를[~임을] 알아채다
go to one's head 자만하다
play it by ear 임기응변으로 대처하다
hold one's tongue 묵묵부답하고 있다
spill the beans 비밀을 폭로하다
live from hand to mouth 겨우 삶을 연명하다

05 정답 ③

정답해설

③ **출제 포인트: 주격 관계대명사절의 동사 수일치**
해당 문장에서 주격 관계대명사 'which'의 선행사는 단수 형태의 명사(구) 'a huge nest'이므로 관계대명사절의 동사에 단수 형태인 'is'를 옳게 사용하였다. 또한 해당 문장에서 'what'은 선행사를 포함하는 관계대명사이며 'he assumes'는 삽입절로 관계대명사절의 동사는 'was'임에 유의해야 한다.

오답해설

① **출제 포인트: 간접의문문/what vs. that**
의문부사 'how'가 이끄는 의문이 주격 보어에 해당하므로 간접의문문임을 알 수 있다. 간접의문문의 어순은 「의문부사+형용사+주어+be동사」이어야 하므로 'how unhappy was the child'를 'how unhappy the child was'로 수정해야 한다. 또한 해당 문장에서 'What'은 선행사를 포함한 관계대명사로 옳게 사용되었다.

② **출제 포인트: 능동태 vs. 수동태/현재분사 vs. 과거분사/가주어 it/명사절을 이끄는 접속사 that**
해당 문장은 'It'과 'that'으로 인해 가주어 'It', 진주어 'that'절로 오해할 수 있으나 문장 내에 4개의 동사가 존재하므로 3개의 연결사가 필요하다는 것을 알 수 있다. 따라서 주어 자리에 온 'It is interesting'은 선행사를 포함하는 관계대명사 'what'을 사용하여 'What is interesting'으로 수정해야한다. 또한 'that' 이하의 문장에서 주격 관계대명사 'what'이 이끄는 절에 불완전타동사 'make'의 수동태가 사용되었으나 이후에 목적어 'you'가 있으므로 틀린 문장이다. 따라서 'is made'를 능동태 'makes'로 수정해야 한다. 또한 'interesting'은 감정 제공 형용사로 주로 사물을 나타내는 명사가 주어로 사용되며, 'interested'는 감정 상태 형용사로 주로 사람을 나타내는 명사가 주어로 사용된다.

④ **출제 포인트: 주어와 동사의 수일치/접속사가 생략되지 않은 분사구문/분사가 생략된 분사구문**
주절의 주어가 단수형태의 명사(구) 'The house'이나 주절의 동사에 복수 형태인 'are'를 사용하였으므로 틀린 문장이다. 따라서 'are'를 단수 형태인 'is'로 수정해야 한다. 또한 해당 문장에서 'though imposing from the outside'는 접속사가 생략되지 않은 분사구문으로 주어 'The house'와 현재분사 'being'이 생략되어 있다. 이때 'imposing'은 현재분사가 아니라 '인상적인'을 뜻하는 형용사임에 유의해야 한다.

해석

① 그녀를 정말로 걱정스럽게 만드는 것은 그 아이가 얼마나 불행했는가였다.
② 그들이 당신을 재미있게 만드는 것에 관심이 있다는 것은 흥미롭다.
③ Tom은 자신이 가정하기에 까치집인 큰 둥지를 찾았다.
④ 그 집은, 겉으로는 인상적이지만, 실은 매우 안락한 크기이다.

06 정답 ③

정답해설

③ **출제 포인트: 접속사의 쓰임**
접속사 'Although'는 '(비록) ~이긴 하지만'을 뜻한다. 해당 문장은 'Although'를 사용하였으며 주어진 해석과 일치하므로 옳은 문장이다.

오답해설

① **출제 포인트: 관용표현(be inconsistent with)**
「be consistent with」는 관용표현으로 '~와 일치하다'를 뜻한다. 해당 문장은 'was consistent with'를 사용하였으나 주어진 해석이 '~에 어긋났다'이므로 틀린 문장이다. 따라서 'was consistent with'를 'was inconsistent with'로 수정해야 한다.

② **출제 포인트: 가정법 과거완료/if 생략 가정법**
가정법 과거완료는 「If+주어+had+과거분사 ~, 주어+would/could/should/might+have+과거분사 ~.」의 구조를 가지며 'If'를 생략할 경우 「Had+주어+과거분사 ~, 주어+would/could/should/might+have+과거분사 ~.」의 구조를 가진다. 해당 문장은 'would have made'와 주어진 해석을 통해 가정법 과거완료가 쓰인 문장임을 알 수 있다. 따라서 종속절인 'If'절에 과거완료를 사용해야 하며 'If'가 생략되어 있으므로 'Did I have'를 'Had I had'로 수정해야 한다. 또한, 해당 문장에 쓰인 'work'는 명사로 '(생계 벌이를 위한) 직장, 일, 직업'을 뜻함에 유의해야 한다.

④ **출제 포인트: By the time+주어+동사 ~, 주어+동사 ~.**
「By the time+주어+동사 ~, 주어+동사 ~.」는 종속절의 동사에 과거 시제를 사용하면 주절의 동사에 과거완료를 사용해야 한다. 해당 문장은 「By the time+주어+동사 ~, 주어+동사 ~.」가 쓰인 문장으로 주절의 동사에 과거완료진행형 'had been looking'을 사용하였으나 종속절의 동사에 과거완료 'had opened'를 사용하였으므로 틀린 문장이다. 따라서 종속절의 동사를 과거완료시제인 'had opened'에서 과거시제인 'opened'로 수정해야 한다.

07 정답 ①

정답해설

① **출제 포인트: 수여동사 vs. 완전타동사**
'borrow'는 완전타동사로 '~을 빌리다'의 의미로 사용된다. 해당 문장은 'borrow' 이후에 간접목적어 'him'과 직접목적어 'ten pounds'를 사용하였으므로 틀린 표현이다. 따라서 'borrow'를 수여동사 'lend'로 수정해 'lend+간접목적어(대상)+직접목적어(사물)'로 '그에게 10파운드를 빌려주어야 한다'는 의미에 맞게 수정해야 한다.

오답해설

② **출제 포인트: 관용표현(not much of)**
「not much of」는 관용표현으로 '대단한 ~이 아닌'을 뜻한다. 해당 문장은 'not much of'가 쓰인 문장으로 주어진 해석과 일치하므로 옳은 문장이다.

③ **출제 포인트: 관용표현(crack down on)**
「crack down on」은 관용표현으로 '~을 단속하다'를 뜻한다. 해당 문장은 'crack down on'이 쓰인 문장으로 주어진 해석과 일치하므로 옳은 문장이다.

④ **출제 포인트: 관용표현(be anxious about)**
「be anxious about」은 관용표현으로 '~에 대해 걱정하다'를 뜻한다. 해당 문장은 'be anxious about'이 쓰인 문장으로 주어진 해석과 일치하므로 옳은 문장이다. 또한 'admitted'와 'she' 사이에는 목적어 절을 이끄는 접속사 'that'이 생략되어 있다.

오답률 TOP 1

08 정답 ④

정답해설

주어진 문장에서는 '거짓 진술을 통해 돈을 빌리려는 사람의 경우'에 대해 설명하고 있다. 주어진 문장에서 언급된 '거짓에 기반해 돈을 빌리는 행위'를 (C)의 'this action(이 행위)'이 가리키고 있으므로, 주어진 문장 이후에 (C)가 이어지는 것이 적절하다. (C) 후반부에 언급된 "making this maxim into a universal law would be clearly self-defeating(이러한 행동 원리를 보편 법칙으로 만드는 것은 분명히 문제를 오히려 키우는 것일 것이다)."의 내용으로 보아, '거짓말을 하는 것이 문제를 해결해 주는 것이 아니라 오히려 문제를 만드는 격이 된다'는 것을 알 수 있으므로, '거짓말이 효과적인 방법이 될 수 없다'고 설명하는 (A)가 이어지는 것이 적절하다. 마지막으로, 앞서 언급된 '필요하다면 거짓 약속을 통해 돈을 빌려도 된다'는 것이 보편적 원리가 된다면, '돈을 빌려주는 사람 누구도 돈을 상환하겠다는 약속을 믿지 않을 것이며, 결국에는 돈을 전혀 빌릴 수 없게' 되는 것이므로, 마침내 이러한 보편적 원리가 보편적으로 통용되지 않는 상황에 이르게 되는 '모순적인' 특징을 가지고 있다는 것을 알 수 있다. 따라서 "Since the universalized maxim is contradictory in and of itself(그 보편화 된 원리가 본질적으로 그리고 자연적으로 모순되기 때문에)"라고 언급하는 (B)가 이어지는 것이 적절하다. 그러므로 정답은 '④ (C) - (A) - (B)'이다.

오답해설
나머지 보기는 문맥상 어색하므로 오답이다.

해석
실제로는 그렇게 할 의도가 없지만, 미래에 상환할 것을 약속하며 타인에게 돈을 빌려 재정적 위기를 완화하려고 생각하는 사람의 경우를 생각해보라.
(C) 이 행위의 행동 원리는 당신이 정말로 그것이 필요하다면 사실이 아닌 진술을 통해 돈을 빌리는 것이 허용된다는 것이다. 그러나 Kant가 지적했듯이, 이러한 행동 원리를 보편 법칙으로 만드는 것은 분명 문제를 오히려 키우는 것일 것이다.
(A) 약속을 전제로 돈을 빌려주는 전체의 관행은 적어도 상환을 하려는 정직한 의도를 상정한다. 만일 이러한 조건이 보편적으로 무시된다면, 거짓된 약속은 돈을 빌리는 방법으로서 전혀 효과적이지 않을 것이다.
(B) 그 보편화된 행동 원리가 본질적으로 그리고 자연적으로 모순되기 때문에, 아무도 그것이 법칙이 되길 원하지 않을 것이다. 그리고 Kant는 우리가 이러한 방식으로 행동하지 않을 (절대 어떤 예외도 있을 수 없는) 완전한 의무를 가지고 있다고 결론지었다.

어휘
contemplate 고려하다, 생각하다
repay 갚다, 상환하다
universalize 일반화하다, 보편화하다
contradictory 모순되는
of itself 자연히, 저절로
whatsoever 전혀, 어떤 종류의 것도
false pretense 사실이 아닌 진술, 거짓 진술, 사기
universal law 보편적 법칙
self-defeating (문제를 해결하기커녕) 문제를 오히려 키우는[골치 아프게 만드는], 자멸적인
relieve 완화하다, 줄이다
presuppose 상정[추정]하다
maxim 행동 원리, 주의, 격언
in itself 그것 자체가[본질적으로]
will 원하다, 좋아하다
permissible 허용되는, 무방한

09 정답 ②

정답해설
(A) 이전에는 파충류가 단단한 껍질을 낳을 수 없다면 부드러운 껍질의 알을 낳을 수 있다고 언급하며 부드러운 알의 특징으로 '산란 후 팽창할 수 있음'을 설명하고 있다. (A) 이후에는 앞서 언급한 부드러운 껍질 알의 특징과는 다른 특징인 '수분을 흡수할 수 있는 능력'에 대한 내용으로 부드러운 껍질 알의 추가적인 특징을 첨가해주고 있다. 따라서 빈칸에는 '첨언'의 접속부사인 'Additionally(게다가)' 또는 'Besides(게다가)'가 적절하다.
(B) 이전에서 '새가 알을 부화시키는 방법'에 대해 언급한 후, (B) 이후에서 앞서 언급된 새의 방법과는 다른 '파충류의 부화 방법'이 언급되고 있다. 즉, 서로 다른 '역접, 대조' 관계에 있는 내용이 연결되고 있으므로, 빈칸에는 'by contrast(대조적으로)', 'on the other hand(반면에)'가 들어가는 것이 자연스럽다.
따라서 정답은 '② Additionally(게다가) - on the other hand(반면에)'이다.

오답해설
① (A) 전후 내용이 '인과' 관계를 나타내고 있지 않기 때문에, 'Thus(그래서)'는 빈칸에 적절하지 않다.
④ (B) 전후 내용이 '역접' 관계이므로, '첨가'를 나타내는 'furthermore(더욱이)'는 빈칸에 적절하지 않다.
나머지 보기는 문맥상 어색하므로 오답이다.

해석
새는 단단한 껍질이 있는 알을 낳는 반면, 일부 파충류 종은 껍질이 부드러운 알을 낳는다. 왜 이것이 사실일까? 만일 어미가 완전한 크기의 단단한 껍질의 알을 낳을 수 없다면, 대신에 그것은 알이 산란 후 팽창할 수 있도록 하는 부드러운 껍질의 알을 낳을 수 있을 것이다. (A) 게다가, 부드러운 껍질은 대기와 지면으로부터 수분을 흡수할 수 있는 능력이 있다. 어떠한 이유로, 새는 그들의 알이 추가적인 수분이 필요하지 않도록 그렇게 진화해왔으나, 그것은 일부 파충류 종에게는 사실이 아니다. 일부 파충류가 껍질이 부드러운 알을 낳은 또 하나의 이유는 그것들이 부화하는 방식 때문이다. 새는 그들의 알 위에 앉아 자신들의 체온을 이용한다; (B) 반면에 파충류는 알을 부화시키기 위해 초목 또는 지면의 자연적인 열을 이용한다. 파충류의 알이 부모의 전체 체중으로부터 태어나지 않은 내용물을 보호할 만큼 충분히 강할 필요가 없기 때문에, 그것들은 껍질이 부드러울 수 있다.

(A)	(B)
① 그래서	대조적으로
② 게다가	반면에
③ 그러나	그에 따라
④ 게다가	더욱이

어휘
case 실정, 사실
absorb 흡수하다
incubate (알을) 부화하다, 품다
utilize 이용하다, 활용하다
earth 땅, 지면, 흙
capacity 능력
moisture 수분, 습기
warmth 온기, 따뜻함
vegetation 초목, 식물
unborn 아직 태어나지 않은

10 정답 ③

정답해설
(A) 이전에서 '농장 동물들이 사람에게 질병을 옮길 수 있다'고 언급한 후, (A) 이후에는 '농장에서 동물 또는 동물과 접촉한 물건을 만진 후에 손을 씻어야 할 필요성'에 대해 설명하고 있다. 즉, (A) 이후에 언급된 행위의 원인이 (A) 이전에 등장하므로, (A) 전후의 내용은 '인과' 관계임을 알 수 있다. 따라서 빈칸에는 'Therefore(그러므로)' 또는 'Hence(이런 이유로)'가 적절하다.
(B) 이전에는 '다른 유형의 동물들이 다른 질병을 옮긴다'고 언급한 후, (B) 이후에서 구체적으로 특정 동물이 어떤 질병을 옮기는지 예를 들어 설명하고 있으므로, (B) 이하는 (B) 이전 문장의 '예시'임을 알 수 있다. 따라서 빈칸에는 'For instance(예를 들어)'가 가장 적절하다.
따라서 정답은 '③ Therefore(그러므로) - For instance(예를 들어)'이다.

오답해설
나머지 보기는 문맥상 어색하므로 오답이다.

해석
그들은 가정의 반려동물과 같지 않으며, 대소변을 배설하는 곳에서 떨어진 휴식 또는 식사 공간을 가지고 있지 않기 때문에, 소, 양, 돼지, 닭, 그리고 염소를 포함한 농장 동물들은 사람들에게 질병을 옮길 수 있다. (A) 그러므로, 당신은 그들과 접촉한 후 또는 울타리, 양동이, 잠자리용 짚단과 같은 농장 동물들과 접촉했던 사물을 만진 후에 흐르는 물과 비누를 이용해 당신의 손을

철저하게 씻어야 하며, 어른들은 농장을 방문하는 아이들을 주의 깊게 살펴야 하고 그들이 손을 잘 씻도록 도와야 한다. 다른 유형의 농장 동물들은 다른 질병을 옮길 수 있다. (B) 예를 들어, 소와 송아지는 종종 E. coli라고 불리는 Escherichia coli라는 박테리아를 옮길 수 있다. 이 균은 사람들에게 피가 섞인 설사를 유발할 수 있다. 게다가 아이들은 E. coli 감염으로 인해 신부전이 발생할 수도 있다. 돼지는 예르시니아증이라는 질병을 유발하는 Yersinia enterocolitica라는 박테리아를 옮길 수 있다. 닭은 Salmonella와 같은 박테리아를 옮길 수 있는데, 이것이 살모넬라증이라는 질병을 유발한다. 이러한 균들 중 다수가 농장 동물의 거름에 있다.

(A)	(B)
① 그러나	유사하게
② 즉	게다가
③ 그러므로	예를 들어
④ 더욱이	반면에

어휘

excrete 배설하다, 배출하다 feces 대변
urine 오줌, 소변 carry (병을) 옮기다
calf 송아지
bacterium 박테리아, 세균 (bacteria의 단수형)
diarrhea 설사 kidney failure 신부전
manure (동물의 배설물로 만든) 거름[천연 비료]

Day 38

결국엔 성정혜 영어 하프모의고사
기적사 DAY 39

| 01 | ① | 02 | ② | 03 | ② | 04 | ③ | 05 | ① |
| 06 | ① | 07 | ① | 08 | ② | 09 | ② | 10 | ② |

오답률 TOP 1
01 정답 ①

정답해설

문맥상 조직 전체를 '단합'으로 시킬 수 있는 원인에 해당되는 선지를 선택해야 한다. 따라서 가장 적절한 것은 '감정 이입, 공감'의 의미를 지닌 ① empathy이다.

해석

공감은 전체 조직이 문제해결에 집중하도록 단합시킨다.
① 감정 이입
② 격통
③ 불안, 공포
④ 안전

어휘

empathy 감정 이입 anguish 격통
angst 불안, 공포 security 안전

02 정답 ②

정답해설

밑줄 친 'dilapidated'는 '파손된, 황폐한'의 뜻으로 ② devastated와 의미가 가장 가깝다.

해석

한때 **파손된** 지역은 이와 같이 "예술가들의 거리"로 다시 태어났다.
① 촉각의
② 큰 타격을 받은, 황폐한
③ 연약한, 섬세한, 정교한
④ 확장된, 쭉 뻗은, 연장한

어휘

dilapidate 황폐케 하다, 파손하다 tactile 촉각의
devastate 황폐시키다 delicate 연약한, 섬세한, 정교한
extend 확장하다, 쭉 뻗다, 연장하다

03 정답 ②

정답해설

밑줄 친 부분에 들어갈 표현은 '경쟁하다'의 의미를 가진 ② compete를 사용하여 '패스트푸드 산업이 시장에서 경쟁한다'고 하는 것이 문맥상 가장 자연스럽다.

해석

패스트푸드 산업은 굉장히 변화무쌍한 시장에서 **경쟁해야** 한다.
① 던지다
② 경쟁하다
③ 위조품을 만들다
④ 약속하다, (범죄를) 저지르다

어휘

volatile 변덕스러운, 휘발성의
cast 던지다
compete 경쟁하다
counterfeit 위조품을 만들다
commit 약속하다, (범죄를) 저지르다

04 정답 ③

정답해설

어버이날 무엇을 했는지에 대해 Andy와 Hannah가 대화를 나누는 지문이다. '부모님에게 받은 것을 그저 돌려드리는 거야'라는 Andy의 말에 Hannah는 좋은 생각이라며 '~하지 말아야겠다는 것을 깨달았다.'라고 말한다. 따라서 빈 칸에 들어갈 가장 적절한 것은 ③ 'take it for granted(당연하게 받아들이다)'이다.

오답해설

① Hannah는 어버이날 부모님에 대해 깨달은 점을 이야기하며 자신이 '나잇 값을 하지 (act my age)' 말아야겠다고 생각했다는 것은 문맥상 빈칸에 들어갈 말로 어색하다.
② Andy가 부모님들로부터 받은 것을 그저 돌려드리는 것이라고 이야기하자 Hannah는 자신이 '최고조에 오르면(go high gear)' 안 되겠다는 것을 깨달았다고 말한다. 이는 대화의 흐름을 고려했을 때 빈칸에 들어갈 말로 부자연스럽다.
④ Andy가 어버이날 부모님을 모시고 외식한 것이 부모님께 받은 것을 그저 돌려드리는 것뿐이라고 말하자 Hannah는 자기도 '운에 맡겨 해보면(take a long chance)' 안 되겠다는 점을 깨달았다고 이야기하는 것은 맥락상 적절하지 않다.

해석

Andy: 안녕, Hannah. 너 어버이날 뭐 했어?
Hannah: 안녕, Andy. 나는 부모님을 위해 케이크와 선물을 샀어. 너는?
Andy: 나는 부모님을 모시고 멋진 레스토랑에서 저녁에 외식을 했어.
Hannah: 부모님이 좋아하셨어?
Andy: 응, 부모님이 그런 건 전혀 예상하지 못했다고 하셨어. 나는 그들에게 받은 것을 그저 돌려드리는 거야.
Hannah: 되게 좋은 생각이다! 나 역시도 그런 것을 <u>당연하게 받아들이지 말</u> 아야겠다는 것을 깨달았어.
Andy: 나도. 나는 그들의 희생에 굉장히 감사해.
① 나잇값을 하다
② 최고조에 오르다
③ ~을 당연하게 받아들이다
④ 운에 맡겨 해보다

어휘

act one's age 나잇값을 하다
go high gear 최고조에 오르다
take it for granted ~을 당연히 받아들이다
take a long chance 운에 맡겨 해보다

05 정답 ①

정답해설

① **출제 포인트: what vs. that**
'what'은 선행사를 포함한 관계대명사로 선행사가 없으며 뒤따라오는 문장이 불완전하다. 해당 문장은 'what'의 선행사가 없으며 'what'이 이끄는 절이 불완전타동사 'call'의 목적어가 없는 불완전한 형태이므로 관계대명사 'what'이 옳게 사용되었다.

오답해설

② **출제 포인트: 타동사로 착각하기 쉬운 완전자동사/수동태 불가동사**
'correspond'는 완전자동사로 전치사 없이 목적어를 가질 수 없다. 해당 문장은 'correspond' 이후에 전치사 없이 목적어 'the witness's version'을 사용하였으므로 틀린 문장이다. 따라서 'correspond'를 'correspond with' 또는 'correspond to'로 수정해야 한다. 또한 해당 문장에서 'what'은 선행사를 포함한 관계대명사로 선행사가 없으며 뒤따라오는 문장이 주어가 없는 불완전한 형태이므로 옳게 사용되었다. 'what'이 이끄는 절의 동사 'happened'는 완전자동사이므로 수동태로 사용할 수 없다.

③ **출제 포인트: 수동태 불가동사/접속사가 생략되지 않은 분사구문/분사가 생략된 분사구문**
'appear'는 자동사이므로 수동태로 사용할 수 없다. 해당 문장은 불완전자동사 'appear'를 수동태로 사용하였으므로 틀린 문장이다. 따라서 'is appeared'를 능동태 'appears'로 수정해야 한다. 또한 해당 문장에서 'though sacred in the eyes of their ancestors'는 접속사가 생략되지 않은 분사구문으로 주어 'This practice'와 현재분사 'being'이 생략되어 있다. 이때 'sacred'는 과거분사가 아니라 '신성한, 성스러운'을 뜻하는 형용사임에 유의해야 한다.

④ **출제 포인트: 주격 관계대명사절의 동사 수일치**
문맥상 '악령이 더 이상 그곳에서 살 수 없다'가 자연스러우므로 주격 관계대명사 'which'의 선행사는 복수형태의 명사(구) 'the evil spirits'임을 알 수 있다. 따라서 관계대명사절의 동사 'was'를 복수 형태인 'were'로 수정해야 한다.

해석

① 그들이 재미있는 상황이라고 부르는 것은 사실 재미있는 상황이 아니다.
② 그날 밤 일어난 일에 대한 그녀의 이야기는 증인의 설명과 일치하지 않았다.
③ 이러한 관습은, 그들의 조상들 눈에는 신성하지만, 그들에게는 우스꽝스럽게 보인다.
④ William은 악령들이 더 이상 그곳에서 살 수 없는 악령의 집에서 밤을 보냈다.

오답률 TOP 3

06 정답 ①

정답해설

① **출제 포인트: 관용표현(be particular about)/수동태**
「be particular about」은 관용표현으로 '~에 대해 까다로운'을 뜻하며 적절하게 사용되었다. 또한 run은 타동사로 '~을 운영하다'의 의미로 쓰일 때 수동형인 'be run'으로 나타낼 수 있으므로 'is run'은 옳게 사용되었다. 'run'의 과거분사 형태가 'run'임에 주의해야한다.

오답해설

② **출제 포인트: 사역동사의 목적격 보어/가정법 과거완료**
사역동사 'have'는 목적격 보어로 목적어와 능동관계인 경우 원형부정사 또는 현재분사를 가진다. 해당 문장은 사역동사 'have'가 과거분사로 사용되었으며 주어진 해석을 통해 목적어와 목적격 보어가 능동관계임을 알 수 있다. 따라서 목적격 보어에 원형부정사 또는 현재분사를 사용해야 하므로 to부정사 'to work'를 원형부정사 'work' 또는 현재분사 'working'으로 수정해야 한다. 또한 해당 문장은 가정법 과거완료가 쓰인 문장으로 「If+주어+had+과거분사 ~, 주어+would/could/should/might+have+과거분사 ~.」의 구조를 가진다.

③ **출제 포인트: 이중부정 금지**
'unless'는 '~하지 않는다면'의 의미로 부정을 뜻을 포함하는 접속사이다. 따라서 'unless'가 이끄는 절에는 부정부사 'not'을 사용하지 않는다. 해당

문장은 'unless'가 이끄는 절에 부정부사 'not'을 사용하였으므로 틀린 문장이다. 따라서 'not'을 삭제해야 한다. 또는 'Unless'를 'If'로 수정해 'If you are not~'으로 사용하는 것도 옳다.

④ 출제 포인트: By the time+주어+동사 ~, 주어+동사 ~.
「By the time+주어+동사 ~, 주어+동사 ~.」는 종속절의 동사에 과거시제를 사용하면 주절의 동사에 과거완료를 사용해야 한다. 해당 문장은 「By the time+주어+동사 ~, 주어+동사 ~.」가 쓰인 문장으로 종속절의 동사에 과거시제를 사용하였으나 주절의 동사에 과거진행 'was operating'을 사용하였으므로 틀린 문장이다. 따라서 'was operating'을 과거완료진행형 'had been operating'으로 수정해야 한다. 또한 'operate'가 완전자동사의 의미로 사용되는 경우 전치사 'on'과 함께 쓰여 '~을 수술하다'의 의미를 가진다.

오답률 TOP 2

07 정답 ①

정답해설

① 출제 포인트: 시간의 부사구/관용표현(come into force)
'last week'은 시간의 부사구로 과거시제 동사와 함께 사용한다. 해당 문장은 'last week'을 사용하였으나 동사에 현재완료시제인 'have come'을 사용하였으므로 틀린 문장이다. 따라서 'have come'을 과거시제 'came'으로 수정해야 한다. 또한 「come into force」는 관용표현으로 '시행되다'를 뜻한다.

오답해설

② 출제 포인트: 관용표현(never so much as)/자동사로 착각하기 쉬운 완전타동사
「never so much as ~」는 관용표현으로 '~조차하지 않다'를 뜻한다. 해당 문장은 'never so much as'가 쓰인 문장으로 주어진 해석과 일치하므로 옳은 문장이다. 또한 해당 문장에서 'mentioned'는 완전타동사 'mention'의 과거형으로 이후에 목적어 'it'을 옳게 사용하였다.

③ 출제 포인트: 수여동사
해당 문장에서 'forgive'는 수여동사이므로 이후에 간접목적어 'you'와 직접목적어 'anything'을 옳게 사용하였다. 또한 'except (for)'는 전치사로 '~을 제외하면, ~이 없으면'을 뜻한다.

④ 출제 포인트: 관용표현(be ashamed of)/목적격 관계대명사의 생략
「be ashamed of」는 관용표현으로 '~을 부끄럽게 여기다'를 뜻한다. 해당 문장은 'be ashamed of'가 쓰인 문장으로 주어진 해석과 일치하므로 옳은 문장이다. 또한 해당 문장에서 'something'과 'we' 사이에는 목적격 관계대명사 'that'이 생략되어 있으며 전치사 'of'와 'about'의 목적어가 없으므로 목적격 관계대명사를 사용하는 것이 옳다.

08 정답 ②

정답해설

본문은 'Sarah Holtman에 의한 Kant의 정의 이론의 적용'에 관한 내용이다. 본문 중반 "It's a question that Holtman seeks to answer, relating Kant's theory of justice to issues that Kant himself never considered, such as civic virtue, the prison system, and the death penalty(그것이 Holtman이 Kant의 정의 이론을 Kant 자신이 결코 생각해보지 않았을 시민적 덕성, 감옥 시스템, 그리고 사형과 같은 문제들과 관련시키면서 답하려고 시도하는 질문이다)."을 통해 '현대의 문제에 Kant의 이론을 관련시킨다'고 언급하고, 이후 "Through the application of the general principles of Kant's theory of justice to these issues(Kant의 정의 이론의 일반 법칙들을 이러한 문제에 적용하는 것을 통해),"를 통해, '이러한 문제들에 Kant 이론의 일반 원리를 적용시킨다'고 언급하고 있으므로, 글의 주제로 가장 적절한 것은 '② Applying Kant's theory today(오늘날 Kant의 이론을 적용하는 것)'이다.

오답해설

① 본문에서 언급된 현대의 문제들 중, '감옥 시스템, 사형'이 언급되기는 하였으나, 전체 글의 내용은 '범죄자를 위한 정의 실현'과는 관련이 없으므로, 글의 주제로 적절하지 않다.
③ 본문과 관련 없는 내용이다.
④ Holtman은 Kant의 이론을 현대의 문제에 적용하며 연구하는 인물로, 두 사람의 이론을 각각 비교하는 내용이 아니므로 오답이다.

해석

철학 교수인 Sarah Holtman은 Kant의 정치 철학을 특정 규칙을 규정하려는 시도가 아닌, 오히려 정의로 간주되는 것을 결정하기 위한 법칙의 일반적 틀로 바라본다. 그녀는 "정의로 간주되는 것은 변하지 않는다. 그러나 우리가 어떻게 정의를 실현하는가는 시간이 지남에 따라 그리고 다른 상황에서 달라질 것이다."라고 말한다. 하지만 우리가 오늘날 어떻게 Holtman이 Kant의 것이라 여기는 정의 이론에 입각해 정의를 실현할 수 있을까? 그것이 Holtman이 Kant의 정의 이론을 Kant 자신이 결코 생각해보지 않았을 시민적 덕성, 감옥 시스템, 그리고 사형과 같은 문제들과 관련시키면서 답하려고 시도하는 질문이다. Kant의 정의 이론의 일반 법칙을 이러한 문제에 적용하는 것을 통해, Holtman은 사람들이 구식이 아닌 생산적이고 감탄할 만한 신념을 가지고 돌아간다고 생각한다. Holtman에 따르면, Kant의 정치적 저술들은 단지 18세기의 인공 유물에 불과한 것이 아니라, 21세기 문제들을 해결하려는 노력에 대한 흥미로운 이론을 제공한다.

① 범죄자들을 위한 정의를 실현하는 것
② 오늘날 Kant의 이론을 적용하는 것
③ Kant의 정의 이론 비판하는 것
④ Kant와 Holtman의 이론을 비교하는 것

어휘

prescribe 규정하다, 정하다 count as …이라 간주되다[간주하다]
realize 실현[달성]하다
attribute A to B A를 B(사람·시대 등)의 작품[것]이라고 생각하다
seek to 동사원형 ~하도록 시도하다
civic 시민의 virtue 덕, 공덕
come away with (어떤 인상·느낌을) 갖고 떠나다
conception 신념, 이해 antiquated 구식인
laudable 칭찬[감탄]할 만한 far from 전혀[결코] …이 아닌
mere 겨우 …의, (한낱) …에 불과한 artifact 인공 유물, 인공품
appealing 흥미로운, 매력적인
grapple with …을 해결하려고 노력하다

09 정답 ②

정답해설

본문은 '포유류와는 달리 새가 알을 낳는 이유'에 대해 설명하고 있다. 본문에 따르면, '태생'은 '암컷의 생산성을 저하시키고 무게 증가로 인한 위험성을 높이며, 수컷의 역할을 박탈할 수 있고, 또한 암컷의 높은 신체 온도가 알의 성장을 저해'할 수 있다. 따라서 비록 새끼를 낳는 것이 진화적인 측면에서 더욱 발달한 것이라고 여겨질 수 있으나, 새의 입장에서는 태생을 하는 것이 오히려 더 비효율적인 번식 방법으로 회귀하는 셈이 되는 것이다. 그러므로 글의 요지로 가장 적절한 보기는 '② It is more effective for birds to lay eggs than live-bearing(새들이 알을 낳는 것이 태생보다 더 효율적이다).'이다.

오답해설

① 새가 알을 돌보는 방법에 대해서는 본문에 구체적으로 언급되지 않는다.

③ 본문은 조류와 포유류의 번식 방법의 차이에 대해 언급하고 있으므로, 글의 요지와 적절하지 않다.
④ 첫 문장 "Why have birds not "advanced" beyond egg laying and begun to bear their young alive like mammals?(왜 새는 알을 낳는 것 이상으로 "발달하지" 않았으며 포유류처럼 그들의 새끼를 살아있는 상태로 낳기 시작하지 않았을까?)"를 통해, '태생을 하는 포유류가 더 많이 진화한 것'이라는 것을 유추할 수는 있으나, 이것이 글 전체를 아우르는 요지는 아니므로, 오답이다.

해석

왜 새는 알을 낳는 것 이상으로 "발달하지" 않았으며 포유류처럼 그들의 새끼를 살아있는 상태로 낳기 시작하지 않았을까? 사람들은 태생(胎生)이 비행과 양립할 수 없다고 주장해왔지만, 박쥐는 그 가설이 틀렸음을 입증한다. Vanderbilt University의 Daniel Blackburn과 Cornell의 Howard Evans는 태생으로의 진화 경로는 보통 그것들이 암컷의 몸에서 마침내 부화할 때까지 알을 더욱더 긴 기간 동안 보유하는 것을 수반했다는 점을 지적했다. Blackburn과 Evans는 알을 보유하고 있는 것이 새에게 이익은 거의 주지 않고 몇몇의 불이익을 준다고 주장한다. 암컷들은 명백히 알이 부화할 때까지 많은 알을 보유하고 있을 수 없기 때문에 – 생산성의 손실과 추가적인 무게 부담과 관련되어 어미에게 주어지는 증가된 위험이 후자에 포함된다. 게다가, 많은 종에서, 새끼 양육에 대한 수컷의 기여가 사라질 것이고, 최근 암컷 새의 몸이 적절한 알의 성장에 있어서 너무 뜨거울 수도 있다는 것도 알려졌다. 그러므로, 태생을 발달시키는 것은 새들에게 후퇴나 다름없는 것 같다.
① 다른 새들은 다른 방식으로 자신들의 알을 돌본다.
② 새들이 알을 낳는 것이 태생보다 더 효율적이다.
③ 조류와 포유류는 몇 가지 공통적인 특징이 있다.
④ 알을 낳는 번식 방법은 태생보다 더 원시적이다.

어휘

bear 낳다	young 새끼
viviparity 태생(胎生)	live-bearing 태생(胎生)
incompatible 양립할 수 없는, 공존할 수 없는	
disprove 틀렸음을 입증하다	hypothesis 가설
argue 주장하다	retention 보유, 간직
latter 후자	retain 보유하다, 간직하다
burden 부담	contribution 기여, 공헌
offspring 새끼, 자식	evolve 진화[발달]시키다

10 정답 ②

정답해설

본문은 '미생물(균)과 인간의 건강의 관계'에 대해 설명하고 있다. 세 번째 문장 "that cloud of dog-borne microbes may be working to keep us healthy."를 통해, '개(반려동물)로 인해 실내로 유입된 미생물이 우리를 건강하게 해준다'고 언급하며, '다양한 균과의 접촉으로 인해 적절한 면역력이 발생할 수 있다'는 것을 암시하고 있다. 또한, 마지막 문장 "According to the so-called hygiene hypothesis, spending over 90 percent of our time in the bacteria-poor environment indoors, as we do (especially early in life, when our immune systems are being formed), can cause our bodies to overreact to harmless substances later on, making us sick(이른바 위생 가설에 따르면, (특히 우리의 면역 체계가 형성되는 시기인 어린 시절에) 우리가 그러하듯이, 박테리아가 적은 실내 환경에서 일생의 90퍼센트 이상을 보내는 것은 향후 우리의 신체가 무해한 물질에도 과민 반응하도록 만들 수 있고, 이것이 우리를 아프게 만든다)."를 통해 '미생물에 충분히 노출되지 않으면, 유해하지 않은 물질에조차도 과민 반응을 일으켜, 이는 질병으로 이어진다'고 설명하며, '미생물(균)에의 적절한 노출의 필요성'을 역설하고 있다. 따라서 글의 요지로 가장 적절한 것은 '② Exposure to a rich array of indoor germs may actually be salutary(풍부한 실내의 균에 노출되는 것이 실제로 유익할 수 있다).'이다.

오답해설

① 본문에서는 '개로 인해 외부에서 유입된 다양한 미생물로 인해 우리의 면역 체계가 강해져 더욱 건강해질 수 있다'고 설명하고 있다. 따라서 글의 내용과 일치하지 않는 보기이므로, 글의 요지로 적절하지 않다.
③ 마지막 문장 "According to the so-called hygiene hypothesis, spending over 90 percent of our time in the bacteria-poor environment indoors, as we do (especially early in life, when our immune systems are being formed), can cause our bodies to overreact to harmless substances later on, making us sick(이른바 위생 가설에 따르면, (특히 우리의 면역 체계가 형성되는 시기인 어린 시절에) 우리가 그러하듯이, 박테리아가 적은 실내 환경에서 일생의 90퍼센트 이상을 보내는 것은 향후 우리의 신체가 무해한 물질에도 과민 반응하도록 만들 수 있고, 이것이 우리를 아프게 만든다)."에서, '실내 환경이 너무 깨끗한 것이 오히려 우리를 아프게 만든다'고 언급하고 있으므로, 본문의 요지와 반대되는 내용이다.
④ 본문과 관련 없는 내용이다.

해석

개들은 진흙에서 구른다. 그들은 배설물과 다른 의심스러운 물질들의 냄새를 맡는다. 그리고 나서 그들은 발, 코, 그리고 털에 수많은 균을 묻혀 우리의 집 안에 들인다. 그리고, 만일 반려동물과 인간의 건강에 대한 최근의 연구가 옳다면, 개로 인해 전달된 그 미생물들 무리는 우리를 건강하게 해주기 위해 작용할지도 모른다. 유행병학 연구는 개를 기르는 가정에서 자란 어린이들은 천식과 알레르기와 같은 자가면역 질병에 걸릴 위험이 더 적다는 것과, 이것이 이 동물들이 우리의 집 안으로 들여오는 미생물의 다양성의 결과일지도 모른다는 것을 보여준다. 이른바 위생 가설에 따르면, (특히 우리의 면역 체계가 형성되는 시기인 어린 시절에) 우리가 그러하듯이, 박테리아가 적은 실내 환경에서 일생의 90퍼센트 이상을 보내는 것은 향후 우리의 신체가 무해한 물질에도 과민 반응하도록 만들 수 있고, 이것이 우리를 아프게 만든다.
① 개들은 사람에게 질병을 일으키는 해로운 박테리아를 옮길 수 있다.
② 풍부한 다수의 실내 균에 노출되는 것이 실제로 유익할 수 있다.
③ 당신들의 아이들을 건강하게 키우기 위해서 집을 가능한 한 깨끗하게 유지하는 것이 중요하다.
④ 천식과 알레르기와 같은 질병들은 간단한 민간요법을 이용함으로써 예방될 수 있다.

어휘

feces 대변, 똥, 배설물	substance 물질, 물체
track (눈·진흙 등을) 발에 묻혀 들이다	
snout 코, 주둥이	cloud 무리, 떼, 집단
-borne -으로 운반된[전달된]	microbe 미생물
epidemiological 전염병학의	autoimmune 자가면역의
asthma 천식	diversity 다양성
hygiene hypothesis 위생 가설 (어렸을 때 먼지, 박테리아 등 전염병을 발생시키는 물질에 노출되지 않으면 면역 체계가 약해져서 알레르기나 천식에 걸릴 가능성이 오히려 커진다는 이론)	
immune 면역의	overreact 과잉[과민] 반응을 보이다
carry 옮기다	rich 풍부한
an array of 다수의	salutary 유익한
home remedy 민간요법, 가정 치료법	

기적사 DAY 40

01	①	02	②	03	③	04	④	05	②
06	③	07	④	08	④	09	③	10	③

01 정답 ①

정답해설

문맥상 '예산'을 뜻하는 ① budget을 사용하여 '경기침체로 예산을 감축했다'고 하는 것이 가장 자연스럽다.

해석

경기침체로 인해, 많은 학군들이 그들의 **예산** 감축을 겪어 왔다.
① 예산
② 장수
③ 가소성, 적응성
④ 유전, 상속

어휘

recession 불경기, 불황 budget 예산
longevity 장수 plasticity 가소성, 적응성
heredity 유전, 상속

02 정답 ②

정답해설

밑줄 친 'available'은 '이용할 수 있는'의 뜻을 가지고 있다. 주어진 문맥상 '이용할 수 있는'의 의미는 ② attainable과 의미가 가장 가깝다.

해석

요즘에는 **이용 가능한** 교육적인 컴퓨터 프로그램, 게임, 그리고 도구가 많이 있다.
① 유사한
② 달성할 수 있는, 획득할 수 있는
③ 방수의
④ 신경학상의

어휘

available 이용 가능한 similar 유사한
attainable 달성할 수 있는, 획득할 수 있는, 이룰 수 있는
waterproof 방수의 neurological 신경학상의

03 정답 ③

정답해설

'나는 화가 나서 그것을 받아들일 수 없었다'고 했고, 여기서 빈칸은 '그것'에 해당하므로 문맥상 '사과하다'의 'apologize'가 가장 적절하다. 따라서 정답은 'apologize'의 과거형인 ③ apologized가 가장 적절하다.

해석

그는 나에게 오늘 아침에 **사과했는데**, 난 너무 화가 나서 그것을 받아들일 수 없었다.
① 고발했다
② 포함했다
③ 사과했다
④ 소유했다

어휘

accuse 고발하다 cover 포함하다
apologize 사과하다 possess 소유하다

04 정답 ④

정답해설

지난 주말에 콘서트에 다녀온 일에 대해 Lena와 Jake가 대화를 나누는 지문이다. '콘서트에서 군중과 함께 노래를 따라 불렀다'라는 Lena의 말에 Jake가 '너의 목소리가 다르게 들리며 ~한 거 같다'라고 말한다. 따라서 빈칸에 들어갈 가장 적절한 것은 ④ have a frog in your throat(네 목이 쉬다)이다.

오답해설

① Jake는 공연장을 다녀온 Lena의 목소리가 다르게 들린다며, 그녀가 '해고된(get the ax)' 것 같다고 말하는 것은 대화의 흐름상 부적절하다.
② 공연장을 다녀온 Lena에게 Jake가 목소리가 달라진 것 같다면서 그녀가 '눈치 챈(smell a rat)' 것 같다고 얘기하는 것은 문맥상 빈칸에 들어갈 말로 어색하다.
③ Lena가 공연장을 다녀온 후로 '목소리가 달라진 듯하다'면서, Jake는 그녀에게 '패배한(lose the day)' 것 같다고 말하는 것은 맥락상 자연스럽지 않다.

해석

Jake: 난 네가 지난 주말에 공연을 다녀왔다고 들었어.
Lena: 응 맞아. 굉장히 멋졌어. 나는 그곳에 혼자 갔지만 내가 간 공연들 중에 가장 재미있었어.
Jake: 네가 즐겼다니 다행이야. 전혀 외롭지 않았어?
Lena: 내가 거기에 처음 도착했을 때는 살짝 외로웠어. 근데 공연이 시작했을 때, 나는 군중과 함께 노래를 계속 따라 불렀어.
Jake: 어쩐지 네 목소리가 다르게 들리더라. 너 목이 쉰 것처럼 보여.
Lena: 맞아. 나 계속 위아래로 뛰면서 군중 속에서 세 시간 가까이 소리 질렀어.
Jake: 우와! 너 공연을 되게 즐겼나 보네!
Lena: 아주 많이 즐겼어!
① 해고당하다
② 눈치채다
③ 패배하다
④ 목이 쉬다

어휘

get the ax 해고당하다 smell a rat 눈치채다
lose the day 패배하다
have a frog in one's throat 목이 쉬다

오답률 TOP 1

05 정답 ②

정답해설

② **출제 포인트: 주격 보어로 쓰인 to부정사에서 to의 생략/what vs. that**

주어로 쓰인 'what'절이 'do'로 끝나는 경우 주격 보어로 쓰인 'to+동사원형'에서 'to'를 생략할 수 있다. 따라서 주격 보어로 쓰인 'make'는 옳은 표현이다. 이때 'What'은 선행사를 포함한 관계대명사로 선행사가 없고 뒤따라오는 문장이 'to do'의 목적어가 없는 불완전한 형태이므로 옳게 사용되었다.

오답해설

① **출제 포인트: 가정법 과거완료/what vs. that**
해당 문장은 주절의 'could have helped'를 통해 가정법 과거완료가 사용되었음을 알 수 있다. 따라서 종속절인 if절의 과거시제 동사 'told'를 과거완료인 'had told'로 수정해야 한다. 또한 해당 문장에서 'what'은 선행사를 포함한 관계대명사로 선행사가 없고 이후의 문장에 주어가 없는 불완전한 형태이므로 옳게 사용되었다. 또한 해당 문장에서 주절에 쓰인 'help'는 자동사로 쓰였다.

③ **출제 포인트: 타동사구/능동태 vs. 수동태**
'cut off'는 타동사구이므로 목적어가 있어야 한다. 해당 문장은 'cut off' 이후에 목적어가 없으므로 틀린 문장이다. 따라서 'cut off'를 수동태 'be cut off'로 수정해야 한다. 이때 'cut'의 과거분사 형태가 'cut'임에 주의해야 한다.

④ **출제 포인트: what vs. that/현재분사 vs. 과거분사**
해당 문장은 'that'이 이끄는 절에 'have known'의 목적어가 없으며 관계대명사 'that' 앞에 선행사가 없으므로 틀린 문장이다. 따라서 'that'을 선행사를 포함하는 관계대명사 'what'으로 수정해야 한다. 또한 해당 문장에서 'though too often telling us what we have known already'는 접속사가 생략되지 않은 분사구문으로 생략된 주어 'Tom'과 능동관계이므로 현재분사 'telling'은 옳은 표현이다.

해석

① 네가 나에게 무엇이 잘못되었는지 말해주었더라면, 나는 도울 수 있었을 텐데.
② 그녀가 할 필요가 있는 일은 유용한 전화번호 목록을 만드는 것이다.
③ 너는 집의 나머지 부분에서 단절될 수 있는 자신만의 작업 공간을 가지고 있어야 한다.
④ Tom은 우리가 이미 알고 있는 것을 우리에게 너무 자주 이야기하지만, 그의 일에 능숙했다.

오답률 TOP 3

06 정답 ③

정답해설

③ **출제 포인트: By the time+주어+동사 ~, 주어+동사 ~.**
「By the time+주어+동사 ~, 주어+동사 ~.」는 종속절의 동사에 과거시제를 사용하면 주절의 동사에 과거완료를 사용해야 한다. 해당 문장은 「By the time+주어+동사 ~, 주어+동사 ~.」가 쓰인 문장으로 종속절의 동사에 과거시제 'became'을, 주절의 동사에 과거완료 'had decided'를 옳게 사용하였다.

오답해설

① **출제 포인트: 현재분사 vs. 과거분사/관용표현(be liable for)**
현재분사 'wasting'은 수식하는 대상 'costs'와 수동관계이므로 과거분사 'wasted'로 수정해야 한다. 또한 해당 문장에서 'is liable for'는 관용표현 「be liable for」의 현재형으로 '~에 대해 책임이 있음'을 뜻한다.

② **출제 포인트: 가정법 과거완료/해석 주의**
가정법 과거완료가 쓰인 문장으로 「If+주어+had+과거분사 ~, 주어+would/could/should/might+have+과거분사 ~.」를 옳게 사용하였으나 주어진 해석이 '몰랐을 텐데'이므로 'would have known'을 'would not have known'으로 수정해야 한다.

④ **출제 포인트: 접속사의 쓰임**
접속사 'although'는 '(비록) ~이긴 하지만'을 뜻한다. 해당 문장은 'although'를 사용하였으나 주어진 해석이 '~한다면'이므로 틀린 문장이다. 따라서 'although'를 'if'로 수정해야 한다.

07 정답 ④

정답해설

④ **출제 포인트: 관용표현(be consistent with)/해석 주의**
「be inconsistent with」는 관용표현으로 '~와 일치하지 않다'를 뜻한다. 해당 문장은 'be inconsistent with'를 사용하였으나 주어진 해석이 '~과 일치한다'이므로 틀린 문장이다. 따라서 'inconsistent'를 'consistent'로 수정해야 한다.

오답해설

① **출제 포인트: 관용표현(not so much as)**
「not so much as」는 관용표현으로 '~조차도 않는'을 뜻한다. 해당 문장은 'not so much as'가 쓰인 문장으로 주어진 해석과 일치하므로 옳은 문장이다.

② **출제 포인트: 수여동사**
해당 문장에서 'left'는 수여동사 'leave'의 과거 형태로 이후에 간접목적어 'all her children'과 직접목적어 'a small sum of money'를 옳게 사용하였다.

③ **출제 포인트: 관용표현(make up for)/관용표현(be anxious to+동사원형)/현재분사 vs. 과거분사**
「make up for」는 관용표현으로 '~을 보상하다, 만회하다'를 뜻하며 「be anxious to+동사원형」은 '~하기를 갈망하다'를 뜻한다. 해당 문장은 'make up for'와 'be anxious to+동사원형'이 쓰인 문장으로 주어진 해석과 일치하므로 옳은 문장이다. 또한 해당 문장에서 'disappointing'은 현재분사형태의 감정 제공 형용사로 명사 'start'를 수식하고 있다.

오답률 TOP 2

08 정답 ④

정답해설

본문은 'Kant가 강조한 자유, 평등, 독립성에 기초한 "정당한 법칙(권리)의 필요성"'에 대한 글이다. ①에서 Kant가 주장한 세 가지 법칙에 대해 설명한 후, ②에서는 해당 법칙의 흥미로운 특징에 대해 언급한 뒤, ③에서 앞서 언급된 사실에 따른 Kant의 주장을 설명하고, 마지막에 Kant의 주장을 뒷받침하는 근거를 제시하는 것이 자연스럽다. 그런데 ④에서는, '모든 사람이 동일한 권리를 갖는' 평등'에 관한 내용을 설명하고 있으므로, '세 가지 원리의 필요성'에 대해 언급하고 있는 ③ 이후에 위치하는 것은 문맥상 어색하다. 따라서 정답은 ④이다.

오답해설

나머지 보기는 문맥상 자연스러우므로 오답이다.

해석

Immanuel Kant는 국가에 의해 기본적 권리, 법, 자격이 주어지고 향상될 경우에만 국가와 관련하여 사회가 정치적으로 기능할 수 있다고 강조했다. ① Kant가 가르치듯이, 이러한 "정당한 법칙"은 세 가지 합리적인 원리에 기반한다: (1) 모든 사회구성원의 인간으로서의 자유, (2) 모든 사회구성원의 국민으로서의 모든 다른 사람과의 평등, (3) 국가의 모든 구성원의 시민으로서의 독립성. ② 이러한 원리의 흥미로운 점은 그것들이 국가에 의해 주어지는 것이 아니라, 국가의 국민에 의한 국가의 형성과 수용에 있어서 필수적이라는 것이다. ③ 이런 의미에서, Kant는 "정당한 법칙" 확립을 위해서 뿐만 아니라, 애초에 국가가 역할을 하기 위해서도 이러한 원리가 무엇보다도 필요하다고 생각했다. ④ 모두에게 법이 동일하고 "평등한" 방식으로 평가되고 적용될 수 있도록 모든 사람은 국가 내에서 동일한 권리를 가져야 할 필요가 있다. 이는 국민의 수용이 없이 한 국가는 존재하지 않을 것이며, 그러므로 국가에 대한 국민들의 지지를 유지하기 위해 국가 내에 권리가 필요하기 때문에 그렇다.

어휘

stress 강조하다
fundamental 근본[본질]적인; 필수적인, 핵심적인
entitlement 자격, 권리
righteous 정당한, 당연한, 옳은
rational 합리적인, 이성적인
subject 국민
independence 독립, 자립
commonwealth 국가, 공화국, 민주국가
creation 창조, 발생
acceptance 수용, 승인
above all 무엇보다도

09 정답 ③

정답해설

본문은 '새와 파충류의 관계'에 대해 언급하며, 이를 설명하기 위해 '파충류의 진화 역사'에 대해 서술하고 있다. 빈칸 바로 이전에는 파충류가 진화되어 온 과정 중, 공룡 멸종 단계에 대해 언급하고 있는데, '한 집단을 제외하고 모든 공룡이 멸종했다'고 설명한다. 이후, "These evolved over the next 65 million years into modern birds(이것들은 이후 6천 5백만 년 동안 현대의 새로 진화했다)."라고 언급하며, 살아남은 공룡들이 현대의 새로 진화했다는 것을 설명하고 있다. 따라서 살아남은 공룡들은 새들의 조상, 즉, '깃털이 있는(feathered)' 집단이었음을 유추할 수 있다. 그러므로 정답은 '③ feathered(깃털이 있는)'이다.

오답해설

①, ④ 본문에는 살아남은 공룡의 '크기'에 대해 언급하고 있지 않으므로, 빈칸에 적절하지 않다.
나머지 선지는 문맥상 빈칸에 적절하지 않다.

해석

새는 파충류와 밀접한 관련이 있으며, 악어와 가장 밀접한 관련이 있다. 이것을 이해하기 위해, 우리는 약간의 역사를 검토해야 한다. 첫 번째 파충류 집단은 약 3억 년 전에 진화했다. 약 4천만 년 이후(지질학적 기준에 따르면 매우 빨리), 수궁류라 불리는 파충류 집단이 갈라져 나왔고, 이것들이 결국 현대의 포유류가 되었다. 다른 파충류 집단은 이후 1억 2천만 년 동안 분리되었고, 공룡이라 불린 한 집단은 매우 번성했다. 이 공룡들은 다른 시대에 갈라진 집단인 현대의 뱀, 도마뱀, 그리고 거북이와 오직 먼 관계에 있을 뿐이다. 그러나, 6천 5백만 년 전, 대량 멸종 사건이 있었으며, <u>깃털이 있는</u> 공룡 한 집단을 제외한 모든 공룡이 죽었다. 이것들은 이후 6천 5백만 년 동안 현대의 새로 진화했다. 그러므로 새는 단지 공룡과 밀접한 관련이 있는 것만이 아니다. 그들은 진정한 공룡인 것이다!
① 거대한
② 비늘이 있는
③ 깃털이 있는
④ 자그마한

어휘

geologic 지질학의
therapsid 수궁류
branch off 갈라지다, 나뉘다
split off 분리되다[갈라지다]
branch 가지, 파생물, 하위 범주
successful 번영하는, 번성하는, 성공적인
distantly 먼
extinction 멸종
gigantic 거대한
feathered 깃털이 있는, 깃털로 덮인
petite 자그마한

10 정답 ③

정답해설

본문은 'Zoonotic diseases(동물 매개 감염병)'에 대한 글이다. 본문 중반 "The World Health Organization (WHO) estimates that 61 percent of all human diseases are zoonotic in origin, while 75 percent of new diseases discovered in the last decade are zoonotic(세계 보건 기구(WHO)는 모든 인간 질병의 61퍼센트의 기원이 동물 매개이며, 한편 지난 10년 동안 발견된 새로운 질병 중 75퍼센트가 동물 매개라고 추정한다)."에 따르면, '모든 인간 질병 61퍼센트의 기원이 동물 매개이며, 지난 10년간 발견된 새로운 질병들 중 75퍼센트가 동물 매개이다.' 본문의 해당 문장에서 언급된 75%는 10년 동안 발견된 '새로운' 질병에 대한 원인으로서 'zoonotic'을 제시한 경우이고, 선지에서 언급된 70% 이상은 '새로운' 질병이 아니라 'human diseases(인간 질병들)'의 수치로 제시한 경우에 해당된다. 즉, 질병의 수치 이전에 어떤 '대상'에 대한 수치인지를 꼭 확인해야겠다. 따라서 '③ Over seventy percent of human diseases were originated from animals(인간 질병의 70퍼센트 이상이 동물로부터 비롯되었다).'는 본문의 내용과 일치하지 않는다.

오답해설

① 첫 문장 "Many different types of animals can carry harmful germs, such as bacteria, fungi, parasites, and viruses(많은 다른 유형의 동물들이 박테리아, 곰팡이 균류, 기생충, 그리고 바이러스와 같은 해로운 균을 옮길 수 있다)."와 두 번째 문장 "These are then shared with humans and cause illness(그러면 이것들은 인간과 공유가 되고 질병을 일으킨다)."를 통해 본문의 내용과 일치하는 것을 알 수 있다.
② 세 번째 문장 "Zoonotic diseases, also called zoonoses, range from mild to severe, and some can even be fatal(동물원성(原性) 감염증이라고도 불리는 동물 매개 감염 질병은 가벼운 것부터 심각한 것까지 다양하며, 일부는 심지어 치명적일 수도 있다)."에서 '일부 동물 매개 감염 질병은 치명적'이라고 언급하고 있으며, 본문 후반에서도 '동물 매개 감염 질병이 수백만 건의 사망을 야기했다'고 언급하고 있으므로, 글의 내용과 일치한다.
④ 본문 후반 "Before the introduction of new hygiene regulations about 100 years ago, zoonotic diseases such as bovine tuberculosis, bubonic plague, and glanders caused millions of deaths(약 100년 전 새로운 위생 규정을 도입하기 전에는 소결핵증, 림프절 페스트, 마비저와 같은 동물 매개 감염 질병은 수백만 건의 사망을 야기했다)."를 통해, '약 100년 전부터 새로운 위생 규정이 도입되었음'을 알 수 있으므로, 글의 내용과 일치한다.

해석

많은 다른 유형의 동물들이 박테리아, 곰팡이 균류, 기생충, 그리고 바이러스와 같은 해로운 균을 옮길 수 있다. 그리고 이것들은 인간과 공유가 되고 질병을 일으킨다. 동물원성(原性) 감염증이라고도 불리는 동물 매개 감염 질병은 가벼운 것부터 심각한 것까지 다양하며, 일부는 심지어 치명적일 수도 있다. 동물 매개 감염 질병은 미국과 전 세계에 모두 널리 퍼져있다. 세계 보건 기구(WHO)는 모든 인간 질병의 61퍼센트의 기원이 동물 매개인 한편 지난 10년 동안 발견된 새로운 질병 중 75퍼센트가 동물 매개라고 추정한다. 약 100년 전 새로운 위생 규정을 도입하기 전에는 소결핵증, 림프절 페스트, 마비저와 같은 동물 매개 감염 질병은 수백만 건의 사망을 야기했다. 그것들은 개발도상국에서 여전히 주요 문제이다.
① 다양한 동물들이 인간에게 질병을 옮길 수 있다.
② 특정 동물 매개 감염 질병은 인간 사망자를 발생시킬 수 있다.
③ 인간 질병의 70퍼센트 이상이 동물로부터 비롯되었다.
④ 위생 문제를 다루기 위해 조치가 취해진 지 약 한 세기가 지났다.

어휘

carry 옮기다
fungus 균류, 곰팡이류 (pl. fungi)
zoonotic disease 동물 매개 감염 질병
zoonosis 동물원성(原性) 감염증 (동물로부터 사람에게 전염되는 질병)
　　　(pl. zoonoses)
fatal 죽음을 초래하는, 치명적인　　estimate 추정하다
hygiene 위생　　bovine tuberculosis 소결핵증
bubonic plague 가래톳페스트, 림프절페스트
glanders 마비저(馬鼻疽)　　transmit 옮기다
address 다루다; 연설하다

결국엔 성정혜 영어 하프모의고사
기적사 복습 모의고사 4회

01	③	02	④	03	③	04	①	05	①
06	①	07	③	08	③	09	④	10	③
11	④	12	③	13	③	14	③	15	③
16	①	17	③	18	④	19	②	20	④

01 정답 ③　　　　　　　　　　　　　　Day 36-02

정답해설

밑줄 친 'analogous'는 '유사한'을 뜻하며 ③ similar와 의미가 가장 가깝다.

해석

세포의 물질대사 조직은, 그것 나름대로의 종합 계획, 작용하는 청사진, 이동 매개체, 그리고 다른 나머지 등에서 완전히 **유사한** 방식으로 작용한다.
① 섬세한, 연약한
② 이상한
③ 유사한, 비슷한
④ 새로운

02 정답 ④　　　　　　　　　　　　　　Day 38-02

정답해설

'specious'는 '그럴듯한, 겉만 번드르르한'의 뜻으로 ④ superficial과 의미가 가장 가깝다.

해석

그의 주장은 나에게 있어 완전히 **그럴듯했**다.
① 새로운
② 부족한, 희귀한, 드물게, 적은
③ 엄중한, 강경한
④ 외관상의, 피상적인, 실체 없는

03 정답 ③　　　　　　　　　　　　　　Day 35-02

정답해설

문맥상 '고통을 받다'를 뜻하는 'suffer'를 활용한 ③ suffered가 빈칸에 들어가기에 가장 적절하다.

해석

한국인들은 일본의 잔인함에 **고통을 받았고**, 독립운동가들은 투옥되고, 고문을 받거나 죽임을 당했다.
① 의지했다
② 뺐다, 공제했다
③ 고통받았다
④ (대사를) 상기시켜 줬다

04 정답 ①　　　　　　　　　　　　　　Day 31-01

정답해설

마지막 문장에서 '핵 테러와 대규모 살상 무기의 확산을 막는다(prevent the spread of weapons of mass destruction and nuclear terrorism)'고

했으므로, 빈칸 다음에 있는 '다각적인 핵 안보와 안전(the multilateral nuclear security and safety)'을 ① 강화한다(beef up)고 하는 것이 문맥상 적절하다.

해석
사무총장은 UN이 다각적인 핵 안보와 안전을 **강화하기** 위한 여러 가지 행동 계획을 제안할 것이라고 말했다. 그는 강력한 경제적 제재가 핵 테러와 대규모 살상 무기의 확산을 막는 데에 필수적이라고 말했다.
① ~을 강화하다, 보강하다
② ~을 생략하다, 없애다, 면제시키다
③ ~을 줄이다, 끄다
④ ~에서 지우다

05 정답 ① — Day 33-02

정답해설
문맥상 '자제하다, 삼가다'를 뜻하는 ① refrain을 사용하여 '먹거나 마시는 것을 삼간다'라고 하는 것이 가장 자연스럽다.

해석
라마단 기간 동안에, 무슬림 사람들은 낮 시간 동안에 먹거나 마시는 것을 **삼간다**.
① 자제하다, 삼가다
② 숙고하다, 응시하다
③ 중재하다, 조정하다
④ 관련되다, 간주하다

06 정답 ① — Day 39-07

정답해설
① 출제 포인트: 시간의 부사구/관용표현(come into force)
'last week'은 시간의 부사구로 과거시제 동사와 함께 사용한다. 해당 문장은 'last week'을 사용하였으나 동사에 현재완료시제인 'have come'을 사용하였으므로 틀린 문장이다. 따라서 'have come'을 과거시제 'came'으로 수정해야 한다. 또한 「come into force」는 관용표현으로 '시행되다'를 뜻한다.

07 정답 ③ — Day 36-06

정답해설
③ 출제 포인트: 가정법 과거완료/If 생략 가정법
가정법 과거완료는 「If+주어+had+과거분사 ~, 주어+would/could/should/might+have+과거분사 ~.」의 구조이며 'If'를 생략할 경우 「Had+주어+과거분사 ~, 주어+would/could/should/might+have+과거분사 ~.」의 구조이다. 해당 문장은 'If'를 생략한 가정법 과거완료가 쓰인 옳은 문장이다.

08 정답 ③ — Day 38-05

정답해설
③ 출제 포인트: 주격 관계대명사절의 동사 수일치
해당 문장에서 주격 관계대명사 'which'의 선행사는 단수 형태의 명사(구) 'a huge nest'이므로 관계대명사절의 동사에 단수 형태인 'is'를 옳게 사용하였다. 또한 해당 문장에서 'what'은 선행사를 포함하는 관계대명사이며 'he assumes'는 삽입절로 관계대명사절의 동사는 'was'임에 유의해야 한다.

해석
① 그녀를 정말로 걱정스럽게 만드는 것은 그 아이가 얼마나 불행했는가였다.
② 그들이 당신을 재미있게 만드는 것에 관심이 있다는 것은 흥미롭다.
③ Tom은 자신이 가정하기에 까치집은 큰 둥지를 찾았다.
④ 그 집은, 겉으로는 인상적이지만, 실은 매우 아늑한 크기이다.

09 정답 ④ — Day 32-09

정답해설
본문은 'bisphenol A (BPA)에의 노출이 미치는 영향'에 대한 다양한 연구 결과를 소개하고 있다. 본문에서 언급된 BPA의 영향에는 '비정상적 난자 성숙(abnormal egg maturation), 사춘기와 배란에의 영향 및 그로 인한 불임(~ affect puberty and ovulation, and that it may lead to infertility), 남성 발기부전(Male impotence), 발기부전과 성욕 및 사정 문제의 위험성 증가(increase the risk of erectile dysfunction and problems with sexual desire and ejaculation)' 등이 있으며, 모두 인간의 생식 작용에 관한 내용이고, 부정적인 영향임을 알 수 있다. 따라서 글의 제목으로 가장 적절한 것은 '④ Relation Between Exposure to BPA and Reproductive Disorders(BPA에의 노출과 생식 장애들의 관계)'이다.

해석
2013년 Brigham and Women's Hospital의 과학자들이 bisphenol A (BPA)에의 노출이 인간의 비정상적인 난자 성숙을 일으킬 수 있다는 것을 보여주는 결과를 발표했다. 2015년에 발표된 이전 연구들의 한 리뷰는 BPA가 시상하부와 뇌하수체를 수반하는 내분비 기능을 방해할 수 있다는 증거를 발견했다. 연구원들은 이러한 유형의 효과가 사춘기와 배란에 영향을 미칠 수 있고, 그것이 불임을 야기할 수 있다고 말했다. 저자들은 "생식 작용에 미치는 해로운 영향은 일생동안 지속되며 세대를 망라할 수도 있다"고 덧붙인다. 직장에서의 남성의 BPA에의 노출의 영향을 살펴본 연구에 따르면 남성 발기부전이 영향을 받을 수도 있다. 결과는 높은 수준의 노출은 발기부전과 성욕 및 사정 문제의 위험성을 증가시킬 수 있다는 것을 보여주었다.
① 없이는 우리가 살 수 없는 화학물질: BPA
② BPA에 의해 야기될 수 있는 남성 건강 문제
③ BPA가 인간에게 미치는 긍정적 그리고 부정적 영향
④ BPA에의 노출과 생식 장애들의 관계

10 정답 ③ — Day 31-10

정답해설
주어진 문장 다음으로 도입을 의미하는 (B)가 오는 것이 적절하다. 또한 (A) 초반에 언급된 'These are three of the key aspects~'의 맨 첫 번째 단어 'These'는 (C) 마지막의 'perception, memory, and emotion'을 가리키므로 (C)다음에 (A)가 와야 적절하다. 따라서 정답은 ③이 적절하다.

해석
모든 동물들은 사람처럼 자는 동안 같은 종류의 뇌 활동을 한다. 그들이 꿈을 꾸는지 안 꾸는지는 다른 문제이다, 그것은 단지 또 다른 질문을 취하면서 풀릴 수 있기 때문이다: 동물들은 자각 의식을 가지고 있을까?
(B) 오늘날 많은 과학자들은 동물들이 아마도 계획적이거나 상징적인 생각을 위한 언어와 능력이 부족하다는 관점에서 우리와는 꽤나 다른 제한된 형태의 자각 의식을 가진다고 추측한다.
(C) 동물들은 꿈을 진짜 꾸더라도 당연히 꿈에 대해서 보고 하지 못한다. 그러나 어떤 애완동물 주인이 그들의 가장 친한 동물 친구가 자각과 기억 그리고 감정이 있다는 것에 대해 의심할까?
(A) 이러한 것들은 자각 의식의 세 가지 중요한 면들이다. 그리고 그것들은

동물들이 우리들처럼 구두의 언어를 하든 하지 않든 상관없이 체험할 수 있다. 동물의 뇌가 잠을 잘 동안 활동할 때, 동물들이 일종의 지각의, 감정의, 그리고 기억의 경험을 한다고 왜 추정하지 않겠는가?

11 정답 ④ Day 31-04

정답해설

과속 제한에 걸리면 현장에서 (경찰관에 의해 직접) 벌금을 지불할 것을 요구받았을 수 있는데 그러지 않은 이유를 A가 B에게 묻고 있다. 빈칸 이후의 대화에서 감시 카메라를 더 조심하라고 했기 때문에, (무인) 감시 카메라에 찍혔다는 응답인 ④ 'Because I was photographed by one of speed cameras(속도 감시 카메라 중 하나에 내가 찍혔기 때문이야)'가 가장 적절하다.

해석

A: 이 편지 좀 봐.
B: 아 그래, 공문서 같은 거라고 생각했어. 과속 제한에 걸려서 네가 벌금을 내야 한다고 쓰여 있어. 왜 현장에서 벌금을 부과받지 않았니?
A: 속도 감시 카메라들 중 하나에 내가 찍혔기 때문이야.
B: 점점 더 많은 카메라들이 여기 주위로 설치되고 있어. 넌 앞으로 더 조심해야 할 거야.
A: 농담 아냐. 벌금이 60달러야.
① 그 장소가 너무 붐벼서 벌금을 부과받지 않았기 때문이야
② 그것을 찍을 어떠한 카메라도 찾을 수 없었기 때문이야
③ 벌금을 부과받았을 때 이미 지불했기 때문이야
④ 속도 감시 카메라들 중 하나에 내가 찍혔기 때문이야

12 정답 ③ Day 38-04

정답해설

(A) 대화를 통해 John이 Danny를 위한 깜짝 생일파티를 열어주기 위해 준비하고 있으며 Nina도 동참하게 된 상황임을 알 수 있다. 이때 Nina가 '누군가 무엇을 하고 있는지 물어보면 Danny가 사실을 알아채지 못하게끔 ~할 것이다'라고 이야기하므로 빈칸 (A)에 들어갈 가장 적절한 것은 'hold my tongue(묵묵부답하다)'이다.
(B) '누군가 ~한다면, Danny는 바로 알게 될 것이다.'라고 John이 말하고 있으므로 빈칸 (B)에 들어갈 가장 적절한 것은 'spills the beans(비밀을 폭로하다)'이다.

해석

Nina: 너희들 여기서 뭐 해?
John: 이건 비밀이야. Danny를 위한 깜짝 생일파티를 준비 중이야.
Nina: 우와 Danny가 이것에 대해 모두 알게 되면 아주 기쁘겠다.
John: 정말 그랬으면 좋겠어. 우리는 이것을 두 주 넘게 계획했어. 너도 동참할래?
Nina: 물론이지, 난 아주 좋아. 누군가 우리가 뭐 하고 있는지 묻는다면 난 그냥 Danny가 사실을 알게 되지 않게끔 (A) 묵묵부답할게.
John: 난 널 믿어. 누구든 (B) 비밀을 폭로하면 Danny는 바로 알게 될 거야.
① (A) 자만하다 (B) 임기응변으로 대처하다
② (A) 묵묵부답하고 있다 (B) 임기응변으로 대처하다
③ (A) 묵묵부답하고 있다 (B) 비밀을 폭로하다
④ (A) 겨우 삶을 연명하다 (B) 비밀을 폭로하다

13 정답 ③ Day 40-10

정답해설

본문은 'Zoonotic diseases(동물 매개 감염병)'에 대한 글이다. 본문 중반 "The World Health Organization (WHO) estimates that 61 percent of all human diseases are zoonotic in origin, while 75 percent of new diseases discovered in the last decade are zoonotic(세계 보건 기구(WHO)는 모든 인간 질병의 61퍼센트의 기원이 동물 매개이며, 한편 지난 10년 동안 발견된 새로운 질병 중 75퍼센트가 동물 매개라고 추정한다)."에 따르면, '모든 인간 질병 61퍼센트의 기원이 동물 매개이며, 지난 10년간 발견된 새로운 질병들 중 75퍼센트가 동물 매개이다.' 본문의 해당 문장에서 언급된 75%는 10년 동안 발견된 '새로운' 질병에 대한 원인으로서 'zoonotic'을 제시한 경우이고, 선지에서 언급된 70% 이상은 '새로운' 질병이 아니라 'human diseases(인간 질병들)'의 수치로 제시한 경우에 해당된다. 즉, 질병의 수치 이전에 어떤 '대상'에 대한 수치인지를 꼭 확인해야겠다. 따라서 '③ Over seventy percent of human diseases were originated from animals(인간 질병의 70퍼센트 이상이 동물로부터 비롯되었다).'는 본문의 내용과 일치하지 않는다.

해석

많은 다른 유형의 동물들이 박테리아, 곰팡이 균류, 기생충, 그리고 바이러스와 같은 해로운 균을 옮길 수 있다. 그리고 이것들은 인간과 공유가 되고 질병을 일으킨다. 동물원성(原性) 감염증이라고도 불리는 동물 매개 감염 질병은 가벼운 것부터 심각한 것까지 다양하며, 일부는 심지어 치명적일 수도 있다. 동물 매개 감염 질병은 미국과 전 세계에 모두 널리 퍼져있다. 세계 보건 기구(WHO)는 모든 인간 질병의 61퍼센트의 기원이 동물 매개인 한편 지난 10년 동안 발견된 새로운 질병 중 75퍼센트가 동물 매개라고 추정한다. 약 100년 전 새로운 위생 규정을 도입하기 전에는 소결핵증, 림프절 페스트, 마비저와 같은 동물 매개 감염 질병은 수백만 건의 사망을 야기했다. 그것들은 개발도상국에서 여전히 주요 문제이다.
① 다양한 동물들이 인간에게 질병을 옮길 수 있다.
② 특정 동물 매개 감염 질병은 인간 사망자를 발생시킬 수 있다.
③ 인간 질병의 70퍼센트 이상이 동물로부터 비롯되었다.
④ 위생 문제를 다루기 위해 조치가 취해진 지 약 한 세기가 지났다.

14 정답 ③ Day 35-08

정답해설

본문은 '작동 기억(working memory)과 아이들의 학업 성과(academic performance) 간의 관계'에 대해 설명하고 있다. 본문 중반 ② 문장부터 본문의 마지막까지 '작동 기억'을 '양동이(bucket)'에 비유하여 설명하고 있는데, 중간에 ③ 문장에서 '작동 기억을 향상시킬 수 있는 방법'이 언급되는 것은 문맥상 부자연스럽다. 따라서 정답은 ③이다.

해석

작동 기억은 실행 기능(예를 들어, 계획하기, 착수하기, 과제 관찰하기, 조직하기 등)의 중요한 부분이기 때문에 학업 성과에 있어서 매우 중요하다. 학교에서 빈약한 작동 기억에 의해 크게 영향을 받는 학습 영역은: 수학, 독해, 복잡한 문제해결, 그리고 시험을 보는 것이다. ① 학업에 미치는 가장 큰 영향은 첫 두 영역에서의 어려움으로부터 발생한다. ② 작동 기억은 물 한 컵을 이용해 당신이 계속해서 채울 수 있는 양동이와 매우 유사하다. ③ <u>그것은 단순한 게임과 매일 행해지는 활동을 통해 향상될 수 있다.</u> ④ <u>당신이 추가하는 모든 물방울은 시간이 지나 기억의 반복된 사용의 부족을 통해 증발해버리지 않는 한 양동이 안에 남아 있다.</u> 빈약한 작동 기억을 지닌 아이들에게는, 양동이 바닥에 구멍이 있는 것과 매우 유사하다. 당신은 계속해서 컵 속의 물(정보/지식)을 따라 넣을 수 있지만, 그것은 지속적으로 흘러나간다.

15 정답 ④
Day 33-07

정답해설

④ 출제 포인트: 형용사 vs. 부사
불완전자동사 'remain'의 주격 보어는 형용사 'traditional'이며 밑줄 친 'thorough'는 형용사로 '철저한, 완전한'을 뜻한다. 따라서 'thorough'는 'traditional'을 수식해야 하므로 부사 'thoroughly'로 수정해야 한다.

해석

일부 조직들은 남성들이나 여성들에게 아이를 돌보기 위해 직업 휴식(육아휴직)을 취하는 것을 허락하는 정책들을 가지고 있다. 그러나, 매우 소수의 아버지들만이 이러한 기회들을 스스로 활용할 뿐 아니라, 그런 선택을 한 사례는 그들이 그렇게 하는 경우 그들의 경력을 평생 '망치는' 결과가 될 수 있음을 보여준다. 정말로, 이러한 사실은 남성들의 해당 제도 이용 비율이 낮은 원인이 되는 것이 당연하다. 그러므로, 조직들은 경력을 보다 유연하게 운영할 수 있는 구조를 갖추어야 할 뿐만 아니라, 전형적으로 완전히 전통적인 상태로 남아 있는 태도들을 변화시켜야 한다.

16 정답 ①
Day 36-08

정답해설

빈칸에 들어갈 말은 Kant가 생각하는 도덕적인 행동의 의미를 찾으면 된다. 빈칸 이후에 자세히 설명이 되어 있는 것처럼 Kant는 도덕적인 행동은 '행위 자체의 실행'으로 도덕적인 게 아니라 '행위의 이유'로 판단해야만 한다고 하였다. 게다가 도덕적 행동의 이유는 '동정심'이 아니라 '이성'에서 비롯된 '의무감' 때문이어야만 한다는 것이다. 글의 전반부에서 당신이 도움을 필요로 하는 남자를 애석하게 여겨서 도움을 주었다면 Kant의 입장에서는 도덕적인 행동이 아닌 것이다. 따라서 빈칸에 들어갈 가장 적절한 것은 ① 'that wouldn't be a moral action at all (그것은 도덕적인 행동이 전혀 아니다)' 이다.

해석

당신의 문에 노크 소리가 들린다. 당신 앞에 서 있는 것은 도움을 필요로 하는 젊은 남성이다. 그는 부상을 입었고 피를 흘리고 있다. 당신은 그를 데려와서 그를 도와주고, 그를 편안하게 해주고 안전하게 느끼게 해준다, 그리고 앰뷸런스를 불러준다. 이것은 옳은 일임이 분명하다. 그러나 Immanuel Kant에 의하면 만약 당신이 그에게 애석한 기분이 들었기 때문에 그를 도왔다면, 그것은 도덕적인 행동이 전혀 아니다. 당신의 동정심은 당신의 행동의 도덕성과는 관련이 없다. 그것은 당신의 성격의 일부이지만, 옳거나 그른 것과는 관계가 없다. Kant에게 도덕성은 그저 당신이 무엇을 하는 것이 아니라, 당신이 그것을 왜 하는 것이었다. 옳은 행동을 하는 사람들은 단순히 그들이 어떻게 느끼는 지 때문에 그것을 하지 않는다: 그 결정은 어떻게 당신이 느끼게 되어버린 지와 관계없이 당신의 의무가 무엇인지 말해주는 이성에서 기반 해야만 한다.
① 그것은 도덕적인 행동이 전혀 아니다
② 당신의 행동은 이성에서 비롯된다
③ 그렇다면 당신은 도덕적인 행동을 보여주고 있다
④ 당신은 그를 정직한 사람이 되도록 격려하고 있다

17 정답 ③
Day 32-10

정답해설

본문은 '의식(consciousness)'에 대한 서양의 철학자 및 과학자들의 인식 변화에 대해 설명하고 있다. 과거에 동물들은 감정이 없는 것으로 인식되었으며, 의식은 인간만의 고유한 영역으로 여겨졌다. Darwin의 진화론이 대두된 이후에도, 과학자들은 인간들이 침팬지로부터 진화한 이후에야 의식을 가지기 시작했다고 믿었다. 그러나 본문 후반 "This notion that consciousness was of recent vintage began to change in the decades following the Second World War, when more scientists were systematically studying the behaviors and brain states of Earth's creatures(의식이 최근의 형태라는 개념은 더 많은 과학자들이 지구의 생물들의 행동과 뇌의 상태를 체계적으로 연구하던 제2차 세계대전 이후 수십 년 동안 변화하기 시작했다)."에 따르면, '기존의 개념이 변화하기 시작하였다'고 언급하고 있으며, '지구상의 여러 생물에 관한 체계적인 연구가 실시되어 왔음'을 알 수 있다. 이러한 변화로 인해, 인간만이 가지고 있다고 여겨졌던 '의식'에 대한 인식 변화가 나타났다는 것을 유추할 수 있으므로, 빈칸에 가장 적절한 표현은 '③ a great many animals are conscious like humans(매우 많은 동물들이 인간과 같이 의식이 있다)'이다.

해석

서양에서 의식은 오랫동안 오직 인간에게 부여된 신성한 선물로 여겨졌다. 역사적으로 서양 철학자들은 인간이 아닌 동물들을 무감정의 기계적으로 행동하는 동물로 생각했다. 심지어 Darwin이 동물과 우리의 친족 관계를 입증한 후에도, 많은 과학자들은 의식의 진화는 최근의 사건이라고 생각했다. 그들은 최초의 지성은 우리가 침팬지와 난쟁이 침팬지로부터 분열되고 얼마 후 자각이 발생했다고 생각했다. 의식이 최근의 형태라는 개념은 더 많은 과학자들이 지구의 생물들의 행동과 뇌의 상태를 체계적으로 연구하던 제2차 세계대전 이후 수십 년 동안 변화하기 시작했다. 이제 매년, 종합하면, 매우 많은 동물들이 인간과 같이 의식이 있다는 것을 시사하는 많은 새로운 연구 논문이 발행된다.
① 인간은 영장류와 밀접한 관련이 있다
② 의식은 인간의 배타적인 특징이다
③ 매우 많은 동물들이 인간과 같이 의식이 있다
④ 심지어 인간도 최근까지는 의식이 없었다

18 정답 ④
Day 34-08

정답해설

본문 첫 문장 "New research on children with attention deficit hyperactivity disorder(ADHD) might show some tasks can improve working memory in general, and could help children with the condition(주의력 결핍 과잉 행동 장애(ADHD)를 앓는 아이들에 대한 새로운 연구는 어떤 과제들이 전반적으로 작동 기억을 향상시킬 수 있으며, 그 질환을 앓는 아이들에게 도움이 될 수 있다는 것을 보여줄 수 있다)"을 통해 전체 글의 요지를 파악할 수 있다. 또한 이후 언급되는 실험의 결과(작동 기억 향상 → 과잉 활동과 부주의의 감소)로 더욱 구체적으로 정답의 힌트를 획득할 수 있다. 즉, 작동 기억 능력이 증가된 아이들은 ADHD 증상의 완화를 경험하였으므로, 작동 기억 능력의 증가가 아이들에게 긍정적인 영향을 미친 것을 알 수 있다. 따라서 정답은 '④ Increasing working memory capacity can have a positive impact on kids with ADHD(작동 기억 능력을 증가시키는 것이 ADHD를 앓는 아이들에게 긍정적인 영향을 미칠 수 있다)'이다.

해석

주의력 결핍 과잉 행동 장애(ADHD)를 앓는 아이들에 대한 새로운 연구는 어떤 과제들이 전반적으로 작동 기억을 향상시킬 수 있으며, 그 질환을 앓는 아이들에게 도움이 될 수 있다는 것을 보여줄 수 있다. Torkel Klingberg는 ADHD를 앓는 53명의 아이들을 대상으로 참가자의 절반은 난도가 점차 증가하는 작동 기억 과제를 연습하는 무작위 대조 실험을 실시했다. 나머지 절반은 아이들이 과제를 더 잘하게 되었을 때 더 어려워지지 않는 과제를 풀었다. 점점 더 어려워지는 기억 과제를 수행한 아이들이 연습 과제와는 다른 두 가지 작동 기억 테스트에서 대조군보다 더 나은 성과를 보였다. 게다가, 기억 훈련을 한 아이들의 부모들은 교육 활동을 마친 3개월 후 그들의 아이들의 과잉 활동과 부주의의 감소를 보고한 반면, 대조군 참가자들의 부모들은 그렇지 않았다.

① ADHD는 아이들이 빈약한 작동 기억을 갖도록 유발할 수 있다.
② ADHD 증상은 약물을 통해 효과적으로 줄일 수 있다.
③ ADHD 환자들은 과제를 마치는 데 어려움을 겪는 경향이 있다.
④ 작동 기억 능력을 증가시키는 것이 ADHD를 앓는 아이들에게 긍정적인 영향을 미칠 수 있다.

19 정답 ② Day 38-09

정답해설

(A) 이전에는 파충류가 단단한 껍질을 낳을 수 없다면 부드러운 껍질의 알을 낳을 수 있다고 언급하며 부드러운 알의 특징으로 '산란 후 팽창할 수 있음'을 설명하고 있다. (A) 이후에는 앞서 언급한 부드러운 껍질 알의 특징과는 다른 특징인 '수분을 흡수할 수 있는 능력'에 대한 내용으로 부드러운 껍질 알의 추가적인 특징을 첨가해주고 있다. 따라서 빈칸에는 '첨언'의 접속부사인 'Additionally(게다가)' 또는 'Besides(게다가)'가 적절하다.

(B) 이전에서 '새가 알을 부화시키는 방법'에 대해 언급한 후, (B) 이후에서 앞서 언급된 새의 방법과는 다른 '파충류의 부화 방법'이 언급되고 있다. 즉, 서로 다른 '역접, 대조' 관계에 있는 내용이 연결되고 있으므로, 빈칸에는 'by contrast(대조적으로)', 'on the other hand(반면에)'가 들어가는 것이 자연스럽다.

따라서 정답은 '② Additionally(게다가) - on the other hand(반면에)'이다.

해석

새는 단단한 껍질이 있는 알을 낳는 반면, 일부 파충류 종은 껍질이 부드러운 알을 낳는다. 왜 이것이 사실일까? 만일 어미가 완전한 크기의 단단한 껍질의 알을 낳을 수 없다면, 대신에 그것은 알이 산란 후 팽창할 수 있도록 하는 부드러운 껍질의 알을 낳을 수 있을 것이다. (A) 게다가, 부드러운 껍질은 대기와 지면으로부터 수분을 흡수할 수 있는 능력이 있다. 어떠한 이유로, 새는 그들의 알이 추가적인 수분이 필요하지 않도록 그렇게 진화해왔으나, 그것은 일부 파충류 종에게는 사실이 아니다. 일부 파충류가 껍질이 부드러운 알을 낳은 또 하나의 이유는 그것들이 부화하는 방식 때문이다. 새는 그들의 알 위에 앉아 자신들의 체온을 이용한다; (B) 반면에 파충류는 알을 부화시키기 위해 초목 또는 지면의 자연적인 열을 이용한다. 파충류의 알이 부모의 전체 체중으로부터 태어나지 않은 내용물을 보호할 만큼 충분히 강할 필요가 없기 때문에, 그것들은 껍질이 부드러울 수 있다.

	(A)	(B)
①	그래서	대조적으로
②	게다가	반면에
③	그러나	그에 따라
④	게다가	더욱이

20 정답 ④ Day 37-08

정답해설

본문은 'Kant 시대의 사람들의 도덕적 규율'에 대해 설명하고 있다. 본문은 'Kant 시대의 도덕적 신념과 관례는 종교에 기반을 둔 것이었으며, 종교의 계율이 도덕적인 행동강령을 제시했다'고 설명한다. 주어진 문장의 'Moreover(게다가)'로 보아, 해당 문장 이전에 규율을 따르는 이유에 관한 내용이 먼저 등장해야 함을 알 수 있다. 또한, "everyone had an incentive to obey such rules(모든 사람들이 이러한 강령을 준수하게 하는 유인이 있었다)"로 보아, 주어진 문장 이후에는 '규율을 따르는 것을 통해 받을 수 있는 이득'을 설명하는 내용이 등장하는 것이 자연스럽다는 것을 알 수 있다. ④ 이후 문장에서 "If you "walked in the ways of the Lord," you would be rewarded, either in this life or the next(만일 당신이 "하느님의 길을 걷는다면", 당신은 이생 또는 후생에 보상을 받을 것이다)."라고 '규율을 따르는 것에 의한 보상'에 대해 언급하고 있으므로, 주어진 문장의 'incentive(유인, 동기, 이득)'가 ④ 이후 문장에서 구체적으로 언급되고 있음을 알 수 있다. 따라서 정답은 ④이다.

해석

Kant의 도덕 철학을 이해하기 위해, 그와 그의 시대의 다른 사상가들이 다루었던 문제들에 친숙해지는 것이 중요하다. 가장 초기에 기록되었던 역사에서부터, 사람들의 도덕적 신념과 관례는 종교에 근거를 두고 있었다. (①) 성경, 쿠란과 같은 성서들은 신자들이 신으로부터 전해진 것으로 생각하던 도덕적 규율(살인하지 말라. 도둑질하지 말라. 간음하지 말라 등)을 나열해 놓았다. (②) 그것들이 아마도 지성의 신성한 근원으로부터 온 것이라는 사실이 그것들에 권위를 부여했다. (③) 그것들은 단순히 누군가의 독단적인 의견이 아니었다; 그것들은 신의 의견이었으며, 신의 의견으로서 인류에게 객관적으로 유효한 행동강령을 제공했다. (④ **게다가, 모든 사람들이 이러한 강령을 준수하게 하는 유인이 있었다.**) 만일 당신이 "하느님의 길을 걷는다면", 당신은 이생 또는 후생에 보상을 받을 것이다. 만일 당신이 율법을 위반한다면, 당신은 벌을 받을 것이다. 그 결과, 이러한 신앙을 가지고 자란 분별 있는 사람은 그들의 종교가 가르친 도덕적 규율을 준수하곤 했다.

결국엔 성정혜 영어 하프모의고사
기적사 DAY 41

| 01 | ① | 02 | ① | 03 | ④ | 04 | ④ | 05 | ① |
| 06 | ② | 07 | ① | 08 | ① | 09 | ① | 10 | ② |

01 정답 ①
17 지방직

정답해설

접속사 'but'으로 보아 맛이 없었던 음식에 양념을 쳐서 '맛있게' 만들었다는 흐름이 알맞음을 유추할 수 있다. 따라서 빈칸에 들어갈 가장 적절한 것은 ① palatable이다.

해석

우리의 메인 음식은 그다지 맛있지 않았지만, 나는 양념을 첨가하여 그것을 더 **맛있게** 만들었다.
① 맛있는, 맛 좋은
② 분해할 수 있는
③ 마셔도 되는
④ 예민한

어휘

flavor 맛, 풍미
palatable 맛있는, 맛 좋은
potable 마셔도 되는
condiment 양념, 향신료
dissolvable 분해할 수 있는
susceptible 예민한

02 정답 ①
17 지방직

정답해설

밑줄 친 'subsidies'는 'subsidy'의 복수형으로 '보조금[장려금]'이라는 의미이다. 따라서 ① financial support와 의미가 가장 가깝다.

해석

두 차례의 세계전쟁 동안, 정부 **보조금**과 새로운 항공기에 대한 수요가 그들의 설계와 구조를 위한 기술을 상당히 발전시켰다.
① 재정적 지원
② 장기간 계획
③ 기술적 보조
④ 비 제한적 정책

어휘

subsidy 보조금[장려금]
vastly 매우; 광대하게
construction 구조, 건설
support 지원, 지지; 지지하다
planning 계획, 입안
assistance 도움, 원조, 지원
policy 정책, 방침
demand 수요, 요구; 요구하다
improve 향상시키다, 개선하다
financial 재정의, 금전상의
long-term 장기간의
technical 기술적인, 기술상의
non-restrictive 비 제한적인

03 정답 ④
16 지방직

정답해설

두 문화가 완전히 '다르기' 때문에 그녀가 한 문화에서 다른 문화로 적응하기 힘들었다고 하는 것이 흐름상 적절하므로 가장 적절한 것은 ④ disparate이다.

해석

두 문화가 아주 완전히 **달라서** 그녀는 한 문화에서 다른 문화로 적응하기 힘들다는 것을 발견했다.
① 겹쳐진
② 동등한, 맞먹는
③ 연합의, 결합하기 쉬운
④ 다른, 공통점이 없는

어휘

utterly 완전히, 아주
overlap 겹치다
associative 연합의, 결합하기 쉬운
adapt 적응하다, 맞추다
equivalent 동등한, 맞먹는
disparate 다른, 공통점이 없는

04 정답 ④
19 지방직

정답해설

④에서 A가 '당신의 전화를 못 받았다'고 했는데 B가 '메시지를 남기실 건가요?'라고 대답하는 것은 문맥상 적절하지 않다. 따라서 정답은 ④이다.

오답해설

① A는 B에게 '몇 시에 점심을 먹냐'고 이야기하자 B는 '정오 전에 준비된다'고 말한다. B의 대답은 A의 말에 대한 반응으로 적합하다.
② A는 '몇 번이나 전화했다'고 얘기하며 전화를 받지 않은 이유에 대해 묻는다. 이에 B는 '휴대전화가 꺼져 있었던 것 같아'라고 대답한다. A의 물음에 대한 B의 반응은 적절하다.
③ A는 B에게 '이번 겨울에 휴가를 갈 건지' 묻고 있다. A의 물음에 B는 '그럴지도'라고 하며 '아직 결정을 못 했다'고 대답한다. 이는 자연스러운 대화의 흐름이다.

해석

① A: 우리 몇 시에 점심 먹어?
 B: 정오 전에 준비될 거야.
② A: 너한테 몇 번이나 전화했어. 왜 안 받았어?
 B: 아, 내 휴대전화가 꺼져 있었던 것 같아.
③ A: 이번 겨울에 휴가 갈 거야?
 B: 그럴지도. 아직 결정 못 했어.
④ A: 안녕하세요. 당신의 전화를 못 받아서 죄송합니다.
 B: 메시지 남기시겠어요?

어휘

turn off 끄다
decide 결정하다, 결심하다
miss 놓치다; 그리워하다
vacation 휴가, 방학
I might. 그렇게 할지도 몰라요.
leave 남기다; 떠나다

오답률 TOP 2

05 정답 ①
19 지방직

정답해설

① **출제 포인트: 동사 관용표현(be supposed to+동사원형)/사역동사/시제 일치**

'be supposed to 동사원형'은 '~하기로 하다, 되어있다'라는 뜻을 가진 표현이다. 문장에서 '전화해서 알렸어야 했다'라고 하였으므로 'You were supposed to phone~'은 영어로 알맞게 바꾼 표현이다. 덧붙여 'let'은 사역동사로 'let + 목적어 + 목적격보어[동사원형]' 순으로 오는 것이 적절한 표현인데 'let me know'라고 적절하게 바꾸었으므로 옳은 표현이다. 또한 문장의 주절의 시제가 과거이므로 종속절의 'you were going to be late for work'(일에 늦을 것이다)라고 시제일치를 하였으며 주절의 동사로 쓰인 'let'의 과거형은 'let'임에 주의해야한다. 따라서 영어로 가장 올바르게 옮긴 문장은 ①이다.

오답해설

② **출제 포인트: 시제 일치**
'While I watched a soccer match'는 과거 시제인데 주절의 동사에 현재완료 시제인 'has watched'를 사용하였으므로 시제가 일치하지 않는다. 따라서 'has watched'를 'watched'나 'was watching'으로 수정해야 한다.

③ **출제 포인트: to부정사의 부사적 용법(so as to+동사원형)**
'so as not'은 다음에 to부정사가 와야 한다. 따라서 'so as not hurting her feelings'에서 'so as not to hurt her feelings'가 되어야 한다. 이때 「so as not to+동사원형」은 to부정사의 부사적 용법에 해당하며 '~하지 않기 위해'를 뜻한다.

④ **출제 포인트: 이중부정금지**
'there is no way'는 '~할 방법이 없다'라는 의미로 이미 표현에 부정이 포함되어 있다. 따라서 '~끝낼 수 없다'라는 한국말을 영어로 적절하게 바꾸려면 'can't get'을 'can get'으로 수정해야한다. '~there is no way we can get this project done~'이 적절한 표현이다.

오답률 TOP 1

06 정답 ②
19 지방직

정답해설

② **출제 포인트: 주어와 동사의 수일치**
'while' 이후의 문장 'ones run by the New School in New York City'에서 'run'은 문장의 동사가 아니라 주어인 'ones'를 수식하는 과거분사이다. 동사는 'offers'로 현재시제 3인칭 단수 주어에 맞는 동사가 쓰였으므로 주어는 복수명사 'ones'가 아니라 단수명사 'one'이 오는 것이 어법상 적절하다.

오답해설

① **출제 포인트: 완전타동사+목적어[to부정사 vs. 동명사]/전치사+관계대명사**
'elect'는 목적어로 to부정사를 받는 동사이므로 'elect to do'는 적절한 표현이다. 'in which'는 '전치사 + 관계대명사' 형태로 이후의 문장은 완전한 형태이어야 한다. 'in which' 이후의 문장에서 밑줄 친 'to do'의 목적어로 'a service project'가 왔으므로 능동형으로 쓰인 'to do'는 옳게 사용되었다.

③ **출제 포인트: 현재분사 vs. 과거분사**
해당 문장에서 'gain'은 타동사로 사용되었으며 'gain'의 현재분사 형태인 'gaining' 이후에 목적어인 'more traction'이 있으므로 능동태를 의미하는 현재분사는 옳게 사용되었다.

④ **출제 포인트: 현재분사 vs. 과거분사**
'admit'은 '입학을 허가하다'라는 뜻을 가진 완전타동사로 사용되었다. 문장에서 밑줄 친 'admitted' 다음에 목적어가 아닌 'to selective colleges and universities'라는 전명구가 위치했으므로 수동태를 의미하는 과거분사 형태인 'admitted'가 적절한 표현인 것을 알 수 있다.

해석

프린스턴 대학교는 학생들이 미국 바깥에서 봉사 프로젝트를 하는 것을 선택할 수 있게 하는 학비가 무료인 9개월간의 "Bridge Year"를 제공한다. 채플힐 노스 캐롤라이나 대학교와 터프츠 대학교도 비슷한 프로그램을 가지고 있고, 반면에 뉴욕시의 New School에 의해 운영되는 것은 참가자들에게 일 년 치에 해당하는 학점까지 제공하고 있다. 하지만 최근 5년 동안, 그 아이디어는 미국 내에서 더 많은 견인(매력)을 얻고 있는 중이다. - 특히 선택할 수 있는 단과 대학들과 종합 대학들의 입학 허가를 받은 미국인들 사이에서 말이다.

어휘

tuition 학비
academic credit 학점
traction 견인
selective 선택적인, 선택할 수 있는
elect 선택하다
participant 참가자
admit 입학 허가하다

07 정답 ①
19 지방직

정답해설

① **출제 포인트: 부정부사 도치**
부정어 'Little(거의 ~하지 않은)'이 문두에 위치하면서 주어와 동사가 도치된 구문이다. 일반동사 'think'는 바로 주어 앞에 위치하는 것이 아니라 '조동사(do, does, did) + 주어 + 동사원형'의 일반동사의 의문문 형태를 갖는다. 따라서 문장의 시제는 'ago(~전에)'로 과거인 것을 알 수 있으므로 "We thought little three months ago ~."가 "Little did we think three months ago ~."로 올바르게 도치되었으므로 어법상 맞은 문장이다. 따라서 정답은 ①이다.

오답해설

② **출제 포인트: 가정법 미래/가정법 현재(단순조건문)**
가정법 미래 형태는 '미래의 일어나기 어려운, 또는 드문 사건에 대한 조건'을 나타내는 표현으로 'If + 주어 + should + 동사원형, 주어 + 조동사의 현재형/과거형 + 동사원형'의 구조를 갖는다. 따라서 'will have finished'를 'should finish'로 고치는 것이 어법상 올바르다. 또는 가정법 현재 즉, 단순 조건절로 보아 종속절 동사의 미래완료시제를 현재완료 시제로, 주절의 동사는 「will+동사원형」의 형태로 수정하여, 'I will love to see you tonight if you have finished your work.'로 나타낼 수 있다.

③ **출제 포인트: 간접의문의 어순**
간접의문문 구조는 일반 의문문과 다르게 「의문사 + 주어 + 동사」의 구조이다. 따라서 'who should I go and talk to'가 아니라 'who I should go and talk to'가 어법상 맞은 표현이다. 단, 주어진 간접의문문에서는 의문사가 주격이 아닌 목적격으로 사용되어야 하므로 'whom I should go and talk to'가 정확한 표현이다. 현대영어에서는 의문사 목적격 'whom' 대신에 해당 문장처럼 의문사 주격 'who'를 사용하는 경우도 있으므로 이에 주의해야한다.

④ **출제 포인트: 부가의문문**
부가의문문은 주절에 사용된 동사와 시제가 일치해야 하며 주절이 긍정문인 경우 부가의문문에는 부정형을, 주절이 부정문인 경우 부가의문문에는 긍정형을 사용해야 한다. 따라서 해당 문장의 경우 주절에 'hasn't come'이 사용돼 시제가 현재완료이며 부정문이므로 부가의문문 'is it?'을 'has it?'으로 수정해야 한다.

해석

① 우리는 3개월 전에 우리가 함께 일하게 될 것이라고는 거의 생각하지 않았다.
② 만약 네가 일을 끝마쳤다면 나는 오늘 밤에 너를 만나고 싶다.
③ 새 아파트에 문제가 생겼을 때, 나는 누구에게 가서 이야기를 해야 할지 궁금했다.
④ 이 책은 몇 주 동안 베스트셀러였지만, 아직 어떤 종이책도 나오지 않았어, 그렇지?

08 정답 ②
18 지방직

정답해설

본문 중반부의 'But' 이후부터 요지가 담겨있다. 필자는 중요한 사람들과의 '(인적)관계'를 형성하기 위해서는 '개인의 성과'가 중요함을 서술하고 있다. 이는 성과가 당신이 기여할 수 있는 바를 보여주기 때문이며 일을 더 잘 해낼수록 (인적) 관계를 만들어 내기 쉽다고 언급하고 있다. 따라서 글의 요지로 가장 적절한 것은 '② Building a good network starts from your accomplishments.(좋은 관계망을 형성하는 것은 당신의 성과로부터 시작된다.)'이다.

오답해설

① 중요한 사람들을 만나는 것에 대한 이야기이지, '후원(sponsorship)'에 대한 글이 아니다.
③ 인맥을 구축하는 것이 인생에서 도움이 된다는 내용은 있으나 그것이 성공의 '전제 조건(prerequisite)'이라는 내용은 찾아볼 수 없다.
④ 본문을 통해 인적 관계 형성의 전문가가 되는 것과 개인의 '통찰력(insight)' 및 '결과(output)'와의 관계를 추론해낼 수 없다.

해석

나의 학생들은 만약 단순하게 그들이 중요한 인물들을 더 많이 만난다면, 그들의 성과가 향상될 것이라고 종종 믿는다. 그러나 당신이 이미 그 세계에 가치 있는 어떤 것들을 내어놓지 않는 이상 그러한 사람들과 어울리는 것은 매우 어렵다. 그것은 조언자들과 후원자들의 호기심을 불쾌하게 만드는 것이다. 성과는 당신이 오로지 취하는 것만이 아니라, 무언가 기여할 수 있는 바가 있음을 보여준다. 인생에서, 올바른 사람을 아는 것은 확실히 도움이 된다. 그러나 그들이 당신을 위해 얼마나 열심히 돕는지, 그들이 당신을 위해 얼마나 큰 위험을 감수하는지는 당신이 제공하는 것에 달려 있다. 강력한 관계를 구축하는 것은 당신이 관계 형성의 전문가가 되기를 요구하지 않는다. 그것은 단지 당신이 어떤 것의 전문가가 되기만을 요구할 뿐이다. 만약 당신이 좋은 관계들을 만들어 낸다면, 그것들은 당신의 커리어를 아마 진전시킬 것이다. 만약 당신이 일을 잘 해내면, 그러한 관계들은 만들어 내기 더 쉬워질 것이다. 당신의 명함이 아닌 당신의 통찰력과 당신의 결과가 이야기를 하게 하라.
① 성공적인 경력을 위해 후원은 필수이다.
② 좋은 (인적) 관계를 형성하는 것은 당신의 성과로부터 시작된다.
③ 강력한 (인적) 관계는 당신의 성공을 위한 전제 조건이다.
④ 당신이 관계 형성의 전문가가 됨에 따라 당신의 통찰력과 결과가 성장한다.

어휘

remarkably 두드러지게, 현저하게 engage 관계를 맺다
pique 불쾌하게 하다, 언짢게 하다 go to bat for ~을 도와주다
stick one's neck out 위험을 자초하다, 무모한 짓을 하다
prerequisite 전제 조건

09 정답 ①
18 지방직

정답해설

본문은 시험장에 늦어 당황한 상태로 허둥지둥 시험에 임하고 있는 화자의 상황을 묘사하고 있다. 따라서 ① nervous and worried(긴장하고 걱정되는)가 화자의 심경으로 가장 적절하다. 본문의 'in an absolute panic(완전한 패닉 상태)', 'got so confused(너무 혼란스러워서)', 'desperately(필사적으로)' 등을 통해서도 심경을 유추할 수 있다.

해석

내 얼굴은 백지장처럼 하얘졌다. 나는 내 손목시계를 보았다. 시험은 지금이면 거의 끝났을 것이다. 나는 완전한 패닉 상태에서 그 시험장에 도착했다. 나는 자초지종을 설명하려고 시도했지만, 나의 문장과 설명하는 몸짓은 너무 혼란스러워서 사람의 감정 폭발의 아주 확실한 버전에 불과한 것을 전달했다. 나의 산만한 설명을 관두게 하려는 시도로, 그 시험 감독관은 나를 빈자리에 데려가 시험 책자를 내 앞에 놓았다. 그는 의문스러운 듯이 나와 시계를 보다가 가버렸다. 나는 필사적으로 잃어버린 시간을 보충하려 노력했고, 미친 듯이 허둥지둥 비유와 문장의 완성들을 간신히 해나갔다. "15분 남았습니다." 비운의 목소리가 교실 앞에 퍼졌다. 대수 방정식, 산술 계산, 기하학 도형들이 내 눈앞을 헤엄쳐 갔다. "그만! 연필을 내려놓으세요."
① 긴장하고 걱정되는
② 흥분되고 기운찬
③ 차분하고 확고한
④ 안전하고 느긋한

어휘

white as a sheet 백지장처럼 하얀, 창백한, 핏기가 없는
panic 공황, 극심한 공포 descriptive 묘사하는
nothing more than ~에 불과한, ~에 지나지 않는
convincing 설득력 있는, 확실한
tornado 토네이도; (감정·활동 따위의) 격발, 폭발
in an effort to ~해보려는 노력으로
curb 억제하다, 제한하다 distracting 마음을 산란케 하는
proctor 시험 감독관 desperately 필사적으로
make up for ~에 대해 보상하다, 보충하다
scramble 재빨리 움직이다, 허둥지둥 (간신히) 해내다
analogy 비유, 유사점, 유추 doom 죽음, 파멸, 비운
algebraic 대수의, 대수적인 arithmetic 산수, 연산
geometric 기하학의, 기하학적인

오답률 TOP 3
10 정답 ②
18 지방직

정답해설

주어진 문장은 '건강을 감시, 추적하는 장치들이 전 연령에서 인기가 있다'는 내용인데, 이 이후에는 'However(그러나)'로 시작하며 '이 기술이 특히 노인들에게 효과적'이라는 내용인 (B)가 이어지는 것이 알맞다. (A)의 'Fall alerts(낙상 경보)'는 (B)의 예이므로 (B) 이후에 오는 것이 적절하며, (A) 마지막에 낙상 경보에 진전이 있었다고 말하고 있고 그 진전된 내용이 (C)에서 언급되고 있다. 따라서 정답은 ② '(B) - (A) - (C)'이다.

해석

당신의 건강을 감시하고 추적하는 장치들은 모든 연령대들 사이에서 점점 더 인기를 얻고 있다.
(B) 그러나, 자신의 집에서 나이 들어가는 고령자들에게, 특히 집에 관리인이 없는 이들에게, 이러한 기술들은 생명을 구할 수도 있다.
(A) 예를 들어, 낙상은 65세 이상의 성인들의 주요 사망 원인이다. 낙상 경보는 수년간 있어왔던 대중적인 양로 기술이지만 이제야 진전되었다.
(C) 이 단순한 기술은 노인이 낙상하는 그 순간 자동적으로 911 혹은 가까운 가족에게 경보를 줄 수 있다.

어휘

track 추적하다 alert 경계 태세, 경계경보
senior 연장자, 고령자 caretaker 경비원, 관리인
lifesaving 생명을 구하는 automatically 자동적으로

결국엔 성정혜 영어 하프모의고사
기적사 DAY 42

01	④	02	②	03	③	04	②	05	②
06	③	07	②	08	②	09	③	10	③

오답률 TOP 2

01 정답 ④

정답해설

밑줄 친 'palatable'은 '맛있는, 입에 맞는'을 뜻하는 형용사로 ④ delectable과 의미가 가장 가깝다.

해석

백설탕과 흑설탕과 같은 설탕의 여러 형태들은 음식을 **맛있게** 만들고 커피와 같은 쓴 음료에 부드러운 풍미를 더한다.
① 소금이 든, 염분이 함유된
② 맛이 없는
③ 얼얼하게 매운, 신랄한
④ 아주 맛있는; 매력이 넘치는

어휘

palatable 맛있는, 입에 맞는   smooth 부드러운, 매끄러운
bitter [맛이] 쓴; 격렬한   saline 소금이 든, 염분이 함유된
insipid 맛이 없는   pungent 얼얼하게 매운, 신랄한
delectable 아주 맛있는; 매력이 넘치는

02 정답 ②

정답해설

밑줄 친 'support'는 '지원'을 뜻하는 명사로 ② backing과 의미가 가장 가깝다.

해석

서울 시장은 최근에 시가 법률상의 허점 때문에 중앙 정부의 **지원**을 받는 데 실패한 대략 5만여 명의 시민들에게 생활비를 제공할 것이라고 발표했다.
① 교섭, 협상
② 지원
③ 결렬, 불화
④ 기부

어휘

mayor 시장   announce 발표하다
provide 제공하다   allowance 비용, 수당, 용돈
approximately 대략   support 지원, 지지; 지지하다
loophole (법률·계약서 등의 허술한) 구멍
parley 교섭, 협상   backing 지원
rupture 결렬, 불화   endowment 기부

03 정답 ③

정답해설

밑줄 친 'equal'은 '동등한, 동일한'을 뜻하는 형용사로 ③ equivalent와 의미상 가장 가깝다.

해석

민주주의를 채택한 나라들은 이 이상을 따르고 그들의 사회에서 **동등한** 기회들을 제공하고자 노력한다.
① 가치 없는, 부당한
② 한쪽으로 치우친, 일방적인, 편파적인
③ 동등한
④ 유사한

어휘

adopt 채택하다; 입양하다   democracy 민주주의
ideal 이상; 이상적인   equal 동등한, 동일한
indign 가치 없는, 부당한
lopsided 한쪽으로 치우친, 일방적인, 편파적인
equivalent 동등한   analogous 유사한

04 정답 ②

정답해설

A는 B에게 '부탁을 하나 해도 되는지' 묻는다. 그러자 B는 자신이 '가장 좋아하는 책이 해리포터'라고 대답한다. 이는 A의 질문에 대한 적절한 대답이 아니다.

오답해설

① A가 B에게 '다리 전체에 멍이 들었다'고 이야기하자 B는 '무슨 일이냐'라며 '무엇에 걸려 넘어졌는지' 물어본다. B의 되물음은 A의 말에 대한 반응으로 적합하다.
③ A가 '마을 전체에 소방차가 왔다'라고 얘기하자, B는 '몇 분 전에 사이렌 소리를 들었다'라고 대답한다. A의 말에 대한 B의 반응은 적절하다.
④ A가 '오늘 아침에 기상 예보를 확인했다'라고 말하자 B는 '오늘 비가 오는지' 질문한다. 이는 자연스러운 대화의 흐름이다.

해석

① A: 나는 다리 전체에 멍이 들었어.
   B: 무슨 일이야? 너 뭐에 걸려 넘어졌어?
② A: 내 부탁 하나만 들어줄 수 있어?
   B: 내가 가장 좋아하는 책은 해리포터야.
③ A: 마을 전체에 소방차가 있어.
   B: 나는 몇 분 전에 사이렌 소리를 들었어.
④ A: 나는 오늘 아침에 기상 예보를 확인했어.
   B: 잘했어! 오늘 비와?

어휘

bruise 멍, 타박상; 멍이 생기다   trip over …에 발이 걸려 넘어지다
favor 부탁, 호의, 친절   forecast 예측, 예보; 예측하다

05 정답 ②

정답해설

② **출제 포인트: 동사 관용표현(make it a rule)/to부정사의 부사적 용법(so as not to+동사원형)**

「make it a rule to+동사원형」과 「so as not to+동사원형」은 관용표현으로 각각 '~하는 것을 규칙으로 삼다'와 '~하지 않기 위해'를 뜻한다. 이때 「so as not to+동사원형」은 to부정사의 부사적 용법에 해당한다. 따라서 해당 문장은 옳은 문장이다.

오답해설

① 출제 포인트: 시제 일치/시간의 부사(구) 및 부사절
시간의 부사구 'in the last+숫자+단위 복수[years/weeks/months 등]' 가 오는 경우 동사에 현재완료를 사용한다. 따라서 해당 문장의 'increases'를 'has increased'로 수정해야 한다.

③ 출제 포인트: 이중부정 금지
'scarcely'는 부정을 뜻 가지는 빈도부사로 다른 부정부사와 함께 사용할 수 없다. 해당 문장은 부정의 뜻을 가진 'scarcely'와 'not'이 함께 쓰여 이중부정이 되었으므로 틀린 문장이다. 따라서 주어진 해석에 맞게 'not'을 삭제해 'could not scarcely'를 'could scarcely'로 수정해야한다. 또한 'notebook'은 '노트, 공책, 노트북 컴퓨터'를 나타내며 문맥상 '노트북 컴퓨터(laptop)'를 나타낸다.

④ 출제 포인트: 동사 관용표현(have access to)
'have access to'는 관용표현으로 '~에 접근하다'를 뜻하며, 이때 'access'는 불가산명사이므로 앞에 부정관사를 사용할 수 없다. 따라서 해당 문장의 'have an access to'를 'have access to'로 수정해야 한다.

06 정답 ③

정답해설

③ 출제 포인트: 혼동하기 쉬운 동사(rise vs. raise)
밑줄 친 'rising'은 완전자동사 'rise'의 동명사 형태이므로 이후에 목적어가 올 수 없다. 따라서 문맥상 '가족을 부양하다'가 자연스러우므로 'rising'을 완전타동사 'raise'의 동명사 형태인 'raising'으로 수정해야 한다.

오답해설

① 출제 포인트: 완전타동사+목적어[to부정사 vs. 동명사]
'expect'는 완전타동사인 경우 to부정사를 목적어로 가지므로 'expect'의 목적어로 온 to부정사 'to live'는 옳은 표현이다.

② 출제 포인트: 주어와 동사의 수일치
밑줄 친 'pressures'는 'since'가 이끄는 종속절의 주어에 해당하므로 종속절의 동사를 확인해야 한다. 종속절의 동사가 복수 형태인 'are'이므로 복수 형태의 주어 'pressures'는 옳은 표현이다. 주어와 동사 사이의 'of earning ~ a family'는 전명구에 해당한다. 이처럼 주어와 동사 사이의 거리가 먼 경우 수일치에 주의해야한다.

④ 출제 포인트: 완전타동사+목적어[to부정사 vs. 동명사]/목적격 관계대명사 생략
완전타동사 'hope'는 to부정사를 목적어로 사용할 수 있다. 해당 문장은 'hope'의 목적어로 to부정사를 사용하였으므로 밑줄 친 'to do'는 옳다. 이때 to부정사 'to do'의 목적어는 'the things'로 'the things'와 'they had always hoped to do' 사이에 목적격 관계대명사 'which' 또는 'that'이 생략되어 있다.

해석

나이 60세에 건강 상태가 꽤 괜찮은 사람들은 이제 거의 30년을 더 살 것으로 기대할 수 있다. 생활비를 벌고, 경력을 쌓고, 가족을 부양하는 부담을 뒤로하게 되기 때문에, 이때는 그들 인생의 가장 행복한 세월이 될 수 있다. 근로자들은 항상 하고 싶어 했지만 주당 40시간이 넘는 근무 시간 때문에 할 기회를 결코 가질 수 없었던 일들 중 많은 것을 하기 위해 그들의 "황금기"를 이용할 수 있다.

어휘

reasonably 꽤, 제법
raise a family 가족을 부양하다
earn a living 생활비를 벌다
workweek 주당 근무 시간

오답률 TOP 3

07 정답 ②

정답해설

② 출제 포인트: 간접의문문
의문문이 문장의 요소로 사용되는 경우 간접의문문이 되어 「의문사+주어+동사」의 어순을 가지게 된다. 해당 문장의 경우 의문문 'where you stand'가 'know'의 목적어로 사용되었으므로 간접의문문에 해당한다. 따라서 'where you stand'는 옳은 표현이다.

오답해설

① 출제 포인트: 부가의문문
부가의문문은 주절에 사용된 동사와 시제가 일치해야 하며 주절이 긍정문인 경우 부가의문문에는 부정형을, 주절이 부정문인 경우 부가의문문에는 긍정형을 사용해야 한다. 해당 문장의 경우 주절의 동사가 'has been'으로 현재완료시제이며 긍정문이므로 부가의문문 'has it'을 'hasn't it'으로 수정해야 한다.

③ 출제 포인트: another+단수명사/가정법 미래
'another' 이후에 오는 명사는 단수 형태이다. 따라서 해당 문장의 경우 'another chances'를 'another chance'로 수정해야 한다. 또한 해당 문장은 가정법 미래 「If+주어+should+동사원형 ~, 주어+would+동사원형~.」이 사용되었다.

④ 출제 포인트: 부정부사 도치
부정부사 'Little'이 문두에 오고 일반동사인 경우 「Little+조동사 do(does/did)+주어+동사원형」의 어순을 가진다. 따라서 해당 문장의 경우 'Tom knew'를 'did Tom know'로 수정해야 한다.

해석

① 여러분이 함께 공연을 한 지가 30년이 넘었네요, 그렇지 않나요?
② 월급을 협상하기 전에, 먼저 자신의 입지를 알아야 한다.
③ 이번에 구직에 실패한다면, 내년에 또 다른 기회가 없을 것이다.
④ Tom은 그것이 한국의 대중문화를 대표하는 것들 중 하나일 것이라고는 전혀 알지 못했다.

오답률 TOP 1

08 정답 ②

정답해설

본문은 성공한 사람들에게 있어서 중요한 것은 '인맥(connections)'이 아닌 '일의 성과(the results of work)'라는 것을 설명하고 있다. 빈칸에는 'producing good work(좋은 성과를 내는 것)'가 'most of the need to network(인맥 형성의 필요성)'를 어떻게 변화시켜 주는지 설명하는 단어가 들어가는 것이 가장 적절하다. 본문 마지막 문장 "It's the results of work — and not necessarily exposing yourself to as many people as possible — that attracts more and varied opportunities outside of that work(그 업무 외부에서 더 많고 다양한 기회를 이끌어주는 것은, 반드시 가능한 한 많은 사람들에게 자신을 노출하는 것이 아니라, 바로 업무의 결과이다.)"를 통해 '업무의 성과를 통해 더 많은 기회에 접근할 수 있다'는 것을 알 수 있으므로, 빈칸에는 '줄이다, 완화하다'라는 의미의 단어가 들어가는 것이 가장 적절하다. 따라서 정답은 ② 'attenuate(줄이다, 약하게 하다)'이다.

해석

인맥 형성하는 것을 좋아하지 않는 사람들은 어떻게 그들의 직종에서 성공을 할까? 훌륭한 업무를 수행하는 것이 인맥을 형성할 필요성의 대부분을 여하튼 줄여준다는 – 몇몇 증거로 뒷받침되는 – 희망이 있다. 지식 기반 직종에서 사람들이 어떻게 엘리트 수준에 도달하는지 탐구하는 컴퓨터 공학자인 Cal

Newport는 그의 연구를 하는 동안 몇몇의 로즈 장학생들을 인터뷰했고, 그들 중 많은 이들의 성공으로의 경로가 종종 잘못 알려져 있다는 것을 발견했다. 그는 "로즈 장학생들은 인맥 또는 운에 의존하기보다는 적은 수의 일(보통 두 가지)을 굉장히 잘하는 것에 많은 양의 에너지를 투자한다"고 적었다. 그 업무 외부에서 더 많고 다양한 기회를 이끌어주는 것은 – 반드시 가능한 한 많은 사람들에게 자신을 노출하는 것이 아니라 – 바로 업무의 결과이다.

① 심화시키다
② 줄이다, 약하게 하다
③ 경각시키다
④ 죽이다

어휘

be fond of ~을 좋아하다
network 인적 네트워크[정보망]를 형성하다
get ahead 출세하다, 성공하다   at all (긍정문) 여하튼, 어쨌든 간에
in the course of …동안   misreport 틀리게 보도하다, 오보하다
varied 다양한, 갖가지의   aggravate 심화시키다, 악화시키다
attenuate 약하게 하다, [힘·효력·가치 따위를] 줄이다
awaken 경각시키다   slay 죽이다

09 정답 ③

정답해설

본문은 '시험에 늦었을 경우의 규정'에 대한 글이다. 본문 초반에는 시험 시작한 시간 이내에 도착한 경우에 대해 설명하고, 이어서 한 시간 이후 도착한 경우에는 시험 연기를 신청해야 한다고 언급한 후, 마지막으로 시험 연기를 신청하는 방법에 대해 설명하는 것으로 글을 마무리하고 있다. 따라서 전체 글의 주제로 가장 적절한 보기는 '③ Exam policy for late arrivals(지각에 대한 시험 정책)'이다.

오답해설

① 본문에 언급된 "To apply, you must complete the examination deferral form(신청하기 위해, 당신은 시험 연기 양식을 작성해야 한다)."은 '시험 연기'를 신청하는 방법에 대한 언급이며, '시험을 신청하는 방법'에 대해 설명하는 글이 아니므로 오답이다.
② 본문과 관련 없는 내용이다.
④ 본문에서 '지각'에 관한 내용이 언급되지만, 이에 따른 '불이익(penalty)'에 초점을 맞추어 설명하고 있는 것은 아니다. 따라서 글의 주제로 적절하지 않다.

해석

당신은 공식 시작 시간 한 시간 이내에 시험 감독관의 승인 하에 시험장에 입장할 수 있다. 그러나 지각생들에게는 시험을 위해 예정된 종료 시간 이상의 추가 시간은 주어지지 않을 것이다. 만일 당신이 한 시간 이후에 도착한다면 당신은 시험장 입장이 허용되지 않을 것이다. 이러한 상황에서 당신은 당신의 시험 연기를 신청할 수 있다; 그러나 연기된 시험은 질병 또는 당신이 통제할 수 없는 상황과 같은 극히 예외적인 상황 하에서만 승인될 것이다. 신청하기 위해, 당신은 시험 연기 양식을 작성해야 한다. 양식은 당신의 시험 일자로부터 대학 근무일 3일 이내 또는 늦어도 3일까지 제출되어야 한다. 당신의 신청서는 적절한 증빙 서류들을 포함해야 한다.

① 시험에 지원하는 방법
② 시험 규정 위반들
③ 지각에 대한 시험 정책
④ 시험 지각에 대한 처벌들

어휘

permission 승인   supervisor 감독관
defer 연기하다, 미루다   grant 허락[승인]하다
exceptional 극히 예외적인   deferral 연기
submit 제출하다   no later than 늦어도 …까지
application 신청서   appropriate 적절한
breach 위반   penalty 처벌

10 정답 ③

정답해설

(A) '살던 곳에서 노후를 맞이하는 것(aging in place)'이 노인들 사이에서 인기가 있지만, (A) 이후의 내용 "there are considerable risks to elderly people's health and safety"에 따르면 실제로는 '살던 곳에서 노후를 맞이하는 것'에 상당한 위험이 있다. 즉, 앞서 언급한 긍정적 내용과는 대조적인 부정적 내용이 제시되고 있으므로, (A)에 적절한 것은 'However(그러나)'이다.

(B) 이전 "Accidents and falls are a major concern for elderly people living alone(사고와 낙상은 홀로 사는 노인들에게 큰 근심거리이다)."을 통해, '노인의 주요 걱정거리'에 대해 언급한 후, (B) 이후에서 '노인을 위한 양로 기술(gerontechnology)'이 그러한 걱정거리를 줄여줄 수 있다고 설명하고 있다. 즉, 앞서 언급한 부정적인 내용과 대조적인 긍정적인 내용이 제시되고 있으므로, (B)에 가장 적절한 표현은 'Fortunately(다행히도)'이다.

따라서 정답은 '③ However(그러나) – Fortunately(다행히도)'이다.

오답해설

나머지 보기는 문맥상 어색하므로 오답이다.

해석

American Association of Retired Persons(AARP)에 따르면, 거의 90%의 노인들이 나이가 들어가는 동안 자신들의 집에 머무르고 싶어 한다. 일반적으로 요양 환경에서가 아니라 당신이 이미 사는 곳에서 나이를 먹는 것인, 살던 곳에서 노후 맞기라는 이 아이디어는 많은 도움 없이 살 수 있는 노인들 사이에서 계속해서 인기 있는 선택지가 되고 있다. (A) 그러나, 이 인구가 그들의 기존 생활방식을 위해 설계된 집에서 나이를 먹기 때문에, 노인들의 건강과 안전에 상당한 위험이 존재한다. 살던 곳에서 노후를 맞는 많은 노인들은 간병인 또는 보건 전문가를 매일 접견할 수 없을지 모른다. 사고와 낙상은 홀로 사는 노인들에게 큰 근심거리이다. (B) 다행히도, 오늘날의 노인을 위한 양로 기술은 노인들이 자신들의 집에서 쉽고 안전하게 살도록 도와줄 수 있다. 이것은 스마트 홈 자동화, 웨어러블 기술, 그리고 움직임 감지기 등을 포함할 수 있다.

	(A)	(B)
①	그에 따라	다시 말해
②	비슷하게	예를 들어
③	그러나	다행히도
④	결과적으로	그래서

어휘

senior 연장자, 고령자, 노인   assistance 지원, 원조, 보조
population (특정 범주에 속하는) 인구
considerable 상당한, 많은   elderly 나이가 지긋한; 노인층
have access to …에게 접근[출입]할 수 있다, …을 면회할 수 있다
caretaker 돌보는 사람, 관리인   professional 전문의, 직업의
day-to-day 일상의, 나날의   automation 자동화
wearable 입을 수 있는, 착용하기 알맞은
accordingly 그에 따라   in a word 다시 말해
hence 그래서, 그러므로

결국엔 성정혜 영어 하프모의고사
기적사 DAY 43

01	②	02	②	03	③	04	③	05	③
06	④	07	①	08	③	09	②	10	④

01 정답 ②

정답해설

밑줄 친 'dissolvable'은 '용해될 수 있는'을 뜻하는 형용사로 ② resolvable과 의미상 가장 가깝다.

해석

새로운 기술은 **용해될 수 있는** 물질로 이루어져 있으며, 그것이 피부에 놓여 있을 때 즉시 용해될 것이라는 것을 의미한다.
① 침식 가능한
② 용해할 수 있는
③ 응고 되어진
④ 기화시킬 수 있는, 증발시킬 수 있는

어휘

dissolvable 용해될 수 있는
dissolve 용해시키다, 녹이다
erodible 침식 가능한
resolvable 용해할 수 있는
solidify 굳어지다; 굳히다
vaporizable 기화시킬 수 있는, 증발시킬 수 있는

02 정답 ②

정답해설

밑줄 친 'scheme'은 명사로 사용되어, '계획, 음모'의 의미를 가지고 있다. 해당 문장에서는 '계획'이라는 의미로 쓰여 ② planning과 의미가 가장 가깝다. 또한 'scheme'은 동사로는 '계획하다'의 의미도 가지고 있으므로 주의해야 한다.

해석

"Seoul Digital Basic Plan 2020"은 2016년에 시작하는 그 시의 5개년 디지털 정책 비전과 **계획**을 포함할 것이다.
① 고시, 공고
② 계획, 입안
③ 약속, 약혼
④ 즉흥, 즉석에서 만듦

어휘

include 포함하다
scheme 계획, 음모
bulletin 고시, 공고
planning 계획, 입안
engagement 약속, 약혼
extemporization 즉흥, 즉석에서 만듦

03 정답 ③

정답해설

밑줄 친 'stacked'는 'stack(겹겹이 쌓다, 쌓아 올리다)'의 과거분사로 해당 문장에서는 'when they are stacked'로 쓰여 'when' 이후에 '주어+be동사'인 'they are'이 생략되었다. 따라서 'stacked'는 'overlap(겹치다)'의 과거분사인 ③ overlapped와 의미상 가장 가깝다.

해석

형형색색의 플라스틱 블록들은 매우 간단하지만, 함께 **쌓일** 때는 끝없는 가능성들을 가지게 된다.
① 뒤집힌
② 분리된
③ 겹쳐진
④ 나눠진

어휘

brick 블록, 벽돌
endless 끝없는, 무한한
stack 겹겹이 쌓다, 쌓아 올리다
reverse ~을 뒤집다, 역으로[거꾸로] 하다
separate 분리하다, 떼어놓다
overlap 겹치다
segment 나누다, 구분하다

04 정답 ③

정답해설

A가 B에게 "기차역으로 가는 가장 빠른 경로를 안다"라고 말하자, B는 "지도는 가장 빠른 경로를 보여주지 않아"라고 대답한다. 이는 A의 말에 대한 적절한 답변이 아니다.

오답해설

① A가 B에게 '양말을 어디에 뒀는지' 물어보자 B는 "세탁실에 있어. 왜 물어봐?"라고 대답한다. B의 답변은 A의 질문에 대한 답으로 적절하다.
② A가 B에게 "새 옷을 입은 것을 보고 싶다"라고 이야기하자 B는 "날씨가 더 따뜻해지면 입어 보겠다"라고 답변한다. 이는 A의 발언에 대한 적절한 반응이다.
④ A가 B에게 '왜 계속 재채기하나'면서, '고양이 알레르기가 있는지' 물어본다. 이에 대해 B는 "어렸을 때부터 있었어."라고 말한다. 이는 자연스러운 대화의 흐름이다.

해석

① A: 너 양말 어디에 뒀어?
   B: 세탁실에 있어. 왜 물어봐?
② A: 나는 네가 새 옷을 입은 것을 보고 싶어.
   B: 날씨가 더 따뜻해지면 입어 볼게.
③ A: 나는 기차역으로 가는 가장 빠른 경로를 알아.
   B: 지도는 가장 빠른 경로를 보여주지 않아.
④ A: 너 왜 계속 재채기해? 너 고양이 알레르기 있어?
   B: 나 어렸을 때부터 알레르기가 있었어.

어휘

laundry 세탁소; 세탁물
route 경로, 길, 노선
sneeze 재채기하다; 재채기
allergic 알레르기의

05 정답 ③

정답해설

③ 출제 포인트: 시제 일치/주장, 요구, 명령, 제안 동사+(that)+주어+(should)+동사원형

시간의 부사구 '숫자+단위 복수[years/weeks/months 등]+ago'가 오는 경우 동사에 과거시제를 사용한다. 해당 문장은 과거시제를 나타내는 시간의 부사구 '65 million years ago'가 쓰인 종속절에 과거시제 동사 'prospered'와 'appeared'가 옳게 사용되었다. 또한 'prospered'와 'appeared'는 자동사로 사용되었음에 유의해야한다. 해당 문장에서

'suggest'는 문맥상 '제안하다'의 의미가 아닌 '(넌지시) 말하다, 암시하다'의 의미로 사용되었으므로 종속절에 시제를 적용해야 한다.

오답해설

① 출제 포인트: 이중부정 금지/관용표현(make haste)
'lest'는 '~하지 않도록'이라는 부정의 뜻을 가지는 접속사로 이후에 오는 절에 부정부사 'not'을 사용하지 않는다. 해당 문장은 부정의 뜻을 나타내는 'lest'와 부정부사 'not'이 함께 사용되어 이중부정이 되었으므로 틀린 문장이다. 따라서 해당 문장의 'not'을 삭제해 'should not be late'를 'should be late'로 수정해야한다. 또한 'make haste'는 관용표현으로 '서두르다'를 뜻한다.

② 출제 포인트: to부정사의 부사적 용법(so as not to+동사원형)
「so as not to+동사원형」은 관용표현으로 '~하지 않기 위해'를 뜻하며 to부정사의 부사적 용법에 해당한다. 해당 문장은 동사원형의 자리에 -ing 형태인 'being'을 사용하였으므로 틀린 문장이다. 따라서 'being'을 동사원형 'be'로 수정해야 한다.

④ 출제 포인트: 동사 관용표현(be cut out to+동사원형)
'be cut out to+동사원형'은 관용표현으로 '~의 자질이 있다'를 뜻한다. 해당 문장은 동사원형 자리에 -ing 형태인 'being'을 사용하였으므로 틀린 문장이다. 따라서 'being'을 동사원형 'be'로 수정해야 한다. 또한 'be poor at+목적어'는 관용표현으로 '~에 서툴다'를 뜻하며, 이때 'helping'은 전치사 'at'의 목적어로 쓰인 동명사이다.

오답률 TOP 2
06 정답 ④

정답해설

④ 출제 포인트: 가목적어 it/to부정사의 명사적 용법/to부정사의 의미상 주어/불완전타동사 make
밑줄 친 'a predator'는 불완전타동사 'makes'의 목적어로 볼 수 있으나, 문맥상 '이것은 포식자가 사냥할 한 마리의 동물에 집중하는 것을 더 어렵게 만든다'가 자연스러우므로 밑줄 친 'a predator'를 'harder' 뒤로 이동하면서 'for a predator'로 수정하고 기존의 'a predator'가 있던 자리에는 가목적어 'it'을 사용해야 한다. 즉, 해당 문장은 'This makes it harder for a predator to focus on one animal to catch.'가 옳은 문장이며 'for a predator'는 to부정사의 의미상 주어로 사용된 것임을 알 수 있다.

오답해설

① 출제 포인트: 완전자동사 vs. 완전타동사
'rely'는 완전자동사이므로 전치사를 통해 목적어를 가진다. 해당 문장은 'rely on' 이후에 목적어 'their own senses'가 있으므로 밑줄 친 'rely on'은 옳은 표현이다.

② 출제 포인트: 현재분사 vs. 과거분사
밑줄 친 'picked out'은 'pick out'의 과거분사로, 수식하는 대상 'the unlucky individual'과 수동관계이며 이후에 목적어가 아닌 「by+행위자」인 'by a predator'가 왔으므로 'picked out'은 옳은 표현이다.

③ 출제 포인트: a group of + 복수명사
'a group of' 이후에는 복수명사가 온다. 따라서 밑줄 친 'animals'는 옳은 표현이다.

해석

홀로 사는 동물들은 자신을 방어하기 위해 자신들의 감각에 의존하지만, 무리에 있는 동물은 위험을 경계하는 많은 다른 동물들의 눈, 귀, 코를 갖게 됨으로써 득을 본다. 무리에 있는 동물은 또한 포식자에 의해 선택받는 불운한 개체가 될 가능성이 더 적다. 게다가, 포식자에게서 달아나는 동물 무리는 혼란을 일으킬 수 있다. 이것은 포식자가 사냥할 한 마리의 동물에 집중하는 것을 더 어렵게 만든다.

어휘

rely on ~에 의존하다
on the alert 경계하여
pick out ~을 선택하다
flee 달아나다
defend 방어하다, 지키다
unlucky 불운한
predator 포식자, 육식동물
confusion 혼란

오답률 TOP 1
07 정답 ①

정답해설

① 출제 포인트: 부가의문문
부가의문문은 주절이 긍정문이면 부정의문문의 형태를, 주절이 부정문이면 긍정의문문의 형태를 사용해야 한다. 해당 문장의 경우 주절에 부정부사 'hardly'가 있으므로 부정문임을 알 수 있다. 따라서 부가의문문에 긍정의문문의 형태인 'is he?'를 사용하는 것이 옳다.

오답해설

② 출제 포인트: 부정부사 도치
부정부사 'Hardly'가 문두에 오고 동사의 시제가 현재완료인 경우 「Hardly+have/has+주어+과거분사」의 어순을 가진다. 따라서 해당 문장의 경우 'the whole process has been'을 'has the whole process been'으로 수정해야 한다.

③ 출제 포인트: 간접의문문의 어순
의문문이 문장의 요소로 사용되는 경우 간접의문문이 되어 「의문사+주어+동사」의 어순을 가지게 된다. 따라서 해당 문장의 경우 'why do we tolerate'를 'why we tolerate'로 수정해야 한다. 이때 'why we tolerate ~'는 선행사 'the reason'이 생략된 관계부사절로 보아도 된다.

④ 출제 포인트: 타동사구[완전타동사+목적어+전치사+목적어]/가정법 미래
'provide'는 「provide+목적어[대상]+with+목적어[사물]」 또는 「provide+목적어[사물]+to/for+목적어[대상]」의 구조를 가진다. 따라서 해당 문장의 경우 'with'를 'to' 또는 'for'로 수정하거나, 'more money'와 'local government'의 위치를 바꾸어 'provide local government with more money'로 수정해야한다. 또한 해당 문장은 가정법 미래 「If+주어+were to+동사원형 ~, 주어+would+동사원형~.」이 사용되었다.

해석

① Tom은 자신이 틀렸음을 좀처럼 인정할 것 같지 않아, 그렇지?
② 그 전체 과정은 중앙 정부의 안정에 거의 도움이 되지 않는다.
③ 몇몇 사람들은 왜 우리가 폭력과 타락을 찬양하는 대중문화를 용인하는 것이냐고 묻는다.
④ 만약에 우리가 지방 정부에 돈을 더 제공한다면, 지방 정부는 이 문제를 더 쉽게 해결할 것이다.

08 정답 ③

정답해설

본문은 '일자리 탐색 측면에서의 인맥의 중요성'에 대해 설명하고 있다. 빈칸 이전의 "Today, studies have shown that up to 80 percent of jobs are never advertised; instead, they are filled by word of mouth(오늘날, 연구들은 일자리의 최대 80퍼센트가 절대 광고되지 않는다는 것을 보여주었다; 대신에, 그것들은 구두로 채워진다)."를 통해, 많은 일자리가 구두, 즉 인맥을 통해 채워진다는 것을 알 수 있으며, 빈칸이 포함된 문장의 'Thus(따라서)'로 보아, 빈칸에는 앞서 언급된 내용과 '인과관계'에 있는 표현이 들어가야 한다. 따라서 '많은 일자리가 인맥으로 채워지므로, 중요한 것은 인맥이다'라는 구조가 자연스러우므로, 보기 중 빈칸에 가장 적절한 것은 '③ who you know and who knows you(당신이 누구를 아는가와 누가 당신을 아는가)'이다. 또한 밑줄 친 부분이 포함된 문장은 'it ~ that' 강조 용법이 사용된 문장으로 빈칸에 들어가는 'who you know and who knows you'는 강조 대상에 해당하며, 필자는 이를 하나의 개념으로 보아 단수 취급하고 있음에 주의하자.

오답해설

① 마지막 문장 'one of the greatest ways to connect with people in your field(당신의 분야의 사람들과 소통하는 가장 좋은 방법들 중 하나이다)'로 보아, 본문에서 다루는 인맥은 '자신의 분야의 모든 사람들'로, 함께 일하는 사람들에 국한된 것만이 아니므로 빈칸에 적절하지 않다.
② 본문과 관련 없는 내용이다.
④ 앞서 언급된 '일자리가 인맥을 통해 형성된다'는 내용의 결론으로 '인맥 형성의 장소와 방법'이 언급되는 것은 부자연스럽다. 그리고 본문은 '직업에 관련된(professional) 인맥 형성'에 대한 내용으로, 막연히 '새로운 사람들(new people)'을 만나는 것에 대해 언급하는 것 또한 본문의 내용과 어울리지 않는다.

해석

오늘날 인맥 형성은 당신의 일자리 탐색에 있어서 필수적인 측면이 되었다. 비록 당신이 현재의 직업에 기반이 잘 잡혀있고, 조만간 진로를 바꾸거나 발전시킬 계획이 없다 하더라도, 인맥 형성은 귀중한 수단임이 드러났다. 오늘날, 연구들은 일자리의 최대 80퍼센트가 절대 광고되지 않는다는 것을 보여주었다; 대신에, 그것들은 구두로 채워진다. 따라서 중요한 것은 당신이 누구를 아는가와 누가 당신을 아는가이다. 당신이 당신의 경력을 발전시킬 더 많은 기회를 가질 수 있도록 당신은 관계와 인맥을 형성해야만 한다. 당신의 전문 분야의 단체가 주관하는 회의와 사교 행사에 참가하는 것은 당신의 분야의 사람들과 소통하는 가장 좋은 방법들 중 하나이다.
① 당신이 누구와 함께 그리고 누구를 위해 일하는가
② 당신이 무엇을 하고 그것을 어떻게 하는가
③ 당신이 누구를 아는가와 누가 당신을 아는가
④ 당신이 어디에서 어떻게 새로운 사람들을 만나는가

어휘

well established (성공 등을 통해) 자리를 확실히 잡은
advance 나아가게 하다, 전진시키다 prove (…임이) 드러나다[판명되다]
fill (어떤 일자리에 사람을) 채우다 association 협회, 단체

09 정답 ②

정답해설

본문은 '시험에 참석하지 못한 학생이 지켜야 할 규정'에 대해 설명하고 있다. 두 번째 문장 "If the student fails to notify a dean within 24 hours of the scheduled start time of the examination, the student will not be allowed to take the examination and will receive an "F" on the examination(만일 그 학생이 시험의 예정된 시작 시간 후 24시간 이내에 학과장에게 통지하지 못한다면, 그 학생은 시험을 치르는 것이 허용되지 않을 것이며, 시험에서 "F"를 받을 것이다)"을 통해, '시험에 참석하지 못한 학생은 시험 시작 시간 후 24시간 이내에 학장에게 알려야 한다'는 것을 알 수 있다. 따라서 ②의 'earlier'는 'later'가 되어야 문맥상 자연스럽다. 'no later than'은 '늦어도 ~까지, ~이내에'라는 의미이다. 'no earlier than'은 '~이 지난 후, ~이후'라는 의미로, '24시간이 지난 이후에 연락을 해야 한다'는 뜻이 되므로 문맥상 어색하다.

오답해설

① "If a student does not appear during the scheduled examination period(만일 학생이 예정된 시험 기간 중에 나타나지 않거나)~"로 보아, '시험에 참석하지 못한 학생'에 관한 내용이라는 것을 알 수 있으므로, '시험을 치르지 못한'이라는 의미가 되는 'unable'은 문맥상 자연스럽다.
③ 주어진 기간 이외에 '개별적으로, 별도로' 시험에 참석하지 못한 특수한 상황에 대한 설명을 해야 한다는 의미이므로, 'separate'는 문맥상 자연스럽다.
④ 학장이 설명된 이유가 지연된 통지를 '정당화한다'고 생각하지 않는 한, 시험의 기회가 주어지지 않을 것이기 때문에 'justifying'은 빈칸에 적절하다.

해석

만일 학생이 예정된 시험 기간 중에 나타나지 않거나 예정된 시험 시간 동안 시험을 치를 수 ① 없다면, 그 학생은 가능한 한 빨리, 그러나 늦어도 시험의 예정된 시작 시간 이후 24시간이 ② 지나고 나서(→ 이내에) 학과장에게 통지해야 한다. 만일 그 학생이 시험의 예정된 시작 시간 후 24시간 이내에 학과장에게 통지하지 못한다면, 학생이 자신의 통제 밖에 있는 특수한 상황에 대한 ③ 별도의 설명을 하고 학과장이 그 이유가 그러한 지연된 통지를 ④ 정당화한다고 생각하지 않는 한 그 학생은 시험을 치르는 것이 허용되지 않을 것이며, 시험에서 "F"를 받을 것이다. 여기에서 사용된 "학생의 통제 밖에 있는 특수한 상황"이라는 용어는 건강상의 위급 상황 또는 직계 가족의 위급 상황을 포함하며 이에 국한되지 않는다.

어휘

dean 학과장, 학장 separate 단독의, 독립된, 개별적인
showing (사실 따위의) 설명, 표시
extraordinary 특별한, 특수한, 보통이 아닌
justify 정당화하다
herein 여기에(서), 이 문서 [진술/사실]에서
immediate (관계가) 직접적인, 직접 관련이 있는

오답률 TOP 3

10 정답 ④

정답해설

본문은 다양한 '노후 지원 기술'에 대해 설명하는 글이며, 빈칸에는 이러한 기술들이 광범위하게 시행되고 있지 못하는 이유를 설명하는 표현이 들어가야 한다. 마지막 문장 "On the one hand, they recognize that such technologies could support independent living of the older population, while on the other hand, they do not feel that they themselves personally need them(한편으로는, 그들은 그러한 기술이 고령 인구의 독립적인 삶을 지원해줄 수 있다는 것을 인식하지만, 반면 다른 한편으로는, 그들 자신이 개인적으로 그것들이 필요하다고 생각하지 않는다)."을 통해, '노인들이 기술의 이점을 인정하지만, 실제로 자신들에게 필요하다고는 생각하지 않는 것'에 대해 언급하고 있으므로, '기술에 대한 양면적 태도'를 지니고 있다는 것을 알 수 있다. 따라서 빈칸에 가장 적절한 것은 '④ ambivalent attitude towards(~에 대한 양면적인 태도)'이다.

오답해설

③ 마지막 문장을 통해 '노인들이 기술에 대해 인식을 하고는 있으나, 단순히 자신들이 사용할 필요성을 느끼지 못한다'는 것을 알 수 있다. 따라서 노인들의 '무지(ignorance)'에 의해 기술 시행이 저해되는 것이 아니므로 빈칸에 적절하지 않다.
나머지 보기는 문맥상 어색하므로 오답이다.

해석

응급 구호 시스템, 활력 징후 모니터링, 낙상 감지 시스템과 같은 다양한 유형의 기술이 살던 곳에서 노후를 맞는 것을 돕기 위해 특별히 설계되었다. 이러한 기술들은 때때로 스마트 홈 기술이라고 일컬어진다. 또한, 고령자의 만성

질환 자가 관리를 돕기 위한 온라인 도구를 포함한 광범위한 기술을 망라하는 e-Health도 있다. 그러나 이러한 기술들은 다양한 이유로 인해 대규모로 시행되어오고 있지 못하다. 그 이유 중 하나는 고령자들의 기술의 이러한 유형에 대한 양면적인 태도이다. 한편으로는, 그들은 그러한 기술이 고령 인구의 독립적인 삶을 지원해줄 수 있다는 것을 인식하지만, 반면 다른 한편으로는, 그들 자신이 개인적으로 그것들이 필요하다고 생각하지 않는다.

① ~에 대한 빈틈없는 접근
② ~에 대한 일반적인 선호
③ ~에 대한 만연한 무지
④ ~에 대한 양면적인 태도

어휘

vital sign 바이탈 사인, 활력 징후(사람이 살아 있음을 보여주는 호흡, 체온, 심장 박동 등의 측정치)
be referred to as ~로 불리다
encompass (많은 것을) 포함[망라]하다, 아우르다
implement 시행하다
vigilant 바짝 경계하는, 조금도 방심하지 않는
prevalent 일반적인[널리 퍼져 있는], 만연한
ignorance 무지, 무식
ambivalent 상반[모순]되는 감정을 가진, 양면적인

결국엔 성정혜 영어 하프모의고사
기적사 DAY 44

| 01 | ① | 02 | ④ | 03 | ③ | 04 | ① | 05 | ① |
| 06 | ② | 07 | ④ | 08 | ② | 09 | ④ | 10 | ③ |

01 정답 ①

정답해설

밑줄 친 'drinkable'은 '마실 수 있는'을 뜻하는 형용사로 ① potable과 의미상 가장 가깝다.

해석

그들은 하루에 10만 갤런 이상의 **마실 수 있는** 물을 생산할 수 있는 정수 장비와 증발기를 갖추고 있다.
① 마셔도 되는
② 찔 수 있는
③ 소화할 수 있는
④ 먹을 수 있는

어휘

purification 정화, 정제
drinkable 마실 수 있는
stewable 찔 수 있는
comestible 먹을 수 있는
evaporator 증발기
potable 마셔도 되는
digestible 소화할 수 있는

오답률 TOP 1
02 정답 ④

정답해설

밑줄 친 'assistance'는 '도움, 원조, 지원'이라는 뜻의 명사로 ④ succor와 의미가 가장 가깝다.

해석

이 단체들은 사람들이 게을러지지 않도록 적당량의 **지원**을 제공할 수 있기 때문에 이러한 방식으로 가난한 사람들을 지원하는 것이 더 낫다.
① 중단, 멈춤
② 공물, 헌사
③ 압수, 몰수
④ 도움, 구제, 원조

어휘

organization 조직, 단체
assistance 도움, 원조, 지원
lazy 게으른
tribute 공물, 헌사
succor 도움, 구제, 원조
provide 제공하다, 공급하다
encourage 장려하다; 격려하다
halt 중단, 멈춤
seizure 압수, 몰수

오답률 TOP 2
03 정답 ③

정답해설

밑줄 친 'associative'는 '연상의, 연합의'라는 뜻의 형용사로 ③ reminiscent와 의미가 가장 가깝다.

해석

과제들 중 일부는 개들의 **연상** 학습 능력을 시험했고 반면에 다른 것들은 문제 해결에 있어 개들의 독창력을 시험했다.
① 가슴 아픈, 저미는
② 근절할 수 있는
③ 연상시키는, ~을 생각나게 하는
④ 구체화할 수 있는, 결정체를 이룰 수 있는

어휘

associative 연상의, 연합의
creativity 창조성, 독창력
poignant 가슴 아픈, 저미는
eradicable 근절할 수 있는
reminiscent 연상시키는, ~을 생각나게 하는
crystallizable 구체화할 수 있는; 결정체를 이룰 수 있는

04 정답 ①

정답해설

A가 B에게 "두통이 있다"라고 말하자 B는 "편두통은 두통의 종류 중 하나이다"라고 답변한다. 이러한 대화의 흐름은 자연스럽지 않다.

오답해설

② A는 B에게 '셔츠를 빌려도 되는지' 물어보고, B는 "물론이지"라고 대답하면서 셔츠가 A에게 "맞을지 잘 모르겠다"라고 덧붙인다. 이는 문맥상 자연스럽다.
③ A는 B에게 '양말을 모두 다 쌌는지' 질문하고, B는 "일어나자마자 양말을 쌌다"라고 대답한다. B의 답변은 A의 말에 대한 적합한 반응이다.
④ A는 "엄마와 남은 주말을 함께 보내고 싶다"라고 얘기한다. 그러자 B는 "엄마와 같이 계획을 세워 놓았는지" 되묻는다. 이는 내용상 적절하다.

해석

① A: 나 두통이 있어.
   B: 편두통은 두통의 한 종류야.
② A: 나 네 셔츠 좀 빌려도 돼?
   B: 물론이지, 근데 너에게 맞을지 모르겠어.
③ A: 너 벌써 네 양말을 모두 다 쌌어?
   B: 난 일어나자마자 짐 쌌어.
④ A: 나는 엄마와 남은 주말을 같이 보내고 싶어.
   B: 엄마와 같이 계획 세워 놨어?

어휘

migraine 편두통

05 정답 ①

정답해설

① **출제 포인트: to부정사의 부사적 용법(in order not to+동사원형)**

「in order not to+동사원형」은 관용표현으로 '~하지 않기 위해'를 뜻하며 to부정사의 부사적 용법에 해당한다. 해당 문장은 주어진 해석과 일치하므로 옳은 문장이다. 또한「in order not to+동사원형」은「so as not to+동사원형」과 바꾸어 사용할 수 있다.

오답해설

② **출제 포인트: 유사관계대명사 but/이중부정 금지**

유사 관계대명사 'but'은 부정의 뜻을 포함하므로 뒤따라오는 절에 부정부사 'not'을 사용할 수 없다. 따라서 'but doesn't know'에서 'not'을 삭제해 'but knows'로 수정하거나 'but'을 'that'으로 수정해 'that doesn't know'로 수정해야 한다.

③ **출제 포인트: 시제 일치/시간의 부사(구) 및 부사절**

시간의 부사절 'since+주어+과거시제 동사'가 오는 경우 주절의 동사에 현재완료시제를 사용한다. 따라서 해당 문장의 'was saving'을 'has been saving'으로 수정해야 한다.

④ **출제 포인트: 동사 관용표현(make up to/make up for)**

'make up to'와 'make up for'는 관용표현으로 각각 '~에게 아첨하다'와 '~을 보충하다, 보상하다'를 뜻한다. 해당 문장의 경우 주어진 해석 '~을 보충하다'와 일치해야 하므로 'make up to'를 'make up for'로 수정해야 한다.

06 정답 ②

정답해설

② **출제 포인트: 능동태 vs. 수동태/관용표현(be supposed to+동사원형)**

'happen'은 완전자동사이므로 수동태를 사용할 수 없다. 따라서 밑줄 친 'be happened'를 'happen'으로 수정해야 한다. 또한 'be supposed to+동사원형'은 '~하기로 되어있다, ~해야 한다'를 뜻한다. 'be supposed to'의 'to'는 전치사가 아닌 to부정사의 'to'임에 유의해야한다.

오답해설

① **출제 포인트: 현재분사 vs. 과거분사**

밑줄 친 'causing'은 불완전타동사 'cause'의 현재분사로, 생략된 주어 'a planning discussion'과 능동관계이므로 옳은 표현이다.

③ **출제 포인트: 현재분사 vs. 과거분사**

밑줄 친 'stapled'는 완전타동사 'staple'의 과거분사로, 수식하는 대상 'the report'와 수동관계이다. 또한 해석상 '스테이플러로 고정된 보고서'가 자연스러우므로 과거분사 'stapled'는 옳은 표현이다.

④ **출제 포인트: 주격 관계대명사 that**

밑줄 친 'that'을 포함한 문장 'that ~ problem'은 'anything'을 선행사로 하는 주격 관계대명사이다. 앞에 있는 전치사 'about'으로 인해 선행사를 포함하는 관계대명사 'what'을 사용해야 하는 것으로 오해하지 않도록 주의해야 한다. 또한 해당 문장에서 선행사 'anything'을 수식하는 관계대명사 절은 목적격 관계대명사 절 'that ~ talked about'과 주격 관계대명사 절 'that ~ a problem'이므로 구조 분석에 유의해야 한다.

해석

계획 토론은 꽤 복잡하고 빠를 수 있어서 우리가 할 일을 잊어버리게 한다. 무슨 일이 일어날지를 요약하는 데 시간을 써라. 그것은 이런 것처럼 들릴 수 있다. "내가 이것을 제대로 이해했는지 알아보죠. Tom, 화요일 오후 2시 회의를 위해 당신은 회사 정규 표지와 함께 스테이플러로 고정된 보고서 아홉 부를 준비해야 합니다. 맞죠?" Tom은 아마도 "맞습니다."라고 대답할 것이다. 그리고 나서 여러분은 그에게 문제를 일으킬 수도 있는데 말하지 않은 그 밖에 다른 것이 있는지 물어볼 수 있다.

어휘

summarize 요약하다
be supposed to+동사원형 ~하기로 되어있다, ~해야 한다
staple 스테이플러로 고정하다
cover sheet 표지

07 정답 ④

정답해설

④ **출제 포인트: 가정법 미래**

해당 문장은 가정법 미래가 쓰인 문장으로 「If+주어+were to+동사원형~, 주어+would+동사원형~.」이 옳게 사용되었다.

오답해설

① **출제 포인트: 주요 조동사 표현/간접의문문의 어순**

「cannot help but+동사원형」은 관용표현으로 '~하지 않을 수 없다'를 뜻한다. 'couldn't help but'은 'cannot help but'의 과거형으로 해당 문장의 'wondering'을 'wonder'로 수정해야 한다. 또한 'what Tom was thinking'은 간접의문문에 해당하며 'wonder'의 목적어로 사용되었다.

② **출제 포인트: 완전자동사 listen/부정부사 도치**

관계대명사 'what'은 선행사를 포함한 관계대명사이며 뒤따라오는 문장은 불완전하다. 또한 완전자동사 'listen'은 전치사 'to'를 통해 목적어를 가진다. 따라서 해당 문장의 경우 관계대명사 'what' 이후에 오는 절에 쓰인 'had listened'를 'had listened to'로 수정해야 한다. 덧붙여 부정부사 (구) 'Not only'가 문두에 오고 일반동사가 사용된 경우 「Not only+조동사 do(does/did)+주어+동사원형」의 어순을 가진다.

③ **출제 포인트: 부가의문문**

부가의문문은 주절에 사용된 동사와 시제가 일치해야 한다. 따라서 해당 문장의 경우 주절의 동사 'begins'의 시제가 현재이며 일반동사를 사용하였으므로 부가의문문 'hasn't it?'을 'doesn't it?'으로 수정해야 한다.

해석

① Jane은 Tom이 무슨 생각을 하는지 궁금하지 않을 수 없었다.
② 그는 그 음악을 들었을 뿐만 아니라, 들었던 것을 작성했다.
③ William 씨와 함께하는 리더십 교육이 11시에 시작합니다, 그렇지 않나요?
④ 나의 현재 업무를 계속하게 된다면, 노사 사이의 협상에 관한 더 많은 경험을 얻을 것이다.

08 정답 ②

정답해설

본문은 우리가 흔히 '인맥 형성(networking)'을 위해 하는 실수에 대해 설명하고 있다. 본문 중반 "You throw a lot of activity at the issue and hope for the best(당신들은 그 문제에 많은 행위를 투입하고 최선을 바란다)."에서 '많은 활동'을 한다고 언급한 후, 그에 대한 구체적인 예시로, 다수의 회의 및 행사 참석, 명함 수집, 온라인 팔로워 구축 등을 제시한다. 그리고 "Unfortunately, these don't result in the type of network that supports your career advancement because they have no specific and clear purpose or intention(안타깝게도, 이것들은 구체적이고 명확한 목적 또는 의도를 가지고 있지 않기 때문에 당신의 경력 발전을 도와주는 인맥의 유형이 되지는 않는다)."라고 설명하며, 무작정 다수의 사람들과의 인맥 형성이 바람직하지 않다는 것을 언급한다. 마지막으로 "To create the type of network that supports your ambitions, your networking activity needs to be strategic and focused and your efforts must be purposeful and intentional(당신들의 야망을 뒷받침해주는 인맥의 유형을 형성하기 위해, 당신의 인맥 형성 행위는 전략적이고 집중적이어야 하며, 당신의 노력은 목적의식이 있고 의도적이어야 한다)."을 통해, '전략적이고 집중적'인 인맥 형성 활동의 필요성을 언급하고 있으므로, 전체적인 글의 내용으로 살펴볼 때, 필자는 '인맥의 양보다는 질이 중요하다'는 것을 강조하고 있다는 것을 알 수 있다. 따라서 정답은 '② When networking, quality is more important than quantity (인맥 형성을 할 때, 양보다 질이 더 중요하다).'이다.

오답해설

① 본문에서는 효과적인 인맥 형성의 '방법'에 대해 언급하고 있으며, 성공에 있어서 인맥의 '필요성'이 주요 주제가 아니므로, 필자의 주장으로 적절하지 않다.

③ 본문 초반 "when you throw enough activity or ideas at a situation or problem, eventually something will stick; that is, eventually you will find the answer(당신이 상황이나 문제에 충분한 행위 또는 아이디어를 투입할 때, 결국 무언가가 붙을 것이다; 즉, 결국 당신은 해답을 찾을 것이다)."에서 '꾸준히 포기하지 않는 것의 중요성'에 대해 언급되기는 하지만, 이는 '꾸준하고 막연히 인맥 형성을 시도하는 접근법'을 설명하기 위한 예시일 뿐이며, 본문 전체를 아우르는 내용이 아니므로 오답이다.

④ 필자의 주장은 '전략적이고 집중적'인 인맥 형성이 필요하다는 것이므로, '폭넓은 인맥 형성'의 필요성을 언급하는 해당 보기는 필자의 주장과는 거리가 멀다.

해석

만일 당신이 스파게티를 벽에 던져서 그것이 벽에 붙으면, 그 파스타는 익은 것이다라는 오래된 격언이 있다. 수년 동안 이 구절은 당신이 상황이나 문제에 충분한 행위 또는 아이디어를 투입할 때, 결국 무언가가 붙을 것이다; 즉, 결국 당신은 해답을 찾으리라는 것을 의미하도록 진화해 왔다. 그래서 당신들이 성공하는 데 도움이 되기 위해 인맥을 형성할 필요가 있다는 것을 들을 때, 당신들 중 야망이 있는 사람들은 이러한 접근법으로 문제에 착수한다. 당신들은 그 문제에 많은 행위를 투입하고 최선을 바란다. 당신들은 많은 인맥 형성 행사와 회의에 가고, 수백 장의 명함을 모으고 나누어 준다. 당신들은 온라인상의 입지를 확립하고 수많은 팔로워를 형성한다. 안타깝게도, 이것들은 구체적이고 명확한 목적 또는 의도를 가지고 있지 않기 때문에 당신의 경력 발전을 도와주는 인맥의 유형이 되지는 않는다. 당신들의 야망을 뒷받침해주는 인맥의 유형을 형성하기 위해, 당신의 인맥 형성 행위는 전략적이고 집중적이어야 하며, 당신의 노력은 목적의식이 있고 의도적이어야 한다.

① 신뢰할 수 있는 인맥은 성공을 위한 필수 요소이다.
② 인맥 형성을 할 때, 양보다 질이 더 중요하다.
③ 만일 당신이 포기하지 않는다면, 당신은 결국 당신이 원하는 것을 얻을 것이다.
④ 당신은 인맥을 본인 분야의 인물들로만 국한하지 말아야 한다.

어휘

adage 격언, 속담
tackle (곤란한 문제·일 등에) 달라붙다, 착수하다
presence 진출, 출석, 영향력, 입지
strategic 전략적인
intentional 의도적인
quality 특성, 특질; 품질, 질
give up 포기하다
advancement 발전, 진보, 출세
purposeful 목적의식이 있는
must 절대로[반드시] 필요한 것
quantity 양, 수량
in the end 결국, 마침내

오답률 TOP 3

09 정답 ④

정답해설

(A) 이전 문장에서는 '시험'에 대한 부정적 인식이 언급되고 있다. (A) 이후 문장에서도 "critics often argue that exams promote a superficial understanding of topics, and that they are inauthentic: in other words, they fail to represent the kinds of things students will be asked to do "in the real world"(비평가들은 시험이 주제에 대한 깊이 없는 이해를 촉진시키고, 그것들이 인위적이라고; 다시 말해, 그것들이 학생들이 "실제 세계"에서 수행하도록 요청될 것들의 종류들을 대표하지 못한다고 종종 주장한다)."라고 언급하며, '시험에 대한 부정적 견해'를 소개하고 있으므로, 빈칸에는 '첨가'를 나타내는 'Also(또한)'가 들어가는 것이 자연스럽다.

(B) 이전에서는 모두 '시험에 대한 부정적 견해'가 언급되고 있으나, (B) 이후에서는 앞서 언급된 '시험에 대한 부정적 인식'이 '편협한 관점'이라고 서술하며 '시험의 이점'에 대해 설명하고 있다. 좋은 평가 시스템의 역할에 대해 설명하고, 시험 폐지 대신 적절한 평가 시스템 도입의 필요성을 역설하고 있으므로, (B)에는 '역접'을 나타내는 'But(그러나)' 또는 'However(그러나)'가 들어가는 것이 자연스럽다.

따라서 정답은 '④ Also(또한) - However(그러나)'이다.

오답해설

① (A) 빈칸 이후의 내용이 (A) 이전 내용의 반대 사실을 가정하고 있지 않으므로, 'Otherwise(그렇지 않으면)'는 (A) 빈칸에 적절하지 않다.
나머지 보기는 모두 문맥상 어색하므로 오답이다.

해석

2011년, Macquarie University는 시험 폐지, 즉, 어느 학년의 어느 과목에서든지 무시험을 논의한 최초의 호주 대학이었다. 당시, 시험은 "탐구적이고 자립심 있는 학습자들"을 성장시키지 못한다는 주장이 제기되었다. (A) 또한, 비평가들은 시험이 주제에 대한 깊이 없는 이해를 촉진시키고, 그것들이 인위적이라고; 다시 말해, 그것들이 학생들이 "실제 세계"에서 수행하도록 요청될 것들의 종류들을 대표하지 못한다고 종종 주장한다. (B) 그러나 이는 시험의 이점에 대한 편협한 관점을 취하는 것이다. 훌륭한 평가 프로그램은 각 학생에 대한 균형 잡히고 공정한 평가를 제공할 수 있다. 시험을 폐지하기보다, 우리는 대신에 평가 과제의 어떠한 조합이 각각의 과목에 가장 적합한지를 질문해야 한다.

(A)	(B)
① 그렇지 않으면	그러나
② 그럼에도 불구하고	게다가
③ 예를 들어	그 결과
④ 또한	그러나

어휘

debate 논의하다, 논쟁하다 abolition 폐지
self-sufficient 자급자족하는, 자립심 있는
argue 주장하다
superficial 표면적인, 깊이 없는, 얄팍한
inauthentic 진짜[진품/정통]가 아닌 assessment 평가
evaluation 평가 appropriate 적합한, 적절한
otherwise 그렇지 않으면

10 정답 ③

정답해설

본문은 '노인을 위한 양로 기술(gerontechnology)이 이제 신체 건강뿐만 아니라 정신 건강 관리에도 도움을 주도록 변화하고 있다'고 설명한다. 본문 후반 "older adults care more about being connected to family(고령자들은 가족과 연결되어 있는 것에 더 관심을 가진다)"를 통해, 노인의 정신 건강은 '가족들과의 연결성'과 관련이 있다는 것을 유추할 수 있다. 따라서 "By ③ diminishing seniors' social life and connectivity, gerontechnology are helping seniors avoid depression, boredom, and loneliness(고령자들의 사회생활과 연결성을 ③ 약화시킴으로써, 노인을 위한 양로 기술은 고령자들이 우울증, 지루함 그리고 외로움을 피하도록 돕고 있다)."에서, '노인들이 우울, 지루함, 외로움을 피할 수 있도록 해주는 방법'은 '사회생활과 연결성을 '약화시키는 것'이 아니라 '강화시키는 것'임을 알 수 있다. 따라서 '③ diminishing'은 'enhancing' 또는 'improving' 등으로 바뀌어야 자연스럽다.

오답해설

① 'medication monitoring apps and safety alert systems' 등은 '신체 건강'을 관리하기 위한 기술이므로, 'physical'은 문맥상 자연스럽다.
② 본문 초반에서는 '노인을 위한 양로 기술이 전통적으로 신체 건강에 초점을 맞추었다'고 언급한 후, 최근 '정신 건강을 증진시키는 방향'으로 '변화'하였다고 설명하고 있으므로 'shift'는 문맥상 자연스럽다.
④ 본문 초반에서는 양로 기술이 '신체적 건강'에 초점이 맞추어져 있었다는 사실을 언급하고 있으며, 이후 '정신적 건강 케어'로의 변화를 소개하고 있다. 이를 통해 사람들이 기존에는 '건강'을 의학적인 치료를 요하는 신체적 문제로 보았다는 사실을 유추할 수 있으므로, '사람들이 건강을 '의료화하는 것(medicalizing)'에서 벗어나려 한다'는 의미가 되는 것은 문맥상 자연스럽다.

해석

노인을 위한 양로 기술은 약물치료 모니터링 앱과 안전 경고 시스템의 개발 및 증진과 함께 전통적으로 ① 신체 건강을 향상시키는 것에 초점을 맞추어 왔다. 그러나 최근 몇 년 안에, 정신 건강을 촉진하는 것과 노화에 대한 거시적인 접근법을 채택하는 ② 변화가 있었다. 고령자들의 사회생활과 연결성을 ③ **약화시킴으로써(→강화시킴으로써)**, 노인을 위한 양로 기술은 고령자들이 우울증, 지루함 그리고 외로움을 피하도록 돕고 있다. AgeLab의 연구원인 Chaiwoo Lee는 사람들은 건강을 ④ 의료화 하는 것에서 벗어나려 하고 있고, "고령자들은 가족과 연결되어 있는 것과 생산적인 상태로 남아 있는 것에 더 관심을 가진다"라고 언급한다. 간병인들을 대상으로 한 그녀의 연구를 통해, Chaiwoo는 그들이 가장 시간을 많이 소비하는 업무 중 하나는 "고령자들의 말동무가 되어 주는 것과 감정적 부담을 관리해주는 것"이라는 것을 발견했다.

어휘

shift 변화 adopt 채택하다, 취하다, 쓰다
holistic approach 거시적 접근법 diminish 약화시키다, 줄이다
medicalize 치료하다, 환자로 받아들이다, 의료화하다
productive 생산적인
time-consuming (많은) 시간이 걸리는
keep somebody company …의 곁에 있어 주다[친구가 되어 주다]
burden 짐, 부담

결국엔 성정혜 영어 하프모의고사
기적사 DAY 45

01	④	02	②	03	④	04	④	05	①
06	①	07	①	08	②	09	④	10	④

01 정답 ④

정답해설
밑줄 친 'susceptible'은 '민감한, 예민한'이라는 뜻의 형용사로 ④ impressionable 과 의미가 가장 가깝다.

해석
그 나라의 노인 인구도 또한 요인이 되는데, 이는 나이 든 사람들이 공기의 질과 관련된 질병에 더욱 **민감하기** 때문이다.
① 둔한, 따분한
② 민첩한, 날렵한
③ 아주 약한, 미미한
④ 민감한, 감수성이 풍부한

어휘
susceptible 민감한, 예민한
dull 둔한, 따분한
feeble 아주 약한, 미미한
impressionable 민감한, 감수성이 풍부한
illness 질병, 아픔
nimble 민첩한, 날렵한

02 정답 ②

정답해설
밑줄 친 'policy'는 '정책, 방침'이라는 뜻의 명사로 ② doctrine과 의미가 가장 가깝다.

해석
이러한 동향은 일부 정치가들이 징병 **정책**에서 여성을 포함하지 않는 한국의 정책의 가치에 질문을 하도록 한다.
① 전략, 전술
② 정책, 교리, 학설
③ 교화, 의식 고양
④ 책략, 술수

어휘
politician 정치가
policy 정책, 방침
compulsory 의무적인, 강제적인, 필수의
tactic 전략, 전술
edification 교화, 의식 고양
question 질문하다; 질문, 의문
doctrine 정책, 교리, 학설
stratagem 책략, 술수

오답률 TOP 3
03 정답 ④

정답해설
밑줄 친 'disparate'는 '이질적인, 서로 전혀 다른'이라는 뜻의 형용사로 ④ heterogeneous와 의미가 가장 가깝다.

해석
그들은 **다른** 정보를 연결하고, 증권 분석가가 예측하지 못하는 방법으로 그것을 합친다.
① 단순한, 약한
② 복잡한, 미묘한
③ 동종의, 동질의
④ 이질적인, 이종의

어휘
disparate 이질적인, 서로 전혀 다른
seely 단순한, 약한
homogeneous 동종의, 동질의
security analyst 증권 분석가
intricate 복잡한, 미묘한
heterogeneous 이질적인, 이종의

04 정답 ④

정답해설
A는 B에게 "옆집에 사는 여성이 새로운 사업을 시작하는 것을 생각 중이라고 말했다"라고 이야기하자, B는 "사람들이 폐업하고 있다"라고 말하며, "왜인지는 모르겠다"라고 덧붙인다. B의 대답은 A의 말에 대한 적절한 반응이 아니다.

오답해설
① A가 B에게 "목이 무척 마르다"라고 얘기하자 B는 '정수기(water fountain)'의 위치를 알려준다. 이는 자연스러운 대화의 흐름이다.
② A가 '모임의 회비가 얼마인지' B에게 질문하자 B는 "매년 30달러를 지불해야한다"며 모임 회비의 가격을 알려준다. B의 답변은 A의 물음에 대한 대답으로 적합하다.
③ A는 B에게 "고속도로에서 너무 속도 내지 말라"라고 주의하라고 한다. B는 "명심하겠다"라고 대답하면서 "걱정하지 마"라는 말로 A를 안심시키고자 한다. 이는 문맥상 적절하다.

해석
① A: 나는 정말 목이 말라.
   B: 복도에 정수기가 하나 있어.
② A: 이 모임 회비가 얼마야?
   B: 매년 30달러를 지불해야 해.
③ A: 고속도로에서 너무 빨리 운전하지 마!
   B: 명심할게. 걱정하지 마!
④ A: 옆집에 사는 여성이 새로운 사업을 시작할지 생각 중이라고 말했어.
   B: 요즘에 사람들은 폐업하고 있어. 근데 나도 왜 그런지는 모르겠어.

어휘
thirsty 목이 마른; 갈망하는
water fountain 분수식의 물 마시는 곳; 냉수기
hallway 복도; 현관
annually 매년
run out of …을 다 써버리다, 다 하다
fee 요금, 수수료
highway 고속도로

05 정답 ①

정답해설
① 출제 포인트: 시제 일치
해당 문장은 'while'은 '~하는 동안에'라는 의미의 시간을 나타내는 부사절 접속사로 옳게 사용되었다. 'while'이 이끄는 절의 동사는 과거진행시제, 주절의 시제는 과거시제로 문맥상 올바르게 사용되었다. 또한 'sail'은 해당 문장에서 자동사로 사용되었다.

get one's call through 전화를 연결하다
render 제공하다　　　　　　　courtesy 예의
consideration 배려, 고려

07 정답 ①

정답해설

① 출제 포인트: 부가의문문

부가의문문은 주절에 사용된 동사와 시제가 일치해야 하며 주절이 긍정문인 경우 부가의문문에는 부정형을, 주절이 부정문인 경우 부가의문문에는 긍정형을 사용해야 한다. 해당 문장의 경우 주절의 동사 'get'이 3인칭 단수 현재시제이며 긍정문이므로, 부가의문문에 부정의문 형태인 'doesn't it?'을 사용하는 것이 옳다.

오답해설

② 출제 포인트: 이중부정/부정부사 도치

'seldom'은 '거의 ~않다'의 의미로 부정의 의미를 포함하고 있다. 해당 문장은 부정부사 'seldom'과 'not'을 같이 사용하였으므로 틀린 문장이다. 따라서 'not'을 삭제하고 'Seldom are books returned~'로 수정해야 한다. 또한 부정부사 'seldom'이 문두에 오고 동사가 be동사인 경우 「Seldom+be(is/are/was/were)+주어+~」의 어순을 가진다.

③ 출제 포인트: 간접의문문/등위접속사 for

의문문이 문장의 요소로 사용되는 경우 간접의문문이 되어 「의문사+주어+동사」의 어순을 가지게 된다. 따라서 해당 문장의 경우 직접의문문 어순인 'why did the animals follow him'을 'why the animals followed him'으로 수정해야 한다. 또한 해당 문장에서 'for'는 등위접속사로 절을 이끌며 '왜냐하면 ~때문이다'를 뜻한다.

④ 출제 포인트: want vs. hope/가정법 미래

'hope'는 5형식으로 사용될 수 없는 동사이나 해당 문장에서 5형식으로 사용하였으므로 옳지 않다. 따라서 'hope'를 'want'로 수정해야 한다. 또한 해당 문장은 가정법 미래 문장으로 「If+주어+should+동사원형 ~, 주어+would+동사원형~.」이 옳게 사용되었다.

해석

① 일 년 중 이맘때 거기 진짜 춥잖아, 안 그래?
② 책들은 좀처럼 선반 위의 올바른 위치에 갖다 놓인 적이 없다.
③ Tom은 왜 동물들이 자기를 따라오는지 몰랐다, 왜냐하면 그는 그들에게 줄 것을 좀처럼 가지고 있지 않기 때문이다.
④ 만약 네가 그 부서로 간다면, William은 네가 원래 부서로 돌아가기를 바랄 것이다.

오답률 TOP 1

08 정답 ②

정답해설

본문의 요지는 '(인적) 관계는 그것이 필요하기 전에 미리 수립해놓는 것이 바람직하며, 오직 필요한 순간에만 인맥에 의지하려 하는 것은 잘못된 방식이다'라는 것이다. 즉, 항상 인맥 관리를 꾸준히 그리고 미리 해 놓는 것이 중요하다는 내용이다. 그런데 ②에서는 '부탁을 하는 방식'에 대해 설명하고 있으므로, 글 전체의 흐름에 부합하지 않는다. 따라서 글의 흐름상 어색한 것은 ②이다.

오답해설

① 이후의 문장 "This is the wrong way to lean on a network(이것은 인맥에 의지하는 잘못된 방식이다)."에서 'This'가 가리키는 것이 ①에서 제시된 '부탁을 위해 안부를 묻는 체하는 이메일을 전송하는' 행위에 대해 설명하는 것이므로, 흐름상 적절하다.

오답해설

② 출제 포인트: 이중부정 금지

해당 문장의 'There is no way(~할 수가 없다)'에는 이미 부정의 뜻이 포함되어 있으나 'can't criticize'를 통해 또 한 번 부정의 의미를 나타내고 있으므로 이중부정이 되어 옳지 않은 문장이다. 따라서 '~ 비난할 수 없을 것이다'라는 한국말을 영어로 적절하게 바꾸려면 'There is no way other countries can't criticize ~'를 'There is no way other countries can criticize ~'로 수정해야 한다.

③ 출제 포인트: 동사 관용표현(crack down on)

「crack down on+목적어」는 관용표현으로 '~을 단속하다'를 뜻한다. 해당 문장은 'crack down on'이 아닌 'crack down for'가 사용되었으므로 옳지 않은 문장이다. 따라서 'crack down for'를 'crack down on'으로 수정해야 한다. 또한 'saying ~ power'는 분사구문으로 현재분사로 쓰인 'saying'은 생략된 주어 'the international airline'과 능동 관계이므로 옳게 사용되었다.

④ 출제 포인트: 주요 조동사 표현/to부정사의 부사적 용법(so as not to+동사원형)

「had better+동사원형」은 관용표현으로 '~하는 편이 낫다'를 뜻한다. 해당 문장은 동사원형의 자리에 to부정사인 'to take'를 사용하였으므로 옳지 않은 문장이다. 따라서 해당 문장의 'had better to take'를 'had better take'로 수정해야 한다. 또한 「so as not to+동사원형」은 관용표현으로 '~하지 않기 위해'를 뜻하며, to부정사의 부사적 용법으로 사용되었다.

06 정답 ①

정답해설

① 출제 포인트: 접속사의 쓰임(if vs. whether)

접속사 'if'는 바로 뒤에 'or not'을 사용할 수 없다. 따라서 밑줄 친 'if'를 'whether'로 수정해야 한다.

오답해설

② 출제 포인트: that vs. what

관계대명사 'what'은 선행사를 포함한 관계대명사이며 뒤따라오는 문장은 불완전하다. 밑줄 친 'what'은 목적어 역할을 하는 관계대명사로 앞에 선행사가 없으며, 이후에 오는 절에서 동사 'want'의 목적어가 없으므로 옳은 표현이다.

③ 출제 포인트: 현재분사 vs. 과거분사

밑줄 친 'rendered'는 완전타동사 'render'의 과거분사로, 수식하는 대상 'the service'와 수동관계이며 해석상 '서비스가 그들에게 제공되도록 하다'가 자연스러우므로 과거분사 'rendered'는 옳은 표현이다.

④ 출제 포인트: 등위상관접속사

'not only A but (also) B'는 'A뿐만 아니라 B도'의 의미를 갖는다. 밑줄 친 'but'은 등위상관접속사 'not only A but (also) B'의 'but'에 해당하므로 옳은 표현이며 'A'와 'B'의 병렬구조에 유의해야 한다.

해석

분명하게, 대중들이 우리에 관해서 갖는 판단들 중 하나는 우리의 전화 서비스가 좋은지 아닌지이다. 엄밀히 말하면, 그들이 그들의 전화를 효율적으로 그리고 즉시 연결한다면, 그들은 그들이 원하는 것을 얻는 것이다. 그러나 그것이 그들이 원하는 전부는 아니다. 그들은 그들을 기쁘게 하는 방식으로 그들에게 제공되는 서비스를 갖기를 원한다; 그들은 효율성뿐만 아니라 예의와 배려를 원한다; 그리고 그들이 그들이 원하는 것을 얻을 수 있는 위치에 있다.

어휘

obviously 분명하게　　　　　technically 엄밀히 말하면

나머지 문장은 문맥상 자연스러우므로 오답이다.

해석

지구상에서 가장 성공한 팟캐스터 중 한 사람인 Jordan Harbinger는 당신이 미리 관계를 수립해야 할 필요가 있다고 말한다. ① 우리는 모두, 그 사람이 단지 부탁을 하기 위해 당신에게 아첨을 할 때, 당신의 안부를 묻는 "척하는" 이메일의 수신자가 되어본 적이 있다. 이것은 인맥에 의지하는 잘못된 방식이다. 올바른 방식은 사회적 자본을 오랜 시간 동안 축적하는 것이다. ② **당신의 인맥 내의 누군가에게 부탁을 할 때, 이메일을 통하지 않고 직접 대면하여 그렇게 하는 것이 더 낫다.** 단지 당신이 무언가를 필요로 할 때뿐만이 아니라, 지속적으로 사람들과 연락하라. 당신이 그들을 필요로 할 때 사람들을 찾기 시작하면 너무 늦는다. ③ 관계는 오랜 시간 동안 더 깊어지므로, 씨를 빨리 심는 것이 모든 차이를 만든다. Harbinger는 "당신이 필요하기도 전에 관계를 확립하는 것이 핵심이다."라고 말한다. ④ 사실, 그는 당신이 그것들을 결코 필요로 하지 않을 것이라고 가정할 것을 추천한다. "그것은 마치 당신의 타이어가 펑크가 나기 전에 당신의 자동차의 트렁크에 타이어를 넣는 것과 같다"고 그는 말한다. 당신은 타이어 펑크를 계획하지 않는다. 그리고 최선의 시나리오에서, 당신은 스페어타이어를 결코 사용하지 않는다.

어휘

beforehand 미리, 사전에
receiving end 받는 쪽, 수신자
check on (이상이 없는지를) 확인하다[살펴보다]
butter … up …에게 아부[아첨]를 하다
lean on 기대다, 의지하다
check in with 연락하다
consistently 지속적으로
key 가장 중요한, 핵심적인, 필수적인
spare (특히 자동차 타이어) 스페어, 여분

09 정답 ④

정답해설

본문은 '고부담 시험(high-stakes exam)'이 학생, 교사, 부모, 나아가 학교 교육에 미치는 영향'에 대해 설명하고 있다. 본문 초반의 내용을 통해 '고부담 시험은 인생에서의 더 나은 방향으로의 전환을 가능케 하며, (성공적으로 치른다면), 재정, 인식, 평판에도 좋은 영향을 미칠 수 있다'는 것을 유추할 수 있다. 그러나 본문은 이러한 '중요성'으로 인해, 교육의 진정한 목적과 본질이 변질될 수 있으며, 학생들은 오직 시험 준비만을 위한 학습에 매진하여 스트레스, 불안, 우울함에 빠지고 극단적인 경우에는 학교 폭력 또는 자살에 이를 수도 있다는 사실을 명시하고 있다. 따라서 글의 요지로 가장 적절한 보기는 '④ Although high-stakes exams have some advantages, they also can produce negative effects(고부담 시험이 이점이 있지만, 그것은 또한 부정적인 영향을 초래할 수도 있다).'이다.

오답해설

① 본문 중후반 내용을 통해 '고부담 시험이 교육의 본질을 약화시키고, 학생들에게 정신적 문제를 일으킬 수 있다'는 것을 알 수 있으므로, '고부담 시험이 교육과 학습을 향상시킨다'는 것은 본문의 주장과는 거리가 멀다.

② 본문 후반에서 '고부담 시험의 부정적 효과'에 대해 언급하고 있지만, 본문 어디에도 '고부담 시험이 폐지되어야 한다'는 주장은 언급되고 있지 않으므로 오답이다.

③ 첫 번째 문장 "High-stakes exams often determine the future of learners: transition, graduation, or entrance to higher education, to better schools, or to better jobs(고부담 시험은 종종 학습자의 미래를 결정한다: 이동, 졸업, 또는 고등 교육, 더 나은 학교 또는 더 나은 직종으로의 진입을 말한다)."를 통해, '고부담 시험이 학습자의 미래를 결정한다' 내용을 언급하고 있으나, 이후 고부담 시험이 야기하는 부정적 효과를 설명하고 있으므로, 글 전체의 요지로는 적절하지 않다.

해석

고부담 시험은 종종 학습자의 미래를 결정한다: 이동, 졸업, 또는 고등 교육, 더 나은 학교 또는 더 나은 직종으로의 진입을 말한다. 시험 결과가 재정, 인식, 그리고 명성에 영향을 미칠 수 있기 때문에, 이러한 시험들은 학생들에게 뿐만 아니라, 교사, 학교 그리고 가족에게도 큰 부담이 된다. 일부의 경우에, 부담이 너무 커서 시험들이 학교 교육의 목적과 본질에 대한 사고를 지배할 수 있다. 학생들은 끊임없이 시험을 준비하고, 학생들과 부모는 계속해서 학업적 성공에 대해 염려하며, 학생들에게 가해지는 잘해야 한다는 압박은 학교 폭력뿐만 아니라 스트레스, 불안, 우울함 그리고 심지어 자살로 이어질 수 있다. 게다가, '고득점'에 맞추어진 초점은 테스트와 시험에서 종종 얻어지지 않는 학습의 여타 기본적인 측면과 교육 시스템이 교육의 진정한 가치와 목적을 잃은 것은 아닌지에 대한 의문들을 약화시키고 있을지도 모른다.
① 고부담 시험은 효과적이며 학교 교육과 학습을 향상시키기 위해 필요하다.
② 고부담 시험은 많은 문제를 야기하고 있기 때문에 폐지되어야 한다.
③ 고부담 시험에서 점수를 잘 받는 것이 한 학생의 미래에 큰 차이를 만들 수 있다.
④ 고부담 시험이 몇몇의 이점이 있지만, 그것은 또한 부정적인 영향을 초래할 수도 있다.

어휘

high-stakes 위험(부담이) 큰
transition 전환, 변화
high stakes 중대한 이해관계
reputation 명성
stake 이해관계
undermine (토대를) 약화시키다
lose sight of …을 잃다[잊다], 간과하다
abandon 버리다, 폐기하다, 포기하다

오답률 TOP 2

10 정답 ④

정답해설

본문은 '노인을 위한 양로 기술(gerontechnology) 적용에 대한 난제(challenge)'를 세 가지 제시하고 있다. 첫째는 노인들이 카메라와 마이크 설치를 꺼리는 것, 두 번째는 노인들이 사용하기에 기술이 복잡한 것, 세 번째는 비용이 많이 드는 것이다. 주어진 문장 "Furthermore, physical and mental decline might make it even more difficult for them to use these new technologies(게다가, 신체적 그리고 정신적 쇠퇴는 그들이 이러한 신기술을 사용하는 것을 훨씬 더 어렵게 할지도 모른다)."는 '사용상의 어려움'에 관한 내용이므로 두 번째 난제에 해당하는 것임을 알 수 있다. 그런데, '첨가'를 나타내는 'Furthermore'가 사용된 것으로 보아, 주어진 문장 이전에 다른 이유가 먼저 언급되어야 한다는 것을 알 수 있다. 따라서 주어진 문장이 가장 적절한 곳은 두 번째 난제를 설명한 후, 그 난제에 대한 첫 번째 이유가 설명된 이후인 ④이다.

오답해설

③ 두 번째 난제인 "Secondly, the technologies might be too complex for older people to handle(둘째, 기술은 노인들이 다루기에 너무 복잡할지도 모른다)."이 소개된 후, 그러한 난제가 발생하는 이유가 제시되는 것이 자연스러운데, 주어진 문장의 'Furthermore'로 보아 ③ 이후의 "Today's older people grew up in a time, where technology use was less computerized and less complicated(오늘날의 노인들은 기술사용이 덜 컴퓨터화 되고 덜 복잡하던 시대에 자랐다)."가 먼저 등장한 후, 주어진 문장이 등장하는 것이 문맥상 더 자연스럽다. 따라서 ③은 오답이다.

나머지 보기는 문맥상 어색하므로 오답이다.

해석

노인을 위한 양로 기술 적용에 대한 관련된 난제들이 있다. 첫째, 노인들에 의한 신기술 수용에 의문이 제기된다. 모든 노인들이 욕실 또는 침실에 카메라와 마이크를 설치하는 것에 열광적이지는 않을 것이다. 물론, 이러한 카메라와 마이크는 녹화 기능이 없는, 그들의 자료를 즉각적으로 분석할 단지 센서일 뿐이다. (①) 그러나 감시당하고 있다는 느낌 (그리고 현실에서 기술이 무엇을 하고 있는지에 대한 불확실성)은 상당히 불안할 수 있다. (②) 둘째, 그 기술은 노인들이 다루기에 너무 복잡할지도 모른다. (③) 오늘날의 노인들은 기술사용이 덜 컴퓨터화 되고 덜 복잡하던 시대에 자랐다. (④ **게다가, 신체적 그리고 정신적 쇠퇴는 그들이 이러한 신기술을 사용하는 것을 훨씬 더 어렵게 할지도 모른다.**) 셋째, 기술들은 십중팔구 비싸다, 그래서 많은 사람들이 그러한 기술을 구매할 수 없을 것이며, 만일 그렇게 하더라도[구매하더라도], 유지비용 또한 상당히 높을 것이다. 그러므로 이러한 신기술들은 이미 존재하는 사회적 불평등을 악화시킬 수도 있다.

어휘

concerning …에 관한[관련된]
maintenance 유지, 보수
exacerbate 악화시키다
uneasy 불안한, 우려되는
rather 상당히, 꽤

기적사 DAY 46

| 01 | ④ | 02 | ④ | 03 | ① | 04 | ④ | 05 | ④ |
| 06 | ③ | 07 | ③ | 08 | ④ | 09 | ③ | 10 | ① |

01 정답 ④
18 서울시

정답해설

동의어 문제가 아닌 의미가 가장 먼 것을 찾는 다소 생소한 문항이다. 밑줄 친 'essential'은 '아주 중요한'을 뜻하며 'crucial(중대한), indispensable(필수적인), requisite(필요한)'과 의미가 동일하다. ④ omnipresent의 경우 접두어 omni는 all(全)에 해당되는 표현으로 「omni + competent(전(全)권을 가지는)」와 「omni + potent(전(全)지전능한)」의 의미를 갖는다. 따라서 '어디에나 있는'의 뜻으로, '아주 중요한'의 의미인 'essential'과는 의미가 멀다.

해석

수정의 전제 조건으로서, 수분 작용은 과일과 씨앗용 작물들의 생산에 **아주 중요하고**, 번식으로 식물을 개선시키기 위해 만들어진 프로그램에서 중요한 역할을 한다.
① 중대한
② 필수적인
③ 필요한
④ 어디에나 있는, 편재하는

어휘

prerequisite 전제 조건
pollination [식물] 수분 (작용)
improve 개선하다, 향상시키다
crucial 중대한
requisite 필요한
fertilization 수정; 다산화, 비옥화
essential 아주 중요한, 필수적인
breeding 번식, 사육
indispensable 필수적인
omnipresent 어디에나 있는, 편재하는

02 정답 ④
18 서울시

정답해설

빈칸은 Johnson이 제안에 반대하는 이유에 해당하므로 모두 부정적인 형용사가 적합하다. 따라서 의미상 빈칸에는 ④ wrong – inconvenient가 알맞다.

해석

Johnson 씨는 그것이 **잘못된** 원칙 위에 기초를 두었고 또한 때로는 **불편했기** 때문에 그 제안에 반대했다.
① 흠 있는 – 바람직한
② 긴요한 – 합리적인
③ 순응하는 – 비참한, 개탄스러운
④ 잘못된 – 불편한

어휘

object to ~에 반대하다
faulty 흠 있는
conforming 순응하는
desirable 바람직한
deplorable 비참한, 개탄스러운
proposal 제안, 제의; 청혼
imperative 긴요한, 필수의; 위엄 있는
wrong 잘못된
reasonable 합리적인
inconvenient 불편한

오답률 TOP 2
03 정답 ①
18 서울시

정답해설

회사와 노조가 비우호적인 사업 환경 속에서 임금 협상에 대한 합의를 이끌었다고 서술하고 있다. 이 배경에는 회사와 노조가 다른 입장을 지녔음에도 불구하고, '악화되는' 이유로 인해 의견이 공통적으로 모아졌기 때문임을 유추할 수 있다. 따라서 빈칸에 들어갈 말로 가장 적절한 것은 ① deteriorating 이다.

해석

회사와 노조는 올해의 임금 협상에 대한 잠정적인 합의에 도달했는데, 양측이 비우호적인 사업 환경 속에서 회사의 **악화되는** 영업 이윤을 심각하게 받아들였기 때문이다.
① 악화되는
② 향상하는, 강화하는
③ 개선하는, 좋아지는
④ 균일화된, 평등화된

어휘

tentative 잠정적인, 임시의 deteriorate 악화되다, 퇴폐하다
enhance 향상시키다, 강화하다 ameliorate 개선하다; 좋아지다
level 평평하게 하다; 평등하게 하다, 균일화하다
amid ~가운데(중)에, ~의 (한)복판에

04 정답 ④
17 서울시

정답해설

A는 B에게 오늘 점심 식사를 자신이 사겠다고 제안하고 있으므로, 빈칸에는 수락 또는 거절하는 응답이 와야 한다. 따라서 '④ Wish I could but I have another commitment today(그럴 수 있다면 좋겠지만 저는 오늘 다른 약속이 있어요)'는 A의 제안을 거절하는 내용으로 대화의 흐름에 적절하다.

오답해설

② A가 '오늘 점심 식사를 자신이 사겠다'고 제안하고 있는 상황에서 B가 '잊지 않도록 달력에 적어두겠다'는 대답은 오늘이 아닌 이후 약속에 대한 선약을 잡는 경우에 할 법한 응답으로서 자연스럽지 않다.
나머지 선지는 문맥상 적절하지 않다.

해석

A: 김씨, 제가 오늘 점심을 사는 게 어떨까요?
B: 그럴 수 있다면 좋겠지만 저는 오늘 다른 약속이 있어요.
① 아뇨, 저는 아니에요. 제게 그 시간이 좋을 것 같아요
② 좋아요. 잊지 않도록 제 달력에 적어둘게요
③ 네, 월요일에 문의 할게요
④ 그럴 수 있다면 좋겠지만 저는 오늘 다른 약속이 있어요

어휘

commitment 약속, 위임

05 정답 ④
19 서울시

정답해설

④ 출제 포인트: 비교 대상 일치

비교 대상을 일치하는 문제로 비교급 'than'을 사이에 두고 비교 대상이 동일한 품사 성격을 가져야 한다. 문맥상 해당 문장은 '편한 옷을 입고 집에 있는 것'과 '비즈니스 미팅을 위해 옷을 차려입는 것'을 비교하고 있다. 따라서 'to stay'와 내용상 병렬을 이루므로, 'getting dressed'를 'to get dressed'로 수정해야 한다.

오답해설

① 출제 포인트: 동명사의 사용
전치사로 사용된 'than'의 목적어로 동명사 'maintaining'은 적합한 표현이다. 또한 'maintaining' 이후에 동명사의 목적어 'the cities'가 있으므로 동명사의 능동형으로 쓰인 것도 옳다.

② 출제 포인트: 비교급 비교
글의 내용상 '더 편안해질수록 덜 사회적이 된다'라고 하였으므로 'more' 가 아닌 'less'를 사용한 'less social'은 옳은 표현이다.

③ 출제 포인트: 비교급 비교
문장 후반부에 'than'으로 비교급을 나타내고 있으므로, 비교급 형용사 'easier'는 올바른 표현이다.

해석

도시를 유지하는 것보다 더 심각한 문제가 있다. 사람들이 혼자 일하는 것이 더 편안해질수록, 그들은 덜 사교적이 될 수도 있다. 또 다른 이어지는 비즈니스 미팅에서 옷을 차려입는 것보다 편안한 운동복이나 목욕용 가운을 입고 집에 있는 것이 더 쉽다!

어휘

serious 심각한 maintain 유지하다
comfortable 편안한, 쾌적한 bathrobe 목욕용 가운

오답률 TOP 1
06 정답 ③
19 서울시

정답해설

③ 출제 포인트: 수동태 불가동사
'suffice'는 완전자동사이므로 수동태를 사용할 수 없다. 따라서 밑줄 친 'be sufficed'를 'suffice'로 수정해야 한다.

오답해설

① 출제 포인트: 동사 관용표현(trust to)
'trust to'는 '~에게 맡기다'라는 의미로 알맞게 쓰였다. 'trust'가 자동사로 쓰였음에 유의해야한다.

② 출제 포인트: 부사 관용표현(no doubt)
'no doubt'는 '틀림없이'라는 뜻으로 부사 관용표현이다. 밑줄 친 'doubt' 는 'No'와 함께 문맥에 맞게 사용되었으므로 옳게 사용되었다.

④ 출제 포인트: 능동태 vs. 수동태
'adduce'는 타동사로 '제시하다'라는 뜻이다. 밑줄 친 'adduced' 이후에 목적어가 없고 문맥상 수동형이 적절하므로 'be adduced'는 적절한 표현이다.

해석

내가 지금 출간하는 이 개요는 필연적으로 불완전함이 틀림없다. 나는 나의 몇몇 진술들에 대한 참고문헌과 근거들을 여기에서 제공할 수 없다; 그리고 나는 내 정확성에 대한 일부 확신을 다시 놓는 것을 독자들에게 맡겨야만 한다. 훌륭한 근거들에게 맡기는데 있어 나는 항상 주의해왔음을 희망하지만 틀림없이 오류들이 살며시 스며들 것이다. 나는 여기에서 참고용으로 몇몇 사실들과 함께 내가 도달한 일반적인 결론들만을 제공할 수 있지만, 희망컨대, 대부분의 경우 그것들이면 충분할 것이다. 내 결론들이 근거를 둔 참고문헌들과 함께, 모든 사실들을 상세하게 이후에 출간할 것의 필요를 나보다 더 인지할 수 있는 사람은 없다; 그리고 나는 장래 작업에서 이것을 하기를 희망한다. 사실들이 제시될 수 없는 이 책에서는 한 가지 포인트만 논의될 수는 거의 없다는 것을 나는 잘 알기 때문에, 종종 분명히 내가 도달했던 것과는

직접적으로 반대인 결론들로도 이끌어 갈 것이다. 온당한 결과는 각 질문의 양면 모두에 대한 사실들과 주장들을 완전히 진술하고 균형을 잡음으로써만 얻어질 수 있다; 그리고 이것은 도저히 여기에서는 이루어질 수 없다.

어휘

abstract 개요, 요약본; 추상적인
authority 근거, 권위, 권한
repose 다시 놓다
cautious 신중한, 조심스러운
suffice 충분하다
sensible 인지하고 있는, 분별력 있는, 현명한
hereafter 이후로, 장차
ground A on B (A를 B에 근거하도록 하다)
scarcely 거의 ~않다, 드물게
apparently 분명히, 명백히
reference 참고 (문헌)
trust to ~에게 맡기다
creep in 살며시 접근하다
in illustration 참고로, 예증으로
in detail 상세하게
adduce 제시하다
opposite to ~와 반대인

오답률 TOP 3

07 정답 ③ 19 서울시

정답해설

③ 출제 포인트: 능동태 vs 수동태

문장의 주어인 'Hangul(한글)'이 수동이 아닌 능동의 의미인 '더 중요해지다'가 문맥상 가장 적절하므로 'been taken over'가 아니라 'taken over'가 어법상 적절하다. 따라서 정답은 ③이다. 'take over'가 '더 중요해지다, 우세해지다'의 의미로 사용되는 경우 자동사임에 유의해야한다.

오답해설

① 출제 포인트: 동사의 수일치/능동태 vs. 수동태

주어가 'it'이고 'symbolizes' 다음에 목적어인 'the speech sounds'가 있으므로 3인칭 단수 능동 형태로 쓰인 'symbolizes'는 어법상 적절하다.

② 출제 포인트: 현재분사 vs. 과거분사

'sophisticated'가 명사인 'way'를 수식하고 있다. 문맥상 방법은 '정교하게 되는 것'이 적절하므로 'sophisticated'는 옳게 사용되었다.

④ 출제 포인트: 수동태 불가동사

'occur'는 자동사로 수동태로 사용할 수 없다. 따라서 능동태로 쓰인 'occur'는 어법상 적절하다.

해석

15세기에, 자음과 모음이 있는 한국어 글자가 발명되었다. 언어학자들은 그것이 말소리를 정교하고 매우 우아한 방법으로 상징하고 있어서 그것을 찬양한다. 한글로 불리는 이 글자는 한자와 함께 사용될 수 있지만 그것들을 완전히 대체할 수도 있다. 천천히, 한글이 더 중요해지게 되었다. 북한에서는, 한글만 사용하는 반면, 남한에서는, 여전히 특정 문맥에서 한자가 나타난다.

어휘

alphasyllabic 자음 모음과 관련된
linguist 언어학자
symbolize 상징하다
in tandem with ~와 나란히, ~와 나란히
altogether 모두, 한번에, 모두 합하여
take over 더 중요해지다, 더 커지다; 인수하다, 인계받다
occur 존재하다, 발견되다, 일어나다
script 문자; 대본
admire 칭송하다
sophisticated 세련된, 정교한

08 정답 ④ 18 지방직

정답해설

본문은 성공한 사람들을 예로 들며 한 가지 일에 몰두하는 방법으로 '우선순위(priorities)'를 정해 일을 하라고 조언하고 있다. 빈칸은 이전 문장 "And this order is quite simple(그리고 이러한 순서는 꽤 단순하다)"에 부가적인 설명을 더하는 자리이다. 따라서 선지 중에 우선순위를 정하는 것에 대한 부연 설명으로 이용될 수 있는 것을 찾으면 정답은 ④ 'the most important thing first(가장 중요한 일을 첫 번째로 하는 것이다)'가 된다.

오답해설

① 주어진 글은 일을 처리하는 '우선순위'에 대한 글이지 '속도'에 관한 글이 아니므로 빈칸에 들어갈 말로 적절하지 않다.
나머지 선지는 문맥상 어색하므로 옳지 않다.

해석

성공하는 사람들의 비결은 보통 그들이 한 가지 일에 온전히 집중할 수 있다는 것이다. 그들의 머릿속에 많은 것들이 들어 있을지라도, 그들은 그 많은 책무들이 서로를 방해하지 않고, 대신 좋은 내적 순서를 배당받는 방법을 찾아낸다. 그리고 이러한 순서는 꽤 단순하다: 가장 중요한 일을 첫 번째로 하는 것이다. 이론상, 이는 아주 명확해 보이지만, 일상에서는 다소 어렵다. 당신은 아마 우선순위를 정하려 노력했을지도 모르지만, 일상의 사소한 일들이나 모든 예측 불가능한 방해물들로 인해 실패해왔다. 예를 들어, 다른 사무실로 피해 들어가, 방해되는 어떤 방해물들도 끼어들지 못하도록 함으로써 방해 요소들을 분리해내라. 당신이 우선순위의 한 가지 업무에 집중할 때, 당신은 심지어 당신이 가지고 있는지도 알지 못했던 에너지를 가지고 있다는 것을 알게 될 것이다.

① 더 빠를수록 더 낫다
② 늦더라도 하는 것이 안 하는 것보다 낫다
③ 눈에서 멀어지면, 마음에서도 멀어진다
④ 가장 중요한 일을 첫 번째로 하는 것이다

어휘

commitment 전념, 헌신, 책무
priority 우선 사항
unforeseen 예측하지 못한, 뜻밖의
get in the way 방해되다
impede 지연시키다, 방해하다
trivial 사소한, 하찮은
distraction 집중을 방해하는 것, 방해물

09 정답 ③ 18 지방직

정답해설

첫 문장에서 어업을 지속하기 위해서 과학의 도움이 필요하다고 제시했고, 어떻게 어업이 과학의 도움을 받을 수 있는지에 대한 내용이 전개되고 있다. 즉, 포획하는 물고기의 개체 수를 꼭 알맞게 유지해야 물고기 개체 수 고갈 없이 어업을 지속해나갈 수 있으며, 이를 돕는 연구가 계속 진행되고 있다고 하였으므로 글의 제목으로 가장 적절한 것은 ③ 'Why Does the Fishing Industry Need Science(왜 어업에 과학이 필요한가)?'이다.

오답해설

④ 해당 지문은 '어업과 과학'의 관계를 설명하는 글이며 '남획과 불법 어업'의 관계를 서술하고 있지 않으므로 적절하지 않다.
나머지 선지는 문맥상 적절하지 않다.

해석

과학자의 도움으로, 상업성을 띠는 어업은 그것이 계속되어야 한다면 어업이 과학적으로 행해져야 함을 깨달았다. 물고기 개체 수에 대한 어떠한 어업 압력이 없다면, 물고기의 수는 예상 가능한 풍부한 수준에 도달하여 머무를 것이다. 유일한 변동성은 먹이의 이용 가능성, 적절한 온도와 같은 자연 환경적인 요소들에 기인할 것이다. 만약 어장이 이러한 물고기들을 잡도록 발달된다면, 그것들의 개체 수는 어획량이 적은 한 유지될 수 있을 것이다. 북해의 고등어가 좋은 예이다. 만약 우리가 어장을 늘려 매년 더 많은 물고기를 잡아들인다면, 우리는 우리가 매년 잡는 물고기 전체를 대체할 수 있는 이상적인 지점 아래로 개체 수를 감소시키지 않도록 주의해야만 한다. 우리가 최대 유지

생산량이라고 불리는 이 수준에서 포획한다면, 우리는 매년 가능한 최대 생산량을 유지할 수 있다. 만약 우리가 너무 많이 포획해 버리면, 물고기의 수는 매년 줄어 어업을 할 수 없을 수준이 될 것이다. 과도하게 남획된 동물의 예로 남극의 대왕고래와 북대서양의 넙치가 있다. 매해 최대치의 생산량을 유지하기 위해 꼭 맞는 양만 포획하는 것은 과학이자 예술이다. 우리가 물고기 개체 수를 이해하도록 하고 어떻게 개체 수의 고갈 없이 최대한으로 그것을 이용할 수 있는지를 이해하도록 돕기 위한 연구는 계속해서 진행되고 있다.

① 상업적인 어업에 반대하라
② 어업으로 간주되는 바다 양식업
③ 왜 어업에 과학이 필요한가?
④ 남획된 동물들: 불법 어업의 사례들

어휘
predictable 예측할 수 있는　　abundance 풍부
fluctuation 변동, 오르내림, 파동　　fishery 어장
mackerel 고등어　　sustainable 지속 가능한
yield 산출량, 총수익　　severely 심각하게
overfish 물고기를 남획하다, 다 잡아 버리다
Antarctic 남극의, 남극 지방　　halibut 큰 넙치
deplete 대폭 감소시키다, 고갈시키다

10 정답 ①　　18 지방직

정답해설
(A) 빈칸 이전의 '9/11 테러는 전 세계 언론의 중심에서 일어난 공격을 포함했다'는 사실과 이후의 '9/11 사건의 도달 가능한 가장 넓은 범위를 확보했다'는 사실은 서로 인과관계에 있다. 따라서 'thereby(그렇게 함으로써, 그로 인해)'가 적절하다.
(B) 빈칸 이전에 진주만 공격과 9/11 공격이 또 다른 국면에서 유사하다고 했고, 빈칸 앞뒤로 각각 진주만 공격과 9/11 공격에 대한 서술이 등장하며 두 공격 모두 전략적으로 실패했다고 언급하고 있다. 따라서 빈칸에 가장 알맞은 것은 'Similarly(유사하게)'이다.

오답해설
나머지 선지는 문맥상 적절하지 않다.

해석
테러리즘은 과연 유효할까? 9/11 테러는 알카에다로서는 막대한 전략적 성공이었는데, 부분적으로 그것은 전 세계 언론의 중심지이자 미국의 실질적인 수도에서 일어난 공격을 포함했고, (A) 그렇게 함으로써 그 사건의 도달 가능한 가장 넓은 범위를 확보했기 때문이다. 만약에 테러리즘이 당신이 많은 사람들이 보길 바라는 영화관의 형태라면, 인류 역사에서 9/11 공격보다 더 많은 전 세계의 청중이 시청한 사건은 없을 것이다. 당시에, 어떻게 9/11 테러가 진주만 공격과 유사했는지에 대한 논의가 활발했다. 그것들은 모두 미국을 큰 전쟁으로 끌어들인 습격이라는 점에서 매우 비슷했다. 그러나 그 둘은 다른 양상에서 또한 유사했다. 진주만은 제국주의 일본의 거대한 전략적인 성공이었지만, 그것은 또한 더 큰 전략적인 실패를 이끌었다: 진주만 공격 이후 4년 이내에 일본 제국은 폐허가 되었고, 완전히 패배했다. (B) 유사하게, 9/11 공격은 알카에다에게는 거대한 전략적 성공이었지만, 오사마 빈 라덴에게는 거대한 전략적 실패로 드러났다.

	(A)	(B)
①	그렇게 함으로써	유사하게
②	반면에	그러므로
③	반면에	운이 좋게도
④	그렇게 함으로써	반대로

어휘
enormous 막대한, 거대한, 어마어마한
tactical 작전의, 전술의, 전략적인
take place (일이) 발생하다, 일어나다
coverage 범위　　imperial 제국의
strategic 전략적인　　utterly 완전히, 순전히
defeat 패배시키다

결국엔 성정혜 영어 하프모의고사
기적사 DAY 47

| 01 | ④ | 02 | ② | 03 | ② | 04 | ② | 05 | ③ |
| 06 | ③ | 07 | ④ | 08 | ④ | 09 | ④ | 10 | ② |

01 정답 ④

정답해설

밑줄 친 'crucial'은 '중대한, 결정적인'이라는 뜻의 형용사로 ④ momentous 와 의미가 가장 가깝다.

해석

한 국가의 법적인 투표 나이는 시민들이 그들의 국가를 위해 **중대한** 결정들을 할 정치적인 지도자들에게 투표를 시작할 수 있는 나이를 의미한다.
① 하찮은, 사소한
② 고유한, 본질적인
③ 중요하지 않은, 무형의
④ 중요한, 중대한

어휘

legal 법률과 관련된, 합법적인
trifling 하찮은, 사소한
immaterial 중요하지 않은, 무형의
crucial 중대한, 결정적인
intrinsic 고유한, 본질적인
momentous 중요한, 중대한

오답률 TOP 2
02 정답 ②

정답해설

밑줄 친 'faulty'는 '잘못된, 흠이 있는'이라는 뜻의 형용사로 ② unsound와 의미가 가장 가깝다.

해석

Jane이 **잘못된** 가정을 했다는 것을 보여줌으로써, John의 모든 주장들이 더 설득력을 갖추게 되었다.
① 틀림없는, 정확한
② 오류가 있는, 부적절한
③ 손상된, 제 기능을 못 하는
④ 회복할 수 있는, 되찾을 수 있는

어휘

faulty 잘못된, 흠이 있는
argument 주장, 논의, 논쟁
unerring 틀림없는, 정확한
impaired 손상된, 제 기능을 못 하는
regainable 회복할 수 있는, 되찾을 수 있는
assumption 가정, 상정
convincing 설득력 있는
unsound 오류가 있는, 부적절한

03 정답 ②

정답해설

밑줄 친 'deteriorating'은 '악화되다, 더 나빠지다'를 뜻하는 'deteriorate'의 현재분사 형태로 ② aggravating과 의미가 가장 가깝다.

해석

생태계와 자연보호에 대한 그들의 중대한 기여는 급속하게 **악화 중인** 생태계에 엄청난 변화를 가져왔고 야생동물 서식지들을 복원시켰다.
① 다치지 않은, 아무 탈 없는
② 악화하는
③ 쇠퇴하는, 퇴화하는
④ 개량의, 개선적인

어휘

significant 중대한, 중요한
ecology 생태(계), 생태학
rapidly 급속히, 신속하게
restore 회복시키다
unscathed 다치지 않은, 아무 탈 없는
obsolesce 쇠퇴하다, 퇴화하다
contribution 기여, 기부
conservation 보호, 보존, 관리
deteriorate 악화되다, 더 나빠지다
habitat 서식지
aggravate 악화시키다, 화나게 하다
ameliorative 개량의, 개선적인

04 정답 ②

정답해설

A와 B는 비가 많이 오는 바깥을 보며 대화를 한다. B가 '손전등(flashlight)' 을 준비해야겠다는 것으로 보아, A가 '비가 이만큼 많이 오면, 오늘 조만간 정전(black out)이 있을 수도 있겠다'라고 이야기하는 것이 적절하다. 따라서 정답은 ② 'black out(정전)'이다.

오답해설

나머지 선지는 문맥상 적절하지 않다.

해석

A: 오, 세상에! 밖에 비가 엄청 많이 와!
B: 우와! 비가 이렇게 많이 내린 지 몇 년 된 것 같아.
A: 맞아. 사람들은 가뭄일까 봐 걱정했어.
B: 그러니까. 하지만 나쁜 소식은 내가 우산을 가져오는 것을 까먹었다는 거야. 오늘 아침에 기상 예보를 확인하지 않았어.
A: 걱정하지 마. 나 우산 두 개 있어. 내 것을 빌려도 돼.
B: 진짜 고마워! 넌 내 구원자야.
A: 오, 천만에. 그나저나, 이렇게 비가 많이 오면, 오늘 조만간 정전이 있을 수도 있겠다.
B: 저런! 내 손전등을 준비해놓아야겠다.
① 크거나 중요한 일
② 정전
③ 정면 대결
④ 쓸데없이 간섭하는 사람

어휘

drought 가뭄
big deal 크거나 중요한 일
showdown 정면 대결
backseat driver 쓸데없이 간섭하는 사람
savior 구원자
black out 정전

05 정답 ③

정답해설

③ 출제 포인트: 비교 대상 일치/대명사의 수일치

비교급이 쓰인 문장으로 'than' 이후에 오는 목적어는 비교 대상과 일치해야 한다. 이때 문맥상 목적어에 해당하는 밑줄 친 대명사 'those'가 가리키는 대상은 단수형태의 명사(구) 'the life expectancy'이다. 따라서 'those'를 'that'으로 수정해야 한다.

> 오답해설

① **출제 포인트: 현재분사 vs. 과거분사**
밑줄 친 'selected'는 완전타동사 'select'의 과거분사로, 수식하는 대상 'countries'와 수동관계이며 해석상 '선택된 국가들'이 자연스러우므로 'selected'는 옳은 표현이다.

② **출제 포인트: 명사절을 이끄는 접속사 that**
밑줄 친 'that'은 명사절을 이끄는 접속사로 해당 문장에서 진주어 역할을 하므로 옳게 사용되었다.

④ **출제 포인트: 현재분사 vs. 과거분사/분사구문**
밑줄 친 'followed'는 완전타동사 'follow'의 과거분사로, 생략된 주어 'life expectancy in the Republic of Korea'와 수동관계이며 이후에 목적어가 아닌 'by+행위자'인 'by that in Austria'가 오므로 'followed'는 옳은 표현이다.

> 해석

선택된 5개국 각각에서, 여성의 기대 수명은 남성의 기대 수명보다 더 높을 것으로 예측된다. 여성의 경우, 대한민국의 기대 수명은 5개국 중에서 가장 높을 것으로 예상되며, 오스트리아의 기대 수명이 그 다음일 것이다.

> 어휘

life expectancy 기대 수명

오답률 TOP 1

06 정답 ③

> 정답해설

③ **출제 포인트: 능동태 vs. 수동태/부정부사(구) 도치**
'restrict'는 완전타동사이므로 이후에 목적어가 온다. 밑줄 친 'do they restrict'의 경우 이후에 목적어가 아닌 수식어(구) 'to their immediate locale'이 왔으므로 해당 문장이 수동태임을 알 수 있다. 따라서 'do they restrict'를 수동태로 수정해야 하며, 이때 문두에 부정부사(구) 'No longer'가 있으므로 'are they restricted'로 수정해야 한다.

> 오답해설

① **출제 포인트: 주어와 동사의 수일치**
밑줄 친 'is'는 단수형태의 동사이며 단수형태의 주어 'Parental enthusiasm'과 수일치하므로 옳은 표현이다.

② **출제 포인트: 수여동사의 수동태/능동태 vs. 수동태**
밑줄 친 'are granted'의 경우 이후에 직접목적어 'an entirely different perspective'가 있으므로 수여동사 'grant'의 수동태임을 알 수 있다. 따라서 'are granted'는 옳은 표현이다.

④ **출제 포인트: 타동사구[완전타동사+목적어+전치사+목적어]**
'provide'는 완전타동사의 경우 「provide+목적어[대상]+with+목적어[사물]」 또는 「provide+목적어[사물]+to/for+목적어[대상]」의 형태로 사용한다. 밑줄 친 'with'의 경우 앞에 'provide'와 대상을 나타내는 목적어 'the infant'가 있으며 이후에 사물을 나타내는 목적어 'a growing sense'가 왔으므로 옳은 표현이다.

> 해석

부모는 자신들의 유아가 고개를 들고, 물건을 집으러 손을 뻗고, 스스로 앉고 혼자서 걷자마자 친구와 친척들에게 알리는데 빠르다. 이러한 운동 기능의 성취에 대한 부모의 열성은 전혀 잘못된 것이 아닌데, 왜냐하면 그것들은 실제로 발달의 중요한 단계들이기 때문이다. 각각의 추가적인 기술로 아기들은 새로운 방식으로 자신들의 신체와 환경에 대한 통제력을 얻는다. 혼자서 앉을 수 있는 유아는 하루의 많은 부분을 눕거나 엎드려 보내는 유아들에 비해 세상에 대한 완전히 다른 시각을 부여받게 된다. 근육의 공동 작용에 의한 뻗치기는 사물의 탐구에 대한 온전히 새로운 길을 열어 주며, 아기들이 돌아다닐 수 있을 때 독립적인 탐구와 조작을 위한 기회는 크게 증가된다. 그들은 이제 더 이상 자신들에게 가까운 장소와 다른 사람들이 그들의 앞에 놓아두는 사물들에만 제한되어 있지 않다. 환경을 통제하는 새로운 방식이 성취되면서, 운동 능력의 발달은 유아에게 능력과 숙달에 대한 증가하는 인식을 제공하고 그것은 세상에 대한 유아의 지각 및 인지적 이해에 중요한 방식으로 기여한다.

> 어휘

enthusiasm 열성, 열의	motor 운동 (능력)의
misplaced 잘못된	milestone 중요한 단계
grant+목적어[대상]+목적어[사물] ~에게 ~을 부여하다	
coordinated 근육의 공동작용에 의한	manipulation 조작, 교묘한 처리
contribute to ~에 기여하다	perceptual 지각의
cognitive 인지의	

07 정답 ④

> 정답해설

④ **출제 포인트: 자릿값(동사 vs. 준동사)**
밑줄 친 'improving'을 명사 'music'을 수식하는 현재분사로 오해할 수 있으나 접속사 'that'이 이끄는 명사절에 동사가 없으므로 'improving'은 동사로 사용해야 함을 알 수 있다. 따라서 'improving'을 시제에 맞게 동사 'improved'로 수정해야 한다. 이때 'learned'는 주격 관계대명사 'who'가 이끄는 절의 동사이며, 'read'는 'to play'와 병렬을 이루어 'learned'의 목적어로 쓰인 to부정사의 동사원형에 해당한다.

> 오답해설

① **출제 포인트: 동격의 접속사 that**
밑줄 친 'that'은 'evidence'와 명사절 'children perform better in mathematics if music is incorporated in it'이 동격 관계임을 나타내는 동격 접속사로 옳은 표현이다.

② **출제 포인트: 능동태 vs. 수동태**
해당 문장에서 'It'은 가주어이며 진주어는 접속사 'that'이 이끄는 절이므로 밑줄 친 수동태 'been shown'은 옳은 표현이다. 'that'절을 목적어 절로 오해하지 않도록 주의해야한다.

③ **출제 포인트: 동사 관용표현(put 목적어 to good use)**
'put 목적어 to good use'는 관용표현으로 '~을 잘 활용하다, ~을 유효하게 이용하다'를 뜻한다. 따라서 밑줄 친 'to good use'는 옳은 표현이다.

> 해석

음악이 수학에 통합되면 어린이들이 수학을 더 잘한다는 강력한 연구 증거가 있다. 수학이 알려진 다양한 방면에서 음악과 너무나도 관련이 있어서 학교 안팎에서 그 관계를 잘 이용하지 않는 것은 우리에게 불리할 뿐일 수 있다는 것이 밝혀졌다. 로스앤젤레스의 한 대학의 연구원들은 피아노를 치는 법을 배우고 악보를 읽는 법을 배운 136명의 초등학교 2학년 학생들이 그들의 수리 감각 기술들을 향상시켰다는 것을 발견했다.

> 어휘

incorporate 포함하다, 통합시키다
put 목적어 to good use ~을 잘 활용하다, ~을 유효하게 이용하다
to one's disadvantage ~에게 불리한
numeracy 산술 능력, 수리 감각

오답률 TOP 3
08 정답 ④

정답해설

주어진 문장의 'Nor(…도 (또한) 아니다)'로 보아, 이전에 등장하는 문장이 '부정의 의미'를 가지고 있다는 것을 알 수 있다. 본문 중 ④ 이전 문장 "Chances are, the most important thing is not browsing YouTube for the latest silly cat video(아마 가장 중요한 일이 최신의 유치한 고양이 영상을 찾아 YouTube를 검색하는 것은 아닐 것이다)."에서 부정어를 이용해 추측하며 언급하고 있으므로, 이어서 '가능성 및 부정을 동시에 나타내는 표현(Nor is it likely to be ~)'을 이용한 주어진 문장이 이어지는 것이 자연스럽다. 따라서 정답은 ④이다.

오답해설

나머지 위치는 문맥상 어색하므로 오답이다.

해석

우리는 집중을 방해하는 것, 짧은 주의 지속 시간, 그리고 변화무쌍한 우선순위의 세상에 산다. 소용돌이치는 하찮은 일의 홍수의 희생자가 되지 말라. (①) 임의의 접선과 중요치 않은 업무의 수풀 속에서 길을 잃지 말라. (②) 하루의 방향을 찾을 때, "가장 중요한 것은 무엇인가?"라고 스스로에게 질문하라. (③) 아마 가장 중요한 일이 최신의 유치한 고양이 영상을 찾아 YouTube를 검색하는 것은 아닐 것이다. (④ **당신의 가족에게 감사받지 못할, 당신의 연간 목표에 반영되지 않을, 또는 당신 자신 외에 누구도 알아차리지 못할 집 또는 직장에서의 많은 임의의 바쁜 임무들 또한 그것이 아닐 것이다.**) 가장 중요한 것은 가장 큰 차이를 만들고 당신 자신 또는 타인에게 가장 큰 가치를 가져다주는 모든 것이다. 인생에 보장은 없으나, 가장 중요한 것을 하는 것이 우리가 할 수 있는 최선이며, 가장 중요한 것을 지향하여 노력하는 것이 종종 우리에게 최선의 것을 가져다준다.

어휘

distraction (주의) 집중을 방해하는 것
span (어떤 일이 지속되는) 기간(시간)
ever-changing 늘 변화하는, 변화무쌍한
priority 우선순위   fall victim to …의 희생(물)이 되다
swirl 소용돌이치다   deluge 폭우, 범람, 홍수
triviality 사소함, 하찮은 것   weed 잡초, 수초, 수풀
tangent 접선, 옆길
(The) chances are (that…) 아마 …일 것이다; …할 가능성이 충분하다

09 정답 ④

정답해설

(A) 이전에는 "In future decades ocean warming and acidification can affect growth and reproduction processes of many marine organisms, which may reduce stocks available for many significant commercial species(장차 몇십 년 후, 해양 온난화와 산성화는 많은 해양 생물의 성장 및 번식 과정에 영향을 미칠 수 있으며, 이것이 상업 종으로 이용 가능한 중요한 개체군 다수를 감소시킬 수도 있다)."라고 언급하며, '해양 산성화가 개체군 감소를 야기할 수 있다'고 설명한다. 이어서 개체군 감소가 가능한 '산성화'에 민감한 특정 생물을 구체적으로 예시를 들어 제시하고 있으므로, (A)에 가장 적절한 표현은 'As an example' 또는 'For instance'이다.

(B) 이전에는 '기후 변화'가 해양에 미치는 부정적 영향에 대해 설명하고 있다. 이어서 (B) 이후에서 이러한 '기후 변화'에 대응하지 않고 계속하여 온실가스를 배출한다면 발생할 결과에 대해 언급하고 있다. 따라서 (B)에는 '결과'를 나타내는 'Eventually'가 들어가는 것이 자연스럽다.

따라서 정답은 '④ For instance(예를 들어) – Eventually(결국)'이다.

오답해설

③ (B) 전후의 내용이 '양보' 또는 '역접' 관계가 아니기 때문에 '그럼에도 불구하고'라는 의미의 'Nevertheless'가 들어가는 것은 어색하다.

나머지 보기는 문맥상 어색하므로 오답이다.

해석

과학 연구는 기후 변화가 해양에 미치는 영향이 이미 어장에 영향을 미쳤다는 것을 보여준다. 몇몇 냉수종의 풍부함이 감소하고 있는 반면, 일부 열대 종이 우리의 해안에 나타나고 있다. 장차 몇십 년 후, 해양 온난화와 산성화는 많은 해양 생물의 성장 및 번식 과정에 영향을 미칠 수 있으며, 이것이 상업 종으로 이용 가능한 중요한 개체군 다수를 감소시킬 수도 있다. (A) 예를 들어, 굴과 홍합과 같은 조개류는 특히 산성화에 민감하다. 기후 변화는 또한 해양 먹이 사슬의 핵심인 박테리아와 식물성 플랑크톤 군락에 영향을 미칠 것이다. (B) 결국 만일 우리가 현 속도로 계속 온실가스를 발생시킨다면, 생물 다양성 측면에서 세기말 전에 예상되는 변화들은 과거 2천만 년 또는 3천만 년 전 발생했던 변화와 유사할 수도 있다.

(A)	(B)
① 결과적으로	대조적으로
② 즉	그러나
③ 예를 들어	그럼에도 불구하고
④ 예를 들어	결국

어휘

fishery 어장   abundance 풍부
acidification 산성화   reproduction 번식, 생식
stock 군체, 군락; 비축분, 저장 oyster 굴
mussel 홍합   phytoplankton 식물성 플랑크톤
in terms of … 면에서   biodiversity 생물의 다양성

10 정답 ②

정답해설

빈칸에는 '연구의 목적'을 나타내는 표현이 들어가는 것이 적절하다. 마지막 두 문장 "Through our research, we found only six of the 45 terror groups – that's 13.3 percent – accomplished their broader goals; the others did not. Meanwhile, among the 45 groups that chose not to use terrorism, 26 – or 57.8 percent – reached their objectives(우리의 연구를 통해, 우리는 45개의 테러 집단 중 오직 6 집단 – 그것은 13.3%이다 – 만이 그들의 더 넓은 목표를 성취했고; 나머지는 그렇지 못했다는 것을 알아냈다. 한편, 테러리즘을 이용하지 않기로 선택했던 45개의 집단 중 26 집단 – 또는 57.8% – 이 그들의 목적을 달성했다)."를 통해, '테러리즘을 이용한 집단과 테러리즘을 이용하지 않은 집단의 목표 달성률의 차이'를 비교하고 있으므로, 연구의 목적은 '테러리즘이 목표 달성에 도움이 되는지'에 관한 것임을 유추할 수 있다. 따라서 빈칸에 가장 적절한 표현은 '② terrorism works to achieve a group's goals(테러리즘이 집단의 목표를 달성하는 데 효과가 있는지)'이다.

오답해설

① 본문과 관계없는 내용이므로 오답이다.
③ 본문과 관계없는 내용이므로 오답이다.
④ 본문에는 '테러리스트의 심리적, 정신의학적 특성'에 관해서는 언급되지 않는다.

해석

우리는 테러리즘이 집단의 목표를 달성하는 데 효과가 있는지 알아보기 위해 90개의 집단을 조사했다. 우리가 연구한 집단의 절반은 그들의 목적을 달성하기 위해 테러리즘을 이용했고, 다른 절반은 평화적인 수단을 이용했다. 90개

의 집단을 선택하기 위해, 우리는 동일 국가 또는 지역에서 비교적 동일한 기간에 활동한 45쌍의 집단을 찾았다. 예를 들어, 칠레에서 흉포한 독재자 Augusto Pinochet의 통치 기간 중인 1973년부터 1990년까지, 사람들은 그의 통치를 종식시키려 단체를 조직했다. 한 단체인 Chile's Concertación은 국민 투표를 이용해 Pinochet을 사임시키려 했다. 한편, Manuel Rodriguez Patriotic Front는 폭격, 총격, 납치, 그리고 암살로 Pinochet에게 대항했다. 우리의 연구를 통해, 우리는 45개의 테러 집단 중 오직 6 집단 - 그것은 13.3%이다 - 만이 그들의 더 넓은 목표를 성취했고; 나머지는 그렇지 못했다는 것을 알아냈다. 한편, 테러리즘을 이용하지 않기로 선택했던 45개의 집단 중 26 집단 - 또는 57.8% - 이 그들의 목적을 달성했다.
① 테러리즘이 정당화될 수 있다
② 테러리즘이 집단의 목표를 달성하는 데 효과가 있다
③ 테러리스트 공격이 사전에 예방될 수 있다
④ 테러리스트들이 특정한 심리적 또는 정신의학적 특성을 공유하고 있다

어휘

determine 알아내다, 밝히다 end 목표, 목적
means 수단 autocratic 흉포한, 독재의
dictator 독재자 referendum 국민[주민] 투표
psychiatric 정신 의학[질환]의

결국엔 성정혜 영어 하프모의고사
기적사 DAY 48

| 01 | ④ | 02 | ② | 03 | ② | 04 | ③ | 05 | ③ |
| 06 | ① | 07 | ③ | 08 | ③ | 09 | ② | 10 | ② |

01 정답 ④

정답해설

밑줄 친 'indispensable'은 '필수적인, 없어서는 안 될'이라는 뜻의 형용사로 ④ imperative와 의미가 가장 가깝다.

해석

콩은 2001년 경제 위기에서 그 나라를 건져 낸 주요한 요인으로서 여겨지는 아르헨티나 경제의 **필수적인** 부분이다.
① 사소한, 하찮은
② 시시한, 따분한
③ 결정적인, 흔들리는
④ 필수적인, 긴급한

어휘

soy 콩; 간장
indispensable 필수적인, 없어서는 안 될
petty 사소한, 하찮은 banal 시시한, 따분한
swing 결정적인, 흔들리는 imperative 필수적인, 긴급한

오답률 TOP 2

02 정답 ②

정답해설

밑줄 친 'reasonable'은 '합리적인, 사리를 아는'이라는 뜻의 형용사로 ① sane과 의미가 가장 가깝다.

해석

제한속도는 도로와 고속도로에서 안전하고 **합리적인** 운전 환경을 제공하기 때문에 존재한다.
① 사리 분별이 있는, 건전한
② 일치하는; 자음(자)
③ 외설적인, 적절하지 못한
④ 현명하지 못한, 경솔한

어휘

reasonable 합리적인, 사리를 아는 sane 사리 분별이 있는, 건전한
consonant 일치하는; 자음(자) indecent 외설적인, 적절하지 못한
imprudent 현명하지 못한, 경솔한

03 정답 ②

정답해설

밑줄 친 'enhancing'은 '강화하다, 향상시키다'를 뜻하는 'enhance'의 현재분사로 ② intensifying과 의미가 가장 가깝다.

해석

두 체조 선수, 양학선과 손연재는 런던에서 돌아온 후로, 특정한 회사들의 이미지를 **강화하는** 캠페인 광고를 촬영하느라 바쁘다.

① 고정시키는
② 강화하는
③ 다시 채우는, 보충하는
④ 약화시키는

어휘

gymnast 체조 선수
enhance 강화하다, 향상시키다
fixate 고정[정착]시키다
replenish 다시 채우다, 보충하다
be busy ~ing ~하느라 바쁘다
commercial 상업[광고] 방송; 상업의
intensify 강화하다
undermine 약화시키다

04 정답 ③

정답해설

아들과 엄마는 부엌의 오븐에서 구워지고 있는 사과파이에 관해 대화를 나눈다. 아들이 부엌에서 나는 냄새를 맡고 오븐 안을 궁금해하면서 만지려고 하자, 엄마는 "조심해!"라고 말하며 '③ Curiosity killed the cat(많이 알려고 하면 다친다)'라고 말한다.

오답해설

① 아들이 사과파이 냄새를 맡고 오븐 안을 궁금해하며 만지려고 하는 상황에서 엄마가 아들에게 '계속 이대로 둘 수는 없다[더 이상은 안 된다](Enough is enough)'라고 단호하게 이야기하는 것은 맥락상 부자연스럽다.
② 아들이 오븐 안에 있는 사과파이가 잘 구워지고 있는지 궁금해하면서 뜨거운 오븐을 만지려고 하자 엄마가 '드디어 이야기가 되네(Now you're talking)'라고 말하는 것은 문맥상 어색하다.
④ 뜨거운 오븐 안에 있는 사과파이가 잘 구워지고 있는지 궁금해하는 아들에게 엄마가 아들이 "다치지 않기를 바란다"라고 말하며, '정말 그래(You can say that again)'라고 반응하는 것은 대화의 흐름상 빈칸에 들어갈 말로 적절하지 않다.

해석

아들: 엄마, 이 냄새 부엌에서 나는 거예요? 사과파이 냄새 같아요.
엄마: 너 오늘 집에 늦게 오는 줄 알았는데. 그래서 널 깜짝 놀래 주기 위해 이것을 구우려고 했어.
아들: 고마워요, 엄마! 전 엄마가 만든 사과파이가 정말 좋아요! 아직 오븐 안에 있어요?
엄마: 응, 아직 준비가 안 됐어. 내가 계획한 대로 널 놀래줄 수 없어서 아쉽구나.
아들: 저에게는 깜짝 선물 같아요. 빨리 맛보고 싶어요!
엄마: 조심해! 오븐 만지지 마, 되게 뜨거워!
아들: 오, 저 오븐을 거의 만질 뻔했어요! 파이가 잘 구워지고 있는지 보려고 안을 보고 싶어요.
엄마: 많이 알려고 하면 다친다. 난 네가 다치지 않길 원해.
① 계속 이대로 둘 수는 없다[더 이상은 안 된다]
② 드디어 이야기가 되네
③ 많이 알려고 하면 다친다
④ 정말 그래

어휘

Enough is enough. 계속 이대로 둘 수는 없다[더 이상은 안 된다].
Now you're talking. 드디어 이야기되네.
Curiosity killed the cat. 많이 알려고 하면 다친다.
You can say that again. 정말 그래.

05 정답 ③

정답해설

③ **출제 포인트: 목적격 관계대명사**
해당 문장은 'you're good' 앞의 관계대명사 'which'가 목적격 관계대명사로 쓰여야 하는 경우이다. 이는 'which' 이후의 문장이 완전하므로 먼저 옳지 않은 문장임을 파악한 후, 문맥을 통해 선행사인 'things'를 수식함을 파악해야 한다. 따라서 관계사절에 'be good at'을 이용해 선행사 'things'를 수식한 '여러분이 잘하는 것들'이라는 해석이 적절하므로 'good' 이후에 'at'을 추가해 'good at'으로 수정해야한다.

오답해설

① **출제 포인트: more vs. less/비교급 비교**
문맥상 '여러분의 강점이 여러분의 열정보다 더 중요하다'가 자연스러우므로 밑줄 친 'more'는 옳은 표현이다. 이때 'more'는 'important'의 비교급을 나타내기 위해 사용된 부사이다.
② **출제 포인트: to부정사의 태(수동태 vs. 능동태)**
밑줄 친 'be grounded'는 to부정사의 동사원형에 해당하며 수동태로 사용되었다. 'be grounded' 이후에 목적어가 아닌 수식어(구) 'in things'가 오므로 'be grounded'는 옳은 표현이다.
④ **출제 포인트: that vs. what/주격 관계대명사**
밑줄 친 'that'은 주격 관계대명사로, 'a career path'가 선행사이며 이후에 오는 절의 주어가 없으므로 'that'은 옳은 표현이다.

해석

여러분의 강점이 여러분의 열정보다 더 중요하다. 가장 좋은 직업 선택은 여러분이 잘하는 것에 기초를 두는 경향이 있는데, 여러분의 관심사와 열정(에 기초를 두는 것)보다 더 그러하다는 것을 연구는 보여준다. 이상적으로는, 수요가 있는 진로에서 여러분의 강점과 가치관의 합류점을 발견하기를 원하는 것이다.

어휘

strength 강점
be grounded in ~에 기초를 두다
passion 열정
convergence 집합점, 합류점

오답률 TOP 3

06 정답 ①

정답해설

① **출제 포인트: 목적격 관계대명사**
해당 문장에서 'which ~ person'은 선행사 'the degree'를 수식하는 관계대명사 절이나 'which' 이후의 절이 완전한 형태의 문장이므로 옳지 않다. 따라서 밑줄 친 'take it on'에서 목적어 'it'을 삭제하고 'which'는 문맥상 목적격 관계대명사로 판단해야 옳다.

오답해설

② **출제 포인트: 동사 관용표현(engage in)**
밑줄 친 'engage in'은 관용표현으로 '~에 참여하다'를 뜻하므로 문맥상 옳게 사용되었다.
③ **출제 포인트: 능동태 vs. 수동태**
'raise'는 완전타동사이므로 이후에 목적어가 온다. 밑줄 친 'been raised'는 'raise'의 수동태이며 이후에 목적어가 없으므로 옳은 표현이다.
④ **출제 포인트: 등위상관접속사(not A but B)**
밑줄 친 'but'은 등위상관접속사 'not A but B'의 'but'으로 A와 B에 종속접속사 'because'가 이끄는 절이 병렬구조를 이루고 있으므로 옳게 사용되었다.

해석

우리가 행복한 얼굴 (또는 화가 난 얼굴)을 볼 때, 그 행위는 미묘하게 우리 안에 그에 상응하는 감정을 만들어 낸다. 우리가 다른 사람의 걸음 속도, 자세, 그리고 얼굴 표정을 인식하는 정도까지, 우리는 그들의 감정적 공간에 머무르기 시작한다; 우리의 신체가 다른 사람의 신체를 모방하면서, 우리는 감정적 일체감을 경험하기 시작한다. 우리의 신경 체계는 자동적으로 이러한 감정적 공감에 참여하도록 맞춰진다. 하지만 우리가 얼마나 이 능력을 잘 사용할 수 있는지는 주로 학습된 능력에 달려 있다. 극도의 사회적 고립 속에서 길러진 동물들—그리고 사람들—은 그들 주변의 사람들의 감정적 단서를 잘 읽어내지 못하는데, 그들이 공감을 위한 기본 회로가 부족해서 이기 때문이 아니라, 감정적 스승이 없어서 그들이 이러한 메시지에 관심을 가지는 법을 배운 적이 없고, 따라서 이런 기술을 연습하지 못했기 때문이다.

어휘

corresponding 해당하는, 상응하는
pace (걸음 달리기 움직임의) 속도
posture 자세
engage in 참여하다
isolation 고립
circuitry (전기) 회로

오답률 TOP 1

07 정답 ③

정답해설

③ 출제 포인트: 형용사 vs. 부사/등위접속사의 병렬구조

밑줄 친 'poor'와 등위접속사 'or'를 통해 병렬구조를 이루고 있는 'wrong'은 동사 'do'를 수식하는 부사이다. 따라서 형용사 'poor'를 부사 'poorly'로 수정해야 한다.

오답해설

① 출제 포인트: 동사 관용표현(keep -ing)

'keep -ing'는 관용표현으로 '계속해서 ~하다'를 뜻한다. 따라서 밑줄 친 'delaying'은 옳은 표현이다.

② 출제 포인트: 주어와 동사의 수일치

밑줄 친 'is'는 단수 형태의 동사이며 단수 형태의 주어 'One reason'과 수일치하므로 옳은 표현이다. 주어 'One reason'과 동사 'is' 사이의 'many people ~ do'는 주어 'One reason'을 수식하는 관계부사절로 관계부사 'why' 또는 'that'이 'One reason'과 'many people' 사이에 생략되어있다. 또한 관계부사절 내의 'they should do'는 'things'를 수식하는 목적격 관계대명사절로 'things'와 'they' 사이에 목적격 관계대명사 'which' 또는 'that'이 생략되어있다. 이처럼 주어와 동사 사이의 거리가 먼 경우 수일치에 주의해야한다.

④ 출제 포인트: 현재분사 vs. 과거분사

글을 쓰는 주체를 일반인 주어인 'you[people]'로 보고, 분사구문으로 제시된 문장이다. 일반인 주어인 경우 분사구문에서 주절의 주어와 일치하지 않더라도 예외적으로 생략이 가능하다. 밑줄 친 현재분사 'getting'은 이후에 목적어 'your thoughts'가 있으며 해석상 '당신의 생각을 옮겨적다'를 뜻하는 능동의 의미이므로 옳은 표현이다.

해석

사람들이 그들이 해야만 하는 일들을 계속해서 미루는 한 가지 이유는 그들이 그 일들을 잘못하거나 제대로 못 하는 것을 두려워하기 때문인데, 그래서 그들은 그 일들을 아예 하지 않는다. 예를 들어, 책을 쓰는 최고의 방법들 중 하나는 문체는 고려하지 않고 당신의 생각을 종이에 옮겨 적으면서 그것을 가능한 한 빨리 쓰는 것이다. 그리고 나서, 당신은 당신의 글을 개정하고 다듬기 위해 되돌아갈 수 있다.

어휘

keep -ing 계속해서 ~하다
not at all 전혀 ~ 아니다
delay 연기하다
without regard to ~와 상관없이

---

08 정답 ③

정답해설

본문은 '인생에서 중요한 일은 큰 돌(big rocks), 덜 중요한 일은 모래(sand), 인생을 항아리(jar)'에 비교하고 있다. 본문 마지막에 글의 요지가 등장하는데, "When you tackle life's "big rocks" first, you end up having time for everyday life maintenance tasks, as well as for relaxation and fun. But when you put the sand first, the more important things in life get crowded out(당신이 인생의 "큰 돌"을 먼저 대처할 때, 당신은 결국 휴식과 즐거움뿐만 아니라 일상생활 유지 업무를 위한 시간을 가지게 될 것이다. 그러나 당신이 모래를 먼저 채울 때, 인생에서 더 중요한 일들은 밀려나게 된다)."라고 언급하며, '가장 중요한 일을 먼저 처리하면 나머지를 위한 시간이 따라온다'라고 설명하고 있다. 반면, 덜 중요한 일을 먼저 처리한다면, 정작 더 중요한 일은 밀려날 것이라고 언급한다. 그러므로 글의 요지로 가장 적절한 것은 '③ Take care of the most important things first and the rest will follow(가장 중요한 일을 먼저 하라, 그러면 나머지는 따라올 것이다).'이다.

오답해설

① 본문과 관련 없는 내용이다.
② 본문 중반에서 "The sand is the urgent, but less important things in your life(모래는 당신의 인생에서 긴급하지만 덜 중요한 일이다)."라고 언급하고 있으므로, '긴급한 일을 즉각적으로 처리하라'는 것은 본문의 요지와는 거리가 먼 내용이다.
④ 본문과 관련 없는 내용이다.

해석

당신이 모래 더미, 큰 돌 더미, 그리고 당신이 그 두 더미를 집어넣어야 할 항아리를 가지고 있다고 상상해보라. 예를 들어 항아리를 모래로 먼저 채웠다고 해보자; 당신은 그것이 너무 많은 공간을 차지해서 결국 큰 돌을 넣을 공간이 없다는 것을 알게 될 것이다. 그러나 예를 들어 당신이 대신에 항아리를 큰 돌로 먼저 채우고 나서 모래를 넣었다고 해보자; 그 퇴적물은 큰 돌의 틈 사이에 자리 잡아, 당신이 두 더미의 모든 것이 들어갈 공간을 만들 수 있도록 해줄 것이다. 당신의 인생이 그 항아리와 같다. 모래는 당신의 인생에서 긴급하지만 덜 중요한 일이다. 큰 돌은 당신의 인생에서 가장 중요한 일: 엄격한 마감 시간이 있지는 않지만 당신의 본질적 목표를 달성할 수 있도록 도와주는 활동들이다. 당신이 인생의 "큰 돌"을 먼저 대처할 때, 당신은 결국 휴식과 즐거움뿐만 아니라 일상생활 유지 업무를 위한 시간을 가지게 될 것이다. 그러나 당신이 모래를 먼저 채울 때, 인생에서 더 중요한 일들은 밀려나게 된다.
① 일과 놀이 사이에서 당신의 삶의 균형을 맞추는 것은 중요하다.
② 긴급한 문제에 당신의 즉각적인 주의를 기울여야 한다.
③ 가장 중요한 일을 먼저 하라, 그러면 나머지는 따라올 것이다.
④ 아무리 복잡하더라도 문제에는 항상 해결책이 있다.

어휘

pile 더미, 무더기
sediment 퇴적물, 앙금
urgent 긴급한
tackle 대처하다, 다루다
ultimately 결국
fit in …이 들어갈 공간을 만들다
principle 원칙, 본질
get[be] crowded out 밀려 나가다

09 정답 ②

정답해설

본문 첫 문장에서 글의 주제문을 찾을 수 있다. "Some kinds of fishing gear can be even more destructive when they become lost or forgotten in the water because they continue to catch animals, a phenomenon known as "ghost fishing"(어떤 낚시 장비의 일종은 심지어 더 파괴적일 수 있는데 그것이 잃어버리거나 물속에서 잊혔을 때 그것들은 동물들을 계속해서 잡기 때문이며 이는 "유령 낚시"라고 알려진 현상이다)."라고 설명하며, '버려지거나 분실된 낚시 기구의 위험성'에 대해 강조한 후, 이어서 이러한 버려진 기구에 의해 희생되는 바다 생물의 구체적인 예시를 제시하며 글을 전개하고 있으므로, 글의 요지로 가장 적절한 것은 '② Derelict fishing equipment is threatening some marine animals(버려진 낚시 장비가 일부 해양 동물을 위협하고 있다).'이다.

오답해설

① 본문에서는 '해양 쓰레기(ocean debris)' 중 '버려지거나 분실된 낚시 기구(fishing gear)'에 대해서만 언급하고 있으므로, 본문의 요지와는 거리가 멀다.
③ 본문의 내용과 관계없으므로 오답이다.
④ 본문에서는 '버려진 꽃게(blue crab)의 통발에 후미거북(diamondback terrapin)이 희생된다'고 설명하고 있으며, 꽃게의 개체수와 후미거북의 개체수는 상관관계가 없으므로 오답이다.

해석

어떤 낚시 장비의 일종은 심지어 더 파괴적일 수 있는데 그것이 잃어버리거나 물속에서 잊혔을 때 그것들은 동물들을 계속해서 잡기 때문이며 이는 "유령 낚시"라고 알려진 현상이다. 그 장비는 거둬들여지거나 어떠한 방식으로든 사용되지 않을 다수의 동물들을 걸려들게 할 수 있기 때문에 이것은 특히 낭비적이고 파괴적이다. 후미거북은 어떻게 유령 낚시가 동물의 인구에 영향을 끼칠 수 있는지에 대한 사례 연구를 제공한다. 이 거북이들은 사람들이 또한 꽃게를 잡는 곳인 East Coast의 해수 소택지에 서식한다. 꽃게는 습지의 바닥에 떨어뜨려져 수면에 떠다니는 부표에 묶인 금속 바구니인 게잡이 통발을 이용해 잡힌다. 만약 부표가 분리된다면, 어부는 그 장비를 찾을 수 없을 것이고 그것은 "유령 통발"이 된다. 중앙에 놓인 미끼에 끌려, 꽃게뿐만 아니라 후미거북도 통발로 수영해 들어온다. 그들이 사회적인 동물이기 때문에, 몇몇 거북이가 한 개의 통발에 있을 때, 그것은 종종 다른 개체를 끌어들이고, 유령 통발이 시간이 지남에 따라 점점 더 많은 거북이를 잡게 된다. Georgia에서 130마리 이상의 죽은 거북이가 들어있는 한 개의 유령 통발이 발견되었다.
① 거북이는 해양 쓰레기의 가장 큰 희생자이다.
② 버려진 낚시 장비가 일부 해양 동물을 위협하고 있다.
③ 최신식의 낚시 장비가 다수의 종을 동시에 포획하는 것을 가능하게 해준다.
④ 후미거북은 꽃게의 개체수 감소로 인해 위험에 처해 있다.

어휘

destructive 파괴적인, 해로운　　phenomenon 현상
ensnare (올가미에 걸리듯) 걸려들게[빠지게] 하다
inhabit 서식하다, 살다
salt marsh (바닷물이 드나드는 해변가의) 해수 소택지
blue crab 꽃게, 바다게　　crab pot 게잡이 통발
marsh 습지　　　　　　　　buoy 부표
surface 표면, 지면, 수면　　detach 분리하다
bait 미끼　　　　　　　　　　deceased 죽은, 사망한

10 정답 ②

정답해설

본문은 '최초의 민간인을 대상으로 한 테러 공격이었던 1894년 2월 12일 발생한 Gare Saint-Lazare의 Café Terminus 폭탄 테러'에 관한 내용이다. 테러가 일어나기 전, 카페에서는 많은 사람들이 오케스트라의 연주를 듣고 있었다. 본문 중반 "He had placed a bomb in a metal workman's lunchbox and hurled it at the orchestra(그는 금속으로 된 노동자의 도시락에 폭탄을 넣고, 그것을 오케스트라를 향해 던졌다)."를 통해, 범인이 연주 중이던 오케스트라에게 금속 도시락에 폭탄을 숨기고 던진 사실을 알 수 있으므로, 글의 내용과 일치하는 것은 '② An attacker threw a hidden bomb at the musicians(공격자는 음악가들을 향해 숨겨진 폭탄을 던졌다).'이다.

오답해설

① 본문 중반 "It was the work of a smartly dressed 20-year-old French accountant called Emile Henry(그것은 Emile Henry라고 불리는 말쑥하게 차려입은 20세의 프랑스인 회계사의 짓이었다)."를 통해, '단체가 아닌 개인에 의한 테러'라는 것을 알 수 있다.
③ 본문 후반 "He was captured at the scene of the bombing(그는 폭탄 테러의 현장에서 체포되었다)."을 통해, 'Emile Henry는 테러 후 현장에서 도망치지 못했음'을 알 수 있다.
④ 본문 후반 "He said he had one regret: that he didn't kill more "bourgeois." If only he had a bomb big enough, he boasted, he would have blown up the whole of Paris(그는 한 가지 후회가 있다고 말했다: 그가 더 많은 "부르주아"를 죽이지 못했다"는 것이다. 만일 그가 충분히 큰 폭탄을 가지고 있었더라면, 그는 파리 전체를 날려버렸을 것이라고 허풍을 쳤다)."를 통해, 'Emile Henry는 무고한 시민을 죽게 만든 것을 전혀 후회하거나 반성하지 않았다'는 것을 알 수 있다.

해석

1894년 2월 12일 해가 질 무렵, 음악이 갑자기 멈추었을 때 Gare Saint-Lazare에 있는 Café Terminus는 오케스트라를 듣고 있는 젊은 파리지앵들로 가득 차 있었다. 불덩이가 시야 안에 있는 모든 것을 삼켰다: 세상은 암흑으로 변했다. 생존자들이 정신을 차렸을 때, 그들 주변에 신체 부위들의 조각이 있었고, 사람들은 화염에 휩싸여 달려가고 비명을 지르고 있었다. 그것은 Emile Henry라고 불리는 말쑥하게 차려입은 20세의 프랑스인 회계사의 짓이었다. 그는 금속으로 된 노동자의 도시락에 폭탄을 넣고, 그것을 오케스트라를 향해 던졌다. 이것은 개인이 민간인을 무차별적으로 날려버린 최초의 일이었다. 그는 폭탄 테러의 현장에서 체포되었다. 그는 한 가지 후회가 있다고 말했다: 그가 더 많은 "부르주아"를 죽이지 못했다"는 것이다. 만일 그가 충분히 큰 폭탄을 가지고 있었더라면, 그는 파리 전체를 날려버렸을 것이라고 허풍을 쳤다. Henry가 21세의 나이에 사형당한 후, 무정부주의자들에 의해 자행된 일련의 보복 폭탄 테러가 프랑스를 휩쓸었다.
① 2월 12일의 공격은 무정부주의자 단체에 의해 수행되었다.
② 공격자는 음악가들을 향해 숨겨진 폭탄을 던졌다.
③ Emile Henry는 잡히지 않고 폭탄 테러 현장을 간신히 빠져나왔다.
④ Emile Henry는 무고한 사람들을 뜻하지 않게 죽인 것을 후회했다.

어휘

abruptly 갑자기
come round 다시 의식을 차리다[정신이 돌아오다]
jigsaw 조각 그림 맞추기 (퍼즐)　　hurl 던지다
bourgeois (자본주의 사회의) 지배 계급의 구성원, 부르주아
boast 큰소리치다, 허풍 치다, 자랑하다
execute 처형[사형]하다　　　anarchist 무정부주의자
rip through …를 거칠게 지나가다　　manage to 동사원형 간신히 ~하다
accidentally 뜻하지 않게, 우발적으로

결국엔 성정혜 영어 하프모의고사
기적사 DAY 49

| 01 | ③ | 02 | ③ | 03 | ① | 04 | ④ | 05 | ② |
| 06 | ④ | 07 | ② | 08 | ② | 09 | ① | 10 | ④ |

오답률 TOP 2
01 정답 ③

정답해설

밑줄 친 'requisite'는 '필요한'을 뜻하는 형용사로 ③ incumbent와 의미가 가장 가깝다.

해석

음악을 처리하고, 평가하고 그것을 즐기기 위해 **필요한** 신경 기제를 우리가 가지고 있다는 것은 참으로 행운이다.
① 구속력 있는, 의무적인
② 까다로운, 가리는
③ 필요한, 재임 중인
④ 필요치 않은, 불필요한

어휘

requisite 필요한
appreciate 평가하다, 인정하다, 인식하다; 가치가 오르다
binding 구속력 있는, 의무적인
incumbent 필요한, 재임 중인
neural 신경(계)의
fastidious 까다로운, 가리는
superfluous 필요치 않은, 불필요한

오답률 TOP 3
02 정답 ③

정답해설

밑줄 친 'deplorable'은 '개탄스러운'을 뜻하는 형용사로 ③ lamentable과 의미가 가장 가깝다.

해석

인종 차별주의는 **개탄스럽고** 그러한 민감한 발언들을 게시한 것에 대해 그 학생이 끔찍한 사람일지라도, 그 학생의 처벌은 옳지 않다.
① 오만한, 거만한
② 자랑하는
③ 한탄스러운, 통탄할
④ 감명 깊은, 훌륭한

어휘

racism 인종 차별(주의)
sensitive 민감한, 예민한
haughty 오만한, 거만한
lamentable 한탄스러운, 통탄할
deplorable 개탄스러운
punishment 벌, 처벌
vaunting 자랑하는; 자랑
magnificent 감명 깊은, 훌륭한

03 정답 ①

정답해설

밑줄 친 'ameliorating'은 '개선하다'를 뜻하는 'ameliorate'의 현재분사로 ① refining과 의미가 가장 가깝다.

해석

현재, 개발자들이 대중교통에 대한 대비와 같은 **개선** 조치나 개발을 제공하거나 지원함으로써 부정적인 영향을 완화하거나 제거할 수 있다.
① 개선하는
② 변형시키는
③ 퇴보하는
④ 악화시키는

어휘

mitigate 완화시키다, 경감시키다
adverse 부정적인, 불리한
provision 준비, 대비; 공급, 제공
deform 변형시키다
aggravate 악화시키다; 화나게 하다
obviate 제거하다
ameliorate 개선하다
refine 개선하다; 정제하다
regress 퇴보하다, 퇴행하다

04 정답 ④

정답해설

Jamie와 Alex는 어제 본 축구 경기에 관해 대화를 나눈다. Alex는 손이 "상대 팀으로부터 공을 빼앗았을 때 (A) '목소리를 높여(at the top of my lungs)' 소리를 질렀다"고 이야기한다. Jamie는 자신도 마찬가지지만 "손이 (B) '숨이 가빠(be short of breath)' 보였다"라면서, "그는 숨을 몰아쉬고 있었다"라고 대답한다. 그런데도 손은 경기장을 계속 뛰어다녀 Alex는 "그의 열정에 놀랐다"라고 말한다. Jamie는 Alex의 말에 동의하면서 그가 의심할 여지 없이 (C) '대단한 인물(a big bug)'이라고 말한다.

오답해설

① (A) Alex는 토트넘을 응원하며 손이 상대 팀으로부터 공을 빼앗았을 때 '예기치 못하게(out of the blue sky)' 소리 질렀다고 얘기하는 것은 문맥상 어색하다. (B) Jamie는 손이 숨을 몰아쉬고 있었다면서 '적자를 낸(be in the red)' 것 같았다고 말하는 것은 내용상 적절하지 않다. (C) 손이 경기장을 뛰어다니는 모습을 보며 그의 열정에 놀랐다는 Alex의 말에 Jamie는 손이 의심할 여지 없이 '귀족 가문(a blue blood)'이라는 것을 깨달았다고 하는 것은 대화의 흐름상 부적합하다.
② (A) Alex는 토트넘을 응원하며 손이 상대 팀으로부터 공을 빼앗았을 때 '예기치 못하게(out of the blue sky)' 소리 질렀다고 얘기하는 것은 문맥상 부자연스럽다.
③ (B) Jamie는 손이 숨을 몰아쉬고 있었다면서 '흑자를 낸(be in the black)' 것 같았다고 말하는 것은 내용상 적합하지 않다. (C) 손이 경기장을 뛰어다니는 모습을 보며 그의 열정에 놀랐다는 Alex의 말에 Jamie는 손이 의심할 여지 없이 '귀족 가문(a blue blood)'이라는 것을 깨달았다고 하는 것은 대화의 흐름상 자연스럽지 않다.

해석

Jamie: Alex, 너 어제 축구 경기 봤어?
Alex: 물론이지! 내가 최근에 본 축구 경기 중에 가장 흥미로웠어. 너도 어제 봤어?
Jamie: 나는 그것을 보기 위해 밤새웠어. 너는 무슨 팀 응원했어?
Alex: 나는 토트넘 응원했어. 손이 상대 팀으로부터 공을 빼앗았을 때, (A) 목소리를 높여 소리 질렀어.
Jamie: 나도 마찬가지야. 근데 손이 (B) 숨이 가빠 보였어. 그는 정말 숨을 몰아쉬고 있었어.
Alex: 나도 그거 봤어. 근데 그는 경기장을 계속 뛰어다녔어. 나는 그의 열정에 놀랐어.
Jamie: 맞아. 나는 그가 (C) 대단한 인물이라는 것을 다시 한번 깨달았어.
Alex: 모든 주요 축구팀들이 그를 스카우트하고 싶어 하는 것은 놀라운 일이 아니야.

① (A) 예기치 못하게 (B) 적자를 내다 (C) 귀족 가문
② (A) 예기치 못하게 (B) 숨이 가쁘다 (C) 대단한 인물
③ (A) 목소리를 높여 (B) 흑자를 내다 (C) 귀족 가문
④ (A) 목소리를 높여 (B) 숨이 가쁘다 (C) 대단한 인물

어휘

out of the blue sky 예기치 못하게
in the red 적자 상태인, 적자로   a blue blood 귀족 가문
be short of breath 숨이 차다   a big bug 대단한 인물
at the top of one's lungs 숨이 가쁘다
in the black 흑자상태인, 흑자로

오답률 TOP 1

05 정답 ②

정답해설

② 출제 포인트: '동사+부사'의 목적어 위치

동사와 부사가 결합한 형태의 타동사구인 'put down'의 목적어로 명사가 오는 경우, '동사+부사+명사' 또는 '동사+명사+부사'의 어순으로 나타낸다. 그러나 대명사가 목적어로 오는 경우 '동사+대명사+부사'의 어순을 가진다. 밑줄 친 'yourself'는 대명사로 어법상 'put down yourself'는 옳지 않으므로 ②는 옳지 않다. 따라서 'yourself'를 'down' 앞으로 이동해 'put yourself down'으로 수정해야 한다.

오답해설

① 출제 포인트: 가주어 it

밑줄 친 'it'은 가주어로 사용된 대명사이며 진주어는 동사 'feels' 이후에 오는 to부정사(구) 'to praise yourself rather than put yourself down'이다. 따라서 밑줄 친 'it'은 옳은 표현이다.

③ 출제 포인트: 비교급 비교

비교급의 구조는 「주어+동사+비교급+than+비교대상」이다. 해당 문장에서 'more'는 'many'의 비교급에 해당하므로 밑줄 친 'than'은 옳은 표현이다.

④ 출제 포인트: 완전타동사+목적어[to부정사 vs. 동명사]

'choose'는 to부정사를 목적어로 가진다. 따라서 밑줄 친 to부정사 'to see'는 옳은 표현이다.

해석

스스로를 깎아내리는 것보다는 칭찬하는 것이 얼마나 더 기분 좋은지를 알게 될 것이다. 이런 좋은 기분으로, 여러분은 자기비판의 부정적인 에너지로 이전에 할 수 있었던 것보다 더 많은 것을 자신과 남을 위해 할 수 있다. 좋은 점을 보는 것을 선택하라. 선택은 여러분 자신의 몫이다.

어휘

put down ~을 깎아내리다   self-criticism 자기비판

06 정답 ④

정답해설

④ 출제 포인트: 주어와 동사의 수일치

동명사(구)가 주어인 경우 단수 취급한다. 밑줄 친 동사 'demand'의 주어는 동명사(구) 'Translating sound'이며 단수로 취급하므로 'demand'를 'demands'로 수정해야 한다. 해당 문장의 주어와 동사 사이에 있는 'for example'은 전명구, 'whether ~ rhymes'는 삽입구에 해당한다. 주어와 동사 사이의 거리가 먼 경우 수일치에 유의해야 한다.

오답해설

① 출제 포인트: one of the 복수명사

밑줄 친 'aspects'는 'one of the 복수명사'에서 '복수명사'에 해당하므로 옳은 표현이다. 'most demanding, and at the same time inspiring'은 'aspects'를 수식하는 수식어이다.

② 출제 포인트: 수동태 불가동사/주격관계대명사 수일치

밑줄 친 'arises'는 완전자동사이므로 수동태로 사용할 수 없다. 또한 'arises'는 선행사 'creativity'를 수식하는 주격관계대명사절의 동사이므로 단수 형태의 선행사에 수일치한 단수 형태의 동사 'arises'의 쓰임은 올바르다.

③ 출제 포인트: 불완전타동사와 목적격 보어(require+목적어+목적격 보어[to부정사])

'require'는 불완전타동사로 사용되는 경우 목적격 보어로 to부정사를 사용할 수 있다. 밑줄 친 'to have'는 불완전타동사 'require'의 목적격 보어에 해당하며 이후에 목적어 'an understanding'이 오므로 옳은 표현이다.

해석

아동을 위한 번역에 있어서 가장 힘들면서 동시에 고무적인 양상 중 하나는 Peter Hollindale이 아동용 텍스트의 '아이다움'이라고 부른 것, 즉 '동적(動的)이며, 상상력이 풍부하며, 실험적이며, 상호작용적이며, 불안정한, 아이 상태의 특성'에서 생기는 그런 창의성의 가능성이다. Hollindale이 언급하는 어린 시절의 '불안정한' 특성은 작가나 번역가에게, 아이의 눈과 귀에 대한 언어의 신선함, 아이의 정서상의 관심 사항, 그리고 초기 어린 시절의 말놀이와 연극놀이에 대한 이해력을 가질 것을 요구한다. 예를 들어, 더 어린 아이들을 위한 책의 낭독 특성이든, 동물의 소리든, 아동용 시나 무의미한 노래든, 글 안의 소리를 번역한다는 것은, 시각자료를 가지고 하는 작업이 정말로 그러는 것처럼 상상력이 풍부한 해결책을 요구한다. 그런 다면적인 창의성은 때때로 아동문학을 상상력이 풍부한 실험의 중심에 가져다 놓았다.

어휘

demanding 힘든, 벅찬   inspiring 고무적인
unstable 불안정한   affective 정서적인
cite 언급하다   concern 관심사
forefront 중심, 가장 중요한 위치

07 정답 ②

정답해설

② 출제 포인트: 감정형 분사(현재분사 vs. 과거분사)

감정 유발 분사는 명사를 수식할 때 감정을 제공하는 경우 '-ing' 형태를 사용하며 감정의 상태를 나타내는 경우 'p.p.' 형태를 사용한다. 밑줄 친 'depressed'는 'doing so'를 수식하며 '그렇게 하는 것'은 문맥상 '우울함을 제공하는 것'이므로 'depressed'가 아닌 'depressing'을 사용해야 한다.

오답해설

① 출제 포인트: 목적격 관계대명사

밑줄 친 'whom'은 뒤따라오는 절의 동명사 'meeting'의 목적어가 없으며 선행사 'someone'을 수식하고 있으므로 목적격 관계대명사로 옳게 사용되었다.

③ 출제 포인트: 동사 관용표현(get to 동사원형)

'get to 동사원형'은 관용표현으로 '~하게 되다'를 뜻한다. 따라서 밑줄 친 'to know'는 옳은 표현이다.

④ 출제 포인트: 불완전타동사의 수동태

불완전타동사 'motivate'는 수동태의 경우 'be motivated to+동사원형'의 형태로 사용된다. 해당 문장은 밑줄 친 'motivated' 앞에 be동사 'are'가 있으며 이후에 to부정사 'to find'가 있으므로 수동태로 사용된 것임을 알 수 있다. 따라서 'motivated'는 옳은 표현이다.

해석
사람들이 다시 만날 것을 예견하지 않는 누군가와 교류할 때, 그들은 긍정적인 특성들을 찾아야 할 이유가 거의 없다. 사실 그렇게 하는 것은 그들이 미래의 교류에서 그 사람을 더 잘 알게 될 기회를 갖지 못할 거라는 점을 고려하면 그들을 울적하게 할 것이다. 실제로, 사람들은 때때로 다시 만날 기대를 하지 않는 사람들에게서 부정적인 특징을 찾도록 동기부여 된다.

어휘
motivate 목적어 to 동사원형 ~이 ~하도록 동기를 부여하다
foresee 예견하다
get to 동사원형 ~하게 되다
given that ~을 고려하면
interaction 교류, 상호작용

08 정답 ②

정답해설
주어진 문장에서는 '과식하는 사람'을 언급하며, '능력보다 더 많은 것을 하려 하는 사람'에 대해 설명하고 있다. 이후 이어질 내용으로 가장 알맞은 것은 '시간 관리 측면'에서 '과식하는 사람'과 같이, '능력치보다 더 많은 업무를 떠맡는 사람'에 대해 언급하고 있는 (A)가 이어지는 것이 자연스럽다. 이후, '이러한 행위(This behavior)'로 시작하며 (A)에서 언급된 행동을 가리키는 (C)가 이어지는 것이 알맞다. 마지막으로 (C)에서 설명한 '비효율적이고 스트레스를 주는 업무 방식'을 바로잡기 위한 방법을 설명하고 있는 (B)가 이어지는 것이 적절하다. 따라서 정답은 '② (A) - (C) - (B)'이다.

오답해설
① (C)의 'This behavior'가 가리키는 대상이 (B)에 등장하지 않기 때문에, (C) 이전에 (B)가 위치하는 것은 어색하다.
나머지 보기는 문맥상 어색하므로 오답이다.

해석
과식하는 사람들은 종종 '위보다 더 큰 눈'을 가지고 있는 것으로 묘사된다.
(A) 시간 관리에서 이와 상당하는 것은 기존의 업무 약속을 완전히 무시한 채 매력적이고 흥미진진해 보이는 점점 더 많은 프로젝트를 떠맡는 사람이다.
(C) 이러한 행동은 Type A 노동 방식의 전형이며, 최종 결과는 '접시돌리기'이다 - 하나의 미완결 업무로부터 다른 것으로 서둘러 이동하며, 짧은 한바탕의 노력을 쏟아내고 아무 접시도 바닥에 깨지지 않길 희망한다. 이는 매우 비효율적인 방식의 노동일뿐만 아니라, 매우 스트레스를 준다.
(B) 당신의 업무량에 대한 통제를 회복하기 위해, 현실 직시는 필수적이다. 당신의 할 일 목록에 있는 모든 일의 우선순위를 정하고 각각의 업무가 완료되기 위해 얼마나 오래 걸리는지 추정하라.

어휘
equivalent 상당하는 것, 동등한 것, 등가[등량]물; 동등한, 상당하는
inviting 유혹[매력]적인, 솔깃한
existing 기존의
workload 업무량
estimate 추산[추정]하다
burst (갑자기) 한바탕 …을 함[터뜨림]
disregard 무시, 묵살
commitment 약속
prioritize 우선순위를 매기다
dash (급히) 서둘러 가다

09 정답 ①

정답해설
본문에서는 '어업 기법 중 하나인 주낙 어업(long-lining)'에 관해 설명하고 있으며, 빈칸에는 주낙 어업과 같은 어업 행위를 특징지어 설명하는 표현이 들어가야 한다. 본문에 따르면, '수십만 개의 미끼가 달린 바늘이 빽빽한 낚싯줄을 이용하는 주낙 어업을 통해 어떠한 동물들이라도 잡히게 되고, 잡히면 익사하거나 과다 출혈로 죽는 경우도 있다. 또한 거대한 물고기류는 낚싯바늘을 보호하기 위해 곡괭이를 이용해 잔인하게 포획된다. 이렇게 불특정 다수의 동물을 겨냥한 잔인한 어업 행위를 묘사하는 표현으로 가장 적절한 것은 보기 중 '① Indiscriminate(무차별적인)'이다.

오답해설
②, ③ "Fishers sink pickaxes into the animals' fins, sides, and even eyes — any part that will allow them to haul the animals aboard without ripping out the hook(어부들은 그 동물들의 지느러미, 측면, 그리고 심지어 눈에, 그들이 그 동물들을 바늘을 뜯어내지 않고 배 위로 끌고 올 수 있게 할 수 있는 어떠한 부위에라도, 곡괭이를 박아 넣는다)."를 통해, 해당 어업 행위가 '동정적인, 동정하는(Sympathetic)' 또는 '세심한, 꼼꼼한, 양심적인(Scrupulous)' 면모는 보이지 않는다는 것을 알 수 있다. 따라서 오답이다.
나머지 보기는 문맥상 어색하므로 오답이다.

해석
주낙 어업은 가장 널리 퍼진 어업 기법들 중 하나이다. 선박들은 수십만 개의 미끼가 달린 바늘이 빽빽하게 달려 있는 최대 50마일의 줄을 푼다. 이것들은 다양한 깊이에서 선박의 뒤에서 끌어당겨지거나 부표에 의해 떠다니며 밤새 남겨져 있으며, 공짜 식사를 하려는 그 주위의 어떤 동물이라도 유혹한다. 일단 바늘에 걸리면, 어떤 동물들은 익사하거나 물속에서 출혈로 죽고, 많은 다른 동물들은 선박이 그들을 낚아 올리기 위해 돌아오기 전까지 수 시간 동안 분투한다. 무게가 각각 수백 파운드에 달하는 황새치와 황다랑어와 같은 거대한 어류는 미끼가 달린 줄에 의해 선박 쪽으로 당겨진다. 어부들은 그 동물들의 지느러미, 측면, 그리고 심지어 눈에, 그들이 그 동물들을 바늘을 뜯어내지 않고 배 위로 끌고 올 수 있게 할 수 있는 어떠한 부위에라도, 곡괭이를 박아 넣는다. 이와 같은 무차별적인 어업 행위가 매년 미국 영역에서만 수십만의 바다거북, 돌고래, 조류, 상어, 다른 목표하지 않은 어류, 그리고 다른 해양 동물들을 죽인다.

① 무차별적인, 무분별한
② 동정적인, 동정하는
③ 세심한, 꼼꼼한, 양심적인
④ 무관심한, 그저 그런

어휘
unreel 실패[얼레]에서 풀다
bait 미끼를 달다
buoy 부표
drown 익사하다
swordfish 황새치
sink 박다
haul (억지로) 끌고 가다[오다]
territory 영토, 영역, (한 국가·통치자가 다스리는) 지역
indiscriminate 무차별적인, 무분별한
scrupulous 세심한, 꼼꼼한, 양심적인
bristle with …이 아주 많다[꽉 차 있다]
afloat 뜬
lure 꾀다, 유혹하다
reel 실패에 감다
yellowfin tuna 황다랑어
pickax 곡괭이
rip out 찢다, 잡아 뜯다
sympathetic 동정적인, 동정하는
indifferent 무관심한, 그저 그런

10 정답 ④

정답해설
본문은 '현재까지도 자살 폭탄 테러가 횡행하는 이유'를 '테러리스트와 그들의 연결망을 제거하는 데 초점을 맞춘 미국 주도의 테러와의 전쟁이 실패했기 때문'이라고 지적한다. 본문 마지막 문장 "The bombings in a place as unlikely as Sri Lanka — a country with no history of radical Islamist terrorism — underscore how far militaristic theology can spread and why the world needs to tackle it at its roots(스리랑카만큼 예상

밖의 장소 – 급진적인 이슬람 테러리즘의 역사가 없는 국가 – 에서의 폭탄 테러는 군국주의 신학이 얼마나 멀리 퍼져나갈 수 있고 왜 세계가 그것의 뿌리에서부터 해결해야 할 필요가 있는지 분명히 보여준다)."를 통해 '국군주의 신학(급진적 이슬람 테러리즘 이념)의 강한 파급력을 강조하며, 세계가 그것의 뿌리에서부터 해결해야 한다고 주장한다. 즉, 테러리즘을 이끄는 이슬람의 이념을 파괴하는 것에 집중해야 한다는 것이다. 따라서 글의 요지로 가장 적절한 것은 '④ The war on terrorism strategy needs to focus on discrediting the ideology that attracts terrorists(테러리즘 전략에 대한 전쟁은 테러리스트를 끌어들이는 이념의 신빙성을 없애는 데 초점을 맞출 필요가 있다).'이다.

오답해설

① 본문에서 '테러리스트의 공격이 계속 발생하고 있다'고 언급하고 있으나, 이를 뿌리 뽑기 위한 전략 또한 제시하고 있으므로, 글 전체의 요지로는 적절하지 않다.
② 본문에서 언급되는 사실의 일부이나, 글 전체를 아우르는 내용이 아니므로 글의 요지로는 부적절하다.
③ 본문에서는 '급진적 지하드 이념'에 유혹되는 대상에 대해서는 구체적으로 언급하고 있지 않다.

해석

부활절 일요일 스리랑카에서의 지하드 폭탄 테러는 이 글로벌 세계에서 누구도 테러리스트 공격에서 자유로울 수 없다는 것을 상기시켜주는 가장 최근의 사건이다. 이러한 테러리스트의 공격이 계속해서 발생하는 한 가지 이유는 미국 주도의 테러와의 전쟁이 실패한 것이다 – 그리고 그것은 전 세계의 자살 공격에 영감을 주는 급진적인 지하드의 이념을 물리치는 것이 아닌 테러리스트와 그들의 연결망을 제거하는데 초점을 맞추어왔기 때문이다. 급진적인 이슬람 테러리즘에 관한 한, 이념적 뿌리는 주로, 사우디아라비아에 의해 활성화된 수니파 이슬람의 극단적 형태인 와하브파의 교리에서부터 시작되었다. 와하브파의 교리는 "신앙심 없는 자들"과의 전쟁을 요구하며 폭력적인 정신적 투쟁을 합법화시킨다. 사우디 무슬림 학자 Ali al-Ahmed에 따르면, 그것은 믿지 않는 사람들이 "증오 되고, 박해받고, 심지어 죽임당해야 한다"고 주장한다. 스리랑카만큼 예상 밖의 장소 – 급진적인 이슬람 테러리즘의 역사가 없는 국가 – 에서의 폭탄 테러는 군국주의 신학이 얼마나 멀리 퍼져나갈 수 있고 왜 세계가 그것의 뿌리에서부터 대처해야 할 필요가 있는지 분명히 보여준다.
① 우리가 아무리 열심히 노력해도 테러리스트 공격이 발생하는 것은 완전히 멈춰질 수 없다.
② 자살 폭탄 테러 공격은 종교적 뿌리와 관계없이 세계 모든 곳에서 발생한다.
③ 전 세계의 젊고 취약한 사람들이 급진적 지하드 이념에 의해 쉽게 유혹된다.
④ 테러리즘 전략에 대한 전쟁은 테러리스트를 끌어들이는 이념의 신빙성을 없애는 데 초점을 맞출 필요가 있다.

어휘

jihadi 지하드(jihad)의 전사
defeat 물리치다, 이기다
legitimize 합법화하다, 정당화하다
jihad (이슬람교에서 종교적·도덕적 법칙을 지키기 위한) 정신적 투쟁
infidel 신앙심 없는 자
persecute 박해하다
radical 급진적인, 과격한
militaristic 군국주의
tackle (해결을 위해) 대처하다, 다루다
lure 꾀다, 유혹하다
discredit 존경심[신임]을 떨어뜨리다, 신빙성을 없애다
eliminate 제거하다
trace 추적하다, 추적하여 밝혀내다
advocate 주장하다
unlikely (일반적인) 예상 밖의
underscore 강조하다, 분명히 보여주다
theology 신학
vulnerable 취약한, 연약한

결국엔 성정혜 영어 하프모의고사
기적사 DAY 50

| 01 | ④ | 02 | ② | 03 | ① | 04 | ④ | 05 | ① |
| 06 | ③ | 07 | ① | 08 | ③ | 09 | ④ | 10 | ③ |

01 정답 ④

정답해설

밑줄 친 'omnipresent'는 '어디에나 있는, 편재하는'을 뜻하는 형용사로 ④ ubiquitous와 의미가 가장 가깝다.

해석

여행 중에, William은 **어디에나 있었는데**, 그가 나를 감시하길 원했기 때문이 아니라 발생한 모든 것에 대해 책임이 있었기 때문이었다.
① 지극히 평범한, 시시한
② 희박한, 드문드문한
③ 독특한, 이상한
④ 어디에나 있는, 아주 흔한

어휘

omnipresent 어디에나 있는, 편재하는
banal 지극히 평범한, 시시한   sparse 희박한, 드문드문한
peculiar 독특한, 이상한   ubiquitous 어디에나 있는, 아주 흔한

오답률 TOP 1

02 정답 ②

정답해설

밑줄 친 'inconvenient'는 '불편한'을 뜻하는 형용사로 ② sticky와 의미가 가장 가깝다.

해석

우리는 모두 일상생활에서 살짝 짜증이 나는 정도부터 매우 **불편한** 정도까지 잘 잊는 경향이 있다.
① 아늑한, 은밀한
② 불편한, 끈적거리는
③ 집요한, 완강한
④ 무관심한, 심드렁한

어휘

be prone to ~하기 쉽다   forgetfulness 잊기 쉬움, 건망증
mildly 다소, 약간; 부드럽게, 온화하게   inconvenient 불편한
cozy 아늑한, 은밀한   sticky 불편한, 끈적거리는
tenacious 집요한, 완강한   apathetic 무관심한, 심드렁한

03 정답 ①

정답해설

밑줄 친 'leveling'은 '(물가, 임금 등이) 안정되다, 평평해지다'를 뜻하는 'level'의 현재분사로 ① equalizing과 의미가 가장 가깝다.

해석

어떤 사람들은 그것이 **안정되고** 있다고 말했지만, 그 다음 날 소위 전문가들이 그들의 마음을 바꾸었고 그것은 다시 급락하고 있다.

① 평등하게 하는, 균일하게 하는
② 굳히는, 강화하는
③ 이상하게 하는, 이상 상태로 만드는
④ 구별하는, 차별하는

어휘

level (물가, 임금 등이) 안정되다, 평평해지다
spiral 나선형으로 (급속히) 움직이다   equalize 평등하게 하다, 균일하게 하다
consolidate 굳히다, 강화하다
abnormalize 이상하게 하다, 이상 상태로 만들다
differentiate 구별하다, 차별하다

04 정답 ④

정답해설

Eugene과 Vanessa는 시내에 사는 할머니의 소식에 관한 이야기를 나눈다. Eugene은 "그녀가 (A) '완전히 파산했다(dead broke).'"면서, Vanessa가 할머니에게 무슨 일이 있었냐고 묻자 "그녀가 (B) '전 재산을 한 곳에 걸었다(put all her eggs in one basket)'라고 이야기한다." 그리고 Eugene은 "그녀가 (C) '역경을 극복하고 살아가길(keeps body and soul together)' 진심으로 바란다"라고 말한다.

오답해설

① (A) Eugene은 시내에 평생을 혼자 살아오신 상당히 부유한 할머니가 'TV를 보며 소파에 앉아 감자를 먹는 게으른 유형의 사람(a couch potato)'이라고 말하는 것은 그녀가 투자를 잘못했다는 흐름의 대화에서 빈칸에 들어갈 말로 어색하다. (C) Eugene은 투자를 잘못한 할머니가 '손해를 보길(lays an egg)' 진심으로 바란다고 하는 것은 문맥상 부자연스럽다.
② (A) Eugene은 시내에 평생을 혼자 살아오신 상당히 부유한 할머니가 'TV를 보며 소파에 앉아 감자를 먹는 게으른 유형의 사람(a couch potato)'이라고 말하는 것은 그녀가 투자를 잘못했다는 흐름의 대화에서 빈칸에 들어갈 말로 적절하지 않다. (C) Eugene은 투자를 잘못한 할머니가 '실망하길(loses heart)' 진심으로 바란다고 하는 것은 문맥상 부적합하다.
③ (B) Eugene은 투자를 잘못한 할머니가 '요점을 정확히 찔렀다(hit the nail on the head)'라고 얘기하는 것은 정확하지 않다.

해석

Eugene: 너 시내에 사는 할머니 얘기 들었어?
Vanessa: 아니, 못 들었어. 누구셔?
Eugene: 그녀는 평생 혼자 살아오신 상당히 부유한 할머니셔. 근데 그녀는 지금 (A) 완전히 파산했어.
Vanessa: 오, 안타깝다. 그녀에게 무슨 일이 있었던 거야? 투자를 잘못하신 거야?
Eugene: 정확해. 그녀는 (B) 전 재산을 한 곳에 걸었어.
Vanessa: 그거 꽤 위험했겠다. 그녀가 분산 투자를 했더라면 더 안전했을 텐데.
Eugene: 맞아. 나는 진심으로 그녀가 (C) 역경을 극복하고 살아가길 바라.
Vanessa: 나도. 나는 그녀가 이 모든 역경을 극복하고 난 후에 더 단단한 사람이 되어있을 거라고 확신해.

① (A) TV를 보며 소파에 앉아 감자를 먹는 게으른 유형의 사람
  (B) 전 재산을 한 곳에 걸었다 (C) 손해를 보다
② (A) TV를 보며 소파에 앉아 감자를 먹는 게으른 유형의 사람
  (B) 전 재산을 한 곳에 걸었다 (C) 실망하다
③ (A) 완전히 파산하여 (B) 요점을 정확히 찔렀다
  (C) 역경을 극복하고 살아가다
④ (A) 완전히 파산하여 (B) 전 재산을 한 곳에 걸었다
  (C) 역경을 극복하고 살아가다

어휘

diversified investment 분산 투자
overcome 극복하다, 이기다
a couch potato TV를 보며 소파에 앉아 감자를 먹는 게으른 유형의 사람
put all one's eggs in one basket 전 재산을 한 곳에 걸다
lay an egg 손해를 보다   lose heart 실망하다
dead broke 완전히 파산하여, 무일푼이 되어
hit the nail on the head 요점을 정확히 찌르다
keep body and soul together 역경을 극복하고 살아가다

오답률 TOP 3

05 정답 ①

정답해설

① **출제 포인트: 비교급 비교**
해당 문장에서 비교급 'more'가 사용되었으므로 비교급 비교가 쓰인 문장임을 알 수 있다. 비교급 비교의 경우 「주어+동사+비교급+than+비교 대상」의 형태를 가지므로 밑줄 친 'as'를 'than'으로 수정해야 한다. 밑줄 친 'as'를 'as if(마치 ~인 것처럼)'의 'as'로 본다면 '마치 병당 10달러라는 말을 듣는 것처럼 와인 한 병이 병당 90달러라는 말을 들으면 소비자들은 그것을 더 좋아한다.'가 되어 문맥상 어색한 해석이 된다.

오답해설

② **출제 포인트: 동격을 나타내는 명사절의 접속사 that**
밑줄 친 'that'은 뒤따라오는 문장이 완전한 형태이므로 명사 'Belief'와 명사절 'the wine is more expensive'가 동격 관계임을 나타내는 동격의 접속사로 옳게 사용되었다.
③ **출제 포인트: 주어와 동사의 수일치**
밑줄 친 'turns'는 단수 형태의 동사이므로 주어와 수일치 하는지 확인해야 한다. 주어가 단수 형태의 명사 'Belief'이므로 'turns'는 옳은 표현이다. 이때 주어 'Belief'와 동사 'turns' 사이의 'that ~ expensive'는 동격절로 이처럼 주어와 동사 사이의 거리가 먼 경우 수일치에 주의해야한다.
④ **출제 포인트: 현재분사 vs. 과거분사**
밑줄 친 'associated'는 완전타동사 'associate'의 과거분사로, 수식하는 대상 'the brain'과 수동관계이며 해석상 '관련된 뇌'가 자연스러우므로 'associated'는 옳은 표현이다.

해석

소비자들은 와인 한 병이 병당 90달러라는 말을 들으면 병당 10달러라는 말을 듣는 경우보다 그것을 더 좋아한다. 그 와인이 더 비싸다는 믿음은 쾌락 감각과 관련된 뇌의 영역인 중앙의 안와 전두 피질의 신경 세포를 작동시킨다.

어휘

turn on ~을 작동시키다   neuron 신경 세포, 뉴런
medial 중간의, 중앙의   orbitofrontal cortex 안와 전두 피질
associate A with B A를 B와 관련시키다

06 정답 ③

정답해설

③ **출제 포인트: 수동태 불가동사**
불완전자동사는 수동태로 사용할 수 없다. 밑줄 친 'is seemed'는 수동태로 사용할 수 없는 불완전자동사 'seem'을 수동태로 사용하였으므로 옳지 않다. 따라서 'is seemed'를 능동태 'seems'로 수정해야 한다.

오답해설

① 출제 포인트: 가주어 it
밑줄 친 'it'은 가주어이며 진주어는 to부정사(구) 'to feel it once and charge through the difficulties of life without hesitation'이다. 따라서 가주어 'it'의 쓰임은 올바르다.

② 출제 포인트: 수여동사
밑줄 친 'grant'는 수여동사로 이후에 간접목적어 'me'와 직접목적어 'unlimited and never-ending confidence'가 왔으므로 옳게 사용되었다.

④ 출제 포인트: 명사절의 접속사 that
밑줄 친 'that'은 명사절을 이끄는 접속사로 명사절 'you are there for yourself, and you're enough to handle the situation'과 결합하여 'prove'의 목적어 역할을 한다. 따라서 명사절을 이끄는 접속사 'that'의 쓰임은 올바르다.

해석

어떤 사람들은 자신감이 타고난 것이거나, 그것을 한 번 느끼고 망설임 없이 인생의 어려움을 헤쳐 나가는 것이 충분하다고 생각할지도 모른다. 그렇지 않다. 자신감은 분명히 타고난 것이 아니고 보편적인 자신감이라는 것은 없다. 실천과 적극적인 반복이 숙련자를 만든다. 한 번 내 자신의 편이 되어 주는 것은 내 안에 변화를 정말로 일으켰지만, 그것이 나에게 무한하고 끝없는 자신감을 주지는 않았다. 그것은 단지 시작이었고, 내가 나 자신을 지지할 수 있다는 증거였다. 만약 여러분이 자신을 지지한다는 이러한 믿음을 갖는다면, 모든 상황이 더욱 견딜 수 있고 성취 가능하며, 내 경우에는 생존 가능하게 보인다. 여러분이 자신을 지지하며 그 상황을 충분히 처리할 수 있다는 것을 스스로에게 여러 번 입증할수록, 여러분은 더 자신감을 갖게 될 것이다.

어휘

innate 타고난, 선천적인
prove 입증하다, 증명하다
proof 증거
stand up for ~을 옹호하다
charge 돌격하다
handle 다루다, 처리하다

07 정답 ①

정답해설

① 출제 포인트: 관계대명사 vs. 관계부사
밑줄 친 관계대명사 'which' 이후에 오는 절 'the person ~ stuck'이 완전한 형태이므로 'which'를 관계부사로 수정해야 하며, 선행사가 'non-progress'이므로 관계부사 'where'가 적절하다.

오답해설

② 출제 포인트: to부정사의 형용사적 용법
밑줄 친 'to represent'는 to부정사의 형용사적 용법으로 명사 'manner'를 수식하고 있으므로 옳게 사용되었다.

③ 출제 포인트: 현재분사 vs. 과거분사
밑줄 친 'unpredicted'는 'unpredict'의 과거분사로, 수식하는 대상 'solution'과 수동관계이며 해석상 '예측되지 않은 해결책'이 자연스러우므로 'unpredicted'는 옳은 표현이다.

④ 출제 포인트: 능동태 vs. 수동태
'It'은 가주어이며 접속사 'that'이 이끄는 절이 진주어에 해당하므로 밑줄 친 수동태 'been claimed'는 옳은 표현이다.

해석

몇몇 심리학자들은, 통찰력이란 사람이 과거의 경험에 너무 정신을 쏟아서 꼼짝 못 하게 되는 것이라고 믿어지는 정체 시기 후에 문제를 재구성하는 것의 결과라고 믿는다. 문제를 표현할 새로운 방식이 갑자기 발견되어 지금까지 예측되지 않은 해결책으로 가는 다른 길로 이어진다는 것이다. 문제 상황에서 통찰력을 얻기 위해서 어떤 특정한 지식이나 경험이 요구되지 않는다고 주장되어 왔다.

어휘

insight 통찰력
get stuck 꼼짝 못 하게 되다
claim 주장하다
restructure 재구성하다
represent 표현하다, 나타내다
specific 특정한

08 정답 ③

정답해설

본문은 '자원으로서의 시간'에 관한 내용이다. "Even though time management is used a great deal, there really is no such thing as ③ it(시간 관리가 많이 언급되지만, ③ 그것과 같은 것이 실제로 존재하는 것은 아니다)."에서 '그것과 같은 것은 없다'고 언급하고 있으므로, ③의 'it'은 앞서 언급된 'time management(시간 관리)'라는 것을 알 수 있다. 나머지 보기는 모두 'time(시간)'을 가리키고 있으므로 정답은 ③이다.

오답해설

① 이전에서 '시간'에 대해 설명한 후, '그것을 목표 달성을 위한 도구 중 하나로 생각하라'라고 언급하고 있으므로, ①의 'it'은 'time'을 가리킨다는 것을 알 수 있다.
② 앞선 문장에서 '시간을 도구로 생각하라'고 언급하고, 이후에는 효율적으로 그 도구를 사용하는 법에 대해 설명하고 있으므로, 마찬가지로 ② 또한 '시간'을 가리킨다는 것을 알 수 있다.
④ 동일한 속도로 흐르는 것은 '시간'이므로 ④는 '시간'을 가리킨다는 것을 알 수 있다.

해석

시간은 모두에게 동일한 양 – 매일 24시간의 선물 – 이 주어진다는 점에서 독특한 자원이다. 당신이 그 선물을 어떻게 투자하느냐가 당신이 당신의 인생에 대해 어떻게 느끼느냐에 있어서 주요한 요소이다. 당신의 목표를 달성하기 위해 당신이 이용할 수 있는 도구 중 하나로써 ① 그것을 생각해라. 많은 도구와 마찬가지로, 만일 당신이 ② 그것을 효과적으로 사용하길 원한다면, 그것은 약간의 훈련 (또는 재훈련), 투자, 그리고 연습을 필요로 할 것이다. 시간 관리가 많이 언급되지만, ③ 그것과 같은 것이 실제로 존재하는 것은 아니다. 시간을 효과적으로 사용하는 것은 사실 당신의 개인적인 관리의 문제이다. 당신이 무엇을 하든지 ④ 그것은 동일한 속도로 흐른다. 당신은 그것을 빠르게 하거나 느리게 할 수 없다. 당신이 관리하는 다른 자원들과는 달리, 그것을 통제할 수 있는 방법은 없다. 당신이 할 수 있는 최선은 시간의 틀 안에서 스스로를 책임지고, 당신의 인생에서 가장 중요한 일들에 스스로를 투자하는 것이다.

어휘

invest 투자하다
as with …와 같이
a great deal 많이, 상당히
available 이용할[구할] 수 있는
determination 투지, 결정
framework 틀; 체제

09 정답 ④

정답해설

주어진 글의 두 번째 문장에서 "세계 어장의 붕괴를 막는 것을 돕기 위해 남획 문제에 대한 다른 접근법"에 대해 언급하고 있으므로, 이러한 접근법에 대한 구체적인 예시를 언급하는 (C)가 가장 먼저 이어지는 것이 자연스럽다. 이후, (C)의 두 번째 문장에서 언급된 '가리비 어업에 대한 엄격한 통제'의 결과를 설명해주는 (A)가 이어지는 것이 적절하며, 마지막으로, 이러한 가리비의 경우와는 달리 다른 종에게는 다른 접근법이 필요하다는 점을 시사해주는 (B)가 이어지는 것이 자연스럽다. 따라서 정답은 '④ (C) – (A) – (B)'이다.

오답해설

나머지 보기는 문맥상 어색하므로 오답이다.

해석

많은 세계의 주요 어업 구역이 이미 그들의 자연적인 한계 이상으로 조업 되어 왔다. 세계 어장의 붕괴를 막는 것을 돕기 위해 남획 문제에 대한 다른 접근법이 고려되고 있다.

(C) 예를 들어, 한때 북대서양에서 가장 비옥한 어장 중 하나였던 Georges Bank는 현재 폐쇄되었으며 상업적으로 쇠퇴하였다고 여겨진다. 이 지역은 1996년 가리비 어업에 엄격한 통제를 받았고, 이는 그 현장의 그 종에게 실행 가능한 구제 방안이라는 것이 증명되었다.

(A) 가리비 개체 수는 본래 개체 수를 능가하는 수준에 도달하며 5년 이내에 회복되었고, 그 만의 일부는 가리비 어업을 위해 재개장될 수 있었다.

(B) 그러나 Georges Bank의 다른 종들은 계속해서 감소하고 있다. 신속하고 직접적인 보충은 성숙하는데 수년이 걸리는 천천히 자라는 종에게는 가능하지 않다.

어휘

overfishing (어업) 남획
under consideration 고려[생각] 중인
collapse 붕괴   fishery 어장
population 개체 수
in excess of ~을 초과하여, ~이상의[으로]
bay 만(灣)   replenishment 보충, 보급
maturity 성숙   fertile 비옥한, 기름진, 풍부한
fishing ground 어장   extinct 쇠퇴한, 활동을 그친
undergo 겪다, 받다   scallop 가리비
viable 실행 가능한, 성공할 수 있는 remedy 구제 방안
locale 현장, 무대

오답률 TOP 2

10 정답 ③

정답해설

주어진 문장은 '테러리즘은 과학적(객관적) 설명보다는 이론적/의견적 설명에 관해 특징지어진다', 즉, 테러리즘의 원인을 규정하는 것이 어렵다고 설명하고 있다. 글의 전체 내용으로 볼 때, ③ 이전까지는 '테러리즘의 원인 정의의 어려움'에 대해 언급하고 있고, ③ 이후부터는 'But'을 이용해, '그렇지만 수많은 심리학자들이 신뢰할만한 자료를 수집하고 있다'고 설명하며, '테러리즘의 원인을 설명할 수 있는 객관적인 자료가 준비되고 있다는 점을 시사하고 있다. 따라서 주어진 문장은 ①, ②, ③ 중 한 곳에 들어가는 것이 자연스럽다는 것을 알 수 있으며, 주어진 문장의 'Given these complexities(이러한 복잡성들을 고려해 볼 때)'로 보아 'these complexities(이러한 복잡성)'가 가리키는 내용이 주어진 문장 이전에 등장하는 것이 자연스럽다는 것을 알 수 있다. 따라서 '테러리즘의 원인을 규정하기 어려운 이유를 나타내는 문장인 "For one thing, terrorists aren't likely to volunteer as experimental subjects, and examining their activities from afar can lead to erroneous conclusions(우선 첫째로, 테러리스트들은 실험의 대상으로서 자원하는 것이 아니며, 멀리서 그들의 행위를 검토하는 것은 잘못된 결론으로 이어질 수 있다)."와 "What's more, one group's terrorist is another group's freedom fighter, as the millions of Arabs who support Palestinian suicide bombers will attest(게다가, 팔레스타인의 자살 폭탄 테러범을 지지하는 수백만의 아랍인들이 증명하듯이, 한 집단의 테러리스트는 다른 집단의 자유의 전사이다)."가 모두 등장한 후 주어진 문장이 제시되는 것이 자연스럽다. 따라서 정답은 ③이다.

오답해설

② 이후의 내용인 '한 집단의 테러리스트가 다른 집단의 자유의 전사일 수도 있다'는 내용 또한 'these complexities'가 가리킬 수 있는 '복잡성'에 해당하므로, 주어진 문장 이전에 등장하는 것이 더 자연스럽다.

나머지 위치는 문맥상 어색하므로 오답이다.

해석

무엇이 사람들을 테러리즘으로 빠지게 하는지 알아내는 것은 쉬운 일이 아니다. (①) 우선 첫째로, 테러리스트들은 실험의 대상으로서 자원하지 않을 것이며, 멀리서 그들의 행위를 검토하는 것은 잘못된 결론으로 이어질 수 있다. (②) 게다가, 팔레스타인의 자살 폭탄 테러범을 지지하는 수백만의 아랍인들이 증명하듯이, 한 집단의 테러리스트는 다른 집단의 자유의 전사이다. (③ **이러한 복잡성들을 고려해 볼 때, 테러리즘의 심리학은 확실한 과학보다는 이론과 의견에 의해 더 많이 특징지어진다고 연구자들은 인정한다.**) 그러나 수많은 심리학자들이 신뢰할 만한 자료를 한데 모으기 시작하고 있다. (④) 그들은 테러리즘을 개인보다는 정치적이고 집단적인 역학과 과정의 관점에서 바라보는 것이 일반적으로 더 유용하다는 것을 밝혀내고 있다. 그리고 우리의 잠재적인 죽음에 대한 공포 및 의미와 개인적 중요성에 대한 우리의 욕구와 같은 보편적 심리학적인 원칙들 또한 테러리스트 행위의 일부 양상과 그것들에 대한 우리의 반응을 설명하는 데 도움이 될지도 모른다.

어휘

given …을 고려해 볼 때   mark 특징[성격] 짓다
good (판단·주장 등이) 사리에 닿는, 타당한, 확실한
determine 밝히다, 알아내다
drive (남을 어떤 상태·행위에) 빠지게[이르게] 하다
for one thing (여러 가지 이유들 중에서) 우선 한 가지 이유는
from afar 멀리서   erroneous 잘못된
attest 증명[입증]하다   in terms of … 면에서[…에 관하여]
principle 원리, 원칙, 법칙   subconscious 잠재의식적인
meaning 의미, 뜻; 목적, 취지   significance 중요성; 의의, 의미

결국엔 성정혜 영어 하프모의고사
기적사 복습 모의고사 5회

01	②	02	④	03	③	04	①	05	④
06	①	07	②	08	③	09	③	10	②
11	③	12	①	13	①	14	③	15	④
16	②	17	④	18	②	19	③	20	②

01 정답 ② — Day 47-03

정답해설

밑줄 친 'deteriorating'은 '악화되다, 더 나빠지다'를 뜻하는 'deteriorate'의 현재분사 형태로 ② aggravating과 의미가 가장 가깝다.

해석

생태계와 자연보호에 대한 그들의 중대한 기여는 급속하게 **악화 중인** 생태계에 엄청난 변화를 가져왔고 야생동물 서식지들을 복원시켰다.
① 다치지 않은, 아무 탈 없는
② 악화하는
③ 쇠퇴하는, 퇴화하는
④ 개량의, 개선적인

02 정답 ④ — Day 46-01

정답해설

동의어 문제가 아닌 의미가 가장 먼 것을 찾는 다소 생소한 문항이다. 밑줄 친 'essential'은 '아주 중요한'을 뜻하며 'crucial(중대한), indispensable(필수적인), requisite(필요한)'과 의미가 동일하다. ④ omnipresent의 경우 접두어 omni는 all(全)에 해당되는 표현으로 「omni + competent(전(全)권을 가지는)」와 「omni + potent(전(全)지전능한)」의 의미를 갖는다. 따라서 '어디에나 있는'의 뜻으로, '아주 중요한'의 의미인 'essential'과는 의미가 멀다.

해석

수정의 전제 조건으로서, 수분 작용은 과일과 씨앗용 작물들의 생산에 **아주 중요하고**, 번식으로 식물을 개선시키기 위해 만들어진 프로그램에서 중요한 역할을 한다.
① 중대한
② 필수적인
③ 필요한
④ 어디에나 있는, 편재하는

03 정답 ③ — Day 49-02

정답해설

밑줄 친 'deplorable'은 '개탄스러운'을 뜻하는 형용사로 ③ lamentable과 의미가 가장 가깝다.

해석

인종 차별주의는 **개탄스럽고** 그러한 민감한 발언들을 게시한 것에 대해 그 학생이 끔찍한 사람일지라도, 그 학생의 처벌은 옳지 않다.
① 오만한, 거만한
② 자랑하는
③ 한탄스러운, 통탄할
④ 감명 깊은, 훌륭한

04 정답 ① — Day 41-01

정답해설

접속사 'but'으로 보아 맛이 없었던 음식에 양념을 쳐서 '맛있게' 만들었다는 흐름이 알맞음을 유추할 수 있다. 따라서 빈칸에 들어갈 가장 적절한 것은 ① palatable이다.

해석

우리의 메인 음식은 그다지 맛있지 않았지만, 나는 양념을 첨가하여 그것을 더 **맛있게** 만들었다.
① 맛있는, 맛 좋은
② 분해할 수 있는
③ 마셔도 되는
④ 예민한

05 정답 ④ — Day 41-03

정답해설

두 문화가 완전히 '다르기' 때문에 그녀가 한 문화에서 다른 문화로 적응하기 힘들었다고 하는 것이 흐름상 적절하므로 가장 적절한 것은 ④ disparate이다.

해석

두 문화가 아주 완전히 **달라서** 그녀는 한 문화에서 다른 문화로 적응하기 힘들다는 것을 발견했다.
① 겹쳐진
② 동등한, 맞먹는
③ 연합의, 결합하기 쉬운
④ 다른, 공통점이 없는

06 정답 ① — Day 43-07

정답해설

① 출제 포인트: 부가의문문
부가의문문은 주절이 긍정문이면 부정의문문의 형태를, 주절이 부정문이면 긍정의문문의 형태를 사용해야 한다. 해당 문장의 경우 주절에 부정부사 'hardly'가 있으므로 부정문임을 알 수 있다. 따라서 부가의문문에 긍정의문문의 형태인 'is he?'를 사용하는 것이 옳다.

해석

① Tom은 자신이 틀렸음을 좀처럼 인정할 것 같지가 않아, 그렇지?
② 그 전체 과정은 중앙 정부의 안정에 거의 도움이 되지 않는다.
③ 몇몇 사람들은 왜 우리가 폭력과 타락을 찬양하는 대중문화를 용인하는 것이냐고 묻는다.
④ 만약에 우리가 지방 정부에 돈을 더 제공한다면, 지방 정부는 이 문제를 더 쉽게 해결할 것이다.

07 정답 ② — Day 48-10

정답해설

본문은 '최초의 민간인을 대상으로 한 테러 공격이었던 1894년 2월 12일 발생한 Gare Saint-Lazare의 Café Terminus 폭탄 테러'에 관한 내용이다. 테러가 일어나기 전, 카페에서는 많은 사람들이 오케스트라의 연주를 듣고 있었다. 본문 중반 "He had placed a bomb in a metal workman's lunchbox and hurled it at the orchestra(그는 금속으로 된 노동자의 도시락에 폭탄을 넣고, 그것을 오케스트라를 향해 던졌다)."를 통해, 범인이 연주 중이던 오케스트라에게 금속 도시락에 폭탄을 숨기고 던진 사실을 알 수 있으므로, 글의 내용과 일치하는 것은 '② An attacker threw a hidden bomb at the musicians(공격자는 음악가들을 향해 숨겨진 폭탄을 던졌다).'이다.

해석

1894년 2월 12일 해가 질 무렵, 음악이 갑자기 멈추었을 때 Gare Saint-Lazare에 있는 Café Terminus는 오케스트라를 듣고 있는 젊은 파리 지앵들로 가득 차 있었다. 불덩이가 시야 안에 있는 모든 것을 삼켰다: 세상은 암흑으로 변했다. 생존자들이 정신을 차렸을 때, 그들 주변에 신체 부위들의 조각이 있었고, 사람들은 화염에 휩싸여 달려가고 비명을 지르고 있었다. 그것은 Emile Henry라고 불리는 말쑥하게 차려입은 20세의 프랑스인 회계사의 짓이었다. 그는 금속으로 된 노동자의 도시락에 폭탄을 넣고, 그것을 오케스트라를 향해 던졌다. 이것은 개인이 민간인을 무차별적으로 날려버린 최초의 일이었다. 그는 폭탄 테러의 현장에서 체포되었다. 그는 한 가지 후회가 있다고 말했다: 그가 더 많은 "부르주아"를 죽이지 못했다"는 것이다. 만일 그가 충분히 큰 폭탄을 가지고 있었더라면, 그는 파리 전체를 날려버렸을 것이라고 허풍을 쳤다. Henry가 21세의 나이에 사형당한 후, 무정부주의자들에 의해 자행된 일련의 보복 폭탄 테러가 프랑스를 휩쓸었다.
① 2월 12일의 공격은 무정부주의자 단체에 의해 수행되었다.
② 공격자는 음악가들을 향해 숨겨진 폭탄을 던졌다.
③ Emile Henry는 잡히지 않고 폭탄 테러 현장을 간신히 빠져나왔다.
④ Emile Henry는 무고한 사람들을 뜻하지 않게 죽인 것을 후회했다.

08 정답 ③ — Day 48-07

정답해설

③ **출제 포인트: 형용사 vs. 부사/등위접속사의 병렬구조**
밑줄 친 'poor'와 등위접속사 'or'를 통해 병렬구조를 이루고 있는 'wrong'은 동사 'do'를 수식하는 부사이다. 따라서 형용사 'poor'를 부사 'poorly'로 수정해야 한다.

해석

사람들이 그들이 해야만 하는 일들을 계속해서 미루는 한 가지 이유는 그들이 그 일들을 잘못하거나 제대로 못 하는 것을 두려워하기 때문인데, 그래서 그들은 그 일들을 아예 하지 않는다. 예를 들어, 책을 쓰는 최고의 방법들 중 하나는 문제는 고려하지 않고 당신의 생각을 종이에 옮겨 적으면서 그것을 가능한 빨리 쓰는 것이다. 그리고 나서, 당신은 당신의 글을 개정하고 다듬기 위해 되돌아갈 수 있다.

09 정답 ③ — Day 46-09

정답해설

첫 문장에서 어업을 지속하기 위해서 과학의 도움이 필요하다고 제시했고, 어떻게 어업이 과학의 도움을 받을 수 있는지에 대한 내용이 전개되고 있다. 즉, 포획하는 물고기의 개체 수를 꼭 알맞게 유지해야 물고기 개체 수 고갈 없이 어업을 지속해나갈 수 있으며, 이를 돕는 연구가 계속 진행되고 있다고 하였으므로 글의 제목으로 가장 적절한 것은 ③ 'Why Does the Fishing Industry Need Science(왜 어업에 과학이 필요한가)?'이다.

해석

과학자의 도움으로, 상업성을 띠는 어업은 그것이 계속되어야 한다면 어업이 과학적으로 행해져야 함을 깨달았다. 물고기 개체 수에 대한 어떠한 어업 압력이 없다면, 물고기의 수는 예상 가능한 풍부한 수준에 도달하여 머무를 것이다. 유일한 변동성은 먹이의 이용 가능성, 적절한 온도와 같은 자연 환경적인 요소들에 기인할 것이다. 만약 어장이 이러한 물고기들을 잡도록 발달된다면, 그들의 개체 수는 어획량이 적은 한 유지될 수 있을 것이다. 북해의 고등어가 좋은 예이다. 만약 우리가 어장을 늘려 매년 더 많은 물고기를 잡아들인다면, 우리는 우리가 매년 잡는 물고기 전체를 대체할 수 있는 이상적인 지점 아래로 개체 수를 감소시키지 않도록 주의해야만 한다. 우리가 최대 유지 생산량이라고 불리는 이 수준에서 포획한다면, 우리는 매년 가능한 최대 생산량을 유지할 수 있다. 만약 우리가 너무 많이 포획해 버리면, 물고기의 수는 매년 줄어 어업을 할 수 없는 수준이 될 것이다. 과도하게 남획된 동물의 예로 남극의 대왕고래와 북대서양의 넙치가 있다. 매해 최대치의 생산량을 유지하기 위해 꼭 맞는 양만 포획하는 것은 과학이자 예술이다. 우리가 물고기 개체 수를 이해하도록 하고 어떻게 개체 수의 고갈 없이 최대한으로 그것을 이용할 수 있는지를 이해하도록 돕기 위한 연구는 계속해서 진행되고 있다.
① 상업적인 어업에 반대하라
② 어업으로 간주되는 바다 양식업
③ 왜 어업에 과학이 필요한가?
④ 남획된 동물들: 불법 어업의 사례들

10 정답 ② — Day 45-08

정답해설

본문의 요지는 '(인적) 관계는 그것이 필요하기 전에 미리 수립해놓는 것이 바람직하며, 오직 필요한 순간에만 인맥에 의지하려 하는 것은 잘못된 방식이다'라는 것이다. 즉, 항상 인맥 관리를 꾸준히 그리고 미리 해 놓는 것이 중요하다는 내용이다. 그런데 ②에서는 '부탁을 하는 방식'에 대해 설명하고 있으므로, 글 전체의 흐름에 부합하지 않는다. 따라서 글의 흐름상 어색한 것은 ②이다.

해석

지구상에서 가장 성공한 팟캐스터 중 한 사람인 Jordan Harbinger는 당신이 미리 관계를 수립해야 할 필요가 있다고 말한다. ① 우리는 모두, 그 사람이 단지 부탁을 하기 위해 당신에게 아첨을 할 때, 당신의 안부를 묻는 "척하는" 이메일의 수신자가 되어본 적이 있다. 이것은 인맥에 의지하는 잘못된 방식이다. 올바른 방식은 사회적 자본을 오랜 시간 동안 축적하는 것이다. ② **당신의 인맥 내의 누군가에게 부탁을 할 때, 이메일을 통하지 않고 직접 대면하여 그렇게 하는 것이 더 낫다.** 단지 당신이 무언가를 필요로 할 때뿐만 아니라, 지속적으로 사람들과 연락하라. 당신이 그들을 필요로 할 때 사람들을 찾기 시작하면 너무 늦는다. ③ 관계는 오랜 시간 동안 더 깊어지므로, 씨를 빨리 심는 것이 모든 차이를 만든다. Harbinger는 "당신이 필요하기도 전에 관계를 확립하는 것이 핵심이다."라고 말한다. ④ 사실, 그는 당신이 그것들을 결코 필요로 하지 않을 것이라고 가정할 것을 추천한다. "그것은 마치 당신의 타이어가 펑크가 나기 전에 당신의 자동차의 트렁크에 타이어를 넣는 것과 같다"고 그는 말한다. 당신은 타이어 펑크를 계획하지 않는다. 그리고 최선의 시나리오에서, 당신은 스페어타이어를 결코 사용하지 않는다.

11 정답 ③ — Day 48-04

정답해설

아들과 엄마는 부엌의 오븐에서 구워지고 있는 사과파이에 관해 대화를 나눈다. 아들이 부엌에서 나는 냄새를 맡고 오븐 안을 궁금해하면서 만지려고 하자, 엄마는 "조심해!"라고 말하며 '③ Curiosity killed the cat(많이 알려고 하면 다친다)'라고 말한다.

해석

아들: 엄마, 이 냄새 부엌에서 나는 거예요? 사과파이 냄새 같아요.
엄마: 너 오늘 집에 늦게 오는 줄 알았는데. 그래서 널 깜짝 놀래 주기 위해 이것을 구우려고 했어.
아들: 고마워요, 엄마! 전 엄마가 만든 사과파이가 정말 좋아요! 아직 오븐 안에 있어요?

엄마: 응, 아직 준비가 안 됐어. 내가 계획한 대로 널 놀래줄 수 없어서 아쉽구나.
아들: 저에게는 깜짝 선물 같아요. 빨리 맛보고 싶어요!
엄마: 조심해! 오븐 만지지 마, 되게 뜨거워!
아들: 오, 저 오븐을 거의 만질 뻔했어요! 파이가 잘 구워지고 있는지 보려고 안 보고 싶어요.
엄마: 많이 알려고 하면 다친다. 난 네가 다치지 않길 원해.
① 계속 이대로 둘 수는 없다[더 이상은 안 된다]
② 드디어 이야기가 되네
③ 많이 알려고 하면 다친다
④ 정말 그래

12 정답 ②
Day 42-04

(정답해설)
A는 B에게 '부탁을 하나 해도 되는지' 묻는다. 그러자 B는 자신이 '가장 좋아하는 책이 해리포터'라고 대답한다. 이는 A의 질문에 대한 적절한 대답이 아니다.

(해석)
① A: 나는 다리 전체에 멍이 들었어.
   B: 무슨 일이야? 너 뭐에 걸려 넘어졌어?
② A: 내 부탁 하나만 들어줄 수 있어?
   B: 내가 가장 좋아하는 책은 해리포터야.
③ A: 마을 전체에 소방차가 있어.
   B: 나는 몇 분 전에 사이렌 소리를 들었어.
④ A: 나는 오늘 아침에 기상 예보를 확인했어.
   B: 잘했어! 오늘 비와?

13 정답 ①
Day 44-05

(정답해설)
① 출제 포인트: to부정사의 부사적 용법(in order not to+동사원형)
「in order not to+동사원형」은 관용표현으로 '~하지 않기 위해'를 뜻하며 to부정사의 부사적 용법에 해당한다. 해당 문장은 주어진 해석과 일치하므로 옳은 문장이다. 또한 「in order not to+동사원형」은 「so as not to+동사원형」과 바꾸어 사용할 수 있다.

14 정답 ③
Day 47-06

(정답해설)
③ 출제 포인트: 능동태 vs. 수동태/부정부사(구) 도치
'restrict'는 완전타동사이므로 이후에 목적어가 온다. 밑줄 친 'do they restrict'의 경우 이후에 목적어가 아닌 수식어(구) 'to their immediate locale'이 왔으므로 해당 문장이 수동태임을 알 수 있다. 따라서 'do they restrict'를 수동태로 수정해야 하며, 이때 문두에 부정부사(구) 'No longer'가 있으므로 'are they restricted'로 수정해야 한다.

(해석)
부모는 자신들의 유아가 고개를 들고, 물건을 집으러 손을 뻗고, 스스로 앉고 혼자서 걷자마자 친구와 친척들에게 알리는데 빠르다. 이러한 운동 기능의 성취에 대한 부모의 열성은 전혀 잘못된 것이 아닌데, 왜냐하면 그것들은 실제로 발달의 중요한 단계들이기 때문이다. 각각의 추가적인 기술로 아기들은 새로운 방식으로 자신들의 신체와 환경에 대한 통제력을 얻는다. 혼자서 앉을 수 있는 유아는 하루의 많은 부분을 눕거나 엎드려 보내는 유아들에 비해 세상에 대한 완전히 다른 시각을 부여받게 된다. 근육의 공동 작용에 의한 뻗치기는 사물의 탐구에 대한 온전히 새로운 길을 열어 주며, 아기들이 돌아다닐 수 있을 때 독립적인 탐구와 조작을 위한 기회는 크게 증가된다. 그들은 이제 더 이상 자신들에게 가까운 장소나 다른 사람들이 그들의 앞에 놓아두는 사물들에만 제한되어 있지 않다. 환경을 통제하는 새로운 방식이 성취되면서, 운동 능력의 발달은 유아에게 능력과 숙달에 대한 증가하는 인식을 제공하고 그것은 세상에 대한 유아의 지각 및 인지적 이해에 중요한 방식으로 기여한다.

15 정답 ④
Day 47-09

(정답해설)
(A) 이전에는 "In future decades ocean warming and acidification can affect growth and reproduction processes of many marine organisms, which may reduce stocks available for many significant commercial species(장차 몇십 년 후, 해양 온난화와 산성화는 많은 해양 생물의 성장 및 번식 과정에 영향을 미칠 수 있으며, 이것이 상업 종으로 이용 가능한 중요한 개체군 다수를 감소시킬 수도 있다)."라고 언급하며, '해양 산성화가 개체군 감소를 야기할 수 있다'고 설명한다. 이어서 개체군 감소가 가능한 '산성화'에 민감한 특정 생물을 구체적으로 예시를 들어 제시하고 있으므로, (A)에 가장 적절한 표현은 'As an example' 또는 'For instance'이다.
(B) 이전에는 '기후 변화'가 해양에 미치는 부정적 영향에 대해 설명하고 있다. 이어서 (B) 이후에서 이러한 '기후 변화'에 대응하지 않고 계속하여 온실가스를 배출한다면 발생할 결과에 대해 언급하고 있다. 따라서 (B)에는 '결과'를 나타내는 'Eventually'가 들어가는 것이 자연스럽다. 따라서 정답은 '④ For instance(예를 들어) - Eventually(결국)'이다.

(해석)
과학 연구는 기후 변화가 해양에 미치는 영향이 이미 어장에 영향을 미쳤다는 것을 보여준다. 몇몇 냉수종의 풍부함이 감소하고 있는 반면, 일부 열대 종이 우리의 해안에 나타나고 있다. 장차 몇십 년 후, 해양 온난화와 산성화는 많은 해양 생물의 성장 및 번식 과정에 영향을 미칠 수 있으며, 이것이 상업 종으로 이용 가능한 중요한 개체군 다수를 감소시킬 수도 있다. (A) 예를 들어, 굴과 홍합과 같은 조개류는 특히 산성화에 민감하다. 기후 변화는 또한 해양 먹이 사슬의 핵심인 박테리아와 식물성 플랑크톤 군락에 영향을 미칠 것이다. (B) 결국 만일 우리가 현 속도로 계속 온실가스를 발생시킨다면, 생물 다양성 측면에서 세기말 전에 예상되는 변화들은 과거 2천만 년 또는 3천만 년 전 발생했던 변화와 유사할 수도 있다.

	(A)	(B)
①	결과적으로	대조적으로
②	즉	그러나
③	예를 들어	그럼에도 불구하고
④	예를 들어	결국

16 정답 ②
Day 42-08

(정답해설)
본문은 성공한 사람들에게 있어서 중요한 것은 '인맥(connections)'이 아닌 '일의 성과(the results of work)'라는 것을 설명하고 있다. 빈칸에는 'producing good work(좋은 성과를 내는 것)'가 'most of the need to network(인맥 형성의 필요성)'를 어떻게 변화시켜 주는지 설명하는 단어가 들어가는 것이 가장 적절하다. 본문 마지막 문장 "It's the results of work — and not necessarily exposing yourself to as many people as possible — that attracts more and varied opportunities outside of that work(그 업무 외부에서 더 많고 다양한 기회를 이끌어주는 것은, 반드시 가능한 한 많은 사람들에게 자신을 노출하는 것이 아니라, 바로 업무의 결과이다.)"를 통해 '업무의 성과를 통해 더 많은 기회에 접근할 수 있다'는 것을 알 수 있으므로, 빈칸에는 '줄이다, 완화하다'라는 의미의 단어가 들어가는 것

이 가장 적절하다. 따라서 정답은 ② 'attenuate(줄이다, 약하게 하다)'이다.

해석

인맥 형성하는 것을 좋아하지 않는 사람들은 어떻게 그들의 직종에서 성공을 할까? 훌륭한 업무를 수행하는 것이 인맥을 형성할 필요성의 대부분을 어떻든 줄여준다는 – 몇몇 증거로 뒷받침되는 – 희망이 있다. 지식 기반 직종에서 사람들이 어떻게 엘리트 수준에 도달하는지 탐구하는 컴퓨터 공학자인 Cal Newport는 그의 연구를 하는 동안 몇몇의 로즈 장학생들을 인터뷰했고, 그들 중 많은 이들의 성공으로의 경로가 종종 잘못 알려져 있다는 것을 발견했다. 그는 "로즈 장학생들은 인맥 또는 운에 의존하기보다는 적은 수의 일(보통 두 가지)을 굉장히 잘하는 것에 많은 양의 에너지를 투자한다"고 적었다. 그 업무 외부에서 더 많고 다양한 기회를 이끌어주는 것은 – 반드시 가능한 한 많은 사람들에게 자신을 노출하는 것이 아니라 – 바로 업무의 결과이다.
① 심화시키다
② 줄이다, 약하게 하다
③ 경각시키다
④ 죽이다

17 정답 ④   Day 43-10

정답해설

본문은 다양한 '노후 지원 기술'에 대해 설명하는 글이며, 빈칸에는 이러한 기술들이 광범위하게 시행되고 있지 못하는 이유를 설명하는 표현이 들어가야 한다. 마지막 문장 "On the one hand, they recognize that such technologies could support independent living of the older population, while on the other hand, they do not feel that they themselves personally need them(한편으로는, 그들은 그러한 기술이 고령 인구의 독립적인 삶을 지원해줄 수 있다는 것을 인식하지만, 반면 다른 한편으로는, 그들 자신이 개인적으로 그것들이 필요하다고 생각하지 않는다)." 을 통해, '노인들이 기술의 이점을 인정하지만, 실제로 자신들에게 필요하다고는 생각하지 않는 것'에 대해 언급하고 있으므로, '기술에 대한 양면적 태도'를 지니고 있다는 것을 알 수 있다. 따라서 빈칸에 가장 적절한 것은 '④ ambivalent attitude towards(~에 대한 양면적인 태도)'이다.

해석

응급 구호 시스템, 활력 징후 모니터링, 낙상 감지 시스템과 같은 다양한 유형의 기술이 살던 곳에서 노후를 맞는 것을 돕기 위해 특별히 설계되었다. 이러한 기술들은 때때로 스마트 홈 기술이라고 일컬어진다. 또한, 고령자의 만성질환 자가 관리를 돕기 위한 온라인 도구를 포함한 광범위한 기술을 망라하는 e-Health도 있다. 그러나 이러한 기술들은 다양한 이유로 인해 대규모로 시행되어오고 있지 못하다. 그 이유 중 하나는 고령자들의 기술의 이러한 유형에 대한 양면적인 태도이다. 한편으로는, 그들은 그러한 기술이 고령 인구의 독립적인 삶을 지원해줄 수 있다는 것을 인식하지만, 반면 다른 한편으로는, 그들 자신이 개인적으로 그것들이 필요하다고 생각하지 않는다.
① ~에 대한 빈틈없는 접근
② ~에 대한 일반적인 선호
③ ~에 대한 만연한 무지
④ ~에 대한 양면적인 태도

18 정답 ④   Day 45-09

정답해설

본문은 '고부담 시험(high-stakes exam)이 학생, 교사, 부모, 나아가 학교 교육에 미치는 영향'에 대해 설명하고 있다. 본문 초반의 내용을 통해 '고부담 시험은 인생에서의 더 나은 방향으로의 전환을 가능하게 하며, (성공적으로 치른다면), 재정, 인식, 평판에도 좋은 영향을 미칠 수 있다'는 것을 유추할 수 있다. 그러나 본문은 이러한 '중요성'으로 인해, 교육의 진정한 목적과 본질이 변질될 수 있으며, 학생들은 오직 시험 준비만을 위한 학습에 매진하여 스트레스, 불안, 우울함에 빠지고 극단적인 경우에는 학교 폭력 또는 자살에 이를 수도 있다는 사실을 명시하고 있다. 따라서 글의 요지로 가장 적절한 보기는 '④ Although high-stakes exams have some advantages, they also can produce negative effects(고부담 시험이 이점이 있지만, 그것은 또한 부정적인 영향을 초래할 수도 있다).'이다.

해석

고부담 시험은 종종 학습자의 미래를 결정한다: 이동, 졸업, 또는 고등 교육, 더 나은 학교 또는 더 나은 직종으로의 진입을 말한다. 시험 결과가 재정, 인식, 그리고 명성에 영향을 미칠 수 있기 때문에, 이러한 시험들은 학생들에게 뿐만 아니라, 교사, 학교 그리고 가족에게도 큰 부담이 된다. 일부의 경우에, 부담이 너무 커서 시험들이 학교 교육의 목적과 본질에 대한 사고를 지배할 수 있다. 학생들은 끊임없이 시험을 준비하고, 학생들과 부모들은 계속해서 학업적 성공에 대해 염려하며, 학생들에게 가해지는 잘해야 한다는 압박은 학교 폭력뿐만 아니라 스트레스, 불안, 우울함 그리고 심지어 자살로 이어질 수 있다. 게다가, '고득점'에 맞추어진 초점은 테스트와 시험에서 종종 얻어지지 않는 학습의 여타 기본적인 측면과 교육 시스템이 교육의 진정한 가치와 목적을 잃은 것은 아닌지에 대한 의문들을 약화시키고 있을지도 모른다.
① 고부담 시험은 효과적이며 학교 교육과 학습을 향상시키기 위해 필요하다.
② 고부담 시험은 많은 문제를 야기하고 있기 때문에 폐지되어야 한다.
③ 고부담 시험에서 점수를 잘 받는 것이 한 학생의 미래에 큰 차이를 만들 수 있다.
④ 고부담 시험이 몇몇의 이점이 있지만, 그것은 또한 부정적인 영향을 초래할 수도 있다.

19 정답 ③   Day 50-10

정답해설

주어진 문장은 '테러리즘은 과학적(객관적) 설명보다는 이론적/의견적 설명에 관해 특징지어진다', 즉, 테러리즘의 원인을 규정하는 것이 어렵다고 설명하고 있다. 글의 전체 내용으로 볼 때, ③ 이전까지는 '테러리즘의 원인 정의의 어려움'에 대해 언급하고 있고, ③ 이후부터는 'But'을 이용해, '그렇지만 수많은 심리학자들이 신뢰할만한 자료를 수집하고 있다'고 설명하며, '테러리즘의 원인을 설명할 수 있는 객관적인 자료가 준비되고 있다는 점을 시사하고 있다. 따라서 주어진 문장은 ①, ②, ③ 중 한 곳에 들어가는 것이 자연스럽다는 것을 알 수 있으며, 주어진 문장의 'Given these complexities(이러한 복잡성들을 고려해 볼 때)'로 보아 'these complexities(이러한 복잡성)'가 가리키는 내용이 주어진 문장 이전에 등장하는 것이 자연스럽다는 것을 알 수 있다. 따라서 '테러리즘의 원인을 규정하기 어려운 이유를 나타내는 문장인 "For one thing, terrorists aren't likely to volunteer as experimental subjects, and examining their activities from afar can lead to erroneous conclusions(우선 첫째로, 테러리스트들은 실험의 대상으로서 자원하는 것이 아니며, 멀리서 그들의 행위를 검토하는 것은 잘못된 결론으로 이어질 수 있다)."와 "What's more, one group's terrorist is another group's freedom fighter, as the millions of Arabs who support Palestinian suicide bombers will attest(게다가, 팔레스타인의 자살 폭탄 테러범을 지지하는 수백만의 아랍인들이 증명하듯이, 한 집단의 테러리스트는 다른 집단의 자유의 전사이다)."가 모두 등장한 후 주어진 문장이 제시되는 것이 자연스럽다. 따라서 정답은 ③이다.

해석

무엇이 사람들을 테러리즘으로 빠지게 하는지 알아내는 것은 쉬운 일이 아니다. (①) 우선 첫째로, 테러리스트들은 실험의 대상으로서 자원하지 않을 것이며, 멀리서 그들의 행위를 검토하는 것은 잘못된 결론으로 이어질 수 있다. (②) 게다가, 팔레스타인의 자살 폭탄 테러범을 지지하는 수백만의 아랍인들이 증명하듯이, 한 집단의 테러리스트는 다른 집단의 자유의 전사이다. (③ **이러한 복잡성들을 고려해 볼 때, 테러리즘의 심리학은 확실한 과학보다는 이론과 의견에 의해 더 많이 특징지어진다고 연구자들은 인정한다.**) 그러나 수많은 심리학자들이 신뢰할 만한 자료를 한데 모으기 시작하고 있다. (④) 그들은 테러리즘을 개인보다는 정치적이고 집단적인 역학과 과정의 관점에서 바라보는 것이 일반적으로 더 유용하다는 것을 밝혀내고 있다. 그리고 우리의 잠재적인 죽음에 대한 공포 및 의미와 개인적 중요성에 대한 우리의 욕구와 같은 보편적 심리학적인 원칙들 또한 테러리스트 행위의 일부 양상과 그것들에 대한 우리의 반응을 설명하는 데 도움이 될지도 모른다.

20 정답 ②
Day 49-08

정답해설
주어진 문장에서는 '과식하는 사람'을 언급하며, '능력보다 더 많은 것을 하려 하는 사람'에 대해 설명하고 있다. 이후 이어질 내용으로 가장 알맞은 것은 '시간 관리 측면'에서 '과식하는 사람'과 같이, '능력치보다 더 많은 업무를 떠맡는 사람'에 대해 언급하고 있는 (A)가 이어지는 것이 자연스럽다. 이후, '이러한 행위(This behavior)'로 시작하며 (A)에서 언급된 행동을 가리키는 (C)가 이어지는 것이 알맞다. 마지막으로 (C)에서 설명한 '비효율적이고 스트레스를 주는 업무 방식'을 바로잡기 위한 방법을 설명하고 있는 (B)가 이어지는 것이 적절하다. 따라서 정답은 '② (A) - (C) - (B)'이다.

해석
과식하는 사람들은 종종 '위보다 더 큰 눈'을 가지고 있는 것으로 묘사된다.
(A) 시간 관리에서 이와 상당하는 것은 기존의 업무 약속을 완전히 무시한 채 매력적이고 흥미진진해 보이는 점점 더 많은 프로젝트를 떠맡는 사람이다.
(C) 이러한 행동은 Type A 노동 방식의 전형이며, 최종 결과는 '접시돌리기'이다 – 하나의 미완결 업무로부터 다른 것으로 서둘러 이동하며, 짧은 한 바탕의 노력을 쏟아내고 아무 접시도 바닥에 깨지지 않길 희망한다. 이는 매우 비효율적인 방식의 노동일뿐만 아니라, 매우 스트레스를 준다.
(B) 당신의 업무량에 대한 통제를 회복하기 위해, 현실 직시는 필수적이다. 당신의 할 일 목록에 있는 모든 일의 우선순위를 정하고 각각의 업무가 완료되기 위해 얼마나 오래 걸리는지 추정하라.

기적사 DAY 51

결국엔 성정혜 영어 하프모의고사

| 01 | ③ | 02 | ① | 03 | ③ | 04 | ① | 05 | ② |
| 06 | ④ | 07 | ④ | 08 | ① | 09 | ④ | 10 | ① |

01 정답 ③
16 지방직

정답해설
페니실린에 알레르기 반응이 있는 사람에게 나타날 효과는 'adverse(부정적인, 반대의)' 효과, 즉 부작용을 가져올 수 있을 것이다. 따라서 정답은 ③ adverse(부정적인, 반대의)이다.

해석
페니실린은 그것에 알레르기가 있는 사람에게는 **부작용**이 있을 수 있다.
① 긍정적인
② 냉담한, 초연한
③ 부정적인, 반대의, 불리한
④ 암시하는, 넌지시 가리키는

어휘
allergic 알레르기가 있는, 알레르기(성)의
affirmative 긍정적인   aloof 냉담한, 초연한
adverse 부정적인, 반대의, 불리한   allusive 암시하는, 넌지시 가리키는

오답률 TOP 2
02 정답 ①
19 지방직

정답해설
밑줄 친 'fluctuate'는 '요동을 치다'라는 뜻을 가진 동사로 유의어 관계에 있는 것은 ① sway(흔들리다)이다. 문장 전반부에 '투자가 편안하게 느껴지는 것은 누구도 쉽지 않다'고 하였으므로 '통화가치가 불안정하다'는 것을 유추할 수 있다.

해석
통화가치가 거의 매일 **요동을 치는** 동안에 어떤 누구도 큰 투자를 하는 것에 편안하지 않다.
① 흔들리다
② 오래 머물다
③ 복제하다
④ 가치가 떨어지다

어휘
currency 통화, (화폐 등의) 유통   fluctuate 요동을 치다
sway 흔들리다   linger 오래 머물다
duplicate 복제하다   depreciate 가치가 떨어지다

오답률 TOP 1
03 정답 ③
18 지방직

정답해설
밑줄 친 'frivolous'는 '가벼운, 시시한'이란 뜻을 가진 형용사이다. 따라서 의미가 가장 가까운 것은 ③ shallow(얕은, 피상적인)이다.

해석
만약 이 설명들이 독자들에게 너무 **시시해** 보인다면, 난 또 다른 대안을 생각할 수밖에 없다.
① 복잡한
② 예의 바른
③ 얕은, 피상적인
④ 포괄적인

어휘
explanation 설명, 설명서
alternative 대안; 대체 가능한
polite 예의 바른
inclusive 포괄적인
frivolous 가벼운, 시시한
complex 복잡한
shallow 얕은, 피상적인

04 정답 ①
18 지방직

정답해설
A와 B는 신혼 여행지에 대해 이야기를 나누고 있다. B가 신혼여행지를 둘 다 가보지 않은 곳으로 가자고 하자 A가 하와이를 제안하고 있다. 이 제안에 대한 B의 대답으로 수락 또는 거절을 하는 표현이 가장 적절하므로 정답은 수락의 의미를 나타내는 ① 'I've always wanted to go there(그곳에 항상 가보고 싶었어요).'이 가장 적절하다.

오답해설
④ 하와이에 가자는 A의 제안이 하와이에 다녀왔음을 유추할 수 있는 근거가 될 수 없으므로 B가 'Oh, you must've been to Hawaii already(오, 당신은 이미 하와이에 다녀왔음이 틀림없군요).'라고 대답하는 것은 옳지 않다.
나머지 선지는 하와이로의 여행을 제안하는 A의 말에 대한 대답으로 적절하지 않다.

해석
A: 당신은 우리 신혼여행으로 어디에 가고 싶어요?
B: 우리 중 누구도 가본 적 없는 곳으로 가요.
A: 그렇다면, 하와이는 어때요?
B: 그곳에 항상 가보고 싶었어요.
① 그곳에 항상 가보고 싶었어요.
② 한국은 살기 좋은 곳이 아닌가요?
③ 좋아요! 그곳에서의 제 마지막 여행은 놀라웠어요!
④ 오, 당신은 이미 하와이에 다녀왔음이 틀림없군요.

어휘
honeymoon 신혼여행; 신혼여행을 하다
amazing 놀라운, 굉장한

오답률 TOP 3
05 정답 ②
19 지방직

정답해설
② 출제 포인트: 주어와 동사의 수일치
밑줄 친 'are'의 주어는 복수 형태의 명사(구) 'the necessary calculations'이므로 'are'는 옳은 표현이다. 'calculations' 이후의 'that we ~ make'는 목적격 관계대명사절, 'about ~ harm'은 전명구, 'resulting from ~ take'는 분사구문이다. 또한 분사구문 내의 'that we take'는 'action'을 수식하는 목적격 관계대명사절로 사용되었다. 이처럼 주어와 동사 사이가 먼 경우 수일치에 유의해야한다.

오답해설
① 출제 포인트: 동격의 접속사 that
'risk is always a factor in any situation where the outcome is not precisely known'은 'sense'와 동격 관계이므로 밑줄 친 'how'를 동격을 나타내는 접속사 'that'으로 수정해야 한다.
③ 출제 포인트: 주어와 동사의 수일치
밑줄 친 'walk'의 주어는 동명사(구) 'making the decision'이다. 동명사(구)는 단수로 취급하므로 복수 형태의 동사 'walk'를 단수 형태의 동사 'walks'로 수정해야 한다.
④ 출제 포인트: what vs. that
밑줄 친 'what'은 선행사를 포함하며 뒤따라오는 문장이 불완전한 관계대명사이나 앞에 선행사 'everything'이 있으므로 관계대명사 'what'을 사용할 수 없다. 따라서 'what' 이후의 문장이 'do'의 목적어가 없는 불완전한 형태이며 선행사 'everything'이 있으므로 선행사를 포함한 관계대명사 'what'을 목적격 관계대명사 'that'으로 수정해야 한다.

해석
위험이 결과가 정확하게 알려지지 않은 어떤 상황에서 항상 요소라는 의미로 위험은 인간의 삶에서 근본적인 요소이다. 게다가, 우리가 취하는 행동으로부터 야기되는 손해의 어떤 형태의 가능성에 대해 우리가 만들어내는 필수적인 계산은 일반적으로 우리의 결정 과정 내에서 기정사실이다. 위험 평가가 주요 기업의 주도권에 대한 결정을 포함하는지 단지 결정을 하는 것이 길을 따라 걷는 것인지 간에, 우리는 항상 포함된 잠재적 위험을 예상하고, 확인하고, 평가하고 있다. 그러한 관점에서, 우리는 우리가 하는 모든 것 안에서 지속적으로 위험을 관리하라는 말을 들을 수 있다.

어휘
fundamental 근본적인
in the sense ~라는 의미에서
calculation 계산
assessment 평가
anticipate 예상하다
constantly 지속적으로
element 요소
factor 요소
given 기정사실
initiative 주도권
evaluate 평가하다

06 정답 ④
19 지방직

정답해설
④ 출제 포인트: 지각동사의 목적격 보어
밑줄 친 'to yawn'은 'seeing(지각동사 see의 동명사 형태)'의 목적격 보어에 해당한다. 따라서 'to yawn'을 동사원형 'yawn' 또는 현재분사 'yawning'으로 수정해야 한다.

오답해설
① 출제 포인트: 현재분사 형태의 형용사
밑줄 친 'catching'은 주격 보어에 해당하는 현재분사 형태의 형용사로 '전염성이 있는'을 뜻한다.
② 출제 포인트: 부사 vs. 형용사
밑줄 친 'easily'는 부사로 이후에 오는 과거분사 'influenced'를 수식하므로 옳게 사용되었다.
③ 출제 포인트: 접속사의 쓰임
밑줄 친 'when'은 종속절 'humans watch other people yawn'을 이끄는 접속사로 'when ~ yawn'은 접속사 'that'이 이끄는 절에서 부사절로 사용되었다.

해석
하품하는 것은 전염성이 있다. 한 사람의 하품은 전체 무리 내의 하품을 촉발할 수 있다. 더 공감력이 뛰어난 사람들은 다른 사람들의 하품에 의해 하품에 더 쉽게 영향을 받는다고 알려져 있다; 뇌 영상법 연구들은 사람들이 다른 사람들이 하품하는 것을 볼 때, 사회적 기능에 관여한다고 알려진 뇌의 영역들이 활성화된다는 것을 보여줘 왔다. 심지어 개들도 그들의 주인 또는 심지어 낯선 사람들이 하품하는 것을 보는 것에 대한 반응으로 하품하며, 전염적인 하품은 다른 동물들에게서도 역시 나타나왔다.

어휘

yawn 하품하다; 하품
trigger 촉발하다
brain imaging 뇌 영상법
catching 전염성이 있는
empathic 공감(감정이입)할 수 있는
contagious 전염성의

07 정답 ④
18 지방직

정답해설

④ 출제 포인트: 독립분사구문

원래 문장은 'Because it was cold outside, I boiled some water to have tea.'이다. 부사절 'Because ~ outside'를 분사구문으로 바꾸며 접속사와 주어가 생략되었으나, 부사절의 비인칭 주어 'it'은 주절의 주어 'I'와 다르므로 생략될 수 없다. 따라서 'Being cold outside'는 'It being cold outside'가 되어야 한다. 이를 독립분사구문이라고 한다.

오답해설

① 출제 포인트: 주어와 동사의 수일치

주어가 'all of 명사(구)'인 경우 동사의 수일치의 기준은 명사(구)이다. 해당 문장에서 동사의 수일치 기준은 'information'으로 불가산명사이며 단수 취급한다. 따라서 3인칭 단수 동사 'was'는 옳게 사용되었다.

② 출제 포인트: 조동사+have+과거분사

「should have + p.p.」는 '~했어야 했는데(하지 못했다)'라는 뜻이다. 해당 문장은 주어진 문장과 해석이 일치하므로 옳다.

③ 출제 포인트: 시제 일치

영화가 시작한 것이 우리가 도착하기 이전에 일어난 일이므로 과거완료 'had already started'가 쓰였다. 또한 부사인 'already'가 과거완료 시제의 동사를 수식하고 있다. 'already'가 완료시제와 함께 쓰이는 경우 보통 'have[has/had]'와 과거분사 사이에 위치한다.

08 정답 ①
18 지방직

정답해설

후반부의 "It recommended a public discussion, and said that doctors should not proceed at this time(그것은 공개적 토론을 권했고, 의사들은 "현시점에서 진행해서는 안 된다"라고 말했다)."에서 의사들은 현시점에서 배아 수정을 진행해서는 안 된다고 했으므로 의사들이 강화를 위한 배아 수정을 즉시 진행하도록 권고받았다는 ①은 일치하지 않는다.

오답해설

② "Last month, in the United States, the scientific establishment weighed in(지난달 미국에서, 과학 기관이 관여했다)."에서 미국 과학 기관이 관여했다고 하고 있으므로 적절하다.

③ "Chinese scientists altered a human embryo to remove a potentially fatal blood disorder(중국 과학자들이 잠재적으로 치명적인 혈액 장애를 제거하기 위해 인간 배아를 변형했다)."를 통해 글의 내용과 일치함을 알 수 있다.

④ 'germline modification'과 'designer babies' 그리고 'eugenics'는 모두 같은 현상을 칭하는 용어들로 소개되었으므로 본문의 내용과 일치한다.

해석

중국 과학자들이 잠재적으로 치명적인 혈액 장애를 단지 그 아기에게서뿐만 아니라 모든 후손으로부터 제거하기 위해 인간 배아를 변형했을 때 우리는 인종으로서 새로운 국면에 진입했다. 연구자들은 이 과정을 "생식 계열의 변형"이라고 일컫는다. 언론은 "designer babies"라는 어구를 좋아한다. 그러나 우리는 그것 그대로 "우생학"이라 불러야만 한다. 그리고 우리 인류는 우리가 그것을 사용하기를 원하는지 아닌지를 결정할 필요가 있다. 지난달, 미국에서, 과학 기관이 관여했다. 국립과학학회와 국립의학연합위원회는 "합리적인 대안"이 없을 때, 심각한 질병을 유발하는 유전자를 겨냥한 배아 수정을 지지했다. 그러나 이것은 이미 건강한 아이들을 더 강하고 키 크게 만드는 것과 같은 "강화"를 위한 수정에 대해 더 경계하는 것이었다. 그것은 공개적 토론을 권했고, 의사들은 "현시점에서 진행해서는 안 된다"라고 말했다. 위원회가 주의를 촉구하는 것에는 그럴만한 이유가 있다. 우생학의 역사는 억압과 고통으로 가득하다.

① 의사들은 강화를 위한 배아 수정을 즉시 진행하도록 권고받았다.
② 최근에, 미국 내 과학 기관은 우생학 토론에 참여했다.
③ 중국 과학자들은 심각한 혈액 장애를 방지하기 위해 인간 배아를 수정했다.
④ "Designer babies"는 생식 계열의 변형 과정에 대한 또 다른 용어이다.

어휘

phase 국면, 양상
alter 바꾸다, 고치다
descendant 자손, 후손
modification 수정, 변경
weigh in (논의, 언쟁, 활동 등에) 끼어들다, 관여하다
endorse 지지하다, 보증하다, 홍보하다
alternative 대안, 대체제
species (생물) 종
embryo 배아
germline 생식 계열
human race 인류
proceed 진행하다, 계속해서 ~을 하다

09 정답 ④
18 지방직

정답해설

강자와 약자를 가려내기 위한 고대 경기 중 극단적인 경기인 '판크라티온'에 대한 글이다. 주어진 문장은 게임의 규칙을 기술하며 'neither'와 'the two'를 제시하고 있으므로, 그 '둘'이 제시된 문장 이후에 위치해야 한다. ④ 이전의 문장에서 "Contenders continued until one of the two collapsed. (참가자는 둘 중 하나가 쓰러질 때까지 게임을 계속한다.)"고 언급하며 'two'를 제시하고 있으므로, 주어진 문장은 ④에 위치하는 것이 알맞다.

오답해설

나머지 보기는 글의 흐름상 적절하지 않다.

해석

고대 올림픽은 마치 현대의 경기들과 같이 선수들에게 그들의 건강과 우월함을 증명할 기회를 제공했다. (①) 고대 올림픽 경기들은 약자를 제거하고 강자를 찬양하기 위해 고안되었다. 우승자들은 벼랑 끝까지 내몰렸다. (②) 현대와 같이, 사람들은 극한 스포츠를 좋아했다. 가장 인기 있는 경기들 중 하나는 33번째 올림피아드에서 추가되었다. 이것은 판크라티온, 즉 레슬링과 복싱이 극단적으로 섞인 것이었다. 그리스어 pakration은 "완전한 힘"을 뜻한다. 남자들은 금속 장신구가 박힌 가죽끈을 착용했고, 그것은 그들의 상대에게 끔찍한 상황을 만들어낼 수 있었다. (③) 이러한 위험한 형식의 레슬링은 시간이나 체급 제한이 없었다. 이 경기에서, 오로지 두 가지 규칙만이 적용되었다. 첫 번째로, 레슬러들은 그들의 엄지손가락으로 상대의 눈을 찌를 수 없었다. 두 번째, 그들은 깨물 수 없었다. 이외의 다른 어떤 것들은 공정한 경기로 여겨졌다. 경기는 복싱 경기와 같은 방식으로 결정되었다. 참가자들은 둘 중 하나가 쓰러질 때까지 계속했다. (④ **둘 중 아무도 항복하지 않으면, 둘 중 하나가 쓰러질 때까지 주먹을 주고받았다**.) 오로지 가장 강한 자와 가장 확신에 찬 선수들만이 이 경기에 시도했다. 상대방의 손가락을 부러뜨려 그의 별명을 얻은 "Mr. Fingertips"와 레슬링 하는 것을 상상해보라!

어휘

surrender 항복하다, 투항하다, 굴복하다
knock out 나가떨어지게 하다
brink (벼랑, 강가 등의) 끝
stud 장신구, 장식용 금속 단추
gouge 찌르다
collapse 쓰러지다, 붕괴되다, 무너지다
glorify 찬양하다
strap 끈
opponent 상대, 반대자
contender 도전자, 경쟁자

10 정답 ①   18 지방직

정답해설

오늘날 과학의 문제점은 인간이 문제들을 선택하는 것이 아니라, 문제들이 인간에게 강요를 하는 현상이라는 내용이다. 즉, 인간이 주체가 아니라 떠밀리고 강요받는 '부록, 부속물 (appendix)'과도 같은 처지가 됨을 알 수 있다. 따라서 빈칸에는 '① makes man its appendix(인간을 그것의 부속물로 만들어버리다)'가 가장 적절하다.

오답해설

② '보안(security)'에 관해 언급되지 않았다.
③ 시스템이 인간으로 하여금, 스스로의 목적을 위해서 '피동적'으로 움직이게 하는 여러 가지 서술로 유추해 보았을 때, '창의적인(creative)' 도전들로 고무시킨다고 할 수 없다.
④ '시장 통제(to control the market)'는 본문과 무관하다.

해석

우리 시대에서, 인간에 대한 고유의 삶과 규칙을 가진 것은 단지 시장의 법칙일 뿐만 아니라, 과학과 기술의 발전이기도 하다. 많은 이유로, 오늘날 과학의 문제점들과 구조는 과학자가 그의 문제들을 선택하지 않는다는 것과 같다; 문제들이 과학자에게 그들 자신을 강요한다. 그는 하나의 문제를 풀고, 그 결과는 그가 더 안심하거나 확신하다는 것이 아니라, 다른 열 가지의 새로운 문제들이 해결된 문제 하나가 있던 자리에 모습을 드러낸다. 그것들은 그에게 해결하라고 강요한다; 그는 계속해서 빨라지는 속도로 진행해야만 한다. 공업 기술에서도 동일하다. 과학의 속도는 기술의 속도를 강요한다. 이론 물리학은 원자 에너지를 우리에게 강요한다; 핵폭탄의 성공적인 생산은 우리에게 수소폭탄의 제조를 강요한다. 우리는 우리의 문제를 선택하지 않는다, 우리는 우리의 생산물을 선택하지 않는다; 우리는 떠밀리고, 우리는 강요당하는 것이다 – 무엇에 의해서? 그것을 초월하는 목적과 목표가 없는, 그리고 인간을 그것의 부속물로 만들어버리는 시스템에 의해서이다.
① 인간을 그것의 부속물로 만들어버리다
② 보안에 대한 잘못된 인식을 창출하다
③ 인간을 창의적인 도전들로 고무시키다
④ 시장을 통제하도록 과학자들에게 권한을 부여하다

어휘

a number of 얼마간의, 다수의
secure 안심하는, 안전한, 확실한
theoretical 이론적인
atomic 원자의
hydrogen 수소
appendix 부록, 부속물
empower 권한을 부여하다
force ~를 강요하다, ~하게 만들다
ever-quickening 계속해서 빨라지는
physics 물리학
fission 핵분열, (세포의) 분열
transcend 초월하다
inspire 고무시키다, 영감을 주다

결국엔 성정혜 영어 하프모의고사
기적사 DAY 52

| 01 | ③ | 02 | ② | 03 | ② | 04 | ④ | 05 | ② |
| 06 | ② | 07 | ② | 08 | ② | 09 | ① | 10 | ① |

01 정답 ③

정답해설

밑줄 친 'affirmative'는 '긍정적인'을 뜻하는 형용사로 ③ sanguine(낙관적인, 자신감이 넘치는)과 의미가 가장 가깝다.

해석

자기 자신을 사랑하는 그녀의 **긍정적인** 사고방식은 다음 세대에게 참된 영감이 되어왔다.
① 암울한, 절망적인
② 회의적인
③ 낙관적인, 자신감이 넘치는
④ 사람을 싫어하는

어휘

affirmative 긍정적인
mindset (흔히 바꾸기 힘든) 사고방식[태도]
inspiration 영감; 고무
bleak 울한, 절망적인
sanguine 낙관적인, 자신감이 넘치는
generation 세대
skeptical 회의적인
misanthropic 사람을 싫어하는

오답률 TOP 1
02 정답 ②

정답해설

밑줄 친 'sway'는 '흔들다, 동요시키다'를 뜻하는 동사로 ② induce(설득하다, 유도하다)와 의미가 가장 가깝다.

해석

정부는 정보 조작을 통해 해당 정부의 사람들의 정신에 영향을 미치고 **흔들어 버릴** 무한한 힘을 받아서는 안 된다.
① 계속하다, 벌이다
② 설득하다, 유도하다
③ 장식하다, 꾸미다
④ 포기하다, 내주다

어휘

sway 흔들다, 동요시키다
wage 계속하다, 벌이다
embellish 장식하다, 꾸미다
manipulation 조작, 속임수
induce 설득하다, 유도하다
relinquish 포기하다, 내주다

오답률 TOP 2
03 정답 ②

정답해설

밑줄 친 'complex'는 '복잡한'을 뜻하는 형용사로 ② fancy(복잡한, 화려한)와 의미가 가장 가깝다.

해석

이제, 과학자들은 특별한 얼굴 인식이 항상 **복잡한** 두뇌를 필요로 하지는 않는다고 믿는다.
① 명쾌한, 알기 쉬운
② 복잡한, 화려한
③ 꾸밈없는, 소박한
④ 복잡하지 않은, 단순한

어휘

facial 얼굴의, 안면의
recognition 인식; (공로 등에 대한) 인정
complex 복잡한   lucid 명쾌한, 알기 쉬운
fancy 복잡한, 화려한   artless 꾸밈없는, 소박한
unfussy 복잡하지 않은, 단순한

04 정답 ④

정답해설

A와 B는 오늘 들은 경제학 강의에 관한 대화를 나눈다. A는 B에게 오늘 경제학 강의가 '자본주의(capitalism)'와 '보이지 않는 손(invisible hand)'에 관한 것이었다고 말하자, B는 자신이 완전히 ④ 'got the wrong end of the stick(잘못 이해했다)'이라고 이야기하며, 자신은 오늘의 강의가 완전히 다른 주제에 관한 것으로 이해했다고 한다.

오답해설

① 오늘 경제학 강의 내용을 이해하기 어려웠다는 B에게 A가 오늘 강의 주제를 이야기해주자, B는 자신이 완전히 '요점으로 들어갔다(got to the point)'라고 말하는 것은 내용상 적절하지 않다.
② B는 오늘 경제학 강의가 어려웠다고 하자, A가 B에게 오늘 경제학 내용을 이야기해준다. 그러자 B가 자신이 완전히 '두각을 보였다(cut a fine figure)'라고 말하는 것은 대화의 흐름상 어색하다.
③ 오늘 경제학 강의 내용이 이해하기 어려웠다는 B는 자신이 완전히 '죽었다(kicked the bucket)'라고 말하는 것은 문맥상 부자연스럽다.

해석

A: 너 오늘 강의 이해했어?
B: 오, 너 경제학 강의 말하는 거지?
A: 응. 그거 꽤 어렵지 않았어?
B: 그거 이해하기 매우 어려웠어. 교수님이 무엇을 설명하려 하신 것인지 이해할 수가 없었어.
A: 그것은 '자본주의'와 자본이 흐르도록 유지해주는 '보이지 않는 손'에 관한 것이었어.
B: '보이지 않는 손'? 나는 완전히 잘못 이해했네. 나는 오늘의 강의가 완전히 다른 주제에 관한 것으로 생각했어.
A: 네가 집에 가서 오늘 배운 것을 복습하면, 네가 다른 학급 친구들을 따라잡을 수 있을 거라 확신해.
① 요점으로 들어갔다
② 두각을 보였다
③ 죽었다
④ 잘못 이해했다

어휘

economics 경제학   get hold of ~을 알게[이해하게] 되다
capitalism 자본주의   invisible 보이지 않는, 볼 수 없는
invisible hand 보이지 않는 손 (Adam Smith의 경제학에서)
capital 자본; 자산; 수도; 대문자
catch up with ~을 따라잡다[따라가다]

get to the point 요점으로 들어가다
cut a fine figure 두각을 보이다
kick the bucket 죽다
get the wrong end of the stick 잘못 이해하다

05 정답 ②

정답해설

② 출제 포인트: 관계대명사+불완전한 형태의 절
선행사 'the modern white wedding dress'와 이후에 'Western cultures' 사이에 목적격 관계대명사가 생략되었음을 먼저 파악해야 한다. 따라서 'use' 이후에 있는 목적어 'it'을 삭제해 선행사인 'the modern white wedding dress'를 수식하여, '서구권 문화에서 사용하는 현대의 흰색 웨딩드레스'라는 문맥으로 사용되어야 자연스럽다.

오답해설

① 출제 포인트: that vs. what
밑줄 친 'that'은 뒤따라오는 문장이 주어가 없는 불완전한 형태이며 선행사 'functions'를 수식하고 있으므로 주격 관계대명사로 옳게 사용되었다.
③ 출제 포인트: sort/kind/type of+무관사 명사
'sort/kind/type of' 이후에 오는 명사는 관사를 사용하지 않는다. 따라서 밑줄 친 'clothing'은 옳은 표현이다.
④ 출제 포인트: 형용사로 고착화된 과거분사
밑줄 친 'specialized'는 형용사로 고착화된 과거분사로 '전문적인, 전문화된'을 뜻한다. 해당 문장은 문맥상 '전문화된 기능'이 자연스러우므로 'specialized'는 옳게 사용되었다.

해석

직물과 의류는 단지 몸을 보호하는 것 이상의 기능이 있다. 옷과 직물은 둘 다 비언어적인 의사소통의 수단으로 사용된다. 명백한 예는 특정한 사회적 역할을 전달하기 위한 제복과 이러한 통과의례를 기념하기 위해 서구권 문화에서 사용하는 현대의 흰색 웨딩드레스의 사용일 것이다. 두 가지 의류 모두는 보는 사람에게 비언어적으로 중요한 정보를 전한다. 그 흰색 드레스를 입은 여자는 이제 결혼할 것이고 사회에서 그녀의 지위와 역할을 바꿀 것이다. 제복을 입은 사람은 사회에서 경찰관과 간호사, 또는 군인과 같이 어떤 전문화된 기능을 갖는다.

어휘

modern 현대의   mark 표시하다
rite of passage 통과의례   onlooker 보는 사람, 구경꾼
be about to 동사원형 막 ~하려고 하다
specialized 전문적인, 전문화된

06 정답 ②

정답해설

② 출제 포인트: 가목적어 it/to부정사의 명사적 용법/의미상 주어/불완전타동사 make
밑줄 친 'teachers'는 불완전타동사 'make'의 목적어에 해당하나 '선생님들을 쉬운 상태로 만들다'로 해석되므로 문맥상 어색하다. 따라서 문맥상 자연스러운 해석을 찾아야 하며, 이때 '선생님들이 심폐 소생술 교육에 참여하는 것을 쉬운 상태로 만들다'가 자연스러우므로 밑줄 친 'teachers'를 'easy' 뒤로 이동하면서 'for teachers'로 수정하고 기존의 'teachers'가 있던 자리에는 가목적어 'it'을 사용해야 한다. 즉, 해당 문장은 'We make it easy for teachers to participate in CPR training at a time to suit your school's schedule.'이 옳은 문장이다. 이때 'for teachers'는 to부정사의 의미상 주어로 사용되었다.

> 오답해설

① 출제 포인트: 부사 vs. 형용사
밑줄 친 'recently'는 부사이며 과거분사 'launched'를 수식하므로 옳은 표현이다.

③ 출제 포인트: that vs. what/목적격 관계대명사
밑줄 친 'that'은 뒤따라오는 문장이 동사 'use'의 목적어가 없는 불완전한 형태이며 선행사 'full life-saving expertise'를 수식하고 있으므로 목적격 관계대명사로 옳게 사용되었다.

④ 출제 포인트: 등위접속사의 병렬구조
밑줄 친 'improve'는 동사원형으로 등위접속사 'and'를 통해 'perform'과 병렬구조를 이루고 있으므로 옳게 사용되었다.

> 해석

저희 회사에서 최근에 출시한 교사용 비상 훈련 프로그램을 소개하게 되어 기쁩니다. 저희의 심폐 소생술 강좌는 학교에서 가장 일반적으로 선택할 수 있는 것입니다. 저희는 선생님들께서 귀교의 일정에 맞는 시간에 심폐 소생술 교육에 참여하기 쉽게 해 드립니다. 저희 강좌는 비상사태에서 생명 유지와 관련된 지원을 하기 위해 그때 사용할 수 있는 완전한 구명 전문 기술을 여러분에게 제공해 드립니다. 적절한 교육으로 여러분은 신속하고 효과적으로 심폐 소생술을 수행할 수 있을 것이고, 환자의 생존 기회를 향상시킬 수 있을 것입니다.

> 어휘

launch 출시하다
option 선택
vital 생명 유지와 관련된; 필수적인
emergency 비상사태
expertise 전문 기술, 전문 지식
proper 적절한

07 정답 ②

> 정답해설

② 출제 포인트: 조동사+have+과거분사

「could+have+p.p.」는 '~했을 수도 있다'를 뜻하며 「should+have+p.p.」는 '~했어야 했는데 (하지 못했다)'를 뜻한다. 해당 문장은 주어진 해석이 '~했을 수도 있다'이나 'should have prevented'를 사용하였으므로 옳지 않은 문장이다. 따라서 'should'를 'could'로 수정해야 한다.

> 오답해설

① 출제 포인트: 주어와 동사의 수일치

주어가 'all of 명사(구)'인 경우 동사의 수일치의 기준은 명사(구)이다. 해당 문장은 'said' 이후에 생략된 접속사 'that'이 이끄는 종속절의 주어가 'all of his children's marriages'이므로 동사의 수일치 기준은 복수 형태의 명사(구) 'his children's marriages'이다. 따라서 종속절의 동사에 복수 형태인 'were'를 사용하는 것이 옳다.

③ 출제 포인트: 시제 일치

William이 실망한 시점보다 배가 떠난 시점이 먼저이며, 주절에 과거시제를 사용하였으므로 종속절에 과거완료시제를 사용한 것은 옳다. 또한 William은 '실망한 상태'이므로 감정 상태를 나타내는 'p.p.' 형태인 과거분사 'disappointed'가 적절하게 사용되었다.

④ 출제 포인트: 독립분사구문/to부정사 관용표현

해당 문장은 주절과 종속절의 주어가 다른 독립분사구문으로 원래 문장은 'As it was twelve o'clock, the chairman was anxious to adjourn the meeting.'이다. 또한 'be anxious to+동사원형'은 관용표현으로 '~하기를 갈망하다'를 뜻한다.

08 정답 ②

> 정답해설

주어진 문장은 '우생학자(Eugenicist)들의 '좋은 혈통(good stock)에 대한 주장'에 대해 언급하고 있다. 이어서 그들의 이러한 주장을 구체적으로 설명하고 있는 (B)가 이어지는 것이 자연스럽다. (B) 후반에서 "despite an obvious lack of evidence and scientific proof(증거와 과학적 근거의 명백한 부족에도 불구하고 말이다)"라고 언급하며, '증거와 과학적 근거가 부족한 주장'임을 명시하고 있는데, 이어서 (A)에서 'However(그러나)'를 이용해, '근거가 부족하지만 지지를 확보하는 데 성공했다'는 내용이 이어지는 것이 알맞다. 마지막으로, (A)에서 언급된 성과에 대해 구체적으로 설명하고 있는 (C)가 이어지는 것이 적절하다. 따라서 정답은 '② (B) - (A) - (C)'이다.

> 오답해설

③ (A)는 '역접'을 나타내는 접속부사인 'However'로 시작하는데, (A)의 내용은 '우생학자들이 지지를 얻었다'는 내용이므로, '우생학이 지지를 얻었다'는 유사한 내용인 (C) 이후에 이어지는 것은 문맥상 적절하지 않다. 따라서 ③은 오답이다.
나머지 보기는 문맥상 어색하므로 오답이다.

> 해석

우생학자들은 "좋은 혈통"에서 온 부모들은 더 건강하고 지적으로 우수한 아이들을 낳는다고 주장했다.
(B) 그들은 빈곤, 무기력, 범죄성, 그리고 빈약한 직업윤리와 같은 "특징"이 유전된 것이며 북방 인종을 조상으로 둔 사람들이 본질적으로 다른 민족보다 우수하다고 생각했다. 증거와 과학적 근거의 명백한 부족에도 불구하고 말이다.
(A) 그러나, 우생학자들은 Carnegie Institution과 일류대학교들이 그들의 연구를 지지하도록 설득할 수 있었고, 그렇게 하여 그것을 정당화하고 그들의 철학이 사실은 과학이라는 인식을 창조했다.
(C) 우생학 운동은 사회를 개선시킬 정당한 방식으로 널리 여겨지게 되었고, Winston Churchill, Margaret Sanger, Theodore Roosevelt 그리고 John Harvey Kellogg와 같은 사람들에 의해 지지되었다. 우생학은 또한 Harvard University를 포함한 많은 유명 대학에서 학과가 되었다.

> 어휘

eugenicist 우생학자
prestigious 명망 있는, 일류의
thus (앞서 말한 바를 가리켜) 이렇게, 그렇게
legitimize 정당화하다, 합법화하다
trait 특징, 특성
criminality 범죄성
inherited 유전된
ancestry 조상, 기원
people 민족, 인종
legitimate 정당한, 적법의
prominent 유명한
good stock 좋은 혈통
perception 인식
shiftlessness 무기력
work ethic 직업윤리
Nordic 북방 인종의
inherently 본질적으로, 생득적으로
eugenics 우생학
academic discipline 학과, 교과

오답률 TOP 3

09 정답 ①

> 정답해설

본문은 '고대 올림픽 경기와 여성'에 대한 내용이다. 본문 초반 "Only men, boys and unmarried girls were allowed to watch the Olympic Games. Married women were barred(오직 남자, 소년, 그리고 미혼의 소녀들만이 고대 올림픽 경기를 관람할 수 있었다. 기혼 여성들은 금지되었다)."를 통해, '기혼 여성은 올림픽을 볼 수 없었으나, 미혼 소녀들은 볼 수 있었음을 알 수

있다. 따라서 글의 내용과 일치하는 것은 '① Some females were able to spectate at the Olympic Games(몇몇 여인들은 올림픽 게임을 구경할 수 있었다).'이다.

오답해설

② 본문 초반 "However, married women could still own horses in the chariot races at the Olympics(그러나, 기혼 여성들은 여전히 올림픽의 전차 경주용 말을 소유할 수는 있었다)."에 따르면 기혼 여성은 말 소유권을 보유할 수는 있지만, 게임에 참여할 수는 없었으므로 오답이다.
③ 본문 중반 "one story tells of a mother so keen to see her son compete that she broke the no-women rule and got in disguised as a man(한 이야기는 아들이 경기하는 것을 간절히 보고 싶어서 여성 금지 규칙을 깨고 남자로 변장해 들어간 한 엄마에 대해 말해준다)."을 통해, 경기에 참가하기 위한 것이 아닌 아들이 경기하는 모습을 보기 위해 변장하여 숨어들었음을 알 수 있다.
④ 본문 후반 "Meanwhile, unmarried women had their own festival at Olympia. This was called the Heraia(한편, 미혼 여성들은 Olympia에서 자신들만의 축제를 열었다. 이것은 Heraia라고 불렸고)"를 통해, Heraia는 미혼 여성들만의 축제였음을 알 수 있다.

해석

오직 남자, 소년, 그리고 미혼의 소녀들만이 고대 올림픽 경기를 관람할 수 있었다. 기혼 여성들은 금지되었다. 만일 그들이 몰래 숨어들어온 것이 발각된다면, 그들은 형벌로 산 옆으로 내던져질 수 있었다. 그러나 기혼 여성들은 여전히 올림픽의 전차 경주용 말을 소유할 수는 있었다. 비록 기혼 여성이 올림픽 경기에 허용되지는 않았지만, 한 이야기는 아들이 경기하는 것을 간절히 보고 싶어서 여성 금지 규칙을 깨고 남자로 변장해 들어간 한 엄마에 대해 말해준다. 한편, 미혼 여성들은 Olympia에서 자신들만의 축제를 열었다. 이것은 Heraia라고 불렸고, Zeus의 아내인 Hera를 기념하여 4년마다 열렸다. Heraia 경기의 우승자들은 남자들과 마찬가지로 신성한 올리브 가지 왕관을 수여받았다.
① 몇몇 여인들은 올림픽 게임을 구경할 수 있었다.
② 말을 보유한 여성들은 전차 경주에서 경쟁할 수 있었다.
③ 한 여성이 올림픽 게임에서 경기하기 위해 남자로 변장했다.
④ 모든 여성이 Heraia 경기에 참가할 수 있었다.

어휘

bar 금(지)하다
chariot race 전차 경주
keen 간절히 …하고 싶은, …을 열망하는
disguised 변장한
sneak in 살짝[몰래] 들어가다
sacred 신성한, 성스러운

10 정답 ①

정답해설

본문 초반에서, '집단적 규칙으로서의 과학의 역할'에 대해 언급한 후, "Classically, science's main goal has been building knowledge and understanding(고전적으로, 과학의 주요 목표는 지식과 이해를 구축하는 것이었다)."라고 언급하며, 과학의 전통적 목적에 대해 설명하고 있다. 이어서, 응용과학 분야에 들어서는 "scientific research is undertaken with the explicit goal of solving a problem or developing a technology(과학적 연구는 문제 해결 또는 기술 발전의 명백한 목표와 함께 수행되었고)"라고 '문제 해결 또는 기술 개발 등이 목적'이 되었다고 설명하고 있으므로, 전체적인 글의 내용은 과학이 어떠한 목적을 추구해 왔는지 단계적으로 설명하고 있다는 것을 알 수 있다. 따라서 글의 제목으로 가장 적절한 것은 '① The Aims of Science(과학의 목적)'이다.

오답해설

나머지는 본문과 관련 없는 내용이므로 오답이다.

해석

집단적 규칙으로서의 과학은 어떻게 자연 세계가 작용하는지, 그것의 구성 요소가 무엇인지, 그리고 어떻게 세계가 현재의 모습이 되었는지에 대한 점점 더 정확한 자연적 설명을 만들어내는 것에 집중한다. 고전적으로, 과학의 주요 목표는 그것의 잠재적인 응용 분야에 관계없이 지식과 이해를 구축하는 것이었다. - 예를 들면, 유기 화합물의 구조에 대해 알아보기 위해 그것이 발생하는 화학 반응을 연구하는 것. 그러나 점점 더 과학적 연구는 문제 해결 또는 기술 발전의 명백한 목표와 함께 수행되었고, 그 목표를 향해 가는 길을 따라 새로운 지식과 설명들이 구축되었다. 예를 들어, 화학자는 항말라리아약을 합성적으로 생산하려 할지도 모르고, 그 과정에서 다른 화학 물질을 생성하는 데 응용될 수 있는 결합을 형성하는 새로운 방법을 발견할지도 모른다.
① 과학의 목적
② 과학의 영향
③ 과학의 필요성
④ 과학의 수수께끼

어휘

collective 집단의, 공통의
component (구성) 요소, 부품
undergo 겪다, 받다, 경험하다
explicit 분명한, 명백한, 명쾌한
synthetically 합성적으로
institution (확립된) 규칙, 법, 관습
organic compound 유기 화합물
undertake 착수하다[하다]
antimalarial 말라리아 예방[치료]의
bond 결합

결국엔 성정혜 영어 하프모의고사
기적사 DAY 53

01	③	02	①	03	②	04	①	05	①
06	④	07	②	08	②	09	②	10	③

01 정답 ③

정답해설
밑줄 친 'aloof'는 '냉담한'을 뜻하는 형용사로 ③ callous(냉담한)와 의미가 가장 가깝다.

해석
몇몇 사람들은 너와 가까워지길 원했지만 그들은 네가 **냉담하다고** 느꼈다.
① 친한, 사이가 좋은
② 명시적인, 공공연한
③ 냉담한
④ 비밀리에 하는, 은밀한

어휘
aloof 냉담한 pally 친한, 사이가 좋은
overt 명시적인, 공공연한 callous 냉담한
clandestine 비밀리에 하는, 은밀한

오답률 TOP 1

02 정답 ①

정답해설
밑줄 친 'linger'는 '오래 머물다, 오래 남아 있다'를 뜻하는 동사로 ① abide(머무르다, 참다)와 의미가 가장 가깝다.

해석
온실가스 배출은 수백 년간 공기 속에 **오래 남아 있을** 것이고 이산화탄소는 열을 끌어모아 계속해서 공기를 따뜻하게 하기 때문에 장기적으로 해롭다.
① 머무르다, 참다
② 흔들리다, 흔들다
③ 벗어나다, 일탈하다
④ 덫에 걸리게 하다, 함정에 빠뜨리다

어휘
emission (빛·열·가스 등의) 배출, 방사, 발산
greenhouse gas 온실가스 detrimental 해로운
linger 오래 머물다, 오래 남아 있다 carbon dioxide 이산화탄소
continuously 계속해서, 연속적으로, 끊임없이
trap ~을 끌어모으다, 가두다; 덫, 올가미
abide 머무르다, 참다 wobble 흔들리다, 흔들다
deviate 벗어나다, 일탈하다
ensnare 덫에 걸리게 하다, 함정에 빠뜨리다

03 정답 ②

정답해설
밑줄 친 'polite'는 '예의 바른, 공손한, 정중한'을 뜻하는 형용사로 ② complaisant(공손한, 정중한)와 의미가 가장 가깝다.

해석
요르단에서는, 대체로 식사 제안을 수락하기 전에 그것을 세 번 거절하는 것이 **예의 바른** 태도이다.
① 아주 멋진, 훌륭한
② 공손한, 정중한
③ 무례한, 버릇없는
④ 감정에 좌우되지 않는

어휘
polite 예의 바른, 공손한, 정중한 attitude 태도[자세]
decline 거절하다, 감소하다; 감소
offer 제안[제의]; 제안[제의]하다, 제공하다
accept 수락하다, 받아들이다, 인정하다
splendid 아주 멋진, 훌륭한 complaisant 공손한, 정중한
impertinent 무례한, 버릇없는 dispassionate 감정에 좌우되지 않는

04 정답 ①

정답해설
Wendy와 Max는 친구들의 소식에 관한 대화를 나눈다. Wendy가 Alex의 근황을 물어보자 Max는 '그에 대해 전혀 모른다(do not know beans about)'라고 답한다. Wendy는 Alex가 군 장교가 되었다고 말하며 '자신도 Nancy를 통해 들었기 때문에 사실인지 모르겠다'고 하자 Max는 'Nancy를 기억한다'라고 얘기하며 '고등학교 친구들과 연락하고 지내야겠다'라고 말한다. 그러자 Wendy는 '간단한 편지를 보내 보는(drop them a line) 것은 어떻냐'라고 제안한다. 따라서 정답은 ①이다.

오답해설
② (B) "고등학교 친구들과 연락하며 지내야겠다"라고 얘기하는 Max에게 Wendy가 "네 소식을 듣고 그들이 기뻐할 거야"라고 말하며 네가 '신경을 건드린다(get on their nerves)'라고 대답하는 것은 대화의 흐름상 부자연스럽다.
③ (A) Max에게 Alex의 근황을 묻는 Wendy에게 Max는 "그에게 한동안 소식을 듣지 못했다"라고 말하며, 그를 '야단치다(give him a piece of your mind)'라고 하는 것은 문맥상 어색하다.
④ (A) Max에게 Alex의 근황을 묻는 Wendy에게 Max는 "그에게 한동안 소식을 듣지 못했다"라고 말하며, 그를 '야단치다(give him a piece of your mind)'라고 하는 것은 빈칸에 들어갈 말로 부적절하다. (B) "고등학교 친구들과 연락하며 지내야겠다"라고 얘기하는 Max에게 Wendy가 "네 소식을 듣고 그들이 기뻐할 거야"라고 말하며 네가 '신경을 건드린다(get on their nerves)'라고 대답하는 것은 맥락상 적합하지 않다.

해석
Wendy: 너 Alex가 요새 어떻게 지내는지 알아?
Max: 전혀 몰라. 나는 그의 소식을 들은 지 꽤 오래됐기 때문에 그에 (A) 대해 전혀 몰라.
Wendy: 내가 최근에 들은 바로는, 그가 군 장교가 되었대.
Max: 우와! 그건 예상치 못한 소식이다. 근데 그에게 꽤 잘 어울리는 것 같아.
Wendy: 나도. 근데 그 소식이 진짜인지 확실하지 않아. 나는 그저 Nancy에게 들었을 뿐이야.
Max: 난 Nancy 기억해. 나 정말 고등학교 친구들과 연락 좀 하고 지내야 겠다.
Wendy: 네가 (B) 간단한 편지를 보내 보는 것은 어때? 그들이 너에게서 소식을 들어 기뻐할 거라고 확신해
Max: 고마워. 한번 시도해봐야겠다.
① (A) ~에 대해 전혀 모르다 (B) 간단한 편지를 보내다

② (A) ~에 대해 전혀 모르다 (B) 신경을 건드리다
③ (A) 야단치다 (B) 간단한 편지를 보내다
④ (A) 야단치다 (B) 신경을 건드리다

어휘

military 군사의, 무력의; 군대
unexpected 예기치 않은, 예상 밖의, 뜻밖의
keep in touch with ~와 연락[접촉]을 유지하다
do not know beans about ~에 대해 전혀 모르다
drop someone a line ~에게 간단한 편지를 보내다
get on one's nerves 신경을 건드리다
give someone a piece of one's mind 야단치다

05 정답 ①

정답해설

① 출제 포인트: 사역동사의 목적격 보어/등위접속사의 병렬구조

밑줄 친 'affect'는 원형부정사로 사역동사 'let'의 목적격 보어에 해당하며, 'accumulate'와 등위접속사 'and'를 통해 병렬구조를 이루고 있다.

오답해설

② 출제 포인트: that vs. what/목적격 관계대명사

밑줄 친 'what'은 선행사를 포함하는 관계대명사이나, 앞에 선행사 'people'이 있고 전치사 'around'의 목적어가 없으므로 'what'을 목적격 관계대명사 'whom' 또는 'that'으로 수정해야 한다.

③ 출제 포인트: 혼동하기 쉬운 동사(rise vs. raise)/관용표현(rise to the occasion)

밑줄 친 'raise'는 완전타동사이므로 이후에 목적어가 있어야 하나, 목적어가 아닌 수식어(구) 'to the occasion'이 왔으며 문맥상 '위기 상황에 대처하다'가 자연스러우므로 'raise'를 완전자동사 'rise'로 수정해야 한다. 이때 'rise to the occasion'은 관용표현으로 '난국에 대처하다, 수단을 발휘하다'를 뜻한다.

④ 출제 포인트: what vs. that

밑줄 친 'that' 앞에 선행사가 없으므로 접속사로 보아야 하나 이후에 오는 절의 'doing'과 'about'의 목적어가 없으므로 'that'을 선행사를 포함하는 관계대명사 'what'으로 수정해야 한다.

해석

모든 이들은 때때로 이런저런 일들에 대한 의심의 순간이 있는데; 그것은 자연스러운 과정이다. 문제는 그러한 순간들이 쌓이거나 당신의 자기 확신에 영향을 끼치지 않게 하는 것이다. 당신은 항상 다른 이들의 논평과 의견의 도전에 직면할 것이다. 당신이 주변에 있으면 기분 좋게 느끼는 사람들과 당신이 그렇게 느끼지 않는 다른 이들이 있다. 어떤 사람들은 당신을 신뢰하기 때문에 당신에게 긍정적인 에너지를 준다. 당신은 그것을 느끼고 당신은 위기 상황에서 능력을 발휘한다. 다른 이들은 항상 당신이 하고 있는 것이나 말하고 있는 것에 관해 할 수 있는 부정적인 논평을 할 수도 있다. 이러한 논평이 당신 자신에 대한 믿음을 흔들리게 하지 마라.

어휘

doubt 의심
from time to time 때때로
accumulate 쌓이다
rise to the occasion 난국에 대처하다, 수단을 발휘하다

오답률 TOP 2
06 정답 ④

정답해설

④ 출제 포인트: 지각동사의 목적격 보어

밑줄 친 'to tell'은 지각동사 'hear'의 목적격 보어 자리에 해당한다. 지각동사 'hear'는 목적어와 목적격 보어의 관계가 능동인 경우 목적격 보어에 원형 부정사 또는 현재분사를 사용한다. 따라서 'to tell'은 원형부정사 'tell' 또는 현재분사 'telling'으로 수정해야 한다.

오답해설

① 출제 포인트: during vs. for

밑줄 친 'during'은 전치사로 이후에 특정 기간을 나타내는 명사(구)가 온다. 이때 'warm showers'는 특정 기간을 나타내는 명사(구)에 해당하므로 'during'은 옳은 표현이다.

② 출제 포인트: 현재분사 vs. 과거분사

밑줄 친 'well-known'은 부사 'well'과 과거분사 'known'이 결합한 형태로, 수식하는 대상 'psychologist'와 수동관계이며 해석상 '잘 알려진 심리학자'가 자연스러우므로 'well-known'은 옳은 표현이다.

③ 출제 포인트: being이 생략된 분사구문

밑줄 친 'unable'은 형용사로 앞에는 분사 'being'이 생략되어 있다. 이때 생략된 주어는 'we'이며 해당 분사구문을 'and we are unable to check our e-mail'로 바꾸어 사용할 수 있다. 따라서 'unable'은 옳게 사용되었다.

해석

"그것이 매우 많은 통찰이 따뜻한 샤워 동안 발생하는 이유이다"라고 잘 알려진 심리학자 Subhra Bhattacharya는 말한다. "많은 사람들에게, 그것은 그날의 가장 편안한 순간이다." 우리가 따뜻한 물로 마사지 받고 있느라 이메일을 확인할 수 없는 때가 되서야, 우리는 마침내 머리의 뒤편에서 우리에게 통찰에 관하여 말하고 있는 조용한 목소리를 들을 수 있다.

어휘

relaxing 편안한
insight 통찰

07 정답 ②

정답해설

② 출제 포인트: 독립분사구문

'snow'는 비인칭대명사 'it'을 주어로 하는 동사이다. 해당 문장을 원래 문장으로 고치면 'As he snowed heavily yesterday, he stayed at home all day long.'이 되며 이때 'snow'의 주어가 'he'이므로 비문임을 알 수 있다. 따라서 원래 문장을 'As it snowed heavily yesterday, he stayed at home all day long.'으로 수정한 후에 분사구문으로 고치면 'It snowing heavily yesterday, he stayed at home all day long.'이 되므로 주어진 문장의 'Snowing'을 'It snowing'으로 수정해야한다.

오답해설

① 출제 포인트: 조동사+have+과거분사

「must+have+p.p.」는 '~이었음에 틀림없다'를 뜻한다. 해당 문장은 주어진 해석이 '~이었음에 틀림없다'이므로 'must have been burgled'는 옳은 표현이다.

③ 출제 포인트: 주어와 동사의 수일치

주어가 'most of 명사(구)'인 경우 동사의 수일치의 기준은 명사(구)이다. 해당 문장은 주어가 'Most of their work'이므로 동사의 수일치 기준은 단수 형태의 명사(구) 'their work'이다. 따라서 동사에 단수 형태인 'involves'를 사용하는 것이 옳다. 또한 'catering'은 해당 문장에서 명사로 쓰였으며 '음식 공급'을 뜻한다.

④ 출제 포인트: 시제 일치
우리가 작업을 하는 시점보다 범위가 정해진 시점이 먼저이며, 주절에 과거시제를 사용하였으므로 종속절에 과거완료시제를 사용한 것은 옳다.

오답률 TOP 3
08 정답②

정답해설

본문은 '세계 최초의 디자이너 아기인 Adam Nash'에 관한 글이다. 두 번째 문장 "When Adam was still an embryo, living in a dish in the lab, scientists tested his DNA to make sure it was free of Fanconi anemia, the rare inherited blood disease from which his sister Molly suffered(Adam이 여전히 실험실의 접시에 살고 있는 배아였을 때, 과학자들은 그의 누나 Molly가 앓고 있던 희귀 유전 혈액 질환인 Fanconi 빈혈이 없다는 것을 확실히 하기 위해 그의 DNA를 검사했다)."를 통해, 'Adam Nash의 DNA에 Fanconi 빈혈 유전자가 없기 때문에 Adam이 태어날 수 있었다'는 것을 알 수 있다. 따라서 글의 내용과 일치하지 않는 것은 '② Adam Nash had the genes for Fanconi anemia(Adam Nash는 Fanconi 빈혈 유전자를 가지고 있었다).'이다.

오답해설

① 본문 첫 문장 "Adam Nash is considered to be the first designer baby, born in 2000 using in vitro fertilization with pre-implantation genetic diagnosis, a technique used to choose desired characteristics(희망하는 특징을 선택하기 위해 사용되는 시술인 착상 전 유전 진단과 함께 체외수정을 이용해 2000년에 태어난 Adam Nash는 최초의 디자이너 아기로 여겨진다)."를 통해 '희망하는 특징'이 선택되어진 '디자이너 아기'라는 것을 언급하고 있으므로, 글의 내용과 일치한다.

③ 본문 후반 "Molly needed a donor match for stem cell therapy, and her parents were determined to find one(Molly는 줄기세포 치료를 위해 일치하는 기증자가 필요했고, 그녀의 부모는 한 사람을 찾기로 결정했다)."을 통해, 'Molly의 부모가 일치하는 기증자를 찾기 위해 Adam을 낳았다'는 것을 알 수 있으므로, Adam을 낳기 전에는 일치하는 기증자가 없었다는 것을 유추할 수 있다. 따라서 오답이다.

④ "Adam was conceived so the stem cells in his umbilical cord could be the lifesaving treatment for his sister(Adam은 그의 탯줄에 있는 줄기세포가 그의 누나의 생명을 살리는 치료제가 될 수 있도록 임신되었다)."를 통해 글의 내용과 일치함을 알 수 있다.

해석

희망하는 특징을 선택하기 위해 사용되는 시술인 착상 전 유전 진단과 함께 체외수정을 이용해 2000년에 태어난 Adam Nash는 최초의 디자이너 아기로 여겨진다. Adam이 여전히 실험실의 접시에 살고 있는 배아였을 때, 과학자들은 그의 누나 Molly가 앓고 있던 희귀 유전 혈액 질환인 Fanconi 빈혈이 없다는 것을 확실히 하기 위해 그의 DNA를 검사했다. 그들은 또한 그가 동일한 조직 유형을 공유하는지 아닌지 밝혀줄 유전자 표지를 위해 그의 DNA를 확인했다. Molly는 줄기세포 치료를 위해 일치하는 기증자가 필요했고, 그녀의 부모는 한 사람을 찾기로 결정했다. Adam은 그의 탯줄에 있는 줄기세포가 그의 누나의 생명을 살리는 치료제가 될 수 있도록 임신되었다. Adam의 임신과 탄생은 윤리적 문제 때문에 찬사와 비판을 모두 받았다.
① Adam Nash의 유전자는 부모에 의해 선택되었다.
② Adam Nash는 Fanconi 빈혈 유전자를 가지고 있었다.
③ Molly는 Adam이 태어날 때까지 일치하는 기증자가 없었다.
④ Molly의 부모는 딸을 살리기 위해 그의 탯줄을 이용하고자 Adam을 낳았다.

어휘

in vitro fertilization 체외수정
pre-implantation genetic diagnosis 착상 전 유전 진단
embryo 배아   anemia 빈혈증
inherited 유전의
marker 유전자 표지(유전학적 해석에서 표지로 사용되는 유전자)
reveal 드러내다, 밝히다   tissue 조직
donor (장기) 기증자, 제공자
match (성질·능력 등에서) […과] 대등한 사람[것], 공통적인 사람[것]
conceive 임신하다   umbilical cord 탯줄

09 정답②

정답해설

본문은 '고대 올림픽 선수들이 알몸으로 경기 및 훈련을 했다'고 설명하며 그로 인해 '위생과 몸 관리에 철저했다'고 언급하고 있다. ①에서는 남성 운동선수가 몸 관리를 배우기 시작한다는 내용을 언급하고 ③에서 관리 과정(whole process)에 대해 설명하고 있는데, ②에서는 '여성이 경기를 관람하는 것'에 대해 언급하고 있으므로, 문맥상 적절하지 않다. 따라서 정답은 ②이다.

오답해설

④의 It은 ③에서 언급된 '관리 과정'을 가리키고 있으므로, 문맥상 자연스럽다. 나머지 보기는 문맥상 자연스러우므로 오답이다.

해석

고대 올림픽의 참가자들은 항상 알몸이었다. 그들의 신체는 훈련을 통해 완벽해지도록 되어있었고, 노출은 신체와 영혼의 공생뿐만 아니라 영원한 미를 상징했다. 또한, 운동선수들은 흠잡을 데 없는 위생과 몸 관리를 유지했다. 이것은 거의 알려지지 않은 사실이다. ① 그들은 알몸이었기 때문에, 그들이 학습하고 지도를 받는 기관인 고등학교에 입학할 때부터 그들은 그들의 위생을 관리하는 것을 배우기 시작하곤 했다. ② *오직 남자들만이 게임에서 경쟁할 수 있었고, 참가자들이 알몸이었기 때문에 여자들은 게임을 관람하는 것이 금지되었다.* ③ 전체 과정은 올리브 오일과 운동선수들이 피부에 문질렀던 고운 모래로 된 가루 층을 포함했다. ④ 그것은 태양으로부터 뿐만 아니라, 그들이 조별 훈련을 받을 때 코치로부터의 이따금씩의 타격에서도 그들을 보호했다. 훈련이 끝났을 때, 그 층은 물과 스펀지를 이용해 벗겨져야 했다. 그리고 이것은 또한 경기 이전에도 각각 행해졌다.

어휘

naked 벌거벗은, 나체의   eternal 영원한
symbiosis 공생   impeccable 흠잡을 데 없는
hygiene 위생   institution 기관, 협회
occasional 가끔의

10 정답③

정답해설

주어진 문장에서는 'many excellent science studies(많은 훌륭한 과학 연구들)'에 대해 언급하고 있으므로, 이어서 이러한 '긍정적인 측면의 과학'과는 비교되는 '나쁜 과학(bad science)'에 대해 언급하고 있는 (B)가 등장하는 것이 자연스럽다. 이후에는 이러한 '나쁜 과학'이 발생하는 일반적인 이유를 과학자들의 측면에서 설명하는 (C)가 이어진 후, 마지막으로, 과학자들의 측면이 아닌 미디어 측면에서 '나쁜 과학'이 발생하는 과정을 설명해주는 (A)가 이어지는 것이 가장 자연스럽다. 따라서 정답은 '③ (B) - (C) - (A)'이다.

오답해설

② (A)의 "Sometimes this is not the fault of the scientists"로 보아, (A) 이전에 '과학자의 잘못'이라는 내용이 언급되는 것이 자연스러우므로, (C)가 (A) 이전에 등장하는 것이 적절하다. 따라서 오답이다.
나머지 보기는 문맥상 어색하므로 오답이다.

해석

잘 설계된 실험에 기반하고 결집된 실험적 데이터에 근거한 조리 정연한 주장을 하는 많은 훌륭한 과학 연구들이 있다.
(B) 매년 발행되는 과학적 결론들과 논문들의 대부분은 유효한 발견을 제공하고 지식 체계에 공헌을 하는 반면, 안타깝게도, 그곳에 많은 경우의 나쁜 과학이 있다.
(C) 나쁜 과학에는 다수의 이유가 있다: 빈약한 연구, 빈약하게 설계된 실험, 연구자들의 비행, 그리고 우연한 또는 고의의 데이터 오역.
(A) 미디어가 가능성과 같은 신중한 방식으로 적힌 사소한 관측 또는 진술을 채택하고 이것을 정립된 사실로 바꿔버리기 때문에, 때때로 이것은 과학자의 잘못이 아니다. 예를 들어, "암의 모든 유형을 위한 치료제"는 가장 흔한 (그리고 오도하는) 헤드라인 중 하나이다.

어휘

reasoned 조리 정연한
for (왜냐하면) …니까
established 확립된, 정립된
misleading 호도[오도]하는, 오해의 소지가 있는
finding 발견(물), 조사[연구] 결과
body 본체, 중심부
misconduct (특히 전문직 종사자의) 비행, 위법[불법] 행위
deliberate 고의의
assembled 모인, 집합된, 결집한
guarded 조심스러운, 신중한
contribution 공헌
misinterpretation 오역

기적사 DAY 54

| 01 | ② | 02 | ③ | 03 | ① | 04 | ③ | 05 | ③ |
| 06 | ② | 07 | ④ | 08 | ② | 09 | ① | 10 | ④ |

오답률 TOP 1
01 정답 ②

정답해설

밑줄 친 'adverse'는 '부정적인'을 뜻하는 형용사로 ② cynical(부정적인, 냉소적인)과 의미가 가장 가깝다.

해석

낮은 출산율에 대한 **부작용**이 매년 계속 나타나는 것처럼 보인다.
① 답답한
② 부정적인, 냉소적인
③ 긍정적인, 낙관적인
④ 해로운

어휘

adverse 부정적인
stuffy 답답한
upbeat 긍정적인, 낙관적인
birthrate 출생률, 출산율
cynical 부정적인, 냉소적인
detrimental 해로운

02 정답 ③

정답해설

밑줄 친 'duplicate'는 '복제하다, 복사하다'를 뜻하는 동사로 ③ replicate(복제하다, 모사하다)와 의미가 가장 가깝다.

해석

최신 과학 장비와 현대 기술의 도움에도 불구하고 과학자들은 그 과정을 **복제**할 수 없었다.
① 꾸물거리다, 미적거리다
② 모방하다
③ 복제하다, 모사하다
④ 변동을 거듭하다

어휘

state-of-the-art 최신식의, 최첨단의
duplicate 복제하다, 복사하다
emulate 모방하다
fluctuate 변동을 거듭하다
dally 꾸물거리다, 미적거리다
replicate 복제하다, 모사하다

오답률 TOP 2
03 정답 ①

정답해설

밑줄 친 'shallow'는 '얕은'을 뜻하는 형용사로 ① shoal(얕은, 얕은 수심에서 뜨는)과 의미가 가장 가깝다.

해석

한 가지 가설은 **얕은** 물이 고래들을 혼란시키고 그들의 항해 능력을 방해할 수 있다고 예측한다.

① 얕은, 얕은 수심에서 뜨는
② 내용이 부족한, 시시한; (빛·목소리 등이) 희미한
③ 비비 꼬인, 비틀린
④ 이종의, 이질적인

어휘

hypothesis 가설, 추정, 추측
shallow 얕은
disturb 방해하다
shoal 얕은, 얕은 수심에서 뜨는
feeble 내용이 부족한, 시시한; (빛·목소리 등이) 희미한
tortuous 비비 꼬인, 비틀린
predict 예측[예견]하다
confuse 혼동하다, 혼란시키다
navigational 항해의, 비행의
heterogeneous 이종의, 이질적인

04 정답 ③

정답해설

A와 B는 조별 과제의 같은 조의 조원으로서, 주제를 무엇으로 정할지를 논의 중이다. A와 B는 '4차 산업 혁명'과 '인공지능'을 주제로 정하기로 하고, A는 "새로운 발전에 관한 발표를 함으로써 '대세에 따라야(jump on the bandwagon) 한다"라고 주장한다. 따라서 정답은 ③이다.

오답해설

① 조별 과제의 발표 주제를 '4차 산업 혁명'과 '인공지능'으로 정하기로 하고, A는 새로운 발전을 발표함으로써 '싸움을 그만둬야(bury the hatchet)' 한다고 하는 것은 문맥상 어색하다.
② A와 B는 새로운 발전에 대해 발표함으로써 '마감에 맞추려고 해야(work against the clock)' 한다고 말하는 것은 대화의 흐름상 빈칸에 들어갈 말로 적절하지 않다.
④ A와 B는 '4차 산업 혁명'과 '인공지능'을 조별 과제의 주제로 정하기로 한 후, A가 새로운 발전에 대해 발표함으로써 '주객이 전도돼야(put the cart before the horse)' 한다고 이야기하는 것은 내용상 자연스럽지 않다.

해석

A: 이 팀 과제의 파트너로서, 우리가 무엇을 주제로 원하는지 논의해야 해.
B: 음, 나는 주말 동안 그것에 대해 생각해 봤고 '4차 산업 혁명'에 관한 생각을 떠올렸어.
A: 그거 굉장히 흥미로운 주제네! '인공지능'도 언급해보는 게 어때?
B: 좋은 생각이야! 요즘 그런 기술 발전에 관련된 소식이 아주 많아.
A: 그러니까. 우리는 최근의 발전에 대해 발표함으로써 대세에 따라야 해.
B: 응, 그것은 대세를 따를 수 있는 좋은 방법이야.
① 싸움을 그만두다
② 마감에 맞추려고 하다
③ 대세에 따르다
④ 주객이 전도되다

어휘

come up with ~을 생각하다; ~을 따라잡다
industrial revolution 산업 혁명   artificial intelligence(AI) 인공지능
technological (과학) 기술(상)의   presentation 발표; 제출
keep up with ~의 시류[유행]를 따르다; (할부금 등을) 계속 내다; ~을 정기적으로 하다
bury the hatchet 싸움을 그만두다, 화해하다
work against the clock 마감에 맞추려고 하다
jump on the bandwagon 대세에 따르다
put the cart before the horse 주객이 전도되다

05 정답 ③

정답해설

③ **출제 포인트**: help+목적어[to부정사/원형부정사]
'help'는 원형부정사 또는 to부정사를 목적어로 가진다. 밑줄 친 'support'는 원형부정사이며 'help'의 목적어로 사용되었으므로 옳은 표현이다.

오답해설

① **출제 포인트**: 수동태 불가동사
'take place'는 수동태로 사용할 수 없는 동사구이다. 밑줄 친 'be taken place'는 'take place'의 수동태이므로 능동태 'take place'로 수정해야 한다.
② **출제 포인트**: 현재분사 vs. 과거분사
밑줄 친 'designating'은 완전타동사 'designate'의 현재분사이나 이후에 목적어가 아닌 수식어 'for donations'가 왔으며 수식하는 대상 'two locations'와 수동관계이므로, 'designating'을 과거분사 'designated'로 수정해야 한다.
④ **출제 포인트**: 선행사에 따른 관계대명사의 쓰임
밑줄 친 'which'는 'our community(지역 사회)'를 선행사로 하는 주격 관계대명사처럼 보이나, 문맥상 도서를 살 여유가 없을지도 모르는 주체는 '지역 사회'가 아닌 '아이들'이므로 선행사가 'children(아이들)'임을 알 수 있다. 따라서 사물인 선행사를 수식하는 'which'를 사람인 선행사를 수식하는 주격 관계대명사 'who' 또는 'that'으로 수정해야 한다.

해석

저희의 도서 기부 운동을 위해 아동 도서를 기부하는 방법에 대한 귀하의 질문에 감사드립니다. 이 행사는 9월 10일부터 16일까지 일주일간 열릴 것입니다. 이 기간 동안 하루 24시간 도서를 가져다주실 수 있습니다. 기부를 위해 지정된 장소로는 Adams 어린이 도서관과 Aileen 주민 센터 두 군데가 있습니다. 각 장소마다 정문에 파란색 기부 상자가 있습니다. 귀하께서 이곳을 방문하실 수 없다면, 도서를 저희 기관에 우편으로 직접 보내실 수 있습니다. 귀하의 기부는 도서를 살 여유가 없을지도 모르는 저희 지역 사회의 아이들을 지원하는 데 도움이 될 것입니다. 저희는 이 정보가 귀하의 기부를 더 용이하게 하기를 바랍니다.

어휘

donate 기부하다   book drive 도서 기부 운동
drop off ~을 가져다주다   designate 지정하다
directly 바로, 직접   afford (~을 할 금전적) 여유가 되다

06 정답 ②

정답해설

② **출제 포인트**: 이중부정 금지
밑줄 친 부분이 포함된 문장의 주어가 부정어를 포함한 부정대명사 'none'이므로 부정부사 'not'을 사용하면 이중부정이 되어 옳지 않다. 따라서 밑줄 친 'didn't have'를 'had'로 수정해야 한다.

오답해설

① **출제 포인트**: 관계부사 vs. 관계대명사
밑줄 친 'why'는 선행사 'the reason'이 생략된 관계부사이며 이후에 오는 절이 완전한 형태이므로 옳게 사용되었다.
③ **출제 포인트**: 현재분사 vs. 과거분사/분사구문
밑줄 친 'wait'은 완전자동사 'wait'의 현재분사이며 생략된 주어 'he'와 능동관계이므로 옳게 사용되었다.

④ 출제 포인트: 현재분사 vs. 과거분사

밑줄 친 'discarded'는 완전타동사 'discard'의 과거분사로, 수식하는 대상 'book'과 수동관계이며 해석상 '버려진 책'이 자연스러우므로 'discarded'는 옳은 표현이다.

해석

1972년 여름, 배우 Anthony Hopkins는 George Feifer의 소설 *The Girl from Petrovka*를 바탕으로 한 영화에서 주연을 맡기로 계약했다. 그것이 그가 그 소설책 한 권을 사기 위하여 런던으로 간 이유이다. 불행하게도, 런던의 주요 서점 어디에도 그 책은 한 권도 없었다. 그 후 집으로 돌아오는 길에, Leicester Square 지하철역에서 지하철을 기다리던 중 그는 그의 옆에 있던 의자 위에 놓여 있는 버려진 책을 보았다.

어휘

sign 계약을 체결하다
leading role 주연
underground train 지하철
discard 버리다, 폐기하다

07 정답 ④

정답해설

④ 출제 포인트: 주어와 동사의 수일치/many a+단수가산명사 vs. many+복수가산명사

'many a' 이후에는 단수가산명사가 오며 'many a+단수가산명사'가 주어인 경우 동사에 단수 형태를 사용한다. 해당 문장은 주어가 'many a man'이나 동사에 복수 형태인 'have'를 사용하였으므로 틀린 문장이다. 또한 주절과 종속절의 시제를 확인해보면 배가 들어온 시점은 과거시제인 'came'이고 부두를 떠난 시점은 이전의 사건이므로 'have left'를 'had left'로 고쳐야 옳다. 종속절의 시제가 과거이고 주절이 이전의 시점이므로 시제를 반영해서 주절의 시제를 과거완료인 'had left'로 수정해야 함에 유의하자.

오답해설

① 출제 포인트: 독립분사구문
해당 문장은 주절과 종속절의 주어가 다른 독립분사구문으로 원래 문장은 'As the sea was calm, we decided to go diving.'이다.

② 출제 포인트: 시제 일치
내가 기다리는 시점과 찬물 한 잔을 들이킨 시점이 일치하며, 주절에 과거시제를 사용하였으므로 종속절에 과거시제를 사용한 것은 옳다.

③ 출제 포인트: 조동사+have+과거분사
「need+not+have+p.p.」는 '~할 필요는 없었는데 (했다)'를 뜻한다. 해당 문장은 주어진 해석이 '~할 필요는 없었는데 (했다)'이므로 'need not have participated'는 옳은 표현이다. 또한 'participate'는 완전자동사로 전치사 'in'과 함께 쓰여 목적어를 가진다.

오답률 TOP 3

08 정답 ②

정답해설

본문 첫 문장에서 주제가 나타난다. "Today, the World Anti-Doping Agency (WADA) has a new hurdle to overcome — that of gene doping(오늘날, World Anti-Doping Agency (WADA)는 극복해야 할 새로운 장애물을 가지고 있다. 바로 유전자 도핑이다.)"이라고 '새로운 유형의 도핑인 유전자 도핑'에 관해 소개하고 있다. '유전자 도핑은 적발하기 어렵다'는 것을 본문을 통해 알 수 있고, 이로 인해 '스포츠의 정정당당한 승부에 위협이 된다'는 점을 유추할 수 있다. 따라서 글의 제목으로 가장 적절한 것은 '② A New Threat to Fair Play in Sport(스포츠에서 공정한 경기에 대한 새로운 위협)'이다.

오답해설

① 본문에서는 도핑이 이용되는 특정 종목에 관해 언급하지 않고 있으며, 특히 '유전자 도핑'에 초점을 맞추고 있으므로, 글의 제목으로 적절하지 않다.
③ '도핑 검사가 필요한 이유'는 본문에 언급되지 않는다.
④ '유전자 도핑의 장, 단점'에 관해서는 본문에 언급되지 않는다.

해석

오늘날, World Anti-Doping Agency (WADA)는 극복해야 할 새로운 장애물을 가지고 있다 - 바로 유전자 도핑이다. 이 관행은 운동 기록을 향상시키기 위해 세포, 유전자 또는 유전적 요소의 비 치료적인 사용으로 정의된다. 유전자 도핑은 질병을 치료하거나 예방하기 위해 유전자 물질의 인간 세포로의 이전을 포함하는 유전자 치료의 최첨단 연구를 이용한다. 유전자 도핑이 세포가 일반적으로 만드는 단백질과 호르몬의 양을 증가시키기 때문에, 유전적 기록 향상제를 검사하는 것은 매우 어려울 것이고, 이러한 형식의 도핑을 적발하는 방법을 개발하기 위한 새로운 경쟁이 진행 중이다. 더 나은 운동선수를 만들기 위해 유전자를 바꿀 가능성은 1990년대 후반 소위 "Schwarzenegger 쥐"의 발명과 함께 즉각적으로 실현되었다. 이 쥐들은 증가된 근육 성장과 힘을 가지도록 유전적으로 설계되었기 때문에 이 별명을 얻었다.

① 다양한 스포츠에서의 도핑
② 스포츠에서 공정한 경기에 대한 새로운 위협
③ 운동선수들이 도핑 검사를 받아야 하는 이유
④ 유전자 도핑: 장점과 단점

어휘

overcome 극복하다
doping 도핑, 금지 약물 복용[사용]
nontherapeutic 비 치료적인
athletic performance 운동 기록
take advantage of 이용하다, 편승하다
cutting-edge 최첨단의
alter 바꾸다, 고치다
realize 실현하다

09 정답 ①

정답해설

본문에서 언급된 '이국적인 고기 섭취(ate exotic meats), 여성이 남성인 척 하는 것(pretending to be men), 아편틴크 사용(used laudanum), 스트리크닌 복용(downed several doses of strychnine)' 등은 모두 정상적인 경쟁이 아닌 '부정행위'에 해당한다. 따라서 빈칸에 가장 적절한 표현은 '① there has been cheating(부정행위가 있어왔다)'이다.

오답해설

② 본문에서 언급된 '코치' 혹은 '트레이너'는 본문 후반의 'Charles Lucas' 뿐이므로, 글 전체를 아우르는 내용이 '코칭'에 대한 것이 아님을 알 수 있다. 따라서 오답이다.
나머지 보기는 본문과 관련 없는 내용이므로 오답이다.

해석

스포츠가 존재하는 한, 부정행위가 있어왔다. 고대 올림픽에서 참가자들은 그들에게 아마도 힘을 주었던 이국적인 고기를 섭취했다. 염색체 검사 이전, 그리스인들은 여성이 남성인 척하는 것을 방지하기 위해 알몸으로 경쟁했다. 1807년, Abraham Wood는 위대한 Captain Barclay에 대항해 경보 경기를 하는 중 24시간 동안 깨어있기 위해 아편틴크를 사용했다고 주장했다. 1904년 올림픽 마라톤에서, 미국인 Thomas J. Hicks는 그의 "트레이너" Charles Lucas가 준 다량의 스트리크닌과 계란 흰자를 마신 후, 큰 잔의 브랜디를 마셨다. 그가 비록 2등으로 완주했으나, 1등 완주자인 Fred Lorz가 적어도 3마일을 차로 이동했다는 것이 밝혀졌을 때, 그는 우승자로 선언되었다. 이후, Lucas는 "그 마라톤 경주가 도로에서는 약물이 선수들에게 매우 이롭다는 것을 증명했다"라고 떠벌렸다.

① 부정행위가 있어왔다
② 코칭이 있어왔다
③ 스포츠 팬이 있어왔다
④ 스포츠 도박이 있어왔다

어휘

exotic 이국적인, 외국의
supposedly 아마, 정황상
chromosome 염색체
laudanum 아편틴크(아편으로 만든 약물)
racewalk 경보 경기하다
down 급히 다 먹다[마시다], 죽 들이켜다
dose (어느 정도의) 양, 약간, 복용량
strychnine 스트리크닌(극소량이 약품으로 이용되는 독성 물질)
brag (심하게) 자랑하다, 떠벌리다

10 정답 ④

정답해설

본문은 '과학 부정론자(Science denialists)'에 대한 글로써 과학과는 달리 그들의 주장은 증명된 근거에 뒷받침되지 않는다고 말한다. 주어진 문장에서, 가정법을 이용해 '사실과 반대되는 내용'을 설명하고 있으므로, 실제로 '부정론자들은 지구 온난화 또는 진화를 반박할 근거를 가지고 있지 않다'는 것을 알 수 있다. ④ 이후 문장에서 "But, knowing their arguments don't hold water(그러나, 그들의 주장이 타당하지 않다는 것을 알기 때문에)"라고 언급하며, 앞서 주어진 문장에서 유추할 수 있는 내용을 재차 언급해주고 있으므로, 해당 문장 이전에 주어진 문장이 등장하는 것이 문맥상 자연스럽다. 따라서 정답은 ④이다.

오답해설

③ 이후 문장의 "thousands of peer-reviewed journal articles"가 ③ 이전 문장의 'overwhelming evidence(압도적인 증거)'를, ③ 이후 문장의 "opinion polls and talk radio(여론조사와 라디오의 전화 토론 프로그램)"가 ③ 이전 문장의 "a few hoaxes(날조된 것)"를 각각 직간접적으로 가리키고 있으므로, 두 문장이 서로 연달아 이어지는 것이 문맥상 자연스럽다. 따라서 오답이다.

나머지 위치는 문맥상 어색하므로 오답이다.

해석

진화에서부터 지구 온난화와 백신까지, 과학은 잘 실험된 과학적 지식을 단지 많은 경쟁하고 있는 이념들 중 하나로 일축하는 사람들인 부정론자들로부터의 공격을 받고 있다. 과학은 자연이 어떻게 작용하는지에 대한 결론이 증거에 기반 한 실험에 기초할 것을 요구한다. 때때로 진행은 더디다. 그러나 어렵고 종종 좌절감을 주는 과정을 통해, 우리는 세계에 대해 더 많이 배울 수 있다. (①) 과학 부정주의는 다르게 작용한다. 창조론자들은 화석, 분자, 그리고 진화의 해부학적 증거의 풍부함에 흔들리지 않는다. 지구 온난화 부정론자들은 산더미 같은 기후 자료에 감명받지 않는다. (②) 부정론자들은 압도적인 증거를 무시하고, 대신에 날조된 것에 집중한다. (③) 부정론자들에게는 여론조사와 라디오의 전화 토론 프로그램이 수천 개의 동료 심사를 받은 학술지 기사들보다 더 중요하다. (④ **만일 부정론자들이 지구 온난화 또는 진화를 반박하는 증거를 가지고 있다면, 과학자들에 의한 분석을 요청하면서, 그들은 과학 학회와 학술지에 그것을 제출했을 것이다.**) 그러나 그들의 주장이 타당하지 않다는 것을 알기 때문에, 그들은 전문적인 철저한 검토의 대상이 아닌 대량 판매용의 도서, 신문, 라디오의 전화 토론 프로그램, 그리고 블로그와 같은 활동 무대에서 잘못된 정보를 퍼뜨린다.

어휘

assault 공격, 도전, 폭행
denialist 부정론자
dismiss (고려할 가치가 없다고) 묵살[일축]하다
merely 단지
unmoved by …에 무감동한, 마음이 흔들리지 않는
molecular 분자
anatomical 해부학적인
unimpressed by …에 감명받지 않는, …이 대단하다고 생각하지 않는
mountain 산더미
hoax 거짓말, 날조, 조작, 장난질
opinion poll 여론조사
talk radio (라디오의) 전화 토론 프로그램
peer-reviewed 동료 심사를 받은
disprove 반박하다, 틀렸음을 입증하다
argument 주장
hold water 타당하다, 이치에 맞다
arena (각축전이 벌어지는) 무대
subject to …의 대상인
scrutiny 정밀 조사, 철저한 검토
mass-market 일반 대중을 대상으로 한, 대량 판매 시장용의

기적사 DAY 55

01	③	02	②	03	①	04	④	05	②
06	③	07	③	08	②	09	④	10	②

01 정답 ③

정답해설

밑줄 친 'allusive'는 '암시적인'을 뜻하는 형용사로 ③ connotative(암시하는, 함축적인)와 의미가 가장 가깝다.

오답해설

① 직설적인, 무딘
② 의기양양한, 우쭐해하는
③ 암시하는, 함축적인
④ 거만한, 남을 얕보는

해석

그의 시는 매우 **암시적**이고 많은 다른 해석들을 할 수 있다.

어휘

allusive 암시적인
capable (능력·특질 상) ~을 할 수 있는; 유능한
interpretation 해석; 연출; 통역　　blunt 직설적인, 무딘
smug 의기양양한, 우쭐해하는　　connotative 암시하는, 함축적인
supercilious 거만한, 남을 얕보는

오답률 TOP 2
02 정답 ②

정답해설

밑줄 친 'depreciate'는 '가치가 하락하다'를 뜻하는 동사로 ② detract(가치가 떨어지다)와 의미가 가장 가깝다.

해석

G-20 회의의 합의가 기존 원칙을 재확인하는 것이었기 때문에, 전문가들은 엔화 **가치가 더 하락할** 것으로 예측했다.
① 평가 절상하다
② 가치가 떨어지다
③ 의문을 제기하다
④ 폄하하다

어휘

reconfirm 재확인하다　　principle 원칙, 원리
predict 예측[예견]하다　　yen 엔화(일본의 화폐 단위)
depreciate 가치가 하락하다　　further 더; 더 멀리에
revalue 평가 절상하다　　detract 가치가 떨어지다
impugn 의문을 제기하다　　disparage 폄하하다

오답률 TOP 1
03 정답 ①

정답해설

밑줄 친 'inclusive'는 '포괄적인, 폭넓은'을 뜻하는 형용사로 ① sweeping(포괄적인, 전면적인)과 의미가 가장 가깝다.

해석

포괄적이고 지속 가능한 세계 경제 성장을 위해 국제사회 내부에의 협력은 매우 중요하다.
① 포괄적인, 전면적인
② 말을 잘 듣는
③ 확정적인, 확실한
④ 극히 추상적인, 난해한

어휘

cooperation 협력, 합동, 협동　　inclusive 포괄적인, 폭넓은
sustainable 지속[유지] 가능한　　sweeping 포괄적인, 전면적인
amenable 말을 잘 듣는　　determinate 확정적인, 확실한
metaphysical 극히 추상적인, 난해한

오답률 TOP 3
04 정답 ④

정답해설

Serena는 자신이 아르바이트하는 카페의 사장에 대해 Jaden에게 말한다. 사장으로 인해 스트레스를 많이 받는다고 말하며, 자신의 사장이 '심술 맞은 사람(a dog in the manger)'이라고 이야기한다. 따라서 정답은 ④이다.

오답해설

① Serena는 자신의 아르바이트 상사에 대한 불만을 Jaden에게 털어놓으면서 상사가 '이익을 불러오는 사업(a cash cow)'이라고 하는 것은 문맥상 부자연스럽다.
② Serena는 "자신이 아르바이트 상사를 좋아하지 않는다"라고 말하며 상사를 '생계 수단(bread and butter)'이라고 부르는 것은 대화의 흐름상 빈칸에 들어갈 말로 어색하다.
③ Serena가 Serena의 아르바이트 상사에 관해 이야기하며, 상사가 '회의론자(doubting Thomas)'이기 때문에 별로 좋아하지 않는다고 얘기하는 것은 대화의 내용을 고려했을 때 적절하지 않다.

해석

Serena: 난 너무 지쳤어! 나는 정말 쉴 시간이 필요해.
Jaden: 너 오늘 되게 힘든 하루를 겪은 것처럼 보여. 무슨 일이야?
Serena: 나는 최근에 카페에서 아르바이트를 구했는데 내가 상사를 정말 별로 안 좋아해.
Jaden: 너 되게 스트레스 많이 받겠다. 너에게 무슨 일을 한 거야?
Serena: 이 말은 정말 하고 싶지 않았는데, 내 상사는 심술 맞은 사람이야.
Jaden: 그가 불친절하고 욕심에 가득 찬 사람 같이 들리네. 내가 맞아?
Serena: 맞아. 그는 우리가 일할 때 절대 앉도록 허락해주지 않아. 근데 그는 앉아 있고 우리가 일하는 곳 바로 뒤에서 우리를 계속 항상 지켜보고 있어.
Jaden: 오, 내가 상상했던 것보다 훨씬 스트레스를 많이 받겠다.
① 이익을 불러오는 사업
② 생계 수단
③ 회의론자
④ 심술 맞은 사람

어휘

exhausted 기진맥진한, 탈진한; 고갈된
harsh 가혹한, 냉혹한　　unfriendly 불친절한, 비우호적인
greed 탐욕; 식탐　　a cash cow 이익을 불러오는 사업
bread and butter 생계 수단　　doubting Thomas 회의론자
a dog in the manger 심술 맞은 사람

05 정답 ②

정답해설

② 출제 포인트: 주어와 동사의 수일치
밑줄 친 'are'는 복수형태의 동사이므로 주어와 수일치 하는지 확인해야 한다. 주어가 복수형태의 명사(구) 'Parents and children'이므로 'are'는 옳은 표현이다.

오답해설

① 출제 포인트: want vs. hope
'hope'는 목적어로 'that+절'을 가질 수 있으나 'want'는 목적어로 'that+절'을 가질 수 없다. 해당 문장은 밑줄 친 'want' 이후에 'that+절'이 목적어로 왔으므로 옳지 않다. 따라서 'want'를 'hope'로 수정해야 한다.

③ 출제 포인트: 가주어 It
밑줄 친 'That'은 대명사이나 문맥상 가리키는 대상이 to부정사(구) 'to check the garden for potential dangers'이므로 'That'을 대명사 'It'으로 수정해야 한다. 이때 'It'은 가주어이며 'to check the garden for potential dangers'는 진주어에 해당한다.

④ 출제 포인트: 접속사 vs. 전치사(make sure that vs. make sure of)
'make sure of'는 이후에 명사(구)가 오며 'make sure that'은 이후에 명사절이 온다. 해당 문장은 'make sure of' 이후에 명사절 'all dangerous equipment and machinery are safely stored'가 왔으므로 밑줄 친 'of'를 'that'으로 수정해야 한다.

해석

다음 주 월요일에, Nature's Beauty Gardens에서는 매년 열리는 'Toddler Trek' 행사를 위해 매우 중요한 고객들을 즐거운 마음으로 초대할 것입니다. 저희는 이 행사가 걸음마를 배우는 아이들에게 재미있고, 교육적이고, 그리고 가장 중요하게는 안전하기를 희망합니다. 이 행사에 참여하는 부모와 아이들은 야외 활동을 즐기고 점심 도시락을 들면서 시간을 보낼 것입니다. 따라서 잠재적인 위험에 대비해 정원을 점검하는 것이 매우 중요합니다. 각 부서의 관리자들은 모든 위험한 장비와 기계들이 안전하게 보관되어 있는지 확실하게 해야 합니다.

어휘

toddler 걸음마를 배우는 아이 outdoor 야외의
potential 잠재적인 department 부서
equipment 장비 machinery 기계(류)

06 정답 ③

정답해설

③ 출제 포인트: what vs. that
해당 문장에서 동사 'see'의 목적어가 명사절 'health is not linearly related to control'임을 알 수 있다. 관계대명사 'what'은 선행사를 포함하며 뒤따라오는 문장이 불완전한 형태이나 밑줄 친 'what' 이후의 문장 'health ~ control'은 완전한 문장이므로 관계대명사 'what'을 사용할 수 없다. 따라서 관계대명사 'what'을 접속사 'that'으로 수정해야 한다.

오답해설

① 출제 포인트: 접속사의 쓰임
밑줄 친 'when'은 접속사로 종속절 'people who feel helpless fail to take control'을 이끌며, 접속사 'that'이 이끄는 명사절 'they experience negative emotional states such as anxiety and depression'의 동사 'experience'를 수식하는 부사 역할을 한다.

② 출제 포인트: 전치사의 쓰임
밑줄 친 'Like'는 전치사이며 이후에 목적어 'stress'가 왔으므로 옳은 표현이다.

④ 출제 포인트: 불완전타동사와 목적격 보어/불완전타동사의 수동태
불완전타동사 'encourage'는 목적격 보어로 to부정사를 가진다. 해당 문장은 불완전타동사 'encourage'의 수동태가 쓰인 문장이며 밑줄 친 'to take'는 'encourage'의 목적격 보어에 해당하므로 옳은 표현이다.

해석

연구는 무력함을 느끼는 사람들이 통제하는 데 실패할 때, 그들이 불안과 우울증과 같은 부정적인 감정 상태를 경험한다는 것을 보여주었다. 스트레스처럼, 이런 부정적인 감정들은 면역 반응을 손상할 수 있다. 이것으로부터 우리는 건강이 통제와 곧장 연결되어 있지 않다는 것을 알 수 있다. 최적의 건강을 위해, 사람들은 어느 정도까지 통제하지만 더 이상의 통제가 불가능한 때를 인식하도록 권장되어야 한다.

어휘

helpless 무력한 depression 우울증
immune response 면역 반응 linearly 곧장, 직선으로

07 정답 ③

정답해설

③ 출제 포인트: 조동사+have+과거분사
「should+have+p.p.」는 '~했어야 했는데 (하지 못했다)'를 뜻하며 「could+have+p.p.」는 '~했을 수도 있다'를 뜻한다. 해당 문장은 주어진 해석이 '~했어야 했는데 (하지 못했다)'이나 'could have been'을 사용하였으므로 옳지 않다. 따라서 'could'를 'should'로 수정해야 한다.

오답해설

① 출제 포인트: 독립분사구문
해당 문장은 주절과 종속절의 주어가 다른 독립분사구문으로 원래 문장은 'As there was no taxi, I couldn't go home yesterday.'이다. 이때 'there was no taxi'는 유도부사구문으로 주어는 'no taxi'이다.

② 출제 포인트: 시제 일치
사람들이 흩어진 시점보다 유명 가수가 떠난 시점이 먼저이며, 주절에 과거시제를 사용하였으므로 종속절에 과거완료시제를 사용한 것은 옳다.

④ 출제 포인트: 주어와 동사의 수일치
'curry and rice'는 두 개의 명사이지만 하나의 개념이므로 단수로 취급한다. 따라서 해당 문장의 동사에 단수 형태인 'is'를 옳게 사용하였다.

08 정답 ②

정답해설

(A) 이전 문장 "However, the rapid advancement of technology before and after the turn of the twenty-first century makes designer babies an increasingly real possibility(그러나 21세기로의 전환 전후의 빠른 기술의 진보가 디자이너 아기를 점점 더 현실성 있는 가능성으로 만들어준다)."에서, '디자이너 아기 탄생의 현실성이 점점 더 커지고 있음'을 언급하고 있으며, (A) 이후에서는 '디자이너 아기가 생명 윤리 논쟁에서 중요한 주제'가 되었음을 설명하고 있다. 즉, '이전에는 비현실적인 사안이었으므로, 논쟁이 적었던 반면, 현재는 실현 가능성이 커졌기 때문에, 결과적으로 생명 윤리 논쟁 또한 격렬해지고 있다'는 내용이 되는 것이 자연스러우므로, 빈칸에는 '결과, 인과'를 나타내는 'As a result(결과적으로)'가 들어가는 것이 자연스럽다.

(B) 이전 내용은 '디자이너 아기는 (아직은) 실현되지 않은 학문 분야일 뿐'이라는 것이고, (B) 이후의 내용은, '(아직 현실이 되지 않았지만) 이미 규제에 관한 우려를 이끌어내고 있다'는 것이다. 따라서 빈칸에는 '양보'를 나타내는 'nonetheless'가 들어가는 것이 가장 적절하다.
따라서 정답은 '② As a result(결과적으로) – nonetheless(그럼에도 불구하고)'이다.

오답해설
나머지 보기는 문맥상 어색하므로 오답이다.

해석
디자이너 아기는 특별히 선택된 특징을 위해 체외에서 유전자 조작으로 생성된 아기이며, 이러한 특징은 낮아진 질병의 위험에서부터 성별 선택까지 다를 수 있다. 유전 공학과 체외수정의 출현 이전에, 디자이너 아기는 주로 공상 과학 개념이었다. 그러나 21세기로의 전환 전후의 빠른 기술의 진보가 디자이너 아기를 점점 더 현실성 있는 가능성으로 만들어준다. (A) 결과적으로, 디자이너 아기는 생명 윤리 논쟁에서 중요한 주제가 되었고, 심지어 2004년 "디자이너 아기"라는 용어는 Oxford English Dictionary에 공식으로 수록되었다. 디자이너 아기는 아직 실질적인 현실이 되지 않은 태생학 내의 한 분야를 대표하지만, (B) 그럼에도 불구하고 향후 디자이너 아기에 대한 규제를 시행해야 할 필요가 있을지 없을지에 대한 윤리적인 우려를 이끌어낸다.

(A)	(B)
① 반면에	그렇지 않으면
② 결과적으로	그럼에도 불구하고
③ 게다가	그에 따라
④ 예를 들어	안타깝게도

어휘
in vitro 체외[시험관]에서
advent 출현, 도래
bioethical 생명 윤리의
ethical 윤리적인
limitation 규제, 제약
trait 특성, 특징
in vitro fertilization 체외수정
embryology 태생학
implement 시행하다
regarding …에 관한

09 정답 ④

정답해설
본문은 '마라톤(marathon)의 기원'에 대한 글이며, 주어진 문장은 '현대 마라톤의 거리(distance)가 표준화된 사실'에 대해 언급하고 있으므로, 주어진 문장 전후에 '거리'에 관한 내용이 언급되는 것이 자연스럽다. ④ 이후 문장에서, "It was the exact measurement between Windsor Castle, the start of the race, and the finish line inside White City Stadium(그것은 경주의 시작점인 Windsor Castle과 White City Stadium 내부의 결승선을 정확히 측정한 길이였다)."라고 설명하며, 해당 거리가 어떻게 측정되었는지 구체적으로 설명하고 있으므로, 주어진 문장 이후에 이어지는 것이 가장 자연스럽다. 따라서 정답은 ④이다.

오답해설
② 최초 마라톤의 거리를 언급한 ② 이전의 문장 이후에, 현대 마라톤의 거리를 언급하는 주어진 문장이 등장하는 것이 어색하지는 않지만, 그렇게 된다면 마지막 문장의 'It'이 가리키는 것이 ④ 이전 문장에 존재하지 않게 되므로, 문맥상 자연스럽지 않게 된다. 따라서 ②에 주어진 문장이 들어가는 것은 전체적인 글의 흐름상 적절하지 않다.

나머지 보기는 문맥상 어색하므로 오답이다.

해석
마라톤은 고대 올림픽 경기의 종목이 아니었다. (①) 그것은 Athens에서 열린 1896년 현대 올림픽 경기에서 최초로 도입된 현대 종목으로, 40킬로미터 거리인 Athens의 북동쪽에 있는 Marathon으로부터 올림픽 경기장까지의 경주였다. (②) 그 경주는 전투를 위한 도움을 요청하기 위해 페르시아인들이 기원전 490년에 Marathon에 상륙한 소식을 Sparta에(149마일의 거리) 전한 고대의 "주간 보발"이었던 Pheidippides의 질주를 기념한다. (③) 기원전 5세기 고대 그리스 역사학자 Herodotus에 따르면 Pheidippides는 스파르타인들에게 그 소식을 이튿날 전달했다. (④ **현대 마라톤의 거리는 올림픽 경기가 London에서 개최된 1908년에 26마일 3850야드 또는 42.195km로 표준화되었다.**) 그것은 경주의 시작점인 Windsor Castle과 White City Stadium 내부의 결승선을 정확히 측정한 길이였다.

어휘
event 종목, 경기
runner 사자(使者), 보발(步撥)
standardize 표준화하다
commemorate 기념하다
enlist 요청하다
measurement 치수[크기/길이/양]

10 정답 ②

정답해설
본문은 '과학 연구자들이 겪는 어려움'에 대해 설명하는 글로써, 첫 번째 문장 "Scientific researchers face perpetual struggle to secure and sustain funding(과학 연구원들은 자금을 확보하고 유지하기 위한 끊임없는 투쟁에 직면한다)."을 통해 글의 요지를 엿볼 수 있다. 즉, 과학 연구를 위한 자금이 부족하고, 그로 인해 연구 주제의 폭이 좁아지며, 연구의 질이 떨어진다고 설명하고 있다. 따라서 전체 글의 주제로 가장 적절한 것은 '② The financial short in the field of science(과학계의 재정 부족)'이다.

오답해설
① 본문에서 '자금을 획득하는 것의 어려움'에 관해서는 언급하고 있으나, '자금을 획득하는 방법'에 관해서는 언급하고 있지 않다.
③ 세 번째 문장 "The situation is particularly for early career researchers who find it difficult to compete for funds with senior researchers(그 상황은 특히 선임 연구원들과 자금을 놓고 경쟁하는 것을 어려워하는 신참 연구원들에게 존재한다)."에서 언급된 '경쟁'은 '자금 확보를 위한 경쟁'이고, 보기의 'high competitions'는 더 광범위한 일반적인 '경쟁'을 포함하고 있으므로, 본문의 주제로는 적절하지 않다.
④ 본문과 관련이 적은 내용이다.

해석
과학 연구원들은 자금을 확보하고 유지하기 위한 끊임없는 투쟁에 직면한다. 과학계 종사 인구는 증가하고 있는 반면, 대부분의 국가에서의 자금은 과거 10년 동안 감소해오고 있다. 그 상황은 특히 선임 연구원들과 자금을 놓고 경쟁하는 것을 어려워하는 신참 연구원들에게 존재한다. 이 극단적인 경쟁은 또한 과학이 수행되는 방식에도 영향을 미치고 있다. Vox 설문 조사의 응답자들은 대부분의 보조금이 오직 몇 년 동안만 할당되기 때문에, 연구원들이 단기 프로젝트를 선택하는 경향이 있고, 이는 때때로 복잡한 연구 과제를 연구하기에는 불충분할 수 있다는 점을 지적했다. 이것은 연구원들이 자금 제공원과 그들의 기관을 행복하게 유지할 것에 기반하여 선택을 한다는 것을 의미한다. 그러나 이러한 선택의 결과는 수준 이하의 질과 낮은 연구 영향력을 가진 출판 논문들 수의 증가이다.

① 연구를 위한 자금을 획득하는 방법
② 과학계의 재정 부족
③ 신규 그리고 선임 과학자들 사이의 높은 경쟁
④ 과학 연구와 출판의 중요성

어휘

perpetual (오랫동안) 끊임없이 계속되는, 빈번한
struggle 투쟁, 분투
sustain 유지하다, 지속시키다
early career 초기 경력(자)
allot 할당하다, 배당하다
body (흔히 공공 목적을 위해 함께 일하는) 단체[조직]
substandard 수준 이하의
secure 확보하다
workforce 노동 인구[노동력]
grant 보조금
insufficient 불충분한

기적사 DAY 56

결국엔 성정혜 영어 하프모의고사

| 01 | ④ | 02 | ① | 03 | ④ | 04 | ② | 05 | ① |
| 06 | ① | 07 | ② | 08 | ① | 09 | ③ | 10 | ④ |

01 정답 ④   17 서울시

[정답해설]

밑줄 친 'cardinal'은 '중요한'이라는 뜻으로 ④ principal(주요한, 주된)과 의미가 가장 가깝다.

[해석]

판매원으로서, 당신은 당신의 가장 **중요한** 원칙이 고객을 만족시키기 위해 당신이 할 수 있는 모든 것을 하는 것이라는 것을 기억해야 한다.
① 결정적인
② 거대한
③ 잠재적인
④ 주요한, 주된

[어휘]

salesman 판매원
satisfy 만족시키다; 충족시키다
gigantic 거대한
principal 주요한, 주된
cardinal 중요한; 추기경; 진홍색의
definitive 결정적인
potential 잠재적인

02 정답 ①   17 서울시

[정답해설]

밑줄 친 'surreptitious'는 '비밀리에 하는'을 뜻하며 ① clandestine(비밀리에 하는, 은밀한)과 그 의미가 가장 가깝다.

[해석]

비밀리에 하는 녹음의 오디오는 참가자가 녹음되기를 원하지 않았다는 것을 분명하게 나타낸다.
① 비밀리에 하는, 은밀한
② 법에 명시된, 법으로 정한
③ 솔직한
④ 천사 같은, 맑은, 거룩한

[어휘]

surreptitious 비밀리에 하는
clandestine 비밀리에 하는, 은밀한
forthright 솔직한
indicate 나타내다[보여 주다]
statutory 법에 명시된, 법으로 정한
seraphic 천사 같은, 맑은, 거룩한

오답률 TOP 1
03 정답 ④   17 서울시

[정답해설]

'desultory'는 '두서없는, 종잡을 수 없는'이라는 의미로 ④ disconnected(일관성이 없는)와 의미가 가장 가깝다.

[해석]

3년 동안의 **두서없는** 배회 후에, 그 노인은 스페인 남부에 있는 지역인 Andalusia로 왔다.

① 목적 있는, 결의에 찬
② 비참한
③ 금욕적인
④ 일관성이 없는

어휘

desultory 두서없는, 종잡을 수 없는
purposeful 목적 있는, 결의에 찬
ascetic 금욕적인
wander 돌아다니다, 헤매다
miserable 비참한
disconnected 일관성이 없는; 단절된

04 정답 ②   15 서울시

정답해설

「should have + p.p.」(~했어야 했는데)로 과거의 하지 못한 일을 후회하는 표현이다. B가 미안하다며 어떠한 응답을 하자 A는 '예약을 했어야 했다'고 말하고 있으므로, B는 빈방이 없다고 말했을 것임을 유추할 수 있다. 따라서 정답은 ② 'We're completely booked(방이 모두 예약되었어요).'이다.

오답해설

①, ③, ④ 나머지 선지는 문맥상 적절하지 않다.

해석

A: 빈방 있나요?
B: 죄송해요. 방이 모두 예약되었어요.
A: 예약을 했어야 했는데.
B: 그게 좋았겠죠.
① 일행이 몇 분이시죠?
② 방이 모두 예약되었어요.
③ 방이 많이 있어요.
④ 어떤 방을 찾으시나요?

어휘

vacancy (호텔 등의) 빈방[객실]; 결원, 공석
reservation 예약
company 일행, 동료; 회사

오답률 TOP 2
05 정답 ①   19 서울시

정답해설

① **출제 포인트: '동사+부사'의 목적어 위치**
「go through+목적어」는 관용표현으로 '~을 검토하다, 조사하다'를 뜻하며 이때 'through'는 전치사이므로 'go+목적어+through'의 형태로 사용할 수 없다. 해당 문장은 「go through+목적어」를 'go+목적어+through」의 형태로 사용하였으므로 틀린 문장이다. 따라서 'go the documents through'를 'go through the documents'로 수정해야 한다.

오답해설

② **출제 포인트: 부정부사(구) 도치/주어와 동사의 수일치/the number of vs. a number of**
부정부사(구) 'Not only'가 문두에 오고 동사가 현재완료인 경우 이후에 오는 어순은 「have/has+주어+과거분사」이다. 해당 문장은 문두에 'Not only'를 사용하였으므로 이후에 오는 「have/has+주어+과거분사」 형태인 'has the number of baseball players increased'는 옳은 표현이다. 이때 주어가 「the number of+목적어[복수명사]」인 경우 동사의 수일치 기준은 단수 형태인 'the number'이므로 'has'를 사용하는 것이 옳다. 또한 'but so' 이후에 나오는 문장의 주어는 복수 형태인 'the values'이므로 'have'가 도치되어 주어 전에 위치하는 것은 적절하다.

③ **출제 포인트: 비교급 비교**
불가산명사 'money' 앞에 형용사 'much'의 비교급인 'more'를 사용하였고 비교 대상 앞에 접속사 'than'을 사용하였으므로 해당 문장은 옳은 문장이다.

④ **출제 포인트: 능동태 vs. 수동태**
해당 문장은 완전타동사 'give'가 과거시제 수동태로 쓰인 문장으로 'was given' 이후에 있는 「전치사+목적어[대상]」인 'to a local private university'는 옳은 표현이다. 이때 해당 문장을 능동태로 바꾸면 'The Ministry of Education gave a huge research fund to a local private university.'와 같다.

해석

① 사장님은 이사회가 시작하기 전에 우리 팀이 서류를 검토하는 것을 원한다.
② 야구 선수들의 수가 증가해왔을 뿐만 아니라 선수들의 가치들도 증가해왔다.
③ Bob은 그가 갚을 수 있는 것보다 더 많은 돈을 은행에서부터 빌리는 경향이 있다.
④ 아주 큰 연구 자금은 교육부에 의해 지방의 사립대에 주어졌다.

오답률 TOP 3
06 정답 ①   19 서울시

정답해설

① **출제 포인트: one of the 최상급 복수명사**
'one of the 최상급 복수명사'는 '가장 ~한 것 중에 하나'라는 뜻이다. 밑줄 친 'one of easiest jobs'는 최상급 'easiest' 앞에 'the'가 빠진 형태이므로 옳지 않다. 따라서 'easiest' 앞에 'the'를 추가해 'one of the easiest jobs'로 수정해야한다.

오답해설

② **출제 포인트: 현재분사 vs. 과거분사**
분사구문의 주어를 파악하면 능동 분사구문이 적절한지 수동분사구문이 적절한지 알 수 있다. 'waving his arms in time with the music'의 주어는 분사구문 앞에 위치한 'he'이므로 능동형 분사구문이 어법상 적절한 것을 알 수 있다.

③ **출제 포인트: 보어도치**
'Hidden from the audience ~ novice'가 문두로 강조된, 보어 도치에 해당된다. 어순은 '보어 + 동사 + 주어'로 주어인 'abilities'가 문장의 주어로서 동사는 'are'로 수일치 하므로 적절하게 사용되었다.

④ **출제 포인트: to부정사의 형용사적 용법**
밑줄 친 'to motivate and communicate with all of the orchestra members'는 'the conductor's abilities'를 수식하는 to부정사의 형용사적 용법으로 옳게 사용되었으며, 'to read and interpret', 'to play ~ and understand' 그리고 'to organize and coordinate'와 병렬구조로 사용되었다.

해석

관객석에서 콘서트를 보는 음악 애호가에게, 지휘자는 세상에서 가장 쉬운 직업을 가지고 있다고 믿는 것은 쉬울 것이다. 그는 그곳에 서서, 음악에 맞춰 팔을 흔들고 오케스트라는 찬란한 소리를 내는데, 어느 모로 보나 아주 자연스럽게 보인다. 특히 음악적 초보자들인 청중들로부터 숨겨져 있는 지휘자의 능력은 모든 부분을 한 번에 해석하고 여러 악기를 연주하고 더 많은 것들의 역할을 이해하고, 이질적인 부분들을 조직하고 조율하며, 모든 오케스트라 단원들과 동기부여하고 소통을 하는 능력이다.

어휘

conductor 지휘자
spontaneously 자연스럽게
to all appearances 어느 모로 보나
novice 초보자

capacity 능력, 역할
coordinate 조율하다
disparate 이질적인 부분들로 이뤄진

07 정답 ② 19 서울시

정답해설

㉠ 출제 포인트: 주어와 동사의 수일치
㉠이 포함된 문장의 주어가 복수 형태인 'Supplements'이므로 복수 형태의 동사 'include'를 사용하는 것이 옳다.

㉡ 출제 포인트: 현재분사 vs. 과거분사
㉡ 다음에 목적어인 'natural herbs'가 있으므로 능동의 의미를 갖는 현재분사 'containing'이 적합한 표현이다.

㉢ 출제 포인트: 접속사의 쓰임(whether vs. if)
㉢ 다음에 'the vitamins come from synthetic or natural sources (비타민이 합성물 혹은 천연 원료로부터 온다)'라는 표현이 있으므로 'whether A or B'가 적절한 표현이다. 따라서 ㉢에는 'whether'가 적절하다.

따라서 정답은 ② 'include, containing, whether'이다.

오답해설

㉠ 'includes'는 주어인 'Supplements'와 주술 일치가 되지 않으므로 정답이 될 수 없다.
㉡ 과거분사 'contained'는 빈칸 이후에 타동사 'contain'의 분사 형태인 'containing'이 가져야 할 목적어 'natural herbs'가 있으므로 적절한 표현이 아니다.
㉢ 'if'절은 전치사의 목적어 절로 사용할 수 없다.

해석

오늘날 시판되는 보조식품에는 천연 허브나 합성 재료를 사용한 것들이 포함된다. 전문가들은 복합 비타민 중에서 선택할 때 천연 허브를 함유한 것이 합성 성분을 함유한 것보다 반드시 낫다고는 할 수 없다고 지적한다. 신체는 비타민이 합성물로부터 나오든 천연 원료로부터 나오든 상관없이 그들의 기능을 위해 각각의 비타민과 미네랄의 분자량과 구조를 인식한다.

어휘

supplement 보충제, 보조식품
synthetic 합성의
ingredient 재료
molecular weight 분자량
structure 구조
regardless of ~와 관계없이

08 정답 ① 17 지방직

정답해설

맨 마지막 문장 "As a result of soil being eroded much more rapidly from fields than from the churchyard, the yard now stands like a little island raised 10 feet above the surrounding sea of farmland(교회 경지보다 농지에서 훨씬 급속도로 침식되고 있는 흙의 결과로, 그 경지는 이제 그곳을 둘러싸고 있는 농경지라는 바다 위로 10피트 떠 있는 작은 섬처럼 서 있다)."를 통해 아이오와의 그 교회 경지가 그것을 둘러싼 농경지보다 10피트 더 높이 있다는 것을 알 수 있다. 따라서 정답은 ①이다.

오답해설

② 농작물 생산성은 아이오와의 부연 설명에 불과하다. 흙 형성 속도와 관련된 내용은 찾아볼 수 없다.
③ "Because those soil erosion rates are so much higher than soil formation rates, that means a net loss of soil(그러한 토양의 침식 속도는 토양의 형성 속도보다 훨씬 높기 때문에, 그것은 흙의 순손실을 의미한다)."를 통해 토양의 침식 속도는 토양의 형성 속도보다 빠르다는 것을 알 수 있다.
④ "For instance, about half of the top soil of Iowa, the state whose agriculture productivity is among the highest in the U.S., has been eroded in the last 150 years(예를 들어, 미국에서 농작물 생산성이 가장 높은 주 중 하나인 아이오와의 표층 토양의 약 절반가량은 지난 150년간 침식되어왔다)."를 통해 아이오와는 지난 150년간 표층 토양이 절반가량 침식되어왔다는 것을 알 수 있다.

해석

농작물 재배를 위해 사용되는 농지의 토양은 토양이 형성되는 속도의 10배에서 40배의 속도로, 그리고 삼림지에서 토양이 침식되는 속도의 500배에서 10,000배의 속도로 물과 풍식에 의해 휩쓸려 운반된다. 그러한 토양의 침식 속도는 토양의 형성 속도보다 훨씬 높기 때문에, 그것은 흙의 순손실을 의미한다. 예를 들어, 미국에서 농작물 생산성이 가장 높은 주 중 하나인 아이오와의 표층 토양 중 약 절반가량은, 지난 150년간 침식되어왔다. 아이오와에 가장 최근 방문했을 때, 호스트는 내게 그러한 토양 손실의 예를 극적으로 보여주는 교회 경지를 보여주었다. 교회는 19세기에 농경지 한가운데에 지어졌고, 그 이후로 계속 교회로 유지되어 온 반면, 그곳 주변 땅에서는 농사가 지어졌다. 교회 경지보다 농지에서 훨씬 급속도로 침식되고 있는 흙의 결과로, 그 경지는 이제 둘러싸고 있는 농경지라는 바다 위로 10피트 떠 있는 작은 섬처럼 서 있다.

① 아이오와에 있는 한 교회 경지는 그곳을 둘러싸고 있는 농경지보다 더 높이 있다.
② 아이오와의 농작물 생산성은 그곳의 토양 형성을 가속화해왔다.
③ 농경지에서 토양의 형성 속도는 토양의 침식 속도보다 빠르다.
④ 아이오와는 지난 150년간 표층의 토양을 유지해왔다.

어휘

farmland 농지
carry away 운반해 가다
formation 형성
productivity 생산성
erode 침식시키다, 풍화시키다

09 정답 ③ 17 지방직

정답해설

본문은 처음부터 끝까지 '운동을 하지 않으면 건강 지수가 낮아진다.'고 말하고 있다. 그러나 '근육을 형성하기 위해 더 많은 양의 단백질이 요구된다'는 ③의 문장은 글의 전체적인 흐름에서 벗어난다. 뿐만 아니라, ③의 앞 문장에서 운동을 하지 않으면 몸이 기초 선상으로 돌아간다고 이야기하고 있는데, '근육 형성을 위해 요구되는 단백질'에 관한 내용은 바로 다음으로 나올 내용으로 어울리지 않는다. 따라서 정답은 ③이다.

오답해설

나머지 문장은 문맥상 흐름에 자연스럽다.

해석

당신이 여행을 해오고 있든, 가족에게 집중하든, 또는 직장에서 바쁜 시즌을 보내고 있든, 운동을 14일간 하지 않는 것은 당신의 근육뿐 아니라, 당신의 성과, 뇌, 그리고 수면에도 타격을 끼친다. ① 대부분의 전문가는 만약 당신이 헬스장으로 돌아오지 않는다면, 2주 후에 곤경에 처할 것이라는 것에 동의한다. "운동을 하지 않은 지 2주가 되었을 때 건강 지수의 감소를 자연스럽게 나타내는 다수의 생리학적인 현상이 있다."라고 엘리트 운동선수들과 일하는 뉴욕 기반의 운동 생리학자이자 트레이너인 Scott Weiss는 말한다. ② 결국에는, 이 모든 능력에도 불구하고, 인체(심지어 건강한 인체)는 아주 민감한 시스템이고 트레이닝을 통해 나타나는 생리학적인 변화들(근육의 강도 또는 더 뛰어난 유산소 베이스)은 당신의 운동량이 줄어들면 간단하게 사라질 것이라고 그는 언급한다. 훈련의 요구가 존재하지 않기 때문에, 당신의 몸은 간단하게 기초 선상으로 슬그머니 돌아가는 것이다. ③ **당신의 몸에서 빠른 속도로 근육을 형성하기 위해 더 많은 양의 단백질이 요구된다.** ④ 물론, 얼마나 많이 그리고 얼마나 빠르게 당신의 몸 컨디션을 망가뜨릴지는 당신이 얼마나 건강한지, 당신의 나이, 그리고 얼마나 오래 땀을 흘리는 습관을 가지는지와 같은 여러 요인에 달려있다. "두 달에서 여덟 달 동안 운동을 아예 하지 않는 것은 당신의 건강 지수를 마치 운동을 한 번도 한 적이 없었던 상태로 낮춘다."라고 Weiss는 언급한다.

어휘

take a toll 피해[타격]을 주다
dwindle 줄어들다
at a rapid pace 빠른 속도로
physiological 생리학적인
slink 살금살금 움직이다
a slew of 많은

10 정답 ④ 17 지방직

정답해설

"For learned men, this bordered on heresy. Supernatural powers were never human in origin, nor could witches derive their craft from the tradition of learned magic, which required a scholarly training at the university, a masculine preserve at the time(학자들에게 이것은 이단에 가까운 것이다. 초자연적인 힘은 절대 인간이 타고 나지 않았을뿐더러, 마녀들은 당시에 남자들이 지키고 있던 대학에서 학술적인 훈련을 요구하는 학습된 마법의 전통으로부터 그들의 기술을 얻을 수 없었다)."에서 학자들은 마녀의 힘은 대학의 학문적인 훈련을 통해 얻을 수 있는 것이 아니라고 믿었음을 알 수 있으므로 본문의 내용과 일치하지 않는 것은 ④이다.

오답해설

① 민중은 마녀의 힘의 근원이 '초자연적(supernatural)'이라고 믿었고, 학자들은 마녀의 힘은 '초자연적인 것'이 아닌 '이단(heresy)'에 가까운 것이라고 하였으므로 힘의 근원에 관해 다른 견해를 지녔다는 것을 알 수 있다.
② 본문 중반에 언급된 "the folk belief that the witch had innate supernatural powers not derived from the devil(마녀는 악마로부터 파생된 것이 아닌 타고난 초자연적 힘을 가지고 있다는 민중들의 믿음)"을 통해 알 수 있다.
③ 본문의 첫 번째 문장인 "Before the fifteenth century, ~ and other dissident groups."를 통해 알 수 있는 내용이다.

해석

15세기 이전에, 마녀의 모든 네 가지 특징들(야간 비행, 비밀 회동, 유해한 마법, 그리고 악마와의 조약)은 개인적으로 혹은 교회에 의해 한정된 조합으로 템플 기사단원, 이단자, 훈련된 마법사, 그리고 다른 반체제 집단을 포함한 반대파 탓으로 여겨졌다. 초자연적인 현상에 대한 사람들의 믿음은 마녀재판 동안의 소작농들의 자백에서 나타났다. 마법에 대한 대중적이고 학술적인 견해들 사이에 가장 두드러지는 차이점은 마녀는 악마로부터 파생된 것이 아닌 타고난 초자연적 힘을 가지고 있다는 민중들의 믿음에 있다. 학자들에게 이것은 이단에 가까운 것이다. 초자연적인 힘은 절대 인간이 타고 나지 않았을뿐더러, 마녀들은 당시에 남자들이 지키고 있던 대학에서 학술적인 훈련을 요구하는 학습된 마법의 전통으로부터 그들의 기술을 얻을 수 없었다. 마녀의 힘은 필연적으로 그녀가 악마와 맺은 조약에서 나온 것이다.
① 민중들과 학자들은 마녀의 초자연적인 힘의 근원에 관하여 다른 견해를 지녔다.
② 민중들의 믿음에 의하면, 초자연적인 힘은 마녀의 본질적인 천성에 속했다.
③ 마녀의 네 가지 특징은 교회에 의해 그것의 반체제 집단의 탓으로 돌려졌다.
④ 학자들은 마녀의 힘은 대학의 학문적인 훈련을 통해 얻어진다고 믿었다.

어휘

pact 약속, 협정, 조약
ascribe ~ to … ~을 …의 탓으로 돌리다
adversary 상대방, 적수 heretic 이단자
dissident 반체제 인사 peasant 소작농
confession 자백, 고백 witchcraft 마법, 마술
innate 타고난
border on ~에 아주 가깝다, 거의 ~와 같다
heresy 이단

기적사 DAY 57

결국엔 성정혜 영어 하프모의고사

01	②	02	①	03	②	04	①	05	③
06	③	07	①	08	②	09	③	10	③

01 정답 ②

정답해설

밑줄 친 'definitive'는 '명확한, 한정적인'을 뜻하는 형용사로 ② plain(분명한, 솔직한, 소박한)과 의미가 가장 가깝다.

해석

John은 레오나르도 다빈치가 원래 초상화를 그렸을 때, 모나리자의 속눈썹을 포함시켰었다는 **명확한** 증거를 발견했다.

① 모호한, 흐릿한
② 분명한, 솔직한, 소박한
③ 진흙투성이인, 탁한
④ 이제 시작 단계인

어휘

definitive 명확한, 한정적인
portrait 초상화
plain 분명한, 솔직한, 소박한
inchoate 이제 시작 단계인
proof 증거, 증명
hazy 모호한, 흐릿한
muddy 진흙투성이인, 탁한

오답률 TOP 2

02 정답 ①

정답해설

밑줄 친 'clandestine'은 '은밀한, 비밀리에 하는'을 뜻하는 형용사로 ① furtive(은밀한, 엉큼한)와 의미가 가장 가깝다.

해석

백신 프로그램 또는 방화벽을 피하기 위해 악성 소프트웨어는 계속 진화하기 때문에 더 **은밀한** 방법들이 계속 나타날 것이다.

① 은밀한, 엉큼한
② 노골적인, 뻔한
③ 공개적인, 대중적인
④ 눈에 잘 띄는, 뚜렷한

어휘

clandestine 은밀한, 비밀리에 하는
get around ~을 피하다; 돌아다니다
furtive 은밀한, 엉큼한
exoteric 공개적인, 대중적인
malware 악성 소프트웨어
firewall 방화벽
blatant 노골적인, 뻔한
conspicuous 눈에 잘 띄는, 뚜렷한

오답률 TOP 1

03 정답 ②

정답해설

밑줄 친 'disconnected'는 '무관한, 일관성이 없는'을 뜻하는 형용사로 ② external(무관한, 외부의)과 의미가 가장 가깝다.

해석

정보기술부문에서의 범죄가 다른 분야에서 발생하는 범죄의 다른 유형과 **무관하지** 않다.

① 괜찮은, 예의 바른
② 무관한, 외부의
③ 버릇없는, 꼴불견의
④ 관련 있는, 적절한

어휘

sector 분야[부문]
decent 괜찮은, 예의 바른
indecent 버릇없는, 꼴불견의
disconnected 무관한, 일관성이 없는
external 무관한, 외부의
pertinent 관련 있는, 적절한

04 정답 ①

정답해설

A와 B는 방학 때 여행을 다녀오는 것에 관해 대화를 나누고 있다. B가 A에게 (A) '떠나고(hit the road)' 싶다고 이야기하고, A는 다른 친구들과 함께 떠나는 것을 제안한다. 그리고 "친구들과 여행 간다면 (B) '행복한(in seventh heaven)' 기분이 들 것 같다고 이야기한다. 그러자 B는 (C) "정말 그래(Tell me about it)"라고 이야기하며 동의한다. 따라서 정답은 ①이다.

오답해설

② (B) 개학하기 전에 친구들과 여행을 가고 싶어 하는 A는 친구들과 여행을 가면 자신이 '빙산의 일각(the tip of the iceberg)'인 것처럼 느껴질 것이라고 하는 것은 문맥상 어색하다. (C) 개학하기 전 친구들과 여행 가는 것에 들떠있는 A와 B가 즐겁게 대화를 나누다가 B가 "그만해(Give me a break)"라고 말하며 "여행 내내 잊지 못할 추억을 만들 수 있을 것"이라고 이야기하는 것은 내용상 적절하지 않다.

③ (A) "개학하기 전에 친구들과 여행을 다녀오고 싶다"라는 A의 말에 B는 동의하면서 "나도 '패배하고(lose the day)' 싶다"라고 말하는 것은 문맥상 자연스럽지 않다. (C) 개학하기 전 친구들과 여행 가는 것에 들떠있는 A와 B가 즐겁게 대화를 나누다가 B가 "쥐구멍에도 볕들 날 온다(Every dog has its day)"라고 얘기하는 것은 대화의 흐름을 고려했을 때 적합하지 않다.

④ (A) "개학하기 전에 친구들과 여행을 다녀오고 싶다"라는 A의 말에 B는 동의하면서 "나도 '패배하고(lose the day)' 싶다"라고 말하는 것은 문맥상 자연스럽지 않다. (B) 개학하기 전에 친구들과 여행을 가고 싶어 하는 A는 친구들과 여행을 가면 자신이 '빙산의 일각(the tip of the iceberg)'인 것처럼 느껴질 것이라고 하는 것은 맥락상 부자연스럽다. (C) 개학하기 전 친구들과 여행 가는 것에 들떠있는 A와 B가 즐겁게 대화를 나누다가 B가 "쥐구멍에도 볕들 날 온다(Every dog has its day)"라고 얘기하는 것은 흐름을 고려했을 때 적합하지 않다.

해석

A: 나는 개학하기 전에 친구들과 여행을 다녀오고 싶어.
B: 좋은 생각이야! 나도 정말 (A) 떠나고 싶어.
A: 우리 다른 친구들과 같이 가는 것 어때?
B: 응, 나는 좋아. 나는 이번 방학 때 여행 갈 시간이 전혀 없었어.
A: 나도. 친구들과 여행하면 (B) 행복한 것처럼 느껴질 거야.
B: (C) 정말 그래! 나는 여행 동안 우리가 잊지 못할 기억들을 만들 수 있을 거라고 확신해.
A: 우리 바로 계획을 세워야겠다.
B: 물론이지, 시작하자!

① (A) 떠나다 (B) 행복한 (C) 정말 그래
② (A) 떠나다 (B) 빙산의 일각 (C) 그만해

③ (A) 패배하다 (B) 행복한 (C) 쥐구멍에도 볕들 날 온다
④ (A) 패배하다 (B) 빙산의 일각 (C) 쥐구멍에도 볕들 날 온다

어휘

unforgettable 잊지 못할[잊을 수 없는]
hit the road 떠나다
in seventh heaven 행복한
tell me about it 정말 그래
the tip of the iceberg 빙산의 일각
give me a break 그만해
lose the day 패배하다
every dog has its day 쥐구멍에도 볕들 날 온다

05 정답 ③

정답해설

③ **출제 포인트: the number of vs. a number of/주어와 동사의 수일치/'동사+부사'의 목적어 위치**

주어가 「the number of 목적어[복수명사]」인 경우 동사의 수일치 기준은 단수 형태인 'the number'이므로 동사에 단수 형태를 사용해야 하며, 주어가 「a number of 목적어[복수명사]」인 경우 동사의 수일치 기준은 복수 형태인 목적어[복수명사]이므로 동사에 복수 형태를 사용해야 한다. 해당 문장은 주어에 「the number of 목적어[복수명사]」인 'the number of measures'를 사용하였으나 동사에 복수 형태인 'were'를 사용하였으므로 틀린 문장이다. 이때 문맥상 '많은 조치들이 취해졌을 뿐만 아니라'가 자연스러우므로 'were'를 'was'로 수정하는 것이 아니라 'the number of'를 'a number of'로 수정해야 한다. 또한 'ease off'는 '타동사+부사' 형태의 이어동사이므로, 대명사 목적어의 경우 반드시 '타동사+대명사+부사' 형태여야 한다. 따라서 ease it off로 수정해야 한다.

오답해설

① **출제 포인트: 비교급 비교/주어와 동사의 수일치**
불완전자동사 'was'의 주격 보어로 'high'의 비교급인 'higher'를 사용하였으며 비교 대상 앞에 'than'을 사용하였고 'cost'의 경우 수치 개념이 포함된 명사이므로 'high'의 비교급인 'higher'가 수식하는 것은 옳다. 또한 해당 문장의 주어 'The actual cost'와 동사 'was'는 옳게 수일치 되었다. 주어와 동사 사이의 거리가 먼 경우 수일치에 유의해야한다.

② **출제 포인트: '동사+부사'의 목적어 위치**
「get through+목적어」는 관용표현으로 '~을 통과하다, 합격하다'를 뜻하며 이때 'through'는 전치사이므로 「get+목적어+through」의 형태로 사용할 수 없다. 해당 문장은 「get through+목적어」인 'get through this exam'을 사용하였으므로 옳은 문장이다.

④ **출제 포인트: 능동태 vs. 수동태/수여동사의 수동태**
해당 문장은 수여동사 'give'의 과거시제 수동태로 쓰인 문장으로 'was given' 이후에 있는 'exemption'은 직접목적어로 옳은 표현이다. 이때 해당 문장을 능동태로 바꾸면 다음과 같다.
※ 주어 gave Jane exemption form the final examination as she suffered injury to the left occipital area in a traffic accident. (이때 해당 문장에서 주어는 원문에서 「by+행위자」가 생략되어 있으므로 '주어'로 표기하였다.)

해석

① 허리케인 카트리나로 파괴된 건물을 복구하는 실제 비용은 우리가 예상했던 것보다 더 높았다.
② William은 지난 시험에서 실수를 많이 했기 때문에 이번 시험을 통과하기 위해 열심히 공부해야 했다.
③ 그 문제를 완화시키기 위해 많은 조치들이 취해졌을 뿐만 아니라, 많은 법안들이 통과되었다.
④ 그녀는 교통사고로 좌측 후두부에 손상을 입었기 때문에 최종 시험에서 면제를 받았다.

06 정답 ③

정답해설

③ **출제 포인트: 현재분사 vs. 과거분사**
'새롭게 설립된 London Institution'이 해석상 자연스러우므로 'found(설립하다)'와 수식하는 대상 'London Institution'이 수동관계임을 알 수 있다. 따라서 밑줄 친 현재분사 'founding'을 과거분사 'founded'로 수정해야 한다.

오답해설

① **출제 포인트: one of the 최상급 복수명사**
밑줄 친 'scholars'는 'scholar'의 복수 형태로 앞에 있는 'one of'와 연결된다. 「one of the 최상급 복수명사」에서 'the'의 자리에 소유격을 사용할 수 있음에 유의하도록 한다.

② **출제 포인트: 완전타동사 vs. 완전자동사**
'enter'는 '~에 들어가다'를 뜻하는 경우 완전타동사에 해당한다. 해당 문장에서 밑줄 친 'entered'는 이후에 있는 목적어 'Cambridge University'를 통해 '~에 들어가다'로 사용되었음을 알 수 있다. 따라서 완전타동사로 쓰인 'entered'는 옳게 사용되었다.

④ **출제 포인트: 전치사의 쓰임(during vs. for)**
밑줄 친 'During' 이후에 있는 목적어 'his lifetime'은 특정 기간을 나타내는 명사(구)이므로 전치사 'during'의 쓰임은 올바르다.

해석

영국의 가장 유명한 고전학자 중 한 명인 Richard Porson은 1759년 크리스마스에 태어났다. 그의 재능은 일찍 인정받았고, 그는 부유한 후원자들에 의해 15세에 Eton College로 보내졌다. 4년 후, 그는 케임브리지 대학교에 들어갔다. 그는 그리스어로 된 원문을 상당히 개선했고, Euripides가 쓴 희곡 4편을 편집했다. 1806년에 그는 새롭게 설립된 London Institution에 수석 사서로 선출되었다. 그의 평생 동안, 그는 고전 문학에 관한 수많은 책을 수집했다.

어휘

notable 유명한, 저명한
recognize 인정하다
significantly 상당히

07 정답 ①

정답해설

㉠ **출제 포인트: 현재분사 vs. 과거분사**
'he soon managed to translate his jokes for the American audience'가 주절에 해당하므로 ㉠이 포함된 부분은 종속절에 해당하며 분사구문임을 알 수 있다. 이때 생략된 주어는 'he'이며 ㉠ 이후에 목적어 'English'가 있으므로 ㉠에는 능동을 나타내는 현재분사를 사용해야 한다. 따라서 ㉠에 들어갈 것으로 가장 적절한 것은 'Learning'이다.

㉡ **출제 포인트: 주어와 동사의 수일치/병렬구조**
주어가 'Victor Borge'이며 단수 형태이므로 ㉡에는 단수 형태인 'was'를 사용하는 것이 옳으며 앞선 'became'과 병렬구조를 이루고 있다.

㉢ **출제 포인트: 능동태 vs. 수동태**
해당 문장에서 ㉢ 이후에 있는 'the longest-running one-man show'를 통해 'remain'이 불완전자동사로 사용되었음을 알 수 있으며 불완전자동사는 수동태로 사용할 수 없으므로 ㉢에는 능동태인 'remains'를 사용하는 것이 옳다.

따라서 정답은 '① Learning, was, remains'이다.

해석

영화를 보면서 영어를 배워, 그는 곧 미국 청중들을 위해서 자신의 우스갯소리를 어떻게든 바꿀 수 있었다. 1948년에, Victor Borge는 미국 시민이 되었고 몇 년 후에 자신이 진행하는 프로인 Comedy in Music을 제안받았다. 그 프로는 브로드웨이 역사상 가장 오래 공연된 1인 진행 프로로 남아 있다.

어휘

manage to 동사원형 어떻게든 ~하다
translate 바꾸다, 번역하다

08 정답 ①

정답해설

본문은 '태국의 농부들이 보존 구역에 침입하는 이유와 이 문제를 해결하기 위해 진행된 프로젝트'에 관해 설명하고 있다. 본문 중반 "To address this issue, a recent project compared the physical and chemical properties of soils from farmlands and soils from the conserved area(이 문제를 다루기 위해, 최근 한 프로젝트가 농지의 토양과 보존 구역 토양의 물리적 그리고 화학적 특징을 비교했다)."를 통해, 두 지역의 토양의 특징을 비교함으로써 문제 해결을 꾀했다는 것을 알 수 있으며, 이후 문장에서 '두 지역 토양의 영양 성분이 거의 차이가 나지 않았다'고 밝히고 이러한 사실을 농부들에게 알렸다고 설명하고 있으므로, 농부들이 자신들의 농지 대신 보존 구역의 토양을 이용하려고 했던 이유는 자신들의 농지보다 보존 구역의 영양 성분이 더 풍부하다, 즉 더 '비옥하다'고 생각했기 때문이라는 것을 유추할 수 있다. 따라서 빈칸에 가장 적절한 표현은 '① more fertile(더 비옥한)'이다.

오답해설

나머지 보기는 모두 본문의 내용과는 반대되는 의미가 되므로 오답이다.

해석

태국 농부들은 보통 낮은 정규 교육을 받고 토질 개선과 적절한 비료 사용에 대한 지식의 부족함을 가지고 있다. 몇 년간 농사를 지은 후, 그들의 제한된 농지 공간에서의 토양의 악화와 그들이 자신들의 농장의 토양보다 보존 구역의 토양이 더욱 비옥하다고 믿기 때문에, 그들은 보존된 삼림 구역으로 침입하려고 시도한다. 결과적으로, 그들 중 대부분은 체포되고, 이는 개인 및 가족의 문제를 일으킨다. 이 문제를 다루기 위해, 최근 한 프로젝트가 농지의 토양과 보존 구역 토양의 물리적 그리고 화학적 특징을 비교했다. 결과는 보존 구역으로부터의 토양이 좀 더 많은 유기물과 질소함량을 보유하고 있다는 점을 제외하고, 양쪽으로부터의 토양의 영양분이 분석의 거의 모든 요인에서 크게 차이가 나지 않는다는 것을 보여주었다. 이 분석 자료는 농부들에게 통보되었고 더 높은 생산성을 확보하기 위해 적절한 유기물을 사용하여 그들의 농지를 개선할 것을 그들에게 제안했다.
① 더 비옥한
② 더 척박한
③ 더 황량한
④ 경작에 덜 적합한

어휘

fertilizer 비료
conserve 보존하다, 보호하다
expanse 넓게 퍼진 공간[장소], 구역
nutrient 영양분
nitrogen 질소
fertile 비옥한
barren 황량한, 척박한
trespass 침입하다, 침범하다
deterioration 악화
property 특징
parameter 파라미터, 매개 변수
appropriate 적절한, 알맞은
sterile 척박한, 불모의
arable 경작에 적합한

오답률 TOP 3
09 정답 ③

정답해설

본문은 '운동을 하면 근육이 인슐린을 처리해 에너지 소비를 늘려주고, 반대로 (운동을 하지 않아) 에너지 소비를 줄이면 인슐린 민감도가 떨어져 당을 지방으로 저장하고, 여러 질병의 위험성을 높인다'고 설명하고 있다. 즉, 운동을 하지 않음으로 인해 신체에 발생하는 일에 대해 언급하고 있으므로, 글의 제목으로 가장 적절한 것은 '③ One Thing That Happens When You Quit Working Out(당신이 운동을 중단할 때 발생하는 한 가지 일)'이다.

오답해설

① 본문에서는 '운동을 하면 근육이 인슐린을 처리해 에너지 소비를 늘려준다'고 언급하고 있기 때문에, 근육의 중요성에 대한 글이라고 착각할 수도 있다. 그러나 이후, 운동을 하지 않는 경우 근육은 "your muscles will adapt physiologically to become a little less insulin sensitive(당신의 근육은 생리적으로 인슐린에 조금 덜 민감하게 변할 것)"하게 될 것이라고 설명하고 있으므로, '근육' 자체가 인슐린 처리를 높여주는 것이 아니라, 운동을 하는 것이 근육이 인슐린을 처리하여 에너지를 소비하도록 만든다는 것을 알 수 있다. 따라서 '근육의 중요성'이 글의 제목이 되는 것은 적절하지 않다.
② 본문과 관계없는 내용이므로 오답이다.
④ 본문에는 '인슐린 민감도(Insulin Sensitivity)'가 저하되는 경우에 대해 설명하고 있으며, 이를 향상시키는 방법에 대해서는 언급하지 않는다.

해석

우리가 운동할 때, 우리의 근육은 인슐린을 처리하고 결과적으로 발생하는 포도당을 에너지로 흡수한다. 그러한 에너지 소비를 줄이면, 당신의 근육은 생리적으로 인슐린에 조금 덜 민감하게 변할 것이라고 University of Kansas의 연구원인 John Thyfault는 말한다. 인슐린 민감도를 잃는 것은 당신의 신체가 당신의 움직임에 동력을 공급하기 위해 당을 에너지로 사용하기보다는 그것을 지방으로 전환시킨다는 것을 의미한다. 그리고 그러한 적응이 우리의 수렵·채집인 조상들이 기복이 심한 생활방식을 극복하는 데 도움이 되었던 반면, 부적절한 인슐린 조절은 당신의 세포가 근육 운동에서 사용되지 않는 것의 일부를 지방으로 저장하는 것을 유발할 수 있기 때문에 이것은 현대의 사무직원에게는 나쁜 소식이다. 이러한 변화는 당신을 제2형 당뇨병 및 염증과 같은 다른 질환 발병의 더 커다란 위험에 노출시킨다.
① 왜 근육이 중요한가?
② 더 나은 건강을 위해 에너지 수준을 높이는 방법
③ 당신이 운동을 중단할 때 발생하는 한 가지 일
④ 인슐린 민감도: 그것을 자연적이고 빠르게 향상시키는 방법

어휘

absorb 흡수하다
expenditure 소비, 소모
physiologically 생리(학)적으로
convert 전환하다
ancestor 조상, 선조
feast-or-famine 기복이 심한, 파란만장한, 풍요냐 궁핍이냐의 양극단의
desk jockey 사무직원
Type 2 diabetes 제2형 당뇨병
work out 운동하다
glucose 포도당
adapt to 동사원형 ~하도록 변경하다
sensitive 민감한
hunter-gatherer 수렵·채집인
prompt 유발하다, 촉발하다
inflammation 염증

10 정답 ③

정답해설

본문 초반에 글의 요지가 등장한다. 본문 첫 문장 "There is no question that some of the economic and social, and demographic developments that occurred in early modern Europe aggravated the personal tensions that underlay many witchcraft accusations(초기의 현대 유럽에서 발생한 경제, 사회, 그리고 인구학적 발전의 일부가 마녀재판의 기저를 이루던 개인적인 갈등을 악화시켰다는 것에는 의심의 여지가 없다)."에 따르면, '경제, 사회, 인구학적 발전으로 인해, 개인적인 갈등이 악화되었고', 이러한 갈등이 마녀재판을 더 심화시켰다는 것을 유추할 수 있다. 이후에서는 구체적으로 갈등을 악화시킨 발전(변화)의 예시를 제시하고 있으므로, 글의 요지로 가장 적절한 것은 '③ The European witch-hunts may be considered as the product of social and economic changes(유럽의 마녀사냥은 사회 및 경제 변화의 산물로 여겨질 수 있다).'이다.

오답해설

① 본문에는 종교 또는 미신에 관한 내용은 언급되지 않으므로 오답이다.
② 본문에서는 '유럽의 마녀사냥이 기이한 현상'이라는 평가를 내리지 않고 있으므로 오답이다.
④ 본문에서 마녀사냥으로 인한 고문, 처형 등에 대한 내용은 언급되지 않으므로 오답이다.

해석

초기의 현대 유럽에서 발생한 경제, 사회, 그리고 인구학적 발전의 일부가 마녀재판의 기저를 이루던 개인적인 갈등을 악화시켰다는 것에는 의심의 여지가 없다. 인플레이션, 빈곤의 증가, 증가하는 인구에 의한 한정된 자원 공급에 대한 압박, 미혼 여성 인구의 증가, 그리고 가족 구조의 변화가 모두 마녀재판을 부추기는 데에 있어서 어느 정도 역할을 했다. 일부 여성들은 그들이 이러한 변화에 의해 가장 악영향을 받았기 때문에, 또는 자본주의의 출현과 관련하여, 그것에 가장 저항했기 때문에 마법을 사용한 죄로 기소를 당했을지도 모른다. 게다가, 기근, 전염병의 발병, 그리고 전쟁에 의해 야기된 혼란과 같은 특정 경제 위기가 많은 개별적 마녀사냥을 촉발하는데 일조했을지도 모른다.
① 마녀사냥은 종교와 미신과 같은 많은 이유에 의해 야기될 수 있다.
② 유럽의 마녀사냥은 서구 역사의 가장 기이한 현상 중 하나이다.
③ 유럽의 마녀사냥은 사회 및 경제 변화의 산물로 여겨질지도 모른다.
④ 마녀사냥은 수많은 희생자의 고문과 처형을 야기했으며, 그들 중 대부분은 여성이었다.

어휘

demographic 인구학의 aggravate 악화시키다
tension 긴장[갈등]
underlie (…의) 기저를 이루다[기저가 되다]
witchcraft 마법, 주술 accusation 고발, 기소
unattached 매이지[결혼을 하지] 않은
accuse 고발[기소/비난]하다, 혐의를 제기하다
adversely affect 악영향을 주다 with respect to …에 관하여
advent 출현, 도래 resistant 저항[반대]하는
famine 기근 outbreak 발생
epidemic disease 전염병 dislocation 혼란
trigger 촉발하다, 방아쇠를 당기다 superstition 미신
bizarre 기이한, 이상한 phenomenon 현상
torture 고문 execution 처형

결국엔 성정혜 영어 하프모의고사
기적사 DAY 58

| 01 | ② | 02 | ③ | 03 | ③ | 04 | ② | 05 | ② |
| 06 | ④ | 07 | ② | 08 | ④ | 09 | ② | 10 | ③ |

01 정답 ②

정답해설

밑줄 친 'gigantic'은 '거대한'을 뜻하는 형용사로 ② titanic(거대한, 강력한)과 의미가 가장 가깝다.

해석

캘리포니아에 있는 그 공원은 그곳의 **거대한** 폭포, 깊은 계곡, 그리고 다양한 야생동물과 식물로 잘 알려져 있다.
① 아주 작은, 미약한
② 거대한, 강력한
③ 무력해진, 기운이 빠진
④ 겁이 많은

어휘

gigantic 거대한 waterfall 폭포
valley 계곡 puny 아주 작은, 미약한
titanic 거대한, 강력한 effete 무력해진, 기운이 빠진
timorous 겁이 많은

02 정답 ③

정답해설

밑줄 친 'statutory'는 '법에 명시된, 법으로 정한'을 뜻하는 형용사로 ③ legitimate(합법적인, 타당한)와 의미가 가장 가깝다.

해석

이 행성에 있는 어느 곳에서도 모든 채무자들이 **법에 명시된** 권리인 것을 초과하여 구제를 받은 적은 없다.
① 불법의, 사회 통념에 어긋나는
② 범죄의, 중죄의
③ 합법적인, 타당한
④ 음모의, 공모하는 듯한

어휘

bail out 구제하다, 곤경을 벗어나게 하다
statutory 법에 명시된, 법으로 정한 entitlement 자격[권리]
illicit 불법의, 사회 통념에 어긋나는 felonious 범죄의, 중죄의
legitimate 합법적인, 타당한 conspiratorial 음모의, 공모하는 듯한

03 정답 ③

정답해설

밑줄 친 intended는 문맥상 '의도하는'이라는 의미로 ③ purposeful(목적이 있는)과 의미가 가장 가깝다.

해석

무의미한 고통은 견딜 수 없지만, 그것이 **의도가 있다**고 믿는다면 엄청난 고통도 견딜 수 있다.

① 표류하는, 방황하는
② 무관심한, 심드렁한
③ 목적이 있는
④ 목표가 불분명한, 지시 없는

어휘

intended 의도하는
torment 고통, 고뇌; 괴롭히다
purposeful 목적의식이 있는, 결단력 있는
adrift 표류하는, 방황하는
undirected 목표가 불분명한, 지시 없는
pointless 무의미한, 할 가치가 없는
endure 견디다, 참다, 인내하다
apathetic 무관심한, 심드렁한

오답률 TOP 1

04 정답 ②

정답해설

A와 B는 오랜만에 재회한 상황에서 대화를 나눈다. 서로의 근황을 물어본 후, A는 B에게 "시간이 있냐"고 물으며, "어디 들어가서 '잠시 이야기를 나누자(shoot the breeze)'"라고 B에게 제안한다. 따라서 정답은 ②이다.

오답해설

① A와 B가 오랜만에 우연히 만난 상황에서 이야기를 나누다가 A가 B에게 "시간이 좀 있는지" 물어보며 어디 들어가서 '말만 그럴듯한 말을 하자(talk the talk)'고 제안하는 것은 문맥상 어색하다.
③ A는 B를 오랜만에 우연히 만나 근황을 물어보며 "시간이 있는지"도 묻는다. B는 "여가시간이 있다"라고 답변하자 "어디 들어가서 '빚을 내어 빚을 메꾸자(rob Peter to pay Paul)'"라고 말하는 것은 대화의 흐름상 빈칸에 들어갈 말로 적절하지 않다.
④ B에게 "시간이 좀 있는지" 질문하는 A에게 B는 "여가시간이 있다"라고 대답하고, A는 "어디에 들어가서 '다른 사람과 같은 생각을 갖자(speak the same language)'"라고 이야기하는 것은 흐름상 부자연스럽다.

해석

A: 오랜만이야!
B: 세상에! 널 만난 지 꽤 오래됐어!
A: 그러니까! 너 어떻게 지냈어?
B: 나는 잘 지냈어. 넌 어때? 일 잘돼가?
A: 응, 너 시간 좀 있어?
B: 지금 당장? 응, 나 여가시간 좀 있어. 왜?
A: 음, 그럼 어디 들어가서 <u>잠시 이야기를 나누자</u>.
B: 좋은 생각이야. 우린 얘기할 것들이 많아.
① 말만 그럴듯한 말을 하다
② 잠시 이야기를 나누다
③ 빚을 내어 빚을 메꾸다
④ 다른 사람과 같은 생각을 갖다

어휘

talk the talk 말만 그럴듯한 말을 하다
shoot the breeze 잠시 이야기를 나누다
rob Peter to pay Paul 빚을 내어 빚을 메꾸다
speak the same language 다른 사람과 같은 생각을 갖다

오답률 TOP 3

05 정답 ②

정답해설

② **출제 포인트: 수여동사의 수동태/능동태 vs. 수동태**
해당 문장은 완전타동사 'say'의 과거시제 수동태를 사용하였으나 'was said' 이후에 직접목적어인 'that rest should be imperative for weeks'가 있으므로 틀린 문장이다. 따라서 'was said'는 수여동사 'tell'의 과거시제 수동태인 'was told'로 수정해야 한다.

오답해설

① **출제 포인트: '동사+부사'의 목적어 위치**
해당 문장에서 'out'은 부사로 동사 'get'과 결합하여 「get+목적어+out」의 형태로 사용되었다. 이때 「get+목적어+out」은 '~을 생산해 내다, 펴내다'를 뜻하며 목적어가 일반명사인 경우 「get+out+목적어」의 형태로도 사용할 수 있다.

③ **출제 포인트: 비교급 비교**
불완전자동사 'is'의 주격 보어로 형용사 'expensive'의 비교급인 'more expensive'를 사용하였으며 비교 대상 앞에 'than'을 사용하였으므로 해당 문장은 옳은 문장이다. 또한 'more expensive' 앞에 있는 'much'는 비교급 강조부사로 긍정문에서 주로 'so' 또는 'too'와 결합하여 사용한다.

④ **출제 포인트: 주어와 동사의 수일치/the number of vs. a number of/능동태 vs. 수동태**
주어가 「a number of 목적어[복수명사]」인 경우 동사의 수일치 기준은 복수 형태인 목적어[복수명사]이므로 동사에 복수 형태를 사용해야 한다. 해당 문장은 주어에 「a number of 목적어[복수명사]」인 'a number of simplifications'를 사용하였으므로 동사의 수일치 기준은 복수 형태인 'simplifications'이다. 따라서 복수 형태의 동사 'have'는 옳은 표현이다. 또한 '많은 간소화'는 '이루어지는 것'이므로 현재완료 수동태 'have been made'의 쓰임은 올바르다.

해석

① 우리가 올해 말까지 Milton에 의해 쓰인 이 책을 펴낼 수 있을까요?
② 그 야구 스타는 휴식을 몇 주 동안 반드시 해야 한다는 이야기를 들었다.
③ 귀사의 시스템에 관심이 있지만, 그것은 당신의 경쟁사의 것보다 훨씬 더 비싸다.
④ 많은 시민운동에 의해 복지 제도에 대한 많은 간소화가 이뤄졌다.

---

06 정답 ④

정답해설

④ **출제 포인트: 현재분사 vs. 과거분사/지각동사의 목적격 보어**
지각동사 'hear'는 목적어와 목적격 보어의 관계가 능동인 경우 목적격 보어 자리에 원형 부정사 또는 현재분사를 사용한다. 주어진 문장은 목적어 'any of the babies'와 목적격 보어가 능동 관계이므로 'to cry'를 원형 부정사 'cry' 또는 현재분사 'crying'으로 수정해야 한다.

오답해설

① **출제 포인트: to부정사의 형용사적 용법**
밑줄 친 'to identify'는 명사(구) 'the ability'를 수식하는 to부정사의 형용사적 용법으로 옳게 사용되었다.

② **출제 포인트: 주격 관계대명사절의 동사 수일치**
밑줄 친 'has'는 주격 관계대명사 'that'이 이끄는 절의 동사에 해당하며 이때 'that'의 선행사는 'bonding factors'가 아니라, 단수 형태인 'one'이므로 단수 형태의 동사 'has'의 쓰임은 올바르다. (※ 주의: 주격 관계대명사절의 동사 수일치를 묻는 문제에서 선행사가 「단수명사 of 복수명사」의

형태인 경우 해당 보기에 △표시를 한 후 확실하게 틀린 보기가 있는지를 확인해야 한다.)

③ 출제 포인트: 현재분사 vs. 과거분사
밑줄 친 'living'은 분사구문에 쓰인 현재분사로 생략된 주어 'a mother'와 능동관계이다. 따라서 현재분사 'living'의 쓰임은 올바르다.

해석
자고 있는 엄마는 자기 아기 특유의 울음소리를 식별할 수 있는 능력을 가지고 있다. 이것은 오늘날 우리가 사는 방식 때문에 잊힌 유대감 형성 요인 중의 하나이다. 일반적으로, 이제는 어느 주택이나 아파트에도 신생아가 한 명만 있기 때문에, 이런 능력을 시험해 볼 방법은 없다. 하지만, 소규모 마을 정착지의 작은 움막에 살았던 고대 부족의 엄마는 밤에 우는 어떤 아기의 울음소리도 들을 수 있었을 것이다.

어휘
identify 알아보다, 식별하다
newborn 갓 태어난
hut 움막, 오두막
typically 일반적으로
tribe 부족, 종족
settlement 정착지, 촌락

오답률 TOP 2
07 정답 ②

정답해설

㉠ 출제 포인트: 전치사의 쓰임(for vs. during)
빈칸 이후에 있는 'the wetter summer season'은 특정 기간을 나타내는 명사(구)이므로 ㉠에는 전치사 'during'을 사용하는 것이 옳다.

㉡ 출제 포인트: 등위접속사의 병렬구조
등위접속사 'and'를 통해 「주절, when이 이끄는 종속절, and 주절, when이 이끄는 종속절」형태의 병렬구조를 이루고 있다. 이때 ㉡은 주절의 동사에 해당하며 앞에 있는 주절에서 주어는 'The saola', 동사는 단수 형태인 'stays'를 사용하였으므로 ㉡에는 단수 형태의 동사 'moves'를 사용하는 것이 옳다.

㉢ 출제 포인트: 주어와 동사의 수일치
주어가 'Hunting and the loss'이며 「A and B」형태의 주어는 복수로 취급하므로 ㉢에는 복수 형태인 'threaten'을 사용하는 것이 옳다.
따라서 정답은 '② during, moves, threaten'이다.

해석
saola는 고지대의 개울에 물이 많은 더 습한 여름 동안 고지대에 머무르고, 산의 개울이 말라버리는 겨울에는 저지대로 이동한다. 그것들은 주로 두세 마리씩 무리 지어 다닌다고 알려져 있다. 사냥 그리고 벌목과 농경지로의 전환으로 인한 삼림 서식지의 감소가 그것의 생존을 위협한다.

어휘
elevation 높은 곳
logging 벌목
altitude 고도가 높은 곳
conversion 전환

08 정답 ④

정답해설
본문은 '토양이 발달하는 데는 엄청난 시간이 걸리며, 일단 파괴되면 다시 회복되는데 오랜 기간이 걸린다'고 설명한다. 주어진 문장은 '집과 도로 건설을 위해 토양이 파괴되는 예시'를 보여주고 있다. 따라서 주어진 문장 이전에는 '토양 파괴'에 대한 내용이 언급되는 것이 자연스럽다. 본문에서는 ④ 이전 문장에서 "The soil that took nature thousands of years to develop from its parent material can be destroyed in a matter of hours with excavation equipment(자연이 모재로부터 발달시키는데 수천 년이 걸린 토양은 발굴 장비로 몇 시간 내에 파괴될 수 있다)."라고 '토양이 파괴되는 것'에 대해 최초로 언급되고 있으며, ④ 이후 문장에서는 "Once disturbed and compacted(일단 건드려지고 다져지면)"라고 시작하며, 주어진 문장에서 설명한 'the top soil is stripped and subsoil compacted(표토는 파헤쳐지고 심토는 다져진다)'를 가리키고 있으므로, 주어진 문장이 들어갈 가장 적절한 위치는 ④이다.

오답해설
①, ②, ③ 이전 문장에서는 토양 파괴에 대한 언급이 없으므로, 주어진 문장이 들어가기에는 어색하다.

해석
토양은 수백 년에서 수천 년에 걸쳐 발달한다. (①) 그러나, 그것이 우리의 발밑에 묻혀있기 때문에, 그것의 복잡한 구조와 생태를 보고 제대로 인식하는 것은 어렵다. (②) 식물의 성장을 돕는 생산적인 토양에는 공기와 물을 뿌리, 곤충, 그리고 미생물에게 데려다주는 상호 연결된 길이 있는 공극이 있다. (③) 자연이 모재로부터 발달시키는 데 수천 년이 걸린 토양은 발굴 장비로 몇 시간 내에 파괴될 수 있다. (④ **집과 도로를 건설하기 위해, 표토는 파헤쳐지고, 단단한 토대를 만들기 위해 심토는 다져진다.**) 일단 건드려지고 다져지면, 자연적인 힘이 다른 층, 집합체, 그리고 상호 연결된 토양의 틈새를 새로 만들어내는 데는 수십 년에서 수 세기가 걸린다. 한 무더기의 흙을 쌓는 것이 그것을 토양으로 만드는 것은 아니다.

어휘
appreciate (제대로) 인식하다
pore space 공극(토양 입자와 입자 사이에 공기나 물로 채워질 수 있는 틈새)
microbe 미생물
excavation 발굴, 땅파기
subsoil 심토
compact 다지다, 압축하다, 단단하게 만들다
disturb (제자리에 있는 것을) 건드리다[흩뜨리다]
aggregate 전체, 집합체
a matter of hours 겨우 몇 시간
strip (껍질 등을) 벗기다, 없애다
pile up 쌓다, 쌓아 올리다

09 정답 ②

정답해설
본문은 '운동을 할 때는 기존의 근육의 부피가 증가하는 것이고, 운동을 하지 않을 때는 근육의 부피가 감소하는 것일 뿐 근육 자체가 사라지는 것은 아니며 또한 근육이 지방으로 변하는 것도 아니다'라고 설명하고 있다. 즉, 운동을 하지 않더라도 근육 자체는 동일하게 존재하며, 단지 근육의 크기가 변화하는 것이다. 따라서 글의 요지로 가장 적절한 것은 '② Your muscles do not just go away even if you stop exercising(당신이 운동을 중단하더라도 당신의 근육이 사라지는 것은 아니다).'이다.

오답해설
① 본문 후반에 '지방 형성'에 관해 언급되지만, '지방 섭취'에 관한 내용은 언급되지 않으므로 오답이다.
③ "You may be afraid that muscles turn to fat or disappear if you stop working out, but instead all they do is shrink and decrease in mass(당신은 만일 당신이 운동하는 것을 멈춘다면 근육이 지방으로 바뀌거나 사라질까 봐 두려워할지도 모르지만, 대신에 그것들이 하는 모든 것은 오그라들고 질량이 감소하는 것뿐이다)."에서 '운동 중단의 효과'로 '근육 부피의 감소'를 언급하고 있으며, '체중 증가'에 대해서는 언급하지 않으므로, 글의 요지로 적절하지 않다.
④ '질병'에 관해서는 본문에 언급되지 않으므로 오답이다.

해석

당신이 운동할 때, 당신의 신체가 실제로 새로운 근육을 생성하는 것은 아니다. 대신에, 당신의 기존 근육이 더 커지고 강해지며, 세동맥과 세정맥 간 연결되어 있는 혈관인 모세혈관의 수가 증가한다. 규칙적인 운동과 함께, 근육은 또한 더 많은 미토콘드리아를 발달시킨다 – 이것이 세포에서 호흡과 에너지 생성의 생화학 과정이 발생하는 곳이다. 결과는 더 크고 더 뚜렷한 근육량이며, 새로이 생성된 근육 조직이 아니다. 주로 앉아서 지내는 – 또는 활동적이지 않은 – 생활방식을 채택하는 것은 당신의 근육에 반대의 효과를 미친다. 운동 중 당신의 세포에 연료를 공급하는 데 이전에 필요했던 증가된 혈류량은 더 이상 필요하지 않고, 당신의 신체는 수축하고 당신의 모세혈관의 크기를 감소시키기 시작한다. 당신은 만일 당신이 운동하는 것을 멈춘다면 근육이 지방으로 바뀌거나 사라질까 봐 두려워할지도 모르지만, 대신에 그것들이 하는 모든 것은 오그라들고 질량이 감소하는 것뿐이다. 만일 당신의 식단이 당신이 유지하는 활동의 수준을 위해 필요로 하는 것보다 더 많은 칼로리를 당신의 신체에 제공한다면 지방이 생산될 수는 있지만, 당신의 신체가 마법처럼 근육을 지방으로 변화시키는 것은 아니다.

① 당신은 운동 후 지방 섭취를 피해서는 안 된다.
② 당신이 운동을 중단하더라도 당신의 근육이 사라지는 것은 아니다.
③ 운동을 중단하는 것은 체중 증가와 같은 즉각적인 건강 효과를 줄 수 있다.
④ 적절한 식이와 운동 일정을 유지하는 것은 질병을 막기 위해 필요하다.

어휘

capillary 모세혈관
blood vessel 혈관, 핏줄
arteriole 세동맥, 소동맥
venule 세정맥
biochemical 생화학의
respiration 호흡
define 윤곽[모양/경계]을 분명히 나타내다
mass 질량
tissue 조직
adopt 채택하다, 차용하다
sedentary 주로 앉아서 지내는, 몸을 많이 움직이지 않는
contract 수축하다
shrink 오그라들다, 줄어들다
go away 없어지다, 사라지다
ward off 피하다, 막다, 물리치다

10 정답 ③

정답해설

본문은 '1692년 Massachusetts의 Salem Village에서 발생한 Salem 마녀재판'에 대한 내용이다. 본문 중반 "while more than 150 men, women and children were accused over the next several months(한편 150명 이상의 남성, 여성 그리고 아이들이 이후 몇 개월에 걸쳐 기소되었다)."를 통해, '150명 이상의 남성, 여성, 아이들이 기소되었음'을 알 수 있으므로 '성별, 연령에 관계없는 기소가 이루어졌음'을 알 수 있다. 따라서 글의 내용과 일치하는 보기는 '③ A number of people were accused of witchcraft regardless of gender and age(성별과 나이에 상관없이 수많은 사람들이 기소되었다).'이다.

오답해설

① 본문 첫 문장 "after two young girls in Salem Village, Massachusetts, named Elizabeth Hubbard and Dorothy Good, claimed to be possessed by the devil and accused several local women of witchcraft(Salem Village의 Elizabeth Hubbard와 Dorothy Good라는 두 어린 소녀들이 악마에 사로잡혔다고 주장했고 몇몇 지역 여성들을 주술 혐의로 고발한 이후)."를 통해, 'Elizabeth Hubbard와 Dorothy Good'은 '고발을 당한 것이 아니라 고발을 한 주체'라는 것을 알 수 있다. 따라서 오답이다.

② 본문 중반 "the first convicted witch, Bridget Bishop, was hanged that June. Eighteen others followed Bishop to Salem's Gallows Hill"을 통해, 'Bridget Bishop과 18명의 다른 사람들', 즉 총 19명이 교수형을 당했다는 것을 알 수 있다. 따라서 오답이다.

④ 본문 첫 문장에서 '재판이 1692년 봄에 시작되었음'을 알 수 있으며, 본문 후반 "By September 1692, the hysteria had begun to abate and public opinion turned against the trials(1692년 9월경, 그 히스테리는 누그러들기 시작했고, 여론은 그 재판에 등을 돌렸다)."를 통해, 같은 해 9월 여론이 재판을 지지하지 않게 되었음을 알 수 있다. 따라서 오답이다.

해석

악명 높은 Salem 마녀재판은 Massachusetts, Salem Village의 Elizabeth Hubbard와 Dorothy Good라는 두 어린 소녀들이 악마에 사로잡혔다고 주장했고 몇몇 지역 여성들을 주술 혐의로 고발한 이후 1692년 봄에 시작되었다. 식민지 시대의 Massachusetts 전역에 퍼진 히스테리의 물결로써, 사건을 심리하기 위해 Salem에 특별 법정이 소집되었다; 첫 번째 유죄 선고를 받은 마녀인 Bridget Bishop은 그해 6월에 교수형을 당했다. 18명의 다른 사람들이 Bishop의 뒤를 이어 Salem의 Gallows Hill로 보내졌고, 한편 150명 이상의 남성, 여성 그리고 아이들이 이후 몇 개월에 걸쳐 기소되었다. 1692년 9월경, 그 히스테리는 누그러들기 시작했고, 여론은 그 재판에 등을 돌렸다. 비록 Massachusetts General Court가 이후 고발된 마녀들에 대한 유죄 평결을 무효화했고 그들의 가족에게 보상금을 지급했지만, 그 공동체에 비통함은 지속되었고, Salem 마녀재판의 고통스러운 유산은 수 세기 동안 남아 있을 것이다.

① 재판은 Elizabeth Hubbard와 Dorothy Good이 주술 혐의로 기소당한 이후 시작되었다.
② 18명의 사람들이 교수형에 처해졌다.
③ 성별과 나이에 상관없이 수많은 사람들이 기소되었다.
④ 재판은 수년 동안 일반 대중들의 지지를 받았다.

어휘

infamous 악명 높은, 오명이 난
trial 재판
claim 주장하다
be possessed by 귀신이 들리다[씌우다]
accuse A of B (A를 B의 혐의로) 고발[기소/비난]하다, 혐의를 제기하다
witchcraft 마법, 마술, 주술
hysteria 히스테리
colonial 식민지의, 식민지 시대의
convene 소집하다, 회합하다
hear (법정에서) 심리[공판]를 갖다
convicted 유죄로 결정된
hang 교수형에 처하다, 목을 매달다
abate (강도가) 약해지다, 누그러들다
annul (법적으로) 취소하다[무효하게 하다]
verdict 평결
grant (인정하여 정식으로) 주다, 수여하다
indemnity 배상[보상]금
bitterness 비통함, 쓰라림
linger (예상보다 오래) 남다[계속되다]
legacy (과거의) 유산
endure 오래가다[지속되다]
charge A with B (A를 B의 죄로) 기소하다
regardless of …에 상관없이[구애받지 않고]

결국엔 성정혜 영어 하프모의고사
기적사 DAY 59

01	①	02	②	03	③	04	③	05	②
06	③	07	④	08	②	09	③	10	①

01 정답 ①

정답해설

밑줄 친 'potential'은 '잠재적인, 가능성이 있는'을 뜻하는 형용사로 ① latent(잠재하는, 잠복해 있는)와 의미가 가장 가깝다.

해석

미국 법은 **잠재적인** 안전 결함이 발견됐을 때 자동차 회사가 영업일 5일 안에 정부에 그것을 알리도록 요구한다.
① 잠재하는, 잠복해 있는
② 분명한
③ 의심스러운, 몽롱한
④ 조용한, 잠잠한

어휘

automaker 자동차 회사
potential 잠재적인, 가능성이 있는
latent 잠재하는, 잠복해 있는
equivocal 의심스러운, 몽롱한
notify 알리다[통고/통지하다]
defect 결함, 결점
manifest 분명한
quiescent 조용한, 잠잠한

02 정답 ②

정답해설

밑줄 친 'forthright'는 '기탄없이 말하는, 솔직한'을 뜻하는 형용사로 ② candid(솔직한)와 의미가 가장 가깝다.

해석

대통령에게 직접 보고하는 민정수석비서관은 전적으로 **기탄없이 말해**야 한다.
① 교활한, 음흉한
② 솔직한
③ 즉흥적으로 한
④ 솔직하지 못한

어휘

secretary 비서
forthright 기탄없이 말하는, 솔직한
candid 솔직한
disingenuous 솔직하지 못한
absolutely 전적으로, 틀림없이
sly 교활한, 음흉한
impromptu 즉흥적으로 한

오답률 TOP 1

03 정답 ③

정답해설

밑줄 친 'miserable'은 '비참한'을 뜻하는 형용사로 ③ abject(극도로 비참한, 절망적인)와 의미가 가장 가깝다.

해석

1833년, 그가 그의 이전의 주인에게 돌아갔을 때, 그는 노예들의 **비참한** 삶을 다시 목격했다.

① 희망적인, 장밋빛의
② 혈색이 좋은, 건강한
③ 극도로 비참한, 절망적인
④ 통탄할

어휘

witness 목격하다; 목격자
rosy 희망적인, 장밋빛의
abject 극도로 비참한, 절망적인
miserable 비참한
ruddy 혈색이 좋은, 건강한
grievous 통탄할

04 정답 ③

정답해설

A와 B는 B가 최근 2주 동안 잠을 제대로 자지 못하는 상황에 관한 대화를 하고 있다. A는 B에게 '잠을 잘 자지 못하는 이유가 무엇인지' 물어보자, B는 "일이 너무 많아서 '밤늦게까지 업무를 할(burn the midnight oil)' 수밖에 없었다"라고 답변한다. 따라서 정답은 ③이다.

오답해설

① B가 잠을 제대로 자지 못했던 이유가 일이 너무 많아서 '임시방편을 세울(make a shift)' 수밖에 없었다고 하는 것은 대화의 흐름상 어색하다.
② B는 자신이 지난 2주 동안 충분한 잠을 자지 못해서 피곤하다면서, 그 이유가 일이 너무 많기 때문이라고 말하며, '자신의 소신을 지킬(stick to my guns)' 수밖에 없었다고 이야기하는 것은 맥락상 부자연스럽다.
④ A가 B에게 잠을 제대로 못 잔 이유를 물어보자 B는 "일이 너무 많았다"라고 하면서 '허풍을 떨(blow my own trumpet)' 수밖에 없었다고 얘기하는 것은 내용상 적절하지 않다.

해석

A: 저기, 너 아파 보인다. 너 괜찮아?
B: 나는 내가 완전히 괜찮다고는 못 하겠어. 나는 지금 잠이 덜 깼어.
A: 너 어젯밤에 잠을 잘 못 잤어?
B: 어젯밤만 그런 것이 아니야. 난 지난 2주 동안 충분한 잠을 자지 못했어.
A: 아, 그것이 네가 아파 보이는 이유구나. 너는 왜 잠을 못 잤니?
B: 나는 너무 많은 일에 시달리고 있어. 나는 밤늦게까지 업무를 할 수밖에 없었어.
A: 너는 네 건강을 다른 것들보다 우선시해야 해. 일이 네 건강을 진짜 망칠 수 있어.
B: 맞아. 나는 집에 가서 낮잠을 좀 자야겠어.
① 임시방편을 세우다
② 자신의 소신을 지키다
③ 밤늦게까지 업무를 하다
④ 허풍을 떨다

어휘

prioritize 우선시키다, 우선순위를 매기다
make a shift 임시방편을 세우다
stick to one's guns 자신의 소신을 지키다
burn the midnight oil 밤늦게까지 업무를 하다
blow one's own trumpet 허풍을 떨다

오답률 TOP 2

05 정답 ②

정답해설

② **출제 포인트: 비교급 비교**

비교급 비교의 경우 '비교급 형용사/부사'와 함께 비교 대상 앞에 'than'을

사용한다. 해당 문장은 형용사 'bad'의 비교급인 'worse'를 사용하였으나 비교 대상 앞에 'as'를 사용하였으므로 틀린 문장이다. 따라서 'as'를 'than'으로 수정해야 한다.

오답해설

① 출제 포인트: 능동태 vs. 수동태
해당 문장에서 'It'은 가주어이며 'that people could be possessed by evil spirits'는 진주어에 해당하므로 완전자동사 'believe'의 과거시제 수동태인 'was believed'는 옳은 표현이다. 이때 'that people could be possessed by evil spirits'를 목적어로 오해하지 않도록 주의해야 한다.

③ 출제 포인트: '동사+부사'의 목적어 위치
「put+back+목적어」는 관용표현으로 '~을 지연시키다, 지체시키다'를 뜻하며 이때 'back'은 부사이므로 「put+목적어+back」의 형태로 사용할 수 있다. 해당 문장은 「put+back+목적어」인 'put back our plans'를 사용하였으므로 옳은 문장이다.

④ 출제 포인트: 부정부사(구) 도치
부정부사(구) 'Little'이 문두에 오고 동사가 과거시제 일반동사인 경우 'Little' 이후에 오는 어순은 「did+주어+동사원형」이다. 해당 문장은 문두에 'Little'을 사용하였으므로 이후에 오는 「did+주어+동사원형」형태인 'did she know'는 옳은 표현이다.

해석

① 사람들이 악령에 사로잡힐 수도 있다고 믿어졌다.
② 추운 날씨에 젖은 머리로 외출을 하는 것보다 더 나쁜 것은 없다.
③ 나쁜 거래 수치는 우리의 확장을 위한 계획들을 지연했고 그래서 우리는 그것들을 수정할 수밖에 없다.
④ 그녀는 자신의 딸에게 평생토록 계속될 열정을 불어 넣고 있다는 것을 결코 알지 못했다.

06 정답 ③

정답해설

③ 출제 포인트: one of the 최상급 복수명사
「one of the 최상급 복수명사」표현에서 최상급 앞에 있는 'the'가 빠질 경우 틀린 표현이 된다. 따라서 밑줄 친 'most'를 'the most'로 수정해야 한다.

오답해설

① 출제 포인트: 현재분사 vs. 과거분사
'키우는 동식물들'이 해석상 자연스러우므로 'domesticate'와 수식하는 대상 'plants and animals'가 수동관계임을 알 수 있다. 따라서 밑줄 친 과거분사 'domesticated'는 옳은 표현이다.

② 출제 포인트: 불완전타동사의 목적격 보어/자릿값(형용사 vs. 부사)
불완전타동사 'made'의 목적격 보어로 형용사를 사용하는 것은 옳다. 따라서 밑줄 친 형용사 'dependent'는 옳은 표현이다.

④ 출제 포인트: 능동태 vs. 수동태
형용사 'available'을 통해 밑줄 친 'made'를 수동태 'was made'로 수정해야 한다고 생각할 수 있으나 'available' 이후에 있는 'an abundant new source of food'가 'made'의 목적어에 해당하므로 능동태인 'made'는 옳은 표현이다. 이때 목적어가 긴 경우 목적어가 목적격 보어 뒤로 이동할 수 있음에 유의하도록 한다. 목적어가 목적격 보어 뒤로 이동하는 이유는 「불완전타동사+목적어+목적격 보어」인 'made an abundant new source of food available'로 고치게 되면 'available'이 수식하는 대상이 전치사 'of'의 목적어인 'food'인지 불완전타동사의 목적어인 'source'인지 알 수 없게 되기 때문이다.

해석

비록 농부들은 당시에 그것을 깨닫지 못했지만, 인간인 농부들과 그들이 키우는 동물과 식물들은 원대한 협상을 했다. 옥수수에 대해 생각해 보자. (옥수수의) 재배는 그것을 인간에게 의존하게 만들었다. 그러나 인간과의 연관은 또한 옥수수로 하여금 그리 알려지지 않은 멕시코 벼과 식물로서의 그것의 기원을 훨씬 더 멀리 뛰어넘게 하여 이제 옥수수는 지구상에서 가장 널리 재배되는 농작물 중 하나이다. 한편, 인간의 관점에서 보면 옥수수의 재배는 풍부한 새로운 식량원을 이용할 수 있게 해주었다.

어휘

domesticate 키우다, 재배하다　　association 연관, 제휴
abundant 풍부한

07 정답 ④

정답해설

㉠ 출제 포인트: 주어와 동사의 수일치
주어가 단수 형태인 'The price'이므로 ㉠에는 단수 형태 동사인 'is'를 사용하는 것이 옳다. 'that the farmer ~ wholesaler'는 선행사 'The price'를 수식하는 목적격 관계대명사 절이다.

㉡ 출제 포인트: 자릿값(동사 vs. 준동사)
㉡은 'If'가 이끄는 종속절의 동사 자리에 해당하므로 'leads'가 ㉡에 들어가는 것이 옳다.

㉢ 출제 포인트: 접속사의 쓰임(and vs. but)
문맥상 '슈퍼마켓이 감자에 대해 도매상에게 지급해야 하는 가격은 상승할 것이고, 이것은 그들이 자기 가게의 감자에 매기는 가격에 반영될 것이다'가 자연스러우므로 ㉢에는 등위접속사 'and'가 들어가는 것이 옳다.

오답해설

㉡ 현재분사 'leading'을 사용하게 되면 해당 종속절의 동사가 없으므로 비문이 된다.

㉢ 'but'을 사용하면 '슈퍼마켓이 감자에 대해 도매상에게 지급해야 하는 가격은 상승할 것이지만, 이것은 그들이 자기 가게의 감자에 매기는 가격에 반영될 것이다'가 되어 문맥상 어색하며, 가격 상승과 가격 반영을 반의 관계로 보기 어렵다.

해석

도매상에게서 농부가 받는 가격은 소매상이 소비자에게 부과하는 가격보다 그날그날 훨씬 더 유동적이다. 예를 들어, 악천후가 감자의 흉작을 초래한다면, 슈퍼마켓이 감자에 대해 도매상에게 지급해야 하는 가격은 상승할 것이고 이것은 그들이 자기 가게의 감자에 매기는 가격에 반영될 것이다.

어휘

flexible 유동적인, 융통성이 있는　　wholesale 도매상
reflect 반영하다

08 정답 ③

정답해설

본문은 'The U.S. Natural Resources Conservation Service (NRCS)에 의한 토양의 분류'에 대한 설명이다. 본문 중반 "In general, Class I soils are more arable and suitable for cropland; Class II soils have some limitations that reduce the choice of plants that can be grown, or require moderate conservation practices to reduce the risk of damage when used; Class III soils have severe limitations that reduce the choice of plants, require special conservation practices, or both, but may be productive with careful management(일반적으로 Class I 토양은 더 경작에 적합하고 경지로 알맞다; Class II 토양은 경작될 수 있는 식물의 선택지를 감소시키는 약간의 한계가 있거나, 사용 시 손상의 위험을 줄이기 위한 적당한 보전 처리를 요한다; Class III 토양은 식물의 선택을 감소시키는 심각한 한계가 있거나, 특별한 보전 처리를 요하거나, 또는 둘 다이지만, 세심한 관리를 한다면 생산성이 있을 수도 있다)."에 따르면, Class II 토양은 'moderate conservation practices(적당한 보전 처리)'를 필요로 하고, Class III 토양은 'special conservation practices(특별한 보전 처리)'를 필요로 한다고 언급하고 있으므로, Class III 토양이 Class II 토양보다 더 많은 관리와 처리가 필요하다는 것을 알 수 있다. 따라서 글의 내용과 일치하지 않는 것은 '③ Class II soils require more care and treatment than Class III soils(Class II 토양은 Class III 토양보다 더 많은 관리와 처리를 필요로 한다).'이다.

오답해설

① 두 번째 문장 "The groupings are based upon composition and limitations of the soils, the risk of damage when they are used, and the way they respond to treatment(그 분류 집단은 토양의 구성과 한계, 그것들이 사용되었을 시 손상의 위험, 그리고 그것들이 처리에 대응하는 방식에 기반한 것이다)."를 통해 본문의 내용과 일치하는 것을 알 수 있다.

② "Class I soils are more arable and suitable for cropland(Class I 토양은 더 경작에 적합하고 경지로 알맞다)"를 통해, Class I 토양이 가장 비옥함을 알 수 있고, "Class III soils have severe limitations that reduce the choice of plants, require special conservation practices, or both, but may be productive with careful management(Class III 토양은 식물의 선택을 감소시키는 심각한 한계가 있거나, 특별한 보전 처리를 요하거나, 또는 둘 다이지만, 세심한 관리를 한다면 생산성이 있을 수도 있다)"를 통해, Class III 토양은 작물 선택의 제약이 있을 수 있다는 것을 알 수 있으므로, Class I 토양에서 자랄 수 있는 작물이 Class III 토양에서는 자랄 수 없을 가능성이 있다는 것을 유추할 수 있다.

④ 본문 중반 "Under the NRCS system, there are eight capability classes ranging from Class I to Class VIII(NRCS의 시스템하에, Class I에서 Class VIII의 범위에 이르는 8개의 능력 집단이 있다)."에서 총 8단계로 나누어 있다는 것을 알 수 있다. 그리고 마지막 문장 이전까지 Class I, II, III에 관해 언급한 후, 마지막 문장에서 "The soils in the remaining classes have progressively greater natural limitations for cropland, but may be used for pasture, grazing, woodland, wildlife, recreation, and esthetic purposes(그 외의 집단의 토양은 경지로서는 계속해서 더 커지는 자연적인 한계를 지니고 있으나, 목초지, 방목지, 삼림 지대, 야생 생물, 휴양, 그리고 미적인 목적을 위해서는 사용될지도 모른다)."라고 언급하며, 나머지 그룹은 경지로는 더 큰 한계가 있다고 설명하고 기타 사용처를 제시하고 있으므로, 나머지 5단계의 그룹은 경지로는 권고되지 않는다는 것을 알 수 있다.

해석

U.S. Natural Resources Conservation Service (NRCS)는 토양을 대부분의 종류의 농사에 대한 그들의 일반적인 적합성을 나타내는 능력 집단으로 분류했다. 그 분류 집단은 토양의 구성과 한계, 그것들이 사용되었을 시 손상의 위험, 그리고 그것들이 처리에 대응하는 방식에 기반한 것이다. NRCS의 시스템하에, Class I에서 Class VIII의 범위에 이르는 8개의 능력 집단이 있다. 일반적으로 Class I 토양은 더 경작에 적합하고 경지로 알맞다; Class II 토양은 경작될 수 있는 식물의 선택지를 감소시키는 약간의 한계가 있거나, 사용 시 손상의 위험을 줄이기 위한 적당한 보전 처리를 요한다; Class III 토양은 식물의 선택을 감소시키는 심각한 한계가 있거나, 특별한 보전 처리를 요하거나, 또는 둘 다이지만, 세심한 관리를 한다면 생산성이 있을 수도 있다. 그 외의 집단의 토양은 경지로서는 계속해서 더 커지는 자연적인 한계를 지니고 있으나, 목초지, 방목지, 삼림 지대, 야생 생물, 휴양, 그리고 미적인 목적을 위해서는 사용될 수 있을지도 모른다.

① NRCS는 토양을 분류할 때 다수의 요소를 고려했다.
② Class I 토지에서 자랄 수 있는 일부 작물은 Class III 토지에서 살아남을 수 없을지도 모른다.
③ Class II 토양은 Class III 토양보다 더 많은 관리와 처리를 필요로 한다.
④ 경지로는 권고되지 않는 다섯 가지의 토양 집단이 있다.

어휘

capability 능력, 역량
grouping (흔히 더 큰 집단의 일부인) 그룹[집단], 분류
suitability 적당, 적합 arable 경작에 알맞은
conservation 보존, 보전 remaining 나머지의, 잔여의
progressively 계속해서, 점진적으로 pasture 목초지, 초원
grazing 방목지, 목초지 esthetic 심미적, 미학적
take … into account …를 고려하다

09 정답 ③

정답해설

본문은 'Department of Health and Human Services에서 건강한 성인에게 권고하는 일주일 운동량'에 관한 내용이다. 본문 중반의 "Even small amounts of physical activity are helpful, and accumulated activity throughout the day adds up to providing similar health benefits(적은 양의 신체 활동이라도 도움이 되며, 하루 동안 축적된 활동은 결국 유사한 건강상 이점을 제공하게 된다)."를 통해, '운동은 적은 양도 도움이 되고, 하루에 축적된 운동의 양이 유사한 효과를 줄 수 있다'고 설명하고 있으므로, '연속으로 1시간 운동을 하는 것과, 10분씩 짧은 운동을 6번에 걸쳐 총 1시간을 하는 것이 모두 도움이 된다'는 것을 알 수 있다. 따라서 '③ Doing a ten-minute workout six times a day is less beneficial than exercising nonstop for an hour(하루에 10분짜리 운동을 6번 하는 것은 한 시간 동안 쉬지 않고 운동하는 것보다 덜 이롭다).'는 글의 내용과 일치하지 않는다.

오답해설

① 두 번째 문장 "For most healthy adults, the Department of Health and Human Services recommends at least 140 minutes a week of moderate aerobic activity or 70 minutes a week of vigorous aerobic activity"를 통해, '일주일에 적당한 유산소 운동 140분 또는 격렬한 유산소 운동 70분이 권고된다'는 것을 알 수 있고, 이후 "Examples include running, walking or swimming."에서 '유산소 운동의 예시'로 '수영'을 들고 있으므로, '일주일에 격렬한 70분의 수영은 적당한 140분의 수영에 상당한다'는 것을 알 수 있다.

② "For most healthy adults, the Department of Health and Human Services recommends at least 140 minutes a week of moderate aerobic activity"를 통해, '일주일에 140분 동안 적당한 유산소 운동'을 권하고 있으며, "The guidelines suggest that you spread this exercise throughout the week."에서, '일주일에 걸쳐 분산시킬 것을 제안'하고 있음을 알 수 있다. 즉, 7일 동안 140분의 운동이라면, 하루에 20분에 상당하므로, ②는 글의 내용과 일치한다.

④ 본문 후반 "It also recommends strength training exercises for all major muscle groups at least two times a week. Examples include lifting free weights, using weight machines or doing body-weight training(그것은 또한 모든 주요 근육 그룹을 위해 근력운동을 주당 최소 2번 권고한다. 예시로는 덤벨 들기, 종합 헬스 기구 이용하기, 또는 체중 운동을 하는 것을 포함한다)."을 통해 글의 내용과 일치하는 것을 알 수 있다.

해석

운동과 신체 활동은 좋은 기분을 느끼고, 당신의 건강을 증진시키고, 즐거움을 얻는 훌륭한 방법들이다. 대부분의 건강한 성인들에게 Department of Health and Human Services는 최소 주당 140분의 적당한 유산소 운동 또는 주당 70분의 격렬한 유산소 운동이나, 적당한 운동과 격렬한 운동의 결합을 권고한다. 그 지침은 당신이 이 운동을 일주일에 걸쳐 분산시킬 것을 제안한다. 예시로는 달리기, 걷기, 또는 수영을 포함한다. 적은 양의 신체 활동이라도 도움이 되며, 하루 동안 축적된 활동은 결국 유사한 건강상 이점을 제공하게 된다. 그것은 또한 모든 주요 근육 그룹을 위해 근력운동을 주당 최소 2번 권고한다. 예시로는 덤벨 들기, 종합 헬스 기구 이용하기, 또는 체중 운동을 하는 것을 포함한다. 당신의 활동을 일주일에 걸쳐 분산시켜라. 만일 당신이 체중을 줄이거나, 특정한 신체 단련 목표를 충족시키거나, 훨씬 더 많은 이득을 얻길 원한다면, 당신은 적당한 유산소 운동을 주당 280분 또는 그 이상으로 증가시킬 필요가 있을 것이다.

① 일주일에 70분의 격렬한 수영을 하는 것은 일주일에 140분의 적당한 수영을 하는 것에 상당한다.
② 매일의 20분간의 적당한 걷기는 건강한 성인에게 유익할 수 있다.
③ 하루에 10분짜리 운동을 6번 하는 것은 한 시간 동안 쉬지 않고 운동하는 것보다 덜 이롭다.
④ 체중 운동은 적어도 일주일에 두 번 권고된다.

어휘

moderate 적당한, 보통의, 중간의   aerobic 유산소의
vigorous 격렬한, 활발한   accumulate 축적하다, 모으다
add up to something 결국 …되다
free weight 바벨, 덤벨, 케틀벨 등 외부 장비에 연결되어 있지 않은 근력운동 기구
weight machine 종합 헬스 기구   meet (필요, 요구 등을) 충족시키다
ramp up 늘리다[증가시키다]

오답률 TOP 3

10 정답 ①

정답해설

본문은 '전 세계에 걸쳐 어느 시대에나 주술(witchcraft)의 대상, 또는 주술 고발(witchcraft accusations)의 대상은 친척 또는 이웃인 경우가 많았다'고 설명하고 있다. 본문 중반 "Especially close neighbors with whom people were in everyday contacts represented the most threatening source of harm and the most obvious targets of witchcraft accusations almost everywhere(특히 거의 모든 곳에서 사람들이 일상적으로 접촉하던 가까운 이웃이 가장 위협적인 위해의 근원이자 주술 고발의 가장 명백한 대상에 해당했다)."를 통해, '위해한 주술을 거는 사람도, 위해한 주술을 걸었다고 의심받은 대상도 모두 가까운 이웃이었음'을 알 수 있으며, 이후 두 예시를 통해, 주술 고발이 서로 가까운 관계에 있는 사람들 사이에서 이루어졌다는 것을 설명하고 있다. 따라서 '가까운 사람(이웃)이 (주술을 통해 나에게 위해를 가할 수도 있고, 내가 주술로 위해를 가했다고 의심할 수도 있으므로) 위험하다'는 내용을 함축하고 있으므로, 글의 제목으로 가장 적절한 것은 '① The Enemy near the Door(문 가까이의[집 근처의] 적)'이다.

오답해설

② 두 번째 문장 "Behringer claims that a basic set of beliefs about anti-social people who try to inflict harm by mystical means, mostly on their relatives or neighbors, is common to the ancient world, medieval and early modern Europe and present-day Africa, south-east Asia, Australia and Americas(Behringer는 신령스러운 수단을 통해, 주로 그들의 친척 또는 이웃에게, 위해를 가하려 시도하는 반사회적인 사람들에 대한 기본적인 일련의 믿음은 고대 세계, 중세 그리고 초기 현대 유럽, 그리고 현재의 아프리카, 동남아시아, 호주 그리고 미주에 공통적이라고 주장한다)."에서 '전 세계에 신령스러운 수단을 이용해 위해를 가하는 사람들'에 대한 믿음이 공통적으로 존재한다고 언급하고 있으나, 이는 '그러한 반사회적인 사람들이 주로 친척 또는 이웃과 같은 가까운 사람들에게 해를 가한다는 믿음'에 대해 설명하기 위한 내용이며, 전 세계의 마녀사냥과는 관계없는 내용이므로 글의 제목으로 적절하지 않다.

③ 본문과 관계없는 내용이다.
④ '주술 고발의 역사'에 대해서는 본문에 언급되지 않는다.

해석

사람들은 대개 자신들의 불운에 책임이 있는 범인을 다른 무엇보다도 먼저 자신들에게 아주 가까이에 있는 환경에서 찾는다. Behringer는 신령스러운 수단을 통해, 주로 그들의 친척 또는 이웃에게, 위해를 가하려 시도하는 반사회적인 사람들에 대한 기본적인 일련의 믿음은 고대 세계, 중세 그리고 초기 현대 유럽, 그리고 현재의 아프리카, 동남아시아, 호주 그리고 미주에 공통적이라고 주장한다. 특히 거의 모든 곳에서 사람들이 일상적으로 접촉하던 가까운 이웃이 가장 위협적인 위해의 근원이자 주술 고발의 가장 명백한 대상에 해당했다. Macfarlane은 1560년에서 1599년까지의 Essex 재판에서의 주술 고발은 동일한 마을에서 왔을 뿐만 아니라, 심지어 마을의 동일한 지역에서 살고 서로를 친밀하게 알고 있는 사람들 사이에서 주로 행해졌으며, 고발은 개인 간 강한 관계가 있는 지역에 국한되었다고 주장했다. 또한, 19세기에 Drenthe라는 네덜란드 지방에서, 주술에 대한 혐의는 주로 (여성) 이웃에게 돌아갔다.

① 문 가까이의[집 근처의] 적
② 전 세계의 마녀사냥
③ 이웃과의 분쟁 해결
④ 주술 고발의 역사

어휘

culprit 범인
first and foremost 무엇보다도 먼저
immediate (시간적·공간적으로) 아주 가까이에[바로 옆에] 있는
inflict (괴로움 등을) 가하다[안기다]   mystical 신령스러운
common to …에 공통된   represent (…에) 해당하다
witchcraft 마술, 마법, 주술
accusation 혐의 (제기), 비난, 고발, 기소
trial 재판   intimately 친밀하게
intense 강렬한, 집중적인   suspicion 혐의, 의심
fall on …으로 돌려지다, 쏠리다   dispute 분쟁, 분규

기적사 DAY 60

결국엔 성정혜 영어 하프모의고사

| 01 | ② | 02 | ① | 03 | ④ | 04 | ③ | 05 | ④ |
| 06 | ② | 07 | ③ | 08 | ③ | 09 | ② | 10 | ④ |

01 정답 ②

정답해설

밑줄 친 'principal'은 '주요한, 주된'을 뜻하는 형용사로 ② staple(주된, 주요한)과 의미가 가장 가깝다.

해석

지역의 궁전 소유주 혹은 관리자로서, 그들은 **주요** 지역 사회 명소를 만들고 형성하는 사람들이었다.
① 사소한, 하찮은
② 주된, 주요한
③ 허름한, 부당한
④ 중요하지 않은, 무형의

어휘

principal 주요한, 주된   petty 사소한, 하찮은
staple 주된, 주요한   shabby 허름한, 부당한
immaterial 중요하지 않은, 무형의

오답률 TOP 1

02 정답 ①

정답해설

밑줄 친 'seraphic'은 '거룩한, 천사 같은'을 뜻하는 형용사로 ① sublime(숭고한, 황당한)과 의미가 가장 가깝다.

해석

역사에서 영웅으로 칭송받는 한 남자가 있었고 그의 **거룩한** 희생은 모두에게 알려져 있었다.
① 숭고한, 황당한
② 평민의, 교양 없는
③ 터무니없는, 웃기는
④ 이상한, 기이한

어휘

extol 칭찬[칭송]하다, 극찬[격찬]하다   seraphic 거룩한, 천사 같은
sacrifice 희생   sublime 숭고한, 황당한
plebeian 평민의, 교양 없는   ludicrous 터무니없는, 웃기는
outlandish 이상한, 기이한

오답률 TOP 3

03 정답 ④

정답해설

밑줄 친 'ascetic'은 '금욕적인'을 뜻하는 형용사로 ④ abstinent(금욕적인, 자제하는)와 의미가 가장 가깝다.

해석

William은 학교에서 외향적이고 장난기가 있는 반면에, 그의 남동생인 John은 학교에서 **금욕적**이고 엄격하다.

① 호화로운, 풍성한
② 낭비하는, 방탕한
③ 쾌락의
④ 금욕적인, 자제하는

어휘

extroverted 외향적인, 사교적인   fun-loving 재미를 추구하는
ascetic 금욕적인   strict 엄격한[엄한]
lavish 호화로운, 풍성한   prodigal 낭비하는, 방탕한
sybaritic 쾌락의   abstinent 금욕적인, 자제하는

04 정답 ③

정답해설

Kevin과 Helena는 크리스마스 날 무엇을 했는지에 관한 대화를 나눈다. Kevin은 남동생에게 선물을 줬는지 묻고 Helena는 남동생에게 줄 크리스마스 선물을 숨겨놨는데 남동생이 발견하기 전에는 '시무룩한 표정을 지었다(pulled a long face)'라고 이야기한다. 따라서 정답은 ③이다.

오답해설

① '남동생에게 크리스마스 선물을 줬는지' 묻는 Kevin의 질문에 Helena는 "선물을 크리스마스트리 뒤에 숨겨놓았는데 그가 발견하기 전에 '체면을 차렸다(saved face)'"라고 대답하는 것은 대화의 흐름상 빈칸에 들어갈 말로 부적절하다.
② Helena는 "남동생에게 줄 크리스마스 선물을 트리 뒤에 숨겨놨는데 그가 선물을 발견하기 전에는 '스스로 책임졌다(faced the music)'"라고 이야기하는 것은 문맥상 어색하다.
④ Helena의 남동생이 크리스마스트리 뒤에 있는 선물을 발견하기 전에 '시장을 장악했다(had a corner on the market)'라고 하는 것은 대화의 내용상 자연스럽지 않다.

해석

Kevin: 너 크리스마스 날 뭐했어?
Helena: 나는 가족들과 함께 크리스마스를 보냈어. 넌 뭐했어?
Kevin: 나는 캐나다 여행 중이었어. 거기는 크리스마스 날 눈이 많이 왔어.
Helena: 정말 좋았겠다! 정말 부러워.
Kevin: 나는 그 추억들을 영원히 간직할 거야. 너는 네 남동생에게 크리스마스 선물 줬어?
Helena: 응, 크리스마스트리 뒤에 숨겨놨는데 그가 발견하기 전에 시무룩한 표정을 지었어.
Kevin: 트리 밑의 공간이 빈 것을 봤을 때 그가 실망했음에 틀림없어.
Helena: 그래서 선물이 위치한 곳의 힌트를 그에게 줬어.
① 체면을 차렸다
② 스스로 책임졌다
③ 시무룩한 표정을 지었다
④ 시장을 장악했다

어휘

jealous 질투하는, 시기하는   save face 체면을 차리다
face the music 스스로 책임지다
pull a long face 시무룩한 표정을 짓다
have a corner on the market 시장을 장악하다

05 정답 ④

정답해설

④ **출제 포인트: Only 부사구/절 도치**
문두에 「Only+부사절」이 오고 주절에 조동사가 있는 경우 주절의 어순은 「조동사+주어+동사원형」의 의문문 어순이다. 해당 문장은 「Only+부사절」인 'Only when national security is guaranteed'를 사용하였으나 주절의 어순이 「주어+조동사+동사원형」인 평서문 어순을 사용하였으므로 틀린 문장이다. 따라서 'we can turn'을 'can we turn'으로 수정해야 한다.

오답해설

① **출제 포인트: 능동태 vs. 수동태**
해당 문장에서 'It'은 가주어이며 'that the corruption in the organization is acute'는 진주어에 해당하므로 완전타동사 'say'의 현재시제 수동태인 'is said'는 옳은 표현이다. 이때 'that the corruption in the organization is acute'를 목적어로 오해하지 않도록 주의해야 한다.

② **출제 포인트: '동사+부사'의 목적어 위치**
「put+away+목적어」는 관용표현으로 '~을 치우다'를 뜻하며 이때 'away'는 부사이므로 「put+목적어+away」의 형태로 사용할 수 있다. 해당 문장은 「put+away+목적어」인 'put away foods'를 사용하였으므로 옳은 문장이다.

③ **출제 포인트: 비교급 비교/to부정사의 형용사적 용법**
불완전자동사 'be'의 주격 보어로 형용사 'big'의 비교급인 'bigger'를 사용하였으며 비교 대상 앞에 'than'을 사용하였으므로 해당 문장은 옳은 문장이다. 또한 해당 문장에서 'to be'는 불완전자동사 'proved'의 주격 보어로 to부정사의 형용사적 용법에 해당한다.

해석

① 그 기관 내 부패가 심하다고 한다.
② 음식을 적절하게 준비하고, 조리하고, 치우는 것은 중요하다.
③ 그 언어를 할 줄 모른다는 것은 내가 상상했던 것보다 더 큰 핸디캡인 것으로 드러났다.
④ 국가 안보가 보장될 때만, 우리는 우리의 관심을 시민권의 개념으로 돌릴 수 있다.

06 정답 ②

정답해설

② **출제 포인트: 자릿값(동사 vs. 준동사)/등위접속사의 병렬구조**
'Technological advances ~ and cheaper.'에서 'made'는 등위접속사 'and'를 통해 병렬구조를 이루고 있는 과거시제 동사이다. 그러나 등위접속사 'and'의 앞에 'made'와 병렬구조를 이루는 과거시제 동사가 없으므로 밑줄 친 현재분사 'providing'을 과거시제 동사 'provided'로 수정해야 한다.

오답해설

① **출제 포인트: to부정사의 형용사적 용법/불완전타동사의 목적격 보어**
밑줄 친 'to develop'은 명사(구) 'modern tourism'을 수식하므로 to부정사의 형용사적 용법에 해당하며, 이때 'modern tourism'은 불완전타동사 'allow'의 동명사 형태인 'allowing'의 목적어에 해당하므로 'to develop'은 목적격 보어에 해당함을 알 수 있다.

③ **출제 포인트: 등위상관접속사의 병렬구조**
등위상관접속사 「not only A but also B」를 통해 「과거시제 동사+목적어」가 병렬구조를 이루고 있음을 알 수 있다. 따라서 밑줄 친 과거시제 동사 'prompted'는 옳은 표현이며 'created'와 병렬구조를 이루고 있다.

④ **출제 포인트: 현재분사 vs. 과거분사**
밑줄 친 'considered' 이후에 있는 'a fundamental precondition for tourism'을 보고 과거분사 'considered'를 현재분사 'considering'으로 수정해야 한다고 오해할 수 있으나 'a fundamental precondition for tourism'은 목적격 보어에 해당하므로 밑줄 친 'considered'는 옳은 표현이다. 즉, 해당 문장의 경우 불완전타동사 'consider'의 현재완료 수동태인 「has/have been considered+목적격 보어」가 쓰인 문장이다.

해석

교통의 발전과 향상은 현대의 관광 산업이 대규모로 발전해서 전 세계의 수십억 명의 사람들의 삶의 일상적인 부분이 되도록 하는 데 가장 중요한 요인 중 하나였다. 기술적 진보가 지방과 지역, 그리고 전 세계의 교통망이 폭발적으로 확대되는 토대를 제공했고, 여행을 더 빠르고, 더 쉽고, 더 값싸게 만들었다. 이것은 관광객을 창출하고 받아들이는 새로운 지역을 만들어냈을 뿐만 아니라 숙박시설 같은 관광 산업 기반 시설에서의 여타의 많은 변화를 유발했다. 그 결과 교통 기반 시설과 서비스의 이용 가능성이 관광 산업의 기본적인 전제 조건으로 간주되어왔다.

어휘

explosive 폭발적인   expansion 확대, 팽창
prompt 유발하다, 촉진하다   a host of 많은, 다수의
precondition 전제 조건

07 정답 ③

정답해설

㉠ **출제 포인트: 주격 관계대명사절의 동사 수일치**
㉠은 주격 관계대명사 'who'가 이끄는 절의 동사에 해당하며 선행사는 단수 형태인 'a world-class runner'이므로 ㉠에 단수 형태의 동사 'was'를 사용하는 것이 옳다.

㉡ **출제 포인트: 관용표현(spend+시간+(in)+동명사)**
㉡은 관용표현 「spend+시간+(in)+목적어[동명사/명사(구)]」의 목적어에 해당하는 부분으로 동명사 'collecting'을 사용하는 것이 옳다.

㉢ **출제 포인트: so+형용사/부사+that+절 vs. too+형용사/부사+to+동사원형**
㉢ 이후에 있는 형용사 'complex'와 「that+절」을 통해 「so+형용사+that+절」이 사용된 것임을 알 수 있으므로 ㉢에는 'so'를 사용하는 것이 옳다. 단, too를 사용할 경우 이후에 오는 「that+절」을 「to+동사원형」으로 바꾸어야 한다.

해석

나는 맥박 측정기와 평균 속도 계측기에 끊임없이 자신을 연결하는 어떤 세계 일류 달리기 선수와 훈련하곤 했다. 그는 자신을 향상시키는 데 도움이 될 거라고 생각되는 자료를 수집하며 여러 시간을 보냈다. 사실 그의 운동 시간 중 상당 부분인 25%가 운동이 아닌 외적인 것에 바쳐졌다. 스포츠가 그에게는 아주 복잡해져서 그는 마음껏 즐기는 법을 잊었다.

어휘

world-class 세계 일류의
hook oneself up to 자신을 ~에 연결하다
devote A to B A를 B에 바치다   external 외적인 것, 외부 사항

08 정답 ③

정답해설

본문의 첫 문장 "The earth's soil stores a lot of carbon from the atmosphere, and managing it with the climate in mind may be an important part of reducing greenhouse gas emissions to curb global warming(지구의 토양은 대기로부터의 많은 탄소를 저장하고, 기후를 염두에 두고 그것을 관리하는 것은 지구 온난화를 억제하기 위해 온실가스 배출을 줄이는 것의 중요한 부분이 될지도 모른다)"을 통해, '토양이 탄소를 저장할 수 있고, 이것이 지구 온난화를 억제하는 데 도움을 줄 수 있다'고 언급하고 있다. 특히, "Much of that is locked up in land used for agriculture(그것 중 다수가 농업에 사용되는 토지에 가두어져 있다)."를 통해, 농경지에 흡수된 탄소의 양이 상당하다는 것을 알 수 있다. 즉, 농경지가 지구 온난화 또는 기후 변화에 대처하는 것에 도움이 될 수 있다는 글이므로, 제목으로 가장 적절한 것은 '③ Farmland Could Help To Combat Climate Change(농지가 기후 변화와의 싸움을 도울 수 있다)'이다.

오답해설
① 본문은 '탄소가 토양에 저장된다'고 설명하고 있으며, 탄소가 작물 및 식물에 미치는 영향에 대해서는 언급하지 않는다.
② 농업 생산성에 대해서는 본문에 언급되지 않는다.
④ 토양 오염에 관해서는 언급되지 않는다.

해석
Nature 지에 게재된 한 논문에 따르면, 지구의 토양은 대기로부터의 많은 탄소를 저장하고, 기후를 염두에 두고 그것을 관리하는 것은 지구 온난화를 억제하기 위해 온실가스 배출을 줄이는 것의 중요한 부분이 될지도 모른다. 현재 대기 중에 있는 탄소의 약 3배인 최대 2조 4천억 미터톤이 지구의 토양에 저장되어 있다. 그것 중 다수가 농업에 사용되는 토지에 가두어져 있다. 경지 토양은 거름, 뿌리, 낙엽, 그리고 다른 부패하는 식물의 조각들과 같은 유기적 물질에 대기 중 탄소를 저장한다. 그 연구는 만일 지구의 모든 농부들이 토양이 더 많은 탄소를 저장할 수 있도록 그들의 토지를 관리한다면, 매년 화석 연료를 태우는 것으로부터 배출되는 온실가스의 영향이 절반에서 80% 사이까지 감축될 수 있을 것이라 말한다.
① 작물과 식물에 미치는 탄소의 영향
② 지구 온난화와 농업 생산성
③ 농지가 기후 변화와의 싸움을 도울 수 있다
④ 농부들의 토양 오염과의 지속적인 전쟁

어휘
carbon 탄소
in mind 염두에 두는, 유념하는, 명심하는
curb 억제하다, 제한하다   metric ton 미터 톤(1,000kg)
agriculture 농업   manure 거름
decompose 부패하다   emit 배출하다
fossil fuel 화석 연료
combat (좋지 않은 일의 발생이나 악화를) 방지하다[(방지하기 위해) 싸우다]

오답률 TOP 2
09 정답 ②

정답해설
주어진 문장에서는 '신체변형장애(body dysmorphic disorder)'의 정의에 대해 설명하고 있다. 이후에는 '신체변형장애'를 겪는 사람이 할 수 있는 행동에 대해 설명하는 (A)가 이어지는 것이 자연스럽다. 이어서, (A)에서 설명한 행동을 'this behavior(이러한 행동)'로 가리키며 과도한 운동을 하는 행동에 대한 정당성을 부여하는 '사고방식(thinking)'에 대해 언급하고, 이러한 사고 방식이 야기하는 '행위(activity)'에 대해 설명하는 (C)가 이어지는 것이 알맞다. 마지막으로 (C)에서 설명한 유형의 사고와 행동을 'this type of thinking and activity'로 동시에 가리키며, 이러한 특징이 발생하고 지속되는 시기에 대해 설명해주는 (B)가 이어지는 것이 적절하다. 따라서 정답은 '② (A) – (C) – (B)'이다.

오답해설
① 주어진 문장에서 'thinking(사고)'이 드러나고, (A)에서 'activity(행위)'가 드러난 후, (B)가 이어질 수 있다고 생각할 수 있으나, 나머지 (C)에서 'this behavior(이러한 행동)'가 가리키는 내용이 (B)에 명백하게 드러나지 않고, 또한 (C)에서 '진지한 운동선수라고 생각하며 이러한 행위를 정당화한다'는 내용은 '부상의 위험에도 불구하고 심한 운동을 하는 행위'를 정당화한다고 보는 것이 더 적합하다. 따라서 전체 글의 흐름상 (A)와 (C)가 바로 이어지는 것이 가장 자연스러우므로, ①은 오답이다.
③, ④ 주어진 문장의 내용은 '정신적 장애'이므로, (B)의 'this type of thinking and activity' 중 'thinking(사고)'에만 해당한다고 할 수 있다. 따라서 'activity(행위)'가 가리키는 내용은 주어진 문장에 언급되지 않으므로, 주어진 문장에 (B)가 바로 이어지는 것은 어색하다.

해석
신체변형장애는 당신의 팔 또는 다리 근육이 너무 작거나 당신의 허리선이 충분히 가늘지 않은 것과 같은 당신의 신체적 특징(외모)에서 인지된 결함에 대해 당신이 과도하게 걱정하는 정신장애이다.
(A) 당신의 인지된 결함에 최선을 다하고자 노력하기 위해, 심지어 그것이 당신의 관절 또는 건강의 손상으로 이어지더라도, 당신은 사이클링, 마라톤, 보디빌딩 또는 같은 근육을 계속해서 다시 사용하는 다른 운동에 의지할지도 모른다.
(C) 종종, 당신은 자신이 당신의 운동에서 너무 열심히 또는 너무 오래 운동할 수 없는(아무리 열심히 또는 오래 운동을 해도 지나치지 않은) 진지한 운동선수라고 믿음으로써 이러한 행동을 정당화할지도 모르고 이것은 종종 "결함을 바로잡기" 위한 과도하고 중독적인, 심지어는 사회적으로 고립된 운동으로 이어질 수 있다.
(B) 일반적으로, 이러한 유형의 사고와 활동은 청소년기 또는 초기 성인기에 시작될 수 있으나, 당신이 "완벽한 몸"을 갈망함에 따라, 평생 동안 당신과 함께 머무를 수도 있다.

어휘
excessively 지나치게, 과도하게, 심히
perceive 인지하다, 인식하다, 지각하다
defect 결함   feature 특징, 특성
turn to 의지하다
hammer away at …을 열심히[꾸준히] 하다, …을 거듭해서[집요하게] 하다
come to (특히 좋지 않은 상황이) 되다
detriment 손상   adolescence 청소년기
athlete 운동선수   immoderate 과도한, 터무니없는
addictive 중독적인   isolated 고립된
in an attempt to 동사원형 ~하기 위하여, ~하려는 시도로

10 정답 ④

정답해설
본문은 '동화에서 묘사되는 마녀의 결말'에 대해 설명하고 있다. 본문의 내용을 통해, 일반적으로 마녀는 남자 또는 여자 주인공에 의해 처치되지만, 혈육을 죽여서는 안 된다는 동화의 규율 때문에 'Perrault의 *The Sleeping Beauty in the Woods*에 등장하는 마녀는 자살을 했다'라는 것을 알 수 있다. 주어진 문장의 'That is(즉)'로 보아, 주어진 문장은 앞서 언급된 내용과 유사한 내용을 '재서술'하고 있다는 것을 알 수 있다. 주어진 문장에서 '친부모를 죽여서는 안 된다'라는 내용이 언급되고 있으므로, 본문 중 '혈육을 죽여서는 안 된다(children are not permitted to destroy their own flesh and blood)'는 내용이 제시된 후, 주어진 문장이 이어지는 것이 자연스럽다. 따라서 정답은 ④이다.

오답해설

③ 주어진 문장 또한 'Perrault의 *The Sleeping Beauty in the Woods*에 등장하는 마녀가 자살한 이유에 대해 설명'해주고 있으나, 주어진 문장이 'That is'로 시작되고 있으므로, 주어진 문장 이전에 '이유'에 대해 설명하는 내용이 먼저 등장해야 한다는 것을 알 수 있다. 따라서 '이유가 있다'라고 말한 후, 주어진 문장이 바로 이어지는 것은 적절하지 않다.

나머지 위치는 문맥상 어색하므로 오답이다.

해석

대부분의 이야기에서 마녀는 남자 주인공 또는 여자 주인공의 손에 죽는 반면, Perrault의 *The Sleeping Beauty in the Woods*에 등장하는 마녀는 스스로 목숨을 끊는다. (①) 자신의 악한 계획 실행을 실패한 것에 좌절한 그 시어머니는 "두꺼비, 독사, 뱀들"이 가득 찬 통에 뛰어들어 자살한다. (②) 따라서 Perrault의 이야기는 마녀가 스스로 목숨을 끊는 몇 안 되는 동화 중 하나이다. 이것에는 이유가 있다. (③) 동화의 가장 중요한 규칙은 아이들이 자신들의 혈육을 파괴하는 것이 허락되지 않는다는 것을 명령한다. (④ **즉, 남자 주인공과 여자 주인공이 마녀, 사람을 잡아먹는 거인, 그리고 여자 마법사, 심지어 계모를 죽이는 것이 허락되지만, 그들의 친부모를 죽이는 것은 절대 허락되지 않는다.**) Perrault의 이야기에서 만일 왕자가 마녀를 파괴했다면, 그는 모친 살해를 저지르는 것이었을 것이다. 사람을 잡아먹는 엄마가 스스로 목숨을 끊게 함으로써, Perrault는 젊은 독자들에게 몹시 충격적일지도 모르는 결말을 피한다.

어휘

ogre (이야기 속에 나오는) 사람을 잡아먹는 거인
sorceress (이야기 속의) 여자 마법사
die by one's own hand 자살하다
execute 실행하다, 수행하다 vat 통(액체를 담는 데 쓰는 대형 통)
viper 독사 serpent 뱀
cardinal rule 기본적인[가장 중요한] 규칙
mandate 명령하다 flesh and blood 혈육, 육친, 자손
matricide 모친 살해 ogress ogre의 여성형

결국엔 성정혜 영어 하프모의고사
기적사 복습 모의고사 6회

01	②	02	②	03	①	04	③	05	②
06	④	07	②	08	②	09	①	10	④
11	②	12	②	13	②	14	②	15	③
16	①	17	②	18	③	19	①	20	①

01 정답 ②
Day 53-03

정답해설

밑줄 친 'polite'는 '예의 바른, 공손한, 정중한'을 뜻하는 형용사로 ② complaisant(공손한, 정중한)와 의미가 가장 가깝다.

해석

요르단에서는, 대체로 식사 제안을 수락하기 전에 그것을 세 번 거절하는 것이 **예의 바른** 태도이다.
① 아주 멋진, 훌륭한
② 공손한, 정중한
③ 무례한, 버릇없는
④ 감정에 좌우되지 않는

02 정답 ②
Day 59-02

정답해설

밑줄 친 'forthright'는 '기탄없이 말하는, 솔직한'을 뜻하는 형용사로 ② candid(솔직한)와 의미가 가장 가깝다.

해석

대통령에게 직접 보고하는 민정수석비서관은 전적으로 **기탄없이 말해**야 한다.
① 교활한, 음흉한
② 솔직한
③ 즉흥적으로 한
④ 솔직하지 못한

03 정답 ①
Day 56-02

정답해설

밑줄 친 'surreptitious'는 '비밀리에 하는'을 뜻하며 ① clandestine(비밀리에 하는, 은밀한)과 그 의미가 가장 가깝다.

해석

비밀리에 하는 녹음의 오디오는 참가자가 녹음되기를 원하지 않았다는 것을 분명하게 나타낸다.
① 비밀리에 하는, 은밀한
② 법에 명시된, 법으로 정한
③ 솔직한
④ 천사 같은, 맑은, 거룩한

04 정답 ③
Day 51-01

정답해설

페니실린에 알레르기 반응이 있는 사람에게 나타날 효과는 'adverse(부정적인,

반대의)' 효과, 즉 부작용을 가져올 수 있을 것이다. 따라서 정답은 ③ adverse (부정적인, 반대의)이다.

해석

페니실린은 그것에 알레르기가 있는 사람에게는 **부작용**이 있을 수 있다.
① 긍정적인
② 냉담한, 초연한
③ 부정적인, 반대의, 불리한
④ 암시하는, 넌지시 가리키는

05 정답 ② — Day 58-05

정답해설

② 출제 포인트: 수여동사의 수동태/능동태 vs. 수동태

해당 문장은 완전타동사 'say'의 과거시제 수동태를 사용하였으나 'was said' 이후에 직접목적어인 'that rest should be imperative for weeks'가 있으므로 틀린 문장이다. 따라서 'was said'는 수여동사 'tell'의 과거시제 수동태인 'was told'로 수정해야 한다.

해석

① 우리가 올해 말까지 Milton에 의해 쓰인 이 책을 펴낼 수 있을까요?
② 그 야구 스타는 휴식을 몇 주 동안 반드시 해야 한다는 이야기를 들었다.
③ 귀사의 시스템에 관심이 있지만, 그것은 당신의 경쟁사의 것보다 훨씬 더 비싸다.
④ 많은 시민운동에 의해 복지 제도에 대한 많은 간소화가 이뤄졌다.

06 정답 ④ — Day 59-07

정답해설

㉠ 출제 포인트: 주어와 동사의 수일치

주어가 단수 형태인 'The price'이므로 ㉠에는 단수 형태 동사인 'is'를 사용하는 것이 옳다. 'that the farmer ~ wholesaler'는 선행사 'The price'를 수식하는 목적격 관계대명사 절이다.

㉡ 출제 포인트: 자릿값(동사 vs. 준동사)

㉡은 'If'가 이끄는 종속절의 동사 자리에 해당하므로 'leads'가 ㉡에 들어가는 것이 옳다.

㉢ 출제 포인트: 접속사의 쓰임(and vs. but)

문맥상 '슈퍼마켓이 감자에 대해 도매상에게 지급해야 하는 가격은 상승할 것이고, 이것은 그들이 자기 가게의 감자에 매기는 가격에 반영될 것이다'가 자연스러우므로 ㉢에는 등위접속사 'and'가 들어가는 것이 옳다.

해석

도매상에서 농부가 받는 가격은 소매상이 소비자에게 부과하는 가격보다 그 날그날 훨씬 더 유동적이다. 예를 들어, 악천후가 감자의 흉작을 초래한다면, 슈퍼마켓이 감자에 대해 도매상에게 지급해야 하는 가격은 상승할 것이고 이것은 그들이 자기 가게의 감자에 매기는 가격에 반영될 것이다.

07 정답 ② — Day 53-07

정답해설

② 출제 포인트: 독립분사구문

'snow'는 비인칭대명사 'it'을 주어로 하는 동사이다. 해당 문장을 원래 문장으로 고치면 'As he snowed heavily yesterday, he stayed at home all day long.'이 되며 이때 'snow'의 주어가 'he'이므로 비문임을 알 수 있다. 따라서 원래 문장을 'As it snowed heavily yesterday, he stayed at home all day long.'으로 수정한 후에 분사구문으로 고치면 'It snowing heavily yesterday, he stayed at home all day long.'이 되므로 주어진 문장의 'Snowing'을 'It snowing'으로 수정해야한다.

08 정답 ② — Day 51-05

정답해설

② 출제 포인트: 주어와 동사의 수일치

밑줄 친 'are'의 주어는 복수 형태의 명사(구) 'the necessary calculations'이므로 'are'는 옳은 표현이다. 'calculations' 이후의 'that we ~ make'는 목적격 관계대명사절, 'about ~ harm'은 전명구, 'resulting from ~ take'는 분사구문이다. 또한 분사구문 내의 'that we take'는 'action'을 수식하는 목적격 관계대명사절로 사용되었다. 이처럼 주어와 동사 사이가 먼 경우 수일치에 유의해야 한다.

해석

위험이 결과가 정확하게 알려지지 않은 어떤 상황에서 항상 요소라는 의미로 위험은 인간의 삶에서 근본적인 요소이다. 게다가, 우리가 취하는 행동으로부터 야기되는 손해의 어떤 형태의 가능성에 대해 우리가 만들어내는 필수적인 계산은 일반적으로 우리의 결정 과정 내에서 기정사실이다. 위험 평가가 주요 기업의 주도권에 대한 결정을 포함하는지 단지 결정을 하는 것이 길을 따라 걷는 것인지 간에, 우리는 항상 포함된 잠재적 위험을 예상하고, 확인하고, 평가하고 있다. 그러한 관점에서, 우리는 우리가 하는 모든 것 안에서 지속적으로 위험을 관리하라는 말을 들을 수 있다.

09 정답 ① — Day 57-04

정답해설

A와 B는 방학 때 여행을 다녀오는 것에 관해 대화를 나누고 있다. B가 A에게 (A) '떠나고(hit the road)' 싶다고 이야기하고, A는 다른 친구들과 함께 떠나는 것을 제안한다. 그리고 "친구들과 여행 간다면 (B) '행복한(in seventh heaven)' 기분이 들 것 같다고 이야기한다. 그러자 B는 (C) "정말 그래(Tell me about it)"라고 이야기하며 동의한다. 따라서 정답은 ①이다.

해석

A: 나는 개학하기 전에 친구들과 여행을 다녀오고 싶어.
B: 좋은 생각이야! 나도 정말 (A) 떠나고 싶어.
A: 우리 다른 친구들과 같이 가는 것 어때?
B: 응, 나는 좋아. 나는 이번 방학 때 여행 갈 시간이 전혀 없었어.
A: 나도. 친구들과 여행하면 (B) 행복한 것처럼 느껴질 거야.
B: (C) 정말 그래! 나는 여행 동안 우리가 잊지 못할 기억들을 만들 수 있을 거라고 확신해.
A: 우리 바로 계획을 세워야겠다.
B: 물론이지, 시작하자!
① (A) 떠나다 (B) 행복한 (C) 정말 그래
② (A) 떠나다 (B) 빙산의 일각 (C) 그만해
③ (A) 패배하다 (B) 행복한 (C) 쥐구멍에도 볕들 날 온다
④ (A) 패배하다 (B) 빙산의 일각 (C) 쥐구멍에도 볕들 날 온다

10 정답 ④ — Day 52-04

정답해설

A와 B는 오늘 들은 경제학 강의에 관한 대화를 나눈다. A는 B에게 오늘 경제학 강의가 '자본주의(capitalism)'와 '보이지 않는 손(invisible hand)'에 관한 것이었다고 말하자, B는 자신이 완전히 ④ 'got the wrong end of the stick(잘못 이해했다)'이라고 이야기하며, 자신은 오늘의 강의가 완전히 다른 주제에 관한 것으로 이해했다고 한다.

해석

A: 너 오늘 강의 이해했어?
B: 오, 너 경제학 강의 말하는 거지?
A: 응. 그거 꽤 어렵지 않았어?
B: 그거 이해하기 매우 어려웠어. 교수님이 무엇을 설명하려 하신 것인지 이해할 수가 없었어.
A: 그것은 '자본주의'와 자본이 흐르도록 유지해주는 '보이지 않는 손'에 관한 것이었어.
B: '보이지 않는 손'? 나는 완전히 잘못 이해했네. 나는 오늘의 강의가 완전히 다른 주제에 관한 것으로 생각했어.
A: 네가 집에 가서 오늘 배운 것을 복습하면, 네가 다른 학급 친구들을 따라잡을 수 있을 거라 확신해.

① 요점으로 들어갔다
② 두각을 보였다
③ 죽었다
④ 잘못 이해했다

---

11 정답 ②   Day 60-09

정답해설

주어진 문장에서는 '신체변형장애(body dysmorphic disorder)'의 정의에 대해 설명하고 있다. 이후에는 '신체변형장애'를 겪는 사람이 할 수 있는 행동에 대해 설명하는 (A)가 이어지는 것이 자연스럽다. 이어서, (A)에서 설명한 행동을 'this behavior(이러한 행동)'로 가리키며 과도한 운동을 하는 행동에 대한 정당성을 부여하는 '사고방식(thinking)'에 대해 언급하고, 이러한 사고방식이 야기하는 '행위(activity)'에 대해 설명하는 (C)가 이어지는 것이 알맞다. 마지막으로 (C)에서 설명한 유형의 사고와 행동을 'this type of thinking and activity'로 동시에 가리키며, 이러한 특징이 발생하고 지속되는 시기에 대해 설명해주는 (B)가 이어지는 것이 적절하다. 따라서 정답은 '② (A) - (C) - (B)'이다.

해석

신체변형장애는 당신의 팔 또는 다리 근육이 너무 작거나 당신의 허리선이 충분히 가늘지 않은 것과 같은 당신의 신체적 특징(외모)에서 인지된 결함에 대해 당신이 과도하게 걱정하는 정신장애이다.
(A) 당신의 인지된 결함에 최선을 다하고자 노력하기 위해, 심지어 그것이 당신의 관절 또는 건강의 손상으로 이어지더라도, 당신은 사이클링, 마라톤, 보디빌딩 또는 같은 근육을 계속해서 다시 사용하는 다른 운동에 의지할지도 모른다.
(C) 종종, 당신은 자신이 당신의 운동에서 너무 열심히 또는 너무 오래 운동할 수 없는(아무리 열심히 또는 오래 운동해도 지나치지 않은) 진지한 운동선수라고 믿음으로써 이러한 행동을 정당화할지도 모르고 이것은 종종 "결함을 바로잡기" 위한 과도하고 중독적인, 심지어는 사회적으로 고립된 운동으로 이어질 수 있다.
(B) 일반적으로, 이러한 유형의 사고와 활동은 청소년기 또는 초기 성인기에 시작될 수 있으며, 당신이 "완벽한 몸"을 갈망함에 따라, 평생 동안 당신과 함께 머무를 수도 있다.

---

12 정답 ④   Day 54-10

정답해설

본문은 '과학 부정론자(Science denialists)'에 대한 글로써 과학과는 달리 그들의 주장은 증명된 근거에 뒷받침되지 않는다고 말한다. 주어진 문장에서, 가정법을 이용해 '사실과 반대되는 내용'을 설명하고 있으므로, 실제로 '부정론자들은 지구 온난화 또는 진화를 반박할 근거를 가지고 있지 않다'는 것을 알 수 있다. ④ 이후 문장에서 "But, knowing their arguments don't hold water(그러나, 그들의 주장이 타당하지 않다는 것을 알기 때문에)"라고 언급하며, 앞서 주어진 문장에서 유추할 수 있는 내용을 재차 언급해주고 있으므로, 해당 문장 이전에 주어진 문장이 등장하는 것이 문맥상 자연스럽다. 따라서 정답은 ④이다.

해석

진화에서부터 지구 온난화와 백신까지, 과학은 잘 실험된 과학적 지식을 단지 많은 경쟁하고 있는 이념들 중 하나로 일축하는 사람들인 부정론자들로부터의 공격을 받고 있다. 과학은 자연이 어떻게 작용하는지에 대한 결론이 증거에 기반 한 실험에 기초할 것을 요구한다. 때때로 진행은 더디다. 그러나 어렵고 종종 좌절감을 주는 과정을 통해, 우리는 세계에 대해 더 많이 배울 수 있다. (①) 과학 부정주의는 다르게 작용한다. 창조론자들은 화석, 분자, 그리고 진화의 해부학적 증거의 풍부함에 흔들리지 않는다. 지구 온난화 부정론자들은 산더미 같은 기후 자료에 감명받지 않는다. (②) 부정론자들은 압도적인 증거를 무시하고, 대신에 날조된 것에 집중한다. (③) 부정론자들에게는 여론조사와 라디오의 전화 토론 프로그램이 수천 개의 동료 심사를 받은 학술지 기사보다 더 중요하다. (④ **만일 부정론자들이 지구 온난화 또는 진화를 반박하는 증거를 가지고 있다면, 과학자들에 의한 분석을 요청하면서, 그들은 과학 학회와 학술지에 그것을 제출했을 것이다.**) 그러나 그들의 주장이 타당하지 않다는 것을 알기 때문에, 그들은 전문적인 철저한 검토의 대상이 아닌 대량 판매용의 도서, 신문, 라디오의 전화 토론 프로그램, 그리고 블로그와 같은 활동 무대에서 잘못된 정보를 퍼뜨린다.

---

13 정답 ②   Day 54-08

정답해설

본문 첫 문장에서 주제가 나타난다. "Today, the World Anti-Doping Agency (WADA) has a new hurdle to overcome — that of gene doping(오늘날, World Anti-Doping Agency (WADA)는 극복해야 할 새로운 장애물을 가지고 있다. 바로 유전자 도핑이다)."이라고 '새로운 유형의 도핑인 유전자 도핑'에 관해 소개하고 있다. '유전자 도핑은 적발하기 어렵다'는 것을 본문을 통해 알 수 있고, 이로 인해 '스포츠의 정정당당한 승부에 위협이 된다'는 점을 유추할 수 있다. 따라서 글의 제목으로 가장 적절한 것은 '② A New Threat to Fair Play in Sport(스포츠에서 공정한 경기의 대한 새로운 위협)'이다.

해석

오늘날, World Anti-Doping Agency (WADA)는 극복해야 할 새로운 장애물을 가지고 있다 – 바로 유전자 도핑이다. 이 관행은 운동 기록을 향상시키기 위해 세포, 유전자 또는 유전적 요소의 비 치료적인 사용으로 정의된다. 유전자 도핑은 질병을 치료하거나 예방하기 위해 유전자 물질의 인간 세포로의 이전을 포함하는 유전자 치료의 최첨단 연구를 이용한다. 유전자 도핑이 세포가 일반적으로 만드는 단백질과 호르몬의 양을 증가시키기 때문에, 유전적 기록 향상제를 검사하는 것은 매우 어려울 것이고, 이러한 형식의 도핑을 적발하는 방법을 개발하기 위한 새로운 경쟁이 진행 중이다. 더 나은 운동선수를 만들기 위해 유전자를 바꿀 가능성은 1990년대 후반 소위 "Schwarzenegger 쥐"의 발명과 함께 즉각적으로 실현되었다. 이 쥐들은 증가된 근육 성장과 힘을 가지도록 유전적으로 설계되었기 때문에 이 별명을 얻었다.

① 다양한 스포츠에서의 도핑
② 스포츠에서 공정한 경기에 대한 새로운 위협
③ 운동선수들이 도핑 검사를 받아야 하는 이유
④ 유전자 도핑: 장점과 단점

14 정답 ②
Day 53-09

정답해설

본문은 '고대 올림픽 선수들이 알몸으로 경기 및 훈련을 했다'고 설명하며 그로 인해 '위생과 몸 관리에 철저했다'고 언급하고 있다. ①에서는 남성 운동선수가 몸 관리를 배우기 시작한다는 내용을 언급하고 ③에서 관리 과정(whole process)에 대해 설명하고 있는데, ②에서는 '여성이 경기를 관람하는 것'에 대해 언급하고 있으므로, 문맥상 적절하지 않다. 따라서 정답은 ②이다.

해석

고대 올림픽의 참가자들은 항상 알몸이었다. 그들의 신체는 훈련을 통해 완벽해지도록 되어있었고, 노출은 신체와 영혼의 공생뿐만 아니라 영원한 미를 상징했다. 또한, 운동선수들은 흠잡을 데 없는 위생과 몸 관리를 유지했다. 이것은 거의 알려지지 않은 사실이다. ① 그들은 알몸이었기 때문에, 그들이 학습하고 지도를 받는 기관인 고등학교에 입학할 때부터 그들은 그들의 위생을 관리하는 것을 배우기 시작하곤 했다. ② <u>오직 남자들만이 게임에서 경쟁할 수 있었고, 참가자들이 알몸이었기 때문에 여자들은 게임을 관람하는 것이 금지되었다.</u> ③ 전체 과정은 올리브 오일과 운동선수들이 피부에 문질렀던 고운 모래로 된 가루 층을 포함했다. ④ 그것은 태양으로부터 뿐만 아니라, 그들이 조별 훈련을 받을 때 코치로부터의 이따금씩의 타격에서도 그들을 보호했다. 훈련이 끝났을 때, 그 층은 물과 스펀지를 이용해 벗겨져야 했다. 그리고 이것은 또한 경기 이전에도 각각 행해졌다.

15 정답 ③
Day 59-08

정답해설

본문은 'The U.S. Natural Resources Conservation Service (NRCS)에 의한 토양의 분류'에 대한 설명이다. 본문 중반 "In general, Class I soils are more arable and suitable for cropland; Class II soils have some limitations that reduce the choice of plants that can be grown, or require moderate conservation practices to reduce the risk of damage when used; Class III soils have severe limitations that reduce the choice of plants, require special conservation practices, or both, but may be productive with careful management(일반적으로 Class I 토양은 더 경작에 적합하고 경지로 알맞다; Class II 토양은 경작될 수 있는 식물의 선택지를 감소시키는 약간의 한계가 있거나, 사용 시 손상의 위험을 줄이기 위한 적당한 보전 처리를 요한다; Class III 토양은 식물의 선택을 감소시키는 심각한 한계가 있거나, 특별한 보전 처리를 요하거나, 또는 둘 다이지만, 세심한 관리를 한다면 생산성이 있을 수도 있다)."에 따르면, Class II 토양은 'moderate conservation practices(적당한 보전 처리)'를 필요로 하고, Class III 토양은 'special conservation practices(특별한 보전 처리)'를 필요로 한다고 언급하고 있으므로, Class III 토양이 Class II 토양보다 더 많은 관리와 처리가 필요하다는 것을 알 수 있다. 따라서 글의 내용과 일치하지 않는 것은 '③ Class II soils require more care and treatment than Class III soils(Class II 토양은 Class III 토양보다 더 많은 관리와 처리를 필요로 한다).'이다.

해석

U.S. Natural Resources Conservation Service (NRCS)는 토양을 대부분의 종류의 농사에 대한 그들의 일반적인 적합성을 나타내는 능력 집단으로 분류했다. 그 분류 집단은 토양의 구성과 한계, 그것들이 사용되었을 시 손상의 위험, 그리고 그것들이 처리에 대응하는 방식에 기반한 것이다. NRCS의 시스템하에, Class I에서 Class VIII의 범위에 이르는 8개의 능력 집단이 있다. 일반적으로 Class I 토양은 더 경작에 적합하고 경지로 알맞다; Class II 토양은 경작될 수 있는 식물의 선택지를 감소시키는 약간의 한계가 있거나, 사용 시 손상의 위험을 줄이기 위한 적당한 보전 처리를 요한다; Class III 토양은 식물의 선택을 감소시키는 심각한 한계가 있거나, 특별한 보전 처리를 요하거나, 또는 둘 다이지만, 세심한 관리를 한다면 생산성이 있을 수도 있다. 그 외의 집단의 토양은 경지로서는 계속해서 더 커지는 자연적인 한계를 지니고 있으나, 목초지, 방목지, 삼림 지대, 야생 생물, 휴양, 그리고 미적인 목적을 위해서는 사용될 수 있을지도 모른다.

① NRCS는 토양을 분류할 때 다수의 요소를 고려했다.
② Class I 토지에서 자랄 수 있는 일부 작물은 Class III 토지에서 살아남을 수 없을지도 모른다.
③ Class II 토양은 Class III 토양보다 더 많은 관리와 처리를 필요로 한다.
④ 경지로는 권고되지 않는 다섯 가지의 토양 집단이 있다.

16 정답 ①
Day 52-09

정답해설

본문은 '고대 올림픽 경기와 여성'에 대한 내용이다. 본문 초반 "Only men, boys and unmarried girls were allowed to watch the Olympic Games. Married women were barred(오직 남자, 소년, 그리고 미혼의 소녀들만이 고대 올림픽 경기를 관람할 수 있었다. 기혼 여성들은 금지되었다)."를 통해, '기혼 여성은 올림픽을 볼 수 없었으나, 미혼 소녀들은 볼 수 있었음'을 알 수 있다. 따라서 글의 내용과 일치하는 것은 '① Some females were able to spectate at the Olympic Games(몇몇 여인들은 올림픽 게임을 구경할 수 있었다).'이다.

해석

오직 남자, 소년, 그리고 미혼의 소녀들만이 고대 올림픽 경기를 관람할 수 있었다. 기혼 여성들은 금지되었다. 만일 그들이 몰래 숨어들어온 것이 발각된다면, 그들은 형벌로 산 옆으로 내던져질 수 있었다. 그러나 기혼 여성들은 여전히 올림픽의 전차 경주용 말을 소유할 수는 있었다. 비록 기혼 여성이 올림픽 경기에 허용되지는 않았지만, 한 이야기는 아들이 경기하는 것을 간절히 보고 싶어서 여성 금지 규칙을 깨고 남자로 변장해 들어간 한 엄마에 대해 말해준다. 한편, 미혼 여성들은 Olympia에서 자신들만의 축제를 열었다. 이것은 Heraia라고 불렸고, Zeus의 아내인 Hera를 기념하여 4년마다 열렸다. Heraia 경기의 우승자들은 남자들과 마찬가지로 신성한 올리브 가지 왕관을 수여받았다.

① 몇몇 여인들은 올림픽 게임을 구경할 수 있었다.
② 말을 보유한 여성들은 전차 경주에서 경쟁할 수 있었다.
③ 한 여성이 올림픽 게임에서 경기하기 위해 남자로 변장했다.
④ 모든 여성이 Heraia 경기에 참가할 수 있었다.

17 정답 ②
Day 55-10

정답해설

본문은 '과학 연구자들이 겪는 어려움'에 대해 설명하는 글로써, 첫 번째 문장 "Scientific researchers face perpetual struggle to secure and sustain funding(과학 연구원들은 자금을 확보하고 유지하기 위한 끊임없는 투쟁에 직면한다)."을 통해 글의 요지를 엿볼 수 있다. 즉, 과학 연구를 위한 자금이 부족하고, 그로 인해 연구 주제의 폭이 좁아지며, 연구의 질이 떨어진다고 설명하고 있다. 따라서 전체 글의 주제로 가장 적절한 것은 '② The financial short in the field of science(과학계의 재정 부족)'이다.

해석

과학 연구원들은 자금을 확보하고 유지하기 위한 끊임없는 투쟁에 직면한다. 과학계 종사 인구는 증가하고 있는 반면, 대부분의 국가에서의 자금은 과거 10년 동안 감소해오고 있다. 그 상황은 특히 선임 연구원들과 자금을 놓고 경쟁하는 것을 어려워하는 신참 연구원들에게 존재한다. 이 극단적인 경쟁은 또한 과학이 수행되는 방식에도 영향을 미치고 있다. Vox 설문 조사의 응답자들은 대부분의 보조금이 오직 몇 년 동안만 할당되기 때문에, 연구원들이 단기 프로젝트를 선택하는 경향이 있고, 이는 때때로 복잡한 연구 과제를 연구하기에는 불충분할 수 있다는 점을 지적했다. 이것은 연구원들이 자금 제공원과 그들의 기관을 행복하게 유지할 것에 기반하여 선택을 한다는 것을 의미한다. 그러나 이러한 선택의 결과는 수준 이하의 질과 낮은 연구 영향력을 가진 출판 논문들 수의 증가이다.
① 연구를 위한 자금을 획득하는 방법
② 과학계의 재정 부족
③ 신규 그리고 선임 과학자들 사이의 높은 경쟁
④ 과학 연구와 출판의 중요성

18 정답 ③　　　　　　　　　　　　　　　　　Day 59-09

정답해설
본문은 'Department of Health and Human Services에서 건강한 성인에게 권고하는 일주일 운동량'에 관한 내용이다. 본문 중반의 "Even small amounts of physical activity are helpful, and accumulated activity throughout the day adds up to providing similar health benefits(적은 양의 신체 활동이라도 도움이 되며, 하루 동안 축적된 활동은 결국 유사한 건강상 이점을 제공하게 된다)."를 통해, '운동은 적은 양도 도움이 되고, 하루에 축적된 운동의 양이 유사한 효과를 줄 수 있다'고 설명하고 있으므로, '연속으로 1시간 운동을 하는 것과, 10분씩 짧은 운동을 6번에 걸쳐 총 1시간을 하는 것이 모두 도움이 된다'는 것을 알 수 있다. 따라서 '③ Doing a ten-minute workout six times a day is less beneficial than exercising nonstop for an hour(하루에 10분짜리 운동을 6번 하는 것은 한 시간 동안 쉬지 않고 운동하는 것보다 덜 이롭다).'는 글의 내용과 일치하지 않는다.

해석
운동과 신체 활동은 좋은 기분을 느끼고, 당신의 건강을 증진시키고, 즐거움을 얻는 훌륭한 방법들이다. 대부분의 건강한 성인들에게 Department of Health and Human Services는 최소 주당 140분의 적당한 유산소 운동 또는 주당 70분의 격렬한 유산소 운동이나, 적당한 운동과 격렬한 운동의 결합을 권고한다. 그 지침은 당신이 이 운동을 일주일에 걸쳐 분산시킬 것을 제안한다. 예시로는 달리기, 걷기, 또는 수영을 포함한다. 적은 양의 신체 활동이라도 도움이 되며, 하루 동안 축적된 활동은 결국 유사한 건강상 이점을 제공하게 된다. 그것은 또한 모든 주요 근육 그룹을 위해 근력운동을 주당 최소 2번 권고한다. 예시로는 덤벨 들기, 종합 헬스 기구 이용하기, 또는 체중 운동을 하는 것을 포함한다. 당신의 활동을 일주일에 걸쳐 분산시켜라. 만일 당신이 체중을 줄이거나, 특정한 신체 단련 목표를 충족시키거나, 훨씬 더 많은 이득을 얻길 원한다면, 당신은 적당한 유산소 운동을 주당 280분 또는 그 이상으로 증가시킬 필요가 있을 것이다.
① 일주일에 70분의 격렬한 수영을 하는 것은 일주일에 140분의 적당한 수영을 하는 것에 상당한다.
② 매일의 20분간의 적당한 걷기는 건강한 성인에게 유익할 수 있다.
③ 하루에 10분짜리 운동을 6번 하는 것은 한 시간 동안 쉬지 않고 운동하는 것보다 덜 이롭다.
④ 체중 운동은 적어도 일주일에 두 번 권고된다.

19 정답 ①　　　　　　　　　　　　　　　　　Day 57-08

정답해설
본문은 '태국의 농부들이 보존 구역에 침입하는 이유와 이 문제를 해결하기 위해 진행된 프로젝트'에 관해 설명하고 있다. 본문 중반 "To address this issue, a recent project compared the physical and chemical properties of soils from farmlands and soils from the conserved area(이 문제를 다루기 위해, 최근 한 프로젝트가 농지의 토양과 보존 구역 토양의 물리적 그리고 화학적 특징을 비교했다)."를 통해, 두 지역의 토양의 특징을 비교함으로써 문제 해결을 꾀했다는 것을 알 수 있으며, 이후 문장에서 '두 지역 토양의 영양 성분이 거의 차이가 나지 않았다'고 밝히고 이러한 사실을 농부들에게 알렸다고 설명하고 있으므로, 농부들이 자신들의 농지 대신 보존 구역의 토양을 이용하려고 했던 이유는 자신들의 농지보다 보존 구역의 영양 성분이 더 풍부하다, 즉 더 '비옥하다'고 생각했기 때문이라는 것을 유추할 수 있다. 따라서 빈칸에 가장 적절한 표현은 '① more fertile(더 비옥한)'이다.

해석
태국 농부들은 보통 낮은 정규 교육을 받고 토질 개선과 적절한 비료 사용에 대한 지식의 부족함을 가지고 있다. 몇 년간 농사를 지은 후, 그들의 제한된 농지 공간에서의 토양의 악화와 그들이 자신들의 농장의 토양보다 보존 구역의 토양이 <u>더욱 비옥하다</u>고 믿기 때문에, 그들은 보존된 삼림 구역으로 침입하려고 시도한다. 결과적으로, 그들 중 대부분은 체포되고, 이는 개인 및 가족의 문제를 일으킨다. 이 문제를 다루기 위해, 최근 한 프로젝트가 농지의 토양과 보존 구역 토양의 물리적 그리고 화학적 특징을 비교했다. 결과는 보존 구역으로부터의 토양이 좀 더 많은 유기물과 질소함유량을 보유하고 있다는 점을 제외하고, 양쪽으로부터의 토양의 영양분이 분석의 거의 모든 요인에서 크게 차이가 나지 않는다는 것을 보여주었다. 이 분석 자료는 농부들에게 통보되었고 더 높은 생산성을 확보하기 위해 적절한 유기물을 사용하여 그들의 농지를 개선할 것을 그들에게 제안했다.
① 더 비옥한
② 더 척박한
③ 더 황량한
④ 경작에 덜 적합한

20 정답 ①　　　　　　　　　　　　　　　　　Day 51-10

정답해설
오늘날 과학의 문제점은 인간이 문제들을 선택하는 것이 아니라, 문제들이 인간에게 강요를 하는 현상이라는 내용이다. 즉, 인간이 주체가 아니라 떠밀리고 강요받는 '부록, 부속물 (appendix)'과도 같은 처지가 됨을 알 수 있다. 따라서 빈칸에는 '① makes man its appendix(인간을 그것의 부속물로 만들어버리다)'가 가장 적절하다.

해석
우리 시대에서, 인간에 대한 고유의 삶과 규칙을 가진 것은 단지 시장의 법칙일 뿐만 아니라, 과학과 기술의 발전이기도 하다. 많은 이유로, 오늘날 과학의 문제점들과 구조는 과학자가 그의 문제들을 선택하지 않는다는 것과 같다; 문제들이 과학자에게 그들 자신을 강요한다. 그는 하나의 문제를 풀고, 그 결과는 그가 더 안심하거나 확신하다는 것이 아니라, 다른 열 가지의 새로운 문제들이 해결된 문제 하나가 있던 자리에 모습을 드러낸다. 그것들은 그에게 해결하라고 강요한다; 그는 계속해서 빨라지는 속도로 진행해야만 한다. 공업 기술에서도 동일하다. 과학의 속도는 기술의 속도를 강요한다. 이론 물리학은 원자 에너지를 우리에게 강요한다; 핵폭탄의 성공적인 생산은 우리에게 수소 폭탄의 제조를 강요한다. 우리는 우리의 문제를 선택하지 않는다, 우리는 우리의 생산물을 선택하지 않는다; 우리는 떠밀리고, 우리는 강요당하는 것이다 ― 무엇에 의해서? 그것을 초월하는 목적과 목표가 없는, 그리고 <u>인간을 그것의 부속물로 만들어버리는</u> 시스템에 의해서이다.
① 인간을 그것의 부속물로 만들어버리다
② 보안에 대한 잘못된 인식을 창출하다
③ 인간을 창의적인 도전들로 고무시키다
④ 시장을 통제하도록 과학자들에게 권한을 부여하다

기적사 DAY 61

결국엔 성정혜 영어 하프모의고사

| 01 | ② | 02 | ③ | 03 | ④ | 04 | ③ | 05 | ② |
| 06 | ① | 07 | ④ | 08 | ② | 09 | ② | 10 | ③ |

01 정답 ②
15 지방직

정답해설
'rule out'은 '배제하다'를 뜻하는 동사구로 ② exclude(배제하다)와 유의어 관계이다.

해석
진단을 내리기 전에 당신의 주치의가 **배제할** 일부 질병들이 존재한다.
① 추적하다
② 배제하다
③ 지시하다
④ 조사하다

어휘
rule out 배제하다   diagnosis 진단
trace 추적하다   exclude 배제하다
instruct 지시하다   examine 조사하다

02 정답 ③
15 지방직

정답해설
'made of money'는 '아주 부자인'을 뜻하는 형용사(구)로 ③ wealthy(부유한, 재산이 많은)와 유의어 관계이다.

해석
나는 **아주 부자**가 아니야, 너도 알다시피!
① 가난한, 빈곤한
② 검소한, 절약하는
③ 부유한, 재산이 많은
④ 인색한, 적은

어휘
made of money 아주 부자인
needy 가난한, 빈곤한
thrifty 검소한, 절약하는
wealthy 부유한, 재산이 많은
stingy 인색한, 적은

03 정답 ④
15 지방직

정답해설
'pushy'는 '지나치게 밀어붙이는, 강요하는'을 뜻하는 형용사로 ④ aggressive (대단히 적극적인, 공격적인)와 의미상 가장 가깝다.

해석
숙련된 판매원은 적극적인 것과 **강요하는** 것 사이에는 차이가 있다고 주장한다.
① 오싹한, 흥분된
② 용감한
③ 소심한
④ 공격적인, 대단히 적극적인, 시비조의

어휘
claim 주장하다   assertive 적극적인
pushy 지나치게 밀어붙이는, 강요하는   thrilled 오싹한, 흥분된
brave 용감한   timid 소심한
aggressive 공격적인, 대단히 적극적인, 시비조의

04 정답 ③
17 지방직

정답해설
A가 Ted의 생일 선물로 무엇을 살지 B에게 물어보자, B는 빈칸 다음에서 Ted가 무엇이 필요한지 모르겠다고 A에게 답한다. 따라서 생일 선물을 생각해내기 위해 '머리를 쥐어짠다'라고 말하는 것이 가장 적절하므로 빈칸에 들어갈 말로 가장 적절한 것은 '③ racking my brain(머리를 쥐어짜내고 있는)'이다.

오답해설
①, ②, ④ 나머지 선지는 Ted의 생일 선물을 고민하고 있는 B의 대답으로 적절하지 않다.

해석
A: 이번 Ted의 생일을 위해 어떤 선물을 살 거니? 나는 그에게 두 개의 야구 모자를 선물할 거야.
B: 나는 딱 적당한 선물을 생각해내려고 머리를 쥐어짜고 있어. 그가 무엇이 필요한지 전혀 모르겠어.
A: 그에게 앨범을 선물하는 건 어때? 그는 사진을 많이 가지고 있어.
B: 그거 정말 완벽한 생각이다! 내가 왜 그 생각을 못 했을까? 제안해줘서 고마워!
① 그에게 연락을 받고 있는
② 하루 종일 자고 있는
③ 머리를 쥐어짜고 있는
④ 사진 앨범을 수집하고 있는

어휘
have[get] an inkling of …을 어렴풋이 알다
contact 연락하다; 연락
rack one's brain 지혜를 짜내다, 골똘히 생각하다

오답률 TOP 2
05 정답 ②
18 지방직

정답해설
② 출제 포인트: to부정사의 부사적 용법/주어진 해석과 일치 확인
to부정사의 부사적 용법이 쓰인 문장으로 영어 지문 자체는 문법적으로 옳은 문장이나 영어 지문 '~are using therapy to guide gene tests(유전자 검사를 안내하기 위해 치료법을 이용하고 있다)'와 주어진 해석 '치료법을 안내하기 위해 유전자 검사를 이용하고 있다'가 일치하지 않으므로 틀린 문장이다. 따라서 'therapy'와 'gene tests'의 위치를 서로 바꾸어야 한다. 즉, 'Many clinics are using gene tests to guide therapy.'가 주어진 해석과 일치하는 옳은 문장이다.

오답해설
① 출제 포인트: what vs. that/완전자동사/주어와 동사의 수일치
'What' 이후에 오는 절의 형태가 불완전하며 앞에 선행사가 없으므로 관계대명사 'What'은 옳은 표현이다. 이때 관계대명사절의 동사 'matters'는 완전자동사임에 주의해야 한다. 또한 주절의 동사는 주어와 수일치 해야

하며 해당 문장의 경우 주어가 선행사를 포함하는 관계대명사 'What'이 이끄는 절이므로 주절의 동사에 단수 형태 'is'를 옳게 사용하였다. 또한 'have'는 진행형 불가동사로 'be+ing' 형태로는 사용할 수 없으나, 해당 문장에서는 진행이 아닌 동명사 'having'으로서 be동사의 보어로 사용되어 '갖는 것[두는 것]'의 의미로 사용되었다.

③ 출제 포인트: 비교급 강조부사/불가산명사
'much'는 비교급 강조부사로 해당 문장에서 비교급 형용사 'less'를 수식하고 있다. 또한 'money'는 불가산명사이므로 양을 나타내는 형용사 'little'의 비교급인 'less'의 수식을 받는다.

④ 출제 포인트: 완전타동사 vs. 완전자동사/능동태 vs. 수동태
'reflect'는 '반영하다'를 뜻하는 경우 완전타동사로 사용되며 해당 문장의 경우 'reflects' 이후에 목적어가 오므로 능동태로 사용하는 것이 옳다.

오답률 TOP 3

06 정답 ①
18 지방직

정답해설

① 출제 포인트: 능동태 vs. 수동태/find vs. found
"It also founded that commercial operators—not the middle-class New Yorkers in the ads—were making millions renting spaces exclusively to Airbnb guests."에서 'that'절 이하가 발견된 것이므로 '설립하다'라는 동사 'found'가 아니라 '찾다, 발견하다'라는 뜻의 동사 'find'를 사용해야 문맥상 적절하고 'that'절 이하의 사실이 '발견된' 것이므로 수동태로 동사 형태를 바꾸는 것이 어법상 알맞은 표현이다. 따라서 "It was also found that commercial operators—not the middle-class New Yorkers in the ads—were making millions renting spaces exclusively to Airbnb guests."가 올바른 문장이다. 이때 'It'은 가주어, 'that'절 이하는 진주어이다.

또는 주어 'It'을 'a recent report'로 보아 '보고서가 해당 내용을 발견했다'라고 해석한다면 "It also found that commercial operators—not the middle-class New Yorkers in the ads—were making millions renting spaces exclusively to Airbnb guests."도 역시 가능하다. 'find'와 'found'를 구별하는 출제 포인트에서는 타동사 간의 구별인 만큼 해석에 주의해야 한다.

cf. find-found-found: ~을 발견하다
　　found-founded-founded: ~을 설립하다

오답해설

② 출제 포인트: 현재분사 vs. 과거분사
밑줄 친 'elected'는 'elect'의 과거분사로 이후에 있는 명사 'officials'를 수식하며 해석상 '선출된 공무원들'이 자연스러우므로 옳은 표현이다.

③ 출제 포인트: 주어와 동사의 수일치
주어가 'most of 목적어'인 경우 동사의 수일치 기준은 목적어가 된다. 해당 문장은 'most of 목적어'가 주어이며 동사에 복수 형태인 'were'를 사용하였으므로 목적어에 해당하는 복수 형태의 명사 'hosts'는 옳은 표현이다.

④ 출제 포인트: 등위접속사의 병렬구조
밑줄 친 'stay'는 앞에 있는 등위접속사 'and'를 통해 'to pay'와 병렬구조를 이루고 있다. 'stay'의 경우 'to stay'에서 'to'가 생략된 형태이다.

해석

최근 보고서에 따르면, 뉴욕 안의 Airbnb 목록들 중 3/4이 불법이었다. 광고 안의 중산층 뉴욕 시민들이 아닌 상업적인 사업자들이 독점적으로 Airbnb 투숙객들에게 공간을 대여해주면서 많은 돈을 벌고 있었던 것이 또한 발견되었다. 지난주에 선출된 공무원들에게 보내진 편지에서, Airbnb는 그것의 지역 호스트들 중 대부분은 - 87퍼센트- "그들의 명세서를 지불하고 그들의 집에서 머물기 위해" 그들의 집들을 드물게 대여했던 거주자들이었다고 말했다.

어휘

recent 최근에
illegal 불법의
operator 사업자, 운영자
exclusively 독점적으로
official 공무원, 관리
bill 명세서
listing 목록
commercial 상업적인
rent 임대하다
elected 선출된
infrequently 드물게

07 정답 ④
18 지방직

정답해설

④ 출제 포인트: 등위접속사의 병렬구조/that vs. what/주격 관계대명사절의 동사 수일치
등위접속사 'and'를 통해 to부정사 'to maximize'와 'to reduce'가 병렬구조를 이루고 있으며 주격 관계대명사 'that'의 선행사가 복수 형태인 'bugs'이므로 관계대명사절의 동사에 복수 형태인 'impede'를 옳게 사용하였다.

오답해설

① 출제 포인트: 등위접속사의 병렬구조/주격 관계대명사+be동사 생략
문맥상 '학생들이 이해하는 것을 더 강화하는 것과 더 효과적인 교육 과정을 디자인하는 것에 관심이 있는'이 자연스러우므로 'design'이 등위접속사 'and'를 통해 병렬구조를 이루고 있는 대상이 동명사 'enhancing'임을 알 수 있다. 따라서 'design'을 동명사 'designing'으로 수정해야 한다. 또한 해당 문장에서 'new or veteran'과 'interested'는 모두 'educators'를 수식하며 앞에 「주격 관계대명사+be동사」인 'who are'가 생략되어 있다고 볼 수 있다.

② 출제 포인트: 시제 일치/비교급 강조부사/목적격 관계대명사 생략
시간의 부사구 'at the time'을 통해 접속사 'than' 이후에 온 대동사 'do'의 시제가 과거임을 유추할 수 있다. 따라서 'do'를 과거시제 대동사 'did'로 수정해야 한다. 또한 해당 문장에서 'far'는 비교급 강조부사로 비교급에 해당하는 'less'를 수식하고 있으며 'the various species' 이후에 'collected'의 목적어에 해당하는 목적격 관계대명사가 생략되어 있다.

③ 출제 포인트: 전치사의 쓰임/to부정사의 명사적 용법/관계대명사 what
'despite'는 전치사로 '~에도 불구하고'를 뜻하며 'in spite of'로 바꾸어 사용할 수 있으나 'despite of'는 없는 표현이다. 따라서 해당 문장의 'despite of'를 'despite' 또는 'in spite of'로 수정해야 한다. 또한 해당 문장에서 'to gain'은 to부정사의 명사적 용법으로 불완전자동사 'is'의 주격 보어로 사용되었으며 'what'은 이후에 절이 'mean'의 목적어가 없는 불완전한 형태이며, 선행사가 없으므로 선행사를 포함하는 관계대명사 'what'은 옳게 사용되었다.

해석

① 이 책은 학생들이 이해하는 것을 더 강화하는 것과 더 효과적인 교육 과정을 디자인하는 것에 관심이 있는 신입이거나 베테랑인 교육자들을 위해 의도된 것이다.

② Darwin은 그를 위해 이러한 유기체들을 분류했던 그 시대 영국의 전문가들이 한 것보다 Beagle 여행에서 그가 수집했던 다양한 종들에 대해 훨씬 더 조금 알고 있었다.

③ 글을 읽는 도전은 누군가의 가정들과 편견들의 장벽에도 불구하고, 그 글이 의미하는 것에 대해 깊은 이해를 얻는 것이다.

④ 소프트웨어 개발자는 사용자들의 편의를 최대화하고 결과를 방해하는 버그를 줄이기 위해 작업한다.

08 정답 ①
18 서울시

정답해설

첫 번째 빈칸 이전 문장에서 예술품이 너무 빨리 인정을 받는다고 했고, 빈칸 다음에는 모든 작품들이 빨리 팔리는 것은 아니라고 언급되어 있다. 첫 번째 빈칸 앞과 뒤 문장이 인과관계는 아니므로 첫 번째 빈칸은 'Of course(물론)'가 알맞다. 'Of course(물론)'는 접속사로 볼 수 없으나, 문맥을 연결해주는 역할을 분명히 할 수 있다.

두 번째 빈칸 이전에 예술품 구입의 구체적인 기능인 'adds to their social prestige(사회적 위신의 향상)'가 언급되어 있고, 빈칸 이후에 또 다른 기능인 'investment(투자)'가 언급되기 때문에 첨언의 의미를 가진 'Furthermore(게다가)'가 적절하다.

따라서 정답은 '① Of course – Furthermore'이다.

오답해설

첫 번째 빈칸의 앞과 뒤 문장이 인과관계가 아니기 때문에 인과 관계를 나타내는 'Therefore(그러므로)'는 적절하지 않다. 또한 두 번째 빈칸은 빈칸 앞에서 설명한 '예술품 구입의 구체적 기능'에 뒤이어 빈칸 이후에는 부가적으로 '예술품 구입의 또 다른 기능'을 언급하고 있으므로 역접을 나타내는 'On the other hand(반면에)'나 예시를 나타내는 'For instance(예를 들면)', 'For example(예를 들면)'은 적절하지 않다.

해석

현대 예술은 오늘날의 중산층 사회의 사실상 필수적인 부분이 되었다. 스튜디오에서 금방 나온 예술작품들조차 열광을 마주하게 된다. 그것들은 꽤 빨리 인정을 받는다 – 더 퉁명스러운 문화 비평가들의 취향에는 너무 빠르다. 물론, 모든 예술작품들이 즉시 구입되는 것은 아니지만, 분명히 아주 새로운 예술작품들을 사는 것을 즐기는 사람들이 늘어나고 있다. 빠르고 비싼 자동차들 대신, 그들은 젊은 예술가들의 그림, 조각, 그리고 사진 작품들을 구매한다. 그들은 또한 현대 예술이 그들의 사회적 위신을 높여준다고 생각한다. 게다가, 예술은 자동차와 같은 정도로 마모되지 않기 때문에, 훨씬 더 좋은 투자이다.

① 물론 – 게다가
② 그러므로 – 반면에
③ 그러므로 – 예를 들면
④ 물론 – 예를 들면

어휘

contemporary 동시대의, 현대의   integral 필수적인
enthusiasm 열광   recognition 인정
surly 무례한
undoubtedly 의심할 여지가 없는, 확실한
brand new 아주 새로운   photographic 사진의
prestige 위신
wear and tear (일상적인 사용에 의한) 마모

오답률 TOP 1

09 정답 ②
18 서울시

정답해설

주제문인 첫 문장에서 자신의 국가에서 민주주의를 신봉하는 것과 다른 나라에 동일한 민주주의를 강요하는 것은 다른 문제라고 언급하고 있다. 즉, '같은 민주주의 시스템도 각기 다른 사회 환경에서는 다른 결과가 있을 수 있음'을 의미하는 것으로 볼 수 있다. 따라서 '② One man's food is another's poison(누군가의 음식이 다른 누군가에게는 독일 수 있다).'가 글의 내용과 가장 부합하는 속담이다.

오답해설

나머지 선지는 글의 내용과 부합하는 속담으로 볼 수 없다.

해석

우리의 민주주의 시스템이 가장 좋은 것이라고 믿는 것과 그것을 다른 나라에 강요하는 것은 별개의 일이다. 이것은 독립국가에 대한 내정 불간섭이라는 UN의 정책의 노골적인 위반이다. 서양의 시민들이 그들의 정치 제도를 위해 싸웠듯, 우리는 다른 국가의 시민들도 그들이 원한다면 그렇게 할 것이라고 믿어야 한다. 민주주의는 또한 절대적인 용어가 아니다 – 나폴레옹은 오늘날 서아프리카와 동남아시아의 지도자들이 그러는 것처럼, 그의 권력에 대한 장악을 합법화하기 위해 선거와 국민 투표를 이용했다. 부분적인 민주주의를 가진 국가들은 국내에서의 질서를 유지하는 것을 지나치게 걱정하는 완전히 비선출된 독재보다 종종 더 공격적이다. 상이한 형태들의 민주주의는 어느 기준을 도입할지를 선택하는 것을 불가능하게 만든다. 미국과 유럽 국가들은 정부의 규제 그리고 동의와 대립 사이의 균형이라는 측면에서 모두 다르다.

① 남의 떡이 더 커 보인다.
② 한 사람의 음식이 다른 사람에게는 독이다.
③ 예외가 없는 법칙은 없다.
④ 로마에 가면 로마법을 따른다.

어휘

impose 도입하다   blatant 노골적인, 뻔한
breach 위반, 위반하다   non-intervention 불간섭, 불개입의
affairs 사건, 일   institution 기관; 제도, 관습
legitimize 정당화하다, 합법화하다   partial 부분의, 편파적인
unselected 비 선출된   dictatorship 독재
impose 도입하다; 부과하다   in terms of~ ~에 관하여
restraint 규제   consensus 동의
confrontation 대립   exception 예외

10 정답 ③
18 서울시

정답해설

주어진 지문은 미국에서 공포를 일으켰던 '광대'에 대한 내용이다. 광대가 아이들을 꾀어내는 시도와 겁을 주려고 하는 위협적인 모습으로 보아 광대에 대해 부정적으로 서술하고 있음을 알 수 있다. 따라서 빈칸에는 광대에 대한 부정적인 이미지로 인한 부정적인 결과가 와야 한다. 따라서 빈칸에는 '③ caused a nationwide panic(전국적인 공포를 일으켰다)'이 알맞다.

오답해설

①, ②, ④ 모두 광대에 대한 긍정적인 이미지와 영향에 대한 것이므로 알맞지 않다.

해석

광대가 사람들을 겁먹게 한다는 생각은 미국에서 힘을 얻기 시작했다. 예를 들면, 사우스 캐롤라이나에서 한밤중에 숲이나 도시에 광대 의상을 입은 사람들이 종종 숨어 있다는 것을 봤다고 사람들은 보고했다. 몇몇 사람들은 광대가 빈집이나 숲으로 아이들을 꾀어내는 시도를 했다고 말했다. 곧 아이들과 어른들 모두에게 겁주려고 하는 위협적인 모습을 한 광대에 대한 보고가 있었다. 비록 대개 폭력에 대한 보고는 없었고, 보고된 목격의 대다수가 후에 거짓으로 밝혀졌지만, 이것은 <u>전국적인 공포를 일으켰다</u>.

① 서커스 산업에 이득이 됐다
② 광고에 광대의 사용을 촉진시켰다
③ 전국적인 공포를 일으켰다
④ 행복한 광대의 완벽한 이미지를 형성했다

어휘

clown 광대
costume 의상
lure 꾀어내다
violence 폭력
nationwide 전국적인
frighten 겁먹게 하다
individual 개인
threaten 위협하다
sighting 목격
panic 공포

기적사 DAY 62

| 01 | ④ | 02 | ③ | 03 | ① | 04 | ① | 05 | ③ |
| 06 | ① | 07 | ② | 08 | ③ | 09 | ② | 10 | ③ |

01 정답 ④

정답해설

'trace'는 '추적하다'를 뜻하는 동사로 ④ chase(추적하다, 뒤쫓다)와 유의어 관계이다.

해석

이 프로젝트는 인류의 이동을 **추적하기** 위해 집단유전학과 분자생물학을 결합시킨다.
① 달아나다, 빗장을 지르다
② 쫓아내다, 추방하다
③ 금하다, 제외하다
④ 추적하다, 뒤쫓다

어휘

combine 결합시키다
molecular 분자의, 분자로 된, 분자에 의한
biology 생물학
migration 이주, 이동
expel 쫓아내다, 추방하다
chase 추적하다, 뒤쫓다
genetics 유전학
trace 추적하다
bolt 달아나다, 빗장을 지르다
debar 금하다, 제외하다

02 정답 ③

정답해설

'needy'는 '어려운, 궁핍한'을 뜻하는 형용사로 ③ destitute(궁핍한, 극빈한)와 유의어 관계이다.

해석

그 프로그램을 통해서, 사람들은 **궁핍한** 가족들에게 돈을 기부할 수 있다.
① 우아한, 화려한
② 호화로운, 엄청나게 부유한
③ 궁핍한, 극빈한
④ 치명적인

어휘

donate 기부[기증]하다
posh 우아한, 화려한
destitute 궁핍한, 극빈한
needy 어려운, 궁핍한
opulent 호화로운, 엄청나게 부유한
pernicious 치명적인

오답률 TOP 3

03 정답 ①

정답해설

'thrilled'는 '흥분한, 황홀해하는'을 뜻하는 형용사로 ① hyper(흥분한, 들뜬)와 의미상 가장 가깝다.

해석

그들은 태양을 거의 완전한 불의 고리로 바꾼 이 웅장한 광경을 보게 되어 **흥분**했다.

① 흥분한, 들뜬
② 냉담한
③ 상냥한, 유순한
④ 차분한, 조용한

> 어휘

thrilled 흥분한, 황홀해하는
magnificent 웅장한, 참으로 아름다운[감명 깊은/훌륭한]
hyper 흥분한, 들뜬 callous 냉담한
benign 상냥한, 유순한 sedate 차분한, 조용한

04 정답 ①

> 정답해설

Chloe의 베트남 여행에 대해 '재미있지 않았던 한 가지 이유가 뭐였어?'라는 Charles의 질문에 Chloe는 '현지 시장을 방문했을 때, 물건을 팔려는 상인들이 ~했기 때문'이라고 답하고 있다. 따라서 문맥상 부정적인 내용이 들어가야 하므로 빈칸에 들어갈 가장 적절한 것은 '① rip us off(바가지를 씌우다)'이다.

> 오답해설

② Chloe가 베트남 여행이 재미있지 않았던 단 한 가지 이유를 설명하면서 현지 시장을 방문했을 때 물건을 팔려는 상인들이 '진솔하게 이야기하려고 (talk turkey)' 했다고 말하는 것은 대화의 흐름상 부자연스럽다.
③ Chloe가 Charles에게 베트남에서 좋지 않았던 일에 관해 이야기하며 현지 시장을 방문했을 때 물건을 팔려는 상인들이 '좋은 금광을 찾으려고 (strike it rich)' 했다고 얘기하는 것은 문맥상 어색하다.
④ 베트남 여행에서 단 한 가지 재미있지 않았던 이유를 설명하면서 Chloe가 현지 시장을 방문했을 때 물건을 판매하려는 상인들이 '화해하려고(kiss and make up)' 했기 때문이라고 말하는 것은 맥락상 적절하지 않다.

> 해석

Charles: 너 지난 여름 방학 동안 뭐 했어?
Chloe: 나는 고등학교 친구들과 베트남을 방문했어.
Charles: 재미있었겠네! 어땠어?
Chloe: 단 한 가지를 제외하고는 모든 것이 재밌었어.
Charles: 오, 그 한 가지가 뭐였어?
Chloe: 우리가 현지 시장을 방문했을 때, 물건을 팔려고 하는 상인들이 우리에게 바가지를 씌우려고 했어.
Charles: 와, 진짜? 나쁜 경험이었겠다! 근데 그런 일은 관광객들에게 자주 발생해.
① 바가지 씌우다
② 진솔하게 이야기하다
③ 좋은 금광을 찾다, 일확천금을 하다
④ 화해하다

> 어휘

merchant 상인 rip somebody off 바가지 씌우다
talk turkey 진솔하게 이야기하다
strike it rich 좋은 금광을 찾다, 일확천금을 하다
kiss and make up 화해하다

05 정답 ③

> 정답해설

③ 출제 포인트: what vs. that/주어와 동사의 수일치/등위상관접속사의 병렬구조/주어진 해석과 일치 확인
'what' 이후에 오는 절의 형태가 동사 'need'의 목적어가 없으므로 불완전한 문장이며, 앞에 선행사가 없으므로 관계대명사 'what'은 옳은 표현이다. 또한 동사 'is'의 주어는 선행사를 포함하는 관계대명사 'what'이 이끄는 절이므로 단수 형태의 동사 'is'는 옳은 표현이며, 주격 보어로 사용된 to부정사가 등위상관접속사 'not A but B'를 통해 병렬구조를 이루고 있다. 즉, 해당 보기의 경우 영어 지문 자체는 문법적으로 옳으나 제시된 영어 지문 'not to be defensive but to be offensive(방어적이어야 한다는 것이 아니라 공격적이어야 한다는 것)'와 주어진 해석 '공격적이어야 한다는 것이 아니라 방어적이어야 한다는 것'이 일치하지 않으므로 틀린 문장이다. 따라서 'to be defensive'와 'to be offensive'의 위치를 서로 바꾸어야 한다. 즉, 'Can you say what we need now is not to be offensive but to be defensive?'가 주어진 해석과 일치하는 옳은 문장이다.

> 오답해설

① 출제 포인트: to부정사의 부사적 용법/조동사 관용표현(cannot help but 동사원형)
「cannot help but+동사원형」은 관용표현으로 '~하지 않을 수 없다'를 뜻한다. 해당 문장은 'cannot help but+동사원형'의 과거시제인 'could not help but+동사원형'을 사용하였으며 주어진 해석과 일치하므로 옳은 문장이다. 이때, 해당 문장에서 'to laugh'는 to부정사의 부사적 용법으로 사용되었다.

② 출제 포인트: 주의해야 할 완전자동사/불완전타동사의 수동태(be left to+동사원형)
해당 문장에서 'was left to reflect'는 '~가 ~하도록 두다'를 뜻하는 불완전타동사 'leave'의 수동태로 'to reflect'는 목적격 보어에 해당한다. 또한 해당 문장에서 'reflect'는 '심사숙고하다'를 뜻하는 완전자동사이므로 목적어를 가지기 위해 전치사 'on'을 사용하였으므로 옳은 문장이다.

④ 출제 포인트: 비교급 강조부사
해당 문장에서 'even'은 비교급 강조부사로 동사 'aggravate'를 수식하는 비교급 부사 'further'를 수식하고 있으므로 옳은 문장이다.

06 정답 ①

> 정답해설

① 출제 포인트: 주어와 동사의 수일치/현재분사 vs. 과거분사
형용사 'rigid'와 'social'의 수식을 받으므로 밑줄 친 'controls'는 명사임을 알 수 있다. 이때 'controls'는 주어에 해당하므로 동사와 수일치 해야 하며 단수 형태의 동사인 'was'를 사용하였으므로 복수 형태의 명사인 'controls'는 틀린 표현이다. 따라서 'controls'를 단수 형태인 'control'로 수정해야 한다. 또한 밑줄 친 'required'는 완전타동사 'require'의 과거분사로 명사 'controls'를 수식하고 있으며 이후에 목적어가 없고 해석상 '요구된 통제'가 자연스러우므로 옳은 표현이다.

> 오답해설

② 출제 포인트: 현재분사 vs. 과거분사/형용사 vs. 부사
밑줄 친 'structured'는 완전타동사 'structure'의 과거분사로 명사 'community'를 수식하고 있으며 이후에 목적어가 없고 해석상 '조직된 공동체'가 자연스러우므로 옳은 표현이다. 또한 'loosely'는 과거분사 'structured'를 수식하는 부사이다.

③ **출제 포인트: 능동태 vs. 수동태/불완전타동사의 목적격 보어**
밑줄 친 'allowed' 이후에 「목적어+목적격 보어」인 'science to follow reason'이 왔으므로 불완전타동사임을 알 수 있으며 능동태로 사용하는 것이 옳다. 'allow'는 불완전타동사로 쓰이는 경우 목적격 보어로 to부정사를 가짐에 유의해야 한다.

④ **출제 포인트: 서수+명사[단수 vs. 복수]**
서수 이후에 오는 명사는 단수 형태를 사용한다. 따라서 밑줄 친 'seventeenth-century'는 옳은 표현이다.

해석
일부 제국들은 컸지만, 제국을 하나로 뭉치게 하기 위해 요구된 엄격한 사회적 통제는 그것이 이성에 이롭지 않았던 것과 마찬가지로 과학에도 이롭지 않았다. 과학의 초창기 육성과 이후의 개화는 독창적인 생각과 자유분방한 동기를 지지하는 크고 느슨하게 조직되어 있는 경쟁적인 공동체를 필요로 했다. 상업의 융성과 권위주의적인 종교의 쇠퇴는 17세기 유럽에서 과학이 이성을 따르게 해주었다.

어휘
empire 제국, 왕국　　　　rigid 엄격한, 융통성 없는
nurturing 육성　　　　　flowering 개화
freewheeling 자유분방한

오답률 TOP 1

07 정답 ②

정답해설

② **출제 포인트: that vs. what/주격 관계대명사절의 동사 수일치/등위접속사의 병렬구조/현재분사 vs. 과거분사**
선행사 'a wilderness'를 가지며 이후에 오는 절이 주어가 없는 불완전한 형태이므로 주격 관계대명사 'that'의 쓰임은 올바르며, 이때 선행사 'a wilderness'는 단수 형태이므로 주격 관계대명사절의 동사에 단수 형태인 'was'를 옳게 사용하였다. 또한 과거분사 'untamed'는 등위접속사 'but'을 통해 과거분사 'filled'와 병렬구조를 이루고 있으며 불완전자동사 'was'의 주격 보어에 해당한다. 마지막으로 'having'은 완전타동사 'have'의 현재분사로 이후에 목적어 'no plowed fields, fences, or farm houses'를 가지며 수식하는 대상 'a wilderness'와 능동관계이므로 'having'은 옳은 표현이다. 이때 주의해야 할 점은 'untamed'까지가 주격 관계대명사 'that'이 이끄는 관계대명사 절이며, 'having no plowed fields, fences, or farm houses'는 관계대명사절에 포함되는 분사구문이 아닌 선행사 'a wilderness'를 수식하는 분사구라는 것이다. 즉, 다음과 같이 이해하면 된다.

→ They saw a wilderness <u>that was filled with seemingly infinite abundance, but untamed</u>
　　　　　　　주격관계대명사절
, <u>having no plowed fields, fences, or farm houses</u>.
　　　　　분사구문
관계대명사절과 분사구가 수식어로서 선행사 'a wilderness'를 수식하는 것으로 이해할 수 있다.

오답해설

① **출제 포인트: 전치사의 쓰임(prior to+목적어[명사/동명사])**
'prior to'는 전치사로 '~에 앞서'를 뜻하며 이후에 목적어가 온다. 따라서 'Prior to' 이후에 온 동사원형 'come'을 동명사 'coming'으로 수정해야 한다.

③ **출제 포인트: 접속사의 쓰임/독립분사구문**
절 'more than 3 percent of employees left their jobs each month' 이후에 접속사 없이 또 다른 절인 'most of them took a job with another employer'가 사용되었으므로 틀린 문장이다. 따라서 문맥에 맞게 접속사 and를 사용하거나 두 번째 절의 동사 'took'을 현재분사 'taking'으로 수정하여 독립분사구문으로 고쳐야 한다. 즉, 다음과 같다.

→ According to the statistics, in 2005, more than 3 percent of employees left their jobs each month, <u>and</u> most of them took a job with another employer.
→ According to the statistics, in 2005, more than 3 percent of employees left their jobs each month, most of them <u>taking</u> a job with another employer.

또한, 접속사 'and'와 대명사 'them'이 함께 쓰여 목적격 관계대명사 'whom'으로 접속사와 명사의 역할을 동시에 할 수 있다.

→ According to the statistics, in 2005, more than 3 percent of employees left their jobs each month, most of <u>whom</u> took a job with another employer.

④ **출제 포인트: 주의해야 할 완전자동사/현재분사 vs. 과거분사**
'cope'는 완전자동사이므로 전치사 없이 목적어를 가질 수 없다. 따라서 'cope'와 목적어 'the world' 사이에 전치사 'with'가 들어가야 하며 'cope with'는 '~에 대처하다'를 뜻한다. 또한 'enhancing'은 현재분사로 이후에 목적어 'their ability'가 있으며 생략된 주어 'it'과 능동관계이므로 'enhancing'은 옳은 표현이다.

해석
① 이 병원에 들어오기 전에, 그는 독립 계약자로 일했다.
② 그들은 외견상으로는 무한한 풍요로 채워져 있으나, 길들여지지 않았으며, 경작된 밭이나 울타리 또는 농가가 없는 황무지를 보았다.
③ 통계에 따르면, 2005년, 3% 이상의 노동자들이 매달 그들의 직업을 떠났고, 그들의 대부분이 다른 고용주가 있는 직업을 얻었다.
④ 그것은 현재 세대를 위한 더 나은 삶과 다가올 세대를 위한 생존으로 이끌고, 그들이 물려받을 세계에 대처할 수 있는 그들의 능력을 향상시킨다.

08 정답 ③

정답해설

본문은 '현대 미술의 이점'에 대해 설명하는 글이다. 두 번째 문장 "Through painting, sculpture, and performance art, anyone can reveal themselves in a way that will be safely observable for others(그림, 조각, 그리고 행위예술을 통해, 누구나 타인이 안전하게 관찰할 수 있는 방식으로 자기 자신을 드러낼 수 있다)."를 통해, '현대 미술을 통해 자기 자신을 드러낼 수 있다'는 사실을 언급하고 있으며, 네 번째 문장 "Moreover, just as the making of art is a way to reveal oneself, so is the selection and display of art in someone's office or home décor(게다가, 예술을 창작하는 것이 자신을 드러내는 방식인 것처럼, 누군가의 사무실 또는 집의 실내장식에서 예술의 선택과 전시 또한 그러하다)."를 통해, '미술 창작뿐만 아니라 미술의 선택을 통해서도 자신을 표현할 수 있음'을 언급하고 있다. 따라서 빈칸에 들어가야 할 현대 미술의 이점으로 가장 적절한 것은 '③ a means of personal expression(사적 표현의 수단)'이다.

오답해설

① 본문에서는 '창작된 미술품 또는 장식품으로 이용된 미술품을 통해 개인의 감정과 사고를 이해할 수 있다'고 설명하고 있으므로, 빈칸에 적절하지 않다.
② 본문과 관련 없는 내용이므로 오답이다.
④ 본문 후반에서는 '미술 창작 외에 미술의 선택 또한 자기 자신을 표현하는 수단'이라고 언급하고 있는데, '예술적 기술'을 보여주는 것은 '미술 창작' 시에만 해당하는 것이므로, 빈칸에 적절하지 않다.

해석
현대 미술의 이점 중 하나는 그것이 개인들에게 <u>사적 표현의 수단</u>을 허락해준

다는 것이다. 그림, 조각, 그리고 행위예술을 통해, 누구나 타인이 안전하게 관찰할 수 있는 방식으로 자기 자신을 드러낼 수 있다. 마찬가지로, 드러낸 시각은 예술가의 정신과 사고를 들여다보는 독특한 창을 제공하기 때문에 사회에 가치가 있다. 게다가, 예술을 창작하는 것이 자신을 드러내는 방식인 것처럼, 누군가의 사무실 또는 집의 실내장식에서 예술의 선택과 전시 또한 그러하다. 직접 흥미를 끄는 예술품들을 선택함으로써, 비록 그들이 예술을 창작하는 데 개인적인 예술적 재능 또는 관심은 없더라도, 개인은 자기 자신의 선택을 행사할 수 있고, 자기 자신의 감정과 사고의 요소를 표현할 수 있다. 타인들 또한 예술적 선택에 기반하여 그 사람에 대한 이해를 빠르게 얻을 수 있다.

① 비판이 없는 공간
② 우리의 일상생활을 잠깐 들여다봄
③ 사적 표현의 수단
④ 그들의 예술적 기술을 표현할 수 있는 기회

어휘

contemporary 현대의
observable 식별[관찰]할 수 있는
exhibit 보이다[드러내다]
décor 실내장식, 인테리어
personally 개인적으로, 직접
exercise (권력·권리·역량 등을) 행사[발휘]하다
judgment 비판, 비난
means 수단, 방법
reveal 드러내다, 보여주다, 밝히다
perspective 관점, 시각
display 전시, 진열
appeal 관심[흥미]을 끌다, 매력적이다
glimpse into …을 잠깐 들여다봄

오답률 TOP 2

09 정답 ②

정답해설

본문은 '단순히 민주국가가 되는 것만이 아니라, 높은 수준의 민주국가가 되는 것이 목표가 되어야 한다'고 설명하며, '민주국가에도 높은 수준의 민주국가와 낮은 수준의 민주국가가 있다'는 것을 언급하고 있다. 따라서 전체 글의 요지로 가장 적절한 보기는 '② Not all democracy is the same(모든 민주주의가 동일한 것은 아니다).'이다.

오답해설

① 본문에서 '민주주의가 이롭다'는 내용은 구체적으로 언급되지 않는다.
③ 세 번째 문장에서 "One of the subsequent goals ought to be to establish and maintain a high degree of quality of democracy(이후의 목표 중 하나는 높은 수준의 민주주의의 질을 확립하고 유지하는 것이어야 한다)."라고 '높은 수준의 민주주의에 도달해야 한다'고 설명하고 있으나, 그것이 어렵다고 설명하는 내용은 본문에 존재하지 않는다.
④ 본문 후반에서 '투표'에 관해 언급되기는 하지만, 이는 '민주주의의 수준'에 대해 설명하려는 예시일 뿐, 본문의 요지와는 관계없다.

해석

보편적 관점은 국가들의 주된 목표 중 하나는 민주국가가 되는 것이어야 한다는 것이다. 그러나 국가들은 그들이 민주주의 상태를 달성했을 때 만족해서는 안 된다. 이후의 목표 중 하나는 높은 수준의 민주주의의 질을 확립하고 유지하는 것이어야 한다. 물론, 이 목표는 또한 안정된 민주국가들에게도 적용된다. 민주주의 시스템의 정당성에 있어서, 높은 수준의 민주주의 질은 중요하다는 것이 보여질 수 있고, 낮은 수준의 민주주의 질은 심각한 민주주의적 문제점으로 보여질 수 있다. 예를 들어, 민주주의 시스템에서 투표를 통한 정치 참여는 주춧돌로 여겨질 수 있다. 만약 투표자의 투표율이 낮다면, 그 선거와 민주주의 시스템의 정당성은 문제가 될 수 있다.
① 민주주의는 이로울 수 있다.
② 모든 민주주의가 동일한 것은 아니다.
③ 양질의 민주주의에 도달하는 것은 어렵다.
④ 민주주의 사회에서 투표는 가장 중요한 행위이다.

어휘

democracy 민주(주의)국가, 민주주의
democratic 민주주의의, 민주적인
subsequent 그[이]다음의, 차후의
well-established 확고부동한, 안정된, 정착된
legitimacy 적법[합법] (성), 정당성
participation 참가, 참여
cornerstone 주춧돌[초석]
turnout 투표자의 수, 투표율
come into question 문제가 되다

10 정답 ③

정답해설

본문은 '광대의 직업윤리(행동 강령)'에 관해 설명하는 글이다. ③에서 'they'가 '구체적(detailed)'이라고 언급하고 있으므로, 'they'가 가리키는 것은 '사람'이 아닌 이전 문장에서 언급한 "clown commandments(광대 계율)"라는 것을 유추할 수 있다. 나머지 보기는 모두 'clowns'를 가리키고 있으므로, 정답은 ③이다.

오답해설

① '자신들이 딜레마에 빠지지 않는다'는 의미이므로, '광대들이 딜레마에 빠지지 않는다'는 것이다. 따라서 ① themselves는 'clowns'를 의미한다.
② '규칙을 따라야 하는 것'은 광대들이므로, ② they는 'clowns'를 의미한다.
④ '업무 중에 절대 취해서는 안 되는 것'은 광대들이므로, ④ They는 'clowns'를 의미한다.

해석

많은 직업은 고유의 행동 강령이 있다. 비록 광대들이 좀처럼 ① 자신들이, 가령 의사나 변호사의 윤리적 딜레마에 직면한다고 생각하지는 않으나, ② 그들 또한 일련의 규율을 준수해야 한다. 이 "광대 계율"은 주로 광대를 오로지 웃음을 전파하는 사람으로서 유지시키려고 하는데, 많은 사람들이 광대와 연관하여 가지고 있는 오싹한 연상을 고려해 볼 때, 이것은 중요한 목표이다. ③ 그것들은 꽤 세부적이긴 하지만, 주요 요점은 전문가다운 행동과 외양을 포함한다. 예를 들어, 광대는 광대 복장을 하고 있는 중에 음주나 흡연을 해서는 절대 안 된다. ④ 그들은 업무 중에 절대 취해서는 안 된다. 그들은 광대를 좋지 않게 인식시킬 수 있는 모든 것을 피하기 위해 가능한 한 빨리 의복을 벗어야 한다. 광대는 웃기는 것으로 생계를 꾸릴지 모르지만, 그들은 진지하게 받아들여지지 않는 것에 대해서는 꽤 심각하다.

어휘

profession 직업[직종]
seldom 좀처럼[거의] …않는
ethical 윤리적인
abide by (법률·합의 등을) 따르다, 준수하다
commandment 계율, 계명
seek to 동사원형 ~하도록 시도[추구]하다
preserve 유지하다, 보존하다, 보호하다
exclusively 오로지, 오직, 전적으로
creepy 오싹한, 으스스한
involve 포함하다, 수반하다
intoxicated (술·마약에) 취한
garb 특이한 또는 특정 유형의 사람이 입는) 의복
reflect badly on …이 좋지 않게 비추게[인식되게] 하다
make a living 생계를 꾸리다
codes of conduct 행동 강령[수칙]
face 직면하다, 대면하다
say 이를테면, 말하자면, 가령
considering …을 고려[감안]하면
association 연상, 관계
conduct 행동, 행위

기적사 DAY 63
결국엔 성정혜 영어 하프모의고사

01	①	02	②	03	③	04	④	05	③
06	③	07	①	08	②	09	②	10	③

오답률 TOP 1
01 정답 ①

정답해설

'excludes'는 동사 'exclude'의 단수 형태로 '제외하다'를 뜻한다. 따라서 ① scratches(제외하다, 긁다)와 의미가 가장 가깝다.

해석

그들은 자택에서 교육받는 자녀의 절충적인 교육 과정이 중요 과목들을 종종 **제외한다**고 주장한다.
① 제외하다, 긁다
② 용납하다
③ 포함하다, 포괄하다
④ 비난하다, 규탄하다

어휘

eclectic 절충적인; 다방면에 걸친
scratch 제외하다, 긁다
subsume 포함하다, 포괄하다
exclude 제외하다
condone 용납하다
condemn 비난하다, 규탄하다

오답률 TOP 2
02 정답 ②

정답해설

'thrifty'는 '검소한, 절약하는'을 뜻하는 형용사로 ② spartan(검소하고 엄격한, 스파르타식의)과 의미상 가장 가깝다.

해석

할인점에는 **검소한** 구매자들을 위한 저렴한 제품들을 가지고 있다.
① 약삭빠른, 영리한
② 검소하고 엄격한, 스파르타식의
③ 경솔한, 무분별한
④ 즉석의, 사전 준비 없이 하는

어휘

discount 할인의; 할인; 할인하다
canny 약삭빠른, 영리한
imprudent 경솔한, 무분별한
thrifty 검소한, 절약하는
spartan 검소하고 엄격한, 스파르타식의
offhand 즉석의, 사전 준비 없이 하는

03 정답 ③

정답해설

'brave'는 '용감한, 용기 있는'을 뜻하는 형용사로 ③ gallant(용감한, 용맹한)와 의미상 가장 가깝다.

해석

당신이 **용감하지** 않을 때 당신이 할 수 있는 가장 용기 있는 행동은 용기를 천명하고 그에 맞춰 행동하는 것이다.
① 작고 연약한, 보잘것없는
② 거의 없는, 부족한
③ 용감한, 용맹한
④ 겁이 많은, 비겁한

어휘

brave 용감한, 용기 있는
accordingly 그에 맞춰, 그것에 알맞게
puny 작고 연약한, 보잘것없는
gallant 용감한, 용맹한
profess 천명[공언]하다; 주장하다
scant 거의 없는, 부족한
cowardly 겁이 많은, 비겁한

오답률 TOP 3
04 정답 ④

정답해설

(A) A가 자신만의 옷 가게를 개업하려 했지만 실패해서 '~한 기분이다'라고 말하고 있으므로 빈칸 (A)에 들어갈 가장 적절한 것은 '헛된 노력을 했다(went on a wild goose chase)'이다.
(B) A는 B가 처한 상황에 대해 안타까워하고 있다. B가 옷 가게를 열면 많은 돈을 벌 수 있을 것이라고 생각한다고 말하며 옷 가게를 열지 않으면 '~하는 것과 같다'라고 말하고 있으므로 빈칸 (B)에 들어갈 가장 적절한 것은 '큰 이익이 기대되는 일을 포기하다(killing the goose that laid the golden egg)'이다. 따라서 정답은 ④이다.

오답해설

① (A) B는 자신의 기분이 좋지 않은 이유에 관해 설명하며 자신만의 옷 가게를 개업하기 위해 준비 중이었지만 실패했다고 말한다. 이러한 상황에 대해 자신이 '자제심을 잃은(lost my head)' 것처럼 느껴진다고 말하는 것은 문맥상 자연스럽지 않다. (B) B가 처한 상황에 관해 대화를 나누며, A는 B에게 가게를 열지 않으면 '작은 일을 크게 떠벌리는(making a mountain out of a molehill)' 것과 같다고 이야기하는 것은 맥락상 적합하지 않다.
② (A) B는 자신의 기분이 좋지 않은 이유에 관해 설명하며 자신만의 옷 가게를 개업하기 위해 준비 중이었지만 실패했다고 말한다. 이러한 상황에 대해 자신이 '자제심을 잃은(lost my head)' 것처럼 느껴진다고 말하는 것은 문맥상 어색하다.
③ (B) B가 처한 상황에 관해 대화를 나누며, A는 B에게 가게를 열지 않으면 '작은 일을 크게 떠벌리는(making a mountain out of a molehill)' 것과 같다고 이야기하는 것은 대화의 흐름상 빈칸에 들어갈 말로 부적절하다.

해석

A: 너 아파? 별로 좋아 보이지 않아.
B: 아니, 전혀 아프지 않아. 사실, 심각한 고민을 하고 있기 때문이야.
A: 오, 무슨 일이야? 나는 항상 널 도울 준비가 되어있어.
B: 음, 나는 내 옷 가게를 개업하기 위해 준비하고 있었지만 실패했어. 나는 (A) 헛된 노력을 한 기분이야.
A: 내가 뭐라고 해야 할지 모르겠다. 네가 왜 옷 가게를 개업하지 않는지 물어봐도 될까?
B: 내 부모님은 그 사실에 굉장히 불만족스러워하셔. 내가 공부에 집중하길 원하셔.
A: 난 네가 그 사업으로부터 많은 돈을 벌 수 있을 거라고 생각하는데 너무 안타깝다. 네가 개업하지 않으면 (B) 큰 이익이 기대되는 일을 포기하는 것과 같아.
B: 알아. 근데 슬프게도, 다른 선택지가 없어.
① (A) 자제심을 잃었다 (B) 작은 일을 크게 떠벌리다
② (A) 자제심을 잃었다 (B) 큰 이익이 기대되는 일을 포기하다
③ (A) 헛된 노력을 했다 (B) 작은 일을 크게 떠벌리다
④ (A) 헛된 노력을 했다 (B) 큰 이익이 기대되는 일을 포기하다

어휘

at all 전혀, 조금도
lose one's head 자제심을 잃다
make a mountain out of a molehill 작은 일을 크게 떠벌리다
kill the goose that laid the golden egg 큰 이익이 기대되는 일을 포기하다
go on a wild goose chase 헛된 노력을 하다

05 정답 ③

정답해설

③ **출제 포인트: 주어와 동사의 수일치/불가산명사/비교급 강조부사**

불가산명사가 주어인 경우 동사에 단수 형태를 사용해야 한다. 해당 문장은 유도부사구문으로 주어가 불가산명사 'news'이나 동사에 복수 형태인 'were'를 사용하였으므로 틀린 문장이다. 따라서 'were'를 단수 형태인 'was'로 수정해야 한다. 또한 해당 문장에서 'even'은 비교급 강조부사로 불가산명사 'news'를 수식하는 비교급 형용사 'more'를 수식한다.

오답해설

① **출제 포인트: 수여동사의 문장구조/능동태 vs. 수동태**

'give'는 수여동사의 경우 「give+간접목적어[대상]+직접목적어[사물]」의 형태를 가진다. 해당 문장은 수여동사 'give'의 3인칭 단수 현재시제인 'gives'가 능동태로 쓰인 문장으로 이후에 간접목적어 'them'과 직접목적어 'a huge advantage'가 왔으므로 옳은 문장이다.

② **출제 포인트: to부정사의 부사적 용법**

해당 문장에서 'to protect'는 to부정사의 부사적 용법으로 사용되었으며, 'huddled'는 완전자동사 'huddle(옹송그리며 모이다)'의 과거시제로 옳은 표현이다.

④ **출제 포인트: what vs. that/주어와 동사의 수일치/완전자동사 vs. 완전타동사/가목적어 it**

첫 번째 'What'은 이후의 문장이 불완전타동사 'call'의 목적어가 없는 불완전한 형태이며, 두 번째 'what'은 이후 문장에 주어가 없는 불완전한 형태이다. 또한 첫 번째와 두 번째 'what' 앞에 선행사가 없으므로 선행사를 포함한 관계대명사 'what'은 옳은 표현이다. 덧붙여 동사 'consists'의 주어는 선행사를 포함하는 관계대명사 'what'이 이끄는 절이므로 단수형태의 동사 'consists'는 옳은 표현이며, 이때 'consists'는 완전자동사이므로 목적어를 가지기 위해 전치사 'of'를 사용하였다. 마지막으로 해당 문장에서 'it'은 가목적어이며 진목적어는 to부정사 'to work'로 'for the employees'는 to부정사의 의미상 주어에 해당한다.

06 정답 ③

정답해설

③ **출제 포인트: 관용표현(be inclined to+동사원형)**

'be inclined to'는 관용표현으로 '~할 생각이 있는, ~하는 경향이 있는'을 뜻하며 이후에 동사원형이 온다. 해당 문장은 'be inclined to'의 과거시제 부정형인 'were not inclined to'를 사용하였으나 이후에 동사원형이 아닌 동명사 'updating'을 사용하였으므로 틀린 문장이다. 따라서 'updating'을 동사원형 'update'로 수정해야 한다. 'be inclined to'의 'to'가 전치사가 아닌 to부정사의 'to'임에 유의해야한다.

오답해설

① **출제 포인트: 현재분사 vs. 과거분사**

밑줄 친 'estimated'는 완전타동사 'estimate'의 과거분사로 해석상 '추정된 즐거움'이 자연스러우며 수식 대상인 'pleasure'와 수동관계이므로 'estimated'는 옳은 표현이다.

② **출제 포인트: 현재분사 vs. 과거분사/등위접속사의 병렬구조**

밑줄 친 'decreasing'은 완전타동사 'decrease'의 현재분사로 이후에 목적어 'the expected pleasure'가 있으며 생략된 주어 'the decision'과 능동관계이므로 'decreasing'은 옳은 표현이다. 이때 'decreasing'을 본동사 'decreases'로 고치지 않도록 주의해야 한다. 등위접속사 'and'를 통해 병렬구조를 이루고 있는 것이 본동사라면 앞에 있는 현재분사 'enhancing'도 'enhances'로 고쳐야 하나 'enhancing'에 밑줄이 없으므로 'and'를 통해 'decreasing'이 병렬구조를 이루고 있는 대상이 'enhancing'임을 알 수 있다. 따라서 해당 문장에서 'enhancing ~ option'과 'decreasing ~ option'은 분사구문으로 'and'를 통해 병렬구조를 이루고 있다.

④ **출제 포인트: 접속사의 쓰임**

밑줄 친 'so that'은 목적을 나타내는 접속사로 '~하도록'을 뜻하며 부사절을 이끈다.

해석

선택을 한 후에, 그 결정은 결국 우리의 추정된 즐거움을 변화시키며, 그 선택된 선택사항으로부터 기대되는 즐거움을 향상시키고 거부된 선택사항으로부터 기대되는 즐거움을 감소시킨다. 우리의 선택과 일치하도록 재빨리 선택사항의 가치를 새롭게 할 생각이 없다면, 우리는 뒤늦게 자신을 비판하여 미칠 지경으로 몰고 갈 것이다.

어휘

ultimately 궁극적으로, 결국
decrease 줄다, 감소하다
be inclined to 동사원형 ~하는 경향이 있다
update 갱신하다, 새롭게 하다
second-guess 뒤늦게 비판하다
insanity 정신 이상

07 정답 ①

정답해설

① **출제 포인트: 비교급 비교/시제 일치/little vs. few**

해당 문장은 비교급 형용사 'fewer'와 'less' 그리고 접속사 'than'을 통해 비교급 비교가 쓰인 문장임을 알 수 있으며 이때 'than' 이후에 온 대동사 'do'의 시제는 주절에 쓰인 동사 'get'과 'have' 즉, 현재시제와 일치하므로 옳은 문장이다. 또한 해당 문장에서 'success'는 '성공'을 뜻하는 불가산명사이므로 양을 나타내는 비교급 형용사 'less'의 수식을 받는 것이 옳다.

오답해설

② **출제 포인트: 등위접속사의 병렬구조/동명사의 태/분사구문**

불완전자동사 'are'의 주격 보어에 해당하는 과거분사가 등위접속사 'and'를 통해 「A, B, and C」의 병렬구조를 이루고 있는 문장으로 B에 해당하는 'identify'를 과거분사 'identified'로 수정해야 한다. 또한 'before being packed'의 경우 「전치사+동명사의 수동태」 또는 「접속사+being이 생략되지 않은 분사구문」으로 볼 수 있다. 이때 동명사의 의미상 주어와 being이 생략되지 않은 분사구문의 생략된 주어는 'These finds'이다.

③ **출제 포인트: 시제 일치/recognize A as B의 수동태**

'since then'은 시간의 부사구로 현재완료와 함께 사용한다. 따라서 'was'를 현재완료 'has been'으로 수정해야 한다. 또한 해당 문장은 「recognize A as B」의 수동태인 「A be recognized as B」가 옳게 사용되었다.

④ **출제 포인트: that vs. what**

'what' 이후에 「주어+불완전자동사+보어」 형태의 완전한 절이 왔으므로 'what'은 틀린 표현임을 알 수 있으며 앞에 추상명사 'impression'이 있으므로 동격의 접속사 'that'을 사용해야 한다. 따라서 'what'을 'that'으로 수정해야 한다.

해석
① 그 학생들은 또래들이 하는 것보다 일반적으로 더 적은 연습 기회들을 획득하며 더 적은 성공을 가진다.
② 이러한 발견들은 보통 실험실로 운송되기 위해 포장되기 전 현장에서 세척되고, 식별되고, 목록으로 작성된다.
③ 그때 이후로, 파인애플은 국제적으로 환대의 상징과 친근함, 따뜻함, 격려의 표시로 인식되어졌다.
④ 우리가 특정 문화 체계의 정치 조직을 말할 때, 우리는 정치적 경계와 문화적 경계가 같다는 인상을 받게 된다.

08 정답 ②

정답해설
주어진 글은 '근대미술(Modern art)의 정의'에 대해 설명하고 있다. 이에 이어질 가장 적절한 보기는 '최초의 근대 화가'로 여겨지는 'Édouard Manet'을 언급하고 있는 (A)가 가장 적절하다. (A) 후반부에서 '그가 전통을 거부했다(he broke with tradition)'고 언급하고 있으므로, 이어지는 보기는 'instead(대신에)'를 이용하여, 그가 전통적 기법 대신 사용한 근대미술의 기법을 설명하고 있는 (C)가 이어지는 것이 적절하다. 마지막으로 (C)에서 언급된 그의 기법을 (B)에서 'this'로 가리키고 있으므로, (B)가 마지막에 위치하는 것이 자연스럽다. 따라서 정답은 '② (A) - (C) - (B)'이다.

오답해설
① (B)의 'this'가 가리키는 것이 (A)의 '전통 거부'를 가리킨다고 생각할 수도 있으나, 그렇다면 (C)의 instead와 연결되는 대조되는 내용이 (B)에 언급되어야 하는데, (B)에는 해당 내용이 존재하지 않으므로, 문맥상 어색하다. 따라서 오답이다.
나머지 보기는 문맥상 어색하므로 오답이다.

해석
근대미술(Modern art)은 1860년대와 1960년대 말 사이의 시기에 창작된 것이다. 미술은 "근대적(현대적)"이라고 불렸는데 왜냐하면 그것이 그 이전에 있었던 것에 기반을 두지 않거나 미술 학파들의 사상에 의존하지 않기 때문이다.
(A) 많은 미술 역사가들은 Édouard Manet을 그가 근대 삶의 장면을 묘사했기 때문일 뿐만 아니라 그가 원근법 기교를 통해 현실 세계를 모방하려는 시도를 하지 않았을 때 전통을 거부했기 때문에 최초의 근대 화가로 여긴다.
(C) 대신에, 그는 그의 예술작품이 단순히 평평한 캔버스 위의 물감인 사실과 때때로 구도의 표면에 흔적을 남긴 페인트 붓을 이용해 만들어진 사실에 주의를 끌었다.
(B) 이것이 관중과 비평가들을 놀라게 한 반면, 그것은 그의 동료들과 향후 몇 세대의 미술가들에게 영감을 주었는데, 그들 각각은, 추상 작품에서든지 구상 작품에서든지 간에, 그들의 표현 수단에 어떻게 더 많은 주의를 끌 것인가를 실험했다.

어휘
modern art 근대미술
rely on 의존하다, 의지하다
academy 협회, 학회, 학파
break with 그만두다, 거부하다, 관계를 끊다
mimic 모방하다, 흉내 내다
perspective 원근법
peer 동료, 또래[동배]
representational 구상주의적인
medium (화가, 작가, 음악가의) 표현 수단
composition 구도, 구성
build on …을 기반으로 하다
teaching 교리, 사상, 가르침
depict 묘사하다, 그리다
by way of …로[…을 통해]
trick 기교, 트릭, 비결, 요령
abstract 추상적인
draw attention 주의[관심]를 끌다

09 정답 ②

정답해설
주어진 문장에서는 'not all elections are democratic(모든 선거가 민주적인 것은 아니다)'라고 언급하며, '민주적이지 않은 선거'도 존재함을 언급하고 있으므로, 주어진 문장 이후에는 '민주적이지 않은 선거에 대한 예시'가 언급되는 것이 가장 자연스럽다. ② 이후에서 "Right-wing dictatorships, Marxist regimes, and single-party governments stage elections to give their rule the aura of legitimacy(우익 독재 정부, 마르크스주의 정권, 그리고 단일정당 정부는 그들의 통치에 정당성의 기운을 제공하기 위해 선거를 개최한다)."라고 언급하며, '비민주적인 선거를 하는 정부들'의 예시를 언급한 후, 이후 '비민주적 선거가 치러지는 양상'을 구체적으로 제시하고 있다. 따라서 주어진 문장이 들어갈 가장 적절한 보기는 ②이다.

오답해설
나머지 보기는 문맥상 어색하므로 오답이다.

해석
민주국가에서, 정부의 권한은 오직 피통치자의 동의로부터 나오기 때문에 선거는 대의 민주주의 정부의 중심 제도이다. (①) 그 동의를 정부 권한으로 변환시키는 주요 기제는 자유롭고 공정한 선거의 실시이다. (② **모든 현대 민주국가는 선거를 실시하지만, 모든 선거가 민주적인 것은 아니다.**) 우익 독재 정부, 마르크스주의 정권, 그리고 단일정당 정부는 그들의 통치에 정당성의 기운을 제공하기 위해 선거를 개최한다. (③) 그러한 선거에서는, 대안적 선택 없이, 오직 한 명 또는 한 목록의 후보들만이 존재할 수도 있다. (④) 일부 선거는 각각의 직위에 여러 후보를 제공할 수도 있지만, 위협 또는 조작을 통해 오직 정부에서 승인된 후보만이 선택되도록 만들 수도 있다. 다른 선거는 진정한 선택지를 제공할 수도 있다 - 그러나 오직 재임 중인 당내에서만. 이러한 것들은 민주주의적 선거가 아니다.

어휘
hold 개최하다, 열다
representative 대표제[대의원제]의
derive …에서 비롯되다, …에 기원을 두다, …에서 나오다
solely 오로지, 단독으로
the governed 피통치자, 피치자
mechanism 기제, 방법, 메커니즘
holding 개최
dictatorship 독재 정부[독재 국가]
single-party 단일정당의
rule 통치, 지배
legitimacy 정당성, 타당성, 합법성
alternative 대안의, 대체 가능한
office (권위 있는, 특히 정부의 주요) 지위, 공직, 정권
intimidation 위협, 협박
approve 승인하다, 인가하다
incumbent 재임 중인
institution 제도[관습]
authority 권한, 지휘권
consent 동의, 합의
principal 주요한, 주된
translate (다른 형태로) 바꾸다[옮기다]
right-wing 우익[우파/보수파]의
regime 정권, 제도, 체제
stage 개최하다, 벌이다, 꾸미다
aura 기운, 분위기
candidate 후보
rig (부정한 수법으로) 조작하다
genuine 진짜의, 진정한
party 정당, 당

10 정답 ③

정답해설
본문은 'Cheyenne 부족 고유의 광대'인 'contrary'에 관한 설명이다. 'contrary는 일종의 전사이지만 늘 반대로 말하고 행동함으로써, 부족 내에서 광대의 역할을 한다'고 언급하고 있다. ②에서 '전사가 contrary가 되는 이유'를 '공포 극복'을 위함이라고 언급한 후, ④와 마지막 문장에서 '어떻게 공포를 극복할 수 있는지' 설명하고 있다. 그런데 ③에서는, '일반적으로 전사가 받는 대우'에 대해 설명하고 있으므로, '특별한 전사인 contrary'에 대해 설명하는 글의 중간에 위치하는 것은 문맥상 어색하다. 따라서 정답은 ③이다.

Day 63

오답해설

① 이전 문장에서, '의사소통 이상으로 반전이 확대되었다'고 설명하고 있으므로, 이어서 '반대의 행위'를 나타내는 ①이 이어지는 것은 자연스럽다. 나머지 보기는 문맥상 자연스러우므로 오답이다.

해석

북미의 Cheyenne 부족에서는 *contrary(반대)*라고 불리는 특정 유형의 전사가 어쩌면 그 특정 문화의 광대로 여겨질지도 모른다. contrary들은 항상 반의어로 의사소통했다. 예를 들어, '예'를 의미하기 위해 머리를 흔드는 것과 '아니오'를 의미하기 위해 끄덕이는 것. 만일 그들이 장작의 부족에 대해 경고하길 원한다면, 그들은 "우리는 나무가 많아! 더 이상 가져오지 마."라고 말했다. 이러한 반전은 또한 의사소통 이상으로 확대되었다. ① 그들은 의복을 거꾸로 입고, 흙으로 씻곤 했으며, 심지어 물로 자신들의 몸을 말린 것으로 알려져 있었다. ② 한 전사가 그러한 인물이 되기로 결정하는 이유는 공포를 극복하기 위함이었다. ③ 전사는 사람들에게 전쟁 유발자가 아니라 보호자이자 지도자로서 간주되었으며, 전사들은 전장에서 다양한 용맹의 행위를 수행하고 축적함으로써 높은 지위를 얻었다. ④ contrary는 소지자를 번개가 공격할 수 없도록 만들어준다고 회자된 긴 창을 무기로 사용했다. 따라서 천둥 혹은 번개에 대한 두려움을 가진 사람들은 부족의 광대 전사가 되어 그들의 공포증을 물리칠 수 있었다.

어휘

warrior 전사
opposite 반의어, 반대
reversal (정반대로) 뒤바꿈[뀜], 전환, 반전
extend 확대[확장]하다
figure 인물, 사람
rank (사회적으로) 높은 지위[신분]
bravery 용맹, 용기
bearer 소지자, 운반자
invulnerable to …이 해칠[물리칠] 수 없는, …로부터 안전한, …에 끄떡없는
conquer 물리치다, 이기다, 정복하다
could well 어쩌면 ~일지 모른다
nod 끄덕이다
bathe (몸을) 씻다, 세척하다
overcome 극복하다, 이기다
accumulate 축적하다, 쌓아 올리다
lance 긴 창
phobia 공포증

기적사 DAY 64

결국엔 성정혜 영어 하프모의고사

| 01 | ④ | 02 | ④ | 03 | ② | 04 | ③ | 05 | ④ |
| 06 | ③ | 07 | ② | 08 | ③ | 09 | ④ | 10 | ② |

01 정답 ④

정답해설

'instruct'는 '지시하다, 가르치다'를 뜻하는 동사로 ④ mandate(지시하다, 명령하다)와 유의어 관계이다.

해석

이 자료는 외국에서 싸우는 동포를 지원하는 활동들에 참여하도록 민간인들을 **지시하고** 용기를 북돋는 데 도움이 된다.
① 쫓아내다, 몰아내다
② 무죄를 선고하다
③ 탄핵하다, 고발하다
④ 지시하다, 명령하다

어휘

instruct 지시하다, 가르치다
encourage 격려[고무]하다, 용기를 북돋우다
civilian 민간인
compatriot 동포
acquit 무죄를 선고하다
mandate 지시하다, 명령하다
engage in ~에 관여[참여]하다
oust 쫓아내다, 몰아내다
impeach 탄핵하다, 고발하다

02 정답 ④

정답해설

'wealthy'는 '부유한, 재산이 많은'을 뜻하는 형용사로 ④ opulent(부유한, 호화로운)와 의미상 가장 가깝다.

해석

그녀는 **부유한** 러시아 기업가이자 예술 후원자였다.
① 삭막한, 냉혹한
② 무딘, 직설적인, 솔직한
③ 요령 있는, 눈치 있는
④ 부유한, 호화로운

어휘

wealthy 부유한, 재산이 많은
stark 삭막한, 냉혹한
tactful 요령 있는, 눈치 있는
industrialist 기업가
blunt 무딘, 직설적인, 솔직한
opulent 부유한, 호화로운

오답률 TOP 1

03 정답 ②

정답해설

'timid'는 '소심한, 용기가 없는'을 뜻하는 형용사로 ② mousy(소심한, 내성적인)와 의미상 가장 가깝다.

해석

외향적인 사람은 자극적이지 않은 음식을 좋아하는 반면, **소심한** 사람은 맵고 짠 음식을 좋아한다.

① 약삭빠른, 영리한
② 소심한, 내성적인
③ 상냥한, 사근사근한
④ 교활한, 기묘한

어휘

timid 소심한, 용기가 없는　　　　extrovert 외향적인 사람
bland (맛이) 자극적이지 않은, 특별한 맛이 안 나는; 특징 없는, 단조로운
astute 약삭빠른, 영리한　　　　mousy 소심한, 내성적인
affable 상냥한, 사근사근한　　　cunning 교활한, 기묘한

오답률 TOP 3
04 정답 ③

정답해설

중요한 오디션에 지원한 아들과 엄마의 대화이다. 아들은 다음 날 있을 학교 밴드 오디션에 긴장된다고 하자, 엄마는 아들에게 오디션에서 확실히 '~이 있다'라고 격려한다. 따라서 빈칸에 들어갈 가장 적절한 것은 '③ stand a chance(성공할 가망성이 있다)'이다.

오답해설

① 학교 밴드 오디션을 앞둔 아들에게 엄마는 걱정하지 말라고 이야기하고 있다. '행운을 빌어(break a leg)'라는 표현은 상대방을 응원하는 표현으로 주어진 문장의 주어인 오디션에 참가하는 'You[아들]' 스스로가 '행운을 빈다'라고 하는 것은 문맥상 어색하다.
② 학교 밴드 오디션을 앞둬 긴장한 아들을 엄마가 격려해주며 그에게 오디션에서 확실히 '떼돈을 번다(make a killing)'라고 이야기하는 것은 대화의 흐름상 빈칸에 들어갈 말로 적합하지 않다.
④ 아들은 다음 날 학교 밴드의 리드 싱어 자리 오디션을 앞둬 긴장한 상태이다. 엄마는 아들을 격려하며 그에게 오디션에서 확실히 '변덕을 부린다(blow hot and cold)'라고 말하는 것은 맥락상 어색하다.

해석

엄마: 오늘 기분이 어때?
아들: 조금 긴장되기 시작했어요. 저는 내일 중요한 오디션이 있어요.
엄마: 오, 정말? 그건 몰랐는데. 무슨 오디션 봐?
아들: 아직 아무에게도 이야기하지 않았어요. 학교 밴드의 리드 싱어 자리를 위한 오디션을 받아요.
엄마: 우와! 멋지네! 아들아, 너무 걱정하지 마. 너는 천상의 목소리를 가졌어. 너는 오디션에서 틀림없이 성공할 가망성이 있어.
아들: 감사해요, 엄마. 엄마는 저의 가장 든든한 지원군이에요.
① 행운을 빌어
② 떼돈을 벌다
③ 성공할 가망성이 있다
④ 변덕을 부리다

어휘

audition 오디션을 보다[오디션에 참가하다]
doubtlessly 의심 없이, 틀림없이　　break a leg 행운을 빌어
make a killing 떼돈을 벌다
stand a chance 성공할 가망성이 있다
blow hot and cold 변덕을 부리다

오답률 TOP 2
05 정답 ④

정답해설

④ **출제 포인트: 주의해야 할 완전자동사/능동태 vs. 수동태**
'depend'는 완전자동사이므로 목적어를 가지기 위해 전치사 'on'을 사용한다. 해당 문장은 주어진 문맥상 수동태로 사용할 수 없으나 'depend on'의 수동태인 'be depended on'을 사용하였으므로 틀린 문장이다. 따라서 'be depended on'을 능동태 'depend on'으로 수정해야 한다.

오답해설

① **출제 포인트: to부정사의 부사적 용법/불완전타동사의 구조(find+목적어+목적격 보어[형용사])/관용표현(from abroad)**
해당 문장에서 'to find'는 to부정사의 부사적 용법으로 결과를 나타내며, 이때 'find'는 불완전타동사로 「find+목적어+목적격 보어[형용사]」의 형태를 가진다. 따라서 'the house'는 목적어에 해당하며 'empty'는 목적격 보어에 해당한다. 또한 'from abroad'는 관용표현으로 '해외에서'를 뜻하며 '해외에서 돌아오다'를 나타낼 때 'return from abroad'를 사용함에 주의하도록 하자.
② **출제 포인트: 주어와 동사의 수일치/try+목적어[to부정사 vs. 동명사]/what vs. that**
'The police'가 주어인 경우 동사에는 복수 형태를 사용하므로 복수형태 동사 'are'는 옳은 표현이며, 주어진 해석이 '~하기 위해 애쓰다'이므로 'try'의 목적어로 to부정사를 사용하는 것이 옳다. 또한 'what' 이후에 오는 절이 주어가 없는 불완전한 형태이며 앞에 선행사가 없으므로 관계대명사 'what'은 옳은 표현이다.
③ **출제 포인트: 비교급 강조부사**
해당 문장에서 'even'은 비교급 강조부사로 형용사 'lavish'를 수식하는 비교급 부사 'more'를 수식한다.

06 정답 ③

정답해설

③ **출제 포인트: 능동태 vs. 수동태**
앞에 that이 문장에서 어떤 역할을 하는지 판단하는 것이 관건이다. 해당 문장에서는 문맥상 'the aid'를 선행사로 받는 관계대명사임을 확인할 수 있다. 'the aid'와 'it' 사이에 있는 'that'은 관계대명사이므로 이후에 오는 절은 불완전한 형태이어야 하나 밑줄 친 'is provided'가 수동태이므로 'that' 이후의 문장이 완전한 형태의 절이 되어 'that'은 틀린 표현이 된다. 따라서 'is provided'를 능동태 'provides'로 수정해야 하며 이때 'that'은 'provides'의 목적어가 없으므로 목적격 관계대명사임을 알 수 있다.

오답해설

① **출제 포인트: to부정사를 목적격 보어로 가지는 불완전타동사**
밑줄 친 'to come'은 불완전타동사 'allows'의 목적격 보어에 해당하므로 옳은 표현이다. 이때 불완전타동사 'allow'는 「allow+목적어+목적격 보어[to부정사]」의 형태로 사용됨에 유의하도록 하자.
② **출제 포인트: 관계대명사의 계속적 용법**
밑줄 친 'which' 앞에 콤마(,)가 있고 이후에 오는 절이 주어가 없는 불완전한 형태이므로 'which'가 계속적 용법으로 사용된 주격 관계대명사임을 알 수 있다. 이때 'which'의 선행사는 앞 문장 전체 'They also learn new tastes and ways of thinking'이다.
④ **출제 포인트: 주어와 동사의 수일치/to부정사의 형용사적 용법**
밑줄 친 'opportunity'는 주절의 주어에 해당하며 동사에 단수 형태인 'encourages'를 사용하였으므로 단수형태 'opportunity'는 옳은 표현이다. 또한 'to sell ~ for them'은 'opportunity'를 수식하는 to부정사의

형용사적 용법으로 사용되었다. 이처럼 주어와 동사의 사이가 먼 경우 수 일치에 유의해야한다.

해석

관광은 다른 장소와 다른 문화권으로부터 온 사람들이 함께 모이게 하고, 그리하여 관광객과 지역의 공동체가 서로의 차이점과 유사점에 관해 배우게 된다. 그들은 또한 새로운 취향과 사고방식에 관해 알게 되는데, 그것이 지역 사람들과 관광객들 사이의 보다 나은 이해로 이어질지도 모른다. 관광의 또 다른 긍정적인 효과는 한 사회의 문화, 특히 문화권의 예술 형태의 생존을 위해 제공하는 도움이다. 관광객들에게 전통 미술품을 팔거나, 민속춤을 공연할 기회는 지역 예술가들이 전통적인 예술 형태를 보존하도록 장려한다.

어휘

tourism 관광 similarity 유사점
aid 도움 artwork 미술품
preserve 보존하다

07 정답 ②

정답해설

② 출제 포인트: 현재분사 vs. 과거분사/수동태 불가동사

해당 문장에서 'Thought of as a relationship'은 'think of A as B(A를 B로 여기다)'의 수동태인 「A be thought of as B」가 분사구문으로 쓰인 것으로 생략된 주어 A는 주절의 주어인 'leadership'이다. 또한 주격 관계대명사 'that'이 이끄는 절의 동사 'occurs'는 완전자동사이므로 수동태로 사용할 수 없음에 주의해야 한다.

오답해설

① 출제 포인트: that vs. what

'that' 이후에 오는 절 'North America looks like from the Southern Hemisphere'는 전치사 'like'의 목적어가 없는 불완전한 형태이므로 'that'이 관계대명사임을 알 수 있으나 'that' 앞에 선행사가 없으므로 'that'을 선행사를 포함한 관계대명사 'what'으로 수정해야 한다.

③ 출제 포인트: 전치사 vs. 접속사

'because' 이후에 온 'the unnecessary conflicts it creates'는 관계대명사절과 결합한 명사구이므로 'because'를 전치사 'because of'로 수정해야 한다. 이때 'conflicts'와 'it' 사이에는 'creates'의 목적어가 없으므로 목적격 관계대명사 'which' 또는 'that'이 생략되어 있다.

④ 출제 포인트: 시제 일치

조건절이 미래를 나타내는 경우 현재시제를 사용해야 하나 'If'가 이끄는 조건절에 미래를 나타내는 조동사 'will'을 포함해 동사 'will think'를 사용하였으므로 옳지 않은 문장이다. 따라서 if절의 'will think'를 'think'로 수정해야 한다.

해석

① 연설자는 이것이 남반구에서 본 북미의 모습이라고 재빨리 말했다.
② 관계로 여겨지면, 리더십은 리더들과 추종자들 사이에서 일어나는 협력의 과정이 된다.
③ 불평등은 엘리트를 제외하고 아무에게도 혜택을 제공하지 않으며 그것이 만들어내는 불필요한 갈등 때문에 전체 사회에 해롭다.
④ 만약 우리가 사람들과 관계가 복잡한 기계와 같다고 생각한다면, 우리는 아마 그들의 문제를 기계들에 있는 오작동으로 볼 것이다.

08 정답 ③

정답해설

본문은 '현대 미술'의 한 분야인 'readymade(레디메이드)'의 시초에 관해 설명하는 글이다. 본문 초반에는 '현대 미술'을 받아들이는 우리의 엇갈린 반응에 대해 언급한 후, 그러한 현상이 발생하게 된 이유에 대해 설명하며, '레디메이드'를 최초로 시도한 'Marcel Duchamp'에 대해 언급하며 그러한 그의 시도가 현대 미술에 미친 영향에 대해 설명하고 있다. 그런데 ③에서는 그의 작품이 거절되었다는 내용과 그가 이사회에서 사임했다는 내용이 언급되고 있으므로, 해당 문장은 '그가 현대 미술에 미친 영향'과는 거리가 멀다는 것을 알 수 있다. 또한 ③ 이후 문장 "This was the beginning of the "readymade"(이것이 "레디메이드(readymade)"의 시작이었다)."의 'This'가 가리키는 것이 ②에서 언급된 'Marcel Duchamp's act'라는 것을 통해서도 ③은 문맥상 위치가 부자연스럽다는 것을 알 수 있다. 따라서 정답은 ③이다.

오답해설

나머지 보기는 문맥상 자연스러우므로 오답이다.

해석

누군가 슈퍼마켓에서 10배 저렴하게 찾을 수 있는 물건으로 만들어진 예술작품을 사는 것은 우리들 중 많은 사람들에게 이해할 수 없는 일이다. 일반적으로 두 가지 유형의 반응이 따라온다: 분노 또는 누군가의 판단 능력에 대한 완전한 자기 회의. 그들은 나를 바보라고 생각하는가? 또는: 그것이 결국 예술이 아니라고 말하는 나는 누구인가? ① 우리는 어떻게 그러한 예술과 관객 사이의 고도의 의사소통 오류 상태에 도달하게 되었을까? ② 모두가 잘 알듯이, 이 현상의 기원은 소변기를 거꾸로 뒤집어, 그것을 "샘(fountain)"이라고 칭한 Marcel Duchamp의 행위이다. ③ <u>그러나, 전시 위원회는 그것이 예술이 아니라고 주장했으며, 그것을 전시회에 거부했고, 이것이 Duchamp가 Independent Artists 이사회에서 사임하도록 했다.</u> 이것이 "레디메이드(readymade)"의 시작이었다. ④ 그렇게 함으로써, 그 예술가는 평범한 제조품을 예술품으로 탈바꿈시켰다. 이제, 한 물체는 더 이상, 정물화와 같은 고전 장르에서 그러했던 것과 같이, "상징되지" 않고, 대중에게 직접적으로 "보여진다."

어휘

baffling 이해할 수 없는, 당황하게 하는
self-doubt 자기 회의 capacity 능력
take A for B A를 B로 생각하다 after all 결국
advanced 고도의 miscommunication 의사소통 오류
phenomenon 현상 urinal 소변기
readymade 레디메이드(현대 미술의 오브제; 일상의 기제품(旣製品)을 본래의 용도가 아닌 다른 의미를 부여하여 작품으로 발표한 것)
represent 상징하다, 대표하다 still life 정물화
present 보여주다[나타내다, 묘사하다]

09 정답 ④

정답해설

(A) 첫 번째 문장에서 '아시아의 민주주의 형세에 대한 암울한 그림'에 대해 언급한 후, (A) 이후에서, 여러 국가에서 민주적이지 않은 상황이 벌어지는 예시를 다수 제시하고 있으므로, 빈칸에 가장 적절한 표현은 '예시'를 나타내는 'To take some examples(예를 들어)' 또는 'For instance(예를 들어)'이다.

(B) 이전의 내용은 개별 국가에서 '비민주적인 행태가 자행되는 상황'에 대해 언급하고 있다. 그러나 (B) 이후에서는 '큰 그림, 즉 전체적인 아시아의 민주주의 척도는 오히려 향상된 것으로 보인다'라고 설명하고 있다. (B) 전후의 내용이 '대조'적인 내용이므로, 빈칸에는 'However(그러나)' 또는 'On the other hand(반면에)' 들어가는 것이 자연스럽다.

따라서 정답은 '④ For instance(예를 들어) – On the other hand(반면에)'이다.

오답해설

① (A) 전후가 '인과관계'가 아니기 때문에 'Therefore(그러므로)'는 빈칸에 적절하지 않다.
② (B) 이후의 내용이 (B) 이전 내용의 결과가 아니기 때문에 'As a consequence(결과적으로)'는 빈칸에 적절하지 않다.
나머지 보기는 문맥상 어색하므로 오답이다.

해석

지난 몇 달간 뉴스 보도는 아시아의 민주주의 형세에 대한 암울한 그림을 묘사한다. (A) 예를 들어, 캄보디아에서는 총리에 의해 정치적 반체제 인사에 대한 심각한 탄압이 이루어졌고, 최후의 독립 신문사의 폐쇄는 내년의 총선거 훨씬 이전에 민주주의가 무너지고 있다는 것을 암시한다. 필리핀에서의 Rodrigo Duterte 대통령의 반 마약 운동은 사법 절차에 의하지 않은 빈번한 살인 행위 중 수천 명의 희생자를 낳았다. 그리고 미얀마에서는, 국제사회에서 가장 저명한 민주주의 및 인권 옹호자들 중 한 명인 Aung San Suu Kyi가 계속 진행되고 있는 Rohingya 위기에 조치를 취하지 못한 것에 대해 지구촌 전역에서 가혹한 비판을 받았다. (B) 반면에, 더 큰 그림은 실제로 다른 이야기를 한다. 지난 10년간 순 민주화 진행은 상당히 증가했다. 민주적 개선이 역행을 능가했고, "국민의, 국민에 의한, 국민을 위한 정부"에 대한 안건은 활기를 얻고 있다.

	(A)	(B)
①	그러므로	그러나
②	예를 들어	결과적으로
③	확실히 말하면	요컨대
④	예를 들어	반면에

어휘

bleak 암울한, 절망적인
dissident 반체제 인사
prime minister 총리, 수상
crusade (옳다고 믿는 것을 이루기 위한 장기적이고 단호한) 운동
spate (보통 불쾌한 일의) 빈발
extrajudicial 재판 외의, 사법 절차에 의하지 않는
prominent 유명한, 저명한, 중요한
harsh 가혹한, 냉혹한
progress 진전, 진행
gain 개선, 이득
rollback 역행, 후퇴, 되돌리기
gain momentum 활기를 찾다, 번성하다
crackdown 엄중 단속, 강력 탄압
impose 시행하다, 부과하다
crumble 흔들리다[무너지다]
defender 옹호자
ongoing 계속 진행 중인
significantly 상당히, 크게
surpass 능가하다, 뛰어넘다

10 정답 ②

정답해설

본문은 '병원 광대(Medical clowning)'에 관한 내용이다. 본문에 따르면, '광대 요법'은 환자의 스트레스와 불안을 완화시킬 수 있다고 한다. 일반적으로 두려움을 일으키는 광대와는 달리, '병원 광대'는 농담과 장난을 이용해 웃음을 유발하고, 특히, 이스라엘의 사례에서 비추어 볼 때 광대 요법이 실제로 환자의 치료에 있어서 긍정적인 효과를 발휘한다는 것을 알 수 있다. 따라서 글의 요지로 가장 적절한 보기는 '② Certain clowns are playing positive roles in the medical world(특정 광대들이 의학계에서 긍정적인 역할을 하고 있다).'이다.

오답해설

① 본문과 관련 없는 내용이다.
③ 본문에서는 광대 요법이 '특정 연령'에만 적용된다는 내용이 언급되지 않고, 광대 요법을 적용받는 환자의 연령에 대해서 특별히 언급하고 있지 않으므로 글의 요지로 적절하지 않다.
④ 본문에서 언급되지 않는 내용이므로 오답이다.

해석

당신은 빨간 코의 익살꾼들이 오직 서커스에만 속한다고 생각하는가? 다시 생각해 보라. 전 세계에서 병원 광대는 환자의 전반적 치료를 촉진하고 아이들의 울음을 웃음으로 성공적으로 바꾸고 있다. 웃음은 가장 좋은 형태의 약이다라는 말이 있지 않은가. 새로운 연구가 "광대 요법"이 환자의 스트레스와 불안을 완화시킨다는 것을 보여줌에 따라, 이 아이디어는 현재 병원 진료에 적용되고 있다. 당신의 악몽 속에 있는 색칠된 얼굴과는 달리, 이 광대들은 그들의 환자들에게 웃음을 유발하고 엔도르핀을 분비시키기 위해 농담과 장난을 이용하며, 진통제의 필요성을 감소시키고 전반적인 건강을 향상시킨다. 이스라엘에서 병원 광대는 비웃을 수 없는 인정받는 관례가 되었다. 이 Dream Doctors는 병동 환자들의 힘을 북돋우고 치료하는 것을 도와주며, 심지어 수술 중에도 참석한다. 한 이스라엘 연구는 광대의 참석이 체외수정 불임 치료 중 여성의 임신 가능성을 20.2%에서 36.4%로 증가시키는 데 도움을 준다는 것을 보여주었다.

① 서커스 광대는 그들이 무서울 수 있는 것만큼 재미있을 수도 있다.
② 특정 광대들이 의학계에서 긍정적인 역할을 하고 있다.
③ 광대 요법은 어린이 환자와 성인 환자 모두에게 권장되어야 한다.
④ 병원 광대들은 환자를 돕기 위해 적절히 교육받고 훈련받아야만 한다.

어휘

giggle 피식 웃음, 킥킥[키득/낄낄]거림
practice 행위, 업무; 관례, 관습
anxiety 불안, 염려
provoke 유발하다
established 인정받는, 확실히 자리를 잡은
laugh at 비웃다
terrifying 무서운, 겁나게 하는
pregnant 임신한
indicate 나타내다, 보여주다
prank 장난
endorphin 엔도르핀
hospital ward 병동
presence 존재

결국엔 성정혜 영어 하프모의고사
기적사 DAY 65

| 01 | ③ | 02 | ④ | 03 | ① | 04 | ③ | 05 | ③ |
| 06 | ① | 07 | ① | 08 | ② | 09 | ③ | 10 | ④ |

오답률 TOP 1
01 정답 ③

정답해설

'examine'은 '조사하다, 검토하다'를 뜻하는 동사로 ③ canvass(조사하다, 유세를 하다)와 유의어 관계이다.

해석

그는 연구 결과가 이것을 좀 더 자세히 **조사하기** 위해 사용될 수 있다고 말한다.
① 밀다, 찌르다
② 급락하다, 거꾸러지다
③ 조사하다, 유세를 하다
④ 암시하다, 넌지시 말하다

어휘

examine 조사하다, 검토하다 thrust 밀다, 찌르다
plunge 급락하다, 거꾸러지다 canvass 조사하다, 유세를 하다
insinuate 암시하다, 넌지시 말하다

오답률 TOP 2
02 정답 ④

정답해설

'stingy'는 '인색한'을 뜻하는 형용사로 ④ parsimonious(인색한)와 유의어 관계이다.

해석

그 나라는 교육적인 목적을 위해 재능 있는 외국인 학생들을 유치하는 데 있어 **인색해서는** 안 된다.
① 장래를 준비하는, 앞날에 대비하는
② 현명한
③ 낭비하는, 사치스러운
④ 인색한

어휘

stingy 인색한
provident 장래를 준비하는, 앞날에 대비하는
sagacious 현명한   extravagant 낭비하는, 사치스러운
parsimonious 인색한

오답률 TOP 3
03 정답 ①

정답해설

'aggressive'는 '공격적인, 적극적인'을 뜻하는 형용사로 ① vicious(공격적인, 사나운)와 의미상 가장 가깝다.

해석

하키, 풋볼 그리고 럭비와 같은 충돌 스포츠는 **공격적인** 태클과 극도로 육체적인 종류의 경기를 특징으로 삼는다.
① 사나운, 공격적인
② 긴장한, 초조해하는
③ 앙심을 품은, 보복을 하려는
④ 주변적인, 지엽적인

어휘

collision 충돌 (사고), 부딪침   aggressive 공격적인, 적극적인
vicious 사나운, 공격적인   uptight 긴장한, 초조해하는
revengeful 복수심에 불타는   peripheral 주변적인, 지엽적인

04 정답 ③

정답해설

'북한의 만행을 멈춰야 한다'는 B의 발언에 A는 동의하며 '우리가 더 이상 ~하지 말아야 한다'면서 '우리는 조치를 취해야 한다'라고 말한다. 따라서 문맥상 '형세를 살피지 말아야 한다'가 자연스러우므로 빈칸에 들어갈 가장 적절한 것은 '③ sit on the fence(형세를 살피다)'이다.

오답해설

① 북한의 만행을 멈추기 위해 조치를 취해야 한다고 말하는 B의 말에 A는 동의하면서 더 이상 '물 샐 틈이 없이 정연하지(hold water)' 말아야 한다고 하는 것은 대화의 흐름상 어색하다.
② A가 북한의 만행을 멈추기 위해 조치를 취해야 한다는 것에 동의하며 우리가 더 이상 '오해가 없어지지(clear the air)' 말아야 한다고 이야기하는 것은 문맥상 적합하지 않다.
④ 북한의 만행을 멈추기 위한 조치를 취해야 한다고 말하는 B에게 A는 동의하면서 우리가 더 이상 '수박 겉핥기식으로 하지(scratch the surface)' 말아야 한다고 얘기하는 것은 문맥상 부적절하다.

해석

A: 너 최근 정치적 문제에 대해 들었어?
B: 아니, 오늘 아침에 너무 바빠서 뉴스를 확인하지 못했어. 심각한 문제가 있었어?
A: 지난 늦은 밤에 북한이 남한에 미사일을 발사했어.
B: 뭐라고? 진짜야? 다친 사람 있었어?
A: 다행히, 부상자는 없었어. 근데 뉴스를 듣고 난 정말 화가 났어.
B: 나도 마찬가지야. 우리는 그들의 만행을 멈추기 위해 조치를 취해야 해.
A: 물론이야. 우리는 더 이상 <u>형세를 살피지</u> 말아야 해. 우리가 조치를 취할 때야.
① 물 샐 틈이 없이 정연하다
② 오해가 없어지다
③ 형세를 살피다
④ 수박 겉핥기식으로 하다

어휘

brutality 만행, 잔인한 행위   hold water 물 샐 틈이 없이 정연하다
clear the air 오해가 없어지다   sit on the fence 형세를 살피다
scratch the surface 수박 겉핥기식으로 하다

05 정답 ③

정답해설

③ **출제 포인트: little vs. few/비교급 강조부사/주어와 동사의 수일치/불가산명사**

'fewer'는 불가산명사를 수식할 수 없는 형용사 'few'의 비교급으로 해당 문장에서 불가산명사 'money'를 수식하고 있으므로 옳지 않은 문장이다. 따라서 'fewer'를 불가산명사를 수식할 수 있는 형용사 'little'의 비교급인

'less'로 수정해야 한다. 이때 해당 문장에서 'even'은 비교급 강조부사로 불가산명사 'money'를 수식하는 비교급 형용사 'less'를 수식한다. 또한 해당 문장의 'there ~ account'는 유도부사구문으로 단수형태의 동사 'was'의 경우 주어가 불가산명사 'money'이므로 옳은 표현이다.

오답해설

① 출제 포인트: 가정법 과거/to부정사의 부사적 용법

가정법 과거는 「If+주어+과거시제 동사 ~, 주어+would/should/could/might+동사원형」의 형태를 가진다. 해당 문장은 가정법 과거 'If+주어+과거시제 동사 ~, 주어+would+동사원형'이 쓰인 문장으로 주어진 해석과 일치하는 옳은 문장이다. 이때 해당 문장에서 'to see'는 목적을 나타내는 to부정사의 부사적 용법으로 사용되었다.

② 출제 포인트: 주의해야 할 타동사/능동태 vs. 수동태

'exchange'는 '교환하다'를 뜻하는 완전타동사로 해당 문장의 경우 이후에 목적어 'local currency'가 오므로 능동태로 사용하는 것이 옳다.

④ 출제 포인트: what vs. that/주어와 동사의 수일치/불완전타동사의 구조

'What' 이후에 오는 절이 주어가 없는 불완전한 형태이며 앞에 선행사가 없으므로 관계대명사 'What'은 옳은 표현이다. 또한 주절의 동사는 주어와 수일치 해야 하며 해당 문장의 경우 주어가 선행사를 포함하는 관계대명사 'What'이 이끄는 절이므로 주절의 동사에 단수 형태 'was'를 옳게 사용하였다. 마지막으로 해당 문장에서 'made'는 불완전타동사 'make'의 과거시제로 「make+목적어+목적격 보어[형용사]」의 형태를 가진다. 따라서 'her'는 목적어에 해당하며 'remarkable'은 목적격 보어에 해당한다.

06 정답 ①

정답해설

① 출제 포인트: what vs. that

'what' 이후에 오는 절에 전치사 'against'의 목적어가 없으므로 불완전한 형태의 절임을 알 수 있다. 따라서 'what'은 관계대명사이며 이때 앞에 선행사 'the information overload'가 있으므로 'what'을 목적격 관계대명사 'which' 또는 'that'으로 수정해야 한다. 해당 문장에서 'overload'는 동사가 아닌 '과부하'를 뜻하는 명사임에 유의해야 한다.

오답해설

② 출제 포인트: 현재분사 vs. 과거분사

밑줄 친 부분을 포함한 'When deciding whether to invest in a company'는 접속사가 살아있는 분사구문이다. 'deciding'은 완전타동사 'decide'의 현재분사로 이후에 목적어에 해당하는 「whether+to+동사원형」이 왔으며 생략된 주어 'they'와 능동관계이므로 'deciding'은 옳은 표현이다.

③ 출제 포인트: 능동태 vs. 수동태/관용표현(take up+목적어)

밑줄 친 'take up' 이후에 목적어에 해당하는 명사구 'so much of your working memory'가 왔으므로 능동태인 'take up'을 사용하는 것이 옳다. 이때 'take up+목적어'는 '~을 차지하다'를 뜻하는 관용표현에 해당한다.

④ 출제 포인트: 부사절을 이끄는 접속사

앞에 있는 'so much of your working memory'의 'so much'를 통해 밑줄 친 'that'이 결과를 나타내는 부사절의 접속사로써 사용된 것을 알 수 있다. 따라서 'that'은 옳은 표현이다.

해석

주식 중개인의 책상에서 번쩍이는 화면의 무더기를 본 적이 있다면 그들이 부딪히고 있는 정보 과부하를 알게 된다. 예컨대 회사에 투자해야 할지의 여부를 결정할 때, 그들은 다른 정보들 중에서도, 실권을 가진 사람들; 그 회사 시장의 현재 규모와 잠재적 규모; 순수익; 그리고 그 회사의 과거, 현재 및 미래의 주식 가격 등을 고려할지도 모른다. 이 요인들을 모두 저울질하는 것은 작동 기억의 아주 많은 부분을 차지할 수도 있으므로, 그 작동 기억은 압도당하게 된다.

어휘

take 목적어 into account ~을 고려하다
net profit 순수익   stock value 주식 주가
weigh 저울질하다, 평가하다   take up ~을 차지하다
working memory 작동[심리] 기억

07 정답 ①

정답해설

① 출제 포인트: 등위접속사의 병렬구조/recognize A as B의 수동태

등위접속사 'and'를 통해 절과 절이 병렬구조를 이루고 있으며 「recognize A as B」의 수동태인 「A be recognized as B」를 옳게 사용하였으므로 해당 문장은 옳은 문장이다.

오답해설

② 출제 포인트: 주어와 동사의 수일치/시제 일치

등위접속사 'and'를 통해 동사 'became'과 'were'가 병렬구조를 이루고 있으나 주어가 단수 형태인 'He'이므로 'were'를 'was'로 수정해야 한다. 또한 'in the mid-1850s'는 과거시제와 함께 사용하는 시간의 부사구로 과거시제동사 'became'은 옳은 표현이다.

③ 출제 포인트: 전치사 vs. 접속사/시제 일치

'that sport is a salient part of our daily lives'는 동격절로 'the fact'와 결합한 명사구이므로 접속사 'Although'를 전치사 'Despite' 또는 'In spite of'로 수정해야 한다. 또한 'until recently'는 시간의 부사구로 현재완료와 함께 사용할 수 있다.

④ 출제 포인트: 주어와 동사의 수일치/주격 관계대명사절의 동사 수일치/준사역동사의 목적격 보어

해당 문장에서 'Leaders'는 주격 관계대명사 'who'의 선행사이자 주절의 주어에 해당하며 복수 형태이므로 주격 관계대명사절의 동사와 주절의 동사에 복수 형태를 사용해야 한다. 주격 관계대명사절의 동사에 복수 형태인 'choose'를 사용하였으나 주절의 동사에 단수 형태인 'helps'를 사용하였으므로 틀린 문장이다. 따라서 'helps'를 'help'로 수정해야 한다. 이때 'help'는 준사역동사이므로 목적격 보어에 해당하는 원형부정사인 'increase'는 옳은 표현이다. 또한 해당 문장에서 'which'는 관계대명사가 아닌 'seminars and conferences'를 수식하는 의문형용사임에 유의해야 한다.

해석

① 교육은 젊은 사람들에 대한 투자이며, 보편적으로 국가 책무의 일부로 여겨진다.
② 그는 1850년대 중반에 젊은 예술가들 중 한 명이 되었고, 특히 John과 친했는데, 그는 그의 그림에 영향을 주었다.
③ 스포츠가 우리 일상의 매우 중요한 부분이라는 사실에도 불구하고, 그것은 최근까지도, 사회학자들에 의해 진지하게 연구된 적이 거의 없다.
④ 어떤 세미나 그리고 회의에 참석할지를 주의 깊게 선택하는 리더들은 개인적인 발달 관련 목표에 대한 그들의 기여를 늘리는 데에 그들 자신에게 도움을 준다.

08 정답 ②

정답해설

본문의 요지는 '현대 예술은 외견상 단순해 보일지 모르나, 그것이 함축하고 있는 의미는 결코 단순하지 않으며, 과거의 예술품보다 현대의 상황에 더 잘 부합하는 의의를 관람객에게 전달할 수 있다'는 것이다. 마지막 문장 "In this sense, contemporary art deserves our appreciation and it's time it lost its undeserved bad reputation(이러한 견지에서, 현대 예술은 우리의 감상을 받을 만하며, 이제 그것이 부당한 악명을 떨쳐버릴 때이다)."을 통해, '현대 예술이 감상할 가치가 충분하다'는 점을 드러내고 있으므로, 글의 제목으로 가장 적절한 것은 '② Is Contemporary Art Worth Looking At?(현대 예술은 감상할 가치가 있는가?)'이다.

오답해설

① 본문 초반에서 '현대 예술은 단순해 보인다'고 언급하고 있으나, 그 이후 '현대 예술이 함축하는 의미는 단순하지 않다'고 설명하고 있으므로, '누구나 현대 예술가가 될 수 있다'는 글의 제목으로 적절하지 않다.
③ 본문과 관련 없는 내용이므로 오답이다.
④ 본문에서 '현대 예술이 단순해 보인다'는 언급은 존재하지만, 그 '이유'는 설명하고 있지 않으므로 글의 제목으로 적절하지 않다.

해석

현대 예술은 종종 조금 의미가 없고 기술이 부족한 것으로 치부될 수 있다. 상투적인 "내 5살짜리 아이도 이것을 할 수 있다"는 구절은 만일 예술가의 작품이 너무 단순해 보인다면 언급된다. 그렇다, 많은 현대 예술작품이 언뜻 보기에는 약간 기초적인 것처럼 보인다. 그러나 그것이 그것들이 복잡한 개념을 지니고 있지 않다는 것을 의미하지는 않는다 - 사실, 그러한 작품 내에 담긴 아이디어는 훨씬 오래되었지만 더 인기 있는 그림들에 담긴 것보다 흔히 더 심오하다. 그리고 분명히 예술작품이 더 최신의 것일수록, 메시지가 현대의 관람객에게 더 의의가 있다, 그렇지 않은가? Rachel Maclean의 HOME에서의 최근 전시회가 이것의 한 예이다. 그것은 꽤 단순했으며 모든 사람의 취향에 맞지는 않았다, 그러나 그것이 표현한 소셜 미디어 및 기술과 우리의 관계에 대한 메시지는 정말 심금을 울렸다. 예술은 시각적 즐거움일 뿐이어야 한다는 계속되는 믿음이 있는 것 같다. 그러나 예술은 비록 그것이 아름답고 복잡하지는 않더라도, 감정을 상기시키고 사고를 자극해야 한다. 이러한 견지에서, 현대 예술은 우리의 감상을 받을 만하며 이제 그것이 부당한 악명을 떨쳐버릴 때이다.

① 누구나 현대 예술가가 될 수 있다
② 현대 예술은 감상할 가치가 있는가?
③ 현대 예술이 사회에 어떻게 영향을 미치는가?
④ 현대 예술이 왜 그렇게 단순해 보이는가?

어휘

dismiss 일축하다, 치부하다, 묵살하다
cliched 낡은 투의, 상투적인 문구의
at first glance 처음에는[언뜻 보기에는]
profound 심오한, 깊은   relevant 의의가 있는[유의미한], 관련된
exhibition 전시(회)
to one's taste …의 취향[기호]에 맞는
strike a chord 심금을 울리다, 뭔가 생각나게 하다
ongoing 계속 진행 중인   conjure up 상기시키다[떠올리게 하다]
provoke 유발하다, 자극하다   appreciation 감상
undeserved 받을 만하지 않은, 부당한
reputation 명성, 평판   worth -ing ~할 가치가 있는

09 정답 ③

정답해설

본문은 'Economist Intelligence Unit이 매년 발표하는 민주주의 지수에서 미국이 2016년 최초로 결함 있는 민주국가로 강등되었다'라는 내용이다. 본문 중반 "America's score fell to 7.98 in 2016 from 8.05 in the previous year, below the 8.00 threshold for a full democracy(미국의 점수는 전년도의 8.05에서, 완전한 민주국가가 되기 위한 8.0 경계점 이하인 7.98로 2016년에 떨어졌)."를 통해, '미국은 2015년에 8.05점을 획득하여 완전한 민주국가로 평가되었음'을 알 수 있다. 그리고 마지막 문장 "Other flawed democracies in 2016 included Japan, France, Belgium, South Korea and India, all of which were deemed flawed democracies in 2015 as well(2016년에 다른 결함 있는 민주국가들은 일본, 프랑스, 벨기에, 대한민국 그리고 인도를 포함했고, 이들 국가 모두는 2015년에도 결함 있는 민주국가들로 여겨졌다)."를 통해, '벨기에는 2015년과 2016년 모두 결함 있는 민주국가로 평가되었음'을 알 수 있다. 즉, 2015년에 벨기에는 8.00 이하의 점수를 받았다는 것을 유추할 수 있다. 따라서 '③ In 2015, the U.S. received a lower score than Belgium(2015년에 미국은 벨기에보다 낮은 점수를 받았다).'은 글의 내용과 일치하지 않는다.

오답해설

① 첫 문장 "The U.S. has been demoted from a full democracy to a flawed democracy for the first time(미국은 완전한 민주국가에서 결함 있는 민주국가로 처음으로 강등되었다)"을 통해 '미국이 결함 있는 민주국가로 평가받은 것은 최초'라는 것을 알 수 있으며, 본문 중반 "America's score fell to 7.98 in 2016 from 8.05 in the previous year,(미국의 점수는 2016년에 전년도의 8.05에서 7.98로 떨어졌다)"를 통해, 해당 평가는 2016년에 해당하는 것을 알 수 있다. 따라서 2016년 이전에는 항상 '완전한 민주국가'로 평가받았음을 유추할 수 있으므로, 글의 내용과 일치한다.
② 두 번째 문장 "Every year, the firm's Democracy Index provides a snapshot of global democracy by scoring countries on five categories: electoral process and pluralism; civil liberties; the functioning of government; political participation; and political culture(매년, 그 기업의 민주주의 지수는, 선거 절차 및 다원주의, 시민적 자유, 정부의 기능, 정치 참여, 그리고 정치 문화의 5개 범주에서 국가들에 점수를 매김으로써 전 세계 민주주의에 대한 정보를 제공한다)."에서 '다섯 개의 범주에서 평가'한다고 언급하고 있으므로, 글의 내용과 일치한다.
④ 본문 중후반 "That put the world's largest economy on the same footing as Italy, a country known for its fractious politics(그것이 세계에서 가장 거대한 경제를 괴팍한 정치로 알려진 국가인 이탈리아와 동일한 입장에 놓이게 했다)."를 통해, 미국과 이탈리아가 동일한 유형으로 평가받았음을 유추할 수 있으므로, 이탈리아 또한 결함 있는 민주국가임을 알 수 있다.

해석

Economist Intelligence Unit에 따르면, 미국은 완전한 민주국가에서 결함 있는 민주국가로 처음으로 강등되었다. 매년, 그 기업의 민주주의 지수는, 선거 절차 및 다원주의; 시민적 자유; 정부의 기능; 정치 참여; 그리고 정치 문화의 5개 범주에서 국가들에 점수를 매김으로써 전 세계 민주주의에 대한 정보를 제공한다. 그러면 국가들은 완전한 민주국가, 결함 있는 민주국가, 혼합 체제 그리고 독재 정권의 4가지 유형의 정부로 분류된다. 미국의 점수는 2016년에 전년도의 8.05에서, 완전한 민주국가가 되기 위한 8.0 경계점 이하인 7.98로 떨어졌다. 그것이 세계에서 가장 거대한 경제를 괴팍한 정치로 알려진 국가인 이탈리아와 동일한 입장에 놓이게 했다. 결함 있는 민주국가는 자유 선거가 있는 국가이지만, 약한 통치, 후진적인 정치 문화 그리고 낮은 수준의 정치 참여에 의해 위축된다. 2016년에 다른 결함 있는 민주국가들은 일본,

프랑스, 벨기에, 대한민국 그리고 인도를 포함했고, 이들 국가 모두는 2015년에도 결함 있는 민주국가들로 여겨졌다.
① 미국은 2016년 이전에는 항상 완전한 민주국가로 평가되어 왔다.
② Economist Intelligence Unit은 다수의 범주에서 국가들을 평가한다.
③ 2015년에, 미국은 벨기에보다 낮은 점수를 받았다.
④ 이탈리아는 2016년에 결함 있는 민주국가라는 명칭을 받았다.

어휘

demote 강등[좌천]시키다
snapshot 짤막한 묘사[정보]
pluralism 다원주의, 다원성
classify 분류[구분]하다
regime 정권, 제도, 체제
threshold 한계점
fractious 성[짜증]을 잘 내는, 괴팍한
governance 통치, 관리
flawed 결함[결점/흠]이 있는
electoral 선거의
participation 참여, 참가
hybrid 혼합(물)
authoritarian 독재적인
footing 입장[관계], 지위, 신분
weigh down by …로 내리누르다
multiple 다수의

at the sight of …을 보고
hypothesis 가설
refer to 나타내다, 말하다
exclusively 오로지, 오직
resemble 닮다, 비슷[유사]하다
push 정력적으로[끈기 있게] 노력하다[일하다]
interpret 이해하다, 해석하다
inanimate 무생물의
stem from …에서 생겨나다[기인하다]
instinctive 본능[직감]에 따른, 본능적인
repulsion 역겨움, 혐오감
kick in 효과가 나타나기 시작하다
besides … 외에
feature 이목구비(의 각 부분); 특징, 특성
disturbing 충격적인, 불안감을 주는
probable 있을[사실일] 것 같은, 개연성 있는, 가능한
phenomenon 현상
uncanny 불쾌한, 이상한, 묘한
nature 본질, 특징, 특징
cover 다루다, 포함시키다

plainly 분명히, 명백히
aversion to …을 싫어함[혐오, 반감]

corpse 시체, 송장
figure 모습, 형태, 형상
distorted 비뚤어진, 곡해된, 왜곡된

get over 극복하다

10 정답 ④

정답해설

본문에서는 '광대에 대한 두려움(fear of clowns), 즉 광대 공포증(coulrophobia)'의 원인을 '불쾌한 골짜기 효과(uncanny valley effect)'로 설명하고 있다. '불쾌한 골짜기 효과'란 '인간이 인간이 아닌 대상을 볼 때, 인간과 유사할수록 불쾌함을 느낀다'라는 것이다. 즉, 광대를 '인간과 유사하지만 인간은 아닌 대상'으로 인식하기 때문에, 광대에 대한 공포감이 유발된다는 것이다. 따라서 글의 주제로 가장 적절한 것은 '④ A probable reason why clowns are feared(광대를 두려워하는 가능성 있는 이유)'이다.

오답해설

① 본문과 관련 없는 내용이다.
② 본문에서 로봇이 언급된 이유는 '불쾌한 골짜기 효과'를 설명하기 위한 것이며, 광대와의 공통점을 언급하기 위한 것이 아니므로 오답이다.
③ 첫 문장에 '광대 공포증의 증상'에 대해 간단히 언급되기는 하지만, 글 전체를 아우르는 내용이 아니므로 오답이다.

해석

우리 모두는 일부 사람들이 광대에 대한 두려움, 또는 광대 공포증이 있다는 것을 알고 있으며, 그것은 그 얼굴이 불안하다고 생각하는 것에서부터 그들을 보고 완전한 공포를 느끼는 것까지 다를 수 있다. 연구자들은 이 현상을 설명하려 노력해왔으며, 그에 대한 그들의 주요 가설은 "불쾌한 골짜기" 효과이다. 이 효과는 인간과 거의 유사하지만 인간은 아닌 이미지의 불안한 특성을 말한다. 본래 이것은 오직 사람처럼 보이도록 설계된 로봇만을 포함했다. 단지 명백히 무생물인 로봇 또는 자연적인 인간을 볼 때와 비교하여, 사람을 닮도록 의도된 로봇을 볼 때, 뇌는 그들이 보고 있는 것을 이해하기 위해 더 열심히 노력해야 한다. 그 광경에 대한 반감은 또 하나의 거의 인간과 같은 모습, 즉 시체에 대한 본능적인 혐오감에서 기인할지도 모른다. 불쾌한 골짜기 효과는 그림 또는 비디오게임 캐릭터 – 또는 광대와 같은 로봇 이외의 모습에도 효과가 나타날 수 있다. 당신의 뇌는 인간을 보길 기대하지만, 광대의 왜곡되고 알록달록한 이목구비는 꽤 불안감을 줄 만큼 충분히 인간 같지 않아 보인다.
① 광대 공포증을 극복하는 방법
② 광대와 로봇의 공통점
③ 광대에 대한 두려움의 다양한 증상
④ 광대를 두려워하는 가능성 있는 이유

어휘

coulrophobia 광대 공포증
unsettling 불안하게[동요하게] 만드는
terror (극심한) 두려움[무서움], 공포(심)
vary 달라지다[다르다]
outright 완전한, 전면적인

결국엔 성정혜 영어 하프모의고사
기적사 DAY 66

| 01 | ③ | 02 | ④ | 03 | ① | 04 | ① | 05 | ④ |
| 06 | ③ | 07 | ① | 08 | ② | 09 | ② | 10 | ④ |

01 정답 ③
16 서울시

정답해설

'rebellious'는 '반항적인'을 뜻하는 형용사로 ③ disobedient(반항하는, 거역하는)와 의미상 가장 가깝다.

해석

부모들은 **반항적**으로 행동하거나, 사회적으로 서투른 것처럼 보이는 자녀를 포기해서는 안 된다. 이것은 대부분의 젊은이들이 경험하고 결국 벗어나게 되는 일반적인 단계이기 때문이다.
① 수동적인
② 의식이 혼탁한, 기뻐 날뛰는
③ 반항적인, 복종하지 않는
④ 산발적인, 때때로 일어나는

어휘

rebellious 반항적인
go through ~을 겪다[경험하다]
passive 수동적인
disobedient 반항적인, 복종하지 않는
awkward 서투른; 어색한; 곤란한
outgrow 벗어나다
delirious 의식이 혼탁한, 기뻐 날뛰는
sporadic 산발적인, 때때로 일어나는

02 정답 ④
16 서울시

정답해설

'prodigal'은 '사치스러운'을 뜻하는 형용사로 ④ lavish(낭비하는, 사치스러운)와 의미상 가장 가깝다.

해석

그는 1800년대에 New York의 부유한 가정에서 태어났다. 이러한 환경은 그의 삶 대부분에서 **사치스러운** 생활을 누리도록 해주었다.
① 위증(죄)
② 불안정한
③ 치명적인, 유해한
④ 낭비하는, 사치스러운

어휘

circumstance 상황, 환경
existence 생활; 존재
unstable 불안정한
lavish 낭비하는, 사치스러운
prodigal 사치스러운
perjury 위증(죄)
pernicious 치명적인, 유해한

03 정답 ①
16 서울시

정답해설

'resurgence'는 '부활, 재기'를 뜻하는 명사로 ① comeback(부활, 재개, 복귀)과 의미상 가장 가깝다.

해석

아마도 미국의 고등 교육의 당대 상황에서 가장 밝은 부분은 학생들을 교정을 넘어 시민으로서의 삶에 가담하게 하는 것에 대한 관심의 **부활**이다.
① 부활, 재개, 복귀
② 사라짐
③ 동기, 유도
④ 소수, 소량, 결핍

어휘

contemporary 당대의, 현대의; 동시대의
resurgence 부활, 재기
comeback 부활, 재개, 복귀
motivation 동기, 유도
civic 시민의; 도시의
disappearance 사라짐
paucity 소수, 소량, 결핍

04 정답 ①
13 서울시

정답해설

매일 조깅을 하면 마라톤에 참가할 수 있을 거라는 B의 말에 A는 '지쳐서 그만 한다'고 언급하고 있다. 따라서 빈칸에 들어갈 말로 가장 적합한 것은 ① 'Count me out!(나는 빼줘!)'이 가장 적절하다.

오답해설

②, ③, ④, ⑤ 나머지 선지는 마라톤으로 지쳐 그만두겠다고 말하는 A가 B에게 할 대답으로 적절하지 않다.

해석

A: Kate, 나 너무 피곤해. 겨우 아침 7시 30분밖에 안 됐어! 몇 분만 쉬자.
B: 아직 멈추면 안 돼. 조금만 더 분발해. 내가 조깅을 시작했을 때, 나도 엄청 힘들었어.
A: 그러면 나 좀 봐줘. 이번이 내 첫 번째잖아.
B: 힘내, Mary. 3개월 정도 조깅하고 나면, 마라톤에 나갈 준비가 될 거야.
A: 마라톤! 마라톤이 몇 마일이나 되지?
B: 30마일 정도야. 만약 내가 매일 조깅을 한다면, 두 달 후에는 마라톤에 참가할 수 있을 거야.
A: <u>나는 빼줘!</u> 반 마일만 했는데도 지금 지쳤어. 그만할래.
① 나는 빼줘!
② 왜 내가 마라톤에 참가하면 안 되지?
③ 왜 내가 그 생각을 하지 못했지?
④ 나는 그렇게 생각하지 않아.
⑤ 누가 할 소리(사돈 남 말하네)!

어휘

count somebody out (어떤 활동에서) ~를 빼다
look who is talking 누가 할 소리(사돈 남 말하네)

05 정답 ④
19 서울시

정답해설

④ **출제 포인트: that vs. what**
문맥상 '각 나라가 그것이 가장 잘하는 것을 전문으로 할 때'가 자연스러우므로 'it does best'가 「주어+완전타동사+부사」로 이루어진 불완전한 형태의 절임을 알 수 있다. 따라서 밑줄 친 'that'은 관계대명사이나 앞에 선행사가 아닌 전치사 'in'이 있으므로 선행사를 포함하는 관계대명사 'what'으로 수정해야 한다. 이때 'in'은 관계대명사절에서 상승한 전치사가 아닌 동사 'specializes'와 연결되는 전치사이다.

오답해설

① **출제 포인트: 주어와 동사의 수일치**
주어가 단수 형태인 'The growth'이므로 단수 형태의 동사 'is'의 쓰임은 올바르다. 'of foreign markets and competition'은 전명구로 수식어이

고 'most notably those in China and India'는 삽입구이므로 둘 다 동사의 수일치에 영향을 주지 않는다. 이처럼 주어와 동사의 사이가 먼 경우 수일치에 유의해야 한다.

② **출제 포인트: 접속사의 쓰임**
'whether economic globalization is a good' 이후에 있는 'or'를 통해 접속사 'whether'가 「whether A or B」의 형태로 사용된 것임을 알 수 있으므로 밑줄 친 'whether'는 옳은 표현이다. 이때 'whether'가 이끄는 절 'whether ~ an evil'은 앞에 있는 전치사 'as to'를 통해 목적어로 쓰인 명사절임을 알 수 있다.

③ **출제 포인트: 주격 관계대명사/관계대명사의 계속적 용법**
밑줄 친 'which' 이후에 있는 동사 'holds'를 통해 밑줄 친 'which'가 주격 관계대명사임을 알 수 있으며 이때 'holds'는 'hold'의 단수 형태이므로 'which'가 가리키는 선행사는 'the economic theory of comparative advantage'이다. 또한 'which' 앞에 콤마(,)가 있으므로 계속적 용법으로 사용된 것임을 알 수 있다.

해석
특히 중국과 인도의 시장에서, 해외 시장과 경쟁의 성장은 전 세계적으로 기업들이 사업을 수행하는 방식에 엄청난 영향을 미치고 있다. 실제로, 중국과 인도를 경제지도에 올려놓는 데 기여한 아웃소싱과 오프쇼어링(생산이 미국 이외의 지역으로 이동)의 등장은 미국과 해외에서 경제 세계화가 선인지 악인지에 대해 상당한 논쟁을 불러일으켰다. 그러나 많은 사람들은 세계화가 좋은 것이며, 아웃소싱과 오프쇼어링은 비교우위의 경제이론의 단순한 표현이라고 제시하고 있는데, 이것은 각 나라가 그것이 가장 잘하는 것을 전문으로 할 때 모든 사람이 이득을 얻는다고 주장한다.

어휘

growth 성장	competition 경쟁
notably 특히	tremendous 엄청난
impact 영향, 충격	advent 등장
outsource 외부에 위탁하다	off-shoring 해외 업무 위탁
debate 논쟁하다	globalization 세계화
manifestation 표현, 징후	comparative 비교적인
advantage 이익	gain 이득
specialize 전문화하다	

오답률 TOP 3
06 정답 ③   19 서울시

정답해설
③ **출제 포인트: 접속사의 쓰임/접속사가 살아있는 분사구문**
제시된 글의 문맥상 '방치되지 않았다면'이라는 '조건'이 아니라, '비록 방치되었지만'이라는 '양보'가 자연스럽다. 따라서 'unless(~하지 않았다면)'를 'although(비록~일지라도)'로 수정해야 한다. 또한 이는 접속사가 살아있는 분사구문으로서 원문은 'unless they(=some of the fields) were unattended'에서 접속사를 남겨둔 분사구문에 해당된다.

오답해설
① **출제 포인트: 현재분사 vs. 과거분사**
'Beginning in October'에서 'Beginning'은 완전자동사 'begin(시작하다)'의 현재분사로 생략된 주어는 'the expedition'이며 해석상 '10월에 시작하여'가 자연스러우므로 현재분사로 시작하는 분사구문인 'Beginning in October'는 옳은 표현이다.

② **출제 포인트: 관용표현(make one's way through)**
밑줄 친 'made its way through'는 관용표현 'make one's way through(~로 나아가다)'의 과거시제로 옳은 표현이다.

④ **출제 포인트: 대명사 수일치/과거완료**
'These had once been'에서 'These'는 지시대명사로 가리키는 대상이 'Some of the fields'이며 복수 형태이므로 옳은 표현이다. 또한 문맥상 탐험대가 지나친 시점보다 Arikara 부족이 거주했던 시점이 더 이전이므로 대과거를 뜻하는 과거완료 'had been'은 옳은 표현이다.

해석
10월에 시작하여, 탐험대가 현재의 북부 South Dakota로 나아갔을 때, 밭이 딸린 오두막의 거주지역과 경작된 땅으로 이루어진 수많은 버려진 마을들을 지나쳤다. 몇몇 땅들은 **방치되지 않았다면(→방치되었을지라도)**, 여전히 거기에서 호박과 옥수수가 자라고 있었다. 이것들은 강력한 Akikara 부족에게 한 때 집이었다.

어휘

expedition 탐험, 탐험대	northern 북부의
numerous 수많은	abandon 버리다
earth-lodge 밭이 딸린 오두막	compose of 구성되다
dwelling 마을, 밀집 거주지역	mighty 강력한
tribe 부족	

오답률 TOP 1
07 정답 ①   19 서울시

정답해설
① **출제 포인트: 현재분사 vs. 과거분사**
'frustrated'는 감정 상태 형용사인 과거분사로 수식하는 대상은 '감정을 제공받는 대상'이어야 하나 'situations'는 '감정을 제공하는 주체'에 해당하므로 'frustrated'를 감정 제공 형용사인 현재분사 'frustrating'으로 수정해야 한다.

오답해설
② **출제 포인트: 불완전자동사와 주격 보어**
밑줄 친 'seem intuitive'는 「불완전자동사+주격 보어[형용사]」 형태로 옳은 표현이다.

③ **출제 포인트: 능동태 vs. 수동태**
완전타동사 'provide' 이후에 목적어 'evidence'를 사용하였으므로 능동태에 해당하는 밑줄 친 'provide evidence'는 옳은 표현이다. 이때 이후에 오는 'that ~ anger'는 'evidence'와 동격인 동격절이며, 'that'은 동격절을 이끄는 접속사이다.

④ **출제 포인트: 현재분사 vs. 과거분사**
'irritating'은 감정 제공 형용사인 현재분사로 수식하는 대상은 '감정을 제공하는 주체' 'conditions'이다. 따라서 'irritating'은 옳은 표현이다. 'irritating' 앞에 있는 전치사 'to'는 'adjust'와 결합하여 '~에 적응하다'를 나타낸다.

해석
밤에 단지 한 두 시간의 수면을 잃는 것은 당신을 더 화나게 만든다; 새로운 연구에 따르면 특히 절망적인 상황들에서 말이다. 그 결과가 직관적인 것처럼 보일지 모르지만, 연구는 수면 부족이 분노를 야기한다는 증거를 제공한 첫 번째 것들 중 하나이다. 그 연구는 또한 피곤할 때 화나게 하는 상태에 적응하는 우리의 능력에 대한 새로운 통찰력을 제공한다.

어휘

frustrated 절망스러운	situation 상황
result 결과	intuitive 직관적인
evidence 증거	insight 통찰력
adjust 적응하다	irritating 화나게 하는

오답률 TOP 2
08 정답 ②
18 서울시

정답해설

② 앞 문장에서 현대사회에서 많은 사람들이 행복하지 않다고 서술한다. 따라서 당신이 행복하지 않은 경우를 가정하는 주어진 문장이 ②에 오고 주어진 문장에 뒤이어 당신이 행복한 경우를 가정하는 문장으로 이어지는 것이 흐름상 알맞다. 따라서 주어진 문장이 들어갈 곳으로 가장 적절한 것은 ②이다.

오답해설

나머지 선지는 문맥상 부자연스러우므로 오답이다.

해석

(①) 동물들은 그들이 건강하고 충분하게 먹을 것을 가지고 있는 한 행복하다. 사람들은 인간도 그렇게 되어야 한다고 느끼지만, 그러나 현대 세계에서 그들은 적어도 대다수의 경우에 그렇지 않다. (② **만일 당신이 스스로 행복하지 않다면, 당신은 아마 이 점에서 예외적이지 않다는 것을 인정할 준비가 되어야 할 것이다.**) 만일 당신이 행복하다면, 얼마나 많은 당신의 친구들이 그러한지 물어보아라. (③) 그리고 당신이 친구들을 살필 때, 표정을 읽는 기술을 스스로 터득해라; 일상에서 당신이 마주하는 사람들의 기분을 잘 받아들이도록 하라. (④)

어휘

prepare 준비하다
exceptional 예외적인; 특출한
receptive 수용적인, 선뜻 받아들이는
admit 인정하다
review 재검토하다; 검토
ordinary 보통의, 일상적인, 평범한

09 정답 ②
18 서울시

정답해설

본문은 '담배 산업에 대한 엄격한 규정들은 다른 산업에도 부정적인 도미노 효과를 초래했다'는 것을 서술하고 있다. ①은 제한적인 조치가 어떻게 이루어졌는지에 대해 서술하고 있다. ③은 규제에 대한 결과로 다른 산업에 영향을 주었다고 했으며, ④는 그 영향에 대한 구체적인 설명이다. 하지만 ②는 엄격한 규제가 대중의 건강에 미친 영향과 담배 밀수에 대해 말하고 있으므로 흐름상 적절하지 않다. 따라서 정답은 ②이다.

오답해설

나머지 선지는 문맥상 자연스러우므로 오답이다.

해석

담배 산업에 대한 엄격한 규정들은 술, 탄산음료 및 기타 제품들을 넘어섰고, 그것은 고객의 선택을 제한하고 제품이 더 비싸지도록 했다. ① 국가들은 지난 40년 동안 과세, 그림의 유해 경고 그리고 광고나 홍보의 금지를 포함하여 담배 제품에 반대하는 더 제한적인 조치를 취해왔다. ② *규제 조치들은 대중의 건강을 개선하지 못했고, 담배 밀수를 증가시켰다.* ③ 규제를 우선 담배에, 그리고 다른 소비자 제품들에 적용하는 것은 도미노 효과를 냈고, 다른 산업에서도 소위 "미끄러운 비탈"이라고 불리게 되었다. ④ 미끄러운 이 비탈의 맨 끝에는 평범한 포장이 있는데, 여기에서는 모든 상표와 로고 그리고 브랜드의 특정 색채들이 사라졌으며, 의도치 않은 결과와 지적인 재산권에 심각한 침해를 가져왔다.

어휘

tight 엄격한
taxation 과세, 세금
smuggling 밀수
unintended 의도하지 않은
property right 재산권
restrictive 제한하는, 한정적인
regulatory 규제의, 단속의
slippery slope 미끄러운 비탈
infringement 위반, 침해

10 정답 ④
18 서울시

정답해설

빈칸 이전에는 침입을 당하는 경우에 고국의 언어가 침입자의 언어로 대체될 수도 있다고 서술하고 있다. 그리고 빈칸 이후의 문장에서는 고국의 언어가 지배적인 언어가 되거나, 침입자의 언어와 공존할 수도 있다고 언급하고 있다. 따라서 빈칸을 기준으로 대조되는 내용이기 때문에 연결사는 '④ Alternatively(그 대신에, 그렇지 않으면)'가 들어가는 것이 가장 적절하다.

오답해설

나머지 선지는 문맥상 적절하지 않다.

해석

한 언어의 화자가 다른 언어의 화자들과 접하게 될 때 언어는 변화한다. 이것은, 아마도, 이주 때문일 수도 있다, 그들이 더 비옥한 땅으로 이주를 했기 때문에, 혹은 전쟁이나 가난 또는 질병으로 인해 이동하기 때문이다. 그것은 또한 그들이 침입당하기 때문일 수도 있다. 그 상황에 따라, 고국의 언어는 침입자의 언어에 의해 완전히 소멸할지도 모르며, 우리는 이 경우 대체라고 말한다. <u>그 대신에,</u> 고국의 언어는 침입자의 언어와 나란히 지속 할 수도 있고, 정치적인 상황에 따라, 그것은 지배적인 언어가 될 수도 있다.
① 일반적으로, 전형적으로, 대체로
② 시종일관하여, 지속적으로
③ 비슷하게, 유사하게
④ 그 대신에, 그렇지 않으면

어휘

come into contact 접촉하다, 마주치다
migration 이주, 이동
on account of ~ 때문에
poverty 가난, 빈곤
replacement 교체, 대체
dominant 지배적인, 우위의
fertile 비옥한
invade 침략하다, 침입하다
succumb 죽다, 양보하다
side-by-side 나란히

기적사 DAY 67

결국엔 성정혜 영어 하프모의고사

| 01 | ③ | 02 | ④ | 03 | ① | 04 | ① | 05 | ② |
| 06 | ④ | 07 | ③ | 08 | ③ | 09 | ② | 10 | ② |

오답률 TOP 2

01 정답 ③

정답해설

'passive'는 '소극적인, 수동적인'을 뜻하는 형용사로 ③ privative(소극적인, 결핍의)와 의미상 가장 가깝다.

해석

일반적인 믿음은 남자는 적극적이고 밖에서 일해야 하는 반면에 여자는 **소극적**이며 안에서 일해야 한다는 것이었다.
① 온순한, 온화한
② 혈기 왕성한, 거침없는
③ 소극적인, 결핍의
④ 적극적인, 확신에 찬

어휘

aggressive 적극적인, 공격적인
meek 온순한, 온화한
privative 소극적인, 결핍의
passive 소극적인, 수동적인
feisty 혈기 왕성한, 거침없는
assertive 적극적인, 확신에 찬

02 정답 ④

정답해설

'lavish'는 '호화로운, 풍성한'을 뜻하는 형용사로 ④ sumptuous(호화로운)와 의미상 가장 가깝다.

해석

그 디저트는 예술작품이다: 여러 가지 산딸기류, 으깨진 피스타치오, 다크 초콜릿, 그리고 민트 잎들이 이 **호화로운** 디저트를 정교하게 장식한다.
① 시무룩한, 음침한
② 황량한, 냉혹한
③ 꾸밈없는, 소박한
④ 호화로운

어휘

assorted 여러 가지의, 갖은
garnish 장식하다, 고명을 하다; 고명
dour 시무룩한, 음침한
austere 꾸밈없는, 소박한
delicately 정교하게; 섬세하게
lavish 호화로운, 풍성한
stark 황량한, 냉혹한
sumptuous 호화로운

03 정답 ①

정답해설

'paucity'는 '부족, 결핍'을 뜻하는 명사로 ① dearth(부족, 결핍)와 의미상 가장 가깝다.

해석

교육의 **부족**, 문맹 그리고 운명에 대한 통제 부족 때문에, 그는 조선시대 역사에서 비극적인 인물로 주로 기억되고 있다.

① 부족, 결핍
② 과다
③ 포만감
④ 풍부함

어휘

paucity 부족, 결핍
illiteracy 문맹; 무식
tragic 비극적인, 비극의
dearth 부족, 결핍
satiety 포만감
upbringing 교육, 양육, 훈육
chiefly 주로
figure 인물; 수치; 숫자
surfeit 과다
plenitude 풍부함

04 정답 ①

정답해설

(A) 영화 관람이 취미라고 말하는 Jane에게 Steve는 '그녀가 좋아했던 ~한 영화'를 추천해 줄 수 있는지 묻는다. 따라서 빈칸 (A)에 들어갈 가장 적절한 것은 '최신의(up to date)'이다.
(B) Jane이 Steve에게 〈인셉션〉이라는 영화를 추천해주자 Steve는 그 영화를 관람했다며 영화가 개봉했을 때 '~였다'라고 말한다. 그러므로 빈칸 (B)에 들어갈 가장 자연스러운 것은 '대히트(smash hit)'이다.
따라서 정답은 '① (A) up to date(최신의) - (B) smash hit(대히트)'이다.

오답해설

② (B) 영화 〈인셉션〉을 추천해 준 Jane에게 Steve가 그 영화를 봤다고 말하면서 그것이 개봉했을 때 '최고급(top notch)'이었다고 이야기하는 것은 문맥상 자연스럽지 않다.
③ (A) 영화 관람이 취미라는 Jane에게 Steve가 그녀가 좋아했던 '당근과 채찍(carrot and stick)' 영화를 추천해 줄 수 있는지 물어보는 것은 대화의 흐름상 빈칸에 들어갈 말로 부적절하다.
④ (A) 영화 관람이 취미라는 Jane에게 Steve가 그녀가 좋아했던 '당근과 채찍(carrot and stick)' 영화를 추천해 줄 수 있는지 물어보는 것은 맥락상 빈칸에 들어갈 말로 어색하다. (B) Steve는 Jane이 추천해 준 〈인셉션〉 영화를 관람했다고 말하면서 그것이 개봉했을 때 '판박이처럼 닮은 것(a spitting image)'이었다고 얘기하는 것은 문맥상 어색하다.

해석

Jane: 나는 요새 무척 심심해.
Steve: 오, 난 네가 아르바이트하느라 바쁜 줄 알았어.
Jane: 한 달 전에 아르바이트 그만뒀어. 지금은 그냥 내 취미 생활을 즐기고 있어.
Steve: 잘됐다! 네 취미가 뭐야?
Jane: 나는 영화 보는 것을 좋아해. 그래서 집에서 영화를 많이 보고 있어.
Steve: 네가 좋아했던 (A) 최신 영화 좀 추천해 줄 수 있어?
Jane: 물론이지! 내 추천은 〈인셉션〉이야.
Steve: 나 그 영화 봤어! 그것은 개봉했을 때 (B) 대히트였잖아.
Jane: 사실, 그 영화는 최다 관객을 기록했어.
Steve: 우와! 멋지다. 그것은 내가 가장 좋아하는 영화 중 하나야.
① (A) 최신의 (B) 대히트
② (A) 최신의 (B) 최고급
③ (A) 당근과 채찍 (B) 대히트
④ (A) 당근과 채찍 (B) 판박이처럼 닮은 것

어휘

up to date 최신의
top notch 최고급
a spitting image 판박이처럼 닮은 것
smash hit 대히트
carrot and stick 당근과 채찍

05 정답 ②

정답해설

② 출제 포인트: **sort/kind/type of+무관사(a/an/the)+명사**
'type of' 이후에는 「무관사(a/an/the)+명사」 형태의 목적어가 온다. 해당 문장의 경우 'types of' 이후에 「정관사+명사」 형태의 목적어가 왔으므로 밑줄 친 'the'를 삭제해야 한다.

오답해설

① 출제 포인트: **현재분사 vs. 과거분사/with 분사구문**
밑줄 친 'resolved'는 「with+목적어+분사」 형태의 with분사구문에 쓰인 과거분사로 이후에 「by+행위자」에 해당하는 'by importation and successful establishment of natural enemies'가 왔으며 수식하는 대상 'a number of pest problems'와 수동관계이므로 'resolved'는 옳은 표현이다.

③ 출제 포인트: **등위상관접속사/접속사의 쓰임**
앞에 있는 'not'을 통해 'but'이 「not A but B」의 형태로 사용된 것임을 알 수 있으며 이때 A와 B는 불완전자동사 'is'의 주격 보어에 해당하는 명사구이다. 따라서 밑줄 친 접속사 'but'은 옳은 표현이다.

④ 출제 포인트: **주격 관계대명사절의 동사 수일치**
밑줄 친 'determine'은 주격 관계대명사 'that'이 이끄는 절의 동사로 수일치 기준은 선행사이다. 이때 'that'의 선행사는 복수 형태인 'factors'이므로 복수 형태의 동사 'determine'은 옳은 표현이다.

해석

'생물학적 방제'라는 용어는 모든 범위의 생물학적인 유기체와 생물학적 기반의 제품들을 포함하기 위해 가끔 넓은 맥락에서 사용되어 왔다. 이것은 많은 해충 문제가 천적의 도입과 성공적인 정착에 의해 영구적으로 해결이 되면서, 많은 경우에 있어서 멋지게 성공을 거두어 왔다. 이러한 도입의 성공은 대체로 특정한 유형의 생태계나 다년생의 생태계에 도입된 해충과 같은 해충 상황에 국한되었다. 다른 한편으로는, 이런 접근은 줄뿌림 작물이나 다른 단명 하는 계통의 주요한 해충에서는 제한적인 성공에 맞닥뜨렸다. 이러한 상황에서, 문제는 흔히 효과적인 천적의 부족이 아니라 관리 관행과 특정한 농업 생태계 환경에 있어서 도입 시도의 성공 혹은 실패를 결정하는 요인들에 대한 공동 연구의 부족이다.

어휘

biological control 생물학적 방제
spectacularly 멋지게
resolve 해결하다
perennial 다년생의; 다년생 식물; 영원한
row crop 줄뿌림 작물
concerted 공동의, 통합된
spectrum 범위, 영역
pest 해충
importation 도입, 수입
ephemeral 수명이 짧은, 단명하는
agro-ecosystem 농업 생태계

06 정답 ④

정답해설

④ 출제 포인트: **동명사의 태**
밑줄 친 'of being dropped'에서 'being dropped'는 전치사 'of'의 목적어로 쓰인 동명사의 수동태에 해당하나 이후에 목적어 'anchor'가 있으므로 능동태로 사용해야 한다. 따라서 'being dropped'를 동명사의 능동태인 'dropping'으로 수정해야 한다.

오답해설

① 출제 포인트: **현재분사 vs. 과거분사**
'driven'은 완전타동사 'drive'의 과거분사로 이후에 「by+행위자」에 해당하는 'by the winds'가 왔으며 생략된 주어 'We'와 수동관계이므로 밑줄 친 'driven by the winds'는 옳은 표현이다.

② 출제 포인트: **관용표현(be satisfied with)**
밑줄 친 'be satisfied with'는 관용표현으로 '~에 만족하다'라는 뜻으로 적절히 사용되었다.

③ 출제 포인트: **주격 관계대명사의 동사 수일치**
밑줄 친 'who select'는 「주격 관계대명사+동사」에 해당한다. 이때 주격 관계대명사절의 동사 'select'의 수일치 기준은 선행사인 'Sailors'이며 사람을 나타내고 복수 형태이므로 'who select'는 옳은 표현이다.

해석

우리는 주변 환경의 바람에 의해 몰리고 전통과 관습의 물결에 의해 이리저리 내던져지면서 표류한다. 결국, 대부분의 사람들은 그들이 '폭풍 속의 어떤 항구(궁여지책)'에 만족해야 한다는 것을 발견한다. 그들이 항구로 내몰리기 때문에 그것을 선택하는 선원들은 닻을 내릴 한 번의 기회를 좀처럼 가지지 못할 수 있다.

어휘

toss 흔들리다[흔들리게 하다]
any port in a storm 폭풍 속의 항구(궁여지책)
drop anchor 닻을 내리다

07 정답 ③

정답해설

③ 출제 포인트: **either+단수가산명사**
'either' 이후에 명사가 오는 경우 단수 형태를 사용해야 한다. 따라서 밑줄 친 'either questions'의 'questions'를 단수 형태인 'question'으로 수정해야 한다.

오답해설

① 출제 포인트: **불완전자동사와 주격 보어**
'feel'은 불완전자동사의 경우 주격 보어로 'like+(that)+절'을 사용할 수 있다. 따라서 밑줄 친 'feel like having'의 경우 'like'와 'having' 사이에 접속사 'that'이 생략되어 있으며 'having'은 'that'이 이끄는 절의 주어로 사용된 동명사이다.

② 출제 포인트: **능동태 vs. 수동태**
완전타동사 'crave' 이후에 목적어 'the recognition'을 사용하였으므로 능동태에 해당하는 밑줄 친 'crave the recognition'은 옳은 표현이다.

④ 출제 포인트: **try+목적어[to부정사 vs. 동명사]**
완전타동사 'try'가 목적어로 to부정사를 가지는 경우 '~하려고 애쓰다'를 뜻하며 목적어로 동명사를 가지는 경우 '~해보다'를 뜻한다. 해당 문장은 문맥상 '기분 좋게 느끼려고 애쓰다'가 자연스러우므로 밑줄 친 'trying to feel'은 옳은 표현이다.

해석

예를 들어, 승리자인 자녀를 두는 것이 여러분이 가치 있는 부모라는 것을 증명하는 것처럼 생각되는가? 스타인 선수의 부모로서의 인정을 갈망하는가? 두 질문 중 어느 질문에라도 '예'라고 대답할 수 있다면, 여러분은 자녀의 운동 성취를 통해 스스로에 대해 기분 좋게 느끼려고 애쓰고 있는 것인지도 모른다.

어휘

crave 갈망하다, 열망하다
recognition 인정
worthwhile 가치 있는
accomplishment 성취, 업적

오답률 TOP 1
08 정답 ③

정답해설

(A) 이전에서는 표준 중국어에서 의미하는 '행복'에 대해 설명하고 있다. 그리고 (A) 이후에서 특히 영어 문화에서는 상상할 수 없는 개념의 '행복'이라는 의미에 대해 언급하고 있는 것을 알 수 있다. (A) 이전에서 언급한 내용에 대해 추가적으로 자세한 내용을 덧붙여 설명하고 있으므로, 보기 중 빈칸에 가장 적절한 표현은 'In fact(사실)'이다.

(B) 이전에서는 미국에서 경험하는 '축하' 관련한 행복과는 다른 '덴마크어' 상의 '행복(lykke)'에 관해 언급하고 있다. 그리고 (B) 이후에서도 역시, '축하' 보다는 '평온과 안정'에 더 가까운 것을 의미하는 '홍콩의 광둥어에서의 행복'에 대해 설명하고 있다. (B) 전후 내용이 모두, '미국에서 행복이 경험되는 것과는 다른 방식'에 대해 설명하고 있으므로, 빈칸에는 '유사' 관계를 나타내는 'Likewise(마찬가지로)' 또는 'Similarly(유사하게)'가 가장 적절하다.

따라서 정답은 '③ In fact(사실) – Similarly(유사하게)'이다.

오답해설

① (A) 전후 관계가 '인과' 관계가 아니기 때문에 'Therefore(그러므로)'가 빈칸에 들어가는 것은 어색하다.
나머지 보기는 문맥상 어색하므로 오답이다.

해석

행복이 다른 문화권에서 어떻게 받아들여지는가의 차이는 언어에서 분명하다. '행복(happiness)'과 '행복한(happy)'과 같은 단어들은 동양과 서양 문화에서 다른 함축적 의미를 가지고 있고 항상 직접적으로 번역될 수 있는 것은 아니다. 예를 들어, 표준 중국어는 영어의 개념과 완벽히 동등한 것이 아닌 "행복"을 나타내는 다수의 단어를 가지고 있다, 왜냐하면 그것들은 "좋은 기분"에서부터 "삶에 의미를 지니는 것" 또는 "좋은 인생을 사는 것"까지 어느 것이나 의미할 수 있기 때문이다. (A) 사실, 표준 중국어에서, 행복은 또한 "잘 죽는 것"으로 정의되기도 하는데, 이는 영어권 문화에서는 아주 상상도 할 수 없는 것일 것이다. 게다가, 다른 언어에서 행복이 정의되는 방식은 그것이 문화권 간에서 어떻게 다르게 경험되는지를 가리킨다. 예를 들어, "lykke"라는 덴마크어 개념은 "행복"으로 번역되지만, 행복이 축하의 상태를 포함하는 미국에서 행복이 경험되는 방식과는 거의 관련이 없다. (B) 유사하게, 홍콩의 광둥어에서 행복에 해당하는 단어는 낮은 각성 상태와 연결되어 있고, 그것의 의미는 축하보다는 평온과 안정에 더 가깝다.

	(A)	(B)
①	그러므로	마찬가지로
②	그러나	즉
③	사실	유사하게
④	그에 따라	대조적으로

어휘

variation 차이, 변화 connotation 함축(적 의미)
Mandarin 표준 중국어 multiple 다수의
equivalent 동등한 것, 대응하는 것 define 정의하다
unthinkable 상상도 할 수 없는
have little to do with …와 거의 관련이 없다
involve 수반하다, 포함하다 Cantonese 광둥어
arousal 각성

09 정답 ②

정답해설

본문에서는 "2016년에 미국에서 FDA에 의해 발효된 전자 담배에 대한 규제"에 관해 설명하고 있다. 본문에 따르면, 전자 담배 시장은 점점 성장하고 있었으며, 특히 전자 담배는 기존의 전통 담배와 경쟁하는 구도였다. 그렇기 때문에, 기존의 거대 담배 회사들은 신규 업체들이 시장에 성공적으로 진입하는 것을 막기 위해 전자 담배에 대한 규정을 도입하는 것에 우호적이었다는 것을 알 수 있다. 본문 마지막 문장 "With the new FDA rules, Big Tobacco got just what it wanted(새로운 FDA 규정으로 거대 담배 회사는 그것이 원했던 바로 그것을 얻었다)."을 통해, '거대 담배 회사들은 전자 담배 규정을 원하고 있었다'는 것을 알 수 있으므로, 글의 요지로 가장 적절한 것은 '② The FDA's new e-cigarette regulations were a gift to Big Tobacco(FDA의 새로운 전자 담배 규정은 거대 담배 회사에게 선물이었다).'이다.

오답해설

① 본문에서 언급된 사실이기는 하지만, 본문의 주요 주제는 '전자 담배에 대한 규정'이므로 글 전체의 요지로는 적절하지 않다.
③ 본문에서 이미 전자 담배에 대한 규제가 실시되었음을 언급하고 있으며, 더 강력한 규제의 필요성에 대해서는 본문에 언급되지 않으므로 오답이다.
④ 새로운 규정이 발효된 이후의 상황에 대해서는 언급되지 않으므로 오답이다.

해석

2016년에, 식품 의약품국(Food and Drug Administration)은 전자 담배에 대한 규제 권한을 확고히 하는 규정들을 최종적으로 승인했다. 전자 담배 이용은 주로 현재 그리고 이전 흡연자들에 의해 힘입어 최근 급격히 증가했다. 많은 담배 이용자들이 자신들의 폐에 덜 손상을 입히면서 그들의 니코틴에 대한 갈망을 충족시킬 수 있다는 것을 배웠다. 전자 담배가 전통적인 담배와 경쟁하기 때문에 – 그리고 많은 전자 담배와 불연성 제품들은 소규모 신생 기업에 의해 제조되기 때문에 – (Philip Morris라고도 알려진) Altria와 같은 거대 담배 회사들은 이 시장을 탄압하려고 시도해 왔다. 거대 담배 회사들은 전자 담배 브랜드를 만들거나 인수하는 한편, 또한 소기업들이 경쟁하기 어렵게 만들 규정을 요구해 왔다. 새로운 FDA 규정으로, 거대 담배 회사는 그것이 원했던 바로 그것을 얻었다.

① 전자 담배는 전통 담배와 경쟁해오고 있다.
② FDA의 새로운 전자 담배 규정은 거대 담배 회사에게 선물이었다.
③ FDA는 공공의 건강을 보호하기 위해 전자 담배를 더 강력히 규제해야 한다.
④ 전자 담배 시장은 새로운 규정에도 불구하고 크게 성장해오고 있다.

어휘

finalize 최종적으로 승인하다, 마무리 짓다, 완결하다
assert (자신의 권리·권위 등을) 확고히 하다
regulatory 규제하는 authority 권한
boom 호황을 맞다, 번창[성공]하다
fuel …에 활기를 불어넣다, 부채질하다, 촉진하다
craving 갈망, 열망
vape 불연성 담배에서 나오는 연기를 들이마시다
startup 신규의, 신생의, 스타트업의 tobacco company 담배 회사
seek to 동사원형 ~하려고 시도하다
clamp down on …을 탄압하다[엄하게 단속하다]
Big Tobacco 거대 담배 회사(Philip Morris, RJR Nabisco, U.S. Tobacco 따위)
acquire 사거나 받아서) 획득하다[취득하다]
push for …을 계속 요구하다[조르다]
significantly 상당히, 크게

오답률 TOP 3
10 정답 ②

정답해설

(A) 이전에서는 '인터넷상에서 많은 언어들이 서로 영향을 미친다'고 언급한 후, (A) 이후에는 '소수 특정 언어가 인터넷을 점령하고 더 많은 영향을 미친다'고 설명하고 있으므로, 빈칸에는 '양보'를 나타내는 'Still(그럼에도 불구하고)' 또는 '역접'을 나타내는 'But(그러나)'이 들어가는 것이 자연스럽다.

(B) 이전에서는 '인터넷에서 우위를 점하고 있는 언어들(영어, 러시아어, 한국어, 독일어)'에 대해 언급한 후, (B) 이후에서는 '실제로는 널리 쓰이지만 인터넷상에서는 대표성이 낮은 언어들(스페인어, 아랍어)'에 대해 언급하고 있다. 두 범주의 언어들을 서로 비교하고 있으므로 빈칸에 가장 적절한 표현은 'by comparison(그에 비해)'이다.

따라서 정답은 '② Still(그럼에도 불구하고) - by comparison(그에 비해)'이다. 'still'이 '여전히, 아직도'라는 의미 외에도 '양보'의 의미인 '그럼에도 불구하고'를 뜻함에 유의해야한다.

오답해설

④ (B) 전후 내용이 '유사' 관계가 아니기 때문에 'likewise(유사하게)'가 빈칸에 들어가는 것은 어색하다.
나머지 보기는 문맥상 어색하므로 오답이다.

해석

언어 접촉은 종종 국경을 따라 또는 이주의 결과로 발생한다. 그러나 기술이 진보함에 따라, 그것은 다른 방식으로 발생해오고 있다. 최근 수십 년간, 인터넷은 많은 언어들이 접촉하게 했고, 따라서 그것들은 서로 영향을 미친다. (A) 그럼에도 불구하고, 오직 몇몇 언어들만이 웹을 점령하고, 다른 언어에 크게 영향을 미치고 있다. 러시아어, 한국어, 그리고 독일어와 함께, 영어가 단연 지배적이다. (B) 그에 비해, 스페인어와 아랍어와 같은 수백만의 사람들이 말하는 언어들조차 인터넷에서는 대표성이 거의 없다. 그 결과, 인터넷 사용의 직접적인 결과로서 영어 단어가 전 세계 다른 언어들에 훨씬 높은 비율로 영향을 미치고 있다. 예를 들어, 프랑스에서는, 프랑스어 이용자들이 "informatique en nuage"를 사용하도록 하려는 노력에도 불구하고 "cloud computing"이라는 영어 용어가 일반화되었다.

	(A)	(B)
①	또한	한 마디로
②	그럼에도 불구하고	그에 비해
③	그래서	예를 들어
④	그러나	유사하게

어휘

migration 이주, 이동
bring (특정 상태·장소에) 있게 하다, …하게 하다
still 그럼에도 불구하고, 그런데도; 여전히, 아직도
dominate 지배하다, 군림하다　　by far 단연코, 매우
predominate 두드러지다, 지배적이다, 우위를 차지하다
multiple 다수의, 많은　　by comparison 그에 비해
representation 대표성, 대표
come into common use 일반화하다
adopt 쓰다, 차용하다, 채택하다

기적사 DAY 68

| 01 | ④ | 02 | ② | 03 | ② | 04 | ② | 05 | ③ |
| 06 | ② | 07 | ① | 08 | ② | 09 | ③ | 10 | ③ |

01 정답 ④

정답해설

'delirious'는 '열광적인, 기뻐 날뛰는'을 뜻하는 형용사로 ④ rapturous(열광적인, 황홀해하는)와 의미상 가장 가깝다.

해석

그것은 본머스 전역의 술집에서 수만 명의 **열광적인** 팬들에 의해 공유되는 감정이었다.
① 무기력한, 활기 없는
② 무기력한, 게으른
③ 무기력한, 힘이 없는
④ 열광적인, 황홀해하는

어휘

sentiment 감정, 정서　　delirious 열광적인, 기뻐 날뛰는
torpid 무기력한, 활기 없는　　supine 무기력한, 게으른
listless 무기력한, 힘이 없는　　rapturous 열광적인, 황홀해하는

오답률 TOP 2
02 정답 ②

정답해설

'pernicious'는 '치명적인'을 뜻하는 형용사로 ② capital(치명적인, 중대한)과 의미상 가장 가깝다.

해석

비록 그 문제가 **치명적**이고 인종 차별만큼 다루기 어렵다고 할지라도, 당신은 그 문제를 해결하기 위해 다양한 해결책을 생각하기 시작한다.
① 앙증맞은, 암전한
② 치명적인, 중대한
③ 매우 아름다운, 정교한
④ 즙이 많은, 다육성의

어휘

pernicious 치명적인　　intractable 다루기 힘든
racism 인종 차별 (주의)　　dainty 앙증맞은, 암전한
capital 치명적인, 중대한　　exquisite 매우 아름다운, 정교한
succulent 즙이 많은, 다육성의

03 정답 ②

정답해설

'motivation'은 '자극, 동기부여'를 뜻하는 명사로 ② impetus(자극, 자극제)와 의미상 가장 가깝다.

해석

그들은 그들의 시간을 이러한 꿈들로 채웠고 결과적으로 사람들은 인생에서 일을 하고 그것을 달성하기 위해 더 많은 **동기부여**를 가질 수 있었다.

① 대담성, 대담한
② 자극, 자극제
③ 뻔뻔함
④ 탄력, 가속도

어휘

motivation 자극, 동기부여
impetus 자극, 자극제
momentum 탄력, 가속도
daring 대담성, 대담한
audacity 뻔뻔함

04 정답 ②

정답해설

A와 B는 주식투자에 대해 이야기하고 있다. A는 최근에 투자한 세계적인 IT 기업의 주식 현황을 당일 아침에 확인했을 때 상당히 실망했다고 말한다. B는 A가 실망한 이유를 궁금해하며 주식이 '~했는지' 묻는다. 따라서 빈칸에 들어갈 가장 적절한 것은 '② take a nosedive(폭락하다)'이다.

오답해설

① 오늘 아침에 주식 현황을 확인하고 실망했다는 A에게 B는 이유를 물어보면서 주식이 '강화했는지(beef up)' 질문하는 것은 문맥상 어색하다.
③ A가 아침에 주식 현황을 확인하고 실망한 이유를 궁금해하면서 B는 주식이 '매우 잘 팔렸는지(sell like hot cakes)' 묻는 것은 대화의 흐름상 적절하지 않다.
④ B는 A가 아침에 주식 현황을 확인한 후 실망한 이유를 궁금해하면서 주식이 '폭우가 쏟아졌는지(rain cats and dogs)' 물어보는 것은 맥락을 고려했을 때 빈칸에 들어갈 말로 부적절하다.

해석

A: 너 투자해본 적 있어?
B: 물론이지. 나는 주식투자에 대해 많이 알지는 않지만, 투자 경험은 좀 있어. 투자해볼 생각이야?
A: 음, 나는 최근에 세계적인 IT 기업에 투자했어. 오늘 아침에 투자 현황을 확인했을 때, 나는 굉장히 실망했어.
B: 왜? 그것이 폭락했어?
A: 응 맞아. 다시 오를 때까지 그냥 기다려봐야 할까?
B: 나는 네가 좀 더 기다려보는 것을 추천해.
① 강화하다
② 폭락하다
③ 매우 잘 팔리다
④ 폭우가 쏟아지다

어휘

stock 주식; 재고
take a nosedive 폭락하다
rain cats and dogs 폭우가 쏟아지다
beef up 강화하다
sell like hot cakes 매우 잘 팔리다

05 정답 ③

정답해설

③ 출제 포인트: that vs. what/목적격 관계대명사
밑줄 친 'if'는 'you want'가 아닌 'you want is to get better at tennis'를 이끄는 부사절의 접속사이며 'you want'는 목적어가 없는 불완전한 형태의 절로 'if'가 이끄는 부사절의 주어에 해당한다. 이때 'if' 이후에 선행사가 없으므로 선행사를 포함하는 목적격 관계대명사 'what'을 사용해야 한다. 따라서 'if'를 'if what'으로 수정해야 한다.

오답해설

① 출제 포인트: 현재분사 vs. 과거분사
밑줄 친 'giving'은 수여동사 'give'의 현재분사로 이후에 간접목적어 'you'와 직접목적어 'tennis lessons'가 왔으며 수식하는 대상 'two different tennis pros'와 능동 관계이므로 'giving'은 옳은 표현이다.

② 출제 포인트: 주어와 동사의 수일치
동명사(구)가 주어인 경우 단수 취급하여 단수 형태의 동사를 사용한다. 해당 문장은 주어가 동명사구인 'hearing "good swing"'이므로 밑줄 친 단수 형태의 동사 'gives'는 옳은 표현이다.

④ 출제 포인트: 사역동사와 목적격 보어
밑줄 친 'feel'은 사역동사 'makes'의 목적격 보어에 해당하는 원형부정사로 옳은 표현이다.

해석

당신은 무엇이 당신을 훌륭한 테니스 선수로 만들 수 있다고 생각하는가? 당신에게 테니스 강습을 해주는 두 명의 다른 테니스 프로 선수가 있다고 가정해 보라. 첫 번째 프로 선수는 당신을 격려하려고 "잘 쳤어요"와 "스윙 좋아요" 같은 말을 늘 한다. 두 번째 프로 선수는 당신이 스윙을 잘 할 때만 "스윙 좋아요"라고 말한다. 단지 "스윙 좋아요"라는 말을 듣는 것이 당신에게 보상을 준다면, 당신은 첫 번째 강사를 선호할 것이다. 그러나 당신이 원하는 것이 테니스를 더 잘 치게 되는 것이라면, 당신은 두 번째 강사를 선호할 것이다. 그것은 당신을 향한 두 번째 강사의 피드백이 첫 번째 강사의 것보다 훨씬 더 유익하기 때문이다. 당신은 "스윙 좋아요"라는 보상을 추구하는 것이 아니라, 테니스 경기를 더 잘하게 되는 것을 추구한다. 그래서 단순히 당신을 기분 좋게 만들어주는 피드백은 결국에 당신이 테니스 기술을 발전시키는 데 도움이 되지 않을 것이다.

어휘

pro 프로 선수
be after ~을 추구하다
informative 유익한
in the long run 결국에는

06 정답 ②

정답해설

② 출제 포인트: 주장, 요구, 명령, 제안동사+(that)+주어+(should)+동사원형
'suggest'는 완전타동사이므로 5형식을 사용할 수 없다. 따라서 밑줄 친 'to use bold print'에서 'to use'는 틀린 표현이며 이때 문맥상 'suggest'가 '제안하다'라는 뜻으로 명사절을 이끌 수 있다. 해당 문장에서는 'suggest'와 'you' 사이에 명사절을 이끄는 접속사 'that'이 생략되어 있다고 보고, 명사절에 해당되는 'you ~ box'에서 동사는 'should use' 또는 'should'가 생략된 'use'가 사용되어야 적절하다. 따라서 'to use'를 'should use' 또는 'use'로 수정해야 한다.

오답해설

① 출제 포인트: 현재분사 vs. 과거분사
밑줄 친 'Knowing how dangerous'에서 'Knowing'은 완전타동사 'know'의 현재분사로 이후에 의문사 'how'가 이끄는 절이 목적어로 왔으며 생략된 주어 'I'와 능동관계이므로 'Knowing'은 옳은 표현이다. 또한 'how dangerous'는 불완전자동사 'is'의 보어에 해당하는 「의문부사+형용사」형태의 형용사구 형태로 간접의문문으로 쓰여 'how+형용사+주어+동사'의 어순으로 사용되었다.

③ 출제 포인트: 주어와 동사의 수일치
밑줄 친 'is a warning'은 「불완전자동사+주격 보어」의 형태로 'is'의 수일치 기준은 주어 'the notice'이며 이때 'the notice'는 단수 형태이므로 단수 형태의 동사 'is'는 옳은 표현이다.

④ 출제 포인트: 수동태 불가동사

'occur'는 완전자동사이므로 수동태로 사용할 수 없다. 따라서 밑줄 친 'does not occur'는 옳은 표현이다.

해석

화학 물질 중독이 얼마나 위험한지를 알기에, 저는 그 그릇을 전자레인지에 데우지 말 것을 당신이 소비자들에게 충분히 경고하는 것이 중요하다고 생각합니다. 저는 당신이 상자의 바깥에 굵은 활자체를 사용해야 한다고 제안합니다. 해로운 화학 물질에 대한 알림은 단순히 그 그릇의 특징이 아니라 경고라는 것을 분명히 밝히십시오. 불필요한 중독이 발생하지 않도록 이것을 고려해 주십시오.

어휘

poisoning 중독, 독살 microwave ~을 전자레인지에 데우다
bold 굵은, 용감한 print 활자, 활자체

오답률 TOP 1

07 정답 ①

정답해설

① 출제 포인트: 능동태 vs. 수동태/It(가주어)+be+과거분사+that절(진주어)

'note'는 「It(가주어)+be+과거분사+that절(진주어)」의 형태로 사용할 수 있는 동사이다. 해당 문장의 경우 접속사 'that'이 이끄는 절은 진주어이며 'It'은 가주어이므로 완전타동사 'note'의 목적어가 없음을 알 수 있다. 따라서 밑줄 친 'note'는 수동태인 'be noted'로 수정해야 한다.

오답해설

② 출제 포인트: 주어와 동사의 수일치/능동태 vs. 수동태
밑줄 친 'has reduced'는 완전타동사 'reduce'의 현재완료 형태에 해당하며 이때 주어가 단수 형태인 'no development'이고 이후에 목적어 'the importance'가 왔으므로 'has reduced'는 옳은 표현이다.

③ 출제 포인트: 최상급
밑줄 친 'the most basic'은 형용사 'basic'의 최상급 표현으로 명사 'job'을 수식하고 있다.

④ 출제 포인트: 현재분사 vs. 과거분사
'preferred'는 완전타동사 'prefer'의 과거분사 형태로 해석상 '선호되는 직장'이 자연스러우며 수식하는 대상 'workplace'와 수동관계이므로 밑줄 친 'preferred workplace'는 옳은 표현이다.

해석

하지만 인터넷 직업 시대에서의 어떠한 발전도 가장 기본적인 구직기술, 즉 자기 이해의 중요성을 감소시키지는 않았다는 것에 주목해야 한다. 심지어 인터넷 시대에도, 구직은 개인적인 직업 역량, 분야에 대한 관심, 그리고 선호되는 직장 분위기와 흥미를 확인하는 것과 함께 시작한다.

어휘

self-knowledge 자기 이해

08 정답 ②

정답해설

주어진 문장에서는 '보편적으로 사람들이 행복을 추구하지만, 이러한 행복 추구가 역설적으로 웰빙을 저해시킨다는 연구 결과가 있다'라고 설명하고 있다. 이후 이어질 내용으로 가장 적절한 것은 주어진 문장에서 설명한 연구 결과에 대해 'However(그러나)'를 이용해 반박하고 있는 (B)이다. (B)에서는 '기존의 연구가 주로 미국에서 실시되었으며, 이는 결국 다른 문화권에서는 다른 결과를 낳을 수도 있다는 가능성을 보여준다'라고 설명한다. 이후, (B)에서 언급한 '문화에 달려있는 관계'에 대해 'For instance(예를 들어)'를 이용해 예를 들어 설명하고 있는 (A)가 이어지는 것이 자연스럽다. 마지막으로, (A)에서 언급한 '문화적 차이에 따른 행복 추구와 웰빙과의 관계'를 구체적으로 설명하고 있는 (C)가 연결되는 것이 적절하다. 따라서 정답은 '② (B) - (A) - (C)'이다.

오답해설

③ (C)에서 언급된 'in cultures where happiness is defined in more socially engaged ways(행복이 사회적으로 더 관여된 방식으로 정의되는 문화에서)'는 (A)의 'in collectivist cultures found in regions such as East Asia may be defined in terms of social engagement(동아시아와 같은 지역에서 찾을 수 있는 집단주의 문화에서 사회적 참여라는 측면에서 정의될지도 모른다'에서 언급되고 있으므로 (A)가 (C) 이전에 위치하는 것이 더 자연스럽다.

나머지 보기는 문맥상 어색하므로 오답이다.

해석

사람들이 행복해지길 원한다는 생각은 비전문가들에게는 분명한 것처럼 보이고 비교 문화 실증 연구에서 확인되어왔다. 그러나 역설적으로, 증가하는 연구가 행복을 추구하는 것이 실제로 웰빙을 저해시킨다는 것을 나타낸다.
(B) 그러나 행복과 웰빙 추구에 대한 대부분의 연구가 미국에서 실시되어왔으며, 이는 이러한 관계가 문화에 달려있다는 가능성을 열어둔다.
(A) 예를 들어, 미국과 같은 개인주의 문화에서의 행복은 매우 자기 지향적인 방식으로 정의되는 반면, 동아시아와 같은 지역에서 발견된 집단주의 문화에서의 행복은 사회적 참여라는 측면에서 정의될지도 모른다.
(C) 사회적 연결이 웰빙의 강력한 예측 변수이기 때문에, 행복이 사회적으로 더 관여된 방식으로 정의되는 문화에서는 행복의 추구는 더 높은 웰빙으로 이어질 것이며, 이는 사람들이 행복 추구 과정에서 - 친구 및 가족과 더 많은 시간을 보내는 것과 같은 - 사회 활동에 관여하도록 이끌 것이다.

어휘

layperson (특정 주제에 대한) 비전문가, 문외한
cross-cultural 비교 문화적, 여러 문화가 섞인[혼재된]
empirical 경험[실험]에 따른, 실증적인
paradoxically 역설적으로 body 많은 양[모음]
indicate 나타내다[보여 주다] pursue 추구하다
impair 손상[악화]시키다
well-being 웰빙, (건강과) 행복, 복지[복리]
individualistic 개인주의적인 define 정의하다
self-oriented 자기 지향적인 collectivist 집단주의적인
in terms of … 면에서[…에 관하여] engagement 참여, 관계
pursuit 추구, (원하는 것을) 좇음[찾음]
conduct (특정한 활동을) 하다; 지휘하다
leave A open A를 열어두다 robust 강력한, 튼튼한
predictor 예측 변수 engaged 관여된
engage in 참여하다, 종사하다

오답률 TOP 3

09 정답 ③

정답해설

주어진 문장의 'Now that(~이므로, ~이니까)'으로 보아, 주어진 문장 이전에는 '연방 법으로 제정되기 이전의 상황'에 대해 설명하는 내용이 등장해야 한다는 것을 알 수 있다. ③ 이전 문장 "Nineteen states around the US plus Washington, DC, have already raised the minimum age to buy tobacco to 21(Washington, DC뿐만 아니라 미국의 19개의 주가 담배 구매 연령을 21세로 이미 올렸다)."에서, '해당 법안이 연방 법안으로 제정되기

전 이미 몇몇 주에서 자체적으로 실시하고 있었다'라고 설명하고 있으므로, 이후에 '이제 연방 법이 되었으므로 모든 주가 이를 준수해야 한다'는 내용이 이어지는 것이 자연스럽다. 따라서 정답은 ③이다.

오답해설

② 이전 문장에서 '연방 정부가 여러 주를 모사한다'라고 언급한 후, 바로 해당 주들의 예시가 언급되는 것이 자연스럽다. 따라서 ②에 주어진 문장이 들어가는 것은 어색하다.

나머지 보기는 문맥상 어색하므로 오답이다.

해석

미국 식품 의약품국(Food and Drug Administration)은 공식적으로 담배, 전자 담배, 그리고 니코틴을 함유한 불연성 제품과 같은 담배 제품들을 구매할 수 있는 최소 연령을 18세에서 21세로 올렸다. (①) 담배 제품을 구매할 수 있는 연령을 올림으로써, 연방 정부는 많은 주들이 해오고 있던 것을 모사하고 있다. (②) Washington, DC뿐만 아니라 미국의 19개의 주가 담배를 구매하기 위한 최소 연령을 21세로 이미 올렸다. (③ **이제 이것이 연방 법이기 때문에, 모든 주들은 이를 준수해야 할 것이다.**) 그 변화는 수천의 생명을 구할 수 있을 것이다. (④) 연구는 그들이 가장 중독이 될 가능성이 크기 때문에 십대들이 흡연 또는 니코틴 제품을 피우는 것을 방지하도록 노력하는 것이 중요하다는 것을 보여준다.

어휘

vape 불연성 담배에서 나오는 연기를 들이마시다, 전자 담배를 피우다
federal 연방의
replicate 모사하다, 복제하다
comply 준수하다, 따르다
prevent A from -ing A가 V하는 것을 막다 [방지하다, 예방하다]
addicted 중독된, 습관이 된

10 정답 ③

정답해설

본문에서는 '언어 변화는 화자의 목적이 아니다'라고 설명하며 "the change is not intended by the speakers(그 변화는 화자에 의해 의도된 것은 아니다)"를 통해, 언어 변화는 '의도되지 않은 현상'이라는 것을 언급하고 있다. 이후, 이러한 언어 변화가 발생하는 단계를 '교통 체증(traffic jam)'에 비유하여 설명하고 있다. 따라서 글의 요지로 가장 적절한 것은 '③ Language change is an unintentional process(언어 변화는 의도하지 않은 과정이다).'이다.

오답해설

① 본문에서 언급되지 않는 내용이다.
② 본문에서 언급되지 않는 내용이다.
④ 교통 체증은 언어 변화를 설명하기 위한 예시일 뿐이며, 글의 주요 요지가 아니므로 오답이다.

해석

언어 변화는 화자의 목표가 아니다. 오히려, 그것은 발생하지만 의도한 것은 아닌 이른바 '부수 현상'이다. 언어학 용어에서, 부수 현상은 변화가 내부 또는 외부 요인으로 인해 – 또는 양자의 결합으로 인해 – 발생하지만, 그 변화는 화자에 의해 의도된 것은 아니다. 교통 체증과의 비교가 요점을 설명하는 데 도움이 될지도 모른다: 만일 모든 자동차가 앞에 있는 차와의 충돌을 피하기 위해 브레이크를 밟는다면, 결과는 교통 체증이지만, 그 체증은 어떤 운전자의 목표도 아니다; 그것은 제동과 출발에서 비롯된 교통량 압축의 결과에 의해 발생한다. 그러므로 교통 체증은 운전자의 행위에서 비롯된 부수 현상이다.
① 사회가 변하기 때문에 언어가 변한다.
② 언어 변화는 모든 언어에서 발생한다.
③ 언어 변화는 의도하지 않은 과정이다.
④ 교통 체증은 조심스러운 운전 습관에 의해서 야기될 수 있다.

어휘

rather 오히려, 반대로, 도리어
epiphenomenon 부수 현상
linguistic 언어학의
illustrate 설명하다, 보여주다
arise 생기다, 발생하다
as a consequence of …의 결과로서, …때문에
compression 압축, 압착(된 것)
unintentional 의도하지 않은, 고의가 아닌
what is called 소위, 이른바
intentional 의도적인, 고의적인
comparison 비교
brake 브레이크를 밟다; 브레이크

기적사 DAY 69

01	④	02	①	03	③	04	③	05	②
06	③	07	②	08	②	09	④	10	④

01 정답 ④

정답해설

'disobedient'는 '반항적인, 거역하는'을 뜻하는 형용사로 ④ truculent(반항적인, 약간 공격적인)와 의미상 가장 가깝다.

해석

몇몇 사람들은 교사들이 학교에서 문제가 있거나 **반항적인** 학생들을 통제하는 데 어려움을 겪을 것이라고 우려한다.
① 상냥한, 다정한
② 화기애애한, 다정한
③ 쾌활한, 정감 있는
④ 반항적인, 약간 공격적인

어휘

problematic 문제가 있는[많은]
genial 상냥한, 다정한
amiable 쾌활한, 정감 있는
disobedient 반항적인, 거역하는
cordial 화기애애한, 다정한
truculent 반항적인, 약간 공격적인

오답률 TOP 1

02 정답 ①

정답해설

'unstable'은 '불안정한, 흔들릴 듯한'을 뜻하는 형용사로 ① wobbly(불안정한, 흔들리는)와 의미상 가장 가깝다.

해석

한국의 **불안정한** 경제 및 정치적 상황은 대기업들이 시설에 투자를 하거나 직원을 모집하는 것을 막아왔다.
① 불안정한, 흔들리는
② 파괴적인, 파멸을 가져올
③ 산만한, 종잡을 수 없는
④ 끝없이 계속되는

어휘

unstable 불안정한, 흔들릴 듯한
wobbly 불안정한, 흔들리는
rambling 산만한, 종잡을 수 없는
recruit 모집하다[뽑다]
ruinous 파괴적인, 파멸을 가져올
interminable 끝없이 계속되는

오답률 TOP 2

03 정답 ③

정답해설

'disappearance'는 '소멸, 소실, 사라짐'을 뜻하는 명사로 ③ passing(소멸, 통과)과 의미상 가장 가깝다.

해석

2013년에 발표된 옥스퍼드 대학교의 한 보고서는 향후 20년 안에 현재 직업들의 47%의 **소실**을 예측한다.

① 추방, 망명
② 만료, 만기
③ 소멸, 통과
④ 생략, 누락

어휘

disappearance 소멸, 소실, 사라짐
exile 추방, 망명
omission 생략, 누락
lapse 실수, 경과
passing 소멸, 통과

오답률 TOP 3

04 정답 ③

정답해설

- (A) David가 팀 프로젝트에 참여하지 않는 한 팀원에게 더 책임감을 가지라고 정중하게 말했다고 하자, Clara는 그 말을 들은 후 팀원의 태도가 어땠는지 묻는다. 그러자 David는 그녀가 '~했다'라고 대답하면서 그녀가 왜 화났는지 모르겠다고 대답하고 있으므로, 빈칸 (A)에 들어갈 가장 적절한 것은 'hit the roof(화를 심하게 냈다)'이다.
- (B) David가 진행하는 팀 프로젝트의 팀원과 겪은 갈등에 대한 David의 이야기를 들은 Clara는 팀원이 자신의 책임을 '~하는 사람'처럼 들린다고 말하므로 빈칸 (B)에 들어갈 가장 자연스러운 것은 'makes little of(~을 중요하지 않게 다루다)'이다.
- (C) 팀원에 대해 자신의 책임을 중요하지 않게 다루는 사람 같다고 하는 Clara의 이야기에 동의하며, David는 그녀가 그런 태도로 행동하는 것이 '~해야 한다'라고 말한다. 따라서 빈칸 (C)에 들어갈 가장 적절한 것은 'know better than to(~할 정도로 어리석지는 않다)'이다.

오답해설

① (A) David가 팀 프로젝트에 전혀 참여하지 않은 팀원에게 정중하게 책임감을 느껴달라고 부탁한 후 반응에 대해 묻는 Clara의 질문에, 팀원이 '더치페이했다(went Dutch)'라고 답변하는 것은 문맥상 어색하다. (C) David는 책임감 없는 팀원에 대해 그녀가 그런 태도로 행동하려면 '희생해야(fall prey to)' 한다고 하는 것은 대화의 흐름상 부자연스럽다.
② (C) David는 책임감 없는 팀원에 대해 그녀가 그런 태도로 행동하려면 '희생해야(fall prey to)' 한다고 하는 것은 맥락상 부적절하다.
④ (A) David가 팀 프로젝트에 전혀 참여하지 않은 팀원에게 정중하게 책임감을 느껴달라고 부탁한 후 반응에 대해 묻는 Clara의 질문에, 팀원이 '더치페이했다(went Dutch)'라고 답변하는 것은 문맥상 어색하다. (B) David는 책임감이 부족한 팀원과 갈등하는 상황에서 팀원이 화난 이유를 전혀 모르겠다고 말한다. 그러자 Clara가 그 팀원이 자신의 책임을 '감수하고 받아들이는(comes to terms with)' 사람처럼 들린다고 이야기하는 것은 문맥상 빈칸에 들어갈 말로 적절하지 않다.

해석

Clara: 안녕, 데이비드! 너 화나 보인다.
David: 진행 중인 팀 프로젝트에 문제가 있어서 지금 굉장히 화나.
Clara: 너 되게 스트레스받겠다. 무엇이 널 괴롭히는 거야?
David: 팀원 중 한 명이 아예 참여를 안 해. 그래서 내가 그녀에게 아주 정중하게 더 책임감을 느껴달라고 이야기했어.
Clara: 네가 그렇게 말한 후 그녀가 어떻게 행동했어?
David: 그녀는 (A) 화를 심하게 냈어. 그녀가 왜 화났는지 전혀 모르겠어.
Clara: 오, 네 팀원이 자신의 책임을 (B) 중요하지 않게 다루는 사람처럼 들려.
David: 음, 나도 너와 동의해. 그녀는 그런 식의 태도로 행동할 (C) 정도로 어리석지 않아야 해.

① (A) 더치페이했다 (B) ~을 중요하지 않게 다루다 (C) ~에 희생하다
② (A) 화를 심하게 냈다 (B) ~을 중요하지 않게 다루다
   (C) ~에 희생하다

③ (A) 화를 심하게 냈다 (B) ~을 중요하지 않게 다루다
(C) ~정도로 어리석지 않다
④ (A) 더치페이했다 (B) ~을 감수하고 받아들이다
(C) ~정도로 어리석지 않다

어휘

go Dutch 더치페이하다
make little of ~을 중요하지 않게 다루다
fall prey to ~에 희생하다   hit the roof 화를 심하게 내다
know better than to ~정도로 어리석지 않다
come to terms with ~을 감수하고 받아들이다

05 정답 ②

정답해설

② 출제 포인트: 주어와 동사의 수일치
주어가 동명사(구)인 경우 단수 취급하므로, 해당 문장은 주어가 동명사 'struggling'이므로 동사에 단수 형태를 사용해야 한다. 그러나 해당 문장의 동사는 'inoculate'로 복수 동사 형태를 사용하였으므로 밑줄 친 'inoculate'를 단수 동사 형태인 'inoculates'로 수정해야 한다. 이처럼 주어와 동사 사이의 거리가 먼 경우 수일치에 주의해야한다.

오답해설

① 출제 포인트: that vs. what
문맥상 '우리가 고난 예방 접종이라고 부르는 것에 관심을 갖게 되었다'가 자연스러우므로 'we call hardship inoculation'은 「주어+불완전타동사+목적격 보어」로 목적어가 없는 불완전한 형태의 절임을 알 수 있다. 따라서 밑줄 친 'what'은 선행사를 포함하는 관계대명사에 해당하므로 옳은 표현이다. 이때 앞에 있는 'in'은 관계대명사절에서 상승한 전치사가 아닌 과거분사 'interested'와 연결되는 전치사이다.

③ 출제 포인트: 형용사 vs. 부사
밑줄 친 'difficult'는 비교 대상인 'easy'와 병렬구조를 이루며, 형용사로서 부정대명사 'ones'를 수식하고 있으므로 옳게 사용되었다.

④ 출제 포인트: 명사절을 이끄는 접속사 that
밑줄 친 'that'은 'have found'의 목적어에 해당하는 명사절을 이끄는 접속사로 옳은 표현이다.

해석

2년 전쯤에, 나는 우리가 고난 예방 접종이라고 부르는 것에 관심을 갖게 되었다. 이것은 백신 접종이 질병에 대비해 여러분에게 예방주사를 놓아주는 것처럼 전화번호를 외우려고 노력하거나 긴 일요일 오후에 무엇을 해야 할지를 정하는 것과 같은 정신적인 퍼즐로 고심하는 것이 미래의 정신적인 고난들에 대비하여 여러분에게 예방주사를 놓아주는 개념이다. 적은 양의 정신적인 고난이 우리에게 유익하다는 개념을 뒷받침하는 꽤 많은 증거가 존재한다. 젊은 성인들은 예전에 쉬운 것보다는 어려운 것들을 풀어본 적 있을 때 까다로운 정신적인 퍼즐들을 훨씬 더 잘 푼다. 청소년기의 운동선수들 또한 어려운 일들을 잘 해내는데: 예를 들어, 우리는 대학 농구팀들이 그들의 프리시즌 일정이 더 힘들 때 더 잘 해낸다는 것을 알게 되었다.

어휘

inoculation (예방) 접종   vaccination 백신 접종
inoculate 접종하다, 예방주사를 놓다   dose (어느 정도의) 양, 약간
tricky 힘든, 곤란한   thrive on ~을 잘 해내다
demanding 부담이 큰, 힘든

06 정답 ③

정답해설

③ 출제 포인트: 현재분사 vs. 과거분사
'offered'는 완전타동사 'offer'의 과거분사이나 이후에 목적어 'a transparent screen'이 왔으며 생략된 주어 'high-tech firms'와 능동 관계이므로 'offered'를 현재분사 'offering'으로 수정해야 한다.

오답해설

① 출제 포인트: 관용표현(be based on)
밑줄 친 'is based on'은 관용표현 'be based on(~에 기반을 두다)'의 현재시제로 옳은 표현이다.

② 출제 포인트: 동사 vs. 준동사
'failed'는 'fail'의 과거분사가 아닌 과거시제 동사로 사용되었으며 주어는 'laws'이다. 또한 해당 문장에서 'fail'은 완전자동사로 전치사 'in'과 함께 옳게 사용되었다.

④ 출제 포인트: that vs. what/관용표현(go on)
'what' 이후에 오는 절이 주어가 없는 불완전한 형태의 절이며 'what' 앞에 선행사가 없으므로 선행사를 포함하는 관계대명사 'what'의 쓰임은 올바르다. 이를 의문대명사 'what'으로 보아 간접의문문으로 'what is going on~'으로 사용되었다고 볼 수도 있다. 이때, 'what'은 의문사이자 문장의 주어로 이어서 바로 동사 'is going'이 나오는 점에 유의해야 한다. 덧붙여 문장에 사용된 'go on'은 관용표현으로 '(일이) 일어나다[벌어지다]'를 뜻한다.

해석

이러한 권고는 이 변화가 환영받는다는 가정에 기반을 두고 있지만, 보행 중 문자 보내기를 금지하는 법들은 Toronto, Arkansas, Illinois, Nevada, New Jersey 그리고 New York에서 실패했다. 한편, 첨단 기술 기업들은 문자를 보내는 동안 그들의 앞에서 일어나는 일을 보행자들이 볼 수 있도록 하는 투명 화면을 제공하면서, 그 문제에 대한 기술적 해결책들을 개발하고 있다.

어휘

recommendation 권고   be based on ~에 기반을 두다
transparent 투명한, 명백한   pedestrian 보행자
go on 일어나다, 벌어지다

07 정답 ②

정답해설

② 출제 포인트: 주어와 동사의 수일치
주어가 단수 형태의 명사구 'the growth'이므로 동사에 단수 형태를 사용해야 한다. 따라서 복수 형태의 동사 'were'를 단수 형태인 'was'로 수정해야 한다. 이때 'in the size and complexity of human populations'는 'the growth'를 수식하는 전명구에 해당하며 동사의 수일치에 영향을 주지 않는다.

오답해설

① 출제 포인트: 형용사로 고착화된 분사
'renowned'는 형용사로 고착화된 분사로 '유명한, 명성 있는'을 뜻하며 해당 문장에서 명사구 'French scholar'를 수식하고 있으므로 옳은 표현이다.

③ 출제 포인트: 능동태 vs. 수동태
밑줄 친 'were focused on'은 「focus A on B」의 수동태인 「A be focused on B」의 과거시제에 해당하며 주어가 복수 형태인 'their thoughts'이므로 'were focused on'은 옳은 표현이다.

④ **출제 포인트: to부정사의 형용사적 용법**
밑줄 친 'to reflect and debate'는 명사 'time'을 수식하는 to부정사의 형용사적 용법으로 옳게 사용되었다.

해석

유명한 프랑스 학자에 따르면, 인구의 규모와 복잡성의 증가가 과학 발전의 추진력이었다. 일찍이 소규모 공동체들은 모든 그들의 신체적 그리고 정신적 노력을 생존에 초점을 맞추어야 했고, 그들의 생각은 음식과 종교에 초점이 맞춰졌다. 공동체가 커짐에 따라, 어떤 사람들은 곰곰이 생각하고 토론할 시간을 가졌다.

어휘

renowned 유명한, 명성 있는
concentrate A on B B에 A를 집중시키다
focus A on B B에 A를 집중시키다
reflect 곰곰이 생각하다, 심사숙고하다

08 정답 ②

정답해설

본문에서는 '소셜 미디어에서 보이는 지속적인 행복은 실제로는 불가능한 것이며, 진정한 행복을 느끼기 위해서는 다른 감정을 받아들일 수 있어야 한다'고 설명한다. 본문 마지막 문장 "In the long term, unhappiness might just be the key to happiness(장기적으로, 불행이 바로 행복의 열쇠가 될 수도 있다)."를 통해, '불행을 느끼는 것 또한 이후 진정한 행복을 느끼기 위해 필요하다'라는 것을 알 수 있다. 따라서 필자의 주장으로 가장 적절한 보기는 '② Feeling unhappy can be good for you(불행을 느끼는 것이 당신에게 좋을 수 있다).'이다.

오답해설

① 본문 초반에 '소셜 미디어 속 행복한 모습'에 대해 언급하고, 본문 중반에서 "Not only is it overrated, but it's totally unachievable(그것이 과대평가되어 있을 뿐만 아니라, 완전히 이룩할 수 없는 것이다)."라고 설명하고 있지만, 이는 '행복뿐만 아니라 다른 감정을 느끼는 것의 중요성'을 강조하기 위해 언급한 것이며, 글의 주요 요지는 본문 후반에 언급되고 있다. 따라서 오답이다.
나머지 선지는 본문과 관련이 없는 내용이므로 오답이다.

해석

소셜 미디어를 둘러보고 꿈의 직장을 얻고, 완벽한 가족을 구성하고 해변에서 햇볕을 쬐는 친구들을 직면하는 것은 다른 모든 이들이 어떠한 끝이 없는 상태의 행복감에 젖어 있는 느낌을 만들 수 있다. 그리고 소파에 누워 한 손에는 감자칩 한 봉지를 들고 한 손에는 당신의 휴대폰을 들고 한 시간 동안 스크롤을 하는 시간을 보내는 당신이 거기에 있다. 소셜 미디어는 우리를 불만족스럽게 만든다. 마치 우리 주변의 모든 사람들이 항상 행복한 것처럼 보인다. 그러나 그러한 끊임없는 행복은 과대 평가되어 있다. 그것은 과대 평가되어 있을 뿐만 아니라, 완전히 이룩할 수 없는 것이다. 만일 우리가 끊임없이 행복하길 기대한다면, 우리는 다른 어떤 감정을 느끼는 것이 잘못되었다고 판단하고, 따라서 우리는 우리가 슬픔, 화, 좌절 등을 느끼면 나쁜 것이라고 내면화 한다. 그러나 실제로, 진정으로 행복을 느끼기 위해서 우리는 다른 감정들을 받아들여야 한다. 그것이 슬픔 또는 불행함을 경험하는 것이 때때로 유용할 수도 있는 이유이다. 장기적으로, 불행이 바로 행복의 열쇠가 될지도 모른다.
① 소셜 미디어는 가짜 행복으로 가득하다.
② 불행을 느끼는 것이 당신에게 좋을 수 있다.
③ 당신의 감정을 당신을 사랑하는 사람들에게 표현하라.
④ 행복해지기 위해, 자신을 타인들과 비교하지 말라.

어휘

browse 둘러보다[훑어보다]
be confronted with 직면하다, 마주치다
score (성공 등을) 얻다
sun oneself 햇볕을 쬐다
impression 느낌, 인상
euphoria 행복감, 희열
crisp (감자를 얇고 동그랗게 잘라 튀긴) 감자칩
unsatisfied 만족[충족]하지 않은
constant 끊임없는
overrate 과대평가하다
unachievable 도달할[이룰] 수 없는
constantly 끊임없이
internalize (사상·태도 등을) 내면화하다
frustrated 좌절감을 느끼는, 불만스러워하는
miserableness 불행함, 비참한

09 정답 ④

정답해설

주어진 문장에서는 '2012년 12월 호주에서 제정된 담배에 대한 단순 포장 규정'에 대해 설명하고 있다. 이에 이어질 내용으로 가장 적절한 것은 '해당 규정에 대해 구체적으로 설명'하고 있는 (C)이다. 이어서, 이러한 규정을 통해 얻어진 결과를 통계 조사 결과를 인용해 설명해주는 (A)가 이어지는 것이 적절하다. 마지막으로 (A)에서 언급된 결과에 대해 'however'를 통해 반박하는 내용인 (B)가 이어지는 것이 자연스럽다. 따라서 정답은 '④ (C) - (A) - (B)'이다.

오답해설

나머지 보기는 문맥상 어색하므로 오답이다.

해석

담배 흡연이 예방 가능한 사망의 주요 원인임에 따라, 호주는 사람들이 담배 제품을 사용하는 것을 막기 위해 2012년 12월 담배와 담배 제품에 대한 단순 포장 규정을 제정했다.
(C) 그 규정은 효과를 높이기 위해 포장의 대부분이 건강 경고문으로 뒤덮이도록 했고, 포장이 소비자들에게 덜 매력적으로 보이도록 하기 위해 브랜드명 및 로고를 삭제하도록 했다.
(A) Australian Bureau of Statistics의 National Health Survey 2014-2015에 따르면, 단순 포장 시행을 포함한 수많은 법안들 때문에 그 국가의 흡연율은 2001년(28.2%)과 2015년(16.3%) 사이에 10% 이상 감소했다.
(B) 그러나, 단순 포장의 효과는 그 국가의 주요 담배 회사들에 의해 반박되었다. 그들은 흡연율의 감소는 미미하고 단순 포장이 불법 담배 시장을 조장했다고 주장했다.

어휘

leading 가장 중요한, 선두적인
preventable 막을 수 있는, 방해[예방]할 수 있는
enact 제정하다
plain 단순한, 소박한, 꾸미지 않은
discourage (무엇을 어렵게 만들거나 반대하여) 막다[말리다]
bureau 부서, 국
statistics 통계
decline 감소하다, 하락하다
initiative 새로운 중요 기획[계획], 법안
implementation 실행
refute 반박하다, 부인하다
claim 주장하다
insignificant 사소한, 하찮은
boost 조장하다, 촉진하다, 신장시키다

10 정답 ④

정답해설

본문은 '언어 변화'에 대한 글로서, 본문 초반에는 '우리가 쉽게 인식할 수 있는 언어 변화'에 대해 언급한 후, 빈칸 이후에는 '수백 년이 흐른 후에야 비로소 인지된 언어 변화'의 예시인 'The Great Vowel Shift'를 제시하고 있다. 따라서 빈칸에는 '오랫동안 인지되지 않는 변화'에 대해 언급하는 내용이 들어가는 것이 자연스럽다. 그러므로 빈칸에 가장 적절한 표현은 '④ may not be noticeable for decades or even centuries(수십 년 또는 심지어 수 세기 동안 알아차릴 수 없을 수도 있는)'이다.

오답해설

① 본문에서는 '외국어의 영향'에 관해서는 언급되지 않는다.
② 본문과 관련 없는 내용이므로 오답이다.
③ 본문에서는 언어 변화를 유발하는 요인에 대해서는 언급되지 않는다.

해석

언어가 변한다는 것을 모든 사람이 알고 있다. 오직 최근에 도입된 단어(bromance, YOLO, derp) 또는 구식이 된 문장구조(How do you do? Have you a moment?)를 구분하는 것은 쉽지만, 끊임없이 우리는 수십 년 또는 심지어 수 세기 동안 알아차릴 수 없을지도 모르는 언어 변화의 한복판에 있다. 언어에 있어서 가장 거대하고 가장 오래 지속되는 변화 중 몇몇은 천천히 그리고 알아차릴 수 없게 발생한다. 예를 들어, 대모음 추이(Great Vowel Shift)는 350년에 걸쳐 발생한 일련의 발음 변화이며, 그 이후 100년 이상 동안 별로 알아차려지지 않았다. 그것은 현대와 중세 영어 사이의 명료함의 격차를 야기했고, 영어 발음과 스펠링 사이의 성가신 정렬 불량을 창출해 냈다. 그러나 그것이 진행되고 있는 동안에는 알아차리는 것이 불가능했다.
① 외국어에 의해 영향을 받을 수도 있는
② 오랜 기간 동안 사용되지 않을 수도 있는
③ 사회 그리고 문화적 요소에 의해 유발될 수도 있는
④ 수십 년 또는 심지어 수 세기 동안 알아차릴 수 없을지도 모르는

어휘

pick out 분간하다, 가려내다   introduce 도입하다, 소개하다
bromance 브로맨스(남자들 간의 진한 우정)
YOLO 욜로, You only live once의 약자
derp 이런 바보 같으니라고! 젠장! (어리석음을 한탄하며 말하는 감탄사로 2013년경에 문서에 등장함)
construction 구조, 구성   out of style 유행이 지난
constantly 끊임없이, 거듭   lasting 지속적인, 영속적인
imperceptibly 알아차릴 수 없게, 희미하게, 미세하게
Great Vowel Shift 대모음 추이(推移) (중세 영어에서 현대[근대]영어로의 역사적 음운(音韻) 변화)
pronunciation 발음
intelligibility 명료함, 알 수 있음, 이해할 수 있음
misalignment 정렬 불량, 어긋남, 일렬로 서지 않음
see 간파하다, 알다   trigger 촉발하다, 유발하다
noticeable 알아차릴 수 있는, 뚜렷한, 분명한

결국엔 성정혜 영어 하프모의고사
기적사 DAY 70

| 01 | ② | 02 | ④ | 03 | ② | 04 | ① | 05 | ② |
| 06 | ② | 07 | ③ | 08 | ④ | 09 | ④ | 10 | ③ |

01 정답 ②

정답해설

'sporadic'은 '산발적인, 이따금 발생하는'을 뜻하는 형용사로 ② scattered(산발적인, 산재한)와 의미상 가장 가깝다.

해석

경기 전에 도시의 여러 곳에서 영국과 독일 축구 팬들이 연루된 **산발적인** 충돌이 있었다.
① 말을 잘 듣는
② 산발적인, 산재한
③ 끈질긴, 수그러들지 않는
④ 확고한, 바꿀 수 없는

어휘

sporadic 산발적인, 이따금 발생하는   amenable 말을 잘 듣는
scattered 산발적인, 산재한   relentless 끈질긴, 수그러들지 않는
implacable 확고한, 바꿀 수 없는

오답률 TOP 1

02 정답 ④

정답해설

'perjury'는 '위증'을 뜻하는 명사로 ④ mendacity(거짓말, 허위)와 의미상 가장 가깝다.

해석

정부는 검사들에게 용의자를 강제적으로 소환하고 **위증**을 범한 사람들을 처벌하도록 허용하는 법을 제정할 계획이다.
① 가석방
② 중죄, 흉악 범죄
③ 죄수, 상습범, 전과자
④ 거짓말, 허위

어휘

prosecutor 검사, 검찰관   forcibly 강제로
summon (법원으로) 소환하다   suspect 용의자
punish 처벌하다, 벌주다
commit (그릇된 일·범죄를) 저지르다[범하다]
perjury 위증   parole 가석방
felony 중죄, 흉악 범죄   jailbird 죄수, 상습범, 전과자
mendacity 거짓말, 허위

03 정답 ②

정답해설

'comeback'은 '부흥, 부활, 복귀'를 뜻하는 명사로 ② resurgence(재기, 부활)와 의미상 가장 가깝다.

해석
그것은 억만장자들을 위해 건설되고 있는 거대한 새 주택에 태피스트리가 **부흥**할 것이라고 확신한 한 딜러에 의해 구입되었다.
① 일시적인 중단, 유예, 연기
② 재기, 부활
③ 연기, 거치
④ 연기, 보류, 정학

어휘
convince 납득시키다, 확신시키다
tapestry 태피스트리(여러 가지 색실로 그림을 짜 넣은 직물)
comeback 부흥, 부활, 복귀   billionaire 억만장자, 갑부
respite 일시적인 중단, 유예, 연기   resurgence 재기, 부활
deferment 연기, 거치   suspension 연기, 보류, 정학

오답률 TOP 3

04 정답 ①

정답해설
(A) 교수님은 학생이 처한 상황에 대해 '두 선택 모두에 확실히 ~가 있다'라고 말하고 있으므로 빈칸 (A)에 들어갈 가장 적절한 것은 '장점과 단점(pros and cons)'이다.
(B) 학생이 고민하는 상황에서 교수님의 조언을 듣고 '고민에 대해 ~하겠다'고 말하고 있으므로 빈칸 (B)에 들어갈 가장 적절한 것은 '곰곰이 숙고하다(mull over)'이다.

오답해설
② (A) 학생이 두 가지 선택지 중 어느 것을 택할지 고민하는 상황에서 교수님이 두 선택지 모두에 확실하게 '핵심(the bottom line)'이 있다고 말하는 것은 문맥상 어색하다.
③ (B) 학생은 교수님의 조언을 들은 후, 자신의 고민에 대해 '부족할(run short of)' 것이라고 이야기하는 것은 대화의 흐름상 빈칸에 들어갈 말로 적절하지 않다.
④ (A) 학생이 두 가지 선택지 중 어느 것을 택할지 고민하는 상황에서 교수님이 두 선택지 모두에 확실하게 '핵심(the bottom line)'이 있다고 말하는 것은 맥락상 적합하지 않다. (B) 학생은 교수님의 조언을 들은 후, 자신의 고민에 대해 '부족할(run short of)' 것이라고 이야기하는 것은 대화의 흐름상 빈칸에 들어갈 말로 자연스럽지 않다.

해석
학생: 교수님, 안녕하세요. 지금 교수님의 상담 시간인가요?
교수: 안녕. 응 지금 상담 시간 맞아. 들어와도 좋아.
학생: 감사합니다. 교수님께서 수업 시간에 말씀해주신 인턴십 프로그램에 대해 상담하고 싶습니다.
교수: 오, 다음 학기에 지원하는 것에 관심 있니?
학생: 네. 근데 한 가지 고민이 있어요. 저는 다음 학기에 교환 학생으로 외국에 갈 생각이었어요. 어떤 선택을 해야 할지 고민이에요.
교수: 음, 확실히 두 선택지 모두에 (A) 장점과 단점이 있어. 근데 내가 생각하기로는 인턴십 프로그램이 실무 경험을 하기에 더 나은 기회를 제공할 것 같아.
학생: 교수님 말씀이 맞아요. 이 고민에 대해 (B) 곰곰이 숙고해 보겠습니다. 시간 내주셔서 감사합니다, 교수님.
교수: 천만에. 상담 시간 동안에 언제든 방문해도 좋아.
① (A) 장점과 단점 (B) 곰곰이 숙고하다
② (A) 핵심 (B) 곰곰이 숙고하다
③ (A) 장점과 단점 (B) 부족하다
④ (A) 핵심 (B) 부족하다

어휘
office hours (대학 교수의) 면접 시간, 근무 시간, 영업시간
pros and cons 장점과 단점, 찬반양론
hands-on 실제의, 실지의   mull over 곰곰이 숙고하다
the bottom line 핵심   run short of 부족하다

---

05 정답 ②

정답해설
② **출제 포인트: 접속사의 쓰임/if vs. whether**
접속사 'if' 이후에는 'or not'이 바로 올 수 없으며 전치사의 목적어절을 이끄는 접속사로 사용할 수 없다. 해당 문장은 'if' 이후에 'or not'이 사용되었으며 전치사 'about'의 목적어절을 이끄는 접속사로 사용되었으므로 옳지 않다. 따라서 'if'를 'whether'로 수정해야 한다.

오답해설
① **출제 포인트: 주어와 동사의 수일치**
밑줄 친 'difference'는 단수 형태로 주어에 해당하며 이때 동사가 단수 형태인 'is'이므로 'difference'는 옳은 표현이다. 'difference'와 'is' 사이의 'between ~ out'은 전명구에 해당하며, 이처럼 주어와 동사 사이의 거리가 먼 경우 수일치에 유의해야한다.
③ **출제 포인트: to부정사의 명사적 용법**
밑줄 친 'to listen'은 to부정사의 명사적 용법에 해당하며 진주어로 옳게 사용되었다.
④ **출제 포인트: that vs. what**
밑줄 친 'what' 이후에 오는 절이 목적어가 없는 불완전한 형태이며 'what' 앞에 선행사가 없으므로 선행사를 포함한 관계대명사 'what'은 옳은 표현이다.

해석
흔히 직장에서 성취감을 느끼는 것과 공허함, 상실감, 짜증 그리고 극도의 피로를 느끼는 것 사이의 차이는 여러분이 무언가를 배우고 있는지 아닌지에 관한 것이다. 이것이 경청해야 하는 또 다른 이유이다. 여러분이 잠시 멈추고, 자신의 마음을 진정시키고, 다른 사람들이 말하는 것을 경청할 때 여러분이 얼마나 더 많이 배우는가 하는 것은 놀랍다. 이것은 여러분이 이끄는 바로 그 팀은 물론 여러분의 왼쪽과 오른쪽에 있는 동료들에게도 사실이다. 때때로 특히 만약 여러분이 100퍼센트 동의하지 않는다면, 여러분의 상사나 임원에게 경청하는 것은 어렵다. 어떤 경우에 여러분은 심지어 그들을 좋아하지 않을 수도 있다. 나는 그것을 안다. 그들은 이유가 있어 자신들의 역할을 맡고 있으며, 그들이 몇 가지는 알고 있을지도 모른다는 것을 기억해라. 그들이 말하는 것에 마음을 열고 기꺼이 경청해라. 여러분은 자신이 듣는 모든 것에 동의하지 않을지도 모르지만, 적어도 여러분은 경청했다.

어휘
fulfilled 성취감을 느끼는   pause 잠시 멈추다
executive 간부, 임원   willing 기꺼이 하는, 자발적인

---

06 정답 ②

정답해설
② **출제 포인트: 주어와 동사의 수일치/능동태 vs. 수동태**
밑줄 친 'are determined'는 'determine'의 수동태에 해당하며 이후에 「by+행위자」인 'by our culture'가 왔으므로 수동태 자체는 옳으나 주어가 단수 형태인 'the strength'이므로 복수 형태의 동사 'are'를 단수 형태의 동사 'is'로 수정해야 한다.

오답해설

① 출제 포인트: 현재분사 vs. 과거분사
'projected'는 '투사하다'를 뜻하는 완전타동사 'project'의 과거분사로 해석상 '투사된 경험'이 자연스러우며 수식하는 대상 'experiences'와 수동 관계이므로 밑줄 친 'projected experiences'는 옳은 표현이다.

③ 출제 포인트: 수여동사의 구조/주어와 동사의 수일치
밑줄 친 'give us hints'는 「수여동사+간접목적어+직접목적어」에 해당하며 이때 'give'의 수일치 기준은 접속사 'for'가 이끄는 절의 주어인 'their form and spatial organization'이므로 복수 형태의 동사 'give'는 옳게 사용되었다. 또한 해당 문장에서 'tell'은 완전타동사로 사용되었으며, 접속사 'for'를 전치사 'for'로 오해하지 않도록 유의해야한다.

④ 출제 포인트: 접속사가 생략되지 않은 분사구문
밑줄 친 'unless especially invited'는 접속사가 생략되지 않은 분사구문에 해당하며 이때 생략된 주어는 'we'이다. 문맥상 '특별히 초대받지 않는다면'이 자연스러우므로 'unless especially invited'는 옳은 표현이다.

해석

건물은 이러한 투사된 경험을 통해서 우리 안에 공감할 수 있는 반응을 불러일으키며, 이러한 반응의 강도는 우리의 문화에 의해 결정된다. 그것들은 이야기를 들려준다, 왜냐하면 그것들의 형태와 공간 구성이 그것들이 어떻게 사용되어야 하는지에 대한 힌트를 우리에게 주기 때문이다. 그것들의 물리적 배치는 어떤 사용을 권장하고 다른 사용을 억제한다; 우리는 특별히 초대받지 않는다면 극장의 무대 뒤로 가지 않는다.

어휘

arouse ~을 불러일으키다　　empathic 공감할 수 있는
project 투사하다　　spatial 공간의, 공간적인
layout 배치, 레이아웃

오답률 TOP 2
07 정답 ③

정답해설

③ 출제 포인트: 능동태 vs. 수동태
타동사 'say'의 수동태인 'are said'가 사용되었음에 주의해야 한다. 주어진 문장에서 수동태로 쓰인 'are said'가 전명구 'about a particularly convincing interpretation' 이후에 온 that절 'that a performer ~ composer'를 'say'의 목적어로 갖고 있으므로, 수동태 동사 형태인 'are said'는 옳지 않다. 따라서 밑줄 친 'are said'를 능동태 'say'로 수정해야 한다.

오답해설

① 출제 포인트: 대명사 수일치
'that of an actor'에서 'that'이 가리키는 대상은 단수 형태의 명사 'interpretation'이므로 'that'의 쓰임은 올바르다.

② 출제 포인트: 완전타동사 vs. 수여동사
'project'는 4형식으로 사용할 수 없는 완전타동사이다. 해당 문장에서 'project'의 목적어는 'a mixture ~ intentions'이므로 밑줄 친 'an audience' 앞에 전치사 'to'를 사용해서 'to an audience'를 전명구로 사용하는 것이 옳다.

④ 출제 포인트: 현재분사 vs. 과거분사
'convincing'은 'convince'의 현재분사로 해석상 '설득력 있는 해석'이 자연스러우며 수식하는 대상 'interpretation'과 능동 관계이므로 'convincing'은 옳은 표현이다.

해석

배우의 해석처럼, 그 혹은 그녀의 해석에는 미묘한 타이밍과 음조로 가득하다. 연주자들은 그들 자신의 느낌과 작곡자의 의도를 혼합한 것을 청중에게 전한다. 비평가들은 때때로 특히 설득력 있는 해석에 대해서 연주자가 작품과 그 작품의 작곡자와 동일시된다고 말한다.

어휘

interpretation 해석　　subtle 미묘한
inflection 음조, 어조　　convincing 설득력 있는
composer 작곡가
identify A with B A와 B를 동일시하다

08 정답 ④

정답해설

본문은 '행복이 수명과 관련이 없다'는 내용으로, 마지막 문장 "The findings showed that happiness may not prolong a person's life, and feeling blue doesn't predispose a person to health problems that can cause death(연구 결과는 행복이 한 사람의 수명을 연장시키지 않는다는 것과 울적함을 느끼는 것이 한 사람이 사망을 유발하는 건강 문제를 겪기 쉽게 하도록 하지 않는다는 것을 보여주었다)."를 통해, '행복 또는 우울감이 수명을 연장하거나 질병을 유발하지 않는다'는 점을 시사하고 있다. 여기에서 '행복 또는 우울감'은 '기분(mood)'이라고 할 수 있으므로, 글의 주제로 가장 적절한 보기는 '④ The relationship between someone's mood and his or her lifespan(누군가의 기분과 그 또는 그녀의 수명 사이의 관계)'이다.

오답해설

① 본문은 '정신 건강'이 아니라 '수명'에 관해 설명하고 있으므로 오답이다.
② 본문과 관련이 없는 내용이므로 오답이다.
③ 본문에서 언급되지 않는 내용이다.

해석

새로운 연구가 행복이 한 사람이 얼마나 오래 살 것인가에 영향을 미치지 않는다는 것을 발견했다. 옥스퍼드 대학의 연구원들이 슬픔과 갈등이 나쁜 건강을 야기한다는 보편적인 믿음에 대한 정반대의 결과를 발견했다. 대신에, 그들은 행복과 슬픔 모두 한 사람의 수명에 영향을 미치지 않는다는 것을 발견했다. "많은 사람들이 여전히 스트레스 또는 불행이 직접적으로 질병을 야기할 수 있다고 믿는다, 그러나 그들은 단순히 원인과 결과를 혼동하는 것이다"라고 옥스퍼드 대학의 Richard Peto는 말했다. "물론 아픈 사람들은 건강한 사람들보다 더 불행한 경향이 있지만, UK Million Women Study는 행복과 불행이 사망률에 어떠한 직접적인 영향도 미치지 않는다는 것을 보여준다." 연구 결과는 행복이 한 사람의 수명을 연장시키지 않는다는 것과 울적함을 느끼는 것이 한 사람이 사망을 유발하는 건강 문제를 겪기 쉽게 하도록 하지 않는다는 것을 보여주었다.
① 정신 건강에 미치는 행복의 영향
② 스트레스와 우울의 원인과 결과
③ 치명적인 질병을 피하고 더 오랜 인생을 살기 위한 정보
④ 누군가의 기분과 그 또는 그녀의 수명 사이의 관계

어휘

tension 갈등, 긴장　　lifespan 수명
confuse A and B A와 B를 혼동하다
finding 결과, 결론　　prolong 연장시키다
feel blue 우울한, 울적한
predispose someone to something (특정한 질병에) 취약하게[잘 걸리게] 하다

09 정답 ④

정답해설

(A) 이전 문장에서는 '금연을 원하는 사람들이 많지만, 금연을 쉽다고 생각하지는 않는다'고 설명한다. 그리고 (A) 이후에서 구체적인 수치를 제시하며, 금연에 실패하는 사람들의 비율을 제시하고 있다. 즉, (A) 이전에 설명한 내용에 대한 구체적인 내용을 추가하고 있는 구조이므로, 빈칸에 가장 적절한 것은 'In fact(사실)'이다.

(B) 이전의 내용은 '금연의 어려움'에 대해 설명하고 있다. 흡연의 중독적인 특징 때문에 금연이 어렵기 때문에, (B) 이후에서, '구체적인 치료 계획을 따라야 할 필요'가 있다고 설명하고 있으므로, '인과' 관계를 나타내는 'Therefore(그러므로)' 또는 'Thus(그러므로)'가 빈칸에 가장 적절하다.

따라서 정답은 '④ In fact(사실) - Thus(그러므로)'이다.

오답해설

① (A) 빈칸 전후의 내용이 '역접' 관계가 아니기 때문에 'However(그러나)'가 (A)에 들어가는 것은 부적절하다.

나머지 보기는 문맥상 어색하므로 오답이다.

해석

전 세계에 예방 가능한 사망의 주요 원인으로 알려진 흡연은 사람들을 폐암과 심장병을 포함한 여러 담배 관련 질병의 위험에 처하게 한다. 안타깝게도, 많은 사람들이 담배를 끊길 바라는 반면, 그들은 그렇게 하는 것을 쉽다고 생각하지 않는다. (A) 사실, 연구에 따르면, 흡연자의 최대 70%가 담배를 끊기를 바라고, 최대 50%가 지난해에 금연을 시도했지만 그렇게 하는 것을 실패했다고 보고했다. 이러한 어려움은 흡연의 중독적인 특징 때문이다. (B) 그러므로, 흡연자들은 성공적으로 금연을 하기 위해 흡연 습관을 그만두는 과정을 일컫는 말인 금연을 위한 구체적인 치료 계획을 따를 필요가 종종 있다. 주로 담배를 매우 중독성 있게 만드는 니코틴 함유량 때문에, 담배에 대한 그들의 애착이 더 깊고 오래될수록, 금연의 과정은 더 어려울 것이다.

(A)	(B)
① 그러나	그러므로
② 그 뒤에	즉
③ 게다가	반면에
④ 사실	그러므로

어휘

leading 가장 중요한, 선두적인
preventable 막을 수 있는, 방해[예방]할 수 있는
place (특정한 상황에) 두다[처하게 하다]
attempt 시도하다, 애써 해보다
challenge 과제, 난제, 도전, 어려움
nature 자연, 천성, 특징
smoking cessation 금연
attachment 애착
quit 그만두다, 중지하다
addictive 중독성의
cessation 중단, 중지
refer to 말하다, 지칭하다

10 정답 ③

정답해설

주어진 문장에서는 '언어가 타인과 접촉할 때 변화한다'고 설명한다. 이후에 이어질 내용으로 적절한 것은, '모든 사람은 다르게 말한다'고 언급하며, 이러한 접촉으로 인해 변화가 발생하는 이유를 제시하고 있는 (B)이다. (B)에서는 크게는 지리적으로 다른 지역, 그리고 작게는 작은 공동체 내에서도 말하는 방식의 차이가 존재한다고 설명한다. 이후에는, 더 하위 단위인 '가족' 내에서도 '세대' 간 말의 차이가 존재한다고 설명하는 (A)가 이어지는 것이 적절하다. 마지막으로, 앞서 (B)와 (A)에서 언급된 여러 화자들을 'these different speakers(이러한 다른 화자들)'를 이용해 가리키고 있는 (C)가 이어지는 것이 알맞다. 따라서 정답은 '③ (B) - (A) - (C)'이다.

오답해설

④ (A)의 'Also(또한)'로 보아, (A) 이전에서 유사한 논조의 내용이 먼저 언급되어야 함을 알 수 있다. (A)의 주요 내용은 '사용하는 언어의 차이'이므로, (B)에서 언급된 '성별, 민족성, 사회 및 교육적 배경에 따른 발화 방식의 차이' 이후에 바로 연결되는 것이 문맥상 자연스럽다는 것을 알 수 있다. 따라서 오답이다.

나머지 보기는 문맥상 어색하므로 오답이다.

해석

언어는 화자들이 서로 접촉할 때마다 매우 미묘하게 변화한다.

(B) 동일하게 말하는 두 개인은 없다: 다른 지리적 장소에서 온 사람들은 분명 다르게 말한다, 그러나 심지어 동일한 소규모의 공동체 내에서도 화자의 성별, 민족성, 그리고 사회 및 교육적 배경에 따라 차이가 있다.

(A) 또한, 만일 당신의 가족이 동일한 지역에서 수 세대 동안 살아왔다 하더라도, 당신은 아마 당신이 사용하는 언어와 당신의 조부모님이 말하는 방식 사이의 수많은 차이를 알아차릴 수 있을 것이다.

(C) 이러한 다른 화자들과의 상호 작용을 통해, 우리는 새로운 단어, 표현 그리고 발음을 접하고 우리 자신의 화법에 그것들을 통합시킨다. 이러한 방식으로, 우리는 언어 변화에 우리 자신의 작은 기여를 하고 있는 것이다.

어휘

subtly 미묘하게
identify 찾다, 발견하다, 알아보다
geographical 지리적인
ethnicity 민족성
pronunciation 발음
speech 말투, 화법, 담화
come into contact 접촉하다
identically 꼭 같게, 동일하게
variation 차이, 변화
encounter 접하다[마주치다]
integrate 통합시키다
contribution 기여, 공헌

기적사 복습 모의고사 7회

결국엔 성정혜 영어 하프모의고사

01	①	02	③	03	②	04	④	05	②
06	②	07	①	08	②	09	③	10	④
11	③	12	③	13	②	14	②	15	③
16	④	17	①	18	③	19	③	20	③

01 정답 ①   Day 63-01

정답해설

'excludes'는 동사 'exclude'의 단수 형태로 '제외하다'를 뜻한다. 따라서 ① scratches(제외하다, 긁다)와 의미가 가장 가깝다.

해석

그들은 자택에서 교육받는 자녀의 절충적인 교육 과정이 중요 과목들을 종종 **제외한다**고 주장한다.
① 제외하다, 긁다
② 용납하다
③ 포함하다, 포괄하다
④ 비난하다, 규탄하다

02 정답 ③   Day 66-01

정답해설

'rebellious'는 '반항적인'을 뜻하는 형용사로 ③ disobedient(반항하는, 거역하는)와 의미상 가장 가깝다.

해석

부모들은 **반항적**으로 행동하거나, 사회적으로 서툴러 보이는 자녀를 포기해서는 안 된다. 이것은 대부분의 젊은이들이 경험하고 결국 벗어나게 되는 일반적인 단계이기 때문이다.
① 수동적인
② 의식이 혼탁한, 기뻐 날뛰는
③ 반항적인, 복종하지 않는
④ 산발적인, 때때로 일어나는

03 정답 ②   Day 68-02

정답해설

'pernicious'는 '치명적인'을 뜻하는 형용사로 ② capital(치명적인, 중대한)과 의미상 가장 가깝다.

해석

비록 그 문제가 **치명적**이고 인종 차별만큼 다루기 어렵다고 할지라도, 당신은 그 문제를 해결하기 위해 다양한 해결책을 생각하기 시작한다.
① 앙증맞은, 얌전한
② 치명적인, 중대한
③ 매우 아름다운, 정교한
④ 즙이 많은, 다육성의

04 정답 ④   Day 61-03

정답해설

'pushy'는 '지나치게 밀어붙이는, 강요하는'을 뜻하는 형용사로 ④ aggressive(대단히 적극적인, 공격적인)와 의미상 가장 가깝다.

해석

숙련된 판매원은 적극적인 것과 **강요하는** 것 사이에는 차이가 있다고 주장한다.
① 오싹한, 흥분된
② 용감한
③ 소심한
④ 공격적인, 대단히 적극적인, 시비조의

05 정답 ②   Day 62-09

정답해설

본문은 '단순히 민주국가가 되는 것만이 아니라, 높은 수준의 민주국가가 되는 것이 목표가 되어야 한다'고 설명하며, '민주국가에도 높은 수준의 민주국가와 낮은 수준의 민주국가가 있다'는 것을 언급하고 있다. 따라서 전체 글의 요지로 가장 적절한 보기는 '② Not all democracy is the same(모든 민주주의가 동일한 것은 아니다).'이다.

해석

보편적 관점은 국가들의 주된 목표 중 하나는 민주국가가 되는 것이어야 한다는 것이다. 그러나 국가들은 그들이 민주주의 상태를 달성했을 때 만족해서는 안 된다. 이후의 목표 중 하나는 높은 수준의 민주주의의 질을 확립하고 유지하는 것이어야 한다. 물론, 이 목표는 또한 안정된 민주국가들에게도 적용된다. 민주주의 시스템의 정당성에 있어서, 높은 수준의 민주주의의 질은 중요하다는 것이 보여질 수 있고, 낮은 수준의 민주주의의 질은 심각한 민주주의적 문제점으로 보여질 수 있다. 예를 들어, 민주주의 시스템에서 투표를 통한 정치 참여는 주춧돌로 여겨질 수 있다. 만약 투표자의 투표율이 낮다면, 그 선거와 민주주의 시스템의 정당성은 문제가 될 수 있다.
① 민주주의는 이로울 수 있다.
② 모든 민주주의가 동일한 것은 아니다.
③ 양질의 민주주의에 도달하는 것은 어렵다.
④ 민주주의 사회에서 투표는 가장 중요한 행위이다.

06 정답 ②   Day 64-07

정답해설

② 출제 포인트: 현재분사 vs. 과거분사/수동태 불가동사

해당 문장에서 'Thought of as a relationship'은 'think of A as B(A를 B로 여기다)'의 수동태인 「A be thought of as B」가 분사구문으로 쓰인 것으로 생략된 주어 A는 주절의 주어인 'leadership'이다. 또한 주격 관계대명사 'that'이 이끄는 절의 동사 'occurs'는 완전자동사이므로 수동태로 사용할 수 없음에 주의해야 한다.

해석

① 연설자는 이것이 남반구에서 본 북미의 모습이라고 재빨리 말했다.
② 관계로 여겨지면, 리더십은 리더들과 추종자들 사이에서 일어나는 협력의 과정이 된다.
③ 불평등은 엘리트를 제외하고 아무에게도 혜택을 제공하지 않으며 그것이 만들어내는 불필요한 갈등 때문에 전체 사회에 해롭다.
④ 만약 우리가 사람들과 관계가 복잡한 기계와 같다고 생각한다면, 우리는 아마 그들의 문제를 기계들에 있는 오작동으로 볼 것이다.

07 정답 ①
Day 68-07

정답해설

① 출제 포인트: 능동태 vs. 수동태/It(가주어)+be+과거분사+that절(진주어)

'note'는 「It(가주어)+be+과거분사+that절(진주어)」의 형태로 사용할 수 있는 동사이다. 해당 문장의 경우 접속사 'that'이 이끄는 절은 진주어이며 'It'은 가주어이므로 완전타동사 'note'의 목적어가 없음을 알 수 있다. 따라서 밑줄 친 'note'는 수동태인 'be noted'로 수정해야 한다.

해석

하지만 인터넷 직업 시대에서의 어떠한 발전도 가장 기본적인 구직기술, 즉 자기 이해의 중요성을 감소시키지는 않았다는 것에 주목해야 한다. 심지어 인터넷 시대에도, 구직은 개인적인 직업 역량, 분야에 대한 관심, 그리고 선호되는 직장 분위기와 흥미를 확인하는 것과 함께 시작한다.

08 정답 ②
Day 65-08

정답해설

본문의 요지는 '현대 예술은 외견상 단순해 보일지 모르나, 그것이 함축하고 있는 의미는 결코 단순하지 않으며, 과거의 예술품보다 현대의 상황에 더 잘 부합하는 의미를 관람객에게 전달할 수 있다'는 것이다. 마지막 문장 "In this sense, contemporary art deserves our appreciation and it's time it lost its undeserved bad reputation(이러한 견지에서, 현대 예술은 우리의 감상을 받을 만하며, 이제 그것이 부당한 악명을 떨쳐버릴 때이다)."을 통해, '현대 예술이 감상할 가치가 충분하다'는 점을 드러내고 있으므로, 글의 제목으로 가장 적절한 것은 '② Is Contemporary Art Worth Looking At?(현대 예술은 감상할 가치가 있는가?)'이다.

해석

현대 예술은 종종 조금 의미가 없고 기술이 부족한 것으로 치부될 수 있다. 상투적인 "내 5살짜리 아이도 이것을 할 수 있다"는 구절은 만일 예술가의 작품이 너무 단순해 보인다면 언급된다. 그렇다, 많은 현대 예술작품이 언뜻 보기에는 약간 기초적인 것처럼 보인다, 그러나 그것이 그것들이 복잡한 개념을 지니고 있지 않다는 것을 의미하지는 않는다 - 사실, 그러한 작품 내에 담긴 아이디어는 훨씬 오래되었지만 더 인기 있는 그림들에 담긴 것들보다 흔히 더 심오하다. 그리고 분명히 예술작품이 더 최신의 것일수록, 메시지가 현대의 관람객에게 더 의미가 있다, 그렇지 않은가? Rachel Maclean의 HOME에서의 최근 전시회가 이것의 한 예이다. 그것은 꽤 단순했으며 모든 사람의 취향에 맞지는 않았다, 그러나 그것이 표현한 소셜 미디어 및 기술과 우리의 관계에 대한 메시지는 정말 심금을 울렸다. 예술은 시각적 즐거움일 뿐이어야 한다는 계속되는 믿음이 있는 것 같다. 그러나 예술은 비록 그것이 아름답고 복잡하지는 않더라도, 감정을 상기시키고 사고를 자극해야 한다. 이러한 견지에서, 현대 예술은 우리의 감상을 받을 만하며 이제 그것이 부당한 악명을 떨쳐버릴 때이다.

① 누구나 현대 예술가가 될 수 있다
② 현대 예술은 감상할 가치가 있는가?
③ 현대 예술이 사회에 어떻게 영향을 미치는가?
④ 현대 예술이 왜 그렇게 단순해 보이는가?

09 정답 ③
Day 61-10

정답해설

주어진 지문은 미국에서 공포를 일으켰던 '광대'에 대한 내용이다. 광대가 아이들을 꾀어내는 시도와 겁을 주려고 하는 위협적인 모습으로 보아 광대에 대해 부정적으로 서술하고 있음을 알 수 있다. 따라서 빈칸에는 광대에 대한 부정적인 이미지로 인한 부정적인 결과가 와야 한다. 따라서 빈칸에는 '③ caused a nationwide panic(전국적인 공포를 일으켰다)'이 알맞다.

해석

광대가 사람들을 겁주게 한다는 생각은 미국에서 힘을 얻기 시작했다. 예를 들면, 사우스 캐롤라이나에서 한밤중에 숲이나 도시에 광대 의상을 입은 사람들이 종종 숨어 있었다는 것을 봤다고 사람들은 보고했다. 몇몇 사람들은 광대가 집이나 숲으로 아이들을 꾀어내는 시도를 했다고 말했다. 곧 아이들과 어른들 모두에게 겁주려고 하는 위협적인 모습을 한 광대에 대한 보고가 있었다. 비록 대개 폭력에 대한 보고는 없었고, 보고된 목격의 대다수가 후에 거짓으로 밝혀졌지만, 이것은 전국적인 공포를 일으켰다.

① 서커스 산업에 이득이 됐다
② 광고에 광대의 사용을 촉진시켰다
③ 전국적인 공포를 일으켰다
④ 행복한 광대의 완벽한 이미지를 형성했다

10 정답 ④
Day 69-10

정답해설

본문은 '언어 변화'에 대한 글로서, 본문 초반에는 '우리가 쉽게 인식할 수 있는 언어 변화'에 대해 언급한 후, 빈칸 이후에는 '수백 년이 흐른 후에야 비로소 인지된 언어 변화'의 예시인 'The Great Vowel Shift'를 제시하고 있다. 따라서 빈칸에는 '오랫동안 인지되지 않는 변화'에 대해 언급하는 내용이 들어가는 것이 자연스럽다. 그러므로 빈칸에 가장 적절한 표현은 '④ may not be noticeable for decades or even centuries(수십 년 또는 심지어 수 세기 동안 알아차릴 수 없을 수도 있는)'이다.

해석

언어가 변한다는 것을 모든 사람이 알고 있다. 오직 최근에 도입된 단어(bromance, YOLO, derp) 또는 구식이 된 문장구조(How do you do? Have you a moment?)를 구분하는 것은 쉽지만, 끊임없이 우리는 수십 년 또는 심지어 수 세기 동안 알아차릴 수 없을지도 모르는 언어 변화의 한복판에 있다. 언어에 있어서 가장 거대하고 가장 오래 지속되는 변화 중 몇몇은 천천히 그리고 알아차릴 수 없게 발생한다. 예를 들어, 대모음 추이(Great Vowel Shift)는 350년에 걸쳐 발생한 일련의 발음 변화이며, 그 이후 100년 이상 동안 별로 알아차려지지 않았다. 그것은 현대와 중세 영어 사이의 명료함의 격차를 야기했고, 영어 발음과 스펠링 사이의 성가신 정렬 불량을 창출해 냈다. 그러나 그것이 진행되고 있는 동안에는 알아차리는 것이 불가능했다.

① 외국어에 의해 영향을 받을 수도 있는
② 오랜 기간 동안 사용되지 않을 수도 있는
③ 사회 그리고 문화적 요소에 의해 유발될 수도 있는
④ 수십 년 또는 심지어 수 세기 동안 알아차릴 수 없을지도 모르는

11 정답 ③
Day 64-04

정답해설

중요한 오디션에 지원한 아들과 엄마의 대화이다. 아들은 다음 날 있을 학교 밴드 오디션에 긴장된다고 하자, 엄마는 아들에게 오디션에서 확실히 '~이 있다'라고 격려한다. 따라서 빈칸에 들어갈 가장 적절한 것은 '③ stand a chance(성공할 가망성이 있다)'이다.

해석

엄마: 오늘 기분이 어때?
아들: 조금 긴장되기 시작했어요. 저는 내일 중요한 오디션이 있어요.
엄마: 오, 정말? 그건 몰랐는데. 무슨 오디션 봐?
아들: 아직 아무에게도 이야기하지 않았어요. 학교 밴드의 리드 싱어 자리를 위한 오디션을 받아요.

엄마: 우와! 멋지다! 아들아, 너무 걱정하지 마. 너는 천상의 목소리를 가졌어. 너는 오디션에서 틀림없이 성공할 가망성이 있어.
아들: 감사해요, 엄마. 엄마는 저의 가장 든든한 지원군이에요.
① 행운을 빌어
② 떼돈을 벌다
③ 성공할 가망성이 있다
④ 변덕을 부리다

12 정답 ③   Day 69-04

정답해설

(A) David가 팀 프로젝트에 참여하지 않는 한 팀원에게 더 책임감을 가지라고 정중하게 말했다고 하자, Clara는 그 말을 들은 후 팀원의 태도가 어땠는지 묻는다. 그러자 David는 그녀가 '~했다'라고 대답하면서 그녀가 왜 화났는지 모르겠다고 대답하고 있으므로, 빈칸 (A)에 들어갈 가장 적절한 것은 'hit the roof(화를 심하게 냈다)'이다.

(B) David가 진행하는 팀 프로젝트의 팀원과 겪은 갈등에 대한 David의 이야기를 들은 Clara는 팀원이 자신의 책임을 '~하는 사람'처럼 들린다고 말하므로 빈칸 (B)에 들어갈 가장 자연스러운 것은 'makes little of(~을 중요하지 않게 다루다)'이다.

(C) 팀원에 대해 자신의 책임을 중요하지 않게 다루는 사람 같다고 하는 Clara의 이야기에 동의하며, David는 그녀가 그런 태도로 행동하는 것이 '~해야 한다'라고 말한다. 따라서 빈칸 (C)에 들어갈 가장 적절한 것은 'know better than to(~할 정도로 어리석지는 않다)'이다.

해석

Clara: 안녕, 데이비드! 너 화나 보인다.
David: 진행 중인 팀 프로젝트에 문제가 있어서 지금 굉장히 화나.
Clara: 너 되게 스트레스받겠다. 무엇이 널 괴롭히는 거야?
David: 팀원 중 한 명이 아예 참여를 안 해. 그래서 내가 그녀에게 아주 정중하게 더 책임감을 느껴달라고 이야기했어.
Clara: 네가 그렇게 말한 후 그녀가 어떻게 행동했어?
David: 그녀는 (A) 화를 심하게 냈어. 그녀가 왜 화났는지 전혀 모르겠어.
Clara: 오, 네 팀원이 자신의 책임을 (B) 중요하지 않게 다루는 사람처럼 들려.
David: 음, 나도 너와 동의해. 그녀는 그런 식의 태도로 행동할 (C) 정도로 어리석지 않아야 해.

① (A) 더치페이했다 (B) ~을 중요하지 않게 다루다 (C) ~에 희생하다
② (A) 화를 심하게 냈다 (B) ~을 중요하지 않게 다루다
   (C) ~에 희생하다
③ (A) 화를 심하게 냈다 (B) ~을 중요하지 않게 다루다
   (C) ~정도로 어리석지 않다
④ (A) 더치페이했다 (B) ~을 감수하고 받아들이다
   (C) ~정도로 어리석지 않다

13 정답 ②   Day 70-05

정답해설

② **출제 포인트: 접속사의 쓰임/if vs. whether**

접속사 'if' 이후에는 'or not'이 바로 올 수 없으며 전치사의 목적어절을 이끄는 접속사로 사용할 수 없다. 해당 문장은 'if' 이후에 'or not'이 사용되었으며 전치사 'about'의 목적어절을 이끄는 접속사로 사용되었으므로 옳지 않다. 따라서 'if'를 'whether'로 수정해야 한다.

해석

흔히 직장에서 성취감을 느끼는 것과 공허함, 상실감, 짜증 그리고 극도의 피로를 느끼는 것 사이의 차이는 여러분이 무언가를 배우고 있는지 아닌지에 관한 것이다. 이것이 경청해야 하는 또 다른 이유이다. 여러분이 잠시 멈추고, 자신의 마음을 진정시키고, 다른 사람들이 말하는 것을 경청할 때 여러분이 얼마나 더 많이 배우는가 하는 것은 놀랍다. 이것은 여러분이 이끄는 바로 그 팀은 물론 여러분의 왼쪽과 오른쪽에 있는 동료들에게도 사실이다. 때때로 특히 만약 여러분이 100퍼센트 동의하지 않는다면, 여러분의 상사나 임원에게 경청하는 것은 어렵다. 어떤 경우에 여러분은 심지어 그들을 좋아하지 않을 수도 있다. 나는 그것을 안다. 그들은 이유가 있어 자신들의 역할을 맡고 있으며, 그들이 몇 가지는 알고 있을지도 모른다는 것을 기억해라. 그들이 말하는 것에 마음을 열고 기꺼이 경청해라. 여러분은 자신이 듣는 모든 것에 동의하지 않을지도 모르지만, 적어도 여러분은 경청했다.

14 정답 ②   Day 61-05

정답해설

② **출제 포인트: to부정사의 부사적 용법/주어진 해석과 일치 확인**

to부정사의 부사적 용법이 쓰인 문장으로 영어 지문 자체는 문법적으로 옳은 문장이나 영어 지문 '~are using therapy to guide gene tests(유전자 검사를 안내하기 위해 치료법을 이용하고 있다)'와 주어진 해석 '치료법을 안내하기 위해 유전자 검사를 이용하고 있다'가 일치하지 않으므로 틀린 문장이다. 따라서 'therapy'와 'gene tests'의 위치를 서로 바꾸어야 한다. 즉, 'Many clinics are using gene tests to guide therapy.'가 주어진 해석과 일치하는 옳은 문장이다.

15 정답 ③   Day 65-09

정답해설

본문은 'Economist Intelligence Unit이 매년 발표하는 민주주의 지수에서 미국이 2016년 최초로 결함 있는 민주국가로 강등되었다'라는 내용이다. 본문 중반 "America's score fell to 7.98 in 2016 from 8.05 in the previous year, below the 8.00 threshold for a full democracy(미국의 점수는 전년도의 8.05에서, 완전한 민주국가가 되기 위한 8.0 경계점 이하인 7.98로 2016년에 떨어졌다)."를 통해, '미국은 2015년에 8.05점을 획득하여 완전한 민주국가로 평가되었음'을 알 수 있다. 그리고 마지막 문장 "Other flawed democracies in 2016 included Japan, France, Belgium, South Korea and India, all of which were deemed flawed democracies in 2015 as well(2016년에 다른 결함 있는 민주국가들은 일본, 프랑스, 벨기에, 대한민국 그리고 인도를 포함했고, 이들 국가 모두는 2015년에도 결함 있는 민주국가들로 여겨졌다)."를 통해, '벨기에는 2015년과 2016년 모두 결함 있는 민주국가로 평가되었음'을 알 수 있다. 즉, 2015년에 벨기에는 8.00 이하의 점수를 받았다는 것을 유추할 수 있다. 따라서 '③ In 2015, the U.S. received a lower score than Belgium(2015년에 미국은 벨기에보다 낮은 점수를 받았다).'은 글의 내용과 일치하지 않는다.

해석

Economist Intelligence Unit에 따르면, 미국은 완전한 민주국가에서 결함 있는 민주국가로 처음으로 강등되었다. 매년, 그 기업의 민주주의 지수는, 선거 절차 및 다원주의; 시민적 자유; 정부의 기능; 정치 참여; 그리고 정치 문화의 5개 범주에서 국가들에 점수를 매김으로써 전 세계 민주주의에 대한 정보를 제공한다. 그러면 국가들은 완전한 민주국가, 결함 있는 민주국가, 혼합 체제 그리고 독재 정권의 4가지 유형의 정부로 분류된다. 미국의 점수는 2016년에 전년도의 8.05에서, 완전한 민주국가가 되기 위한 8.0 경계점 이하인 7.98로 떨어졌다. 그것이 세계에서 가장 거대한 경제를 괴팍한 정치로 알려진 국가인 이탈리아와 동일한 입장에 놓이게 했다. 결함 있는 민주국가는 자유 선거가 있는 국가이지만, 약한 통치, 후진적인 정치 문화 그리고 낮은 수준의 정치 참여에 의해 위축된다. 2016년에 다른 결함 있는 민주국가들은 일본, 프랑스, 벨기에, 대한민국 그리고 인도를 포함했고, 이들 국가 모두는 2015년

에도 결함 있는 민주국가들로 여겨졌다.
① 미국은 2016년 이전에는 항상 완전한 민주국가로 평가되어 왔다.
② Economist Intelligence Unit은 다수의 범주에서 국가들을 평가한다.
③ 2015년에, 미국은 벨기에보다 낮은 점수를 받았다.
④ 이탈리아는 2016년에 결함 있는 민주국가라는 명칭을 받았다.

16 정답 ④ — Day 70-08

정답해설

본문은 '행복이 수명과 관련이 없다'는 내용으로, 마지막 문장 "The findings showed that happiness may not prolong a person's life, and feeling blue doesn't predispose a person to health problems that can cause death(연구 결과는 행복이 한 사람의 수명을 연장시키지 않는다는 것과 울적함을 느끼는 것이 한 사람이 사망을 유발하는 건강 문제를 겪기 쉽게 하도록 하지 않는다는 것을 보여주었다)."를 통해, '행복 또는 우울감이 수명을 연장하거나 질병을 유발하지 않는다'는 점을 시사하고 있다. 여기에서 '행복 또는 우울감'은 '기분(mood)'이라고 할 수 있으므로, 글의 주제로 가장 적절한 보기는 '④ The relationship between someone's mood and his or her lifespan(누군가의 기분과 그 또는 그녀의 수명 사이의 관계)'이다.

해석

새로운 연구가 행복은 한 사람이 얼마나 오래 살 것인가에 영향을 미치지 않는다는 것을 발견했다. 옥스퍼드 대학의 연구원들이 슬픔과 갈등이 나쁜 건강을 야기한다는 보편적인 믿음에 대한 정반대의 결과를 발견했다. 대신에, 그들은 행복과 슬픔 모두 한 사람의 수명에 영향을 미치지 않는다는 것을 발견했다. "많은 사람들이 여전히 스트레스 또는 불행이 직접적으로 질병을 야기할 수 있다고 믿는다, 그러나 그들은 단순히 원인과 결과를 혼동하는 것이다"라고 옥스퍼드 대학의 Richard Peto는 말했다. "물론 아픈 사람들은 건강한 사람들보다 더 불행한 경향이 있지만, UK Million Women Study는 행복과 불행이 사망률에 어떠한 직접적인 영향도 미치지 않는다는 것을 보여준다." 연구 결과는 행복이 한 사람의 수명을 연장시키지 않는다는 것과 울적함을 느끼는 것이 한 사람이 사망을 유발하는 건강 문제를 겪기 쉽게 하도록 하지 않는다는 것을 보여주었다.
① 정신 건강에 미치는 행복의 영향
② 스트레스와 우울의 원인과 결과
③ 치명적인 질병을 피하고 더 오랜 인생을 살기 위한 정보
④ 누군가의 기분과 그 또는 그녀의 수명 사이의 관계

17 정답 ③ — Day 67-08

정답해설

(A) 이전에서는 표준 중국어에서 의미하는 '행복'에 대해 설명하고 있다. 그리고 (A) 이후에서 특히 영어 문화에서는 상상할 수 없는 개념의 '행복'이라는 의미에 대해 언급하고 있는 것을 알 수 있다. (A) 이전에서 언급한 내용에 대해 추가적으로 자세한 내용을 덧붙여 설명하고 있으므로, 보기 중 빈칸에 가장 적절한 표현은 'In fact(사실)'이다.

(B) 이전에서는 미국에서 경험하는 '축하' 관련한 행복과는 다른 '덴마크어' 상의 '행복(lykke)'에 관해 언급하고 있다. 그리고 (B) 이후에서도 역시, '축하' 보다는 '평온과 안정'에 더 가까운 것을 의미하는 '홍콩의 광둥어에서의 행복'에 대해 설명하고 있다. (B) 전후 내용이 모두, '미국에서 행복이 경험되는 것과는 다른 방식'에 대해 설명하고 있으므로, 빈칸에는 '유사' 관계를 나타내는 'Likewise(마찬가지로)' 또는 'Similarly(유사하게)'가 가장 적절하다. 따라서 정답은 '③ In fact(사실) - Similarly(유사하게)'이다.

해석

행복이 다른 문화권에서 어떻게 받아들여지는가의 차이는 언어에서 분명하다. '행복(happiness)'과 '행복한(happy)'과 같은 단어들은 동양과 서양 문화에서 다른 함축적 의미를 가지고 있고 항상 직접적으로 번역될 수 있는 것은 아니다. 예를 들어, 표준 중국어는 영어의 개념과 완벽히 동등한 것이 아닌 "행복"을 나타내는 다수의 단어를 가지고 있는데, 왜냐하면 그것들은 "좋은 기분"에서부터 "삶에 의미를 지니는 것" 또는 "좋은 인생을 사는 것"까지 어느 것이나 의미할 수 있기 때문이다. (A) 사실, 표준 중국어에서, 행복은 또한 "잘 죽는 것"으로 정의되기도 하는데, 이는 영어권 문화에서는 아주 상상도 할 수 없는 것일 것이다. 게다가, 다른 언어에서 행복이 정의되는 방식은 그것이 문화권 간에서 어떻게 다르게 경험되는지를 가리킨다. 예를 들어, "lykke"라는 덴마크어 개념은 "행복"으로 번역되지만, 행복이 축하의 상태를 포함하는 미국에서 행복이 경험되는 방식과는 거의 관련이 없다. (B) 유사하게, 홍콩의 광둥어에서 행복에 해당하는 단어는 낮은 각성 상태와 연결되어 있고, 그것의 의미는 축하보다는 평온과 안정에 더 가깝다.

(A)	(B)
① 그러므로	마찬가지로
② 그러나	즉
③ 사실	유사하게
④ 그에 따라	대조적으로

18 정답 ③ — Day 63-10

정답해설

본문은 'Cheyenne 부족 고유의 광대'인 'contrary'에 관한 설명이다. 'contrary는 일종의 전사이지만 늘 반대로 말하고 행동함으로써, 부족 내에서 광대의 역할을 한다'고 언급하고 있다. ②에서 '전사가 contrary가 되는 이유'를 '공포 극복'을 위함이라고 언급한 후, ④와 마지막 문장에서 '어떻게 공포를 극복할 수 있는지' 설명하고 있다. 그런데 ③에서는, '일반적으로 전사가 받는 대우'에 대해 설명하고 있으므로, '특별한 전사인 contrary'에 대해 설명하는 글의 중간에 위치하는 것은 문맥상 어색하다. 따라서 정답은 ③이다.

해석

북미의 Cheyenne 부족에서는 contrary(반대)라고 불리는 특정 유형의 전사가 어쩌면 그 특정 문화의 광대로 여겨질지도 모른다. contrary들은 항상 반의어로 의사소통했다. 예를 들어, '예'를 의미하기 위해 머리를 흔드는 것과 '아니오'를 의미하기 위해 끄덕이는 것. 만일 그들이 장작의 부족에 대해 경고하길 원한다면, 그들은 "우리는 나무가 많아! 더 이상 가져오지 마."라고 말했다. 이러한 반전은 또한 의사소통 이상으로 확대되었다. ① 그들은 의복을 거꾸로 입고, 흙으로 씻곤 했으며, 심지어 물로 자신들의 몸을 말린 것으로 알려져 있었다. ② 한 전사가 그러한 인물이 되기로 결정하는 이유는 공포를 극복하기 위함이었다. ③ <u>전사는 사람들에게 전쟁 유발자가 아니라 보호자이자 지도자로서 간주되었으며, 전사들은 전장에서 다양한 용맹의 행위를 수행하고 축적함으로써 높은 지위를 얻었다.</u> ④ contrary는 소지자를 번개가 공격할 수 없도록 만들어준다고 회자된 긴 창을 무기로 사용했다. 따라서 천둥 혹은 번개에 대한 두려움을 가진 사람들은 부족의 광대 전사가 되어 그들의 공포증을 물리칠 수 있었다.

19 정답 ③ — Day 68-09

정답해설

주어진 문장의 'Now that(~이므로, ~이니까)'으로 보아, 주어진 문장 이전에는 '연방 법으로 제정되기 이전의 상황'에 대해 설명하는 내용이 등장해야 한다는 것을 알 수 있다. ③ 이전 문장 "Nineteen states around the US plus Washington, DC, have already raised the minimum age to buy tobacco to 21(Washington, DC뿐만 아니라 미국의 19개의 주가 담배 구매 연령을 21세로 이미 올렸다)."에서, '해당 법안이 연방 법안으로 제정되기 전 이미 몇몇 주에서 자체적으로 실시하고 있었다'라고 설명하고 있으므로, 이후에 '이제 연방 법이 되었으므로 모든 주가 이를 준수해야 한다'는 내용이 이어지는 것이 자연스럽다. 따라서 정답은 ③이다.

해석

미국 식품 의약품국(Food and Drug Administration)은 공식적으로 담배, 전자 담배, 그리고 니코틴을 함유한 불연성 제품과 같은 담배 제품들을 구매할 수 있는 최소 연령을 18세에서 21세로 올렸다. (①) 담배 제품을 구매할 수 있는 연령을 올림으로써, 연방 정부는 많은 주들이 해오고 있던 것을 모사하고 있다. (②) Washington, DC뿐만 아니라 미국의 19개의 주가 담배를 구매하기 위한 최소 연령을 21세로 이미 올렸다. (③ **이제 이것이 연방 법이기 때문에, 모든 주들은 이를 준수해야 할 것이다.**) 그 변화는 수천의 생명을 구할 수 있을 것이다. (④) 연구는 그들이 가장 중독이 될 가능성이 크기 때문에 십대들이 흡연 또는 니코틴 제품을 피우는 것을 방지하도록 노력하는 것이 중요하다는 것을 보여준다.

20 정답 ③ Day 70-10

정답해설

주어진 문장에서는 '언어가 타인과 접촉할 때 변화한다'고 설명한다. 이후에 이어질 내용으로 적절한 것은, '모든 사람은 다르게 말한다'고 언급하며, 이러한 접촉으로 인해 변화가 발생하는 이유를 제시하고 있는 (B)이다. (B)에서는 크게는 지리적으로 다른 지역, 그리고 작게는 작은 공동체 내에서도 말하는 방식의 차이가 존재한다고 설명한다. 이후에는, 더 하위 단위인 '가족' 내에서도 '세대' 간 말의 차이가 존재한다고 설명하는 (A)가 이어지는 것이 적절하다. 마지막으로, 앞서 (B)와 (A)에서 언급된 여러 화자들을 'these different speakers(이러한 다른 화자들)'를 이용해 가리키고 있는 (C)가 이어지는 것이 알맞다. 따라서 정답은 '③ (B) - (A) - (C)'이다.

해석

언어는 화자들이 서로 접촉할 때마다 매우 미묘하게 변화한다.
(B) 동일하게 말하는 두 개인은 없다: 다른 지리적 장소에서 온 사람들은 분명 다르게 말한다, 그러나 심지어 동일한 소규모의 공동체 내에서도 화자의 성별, 민족성, 그리고 사회 및 교육적 배경에 따라 차이가 있다.
(A) 또한, 만일 당신의 가족이 동일한 지역에서 수 세대 동안 살아왔다 하더라도, 당신은 아마 당신이 사용하는 언어와 당신의 조부모님이 말하는 방식 사이의 수많은 차이를 알아차릴 수 있을 것이다.
(C) 이러한 다른 화자들과의 상호 작용을 통해, 우리는 새로운 단어, 표현 그리고 발음을 접하고 우리 자신의 화법에 그것들을 통합시킨다. 이러한 방식으로, 우리는 언어 변화에 우리 자신의 작은 기여를 하고 있는 것이다.

기적사 DAY 71
결국엔 성정혜 영어 하프모의고사

01	①	02	①	03	④	04	②	05	④
06	④	07	③	08	③	09	③	10	③

01 정답 ① 15 지방직

정답해설

'immutable'은 '변경할 수 없는, 불변의'를 뜻하는 형용사로 ① unchanging(불변의, 늘 변치 않는)과 의미상 가장 가깝다.

해석

텔레비전의 **불변의** 법칙 중 하나는 낮은 시청률은 반드시 취소로 이어진다는 것이다.
① 불변의, 늘 변치 않는
② 임시의, 일시적인
③ 과감한, 극단적인
④ 무책임한

어휘

immutable 변경할 수 없는, 불변의
cancellation 취소
provisional 임시의, 일시적인
irresponsible 무책임한
inevitably 필연적으로, 반드시
unchanging 불변의, 늘 변치 않는
drastic 과감한, 극단적인

오답률 TOP 1
02 정답 ① 15 지방직

정답해설

'canny'는 '약삭빠른, 영리한'을 뜻하는 형용사로 ① shrewd(상황 판단이 빠른, 기민한)와 의미상 가장 가깝다.

해석

영리한 투자자들은 주식 시장이 급격히 폭락하게 될 수 있다는 것을 걱정하기 시작한다.
① 상황 판단이 빠른, 기민한
② 명망 있는, 일류의
③ 무례한, 경솔한
④ 궁금한, 호기심이 많은

어휘

canny 약삭빠른, 영리한
shrewd 상황 판단이 빠른, 기민한
impudent 무례한, 경솔한
due [~을] 하기로 되어있는, ~할 예정인
prestigious 명망 있는, 일류의
curious 궁금한, 호기심이 많은

03 정답 ④ 14 지방직

정답해설

'unquenchable'은 '만족할 수 없는, 채울 수 없는'을 뜻하는 형용사로 ④ insatiable(만족할 줄 모르는)과 의미상 가장 가깝다.

해석

전기차는 또한 수입된 석유와 가스에 대한 **만족할 수 없는** 욕구를 억제하기 위한 중국의 노력 중 주요한 한 부분으로, 공산주의 지도자들은 이것을 전략적인 약점으로 여긴다.

① 결코 틀리지 않는, 확실한
② 미적인, 미학의
③ 청소년의
④ 만족할 줄 모르는

어휘
curb 억제[제한]하다
unquenchable 만족할 수 없는, 채울 수 없는
appetite 욕구; 식욕
import 수입하다; 수입
communist 공산주의의; 공산주의자
strategic 전략적인
infallible 결코 틀리지 않는, 확실한
aesthetic 미적인, 미학의
adolescent 청소년의
insatiable 만족할 줄 모르는

04 정답 ② 　　　　　　　　　　　　　　17 지방직

정답해설
빈칸 이전에서 B는 현재 직장에서 만족하고 있다고 답했는데, 빈칸 바로 이후에 B는 정규적(안정적)인 환경에서 일하고 싶다고 자신의 생각을 전하고 있다. 따라서 빈칸에는 현재 직장에 만족하는데 왜 이 직무에 지원하는지를 묻는 내용이 들어가는 것이 적절하므로 정답은 '② Then, why are you applying for this job(그렇다면, 왜 이 직무에 지원하시는 거죠?)'이다.

오답해설
①, ③, ④ 나머지 선지는 빈칸 이후 B의 대답을 위한 A의 질문으로 적절하지 않다.

해석
A: 그래서 Wong씨, 뉴욕시에서는 얼마나 오래 거주하셨습니까?
B: 이곳에서 약 7년 동안 살고 있습니다.
A: 당신의 직장 경력에 대해 말씀해주시겠어요?
B: 지난 3년간 피자 가게에서 일했습니다.
A: 그곳에서 어떤 일을 하시죠?
B: 손님들에게 자리를 안내하고 서빙을 합니다.
A: 그 일에 대해 어떻게 생각하세요?
B: 좋습니다. 모두 좋은 사람들입니다.
A: 그렇다면, 왜 이 직무에 지원하시는 거죠?
B: 저는 단지 조금 더 정규적(안정적)인 환경에서 일을 하고 싶기 때문입니다.
A: 알겠습니다. 다른 덧붙일 말씀이 있나요?
B: 저는 사람들과 잘 지냅니다. 그리고 또한 이탈리아어와 중국어를 할 수 있습니다.
A: 알겠습니다. 감사합니다. 곧 연락드리겠습니다.
B: 곧 소식을 듣기를 바랍니다.
① 그래서, 그곳 환경은 어떻습니까?
② 그렇다면, 왜 이 직무에 지원하시는 거죠?
③ 그런데 능숙하신 다른 외국어가 있습니까?
④ 그리고 이곳에서 일하기 위해 어떤 자질이 필요하다고 생각하십니까?

어휘
wait on (특히 식사) 시중을 들다, (손님에게) 응대하다
formal 정규적인; 공식적인
be in touch 연락하다
apply for ~에 지원하다
be good at ~에 능숙하다

05 정답 ④ 　　　　　　　　　　　　　　18 지방직

정답해설
④ 출제 포인트: '~하자마자 …했다' 구문
해당 문장은 주어진 우리말 해석처럼 영작하려면, 'hardly'가 문두로 강조되면서 이후에 문장은 의문문 어순으로 도치되어야 하며 이는 옳게 사용되었다. 단 접속사 'before'가 아닌 타동사 'dream'이 이끄는 명사절에 해당하는 'he ~ musician'을 이끄는 명사절 접속사 'that'을 사용해야 적절하다. 또한 주어진 우리말 해석과 다르게 주어진 영작문에 'hardly'와 'before'를 이용해서 '~하자마자 …했다'의 의미에 구문 표현으로 수정할 수 있는 점도 참고하자. 주어진 우리말 표현에서 '유명한 음악가가 된 것'과 '생각지 못했던 것'은 각각 대과거와 과거로 표현되어야만 하므로 「Hardly+had+주어+과거분사~, when/before+주어+과거시제 동사....」의 형태를 사용한다. 'hardly'는 '거의 ~하지 않다'라는 뜻인 부사로서 'hardly'가 문장 제일 앞에 위치하면 주어와 동사의 도치가 반드시 일어난다. 즉, "Hardly had I dreamed before he became such a famous musician."이 올바르므로 'did I dream'을 'had I dreamed'로 수정하는 방법도 있다. 단 해당되는 경우는 우리말 해석이 '내가 꿈꾸자마자, 그는 그렇게 유명한 음악가가 되었다'라는 의미로 쓰여야 한다.

오답해설
① 출제 포인트: 관용표현(be sure to+동사원형)
'be sure to~'는 '반드시 ~을 하다'라는 표현으로 문장에서 적절하게 사용되었다. 'be sure to'의 'to'는 전치사 'to'가 아닌 to부정사의 'to'임에 유의해야한다.

② 출제 포인트: 관용표현(manage to+동사원형)/관용표현(get by)
'manage to~'는 '간신히 ~을 하다'라는 뜻을 가진 표현으로 문장에서 적합하게 사용되었다. 'manage to'의 'to'는 전치사 'to'가 아닌 to부정사의 'to'임에 유의해야한다. 또한 'get by'는 관용표현으로 '그럭저럭해[살아] 나가다'를 뜻하며 해당 표현에서 'get'은 자동사, 'by'는 부사로 사용되었음에 유의해야한다.

③ 출제 포인트: 해석 일치 주의/관용표현(vice versa)
주어진 해석이 '수요가 공급을 초과하면'이므로 'demand'와 'supply'의 위치는 적절하다. 또한 'vice versa'는 관용표현으로 '거꾸로, 반대로, 역(逆)도 또한 같음'이라는 의미로 주어진 해석과 일치하므로 옳게 사용되었다.

06 정답 ④ 　　　　　　　　　　　　　　18 지방직

정답해설
④ 출제 포인트: 현재분사 vs. 과거분사
'spending'은 'spend'의 현재분사이나 해석상 '사용된 연료'가 자연스러우며 수식하는 대상 'fuel'과 수동관계이므로 'spending'을 과거분사 'spent'로 수정해야 한다.

오답해설
① 출제 포인트: 등위상관접속사(either A or B)
'either now' 이후에 있는 'or'를 통해 밑줄 친 'either'가 'either A or B'의 형태의 등위상관접속사로 사용된 것임을 알 수 있다. 따라서 'either'는 옳은 표현이며 'either A or B'의 A 자리에 위치한 시간의 부사 'now'와 B자리에 위치한 'in the future'는 시간을 나타내는 부사구로 병렬구조를 이루고 있다.

② 출제 포인트: 완전타동사+목적어[to부정사 vs. 동명사]
'try'는 목적어로 to부정사가 오는 경우 '~하려고 노력하다'를 뜻하며 목적어로 동명사가 오는 경우 '~해보다'를 뜻한다. 해당 문장의 경우 문맥상 '찾으려고 노력하다'가 자연스러우므로 'have tried'의 목적어에 해당하는 밑줄 친 'to find'는 옳은 표현이다.

③ 출제 포인트: 관계대명사 vs. 관계부사
선행사가 'countries'이며 밑줄 친 'where' 이후에 오는 절이 완전한 형태의 절이므로 밑줄 친 관계부사 'where'는 옳은 표현이다.

해석

환경운동가들은 지금이든 미래에서든 어떤 폐기물 처리 체제도 절대적으로 안전할 수는 없다고 주장한다. 정부와 원자력 산업은 수용될 수 있는 해결책을 찾으려고 노력해 왔다. 그러나 여론이 고려되는 국가에서는, 서로가 받아들일 수 있는 해결책이 전혀 발견되지 않았다. 그 결과, 대부분의 사용된 연료는 그것이 생산되었던 핵발전소에 저장되어왔다.

어휘

environmentalist 환경운동가   mutually 서로, 상호 간에
acceptable 받아들여지는, 용인되는

오답률 TOP 2
07 정답 ③
18 지방직

정답해설

③ 출제 포인트: 능동태 vs. 수동태
'~을 위치시키다'를 뜻하는 'locate'는 완전타동사이므로 이후에 목적어가 있어야 한다. 해당 문장의 경우 'locates' 이후에 전명구 'in the center of Gulf National Park'가 왔으며 해석상 '그 화산은 Gulf National Park의 중심에 위치되어 있다'가 자연스러우므로 'locates'를 수동태 'is located'로 수정해야 한다.

오답해설

① 출제 포인트: 전치사 vs. 접속사
'its perfect cone shape and proximity to the beautiful Albay Gulf'는 전명구인 수식어 'to the beautiful Albay Gulf'와 결합한 명사구에 해당하며 전치사 구 'Because of'의 목적어로 쓰였으므로 옳게 사용되었다.

② 출제 포인트: 「기수+측정 단위명사+형용사」
'80 miles wide'는 「기수+측정 단위명사+형용사」의 형태에 해당하며 불완전자동사 'is'의 주격 보어로 사용되었으므로 이때 측정 단위명사에는 복수 형태를 사용하는 것이 옳다. 따라서 '80 miles wide'는 옳은 표현이다.

④ 출제 포인트: 완전타동사 help의 목적어
완전타동사 'help'는 목적어로 to부정사와 원형부정사를 사용할 수 있다. 따라서 해당 문장의 'avoid'는 완전타동사 'help'의 목적어에 해당하는 원형부정사로 옳은 표현이다.

해석

① 그것의 완벽한 원뿔 모양과 아름다운 Albay Gulf에 대한 근접성 때문에, Tarn 산은 인기 있는 관광 명소이다.
② 그것의 토대는 둘레가 80마일이며, 높이는 극적인 8,077피트이다.
③ 그 화산은 많은 사람들이 캠핑하고 오르기 위해 오는 Gulf National Park의 중심에 위치되어 있다.
④ 정부 기관들은 초기 경고를 보냄으로써, 그들이 주요 파괴와 위험을 피하는 것을 도와주길 희망한다.

오답률 TOP 3
08 정답 ③
18 서울시

정답해설

빈칸 이후의 문장에서 우리는 실제 세계에서 브랜드와 가격 등을 보지 않은 채 상품을 제대로 평가할 수 없다고 서술한다. 그러므로 브랜드를 붙이는 것 없이 테스트 된 제품이 객관적으로 평가된다는 개념은 '잘못된' 것이라는 내용으로 빈칸에 가장 적절한 것은 '③ misguided(잘못된)'이다.

오답해설

①, ②, ④ 빈칸 이후에 '우리는 브랜드, 제품이 담긴 상자의 외형과 느낌, 가격 등을 무시한 채로 제품을 평가할 수 없다'고 서술하고 있다. 따라서 브랜드를 붙이는 것 없이 테스트 된 제품이 객관적으로 평가된다는 개념이 '정확한(correct)', '믿을 만한(reliable)', '편견 없는, 공정한(unbiased)' 것이라고 할 수 없으므로 빈칸에 들어갈 말로 적절하지 않다.

해석

브랜드를 붙이는 것 없이 테스트 된 제품이 다소 더 객관적으로 평가된다는 개념은 완전히 잘못된 것이다. 실제 세계에서, 우리가 눈을 감고 코를 잡은 채로 어떤 것들을 평가할 수 없는 것처럼 우리는 우리가 구입하는 제품에 찍혀진 브랜드, 그것이 담긴 상자의 외형과 느낌, 요구된 가격을 무시한 채로 평가할 수는 없다.
① 정확한
② 믿을 만한
③ 잘못된
④ 편견 없는, 공정한

어휘

somehow 어쨌든   objectively 객관적으로
appraise 평가하다, 감정하다   entirely 완전히, 전적으로
correct 정확한   reliable 믿을 만한
misguided 잘못된   unbiased 편견 없는, 공정한

09 정답 ③
18 서울시

정답해설

본문은 휴양을 사업 약속처럼 계획하며 실천하는 미국인들에 대한 내용이다. 미국의 많은 방문객들이 미국인들은 여가를 너무 진지하게 생각한다고 하며 미국인들은 여가가 건강과 신체적 건강함에 기여한다고 생각한다고 서술하고 있다. 따라서 미국인들은 휴양에 대한 다른 관점을 가지고 있는 것이므로 글의 제목으로 가장 적절한 것은 '③ The American approach to recreation(휴양에 대한 미국인들의 접근)'이다.

오답해설

① 본문은 '미국인이 가지고 있는 운동과 여가시간에 대한 관점'에 대해 서술하고 있다. 이것은 ①에서 제시한 '건강과 운동(Health and fitness)'이라는 범위와 맞지 않으며, 글의 후반부에 언급된 '건강함'도 결국은 운동에 대한 가치를 설명하기 위해 일부 인용된 내용이므로 글 전체를 다루고 있지 않은 소재임에 주의해야 한다.
② 미국의 '인기 있는' 여가 활동에 대해서는 언급되어 있지 않다.
④ 본문에 언급되어 있지 않은 내용이므로 제목으로 적절하지 않다.

해석

미국의 많은 방문객들은 미국인들이 그들의 운동과 여가시간의 활동을 너무 진지하게 한다고 생각한다. 미국인들은 종종 그들의 휴양을 마치 그들의 사업 약속이 예정된 것처럼 계획을 만든다. 그들은 매일 같은 시간에 조깅을 하러 가고, 일주일에 두세 번 테니스를 치고, 매주 목요일마다 수영을 한다. 외국인들은 이러한 종류의 휴양은 휴식보다 일처럼 들린다고 종종 생각한다. 그러나 많은 미국인들에게 그들의 여가 활동은 휴식이고 즐길만하며, 적어도 그럴만한 가치가 있는데, 왜냐하면 그것들은 건강과 신체적 건강함에 기여하기 때문이다.
① 건강과 운동
② 미국의 인기 있는 휴양 활동들
③ 휴양에 대한 미국인들의 접근
④ 휴양의 정의

어휘

seriously 심(각)하게; 진지하게
schedule 일정[시간 계획]을 잡다, 예정하다; (작업) 일정, 스케줄
recreation 휴양, 기분 전환, 오락
appointment 약속, 임명, 지명
relaxation 휴식; 완화
recreational 휴양의, 오락의
worthwhile 가치[보람] 있는, ~할 가치가 있는
fitness 건강함, (몸의) 좋은 컨디션

10 정답 ③

18 서울시

정답해설

우리의 감정은 마음의 기반이라고 하면서 수많은 감정을 음악적 상태와 비유하며 설명하고 있다. 따라서 글의 요지로 적절한 것은 '③ Feelings are ubiquitous in our minds(감정은 우리 마음속에 어디에나 존재한다).'이다.

오답해설

① 우리의 마음을 음악과 비유해서 설명했을 뿐 전체적인 요지로 보기에는 무리가 있다.
② 감정이 고통과 기쁨 등으로 구성되어 있다고 했으나 이것 자체가 요지가 될 수는 없다.
④ 본문에 잠깐 언급되었으나 요지가 되기에는 지엽적이다.

해석

고통이나 기쁨, 또는 그사이의 몇몇 속성에 대한 감정은 우리 마음의 기반이다. 우리는 종종 이 단순한 현실을 인지하는 것을 실패하는데 이것은 우리를 둘러싼 물체와 사건에 대한 정신적인 이미지가 그것들을 묘사하는 말과 문장의 이미지와 함께 우리의 과도한 관심을 다 사용하기 때문이다. 그러나 거기에서 그것들은 수많은 감정과 관련된 상태의 감정, 지속적인 우리의 마음의 음악적인 상태, 오직 우리가 잘 때 차츰 잦아드는 막을 수 없는 가장 보편적인 선율의 콧노래, 우리가 기쁨에 사로잡혔을 때 완전한 노래로 변하는 콧노래, 슬픔이 장악할 때의 애절한 진혼곡이다.
① 감정은 음악과 밀접하게 관련되어 있다.
② 감정은 고통과 기쁨으로 이루어진다.
③ 감정은 우리의 마음속에 어디에서나 존재한다.
④ 감정은 물체와 사건에 대한 정신적인 이미지와 관련되어 있다.

어휘

bedrock 기반
overburden 과중한 부담을 주다
continuous 계속되는, 지속적인
humming 콧노래
die down 차츰 잦아들다[약해지다/희미해지다]
all-out 완전한, 철저한
requiem 진혼곡, 레퀴엠
ubiquitous 어디에나 있는, 아주 흔한
along with ~와 함께, ~에 따라
myriad 무수함, 무수히 많은
unstoppable 막을[제지할] 수 없는
mournful 애절한
take over 장악[탈취]하다; 인계받다

기적사 DAY 72

01	③	02	③	03	④	04	④	05	①
06	③	07	④	08	②	09	②	10	③

01 정답 ③

정답해설

'irresponsible'은 '무책임한'을 뜻하는 형용사로 ③ feckless(무책임한, 무기력한)와 의미상 가장 가깝다.

해석

William은 노점상들이 위험할 뿐만 아니라 **무책임하다**고 격렬하게 주장했다.
① 무기력한, 활기 없는
② 나태한
③ 무책임한, 무기력한
④ 몹시 힘든, 불굴의

어휘

passionately 열렬하게; 격렬하게
irresponsible 무책임한
slothful 나태한
strenuous 몹시 힘든, 불굴의
vendor 노점상[행상인]
torpid 무기력한, 활기 없는
feckless 무책임한, 무기력한

02 정답 ③

정답해설

'curious'는 '궁금한, 호기심이 많은'을 뜻하는 형용사로 ③ inquisitive(호기심이 많은, 탐구심이 많은)와 의미상 가장 가깝다.

해석

헛간에서 이상한 것을 발견한 양치기들은 그것의 부드러움에 대하여 **호기심이 생겼다**.
① 냉담한, 냉랭한
② 고르지 못한, 균등하지 않은
③ 호기심이 많은, 탐구심이 많은
④ 무표정한, 아무런 감정이 없는

어휘

shepherd 양치기
curious 궁금한, 호기심이 많은
stony 냉담한, 냉랭한
inquisitive 호기심이 많은, 탐구심이 많은
impassive 무표정한, 아무런 감정이 없는
shed 헛간, 창고; 흘리다; 버리다
softness 부드러움
uneven 고르지 못한, 균등하지 않은

03 정답 ④

정답해설

'insatiable'은 '만족할 줄 모르는'을 뜻하는 형용사로 ④ unappeasable(만족시킬 수 없는, 채울 수 없는)과 의미상 가장 가깝다.

해석

의회의 양당 의원들은 유럽 문제를 논의하는 것에 대해 **만족할 줄 모르는** 욕구를 보이는 것 같다.

① 순결한, 순수한
② 괜찮은, 품위 있는
③ 엄청난, 굉장한
④ 만족시킬 수 없는, 채울 수 없는

어휘

insatiable 만족할 줄 모르는　　appetite 욕구; 식욕
chaste 순결한, 순수한　　decent 괜찮은, 품위 있는
prodigious 엄청난, 굉장한
unappeasable 만족시킬 수 없는, 채울 수 없는

04 정답 ④

정답해설

밑줄 친 부분 전 대화에서 A는 B에게 음식을 맛있게 먹었냐고 묻자 B는 '~했다고 하면서 많이 먹어서 아주 배불렀다'라고 답하므로 빈칸에 '④ my eyes were bigger than my stomach(과욕을 냈다)'가 들어가는 것이 문맥상 가장 적절하다.

오답해설

① 어제 다녀온 뷔페 음식을 맛있게 먹었는지 묻는 A에게 B는 많이 먹어 배가 불렀다고 답하면서 '냉정을 유지했다(kept my shirt on)'라고 이야기하는 것은 문맥상 어색하다.
② B는 어제 뷔페에서 음식을 맛있게 먹었다고 A의 질문에 대답하면서 많이 먹어 배가 아주 불렀다고 말한다. 그러므로 B가 '큰 손실을 봤다(burned my fingers)'라고 말하는 것은 대화의 흐름상 빈칸에 들어갈 말로 부자연스럽다.
③ B는 어제 단짝 친구의 생일파티가 뷔페에서 열려 음식을 맛있게 먹었으며 많이 먹어서 아주 배가 불렀다고 한다. 따라서 맥락상 빈칸에 '가슴이 철렁철렁했다(had butterflies in my stomach)'가 들어가는 것은 어색하다.

해석

A: 너 어제 뭐 했어?
B: 내 단짝 친구의 생일을 축하해주러 갔었어. 파티가 뷔페에서 열렸어.
A: 오, 되게 재미있었겠다! 음식은 맛있게 먹었어?
B: 응, 과욕을 냈어. 너무 많이 먹어서 아주 배불렀어.
A: 확실히 네가 정말 맛있는 식사를 한 것처럼 들려.
B: 맞아. 특히 스파게티와 치킨이 맛있었어.
① 냉정을 유지했다
② 큰 손실을 봤다
③ 가슴이 철렁철렁했다
④ 과욕을 냈다

어휘

celebrate 축하하다, 기념하다
keep one's shirt on 냉정을 유지하다
burn one's fingers 큰 손실을 보다
have butterflies in one's stomach 가슴이 철렁철렁하다
one's eyes are bigger than one's stomach 과욕을 내다

05 정답 ①

정답해설

① **출제 포인트: 부사절을 이끄는 접속사 that(so+형용사/부사+that+절)/to부정사의 명사적 용법**

주어진 해석 '매우 ~해서 ~하다'와 해당 문장 후반부의 'that+절'을 통해 「so+형용사+that+절」이 쓰인 문장임을 알 수 있다. 따라서 'too dangerous'를 'so dangerous'로 수정해야 한다. 또한 'dangerous' 이후에 온 'to exceed the recommending dose'는 to부정사의 명사적 용법으로 사용되었으며 해당 문장의 진주어이다. 해당 문장을 「too+형용사+to+동사원형」으로 오해하지 않도록 주의해야 한다.

오답해설

② **출제 포인트: '~하자마자 …했다' 구문**

주어진 해석이 '~하자마자 …했다'이며 「Hardly+had+주어+과거분사~, when/before+주어+과거시제 동사….」의 형태를 사용하였으므로 옳은 문장이다.

③ **출제 포인트: 불완전자동사와 주격 보어/관용표현(be sure to+동사원형)**

'seem'은 불완전자동사의 경우 'like+명사(구)'를 주격 보어로 사용할 수 있다. 따라서 'seems like a very good idea'는 옳은 표현이다. 또한 'are sure to be'는 관용표현 'be sure to+동사원형(반드시 ~하다)'의 현재시제에 해당한다. 'be sure to'의 'to'는 전치사 'to'가 아닌 to부정사의 'to'임에 유의해야한다.

④ **출제 포인트: 관용표현(manage to+동사원형)/관용표현(get by)**

해당 문장은 관용표현 'mange to+동사원형(간신히 ~하다)'과 관용표현 'get by(그럭저럭 살아가다)'가 쓰인 문장으로 옳은 문장이다. 'manage to'의 'to'는 전치사 'to'가 아닌 to부정사의 'to'임에 유의해야 한다.

06 정답 ③

정답해설

③ **출제 포인트: 관계부사 how vs. 관계부사 that**

관계부사 'how'와 선행사 'way'는 함께 쓰일 수 없다. 밑줄 친 'how'는 이후에 오는 절이 완전한 형태이나 앞에 선행사 'ways'가 있으므로 옳지 않다. 따라서 밑줄 친 관계부사 'how'를 삭제하거나 'how'를 관계부사 'that'으로 수정해야 한다.

오답해설

① **출제 포인트: 관계대명사 vs. 관계부사**

장소를 나타내는 명사구 'Disney's "Soaring Over California"'를 선행사로 가지며 'where' 이후에 오는 절이 완전한 형태의 절이므로 밑줄 친 관계부사 'where'는 옳은 표현이다.

② **출제 포인트: 접속사가 살아있는 분사구문/현재분사 vs. 과거분사/관용표현(while + ~ing)**

'while ② enjoying a simulated hang-gliding experience across the countryside'는 접속사가 살아있는 분사구문이다. 밑줄 친 'enjoying'은 'enjoy'의 현재분사로 이후에 목적어 'a simulated hang-gliding experience'가 왔으며 생략된 주어 'audiences'와 능동 관계이므로 'enjoying'은 옳은 표현이다. 또한 관용표현 'while + 현재분사'로 '~하는 동안'의 의미로 사용되었다고 보아도 옳게 사용되었다.

④ **출제 포인트: 동명사의 쓰임/동명사의 태**

밑줄 친 'stimulating'은 전치사 'by'의 목적어로 사용된 동명사로 이때 「by+동명사」는 '~함으로써'를 뜻한다. 또한 이후에 목적어 'our senses'가 있으므로 동명사의 능동태에 해당하는 'stimulating'은 옳은 표현이다.

해석

새로운 매체는 또한 캘리포니아 모험 테마파크에 있는 명물인 디즈니의 'Soaring Over California'와 같은 향기를 포함할 수도 있는데, 거기에서 시골을 가로지르는 가상의 행글라이딩 체험을 즐기는 동안 관객들은 오렌지 과수원과 소나무 숲의 냄새를 맡는다. 새롭게 등장하는 형태의 오락을 제작하는 사람들은 우리의 감각을 자극함으로써 그들이 현실을 가장하고 조작할 수 있는 방식으로 아마 계속해서 실험할 것이다.

어휘

aroma 향기, 방향
orchard 과수원
simulate …한 체[척]하다, 가장하다
manipulate 조작하다; 조종하다
attraction 명물
pine 소나무
countryside 시골, 전원 지대
stimulate 자극[격려]하다

오답률 TOP 3
07 정답 ④

정답해설
④ 출제 포인트: 기수-측정단위명사-형용사
'35-years-old'는 「기수-측정 단위명사-형용사」에 해당하며 명사 'captain'을 수식하는 수식어로 사용되었다. 이때 수식어로 사용되는 측정 단위명사는 단수 형태이어야 하므로 복수 형태인 'years'를 단수 형태인 'year'로 수정해야 한다.

오답해설
① 출제 포인트: 준사역동사의 목적격 보어/불완전타동사의 목적격 보어/관계대명사 what
'get'은 준사역동사로 목적격 보어에 현재분사와 to부정사를 사용할 수 있으며 'want'는 불완전타동사로 목적격 보어에 to부정사를 사용한다. 따라서 해당 문장의 'to do'는 'get'의 목적격 보어와 'wanted'의 목적격 보어에 해당하는 to부정사로 옳은 표현이다. 또한 'what'은 선행사를 포함한 관계대명사로 'what' 이후의 문장이 부정사로 쓰인 'to do'의 목적어가 없는 불완전한 형태이며 'what' 이전에 선행사가 없으므로 관계대명사 'what'은 옳게 사용되었다.

② 출제 포인트: 능동태 vs. 수동태
'voiced'는 완전타동사 'voice'의 과거시제에 해당하며 이후에 목적어 'his or her own complaints'가 있으므로 능동태인 'voiced'는 옳은 표현이다.

③ 출제 포인트: 접속사의 쓰임/전치사 vs. 접속사
'that although'가 「접속사+접속사」의 형태이므로 이상하다고 생각할 수 있으나 'although'는 부사절 'the team would lose'를 이끌며, 'that'은 부사절을 포함하는 명사절 'although the team would lose, they played with tremendous spirit'을 이끈다. 따라서 'that although'는 옳은 표현이다.

해석
① 나는 그가 하기를 원하는 것을 하게 할 수 없었다.
② 학생들은 각자의 불만을 토로했다.
③ 비록 팀은 졌지만, 그들이 엄청난 기백을 가지고 경기를 했다는 것을 Tom은 알고 있었다.
④ 35세의 국가 대표팀 주장은 뉴욕에서의 10년 후 그가 새로운 도전이 필요하다고 말한다.

08 정답 ②

정답해설
주어진 문장은 '브랜드 자산(Brand equity)'의 정의에 대해 설명하고 있다. (A)의 주어 'The simplest way to understand what it is'에서 'it(그것)'이 주어진 문장의 '브랜드 자산(Brand equity)'을 가리키고 있으므로, (A)가 주어진 문장에 바로 이어지는 것이 자연스럽다. 이후, (A)에서 언급된 테스트의 종류 중 하나의 예시인 'blind taste test(맛 블라인드 테스트)'를 제시해주는 (C)가 이어진 후, 마지막으로 (C)에서 언급된 '맛 블라인드 테스트'의 결과를 통해 얻을 수 있는 결론을 설명해주고 있는 (B)가 위치하는 것이 가장 적절하다. 따라서 정답은 '② (A) - (C) - (B)'이다.

오답해설
① (C)의 'One such test'가 가리키는 내용이 (A)에 등장하므로, (A) 이후에 (C)가 바로 이어지는 것이 문맥상 더 자연스럽다. 따라서 오답이다. 나머지 보기는 문맥상 어색하므로 오답이다.

해석
브랜드 자산은 브랜드에 대한 마케팅 활동에의 과거 투자의 결과로서 한 제품이 얻는 부가 가치이다.
(A) 그것이 무엇인지 이해하는 가장 간단한 방법은 제품 샘플링과 비교 테스트의 전형적인 결과를 이해하는 것이다.
(C) 그러한 한 가지 테스트는 소비자들이 그들이 먹는 브랜드를 알지 못한 채 제품을 시식해본 후, 동일 제품을 브랜드를 알고 먹어보는 맛 블라인드 테스트이다.
(B) 소비자들이 동일한 제품에 대해 브랜드명이 있는 버전과 브랜드명이 없는 버전에 대해 다른 의견을 보고할 때, 그것은 브랜드에 대한 지식이 그들의 인식을 변화시킨 경우임이 틀림없다, 왜냐하면 제품 성능에 대한 소비자들의 인식은 그것과 함께 따라오는 브랜드에 대한 그들의 인상에 크게 의존하기 때문이다.

어휘
brand equity 브랜드 자산[가치]
identical 동일한, 똑같은
must (틀림없이) …일 것이다[…임에 틀림없다]
perception 인식, 인지
dependent 의존하는, 의지하는
sample 시음[시식]하다
acquire 획득하다, 얻다
performance 성능, 효율
impression 인상, 느낌
consume 먹다, 섭취하다, 소비하다

오답률 TOP 2
09 정답 ②

정답해설
(A) 본문 두 번째 문장 "A new RAND Corporation study finds that Americans average more than 5 hours of free time each day(새로운 RAND Corporation의 연구는 미국인들은 매일 평균 5시간 이상의 자유 시간을 갖는다는 것을 알아냈다)."와 세 번째 문장 "But instead of being physically active during their free hours, Americans report they spend most of that time looking at screens (televisions, phones or other devices)(그러나, 그들의 자유 시간 동안 신체적으로 활동적이 되는 것 대신에, 미국인들은 스크린(텔레비전, 휴대폰 또는 다른 기기)을 보며 그 시간의 대부분을 보낸다고 보고한다)."를 통해, '미국인들은 충분한 자유 시간이 있음에도 불구하고, 운동을 하지 않는다'는 것을 알 수 있다. 따라서 (A)에는 '너무 바빠서 운동을 하지 않는 것이 아니다'라는 의미가 되는 어휘가 들어가는 것이 적절하다. 그러므로 빈칸에는 'busy(바쁜)' 또는 'occupied(바쁜)'가 알맞다.
(B) 본문 초반에서 '미국인들은 하루에 평균 5시간 이상이 자유 시간이다'라고 언급하고 있으므로, '하루에 적어도 20~30분의 신체 활동을 하도록 하는 것이 '가능하다''는 의미가 되는 것이 문맥상 자연스럽다. 따라서 빈칸에는 'feasible(가능한)' 또는 'possible(가능한)'이 적절하다.
따라서 정답은 '② busy(바쁜) - feasible(가능한)'이다.

오답해설
③ (B) 'inevitable'은 '필연적인, 불가피한'이라는 의미이므로, 문맥상 빈칸에 적절하지 않다.
④ (A) lazy는 '게으른'이라는 의미이므로, 문맥상 빈칸에 적절하지 않다.
나머지 보기는 문맥상 어색하므로 오답이다.

해석

미국인들이 어쨌든 너무나도 (A) 바빠서 운동을 못 하는 것은 아닐지도 모른다. 새로운 RAND Corporation의 연구는 미국인들은 매일 평균 5시간 이상이 자유 시간이라는 것을 알아냈다. 그러나 그들의 자유 시간 동안 신체적으로 활동적이 되는 것 대신에, 미국인들은 스크린(텔레비전, 휴대폰 또는 다른 기기)을 보며 그 시간의 대부분을 보낸다고 보고한다. "대중들 그리고 심지어 공중 보건 전문가들 사이에서도 여가시간의 부족이 미국인들이 충분한 신체 활동을 하지 못하는 주요 이유라는 일반적인 인식이 있다"고 연구의 공저자인 Deborah Cohen 박사는 말했다. "그러나 우리는 그러한 믿음에 대한 증거가 없다는 것을 발견했다." 이러한 결과는 미국인들이 매일 최소 20 또는 30분을 신체 활동에 사용하도록 하는 것이 (B) 가능하다는 것을 시사한다. 그들이 실제로 어떻게 그들의 시간을 사용하는지에 대한 대중의 의식을 고취시키고 미국인들이 그들의 스크린을 보는 시간을 줄이도록 장려하는 메시지를 만드는 것이 사람들이 신체적으로 더 활동적이 되도록 도울 수 있을 것이다.

(A)	(B)
① 나태한	이상적인
② 바쁜	(실현) 가능한
③ 바쁜	불가피한
④ 게으른	가능한

어휘

average 평균 …이 되다   instead of ~대신에
perception 인지, 인식   leisure 여가
devote 쏟다, 기울이다, 헌신하다   awareness 의식, 관심
feasible 실현 가능한   indolent 게으른, 나태한
ideal 이상적인, 가장 알맞은, 완벽한   inevitable 불가피한, 필연적인

오답률 TOP 1

10 정답 ③

정답해설

주어진 문장은 '생각하는 것(기분)이 감정을 유발하는 것의 예'에 대해 설명하고 있다. 따라서 주어진 문장은, '기분이 감정에 영향을 미친다'는 내용 이후에 들어가는 것이 적절하다. ② 이전 문장 "They are sparked by emotions and colored by the thoughts, memories, and images that have become subconsciously linked with that particular emotion for you(그것들을 감정에 의해 촉발되고, 사고, 기억, 그리고 잠재적으로 당신의 특정한 그 감정과 연결된 이미지들에 의해 색채를 입는다)."에서는 '기분이 감정 등 다른 요소에 의해 영향을 받는다'라고 설명한 후, ③ 이전 문장에서 "But it works the other way around too(그러나 또한 반대로도 작용한다)."라고 설명하며, '즉, 감정이 기분에 영향을 받기도 한다'라고 언급하고 있다. 그러므로 '기분이 감정을 유발하는 것의 예시'인 주어진 문장은 ③에 들어가는 것이 문맥상 자연스럽다.

오답해설

나머지 위치는 문맥상 어색하므로 오답이다.

해석

기분은 당신이 감정을 느낄 때 당신의 신체에 무엇이 일어나는가에 대한 정신적 묘사이고 당신의 뇌가 그 감정에 대한 의미를 감지하고 지정하는 것의 부산물이다. 기분은 감정을 가진 후 발생하는 다음의 것이고, 대개 잠재 의식적인 인지적 입력을 수반하며, 정확히 측정될 수 없다. (①) 그것들은 감정에 의해 촉발되고, 사고, 기억 그리고 잠재적으로 당신의 특정한 그 감정과 연결된 이미지들에 의해 색채를 입는다. (②) 그러나 또한 반대로도 작용한다. (③ **예를 들어, 단지 위협적인 무언가를 생각하는 것은 감정적 공포 반응을 유발할 수 있다.**) 개별 감정은 일시적인 반면, 그것들이 유발하는 기분은 지속될 수 있고 일생에 걸쳐 커질 수 있다. (④) 감정이 결과적으로 특정 감정을 일으키는 잠재적인 기분을 야기할 수 있고 이것이 계속해서 이어지기 때문에, 당신의 인생은 부정적인 기분을 자아내는 고통스럽고 혼란스러운 감정의 순환이 될 수 있고, 이것은 더 많은 부정적 감정을 유발한다.

어휘

portrayal 묘사   byproduct 부산물
perceive 감지[인지]하다   assign 배정하다
cognitive 인지의   input 입력
subconscious 잠재 의식적인, 잠재적인
precisely 정확하게   subconsciously 잠재적으로
the other way around 반대로, 거꾸로
threatening 위협적인   trigger 촉발하다, 유발하다
evoke 유발하다, 떠올려 주다[환기시키다]
persist (없어지지 않고) 계속[지속]되다
in turn 결국, 결과적으로   initiate 일으키다, 시작하다, 개시하다

결국엔 성정혜 영어 하프모의고사
기적사 DAY 73

01	③	02	①	03	③	04	③	05	②
06	①	07	②	08	①	09	④	10	④

오답률 TOP 1
01 정답 ③

정답해설

'drastic'은 '극단적인, 과감한'을 뜻하는 형용사로 ③ sublime(극단적인, 황당한)과 의미상 가깝다.

해석

이것은 기후, 생물의 다양성, 그리고 세계 경제에 **극단적인** 결과로 이어질 수 있다.
① 아주 높은, 고결한
② 온순한, 온화한
③ 극단적인, 황당한
④ 순종적인, 고분고분한

어휘

drastic 극단적인, 과감한
lofty 아주 높은, 고결한
sublime 극단적인, 황당한
biodiversity 생물의 다양성
meek 온순한, 온화한
submissive 순종적인, 고분고분한

오답률 TOP 2
02 정답 ①

정답해설

'impudent'는 '경솔한, 무례한'을 뜻하는 형용사로 ① rash(경솔한, 성급한)와 의미상 가장 가깝다. 이때 'impudent'는 사람의 성격과 관련된 형용사이므로 to부정사의 의미상 주어로 「of+목적어」를 사용하였음에 유의해야 한다. 더해서 'impudent'와 철자가 유사한 'imprudent' 또한 '경솔한, 현명하지 못한'을 뜻하므로 참고하도록 하자.

해석

당신을 도울 수 있는 사람들을 적으로 만드는 것은 **경솔한** 짓이다.
① 경솔한, 성급한
② 경계하는, 조심하는
③ 태만한, 게으른
④ 근면 성실한

어휘

impudent 경솔한, 무례한
wary 경계하는, 조심하는
assiduous 근면 성실한
rash 경솔한, 성급한
remiss 태만한, 게으른

03 정답 ③

정답해설

'adolescent'는 '청소년(기)의, 젊은; 청소년'을 뜻하는 형용사로 ③ juvenile(청소년의)과 의미상 가장 가깝다.

해석

보고서에 따르면, **청소년기의** 아이들이 있는 70% 이상의 부모들이 서로 좋은 관계를 지니고 있다.
① 부드러운, 온화한, 그윽한
② 신랄한, 부식성의
③ 청소년의
④ 톡 쏘는 듯한, 날카로운, 신랄한

어휘

adolescent 청소년(기)의, 젊은; 청소년
mellow 부드러운, 온화한, 그윽한   caustic 신랄한, 부식성의
juvenile 청소년의
pungent 톡 쏘는 듯한, 날카로운, 신랄한

04 정답 ③

정답해설

엄마는 딸에게 운동이 어땠는지 질문하고, 딸은 자신이 '~했다고 말하면서, 이제 힘이 없다'라고 대답하고 있다. 따라서 빈칸에 들어갈 가장 적절한 것은 '③ burned myself out(다 소진됐다)'이다.

오답해설

① 딸에게 체육관에서 운동한 것이 어땠는지 묻자 딸은 이제 힘이 없다고 말하면서 자신이 '격분했다(blew my top)'라고 하는 것은 문맥상 적절하지 않다.
② 딸이 체육관에서 운동을 하고 온 후 운동한 것에 대해 질문하는 엄마에게 이야기하며, 자신이 '인기를 얻었다(caught on fire)'라고 하는 것은 대화의 흐름상 빈칸에 들어갈 말로 어색하다.
④ 엄마가 딸에게 체육관에서 운동하고 온 것이 어땠는지 물어보자 딸은 이제 힘이 없다고 대답하면서 자신이 '정신을 차렸다(came to my senses)'라고 얘기하는 것은 맥락을 고려했을 때 빈칸에 들어갈 말로 적합하지 않다.

해석

엄마: 널 찾고 있었어! 어디 있었어?
딸: 저는 체육관에 아침 운동 하러 다녀왔어요. 뭐 필요하세요?
엄마: 아니, 네 방에 갔는데 네가 침대에 없는 것을 봤어. 그냥 걱정했어.
딸: 아, 집을 나갈 때 엄마를 깨우고 싶지 않았어요. 걱정시켜서 미안해요.
엄마: 괜찮아. 체육관에서 운동한 건 어땠니?
딸: 저는 다 소진되었어요. 이제 힘이 없어요.
① 격분했다
② 인기를 얻었다
③ 다 소진됐다
④ 정신을 차렸다

어휘

blow one's top 격분하다   catch on fire 인기를 얻다
burn oneself out 다 소진되다
come to one's senses 정신을 차리다

05 정답 ②

정답해설

② 출제 포인트: 해석 일치 주의

주어진 해석을 통해 수동태 'will be developed'가 쓰인 문장의 주어가 'the product(상품)'이고 'in response to'의 목적어가 'customer demand(고객의 요구)'임을 알 수 있다. 따라서 'Customer demand

(고객의 요구)'와 'the product(상품)'의 위치를 서로 바꾸어 'The product will be developed in response to customer demand.'로 수정해야 한다.

> 오답해설

① **출제 포인트: '~하자마자 ...했다' 구문**
주어진 해석이 '~하자마자 ...했다'이며 「주어+had+scarcely+과거분사~, when/before+주어+과거시제 동사....」의 형태를 사용하였으므로 옳은 문장이다.

③ **출제 포인트: 가정법 현재/관용표현(manage to+동사원형)**
해당 문장은 가정법 현재 즉, 조건문으로 사용되었으며, 미래시제를 나타내는 경우 if절의 동사에 현재시제를 사용한다. 따라서 if절에 쓰인 현재시제 동사 'play'는 옳은 표현이며 해당 문장에서 'play'는 자동사로 사용되었다. 또한 'manage to stop'은 관용표현 'mange to+동사원형(간신히 ~하다)'에 해당한다.

④ **출제 포인트: 가정법 현재/to부정사의 태/관용표현(be sure to+동사원형)**
해당 문장은 가정법 현재 즉, 조건문으로 사용되었으며 주절에는 명령문을 사용하였다. 이때 명령문에 쓰인 'be sure to factor in'은 관용표현 'be sure to+동사원형(반드시 ~하다)'에 해당한다. 또한 'to be delivered'는 to부정사의 수동태로 주어진 해석 '우편이 배달되는'을 통해 옳은 표현임을 알 수 있으며 'for the mail'은 'to be delivered'의 의미상 주어에 해당한다.

06 정답 ③

> 정답해설

③ **출제 포인트: 관계대명사+불완전한 형태의 절**
'The view'를 선행사로 하는 관계대명사 'which'가 이끄는 절인 'the wearer ~ sees it'은 불완전한 형태이어야 하나 완전한 형태이므로 옳지 않다. 따라서 선행사를 고려해 문맥상 'sees'의 목적어에 해당하는 밑줄 친 'it'을 삭제해야 한다. 이때 'which'는 'The view'를 수식하는 목적격 관계대명사이다.

> 오답해설

① **출제 포인트: 전치사의 쓰임**
밑줄 친 'such as'는 전치사 구로 '~와 같은'을 뜻하며, 이후에 목적어인 'TV and film'이 왔으므로 옳게 사용되었다.

② **출제 포인트: 주어와 동사의 수일치**
주어가 복수 형태인 'Some forms'이므로 밑줄 친 복수 형태의 동사 'engage'는 옳은 표현이다.

④ **출제 포인트: 현재분사 vs. 과거분사**
밑줄 친 'immersed'는 '~에 몰두하다'를 뜻하는 완전타동사 'immerse'의 과거분사로 불완전자동사 'become'의 주격 보어에 해당하며 수식하는 대상인 주어 'Wearers'와 수동관계이므로 'immersed'는 옳은 표현이다.

> 해석

지금껏 여러 해 동안, TV와 영화와 같은 매체에 의한 오락은 볼거리와 소리로 우리의 시각과 청각을 자극할 수 있었다. 그러나 새로운 매체의 일부 형태는 심지어 우리의 촉각과 후각까지 관여시킨다. 어떤 특수 장치를 착용하는 사람이 보는 광경이 그의 뒤에 있는 스크린에 투사된다. 장치를 착용한 사람들은 컴퓨터로 구현된 장면에 빠져들고 가상의 물체를 집고 이동시키기 위해 장갑을 사용한다.

> 어휘

mediated 중개된, 매개된
project 투사하다
stimulate 자극하다
immerse ~에 몰두하다

07 정답 ②

> 정답해설

② **출제 포인트: 전치사 vs. 접속사/시간, 조건의 부사절**
'In case of'는 전치사이므로 이후에 명사(구)가 와야 한다. 해당 문장의 경우 'In case of' 이후에 절이 왔으므로 'In case of'를 'In case that'으로 수정해야 한다. 또한 주절 'their life will be affected'를 통해 조건의 부사절도 미래시제라는 것을 알 수 있으며 이 경우 현재시제 동사 'continue'로 미래를 나타내고 있다.

> 오답해설

① **출제 포인트: 부사절의 접속사 that(so+형용사/부사+that+절)/이어동사 대명사 목적어의 위치**
「so+부사+that+주어+동사」는 '~해서 ...하다'의 의미로 이때 'that'은 부사절을 이끄는 접속사에 해당한다. 또한 'take it off'의 경우 「완전타동사+목적어+부사」 형태의 이어동사이며 이때 목적어에 해당하는 'it'은 대명사이므로 완전타동사와 부사 사이에 위치하여야 한다.

③ **출제 포인트: 주의해야 할 완전타동사/불완전타동사의 목적격 보어/불완전자동사의 주격 보어**
해당 문장에서 'enter'는 목적어를 가지는 완전타동사로 사용되었으며 'found'는 불완전타동사로 'find+목적어+형용사[분사]'로 사용이 가능하다. 해당 문장에서는 현재분사 'lying'을 목적격 보어로 사용하고 있다. 이때 'lie'의 현재분사 형태인 'lying' 이후에 있는 형용사 'motionless'는 불완전자동사 'lie(~한 상태로 있다)'의 주격 보어로 볼 수 있다.

④ **출제 포인트: 불가산명사/주어와 동사의 수일치/현재분사 vs. 과거분사**
해당 문장은 유도부사구문이 사용된 문장이다. 'news'는 불가산명사에 해당하므로 단수로 취급한다. 따라서 단수 형태의 동사 'was'는 옳은 표현이다. 또한 'interesting'은 감정 제공 형용사인 현재분사로 수식하는 대상은 감정을 제공하는 주체에 해당한다. 따라서 'interesting news'는 옳은 표현이다.

> 해석

① Jane은 그녀의 새 모자를 매우 많이 좋아해서 벗으려 하지 않았을 것이다.
② 그들이 환경 파괴를 지속할 경우, 그들의 삶은 영향을 받을 것이다.
③ Tom이 방으로 들어갔을 때, 고양이가 바닥에 꼼짝도 하지 않는 상태로 있는 것을 발견했다. (또는 Tom이 방으로 들어갔을 때, 고양이가 꼼짝도 하지 않고 바닥에 누워 있는 것을 발견했다.)
④ 오늘 아침 그 지진에 대하여 라디오에서 매우 흥미 있는 뉴스가 있었다.

08 정답 ③

> 정답해설

본문은 'Pepsi와 Coca-Cola 사이의 맛 블라인드 테스트 결과 및 현 시장 상황'을 예시로 들며, 브랜드와 제품의 질이 소비자의 선택에 미치는 영향에 대해 설명하는 글이다. 본문에 따르면 맛 블라인드 테스트 결과 Pepsi가 Coca-Cola보다 제품의 질이 뛰어나다는 것이 밝혀졌지만, 그럼에도 불구하고 Coca-Cola 브랜드에 대한 소비자들의 인식이 Pepsi보다 더 우위에 있기 때문에 Coca-Cola가 시장 점유율이 더 높은 것이다. 본문 마지막 문장 "At that point he concluded that brain was recalling ideas from Coke's commercials, and the emotions attached with the brand were overriding the product's actual quality(그 시점에서 그는 뇌가 Coke의 광고로부터 얻은 생각을 상기시키고 있다는 것과, 브랜드에 고착된 감정이 그 제품의 실제 품질보다 더 중요하다는 결론을 내렸다)."를 통해, '브랜드에 대한 감정이 제품의 품질보다 더 중요하다'는 것이 글의 요지임을 알 수 있다. 따라서 정답은 '③ A positive brand image may be more important than a product's high quality(긍정적인 브랜드 이미지가 제품의 좋은 품질보다 더 중요할지도 모른다).'이다.

오답해설
① 본문과 관련 없는 내용이므로 오답이다.
② 본문에서 언급된 사실일 뿐, 본문 전체를 아우르는 글의 요지로는 적절하지 않다.
④ 본문에서 Coca-Cola가 맛을 향상시켰다는 내용은 언급되지 않는다.

해석
1975년, 많은 참가자들이 Pepsi와 Coca-Cola 사이의 맛 블라인드 테스트에 초대되었고, 그들이 Pepsi가 더 달콤하다고 생각함에 따라, 놀랄 것도 없이 사람들은 Pepsi를 선택했다; 그러나 2003년, 신경 과학자인 Read Montague는 의문을 제기했다: 만일 대부분의 사람들이 Pepsi를 선호한다면, 왜 그것의 판매량이 시장을 지배하고 있지 않은가? 이것의 진짜 이유를 알아내기 위해, 그는 몇몇 소비자들을 소집하고 뇌 활동을 추적하기 위해 그들이 MRI 촬영을 받게 했다. 참가자 중 절반은 Pepsi를 선호한다고 말했다. 그의 팀은 사람들이 좋아하는 음료를 마실 때 보상을 추구하는 것과 관련된 배 쪽 피각이라 불리는 뇌의 부분이 활성화된다는 것을 발견했다. 그러나 소비자들이 그들이 무엇을 마시고 있는지 들었을 때, 사정은 변했다. 비율은 3 대 1로 Coke가 우세한 쪽으로 변화했다. 이번에 그들은 뇌의 다른 부분이 활성화되었다는 것을 알아차렸다 – 고차원적 사고와 연관된 내측 전전두피질. 그 시점에서 그는 뇌가 Coke의 광고로부터 얻은 생각을 상기시키고 있다는 것과, 브랜드에 고착된 감정이 그 제품의 실제 품질보다 더 중요하다는 결론을 내렸다.
① 브랜드 마케팅의 중요성은 간과되어서는 안 된다.
② Pepsi가 맛 블라인드 테스트에서 이겼음에도 불구하고, Coke가 여전히 시장을 지배하고 있다.
③ 긍정적인 브랜드 이미지가 제품의 좋은 품질보다 더 중요할지도 모른다.
④ Coca-Cola는 맛을 개선함으로써 Pepsi에 대항하여 시장 점유율을 지켜냈다.

어휘
neuroscientist 신경 과학자
get to the bottom of …의 진짜 이유[원인]를 알아내다
call up 소집하다
things (어떤 사람에게 영향을 미치는) 상황[사정/형편]
ratio 비율, 비
in favor of …에 우호적인[지지하는]
from ~에게서 (온/받은)
overlook 간과하다
dominate 지배하다, 우세하다
shift 변화하다, 이동하다
commercial 광고
override …보다 더 중요하다[우선하다]
market share 시장 점유율

09 정답 ④

정답해설
본문은 '미국인의 TV 시청 시간'에 대한 통계 자료를 제시하고 있다. 본문 중반 "Older people took more time out of their day for TV — those 65 and older watched more than four hours daily on average(나이 든 사람들은 하루 중 더 많은 시간을 TV를 위해 사용했다 – 65세 이상인 사람들은 하루에 평균 4시간 이상을 시청했다)."를 통해, 65세 이상 집단은 하루에 평균 4시간 이상 TV를 시청한다는 것을 알 수 있고, 본문 후반 "The unemployed also spent more time watching daily on average — 3.78 hours — than those with either full-time or part-time jobs on average — 2.10 hours(또한, 실업자들은 정규직 또는 시간제 직업을 가진 사람들보다(2.10시간) 하루에 평균적으로 더 많은 시간을 시청하는데 보냈다(3.78시간))."를 통해, 실업자 집단은 하루에 평균 3.78시간 TV를 시청한다는 것을 알 수 있다. 즉, 단순 시간 비교를 할 때, 65세 이상 집단이 실업자 집단보다 더 많은 시간을 TV를 시청하며 보낸다는 것을 알 수 있다. 따라서 '④ The 65 and older age group watched less hours than the unemployed group(65세 이상 집단이 실업자 집단보다 더 적은 시간을 시청했다).'은 글의 내용과 일치하지 않는다.

오답해설
① 두 번째 문장 "Sitting in front of a television took up 2.7 hours daily, or just over half of the total free time Americans have each day(텔레비전 앞에 앉아있는 것이 미국인이 매일 갖는 전체 자유 시간의 절반을 약간 상회하는 시간인 하루에 2.7시간을 차지했다)."에서, '2.7시간이 미국인의 하루 자유 시간의 절반 이상'이라고 언급하고 있으므로, 미국인의 하루 평균 자유 시간은 6시간을 넘지 않는다는 것을 유추할 수 있다. 따라서 글의 내용과 일치한다.
② 세 번째 문장 "The survey found that American men spend 5.5 hours watching TV on an average day — compared to women who spent 4.8 hours doing so(그 조사는 TV를 시청하며 4.8시간을 보내는 여성과 비교하여, 미국인 남성은 하루 평균 5.5시간을 TV를 시청하며 보낸다는 것을 발견했다)."를 통해 글의 내용과 일치하는 것을 알 수 있다.
③ 본문 중후반 "On the other hand, the 15-44 age group watched the least, about two hours daily on average(반면, 15-44세 집단은 하루에 평균 약 2시간으로, 가장 적게 시청했다)."에서, '15-44세 집단이 (연령 집단 중) 가장 적은 시간 TV를 시청한다'라고 언급하고 있으므로, 15세 미만 집단이 그보다 더 많은 시간을 TV 시청에 할애한다는 점을 유추할 수 있다. 따라서 글의 내용과 일치한다.

해석
Census Bureau의 자료에 따르면, TV를 시청하는 것이 미국이 가장 좋아하는 여가 활동이다. 텔레비전 앞에 앉아 있는 것이 미국인이 매일 갖는 전체 자유 시간의 절반을 약간 상회하는 시간인 하루에 2.7시간을 차지했다. 그 조사는 TV를 시청하며 4.8시간을 보내는 여성과 비교하여, 미국인 남성은 하루 평균 5.5시간을 TV를 시청하며 보낸다는 것을 발견했다. 또한 조사는 연령, 고용 상태, 그리고 기타를 기준으로 사람들이 얼마나 오래 시청했는지를 세분화했다. 나이 든 사람들은 그들의 하루 중 더 많은 시간을 TV를 위해 사용했다 – 65세 이상인 사람들은 하루에 평균 4시간 이상을 시청했다. 반면, 15-44세 집단은 하루에 평균 약 2시간으로, 가장 적게 시청했다. 또한, 실업자들은 정규직 또는 시간제 직업을 가진 사람들보다(2.10시간) 하루에 평균적으로 더 많은 시간을 시청하는데 보냈다(3.78시간). 이것은 심지어 직업을 가진 사람들조차, 평균적으로, 그들의 자유 시간 중 많은 시간을 어떤 종류의 텔레비전 쇼를 보는 데 보낸다는 것을 의미한다.
① 미국인들은 평균적으로 매일 6시간 이하의 자유 시간을 가진다.
② 남성이 여성들보다 더 많은 시간을 TV 시청하는 데 보낸다.
③ 15세 미만의 어린이들이 15세와 44세 사이의 사람들보다 더 많이 TV를 보았다.
④ 65세 이상 집단이 실업자 집단보다 더 적은 시간을 시청했다.

어휘
leisure 여가
bureau 부서, 국
break down 분해하다, 쪼개다
unemployed 실직한, 실업자인
census 인구 조사, 호구 조사
compared to …와 비교하여
employment 고용, 직장

오답률 TOP 3
10 정답 ④

정답해설

본문은 '직감(gut feeling)'에 대해 설명하는 글이다. "④ It, of course, makes perfect sense."에서 '그것이 일리가 있다'라고 하는 것은 앞서 언급된 직감에 대해 설명하는 주장 내용인 "Some suggest it can be explained by our previous experiences. It is like all of a sudden all your knowledge and experience manifests with no effort from your side(몇몇은 그것이 우리의 이전 경험에 의해 설명될 수 있다고 말한다. 그것은 마치 당신의 모든 지식과 경험이 당신 쪽의 노력이 없이 별안간 드러나는 것과 같다)."를 가리키는 것이다. 나머지 보기는 모두 '직감(gut feeling)'을 가리키는 것이므로, 정답은 ④이다.

오답해설

① 네 번째 문장 "You might feel you can trust someone without actually knowing them, or you might feel in danger when, rationally speaking, there is no reasons to be afraid(당신은 그들을 실제로 알지 못한 채로 누군가를 신뢰할 수 있다고 느낄지도 모르거나, 이성적으로 말해서 두려워할 이유가 전혀 없을 때 위험을 느낄지도 모른다)."에서 '직감이 긍정적인 역할을 하는 경우와 부정적인 역할을 하는 경우'에 대해 언급하고 있으므로, "① It can be either positive or negative(① 그것은 긍정적일 수도 있고 부정적일 수도 있다)."의 It은 '직감'을 가리킨다는 것을 알 수 있다.

② "The weirdest part is that sometimes ② it is actually right(가장 기이한 점은 때때로 ② 그것이 실제로 정확하다는 것이다)."에서 본문의 내용상 '때때로 정확할 수 있는 것은 '직감'이므로, it은 '직감'을 가리킨다는 것을 알 수 있다.

③ 본문 중반 "Many attempts have been made to explain gut feeling(직감을 설명하기 위해 많은 시도가 행해져 왔다)."에서 '직감에 대해 설명하려는 시도'에 대해 언급하고, 이후 "Some suggest ③ it can be explained by our previous experiences(몇몇은 ③ 그것이 우리의 이전 경험에 의해 설명될 수 있다고 말한다)."라고 '직감이 설명될 수 있는 방식'을 제시하고 있으므로, it은 '직감'을 가리킨다는 것을 알 수 있다.

해석

기분과 감정의 개념은 그것만으로도 매력적이지만, 그것의 가장 흥미로운 부분 중 하나는 직감이라는 현상이다. 직감은 무의식적이고, 비합리적이며, 직관적이다. ① 그것은 긍정적일 수도 있고 부정적일 수도 있다. 당신은 그들을 실제로 알지 못한 채로 누군가를 신뢰할 수 있다고 느낄지도 모르거나, 이성적으로 말해서 두려워할 이유가 전혀 없을 때 위험을 느낄지도 모른다. 가장 기이한 점은 때때로 ② 그것이 실제로 정확하다는 것이다. 직감을 설명하기 위해 많은 시도가 행해져 왔다. 몇몇은 ③ 그것이 우리의 이전 경험에 의해 설명될 수 있다고 말한다. 그것은 마치 당신의 모든 지식과 경험이 당신 쪽의 노력이 없이 별안간 드러나는 것과 같다. 물론, ④ 그것은 완전히 일리가 있다. 그렇긴 해도, 아마도 당신은 또한 직감이, 그것이 정확할 때, 과거의 경험을 한 것으로는 설명될 수 없는 경우에 대해 생각해 볼 수 있을 것이다.

어휘

fascinating 대단히 흥미로운, 매력적인
by itself 그것만으로
gut feeling 직감
irrational 비합리적인, 비이성적인
rationally 이성적으로, 합리적으로
all of a sudden 별안간, 갑자기
having said that 그렇긴 해도, 그러나
phenomenon 현상
unconscious 무의식적인
intuitive 직감[직관]에 의한
weird 기이한, 기묘한, 이상한
manifest 나타나다, 분명해지다

기적사 DAY 74

| 01 | ① | 02 | ④ | 03 | ② | 04 | ② | 05 | ③ |
| 06 | ① | 07 | ① | 08 | ① | 09 | ④ | 10 | ② |

오답률 TOP 2
01 정답 ①

정답해설

'provisional'은 '임시의, 일시적인'을 뜻하는 형용사로 ① casual(임시의, 평상시의)과 의미상 가장 가깝다.

해석

티베트에서 독립운동을 이끄는 것이 불가능해졌을 때, Dalai Lama는 인도로 떠나 **임시**정부를 세웠다.
① 임시의, 평상시의
② 냉담한
③ 지속적인, 변치 않는
④ 수명이 짧은, 단명하는

어휘

independence 독립; (개인의) 자립
casual 임시의, 평상시의
abiding 지속적인, 변치 않는
provisional 임시의, 일시적인
callous 냉담한
ephemeral 수명이 짧은, 단명하는

02 정답 ④

정답해설

'prestigious'는 '명망 있는, 일류의'를 뜻하는 형용사로 ④ prominent(유명한, 중요한)와 의미상 가장 가깝다.

해석

그 설계자는 MIT의 매우 **명망 있는** 연례 과학 설계 경연에서 1위를 차지했다.
① 사소한, 하찮은
② 임시의, 잠정적인
③ 진짜인, 정확한
④ 유명한, 중요한

어휘

prestigious 명망 있는, 일류의
petty 사소한, 하찮은
authentic 진짜인, 정확한
annual 연례의, 매년의
interim 임시의, 잠정적인
prominent 유명한, 중요한

오답률 TOP 3
03 정답 ②

정답해설

'aesthetic'은 '심미적인, 미학적인'을 뜻하는 형용사로 ② tasteful(심미안이 있는, 우아한)과 의미상 가장 가깝다.

해석

최근, 독일의 연구원들은 유럽에 있는 유명한 역사적 건축물들의 가치를 알아보기 위해 이미지와 **미적** 특징을 연구했다.

① 날카로운, 새된
② 심미안이 있는, 우아한
③ 달콤한, 감미로운
④ 불협화음의, 귀에 거슬리는

어휘

aesthetic 심미적, 미학적
shrill 날카로운, 새된
mellifluous 달콤한, 감미로운
cacophonous 불협화음의, 귀에 거슬리는
determine 알아내다, 밝히다; 결정하다
tasteful 심미안이 있는, 우아한

오답률 TOP 1

04 정답 ②

정답해설

밑줄 친 부분 전 대화에서 A는 B에게 자신이 이틀 전 새로 산 드레스를 입고 더 뚱뚱해 보이지 않는지 묻고 있다. 이에 B는 '멋져 보인다고 말하면서 자신이 ~이다'라고 이야기한다. 따라서 빈칸에 '② mean business(진심이다)'가 들어가는 것이 문맥상 가장 적절하다.

오답해설

① 이틀 전에 새로 구매한 드레스를 입고 자신이 더 뚱뚱해 보이지 않는지 묻는 A의 질문에 B가 A의 말을 부정하고 멋지다고 말하는 상황에서 자신이 '서두른다(step on it)'라고 이야기하는 것은 맥락상 어색하다.
③ A가 B에게 이틀 전에 새로 구매한 드레스를 입은 자신의 모습이 더 뚱뚱해 보이지 않는지 묻자, B는 A의 말을 부정하면서 멋지다고 얘기한다. 그리고서는 자신이 '화낸다(lose my temper)'라고 하는 것은 대화의 흐름상 빈칸에 들어갈 말로 부적합하다.
④ A가 이틀 전에 새로 구매한 드레스를 입은 자신의 모습에 대해 더 뚱뚱해 보이지 않는지 B에게 질문한다. B는 A의 말을 부정하면서 멋있어 보인다고 이야기하고, 자신이 '목표를 달성한다(hit the bull's eye)'고 말하는 것은 문맥상 자연스럽지 않다.

해석

A: 나 이 드레스 입은 모습 어때?
B: 아름다워 보여! 색이 너에게 정말 잘 어울린다.
A: 정말 고마워. 이 옷을 이틀 전에 샀는데, 내게 잘 어울리는지 확실히 모르겠어.
B: 너 아주 괜찮아 보여. 자신감을 더 가져.
A: 더 뚱뚱해 보이지 않아?
B: 전혀 그렇지 않아. 날 믿어, 너 멋있어. 나는 <u>진심이야</u>.
① 서두르다
② 진심이다
③ 화내다
④ 목표를 달성하다

어휘

confidence 자신감
mean business 진심이다
hit the bull's eye 목표를 달성하다
step on it 서두르다
lose one's temper 화내다

05 정답 ③

정답해설

③ 출제 포인트: 불완전타동사의 수동태/few+복수명사/관용표현(manage to+동사원형)

'consider' 이후에 형용사가 오는 경우는 불완전타동사 'consider'의 수동태인 「be considered+목적격 보어[형용사]」뿐이다. 따라서 'consider'를 수동태인 'are considered'로 수정해야 한다. 또한 'few people'에서 'few'는 수를 나타내는 형용사로 복수가산명사를 수식하며 'manage to maintain'은 관용표현 'manage to+동사원형(간신히 ~하다)'에 해당한다.

오답해설

① 출제 포인트: '~하자마자 …했다' 구문
주어진 해석이 '~하자마자 …했다'이며 「No sooner+had+주어+과거분사~, than+주어+과거시제 동사....」를 사용하였으므로 옳은 문장이다.

② 출제 포인트: 수동태 불가동사/주의해야 할 자동사/간접의문문
'vary'는 완전자동사이므로 이후에 목적어가 오지 않으며 수동태로 사용할 수 없다. 또한 'depending on'은 전치사 구로 '~에 따라'를 뜻하며 해당 문장의 경우 의문사절을 목적어로 사용하고 있다. 이때 의문사절은 「의문사+주어+동사」인 간접의문문의 어순을 사용한다.

④ 출제 포인트: 목적격 관계대명사 생략/관용표현(be sure to+동사원형)
해당 문장의 'the doctor told you about at the hospital'에서 전치사 'about'의 목적어가 없으므로 'the restrictions'와 'the doctor' 사이에 목적격 관계대명사 'which' 또는 'that'이 생략되어 있음을 알 수 있다. 또한 'be sure to observe'는 관용표현 'be sure to+동사원형(반드시 ~하다)'에 해당하므로 옳게 사용되었다.

06 정답 ①

정답해설

① 출제 포인트: 불가산명사
'information'은 불가산명사이므로 복수 형태를 사용할 수 없으나 밑줄 친 'informations'는 복수 형태이므로 옳지 않다. 따라서 복수 형태인 'informations'를 단수 형태인 'information'으로 수정해야 한다.

오답해설

② 출제 포인트: 가주어 it/이성적, 감성적 판단의 형용사
밑줄 친 'It'은 가주어이며 진주어는 접속사 'that'이 이끄는 명사절 'we pay attention to these signals instead of viewing them as burdens in our life'이다. 이때 'that' 앞에 있는 형용사가 'necessary'인 경우 'that'이 이끄는 절의 동사에 'should+동사원형' 또는 '동사원형'을 사용해서 'It+be동사+necessary+that+주어+(should)+동사원형'으로 사용될 수 있음에 유의하자.

③ 출제 포인트: 동명사의 쓰임/동명사의 태
밑줄 친 'viewing'은 전치사 구 'instead of'의 목적어로 쓰인 동명사이며 이후에 목적어 'them'을 가지고 있으므로 동명사의 능동태 'viewing'은 옳은 표현이다.

④ 출제 포인트: 접속사의 쓰임
문맥상 '~때문에'를 뜻해야 하므로 밑줄 친 접속사 'as'는 옳은 표현이다. 앞선 비교급 'louder and more extreme'은 비교급 병렬구조로 옳게 사용되었고, 접속사로 쓰인 'as'와 함께 쓰이는 비교급 표현이 아님에 유의해야 한다.

해석

그 조화가 깨질 때, 신체는 우리에게 정보, 신호 그리고 증상을 매우 직접적이고 분명한 방식으로 보낸다. 이러한 신호들을 생활의 부담으로 보는 것 대신에 이런 신호들에 주의를 기울이는 것이 필요하다. 우리가 건강상의 증상을 무시하거나 억제한다면, 신체가 우리의 주목을 끌려고 시도하기 때문에 그것들은 계속해서 더 시끄러워지고 더 극단적이 될 것이다.

어휘

harmony 조화
pay attention to ~에 주의를 기울이다
capture ~의 관심을 끌다
symptom 증상

07 정답 ①

정답해설

① **출제 포인트: 주어와 동사의 수일치/a number of 복수명사**
'a number of' 이후에 오는 명사는 복수 형태이며 주어로 사용할 경우 동사에 복수 형태를 사용해야 한다. 해당 문장은 주어가 'A number of people'이나 동사에 단수 형태인 'lives'를 사용하였으므로 틀린 문장이다. 따라서 'lives'를 복수 형태 동사 'live'로 수정해야 한다.

오답해설

② **출제 포인트: 주어와 동사의 수일치/현재분사 vs. 과거분사**
해당 문장에서 'Doing'은 동명사로서 목적어 'fieldwork'를 가지며 'Doing fieldwork'는 문장에서 주어의 역할을 하고 있다. 동명사 주어는 단수 취급하므로 단수 형태의 동사 'was'는 옳은 표현이다. 또한 'used'는 완전타동사 'use'의 과거분사로 이후에 「by+행위자」인 'by anthropologists'가 왔으며 수식하는 대상 'the common methods'와 수동관계이므로 'used'는 옳은 표현이다.

③ **출제 포인트: 접속사 vs. 전치사/주의해야 할 완전자동사/시제 일치**
'he had worked late the night before'는 절이므로 접속사 'because'의 쓰임은 올바르며 'arrive on time'에서 'arrive'는 완전자동사에 해당한다. 또한 'William이 도착하지 못한 시점'보다 '일한 시점'이 먼저이며 이때 도착하지 못한 시점이 과거시제이므로 일한 시점에 과거완료인 'had worked'를 사용한 것은 옳다.

④ **출제 포인트: 시간의 부사(구) 및 부사절/완전타동사+목적어[to부정사 vs. 동명사]/수동태 불가동사**
'For many decades'는 시간의 부사구로 현재완료와 함께 사용한다. 따라서 현재완료 진행형인 'have been trying'은 옳게 사용되었다. 또한 문맥상 '알아내려고 노력하다'가 자연스러우므로 'trying'의 목적어로 to부정사인 'to find out'을 사용하는 것은 옳다. 마지막으로 'exists'는 완전자동사에 해당하므로 이후에 목적어가 없으며 수동태로 사용할 수 없다.

해석

① 망명 중인 많은 사람들이 암살의 위협 아래 살아간다.
② 현장 연구는 인류학자들에 의해 이용되는 일반적인 방법 중 하나였다.
③ William은 전날 밤늦게까지 일했기 때문에 제시간에 도착하지 못했다.
④ 몇십 년 동안, 사람들은 외계인이 실제로 존재하는지를 알아내려고 노력해 왔다.

08 정답 ①

정답해설

본문은 '블라인드 테스트의 목적'에 대해 설명하는 글이다. 첫 문장 "Blind testing aims to assess a product based on its intrinsic merits by hiding any reference to the wider brand(블라인드 테스트는 더 폭넓은 브랜드에 대한 언급을 숨김으로써 그것의 본질적인 가치에 기반을 두고 제품을 평가하는 것을 목표로 한다)."에서 글의 주제를 확인할 수 있고, 이어서 다양한 상황에서 블라인드 테스트를 통해 얻을 수 있는 효과에 대해 설명해주고 있다. 따라서 전체 글의 제목으로 가장 적절한 것은 '① What Is Blind Testing for?(블라인드 테스트는 무엇을 위한 것인가?)'이다.

오답해설

② 본문에서는 '블라인드 테스트의 효과'를 긍정적으로 평가하고 있으므로, 본문과 어울리지 않는 제목이다.
③ 본문에서는 블라인드 테스트가 수행되는 방법 또는 절차에 대해서는 언급되지 않는다.
④ 본문에서는 블라인드 테스트에 관해서만 언급하고 있으며, 브랜드 테스트에 관해서는 언급되지 않으므로 오답이다.

해석

블라인드 테스트는 더 폭넓은 브랜드에 대한 언급을 숨김으로써 그것의 본질적인 가치에 기반을 두고 제품을 평가하는 것을 목표로 한다. 이것은 이전 경험에 의해 생성된 어떤 후광 효과 또는 부정적 연상에 의한 영향을 받은 결과를 방지한다. 이러한 접근은 시장 연구가들에게 경쟁사의 제품 또는 그 제품의 이전 버전들과 비교하여, 테스트 제품의 절대적인 매력에 대한 확실한 묘사를 해주는 데 효과적이다. 매력을 위해 분투하는 브랜드들에게, 이것은 문제가 브랜드의 이미지에 원인이 있는지 또는 제품 자체에 원인이 있는지 분명히 하는 데 유용할 수 있다. 높은 매력을 가지고 있는 브랜드들에게, 이것은 그들의 제품이 실제로 '우수한'지 또는 평가가 브랜드 후광 효과에 의해 돋보여진 것인지 이해하는 데 도움이 된다.

① 블라인드 테스트는 무엇을 위한 것인가?
② 블라인드 테스트는 왜 무의미한가?
③ 블라인드 테스트는 어떻게 수행되는가?
④ 블라인드 테스트와 브랜드 테스트는 어떻게 다른가?

어휘

assess 평가하다
merit 가치, 요소, 장점
avoid 방지하다
association 연상, 연관
appeal 매력, 마음을 끄는 것
relative to …에 비례하여, …에 관련하여
competitor 경쟁자
establish 입증하다, 분명히 하다
flatter 돋보이게 하다, 아첨하다
pointless 무의미한, 적절치 못한
intrinsic 본질적인, 고유한
reference to …에 대한 언급, 참조
halo effect 후광 효과
absolute 절대적인, 확실한, 완전한
struggle for …을 향하여 애쓰다
be rooted in …에 원인이 있다
halo 후광, 영광

09 정답 ④

정답해설

본문은 '미국과 비교하여, 유럽에서는 노동자들의 여가시간을 보장해주는 정책이 더욱 적극적으로 시행되고 있다'고 설명하고 있다. 본문 중반 'For instance(예를 들어)' 이후부터 유럽과 미국 노동자들의 노동 및 여가 시간 실태를 구체적인 수치를 제시하며 비교 설명하고 있다. 그런데 ④에서는 '미국인들과 유럽인들이 여가시간을 보내는 방법'에 대해 언급하고 있으므로, 문맥상 어색하다. 따라서 정답은 ④이다.

오답해설

나머지 보기는 문맥상 자연스러우므로 오답이다.

해석

프랑스 정부가 2017년에 직원들이 사무실에 있지 않는 동안 업무 이메일로부터 접속을 끊는 것을 허용해주는 정책을 도입했을 때, 많은 미국인 노동자들은 질투심을 가지고 바다 너머를 바라봤을지도 모른다. ① 비록 그 새로운 프랑스의 법이 엄한 규칙을 지정하지는 않았지만, 그것은 노동자들이 업무 이메일로 여가시간을 침해하는 시간의 양을 제한하도록 돕기 위해 고안되었다. ② 그것은 유럽의 노동자들에게 그들의 미국의 상대방보다 더 고른 일과 삶의 균형을 주는 경향이 있는 많은 노동법과 규범의 한 예일 뿐이다. 예를 들어, 2015년에, 프랑스인들은 1년에 평균 1,482시간을 일한 반면, 미국인 노동자들은 약 1,790시간을 일했다. ③ 한편, 연간 약 15일의 휴가를 받는 미국인 노동자들은 또한 약 30일을 받는 유럽인 상대방보다 더 적은 휴가 시간을 얻는다. ④ 또한, 미국인 노동자들은 그들의 여가시간조차도 생산적인 무언가를 하면서 보내는 것을 좋아하는 반면, 유럽인들은 재미있고 스트레스가 없는 무언가를 하기를 선호한다. 게다가, 미국인 직원들은 할당된 휴가 시간 중 약 73%만을 사용하는 반면, 독일과 프랑스 노동자들은 허용되는 거의 모든 휴가 시간을 사용한다.

어휘
institute 도입하다, 시작하다
hard-and-fast 엄중한, 변경을 허락지 않는
infringe upon …을 침해하다
leisure 여가
norm 규범
even 고른, 평평한
counterpart 상대, 대응 관계에 있는 사람[것]
productive 생산적인
what's more 게다가, 한술 더 떠서
allot 할당하다

10 정답 ②

정답해설
본문은 "감정(emotions)"과 "기분(feelings)"의 미묘한 차이에 대해 설명하고 있다. 본문 후반 "Whereas emotions are inborn and common to us all, the meanings they acquire and the feelings they prompt are very personal. Feelings are shaped by individual temperament and experience; they vary enormously from person to person and from situation to situation(감정이 선천적이고 우리 모두에게 보편적인 반면, 그것들이 얻는 의미와 그것들이 촉발하는 기분은 매우 개인적이다. 기분은 개별적 기질과 경험에 의해 형성된다; 그것들은 사람마다 그리고 상황마다 대단히 다르다)."을 통해, '감정은 타고난 것이며, 기분은 후천적인 요소이다'라는 것을 알 수 있다. 따라서 필자의 주장으로 가장 적절한 것은 '② Emotions are instinctual and feelings are acquired(감정은 선천적이고 기분은 후천적이다).'이다.

오답해설
① 본문 후반의 내용에 따르면, '감정은 보편적이고, 기분은 개인적'이므로, '감정은 객관적(objective)이고 기분은 주관적(subjective)'이라는 것을 유추할 수 있다. ①은 본문의 주장과는 반대되는 내용이므로 오답이다.
③ 본문과 관련이 없는 내용이므로 오답이다.
④ 본문 초반 "One side of the coin is an emotion: a physical response to change that is almost hard-wired and universal. The other side of the coin is your feeling: mental associations and other reactions to an emotion that are personal and gained through experience(동전의 한 면은 감정이다: 변화에 대한 거의 내재되어 있고 보편적인 신체적 반응. 동전의 다른 면은 당신의 기분이다: 감정에 대한 개인적이고 경험을 통해 획득되는 정신적 연상 및 기타 반응)."를 통해, '감정은 신체적 반응이고, 기분은 정신적 반응'이라는 것을 알 수 있다. ④는 본문과는 반대되는 내용이므로 오답이다.

해석
우리는 동일한 것을 의미하기 위해 "감정(emotions)"과 "기분(feelings)"이라는 단어를 교체하여 사용한다. 그러나 감정과 기분은 다르다. 그것들은 단지 같은 동전의 양면처럼 매우 밀접하게 관련된 것이다. 동전의 한 면은 감정이다: 변화에 대한 거의 내재되어 있고 보편적인 신체적 반응. 동전의 다른 면은 당신의 기분이다: 감정에 대한 개인적이고 경험을 통해 획득되는 정신적 연상 및 기타 반응. 동일해 보임에도 불구하고, 실제로는 감정이 기분으로 나아가는 것이다. 감정은 종종 특유하고 혼동을 주는 기분보다 더 예측 가능하고 쉽게 이해된다. 감정이 선천적이고 우리 모두에게 보편적인 반면, 그것들이 얻는 의미와 그것들이 촉발하는 기분은 매우 개인적이다. 기분은 개별적 기질과 경험에 의해 형성된다; 그것들은 사람마다 그리고 상황마다 대단히 다르다. 하나의 특정한 감정을 느끼는 매우 많은 방식들이 있다.
① 감정은 주관적이고 기분은 객관적이다.
② 감정은 선천적이고 기분은 후천적이다.
③ 감정과 기분은 문화 전반에 걸쳐 보편적이다.
④ 감정은 정신적 상태이고 기분은 신체적 감각이다.

어휘
interchangeably 교체하여, 교환하여
distinct 다른, 별개의
hard-wired 내재된
universal 보편적인, 일반적인
association 연상, 연관성
acquire 얻다, 획득하다
proceed to …으로 나아가다, …에 이르다
predictable 예측[예견]할 수 있는
idiosyncratic (개인에게) 특유한
inborn 선천적인, 타고난
prompt 촉발하다
temperament 기질
enormously 엄청나게, 대단히
subjective 주관적인
objective 객관적인
instinctual (학습한 것이 아니라) 본능에 따른, 타고난, 선천적인
acquired 후천적인

기적사 DAY 75

결국엔 성정혜 영어 하프모의고사

| 01 | ③ | 02 | ② | 03 | ② | 04 | ③ | 05 | ① |
| 06 | ③ | 07 | ③ | 08 | ③ | 09 | ② | 10 | ② |

01 정답 ③

정답해설
'unchanging'은 '불변의, 늘 변치 않는'을 뜻하는 형용사로 ③ perdurable (불변의, 영속하는)과 의미상 가장 가깝다.

해석
큰 생활 변화가 있을 때, **변하지 않는** 전통은 여러분이 강한 상태를 유지하고 계속 움직이도록 도와줄 수 있다.
① 변덕스러운, 불안한
② 격동의, 격변의
③ 불변의, 영속하는
④ 열렬한, 격정적인

어휘
unchanging 불변의, 늘 변치 않는 carry on 계속 움직이다[가다]
volatile 변덕스러운, 불안한 turbulent 격동의, 격변의
perdurable 불변의, 영속하는 tempestuous 열렬한, 격정적인

오답률 TOP 2
02 정답 ②

정답해설
'shrewd'는 '상황 판단이 빠른, 기민한, 약삭빠른'을 뜻하는 형용사로 ② astute(약삭빠른, 영악한)와 의미상 가장 가깝다.

해석
그녀가 어렸을 때 이후로 매우 많은 어려움을 겪어 와서 그녀는 **상황 판단이 빨라**졌다.
① 둔한, 흐릿한
② 약삭빠른, 영악한
③ 흐린, 어두운
④ 빛나는, 환한

어휘
suffer 겪다, 당하다 hardship 어려움[곤란]
shrewd 상황 판단이 빠른, 기민한, 약삭빠른
dim 둔한, 흐릿한 astute 약삭빠른, 영악한
murky 흐린, 어두운 radiant 빛나는, 환한

오답률 TOP 1
03 정답 ②

정답해설
'infallible'은 '확실한, 결코 틀리지 않는'을 뜻하는 형용사로 ② strong(확실한, 강력한)과 의미상 가장 가깝다.

해석
나는 그녀가 지나치게 흥분한다면 주의를 딴 데로 돌릴 **확실한** 방법을 곧 발견했다.
① 솜씨 없는, 서투른
② 확실한, 강력한
③ 서투른, 어설픈
④ 효과적인

어휘
infallible 확실한, 결코 틀리지 않는
draw a red herring across the path[track] 주제와는 관계가 없는 것을 꺼내어 남의 주의를 딴 데로 돌리다
inept 솜씨 없는, 서투른 strong 확실한, 강력한
clumsy 서투른, 어설픈 efficacious 효과적인

04 정답 ③

정답해설
지갑에 있던 돈을 도둑맞은 Evan에게 Adele은 돈을 가져간 사람이 '~을 좀 가져야 한다'라고 말하고 있다. 따라서 빈칸에 들어갈 가장 적절한 것은 '③ the pang of conscience(양심의 가책)'이다.

오답해설
① Evan이 지갑 안에 들어있던 100달러의 돈을 도둑맞은 상황에 대해 Adele은 현금을 가져간 사람이 '위험한 상황(a close call)'을 좀 가져야 한다고 말하는 것은 문맥상 어색하다.
② Evan의 지갑에 들어있던 현금을 모두 가져간 사람에 대해 Adele이 그는 '예상치 못한 상황에 대한 늦은 반응(a double take)'을 좀 가져야 한다고 이야기 하는 것은 대화의 흐름상 부자연스럽다.
④ Adele이 Evan의 지갑에 있던 현금을 모두 가져가 버린 사람이 '문제의 본질(the long and short of it)'을 좀 가져야 한다고 얘기하는 것은 맥락 상 빈칸에 들어갈 말로 적절하지 않다.

해석
Adele: Evan, 너 되게 걱정 많아 보여!
Evan: 나는 지갑을 잃어버렸고 오늘 아침에 돌려받았어. 근데 누군가가 지갑 안에 들어있던 현금을 모두 가져갔어.
Adele: 어쩌지, 정말 나쁜 사람이다! 지갑에 현금이 얼마나 들어있었어?
Evan: 100달러 정도 들고 다녔어. 교재 살 돈이었어.
Adele: 정말 안타까워. 돈을 가져간 사람은 <u>양심의 가책</u>을 좀 가져야 해.
Evan: 그러길 바라.
① 위험한 상황
② 예상치 못한 상황에 대한 늦은 반응
③ 양심의 가책
④ 문제의 본질

어휘
a close call 위험한 상황
a double take 예상치 못한 상황에 대한 늦은 반응
the pang of conscience 양심의 가책
the long and short of it 문제의 본질

05 정답 ①

정답해설

① 출제 포인트: '~하자마자 ...했다' 구문(주어+had+no sooner+과거분사 ~, than+주어+과거시제 동사....)

'~하자마자 ...했다' 구문은 「주어+had+no sooner+과거분사 ~, than+주어+과거시제 동사....」로 사용한다. 해당 문장은 주어진 문장의 해석이 '~하자마자 ...했다'이며 주절에 'no sooner'를 사용하였으나 종속절에 'when'을 사용하였으므로 틀린 문장이다. 따라서 'when'을 'than'으로 수정해야 한다.

오답해설

② 출제 포인트: 관용표현(be sure to+동사원형)/불완전타동사의 목적격 보어

해당 문장에서 'is sure to make'는 관용표현 'be sure to+동사원형(반드시 ~하다)'에 해당하며 이때 'make'는 불완전타동사로 「make+목적어+목적격 보어[형용사]」의 형태로 사용되었다.

③ 출제 포인트: 능동태 vs. 수동태

'cut off'의 수동태가 쓰인 문장으로 이후에 「by+행위자」인 'by Hurricane Sandy'가 왔으며 주어진 해석인 '끊긴 상태'와 일치하므로 옳은 문장이다.

④ 출제 포인트: 관용표현(manage to+동사원형)/to부정사의 태

해당 문장에서 'managed to be declared'는 관용표현 'mange to+동사원형(간신히 ~하다)'에 해당한다. 이때 'to be declared'는 to부정사의 수동태로 주어진 해석 '파산 선고를 받다'와 일치하므로 옳게 사용되었다.

06 정답 ③

정답해설

③ 출제 포인트: 주장, 요구, 명령, 제안동사+(that)+주어+(should)+동사원형

문맥상 'the latest evidence'를 주어로 갖는 동사 'suggests'가 '제안하다'가 아닌 '암시하다, 시사하다'를 뜻하므로 'suggests'의 목적어에 해당하는 that절의 동사에 시제를 적용해야 한다. 이때 주어가 'it'이고 종속절 'while it isn't ideal'이 현재시제이므로 'help'를 'helps'로 수정해야 한다. 해당 문장에서 'help'는 완전자동사로 쓰였음에 유의해야 한다.

오답해설

① 출제 포인트: 접속사의 쓰임

밑줄 친 'Whether' 이후에 'or not'이 있으므로 밑줄 친 접속사 'Whether'는 옳은 표현이다.

② 출제 포인트: 주어와 동사의 수일치

주어는 접속사 'Whether'가 이끄는 명사절 'Whether ~ the weekend'이며 명사절은 단수 취급한다. 따라서 동사에 단수 형태인 'is'를 사용하는 것이 옳다.

④ 출제 포인트: 전치사+관계대명사+완전한 형태의 절

'전치사 + 관계대명사' 이후의 문장은 완전하다. 해당 문장은 'during which' 이후의 문장이 완전하며 선행사 'a weekend of sleep'을 수식하고 있으므로 밑줄 친 관계대명사 'which'의 쓰임은 올바르다.

해석

우리가 잠을 주말에 보충할 수 있는지 없는지는 수면 연구원들 사이에서 뜨겁게 논의되는 주제이다; 가장 최근의 증거는 그것이 이상적이지는 않지만, 도움이 된다는 것을 시사한다. UCLA 수면 연구원 Peter Liu가 만성적으로 수면에 제한을 받은 사람들을 하룻밤에 약 10시간씩 수면을 취하는, 잠자는 주말을 위해 연구실로 데려왔을 때, 그들은 혈당을 처리하는 인슐린 기능에서 호전을 보였다.

어휘

catch up on ~을 따라잡다, 보충하다
hotly 뜨겁게
chronically 만성적으로
blood sugar 혈당

07 정답 ③

정답해설

③ 출제 포인트: 시간의 부사(구) 및 부사절/능동태 vs. 수동태

'Since the business was known to everybody'는 시간의 부사절로 현재완료와 함께 사용하나 주절의 동사에 과거완료인 'had been opened'를 사용하였으므로 틀린 문장이다. 따라서 'had been opened'를 현재완료 'have been opened'로 수정해야 한다. 또한 문맥상 '~에게 알려지다'가 자연스러우므로 수동태 'was known to'는 옳은 표현이다.

오답해설

① 출제 포인트: what vs. that/접속사의 쓰임

해당 문장의 'you're doing'은 목적어가 없는 불완전한 형태의 절이며 'know' 이후에 선행사에 해당하는 명사(구)가 없으므로 선행사를 포함하는 관계대명사 'what'의 쓰임은 올바르다. 또한 문맥상 '~하지 않는 한'이 자연스러우므로 접속사 'unless'를 사용하는 것이 옳다.

② 출제 포인트: 완전타동사+목적어[동명사 vs. to부정사]/관용표현(spend+시간/돈+on+목적어)

'mind'는 완전타동사로 목적어에 동명사를 사용한다. 따라서 동명사 'spending'은 옳은 표현이며 이때 'spending money on training'은 관용표현 'spend+시간/돈+on+목적어(~에 시간/돈을 쓰다)'에 해당한다.

④ 출제 포인트: 주격 관계대명사절의 동사 수일치/주어와 동사의 수일치/능동태 vs. 수동태

'A novel'은 주절의 주어이자 주격 관계대명사 'that'의 선행사에 해당하며 단수 형태이므로 주절의 동사에 단수 형태인 'is'를, 주격 관계대명사절의 동사에 단수 형태인 'was'를 옳게 사용하였다. 또한 문맥상 '연재되다'와 '출간되다'가 자연스러우므로 수동태 'was serialized'와 'be published'는 옳은 표현이다.

해석

① 당신이 하고 있는 것이 무엇인지 알지 못한다면 어떤 것도 만져서는 안 된다.
② 생산성을 향상한다면, 그녀는 교육에 돈을 쓰는 것을 신경 쓰지 않는다.
③ 그 사업이 모든 사람들에게 알려진 이래로, 많은 비슷한 가게들이 생겼다.
④ 신문에 연재되던 소설이 단행본으로 출간될 예정이다.

08 정답 ③

정답해설

본문은 '소비자들이 제품 또는 서비스에 대한 선호를 결정짓는 데 영향을 미치는 요소'에 대해 설명하는 글이다. 본문 중반 "Examples of such factors include the personal characteristics of the purchaser like socio-economic level, individual characteristics like personality and situational characteristics like the purpose of the purchase(그러한 요소의 예는 사회 경제적 수준과 같은 구매자의 개인적 특성, 성격과 같은 개별적 특성, 그리고 구매의 목적과 같은 상황적 특성을 포함한다)."를 통해, '구매 결정에 관련된 요소는 특정 구매자에게만 해당하는 '특수성'을 포함한다'는 것을 알 수 있다. 그런데 "The decision also involves the ③ indistinctiveness of the purchaser(또한 그 결정은 구매자의 ③ 비 특수성을 포함한다)."에서는 구매자의 '비 특수성'을 포함한다고 진술하고 있으므로, 문맥상 어색하다. 따라서 ③ indistinctiveness (비 특수성)'는 'distinctiveness(특수성)'가 되어야 문맥상 자연스럽다.

오답해설

① 제품 또는 서비스의 선호도를 결정하는 데 영향을 미치는 요소들을 여러 가지 제시하고 있으므로, 'various(다양한)'는 문맥상 자연스럽다.
② 'face'는 동사로 '(상황 등에) 직면하다'라는 의미이므로, 문맥상 '관련된 선택 상황에 처할 때'라는 뜻이 된다. 따라서 글의 흐름상 적절하다.
④ 여러 가지 요소가 얽혀 구매 결정에 서로 영향을 미치는 것이므로, '상호작용'이라는 의미의 'interaction'은 문맥상 적절하다.

해석

소비자들은 제품과 서비스에 대한 그들의 선호를 제품의 특성과 그 제품에 대한 그들의 개인적 태도와 같은 ① 다양한 요소에 기반하여 결정한다. 그러나 중요한 역할을 하는 또 다른 요소는 그들이 ② 직면하는 관련된 선택 집합에서의 제품의 공유되는 측면과 독특한 측면이다. 따라서 어떤 제품을 구매할지를 결정하는 과정은 그것의 품질과 같은 제품의 공유된 특성과 브랜드명과 같은 그것의 독특한 특성을 고려한다. 또한 그 결정은 구매자의 ③ 비 특수성(→특수성)을 포함한다. 그러한 요소의 예는 사회 경제적 수준과 같은 구매자의 개인적 특성, 성격과 같은 개별적 특성, 그리고 구매의 목적과 같은 상황적 특성을 포함한다. 게다가, 이러한 특성들의 ④ 상호작용 또한 이 선택에 영향을 미칠 수 있다. 이러한 제품을 선택하는 일은 많은 다른 유형의 특성들이 관련될 때 훨씬 더 복잡할 수 있다.

어휘

attribute 특성
attitude 태도
relevant 관련 있는, 연관된
take into account 고려하다, 참작하다
characteristic 특성
indistinctiveness 비 특수성, 특색이 없음
socio-economic 사회 경제적인
situational 상황적인
interaction 상호작용

09 정답 ②

정답해설

본문은 '미국인들의 운동 부족 실태'에 대해 설명하는 글이다. 사회가 변모함에 따라 신체 활동을 요하는 업무가 줄어들게 된 것을 운동량 감소의 원인 중 하나로 언급하고 있다. 본문 중반 "About 30 percent of adults are entirely sedentary and another 45 percent don't get enough physical activity, which means only a quarter of all Americans get the exercise they need(성인 중 약 30%가 완전히 비활동적이며, 다른 45%는 충분한 신체 활동을 하지 않는데, 이는 모든 미국인 중 오직 4분의 1만이 그들이 필요한 운동량을 채운다는 것이다)."에서 '대부분의 미국인이 운동량이 부족한 상태'임을 언급하고, 이후 구체적인 조사 결과를 통해 그에 대한 근거를 제시하고 있으므로, 전체 글의 요지로 가장 적절한 보기는 '② Generally speaking, people in the U.S. are not physically active enough(일반적으로 말해서, 미국의 사람들은 신체적으로 충분히 활동적이지 않다).'이다.

오답해설

① 본문과 관련이 없는 내용이다.
③ 마지막 문장 "Even people who report intense activity often overstate their efforts(격렬한 활동을 한다고 보고하는 사람들조차도 종종 자신들의 노력을 과장한다)."를 통해, '사람들이 자신들의 노력을 과장한다'는 내용을 언급하고는 있으나, 본문 전체적으로는 '전혀 운동을 하지 않는 사람들'에 대해서도 언급하고 있으므로, 글 전체를 아우르는 요지라고 볼 수 없다.
④ 본문 초반 '미국의 노동력이 변화하였다'는 내용이 언급되기는 하나, 이는 '운동이 부족해진 이유'에 대해 설명하기 위한 내용이므로, 글 전체의 요지로는 부적절하다.

해석

19세기만큼 최근, 미국의 일터에서 사용된 모든 에너지의 30%는 인간 근육의 힘에 의해 제공되었다; 오늘날, 그 비율은 극소이다. 대부분의 방식에서, 농업 경제로부터 산업 사회, 그리고 오늘날의 정보 시대로의 전환은 매우 요긴한 것이었다. 그러나 또한 무언가가 상실되었다. 미국은 관중의 국가가 되었다. 성인 중 약 30%가 완전히 비활동적이며, 다른 45%는 충분한 신체 활동을 하지 않는데, 이는 모든 미국인 중 오직 4분의 1만이 그들이 필요한 운동량을 채운다는 것이다. 실제 상황은 훨씬 더 나쁠지도 모른다. 자신들이 운동을 한다고 말하는 대부분의 사람들은 자신들의 유일한 규칙적인 신체 활동으로 걷기를 말한다. 그러나 CDC의 연구원들이 자신들이 걷는다고 말한 1,500명 이상의 사람들을 평가했을 때, 그들은 오직 6%만이 건강을 위한 현재의 기준을 충족시킬 만큼 충분히 자주, 충분히 멀리, 또는 충분히 힘차게 걷는다는 것을 발견했다. 격렬한 활동을 한다고 보고하는 사람들조차도 종종 자신들의 노력을 과장한다.

① 걷는 것은 미국에서 대부분의 사람들에게 이상적인 운동이다.
② 일반적으로 말해서, 미국에 있는 사람들은 신체적으로 충분히 활동적이지 않다.
③ 대부분의 사람들은 실제로 자신들이 그들이 하고 있다고 생각하는 만큼 격렬하게 운동하지는 않는다.
④ 미국의 노동력은 19세기 이래로 극적으로 변화해왔다.

어휘

minuscule 극소의
transition 변이, 변천, 과도
agricultural 농업의
boon 요긴한 것
spectator 관중
sedentary 주로 앉아서 지내는, 몸을 많이 움직이지 않는
evaluate 평가하다
briskly 힘차게, 씩씩하게, 활발하게
meet 충족시키다
intense 격렬한, 극심한
overstate 과장하다

오답률 TOP 3

10 정답 ②

정답해설

본문은 'Antonio Damasio의 뇌의 전두엽 손상과 행동적 변화에 대한 사례 연구'에 대한 글이다. 첫 번째 사례인 Phineas Gage는 머리에 부상을 당하고, 이후 회복하였으나, "He became irascible, moody, and impatient(그는 화를 잘 내고, 감정 기복이 심해졌으며, 성급하게 되었다)."에 언급되어 있듯이 감정적인 측면에서 변화를 겪었다. 두 번째 사례자 Elliot 또한, 뇌수술 이후 Gage와 마찬가지로, 감정적으로 자신 및 타인들에게 무관심해지는 변화를 겪었다. 두 예시 모두에서 공통적으로 나타나는 변화의 특징은 전부 '감정'과 관련된 변화라는 것을 알 수 있으므로, 빈칸에 가장 적절한 표현은 '② connected to emotions(감정과 연결된)'이다.

오답해설

① Elliot의 예시에서 "Intellectually he was brilliant as always(지적으로 그는 언제나와 같이 훌륭했다)"라고 언급하며, 그의 지성에는 변화가 없었다는 것을 나타내고 있다. 따라서 빈칸에 적절하지 않다.
③ 기억력에 대해서는 본문에 언급되지 않는다.
④ Phineas Gage의 예시에서 "although he was able to recover most of his mental functions(그가 대부분의 그의 정신 기능을 회복할 수 있었음에도 불구하고)"라고 언급하며, 그가 정신 기능을 대부분 회복했다는 것을 알 수 있다. 따라서 빈칸에 적절하지 않다.

해석

수년 동안, Antonio Damasio는 추론, 집중, 계획, 배열, 그리고 행위의 전환과 관련된 업무를 관장하는 부위인 전두엽에 부상을 입고, 감정과 연결된 행동적 측면에 변화를 겪은 환자들을 연구했다. 예를 들어, Phineas Gage는 철도 산업에서 근무했다. 어느 날, 철봉 하나가 그의 얼굴 왼편에 박혔고, 그의 전두엽 일부를 파괴했다. 놀랍게도, 그는 이 경험에서 살아남았고, 그가 대부분의 그의 정신 기능을 회복할 수 있었음에도 불구하고, 그는 더 이상 그 자신이 아니었다. 그는 화를 잘 내고, 감정 기복이 심해졌으며, 성급하게 되었다. 또한, 성공적인 변호사인 Elliot은 그의 이마 상부에 뇌종양을 앓고 있었다. 그것이 외과적으로 제거되었으나, Gage와 유사하게, 그의 행동에 급격한 변화가 있었다. 지적으로 그는 언제나와 같이 훌륭했지만, 그는 그에게 발생한 것뿐만 아니라 일반적인 비극들에 대해서도 완전히 무관심해졌다.

① 지성과 연관된
② 감정과 연결된
③ 기억과 연관된
④ 정신 기능과 관련된

어휘

investigate 연구하다, 조사하다
reasoning 추리, 추론
reorientation 방향 전환
drive into …를 들이박다
function 기능
moody 기분 변화가 심한
brain tumor 뇌종양
drastic 급격한, 극단적인
indifferent 무관심한
sustain (피해 등을) 입다[당하다]
sequence 차례[순서]대로 배열하다
rod 봉, 막대
recover 회복하다, 복구하다
irascible 화를 잘 내는
impatient 성급한, 안달하는
surgically 외과적으로
intellectually 지적으로
tragedy 비극

결국엔 성정혜 영어 하프모의고사
기적사 DAY 76

| 01 | ④ | 02 | ① | 03 | ② | 04 | ④ | 05 | ④ |
| 06 | ① | 07 | ② | 08 | ③ | 09 | ② | 10 | ③ |

01 정답 ④ 16 서울시

정답해설

'withdrawal'은 '철수, 철회, 취소'를 뜻하는 명사로 ④ retreat(후퇴, 철수)과 의미상 가장 가깝다.

해석

England라는 이름은, 409년에 로마인들의 마지막 **철수** 이후, 5세기에 lowland Britain에서 군주국들을 설립했던 게르만 부족들 중 하나인 앵글족에서 유래했다.

① 붕괴, 실패
② 침략, 침입
③ 항복, 굴복
④ 후퇴, 철수

어휘

monarchy 군주국
collapse 붕괴, 실패
surrender 항복, 굴복
withdrawal 철수, 철회, 취소
invasion 침략, 침입
retreat 후퇴, 철수

02 정답 ① 16 서울시

정답해설

'jettison'은 '버리다, 폐기하다'를 뜻하는 동사로 ① discard(버리다, 폐기하다)와 유의어 관계이다.

해석

그 유명한 여자 사업가는 그녀의 하류 내지는 중산 계급 편견들을 **버릴** 수가 없는 자신을 발견했다.

① 버리다, 폐기하다
② 주제에서 벗어나다
③ 비난하다, 고발하다
④ 부인하다, 부정하다

어휘

distinguished 유명한, 성공한; 기품[위엄] 있는
jettison 버리다, 폐기하다
discard 버리다, 폐기하다
denounce 비난하다, 고발하다
prejudice 편견
digress 주제에서 벗어나다
deny 부인하다, 부정하다

03 정답 ② 16 서울시

정답해설

보통 스컹크들이 모여 산다고 했지만, 역접의 접속부사인 'however(그러나)'가 있으므로 빈칸에는 'however' 이전에 제시된 'live together(모여 산다)'와 반대의 의미인 'solitary(혼자의, 고립의)'가 적절하다.

해석

보통 몇몇 스컹크들은 모여 산다; 그러나, 성체가 된 수컷 줄무늬 스컹크들은 여름 동안 **혼자**이다.

① 야행성의
② 혼자의
③ 약탈하는
④ 잠자는, 휴면 중인

어휘

nocturnal 야행성의 solitary 혼자의
predatory 약탈하는 dormant 잠자는, 휴면 중인

04 정답 ④
13 서울시

정답해설

겨울 스포츠를 좋아한다는 A의 말에 'A가 부럽다'는 B의 대답은 자연스럽지 못하다. 따라서 정답은 ④이다.

오답해설

⑤에서 문맥상 'seconds'는 두 번째(음식)를 나타내며, 이에 대한 허락을 묻는 A에게 B가 '마음껏 드세요(Help yourself)'라고 응답하는 것은 적절하다.

해석

① A: 나 다음 달에 중국에 갈 예정이야.
　B: 중국 어디?
② A: 좋은 소식이 있어.
　B: 뭔데?
③ A: 브라질 여행 갔다 올 때 와인 좀 사다 줘.
　B: 물론이지.
④ A: 나는 겨울 스포츠를 좋아해.
　B: 네가 부럽다.
⑤ A: 한 접시 더 먹어도 될까요?
　B: 마음껏 드세요.

어휘

You bet. 물론이지[당연하죠].　　Help yourself. 마음껏 드세요.

05 정답 ④
18 서울시

정답해설

④ **출제 포인트: 주어와 동사의 수일치**

주어가 단수 형태의 명사구 'The existence'이므로 동사에 단수 형태를 사용해야 하나 복수 형태의 동사인 'are'를 사용하였으므로 옳지 않다. 따라서 복수 형태의 동사 'are'를 단수 형태의 동사 'is'로 수정해야 한다.

오답해설

① **출제 포인트: 관계대명사+불완전한 형태의 절/관용표현(adjust to)**

'a new country and a new culture'를 선행사로 하며 이후에 오는 절이 주어가 없는 불완전한 형태이므로 주격 관계대명사 'which'의 쓰임은 올바르다. 또한 'adjust to'는 관용표현으로 '~에 적응하다'를 뜻하며 'adjusting'은 해당 문장에서 전치사 'of'의 목적어에 해당하는 동명사로 사용되었다.

② **출제 포인트: 주어와 동사의 수일치/준사역동사의 목적격 보어**

접속사 'that'이 이끄는 절의 주어가 동명사 'listening'으로 단수 취급하므로 'that'이 이끄는 절의 동사에 단수 형태인 'helps'를 옳게 사용하였다. 이때 'helps'는 준사역동사로 사용되어 목적격 보어에 원형부정사인 'cope'를 옳게 사용하였다.

③ **출제 포인트: 완전타동사 help의 목적어**

'help'가 완전타동사인 경우 목적어로 원형부정사 또는 to부정사를 사용할 수 있다. 따라서 해당 문장의 'minimize'는 'help'의 목적어로 쓰인 원형부정사로 옳게 사용되었다.

해석

① 문화 충격은 자신의 것들과 상당히 다를지도 모르는 새로운 국가나 새로운 문화에 적응하는 것에 대한 정신적 충격이다.
② 최근 연구는 수술 전과 후에 음악을 듣는 것이 환자들이 관련된 스트레스에 대처하는 것을 돕는다는 것을 발견한다.
③ 하루에 적어도 두 번 양치하는 것과 매일 치실질을 함으로써, 당신은 플라그가 쌓이는 것을 최소화하게 도울 것이다.
④ 교사가 학급을 효율적으로 운영하기를 원한다면, 일관성 있는 규칙들의 존재가 중요하다.

06 정답 ①
18 서울시

정답해설

① **출제 포인트: 능동태 vs. 수동태/수여동사의 수동태**

'convince' 이후에 that절이 오는 경우는 수여동사 'convince'의 수동태인 「be convinced that+절」뿐이다. 따라서 밑줄 친 'convinced'를 수동태 'was convinced'로 수정해야 한다. 만약 능동태로 사용하고 싶다면 밑줄 친 'convinced'와 'that' 사이에 대상에 해당하는 목적어가 있어야 한다.

오답해설

② **출제 포인트: 관용표현(from scratch)**

밑줄 친 'from'은 이후에 있는 'scratch'와 결합하여 '처음부터(from scratch)'를 나타내는 관용표현이므로 옳게 사용되었다.

③ **출제 포인트: 비교급 강조부사**

밑줄 친 'even'은 이후에 비교급 형용사 'easier'를 수식하는 비교급 강조부사로 옳은 표현이다.

④ **출제 포인트: 비교 대상 일치**

밑줄 친 'making'은 「비교급+than」 이후에 위치한 비교 대상으로 앞에 있는 'making pumpkin cake'와 병렬구조로 옳게 사용되었다.

해석

나는 처음부터 호박 케이크를 만드는 것이 상자로부터 케이크를 만드는 것보다 훨씬 쉬울 것이라는 것을 납득하였다.

어휘

convince+목적어[대상]+that+절 ~에게 ~을 납득시키다
from scratch 처음부터

오답률 TOP 3

07 정답 ②
18 서울시

정답해설

② **출제 포인트: 능동태 vs. 수동태**

'he widely acclaimed as a violinist'에서 'acclaimed'는 완전타동사이므로 이후에 목적어가 있어야 하나 전명구 'as a violinist'가 왔으므로 해당 문장은 틀린 문장이다. 따라서 'he widely acclaimed as a violinist'를 수동태 'he was widely acclaimed as a violinist'로 수정해야 한다.

오답해설

① **출제 포인트: 현재분사 vs. 과거분사/one of 명사(구)[복수형태]**

'Born'은 '~을 낳다'를 뜻하는 완전타동사 'bear'의 과거분사로 이후에 전명구 'in Genoa'가 왔으며 생략된 주어 'Piccolo Paganini'와 수동관계이므로 'Born'은 옳은 표현이다. 또한 'one of' 이후에는 복수 형태의 명사(구)가 오므로 'the greatest composers'는 옳은 표현이다.

③ 출제 포인트: 시간의 부사(구) 및 부사절/완전타동사+목적에[to부정사 vs. 동명사]
'in his last years'는 시간의 부사구로 과거시제와 함께 사용한다. 따라서 과거시제 동사 'began'은 옳은 표현이며 이때 'began'은 목적어로 to부정사 또는 동명사를 사용할 수 있으므로 to부정사 'to practice' 또한 옳은 표현이다.

④ 출제 포인트: 능동태 vs. 수동태/관용표현(above all)
'left'는 '~을 남기다'를 뜻하는 완전타동사 'leave'의 과거시제로 이후에 목적어 'many beautiful scores'가 왔으므로 옳은 표현이다. 또한 'above all'은 관용표현으로 '무엇보다도, 특히'를 뜻한다.

해석

이탈리아 제노바에서 태어난 Piccolo Paganini는 19세기의 가장 위대한 작곡가들 중 한 명이다. 그는 바이올리니스트로 널리 칭송되어진 반면, Paganini는 조율, 편곡 그리고 작곡을 포함한 다른 음악적 재능도 가지고 있었다. 자주, 그는 비올라와 피아노를 다루었고, 그의 마지막 몇 해 동안은 오케스트라 지휘자로 활동하기 시작했다. 하지만 무엇보다도 그는 바이올린 협주곡을 위한 많은 아름다운 악보들을 남겼다.

어휘

composer 작곡가 acclaim 칭송하다
above all 무엇보다도, 특히
tune (악기의) 음을 맞추다, 조율하다; 준비하다, 조정하다
arrange 편곡하다; 배열하다, 정리하다
compose 작곡하다; 구성하다 score 악보
concerto 협주곡

08 정답 ③ 18 서울시

정답해설

필자는 자신이 소년일 때 놀았던 운동장에 갔지만 아무도 없었다. 필자 주변의 콘크리트 위에는 자갈, 병 그리고 맥주 캔만이 있을 뿐이다. 따라서 글의 분위기로 가장 적절한 것은 '③ desolate and lonely(황량하고 외로운)'이다.

오답해설

나머지 선지는 글의 분위기로 적절하지 않다.

해석

나는 게임에 참여하기를 바라면서, 동네의 학교 운동장에 갔다. 그러나 거기에는 아무도 없었다. 그물이 없는 농구 골대 아래에서 낙담한 채 모두 어디에 있는지 궁금해하며 근처에서 몇 분 정도 멍하니 있다가, 나를 기다리고 있다고 예상되는 사람들의 이름이 내 마음을 채우기 시작한다. 나는 몇 년 동안 여기와 같은 장소에서 경기를 하지 않았다. 그것이 무엇이었는가? 여기로 오면서 내가 생각하는 것이 무엇이었는가? 내가 어린아이, 소년이었을 때, 나는 놀기 위하여 운동장에 갔다. 오래전이었다. 여기에 있는 아이들은 나를 모를 것이다. 포장도로 밖으로 시끄러운 소음이 할퀴면서, 내 주변에 콘크리트는 자갈, 병들, 그리고 내가 차는 맥주 캔을 제외하고는 텅 비어 있다.
① 차분하고 평화로운
② 흥겹고 즐거운
③ 황량하고 외로운
④ 끔찍하고 무서운

어휘

deject 낙담시키다, 풀이 죽게 하다 hoop (농구의) 링; 테, 고리
wonder 궁금하다, 궁금해하다 pebble 조약돌, 자갈
claw 할퀴다[긁다]
festive 축제적인, 축제의; 흥겨운, 즐거운
merry 즐거운, 명랑한 desolate 황량한, 적막한

오답률 TOP 1

09 정답 ② 18 서울시

정답해설

해당 지문은 미국과 멕시코의 국경에 대한 기원에 대해서 서술하고 있다. "Victorious in the Mexican ~ any plan of nature."를 통해서 '인간은 전쟁 등을 통해 국경이라는 임의적인 경계를 만들어왔다'라는 것을 알 수 있다. 반면 "The one line that nature did provide — the Rio Grande— was a river that ran through but did not really divide continuous terrain(자연이 제공했던 하나의 경계인 Rio Grande 강은 그 사이를 흐르는 강이었지만, 실제로 연속적인 지형을 나눠놓지는 않았다)." 부분 등으로 보아 자연은 경계를 흐르기만 할 뿐, 지형을 나누지 않았다는 것을 알 수 있다. 따라서 '② While nature did not draw lines, human society certainly did(자연은 경계를 만들지 않는 반면에, 인류 사회는 경계를 만들었다).'가 글의 내용과 일치한다.

오답해설

① 본문 중반에 언급된 "it is one thing to draw an arbitrary geographical line between two spheres of sovereignty; it is another to persuade people to respect it(두 지역의 통치권 사이의 임의적인 지리적 경계를 그리는 것과 사람들이 이것을 존중하도록 설득하는 것은 또 다른 이야기라는 것이다)."로 보아 미국과 멕시코가 하나의 통치권이라고 볼 수 없으므로 글의 내용과 일치하지 않는다.

③ 본문 중반에 언급된 "it is one thing to draw an arbitrary geographical line between two spheres of sovereignty; it is another to persuade people to respect it(두 지역의 통치권 사이의 임의적인 지리적 경계를 그리는 것과 사람들이 이것을 존중하도록 설득하는 것은 또 다른 이야기라는 것이다)."으로 보아 경계를 그리는 것과 사람들이 경계를 존중하도록 설득하는 것은 다른 이야기라고 언급하고 있으므로, ③에서 언급된 '사람들이 경계를 존중하는 것을 가능하게 만들었다'고 할 수 없으므로, 글의 내용과 일치하지는 않는다.

④ 본문 후반에 언급된 "The one line that nature did provide — the Rio Grande — was a river that ran through but did not really divide continuous terrain(자연이 제공했던 하나의 경계인 Rio Grande 강은 흐르지만, 실제로 연속적인 지형을 나눠놓지는 않았다)."를 통해서 Rio Grande 강은 경계를 흐르는 강일 뿐, 실제로 연속적인 지형을 나눠놓지는 않았으므로 ④에서 언급된 '지리학적인 경계로 여겨져 왔다'라고 할 수 없다. 따라서 글의 내용과 일치하지 않는다.

해석

이전에 멕시코 북부였던, 미국의 남서부에서, Anglo-America는 Hispanic America와 충돌했다. 그 만남은 언어, 종교, 인종, 경제 그리고 정치 변수들과 관련되었다. Hispanic America와 Anglo-America 사이의 경계는 시간이 지남에 따라 변화했으나, 한 가지 사실은 변하지 않았다; 두 지역의 통치권 사이의 임의적인 지리적 경계를 그리는 것과 사람들이 이것을 존중하도록 설득하는 것은 또 다른 이야기라는 것이다. 1848년 멕시코-미국 전쟁에서 승리한 미국은 멕시코의 절반을 차지했다. 그 결과로 초래된 분열은 어떠한 자연의 계획도 인정하지 않았다. 국경 지방들은 생태학적으로 한 덩어리였다; 즉, 북동부의 멕시코 사막은 남동부의 미국의 사막과 민족주의의 형상화 없이 섞이게 되었다. 자연이 제공했던 하나의 경계인 Rio Grande 강은 흐르지만, 실제로 연속적인 지형을 나눠놓지는 않았다.
① 미국과 멕시코 사이의 경계는 하나의 통치권의 오랜 역사를 의미한다.
② 자연은 경계를 만들지 않는 반면에, 인류 사회는 확실히 경계를 만들었다.
③ 멕시코-미국 전쟁은 사람들이 경계를 존중하는 것을 가능하게 만들었다.
④ Rio Grande는 임의의 지리학적인 경계로 여겨져 왔다.

어휘

run into 충돌하다
arbitrary 임의의, 독단적인, 제멋대로인
sphere 영역, 분야
ratify 승인하다, 인정하다
border 국경, 경계
sovereignty 주권, 영유권, 통치권
borderland 국경 지방, 경계지

오답률 TOP 2
10 정답 ③
18 서울시

정답해설

ⓐ은 난폭 운전의 정의와 예시에 대해 나열하고 있으므로 가장 먼저 위치해야 한다. 이후에 난폭 운전의 계기가 혼잡한 교통 속에서 일정을 맞춰야 하는 것이라는 ㉠이 이어지는 것이 알맞다. 'As a result'로 시작되는 ㉢이 ㉠의 결과이므로 이 뒤에 온다. 마지막으로, 난폭 운전의 결과에 대해 서술하는 ㉡이 오는 것이 적절하다. 따라서 정답은 ③이다.

오답해설

나머지 선지는 문맥상 어색하므로 오답이다.

해석

ⓐ 난폭 운전은 너무 가깝게 따라가기, 과속, 안전하지 않은 차선 변경, 차선을 변경하기 위해 신호 무시하기, 그리고 다른 형태의 태만하거나 조심성 없는 운전과 같은 하나 또는 그 이상의 위반들을 말한다.
㉠ 공격적인 운전자를 유발하는 것은 대개 거의 맞추기 불가능한 일정과 겹쳐진 교통 혼잡이다.
㉢ 그 결과, 공격적인 운전자는 시간을 만들어내기 위한 시도로 보통 여러 개의 위반을 저지른다.
㉡ 불행하게도, 이러한 행동들은 우리의 나머지를 위험에 빠지게 한다. 예를 들어, 지나가기 위해 도로 갓길을 사용하는 것에 의지하는 공격적인 운전자는 다른 운전자들을 깜짝 놀라게 할지도 모르고 그들이 더 큰 위험이나 심지어 충돌을 유발하는 종잡을 수 없는 행동을 하게 할지도 모른다.

어휘

trigger 계기
congestion 혼잡
resort to ~에 의지하다
startle 깜짝 놀라게 하다
crash 충돌
traffic offense 교통 위반
negligent 무관심한, 태만한
aggressive 공격적인
couple with ~와 연결하다
roadway shoulder 도로 갓길
evasive 종잡을 수 없는
violation 위반
combination 조합

기적사 DAY 77

| 01 | ③ | 02 | ④ | 03 | ④ | 04 | ② | 05 | ① |
| 06 | ③ | 07 | ④ | 08 | ③ | 09 | ② | 10 | ② |

01 정답 ③

정답해설

'collapse'는 '붕괴, 실패'를 뜻하는 명사로 ③ disruption(붕괴, 분열)과 의미상 가장 가깝다.

해석

New York Times에 실린 그 기사는 시장 **붕괴**가 달러의 약화에 의해 야기되었다고 단정하고 있다.
① 휴전
② 혼란, 소란
③ 붕괴, 분열
④ 지연, 저지, 방해

어휘

predicate 단정하다, 근거를 두다
truce 휴전
disruption 붕괴, 분열
collapse 붕괴, 실패
turmoil 혼란, 소란
retardation 지연, 저지, 방해

오답률 TOP 3
02 정답 ④

정답해설

'deny'는 '부인하다, 부정하다'를 뜻하는 동사로 ④ repudiate(부인하다, 거부하다)와 유의어 관계이다.

해석

비록 그들은 다른 이념들에 의해 나뉘었지만, 그들의 공통의 민족성은 **부인하지** 않았다.
① 폐지하다, 철회하다
② 피하다, 삼가다
③ 그만두다, 포기하다
④ 부인하다, 거부하다

어휘

divide ~을 나누다, 분할하다
deny 부인하다, 부정하다
rescind 폐지하다, 철회하다
forswear 그만두다, 포기하다
ideology 이념, 관념
ethnicity 민족성
eschew 피하다, 삼가다
repudiate 부인하다, 거부하다

03 정답 ④

정답해설

'nocturnal'은 '야행성의'를 뜻하는 형용사로 ④ noctivagant(야행성의, 밤에 돌아다니는)와 유의어 관계이다.

해석

과학자들은 그 당시의 다른 포유동물들이 (야행성으로) 생각되는 것처럼, 이 동물도 **야행성**이었을 것으로 믿는다.

① 어스름한, 탁한
② 주행성의, 하루 동안의
③ 야광의, 빛을 발하는
④ 야행성의, 밤에 돌아다니는

어휘

nocturnal 야행성의
dusky 어스름한, 탁한
diurnal 주행성의, 하루 동안의
luminous 야광의, 빛을 발하는
noctivagant 야행성의, 밤에 돌아다니는

04 정답 ②

정답해설

A가 B에게 연필깎이를 빌릴 수 있는지 물어보자 B는 물건을 건네주면서 자신의 연필이라고 이야기한다. 이는 연필깎이를 빌리고 싶어 하는 A의 말에 대한 적절한 대답이 아니다. 따라서 정답은 ②이다.

오답해설

① A는 B에게 지지해준 것에 대한 감사를 표하고 B는 대단한 일이 아니라고 대답한다. 이는 문맥상 자연스러운 대화의 흐름이다.
③ A는 날씨가 아주 좋다고 언급하며 소풍이 가고 싶다고 말한다. 그러자 B는 A의 말에 동의하며 소풍갈 때 음식과 음료수 좀 가져가는 것 어떻겠냐고 제안한다. B의 대답은 A의 말에 대한 대답으로 적절하다.
④ A는 문제가 발생한다면 자신에게 바로 연락을 달라고 B에게 부탁하고, B는 A를 안심시키며 모든 것이 잘 될 수 있도록 하겠다고 이야기한다. 이는 대화의 맥락상 적합하다.

해석

① A: 지지해주셔서 감사합니다.
   B: 대단한 일은 아닙니다.
② A: 네 연필깎이를 빌릴 수 있을까?
   B: 여기 있어. 내 연필이야.
③ A: 날씨가 아주 좋아! 나는 소풍을 가고 싶어.
   B: 나도 그렇게 생각해. 우리 소풍갈 때 음식과 음료수 좀 가져가는 것 어때?
④ A: 문제가 발생한다면, 바로 저에게 연락해 주세요.
   B: 걱정 마세요. 모든 것이 잘되도록 하겠습니다.

어휘

appreciate 고마워하다; 인정하다; 가치가 오르다
contact 연락하다; 연락; 접촉

05 정답 ①

정답해설

① **출제 포인트: 관용표현(It takes+사람+시간+to+동사원형, It takes+시간+for+사람+to+동사원형)**

'It takes+사람+시간+to+동사원형'은 관용표현으로 '사람이 ~하는 데 시간이 걸리다'를 뜻한다. 사람을 나타내는 목적어가 시간을 나타내는 목적어 뒤로 이동할 경우 전치사 'for'와 결합하여 'It takes+시간+for+사람+to+동사원형'이 되며, 이때 'for+사람'은 to부정사의 의미상 주어이다. 해당 문장은 사람을 나타내는 목적어 'him'이 시간을 나타내는 목적어 'a while' 앞에 위치하고 있으나 'him' 앞에 전치사 'for'를 사용하였으므로 틀린 문장이다. 따라서 'for'를 삭제해 'takes him a while'로 수정하거나 'for him'을 'a while' 뒤로 옮겨 'takes a while for him'으로 수정해야 옳다.

오답해설

② **출제 포인트: 완전타동사 help의 목적어/능동태 vs. 수동태**

완전타동사 'help'는 목적어로 to부정사 또는 원형부정사를 사용할 수 있다. 따라서 'help'의 목적어이자 원형부정사인 'rescue'는 옳은 표현이다. 또한 해당 문장에서 'was scrambled'는 '긴급 이륙시키다'를 뜻하는 완전타동사 'scramble'의 수동태로 옳게 사용되었다.

③ **출제 포인트: 주장, 요구, 명령, 제안동사+(that)+주어+(should)+동사원형/주어와 동사의 수일치**

해당 문장에서 'suggest'는 문맥상 '암시하다'를 뜻하므로 목적어에 해당하는 접속사 'that'이 이끄는 명사절의 동사에 시제를 적용한다. 이때 해당 명사절의 주어가 동명사 'listening'이며 동명사 주어는 단수 취급하므로 동사에 단수 형태인 'is'를 사용하는 것이 옳다.

④ **출제 포인트: 주어와 동사의 수일치/관용표현(be conscious that+절)/관용표현(be conscious of+명사(구))**

주어가 to부정사인 경우 단수로 취급한다. 따라서 해당 문장의 경우 주어가 to부정사이므로 동사에 단수 형태인 'is'를 옳게 사용하였다. 또한 'be conscious that+절'과 'be conscious of+명사(구)'는 관용표현으로 '~을 의식하다'를 뜻한다.

해석

① 그는 혼자 사는 것에 적응하는 데 시간이 좀 걸린다.
② 젊은 등반가 다섯 명을 구조하는 것을 돕기 위해 헬리콥터 한 대를 긴급 이륙시켰다.
③ 그 연구는 운전하는 동안 졸음이 오는 음악을 듣는 것은 위험하다는 것을 암시한다.
④ 인지하고 있거나 생각하고 있음을 의식하는 것은 우리 자신의 존재를 의식하는 것이다.

06 정답 ③

정답해설

③ **출제 포인트: 주어와 동사의 수일치**

문장의 맨 앞에 유도부사인 'There'가 있으므로 주어와 동사가 도치된 문장임을 알 수 있으며 주어가 복수 형태인 'some forms of guides and filters'이므로 단수 형태 동사 'needs'를 복수 형태 동사인 'need'로 수정해야 한다.

오답해설

① **출제 포인트: 능동태 vs. 수동태/수여동사의 수동태**

'convince' 이후에 that절이 오는 경우는 수여동사 'convince'의 수동태인 「be convinced that+절」뿐이다. 해당 문장의 경우 'that' 앞에 'convince'의 수동태인 'am also convinced'를 사용하였으므로 밑줄 친 'convinced'는 옳은 표현이다.

② **출제 포인트: 전치사의 쓰임**

문맥상 '오염된 지식으로부터 보호받아야 한다'가 자연스러우므로 밑줄 친 전치사 'from'은 옳은 표현이다.

④ **출제 포인트: 현재분사 vs. 과거분사**

밑줄 친 'provided'는 완전타동사 'provide'의 과거분사로 이후에 「by+행위자」인 'by responsible individuals and organizations'가 왔으며 수식하는 대상 'guides and filters'와 수동관계이므로 'provided'는 옳은 표현이다.

해석

나는 또한 사용자들이 중개 서비스에 의해 부패한 지식으로부터 보호를 받아야 한다고 확신한다. 책임 있는 개인과 단체에 의해 제공되는 여러 형태의 지침과 여과 장치가 있어야 한다.

어휘

convince+목적어[대상]+that+절 ~에게 ~을 납득시키다
intermediary 중개의　　　　　corrupt 부패한, 타락한, 오염된

오답률 TOP 1
07 정답 ④

정답해설

④ 출제 포인트: which vs. who

해당 문장에서 'which'의 선행사는 'leaders'이며 사람을 나타내므로 'which'를 관계대명사 'who'로 수정해야 한다. 이때 주의할 점은 선행사를 'negative emotional states of mind'로 보지 않도록 해야 한다는 것이다. 'which'의 선행사를 'negative emotional states'로 가정해서 본다면 '부정적인 감정 상태' 자체가 '짜증을 내고 위세를 부린다'라는 표현이 되어 어색하다. '짜증을 내고 위세를 부린다'는 것의 주체는 'somebody(사람)'가 적절하다. 따라서 'negative emotional states'는 'which'의 선행사가 될 수 없다.

오답해설

① 출제 포인트: 주어와 동사의 수일치

주어가 복수 형태인 'Leaders'이므로 동사에 복수 형태인 'are'를 사용하는 것이 옳다. 또한 'like human magnets'는 'like+명사구'의 형태로 주어를 수식하고 있다.

② 출제 포인트: 완전타동사+목적어[to부정사 vs. 동명사]

해당 문장에서 'gravitate'는 자동사로 사용되었으며 'want'는 완전타동사의 경우 to부정사를 목적어로 가진다. 따라서 해당 문장의 'to follow'는 'want'의 목적어로 사용된 to부정사로 옳게 사용되었다.

③ 출제 포인트: 등위접속사의 병렬구조

절과 절이 등위접속사 'and'를 통해 연결되어 있으며 'inspire'와 'attract'가 병렬구조로 옳게 사용되었다.

해석

긍정적인 감정적 마음의 상태를 갖고 있는 지도자는 인간 자석 같다. 사람들은 자연히 그들에게 끌리고 그들을 따르고 싶어 한다. 그러한 지도자들은 그들의 조직에 열정을 불어넣고 최고의 사람들이 그들을 위해 일하도록 끌어들인다. 반대로 짜증을 내고 위세를 부리는, 부정적인 감정적 마음의 상태를 내뿜는 지도자들은 사람들을 쫓아버리고 추종자를 거의 갖지 못한다.

어휘

magnet 자석　　　　　　　　inspire 불어넣다
enthusiasm 열정　　　　　　repel 쫓아버리다

오답률 TOP 2
08 정답 ③

정답해설

본문에서 화자는 밤중에 한가로이 자신이 살던 옛 마을을 돌아다니며 어린 시절의 추억을 회상하고 행복을 느끼고 있다. 본문에 따르면 보통 어린 시절의 좋은 시절에 돌아가고 싶은 마음은 모두 같지만, 실제로 그러한 시간을 갖는 것은 매우 어려우며 좋았던 시절을 잊고 사는 것이 보편적이다. 하지만 화자는 옛 마을을 홀로 돌아다니며 좋은 시절을 떠올릴 수 있는 기회를 가질 수 있었다는 것이 글 전체의 내용이다. 따라서 화자의 심경으로 가장 적절한 것은 '③ pleased and delighted(기쁘고 즐거운)'이다.

오답해설

② 본문에서 화자가 홀로 어두운 거리를 돌아다니는 모습이 외롭다고 느껴질 수 있으나, 그러한 혼자만의 시간을 보내면서 어린 시절의 추억을 떠올릴 수 있는 좋은 시간이 되었다는 내용이므로, 화자의 심경은 '외롭고 우울하다' 보다는 오히려 '행복했다'는 것이 더 적절하다.

나머지 보기는 문맥상 부적절하므로 오답이다.

해석

나의 옛 마을을 돌아다니고, 문 닫힌 상점들을 들여다보고, 적막한 운동장과 공원을 느긋하게 걷고, 시간이 지남에 따라 위층 창문의 불빛들이 천천히 꺼지는 것을 바라보는 것은 내게 묘한 경험이었다. 한 사람의 인생을 이루는 너무나도 많은 순간들이 있고, 그것들은 매초가 지나면서 축적되지만, 우리들 중 얼마나 많은 사람들이 기억의 보드라운 주름 속에서 머무르는 시간을 보내는가? 우리들 중 얼마나 많은 사람들이 진정으로 그러하길 원하는가? 나는 우리 모두가 그렇다고 생각한다. 나는 어딘가에 항상 당신이 계속해서 다시 체험하고 싶어 하는 순간으로 가득 찬 작은 상자가 존재한다고 생각한다. 그러나 우리가 그것 안에 맞출 수 있도록 우리가 우리 자신을 알맞은 크기에 맞추어 줄어들게 해본 적이 있는가? 우리들 대부분은 그렇지 않다. 우리는 매년 더 크고 더 복잡하게 자란다, 그리고 그 상자는 어느 날 그것을 찾는 것이 불가능해질 때까지 점점 더 작아 보이게 되고, 결국 영원히, 그러나 모르는 사이에 봉해지면서 끊임없는 인생과 시간의 변화 속에서 사라지게 된다. 그러나 그날 밤 나는 나의 모든 작은 상자들을 찾은 것과 같은 기분을 느꼈고, 그것들을 모두 열어보고 싶은 기분이었다.

① 회의적이고 경계하는
② 외롭고 우울한
③ 기쁘고 즐거운
④ 두려워하고 괴로워하는

어휘

wander 거닐다, 돌아다니다　　　peer into 자세히 들여다보다
saunter 한가로이[느긋하게] 걷다　desolate 적막한, 황량한
extinguish (불을) 끄다　　　　　tick by 째깍째깍 흘러가다
extraordinary 묘한, 엄청난, 보통이 아닌; 기이한, 놀라운
with each passing second 매초가 지나면서, 매초마다
languish in …에 머물다　　　　cottony 보드라운
fold 주름, 접힌 것　　　　　　relive (상상 속에서) 다시 체험하다
shrink 줄어들게 하다　　　　　to size 맞는 크기로, 원하는 크기로
until …할 만큼, …하여 결국　　permanently 영구히, 영원히
unknowingly 모르고, 알아채지 못하고
file away 봉하다, 보관하다　　constant 끊임없는, 계속되는
reshuffle 바꾸다, 전환시키다, 개편하다

09 정답 ②

정답해설

주어진 문장에서는 역사상 실제로 발생했던, 그러나 세부적인 내용은 잘 알려지지 않은 '싸움(dispute)'에 관해 언급하고 있다. 이에 바로 이어질 내용으로 가장 적절한 것은, 사건이 발생한 시기와 사건에 연루된 인물들이 최초로 언급되는 (B)이다. 이후 (B)에서 언급된 인물들 사이의 싸움에 대한 구체적인 내용이 언급되는 (A)가 이어지는 것이 적절하며, 마지막으로 (A)에서 발생한 사건을 'This dispute(이 싸움)'를 이용해 가리키고 있는 (C)가 이어지는 것이 자연스럽다. 따라서 정답은 '② (B) - (A) - (C)'이다.

오답해설

③, ④ (C)의 "Finally, a line had been drawn, but the border was far from settled(마침내, 하나의 선이 그려졌지만, 국경은 자리를 잡은 것과는 거리가 멀었다)."는 '국경선이 그려졌다'라고 설명하고 있는데, (A)에서는 '국경 측량'이 아직 진행되고 있는 상황(The border survey, less than a year old, was a mess.)이 언급되고 있으므로, (C) 이후에 (A)가 이어지는 것은 시간상 연결이 자연스럽지 않다. 따라서 오답이다.

나머지 보기는 문맥상 어색하므로 오답이다.

해석

역사는 세부 사항을 희미하게 만들었지만, 이야기는 만취 상태의 싸움, 말다툼, 실랑이, 그리고 총격을 여전히 말해준다.
(B) 그것은 1849년 10월이었다. John Weller 장관과 측량사인 Andrew Gray가 지도에만 존재하던 선을 표시하기 위해 미국과 멕시코의 국경으로 파견되었고, 그 업무는 잘 진행되지 않았다.
(A) 몇몇은 John Weller가 Andrew Gray의 턱을 가격했다고 말한다; 다른 사람들은 그가 Andrew Gray의 목을 조르려 했다고 하지만, 두 이야기 모두에서, Andrew Gray는 John Weller의 허벅지를 총으로 쐈다. 1년도 채 안 된 국경 측량은 엉망진창이었다.
(C) 이 싸움은 멕시코-미국 전쟁 이후 미국이 남쪽 국경을 규정하려고 분투하는 동안 발생했던 여러 문제들 중 하나일 뿐이었다. 마침내, 하나의 선이 그려졌지만, 국경은 자리를 잡은 것과는 거리가 멀었다.

어휘

blur 흐릿하게[희미하게] 하다	tale 이야기
hang (달라붙어서) 떨어지지 않다; 정체해 있다	
boozy 술 취한, 만취한	dispute 싸움, 언쟁, 분쟁
scuffle 실랑이, 옥신각신함	strike 치다, 때리다
strangle 목을 조르다	account 이야기, 말, 설명
survey 측량	commissioner 장관
surveyor 측량사	border 국경
crop up 불쑥 나타나다[발생하다]	define 규정하다, 정하다
settled 자리를 잡은, 안정된	

10 정답 ②

정답해설

본문은 '난폭 운전을 하는 원인'에 대해 설명하는 글이다. "Many psychological factors are at play in aggressive driving(많은 심리학적 요인이 난폭 운전에 작용한다)."라고 '난폭 운전을 야기하는 심리학적 요인'에 대해 언급하며, '세력권 의식, 자기 방위, 힘 과시, 경쟁 본능' 등의 예시를 들고 있다. 따라서 글의 제목으로 가장 적절한 것은 '② What Causes Aggressive Driving(무엇이 난폭 운전을 야기하는가)?'이다.

오답해설

① 두 번째 문장 "Most people drive aggressively from time to time and many drivers are not even aware they are doing it(대부분의 사람들은 이따금 난폭하게 운전을 하고, 많은 운전자들이 그들이 그것을 하고 있다는 것을 인식조차 하지 못한다)."에서, 난폭 운전을 하는 사람들에 대해 언급하기는 하지만, 글 전체를 아우르는 내용이 아니므로, 글의 제목으로 적절하지 않다.
③ 첫 번째 문장 "The National Highway Traffic Safety Administration defines aggressive driving as occurring when "an individual commits a combination of moving traffic offenses so as to endanger other persons or property."(National Highway Traffic Safety Administration은 난폭 운전을 "개인이 타인 또는 재산을 위험에 처하게 하기 위해 여러 가지 주행 중 교통 법규 위반을 저지를" 때 발생하는 것으로 정의한다.)"에서 '난폭 운전의 정의'에 대해 언급하고 있지만, 글 전체를 아우르는 내용은 아니므로, 글의 제목으로 적절하지 않다.
④ 본문에 언급되지 않는 내용이다.

해석

National Highway Traffic Safety Administration은 난폭 운전을 "개인이 타인 또는 재산을 위험에 처하게 하기 위해 여러 가지 주행 중 교통 법규 위반을 저지를" 때 발생하는 것으로 정의한다. 대부분의 사람들은 이따금 난폭하게 운전을 하고, 많은 운전자들이 그들이 그것을 하고 있다는 것을 인식조차 하지 못한다. 많은 심리학적 요인이 난폭 운전에 작용한다. 인간은 자연적으로 세력권 의식의 경향이 있고, 그들의 차량을 자신들의 사적 영역의 연장으로 보는 성향이 있다. 그들은 다른 차량에 의해 위협을 느끼고 난폭하게 또는 자기 방위의 본능에 의해 반응한다. 또한 운전은 몇몇 사람들이 핸들 뒤에서 힘의 감각을 느끼도록 하기도 한다. 보통 때에 정중하고 예의 바른 사람이 운전할 때 난폭해질 수 있다. 우리의 자연적인 경쟁 본능 또한 난폭 운전의 요인이 될 수 있다. 일부 운전자들은 다른 차량에 의해 추월당하는 것에 대해 도전이라고 반응한다. 이것이 결과적으로 운전자들이 위험한 추월 행위를 하도록 만들지도 모른다.

① 누가 난폭하게 운전하는가?
② 무엇이 난폭 운전을 야기하는가?
③ 난폭 운전은 어떻게 정의되는가?
④ 난폭 운전은 왜 위험한가?

어휘

define 정의하다, 규정하다	aggressive driving 난폭 운전
commit 저지르다, 범하다	combination 조합, 결합
moving 주행 중인, 이동하는	traffic offense 교통 법규 위반
so as to 동사원형 ~하기 위하여	
endanger 위험에 빠뜨리다, 위태롭게 만들다	
property 재산, 소유물	aggressively 난폭하게, 공격적으로
from time to time 이따금, 가끔	aware 알고[의식/자각하고] 있는
psychological 심리학적인	play 영향, 작용
prone to …을 잘하는, …의 경향이 있는	
territoriality 세력권 의식, 텃세	tendency 성향, 경향, 기질
extension 연장	domain 영역, 범위, 영토, 소유지
out of (동기·원인) …에서, …로 인해	instinct 본능
self-protection 자기 방위	wheel (자동차의) 핸들
courteous 공손한, 정중한	competitive 경쟁적인
overtake 추월하다, 앞지르다	in turn 결국[결과적으로]
maneuver 작전, (교묘한) 행동, 책략	

기적사 DAY 78

결국엔 성정혜 영어 하프모의고사

| 01 | ④ | 02 | ④ | 03 | ① | 04 | ④ | 05 | ③ |
| 06 | ③ | 07 | ③ | 08 | ③ | 09 | ④ | 10 | ③ |

오답률 TOP 3

01 정답 ④

정답해설

'invasion'은 '침략, 침입'을 뜻하는 명사로 ④ encroachment(침략, 침해)와 의미상 가장 가깝다.

해석

그는 조선시대에 임진왜란 동안 일본의 **침략**으로부터 한국을 구한 영웅으로 기억된다.
① 쿠데타, 대단한 성취
② 틈
③ 파열
④ 침략, 침해

어휘

invasion 침략, 침입
chink 틈
encroachment 침략, 침해
coup 쿠데타, 대단한 성취
rupture 파열

02 정답 ④

정답해설

'denounce'는 '비난하다, 고발하다'를 뜻하는 동사로 ④ condemn(비난하다, 규탄하다)과 의미상 가장 가깝다.

해석

서울 광장은 과거에 민주주의를 추구하는 데 있어 권위주의 정권을 **비난하기** 위해 사용된 시민들의 장소이다.
① 퇴학시키다, 추방하다, 배출하다
② 무죄를 선고하다
③ 이야기하다, 말하다
④ 비난하다, 규탄하다

어휘

denounce 비난하다, 고발하다
regime 정권; 제도, 체제
democracy 민주주의
acquit 무죄를 선고하다
condemn 비난하다, 규탄하다
authoritarian 권위주의적인, 독재적인
quest 추구, 탐구, 탐색
expel 퇴학시키다, 추방하다, 배출하다
recount 이야기하다, 말하다

03 정답 ①

정답해설

'solitary'는 '혼자 하는, 단 하나의'를 뜻하는 형용사로 ① sole(혼자의, 유일한)과 의미상 가장 가깝다.

해석

친구 없이 **혼자 하는** 음주는 당신을 더욱 슬프고 혼란스럽게 만들 수 있다.
① 혼자의, 유일한
② 불친절한, 무례한
③ 의심하는, 불확실한
④ 명랑한, 유쾌한

어휘

solitary 혼자 하는, 단 하나의
sole 혼자의, 유일한
dubious 의심하는, 불확실한
drinking 음주
surly 불친절한, 무례한
convivial 명랑한, 유쾌한

04 정답 ④

정답해설

A는 B에게 얼음 위를 걷지 말라고 충고하면서 얼음이 언 것처럼 보여도 얼지 않았을 수 있다고 말한다. 하지만 B는 자신이 얼음 위를 걷는 것을 좋아한다고 대답한다. 이는 자연스러운 대화의 흐름이 아니다. 따라서 정답은 ④이다.

오답해설

① A는 B에게 다음 날 일찍 일어나야 한다고 말하자 B는 A에게 다음 날 일찍 일정이 있는지 물어본다. B의 반응은 A의 말에 대한 적절한 반응이다.
② A는 창문 밖을 보라며, 눈이 내리고 있다고 이야기한다. B는 감탄하면서 올해의 첫눈이라고 한다. 이는 문맥상 자연스럽다.
③ A는 자신이 있는 장소가 너무 어둡다고 얘기하며, B에게 불을 켜줄 수 있는지 묻는다. 그러자 B는 긍정적으로 답하며 스위치가 어디에 있는지 되묻는다. 이는 대화의 흐름상 적합하다.

해석

① A: 나는 내일 일찍 일어나야 해.
   B: 너 내일 일찍 일정이 있어?
② A: 창문 밖을 봐! 눈이 내리고 있어!
   B: 우와! 올해의 첫눈이야.
③ A: 여기 너무 어두워. 불 좀 켜줄 수 있어?
   B: 물론이지. 스위치 어디 있어?
④ A: 얼음 위를 걷지 마. 그렇게 보일지라도, 얼지 않았을 수 있어.
   B: 나는 얼어있는 얼음 위를 걷는 것을 좋아해.

어휘

dim 어둑한[밝지 않은]
frozen 언, 결빙된; 몹시 추운
turn on 켜다

05 정답 ③

정답해설

③ 출제 포인트: 지각동사의 수동태/관계부사의 생략

지각동사 'see'의 수동태의 경우 목적격 보어에 to부정사 또는 현재분사를 사용할 수 있으나 원형부정사는 사용할 수 없다. 해당 문장은 지각동사 'see'의 수동태를 사용하였으나 목적격 보어에 원형부정사인 'enter'를 사용하였으므로 틀린 문장이다. 따라서 'enter'를 to부정사 'to enter' 또는 현재분사 'entering'으로 수정해야 한다. 또한 'the time' 이후에는 관계부사 'when' 또는 'that'이 생략되어 있으며 이후에 오는 'the crime was committed'는 완전한 형태의 절이다.

오답해설

① 출제 포인트: every+명사[단수형태]/주어와 동사의 수일치/what vs. that

'every' 이후에 오는 명사는 단수 형태이며 'every+명사[단수형태]'가 주어인 경우 동사에 단수 형태를 사용한다. 따라서 해당 문장의 경우 'Every'

이후에 온 단수 형태의 명사 'person'과 단수 형태의 동사 'has'는 옳은 표현이다. 또한 'what' 앞에 'decide'의 목적어에 해당하는 선행사가 없으며 이후에 오는 절은 주어가 없는 불완전한 형태이므로 선행사를 포함하는 관계대명사 'what'의 쓰임은 적절하다.

② **출제 포인트: 주격 관계대명사/수동태 불가동사/능동태 vs. 수동태**
'resulted in'은 'result in'의 과거시제로 수동태로 사용할 수 없는 동사이다. 따라서 'resulted in'은 옳은 표현이다. 또한 주격 관계대명사 'which'가 이끄는 절의 동사 'spanned'는 '~에 걸치다'를 뜻하는 완전타동사 'span'의 과거시제로 이후에 목적어 'eleven countries'가 왔으므로 'spanned'는 옳은 표현이다.

④ **출제 포인트: 불완전타동사의 목적격 보어/가목적어 it/to부정사의 명사적 용법/의미상 주어**
해당 문장에서 'it'은 가목적어이며 'to think of becoming a professional baseball player'가 진목적어에 해당한다. 또한 'impossible'은 목적격 보어로 쓰인 형용사이며 'for him'은 to부정사의 의미상 주어에 해당한다. 따라서 해당 문장은 옳은 문장이다.

해석
① 모든 사람은 그 또는 그녀에게 적합한 것이 무엇인지 결정해야 한다.
② 11개국에 걸친 그 작전 결과 300명의 구류자를 초래했다.
③ 그 범행이 저질러질 무렵 그녀가 그 건물에 들어가는 것이 목격되었다.
④ 그 부상은 그가 프로야구선수가 되는 것에 대해 생각하는 것을 불가능하게 만들었다.

06 정답 ③

정답해설

③ **출제 포인트: 비교급 강조 부사**
'very'는 원급 또는 최상급을 수식하는 강조 부사로 비교급을 수식할 수 없다. 해당 문장은 'very' 이후에 'much'의 비교급인 'more'가 있으므로 'very'를 비교급 강조 부사인 'even, much, still, a lot, (by) far' 등으로 수정해야 한다.

오답해설

① **출제 포인트: 주격 관계대명사절의 동사 수일치**
밑줄 친 'is'는 주격 관계대명사 'which'가 이끄는 절의 동사에 해당하며 선행사가 단수 형태인 'this land'이므로 단수 형태의 동사 'is'는 옳은 표현이다.

② **출제 포인트: 원급 비교**
원급 비교인 「as+원급[형용사/부사]+as」가 사용되었으므로 밑줄 친 접속사 'as'는 옳은 표현이다.

④ **출제 포인트: 비교급 비교**
앞에 있는 비교급 형용사 'more'를 통해 비교급 비교가 쓰인 문장임을 알 수 있으며 밑줄 친 'than'은 비교 대상 앞에 놓인 접속사로 옳은 표현이다.

해석
만약 네가 너의 소유인 이 땅으로부터 매일 너의 게으른 몸으로 덮을 수 있을 만큼의 땅을 경작한다면, 너는 매년 네가 여기 수레에서 보는 것보다 더욱더 많은 옥수수를 거둘 것이다.

어휘
cultivate 경작하다   reap 거두다, 수확하다

오답률 TOP 1

07 정답 ③

정답해설

③ **출제 포인트: 능동태 vs. 수동태**
해당 문장에서 'uses'는 완전타동사이므로 이후에 목적어가 있어야 하나 이후에 to부정사 부사적 용법의 목적을 나타내는 to부정사구 'to survive the natural world'가 왔으며 주어인 'culture'는 '사용하는 주체'가 아닌 '사용되는 대상'에 해당하므로 'uses'를 수동태 'is used'로 수정해야 한다.

오답해설

① **출제 포인트: 관용표현/형용사로 고착화된 분사**
해당 문장에서 'isn't well suited to'는 관용표현 'be suited to+목적어 (~에 적합하다)'의 부정형에 해당하며 'insulating'은 형용사로 고착화된 분사로 '열을 차단하는'을 뜻한다. 따라서 해당 문장은 옳은 문장이다.

② **출제 포인트: 전치사+관계대명사/등위접속사 병렬구조**
해당 문장에서 'with which'는 「전치사+관계대명사」의 형태로 이후에 오는 절 'we hunt and defend ourselves'는 완전한 형태이다. 또한 'make'의 목적어가 등위접속사 'and'를 통해 「A, B, and C」의 병렬구조인 'fur clothing, shelters ~, and weapons'를 이루고 있다. 따라서 해당 문장은 옳은 문장이다.

④ **출제 포인트: 명사절을 이끄는 접속사 that/목적격 관계대명사의 생략**
해당 문장에서 'that'은 접속사로 'keep'의 목적어에 해당하는 명사절을 이끈다. 또한 'the cultural world'와 'they inhabit' 사이에는 목적격 관계대명사 'which' 또는 'that'이 생략되어 있다.

해석
우리는 북극곰의 털이나 해양 포유류들의 열을 차단하는 두꺼운 지방을 가지고 있지 않기 때문에 본질적으로 아열대성인 우리의 몸은 북극에서의 생활에 적합하지 않다. 그러나 우리는 온기를 담을 수 있는 털옷과 주거지, 그리고 사냥을 하고 우리 자신을 방어하는 무기를 만들 수 있다. 이러한 물건들은 문화적 적응의 좋은 예로 그것들은 자연에서 생존하기 위해 문화가 어떻게 사용되는지 보여준다. 그러나 사람들은 그들이 사는 문화적 세계에서도 생존해야 한다는 것을 명심하라.

어휘
subtropical 아열대의   insulating 열을 차단하는
adaptation 적응, 각색

08 정답 ③

정답해설

본문에서는 '아이들에게 충분한 야외 놀이 시간과 장소가 필요한데, 그 이유는 야외 놀이에는 다양한 장점이 있기 때문이다'라고 주장하고 있다. 본문 중반 "However, giving children the space and freedom to play outdoors will bring many benefits such as health benefits and opportunities to build various relationships and appreciate nature(하지만, 아이들에게 야외에서 놀 공간과 자유를 주는 것은 건강상의 이점 및 다양한 관계 형성과 자연을 감상할 수 있는 기회와 같은 다양한 혜택을 가져다 줄 것이다)."에서 글의 요지를 찾을 수 있다. 따라서 정답은 '③ There are advantages to children playing outside(아이들이 야외에서 노는 것에는 장점이 있다).'이다.

오답해설

① 본문에서 '야외 놀이의 장점' 중 하나로 '관계 수립'에 대해 언급되기는 하지만, 글 전체를 아우르는 내용은 아니므로 오답이다.
② 본문에서 '아이들이 놀 장소가 부족하다'고 언급되고 있으나, '대도시에서

녹지가 부족하다'는 것은 이보다 광범위한 내용을 아우르는 문장이므로, 본문의 요지로는 적절하지 않다.
④ 본문에서 언급된 '사실'일 뿐이며, 글 전체의 요지로는 적절하지 않다.

해석

우리들 대부분은 야외에서 놀던 기억을 가지고 있다. 비록 도시에서 자라더라도, 보통 아이들이 놀고 그들의 상상력을 사용하기 위해 모일 수 있는 공원 또는 녹지가 있었다. 안타깝게도, 새로운 개발지들이 들어섬에 따라, 우리의 아이들이 잊혀져가고 있는 것 같다. 요즘 아이들은 집과 학교, 그리고 그 두 사이를 이동하는 자동차 내부처럼 폐쇄된 공간에서 많은 시간을 보내지만, 그들은 또한 야외에서 노는 것을 즐길 더 적은 자유 시간이 있는 더 엄격한 시간 계획표상에 있다. 하지만, 아이들에게 야외에서 놀 공간과 자유를 주는 것은 건강상의 이점 및 다양한 관계 형성과 자연을 감상할 수 있는 기회와 같은 많은 혜택을 가져다줄 것이다. 아이들은 경험과 그들의 감각을 통해 학습한다. 실내에 있을 때, 아이들의 감각은 시각과 청각으로 더 제한되어 있다, 그러나 야외에 있을 때, 그들의 발달과 교육적 잠재력은 최대화될 수 있다. 이것이 우리가 우리의 지역 근처에 우리의 아이들이 가서 야외를 즐길 수 있는 녹지, 공원 그리고 정원을 필요로 하는 이유이다.
① 놀이를 통해, 아이들은 진정한 친구를 사귈 수 있다.
② 대도시들은 빌딩 때문에 녹지가 부족하다.
③ 아이들이 야외에서 노는 것에는 장점이 있다.
④ 과거와 비교해, 오늘날의 아이들은 주로 실내에서 논다.

어휘

congregate 모이다
development (신축 건물이 들어선) 개발지; 발달, 성장
enclosed 폐쇄된, 밀폐된   various 다양한
appreciate 감상하다, 인식하다   potential 가능성, 잠재력
neighborhood 근처, 인근; 이웃   mostly 주로, 일반적으로

오답률 TOP 2

09 정답 ④

정답해설

본문은 '미국-멕시코 국경에 계획된 장벽 건설로 인해 예상되는 홍수 피해'에 대해 설명하는 글이다. "Now, with a steel border fence as high as 30 feet slated to be built between the city and the Rio Grande — which in Texas doubles as the U.S.-Mexico border — locals worry that flooding will worsen, just as it has in other border communities where fences and waterways intersect(현재, 그 도시와 텍사스에서 미국-멕시코 국경으로도 사용되는 Rio Grande 사이에 30피트 높이의 강철 국경 담장이 건설될 것으로 계획됨에 따라, 담장과 수로가 교차하는 다른 국경 지역 사회에서 그랬듯이, 주민들은 홍수가 악화될 것을 걱정한다)."를 통해, '홍수가 더 악화될 것을 우려하고 있다는 것을 알 수 있으므로, 글의 제목으로 가장 적절한 보기는 '④ Planned Barriers Could Cause More Severe Flooding(계획된 장벽이 더 심각한 홍수를 야기할 수 있다)'이다.

오답해설

① 특정 지역에 예상되는 홍수 상황에 대해 설명하는 글이므로, 일반적인 홍수로 인한 물의 위험성에 대한 제목은 본문과 어울리지 않는다.
② 홍수에 대비하는 방법에 대해서는 본문에 언급되지 않는다.
③ 본문에서 장벽이 세워질 것이라는 사실은 언급되고 있으나, 그로 인해 예상되는 홍수 피해가 글의 주제이므로, 본문의 제목으로 부적절하다.

해석

비가 내리고 시내의 수위가 올라갈 때, 그 주의 남부에 있는 이 작은 도시의 주민들은 홍수로 불어난 물이 단지 몇백 피트 내리막에 위치한 도시와 이름이 같은 강을 향해 흘러감에 따라 어떤 거리를 피해야 하는지 알고 있다. 현재, 그 도시와 텍사스에서 미국-멕시코 국경으로도 사용되는 Rio Grande 사이에 30피트 높이의 강철 국경 담장이 건설될 것으로 계획됨에 따라, 담장과 수로가 교차하는 다른 국경 지역 사회에서 그랬듯이, 주민들은 홍수가 악화될 것을 걱정한다. 폭우 동안에, 시내는 잔해와 쓰레기를 이동시킨다. 담장은 이 물질을 가두어 모아, 물의 자연적 방향을 막고, 그것을 거리와 집 안으로 보낼 수도 있다. 가능한 피해를 연구해 온 과학자들은 특히 미국-멕시코 국경 전체의 1,954마일을 따라 가장 생태적으로 다양한 지역 중 하나이며, 수많은 농장과 마을의 발상지인 Lower Rio Grande Valley에 미치는 영향에 대해 우려한다. 결과는 지역 경제와 환경 모두에 끔찍할 수도 있다.
① 홍수로 인한 물에는 숨겨진 위험들이 담겨있다
② 텍사스에서 갑작스러운 홍수에 대비하는 법
③ 국경을 따라, 담장이 설립되고 있다
④ 계획된 장벽이 더 심각한 홍수를 야기할 수 있다

어휘

creek 시내, 개울   floodwater 홍수로 인한 물
namesake (다른 것·사람과) 이름이 같은 것[사람]
downslope 내리막   border 국경
slate 계획하다
double as (주된 용도 외에) …로도 쓰이다
intersect 교차하다, 만나다   debris 잔해, 쓰레기
ecologically 생태학적으로   diverse 다양한
score (복수로) 다수, 많음   consequence 결과
dire 끔찍한, 몹시 나쁜
flash flooding 갑작스러운 홍수, 갑자기 불어난 물
erect 세우다, 건립하다   barrier 장벽, 벽

10 정답 ③

정답해설

본문은 '자기 도취자들이 난폭 운전을 할 가능성이 높다'고 설명하고 있다. 마지막 문장 "Specifically, narcissists are more likely to drive aggressively and engage in dangerous driving behaviors(특히, 자기 도취자들은 난폭하게 운전하고 위험한 운전 행위에 참여할 가능성이 더 높다)."를 통해 전체 글의 주제는 '③ the connection between narcissism and aggressive driving(자기 도취증과 난폭 운전 사이의 관련성)'이라는 것을 알 수 있다.

오답해설

① 본문에서 '자기 도취자들의 특징과 행위'에 대해 언급되기는 하지만, 특히 이러한 특징이 운전과 관련되어 어떻게 발현되는가에 초점을 맞추고 있으므로, 글의 주제로는 부적절하다.
② 본문에서는 '자기 도취자들이 난폭 운전을 할 가능성이 높다'는 사실관계만 제시하고 있을 뿐, 그들을 피해야 한다는 주장은 언급되지 않는다.
④ 본문과 관련 없는 내용이다.

해석

자기 도취자들이 자신들의 욕구가 충족되지 않았다고 느낄 때, 그들이 수치스럽거나 비난을 받았다고 느낄 때, 또는 타인의 행위가 어떤 점에서 자신들을 위압한다고 느낄 때, 이것이, 심지어 도로 위에서도, "자기 도취적 분노"로 일컬어지는 것을 촉발할 수 있다. 비록 우리 모두가 교통(체증)에 앉아 있을 때, 또는 우리가 서두르는 데 누군가가 우리 앞에서 너무 천천히 운전하고 있을 때, 불만을 느끼거나 화가 날 수 있지만, 대부분의 사람들에게 있어서 불만은

일시적이다. 또한 그것은 우리 주변의 사람들을 벌해야겠다는 욕구가 동반되지도 않는다. 그리고 일시적인 분노 또는 불만에도 불구하고, 대부분의 사람들은 복수에 대한 갈망 위에 그들의 안전을 둘 만큼 충분히 그들의 동승자들을 신경 쓴다. 그러나 이것은 자기도취적인 운전자들의 경우에는 이렇지 않다. 일반적으로 자기 도취자들은 공감 능력이 부족하고, 오만불손하며, 자신들이 일반적인 규율에 얽매이지 않는다고 믿는다; 이러한 특징들이 자기 도취자들의 운전 행위에까지 미친다. 특히, 자기 도취자들은 난폭하게 운전하고 위험한 운전 행위에 참여할 가능성이 더 높다.

① 자기 도취자들의 특징과 습성
② 당신이 자기도취적인 운전자들을 피해야 하는 이유
③ 자기도취증과 난폭 운전 사이의 관련성
④ 자기도취증과 자기애적 인격 장애의 원인

어휘

narcissist 자기 도취자, 나르시시스트 need 욕구
meet 충족시키다 impose on …을 위압하다, 속이다
trigger 촉발하다, 유발하다 be referred to as …로 불리다
narcissistic 자기도취적인 rage 분노
frustrated 불만스러워하는 frustration 불만, 좌절
unaccompanied by …이 동반되지 않는
thirst 갈망, 열망 vengeance 복수, 앙갚음
empathy 공감, 감정이입 insolent 오만불손한, 거만한, 무례한
be bound by …에 얽매이다 quality 특징, 특성
extend to …까지 미치다 aggressively 난폭하게, 공격적으로
engage in 참여하다 behavior [심리] 행동, 습성
narcissistic personality disorder 자기애적 인격 장애

기적사 DAY 79

| 01 | ③ | 02 | ③ | 03 | ① | 04 | ④ | 05 | ② |
| 06 | ④ | 07 | ① | 08 | ① | 09 | ③ | 10 | ③ |

오답률 TOP 3

01 정답 ③

정답해설

'surrender'는 '항복, 굴복'을 뜻하는 명사로 ③ capitulation(조건부 항복, 항복 문서)과 의미상 가장 가깝다.

해석

1979년에 출판된 교과서는 독립은 일본의 **항복**뿐만 아니라, 독립 투사들의 노력의 결과였다고 구체적으로 명시했다.
① 허가, 승인, 제재
② 사직, 사임
③ 조건부 항복, 항복 문서
④ 묵인

어휘

specify (구체적으로) 명시하다 independence 독립; (개인의) 자립
surrender 항복, 굴복 sanction 허가, 승인, 제재
resignation 사직, 사임 capitulation 조건부 항복, 항복 문서
acquiescence 묵인

02 정답 ③

정답해설

'digress'는 '주제에서 벗어나다'를 뜻하는 동사로 ③ deviate(벗어나다)와 의미상 가장 가깝다.

해석

당신이 내가 잠깐 **주제에서 벗어나는** 것을 허락한다면, 이전에 무슨 일이 일어났었는지 설명하겠다.
① 다듬다, 손질하다
② 꾸미다, 장식하다
③ 벗어나다
④ 걷다, 거닐다, 횡설수설하다

어휘

digress 주제에서 벗어나다 trim 다듬다, 손질하다
deck 꾸미다, 장식하다 deviate 벗어나다
ramble 걷다, 거닐다, 횡설수설하다 previously 이전에

오답률 TOP 2

03 정답 ①

정답해설

'predatory'는 '포식성의, 육식하는'을 뜻하는 형용사로 ① raptorial(육식의, 생물을 잡아먹는)과 유의어 관계이다.

해석

백상아리는 5천 만 년 전 이상으로 거슬러 올라가며 세계에서 가장 큰 **육식** 물고기이다.

① 육식의, 생물을 잡아먹는
② 탐욕스러운
③ 초식성의
④ 잡식성의

어휘

predatory 포식성의, 육식하는
raptorial 육식의, 생물을 잡아먹는
rapacious 탐욕스러운
herbivorous 초식성의
omnivorous 잡식성의

04 정답 ④

정답해설

남자가 여자에게 그녀의 어린 시절 사진들을 보고 싶다고 이야기하자 여자는 자신이 어릴 적 많은 일을 겪었다고 대답한다. 이는 남자의 말에 대한 적절한 답변이 아니다. 따라서 정답은 ④이다.

오답해설

① 남자는 여자에게 수영할 줄 아는지 물어보자 여자는 사실 자신이 수영을 정말 잘한다고 대답한다. 남자의 질문에 대한 여자의 답변은 자연스럽다.
② 남자는 여자에게 자신이 어디에 옷을 걸어 놓아야 할지 묻는다. 그러자 여자는 베란다에 걸면 된다고 대답한다. 이는 문맥상 자연스러운 대화이다.
③ 남자는 점심으로 무엇을 먹고 싶은지 여자에게 물어본다. 여자는 자신이 요즘 입맛이 없다면서 남자에게 그가 메뉴를 고르라고 대답한다. 여자의 답변은 남자의 물음에 대한 반응으로 적합하다.

해석

① 남자: 너 수영할 줄 알아?
   여자: 나 사실 수영 정말 잘해.
② 남자: 내가 옷을 어디에 걸어야 할까?
   여자: 베란다에 걸면 돼.
③ 남자: 너 점심으로 뭐 먹고 싶어?
   여자: 나는 요새 입맛이 없어. 네가 메뉴를 골라.
④ 남자: 나는 네 어린 시절 사진들을 정말 보고 싶어.
   여자: 나는 어린 시절 많은 일을 겪었어.

어휘

be good at ~에 능숙한
appetite 식욕; 욕구
childhood 어린 시절

오답률 TOP 1

05 정답 ②

정답해설

② 출제 포인트: 불가산명사/주어와 동사의 수일치/불완전타동사의 목적격 보어
'clothing'은 불가산명사이므로 복수 형태로 사용할 수 없다. 따라서 'clothings'를 단수 형태 'clothing'으로 수정해야 하며 'allow'를 단수 형태 동사 'allows'로 수정해야 한다. 이때 'allow'는 불완전타동사로 목적격 보어에 to부정사를 사용하므로 'to breathe'는 옳은 표현이다.

오답해설

① 출제 포인트: 주어와 동사의 수일치
주어가 동명사(구)인 경우 단수 취급한다. 해당 문장은 동명사구 'Keeping ~ hours'가 주어로 쓰였으므로 단수 형태의 동사 'is'는 옳은 표현이다.

③ 출제 포인트: 대명사 수일치
복수 형태의 대명사 'those'가 가리키는 대상이 복수 형태의 명사 'fashions'이므로 'those'는 옳은 표현이다.
④ 출제 포인트: 이성적, 감성적 판단의 형용사/가주어 it/명사절을 이끄는 접속사 that
해당 문장에서 'It'은 가주어이며 진주어는 접속사 'that'이 이끄는 명사절이다. 이때 'that' 앞의 형용사가 'essential'인 경우 'It+be동사+essential+that+주어+(should)+동사원형'으로 쓰여, 'that'이 이끄는 절의 동사에 'should+동사원형' 또는 '동사원형'을 사용해야 한다는 점에 유의해야 한다.

해석

① 일찍 자고 일찍 일어나는 것은 건강으로 향하는 비결이다.
② 면직물은 당신의 피부가 호흡 할 수 있게 해준다.
③ 올해의 패션들은 작년의 것들과는 전혀 다르다.
④ 융자 신청서에 당신의 서명이 있어야 한다는 것은 필수적이다.

06 정답 ④

정답해설

④ 출제 포인트: 수동태 불가동사
'arise'는 완전자동사이므로 수동태로 사용할 수 없으나 수동태로 사용하였으므로 옳지 않다. 따라서 밑줄 친 'is arisen'을 능동태 'arises'로 수정해야 한다.

오답해설

① 출제 포인트: 형용사 vs. 부사
밑줄 친 'lovely'는 형용사로 쓰여 명사 'gift'를 수식하고 있으므로 옳은 표현이다. 해당 문장에서 '~ly' 형태의 'lovely'를 부사로 판단하지 않도록 유의해야 한다.
② 출제 포인트: 수여동사의 문장구조/능동태 vs. 수동태
밑줄 친 'reminded'는 수여동사 'remind'의 과거시제로 이후에 간접목적어 'me'와 직접목적어인 'that+절'이 왔으므로 옳은 표현이다.
③ 출제 포인트: 형용사로 고착화된 분사
밑줄 친 'helping'은 형용사로 사용되어 '도움이 되는 손길'의 의미로 수식하는 대상 'hand'를 꾸며주고 있으므로 옳게 사용되었다.

해석

내 아들과 나에게 그 일은 새해를 시작하는 멋진 선물이었다. 그녀는 기회가 생길 때 도움의 손길을 주지 않기에는 인생은 너무 짧다는 것을 나에게 상기시켰다.

어휘

remind+목적어[대상]+that+절 ~에게 ~을 상기시키다
arise 생기다, 발생하다

07 정답 ①

정답해설

① 출제 포인트: 현재분사 vs. 과거분사/주어와 동사의 수일치
해당 문장에서 'designing'은 'design'의 현재분사이나 해석상 '고안된 저장조'가 자연스러우며 수식하는 대상 'storage ponds'와 수동관계이므로 'designing'을 과거분사 'designed'로 수정해야 한다. 또한 'as'가 이끄는 부사절의 주어가 복수 형태인 'storage ponds'이므로 부사절의 동사에 복수 형태인 'become'을 사용하는 것이 옳다. 이때 'become'은 불완전자동사이며 과거분사 'filled'와 현재분사 'overflowing'은 주격 보어에 해당한다.

오답해설

② 출제 포인트: 주격 관계대명사절의 동사 수일치/주어와 동사의 수일치/능동태 vs. 수동태/현재분사 vs. 과거분사

주절의 주어이자 선행사인 'One avenue'는 단수 형태이므로 주격 관계대명사절의 동사에 단수 형태인 'has'를, 주절의 동사에 단수 형태인 'is'를 옳게 사용하였다. 이때 'avenue(방안)'는 탐색 되어 온 것이므로 주격 관계대명사절에 사용된 현재완료 수동태 'has been explored'는 옳은 표현이다. 또한 'spent'는 'spend'의 과거분사로 해석상 '소비된 연료'가 자연스러우며 수식하는 대상 'fuel'과 수동관계이므로 'spent'는 옳은 표현이다.

③ 출제 포인트: 현재분사 vs. 과거분사/능동태 vs. 수동태

'recovered'는 'recover'의 과거분사로 해석상 '복구된 물질'이 자연스러우며 수식하는 대상 'material'과 수동관계이므로 'recovered'는 옳은 표현이다. 또한 해석상 '복구된 물질 일부가 재활용될 수 있다'가 자연스러우므로 수동태 'be recycled'는 옳은 표현이다.

④ 출제 포인트: 형용사 vs. 부사

'safely'는 과거분사 'stored'를 수식하는 부사이며 'inactive'는 불완전자동사 'become'의 주격 보어로 사용된 형용사이다. 따라서 해당 문장은 옳은 문장이다.

해석

몇 년간의 폐기물을 저장하기 위해 고안된 저장조가 가득 차거나 넘쳐나면서 이것이 이제 그 자체의 문제를 일으키고 있다. 탐색 되어 온 한 가지 방안은 활성 성분을 제거하기 위해 소비된 연료를 재처리하는 것이다. 복구된 물질의 일부는 연료로 재활용될 수 있다. 나머지는 그것이 비활성화될 때까지 안전하게 저장되어야 한다.

어휘

storage 저장	overflow 넘치다
avenue 방안	reprocessing 재처리

08 정답 ④

정답해설

본문은 '아이들의 야외 놀이 시간이 감소한 원인'에 대해 설명하는 글로, 빈칸에는 그러한 현상이 발생하게 된 원인을 설명하는 내용이 들어가야 한다. 두 번째 문장에서 '외부 환경을 위험하거나 유해하게 인식한다'고 설명하고, 세 번째 문장에서 'such overprotectiveness(이러한 과잉보호)'라고 언급하며, '부모가 아이들을 과잉보호한다, 즉, 부모가 아이들에 대해 지나치게 걱정한다'라는 것을 설명하고 있다. 따라서 빈칸에 가장 적절한 표현은 '④ to be overly solicitous about their children's safety(자신들의 아이들의 안전에 대해 과도하게 염려하는)'이다.

오답해설

① 부모가 자기 자신들을 과도하게 보호하는 것이 아니라, 아이들을 과도하게 보호하려 한다는 내용이므로, 빈칸에 적절하지 않다.
② 부모가 아이들과 함께하기 위해 아이들의 야외 놀이를 허락하지 않는다는 내용은 본문에 언급되지 않는다.
③ 본문의 내용은 아이들을 과잉보호하고 안전하게 양육하려는 부모의 태도에 대해 언급하고 있으므로, 아이들을 자연스럽고 단순하게 키운다는 내용과는 거리가 멀다.

해석

아이들의 놀이 기회에 부정적으로 영향을 미치는 주요한 사회 문화적 요소 중 하나는 부모들 사이에 자신들의 아이들의 안전에 대해 과도하게 염려하는 증가 추세이다. 그들이 다양한 이유로 외부 환경을 위험하거나 해롭다고 인식함에 따라, 그들은 아이들을 실내에 머무르게 하거나, 그들이 학교 운동장 또는 특정 놀이터와 같은 안전하다고 알려진 사전에 지정된 장소에서만 놀도록 허락함으로써 위험 회피형 태도를 채택한다. 이러한 과잉보호의 이유는 장소에 따라, 그리고 부모에 따라 그 정도가 다를 수 있다. 그러나 Singer 등은 아시아, 유럽, 아프리카, 북미, 그리고 남미의 16개국의 어머니들을 대상으로 한 조사를 통해 자동차 사고, 세균, 폭력, 불량배, 그리고 납치 가능성에 대한 공포가 전 세계의 어머니들 사이에서 아주 흔하다는 것을 밝혔는데, 그들은 이것을 연구가 진행된 국가에서 지난 20년 동안 아이들의 즉흥적인 놀이가 감소한 가능한 원인으로 꼽았다.

① 자기 자신들을 지나치게 보호하려 하는
② 대부분의 시간 동안 자신들의 아이들과 함께하려는
③ 자신들의 아이들을 자연스럽고 매우 단순하게 키우려는
④ 자신들의 아이들의 안전에 대해 과도하게 염려하는

어휘

sociocultural 사회 문화적인	amongst ~중[사이에]
perceive 여기다, 인식하다	various 다양한
adopt 채택하다, 쓰다	risk averse 위험 회피
attitude 태도	predesignate 미리 지정하다
overprotectiveness 과잉보호	et al. 외, 등
reveal 밝히다, 드러내다	abduction 납치
commonplace 아주 흔한	cite (이유·예를) 들다[끌어대다]
spontaneous 즉흥적인, 자발적인	excessively 지나치게
protective 보호하려고 하는	simplistically 극단적으로 단순하여
overly 너무, 몹시	solicitous 염려하는, 걱정하는

09 정답 ③

정답해설

주어진 문장의 'this policing(이 감시 활동)'과 'them(그들)'이 가리키는 내용이 주어진 문장 이전에 동시에 등장해야 한다. 또한, '그들을 내보내는 것'이 목표가 아니었다고 언급하고 있으므로, 이후에는 그들을 '내부에 머무르게 하려 했다'는 내용이 이어지는 것이 자연스럽다. ③ 이전 문장 "In the decades after, the both official and vigilante groups violently regulated the movement of people across that border — be they Native Americans, escaped slaves, Chinese immigrants, or Mexicans(수십 년 후, 공적 그리고 자경단 단체 모두는, 미국 원주민들, 탈출한 노예들, 중국인 이주민들, 또는 멕시코인들이든 간에 그 국경 지역 사람들의 이동을 폭력적으로 규제했다)."에서, '폭력적으로 규제했다'라는 것이 'this policing'에 해당하고, '미국 원주민들, 탈출한 노예들, 중국인 이주민들, 또는 멕시코인들'이 'them'에 해당한다는 것을 알 수 있다. 또한, ③ 이후에는 '원주민들을 몰아낸 것은 미국인들이 아니라 유럽인들이고, 노예들을 내부에 억류하려 했다'라는 내용이 이어지므로, 주어진 문장 이후에 해당 내용이 이어지는 것이 자연스럽다. 따라서 정답은 ③이다.

오답해설

② 이전 문장 "Texas and American militias used force to establish that border in the 1830s and 1840s, capturing modern-day states like California, Texas, and all of the American southwest from Mexico(텍사스와 미국의 용병대는 1830년대와 1840년대에 그 국경을 확립하기 위해 무력을 사용하고, 멕시코로부터 캘리포니아, 텍사스, 그리고 모든 미국의 남서부와 같은 현재의 주들을 확보했다)."에서 'used force'가 'this policing'에 해당한다고 여길 수 있으나, 'them'에 해당하는 내용은 이 문장에 언급되지 않는다. 'them'이 이 문장에 언급된 'states(주)'를 가리킨다고 보기에는, 'keep them out'이라는 내용이 문맥상 어색하다. 주를 몰아낸다는 것은 불가능하기 때문이다.

나머지 위치는 문맥상 어색하므로 오답이다.

해석

National Guard 부대를 미국-멕시코 국경으로 파견한다는 Donald Trump의 결정은 국경에 대한 미국의 군사화의 오랜 역사 중 가장 최신의 일에 지나지 않는다. 실제로, 미국의 확장과 함께 여러 번 변화한 미국의 남쪽 국경은 거의 틀림없이 폭력을 통해 형성되었다. (①) 텍사스와 미국의 용병대는 1830년대와 1840년대에 그 국경을 확립하기 위해 무력을 사용하고, 멕시코로부터 캘리포니아, 텍사스, 그리고 모든 미국의 남서부와 같은 현재의 주들을 확보했다. (②) 수십 년 후, 공적 그리고 자경단 단체 모두는, 미국 원주민들, 탈출한 노예들, 중국인 이주민들, 또는 멕시코인들이든 간에 그 국경 지역 사람들의 이동을 폭력적으로 규제했다. (③ **사실, 이 감시 활동이 그들을 내보내는 것을 항상 목표로 한 것은 아니었다.**) 텍사스 외부로 내몰려진 미국 원주민들은 유럽인 식민지 개척자들이 폭력적으로 그들을 서쪽으로 몰아내기 전에는 그 지역 또는 더 동쪽에서 살았었다. (④) 아프리카 출신의 노예가 된 사람들은 자경단이 이동을 감시하려고 했던 또 다른 집단이다. 국경을 감시하던 노예 추격자들은 누구도 몰아내려고 하지 않았다 – 그들은 노예가 된 사람들을 내부에 억류하려 했다.

어휘

policing 감시 활동, 치안 유지 활동
border 국경
national boundaries 국경
expansion 확장
militia 민병대, 의용군
immigrant 이주민, 이민자
enslave 노예로 만들다
troop 부대, 군대, 병력
militarization 군사화, 군국화
multiple 다수의
arguably 주장하건대, 거의 틀림없이
vigilante 자경단
colonizer 식민지 개척자
police 감시하다, 치안을 유지하다

10 정답 ③

정답해설

본문은 '방어 운전의 중요성과 방어적인 운전자의 특징'에 대해 설명하는 글이다. 본문 초반에서는 '방어 운전을 해야 하는 이유'에 대해 설명하고, ② 문장부터 방어적인 운전자의 특징에 대해 제시하고 있다. 그런데 ③에서 갑자기 '방어 운전과 난폭 운전과의 경계'가 언급되는 것은 어색하다. 따라서 정답은 ③이다.

오답해설

나머지 보기는 문맥상 자연스러우므로 오답이다.

해석

합법적으로 그리고 조심스럽게 운전하는 것은 우리가 매일 하는 가장 중요한 일 중 하나이다. 우리가 도로를 공유하는 사람들뿐만 아니라 우리의 생명도 우리가 핸들 뒤에서 신중한 결정을 내리는 것에 달려있다. ① 당신은 다른 운전자가 항상 옳은 일을 할 것이라고 결코 확신할 수 없다, 그러므로 때때로 방어적으로 운전하는 것은 안전한 운전자가 되는 것의 중요한 부분이다. ② 방어적인 운전자는 항상 경계하고 예측하지 못한 상황에 적응하기 위해 필요한 조정을 할 준비가 되어있는 사람이다. ③ **방어적인 운전 습관을 사용하는 것은 모든 사람의 안전을 우선으로 여기게 되지만, 때때로 방어 운전과 난폭 운전 사이의 경계가 모호해질 수도 있다.** 방어적인 운전자는 한쪽 벽면이 옆집과 붙어 있는 주택가를 방어적으로 운전할 때와 같이, 언제나 무슨 일이든지 발생할 수 있다는 것을 알고 있다. ④ 교통의 흐름, 날씨, 그리고 노면의 상태는 즉시 변화할 수 있고 운전하는 동안 안전하게 머무르기 위해 즉각적인 조정을 필요로 한다. 방어적인 운전자는 항상 평정을 유지하면서 그러한 변화를 줄 준비가 되어있다. 방어적인 운전자는 또한 다른 운전자의 실수에도 반응할 준비가 항상 되어있다.

어휘

lawfully 합법적으로
wheel (자동차의) 핸들; 바퀴
defensively 방어적으로
alert 경계하는
accommodate 맞추다, 적응하다, 조정하다
unforeseen 예측하지 못한, 뜻밖의
circumstance 상황, 환경
condition 상태, 상황
composure 평정
cautiously 조심스럽게
count on 확신하다, 의존하다, 믿다
aggressive 난폭한, 공격적인
adjustment 조정, 수정
semi 한쪽 벽면이 옆집과 붙어 있는 주택
in an instant 즉시, 당장, 곧

기적사 DAY 80

결국엔 성정혜 영어 하프모의고사

| 01 | ③ | 02 | ① | 03 | ④ | 04 | ④ | 05 | ④ |
| 06 | ② | 07 | ④ | 08 | ③ | 09 | ④ | 10 | ② |

01 정답 ③

정답해설
'retreat'은 '후퇴, 철수'를 뜻하는 명사로 ③ recession(후퇴, 불황)과 의미상 가장 가깝다.

해석
그러나 새롭게 발표된 연구 결과에 따르면, 이러한 진전은 최근에 **후퇴**의 조짐을 보이고 있다고 한다.
① 망명
② 급증
③ 후퇴, 불황
④ 보호, 피난처

어휘
retreat 후퇴, 철수 asylum 망명
upsurge 급증 recession 후퇴, 불황
sanctuary 보호, 피난처

02 정답 ①

정답해설
'discard'는 '버리다, 폐기하다'를 뜻하는 동사로 ① bin(버리다)과 유의어 관계이다.

해석
그것들이 더 이상 뜨겁지 않다면, 껍질을 벗기고, 씨와 줄기를 **버리고**, 세로로 가늘게 잘라라.
① 버리다
② 일축하다, 퇴짜 놓다
③ 간직하다, 보유하다
④ 몹시 싫어하다, 질색하다

어휘
peel (과일·채소 등의) 껍질을 벗기다[깎다]
discard 버리다, 폐기하다 stem (식물의) 줄기; 막다
lengthwise 세로의[로], 긴[길게] bin 버리다
spurn 일축하다, 퇴짜 놓다 retain 간직하다, 보유하다
loathe 몹시 싫어하다, 질색하다

03 정답 ④

정답해설
'dormant'는 '휴면 중의, 활동을 중단한'을 뜻하는 형용사로 '휴면하다'를 뜻하는 완전자동사 'diapause'의 현재분사인 ④ diapausing(휴면 중인)과 유의어 관계이다.

해석
어떤 식물들은 심지어 몇 년 동안이나 **휴면 중일** 수 있는 씨앗으로 건기를 피한다.
① 부수적인; 우연히 일어나는; 주요하지 않은
② 활기 넘치는, 탱탱한
③ 신중한, 판단력 있는
④ 휴면 중인

어휘
evade 피하다, 회피하다 dormant 휴면 중의, 활동을 중단한
incidental 부수적인; 우연히 일어나는; 주요하지 않은
bouncy 활기 넘치는, 탱탱한 judicious 신중한, 판단력 있는
diapause [주로 현재분사형으로] 휴면하다

04 정답 ④

정답해설
A의 '병원을 방문하기 전에 열 기운을 확인해봐'라는 표현은 명령문으로 상대방인 B에게 행동을 권유하는 말이다. 이에 B가 그녀의 상태에 대한 서술로 '그녀가 계속 졸고 있는 것을 보니 춘곤증에 걸린 것이 틀림없어.'라고 답하는 것은 어색하다. 'spring fever'는 '춘곤증'을 뜻한다. 따라서 B의 대답은 A의 말에 대한 적절한 반응이 아니다.

오답해설
① A는 B에게 '과제를 했는지' 질문한다. B는 '과제를 끝내기 위해 밤을 샜다'라고 대답한다. 이는 문맥상 자연스럽다.
② A는 '인터넷으로 숙제를 제출했는지' B에게 물어본다. 그러자 B는 '마감 기한을 겨우 맞췄다'라고 답변한다. 이러한 A와 B의 대화는 적절하다.
③ A는 B에게 '페달을 너무 세게 밟지 말라'라고 주의를 시킨다. B는 '그러지 않겠다'라고 반응하며 '압력을 견디기에는 페달이 너무 약하다'라고 덧붙인다. B의 대답은 A의 말에 대한 적합한 답변이다.

해석
① A: 너 과제 끝냈어?
  B: 나는 그것을 끝내려고 밤을 새웠어.
② A: 너 숙제 인터넷으로 제출했어?
  B: 응, 마감 기한을 겨우 맞췄어.
③ A: 페달을 너무 세게 밟지 마.
  B: 안 그럴게. 압력을 견디기에는 페달이 너무 약해.
④ A: 병원을 방문하기 전에 열 기운을 확인해봐.
  B: 그녀가 계속 졸고 있는 것을 보니 춘곤증에 걸린 것이 틀림없어.

어휘
assignment 과제; 배정 submit 제출하다; 항복[굴복]하다
barely 겨우, 간신히, 가까스로; 거의 ~아니게
withstand 견뎌내다 spring fever 춘곤증
drowsy 졸리는, 나른하게 만드는

05 정답 ④

정답해설
④ 출제 포인트: 관사의 위치/부사절을 이끄는 접속사 that(so+형용사/부사+that+주어+동사)/관용표현(take+목적어+for granted)

'so'가 「부정관사+형용사+단수가산명사」와 결합하는 경우 「so+형용사+부정관사+단수가산명사」의 형태를 사용한다. 해당 문장은 'so'가 「so+부

정관사+형용사+단수가산명사」의 형태를 사용하였으므로 틀린 문장이다. 따라서 'so a familiar thing'을 'so familiar a thing'으로 수정하거나 「such+부정관사+형용사+단수가산명사」를 활용해 'so a familiar thing'을 'such a familiar thing'으로 수정하여도 옳다. 또한 해당 문장은 'so+형용사/부사+that+주어+동사(너무 ~해서 ~하다)'가 사용되었으며 'take it for granted'는 관용표현 'take+목적어+for granted(~을 당연한 일로 여기다)'로 이때 목적어 'it'은 'A test for color blindness(색맹검사)'를 가리킨다.

오답해설

① **출제 포인트: 주어와 동사의 수일치/a variety of+명사[복수형태]**
대명사 'each'가 주어인 경우 동사에 단수 형태를 사용하며 'a variety of' 이후에 오는 명사는 복수 형태이다. 따라서 해당 문장의 경우 동사에 단수 형태인 'has'를, 'a variety of' 이후에 복수 형태의 명사인 'colors and shapes'를 옳게 사용하였다.

② **출제 포인트: 주어와 동사의 수일치/불완전자동사의 주격 보어/목적격 관계대명사의 생략**
주어가 단수 형태인 'The jacket'이므로 동사에 단수 형태인 'looks'를 사용하는 것이 옳으며 이때 'looks'는 불완전자동사이므로 주격 보어에 해당하는 형용사 'nice'의 쓰임은 올바르다. 또한 'the blue tie' 이후에는 'bought'의 목적어에 해당하는 목적격 관계대명사 'which' 또는 'that'이 생략되어 있다.

③ **출제 포인트: 주장, 요구, 명령, 제안동사+(that)+주어+(should)+동사원형**
'demanded'의 목적어로 접속사 'that'이 생략된 명사절이 왔으며 이때 명사절의 동사에 'should'가 생략된 동사원형 'step down'을 사용하였으므로 옳은 문장이다. 해당 문장에서 'involved'는 'the persons'를 수식하는 과거분사로 명사절의 동사로 착각하지 않도록 유의해야한다. 여기서 'persons'는 '사람들'을 나타내는 표현으로 옳게 사용되었다.

해석

① 각각의 장난감은 다양한 색깔과 모양을 가지고 있다.
② 네가 구입한 그 파란 넥타이와 더불어 그 재킷은 정말로 좋아 보인다.
③ 야당은 그 사건에 연루된 자들이 사퇴해야 한다고 요구했다.
④ 색맹검사가 너무 낯익은 것이라서 대부분의 사람들은 이를 당연하게 받아 들인다.

06 정답 ②

정답해설

② **출제 포인트: 대명사 수일치**
밑줄 친 'their'는 대명사의 소유격으로 복수 형태이나 가리키는 대상이 단수 형태인 'a fish'이므로 'their'를 'its'로 수정해야 한다.

오답해설

① **출제 포인트: 현재분사 vs. 과거분사**
밑줄 친 'struggling'은 완전자동사 'struggle'의 현재분사이며 수식하는 대상 'a fish'와 능동 관계이므로 'struggling'은 옳은 표현이다.

③ **출제 포인트: to부정사의 부사적 용법/to부정사의 태**
'to mimic'은 목적을 나타내는 to부정사의 부사적 용법에 해당하며 이후에 목적어 'the ocean'이 있으므로 to부정사의 능동태인 'to mimic'은 옳은 표현이다.

④ **출제 포인트: 주어와 동사의 수일치/능동태 vs. 수동태**
주어가 단수 형태인 'The idea'이므로 동사에 단수 형태인 'reminds'를 사용하는 것이 옳다. 또한 'reminds' 이후에 목적어 'the other great contradiction'이 왔으므로 능동태인 'reminds'는 옳은 표현이다.

해석

바다를 흉내 내기 위해 자기 몸속에 염분을 축적하려고 애쓰는 담수호에 있는 물고기에 관한 생각은 생물권의 다른 거대한 모순을 상기시킨다.

어휘

freshwater lake 담수호 accumulate 축적하다
mimic 흉내 내다 contradiction 모순

07 정답 ④

정답해설

④ **출제 포인트: 능동태 vs. 수동태**
해당 문장에서 'are made'는 불완전타동사 'make'의 수동태로 사용되고 있다. 이런 수동태의 경우 「be made+목적격 보어」의 형태를 사용해야 하나 「be made+목적어+목적격 보어」의 형태를 사용하였으므로 틀린 문장이다. 따라서 'are made'를 능동태인 'make'로 수정해야 한다.

오답해설

① **출제 포인트: 주어와 동사의 수일치**
접속사 'because'가 이끄는 절의 주어가 동명사이므로 단수 취급한다. 따라서 'because'가 이끄는 절에 단수 형태의 동사인 'is'를 사용하는 것이 옳다.

② **출제 포인트: 형용사 vs. 부사**
해당 문장에서 'clear'는 '명료한'을 뜻하는 형용사로 명사 'writing'과 'thinking'을 수식하고 있으므로 옳게 사용되었다.

③ **출제 포인트: 완전타동사+목적어[의문사+to+동사원형]**
'know'는 「의문사+to+동사원형」을 목적어로 가질 수 있다. 따라서 'know how to communicate'는 옳게 사용되었으며, 해당 문장에서 'communicate'는 완전자동사로 사용되었다.

해석

그것은 글을 잘 쓰는 사람이 되는 것이 글쓰기 이상의 것에 관한 것이기 때문이다. 명료한 글쓰기는 명료한 사고의 징후이다. 글을 잘 쓰는 사람들은 어떻게 의사소통하는지를 안다. 그들은 일을 이해하기 쉽게 만든다.

08 정답 ③

정답해설

본문은 '아이들이 스크린을 바라보는 것은 수동적인 형태의 학습이며, 상상력이 풍부하고 창의적인 놀이를 통해서만이 아이들은 근육 및 감각을 건강하고 완전하게 발달시킬 수 있다'고 설명하고 있다. 본문 초반에서는 '스크린을 바라보는 것'에 대해 설명하고 있는데, "This is a very ③ unartificial way of learning and does not engage children in a kinesthetic manner using their entire bodies(이것은 매우 ③ 자연적인 방식의 학습이고, 아이들을 그들의 몸 전체를 사용하는 운동 감각적인 방식으로 끌어들이지 않는다)."에서, '스크린을 보는 것이 '자연적인' 방식의 학습'이라고 하는 것은 문맥상 어색하다. 따라서 ③ unartificial(자연적인)은 artificial(인공적인)이 되는 것이 자연스러우므로, 정답은 ③이다.

오답해설

① '아이들이 스크린을 많이 보는 것'은 양육에 있어서 '우려되는' 점이므로, 'concerning(우려되는)'은 문맥상 적절하다.

② 화면에서 보이는 정보를 받아들이는 것은 일방적인 학습이므로, '수동적인 (passive)'이라는 표현은 적절하다.

④ 본문 초반에서 '스크린을 보는 것은 수동적이고 인공적인 학습법'이라고 했으므로, 이와 비교해 '상상력이 풍부하고 창의적인 놀이'는 '자연스러운 (natural)' 방식이라고 설명하는 것은 자연스럽다.

해석

현재, 아이들 양육하는 것에 있어서 가장 ① 우려되는 측면 중 하나는 그들이 스크린 앞에서 보내는 시간의 양이다. 아이들이 그들의 주의를 스크린에 집중할 때, 이는 매우 ② 수동적인 형태의 학습 또는 오락이다. 세상에 대해 배우고 무언가를 창작하기 위해 그들 자신의 상상력을 이용하는 것 대신에, 아이들은 그저 소근육 운동을 이용하는 반응을 필요로 하거나 필요로 하지 않는 시각 및 청각적 자극의 수신자에 지나지 않는다. 이것은 매우 ③ **자연적인(→ 인공적인)** 방식의 학습이고, 아이들을 그들의 몸 전체를 사용하는 운동 감각적인 방식으로 끌어들이지 않는다. 상상력이 풍부하고 창의적인 놀이가 아이들이 세상을 배우고 정말 몸 전체를 관여시키는 더 ④ 자연스러운 방식이다. 아이들은 다양한 놀이 재료를 조작하고 만진다. 그들은 놀이를 통해 언어적 그리고 비언어적으로 모두 자기 자신을 표현한다. 그들은 돌아다니기 위해 자신들의 모든 근육과 감각을 이용한다. 놀이 중에 활발하게 그들의 다른 감각들뿐만 아니라 그들의 대근육과 소근육을 이용하면서, 아이들은 그들의 뇌에 건강한, 강한, 그리고 완전한 신경 연결을 발달시킨다.

어휘

passive 수동적인, 소극적인
stimulation 자극
artificial 인공적인, 인위적인
kinesthetic 운동 감각의
manipulate 조작하다, 다루다
neurological 신경의
recipient 수신자, 받는 사람
fine motor skill 소근육 운동
engage 끌어들이다, 관여시키다
involve 관련[연루]시키다
verbally 말로, 구두로

09 정답 ④

정답해설

본문은 '영토 분쟁'에 대해 설명하는 글이다. 본문에 따르면, 영토 분쟁은 전쟁의 주요 원인이며, 한 지역에 대해 둘 이상의 국가가 소유권을 주장할 때 발생한다. 인접한 국가끼리의 분쟁일수록 전쟁의 가능성이 더 높고, 가치가 더 높은 지역일수록 폭력을 유발할 가능성이 더 높다. 그런데, "especially if they have ④ agreements over specific pieces of territory(특히 만일 그들이 특정 영토에 대해 ④ 의견 일치가 있다면)."에서, 특정 영토에 대해 '의견 일치'가 있을 때, 전쟁을 할 가능성이 있다는 것은 문맥상 어색하다. 따라서 ④ agreement(의견 일치)는 disagreement(의견 불일치)가 되어야 한다. 따라서 정답은 ④이다.

오답해설

① '공공연하게 또는 분명하게 통치권을 주장한다'는 내용이 들어가야 자연스러우므로, '명백한'이라는 의미의 'explicit'은 문맥상 자연스럽다.
② 본문 첫 문장에서 '영토 분쟁이 전쟁의 주요(leading) 원인'이라고 언급하고 있으므로, '다른 외교 분쟁보다 더 '자주(frequently)' 무력 갈등으로 이어진다는 것은 문맥상 자연스럽다.
③ '인접한(contiguous)' 국경을 공유하는 지역이 멀리 떨어진 지역보다 서로 전쟁을 할 가능성이 더 높으므로, 문맥상 자연스럽다.

해석

역사에서 전쟁의 주요 원인은 Alsace-Lorraine, Kashmir, Golan Heights, 그리고 Beagle Channel을 둘러싼 경쟁과 같은 영토 분쟁과 관련되어 있다. 영토 분쟁은 한 국가의 공적 대표가 다른 국가에 의해 권리가 주장되거나 관리되는 특정 영토에 대한 통치권을 주장하는 ① 명백한 진술을 할 때 발생한다. Issue Correlates of War (ICOW) Project는 1816년 이래 전 세계적으로 800건 이상의 영토 분쟁이 있었음을 확인했다. 영토 분쟁은 다른 유형의 외교 분쟁보다 더 ② 빈번하게 무력 갈등으로 이어진다. ③ 인접 국경을 공유하는 국가들이, 특히 만일 그들이 특정 영토에 대해 ④ 의견 일치(→의견 불일치)가 있다면, 비인접 국가들보다 서로 전쟁을 할 가능성이 더 높다. 천연자원, 종교적 장소, 또는 역사적 발상지라는 주장 때문에 더욱 가치 있는 영토는 더 많은 폭력을 발생시킨다.

어휘

leading 주요한, 선두적인
territorial dispute 영토 분쟁
explicit 명백한, 분명한, 노골적인
territory 영토, 영역
administer 관리하다, 운영하다
conflict 갈등, 충돌
contiguous 인접한, 근접한
generate 발생시키다, 만들어내다
involve 포함하다, 수반하다, 관련시키다
representative 대표, 대변자
sovereignty 통치권
claim (권리를) 주장하다; 차지하다
militarized 무장의, 무력의
diplomatic 외교의
border 국경

10 정답 ②

정답해설

주어진 문장에서는 '난폭 운전의 원인을 '해당 차량의 운전자'로 보는 것이 기존 직원 안전 운전 프로그램의 접근법'이라고 설명하고 있다. 그런데, ② 이후에서는 however(그러나)를 이용해, '대부분은 해당 차량의 운전자들이 난폭 운전의 최초의 원인은 아니다'라고 주어진 문장에서 언급된 내용과 대조적인 내용을 서술해주고 있다. 따라서 주어진 문장이 ②에 들어가는 것이 문맥상 가장 자연스럽다.

오답해설

나머지 보기는 문맥상 어색하므로 오답이다.

해석

우리는 모두 난폭 운전과 보복 운전의 결과를 보았다. 대규모의 차량을 보유한 많은 기업들이 어떤 종류의 운전자 안전 교육을 실시한다. (①) 이러한 차량 안전 프로그램 중 대부분은 운전자 안전의 본질, 장소, 그리고 시기에 초점을 맞춘다. 그러나 너무도 자주 그들은 중요한 질문 하나를 놓친다 – 누구 (때문인가)? (② **많은 직원 안전 운전 프로그램은 난폭 운전이 핸들 뒤에 있는 사람에서 시작하고 끝난다는 접근법을 취한다.**) 그러나 대체로, 트럭 운전자들과 다른 직업 운전자들은 보복 운전의 최초 원인이 아니다. (③) 대신에, 그들이 어떻게 운전하는지는 다른 운전자들에 의해 영향을 받는다. (④) 운전자들은 근무일을 안전하게 운전하고자 하는 최상의 의도를 가지고 출발할지도 모르지만, 하루가 지나감에 따라, 다른 운전자들과의 갈등과 불만이 시작될 수 있다. 이러한 요인들의 조합이 운전자들이 난폭하게 운행하도록 만들 가능성이 훨씬 더 크다.

어휘

approach 접근(법)
effect 결과, 영향
road rage 보복 운전, 운전자 폭행, 로드 레이지
extensive 대규모의, 많은
fleet 전(全) 선박[비행기, 트럭, 버스] 보유 차량
conduct 행하다, 실시하다
where 장소
all too 너무나, 정말
initial 처음의, 초기의
conflict 갈등, 충돌
set in (계속될 기세로) 시작하다[되다]
aggressively 난폭하게, 공격적으로
wheel 핸들
aggressive driving 난폭 운전
what 본질
when 시기, 때
miss out on …을 놓치다
intention 의사, 의도, 목적
frustration 불만

기적사 복습 모의고사 8회

01	④	02	③	03	④	04	①	05	④
06	①	07	④	08	②	09	①	10	②
11	④	12	②	13	③	14	③	15	③
16	③	17	②	18	②	19	②	20	④

01 정답 ④ — Day 77-02

정답해설

'deny'는 '부인하다, 부정하다'를 뜻하는 동사로 ④ repudiate(부인하다, 거부하다)와 유의어 관계이다.

해석

비록 그들은 다른 이념들에 의해 나뉘었지만, 그들의 공통의 민족성은 **부인하지** 않았다.
① 폐지하다, 철회하다
② 피하다, 삼가다
③ 그만두다, 포기하다
④ 부인하다, 거부하다

02 정답 ③ — Day 72-02

정답해설

'curious'는 '궁금한, 호기심이 많은'을 뜻하는 형용사로 ③ inquisitive(호기심이 많은, 탐구심이 많은)와 의미상 가장 가깝다.

해석

헛간에서 이상한 것을 발견한 양치기들은 그것의 부드러움에 대하여 **호기심이 생겼다**.
① 냉담한, 냉랭한
② 고르지 못한, 균등하지 않은
③ 호기심이 많은, 탐구심이 많은
④ 무표정한, 아무런 감정이 없는

03 정답 ④ — Day 76-01

정답해설

'withdrawal'은 '철수, 철회, 취소'를 뜻하는 명사로 ④ retreat(후퇴, 철수)과 의미상 가장 가깝다.

해석

England라는 이름은, 409년에 로마인들의 마지막 **철수** 이후, 5세기에 lowland Britain에서 군주국들을 설립했던 게르만 부족들 중 하나인 앵글족에서 유래했다.
① 붕괴, 실패
② 침략, 침입
③ 항복, 굴복
④ 후퇴, 철수

04 정답 ① — Day 71-02

정답해설

'canny'는 '약삭빠른, 영리한'을 뜻하는 형용사로 ① shrewd(상황 판단이 빠른, 기민한)와 의미상 가장 가깝다.

해석

영리한 투자자들은 주식 시장이 급격히 폭락하게 될 수 있다는 것을 걱정하기 시작한다.
① 상황 판단이 빠른, 기민한
② 명망 있는, 일류의
③ 무례한, 경솔한
④ 궁금한, 호기심이 많은

05 정답 ④ — Day 80-03

정답해설

'dormant'는 '휴면 중의, 활동을 중단한'을 뜻하는 형용사로 '휴면하다'를 뜻하는 완전자동사 'diapause'의 현재분사인 ④ diapausing(휴면 중인)과 유의어 관계이다.

해석

어떤 식물들은 심지어 몇 년 동안이나 **휴면 중일** 수 있는 씨앗으로 건기를 피한다.
① 부수적인; 우연히 일어나는; 주요하지 않은
② 활기 넘치는, 탱탱한
③ 신중한, 판단력 있는
④ 휴면 중인

06 정답 ① — Day 77-05

정답해설

① **출제 포인트: 관용표현(It takes+사람+시간+to+동사원형, It takes+시간+for+사람+to+동사원형)**

'It takes+사람+시간+to+동사원형'은 관용표현으로 '사람이 ~하는 데 시간이 걸리다'를 뜻한다. 사람을 나타내는 목적어가 시간을 나타내는 목적어 뒤로 이동할 경우 전치사 'for'와 결합하여 'It takes+시간+for+사람+to+동사원형'이 되며, 이때 'for+사람'은 to부정사의 의미상 주어이다. 해당 문장은 사람을 나타내는 목적어 'him'이 시간을 나타내는 목적어 'a while' 앞에 위치하고 있으나 'him' 앞에 전치사 'for'를 사용하였으므로 틀린 문장이다. 따라서 'for'를 삭제해 'takes him a while'로 수정하거나 'for him'을 'a while' 뒤로 옮겨 'takes a while for him'으로 수정해야 옳다.

해석

① 그는 혼자 사는 것에 적응하는 데 시간이 좀 걸린다.
② 젊은 등반가 다섯 명을 구조하는 것을 돕기 위해 헬리콥터 한 대를 긴급 이륙시켰다.
③ 그 연구는 운전하는 동안 졸음이 오는 음악을 듣는 것은 위험하다는 것을 암시한다.
④ 인지하고 있거나 생각하고 있음을 의식하는 것은 우리 자신의 존재를 의식하는 것이다.

07 정답 ④　　　　　　　　　　　　　　　　　Day 72-07

정답해설

④ 출제 포인트: 기수-측정단위명사-형용사

'35-years-old'는 「기수-측정 단위명사-형용사」에 해당하며 명사 'captain'을 수식하는 수식어로 사용되었다. 이때 수식어로 사용되는 측정 단위명사는 단수 형태이어야 하므로 복수 형태인 'years'를 단수 형태인 'year'로 수정해야 한다.

해석

① 나는 그가 하기를 원하는 것을 하게 할 수 없었다.
② 학생들은 각자의 불만을 토로했다.
③ 비록 팀은 졌지만, 그들이 엄청난 기백을 가지고 경기를 했다는 것을 Tom은 알고 있었다.
④ 35세의 국가 대표팀 주장은 뉴욕에서의 10년 후 그가 새로운 도전이 필요하다고 말한다.

08 정답 ②　　　　　　　　　　　　　　　　　Day 73-05

정답해설

② 출제 포인트: 해석 일치 주의

주어진 해석을 통해 수동태 'will be developed'가 쓰인 문장의 주어가 'the product(상품)'이고 'in response to'의 목적어가 'customer demand(고객의 요구)'임을 알 수 있다. 따라서 'Customer demand(고객의 요구)'와 'the product(상품)'의 위치를 서로 바꾸어 'The product will be developed in response to customer demand.'로 수정해야 한다.

09 정답 ①　　　　　　　　　　　　　　　　　Day 74-08

정답해설

본문은 '블라인드 테스트의 목적'에 대해 설명하는 글이다. 첫 문장 "Blind testing aims to assess a product based on its intrinsic merits by hiding any reference to the wider brand(블라인드 테스트는 더 폭넓은 브랜드에 대한 언급을 숨김으로써 그것의 본질적인 가치에 기반을 두고 제품을 평가하는 것을 목표로 한다)."에서 글의 주제를 확인할 수 있고, 이어서 다양한 상황에서 블라인드 테스트를 통해 얻을 수 있는 효과에 대해 설명해주고 있다. 따라서 전체 글의 제목으로 가장 적절한 것은 '① What Is Blind Testing for?(블라인드 테스트는 무엇을 위한 것인가?)'이다.

해석

블라인드 테스트는 더 폭넓은 브랜드에 대한 언급을 숨김으로써 그것의 본질적인 가치에 기반을 두고 제품을 평가하는 것을 목표로 한다. 이것은 이전 경험에 의해 생성된 어떤 후광 효과 또는 부정적 연상에 의한 영향을 받은 결과를 방지한다. 이러한 접근은 시장 연구가들에게 경쟁사의 제품 또는 그 제품의 이전 버전들과 비교하여, 테스트 제품의 절대적인 매력에 대한 확실한 묘사를 해주는 데 효과적이다. 매력을 위해 분투하는 브랜드들에게, 이것은 문제가 브랜드의 이미지에 원인이 있는지 또는 제품 자체에 원인이 있는지 분명히 하는 데 유용할 수 있다. 높은 매력을 가지고 있는 브랜드들에게, 이것은 그들의 제품이 실제로 '우수한'지 또는 평가가 브랜드 후광 효과에 의해 돋보여진 것인지 이해하는 데 도움이 된다.
① 블라인드 테스트는 무엇을 위한 것인가?
② 블라인드 테스트는 왜 무의미한가?
③ 블라인드 테스트는 어떻게 수행되는가?
④ 블라인드 테스트와 브랜드 테스트는 어떻게 다른가?

10 정답 ②　　　　　　　　　　　　　　　　　Day 77-09

정답해설

주어진 문장에서는 역사상 실제로 발생했던, 그러나 세부적인 내용은 잘 알려지지 않은 '싸움(dispute)'에 관해 언급하고 있다. 이에 바로 이어질 내용으로 가장 적절한 것은, 사건이 발생한 시기와 사건에 연루된 인물들이 최초로 언급되는 (B)이다. 이후 (B)에서 언급된 인물들 사이의 싸움에 대한 구체적인 내용이 언급되는 (A)가 이어지는 것이 적절하며, 마지막으로 (A)에서 발생한 사건을 'This dispute(이 싸움)'를 이용해 가리키고 있는 (C)가 이어지는 것이 자연스럽다. 따라서 정답은 '② (B) - (A) - (C)'이다.

해석

역사는 세부 사항을 희미하게 만들었지만, 이야기는 만취 상태의 싸움, 말다툼, 실랑이, 그리고 총격을 여전히 말해준다.
(B) 그것은 1849년 10월이었다. John Weller 장관과 측량사인 Andrew Gray가 지도에만 존재하던 선을 표시하기 위해 미국과 멕시코의 국경으로 파견되었고, 그 업무는 잘 진행되지 않았다.
(A) 몇몇은 John Weller가 Andrew Gray의 턱을 가격했다고 말한다; 다른 사람들은 그가 Andrew Gray의 목을 조르려 했다고 하지만, 두 이야기 모두에서, Andrew Gray는 John Weller의 허벅지를 총으로 쐈다. 1년도 채 안 된 국경 측량은 엉망진창이었다.
(C) 이 싸움은 멕시코-미국 전쟁 이후 미국이 남쪽 국경을 규정하려고 분투하는 동안 발생했던 여러 문제들 중 하나일 뿐이었다. 마침내, 하나의 선이 그려졌지만, 국경은 자리를 잡은 것과는 거리가 멀었다.

11 정답 ④　　　　　　　　　　　　　　　　　Day 78-04

정답해설

A는 B에게 얼음 위를 걷지 말라고 충고하면서 얼음이 언 것처럼 보여도 얼지 않았을 수 있다고 말한다. 하지만 B는 자신이 얼음 위를 걷는 것을 좋아한다고 대답한다. 이는 자연스러운 대화의 흐름이 아니다. 따라서 정답은 ④이다.

해석

① A: 나는 내일 일찍 일어나야 해.
　 B: 너 내일 일찍 일정이 있어?
② A: 창문 밖을 봐! 눈이 내리고 있어!
　 B: 우와! 올해의 첫눈이야.
③ A: 여기 너무 어두워. 불 좀 켜줄 수 있어?
　 B: 물론이지. 스위치 어디 있어?
④ A: 얼음 위를 걷지 마. 그렇게 보일지라도, 얼지 않았을 수 있어.
　 B: 나는 얼어있는 얼음 위를 걷는 것을 좋아해.

12 정답 ②　　　　　　　　　　　　　　　　　Day 74-04

정답해설

밑줄 친 부분 전 대화에서 A는 B에게 자신이 이틀 전 새로 산 드레스를 입고 더 뚱뚱해 보이지 않는지 묻고 있다. 이에 B는 '멋져 보인다고 말하면서 자신이 ~이다'라고 이야기한다. 따라서 빈칸에 '② mean business(진심이다)'가 들어가는 것이 문맥상 가장 적절하다.

해석

A: 나 이 드레스 입은 모습 어때?
B: 아름다워 보여! 색이 너에게 정말 잘 어울린다.
A: 정말 고마워. 이 옷을 이틀 전에 샀는데, 내게 잘 어울리는지 확실히 모르겠어.
B: 너 아주 괜찮아 보여. 자신감을 더 가져.

A: 더 뚱뚱해 보이지 않아?
B: 전혀 그렇지 않아. 날 믿어, 너 멋있어. 나는 진심이야.
① 서두르다
② 진심이다
③ 화내다
④ 목표를 달성하다

13 정답 ③   Day 78-06

정답해설

③ 출제 포인트: 비교급 강조 부사

'very'는 원급 또는 최상급을 수식하는 강조 부사로 비교급을 수식할 수 없다. 해당 문장은 'very' 이후에 'much'의 비교급인 'more'가 있으므로 'very'를 비교급 강조 부사인 'even, much, still, a lot, (by) far' 등으로 수정해야 한다.

해석

만약 네가 너의 소유인 이 땅으로부터 매일 너의 게으른 몸으로 덮을 수 있을 만큼의 땅을 경작한다면, 너는 매년 네가 여기 수레에서 보는 것보다 더욱더 많은 옥수수를 거둘 것이다.

14 정답 ③   Day 72-10

정답해설

주어진 문장은 '생각하는 것(기분)이 감정을 유발하는 것의 예'에 대해 설명하고 있다. 따라서 주어진 문장은, '기분이 감정에 영향을 미친다'는 내용 이후에 들어가는 것이 적절하다. ② 이전 문장 "They are sparked by emotions and colored by the thoughts, memories, and images that have become subconsciously linked with that particular emotion for you(그것들은 감정에 의해 촉발되고, 사고, 기억, 그리고 잠재적으로 당신의 특정한 그 감정과 연결된 이미지들에 의해 색채를 입는다)."에서는 '기분이 감정 등 다른 요소에 의해 영향을 받는다'라고 설명한 후, ③ 이전 문장에서 "But it works the other way around too(그러나 또한 반대로도 작용한다)."라고 설명하며, '즉, 감정이 기분에 영향을 받기도 한다'라고 언급하고 있다. 그러므로 '기분이 감정을 유발하는 것의 예시'인 주어진 문장은 ③에 들어가는 것이 문맥상 자연스럽다.

해석

기분은 당신이 감정을 느낄 때 당신의 신체에 무엇이 일어나는가에 대한 정신적 묘사이고 당신의 뇌가 그 감정에 대한 의미를 감지하고 지정하는 것의 부산물이다. 기분은 감정을 가진 후 발생하는 다음의 것이고, 대개 잠재 의식적인 인지적 입력을 수반하며, 정확히 측정될 수 없다. (①) 그것들은 감정에 의해 촉발되고, 사고, 기억 그리고 잠재적으로 당신의 특정한 그 감정과 연결된 이미지들에 의해 색채를 입는다. (②) 그러나 또한 반대로도 작용한다. (③ **예를 들어, 단지 위협적인 무언가를 생각하는 것은 감정적 공포 반응을 유발할 수 있다.**) 개별 감정은 일시적인 반면, 그것들이 유발하는 기분은 지속될 수 있고 일생에 걸쳐 커질 수 있다. (④) 감정이 결과적으로 특정 감정을 일으키는 잠재적인 기분을 야기할 수 있고 이것이 계속해서 이어지기 때문에, 당신의 인생은 부정적인 기분을 자아내는 고통스럽고 혼란스러운 감정의 순환이 될 수 있고, 이것이 더 많은 부정적 감정을 유발한다.

15 정답 ③   Day 79-10

정답해설

본문은 '방어 운전의 중요성과 방어적인 운전자의 특징'에 대해 설명하는 글

이다. 본문 초반에서는 '방어 운전을 해야 하는 이유'에 대해 설명하고, ② 문장부터 방어적인 운전자의 특징에 대해 제시하고 있다. 그런데 ③에서 갑자기 '방어 운전과 난폭 운전과의 경계'가 언급되는 것은 어색하다. 따라서 정답은 ③이다.

해석

합법적으로 그리고 조심스럽게 운전하는 것은 우리가 매일 하는 가장 중요한 일 중 하나이다. 우리가 도로를 공유하는 사람들뿐만 아니라 우리의 생명도 우리가 핸들 뒤에서 신중한 결정을 내리는 것에 달려있다. ① 당신은 다른 운전자가 항상 옳은 일을 할 것이라고 결코 확신할 수 없다. 그러므로 때때로 방어적으로 운전하는 것은 안전한 운전자가 되는 것의 중요한 부분이다. ② 방어적인 운전자는 항상 경계하고 예측하지 못한 상황에 적응하기 위해 필요한 조정을 할 준비가 되어있는 사람이다. ③ **방어적인 운전 습관을 사용하는 것은 모든 사람의 안전을 우선으로 여기게 되지만, 때때로 방어 운전과 난폭 운전 사이의 경계가 모호해질 수도 있다.** 방어적인 운전자는 한쪽 벽면이 옆집과 붙어 있는 주택가를 방어적으로 운전할 때와 같이, 언제나 무슨 일이든지 발생할 수 있다는 것을 알고 있다. ④ 교통의 흐름, 날씨, 그리고 노면의 상태는 즉시 변화할 수 있고 운전하는 동안 안전하게 머무르기 위해 즉각적인 조정을 필요로 한다. 방어적인 운전자는 항상 평정을 유지하면서 그러한 변화를 줄 준비가 되어있다. 방어적인 운전자는 또한 다른 운전자의 실수에도 반응할 준비가 항상 되어있다.

16 정답 ③   Day 77-08

정답해설

본문에서 화자는 밤중에 한가로이 자신이 살던 옛 마을을 돌아다니며 어린 시절의 추억을 회상하고 행복을 느끼고 있다. 본문에 따르면 보통 어린 시절의 좋은 시절에 돌아가고 싶은 마음은 모두 같지만, 실제로 그러한 시간을 갖는 것은 매우 어려우며 좋았던 시절을 잊고 사는 것이 보편적이다. 하지만 화자는 옛 마을을 홀로 돌아다니며 좋은 시절을 떠올릴 수 있는 기회를 가질 수 있었다는 것이 글 전체의 내용이다. 따라서 화자의 심경으로 가장 적절한 것은 '③ pleased and delighted(기쁘고 즐거운)'이다.

해석

나의 옛 마을을 돌아다니고, 문 닫힌 상점들을 들여다보고, 적막한 운동장과 공원을 느긋하게 걷고, 시간이 지남에 따라 위층 창문의 불빛들이 천천히 꺼지는 것을 바라보는 것은 내게 묘한 경험이었다. 한 사람의 인생을 이루는 너무나도 많은 순간들이 있고, 그것들은 매초가 지나면서 축적되지만, 우리들 중 얼마나 많은 사람들이 기억의 보드라운 주름 속에서 머무르는 시간을 보내는가? 우리들 중 얼마나 많은 사람들이 진정으로 그러하길 원하는가? 나는 우리 모두가 그렇다고 생각한다. 나는 어딘가에 항상 당신이 계속해서 다시 체험하고 싶어 하는 순간으로 가득 찬 작은 상자가 존재한다고 생각한다. 그러나 우리가 그것 안에 맞을 수 있도록 우리가 우리 자신을 알맞은 크기에 맞추어 줄어들게 해본 적이 있는가? 우리들 중 대부분은 그렇지 않다. 우리는 매년 더 크고 더 복잡하게 자란다, 그리고 그 상자는 어느 날 그것을 찾는 것이 불가능해질 때까지 점점 더 작아 보이게 되고, 결국 영원히, 그러나 모르는 사이에 봉해지면서 끊임없는 인생과 시간의 변화 속에서 사라지게 된다. 그러나 그날 밤 나는 나의 모든 작은 상자들을 찾은 것과 같은 기분을 느꼈고, 그것들을 모두 열어보고 싶은 기분이었다.
① 회의적이고 경계하는
② 외롭고 우울한
③ 기쁘고 즐거운
④ 두려워하고 괴로워하는

17 정답 ③　　　　　　　　　　　　　　　　Day 71-08

정답해설

빈칸 이후의 문장에서 우리는 실제 세계에서 브랜드와 가격 등을 보지 않은 채 상품을 제대로 평가할 수 없다고 서술한다. 그러므로 브랜드를 붙이는 것 없이 테스트 된 제품이 객관적으로 평가된다는 개념은 '잘못된' 것이라는 내용이므로 빈칸에 가장 적절한 것은 '③ misguided(잘못된)'이다.

해석

브랜드를 붙이는 것 없이 테스트 된 제품이 다소 더 객관적으로 평가된다는 개념은 완전히 잘못된 것이다. 실제 세계에서, 우리가 눈을 감고 코를 잡은 채로 어떤 것들을 평가할 수 없는 것처럼 우리는 우리가 구입하는 제품에 찍혀진 브랜드, 그것이 담긴 상자의 외형과 느낌, 요구된 가격을 무시한 채로 평가할 수는 없다.
① 정확한
② 믿을 만한
③ 잘못된
④ 편견 없는, 공정한

18 정답 ②　　　　　　　　　　　　　　　　Day 72-09

정답해설

(A) 본문 두 번째 문장 "A new RAND Corporation study finds that Americans average more than 5 hours of free time each day(새로운 RAND Corporation의 연구는 미국인들은 매일 평균 5시간 이상의 자유 시간을 갖는다는 것을 알아냈다)."와 세 번째 문장 "But instead of being physically active during their free hours, Americans report they spend most of that time looking at screens (televisions, phones or other devices)(그러나, 그들의 자유 시간 동안 신체적으로 활동적이 되는 것 대신에, 미국인들은 스크린(텔레비전, 휴대폰 또는 다른 기기)을 보며 그 시간의 대부분을 보낸다고 보고한다)."를 통해, '미국인들은 충분한 자유 시간이 있음에도 불구하고, 운동을 하지 않는다'는 것을 알 수 있다. 따라서 (A)에는 '너무 바빠서 운동을 하지 않는 것이 아니다'라는 의미가 되는 어휘가 들어가는 것이 적절하다. 그러므로 빈칸에는 'busy(바쁜)' 또는 'occupied(바쁜)'가 알맞다.
(B) 본문 초반에 '미국인들은 하루에 평균 5시간 이상이 자유 시간이다'라고 언급하고 있으므로, '하루에 적어도 20~30분의 신체 활동을 하도록 하는 것이 '가능하다'는 의미가 되는 것이 문맥상 자연스럽다. 따라서 빈칸에는 'feasible(가능한)' 또는 'possible(가능한)'이 적절하다.
따라서 정답은 '② busy(바쁜) - feasible(가능한)'이다.

해석

미국인들이 어쨌든 너무나도 (A) <u>바빠서</u> 운동을 못 하는 것은 아닐지도 모른다. 새로운 RAND Corporation의 연구는 미국인들은 매일 평균 5시간 이상이 자유 시간이라는 것을 알아냈다. 그러나 그들의 자유 시간 동안 신체적으로 활동적이 되는 것 대신에, 미국인들은 스크린(텔레비전, 휴대폰 또는 다른 기기)을 보며 그 시간의 대부분을 보낸다고 보고한다. "대중들 그리고 심지어 공중 보건 전문가들 사이에서도 여가시간의 부족이 미국인들이 충분한 신체 활동을 하지 못하는 주요 이유라는 일반적인 인식이 있다"고 연구의 공저자인 Deborah Cohen 박사는 말했다. "그러나 우리는 그러한 믿음에 대한 증거가 없다는 것을 발견했다." 이러한 결과는 미국인들이 매일 최소 20 또는 30분을 신체 활동에 사용하도록 하는 것이 (B) <u>가능하다</u>는 것을 시사한다. 그들이 실제로 어떻게 그들의 시간을 사용하는지에 대한 대중의 의식을 고취시키고 미국인들이 그들의 스크린을 보는 시간을 줄이도록 장려하는 메시지를 만드는 것이 사람들이 신체적으로 더 활동적이 되도록 도울 수 있을 것이다.

	(A)	(B)
①	나태한	이상적인
②	바쁜	(실현) 가능한
③	바쁜	불가피한
④	게으른	가능한

19 정답 ②　　　　　　　　　　　　　　　　Day 76-09

정답해설

해당 지문은 미국과 멕시코의 국경에 대한 기원에 대해서 서술하고 있다. "Victorious in the Mexican ~ any plan of nature."를 통해서 '인간은 전쟁 등을 통해 국경이라는 임의적인 경계를 만들어왔다'라는 것을 알 수 있다. 반면 "The one line that nature did provide - the Rio Grande— was a river that ran through but did not really divide continuous terrain(자연이 제공했던 하나의 경계인 Rio Grande 강은 그 사이를 흐르는 강이었지만, 실제로 연속적인 지형을 나눠놓지는 않았다)." 부분 등으로 보아 자연은 경계를 흐르기만 할 뿐, 지형을 나누지 않았다는 것을 알 수 있다. 따라서 '② While nature did not draw lines, human society certainly did(자연은 경계를 만들지 않는 반면에, 인류 사회는 경계를 만들었다).'가 글의 내용과 일치한다.

해석

이전에 멕시코 북부였던, 미국의 남서부에서, Anglo-America는 Hispanic America와 충돌했다. 그 만남은 언어, 종교, 인종, 경제 그리고 정치 변수들과 관련되었다. Hispanic America와 Anglo-America 사이의 경계는 시간이 지남에 따라 변화했으나, 한 가지 사실은 변하지 않았다; 두 지역의 통치권 사이의 임의적인 지리적 경계를 그리는 것과 사람들이 이것을 존중하도록 설득하는 것은 또 다른 이야기라는 것이다. 1848년 멕시코-미국 전쟁에서 승리한 미국은 멕시코의 절반을 차지했다. 그 결과로 초래된 분열은 어떠한 자연의 계획도 인정하지 않았다. 국경 지방들은 생태학적으로 한 덩어리였다; 즉, 북동부의 멕시코 사막은 남동부의 미국의 사막과 민족주의의 형상화 없이 섞이게 되었다. 자연이 제공했던 하나의 경계인 Rio Grande 강은 흐르지만, 실제로 연속적인 지형을 나눠놓지는 않았다.
① 미국과 멕시코 사이의 경계는 하나의 통치권의 오랜 역사를 의미한다.
② 자연은 경계를 만들지 않는 반면에, 인류 사회는 확실히 경계를 만들었다.
③ 멕시코-미국 전쟁은 사람들이 경계를 존중하는 것을 가능하게 만들었다.
④ Rio Grande는 임의적인 지리학적인 경계로 여겨져 왔다.

20 정답 ④　　　　　　　　　　　　　　　　Day 73-09

정답해설

본문은 '미국인의 TV 시청 시간'에 대한 통계 자료를 제시하고 있다. 본문 중반 "Older people took more time out of their day for TV — those 65 and older watched more than four hours daily on average(나이 든 사람들은 하루 중 더 많은 시간을 TV를 위해 사용했다 - 65세 이상인 사람들은 하루에 평균 4시간 이상을 시청했다)."를 통해, 65세 이상 집단은 하루에 평균 4시간 이상 TV를 시청한다는 것을 알 수 있고, 본문 후반 "The unemployed also spent more time watching daily on average — 3.78 hours — than those with either full-time or part-time jobs on average — 2.10 hours(또한, 실업자들은 정규직 또는 시간제 직업을 가진 사람들보다(2.10시간) 하루 평균적으로 더 많은 시간을 시청하는데 보냈다(3.78시간))."를 통해, 실업자 집단은 하루에 평균 3.78시간 TV를 시청한다는 것을 알 수 있다. 즉, 단순 시간 비교를 할 때, 65세 이상 집단이 실업자 집단보다 더 많은 시간을 TV를 시청하며 보낸다는 것을 알 수 있다. 따라서 '④ The 65 and older age group watched less hours than the unemployed group(65세 이상 집단이 실업자 집단보다 더 적은 시간을 시청했다).'은 글의 내용과 일치하지 않는다.

해석

Census Bureau의 자료에 따르면, TV를 시청하는 것이 미국이 가장 좋아하는 여가 활동이다. 텔레비전 앞에 앉아 있는 것이 미국인이 매일 갖는 전체 자유 시간의 절반을 약간 상회하는 시간인 하루에 2.7시간을 차지했다. 그 조사는 TV를 시청하며 4.8시간을 보내는 여성과 비교하여, 미국인 남성은 하루 평균 5.5시간을 TV를 시청하며 보낸다는 것을 발견했다. 또한 조사는 연령, 고용 상태, 그리고 기타를 기준으로 사람들이 얼마나 오래 시청했는지를 세분화했다. 나이 든 사람들은 그들의 하루 중 더 많은 시간을 TV를 위해 사용했다 – 65세 이상인 사람들은 하루에 평균 4시간 이상을 시청했다. 반면, 15-44세 집단은 하루에 평균 약 2시간으로, 가장 적게 시청했다. 또한, 실업자들은 정규직 또는 시간제 직업을 가진 사람들보다(2.10시간) 하루에 평균적으로 더 많은 시간을 시청하는데 보냈다(3.78시간). 이것은 심지어 직업을 가진 사람들조차도, 평균적으로, 그들의 자유 시간 중 많은 시간을 어떤 종류의 텔레비전 쇼를 보는 데 보낸다는 것을 의미한다.

① 미국인들은 평균적으로 매일 6시간 이하의 자유 시간을 가진다.
② 남성이 여성들보다 더 많은 시간을 TV 시청하는 데 보낸다.
③ 15세 미만의 어린이들이 15세와 44세 사이의 사람들보다 더 많이 TV를 보았다.
④ 65세 이상 집단이 실업자 집단보다 더 적은 시간을 시청했다.

기출하프 + 파생하프 + 복습모의고사

성정혜 기적사
하프 모의고사

― 강파이널편 ―

기적사 DAY 01 핵심어휘

01
authorize	허가하다, 승인하다
surrogate	대리인
proxy	대리인
sentry	보초(감시)병
predecessor	전임자
plunderer	약탈자

02
keep one's feet on the ground	현실적이다, 들뜨지 않다
confident	자신 있는, 확신하는
sensible	분별 있는, 현명한
realistic	현실적인, 실제적인

03
on the fence	결정하지 못하여
anguished	번민의, 고뇌에 찬
enthusiastic	열광적인
apprehensive	불안한
undecided	결정하지 못한

04
out of touch with	~와의 접촉 없이
drift apart	사이가 멀어지다
fume	(화가 나서) 씩씩대다

08
high fixed cost	높은 고정비용
marginal cost	한계비용
substantial	상당한
negligible	무시할 수 있는
implication	의미
markup	인상
unit cost	단가

make no sense	말이 되지 않다
production cost	생산비
intellectual property	지적재산

09
claim	권리
fame	명성
blood-sucker	흡혈하는 것
slide	미끄러지다
lash out	후려갈기다
velocity	속도
snap	딱 소리를 내다, 부러지다
secretive	비밀스러운, 숨기는
leaf litter	낙엽
subterranean	지하의

10
wealth	부
central	중심적인
lack	부족
resource	자원
nation-state	국민국가
nevertheless	그럼에도 불구하고
furthermore	더욱이
conversely	역으로
similarly	유사하게

기적사 DAY 02 핵심어휘

01
lurch	비틀거리다
assailant	가해자, 공격자
authority	당국, 권한, 권위
assaulter	공격자, 폭행자

☐ substitute	대용품
☐ avocation	부업, 취미

02

☐ nature	본질
☐ have one's feet on the ground	실제적인
☐ practical	실제적인
☐ dependent	의존하는
☐ seemingly	겉보기에는
☐ groundless	근거 없는

03

☐ crucial	중대한, 결정적인
☐ at this juncture	이 중차대한 시기에, 이 기회에
☐ suspected	의심이 가는, 미심쩍은
☐ debatable	논란의 여지가 있는
☐ enthusiastic	열렬한, 열광적인
☐ significant	중요한, 의미 있는

04

☐ off the wall	기발한, 특이한
☐ aboveboard	정정당당한, 분명히
☐ hat in hand	공손히, 굽실거리며
☐ as easy as making apple pie	누워서 떡 먹기인

08

☐ relatively	상대적으로
☐ package	꾸리다, 포장하다, 제작하다
☐ expertise	전문 지식[기술]
☐ sellable	판매할 수 있는
☐ how-to	입문서의, 초보적인
☐ that is to say	다시 말해서, 즉
☐ vend	판매하다
☐ access	접근[성]
☐ accessible	접근 가능한, 이용하기 쉬운

☐ emerge	나타나다, 드러나다
☐ advent	출현, 도래, 등장

09

☐ simultaneously	동시에
☐ fatality	사망자
☐ ferocity	사나움
☐ determination	투지, 결의
☐ aggressive	공격적인
☐ in quick succession	연달아
☐ venom	독
☐ mandible	아래턱뼈
☐ thrust	찌르다, 쑤셔 넣다
☐ barbless	미늘[바늘]이 없는
☐ appearance	외모
☐ either A or B	A, B 둘 중 하나

10

☐ expenditure	지출
☐ on-the-job	실지[실습]로 배우는
☐ radically	급진적으로
☐ gradually	점진적으로, 차차
☐ acquisition	획득
☐ crucial	중대한, 결정적인
☐ determinant	결정 요인
☐ productivity	생산성
☐ standard of living	생활 수준
☐ utilize	이용하다, 활용하다
☐ further	조장[촉진]하다, 조성[증진]하다
☐ health	(국가·사회 등의) 활력, 번영
☐ craft	공예

기적사 DAY 03 핵심어휘

결국엔 성정혜 영어 하프모의고사

01

☐ lassitude	무기력, 노곤함
☐ weariness	권태, 피로, 지루함
☐ instruction	교육, 지시, 방법, 설명
☐ sentry	보초(감시)병
☐ interrogation	질문, 심문, 의문

02

☐ sensible	분별력 있는
☐ reasonable	합리적인
☐ impartial	치우치지 않는
☐ empirical	경험적인
☐ illogical	비논리적인

03

☐ the dragon and the tiger	용호(龍虎)
☐ almighty	전능한
☐ ambivalent	상반되는
☐ omnipotent	전능한
☐ anguished	번민의, 고뇌에 찬
☐ casual	평상시의, 격의 없는, 우연한

04

☐ adjustment	조정
☐ go bananas	열광하다
☐ beat a dead horse	헛수고하다
☐ change horses in the middle of the stream	어려운 순간에 계획을 바꾸다
☐ look like the cat that swallowed the canary	의기양양하다

08

☐ pricing	가격 책정
☐ stem from	…에서 기인하다
☐ fixed cost	고정비용, 고정 원가
☐ variable cost	변동비용, 변동 원가
☐ characterize	…의 특징이 되다
☐ collectively	집합적으로, 총괄적으로
☐ unit	(제품) 한 개[단위]
☐ virtually	사실상
☐ operating system(OS)	운영 체제
☐ replicate	복제하다

09

☐ be better off ~ing	~하는 것이 더 낫다[좋다]
☐ frown upon	~에 눈살을 찌푸리다 [~을 못마땅해하다]
☐ ban	금지하다
☐ ecological	생태학의
☐ ecosystem	생태계
☐ invasive	침입의
☐ biodiversity	생물 다양성
☐ infamous	악명 높은
☐ red imported fire ant	붉은불개미
☐ native to …	토종의[원산의]
☐ crate	(물품 운송용 대형 나무) 상자
☐ predator	포식자
☐ irreparable	돌이킬 수 없는
☐ prohibit	금지하다
☐ debate	논쟁하다, 논의하다

10

☐ marketization	자유 시장 경제로 전환, 자유 시장화
☐ accelerate	가속화하다
☐ enclosed	단절된, 폐쇄된
☐ running	운영, 경영

☐ -oriented	-지향적인, -중심의
☐ meet	충족시키다
☐ various	다양한
☐ pursuit	추구
☐ competitive	경쟁의, 경쟁이 심한
☐ stimulate	자극하다
☐ adapt	적응하다

결국엔 성정해 영어 하프모의고사
기적사 DAY 04 핵심어휘

01

☐ envy	시기
☐ lust	음욕
☐ gluttony	탐식
☐ sloth	나태
☐ avarice	탐욕
☐ wrath	분노
☐ calling	소명
☐ vocation	직업
☐ avidity	탐욕
☐ plunderer	약탈자

02

☐ confident	자신감 있는, 확신하는
☐ reliant	확신하는
☐ assured	확신하는
☐ convinced	확신하는
☐ confidential	기밀의

03

☐ assiduous	끈기 있는, 근면한, 성실한
☐ ambivalent	상반되는
☐ apprehensive	우려하는, 이해가 빠른
☐ industrious	근면한
☐ avocational	취미의, 여가 활동의

04

☐ a lemon	품질이 좋지 않은 물건
☐ an act of god	불가항력
☐ four-letter word	욕
☐ the best thing since sliced bread	최고의 것

08

☐ significant	주요한
☐ productize	제품화하다
☐ leverage	활용하다, 강화하다
☐ pitfall	위험, 곤란
☐ entrepreneurial	사업가의
☐ burnout	(마음·체력의) 쇠진, (스트레스에 의한) 정신·신경의 쇠약, 기력 소진
☐ ramp up	성장하다, 증가시키다
☐ well-oiled	능률적인, 순조로운
☐ virtual assistant	(인공지능) 가상의 비서
☐ inventory	재고
☐ sales potential	판매 잠재력, 세일즈 포텐셜 (잠재수요 중 기업이 얻을 수 있는 점유율)
☐ maintenance	유지
☐ back-end	말기
☐ manually	수동으로

09

☐ fungus	균류
☐ thereby	그것에 의해
☐ infectious	전염성의
☐ spore	포자
☐ forage	(특히 동물이) 먹이를 찾다
☐ phenomenon	현상
☐ infiltrate	침투시키다
☐ fungal	균성의
☐ snatcher	날치기꾼, (시체) 도둑

understory	(식물 군락의) 하층, 하층 식생
compel	강요하다, 명령하다
vegetation	식물
twig	작은 가지
invasion	침입, 침범
culminate with	…로 끝나다
sprouting	싹 틔움
spore-laden	포자가 가득한[든]
fruiting body	(균류의) 자실체

10

expenditure	지출, 소비, 비용
full-time-equivalent	임의의 업무에 투입된 노동력을 전일 종사, 노동자 수로 측정하는 방법
vice versa	역(逆)도 또한 같음
decline	감소하다, 줄다
generally	대개, 일반적으로

결국엔 성정혜 영어 하프모의고사
기적사 DAY 05 핵심어휘

01

dismay	실망, 경악
euthanasia	존엄사
predecessor	전임자
disappointment	실망
torture	고문

02

realistic	실용적인
meticulous	섬세한, 꼼꼼한
relaxing	편안한, 마음을 느긋하게 해주는
pragmatic	실용적인
infeasible	실행 불가능한

impractical	실행할 수 없는

03

deducted	공제된
subtracted	감해진, 공제된
dedicated	헌신적인, 전념하는
defeated	패배한
undecided	결정하지 못한

04

thumbs up	긍정의 표시
Alpha and Omega	시작과 끝
a pretty kettle of fish	아수라장
a big fish in a little pond	우물 안 개구리

08

somewhat	다소, 약간
substitute	대체재
property	특징, 특성
subsequent	다음의, 그 후의
academic journal	학술지
pose	(질문 등을) 제기하다
pricing	가격 책정
sustain	유지하다, 지탱하다
identical	동일한, 같은
commodity	상품
share	지분, 주식
stock	주식
monopolistic competition	독점적 경쟁
incremental cost	증분 원가[비용]
outcome	결과

09

signify	중요하다, 의미가 되다
predilection	기호, 애호, 매우 좋아함

pile	(쌓아 올린) 더미
rot	썩다, 부패하다
nondestructive	비 파괴적인
cannibalism	카니발리즘, 동족끼리 서로 잡아먹음
larva	유충, 애벌레 (pl. larvae)
nursery	육아실
regurgitate	(삼킨 음식물을 입 안으로 다시) 역류시키다

10

tertiary	제3의, 3차의
peer	또래, 동배
educational attainment	교육 정도[수준]
in respect of	…에 대한
visible	뚜렷한, 두드러지는
counterpart	상대, 대응 관계에 있는 사람
pursue	추구하다

기적사 DAY 06 핵심어휘

01

disobedient	반항하는, 거역하는
muzzle	입막음하다, (말하는 것 등을) 억누르다
nonsense	허튼수작, 터무니없는 생각
express	표현하다
assert	주장하다
suppress	억누르다
spread	펼치다, 퍼뜨리다

02

pompous	(글이나 문체가) 과시적인, 거만한
colloquial	구어의, 일상적인 대화체의
presumptuous	과시하는
casual	평상시의, 우연한
formal	공식적인
genuine	진실된, 진짜의

03

call it a day	하던 일을 그만두다
initiate	시작하다
finish	끝내다
wait	기다리다
cancel	취소하다

04

reservation	예약
certainly	(대답)알았습니다; 물론이지

05

independence	독립
alter	바꾸다
manner	방식, 태도

06

clothes	옷, 의복
fit	맞다
medium	중간의

07

planet	행성
heartbroken	슬픔에 잠긴
documentary	다큐멘터리
extent	정도

08

conscientious	성실한, 양심적인
conscientiousness	성실, 양심
hygiene	위생
factor	요인
tendency	경향
disorganized	체계적이지 못한
unconscientious	성실하지 못한, 비양심적인
root through	찾아 헤매다
inefficient	비효율적인
folk	사람들
setback	좌절
thorough	철저한
norm	표준, 기준
sidestep	회피하다

09

deforestation	삼림 벌채
mass extinction	대량 멸종
biodiversity	생물 다양성
Anthropocene	인류세
underpin	뒷받침하다
exceed	초과하다
ecological	생태학적인
evenly	공평하게
generate	발생하다
Capitalocene	자본론
devastation	황폐화
inequality	불평등
accumulation	축적
viable	실행 가능한

10

tragedy	비극
be haunted by	~에 시달리다
revenger	복수하는 사람
borderline	경계(선)
barbarity	야만(적 행위)

conflicting	상충되는
justice	정의
mercy	자비
exact	요구하다
revenge	복수
vengeance	복수, 보복
take into one's hands	마음대로 하다
moral	도덕적인
perpetrator	가해자
murderous	살인의, 흉악한
deed	행동, 행위
redemption	되찾기, 상환, 구원
depraved	부패한, 타락한
divine	신의, 신성한
atrocity	악행, 포악
depravity	타락, 부패
corrupt	부패한
politician	정치인
accountability	책임, 의무
conscience	양심

결국엔 성정혜 영어 하프모의고사
기적사 DAY 07 핵심어휘

01

document	기록하다
exhume	발굴하다, 파내다
explore	탐험하다
exploit	활용하다, 착취하다
express	표현하다
excavate	발굴하다, 출토하다

02

frigid	몹시 추운
fake	위조의
fallible	잘못을 저지르기 쉬운

☐ formal	공식적인
☐ freezing	몹시 추운, 영하의

03

☐ have emphasis on	강조하다
☐ brisk	활발한
☐ surrender	항복하다, 포기하다, 인도하다
☐ hesitate	주저하다, 망설이다
☐ initiate	시작하다
☐ stress	강조하다, 역설하다

05

☐ end up -ing	결국 ~하게 되다
☐ infant	유아, 아기
☐ pension	연금, 생활보조금
☐ inflation	인플레이션

06

☐ linkage	연결, 결합
☐ infrastructure	기반 시설, 인프라
☐ performance	실행, 수행, 공연, 실적, 성과
☐ follow	~의 뒤를 잇다, ~의 뒤를 따라가다

07

☐ aspect	측면, 양상
☐ including	~을 포함하여
☐ motivation	동기

08

☐ conscientiousness	성실성, 양심
☐ hypothesize	가정하다, 가설을 세우다
☐ conventional	틀에 박힌, 진부한, 전통적인
☐ well-defined	명확한, 알기 쉬운

☐ measure	(판단·평가·비교 따위의) 기준, 표준, 척도
☐ original	독창적인
☐ empirical	경험적인, 실증적인
☐ mixed	엇갈린, 혼합된
☐ conversely	반대로, 역으로
☐ on the whole	전체적으로 보아, 전반적으로

09

☐ Anthropocene	인류세
☐ epoch	시기, 시대, 세
☐ prominently	현저하게, 두드러지게
☐ archaeologist	고고학자
☐ prevalence	널리 퍼짐
☐ fossilized	화석화된
☐ domestication	사육, 가축화
☐ outnumber	…보다 수가 더 많다, 수적으로 우세하다
☐ consequence	결과
☐ not least	특히
☐ emission	배출
☐ vary	다르다, 다양하다
☐ conservative	보수적인, 적게 잡은
☐ anthropogenic	인류 발생의
☐ geological	지질학의
☐ intensive	격렬한, 강한
☐ debate	논쟁
☐ bring about	야기하다

10

☐ school of thought	학설, 학파
☐ punish	벌하다, 응징하다
☐ offender	범죄자
☐ revenge	복수, 보복
☐ trifle with	…을 우습게[하찮게] 보다
☐ dwell on	곱씹다

결국엔 성정혜 영어 하프모의고사
기적사 DAY 08 핵심어휘

01

☐ initiate	시작하다, 착수시키다
☐ dermal	피부의
☐ assert	주장하다
☐ coordinate	조정하다, 조직하다, 협력하다
☐ loiter	빈둥거리다, 게으름 피우다
☐ launch	시작하다, 개시하다

02

☐ innocuous	무해한, 악의 없는
☐ harmless	무해한, 악의 없는
☐ venenose	해로운, 유독한
☐ casual	평상시의, 우연한
☐ malicious	악의 있는

03

☐ make up to	~에게 아첨하다
☐ flatter	아첨하다, 알랑거리다
☐ migrate	이동하다, 이주하다
☐ notify	통보하다, 알리다
☐ cancel	취소하다

04

☐ motivate	~에게 동기부여하다
☐ superstition	미신
☐ catch up with	~을 따라잡다

05

☐ spend+시간+~ing	~하는 데 시간을 보내다
☐ dirt	흙, 먼지, 때
☐ woodland	삼림 지대

06

☐ a little bit	조금
☐ struggle with	~로 분투하다, 노력하다
☐ manageable	관리할 수 있는
☐ inability	무능, 불능
☐ prioritize	우선순위를 매기다

07

☐ conflict	갈등, 충돌
☐ finite	한정된, 유한한
☐ inevitable	불가피한, 필연적인

08

☐ organized	체계적인, 조직적인
☐ conscientiousness	성실함, 양심
☐ continuity	지속성
☐ predictability	예측 가능성
☐ on the fly	급히, 대충 그때그때 봐 가며
☐ pedantry	지나치게 규칙을 찾음 [세세한 것에 얽매임]
☐ neurotic	신경증의
☐ adherence	고수, 집착
☐ painful	성가신, 귀찮은
☐ micro-manager	사소한 일까지 챙기는 사람
☐ improvise	즉석에서[즉흥적으로] 하다
☐ prioritize	우선순위를 정하다
☐ expose	노출시키다, 경험하게[접하게]하다
☐ burnout	번 아웃, 기력 소진, (신체적 또는 정신적인) 극도의 피로

09

☐ Anthropocene	인류세
☐ geological	지질학의
☐ epoch	시기, 세
☐ encapsulate	압축하다, 요약하다

☐ profound	깊은, 극심한
☐ gasket	개스킷(가스·기름 등이 새어 나오지 않도록 파이프나 엔진 등의 사이에 끼우는 마개)
☐ skyrocketing	치솟는
☐ altered	바뀐
☐ unanimous	만장일치의
☐ mistake	오해하다, 잘못 판단하다
☐ anonymous	익명인
☐ misplace	제자리에 두지 않다
☐ continuous	끊임없는
☐ misbelieve	의심하다, 믿지 않다
☐ synonymous	같은 뜻의, 동의어의
☐ misunderstand	오해하다, 잘못 이해하다

10

☐ mild-mannered	온화한, 온순한
☐ rampage	광란
☐ double-barrelled	쌍총신인
☐ sawn-off	한쪽 끝을 (톱으로) 잘라 없앤
☐ solicitor	사무 변호사
☐ plot	음모[모의]하다
☐ tax evasion	탈세
☐ taunt	조롱하다, 비웃다
☐ disheveled	단정치 못한, 부스스한
☐ pull up	멈추다, 서다
☐ taxi rank	택시 승강장
☐ beckon	손짓하다, 부르다
☐ cabby	택시 기사
☐ indiscriminately	무차별적으로
☐ passer-by	행인
☐ inquest	조사, 심리
☐ bitter	억울해하는
☐ resentful	분개하는, 분노하는
☐ shortcoming	결점, 결핍
☐ spree	한바탕 저지르기

결국엔 성정혜 영어 하프모의고사
기적사 DAY 09 핵심어휘

01

☐ preliminary	예비의, 최초의,
☐ inquiry	조사, 탐구, 연구
☐ questionable	의심스러운
☐ interrogate	심문하다, 추궁하다
☐ spread	펼치다, 퍼뜨리다
☐ intrigue	음모를 꾸미다, 호기심을 돋우다
☐ question	질문하다, 심문하다
☐ intimidate	~을 협박하다

02

☐ meticulous	꼼꼼한, 세심한
☐ malleable	(금속 등을) 펴 늘릴 수 있는, 가단성의, 적응성이 있는, 유순한
☐ precise	세밀한, 정밀한, 정확한
☐ genuine	진실된, 진짜의
☐ mischievous	짓궂은

03

☐ pass down	~을 물려주다
☐ compel	강요하다, ~하게 하다
☐ wait	기다리다
☐ dispatch	파견하다, 보내다
☐ transfer	넘겨주다, 물려주다

04

☐ sibling	(한 명의) 형제자매[동기]
☐ look for	찾다, 구하다
☐ make sure	(...임을)확인하다
☐ rush hour	혼잡 시간대
☐ traffic jam	교통 체증

05

☐ unknown	알려지지 않은
☐ episode	사건, 에피소드
☐ passion	열정
☐ try to 동사원형	~하려고 하다, ~하려고 애쓰다

06

☐ badly	몹시, 심하게, 서투르게
☐ behave	처신하다, 행동하다
☐ fulfill	충족시키다, 실행하다

07

☐ refuge	피난처, 보호 구역
☐ hike	도보 여행, 하이킹
☐ search for	~를 찾다
☐ learn about	~에 대해 배우다

08

☐ conscientious	성실한, 양심적인
☐ self-discipline	자기 규율[훈련]
☐ determination	투지, 결심
☐ trait	특성
☐ diabetes	당뇨병
☐ stroke	뇌졸중
☐ joint	관절
☐ note	주목하다
☐ conscientiousness	성실함, 양심
☐ consistently	꾸준히, 지속적으로, 일관되게
☐ quality	특성, 특징
☐ adopt	(특정한 방식이나 자세를) 쓰다[취하다]

09

☐ designated	지정된
☐ inescapable	피할 수 없는
☐ atmospheric	대기의
☐ relentless	끊임없는

☐ current	(물, 공기의) 흐름
☐ capacious	널찍한, 큼직한
☐ cargo-hold	화물 적재실, 화물칸
☐ imprint	자국
☐ pristine	자연[원래] 그대로의, 오염되지 않은
☐ permanently	영구히
☐ blink	명멸하다, 스러지다
☐ geographer	지리학자
☐ geologist	지질학자
☐ Holocene	완신세
☐ Anthropocene	인류세

10

☐ at somebody's expense	…의 비용[희생]으로
☐ go along with	동조하다, 따르다
☐ get back at	복수하다
☐ defector	배신자

결국엔 성정해 영어 하프모의고사
기적사 DAY 10 핵심어휘

01

☐ snap	일시적인 한파
☐ persist	계속되다, 지속되다
☐ relieve	안도시키다
☐ refrain	자제하다, 삼가다
☐ persevere	유지하다, 인내하다
☐ suppress	억누르다

02

☐ irritated	짜증나게 하는
☐ trigger	자극 요인
☐ counseling	상담
☐ bothered	괴롭힘당하는, 성가신
☐ interested	흥미가 있는

☐ probed	조사되는, 수사받는
☐ presumptuous	과시하는

03

☐ rely on	기대다, 의존하다
☐ resort	기대다, 의지하다
☐ resume	재개하다
☐ cease	끝내다
☐ regain	되찾다, 회복하다

04

☐ pain killer	진통제
☐ recommendation	추천
☐ hang out	놀다, 어울리다

05

☐ achieve	성취하다, 달성하다
☐ cabbage	양배추

06

☐ recognize	인식하다, 알아보다
☐ first impression	첫인상
☐ commit	저지르다, 범하다
☐ a series of	일련의

07

☐ obstacle	장애, 장애물
☐ overcome	극복하다
☐ crisis	위기
☐ engage A in B	A를 B에 관여하게 하다, 참여하게 하다
☐ missing	빠진, 누락된, 없어진, 실종된

08

☐ trait	특성
☐ get at	…에 도달하다[미치다]
☐ conscientiousness	성실성, 양심
☐ extraversion	외향성

☐ agreeableness	우호성
☐ neuroticism	신경증적 경향
☐ stability	안정성
☐ unexpectedly	뜻밖에
☐ moderate	중간의

09

☐ Anthropocene	인류세
☐ designate	지정하다
☐ epoch	시기, 세
☐ Capitalocene	자본세
☐ catastrophe	재앙, 참사
☐ delusion	망상, 착각
☐ acknowledge	인정하다
☐ feed	부양하다

10

☐ grudge	원한
☐ plot	계획하다, 꾀하다
☐ hardwire	고정화시키다, 굳어버리게 하다
☐ instinctive	본능적인
☐ reprisal	보복, 앙갚음
☐ vengefulness	복수심에 불탐, 앙심을 품음

결국엔 성정혜 영어 하프모의고사
기적사 DAY 11 핵심어휘

01

☐ premiere	초연, 첫날; 개봉하다
☐ convoluted	대단히 난해한[복잡한]
☐ dimension	관점, 차원
☐ ancient	고대의
☐ unrelated	관계없는
☐ complicated	복잡한
☐ otherworldly	저승의, 내세의

02

☐ wind up	마무리 짓다, 끝내다
☐ initiate	시작하다
☐ resume	재개하다
☐ terminate	종결하다
☐ interrupt	방해하다, 간섭하다

03

☐ sergeant	경사, 병장
☐ dismay	당황하게 하다, 깜짝 놀라게 하다
☐ run over	~을 치다
☐ ask out	초대하다
☐ carry out	이행하다
☐ pass over	제외하다

04

☐ neighborhood	지역, 근처, 이웃
☐ drawback	단점, 결점

05

☐ sneeze	재채기하다
☐ caring	배려하는, 보살피는
☐ go away	없어지다

08

☐ name	이름을 붙이다, 명명하다, 이름을 대다
☐ politics	정치(학)
☐ accomplish	성취하다
☐ direction	지시, 설명
☐ assemble	조립하다
☐ material	자료, 재료
☐ scan	훑어보다
☐ come up with	생각해내다
☐ ignore	무시하다
☐ irrelevant	무관한
☐ play	작용, 운용, 영향
☐ metaphor	비유, 은유

☐ register	등록하다, 기록하다
☐ association	연관(성), 연상

09

☐ obligation	의무
☐ belong to	~에 속하다
☐ comprise	~를 구성하다
☐ manifest	나타내다
☐ aspect	측면, 양상
☐ means	수단, 방법
☐ accumulate	축적하다
☐ make a living	생계를 꾸리다
☐ collectivistic	집단주의의
☐ fulfill	이행하다, 달성하다, 완수하다
☐ individualistic	개인주의의
☐ separate	분리시키다
☐ accomplish	달성하다

10

☐ navigate	길을 찾다, 항해하다
☐ emit	내뿜다, 배출하다
☐ high-pitched	고음의
☐ squeak	날카로운 소리
☐ echo off	~에 부딪혀 반향하다
☐ branch	나뭇가지
☐ obstacle	방해물, 장애물
☐ lie	놓여있다
☐ ahead	앞에, 앞서서
☐ instantaneous	즉각적인
☐ object	물체
☐ insect	곤충
☐ spot	발견하다, 찾아내다
☐ prey	먹이
☐ echolocation	반향 위치 측정
☐ sonar	초음파
☐ tell	구별하다
☐ perceive	인식하다, 인지하다
☐ detect	감지하다
☐ avoid	피하다

결국엔 성정혜 영어 하프모의고사
기적사 DAY 12 핵심어휘

01

☐ renowned	유명한, 명성 있는
☐ prestigious	명망 있는, 일류의
☐ relative	상대적인
☐ quarrelsome	싸우기 좋아하는
☐ otherworldly	저승의, 내세의

02

☐ interrogate	심문하다
☐ make away with	~을 훔치다
☐ interrupt	방해하다, 간섭하다
☐ reconcile	조정하다, 조화시키다
☐ steal	훔치다, 도둑질하다
☐ nullify	무효화하다

03

☐ take care of	돌보다, 신경 쓰다
☐ other than	~이외의
☐ look after	돌보다, 주의를 기울이다
☐ run over	~를 치다
☐ make out	이해하다, ~을 만들어 내다
☐ make up for	보충하다, 보상하다

04

☐ plan	계획을 세우다, 계획하다
☐ motivation	동기
☐ set a ceiling on	상한을 규정하다
☐ get the ball rolling	일을 시작하다
☐ drive somebody up the wall	~의 이성을 잃게 하다, 분노하게 하다
☐ have one's back to the wall	곤경에 처하다

05

☐ curiosity	호기심
☐ via	~을 통해
☐ suspense	서스펜스, 긴장감
☐ hostile	적대적인
☐ outsmart	~보다 한 수 앞서다
☐ outlaw	무법자, 도망자

08

☐ celebrated	유명한, 저명한
☐ revisit	다시 논의하다
☐ conceive	고안하다, 구상하다, 생각하다
☐ predominantly	대개, 대부분
☐ prevalent	널리 퍼진, 일반적인
☐ inspectional	점검의
☐ syntopical	주제별
☐ deliberately	의도적으로
☐ denote	의미하다
☐ notion	개념
☐ embeddedness	맞물림, 내재
☐ extraneous	관련 없는
☐ transient	일시적인, 순간적인
☐ relevant	유의미한, 관련 있는
☐ cumulative	누적되는
☐ esoteric	난해한, 소수만이 즐기는

09

☐ individualist	개인주의자(의)
☐ stress	강조하다
☐ collectivist	집단주의자(의)
☐ sacrifice	희생하다
☐ tendency	경향

10

☐ hail	축하하다, 환호하며 맞이하다
☐ superb	대단히 훌륭한, 최고의
☐ navigate	방향을 읽다
☐ towering	우뚝 솟은
☐ canopy	(숲의 나뭇가지들이) 지붕 모양으로 우거진 것
☐ fumble	더듬거리다, 실수하다, 놓치다
☐ foliage	나뭇잎
☐ grab a bite to eat	간단히 먹다
☐ microbat	작은 박쥐류
☐ kin	친족, 동족
☐ flying fox	날여우박쥐
☐ nocturnal	야행성의
☐ squeak	끼익[꽥/찍]하는 소리
☐ peeper	안경, 눈

결국엔 성정혜 영어 하프모의고사
기적사 DAY 13 핵심어휘

01

☐ reticent	말이 없는, 과묵한
☐ prestigious	일류의, 명성 있는, 유명한
☐ ancient	고대의
☐ placid	조용한, 차분한
☐ mutual	상호적인, 서로의

02

☐ make up with	~와 화해하다
☐ flatter	아첨하다, 아부하다
☐ terminate	종결하다
☐ notify	통보하다, 알리다
☐ reconcile	화해시키다, 조화시키다

03

☐ drug abuse	약물 남용
☐ make up to	~에게 아첨하다
☐ mess up	엉망으로 만들다, 다 망치다
☐ pass over	제외하다
☐ pass down	~을 물려주다, 전수하다

04

☐ con artist	신용 사기꾼
☐ rank and file	일반 직원
☐ a man of one's word	자기 말을 지키는 사람
☐ a man of the world	세상 물정에 밝은 사람

05

☐ pony	조랑말
☐ brand-new	최신의, 신제품의, 새로운
☐ saddle	안장
☐ break into tears	울음을 터트리다

08

☐ skim	대충 읽다, 훑어보다
☐ gist	요점
☐ directory	명단, 목록
☐ comprehension	이해
☐ superficial	표면적인, 피상적인

09

☐ individualism	개인주의
☐ collectivism	집단주의
☐ individualistic	개인주의적인
☐ collectivistic	집단주의적인
☐ interdependence	상호 의존
☐ switch	전환하다, 바꾸다
☐ relative	상대적인

10

☐ exhaust	다 써 버리다, 고갈시키다
☐ critical	대단히 중요한
☐ epidemic	전염병, 유행병
☐ devastate	파괴하다, 황폐하게 만들다
☐ culprit	범인
☐ invasive	침습성의
☐ fungus	균류
☐ metabolism	신진대사
☐ hibernation	동면
☐ die-off	종(種)의 급격한 자연 소멸

결국엔 성정혜 영어 하프모의고사
기적사 DAY 14 핵심어휘

01

☐ robust	탄탄한, 튼튼한
☐ affirmative	긍정적인
☐ unrelated	관계없는
☐ sturdy	튼튼한, 견고한
☐ placid	평온한, 조용한, 차분한
☐ mutual	상호적인, 서로의

02

☐ reveal	밝히다, 누설하다
☐ confidential	비밀의, 감추는
☐ punishment	엄벌, 처벌
☐ settle	해결하다, 타협을 보다, 진정시키다
☐ restrain	자제하다
☐ resume	재개하다
☐ disclose	폭로하다, 밝히다

03

☐ compel	강요하다
☐ ask out	초대하다
☐ dispatch	파견하다
☐ obsess	(어떤 생각이 사람의 마음을) 사로잡다, 집착하게 하다

04

☐ bolt from the blue sky	예기치 못한 일
☐ roll out the red carpet	특히 환영하다
☐ yellow journalism	황색지, 선정적인 언론

05

☐ swimming suit	수영복
☐ minimize	최소화하다
☐ resistance	저항, 반대

08

☐ longitudinal	종적인 (무엇의 장기적인 변화 과정을 다룬)
☐ contract	(병에) 걸리다
☐ chronic	만성의
☐ debilitating	쇠약하게 하는
☐ invariably	변함[예외]없이, 언제나
☐ prolonged	오래 계속되는, 장기적인
☐ neurological	신경학적인, 신경의
☐ misfit	부적응자
☐ casualty	피해자

09

☐ assumption	가정
☐ derive	얻다, 끌어내다
☐ individualist	개인주의자(의)
☐ collectivist	집단주의자(의)
☐ orientation	성향

☐ tendency	경향
☐ conservation	보존, 보호
☐ value orientation	가치 지향
☐ et al.	(특히 이름들 뒤에 써서) 외, 등
☐ endorse	지지하다
☐ self-transcendent	자기초월적인
☐ inaction	무대책, 무대응

10

☐ pest	해충
☐ gnat	각다귀, 모기
☐ cucumber beetle	넓적다리잎벌레
☐ codling moth	코들링나방
☐ nocturnal	야행성의
☐ yield	수확량
☐ exterminate	몰살하다, 근절하다, 퇴치하다
☐ drastic	극단적인, 급격한

결국엔 성정혜 영어 하프모의고사
기적사 DAY 15 핵심어휘

01

☐ sedulous	근면한, 정성을 다하는
☐ industrious	부지런한, 근면한
☐ sensual	관능적인, 감각론의
☐ sensible	현명한, 합리적인
☐ complicated	복잡한

02

☐ rule out	배재하다
☐ initiate	시작하다
☐ solicit	부탁하다
☐ exclude	제외하다, 배제하다
☐ leak	새어나오다

03

☐ settle down	정착하다, 문제를 해결하다, 감정을 차분하게 하다
☐ carry out	이행하다
☐ set store by	중시하다
☐ seep out	새어 나오다

04

☐ cut corners	절약했다
☐ a long day	고단한 날
☐ take a break	휴식하다
☐ a soap opera	연속극
☐ stack the deck	부정한 방법을 쓰다
☐ take the French leave	무단으로 결석하다
☐ lead a dog's life	비참하게 살다

05

☐ embarrassment	당황, 곤란
☐ flat	바람 빠진[펑크 난] 타이어
☐ plan on	~할 계획이다

08

☐ involve	포함하다, 수반하다
☐ the way (that)	~하는 방법, 처럼, 이므로
☐ chunk	덩어리로 나누기; 덩어리
☐ articulate	또렷이 말하다, 발음하다
☐ sense group	의미 단위

09

☐ adopt	채택하다, 차용하다
☐ individualistic	개인주의의
☐ qualitatively	질적으로
☐ distance	관여[개입]하지 않게 하다
☐ interdependent	상호 의존의

connotation	함축(적 의미)
perceive	인지[인식]하다, 여기다

10

tuck	밀어 넣다, 집어넣다
pungent	(맛·냄새가) 톡 쏘는 듯한 [몹시 자극적인]
succumb	굴복하다
purported	(사실이 아닐지도 모르지만) …라고 알려진
property	속성, 특성
epilepsy	간질
persist	계속되다, 지속하다
discreetly	신중하게, 사려 깊게
curative	치유력이 있는
groundless	근거 없는

결국엔 성정혜 영어 하프모의고사
기적사 DAY 16 핵심어휘

01

ethical	윤리적인
biotechnology	생명 공학
key	중요한, 주요한, 핵심적인, 필수적인
incidental	우연한, 부차적인, 간접적인
interactive	상호적인
popular	인기 있는, 유명한

02

plasticity	유연성, 적응성
accuracy	정확성
systemicity	체계성, 조직성
obstruction	방해물, 장애물
suppleness	유순함, 유연함

03

signature	서명
contract	계약
remark	언급하다
genuine	진짜의, 진실된
essential	필수의, 본질적인
reciprocal	상호 간의, 상응하는
verbal	구두의, 말의

04

rip off	바가지를 씌우다

05

tongue	혀
twist	구부리다, 꼬다, 비틀다
amusement park	놀이공원

06

foreman	현장 주임, 감독
wound	부상
shard	파편
penetrate	관통하다
abdomen	복부, 배
load A into B	A를 B에 싣다
hopper	개저선

08

sociologist	사회학자
pious	독실한
orthodox	정통파의
religious	종교적인, 독실한
supervision	감독
conception	개념
retain	유지하다
doctrinaire	교조적인
take trouble	수고하다, 수고를 아끼지 않다

09

☐ rapidly	빠르게
☐ satisfy	만족하다
☐ cut down	베다
☐ consequence	결과
☐ destruction	파괴
☐ Industrialized country	선진국
☐ be covered with	덮여있다

10

☐ adopt	입양하다
☐ select	선택하다
☐ adoption agency	입양기관
☐ assist	도와주다
☐ disability	장애
☐ abuse	학대하다
☐ neglect	무시하다, 방임하다
☐ prospective	장래의
☐ fee	요금
☐ foster	아이를 맡아 기르다
☐ domestic	국내의

결국엔 성정해 영어 하프모의고사
기적사 DAY 17 핵심어휘

01

☐ vigilant	경계하는, 방심하지 않는
☐ stormy	폭풍우의, 사나운 날씨의
☐ unsure	불확실한
☐ alert	방심하지 않는, 기민한
☐ popular	인기 있는, 유명한
☐ null	가치 없는

02

☐ violation	위반, 침해
☐ willingly	기꺼이
☐ abandon	포기하다, 버리다
☐ hegemonistic	패권주의의
☐ ambition	야심
☐ infringement	위반, 위배
☐ vulnerability	약점이 있음, 취약성
☐ suppleness	유순한, 유연함
☐ viability	생존력, 실행 가능성

03

☐ cautious	신중한, 조심스러운, 주의를 기울이는
☐ contamination	오염
☐ verbal	구두의, 말의
☐ unsafe	위험한, 불안한
☐ unwitting	모르는, 무의식적인

04

☐ over-the-counter	처방전 없이 살 수 있는
☐ a rip-off	바가지
☐ side effect	부작용
☐ hue and cry	비난의 목소리
☐ a dark horse	유력한 경쟁 상대
☐ a shot in the dark	근거 없는 짐작
☐ chalk and cheese	전혀 관계없는 것

05

☐ stable	안정된, 안정적인
☐ chaos	혼돈, 혼란
☐ entrench	단단히 자리 잡게 하다
☐ constructive	건설적인
☐ unknown	알려지지 않은, 무명의
☐ territory	영역, 영토, 지역

06

☐ harsh	가혹한, 냉혹한

☐ seabird	바닷새
☐ ecological	생태계의
☐ population	개체군, 인구
☐ gone	사라진, 떠난, 끝난

08

☐ enterprise	사업, 기업
☐ be dedicated to	…에 전념하다
☐ promulgation	공표, 선포
☐ doctrine	교리, 주의, 원칙
☐ integral	필수의
☐ succeed	뒤를 잇다, 승계하다
☐ in conjunction with	…와 함께
☐ contribution	기여
☐ pinpoint	정확히 기술[묘사]하다
☐ disregard	무시하다
☐ distinguish	구별하다, 구분하다

09

☐ cost-effective	비용 효율적인
☐ accord	협정
☐ deforestation	삼림 벌채[파괴]
☐ involve	관련[연루]시키다
☐ efficiency	효율성
☐ inform	알리다, 통지하다
☐ conservation	보존, 보호
☐ combat	(방지하기 위해) 싸우다, (좋지 않은 일의 발생이나 악화를) 방지하다
☐ incentive	장려금, 지원금
☐ awareness	인식

10

☐ outgoing	외향적인, 사교적인
☐ introspective	내성적인
☐ Caucasian	백인
☐ embrace	받아들이다, 수용하다

기적사 DAY 18 핵심어휘

01

☐ tussle	난투, 몸싸움
☐ raucous	시끄러운, 소란스러운
☐ interactive	상호적인
☐ uproarious	시끄러운, 소란한
☐ flamboyant	타는 듯한, 현란한
☐ extended	확장된

02

☐ embrace	포용하다
☐ vulnerability	상처받기 쉬움, 취약함
☐ infringement	위반, 침해
☐ weakness	약함, 약점
☐ obstruction	방해물, 장애물
☐ viability	생존력, 실행 가능성

03

☐ regardless of	~에 관계없이
☐ vulnerable	취약한
☐ reciprocal	상호 간의, 상응하는
☐ constant	일정한, 지속적인, 불변의
☐ splendid	화려한, 멋진

04

☐ under fire	공격을 받다
☐ sour grapes	패배를 인정하지 않고 오기를 부리다
☐ cool as a cucumber	침착한
☐ in a nutshell	간단히 말하자면
☐ an apple of discord	분쟁의 화두
☐ behind the eight ball	곤경에 빠진

05

☐ pajamas	잠옷, 파자마
☐ determined	단호한, 단단히 결심한
☐ crumple	구기다

06

☐ gifted	재능이 있는
☐ diploma	졸업장, 수료증
☐ credit	학점, 신용

08

☐ encounter	접하다, 마주치다
☐ illumination	깨달음
☐ sacrifice	제물, 희생
☐ ritual	의식
☐ substantiate	입증하다
☐ ethnographic	민족지적인, 민족학상의
☐ deliver	[…을] 잘 해내다, 기대에 부응하다
☐ intensify	정도를 더하다, 격렬해지다
☐ watchful	감시하는

09

☐ community service	사회[지역]봉사
☐ property	부동산, 토지
☐ prosecutor	검사
☐ probation	보호 관찰
☐ arborist	수목 재배가
☐ authority	당국, 권위자
☐ defendant	피고
☐ scenic	경치가 좋은
☐ deck	덱(집 후면에 마루처럼 달아내어 앉아서 쉴 수 있게 만들어 놓은 곳)
☐ attorney	변호사

10

☐ requirement	(필수) 요건, 필요조건
☐ domestically	국내적으로
☐ face	직면하다, 만나다
☐ lenient	관대한
☐ rigid	엄격한, 융통성 없는
☐ stringent	엄중한, 엄격한
☐ tight	엄격한, 꽉 끼는

결국엔 성정혜 영어 하프모의고사
기적사 DAY 19 핵심어휘

01

☐ impending	임박한, 곧 닥칠
☐ meteorological	기상의, 기상학의
☐ imminent	임박한, 일촉즉발의
☐ incidental	우연한, 부차적인, 간접적인
☐ constant	불변의, 지속적인
☐ splendid	화려한, 멋진

02

☐ enthusiasm	열정
☐ eagerness	열의, 열심
☐ empathy	감정이입
☐ anguish	격통
☐ ardor	열정, 열의, 정열
☐ systemicity	체계성, 조직성

03

☐ hollow	속이 빈
☐ essential	필수의, 본질적인
☐ watertight	방수의
☐ neurological	신경학상의

04

☐ all the way	온 힘을 다해, 줄곧
☐ like water off a duck's back	아무 효과 없는
☐ goose bumps	소름
☐ keep an eye on	~을 관찰하다
☐ in on time	순식간에
☐ the apple of one's eye	매우 소중한 물건
☐ stand up for	~의 편을 들다
☐ at all costs	큰 희생을 치르는 한이 있어도 (반드시)
☐ like a chicken with its head off	정신없이
☐ stand up against	~에 맞서 저항하다

05

☐ school	떼, 무리, 유파, 학교
☐ split	나뉘다, 분열되다
☐ regroup	재편성하다, 재정비하다
☐ herd	떼
☐ stripe	줄무늬

06

☐ comparative	비교적, 상대적인
☐ strike	타격을 주다
☐ refuge	피난(처), 피신(처)
☐ surviving	살아남은

08

☐ tribal	부족의
☐ expectancy	기대
☐ (or) rather	더 정확히 말하면
☐ reciprocate	보답하다, 응답하다, 화답하다
☐ mana	권위, 위광
☐ prestige	위신
☐ derive	끌어내다, 얻다

09

☐ drought	가뭄
☐ thin	(수가) 줄어들다 [줄어들게 하다], 솎다
☐ endure	견디다, 참다
☐ dense	빽빽한, 밀집한
☐ convert	전환시키다
☐ susceptible	민감한, 예민한

10

☐ multitude	다수
☐ arise	생기다, 발생하다
☐ grief	큰 슬픔, 비통
☐ trigger	유발하다, 촉발하다
☐ turbulent	격동의
☐ spouse	배우자

결국엔 성정혜 영어 하프모의고사
기적사 DAY 20 핵심어휘

01

☐ consecutive	연속적인, 연속되는
☐ deserted	버려진, 사람이 살지 않는
☐ archaeological	고고학의
☐ successive	연속적인, 연이은
☐ key	주요한, 중요한

02

☐ apparent	분명한, 명백한
☐ indolence	게으름, 나태
☐ keenly	날카롭게, 강렬하게
☐ alert	기민한; 경계
☐ idleness	게으름, 나태
☐ determinism	결정론
☐ transformation	변화, 변혁
☐ accuracy	정확성

03

☐ continuous	연속적인, 지속적인
☐ isolated	고립된
☐ hollow	속이 빈
☐ genuine	진짜의, 진실된
☐ geological	지질학의

04

☐ sacrifice	희생하다
☐ meaningless	의미가 없는, 무익한
☐ up a tree	곤경에 빠져
☐ six feet under	죽은
☐ for a song	헐값에
☐ on cloud nine	아주 행복한
☐ in the doghouse	어려움에 처한
☐ a turkey shoot	방어가 힘든 쉬운 일
☐ born with a silver spoon in one's mouth	부유하게 태어난
☐ at the eleventh hour	최후의 순간에

05

☐ opportunity	기회
☐ plentiful	풍부한
☐ discrimination	차별

06

☐ macaque	마카크(아프리카·아시아산 원숭이의 하나)
☐ hit upon	~을 생각해내다
☐ sweet potato	고구마

08

☐ overstate	과장하다
☐ assemblage	집합, 모임
☐ factual	사실에 입각한
☐ empirical	경험에 따른, 실증적인
☐ bent	성향, 취향

☐ interpretation	설명, 해석
☐ hierarchy	계층, 계급
☐ aborigine	원주민
☐ methodology	방법론
☐ correspondence	관련성, 연관성
☐ insistence	주장
☐ unity	통일성, 일치
☐ phenomenon	현상
☐ substantial	상당한
☐ contribution	기여, 공헌

09

☐ clear cutting	개벌(완전히 베어냄)
☐ pose	야기하다
☐ pine marten	소나무 담비
☐ caribou	카리부(북미산 순록) (pl. caribou)
☐ interfere	방해하다
☐ seedling	묘목
☐ body of water	물줄기, 수역
☐ forester	삼림 감독관, 수목 관리원
☐ mimic	모방하다, 흉내를 내다
☐ disturbance	교란, 소동
☐ infestation	침략, 침입
☐ sustainable	지속 가능한

10

☐ foster	위탁…
☐ extensive	광범위한
☐ abuse	학대
☐ clearance	(깨끗이) 치우기, (방해물 등의) 제거, 일소
☐ well-off	부유한, 유복한
☐ approval	승인
☐ evaluation	평가
☐ picture	(전반적인) 상황
☐ evaluate	평가하다
☐ adequate	충분한, 적절한

결국엔 성정혜 영어 하프모의고사
기적사 DAY 21 핵심어휘

01

rationalization	합리화
self-deception	자기기만
cheat	속이다, 기만하다
harshly	엄하게
leniently	관대하게
honestly	정직하게
thankfully	고맙게도, 다행히도

02

responsibility	책임, 의무
take over	인수하다
take down	(이야기 등을) 적어두다, (건물 등을) 헐어버리다
take on	(책임을) 지다, (색채 등을) 나타내다, (일 등을) 떠맡다, ~을 고용하다
take off	이륙하다, (옷을) 벗다

03

iron out	해결하다
conceive	생각하다, 임신하다
review	검토하다, 비평하다
solve	해결하다
pose	포즈를 취하다, 제기하다, 주장하다

04

announcement	발표, 소식
anniversary	기념일
compatible	(사람이) 사이좋게 지낼 수 있는, (사물이) 양립할 수 있는

courtship	(결혼 전의) 교제 (기간)
be up to	~에 달려 있다
hang about with	~와 많은 시간을 보내다, ~와 만나다(사귀다)

05

coral	산호, 산호초
foundation	기반, 토대, 설립
ecosystem	생태계
fishing net	고기잡이 그물, 어망

08

likelihood	가능성, 희망
qualification	자격 조건
pleasant	호감이 가는, 상냥한
candidate	지원자, 후보자
ingratiate	마음에 들게 하다, 환심을 사다
charm	매혹하다

09

carve out	베어내다, 잘라내다
stretch	(연속된) 길, 거리, 범위, 일련의 기간
so-called	이른바
course	수업, 과정
scratch	긁다, 할퀴다
scramble	앞을 다투다, 고생하며 나아가다

10

passage	통과, 통로, 복도
womanhood	여성
altar	제단
bouquet	부케, 꽃다발
elaborate	정교한, 정성 들인

기적사 DAY 22 핵심어휘

01

long face	우울한 얼굴, 슬픈 표정
honest	정직한
blue	파란('우울한'의 경우는 'feel blue'라고 표현한다)
sluggish	느린, 부진한, 게으른

02

accompany	동행하다, 반주하다
annihilate	전멸시키다, 무효로 하다
take on	(책임을) 지다, (색채 등을) 나타내다, (일 등을) 떠맡다, ~을 고용하다
take off	이륙하다, (옷을) 벗다

03

referendum	국민투표
abrogate	폐지하다, 철폐하다
administer	관리하다, 집행하다
benefit	도움이 되다
repeal	폐지하다, 철회하다
pose	포즈를 취하다, 제기하다, 주장하다

04

a real McCoy	진짜배기
a walk of life	계층
a wet blanket	분위기를 깨는 사람
an act of God	천재지변

05

file away	~을 정리해 놓다

08

portray	보여주다, 나타내다
candidate	지원자, 후보자
reflect	나타내다, 반영하다
apply for	…에 지원하다
position	직책, 일자리
obedient	순종적인, 복종하는
dedicated	헌신적인, 전념하는
when it comes to	…에 관한 한

09

scrub	(보통 비눗물과 솔로) 문질러 씻다[청소하다]
mop	(대걸레로) 닦다
gig	(특히 임시로 하는) 일[직장]
incongruous	(특정한 상황에서는) 어울리지 않는[이상한]
remark upon	…에 관한 의견을 말하다[발언하다]
dissect	해부[분석]하다
less than	조금도[결코] …아닌, …이라고는 (도저히) 말할 수 없는
prestige	선망을 얻는, 명망 있는; 위신, 명망
set aside	(다시 필요할 때까지) ~을 한쪽으로 치워 놓다
admit	인정하다
broke	무일푼의, 빈털터리의, 파산한
originality	독창성
overestimate	과대평가하다

10

former	전자
latter	후자
coming-of-age ceremony	성인식
marriageable	혼인하기에 알맞은

☐ chignon	쪽, 시뇽(뒤로 모아 틀어 올린 머리 모양)
☐ in place	제자리에
☐ rod	(목재·금속·유리 소재의 기다란) 막대
☐ yin	음
☐ yang	양

결국엔 성정혜 영어 하프모의고사
기적사 DAY 23 핵심어휘

01

☐ firmly	단호하게
☐ harshly	엄하게, 거칠게
☐ audaciously	대담하게, 호기롭게, 넉살 좋게
☐ assiduously	근면하게, 부지런하게
☐ adamantly	단호하게

02

☐ adjust	조절하다, 순응하다, 조정하다
☐ admire	존경하다, 감탄하다
☐ take over	인수하다
☐ take off	이륙하다; (옷을) 벗다, ~을 데려가다

03

☐ adapt	적응하다, 조정하다
☐ readily	쉽게, 기꺼이
☐ acclimate	순응하다
☐ adopt	채택하다, 입양하다
☐ solve	해결하다
☐ pose	포즈를 취하다, 제기하다, 주장하다

04

☐ double date	두 커플이 함께하는 데이트

☐ a blind date	소개팅
☐ a pipe dream	허황된 상상
☐ monkey business	수상한 일

05

☐ solar	태양의
☐ surface	표면, 외관
☐ radiation	방사선, 복사
☐ emit	내뿜다, 방출하다
☐ vaporize	증발시키다

08

☐ novel	(이전에 볼 수 없었던) 새로운
☐ institution	기관, 협회
☐ caveman	원시인
☐ Civil War	(미국의) 남북전쟁
☐ ancestor	조상
☐ folk	사람들, 가족, 친척
☐ serf	농노
☐ likely	아마
☐ workforce	노동 인구, 총노동력
☐ enormous	거대한, 매우 큰
☐ pork belly	삼겹살
☐ rise (up)	(건물이) 세워지다
☐ statistically	통계학적으로
☐ forebear	선조

09

☐ well-documented	문서[기록]에 의해 충분히 입증된
☐ clerk	점원, 직원
☐ paste	(풀로) 붙이다
☐ boot polish	구두약
☐ shilling	실링(영국에서 1971년까지 사용되던 주화)
☐ equivalent	(가치·의미·중요도 등이) 동등한[맞먹는]
☐ recall	상기하다, 기억하다, 떠올리다

□ alongside	함께, 나란히
□ show … around	…에게 (~을) 둘러보도록 안내하다 [구경시켜 주다]
□ biographer	전기 작가
□ take the liberty of ~ing	제멋대로[무단으로, 실례를 무릅쓰고] …하다
□ set out on	…에 착수[시작]하다
□ boot polisher	구두닦이

10

□ indigenous	토착의, 원산의
□ mark	기념하다, 축하하다
□ coming of age	성인, 성년
□ initiation	의식, 의례
□ bullet ant	총알개미 (독개미의 일종)
□ sedate	(진정제로) 진정시키다, 안정시키다
□ solution	용액
□ weave	짜다, 엮다
□ demonstrate	보여주다, 입증하다
□ manhood	(남자) 성인[어른] (인 상태·기간)
□ cry out	비명을 지르다
□ span	기간, 시간
□ rite of passage	통과의례

결국엔 성정혜 영어 하프모의고사
기적사 DAY 24 핵심어휘

01

□ ambivalent	상반되는
□ adept	능숙한
□ lenient	관대한
□ odd	이상한

02

□ readiness	기꺼이 하려는 상태, 준비가 되어 있음
□ reform bill	개혁안
□ appease	달래다, 진정시키다
□ take down	(이야기 등을) 적어두다, (건물 등을) 헐어버리다
□ take off	이륙하다, (옷을) 벗다
□ adopt	채택하다, 입양하다

03

□ administer	관리하다, 운영하다
□ adjust	조절하다, 순응하다, 조정하다
□ review	검토하다, 비평하다
□ apologize	사과하다, 용서를 구하다
□ host	관리하다

04

□ protection	보호
□ environmentally-friendly	환경친화적인, 환경을 해치지 않는
□ preserve	보존하다, 보호하다
□ cut down on	줄이다
□ give in to	~에 패배를 인정하다
□ zero in on	~에 집중하다
□ boil down to	결국 ~으로 요약되다
□ catch up with	~을 따라잡다
□ drop out of	~을 중도에 그만두다

05

□ characteristic	특징; 특유의
□ deep-rooted	깊이 뿌리박힌
□ subgroup	하위집단, 소집단
□ resistant	저항하는
□ alteration	변화, 개조
□ inherent	본래의, 타고난, 선천적인

08

☐ refer to	지칭하다, 나타내다
☐ personality	개성, 성격
☐ overtime	초과[시간 외] 근무, 잔업, 야근
☐ on the dot	정각에
☐ socialize	어울리다, 교제하다
☐ colleague	동료
☐ candidate	지원자, 후보자
☐ fit	어울리다, 조화롭다; 맞는[어울리는] 것
☐ turnover	이직률
☐ process	절차, 과정

09

☐ ambiguous	불명확한, 불분명한, 모호한
☐ nom de plume	필명
☐ sensational	선정적인
☐ subject matter	주제, 소재
☐ deem	여기다, 생각하다
☐ unladylike	숙녀답지 못한, 상스러운
☐ novella	중편 소설
☐ manipulation	조작, 속임수
☐ pseudonym	필명
☐ pen name	필명

10

☐ coming-of-age ritual	성인식
☐ warrior	전사
☐ ritual	의례, 의식
☐ quest	모험 여행, 원정, 탐구[탐색]
☐ scavenger hunt	물건 찾기, 보물찾기
☐ capable	능력 있는
☐ head	가다, 향하다
☐ wilderness	황무지, 황야, 자연
☐ expedition	탐험, 원정, 여행

☐ evoke	이끌어내다, 유발하다, 불러내다
☐ transition	변천[변화]하다
☐ undertake	하다, 착수하다
☐ self-conscious	남의 시선을 의식하는, 자의식이 강한
☐ stand up for	지지하다, 옹호하다
☐ self-reliant	자립적인, 독립적인
☐ self-respecting	자존심이 있는
☐ put up with	참다, 받아들이다
☐ self-satisfied	자기만족에 빠진
☐ get away with	교묘히 모면하다

결국엔 성정혜 영어 하프모의고사 기적사 DAY 25 핵심어휘

01

☐ ambivalent	불확실한, 이중적인, 상반되는
☐ harsh	엄한, 가혹한, 냉혹한
☐ abrasive	벗겨지는, 쓸리는
☐ casual	편한, 가벼운, 형식이 없는

02

☐ retirement	은퇴
☐ bail	(피고를) 보석하다
☐ take down	내리다
☐ take on	흥분하다, 인기를 얻다
☐ afford	~할 여력이 있다

03

☐ appease	달래다, 진정시키다
☐ soothe	달래다, 진정시키다
☐ conceive	생각하다, 임신하다
☐ apologize	사과하다
☐ attempt	시도하다

04

☐ enterprise	기업
☐ once-in-a-lifetime	일생에 단 한 번의
☐ confident	자신 있는, 확신하는
☐ blow it	망치다
☐ call it a day	일과를 마치다
☐ go at full tilt	전력을 다하다
☐ come off second best	2위가 되다
☐ cut from the same cloth	매우 똑같다

05

☐ scenario	시나리오, 각본
☐ commercial	상업의, 상업적인
☐ agriculturalist	농업 경영인

08

☐ cover letter	자기소개서
☐ demand	필요로 하다
☐ application	지원서
☐ committee	위원회
☐ glance through	훑어보다, 휙휙[대충] 읽다
☐ round up	…을 (찾아) 모으다
☐ bunch	(한 무리의) 사람들, 한패
☐ process	과정, 절차
☐ grant	승인하다
☐ stand-by	대기, 예비
☐ innumerable	셀 수 없이 많은, 무수한
☐ golden rule	(행동의) 기본 원리[법칙], 황금률
☐ convenient	편리한

09

☐ bias	편견
☐ reveal	밝히다, 드러내다
☐ sufficient	충분한

☐ assertion	주장
☐ as far as … be concerned	…에 관한 한, …로서는
☐ frustrating	좌절시키는, 절망적인
☐ favor	선호하다
☐ critique	비평[평론]하다
☐ trait	특성
☐ maternal	모성의, 어머니의
☐ defy	저항하다, 반항하다
☐ outnumber	…보다 수가 더 많다, 수적으로 우세하다
☐ counterpart	상대, 대응 관계에 있는 사람[것]
☐ prejudice	편견
☐ to this day	지금[이날]까지도

10

☐ bar mitzvah	바르미츠바(유대교에서 13세가 된 소년의 성인식)
☐ bat mitzvah	바트미츠바(유대교에서 12세가 된 소녀에 대한 성인식)
☐ coming of age ceremony	성인식
☐ respectively	각각
☐ observe	따르다, 준수하다
☐ commandment	계율, 계명
☐ mark	기념[축하]하다
☐ count in	포함시키다, 계산에 넣다
☐ minyan	예배 정족수(유대교의 예배를 하는 데 최저로 필요한 출석자 수)
☐ contact	관계, 연줄
☐ indicate	나타내다, 보여주다
☐ culpability	책임, 질책[비난]받을 일, 유죄성, (범죄, 잘못 등의) 책임을 질 수 있음
☐ responsibility	책임, 의무, 할 일
☐ abide by	따르다, 지키다, …에 따라 행동하다

☐ take part in	참여하다	
☐ maturity	성숙, 성인임	

결국엔 성정혜 영어 하프모의고사
기적사 DAY 26 핵심어휘

01

☐ acknowledge	인정하다
☐ ethical	윤리의, 도덕의
☐ fair	공정한
☐ reasonable	합리적인
☐ greedy	욕심이 많은
☐ altruistic	이타주의적인
☐ weary	지친, 지루한
☐ skeptical	회의적인

02

☐ state	주, 국가, 상태, 정부; 언급하다
☐ enact	시행하다, 제정하다, 입법하다
☐ legislation	법률, 입법 행위
☐ shelve	보류하다
☐ pending	미결의
☐ hasty	서두르는
☐ precise	정확한
☐ divisible	나눌 수 있는

03

☐ sleep on something	~을 하룻밤 자며 생각하다, ~의 결정을 다음날까지 미루다
☐ take a day off	하루 쉬다, 휴가를 내다
☐ take it for granted	당연히 ~일 것이라고 믿다

04

☐ a long face	슬픈 표정, 우울한 얼굴
☐ step into one's shoes	~의 후임이 되다
☐ jump on the bandwagon	시류에 편승하다
☐ play a good hand	멋진 수를 쓰다

05

☐ border	국경
☐ prompt	촉발하다, 유도하다
☐ acting	대행의
☐ interior minister	내무장관
☐ forces	군대
☐ artillery	대포

08

☐ dismally	우울하게, 음울하게; 쓸쓸하게
☐ unselfishness	이타심
☐ submerge	물속에 가라앉히다, 보이지 않게 하다, 매몰시키다
☐ realism	현실주의
☐ ritualistic	의례적인, 관습적인
☐ fortitude	용기, 인내
☐ conservative	보수적인
☐ redeem	되찾다(만회하다), 회복하다
☐ affirmation	확인
☐ sanctity	신성함

09

☐ theatre art	극예술
☐ falter	[용기·결심 등이] 흔들리다, 꺾이다
☐ integrity	성실, 고결
☐ inexhaustible	지칠 줄 모르는
☐ endow	부여하다, 기부하다
☐ exterior	외모, 겉모습, 외부

☐ genuine	진짜의, 성실한
☐ privilege	특권
☐ affluent	부유한, 유복한
☐ upright	정직한, 올바른, 똑바른
☐ competence	능력, 역량

10

☐ interpret	~을 설명하다, 해석하다
☐ hesitant	망설이는, 주저하는
☐ hearten	~을 격려하다, 고무하다
☐ tyranny	가혹행위, 폭정, 횡포
☐ irritable	화를 곧잘 내는
☐ humility	겸손
☐ tremendous	엄청난, 대단한
☐ alliance	동맹, 협력
☐ automatic	반사의, 자동의, 자동적인

결국엔 성정해 영어 하프모의고사
기적사 DAY 27 핵심어휘

01

☐ suspensive	(일시적으로) 중지하는, 미결정의, 확실치 못한
☐ crooked	구부러진, 굽은
☐ eloquent	웅변의, 달변의, 설득력 있는
☐ skeptical	회의적인

02

☐ quarantine	격리하다; 격리
☐ forcibly	힘으로, 강제적으로
☐ suspect	~을 의심하다, (위험·나쁜 일 등을) 알아채다

☐ refuse	거절하다, 사절[사퇴]하다
☐ isolate	~을 떼놓다, 분리하다, 격리하다
☐ competent	유능한
☐ boundless	무한한
☐ dubious	의심하는, 수상쩍은
☐ divisible	나눌 수 있는

03

☐ cope with	처리하다, 대처하다
☐ count on	기대하다, 생각하다, 의지하다, 세다
☐ deal with	처리하다, 다루다
☐ cut at	내려치다
☐ sleep on	~을 하룻밤 자며 생각하다

04

☐ fingernail	손톱
☐ get rid of	~을 없애다
☐ give birth to	~의 원인이 되다
☐ get the better of	~을 넘어서다
☐ keep close tabs on	~을 눈여겨보다

05

☐ homemade	집에서 만든, 손으로 만든
☐ airship	비행선
☐ lawn chair	접이식 의자
☐ weather balloon	기상 관측 기구
☐ a Citizens' Band radio	개인용 주파수대 라디오
☐ pellet gun	공기총
☐ breach	위반하다, 어기다
☐ power line	송전선
☐ blackout	정전

08

☐ cathedral	대성당

☐ obvious	분명한, 명백한, 확실한		☐ constitution	구조
☐ somehow	어떻게든		☐ inborn	선천적인
☐ stake	화형대		☐ acquired	후천적인
☐ hunchback	꼽추, 곱사등이		☐ lay down	정하다
☐ end up	결국 ~이 되다		☐ resistance	저항
☐ spurn	퇴짜 놓다		☐ impulse	자극
☐ despise	경멸하다, 멸시하다		☐ passage	통로, 길
☐ deformity	기형		☐ resultant	결과
☐ disability	장애		☐ inherited	유전의, 계승된
☐ tyrant	폭군, 독재자		☐ genetic	유전적인
☐ sticky	불쾌한, 힘든		☐ accurate	정확한
☐ cynical	냉소적인		☐ upbringing	양육, 훈육
☐ reading	해석, 이해			
☐ freak	괴물, 괴짜			
☐ unattractiveness	매력 없음			
☐ bag	차지하다			
☐ prevail	승리하다, 이기다			

결국엔 성정혜 영어 하프모의고사
기적사 DAY 28 핵심어휘

09

☐ utilize	활용[이용]하다
☐ i.e.	즉
☐ recall	기억
☐ preceding	이전의, 앞선
☐ circumstance	상황, 환경
☐ empathic	감정 이입의
☐ onstage	무대 위에서의, 관객 앞에서의
☐ make-believe	가장, 환상

01

☐ no nonsense	어리석은 짓을 용납하지 않는; 간단명료한
☐ criminal	범죄의; 범인
☐ controversial	논란의, 논쟁의
☐ weary	지친, 지루한
☐ conscientious	양심적인, 성실한

02

☐ dank	눅눅한, 축축한
☐ debatable	논란의 여지가 있는, 논쟁할 수 있는
☐ deciduous	탈락성의, 낙엽성의
☐ precise	정확한
☐ humid	습한, 눅눅한

10

☐ be accustomed to	…에 익숙하다
☐ vicissitude	우여곡절
☐ everyday existence	일상생활
☐ interpret	이해하다, 해석하다
☐ variability	가변성, 변동성
☐ correspondingly	상대적으로, 상응하여
☐ diverse	다른, 다양한
☐ attribute	속성, 자질

03

☐ cut off	중단하다
☐ shut off from	떼어놓다
☐ make a commitment	헌신하다

□ take a day off	하루를 쉬다
□ take time to think about it	그것에 대해 좀 더 생각해 보다

04

□ give somebody a lift	~를 태워주다
□ give somebody a ring	~에게 전화를 하다[걸다]
□ give ~ a shot	~을 시도하다
□ give somebody a hand	~를 도와주다

05

□ theory	이론, 학설
□ statistical	통계의, 통계적인
□ generate	발생시키다, 만들어내다
□ bewildering	혼란스러운
□ precise	정확한, 정밀한
□ debate	논의하다, 토론하다

08

□ sibling	형제자매
□ domineering	고압적인, 지배하려 드는
□ figure	인물
□ allegedly	주장한[전해진] 바에 의하면
□ abusive	폭력적인, 학대하는
□ make ends meet	겨우 먹고 살 만큼 벌다
□ solace	위안, 위로
□ follow suit	선례를 따르다, 남을 흉내 내다
□ reportedly	알려진 바에 따르면

09

□ bring up	양육하다, 기르다
□ immerse	몰두하게 하다
□ pursue	추구하다

□ adopt	쓰다, 채택하다
□ stage name	(배우의) 예명
□ method actor	매서드 배우(자신이 연기할 배역의 생활과 감정을 실생활에서 직접 경험하도록 하는 연기법으로 연기하는 배우), 스타니 슬라프스키 방식으로 연기하는 배우

10

□ virtue	미덕, 덕
□ trait	특성
□ deem	생각하다, 여기다
□ compassion	연민, 동정심
□ integrity	고결함, 정직함
□ obligation	의무
□ one way or another	어떻게 해서든, 어느 쪽이든지
□ perspective	관점
□ holy grail	성배
□ examine	점검하다, 조사하다
□ fundamental	근본적인, 기초적인
□ good	선(善)

기적사 DAY 29 핵심어휘

01

□ debatable	논란의 여지가 있는, 논쟁할 수 있는
□ altruistic	이타주의적인
□ meticulous	세심한, 꼼꼼한, 소심한
□ humid	눅눅한, 습한

02

□ decrepit	노쇠한, 노후한

☐ eloquent	웅변의, 달변의, 설득력 있는
☐ hasty	서두르는
☐ discreet	신중한, 분별력 있는, 사려 깊은
☐ impotent	노쇠한, 무력한

03

☐ go through	겪다, 경험하다
☐ hardship	고난
☐ get above	분수를 넘다, 자만하다, 우쭐하다
☐ take a day off	하루를 쉬다
☐ pass though	경험하다
☐ hand over	인계하다, ~을 양도하다, 양보하다

04

☐ have a say in	~에 발언권이 있다
☐ have a soft spot for	~에 약하다
☐ have had enough of	~에 질리다
☐ have the nerve to do	~하는 용기가 있다

05

☐ institution	기관
☐ in accordance with	~에 따라서
☐ profound	심오한
☐ overlook	간과하다
☐ wire	연결하다
☐ drive	이끌다, 몰다

08

☐ expert	숙련된, 전문적인
☐ craft	(공들여) 만들다
☐ tug at one's heartstrings	…의 감정을 뒤흔들다, 심금을 울리다
☐ struggle	힘든 것[일]

☐ longing	갈망, 열망
☐ literally	문자[말] 그대로
☐ most	거의
☐ mouthpiece	대변자
☐ impression	감명, 인상
☐ empathize	공감하다
☐ utopian	이상적인

09

☐ stand the test of time	세월의 시험을 견디다 [오랜 세월에도 불구하고 건재하다]
☐ inward	내면의, 마음속의
☐ undergo	겪다
☐ to the full	최대한도로
☐ aid	보조 기구, 보조물
☐ volume	책
☐ read	읽을거리
☐ autobiography	자서전

10

☐ demonstrate	입증하다, 보여주다
☐ superiority	거만함
☐ vulgarity	상스러움
☐ id	이드(인간의 원시적·본능적 요소가 존재하는 무의식 부분)
☐ defense mechanism	방어 기제
☐ demean	품위를 손상시키다, 비하하다
☐ disparage	폄하하다
☐ inflate	과장하다, 부풀리다
☐ self-worth	자아 존중감, 자부심
☐ treat	대우하다, 취급하다
☐ undesirable	바람직하지 않은
☐ note	주목[주의]하다
☐ intimacy	친밀함
☐ buffer	완충하다

결국엔 성정혜 영어 하프모의고사
기적사 DAY 30 핵심어휘

01

☐ get credit for	~의 공적을 인정받다, ~으로 명성을 얻다
☐ holiness	신성함
☐ goodness	선량함
☐ virtuous	도덕적인, 고결한
☐ greedy	욕심이 많은
☐ frigid	몹시 추운, 냉담한
☐ executive	행정부의
☐ exceptional	예외적인, 특별한, 이례적일 정도로 우수한

02

☐ you know	말하자면, 그러니까
☐ gratuitous	이유 없는, 불필요한, 쓸데없는
☐ pending	미결의
☐ groundless	근거[이유, 까닭] 없는
☐ gregarious	사교적인
☐ hospitable	대접이 좋은

03

☐ keep close tabs on	~을 면밀히 감시하다
☐ emerge	나타나다, 드러나다
☐ postpone	연기하다, 미루다
☐ launch	개시, 출시; 시작하다, 출간하다
☐ worsen	악화되다, 악화시키다
☐ competitive	경쟁을 하는, 경쟁력 있는
☐ look forward to	~를 학수고대하다
☐ have one's eyes on	~에 신경 쓰다, 주시하다
☐ make against	~에게 불리하게 작용하다
☐ sleep on	~을 하룻밤 자며 생각하다

04

☐ go in for	~을 좋아하다
☐ talk big	중요한 회의를 하다
☐ get along with	~와 좋은 관계를 유지하다
☐ speak out	솔직하게 이야기하다
☐ find fault with	~을 비난하다
☐ pass the buck to	~에 책임을 미루다
☐ get away with	모면하다

05

☐ weep	울다, 눈물을 흘리다
☐ ritual	의례, 의식 절차
☐ mourning	애도
☐ myriad	무수한

08

☐ tabloid press	타블로이드신문
☐ cryogenically	극저온으로
☐ preserve	보존하다
☐ persistent	지속적인, 끈질긴
☐ cryonics	인체 냉동 보존술
☐ cremate	화장하다
☐ ash	유골, 유해, 재
☐ inter	매장하다
☐ mausoleum	묘, 능
☐ cemetery	묘지
☐ cryopreserve	저온 보존하다
☐ great	위대한 인물, 명사

09

☐ device	(특정한 결과·효과를 낳는) 방법
☐ utilize	활용[이용]하다
☐ what if	…면 어쩌지 […라면 어떻게 될까]
☐ let's say	예를 들면, 이를테면
☐ appropriate	적절한

10

☐ quite	지극히, 더없이, 완전히
☐ second	(아주) 잠깐
☐ autobiography	자서전
☐ heredity	유전(적 특징)
☐ accumulate	축적시키다
☐ flit	휙 스치다[지나가다]
☐ pedestal	받침대
☐ matrix	행렬, 매트릭스

결국엔 성정혜 영어 하프모의고사
기적사 DAY 31 핵심어휘

01

☐ multilateral	다각적인, 다자간의
☐ sanction	제재
☐ beef up	~을 강화하다, 보강하다
☐ dispense with	~을 생략하다, 없애다, 면제시키다
☐ damp down	~을 줄이다, 끄다
☐ scratch off	~에서 지우다

02

☐ noxious	유독한, 유해한
☐ cocktail	혼합물
☐ soot	그을음, 검댕
☐ foul	더럽히다, 반칙을 범하다
☐ blot out	~을 가리다, 지우다
☐ pore over	~을 자세히 조사하다
☐ cater to	~을 충족시키다
☐ resort to	~에 의지하다

03

☐ hypnotize	~에 최면술을 걸다, ~을 매료하다
☐ trance	최면상태, 비몽사몽
☐ conscious	의식이 있는
☐ loom on	~에 나타나다
☐ lapse into	~에 빠지다
☐ level at	~에 비슷하게 하다
☐ lap against	~에 철썩거리다

04

☐ official looking	공식(공무상)으로 보이는
☐ exceed	넘어서다, 초과하다, 능가하다
☐ be fined for ~	~때문에 벌금을 부과받다
☐ fine	벌금

05

☐ mercy killing	안락사
☐ strict	엄격한, 엄한
☐ condition	조건, 상태
☐ undergo	겪다, 받다
☐ remission	차도, 완화
☐ consult	상담하다, 상의하다

06

☐ garage	차고, 주차장, 차량 정비소 겸 주유소
☐ come to the realization that+절	~을 깨닫다(=come to realize that+절)
☐ gadget	도구, 장치

07

☐ accomplish	해내다, 성취하다
☐ monitor	감시하다, 관찰하다
☐ supervision	감독, 관리
☐ uphold	옹호하다, 유지시키다
☐ diplomatic	외교의

08

☐ underachieve	자기 능력 이하의 성적을 내다
☐ working memory	작동[심리] 기억
☐ primary school	초등학교
☐ impede	방해하다, 지체하다
☐ rarely	드물게; 좀처럼 …않다
☐ inattentive	부주의한, 태만한

09

☐ compelling	설득력 있는, 강력한, 강제적인
☐ serving	1인분
☐ tenfold	10배의
☐ come under	[비판·공격·영향 등을] 받다
☐ reputation	명성, 평판
☐ exaggerate	과장하다
☐ ingest	섭취하다; 수집하다; 받아들이다

10

☐ activation	활동
☐ consciousness	의식
☐ perceptual	지각의
☐ emotional	감정의, 감정적인
☐ capacity	능력
☐ propositional	계획의, 제기하는
☐ symbolic	상징적인

결국엔 성정혜 영어 하프모의고사
기적사 DAY 32 핵심어휘

01

☐ analyze	분석하다
☐ make up with	~와 화해하다
☐ dispense with	~을 생략하다, 없애다, 면제시키다
☐ damp down	~을 줄이다, 끄다
☐ make out	~을 이해하다, 만들어내다

02

☐ blue rock thrush	바다직박구리
☐ inhabit	살다[거주/서식하다]
☐ cater	음식을 공급하다
☐ perpetrate	가해하다
☐ migrate	이동하다, 이주하다
☐ oblige	강요하다

03

☐ pave	(기반을) 닦다, (길을) 열다
☐ loom on	~에 나타나다
☐ mend	~을 개선하다, 고치다
☐ dispatch	~을 파견하다

04

☐ venerable	존경할 만한, 공경할 만한
☐ hit upon	생각이 나다
☐ live up to	~에 따라 사는
☐ look up to	~을 존경하다, 쳐다보다
☐ out of season	철이 지난

05

☐ acquisition	획득, 습득
☐ gather	모으다
☐ refer to	~을 말하다
☐ convert A into B	A를 B로 바꾸다

06

☐ injure	부상을 입히다, 손상시키다
☐ help	(불가산명사) 도움
☐ ingroup	내집단
☐ either	(둘 중) 어느 하나

07

☐ prior to + 목적어	~에 앞서
☐ contractor	계약자
☐ perception	인식
☐ administrator	관리자
☐ costly	비용이 많이 드는

08

☐ working memory	작동[심리] 기억
☐ come up with	(해답·돈 등을) 찾아내다[내놓다]
☐ zero in on	…에 모든 관심[신경]을 집중시키다
☐ involved in	…에 관련된[연루된]
☐ capacity	능력

09

☐ exposure	노출
☐ egg	난자
☐ maturation	성숙
☐ interfere	방해하다, 지장을 주다
☐ endocrine	내분비의, 호르몬의
☐ involve	포함하다, 수반하다
☐ puberty	사춘기
☐ ovulation	배란
☐ infertility	불임
☐ detrimental	해로운
☐ reproduction	생식(작용), 번식
☐ transgenerational	세대를 망라하는
☐ impotence	(남성의) 발기부전, 무기력
☐ erectile dysfunction	발기부전
☐ ejaculation	(남성의) 사정
☐ reproductive	생식[번식]의
☐ disorder	장애

10

☐ consciousness	의식, 자각

☐ divine	신성한
☐ bestow	부여[수여]하다
☐ conceive of ~	~을 상상하다, 마음에 그리다
☐ automaton	기계적으로 행동하는 [로봇 같은] 사람[동물]
☐ kinship	친척 관계, 혈족 관계
☐ spark	(갑자기) 불꽃을 일으키다[발생하다]
☐ bonobo	난쟁이 침팬지
☐ vintage	(어느 해의) 제품, 제작품
☐ systematically	체계적으로, 조직적으로
☐ a raft of	많은
☐ primate	영장류
☐ exclusive	배타적인
☐ a great many	꽤[아주] 많은

결국엔 성정혜 영어 하프모의고사
기적사 DAY 33 핵심어휘

01

☐ beef up	~을 강화하다, 보강하다
☐ make up	~을 구성하다, 화장하다, 차지하다
☐ damp down	~을 줄이다, 끄다
☐ make over	~을 양도하다, 고치다

02

☐ daylight	낮; 햇빛
☐ refrain	자제하다, 삼가다
☐ pore	숙고하다, 응시하다
☐ mediate	중재하다, 조정하다
☐ regard	관련되다, 간주하다

03

☐ immediately	즉시, 바로

☐ consciousness	의식, 인식, 정신
☐ revoke	취소하다, 철회하다
☐ level at	~에 비슷하게 하다
☐ regain	되찾다, 회복하다
☐ lap against	~에 철썩거리다

04

☐ go off the deep end	자제심을 잃다
☐ get to the point	본론을 말하다
☐ get somewhere	성공하다, 효과가 있다
☐ have a chip on one's shoulder	안 좋은 감정을 갖다
☐ get the picture	상황을 이해하다
☐ boss people around	~를 부려 먹다

05

☐ pray for	~을 간절히 바라다, ~을 기원하다
☐ raise	기르다, 올리다
☐ alternate A with B	A와 B를 번갈아 하다 [교대로 하다]
☐ earn one's way	자립하여 살아가다

06

☐ personality	성격, 개성
☐ speak + O(언어)	(언어)를 말하다
☐ diverge	[의견, 성격, 모양 등이] 갈라지다, 달라지다
☐ reveal	드러내다, 밝히다

07

☐ organization	조직, 단체, 기구
☐ ruin	망치다, 파괴하다
☐ avail	활용하다, ~에 도움이 되다
☐ anecdotal	일화의
☐ may well + 동사원형	~하는 것은 당연하다

08

☐ working memory	작동[심리] 기억
☐ chunk	덩어리
☐ determinate	확정적인, 확실한
☐ only too	매우, 아주
☐ well-versed	정통한, 잘하는
☐ acoustic	음향의
☐ penalize	불리하게 만들다
☐ indeterminate	정확히 규정할 수 없는, 불확정한

09

☐ polycarbonate	폴리카보네이트(창문, 렌즈 등에 쓰이는 투명하고 단단한 합성수지)
☐ epoxy	에폭시 수지 (강력 접착제의 일종)
☐ lining	안감, 내벽
☐ curing	경화
☐ epoxy-lined	에폭시 안감 처리된, 내벽에 에폭시가 덧칠된
☐ formula	유아용 유동식
☐ detect	발견하다, 감지하다

10

☐ relatively	상대적으로
☐ conscious	의식하는
☐ grow to 동사원형	(…하게) 되다 [되어가다]
☐ encompass	망라하다, 아우르다, 포함하다
☐ discipline	학과, 과목, 분야
☐ address	다루다
☐ principle	원리
☐ assessment	평가
☐ application	응용, 적용
☐ evaluate	평가하다
☐ husbandry	(낙농·양계 등을 포함하는) 농업, 축산
☐ slaughter	도축

☐ legislation	입법
☐ applicability	적용[응용] 가능성
☐ conduct	수행하다
☐ in terms of	··· 면에서
☐ automation	자동화
☐ variability	가변성, 변동성
☐ doubtable	불확실한, 의심스러운
☐ contribute	기여하다, 공헌하다

기적사 DAY 34 핵심어휘

01

☐ toxic	유독성의
☐ vapour	증기
☐ victim	피해자, 희생자
☐ cancel	취소하다(cancel-canceled[cancelled]-canceled[cancelled])
☐ seep out	새어나오다
☐ exclude	제외하다
☐ scratch off	~에서 지우다

02

☐ critic	비평가
☐ blot out	막다
☐ pore over	자세히 조사하다
☐ cater to	충족시키다
☐ set store by	~을 중시하다

03

☐ sew	바느질하다
☐ sow	뿌리다
☐ loom on	~에 나타나다
☐ lapse into	~에 빠지다

04

☐ apply for	~에 지원하다
☐ insurance	보험
☐ look forward to	~을 기대하다
☐ be capable of	~할 수 있다
☐ deal with	다루다, 대처하다, 대하다
☐ proficient	능숙한, 숙달한
☐ make believe	~한 척하다
☐ make a scene	난동을 피우다
☐ know the ropes	요령을 알다
☐ pull oneself together	기운을 차리다

05

☐ continuing	계속적인, 연속적인
☐ take action	조치를 취하다
☐ revenue	수익

06

☐ relate A to B	A를 B와 관련시키다
☐ face	~을 직면하다, ~을 마주보다
☐ detect	~을 감지하다, 발견하다
☐ rising	봉기, 폭동
☐ rise	상승, 인상

07

☐ diversity	다양성
☐ groupthink	집단 사고
☐ lead to	~로 이어지다
☐ term + 목적어 + 목적격 보어[명사]	~을 ~라고 칭하다
☐ converge	모여들다, 집중되다
☐ come up with	(해답·돈 등을) 내놓다

08

☐ attention deficit hyperactivity disorder	주의력 결핍 과잉 행동 장애(ADHD)
☐ randomize	임의[무작위] 추출하다
☐ control	(실험 결과를) 대조하다, 조사하여 밝히다
☐ trial	실험, 테스트
☐ control group	대조군
☐ hyperactivity	과잉[과다] 활동
☐ inattention	부주의
☐ intervention	개입, 치료, 교육 활동

09

☐ tolerable	허용할 수 있는, 참을 수 있는
☐ intake	섭취
☐ conservative	보수적인, 적게 잡은
☐ ingest	삼키다, 먹다
☐ appreciable	주목할 만한

10

☐ parallel	아주 유사한[병행하는]
☐ brand	낙인을 찍다
☐ lesser	~ 보다 중요하지 않은, 뒤떨어진
☐ automation	기계적으로 행동하는 [로봇 같은] 사람[동물]
☐ rung	(사회·조직 내 서열상의) 단계
☐ apex	정상, 절정
☐ seeming	외견상의, 겉보기의
☐ persist	지속하다
☐ animist	물활론자, 정령 신앙자
☐ spirituality	정신성, 영성
☐ posit	(주장·논의의 근거로 삼기 위해 무엇을) 사실로 상정하다 [받아들이다]
☐ medieval	중세의
☐ stand trial	재판을 받다

☐ misdemeanor	경범죄, 비행
☐ grant	주다, 수여하다
☐ ambivalence	양면 가치, 이중 경향, 모순
☐ point to	암시하다, 가리키다
☐ confront	직면하게 만들다

결국엔 성정해 영어 하프모의고사
기적사 DAY 35 핵심어휘

01

☐ incident	사건
☐ disappearance	실종, 사라짐, 소멸
☐ jetliner	제트 여객기
☐ spur	박차를 가하다
☐ damp down	줄이다, 끄다
☐ supervise	감시하다, 관리하다
☐ dispense with	생략하다, 없애다

02

☐ brutality	잔인함, 무자비, 만행
☐ independence	독립, 자립
☐ jail	투옥하다; 교도소, 감옥
☐ torture	고문하다, 괴롭히다; 고문
☐ resort	의지하다
☐ subtract	빼다, 공제하다
☐ suffer	고통받다
☐ prompt	(대사를) 상기시켜 주다

03

☐ redevelopment	재개발, 부흥, 재건
☐ resident	거주자[주민], 투숙객
☐ suspend	중단하다, 정지하다, 유예하다
☐ terrify	겁나게 하다

☐ emphasize	강조하다
☐ loom	나타나다

04

☐ celebrate	축하하다
☐ commitment	헌신; 약속; 전념
☐ wrap up	마무리 짓다
☐ break the ice	어색한 분위기를 깨다
☐ buy the farm	갑자기 죽다
☐ come a long way	크게 발전하다

05

☐ organization	조직, 기구
☐ impression	인상, 느낌
☐ boundary	경계
☐ polity	정치
☐ correspond with[to]	~와 일치하다

06

☐ peer	또래, 동료
☐ perceive A as B	A를 B로 여기다
☐ competent	능숙한
☐ persist	지속되다, 계속되다
☐ equitable	공평한, 공정한
☐ skilled	능숙한, 숙련된, 노련한

07

☐ attend	참석하다
☐ upside down	거꾸로
☐ hemisphere	반구
☐ backwards	뒤의; 뒷걸음질하는

08

☐ working memory	작동[심리] 기억
☐ critical	중요한; 비판적인
☐ executive	실행하는, 집행상의
☐ initiate	시작하다, 착수시키다

☐ bucket	양동이
☐ day-to-day	(일이) 매일 행해지는, 그날그날의
☐ evaporate	증발하다, 사라지다
☐ tip	(내용물을) 따르다; 기울어지다; 끝부분; 봉사료
☐ drain	(물을) 빼내다, (액체를) 따라 내다

09

☐ controversial	논란이 많은
☐ compound	합성물, 복합물
☐ limelight	각광, 세상의 이목[관심]
☐ readily	손쉽게, 순조롭게
☐ absorb	흡수하다[빨아들이다]
☐ -laden	…이 가득한
☐ till	(상점의) 계산대
☐ call	요구, 요청
☐ detectable	발견할 수 있는, 탐지할 수 있는
☐ confirm	(특히 증거를 들어) 사실임을 보여주다 [확인해 주다]
☐ dose	(어느 정도의) 양, 약간
☐ have yet to 동사원형	아직 ~하지 않았다
☐ regulator	규제[단속] 기관[담당자]
☐ decisive	단호한, 결단력 있는
☐ abate	약화시키다, 줄이다
☐ fortify	(감정·태도를) 강화하다
☐ dissuade	단념시키다, 만류하다
☐ blunt	약화[둔화]시키다
☐ convince	설득하다

10

☐ partake	참가하다
☐ aerial	공중의, 기생(氣生)의
☐ terrestrial	지상의, 육생(陸生)의

☐ ox	소 (pl. oxen)
☐ aye	네, 응, 그럼
☐ viviparous	태생의
☐ quadruped	네발짐승
☐ sophistication	정교, 세련, 복잡함
☐ off the mark	표적을 빗나간, 예상이 틀린
☐ go about	계속 …을 (바삐) 하다

결국엔 성정해 영어 하프모의고사
기적사 DAY 36 핵심어휘

01

☐ mountainous	산악의, 산이 많은
☐ longevity	장수
☐ security	안전
☐ innovation	혁신
☐ loyalty	충성

02

☐ metabolic	물질[신진]대사의
☐ function	기능; 기능하다, 작용하다
☐ analogous	유사한
☐ in (a) … fashion	… 방식으로
☐ master plan	기본 설계[종합 계획]
☐ blueprints	청사진, 계획
☐ delicate	섬세한, 연약한
☐ weird	이상한
☐ similar	유사한, 비슷한
☐ novel	새로운

03

☐ criticize	비판하다
☐ warranty	보증서, 보증
☐ cover	포함하다, 다루다
☐ cast	던지다, 보내다
☐ charge	요금을 물리다

☐ claim	주장하다

04

☐ Speak of the devil	호랑이도 제 말하면 온다
☐ Money makes the mare go	돈이 있으면 귀신도 부린다

08

☐ sympathy	동정심
☐ irrelevant	관련이 없는
☐ morality	도덕성
☐ character	성격, 특성
☐ regardless of	~와 관계없이
☐ ethical	윤리적인, 도덕적인

09

☐ genus	(생물 분류상의) 속 (pl. genera)
☐ pursuit	추적, 추구
☐ distressed	곤궁에 처해 있는, 고민하고 있는
☐ elongate	연장하다
☐ quill	깃, 가시
☐ hitherto	지금까지
☐ simultaneously	동시에, 일제히
☐ solicitude	염려, 근심
☐ internal	내부의
☐ modification	변경
☐ primitive	초기의, 원시 사회의
☐ independent	독립적인, 독립된
☐ bask	쬐다, 일광욕하다

10

☐ conquest	정복
☐ infectious	전염되는, 전염성의
☐ smallpox	천연두
☐ mutation	돌연변이, 변화, 변형
☐ ancestral	조상의

기적사 DAY 37 핵심어휘

01

☐ implementation	이행, 실행
☐ excellence	우수함, 장점
☐ superstition	미신
☐ supervision	감독, 관리
☐ loyalty	충성

02

☐ suitable	적절한, 적합한
☐ malicious	악의 있는, 심술궂은
☐ strict	엄격한, 엄중한
☐ similar	유사한
☐ appropriate	적절한, 적합한

03

☐ claim	주장하다
☐ trespass	침입하다, 침해하다
☐ take over	인수하다, 양도받다
☐ turn out	밝혀지다, 나타나다

04

☐ in season	제철에
☐ bold as brass	뻔뻔스러운
☐ cut and dried	독창성 없는
☐ off the record	비공식적인

08

☐ ground	근거를 두다, 입각하다
☐ scripture	성서, 경전
☐ Quran	쿠란(코란)(= Koran)
☐ lay out	펼쳐 놓다
☐ adultery	간통, 간음
☐ supposedly	추정 상, 아마
☐ divine	신성한
☐ authority	권위

☐ arbitrary	독단적인, 임의적인
☐ as such	(선행하는 명사를 받아) 그것으로서, 그러한 자격[지위, 기능 (등)]에 있어서
☐ code of conduct	행동강령
☐ incentive	자극, 유인, 동기, 이득, 혜택
☐ obey	따르다, 준수하다
☐ commandment	율법, 계명
☐ sensible	분별[양식] 있는, 합리적인
☐ bring up	기르다, 양육하다
☐ abide by	준수하다, 지키다, …에 따라 행동하다

09

☐ vary	다르다, 다양하다
☐ relatively	상대적으로
☐ suitable	적절한, 알맞은
☐ elaborate	정성 들인, 공들인
☐ bear	낳다, 출산하다
☐ young	새끼
☐ viviparity	태생(胎生)
☐ squamate	비늘이 있는
☐ tuatara	큰 도마뱀
☐ retention	보유, 유지
☐ unshelled	껍질을 벗기지 않은
☐ oviduct	난관
☐ placenta	태반 (pl. placentae)
☐ fetus	태아
☐ placental	태반의
☐ extant	현존[잔존]하는

10

☐ infection	전염병; 감염
☐ protozoa parasite	원생 기생충
☐ pregnant	임신한
☐ fetus	(특히 임신 8주 이후의) 태아
☐ miscarriage	유산

delivery	출산
stillbirth	사산
hydrocephalus	뇌수종
convulsion	경련, 경기
disability	장애

go to one's head	자만하다
play it by ear	임기응변으로 대처하다
hold one's tongue	묵묵부답하고 있다
spill the beans	비밀을 폭로하다
live from hand to mouth	겨우 삶을 연명하다

결국엔 성정혜 영어 하프모의고사
기적사 DAY 38 핵심어휘

01

proof	증거, 증명
excellence	우수함, 장점
superstition	미신
innovation	혁신
antipathy	반감

02

specious	그럴듯한, 겉만 번드르르한
novel	새로운
scarce	부족한, 희귀한, 드물게, 적은
stern	엄중한, 강경한
superficial	외관상의, 피상적인, 실체 없는

03

diner	식사 손님
assuage	완화하다
charge	청구하다, 기소하다, 비난하다
withdraw	철수하다, 취소하다, 인출하다
wait on	응대하다, 시중들다

04

find out about	~의 존재를[~임을] 알아채다

08

contemplate	고려하다, 생각하다
relieve	완화하다, 줄이다
repay	갚다, 상환하다
presuppose	상정[추정]하다
universalize	일반화하다, 보편화하다
maxim	행동 원리, 주의, 격언
contradictory	모순되는
in itself	그것 자체가 [본질적으로]
of itself	자연히, 저절로
will	원하다, 좋아하다
whatsoever	전혀, 어떤 종류의 것도
permissible	허용되는, 무방한
false pretense	사실이 아닌 진술, 거짓 진술, 사기
universal law	보편적 법칙
self-defeating	(문제를 해결하기는커녕) 문제를 오히려 키우는[골치 아프게 만드는], 자멸적인

09

case	실정, 사실
capacity	능력
absorb	흡수하다
moisture	수분, 습기
incubate	(알을) 부화하다, 품다
warmth	온기, 따뜻함
utilize	이용하다, 활용하다
vegetation	초목, 식물

☐ earth	땅, 지면, 흙
☐ unborn	아직 태어나지 않은

10

☐ excrete	배설하다, 배출하다
☐ feces	대변
☐ urine	오줌, 소변
☐ carry	(병을) 옮기다
☐ calf	송아지
☐ bacterium	박테리아, 세균 (bacteria의 단수형)
☐ diarrhea	설사
☐ kidney failure	신부전
☐ manure	(동물의 배설물로 만든) 거름[천연 비료]

결국엔 성정혜 영어 하프모의고사
기적사 DAY 39 핵심어휘

01

☐ empathy	감정 이입
☐ anguish	격통
☐ angst	불안, 공포
☐ security	안전

02

☐ dilapidate	황폐케 하다, 파손하다
☐ tactile	촉각의
☐ devastate	황폐시키다
☐ delicate	연약한, 섬세한, 정교한
☐ extend	확장하다, 쭉 뻗다, 연장하다

03

☐ volatile	변덕스러운, 휘발성의
☐ cast	던지다

☐ compete	경쟁하다
☐ counterfeit	위조품을 만들다
☐ commit	약속하다, (범죄를) 저지르다

04

☐ act one's age	나잇값을 하다
☐ go high gear	최고조에 오르다
☐ take it for granted	~을 당연히 받아들이다
☐ take a long chance	운에 맡겨 해보다

08

☐ prescribe	규정하다, 정하다
☐ count as	…이라 간주되다 [간주하다]
☐ realize	실현[달성]하다
☐ attribute A to B	A를 B(사람·시대 등)의 작품[것]이라고 생각하다
☐ seek to 동사원형	~하도록 시도하다
☐ civic	시민의
☐ virtue	덕, 공덕
☐ come away with	(어떤 인상·느낌을) 갖고 떠나다
☐ conception	신념, 이해
☐ antiquated	구식인
☐ laudable	칭찬[감탄]할 만한
☐ far from	전혀[결코] …이 아닌
☐ mere	겨우 …의, (한낱) …에 불과한
☐ artifact	인공 유물, 인공품
☐ appealing	흥미로운, 매력적인
☐ grapple with	…을 해결하려고 노력하다

09

☐ bear	낳다
☐ young	새끼
☐ viviparity	태생(胎生)
☐ live-bearing	태생(胎生)

결국엔 성정혜 영어 하프모의고사
기적사 DAY 40 핵심어휘

☐ incompatible	양립할 수 없는, 공존할 수 없는
☐ disprove	틀렸음을 입증하다
☐ hypothesis	가설
☐ argue	주장하다
☐ retention	보유, 간직
☐ latter	후자
☐ retain	보유하다, 간직하다
☐ burden	부담
☐ contribution	기여, 공헌
☐ offspring	새끼, 자식
☐ evolve	진화[발달]시키다

10

☐ feces	대변, 똥, 배설물
☐ substance	물질, 물체
☐ track	(눈·진흙 등을) 발에 묻혀 들이다
☐ snout	코, 주둥이
☐ cloud	무리, 떼, 집단
☐ -borne	-으로 운반된[전달된]
☐ microbe	미생물
☐ epidemiological	전염병학의
☐ autoimmune	자가면역의
☐ asthma	천식
☐ diversity	다양성
☐ hygiene hypothesis	위생 가설(어렸을 때 먼지, 박테리아 등 전염병을 발생시키는 물질에 노출되지 않으면 면역 체계가 약해져서 알레르기나 천식에 걸릴 가능성이 오히려 커진다는 이론)
☐ immune	면역의
☐ overreact	과잉[과민] 반응을 보이다
☐ carry	옮기다
☐ rich	풍부한
☐ an array of	다수의
☐ salutary	유익한
☐ home remedy	민간요법, 가정 치료법

01

☐ recession	불경기, 불황
☐ budget	예산
☐ longevity	장수
☐ plasticity	가소성, 적응성
☐ heredity	유전, 상속

02

☐ available	이용 가능한
☐ similar	유사한
☐ attainable	달성할 수 있는, 획득할 수 있는, 이룰 수 있는
☐ waterproof	방수의
☐ neurological	신경학상의

03

☐ accuse	고발하다
☐ cover	포함하다
☐ apologize	사과하다
☐ possess	소유하다

04

☐ get the ax	해고당하다
☐ smell a rat	눈치채다
☐ lose the day	패배하다
☐ have a frog in one's throat	목이 쉬다

08

☐ stress	강조하다
☐ fundamental	근본[본질]적인; 필수적인, 핵심적인
☐ entitlement	자격, 권리
☐ righteous	정당한, 당연한, 옳은
☐ rational	합리적인, 이성적인

☐ subject	국민	
☐ independence	독립, 자립	
☐ commonwealth	국가, 공화국, 민주국가	
☐ creation	창조, 발생	
☐ acceptance	수용, 승인	
☐ above all	무엇보다도	

09

☐ geologic	지질학의
☐ therapsid	수궁류
☐ branch off	갈라지다, 나뉘다
☐ split off	분리되다[갈라지다]
☐ branch	가지, 파생물, 하위 범주
☐ successful	번영하는, 번성하는, 성공적인
☐ distantly	먼
☐ extinction	멸종
☐ gigantic	거대한
☐ feathered	깃털이 있는, 깃털로 덮인
☐ petite	자그마한

10

☐ carry	옮기다
☐ fungus	균류, 곰팡이류 (pl. fungi)
☐ zoonotic disease	동물 매개 감염 질병
☐ zoonosis	동물원성(原性) 감염증 (동물로부터 사람에게 전염되는 질병) (pl. zoonoses)
☐ fatal	죽음을 초래하는, 치명적인
☐ estimate	추정하다
☐ hygiene	위생
☐ bovine tuberculosis	소결핵증
☐ bubonic plague	가래톳페스트, 림프절페스트
☐ glanders	마비저(馬鼻疽)

☐ transmit	옮기다
☐ address	다루다; 연설하다

결국엔 성정혜 영어 하프모의고사
기적사 DAY 41 핵심어휘

01

☐ flavor	맛, 풍미
☐ condiment	양념, 향신료
☐ palatable	맛있는, 맛 좋은
☐ dissolvable	분해할 수 있는
☐ potable	마셔도 되는
☐ susceptible	예민한

02

☐ subsidy	보조금[장려금]
☐ demand	수요, 요구; 요구하다
☐ vastly	매우; 광대하게
☐ improve	향상시키다, 개선하다
☐ construction	구조, 건설
☐ financial	재정의, 금전상의
☐ support	지원, 지지; 지지하다
☐ long-term	장기간의
☐ planning	계획, 입안
☐ technical	기술적인, 기술상의
☐ assistance	도움, 원조, 지원
☐ non-restrictive	비 제한적인
☐ policy	정책, 방침

03

☐ utterly	완전히, 아주
☐ adapt	적응하다, 맞추다
☐ overlap	겹치다
☐ equivalent	동등한, 맞먹는
☐ associative	연합의, 결합하기 쉬운
☐ disparate	다른, 공통점이 없는

04

turn off	끄다
vacation	휴가, 방학
decide	결정하다, 결심하다
I might.	그렇게 할지도 몰라요.
miss	놓치다; 그리워하다
leave	남기다; 떠나다

06

tuition	학비
elect	선택하다
academic credit	학점
participant	참가자
traction	견인
admit	입학 허가하다
selective	선택적인, 선택할 수 있는

08

remarkably	두드러지게, 현저하게
engage	관계를 맺다
pique	불쾌하게 하다, 언짢게 하다
go to bat for	~을 도와주다
stick one's neck out	위험을 자초하다, 무모한 짓을 하다
prerequisite	전제 조건

09

white as a sheet	백지장처럼 하얀, 창백한, 핏기가 없는
panic	공황, 극심한 공포
descriptive	묘사하는
nothing more than	~에 불과한, ~에 지나지 않는
convincing	설득력 있는, 확실한
tornado	토네이도; (감정·활동 따위의) 격발, 폭발
in an effort to	~해보려는 노력으로
curb	억제하다, 제한하다

distracting	마음을 산란케 하는
proctor	시험 감독관
desperately	필사적으로
make up for	~에 대해 보상하다, 보충하다
scramble	재빨리 움직이다, 허둥지둥 (간신히) 해내다
analogy	비유, 유사점, 유추
doom	죽음, 파멸, 비운
algebraic	대수의, 대수적인
arithmetic	산수, 연산
geometric	기하학의, 기하학적인

10

track	추적하다
alert	경계 태세, 경계경보
senior	연장자, 고령자
caretaker	경비원, 관리인
lifesaving	생명을 구하는
automatically	자동적으로

결국엔 성정혜 영어 하프모의고사
기적사 DAY 42 핵심어휘

01

palatable	맛있는, 입에 맞는
smooth	부드러운, 매끄러운
bitter	[맛이] 쓴; 격렬한
saline	소금이 든, 염분이 함유된
insipid	맛이 없는
pungent	얼얼하게 매운, 신랄한
delectable	아주 맛있는; 매력이 넘치는

02

mayor	시장

☐ announce	발표하다
☐ provide	제공하다
☐ allowance	비용, 수당, 용돈
☐ approximately	대략
☐ support	지원, 지지; 지지하다
☐ loophole	(법률·계약서 등의 허술한) 구멍
☐ parley	교섭, 협상
☐ backing	지원
☐ rupture	결렬, 불화
☐ endowment	기부

03

☐ adopt	채택하다; 입양하다
☐ democracy	민주주의
☐ ideal	이상; 이상적인
☐ equal	동등한, 동일한
☐ indign	가치 없는, 부당한
☐ lopsided	한쪽으로 치우친, 일방적인, 편파적인
☐ equivalent	동등한
☐ analogous	유사한

04

☐ bruise	멍, 타박상; 멍이 생기다
☐ trip over	…에 발이 걸려 넘어지다
☐ favor	부탁, 호의, 친절
☐ forecast	예측, 예보; 예측하다

06

☐ reasonably	꽤, 제법
☐ earn a living	생활비를 벌다
☐ raise a family	가족을 부양하다
☐ workweek	주당 근무 시간

08

☐ be fond of	~을 좋아하다

☐ network	인적 네트워크[정보망]를 형성하다
☐ get ahead	출세하다, 성공하다
☐ at all	(긍정문) 여하튼, 어쨌든 간에
☐ in the course of	…동안
☐ misreport	틀리게 보도하다, 오보하다
☐ varied	다양한, 갖가지의
☐ aggravate	심화시키다, 악화시키다
☐ attenuate	약하게 하다, [힘·효력·가치 따위]를 줄이다
☐ awaken	경각시키다
☐ slay	죽이다

09

☐ permission	승인
☐ supervisor	감독관
☐ defer	연기하다, 미루다
☐ grant	허락[승인]하다
☐ exceptional	극히 예외적인
☐ deferral	연기
☐ submit	제출하다
☐ no later than	늦어도 …까지
☐ application	신청서
☐ appropriate	적절한
☐ breach	위반
☐ penalty	처벌

10

☐ senior	연장자, 고령자, 노인
☐ assistance	지원, 원조, 보조
☐ population	(특정 범주에 속하는) 인구
☐ considerable	상당한, 많은
☐ elderly	나이가 지긋한; 노인층
☐ have access to	…에게 접근[출입]할 수 있다, …을 면회할 수 있다

caretaker	돌보는 사람, 관리인
professional	전문의, 직업의
day-to-day	일상의, 나날의
automation	자동화
wearable	입을 수 있는, 착용하기 알맞은
accordingly	그에 따라
in a word	다시 말해
hence	그래서, 그러므로

기적사 DAY 43 핵심어휘

01

dissolvable	용해될 수 있는
dissolve	용해시키다, 녹이다
erodible	침식 가능한
resolvable	용해할 수 있는
solidify	굳어지다; 굳히다
vaporizable	기화시킬 수 있는, 증발시킬 수 있는

02

include	포함하다
scheme	계획, 음모
bulletin	고시, 공고
planning	계획, 입안
engagement	약속, 약혼
extemporization	즉흥, 즉석에서 만듦

03

brick	블록, 벽돌
endless	끝없는, 무한한
stack	겹겹이 쌓다, 쌓아 올리다
reverse	~을 뒤집다, 역으로[거꾸로] 하다
separate	분리하다, 떼어놓다

overlap	겹치다
segment	나누다, 구분하다

04

laundry	세탁소; 세탁물
route	경로, 길, 노선
sneeze	재채기하다; 재채기
allergic	알레르기의

06

rely on	~에 의존하다
defend	방어하다, 지키다
on the alert	경계하여
unlucky	불운한
pick out	~을 선택하다
predator	포식자, 육식동물
flee	달아나다
confusion	혼란

08

well established	(성공 등을 통해) 자리를 확실히 잡은
advance	나아가게 하다, 전진시키다
prove	(…임이) 드러나다[판명되다]
fill	(어떤 일자리에 사람을) 채우다
association	협회, 단체

09

dean	학과장, 학장
separate	단독의, 독립된, 개별적인
showing	(사실 따위의) 설명, 표시
extraordinary	특별한, 특수한, 보통이 아닌
justify	정당화하다

☐ herein	여기에(서), 이 문서 [진술/사실]에(서)
☐ immediate	(관계가) 직접적인, 직접 관련이 있는

10

☐ vital sign	바이탈 사인, 활력 징후(사람이 살아 있음을 보여주는 호흡, 체온, 심장 박동 등의 측정치)
☐ be referred to as	~로 불리다
☐ encompass	(많은 것을) 포함[망라]하다, 아우르다
☐ implement	시행하다
☐ vigilant	바짝 경계하는, 조금도 방심하지 않는
☐ prevalent	일반적인[널리 퍼져 있는], 만연한
☐ ignorance	무지, 무식
☐ ambivalent	상반[모순]되는 감정을 가진, 양면적인

결국엔 성정혜 영어 하프모의고사
기적사 DAY 44 핵심어휘

01

☐ purification	정화, 정제
☐ evaporator	증발기
☐ drinkable	마실 수 있는
☐ potable	마셔도 되는
☐ stewable	찔 수 있는
☐ digestible	소화할 수 있는
☐ comestible	먹을 수 있는

02

☐ organization	조직, 단체
☐ provide	제공하다, 공급하다

☐ assistance	도움, 원조, 지원
☐ encourage	장려하다; 격려하다
☐ lazy	게으른
☐ halt	중단, 멈춤
☐ tribute	공물, 헌사
☐ seizure	압수, 몰수
☐ succor	도움, 구제, 원조

03

☐ associative	연상의, 연합의
☐ creativity	창조성, 독창력
☐ poignant	가슴 아픈, 저미는
☐ eradicable	근절할 수 있는
☐ reminiscent	연상시키는, ~을 생각나게 하는
☐ crystallizable	구체화할 수 있는; 결정체를 이룰 수 있는

04

☐ migraine	편두통

06

☐ summarize	요약하다
☐ be supposed to+동사원형	~하기로 되어있다, ~해야 한다
☐ staple	스테이플러로 고정하다
☐ cover sheet	표지

08

☐ adage	격언, 속담
☐ tackle	(곤란한 문제·일 등에) 달라붙다, 착수하다
☐ presence	진출, 출석, 영향력, 입지
☐ advancement	발전, 진보, 출세
☐ strategic	전략적인
☐ purposeful	목적의식이 있는
☐ intentional	의도적인
☐ must	절대로[반드시] 필요한 것

☐ quality	특성, 특질; 품질, 질
☐ quantity	양, 수량
☐ give up	포기하다
☐ in the end	결국, 마침내

09

☐ debate	논의하다, 논쟁하다
☐ abolition	폐지
☐ self-sufficient	자급자족하는, 자립심 있는
☐ argue	주장하다
☐ superficial	표면적인, 깊이 없는, 얄팍한
☐ inauthentic	진짜[진품/정통]가 아닌
☐ assessment	평가
☐ evaluation	평가
☐ appropriate	적합한, 적절한
☐ otherwise	그렇지 않으면

10

☐ shift	변화
☐ adopt	채택하다, 취하다, 쓰다
☐ holistic approach	거시적 접근법
☐ diminish	약화시키다, 줄이다
☐ medicalize	치료하다, 환자로 받아들이다, 의료화하다
☐ productive	생산적인
☐ time-consuming	(많은) 시간이 걸리는
☐ keep somebody company	…의 곁에 있어 주다 [친구가 되어 주다]
☐ burden	짐, 부담

기적사 DAY 45 핵심어휘

01

☐ susceptible	민감한, 예민한
☐ illness	질병, 아픔
☐ dull	둔한, 따분한
☐ nimble	민첩한, 날렵한
☐ feeble	아주 약한, 미미한
☐ impressionable	민감한, 감수성이 풍부한

02

☐ politician	정치가
☐ question	질문하다; 질문, 의문
☐ policy	정책, 방침
☐ compulsory	의무적인, 강제적인, 필수의
☐ tactic	전략, 전술
☐ doctrine	정책, 교리, 학설
☐ edification	교화, 의식 고양
☐ stratagem	책략, 술수

03

☐ disparate	이질적인, 서로 전혀 다른
☐ security analyst	증권 분석가
☐ seely	단순한, 약한
☐ intricate	복잡한, 미묘한
☐ homogeneous	동종의, 동질의
☐ heterogeneous	이질적인, 이종의

04

☐ thirsty	목이 마른; 갈망하는
☐ water fountain	분수식의 물 마시는 곳; 냉수기
☐ hallway	복도; 현관
☐ fee	요금, 수수료
☐ annually	매년

☐ highway	고속도로
☐ run out of	…을 다 써버리다, 다 하다

06

☐ obviously	분명하게
☐ technically	엄밀히 말하면
☐ get one's call through	전화를 연결하다
☐ render	제공하다
☐ courtesy	예의
☐ consideration	배려, 고려

08

☐ beforehand	미리, 사전에
☐ receiving end	받는 쪽, 수신자
☐ check on	(이상이 없는지를) 확인하다[살펴보다]
☐ butter … up	…에게 아부[아첨]를 하다
☐ lean on	기대다, 의지하다
☐ check in with	연락하다
☐ consistently	지속적으로
☐ key	가장 중요한, 핵심적인, 필수적인
☐ spare	(특히 자동차 타이어) 스페어, 여분

09

☐ high-stakes	위험(부담이) 큰
☐ transition	전환, 변화
☐ high stakes	중대한 이해관계
☐ reputation	명성
☐ stake	이해관계
☐ undermine	(토대를) 약화시키다
☐ lose sight of	…을 잃다[잊다], 간과하다
☐ abandon	버리다, 폐기하다, 포기하다

10

☐ concerning	…에 관한[관련된]
☐ uneasy	불안한, 우려되는
☐ maintenance	유지, 보수
☐ rather	상당히, 꽤
☐ exacerbate	악화시키다

결국엔 성정혜 영어 하프모의고사
기적사 DAY 46 핵심어휘

01

☐ prerequisite	전제 조건
☐ fertilization	수정; 다산화, 비옥화
☐ pollination	[식물] 수분 (작용)
☐ essential	아주 중요한, 필수적인
☐ improve	개선하다, 향상시키다
☐ breeding	번식, 사육
☐ crucial	중대한
☐ indispensable	필수적인
☐ requisite	필요한
☐ omnipresent	어디에나 있는, 편재하는

02

☐ object to	~에 반대하다
☐ proposal	제안, 제의; 청혼
☐ faulty	흠 있는
☐ imperative	긴요한, 필수의; 위엄 있는
☐ conforming	순응하는
☐ wrong	잘못된
☐ desirable	바람직한
☐ reasonable	합리적인
☐ deplorable	비참한, 개탄스러운
☐ inconvenient	불편한

03

tentative	잠정적인, 임시의
deteriorate	악화되다, 퇴폐하다
enhance	향상시키다, 강화하다
ameliorate	개선하다; 좋아지다
level	평평하게 하다; 평등하게 하다, 균일화하다
amid	~가운데(중)에, ~의 (한)복판에

04

commitment	약속, 위임

05

serious	심각한
maintain	유지하다
comfortable	편안한, 쾌적한
bathrobe	목욕용 가운

06

abstract	개요, 요약본; 추상적인
reference	참고 (문헌)
authority	근거, 권위, 권한
trust to	~에게 맡기다
repose	다시 놓다
creep in	살며시 접근하다
cautious	신중한, 조심스러운
in illustration	참고로, 예증으로
suffice	충분하다
sensible	인지하고 있는, 분별력 있는, 현명한
hereafter	이후로, 장차
in detail	상세하게
ground A on B	(A를 B에 근거하도록 하다)
scarcely	거의 ~않다, 드물게
adduce	제시하다
apparently	분명히, 명백히
opposite to	~와 반대인

07

alphasyllabic	자음 모음과 관련된
script	문자; 대본
linguist	언어학자
admire	칭송하다
symbolize	상징하다
sophisticated	세련된, 정교한
in tandem with	~와 나란히, ~와 나란히
altogether	모두, 한 번에, 모두 합하여
take over	더 중요해지다, 더 커지다; 인수하다, 인계받다
occur	존재하다, 발견되다, 일어나다

08

commitment	전념, 헌신, 책무
impede	지연시키다, 방해하다
priority	우선 사항
trivial	사소한, 하찮은
unforeseen	예측하지 못한, 뜻밖의
distraction	집중을 방해하는 것, 방해물
get in the way	방해되다

09

predictable	예측할 수 있는
abundance	풍부
fluctuation	변동, 오르내림, 파동
fishery	어장
mackerel	고등어
sustainable	지속 가능한
yield	산출량, 총수익
severely	심각하게
overfish	물고기를 남획하다, 다 잡아 버리다
Antarctic	남극의, 남극 지방
halibut	큰 넙치

deplete	대폭 감소시키다, 고갈시키다

regainable	회복할 수 있는, 되찾을 수 있는

10

enormous	막대한, 거대한, 어마어마한
tactical	작전의, 전술의, 전략적인
take place	(일이) 발생하다, 일어나다
coverage	범위
imperial	제국의
strategic	전략적인
utterly	완전히, 순전히
defeat	패배시키다

03

significant	중대한, 중요한
contribution	기여, 기부
ecology	생태(계), 생태학
conservation	보호, 보존, 관리
rapidly	급속히, 신속하게
deteriorate	악화되다, 더 나빠지다
restore	회복시키다
habitat	서식지
unscathed	다치지 않은, 아무 탈 없는
aggravate	악화시키다, 화나게 하다
obsolesce	쇠퇴하다, 퇴화하다
ameliorative	개량의, 개선적인

결국엔 성정혜 영어 하프모의고사
기적사 DAY 47 핵심어휘

01

legal	법률과 관련된, 합법적인
crucial	중대한, 결정적인
trifling	하찮은, 사소한
intrinsic	고유한, 본질적인
immaterial	중요하지 않은, 무형의
momentous	중요한, 중대한

04

drought	가뭄
savior	구원자
big deal	크거나 중요한 일
black out	정전
showdown	정면 대결
backseat driver	쓸데없이 간섭하는 사람

05

life expectancy	기대 수명

02

faulty	잘못된, 흠이 있는
assumption	가정, 상정
argument	주장, 논의, 논쟁
convincing	설득력 있는
unerring	틀림없는, 정확한
unsound	오류가 있는, 부적절한
impaired	손상된, 제 기능을 못 하는

06

enthusiasm	열성, 열의
motor	운동 (능력)의
misplaced	잘못된
milestone	중요한 단계
grant+목적어[대상]+목적어[사물]	~에게 ~을 부여하다
coordinated	근육의 공동작용에 의한

manipulation	조작, 교묘한 처리
contribute to	~에 기여하다
perceptual	지각의
cognitive	인지의

07

incorporate	포함하다, 통합시키다
put 목적어 to good use	~을 잘 활용하다, ~을 유효하게 이용하다
to one's disadvantage	~에게 불리한
numeracy	산술 능력, 수리 감각

08

distraction	(주의) 집중을 방해하는 것
span	(어떤 일이 지속되는) 기간[시간]
ever-changing	늘 변화하는, 변화무쌍한
priority	우선순위
fall victim to	…의 희생(물)이 되다
swirl	소용돌이치다
deluge	폭우, 범람, 홍수
triviality	사소함, 하찮은 것
weed	잡초, 수초, 수풀
tangent	접선, 옆길
(The) chances are (that…)	아마 …일 것이다; …할 가능성이 충분하다

09

fishery	어장
abundance	풍부
acidification	산성화
reproduction	번식, 생식
stock	군체, 군락; 비축분; 저장
oyster	굴
mussel	홍합

phytoplankton	식물성 플랑크톤
in terms of	… 면에서
biodiversity	생물의 다양성

10

determine	알아내다, 밝히다
end	목표, 목적
means	수단
autocratic	횡포한, 독재의
dictator	독재자
referendum	국민[주민] 투표
psychiatric	정신 의학[질환]의

기적사 DAY 48 핵심어휘

01

soy	콩; 간장
indispensable	필수적인, 없어서는 안 될
petty	사소한, 하찮은
banal	시시한, 따분한
swing	결정적인, 흔들리는
imperative	필수적인, 긴급한

02

reasonable	합리적인, 사리를 아는
sane	사리 분별이 있는, 건전한
consonant	일치하는; 자음(자)
indecent	외설적인, 적절하지 못한
imprudent	현명하지 못한, 경솔한

03

gymnast	체조 선수
be busy ~ing	~하느라 바쁘다

☐ enhance	강화하다, 향상시키다
☐ commercial	상업[광고] 방송; 상업의
☐ fixate	고정[정착]시키다
☐ intensify	강화하다
☐ replenish	다시 채우다, 보충하다
☐ undermine	약화시키다

04

☐ Enough is enough.	계속 이대로 둘 수는 없다 [더 이상은 안 된다].
☐ Now you're talking.	드디어 이야기되네.
☐ Curiosity killed the cat.	많이 알려고 하면 다친다.
☐ You can say that again.	정말 그래.

05

☐ strength	강점
☐ passion	열정
☐ be grounded in	~에 기초를 두다
☐ convergence	집합점, 합류점

06

☐ corresponding	해당하는, 상응하는
☐ pace	(걸음 달리기 움직임의) 속도
☐ posture	자세
☐ engage in	참여하다
☐ isolation	고립
☐ circuitry	(전기) 회로

07

☐ keep -ing	계속해서 ~하다
☐ delay	연기하다
☐ not at all	전혀 ~ 아니다
☐ without regard to	~와 상관없이

08

☐ pile	더미, 무더기
☐ ultimately	결국
☐ sediment	퇴적물, 앙금
☐ fit in	…이 들어갈 공간을 만들다
☐ urgent	긴급한
☐ principle	원칙, 본질
☐ tackle	대처하다, 다루다
☐ get[be] crowded out	밀려 나가다

09

☐ destructive	파괴적인, 해로운
☐ phenomenon	현상
☐ ensnare	(올가미에 걸리듯) 걸려들게[빠지게] 하다
☐ inhabit	서식하다, 살다
☐ salt marsh	(바닷물이 드나드는 해변가의) 해수 소택지
☐ blue crab	꽃게, 바다게
☐ crab pot	게잡이 통발
☐ marsh	습지
☐ buoy	부표
☐ surface	표면, 지면, 수면
☐ detach	분리하다
☐ bait	미끼
☐ deceased	죽은, 사망한

10

☐ abruptly	갑자기
☐ come round	다시 의식을 차리다 [정신이 돌아오다]
☐ jigsaw	조각 그림 맞추기 (퍼즐)
☐ hurl	던지다
☐ bourgeois	(자본주의 사회의) 지배 계급의 구성원, 부르주아
☐ boast	큰소리치다, 허풍 치다, 자랑하다
☐ execute	처형[사형]하다

☐ anarchist	무정부주의자
☐ rip through	…를 거칠게 지나가다
☐ manage to 동사원형	간신히 ~하다
☐ accidentally	뜻하지 않게, 우발적으로

결국엔 성정혜 영어 하프모의고사
기적사 DAY 49 핵심어휘

01

☐ requisite	필요한
☐ neural	신경(계)의
☐ appreciate	평가하다, 인정하다, 인식하다; 가치가 오르다
☐ binding	구속력 있는, 의무적인
☐ fastidious	까다로운, 가리는
☐ incumbent	필요한, 재임 중인
☐ superfluous	필요치 않은, 불필요한

02

☐ racism	인종 차별(주의)
☐ deplorable	개탄스러운
☐ sensitive	민감한, 예민한
☐ punishment	벌, 처벌
☐ haughty	오만한, 거만한
☐ vaunting	자랑하는; 자랑
☐ lamentable	한탄스러운, 통탄할
☐ magnificent	감명 깊은, 훌륭한

03

☐ mitigate	완화시키다, 경감시키다
☐ obviate	제거하다
☐ adverse	부정적인, 불리한
☐ ameliorate	개선하다
☐ provision	준비, 대비; 공급, 제공

☐ refine	개선하다; 정제하다
☐ deform	변형시키다
☐ regress	퇴보하다, 퇴행하다
☐ aggravate	악화시키다; 화나게 하다

04

☐ out of the blue sky	예기치 못하게
☐ in the red	적자 상태인, 적자로
☐ a blue blood	귀족 가문
☐ be short of breath	숨이 차다
☐ a big bug	대단한 인물
☐ at the top of one's lungs	숨이 가쁘다
☐ in the black	흑자 상태인, 흑자로

05

☐ put down	~을 깎아내리다
☐ self-criticism	자기비판

06

☐ demanding	힘든, 벅찬
☐ inspiring	고무적인
☐ unstable	불안정한
☐ affective	정서적인
☐ cite	언급하다
☐ concern	관심사
☐ forefront	중심, 가장 중요한 위치

07

☐ motivate 목적어 to 동사원형	~이 ~하도록 동기를 부여하다
☐ foresee	예견하다
☐ given that	~을 고려하면
☐ get to	동사원형 ~하게 되다
☐ interaction	교류, 상호작용

08

☐ equivalent	상당하는 것, 동등한 것, 등가[등량]물; 동등한, 상당하는
☐ inviting	유혹[매력]적인, 솔깃한
☐ disregard	무시, 묵살
☐ existing	기존의
☐ commitment	약속
☐ workload	업무량
☐ prioritize	우선순위를 매기다
☐ estimate	추산[추정]하다
☐ dash	(급히) 서둘러 가다
☐ burst	(갑자기) 한바탕 …을 함[터뜨림]

09

☐ unreel	실패[얼레]에서 풀다
☐ bristle with	…이 아주 많다 [꽉 차 있다]
☐ bait	미끼를 달다
☐ afloat	뜬
☐ buoy	부표
☐ lure	꾀다, 유혹하다
☐ drown	익사하다
☐ reel	실패에 감다
☐ swordfish	황새치
☐ yellowfin tuna	황다랑어
☐ sink	박다
☐ pickax	곡괭이
☐ haul	(억지로) 끌고 가다[오다]
☐ rip out	찢다, 잡아 뜯다
☐ territory	영토, 영역, (한 국가·통치자가 다스리는) 지역
☐ indiscriminate	무차별적인, 무분별한
☐ sympathetic	동정적인, 동정하는
☐ scrupulous	세심한, 꼼꼼한, 양심적인
☐ indifferent	무관심한, 그저 그런

10

☐ jihadi	지하드(jihad)의 전사
☐ eliminate	제거하다
☐ defeat	물리치다, 이기다
☐ trace	추적하다, 추적하여 밝혀내다
☐ legitimize	합법화하다, 정당화하다
☐ jihad	(이슬람교에서 종교적·도덕적 법칙을 지키기 위한) 정신적 투쟁
☐ infidel	신앙심 없는 자
☐ advocate	주장하다
☐ persecute	박해하다
☐ unlikely	(일반적인) 예상 밖의
☐ radical	급진적인, 과격한
☐ underscore	강조하다, 분명히 보여주다
☐ militaristic	군국주의
☐ theology	신학
☐ tackle	(해결을 위해) 대처하다, 다루다
☐ vulnerable	취약한, 연약한
☐ lure	꾀다, 유혹하다
☐ discredit	존경심[신임]을 떨어뜨리다, 신빙성을 없애다

결국엔 성정혜 영어 하프모의고사
기적사 DAY 50 핵심어휘

01

☐ omnipresent	어디에나 있는, 편재하는
☐ banal	지극히 평범한, 시시한
☐ sparse	희박한, 드문드문한
☐ peculiar	독특한, 이상한
☐ ubiquitous	어디에나 있는, 아주 흔한

02

☐ be prone to	~하기 쉽다
☐ forgetfulness	잊기 쉬움, 건망증
☐ mildly	다소, 약간; 부드럽게, 온화하게
☐ inconvenient	불편한
☐ cozy	아늑한, 은밀한
☐ sticky	불편한, 끈적거리는
☐ tenacious	집요한, 완강한
☐ apathetic	무관심한, 심드렁한

03

☐ level	(물가, 임금 등이) 안정되다, 평평해지다
☐ spiral	나선형으로 (급속히) 움직이다
☐ equalize	평등하게 하다, 균일하게 하다
☐ consolidate	굳히다, 강화하다
☐ abnormalize	이상하게 하다, 이상 상태로 만들다
☐ differentiate	구별하다, 차별하다

04

☐ diversified investment	분산투자
☐ overcome	극복하다, 이기다
☐ a couch potato	TV를 보며 소파에 앉아 감자를 먹는 게으른 유형의 사람
☐ put all one's eggs in one basket	전 재산을 한 곳에 걸다
☐ lay an egg	손해를 보다
☐ lose heart	실망하다
☐ dead broke	완전히 파산하여, 무일푼이 되어
☐ hit the nail on the head	요점을 정확히 찌르다
☐ keep body and soul together	역경을 극복하고 살아가다

05

☐ turn on	~을 작동시키다
☐ neuron	신경 세포, 뉴런
☐ medial	중간의, 중앙의
☐ orbitofrontal cortex	안와 전두 피질
☐ associate A with B	A를 B와 관련시키다

06

☐ innate	타고난, 선천적인
☐ stand up for	~을 옹호하다
☐ prove	입증하다, 증명하다
☐ charge	돌격하다
☐ proof	증거
☐ handle	다루다, 처리하다

07

☐ insight	통찰력
☐ restructure	재구성하다
☐ get stuck	꼼짝 못 하게 되다
☐ represent	표현하다, 나타내다
☐ claim	주장하다
☐ specific	특정한

08

☐ invest	투자하다
☐ available	이용할[구할] 수 있는
☐ as with	…와 같이
☐ determination	투지, 결정
☐ a great deal	많이, 상당히
☐ framework	틀; 체제

09

☐ overfishing	(어업) 남획
☐ under consideration	고려[생각] 중인
☐ collapse	붕괴
☐ fishery	어장
☐ population	개체 수

☐ in excess of	~을 초과하여, ~이상의[으로]
☐ bay	만(灣)
☐ replenishment	보충, 보급
☐ maturity	성숙
☐ fertile	비옥한, 기름진, 풍부한
☐ fishing ground	어장
☐ extinct	쇠퇴한, 활동을 그친
☐ undergo	겪다, 받다
☐ scallop	가리비
☐ viable	실행 가능한, 성공할 수 있는
☐ remedy	구제 방안
☐ locale	현장, 무대

10

☐ given	…을 고려해 볼 때
☐ mark	특징[성격]짓다
☐ good	(판단·주장 등이) 사리에 닿는, 타당한, 확실한
☐ determine	밝히다, 알아내다
☐ drive	(남을 어떤 상태·행위에) 빠지게[이르게] 하다
☐ for one thing	(여러 가지 이유들 중에서) 우선 한 가지 이유는
☐ from afar	멀리서
☐ erroneous	잘못된
☐ attest	증명[입증]하다
☐ in terms of	… 면에서[…에 관하여]
☐ principle	원리, 원칙, 법칙
☐ subconscious	잠재 의식적인
☐ meaning	의미, 뜻; 목적, 취지
☐ significance	중요성; 의의, 의미

결국엔 성정혜 영어 하프모의고사
기적사 DAY 51 핵심어휘

01

☐ allergic	알레르기가 있는, 알레르기(성)의
☐ affirmative	긍정적인
☐ aloof	냉담한, 초연한
☐ adverse	부정적인, 반대의, 불리한
☐ allusive	암시하는, 넌지시 가리키는

02

☐ currency	통화, (화폐 등의) 유통
☐ fluctuate	요동을 치다
☐ sway	흔들리다
☐ linger	오래 머물다
☐ duplicate	복제하다
☐ depreciate	가치가 떨어지다

03

☐ explanation	설명, 설명서
☐ frivolous	가벼운, 시시한
☐ alternative	대안; 대체 가능한
☐ complex	복잡한
☐ polite	예의 바른
☐ shallow	얕은, 피상적인
☐ inclusive	포괄적인

04

☐ honeymoon	신혼여행; 신혼여행을 하다
☐ amazing	놀라운, 굉장한

05

☐ fundamental	근본적인
☐ element	요소
☐ in the sense	~라는 의미에서

factor	요소
calculation	계산
given	기정사실
assessment	평가
initiative	주도권
anticipate	예상하다
evaluate	평가하다
constantly	지속적으로

06

yawn	하품하다; 하품
catching	전염성이 있는
trigger	촉발하다
empathic	공감(감정이입)할 수 있는
brain imaging	뇌 영상법
contagious	전염성의

08

phase	국면, 양상
species	(생물) 종
alter	바꾸다, 고치다
embryo	배아
descendant	자손, 후손
germline	생식 계열
modification	수정, 변경
human race	인류
weigh in	(논의, 언쟁, 활동 등에) 끼어들다, 관여하다
endorse	지지하다, 보증하다, 홍보하다
alternative	대안, 대체제
proceed	진행하다, 계속해서 ~을 하다

09

surrender	항복하다, 투항하다, 굴복하다
knock out	나가떨어지게 하다
glorify	찬양하다

brink	(벼랑, 강가 등의) 끝
strap	끈
stud	장신구, 장식용 금속 단추
opponent	상대, 반대자
gouge	찌르다
contender	도전자, 경쟁자
collapse	쓰러지다, 붕괴되다, 무너지다

10

a number of	얼마간의, 다수의
force	~를 강요하다, ~하게 만들다
secure	안심하는, 안전한, 확실한
ever-quickening	계속해서 빨라지는
theoretical	이론적인
physics	물리학
atomic	원자의
fission	핵분열. (세포의) 분열
hydrogen	수소
transcend	초월하다
appendix	부록, 부속물
inspire	고무시키다, 영감을 주다
empower	권한을 부여하다

결국엔 성정혜 영어 하프모의고사
기적사 DAY 52 핵심어휘

01

affirmative	긍정적인
mindset	(흔히 바꾸기 힘든) 사고방식[태도]
inspiration	영감; 고무
generation	세대
bleak	암울한, 절망적인

☐ skeptical	회의적인
☐ sanguine	낙관적인, 자신감이 넘치는
☐ misanthropic	사람을 싫어하는

02

☐ sway	흔들다, 동요시키다
☐ manipulation	조작, 속임수
☐ wage	계속하다, 벌이다
☐ induce	설득하다, 유도하다
☐ embellish	장식하다, 꾸미다
☐ relinquish	포기하다, 내주다

03

☐ facial	얼굴의, 안면의
☐ recognition	인식; (공로 등에 대한) 인정
☐ complex	복잡한
☐ lucid	명쾌한, 알기 쉬운
☐ fancy	복잡한, 화려한
☐ artless	꾸밈없는, 소박한
☐ unfussy	복잡하지 않은, 단순한

04

☐ economics	경제학
☐ get hold of	~을 알게[이해하게] 되다
☐ capitalism	자본주의
☐ invisible	보이지 않는, 볼 수 없는
☐ invisible hand	보이지 않는 손 (Adam Smith의 경제학에서)
☐ capital	자본; 자산; 수도; 대문자
☐ catch up with	~을 따라잡다 [따라가다]
☐ get to the point	요점으로 들어가다
☐ cut a fine figure	두각을 보이다
☐ kick the bucket	죽다

☐ get the wrong end of the stick	잘못 이해하다

05

☐ modern	현대의
☐ mark	표시하다
☐ rite of passage	통과의례
☐ onlooker	보는 사람, 구경꾼
☐ be about to 동사원형	막 ~하려고 하다
☐ specialized	전문적인, 전문화된

06

☐ launch	출시하다
☐ emergency	비상사태
☐ option	선택
☐ expertise	전문 기술, 전문 지식
☐ vital	생명 유지와 관련된; 필수적인
☐ proper	적절한

08

☐ eugenicist	우생학자
☐ good stock	좋은 혈통
☐ prestigious	명망 있는, 일류의
☐ thus	(앞서 말한 바를 가리켜) 이렇게, 그렇게
☐ legitimize	정당화하다, 합법화하다
☐ perception	인식
☐ trait	특징, 특성
☐ shiftlessness	무기력
☐ criminality	범죄성
☐ work ethic	직업윤리
☐ inherited	유전된
☐ Nordic	북방 인종의
☐ ancestry	조상, 기원
☐ inherently	본질적으로, 생득적으로
☐ people	민족, 인종

eugenics	우생학
legitimate	정당한, 적법의
academic discipline	학과, 교과
prominent	유명한

09

bar	금(지)하다
sneak in	살짝[몰래] 들어가다
chariot race	전차 경주
keen	간절히 …하고 싶은, …을 열망하는
disguised	변장한
sacred	신성한, 성스러운

10

collective	집단의, 공통의
institution	(확립된) 규칙, 법, 관습
component	(구성) 요소, 부품
organic compound	유기 화합물
undergo	겪다, 받다, 경험하다
undertake	착수하다[하다]
explicit	분명한, 명백한, 명쾌한
antimalarial	말라리아 예방[치료]의
synthetically	합성적으로
bond	결합

결국엔 성정혜 영어 하프모의고사
기적사 DAY 53 핵심어휘

01

aloof	냉담한
pally	친한, 사이가 좋은
overt	명시적인, 공공연한
callous	냉담한

clandestine	비밀리에 하는, 은밀한

02

emission	(빛·열·가스 등의) 배출, 방사, 발산
greenhouse gas	온실가스
detrimental	해로운
linger	오래 머물다, 오래 남아 있다
carbon dioxide	이산화탄소
continuously	계속해서, 연속적으로, 끊임없이
trap	~을 끌어모으다, 가두다; 덫, 올가미
abide	머무르다, 참다
wobble	흔들리다, 흔들다
deviate	벗어나다, 일탈하다
ensnare	덫에 걸리게 하다, 함정에 빠뜨리다

03

polite	예의 바른, 공손한, 정중한
attitude	태도[자세]
decline	거절하다, 감소하다; 감소
offer	제안[제의]; 제안[제의]하다, 제공하다
accept	수락하다, 받아들이다, 인정하다
splendid	아주 멋진, 훌륭한
complaisant	공손한, 정중한
impertinent	무례한, 버릇없는
dispassionate	감정에 좌우되지 않는

04

military	군사의, 무력의; 군대
unexpected	예기치 않은, 예상 밖의, 뜻밖의
keep in touch with	~와 연락[접촉]을 유지하다

☐ do not know beans about	~에 대해 전혀 모르다
☐ drop someone a line	~에게 간단한 편지를 보내다
☐ get on one's nerves	신경을 건드리다
☐ give someone a piece of one's mind	야단치다

05

☐ doubt	의심
☐ from time to time	때때로
☐ accumulate	쌓이다
☐ rise to the occasion	난국에 대처하다, 수단을 발휘하다

06

☐ relaxing	편안한
☐ insight	통찰

08

☐ in vitro fertilization	체외 수정
☐ pre-implantation genetic diagnosis	착상 전 유전 진단
☐ embryo	배아
☐ anemia	빈혈증
☐ inherited	유전의
☐ marker	유전자 표지(유전학적 해석에서 표지로 사용되는 유전자)
☐ reveal	드러내다, 밝히다
☐ tissue	조직
☐ donor	(장기) 기증자, 제공자
☐ match	(성질·능력 등에서) […과] 대등한 사람[것], 공통적인 사람[것]
☐ conceive	임신하다
☐ umbilical cord	탯줄

09

☐ naked	벌거벗은, 나체의
☐ eternal	영원한
☐ symbiosis	공생
☐ impeccable	흠잡을 데 없는
☐ hygiene	위생
☐ institution	기관, 협회
☐ occasional	가끔의

10

☐ reasoned	조리 정연한
☐ assembled	모인, 집합된, 결집한
☐ for	(왜냐하면) …니까
☐ guarded	조심스러운, 신중한
☐ established	확립된, 정립된
☐ misleading	호도[오도]하는, 오해의 소지가 있는
☐ finding	발견(물), 조사[연구] 결과
☐ contribution	공헌
☐ body	본체, 중심부
☐ misconduct	(특히 전문직 종사자의) 비행, 위법[불법] 행위
☐ deliberate	고의의
☐ misinterpretation	오역

결국엔 성정혜 영어 하프모의고사
기적사 DAY 54 핵심어휘

01

☐ adverse	부정적인
☐ birthrate	출생률, 출산율
☐ stuffy	답답한
☐ cynical	부정적인, 냉소적인
☐ upbeat	긍정적인, 낙관적인
☐ detrimental	해로운

02

☐ state-of-the-art	최신식의, 최첨단의
☐ duplicate	복제하다, 복사하다
☐ dally	꾸물거리다, 미적거리다
☐ emulate	모방하다
☐ replicate	복제하다, 모사하다
☐ fluctuate	변동을 거듭하다

03

☐ hypothesis	가설, 추정, 추측
☐ predict	예측[예견]하다
☐ shallow	얕은
☐ confuse	혼동하다, 혼란시키다
☐ disturb	방해하다
☐ navigational	항해의, 비행의
☐ shoal	얕은, 얕은 수심에서 뜨는
☐ feeble	내용이 부족한, 시시한; (빛·목소리 등이) 희미한
☐ tortuous	비비 꼬인, 비틀린
☐ heterogeneous	이종의, 이질적인

04

☐ come up with	~을 생각하다; ~을 따라잡다
☐ industrial revolution	산업 혁명
☐ artificial intelligence(AI)	인공지능
☐ technological	(과학) 기술(상)의
☐ presentation	발표; 제출
☐ keep up with	~의 시류[유행]를 따르다; (할부금 등을) 계속 내다; ~을 정기적으로 하다
☐ bury the hatchet	싸움을 그만두다, 화해하다
☐ work against the clock	마감에 맞추려고 하다

☐ jump on the bandwagon	대세에 따르다
☐ put the cart before the horse	주객이 전도되다

05

☐ donate	기부하다
☐ book drive	도서 기부 운동
☐ drop off	~을 가져다주다
☐ designate	지정하다
☐ directly	바로, 직접
☐ afford	(~을 할 금전적) 여유가 되다

06

☐ sign	계약을 체결하다
☐ leading role	주연
☐ underground train	지하철
☐ discard	버리다, 폐기하다

08

☐ overcome	극복하다
☐ doping	도핑, 금지 약물 복용[사용]
☐ nontherapeutic	비치료적인
☐ athletic performance	운동 기록
☐ take advantage of	이용하다, 편승하다
☐ cutting-edge	최첨단의
☐ alter	바꾸다, 고치다
☐ realize	실현하다

09

☐ exotic	이국적인, 외국의
☐ supposedly	아마, 정황상
☐ chromosome	염색체
☐ laudanum	아편틴크 (아편으로 만든 약물)
☐ racewalk	경보 경기하다

결국엔 성정혜 영어 하프모의고사
기적사 DAY 55 핵심어휘

☐ down	급히 다 먹다[마시다], 죽 들이켜다
☐ dose	(어느 정도의) 양, 약간, 복용량
☐ strychnine	스트리크닌(극소량이 약품으로 이용되는 독성 물질)
☐ brag	(심하게) 자랑하다, 떠벌리다

10

☐ assault	공격, 도전, 폭행
☐ denialist	부정론자
☐ dismiss	(고려할 가치가 없다고) 묵살[일축]하다
☐ merely	단지
☐ unmoved by	…에 무감동한, 마음이 흔들리지 않는
☐ molecular	분자
☐ anatomical	해부학적인
☐ unimpressed by	…에 감명받지 않는, …이 대단하다고 생각하지 않는
☐ mountain	산더미
☐ hoax	거짓말, 날조, 조작, 장난질
☐ opinion poll	여론조사
☐ talk radio	(라디오의) 전화 토론 프로그램
☐ peer-reviewed	동료 심사를 받은
☐ disprove	반박하다, 틀렸음을 입증하다
☐ argument	주장
☐ hold water	타당하다, 이치에 맞다
☐ arena	(각축전이 벌어지는) 무대
☐ subject to	…의 대상인
☐ scrutiny	정밀 조사, 철저한 검토
☐ mass-market	일반 대중을 대상으로 한, 대량 판매 시장용의

01

☐ allusive	암시적인
☐ capable	(능력·특질 상) ~을 할 수 있는; 유능한
☐ interpretation	해석; 연출; 통역
☐ blunt	직설적인, 무딘
☐ smug	의기양양한, 우쭐해하는
☐ connotative	암시하는, 함축적인
☐ supercilious	거만한, 남을 얕보는

02

☐ reconfirm	재확인하다
☐ principle	원칙, 원리
☐ predict	예측[예견]하다
☐ yen	엔화 (일본의 화폐 단위)
☐ depreciate	가치가 하락하다
☐ further	더; 더 멀리에
☐ revalue	평가 절상하다
☐ detract	가치가 떨어지다
☐ impugn	의문을 제기하다
☐ disparage	폄하하다

03

☐ cooperation	협력, 합동, 협동
☐ inclusive	포괄적인, 폭넓은
☐ sustainable	지속[유지] 가능한
☐ sweeping	포괄적인, 전면적인
☐ amenable	말을 잘 듣는
☐ determinate	확정적인, 확실한
☐ metaphysical	극히 추상적인, 난해한

04

☐ exhausted	기진맥진한, 탈진한; 고갈된

☐ harsh	가혹한, 냉혹한
☐ unfriendly	불친절한, 비우호적인
☐ greed	탐욕; 식탐
☐ a cash cow	이익을 불러오는 사업
☐ bread and butter	생계 수단
☐ doubting Thomas	회의론자
☐ a dog in the manger	심술 맞은 사람

05

☐ toddler	걸음마를 배우는 아이
☐ outdoor	야외의
☐ potential	잠재적인
☐ department	부서
☐ equipment	장비
☐ machinery	기계(류)

06

☐ helpless	무력한
☐ depression	우울증
☐ immune response	면역 반응
☐ linearly	곧장, 직선으로

08

☐ in vitro	체외[시험관]에서
☐ trait	특성, 특징
☐ advent	출현, 도래
☐ in vitro fertilization	체외 수정
☐ bioethical	생명 윤리의
☐ embryology	태생학
☐ ethical	윤리적인
☐ implement	시행하다
☐ limitation	규제, 제약
☐ regarding	…에 관한

09

☐ event	종목, 경기
☐ commemorate	기념하다
☐ runner	사자(使者), 보발(步撥)

☐ enlist	요청하다
☐ standardize	표준화하다
☐ measurement	치수[크기/길이/양]

10

☐ perpetual	(오랫동안) 끊임없이 계속되는, 빈번한
☐ struggle	투쟁, 분투
☐ secure	확보하다
☐ sustain	유지하다, 지속시키다
☐ workforce	노동 인구[노동력]
☐ early career	초기 경력(자)
☐ grant	보조금
☐ allot	할당하다, 배당하다
☐ insufficient	불충분한
☐ body	(흔히 공공 목적을 위해 함께 일하는) 단체[조직]
☐ substandard	수준 이하의

기적사 DAY 56 핵심어휘

01

☐ salesman	판매원
☐ cardinal	중요한; 추기경; 진홍색의
☐ satisfy	만족시키다; 충족시키다
☐ definitive	결정적인
☐ gigantic	거대한
☐ potential	잠재적인
☐ principal	주요한, 주된

02

☐ surreptitious	비밀리에 하는
☐ indicate	나타내다[보여 주다]
☐ clandestine	비밀리에 하는, 은밀한

statutory	법에 명시된, 법으로 정한
forthright	솔직한
seraphic	천사 같은, 맑은, 거룩한

03

desultory	두서없는, 종잡을 수 없는
wander	돌아다니다, 헤매다
purposeful	목적 있는, 결의에 찬
miserable	비참한
ascetic	금욕적인
disconnected	일관성이 없는; 단절된

04

vacancy	(호텔 등의) 빈방[객실]; 결원, 공석
reservation	예약
company	일행, 동료; 회사

06

conductor	지휘자
to all appearances	어느 모로 보나
spontaneously	자연스럽게
novice	초보자
capacity	능력, 역할
coordinate	조율하다
disparate	이질적인 부분들로 이뤄진

07

supplement	보충제, 보조식품
synthetic	합성의
ingredient	재료
molecular weight	분자량
structure	구조
regardless of	~와 관계없이

08

farmland	농지
carry away	운반해 가다
formation	형성
productivity	생산성
erode	침식시키다, 풍화시키다

09

take a toll	피해[타격]를 주다
physiological	생리학적인
dwindle	줄어들다
slink	살금살금 움직이다
at a rapid pace	빠른 속도로
a slew of	많은

10

pact	약속, 협정, 조약
ascribe ~ to ⋯	~을 ⋯의 탓으로 돌리다
adversary	상대방, 적수
heretic	이단자
dissident	반체제인사
peasant	소작농
confession	자백, 고백
witchcraft	마법, 마술
innate	타고난
border on	~에 아주 가깝다, 거의 ~와 같다
heresy	이단

결국엔 성정혜 영어 하프모의고사
기적사 DAY 57 핵심어휘

01

definitive	명확한, 한정적인
proof	증거, 증명

☐ portrait	초상화
☐ hazy	모호한, 흐릿한
☐ plain	분명한, 솔직한, 소박한
☐ muddy	진흙투성이인, 탁한
☐ inchoate	이제 시작 단계인

02

☐ clandestine	은밀한, 비밀리에 하는
☐ malware	악성 소프트웨어
☐ get around	~을 피하다; 돌아다니다
☐ firewall	방화벽
☐ furtive	은밀한, 엉큼한
☐ blatant	노골적인, 뻔한
☐ exoteric	공개적인, 대중적인
☐ conspicuous	눈에 잘 띄는, 뚜렷한

03

☐ sector	분야[부문]
☐ disconnected	무관한, 일관성이 없는
☐ decent	괜찮은, 예의 바른
☐ external	무관한, 외부의
☐ indecent	버릇없는, 꼴불견의
☐ pertinent	관련 있는, 적절한

04

☐ unforgettable	잊지 못할 [잊을 수 없는]
☐ hit the road	떠나다
☐ in seventh heaven	행복한
☐ tell me about it	정말 그래
☐ the tip of the iceberg	빙산의 일각
☐ give me a break	그만해
☐ lose the day	패배하다
☐ every dog has its day	쥐구멍에도 볕들 날 온다

06

☐ notable	유명한, 저명한
☐ recognize	인정하다
☐ significantly	상당히

07

☐ manage to 동사원형	어떻게든 ~하다
☐ translate	바꾸다, 번역하다

08

☐ fertilizer	비료
☐ trespass	침입하다, 침범하다
☐ conserve	보존하다, 보호하다
☐ deterioration	악화
☐ expanse	넓게 퍼진 공간[장소], 구역
☐ property	특징
☐ nutrient	영양분
☐ parameter	요인, 특성, 특질
☐ nitrogen	질소
☐ appropriate	적절한, 알맞은
☐ fertile	비옥한
☐ sterile	척박한, 불모의
☐ barren	황량한, 척박한
☐ arable	경작에 적합한

09

☐ absorb	흡수하다
☐ glucose	포도당
☐ expenditure	소비, 소모
☐ adapt to 동사원형	~하도록 변경하다
☐ physiologically	생리(학)적으로
☐ sensitive	민감한
☐ convert	전환하다
☐ hunter-gatherer	수렵·채집인
☐ ancestor	조상, 선조
☐ feast-or-famine	기복이 심한, 파란만장한, 풍요냐 궁핍이냐의 양극단의

☐ desk jockey	사무직원
☐ prompt	유발하다, 촉발하다
☐ Type 2 diabetes	제2형 당뇨병
☐ inflammation	염증
☐ work out	운동하다

10

☐ demographic	인구학의
☐ aggravate	악화시키다
☐ tension	긴장[갈등]
☐ underlie	(…의) 기저를 이루다 [기저가 되다]
☐ witchcraft	마법, 주술
☐ accusation	고발, 기소
☐ unattached	매이지[결혼을 하지] 않은
☐ accuse	고발[기소/비난]하다, 혐의를 제기하다
☐ adversely affect	악영향을 주다
☐ with respect to	…에 관하여
☐ advent	출현, 도래
☐ resistant	저항[반대]하는
☐ famine	기근
☐ outbreak	발생
☐ epidemic disease	전염병
☐ dislocation	혼란
☐ trigger	촉발하다, 방아쇠를 당기다
☐ superstition	미신
☐ bizarre	기이한, 이상한
☐ phenomenon	현상
☐ torture	고문
☐ execution	처형

결국엔 성정혜 영어 하프모의고사
기적사 DAY 58 핵심어휘

01

☐ gigantic	거대한
☐ waterfall	폭포
☐ valley	계곡
☐ puny	아주 작은, 미약한
☐ titanic	거대한, 강력한
☐ effete	무력해진, 기운이 빠진
☐ timorous	겁이 많은

02

☐ bail out	구제하다, 곤경을 벗어나게 하다
☐ statutory	법에 명시된, 법으로 정한
☐ entitlement	자격[권리]
☐ illicit	불법의, 사회 통념에 어긋나는
☐ felonious	범죄의, 중죄의
☐ legitimate	합법적인, 타당한
☐ conspiratorial	음모의, 공모하는 듯한

03

☐ intended	의도하는
☐ pointless	무의미한, 할 가치가 없는
☐ torment	고통, 고뇌; 괴롭히다
☐ endure	견디다, 참다, 인내하다
☐ purposeful	목적의식이 있는, 결단력 있는
☐ adrift	표류하는, 방황하는
☐ apathetic	무관심한, 심드렁한
☐ undirected	목표가 불명한, 지시 없는

04

talk the talk	말만 그럴듯한 말을 하다
shoot the breeze	잠시 이야기를 나누다
rob Peter to pay Paul	빚을 내어 빚을 메꾸다
speak the same language	다른 사람과 같은 생각을 갖다

06

identify	알아보다, 식별하다
typically	일반적으로
newborn	갓 태어난
tribe	부족, 종족
hut	움막, 오두막
settlement	정착지, 촌락

07

elevation	높은 곳
altitude	고도가 높은 곳
logging	벌목
conversion	전환

08

appreciate	(제대로) 인식하다
pore space	공극(토양 입자와 입자 사이에 공기나 물로 채워질 수 있는 틈새)
microbe	미생물
a matter of hours	겨우 몇 시간
excavation	발굴, 땅파기
strip	(껍질 등을) 벗기다, 없애다
subsoil	심토
compact	다지다, 압축하다, 단단하게 만들다
disturb	(제자리에 있는 것을) 건드리다[흩뜨리다]
aggregate	전체, 집합체
pile up	쌓다, 쌓아 올리다

09

capillary	모세혈관
blood vessel	혈관, 핏줄
arteriole	세동맥, 소동맥
venule	세정맥
biochemical	생화학의
respiration	호흡
define	윤곽[모양/경계]을 분명히 나타내다
mass	질량
tissue	조직
adopt	채택하다, 차용하다
sedentary	주로 앉아서 지내는, 몸을 많이 움직이지 않는
contract	수축하다
shrink	오그라들다, 줄어들다
go away	없어지다, 사라지다
ward off	피하다, 막다, 물리치다

10

infamous	악명 높은, 오명이 난
trial	재판
claim	주장하다
be possessed by	귀신이 들리다[씌우다]
accuse A of B	(A를 B의 혐의로) 고발[기소/비난]하다, 혐의를 제기하다
witchcraft	마법, 마술, 주술
hysteria	히스테리
colonial	식민지의, 식민지 시대의
convene	소집하다, 회합하다
hear	(법정에서) 심리[공판]를 갖다
convicted	유죄로 결정된
hang	교수형에 처하다, 목을 매달다
abate	(강도가) 약해지다, 누그러들다

annul	(법적으로) 취소하다 [무효하게 하다]
verdict	평결
grant	(인정하여 정식으로) 주다, 수여하다
indemnity	배상[보상]금
bitterness	비통함, 쓰라림
linger	(예상보다 오래) 남다 [계속되다]
legacy	(과거의) 유산
endure	오래가다[지속되다]
charge A with B	(A를 B의 죄로) 기소하다
regardless of	…에 상관없이 [구애받지 않고]

결국엔 성정혜 영어 하프모의고사
기적사 DAY 59 핵심어휘

01

automaker	자동차 회사
notify	알리다[통고/통지하다]
potential	잠재적인, 가능성이 있는
defect	결함, 결점
latent	잠재하는, 잠복해 있는
manifest	분명한
equivocal	의심스러운, 몽롱한
quiescent	조용한, 잠잠한

02

secretary	비서
absolutely	전적으로, 틀림없이
forthright	기탄없이 말하는, 솔직한
sly	교활한, 음흉한
candid	솔직한
impromptu	즉흥적으로 한
disingenuous	솔직하지 못한

03

witness	목격하다; 목격자
miserable	비참한
rosy	희망적인, 장밋빛의
ruddy	혈색이 좋은, 건강한
abject	극도로 비참한, 절망적인
grievous	통탄할

04

prioritize	우선시키다, 우선순위를 매기다
make a shift	임시방편을 세우다
stick to one's guns	자신의 소신을 지키다
burn the midnight oil	밤늦게까지 업무를 하다
blow one's own trumpet	허풍을 떨다

06

domesticate	키우다, 재배하다
association	연관, 제휴
abundant	풍부한

07

flexible	유동적인, 융통성이 있는
wholesale	도매상
reflect	반영하다

08

capability	능력, 역량
grouping	(흔히 더 큰 집단의 일부인) 그룹[집단], 분류
suitability	적당, 적합
arable	경작에 알맞은
conservation	보존, 보전
remaining	나머지, 잔여의
progressively	계속해서, 점진적으로

09

☐ pasture	목초지, 초원
☐ grazing	방목지, 목초지
☐ esthetic	심미적, 미학적
☐ take … into account	…를 고려하다
☐ moderate	적당한, 보통의, 중간의
☐ aerobic	유산소의
☐ vigorous	격렬한, 활발한
☐ accumulate	축적하다, 모으다
☐ add up to something	결국 …되다
☐ free weight	바벨, 덤벨, 케틀벨 등 외부 장비에 연결되어 있지 않은 근력운동 기구
☐ weight machine	종합 헬스 기구
☐ meet	(필요, 요구 등을) 충족시키다
☐ ramp up	늘리다[증가시키다]

10

☐ culprit	범인
☐ first and foremost	무엇보다도 먼저
☐ immediate	(시간적·공간적으로) 아주 가까이에 [바로 옆에] 있는
☐ inflict	(괴로움 등을) 가하다 [안기다]
☐ mystical	신령스러운
☐ common to	…에 공통된
☐ represent	(…에) 해당하다
☐ witchcraft	마술, 마법, 주술
☐ accusation	혐의 (제기), 비난, 고발, 기소
☐ trial	재판
☐ intimately	친밀하게
☐ intense	강렬한, 집중적인
☐ suspicion	혐의, 의심

☐ fall on	…으로 돌려지다, 쏠리다
☐ dispute	분쟁, 분규

결국엔 성정혜 영어 하프모의고사
기적사 DAY 60 핵심어휘

01

☐ principal	주요한, 주된
☐ petty	사소한, 하찮은
☐ staple	주된, 주요한
☐ shabby	허름한, 부당한
☐ immaterial	중요하지 않은, 무형의

02

☐ extol	칭찬[칭송]하다, 극찬[격찬]하다
☐ seraphic	거룩한, 천사 같은
☐ sacrifice	희생
☐ sublime	숭고한, 황당한
☐ plebeian	평민의, 교양 없는
☐ ludicrous	터무니없는, 웃기는
☐ outlandish	이상한, 기이한

03

☐ extroverted	외향적인, 사교적인
☐ fun-loving	재미를 추구하는
☐ ascetic	금욕적인
☐ strict	엄격한[엄한]
☐ lavish	호화로운, 풍성한
☐ prodigal	낭비하는, 방탕한
☐ sybaritic	쾌락의
☐ abstinent	금욕적인, 자제하는

04

☐ jealous	질투하는, 시기하는
☐ save face	체면을 차리다

☐ face the music	스스로 책임지다
☐ pull a long face	시무룩한 표정을 짓다
☐ have a corner on the market	시장을 장악하다

06

☐ explosive	폭발적인
☐ expansion	확대, 팽창
☐ prompt	유발하다, 촉진하다
☐ a host of	많은, 다수의
☐ precondition	전제 조건

07

☐ world-class	세계 일류의
☐ hook oneself up to	자신을 ~에 연결하다
☐ devote A to B	A를 B에 바치다
☐ external	외적인 것, 외부 사항

08

☐ carbon	탄소
☐ in mind	염두에 두는, 유념하는, 명심하는
☐ curb	억제하다, 제한하다
☐ metric ton	미터 톤(1,000kg)
☐ agriculture	농업
☐ manure	거름
☐ decompose	부패하다
☐ emit	배출하다
☐ fossil fuel	화석 연료
☐ combat	(좋지 않은 일의 발생이나 악화를) 방지하다[(방지하기 위해) 싸우다]

09

☐ excessively	지나치게, 과도하게, 심히
☐ perceive	인지하다, 인식하다, 지각하다
☐ defect	결함

☐ feature	특징, 특성
☐ turn to	의지하다
☐ hammer away at	…을 열심히[꾸준히] 하다, …을 거듭해서 [집요하게] 하다
☐ come to	(특히 좋지 않은 상황이) 되다
☐ detriment	손상
☐ adolescence	청소년기
☐ athlete	운동선수
☐ immoderate	과도한, 터무니없는
☐ addictive	중독적인
☐ isolated	고립된
☐ in an attempt to 동사원형	~하기 위하여, ~하려는 시도로

10

☐ ogre	(이야기 속에 나오는) 사람을 잡아먹는 거인
☐ sorceress	(이야기 속의) 여자 마법사
☐ die by one's own hand	자살하다
☐ execute	실행하다, 수행하다
☐ vat	통(액체를 담는 데 쓰는 대형 통)
☐ viper	독사
☐ serpent	뱀
☐ cardinal rule	기본적인[가장 중요한] 규칙
☐ mandate	명령하다
☐ flesh and blood	혈육, 육친, 자손
☐ matricide	모친 살해
☐ ogress	ogre의 여성형

기적사 DAY 61 핵심어휘

01

rule out	배제하다
diagnosis	진단
trace	추적하다
exclude	배제하다
instruct	지시하다
examine	조사하다

02

made of money	아주 부자인
needy	가난한, 빈곤한
thrifty	검소한, 절약하는
wealthy	부유한, 재산이 많은
stingy	인색한, 적은

03

claim	주장하다
assertive	적극적인
pushy	지나치게 밀어붙이는, 강요하는
thrilled	오싹한, 흥분된
brave	용감한
timid	소심한
aggressive	공격적인, 대단히 적극적인, 시비조의

04

have[get] an inkling of	…을 어렴풋이 알다
contact	연락하다; 연락
rack one's brain	지혜를 짜내다, 골똘히 생각하다

06

recent	최근에

listing	목록
illegal	불법의
commercial	상업적인
operator	사업자, 운영자
rent	임대하다
exclusively	독점적으로
elected	선출된
official	공무원, 관리
infrequently	드물게
bill	명세서

08

contemporary	동시대의, 현대의
integral	필수적인
enthusiasm	열광
recognition	인정
surly	무례한
undoubtedly	의심할 여지가 없는, 확실한
brand new	아주 새로운
photographic	사진의
prestige	위신
wear and tear	(일상적인 사용에 의한) 마모

09

impose	도입하다
blatant	노골적인, 뻔한
breach	위반, 위반하다
non-intervention	불간섭의, 불개입의
affairs	사건, 일
institution	기관; 제도, 관습
legitimize	정당화하다, 합법화하다
partial	부분의, 편파적인
unselected	비 선출된
dictatorship	독재
impose	도입하다; 부과하다
in terms of~	~에 관하여
restraint	규제

☐ consensus	동의
☐ confrontation	대립
☐ exception	예외

10

☐ clown	광대
☐ frighten	겁먹게 하다
☐ costume	의상
☐ individual	개인
☐ lure	꾀어내다
☐ threaten	위협하다
☐ violence	폭력
☐ sighting	목격
☐ nationwide	전국적인
☐ panic	공포

결국엔 성정혜 영어 하프모의고사
기적사 DAY 62 핵심어휘

01

☐ combine	결합시키다
☐ genetics	유전학
☐ molecular	분자의, 분자로 된, 분자에 의한
☐ biology	생물학
☐ trace	추적하다
☐ migration	이주, 이동
☐ bolt	달아나다, 빗장을 지르다
☐ expel	쫓아내다, 추방하다
☐ debar	금하다, 제외하다
☐ chase	추적하다, 뒤쫓다

02

☐ donate	기부[기증]하다
☐ needy	어려운, 궁핍한
☐ posh	우아한, 화려한

☐ opulent	호화로운, 엄청나게 부유한
☐ destitute	궁핍한, 극빈한
☐ pernicious	치명적인

03

☐ thrilled	흥분한, 황홀해하는
☐ magnificent	웅장한, 참으로 아름다운 [감명 깊은/훌륭한]
☐ hyper	흥분한, 들뜬
☐ callous	냉담한
☐ benign	상냥한, 유순한
☐ sedate	차분한, 조용한

04

☐ merchant	상인
☐ rip somebody off	바가지 씌우다
☐ talk turkey	진솔하게 이야기하다
☐ strike it rich	좋은 금광을 찾다, 일확천금을 하다
☐ kiss and make up	화해하다

06

☐ empire	제국, 왕국
☐ rigid	엄격한, 융통성 없는
☐ nurturing	육성
☐ flowering	개화
☐ freewheeling	자유분방한

08

☐ contemporary	현대의
☐ reveal	드러내다, 보여주다, 밝히다
☐ observable	식별[관찰]할 수 있는
☐ perspective	관점, 시각
☐ exhibit	보이다[드러내다]
☐ display	전시, 진열
☐ décor	실내장식, 인테리어

☐ appeal	관심[흥미]을 끌다, 매력이다
☐ personally	개인적으로, 직접
☐ exercise	(권력·권리·역량 등을) 행사[발휘]하다
☐ judgment	비판, 비난
☐ glimpse into	…을 잠깐 들여다봄
☐ means	수단, 방법

09

☐ democracy	민주(주의)국가, 민주주의
☐ democratic	민주주의의, 민주적인
☐ subsequent	그[이]다음의, 차후의
☐ well-established	확고부동한, 안정된, 정착된
☐ legitimacy	적법[합법] (성), 정당성
☐ participation	참가, 참여
☐ cornerstone	주춧돌[초석]
☐ turnout	투표자의 수, 투표율
☐ come into question	문제가 되다

10

☐ profession	직업[직종]
☐ codes of conduct	행동 강령[수칙]
☐ seldom	좀처럼[거의] …않는
☐ face	직면하다, 대면하다
☐ ethical	윤리적인
☐ say	이를테면, 말하자면, 가령
☐ abide by	(법률·합의 등을) 따르다, 준수하다
☐ commandment	계율, 계명
☐ seek to 동사원형	~하도록 시도[추구]하다
☐ preserve	유지하다, 보존하다, 보호하다
☐ exclusively	오로지, 오직, 전적으로
☐ considering	…을 고려[감안]하면

☐ creepy	오싹한, 으스스한
☐ association	연상, 관계
☐ involve	포함하다, 수반하다
☐ conduct	행동, 행위
☐ intoxicated	(술·마약에) 취한
☐ garb	(특이한 또는 특정 유형의 사람이 입는) 의복
☐ reflect badly on	…이 좋지 않게 비추게[인식되게] 하다
☐ make a living	생계를 꾸리다

결국엔 성정해 영어 하프모의고사
기적사 DAY 63 핵심어휘

01

☐ eclectic	절충적인; 다방면에 걸친
☐ exclude	제외하다
☐ scratch	제외하다, 긁다
☐ condone	용납하다
☐ subsume	포함하다, 포괄하다
☐ condemn	비난하다, 규탄하다

02

☐ discount	할인의; 할인; 할인하다
☐ thrifty	검소한, 절약하는
☐ canny	약삭빠른, 영리한
☐ spartan	검소하고 엄격한, 스파르타식의
☐ imprudent	경솔한, 무분별한
☐ offhand	즉석의, 사전 준비 없이 하는

03

☐ brave	용감한, 용기 있는
☐ profess	천명[공언]하다; 주장하다

☐ accordingly	그에 맞춰, 그것에 알맞게	
☐ puny	작고 연약한, 보잘것없는	
☐ scant	거의 없는, 부족한	
☐ gallant	용감한, 용맹한	
☐ cowardly	겁이 많은, 비겁한	

04

☐ at all	전혀, 조금도
☐ lose one's head	자제심을 잃다
☐ make a mountain out of a molehill	작은 일을 크게 떠벌리다
☐ kill the goose that laid the golden egg	큰 이익이 기대되는 일을 포기하다
☐ go on a wild goose chase	헛된 노력을 하다

06

☐ ultimately	궁극적으로, 결국
☐ decrease	줄다, 감소하다
☐ be inclined to 동사원형	~하는 경향이 있다
☐ update	갱신하다, 새롭게 하다
☐ second-guess	뒤늦게 비판하다
☐ insanity	정신 이상

08

☐ modern art	근대미술
☐ build on	…을 기반으로 하다
☐ rely on	의존하다, 의지하다
☐ teaching	교리, 사상, 가르침
☐ academy	협회, 학회, 학파
☐ depict	묘사하다, 그리다
☐ break with	그만두다, 거부하다, 관계를 끊다
☐ mimic	모방하다, 흉내 내다
☐ by way of	…로[…을 통해]
☐ perspective	원근법
☐ trick	기교, 트릭, 비결, 요령

☐ peer	동료, 또래[동배]
☐ abstract	추상적인
☐ representational	구상주의적인
☐ draw attention	주의[관심]를 끌다
☐ medium	(화가, 작가, 음악가의) 표현 수단
☐ composition	구도, 구성

09

☐ hold	개최하다, 열다
☐ institution	제도[관습]
☐ representative	대표제[대의원제]의
☐ authority	권한, 지휘권
☐ derive	…에서 비롯되다, …에 기원을 두다, …에서 나오다
☐ solely	오로지, 단독으로
☐ consent	동의, 합의
☐ the governed	피통치자, 피치자
☐ principal	주요한, 주된
☐ mechanism	기제, 방법, 메커니즘
☐ translate	(다른 형태로) 바꾸다[옮기다]
☐ holding	개최
☐ right-wing	우익[우파/보수파]의
☐ dictatorship	독재 정부[독재 국가]
☐ regime	정권, 제도, 체제
☐ single-party	단일정당의
☐ stage	개최하다, 벌이다, 꾸미다
☐ rule	통치, 지배
☐ aura	기운, 분위기
☐ legitimacy	정당성, 타당성, 합법성
☐ candidate	후보
☐ alternative	대안의, 대체 가능한
☐ office	(권위 있는, 특히 정부의 주요) 지위, 공직, 정권
☐ intimidation	위협, 협박
☐ rig	(부정한 수법으로) 조작하다

approve	승인하다, 인가하다
genuine	진짜의, 진정한
incumbent	재임 중인
party	정당, 당

10

warrior	전사
could well	어쩌면 ~일지 모른다
opposite	반의어, 반대
nod	끄덕이다
reversal	(정반대로) 뒤바꿈[뀜], 전환, 반전
extend	확대[확장]하다
bathe	(몸을) 씻다, 세척하다
figure	인물, 사람
overcome	극복하다, 이기다
rank	(사회적으로) 높은 지위[신분]
accumulate	축적하다, 쌓아 올리다
bravery	용맹, 용기
lance	긴 창
bearer	소지자, 운반자
invulnerable to	…이 해칠[물리칠] 수 없는, …로부터 안전한, …에 끄떡없는
conquer	물리치다, 이기다, 정복하다
phobia	공포증

결국엔 성정혜 영어 하프모의고사
기적사 DAY 64 핵심어휘

01

instruct	지시하다, 가르치다
encourage	격려[고무]하다, 용기를 북돋우다
civilian	민간인
engage in	~에 관여[참여]하다

compatriot	동포
oust	쫓아내다, 몰아내다
acquit	무죄를 선고하다
impeach	탄핵하다, 고발하다
mandate	지시하다, 명령하다

02

wealthy	부유한, 재산이 많은
industrialist	기업가
stark	삭막한, 냉혹한
blunt	무딘, 직설적인, 솔직한
tactful	요령 있는, 눈치 있는
opulent	부유한, 호화로운

03

timid	소심한, 용기가 없는
extrovert	외향적인 사람
bland	(맛이) 자극적이지 않은, 특별한 맛이 안 나는; 특징 없는, 단조로운
astute	약삭빠른, 영리한
mousy	소심한, 내성적인
affable	상냥한, 사근사근한
cunning	교활한, 기묘한

04

audition	오디션을 보다 [오디션에 참가하다]
doubtlessly	의심 없이, 틀림없이
break a leg	행운을 빌어
make a killing	떼돈을 벌다
stand a chance	성공할 가망성이 있다
blow hot and cold	변덕을 부리다

06

tourism	관광
similarity	유사점
aid	도움

☐ artwork	미술품
☐ preserve	보존하다

08

☐ baffling	이해할 수 없는, 당황하게 하는
☐ self-doubt	자기 회의
☐ capacity	능력
☐ take A for B	A를 B로 생각하다
☐ after all	결국
☐ advanced	고도의
☐ miscommunication	의사소통 오류
☐ phenomenon	현상
☐ urinal	소변기
☐ readymade	레디메이드(현대 미술의 오브제; 일상의 기제품(旣製品)을 본래의 용도가 아닌 다른 의미를 부여하여 작품으로 발표한 것)
☐ represent	상징하다, 대표하다
☐ still life	정물화
☐ present	보여주다 [나타내다, 묘사하다]

09

☐ bleak	암울한, 절망적인
☐ crackdown	엄중 단속, 강력 탄압
☐ dissident	반체제인사
☐ impose	시행하다, 부과하다
☐ prime minister	총리, 수상
☐ crumble	흔들리다[무너지다]
☐ crusade	(옳다고 믿는 것을 이루기 위한 장기적이고 단호한) 운동
☐ spate	(보통 불쾌한 일의) 빈발
☐ extrajudicial	재판 외의, 사법 절차에 의하지 않는
☐ prominent	유명한, 저명한, 중요한
☐ defender	옹호자

☐ harsh	가혹한, 냉혹한
☐ ongoing	계속 진행 중인
☐ progress	진전, 진행
☐ significantly	상당히, 크게
☐ gain	개선, 이득
☐ surpass	능가하다, 뛰어넘다
☐ rollback	역행, 후퇴, 되돌리기
☐ gain momentum	활기를 찾다, 번성하다

10

☐ giggle	피식 웃음, 킥킥[키득/낄낄]거림
☐ practice	행위, 업무; 관례, 관습
☐ indicate	나타내다, 보여주다
☐ anxiety	불안, 염려
☐ prank	장난
☐ provoke	유발하다
☐ endorphin	엔도르핀
☐ established	인정받는, 확실히 자리를 잡은
☐ laugh at	비웃다
☐ hospital ward	병동
☐ terrifying	무서운, 겁나게 하는
☐ presence	존재
☐ pregnant	임신한

결국엔 성정혜 영어 하프모의고사
기적사 DAY 65 핵심어휘

01

☐ examine	조사하다, 검토하다
☐ thrust	밀다, 찌르다
☐ plunge	급락하다, 거꾸러지다
☐ canvass	조사하다, 유세를 하다
☐ insinuate	암시하다, 넌지시 말하다

02

☐ stingy	인색한
☐ provident	장래를 준비하는, 앞날에 대비하는
☐ sagacious	현명한
☐ extravagant	낭비하는, 사치스러운
☐ parsimonious	인색한

03

☐ collision	충돌 (사고), 부딪침
☐ aggressive	공격적인, 적극적인
☐ vicious	사나운, 공격적인
☐ uptight	긴장한, 초조해하는
☐ revengeful	복수심에 불타는
☐ peripheral	주변적인, 지엽적인

04

☐ brutality	만행, 잔인한 행위
☐ hold water	물 샐 틈이 없이 정연하다
☐ clear the air	오해가 없어지다
☐ sit on the fence	형세를 살피다
☐ scratch the surface	수박 겉핥기식으로 하다

06

☐ take 목적어 into account	~을 고려하다
☐ net profit	순수익
☐ stock value	주식 주가
☐ weigh	저울질하다, 평가하다
☐ take up	~을 차지하다
☐ working memory	작동[심리] 기억

08

☐ dismiss	일축하다, 치부하다, 묵살하다
☐ clichéd	낡은 투의, 상투적인 문구의

☐ at first glance	처음에는 [언뜻 보기에는]
☐ profound	심오한, 깊은
☐ relevant	의의가 있는 [유의미한], 관련된
☐ exhibition	전시(회)
☐ to one's taste	…의 취향[기호]에 맞는
☐ strike a chord	심금을 울리다, 뭔가 생각나게 하다
☐ ongoing	계속 진행 중인
☐ conjure up	상기시키다 [떠올리게 하다]
☐ provoke	유발하다, 자극하다
☐ appreciation	감상
☐ undeserved	받을 만하지 않은, 부당한
☐ reputation	명성, 평판
☐ worth -ing	~할 가치가 있는

09

☐ demote	강등[좌천]시키다
☐ flawed	결함[결점/흠]이 있는
☐ snapshot	짤막한 묘사[정보]
☐ electoral	선거의
☐ pluralism	다원주의, 다원성
☐ participation	참여, 참가
☐ classify	분류[구분]하다
☐ hybrid	혼합[물]
☐ regime	정권, 제도, 체제
☐ authoritarian	독재적인
☐ threshold	한계점
☐ footing	입장[관계], 지위, 신분
☐ fractious	성[짜증]을 잘 내는, 괴팍한
☐ weigh down by	…로 내리누르다
☐ governance	통치, 관리
☐ multiple	다수의

10

☐ coulrophobia	광대 공포증

기적사 DAY 66 핵심어휘

vary	달라지다[다르다]
unsettling	불안하게[동요하게] 만드는
outright	완전한, 전면적인
terror	(극심한) 두려움[무서움], 공포(심)
at the sight of	…을 보고
phenomenon	현상
hypothesis	가설
uncanny	불쾌한, 이상한, 묘한
refer to	나타내다, 말하다
nature	본질, 특질, 특징
exclusively	오로지, 오직
cover	다루다, 포함시키다
resemble	닮다, 비슷[유사]하다
push	정력적으로[끈기 있게] 노력하다[일하다]
interpret	이해하다, 해석하다
plainly	분명히, 명백히
inanimate	무생물의
aversion to	…을 싫어함 [혐오, 반감]
stem from	…에서 생겨나다 [기인하다]
instinctive	본능[직감]에 따른, 본능적인
repulsion	역겨움, 혐오감
corpse	시체, 송장
kick in	효과가 나타나기 시작하다
figure	모습, 형태, 형상
besides	… 외에
distorted	비뚤어진, 곡해된, 왜곡된
feature	이목구비(의 각 부분); 특징, 특성
disturbing	충격적인, 불안감을 주는
get over	극복하다
probable	있을[사실일] 것 같은, 개연성 있는, 가능한

01

rebellious	반항적인
awkward	서투른; 어색한; 곤란한
go through	~을 겪다[경험하다]
outgrow	벗어나다
passive	수동적인
delirious	의식이 혼탁한, 기뻐 날뛰는
disobedient	반항적인, 복종하지 않는
sporadic	산발적인, 때때로 일어나는

02

circumstance	상황, 환경
prodigal	사치스러운
existence	생활; 존재
perjury	위증(죄)
unstable	불안정한
pernicious	치명적인, 유해한
lavish	낭비하는, 사치스러운

03

contemporary	당대의, 현대의; 동시대의
resurgence	부활, 재기
civic	시민의; 도시의
comeback	부활, 재개, 복귀
disappearance	사라짐
motivation	동기, 유도
paucity	소수, 소량, 결핍

04

count somebody out	(어떤 활동에서) ~를 빼다

☐ look who is talking	누가 할 소리 (사돈 남 말하네)

05

☐ growth	성장
☐ competition	경쟁
☐ notably	특히
☐ tremendous	엄청난
☐ impact	영향, 충격
☐ advent	등장
☐ outsource	외부에 위탁하다
☐ off-shoring	해외 업무 위탁
☐ debate	논쟁하다
☐ globalization	세계화
☐ manifestation	표현, 징후
☐ comparative	비교적인
☐ advantage	이익
☐ gain	이득
☐ specialize	전문화하다

06

☐ expedition	탐험, 탐험대
☐ northern	북부의
☐ numerous	수많은
☐ abandon	버리다
☐ earth-lodge	밭이 딸린 오두막
☐ compose of	구성되다
☐ dwelling	마을, 밀집 거주 지역
☐ mighty	강력한
☐ tribe	부족

07

☐ frustrated	절망스러운
☐ situation	상황
☐ result	결과
☐ intuitive	직관적인
☐ evidence	증거
☐ insight	통찰력
☐ adjust	적응하다

☐ irritating	화나게 하는

08

☐ prepare	준비하다
☐ admit	인정하다
☐ exceptional	예외적인; 특출한
☐ review	재검토하다; 검토
☐ receptive	수용적인, 선뜻 받아들이는
☐ ordinary	보통의, 일상적인, 평범한

09

☐ tight	엄격한
☐ restrictive	제한하는, 한정적인
☐ taxation	과세, 세금
☐ regulatory	규제의, 단속의
☐ smuggling	밀수
☐ slippery slope	미끄러운 비탈
☐ unintended	의도하지 않은
☐ infringement	위반, 침해
☐ property right	재산권

10

☐ come into contact	접촉하다, 마주치다
☐ migration	이주, 이동
☐ fertile	비옥한
☐ on account of	~ 때문에
☐ invade	침략하다, 침입하다
☐ poverty	가난, 빈곤
☐ succumb	죽다, 양보하다
☐ replacement	교체, 대체
☐ side-by-side	나란히
☐ dominant	지배적인, 우위의

기적사 DAY 67 핵심어휘

01

☐ aggressive	적극적인, 공격적인
☐ passive	소극적인, 수동적인
☐ meek	온순한, 온화한
☐ feisty	혈기 왕성한, 거침없는
☐ privative	소극적인, 결핍의
☐ assertive	적극적인, 확신에 찬

02

☐ assorted	여러 가지의, 갖은
☐ delicately	정교하게; 섬세하게
☐ garnish	장식하다, 고명을 하다; 고명
☐ lavish	호화로운, 풍성한
☐ dour	시무룩한, 음침한
☐ stark	황량한, 냉혹한
☐ austere	꾸밈없는, 소박한
☐ sumptuous	호화로운

03

☐ paucity	부족, 결핍
☐ upbringing	교육, 양육, 훈육
☐ illiteracy	문맹; 무식
☐ chiefly	주로
☐ tragic	비극적인, 비극의
☐ figure	인물; 수치; 숫자
☐ dearth	부족, 결핍
☐ surfeit	과다
☐ satiety	포만감
☐ plenitude	풍부함

04

☐ up to date	최신의
☐ smash hit	대히트
☐ top notch	최고급
☐ carrot and stick	당근과 채찍
☐ a spitting image	판박이처럼 닮은 것

05

☐ biological control	생물학적 방제
☐ spectrum	범위, 영역
☐ spectacularly	멋지게
☐ pest	해충
☐ resolve	해결하다
☐ importation	도입, 수입
☐ perennial	다년생의; 다년생 식물; 영원한
☐ row crop	줄뿌림 작물
☐ ephemeral	수명이 짧은, 단명하는
☐ concerted	공동의, 통합된
☐ agro-ecosystem	농업 생태계

06

☐ toss	흔들리다 [흔들리게 하다]
☐ any port in a storm	폭풍 속의 항구 (궁여지책)
☐ drop anchor	닻을 내리다

07

☐ crave	갈망하다, 열망하다
☐ worthwhile	가치 있는
☐ recognition	인정
☐ accomplishment	성취, 업적

08

☐ variation	차이, 변화
☐ connotation	함축(적 의미)
☐ Mandarin	표준 중국어
☐ multiple	다수의
☐ equivalent	동등한 것, 대응하는 것
☐ define	정의하다
☐ unthinkable	상상도 할 수 없는

☐ have little to do with	…와 거의 관련이 없다
☐ involve	수반하다, 포함하다
☐ Cantonese	광둥어
☐ arousal	각성

09

☐ finalize	최종적으로 승인하다, 마무리 짓다, 완결하다
☐ assert	(자신의 권리·권위 등을) 확고히 하다
☐ regulatory	규제하는
☐ authority	권한
☐ boom	호황을 맞다, 번창[성공]하다
☐ fuel	…에 활기를 불어넣다, 부채질하다, 촉진하다
☐ craving	갈망, 열망
☐ vape	불연성 담배에서 나오는 연기를 들이마시다
☐ startup	신규의, 신생의, 스타트업의
☐ tobacco company	담배 회사
☐ seek to 동사원형	~하려고 시도하다
☐ clamp down on	…을 탄압하다 [엄하게 단속하다]
☐ Big Tobacco	거대 담배 회사 (Philip Morris, RJR Nabisco, U.S. Tobacco 따위)
☐ acquire	(사거나 받아서) 획득하다[취득하다]
☐ push for	…을 계속 요구하다 [조르다]
☐ significantly	상당히, 크게

10

☐ migration	이주, 이동
☐ bring	(특정 상태·장소에) 있게 하다, …하게 하다

☐ still	그럼에도 불구하고, 그런데도; 여전히, 아직도
☐ dominate	지배하다, 군림하다
☐ by far	단연코, 매우
☐ predominate	두드러지다, 지배적이다, 우위를 차지하다
☐ multiple	다수의, 많은
☐ by comparison	그에 비해
☐ representation	대표성, 대표
☐ come into common use	일반화하다
☐ adopt	쓰다, 차용하다, 채택하다

기적사 DAY 68 핵심어휘

01

☐ sentiment	감정, 정서
☐ delirious	열광적인, 기뻐 날뛰는
☐ torpid	무기력한, 활기 없는
☐ supine	무기력한, 게으른
☐ listless	무기력한, 힘이 없는
☐ rapturous	열광적인, 황홀해하는

02

☐ pernicious	치명적인
☐ intractable	다루기 힘든
☐ racism	인종 차별 (주의)
☐ dainty	앙증맞은, 얌전한
☐ capital	치명적인, 중대한
☐ exquisite	매우 아름다운, 정교한
☐ succulent	즙이 많은, 다육성의

03

☐ motivation	자극, 동기부여
☐ daring	대담성, 대담한

☐ impetus	자극, 자극제
☐ audacity	뻔뻔함
☐ momentum	탄력, 가속도

04

☐ stock	주식; 재고
☐ beef up	강화하다
☐ take a nosedive	폭락하다
☐ sell like hot cakes	매우 잘 팔리다
☐ rain cats and dogs	폭우가 쏟아지다

05

☐ pro	프로 선수
☐ informative	유익한
☐ be after	~을 추구하다
☐ in the long run	결국에는

06

☐ poisoning	중독, 독살
☐ microwave	~을 전자레인지에 데우다
☐ bold	굵은, 용감한
☐ print	활자, 활자체

07

☐ self-knowledge	자기 이해

08

☐ layperson	(특정 주제에 대한) 비전문가, 문외한
☐ cross-cultural	비교 문화적, 여러 문화가 섞인[혼재된]
☐ empirical	경험[실험]에 따른, 실증적인
☐ paradoxically	역설적으로
☐ body	많은 양[모음]
☐ indicate	나타내다[보여 주다]
☐ pursue	추구하다
☐ impair	손상[악화]시키다

☐ well-being	웰빙, (건강과) 행복, 복지[복리]
☐ individualistic	개인주의적인
☐ define	정의하다
☐ self-oriented	자기 지향적인
☐ collectivist	집단주의적인
☐ in terms of	… 면에서 […에 관하여]
☐ engagement	참여, 관계
☐ pursuit	추구, (원하는 것을) 좇음[찾음]
☐ conduct	(특정 활동을) 하다; 지휘하다
☐ leave A open	A를 열어두다
☐ robust	강력한, 튼튼한
☐ predictor	예측 변수
☐ engaged	관여된
☐ engage in	참여하다, 종사하다

09

☐ vape	불연성 담배에서 나오는 연기를 들이마시다, 전자 담배를 피우다
☐ federal	연방의
☐ replicate	모사하다, 복제하다
☐ comply	준수하다, 따르다
☐ prevent A from -ing	A가 V하는 것을 막다 [방지하다, 예방하다]
☐ addicted	중독된, 습관이 된

10

☐ rather	오히려, 반대로, 도리어
☐ what is called	소위, 이른바
☐ epiphenomenon	부수 현상
☐ intentional	의도적인, 고의적인
☐ linguistic	언어학의
☐ comparison	비교
☐ illustrate	설명하다, 보여주다
☐ brake	브레이크를 밟다; 브레이크

☐ arise	생기다, 발생하다
☐ as a consequence of	…의 결과로서, …때문에
☐ compression	압축, 압착(된 것)
☐ unintentional	의도하지 않은, 고의가 아닌

☐ make little of	~을 중요하지 않게 다루다
☐ fall prey to	~에 희생하다
☐ hit the roof	화를 심하게 내다
☐ know better than to	~정도로 어리석지 않다
☐ come to terms with	~을 감수하고 받아들이다

결국엔 성정혜 영어 하프모의고사
기적사 DAY 69 핵심어휘

01

☐ problematic	문제가 있는[많은]
☐ disobedient	반항적인, 거역하는
☐ genial	상냥한, 다정한
☐ cordial	화기애애한, 다정한
☐ amiable	쾌활한, 정감 있는
☐ truculent	반항적인, 약간 공격적인

02

☐ unstable	불안정한, 흔들릴 듯한
☐ recruit	모집하다[뽑다]
☐ wobbly	불안정한, 흔들리는
☐ ruinous	파괴적인, 파멸을 가져올
☐ rambling	산만한, 종잡을 수 없는
☐ interminable	끝없이 계속되는

03

☐ disappearance	소멸, 소실, 사라짐
☐ lapse	실수, 경과
☐ exile	추방, 망명
☐ passing	소멸, 통과
☐ omission	생략, 누락

04

☐ go Dutch	더치페이하다

05

☐ inoculation	(예방) 접종
☐ vaccination	백신 접종
☐ inoculate	접종하다, 예방주사를 놓다
☐ dose	(어느 정도의) 양, 약간
☐ tricky	힘든, 곤란한
☐ thrive on	~을 잘 해내다
☐ demanding	부담이 큰, 힘든

06

☐ recommendation	권고
☐ be based on	~에 기반을 두다
☐ transparent	투명한, 명백한
☐ pedestrian	보행자
☐ go on	일어나다, 벌어지다

07

☐ renowned	유명한, 명성 있는
☐ concentrate A on B	B에 A를 집중시키다
☐ focus A on B	B에 A를 집중시키다
☐ reflect	곰곰이 생각하다, 심사숙고하다

08

☐ browse	둘러보다[훑어보다]
☐ be confronted with	직면하다, 마주치다
☐ score	(성공 등을) 얻다
☐ sun oneself	햇볕을 쬐다
☐ impression	느낌, 인상

euphoria	행복감, 희열
crisp	(감자를 얇고 동그랗게 잘라 튀긴) 감자칩
unsatisfied	만족[충족]하지 않은
constant	끊임없는
overrate	과대평가하다
unachievable	도달할[이룰] 수 없는
constantly	끊임없이
internalize	(사상·태도 등을) 내면화하다
frustrated	좌절감을 느끼는, 불만스러워하는
miserableness	불행함, 비참한

09

leading	가장 중요한, 선두적인
preventable	막을 수 있는, 방해[예방]할 수 있는
enact	제정하다
plain	단순한, 소박한, 꾸미지 않은
discourage	(무엇을 어렵게 만들거나 반대하여) 막대[말리다]
bureau	부서, 국
statistics	통계
decline	감소하다, 하락하다
initiative	새로운 중요 기획[계획], 법안
implementation	실행
refute	반박하다, 부인하다
claim	주장하다
insignificant	사소한, 하찮은
boost	조장하다, 촉진하다, 신장시키다

10

pick out	분간하다, 가려내다, 고르다
introduce	도입하다, 소개하다
bromance	브로맨스(남자들 간의 진한 우정)

YOLO	욜로, You only live once의 약자
derp	이런 바보 같으니라고! 젠장! (어리석음을 한탄하며 말하는 감탄사로 2013년경에 문서에 등장함)
construction	구조, 구성
out of style	유행이 지난
constantly	끊임없이, 거듭
lasting	지속적인, 영속적인
imperceptibly	알아차릴 수 없게, 희미하게, 미세하게
Great Vowel Shift	대모음 추이(推移) (중세 영어에서 현대[근대]영어로의 역사적 음운(音韻) 변화)
pronunciation	발음
intelligibility	명료함, 알 수 있음, 이해할 수 있음
misalignment	정렬 불량, 어긋남, 일렬로 서있지 않음
see	간파하다, 알다
trigger	촉발하다, 유발하다
noticeable	알아차릴 수 있는, 뚜렷한, 분명한

결국엔 성정혜 영어 하프모의고사
기적사 DAY 70 핵심어휘

01

sporadic	산발적인, 이따금 발생하는
amenable	말을 잘 듣는
scattered	산발적인, 산재한
relentless	끈질긴, 수그러들지 않는
implacable	확고한, 바꿀 수 없는

02

☐ prosecutor	검사, 검찰관
☐ forcibly	강제로
☐ summon	(법원으로) 소환하다
☐ suspect	용의자
☐ punish	처벌하다, 벌주다
☐ commit	(그릇된 일·범죄를) 저지르다[범하다]
☐ perjury	위증
☐ parole	가석방
☐ felony	중죄, 흉악 범죄
☐ jailbird	죄수, 상습범, 전과자
☐ mendacity	거짓말, 허위

03

☐ convince	납득시키다, 확신시키다
☐ tapestry	태피스트리(여러 가지 색실로 그림을 짜 넣은 직물)
☐ comeback	부흥, 부활, 복귀
☐ billionaire	억만장자, 갑부
☐ respite	일시적인 중단, 유예, 연기
☐ resurgence	재기, 부활
☐ deferment	연기, 거치
☐ suspension	연기, 보류, 정학

04

☐ office hours	(대학 교수의) 면접 시간, 근무 시간, 영업시간
☐ pros and cons	장점과 단점, 찬반양론
☐ hands-on	실제의, 실지의
☐ mull over	곰곰이 숙고하다
☐ the bottom line	핵심
☐ run short of	부족하다

05

☐ fulfilled	성취감을 느끼는
☐ pause	잠시 멈추다

☐ executive	간부, 임원
☐ willing	기꺼이 하는, 자발적인

06

☐ arouse	~을 불러일으키다
☐ empathic	공감할 수 있는
☐ project	투사하다
☐ spatial	공간의, 공간적인
☐ layout	배치, 레이아웃

07

☐ interpretation	해석
☐ subtle	미묘한
☐ inflection	음조, 어조
☐ convincing	설득력 있는
☐ composer	작곡가
☐ identify A with B	A와 B를 동일시하다

08

☐ tension	갈등, 긴장
☐ lifespan	수명
☐ confuse A and B	A와 B를 혼동하다
☐ finding	결과, 결론
☐ prolong	연장시키다
☐ feel blue	우울한, 울적한
☐ predispose someone to something	(특정한 질병에) 취약하게[잘 걸리게] 하다

09

☐ leading	가장 중요한, 선두적인
☐ preventable	막을 수 있는, 방해[예방]할 수 있는
☐ place	(특정한 상황에) 두다[처하게 하다]
☐ attempt	시도하다, 애써 해보다
☐ quit	그만두다, 중지하다
☐ challenge	과제, 난제, 도전, 어려움
☐ addictive	중독성의

☐ nature	자연, 천성, 특징
☐ cessation	중단, 중지
☐ smoking cessation	금연
☐ refer to	말하다, 지칭하다
☐ attachment	애착

10

☐ subtly	미묘하게
☐ come into contact	접촉하다
☐ identify	찾다, 발견하다, 알아보다
☐ identically	꼭 같게, 동일하게
☐ geographical	지리적인
☐ variation	차이, 변화
☐ ethnicity	민족성
☐ encounter	접하다[마주치다]
☐ pronunciation	발음
☐ integrate	통합시키다
☐ speech	말투, 화법, 담화
☐ contribution	기여, 공헌

결국엔 성정혜 영어 하프모의고사
기적사 DAY 71 핵심어휘

01

☐ immutable	변경할 수 없는, 불변의
☐ inevitably	필연적으로, 반드시
☐ cancellation	취소
☐ unchanging	불변의, 늘 변치 않는
☐ provisional	임시의, 일시적인
☐ drastic	과감한, 극단적인
☐ irresponsible	무책임한

02

☐ canny	약삭빠른, 영리한

☐ due	[~을] 하기로 되어있는, ~할 예정인
☐ shrewd	상황 판단이 빠른, 기민한
☐ prestigious	명망 있는, 일류의
☐ impudent	무례한, 경솔한
☐ curious	궁금한, 호기심이 많은

03

☐ curb	억제[제한]하다
☐ unquenchable	만족할 수 없는, 채울 수 없는
☐ appetite	욕구; 식욕
☐ import	수입하다; 수입
☐ communist	공산주의의; 공산주의자
☐ strategic	전략적인
☐ infallible	결코 틀리지 않는, 확실한
☐ aesthetic	미적인, 미학의
☐ adolescent	청소년의
☐ insatiable	만족할 줄 모르는

04

☐ wait on	(특히 식사) 시중을 들다, (손님에게) 응대하다
☐ formal	정규적인; 공식적인
☐ be in touch	연락하다
☐ apply for	~에 지원하다
☐ be good at	~에 능숙하다

06

☐ environmentalist	환경 운동가
☐ mutually	서로, 상호 간에
☐ acceptable	받아들여지는, 용인되는

08

☐ somehow	어쨌든
☐ objectively	객관적으로

기적사 DAY 72 핵심어휘

☐ appraise	평가하다, 감정하다
☐ entirely	완전히, 전적으로
☐ correct	정확한
☐ reliable	믿을 만한
☐ misguided	잘못된
☐ unbiased	편견 없는, 공정한

09

☐ seriously	심(각)하게; 진지하게
☐ schedule	일정[시간 계획]을 잡다, 예정하다; (작업) 일정, 스케줄
☐ recreation	휴양, 기분 전환, 오락
☐ appointment	약속, 임명, 지명
☐ relaxation	휴식; 완화
☐ recreational	휴양의, 오락의
☐ worthwhile	가치[보람] 있는, ~할 가치가 있는
☐ fitness	건강함, (몸의) 좋은 컨디션

10

☐ bedrock	기반
☐ along with	~와 함께, ~에 따라
☐ overburden	과중한 부담을 주다
☐ myriad	무수함, 무수히 많음
☐ continuous	계속되는, 지속적인
☐ unstoppable	막을[제지할] 수 없는
☐ humming	콧노래
☐ die down	차츰 잦아들다 [약해지다/희미해지다]
☐ all-out	완전한, 철저한
☐ mournful	애절한
☐ requiem	진혼곡, 레퀴엠
☐ take over	장악[탈취]하다; 인계받다
☐ ubiquitous	어디에나 있는, 아주 흔한

01

☐ passionately	열렬하게; 격렬하게
☐ vendor	노점상[행상인]
☐ irresponsible	무책임한
☐ torpid	무기력한, 활기 없는
☐ slothful	나태한
☐ feckless	무책임한, 무기력한
☐ strenuous	몹시 힘든, 불굴의

02

☐ shepherd	양치기
☐ shed	헛간, 창고; 흘리다; 버리다
☐ curious	궁금한, 호기심이 많은
☐ softness	부드러움
☐ stony	냉담한, 냉랭한
☐ uneven	고르지 못한, 균등하지 않은
☐ inquisitive	호기심이 많은, 탐구심이 많은
☐ impassive	무표정한, 아무런 감정이 없는

03

☐ insatiable	만족할 줄 모르는
☐ appetite	욕구; 식욕
☐ chaste	순결한, 순수한
☐ decent	괜찮은, 품위 있는
☐ prodigious	엄청난, 굉장한
☐ unappeasable	만족시킬 수 없는, 채울 수 없는

04

☐ celebrate	축하하다, 기념하다
☐ keep one's shirt on	냉정을 유지하다
☐ burn one's fingers	큰 손실을 보다

□ have butterflies in one's stomach	가슴이 철렁철렁하다
□ one's eyes are bigger than one's stomach	과욕을 내다

06

□ aroma	향기, 방향
□ attraction	명물
□ orchard	과수원
□ pine	소나무
□ simulate	…한 체[척]하다, 가장하다
□ countryside	시골, 전원 지대
□ manipulate	조작하다; 조종하다
□ stimulate	자극[격려]하다

08

□ brand equity	브랜드 자산[가치]
□ acquire	획득하다, 얻다
□ identical	동일한, 똑같은
□ must	(틀림없이) …일 것이다 […임에 틀림없다]
□ perception	인식, 인지
□ performance	성능, 효율
□ dependent	의존하는, 의지하는
□ impression	인상, 느낌
□ sample	시음[시식]하다
□ consume	먹다, 섭취하다, 소비하다

09

□ average	평균 …이 되다
□ instead of	~대신에
□ perception	인지, 인식
□ leisure	여가
□ devote	쏟다, 기울이다, 헌신하다
□ awareness	의식, 관심
□ feasible	실현 가능한

□ indolent	게으른, 나태한
□ ideal	이상적인, 가장 알맞은, 완벽한
□ inevitable	불가피한, 필연적인

10

□ portrayal	묘사
□ byproduct	부산물
□ perceive	감지[인지]하다
□ assign	배정하다
□ cognitive	인지의
□ input	입력
□ subconscious	잠재 의식적인, 잠재적인
□ precisely	정확하게
□ subconsciously	잠재적으로
□ the other way around	반대로, 거꾸로
□ threatening	위협적인
□ trigger	촉발하다, 유발하다
□ evoke	유발하다, 떠올려 주다[환기시키다]
□ persist	(없어지지 않고) 계속[지속]되다
□ in turn	결국, 결과적으로
□ initiate	일으키다, 시작하다, 개시하다

결국엔 성정혜 영어 하프모의고사
기적사 DAY 73 핵심어휘

01

□ drastic	극단적인, 과감한
□ biodiversity	생물의 다양성
□ lofty	아주 높은, 고결한
□ meek	온순한, 온화한
□ sublime	극단적인, 황당한
□ submissive	순종적인, 고분고분한

02

☐ impudent	경솔한, 무례한
☐ rash	경솔한, 성급한
☐ wary	경계하는, 조심하는
☐ remiss	태만한, 게으른
☐ assiduous	근면 성실한

03

☐ adolescent	청소년(기)의, 젊은; 청소년
☐ mellow	부드러운, 온화한, 그윽한
☐ caustic	신랄한, 부식성의
☐ juvenile	청소년의
☐ pungent	톡 쏘는 듯한, 날카로운, 신랄한

04

☐ blow one's top	격분하다
☐ catch on fire	인기를 얻다
☐ burn oneself out	다 소진되다
☐ come to one's senses	정신을 차리다

06

☐ mediated	중개된, 매개된
☐ stimulate	자극하다
☐ project	투사하다
☐ immerse	~에 몰두하다

08

☐ neuroscientist	신경 과학자
☐ dominate	지배하다, 우세하다
☐ get to the bottom of	…의 진짜 이유[원인]를 알아내다
☐ call up	소집하다
☐ things	(어떤 사람에게 영향을 미치는) 상황[사정/형편]
☐ ratio	비율, 비

☐ shift	변화하다, 이동하다
☐ in favor of	…에 우호적인 [지지하는]
☐ commercial	광고
☐ from	~에게서 (온/받은)
☐ override	…보다 더 중요하다 [우선하다]
☐ overlook	간과하다
☐ market share	시장 점유율

09

☐ leisure	여가
☐ census	인구 조사, 호구 조사
☐ bureau	부서, 국
☐ compared to	…와 비교하여
☐ break down	분해하다, 쪼개다
☐ employment	고용, 직장
☐ unemployed	실직한, 실업자인

10

☐ fascinating	대단히 흥미로운, 매력적인
☐ by itself	그것만으로
☐ phenomenon	현상
☐ gut feeling	직감
☐ unconscious	무의식적인
☐ irrational	비합리적인, 비이성적인
☐ intuitive	직감[직관]에 의한
☐ rationally	이성적으로, 합리적으로
☐ weird	기이한, 기묘한, 이상한
☐ all of a sudden	별안간, 갑자기
☐ manifest	나타나다, 분명해지다
☐ having said that	그렇긴 해도, 그러나

기적사 DAY 74 핵심어휘

01
independence	독립; (개인의) 자립
provisional	임시의, 일시적인
casual	임시의, 평상시의
callous	냉담한
abiding	지속적인, 변치 않는
ephemeral	수명이 짧은, 단명하는

02
prestigious	명망 있는, 일류의
annual	연례의, 매년의
petty	사소한, 하찮은
interim	임시의, 잠정적인
authentic	진짜인, 정확한
prominent	유명한, 중요한

03
aesthetic	심미적, 미학적
determine	알아내다, 밝히다; 결정하다
shrill	날카로운, 새된
tasteful	심미안이 있는, 우아한
mellifluous	달콤한, 감미로운
cacophonous	불협화음의, 귀에 거슬리는

04
confidence	자신감
step on it	서두르다
mean business	진심이다
lose one's temper	화내다
hit the bull's eye	목표를 달성하다

06
harmony	조화
symptom	증상
pay attention to	~에 주의를 기울이다
capture	~의 관심을 끌다

08
assess	평가하다
intrinsic	본질적인, 고유한
merit	가치, 요소, 장점
reference to	…에 대한 언급, 참조
avoid	방지하다
halo effect	후광 효과
association	연상, 연관
absolute	절대적인, 확실한, 완전한
appeal	매력, 마음을 끄는 것
relative to	…에 비례하여, …에 관련하여
competitor	경쟁자
struggle for	…을 향하여 애쓰다
establish	입증하다, 분명히 하다
be rooted in	…에 원인이 있다
flatter	돋보이게 하다, 아첨하다
halo	후광, 영광
pointless	무의미한, 적절치 못한

09
institute	도입하다, 시작하다
hard-and-fast	엄중한, 변경을 허락지 않는
infringe upon	…을 침해하다
leisure	여가
norm	규범
even	고른, 평평한
counterpart	상대, 대응 관계에 있는 사람[것]
productive	생산적인
what's more	게다가, 한술 더 떠서
allot	할당하다

10

☐ interchangeably	교체하여, 교환하여
☐ distinct	다른, 별개의
☐ hard-wired	내재된
☐ universal	보편적인, 일반적인
☐ association	연상, 연관성
☐ acquire	얻다, 획득하다
☐ proceed to	…으로 나아가다, …에 이르다
☐ predictable	예측[예견]할 수 있는
☐ idiosyncratic	(개인에게) 특유한
☐ inborn	선천적인, 타고난
☐ prompt	촉발하다
☐ temperament	기질
☐ enormously	엄청나게, 대단히
☐ subjective	주관적인
☐ objective	객관적인
☐ instinctual	(학습한 것이 아니라) 본능에 따른, 타고난, 선천적인
☐ acquired	후천적인

결국엔 성정혜 영어 하프모의고사
기적사 DAY 75 핵심어휘

01

☐ unchanging	불변의, 늘 변치 않는
☐ carry on	계속 움직이다[가다]
☐ volatile	변덕스러운, 불안한
☐ turbulent	격동의, 격변의
☐ perdurable	불변의, 영속하는
☐ tempestuous	열렬한, 격정적인

02

☐ suffer	겪다, 당하다
☐ hardship	어려움[곤란]
☐ shrewd	상황 판단이 빠른, 기민한, 약삭빠른

☐ dim	둔한, 흐릿한
☐ astute	약삭빠른, 영악한
☐ murky	흐린, 어두운
☐ radiant	빛나는, 환한

03

☐ infallible	확실한, 결코 틀리지 않는
☐ draw a red herring across the path[track]	주제와는 관계가 없는 것을 꺼내어 남의 주의를 딴 데로 돌리다
☐ inept	솜씨 없는, 서투른
☐ strong	확실한, 강력한
☐ clumsy	서투른, 어설픈
☐ efficacious	효과적인

04

☐ a close call	위험한 상황
☐ a double take	예상치 못한 상황에 대한 늦은 반응
☐ the pang of conscience	양심의 가책
☐ the long and short of it	문제의 본질

06

☐ catch up on	~을 따라잡다, 보충하다
☐ hotly	뜨겁게
☐ chronically	만성적으로
☐ blood sugar	혈당

08

☐ attribute	특성
☐ attitude	태도
☐ relevant	관련 있는, 연관된
☐ take into account	고려하다, 참작하다
☐ characteristic	특성
☐ indistinctiveness	비 특수성, 특색이 없음
☐ socio-economic	사회 경제적인

☐ situational	상황적인	
☐ interaction	상호작용	

09

☐ minuscule	극소의
☐ transition	변이, 변천, 과도
☐ agricultural	농업의
☐ boon	요긴한 것
☐ spectator	관중
☐ sedentary	주로 앉아서 지내는, 몸을 많이 움직이지 않는
☐ evaluate	평가하다
☐ briskly	힘차게, 씩씩하게, 활발하게
☐ meet	충족시키다
☐ intense	격렬한, 극심한
☐ overstate	과장하다

10

☐ investigate	연구하다, 조사하다
☐ sustain	(피해 등을) 입다 [당하다]
☐ reasoning	추리, 추론
☐ sequence	차례[순서]대로 배열하다
☐ reorientation	방향 전환
☐ rod	봉, 막대
☐ drive into	···를 들이박다
☐ recover	회복하다, 복구하다
☐ function	기능
☐ irascible	화를 잘 내는
☐ moody	기분 변화가 심한
☐ impatient	성급한, 안달하는
☐ brain tumor	뇌종양
☐ surgically	외과적으로
☐ drastic	급격한, 극단적인
☐ intellectually	지적으로
☐ indifferent	무관심한
☐ tragedy	비극

결국엔 성정혜 영어 하프모의고사
기적사 DAY 76 핵심어휘

01

☐ monarchy	군주국
☐ withdrawal	철수, 철회, 취소
☐ collapse	붕괴, 실패
☐ invasion	침략, 침입
☐ surrender	항복, 굴복
☐ retreat	후퇴, 철수

02

☐ distinguished	유명한, 성공한; 기품[위엄] 있는
☐ jettison	버리다, 폐기하다
☐ prejudice	편견
☐ discard	버리다, 폐기하다
☐ digress	주제에서 벗어나다
☐ denounce	비난하다, 고발하다
☐ deny	부인하다, 부정하다

03

☐ nocturnal	야행성의
☐ solitary	혼자의
☐ predatory	약탈하는
☐ dormant	잠자는, 휴면 중인

04

☐ You bet.	물론이지[당연하죠].
☐ Help yourself.	마음껏 드세요.

06

☐ convince +목적어[대상]+that +절	~에게 ~을 납득시키다
☐ from scratch	처음부터

07

☐ composer	작곡가
☐ acclaim	칭송하다
☐ above all	무엇보다도, 특히
☐ tune	(악기의) 음을 맞추다, 조율하다; 준비하다, 조정하다
☐ arrange	편곡하다; 배열하다, 정리하다
☐ compose	작곡하다; 구성하다
☐ score	악보
☐ concerto	협주곡

08

☐ deject	낙담시키다, 풀이 죽게 하다
☐ hoop	(농구의) 링; 테, 고리
☐ wonder	궁금하다, 궁금해하다
☐ pebble	조약돌, 자갈
☐ claw	할퀴다[긁다]
☐ festive	축제적인, 축제의; 흥겨운, 즐거운
☐ merry	즐거운, 명랑한
☐ desolate	황량한, 적막한

09

☐ run into	충돌하다
☐ border	국경, 경계
☐ arbitrary	임의의, 독단적인, 제멋대로인
☐ sphere	영역, 분야
☐ sovereignty	주권, 영유권, 통치권
☐ ratify	승인하다, 인정하다
☐ borderland	국경지방, 경계지

10

☐ trigger	계기
☐ aggressive	공격적인
☐ congestion	혼잡
☐ couple with	~와 연결하다

☐ resort to	~에 의지하다
☐ roadway shoulder	도로 갓길
☐ startle	깜짝 놀라게 하다
☐ evasive	종잡을 수 없는
☐ crash	충돌
☐ violation	위반
☐ traffic offense	교통 위반
☐ combination	조합
☐ negligent	무관심한, 태만한

결국엔 성정혜 영어 하프모의고사
기적사 DAY 77 핵심어휘

01

☐ predicate	단정하다, 근거를 두다
☐ collapse	붕괴, 실패
☐ truce	휴전
☐ turmoil	혼란, 소란
☐ disruption	붕괴, 분열
☐ retardation	지연, 저지, 방해

02

☐ divide	~을 나누다, 분할하다
☐ ideology	이념, 관념
☐ deny	부인하다, 부정하다
☐ ethnicity	민족성
☐ rescind	폐지하다, 철회하다
☐ eschew	피하다, 삼가다
☐ forswear	그만두다, 포기하다
☐ repudiate	부인하다, 거부하다

03

☐ nocturnal	야행성의
☐ dusky	어스름한, 탁한
☐ diurnal	주행성의, 하루 동안의
☐ luminous	야광의, 빛을 발하는

☐ noctivagant	야행성의, 밤에 돌아다니는

04

☐ appreciate	고마워하다; 인정하다; 가치가 오르다
☐ contact	연락하다; 연락; 접촉

06

☐ convince +목적어[대상]+that +절	~에게 ~을 납득시키다
☐ intermediary	중개의
☐ corrupt	부패한, 타락한, 오염된

07

☐ magnet	자석
☐ inspire	불어넣다
☐ enthusiasm	열정
☐ repel	쫓아버리다

08

☐ wander	거닐다, 돌아다니다
☐ peer into	자세히 들여다보다
☐ saunter	한가로이[느긋하게] 걷다
☐ desolate	적막한, 황량한
☐ extinguish	(불을) 끄다
☐ tick by	째깍째깍 흘러가다
☐ extraordinary	묘한, 엄청난, 보통이 아닌; 기이한, 놀라운
☐ with each passing second	매초가 지나면서, 매초마다
☐ languish in	…에 머물다
☐ cottony	보드라운
☐ fold	주름, 접힌 것
☐ relive	(상상 속에서) 다시 체험하다
☐ shrink	줄어들게 하다

☐ to size	맞는 크기로, 원하는 크기로
☐ until	…할 만큼, …하여 결국
☐ permanently	영구히, 영원히
☐ unknowingly	모르고, 알아채지 못하고
☐ file away	봉하다, 보관하다
☐ constant	끊임없는, 계속되는
☐ reshuffle	바꾸다, 전환시키다, 개편하다

09

☐ blur	흐릿하게[희미하게] 하다
☐ tale	이야기
☐ hang	(달라붙어서) 떨어지지 않다; 정체해 있다
☐ boozy	술 취한, 만취한
☐ dispute	싸움, 언쟁, 분쟁
☐ scuffle	실랑이, 옥신각신함
☐ strike	치다, 때리다
☐ strangle	목을 조르다
☐ account	이야기, 말, 설명
☐ survey	측량
☐ commissioner	장관
☐ surveyor	측량사
☐ border	국경
☐ crop up	불쑥 나타나다 [발생하다]
☐ define	규정하다, 정하다
☐ settled	자리를 잡은, 안정된

10

☐ define	정의하다, 규정하다
☐ aggressive driving	난폭 운전
☐ commit	저지르다, 범하다
☐ combination	조합, 결합
☐ moving	주행 중인, 이동하는
☐ traffic offense	교통 법규 위반
☐ so as to 동사원형	~하기 위하여

기적사 DAY 78 핵심어휘

01

☐ invasion	침략, 침입
☐ coup	쿠데타, 대단한 성취
☐ chink	틈
☐ rupture	파열
☐ encroachment	침략, 침해
☐ endanger	위험에 빠뜨리다, 위태롭게 만들다
☐ property	재산, 소유물
☐ aggressively	난폭하게, 공격적으로
☐ from time to time	이따금, 가끔
☐ aware	알고[의식/자각하고] 있는
☐ psychological	심리학적인
☐ play	영향, 작용
☐ prone to	…을 잘하는, …의 경향이 있는
☐ territoriality	세력권 의식, 텃세
☐ tendency	성향, 경향, 기질
☐ extension	연장
☐ domain	영역, 범위, 영토, 소유지
☐ out of	(동기·원인) …에서, …로 인해
☐ instinct	본능
☐ self-protection	자기 방위
☐ wheel	(자동차의) 핸들
☐ courteous	공손한, 정중한
☐ competitive	경쟁적인
☐ overtake	추월하다, 앞지르다
☐ in turn	결국[결과적으로]
☐ maneuver	작전, (교묘한) 행동, 책략

02

☐ denounce	비난하다, 고발하다
☐ authoritarian	권위주의적인, 독재적인
☐ regime	정권; 제도, 체제
☐ quest	추구, 탐구, 탐색
☐ democracy	민주주의
☐ expel	퇴학시키다, 추방하다, 배출하다
☐ acquit	무죄를 선고하다
☐ recount	이야기하다, 말하다
☐ condemn	비난하다, 규탄하다

03

☐ solitary	혼자 하는, 단 하나의
☐ drinking	음주
☐ sole	혼자의, 유일한
☐ surly	불친절한, 무례한
☐ dubious	의심하는, 불확실한
☐ convivial	명랑한, 유쾌한

04

☐ dim	어둑한[밝지 않은]
☐ turn on	켜다
☐ frozen	언, 결빙된; 몹시 추운

06

☐ cultivate	경작하다
☐ reap	거두다, 수확하다

07

☐ subtropical	아열대의
☐ insulating	열을 차단하는
☐ adaptation	적응, 각색

08

☐ congregate	모이다
☐ development	(신축 건물이 들어선) 개발지; 발달, 성장

☐ enclosed	폐쇄된, 밀폐된
☐ various	다양한
☐ appreciate	감상하다, 인식하다
☐ potential	가능성, 잠재력
☐ neighborhood	근처, 인근; 이웃
☐ mostly	주로, 일반적으로

09

☐ creek	시내, 개울
☐ floodwater	홍수로 인한 물
☐ namesake	(다른 것·사람과) 이름이 같은 것[사람]
☐ downslope	내리막
☐ border	국경
☐ slate	계획하다
☐ double as	(주된 용도 외에) …로도 쓰이다
☐ intersect	교차하다, 만나다
☐ debris	잔해, 쓰레기
☐ ecologically	생태학적으로
☐ diverse	다양한
☐ score	(복수로) 다수, 많음
☐ consequence	결과
☐ dire	끔찍한, 몹시 나쁜
☐ flash flooding	갑작스러운 홍수, 갑자기 불어난 물
☐ erect	세우다, 건립하다
☐ barrier	장벽, 벽

10

☐ narcissist	자기도취자, 나르시시스트
☐ need	욕구
☐ meet	충족시키다
☐ impose on	…을 위압하다, 속이다
☐ trigger	촉발하다, 유발하다
☐ be referred to as	…로 불리다
☐ narcissistic	자기도취적인
☐ rage	분노
☐ frustrated	불만스러워하는

☐ frustration	불만, 좌절
☐ unaccompanied by	…이 동반되지 않는
☐ thirst	갈망, 열망
☐ vengeance	복수, 앙갚음
☐ empathy	공감, 감정이입
☐ insolent	오만불손한, 거만한, 무례한
☐ be bound by	…에 얽매이다
☐ quality	특징, 특성
☐ extend to	…까지 미치다
☐ aggressively	난폭하게, 공격적으로
☐ engage in	참여하다
☐ behavior	[심리] 행동, 습성
☐ narcissistic personality disorder	자기애적 인격 장애

결국엔 성정혜 영어 하프모의고사
기적사 DAY 79 핵심어휘

01

☐ specify	(구체적으로) 명시하다
☐ independence	독립; (개인의) 자립
☐ surrender	항복, 굴복
☐ sanction	허가, 승인, 제재
☐ resignation	사직, 사임
☐ capitulation	조건부 항복, 항복 문서
☐ acquiescence	묵인

02

☐ digress	주제에서 벗어나다
☐ trim	다듬다, 손질하다
☐ deck	꾸미다, 장식하다
☐ deviate	벗어나다
☐ ramble	걷다, 거닐다, 횡설수설하다
☐ previously	이전에

03

☐ predatory	포식성의, 육식하는
☐ raptorial	육식의, 생물을 잡아먹는
☐ rapacious	탐욕스러운
☐ herbivorous	초식성의
☐ omnivorous	잡식성의

04

☐ be good at	~에 능숙한
☐ appetite	식욕; 욕구
☐ childhood	어린 시절

06

☐ remind+목적어[대상]+that+절	~에게 ~을 상기시키다
☐ arise	생기다, 발생하다

07

☐ storage	저장
☐ overflow	넘치다
☐ avenue	방안
☐ reprocessing	재처리

08

☐ sociocultural	사회 문화적인
☐ amongst	~중[사이]에
☐ perceive	여기다, 인식하다
☐ various	다양한
☐ adopt	채택하다, 쓰다
☐ risk averse	위험 회피
☐ attitude	태도
☐ predesignate	미리 지정하다
☐ overprotectiveness	과잉보호
☐ et al.	외, 등
☐ reveal	밝히다, 드러내다
☐ abduction	납치
☐ commonplace	아주 흔한

☐ cite	(이유·예를) 들다 [끌어대다]
☐ spontaneous	즉흥적인, 자발적인
☐ excessively	지나치게
☐ protective	보호하려고 하는
☐ simplistically	극단적으로 단순화하여
☐ overly	너무, 몹시
☐ solicitous	염려하는, 걱정하는

09

☐ policing	감시 활동, 치안 유지 활동
☐ troop	부대, 군대, 병력
☐ border	국경
☐ militarization	군사화, 군국화
☐ national boundaries	국경
☐ multiple	다수의
☐ expansion	확장
☐ arguably	주장하건대, 거의 틀림없이
☐ militia	민병대, 의용군
☐ vigilante	자경단
☐ immigrant	이주민, 이민자
☐ colonizer	식민지 개척자
☐ enslave	노예로 만들다
☐ police	감시하다, 치안을 유지하다

10

☐ lawfully	합법적으로
☐ cautiously	조심스럽게
☐ wheel	(자동차의) 핸들; 바퀴
☐ count on	확신하다, 의존하다, 믿다
☐ defensively	방어적으로
☐ aggressive	난폭한, 공격적인
☐ alert	경계하는
☐ adjustment	조정, 수정

☐ accommodate	맞추다, 적응하다, 조정하다
☐ unforeseen	예측하지 못한, 뜻밖의
☐ circumstance	상황, 환경
☐ semi	한쪽 벽면이 옆집과 붙어 있는 주택
☐ condition	상태, 상황
☐ in an instant	즉시, 당장, 곧
☐ composure	평정

결국엔 성정혜 영어 하프모의고사
기적사 DAY 80 핵심어휘

01

☐ retreat	후퇴, 철수
☐ asylum	망명
☐ upsurge	급증
☐ recession	후퇴, 불황
☐ sanctuary	보호, 피난처

02

☐ peel	(과일채소 등의) 껍질을 벗기다[깎다]
☐ discard	버리다, 폐기하다
☐ stem	(식물의) 줄기; 막다
☐ lengthwise	세로의[로], 긴[길게]
☐ bin	버리다
☐ spurn	일축하다, 퇴짜 놓다
☐ retain	간직하다, 보유하다
☐ loathe	몹시 싫어하다, 질색하다

03

☐ evade	피하다, 회피하다
☐ dormant	휴면 중의, 활동을 중단한
☐ incidental	부수적인; 우연히 일어나는; 주요하지 않은

☐ bouncy	활기 넘치는, 탱탱한
☐ judicious	신중한, 판단력 있는
☐ diapause	[주로 현재분사형으로] 휴면하다

04

☐ assignment	과제; 배정
☐ submit	제출하다; 항복[굴복]하다
☐ barely	겨우, 간신히, 가까스로; 거의 ~아니게
☐ withstand	견뎌내다
☐ spring fever	춘곤증
☐ drowsy	졸리는, 나른하게 만드는

06

☐ freshwater lake	담수호
☐ accumulate	축적하다
☐ mimic	흉내 내다
☐ contradiction	모순

08

☐ passive	수동적인, 소극적인
☐ recipient	수신자, 받는 사람
☐ stimulation	자극
☐ fine motor skill	소근육 운동
☐ artificial	인공적인, 인위적인
☐ engage	끌어들이다, 관여시키다
☐ kinesthetic	운동 감각의
☐ involve	관련[연루]시키다
☐ manipulate	조작하다, 다루다
☐ verbally	말로, 구두로
☐ neurological	신경의

09

☐ leading	주요한, 선두적인
☐ involve	포함하다, 수반하다, 관련시키다

☐ territorial dispute	영토 분쟁
☐ representative	대표, 대변자
☐ explicit	명백한, 분명한, 노골적인
☐ sovereignty	통치권
☐ territory	영토, 영역
☐ claim	(권리를) 주장하다; 차지하다
☐ administer	관리하다, 운영하다
☐ militarized	무장의, 무력의
☐ conflict	갈등, 충돌
☐ diplomatic	외교의
☐ contiguous	인접한, 근접한
☐ border	국경
☐ generate	발생시키다, 만들어 내다

10

☐ approach	접근(법)
☐ wheel	핸들
☐ effect	결과, 영향
☐ aggressive driving	난폭 운전
☐ road rage	보복 운전, 운전자 폭행, 로드 레이지
☐ extensive	대규모의, 많은
☐ fleet	전(全) 선박[비행기, 트럭, 버스] 보유 차량
☐ conduct	행하다, 실시하다
☐ what	본질
☐ where	장소
☐ when	시기, 때
☐ all too	너무나, 정말
☐ miss out on	…을 놓치다
☐ initial	처음의, 초기의
☐ intention	의사, 의도, 목적
☐ conflict	갈등, 충돌
☐ frustration	불만
☐ set in	(계속될 기세로) 시작하다[되다]
☐ aggressively	난폭하게, 공격적으로

MEMO

MEMO

MEMO

MEMO

MEMO